STATE CONSTITUTIONAL LAW
THE MODERN EXPERIENCE

■ ■ ■

By

Randy J. Holland
Justice
Delaware Supreme Court

Stephen R. McAllister
Professor of Law
University of Kansas School of Law

Jeffrey M. Shaman
Vincent de Paul Professor of Law
DePaul University College of Law

Jeffrey S. Sutton
Judge
United States Court of Appeals for the Sixth Circuit

AMERICAN CASEBOOK SERIES®

WEST®
A Thomson Reuters business

Mat #41028006

American Casebook Series is a trademark registered in the U.S. Patent and Trademark Office.

© 2010 Thomson Reuters
    610 Opperman Drive
    St. Paul, MN 55123
    1–800–313–9378
Printed in the United States of America

ISBN: 978–0–314–26449–7

Each of the Co-Authors Dedicates This Book as Follows –

Randy J. Holland
To Ilona E. Holland
Ethan, Jennifer and Aurora (Rori)

Stephen McAllister
To Suzanne Valdez,
Mara, Fiona, Brett, Isabel and Sofia

Jeffrey M. Shaman
To Susan Shaman

Jeffrey Sutton
To Peggy Sutton,
Nathaniel, John and Margaret

FOREWORD

State Constitutional Law – The Modern Experience
Foreword by E. Norman Veasey[*]

As is the case with the weather, lawyers often talk about the constitutions of the various states, but seldom do anything about that subject. Most of the American cases and literature focus on the United States Constitution. State constitutional law is often neglected, but it is a vibrant and significant feature of our jurisprudence. Justice Randy J. Holland, Judge Jeffrey S. Sutton, Professor Steven R. McAllister and Professor Jeffrey M. Shaman have breathed new life into the subject with this outstanding, scholarly casebook.

Lawyers take an oath upon admission to the bar to support the United States Constitution and the constitution of their states of admission. See, e.g., Rule 54, Rules of the Supreme Court of Delaware ("I ... do solemnly swear (or affirm) that I will support the Constitution of the United States and the Constitution of the State of Delaware ..."). But can a lawyer be true to this solemn oath if she has not studied state constitutional law or been examined on her state constitution? Perhaps she can "catch up" in practice with some "on the job training," as the need arises. But that is not a particularly professional approach. This new, epic work on state constitutional law should become an important basis for law school curricula. Moreover, state constitutional law should be considered as a bar examination topic.

The framers of the United States constitution adopted a "'constitutionally mandated balance of power' between the States and the Federal Government ... to ensure the protection of 'our fundamental liberties.'" *Atascadero State Hosp. v. Scanlon*, 473 U.S. 234, 242 (1985) (quoting *Garcia v. San Antonio Metro. Transit Auth.*, 469 U.S. 528 (Powell, J., dissenting)). The preservation of diversity in the legal and governmental systems of each state was expressly contemplated when the United States constitution was framed and adopted. *See* Randy J. Holland, *State Constitutions: Purpose and Function*, 69 Temp. L.Rev. 989, 998-99 (1996). State constitutions are a source of rights independent of the Federal Constitution and may be applied by state courts to grant more extensive protection for individual rights than is recognized under the Federal Constitution.

---

[*] Chief Justice (Ret.) Delaware Supreme Court (1992-2004).

Under the system of dual sovereignty that exists in this nation, a state court is free to interpret its own state constitution in any way it determines, provided it does not contravene federal law. While the Supremacy Clause of the Federal Constitution makes federal law supreme to state law, so long as state constitutional protection does not fall below the federal floor, a state court may interpret its own state constitution as it chooses, irrespective of federal constitutional law. Although decisions of the United States Supreme Court concerning constitutional issues are entitled to respect and may provide guidance on constitutional matters, they are not binding on a state court as it interprets its own state constitutional guarantees. A state court is free as a matter of its own law to grant more expansive rights than those afforded by federal law. The expansion beyond federally guaranteed individual liberties by a state constitution is attributable to a variety of reasons: differences in textual language, legislative history, pre-existing state law, structural differences, matters of particular concern, and state traditions.

As Judge Sutton, one of the co-authors of this work, has written, "... lawyers and clients have two chances, not one, to invalidate [dubious state or local action]. They may invoke the United States Constitution ... or that State's Constitution to strike the law. Yet ... that is not what most lawyers do." Jeffery S. Sutton, *Why Teach — and Why Study — State Constitutional Law*, 34 OKLAHOMA CITY UNIVERSITY LAW REVIEW 165, 166 (2009). A lawyer challenging police action or a dubious state statute should welcome the leverage of two arrows in her quiver.

Indeed, lawyers *should*, in many cases, frame their attacks on the constitutions of both sovereigns. Why? "State constitutional law not only gives the client two chances to win, it will also give the client a *better* chance to win." *Id.* at 173. There are many reasons cited by Judge Sutton showing this to be true, but one overarching reason is that a state supreme court's decision that rests on its application of the state constitution is the last word in the case and cannot be countermanded by the United States Supreme Court. As the late Supreme Court Justice William Brennan has written, "Moreover, the state decisions not only cannot be overturned by, they indeed are not even reviewable by, the Supreme Court of the United States." William J. Brennan, Jr., *State Constitutions and the Protection of Individual Rights*, 90 HARV. L. REV. 489, 501 (1977). This principle is based on the established doctrine that "... if a state ground is independent and adequate to support a judgment, the [U.S. Supreme] Court has no jurisdiction at all over the decision despite the presence of federal issues." *Id.* at 501 n.80.

The law concerning unreasonable searches and seizures reflects differing standards between federal and state constitutions and a labyrinth of factual situations. *See United States v. Cortez*, 449 U.S. 411, 417

(1981). A case in point is the 1999 Delaware Supreme Court decision in *Jones v. State*, 745 A.2d 856 (Del. 1999). There the Court held—arguably in the face of contrary federal and Delaware decisions under the United States Constitution adjudicating similarly worded provisions—that the police did not have a reasonable and articulable basis to make a stop of the defendant and the seizure of controlled substances on his person.

In *Jones* the Court framed the issue as "whether the search and seizure language in the Delaware Constitution means the same thing as the United States Supreme Court's construction of *similar* language in the United States Constitution." *Id.* at 495. The Court then analyzed a number of historical references, including those where similar terms had been used, with differing results. *Id.* at 495-506. Noting that the law concerning unreasonable searches and seizures "reflects differing standards between federal and state constitutions and a labyrinth of factual situations," the Court held:

> If an officer attempts to seize someone before possessing reasonable and articulable suspicion, that person's actions stemming from the attempted seizure may not be used to manufacture the suspicion the police lacked initially."

Id. at 855-56.

State constitutional law, like its federal counterpart, is not limited to issues involving the common law or individual rights. Numerous other areas of law involve the application of state constitutions. The structure and power of state and local governments, the state judicial system, taxation, public finance, and public education are all affected by a state's constitutions and its interpretation. "From its inception of the American republic, federal and state constitutional traditions have been distinct." James E. Henretta, *Foreword: Rethinking the State Constitutional Tradition*, 22 Rutgers L.J. 819, 819-26, 836-39 (1991). The United States Constitution has retained its original character as a document that fixed the basic structure of government and allocated power among its three branches. State constitution-making and amending has been a recurring process within the broader political, social, economic, and historical contexts of time and place. A.E. Dick Howard, *The Values of Federalism*, 1 New. Eur. L. Rev. 241, 145-46 (1993); Lewis B. Kaden, *Politics, Money, and State Sovereignty: The Judicial Role*, 79 Colum. L. Rev. 847-853-57 (1979). *See also* Robert P. Stoker, Reluctant Partners (1991).

This new, richly documented and superbly-analyzed casebook by such distinguished legal scholars is destined to be the seminal authority in this vitally important field. For some lawyers, a system of dual sovereignty means that litigants will have two opportunities, not than just one, to invalidate a state law or otherwise halt state action. And for others, our federal system makes state courts accountable for properly interpreting their own constitutions, without regard to whether those interpretations increase or decrease individual liberty and without regard to whether they follow or break from decisions of the U.S. Supreme Court. But for all lawyers, the independence of the sovereignty of the states makes the study and effective use of state constitutional law an imperative in the twenty-first century, as indicated in the following February 2010 resolution that was passed unanimously by the Conference of Chief Justices.

CONFERENCE OF CHIEF JUSTICES RESOLUTION:
State Constitutional Law Courses

RESOLUTION 1

Encouraging the Teaching of State Constitutional Law Courses

WHEREAS, all lawyers take an oath to support the United States Constitution and the constitution of their state; and

WHEREAS, although all law schools offer a course in constitutional law, the overwhelming majority of those courses are taught from the perspective of the federal Constitution; and

WHEREAS, the United States Constitution creates a dual system of government with two sets of sovereigns whereby all powers not delegated to the federal government are reserved to the states; and

WHEREAS, state constitutions contain different structures of government, unique provisions, and substantive provisions or declarations of rights that are often greater than federally guaranteed individual rights and liberties; and

WHEREAS, being a competent and effective lawyer requires an understanding of both the federal Constitution and state constitutional law;

NOW, THEREFORE, BE IT RESOLVED that the Conference of Chief Justices encourages all law schools to offer a course on state constitutional law.

Adopted as proposed by the Professionalism and Competence of the Bar Committee at the Conference of Chief Justices 2010 Midyear Meeting.

SUMMARY OF CONTENTS

TABLE OF CONTENTS

TABLE OF CASES

Principal cases are in bold type. Non-principal cases are in roman type. References are to Pages.

TABLE OF AUTHORITIES

Books and Articles

Abrahamson, Shirley S., *Divided We Stand: State Constitutions in a More Perfect Union*, 18 HASTINGS CONST. L.Q. 723, 727-28 (1991), 50.

Ackerman, Bruce, *We The People Foundations (Cambridge: Harvard University Press* (1991), 63.

Adams, *First American Constitutions*, 300, 307; James Dealey, *Growth of American State Constitutions* (1915; rpt. New York: Da Capo Press, 1972), 8.

Adams, John, *Thoughts on Government, in* 4 *The Works of John Adams* 200 (Charles Francis Adams ed., 1850-1856), 10.

Adams, John, *Thoughts on Government* (Boston, 1776), in *American Political Writing*, ed. Hyneman and Lutz, 1:407, 16.

Adams, Willi Paul, *The First American Constitutions: Republican Ideology and the Making of the State Constitutions in the Revolutionary Era* 51-52 (1980), 8.

Adrian, *Trends in State Constitutions*, 5 HARV. J. LEGIS. 311, 341 (1968) quoted in William F. Swindler, *State Constitutions for the 20th Century*, 50 NEB. L. REV. 577, 577-78 (1971), 63.

Amar, Akhil Reed, *Of Sovereignty and Federalism*, 96 YALE L.J. 1425, 1429 (1987), 50.

Amar, Akhil Reed, *The Bill of Rights and the Fourteenth Amendment*, 101 YALE L.J. 1193 (1992), 61.

Bayard, James A., *A Brief Exposition of the Constitution of the United States* 3 (2d ed. 1838), 896.

Beck, Phyllis W., *Foreword: Stepping Over the Procedural Threshold in the Presentation of State Constitutional Claims*, 68 TEMP. L. REV. 1035 (1995), 62.

Bernstein, Richard B. with Agel, Jerome, *Amending America* (New York: Times Books 1993), 896.

Billias, George A., *American Constitutionalism and Europe, 1776-1848, in American Constitutionalism Abroad* 13-14, 19-23 (George A. Billias ed. 1990), 14.

Bishop, William B. and Attree, William, *Report of the Debates and Proceedings of the Convention for the Revision of the Constitution of New York, 1846,* (Albany: Evening Atlas, 1846), 40.

Blaustein, A. Blaustein & Sigler, J., *Constitutions That Made History* 20 (1988), 17.

Blum, Callon, Morgan, Schlecinger, Staupp and Woodward, *The National Experience: A History of the United States* (Harcourt, Brace & World, Inc. 1963), 39.

Bodenhamer, David J., *The Pursuit of Justice: Crime and Law in Antebellum Indiana* (New York: Garland, 1986), 44.

Borden, Morton, *Jews, Turks, and Infidels* (Chapel Hill: University of North Carolina Press, 1984), 15.

Botein, Stephen, "*Religious Dimensions of the Early American State*," in *Beyond Confederation: Origins of the Constitution and American National Identity*, ed. Richard Beeman, Sephen Botein, and Edward C. Carter II (Chapel Hill: University of North Carolina Press, 1987), 15.

Brennan, William J., Jr., *State Constitutions and the Protection of Individual Rights*, 90 HARV. L. REV. 489 (1977), 62.

Brennan, William J., Jr., *The Bill of Rights and the States: The Revival of State Constitutions as Guardians of Individual Rights*, 61 N.Y.U. L. REV. 535 (1986), 62.

Briffault, Richard, *The Item Veto In State Courts*, 66 Temple L. Rev. 1171 (1993), 843.

Brown, Samuel W., *The Secularization of American Education as Shown by State Legislation, State Constitutional Provisions and State Supreme Court Decisions* (New York: Bureau of Publications, Teachers College, Columbia University, 1912), 45.

Brunhouse, R., *The Counter-Revolution in Philadelphia 1776-1790* (1942), 16.

Bryce, James, 1 *The American Commonwealth* 434 2d rev., ed. (New York: Macmillan 1981), 7.

Calabresi, Steven G., *The Fatally Flawed Theory of the Unbundled Executive*, 93 Minn. L. Rev. 1696, 1697 (2009), 824.

Carmella, Angela C., *State Constitutional Protection of Religious Exercise: An Emerging Post-Smith Jurisprudence,* 1993 BYU L. REV. 277 (1993), 524.

Cella, *The People of Massachusetts, A New Republic, and the Constitution of 1780: The Evolution of Principles of Popular Control of Political Authority, 1774-1780*, 14 SUFFOLK U.L. REV.975 (1980), 24.

Coleman, *Thomas McKean: Forgotten Leader of the Revolution,* at 203 n. 56, 18.

Colson, Dennis C., *Idaho's Constitution: The Tie That Binds* 1, 4-6, 220-23 (University of Idaho 1991), 28.

Cooley, Thomas M., *A Treatise on the Constitutional Limitations Which Rest Upon the Legislative Power of the States of the American Union* (1868), 255.

Cornelius, Janet, *Constitution Making in Illinois 1818-1970* (Urbana: University of Illinois Press, 1972), 31.

Cornwell, Elmer E., Jr., Goodman, Jay S., and Swanson, Wayne R., *State Constitutional Conventions* (New York: Praeger, 1975); and Charles Press, *"Assessing Policy and Operational Implications of State Constitutional Change,"* Publius: The Journal of Federalism 12 (Winter 1982): 99-111, 67.

Cortner, Richard, *The Supreme Court and the Second Bill of Rights: The Fourteenth Amendment and the Nationalization of Civil Liberties* (Madison: University of Wisconsin Press, 1981), 50.

Crihfield, Brevard & Frank Smothers, *The States in the Federal System*, 34 N.Y.U. L. REV. 1018 (1959), 7.

Cronin, Thomas E., *Direct Democracy: The Politics of Initiative, Referendum, and Recall* (1989).

Curtis, Michael Kent, *No State Shall Abridge: The Fourteenth Amendment and the Bill of Rights* (Durham: Duke University Press, 1986), 31.

Curtis, Michael K., *The Fourteenth Amendment and the Bill of Rights*, 14 CONN. L. REV. 237 (1982), 61.

Dealey, James Q., *Growth of American State Constitutions* 97 (New York: Da Capo Press, 1972), 22.

DeForrest, Mark Edward, *An Overview and Evaluation of State Blaine Amendments: Origins, Scope, and First Amendment Concerns*, 26 HARV. J. L. & PUB. POL'Y 551 (2003), 546.

Devlin, John, *Toward a State Constitutional Analysis of Allocation of Powers: Legislators and Legislative Appointees Performing Administrative Functions*, 66 TEMP. L. REV. 1205 (1993), 30.

Dickson, Brent E., *Lawyers and Judges as Framers of Indiana's 1851 Constitution*, 30 INDIANA L. REV. 397 (1997), 44.

Dixon, Robert G., *Democratic Representation: Reapportionment in Law and Politics* (New York: Oxford University Press, 1968), 64.

Douglass, *Thomas Burke, Disillusioned Democrat*, 26 N.C. HIST. REV. 150, 157 (1950), 18.

Dragich, Martha, *State Constitutional Restrictions on Legislative Procedure: Rethinking the Analysis of Original Purpose, Single Subject, and Clear Title Challenges*, 38 Harv. J. Legis. 103 (2001), 732.

Elazar, Daniel J., *The Principles and Traditions Underlying State Constitutions*, 12 *Publius: the Journal of Federalism* 11, 18-22 (1982), 65.

Erdman, Charles R., *The New Jersey Constitution of 1776* (Princeton, N.J. 1929), 13.

Fairman, Charles, *Does the Fourteenth Amendment Incorporate The Bill of Rights?* 2 STAN. L. REV. 5 (1949), 61.

Fehrenbacher, Don E., *Sectional Crisis and Southern Constitutionalism*, 84, LOUISIANA STATE UNIVERSITY PRESS (1995).

Feldman, Jonathan, *Separation of Powers and Judicial Review of Positive Rights Claims: The Role of State Courts in an Era of Positive Government*, 24 RUTGERS L.J. 1057 (1993), 30.

Few, J. Kendall, *In Defense of Trial by Jury*, 469-76 (1993), 62.

Field, Phyllis F., *The Politics of Race in New York: The Struggle for Black Suffrage in the Civil War Era* (Ithaca: Cornell University Press, 1982), 47.

Finkleman, Paul and Gottlieb, Stephen E., editors *Toward a Usable Part: Liberty Under State Constitutions* (Athens: University of Georgia Press 1991), 895.

Foner, Eric, *Reconstruction: America's Unfinished Revolution, 1863-1877* (Harper Collins Publishers, Inc. 1988), 47.

Friesen, Jennifer, *State Constitutional Law: Litigating Individual Rights, Claims and Defenses* (2006), 331, 545, 546, 642, 667.

Fritz, Mechthild, *Religion in a Federal System: Diversity versus Uniformity*, 38 KAN. L. REV. 39 (1989), 523.

Galie, Peter J. and Bopst, Christopher, *The Constitutional Commission in New York: A Worthy Tradition*, 64 Alb. L. Rev. 1285 (2001), 936.

Goldenziel, Jill, *Blaine's Name in Vain?: State Constitutions, School Choice, and Charitable Choice*, 83 DENV. U. L. REV. 57 (2005), 523.

Grad, Frank P., *The State Constitution: Its Function and Form for Our Time*, 54 VA. L. REV. 928 (1968), 7.

Graves, W. Brooke, *State Constitutional Law: A Twenty-Five Year Summary*, 8 WM. & MARY L. REV. 1, 4 (1966), 31.

Graves, W. Brooke, 14 LA. L. REV. 749-763 (1954), 63.

Green, Fletcher, *Constitutional Development in the South Atlantic States, 1776-1860* (1930), 21.

Green, Thomas F., Jr., *A Malapropian Provision of State Constitutions*, 24 WASH. U. L.Q. 359 (1939), 38.

Grey, Thomas C., *Origins of the Unwritten Constitution: Fundamental Law in American Revolutionary Thought*, 30 STAN. L. REV. 843 (1978), 7.

Griffin, Stephen M., *American Constitutionalism From Theory to Politics*, p. 34 (Princeton University Press 1996), 32.

Gunther, Gerald, *Constitutional Law* 422-40 (11th ed. 1985). *See Barron v. Baltimore*, 32 U.S. (7 Pet.) 243 (1833), 50.

Hall, Kermit L., *"Mostly Anchor and Little Sail," The Revolution of American and State Constitutions* in Paul Finkelman and Stephen E. Gottlieb, eds., *Toward a Usable Past: Liberty Under State Constitutions*, (Athens: University of Georgia Press, 1991), 35.

Hall, Kermit L., *"The Judiciary on Trial: State Constitutional Reform and the Rise of an Elected Judiciary, 1846-1860," Historian* 44 (May 1983), 41.

Hawke, D., *In the Midst of a Revolution* 178 (discussion of Adams's dislike for Pennsylvania Constitution), 18.

Howard, A.E. Dick, *The Road From Runnymede: Magna Carta and Constitutionalism in America 203-15* (1968), 7.

Heise, Michael, *State Constitutions, School Finance Litigation, and the "Third Wave": From Equity to Adequacy*, 68 TEMP. L. REV. 1151 (1995), 32.

Henkin, Louis, *"Selective Incorporation" in the Fourteenth Amendment*, 73 YALE L.J. 74 (1963), 61.

Henretta, James A., *Foreward: Rethinking the State Constitutional Tradition*, 22 RUTGERS L.J. 819, 819-26, 836-39 (1991), 33.

Henretta, James A., *"The Rise and Decline of "Democratic-Republicanism" Political Rights in New York and the Several States*, 1800-1915 in *Toward a Usable Past: Liberty Under State Constitutions*, Paul Finkelman and Stephen E. Gottlieb, 41.

Herget, James E., *The Missing Power of Local Governments: A Divergence Between Text and Practice in Our Early State Constitution*, 62 VA. L. REV. 999, 1001 (1976), 30.

Hoffman, Jonathan M., *Questions Before Answers: The Ongoing Search to Understand the Origins of the Open Courts Clause*, 32 Rutgers L.J. 1005 (2001), 665

Hoffman, R., *A Spirit of Dissention: Economics, Politics and the Revolution in Maryland* 170-183, 269 (1973), 21.

Holliday, Winston David, Jr., *Tipping the Balance of Power: A Critical Survey of the Gubernatorial Line Item Veto*, 50 S.C. L. Rev. 503 (1999), 843.

Holt, Michael F., *The Political Crisis of the 1850s* (1978), 38.

Holt, Wythe, *Virginia's Constitutional Convention of 1901-1902*, at 1-2, 24-25, 30-31, 104-05, 109, 254 (Garland Publishing, Inc. 1990), 43.

Horack, *Special Legislation: Another Twilight Zone*, 12 IND. L.J. 109 (1937), 38.

Howe, Daniel Walker, *The Political Culture of the American Whigs* (Chicago: University of Chicago Press, 1979), 34.

Hubsch, Allen W., *The Emerging Right to Education Under State Constitutional Law*, 65 TEMP. L. REV. 1325 (1992), 30.

Hurst, James Willard, *The Growth of American Law: The Law Makers* (Boston: Little, Brown, 1950), 28.

Jefferson to Samuel Kercheval, July 12, 1816, in Thomas Jefferson, *Writings: Autobiography; A Summary View of the Rights of British American; Notes on the State of Virginia; Public Papers; Addresses, Messages, and Replies; Miscellany; Letters* (New York: Library of America, 1984), 893.

Johnson, Alvin W., *The Legal Status of Church-State Relationships in the United States* (Minneapolis: University of Minnesota Press, 1934), 51.

Johnson, David Alan, *Founding the Far West: California, Oregon, and Nevada, 1840-1890*, at 101-04, 108, 120-21, 138-39, 140, 142, 189-90, 192-93 (University of California Press 1992), 42.

Karasik, Sidney Z., *Equal Protection of the Law Under the Federal and Illinois Constitutions: A Contrast in Unequal Treatment*, 30 DEPAUL L. REV. 263 (1981), 38.

Keller, Morton, *Affairs of State: Public Life in Late Nineteenth Century America* 111-14 (The Belknap Press of Harvard University 1977), 52.

Peters, Ellen A., "State Constitutional Law: Federalism in the Common Law Tradition," MICH. L. REV. 84 (1986), 33.

Peterson, Merrill D., *Democracy, Liberty & Property: The State Constitutional Conventions of the 1820s* (1966), 32.

Pollock, Stewart G., *Adequate and Independent State Grounds as a Means of Balancing the Relationship Between State and Federal Courts*, 63 TEX. L. REV. 977, 979 (1985), 50.

Porter, David O., *The Ripper Clause In State Constitutional Law: An Early Urban Experiment - Part I*, 1969 UTAH L. REV. 287, 306-11 (1969), 54.

Reardon, Paul C., "*The Massachusetts Constitution Marks a Milestone*," *Publius: The Journal of Federalism* 12 (Winter 1982): 45-55, 25.

Rebell, Michael A., "Educational Adequacy, Democracy, and the Courts," *in* National Research Council, Achieving High Educational Standards for All: Conference Summary 218 (Timothy Ready et al. eds., 2002), 570.

Remarks by California's Chief Justice, Ronald M. George, to the American Academy of Arts & Sciences, October 10, 2009 in Cambridge, Massachusetts, 927.

Roesler, Sannon M., *The Kansas Remedy by Due Course of Law Provision: Defining a Right to a Remedy*, 47 Kan. L. Rev. 655 (1999), 624.

Rush, Benjamin, "Thoughts upon the Mode of Education Proper in a Republic," in *Essays on Education in the Early Republic*, ed. Frederick Rudolph (Cambridge, Mass.: Harvard University Press, 1965), 3-23, 29.

Rush, B., *The Autobiography of Benjamin Rush* 113-14 at 153 (G. Corner ed. 1948), 23.

Ruud, Millard H., *No Law Shall Embrace More than One Subject*, 42 Minn.L.Rev. 389 (1958), 38.

Schmidt, David B., *Citizen Lawmakers: The Ballot Initiative Revolution* (1989), 31.

Schuman, David, *The Right to a Remedy,* 65 Temple L. Rev. 1197 (1992), 642, 665.

Selsam, John Paul, *The Pennsylvania Constitution of 1776* (New York: Octagon Books, 1971), 17.

Shaman, Jeffrey M., *Equality and Liberty in the Golden Age of State Constitutional Law* (2008), 179, 300, 331, 732.

Shaman, Jeffrey M., *On the 100th Anniversary of Lochner v. New York*, 72 Tenn. L. R. 455 (2005), 255.

Stevens, *History of Georgia*, II, 388 *quoted in* Fletcher M. Green, *Constitutional Development in the South Atlantic States, 1776-1860* (1930), 26.

Sturm, Albert L., *Methods of State Constitutional Reform*, University of Michigan Press, Ann Arbor (1954), 31.

Sturm, Albert L. and Craig, James B. Jr., *State Constitutional Commissions: Fifteen Years of Increasing Use*, 60.

Sturm, Albert L., "*The Development of American State Constitutions*," *Publius: The Journal of Federalism* 12 (Winger 1982): 57-98, 67.

Sutton, Jeffrey S., *San Antonio Independent School District v. Rodriguez and Its Aftermath*, 94 VA. L. REV. 1963 (2008), 138, 568.

Swindler, William, "Missouri Constitutions: History, Theory and Practice," 23 MISSOURI L. REV. 35-37 (January 1958), 54.

Swindler, William F., "Rights of Englishmen" Since 1776: Some Anglo-American Notes, 124 U. PA. L. REV. 1083 (1976), 7.

Swindler, William F., *State Constitutions for the 20th Century,* 50 NEB. L. REV. 577, 578 (1971), 63.

Tarr, G. Alan, *Constitutional Politics in the States, Contemporary Controversies and Historical Patterns*, p. 8 (Greenwood Press 1996), 39.

Thach, C., Jr., *The Creation of the Presidency, 1775-1789,* at 110-16; E. Douglass, (1955), 24.

The Federalist No. 49, ed. Jacob E. Cooke (Middletown, Conn.: Wesleyan University Press, 1961), 895.

Thompson, Barton H. Jr., *The Environment and Natural Resources* (Chapter Ten) in G. Alan Tarr & Robert E. Williams (eds.) *State Constitutions in the 21st Century* (2006), 731.

Thro, William E., Note, *To Render Them Safe: The Analysis of State Constitutional Provisions in Public School Finance Reform Litigation*, 75 VA. L. REV. 1639, 1661-70 (1989), 30.

Tribe, *American Constitutional Law*, p. 386, 63.

Tyack, David and James, Thomas James and Benavot, Aaron, *Law and the Shaping of Public Education*, 1785-1954 (Madison: University of Wisconsin Press, 1987), 28.

Tyack, David and James, Thomas, "State Government and American Public Education: Exploring the 'Primeval Forest,'" *History of Education Quarterly* 26 (1986): 39-69, 29.

Viteritti, Joseph P., *Blaine's Wake: School Choice, The First Amendment, and State Constitutional Law,* 22 HARV. J. L. & PUB. POL'Y 657 (1998), 565.

Wechsler, Herbert, The Political Safeguards of Federalism: The Role of the States in the Composition and Selection of the National Government, 54 COLUM. L. REV. 543 (1954), 7.

Wheeler, Harvey, *The Rise and Fall of Political Democracy,* p. 16, Center for the Study of Democratic Institutions, Santa Barbara (1966), 60.

Wiecek, William M., *State Protection of Personal Liberty: Remembering the Future, in Toward a Usable Past: Liberty Under State Constitution,* 371, 379-80 (University of Georgia Press 1991), 42.

Williams, Robert F., *Are State Constitutional Conventions Things of the Past? The Increasing Role of the Constitutional Commission in State Constitutional Change,* 1 HOFSTRA L. & POLY'S SYMP. 1 (1996), 30.

Williams, Robert F., *State Constitutional Law: Cases and Materials* 76-77 (2d ed. 1993) *citing* Chapter 180, *Fiftieth Congress,* Second Session 1889, 29.

Williams, Robert F., *State Constitutional Law Processes,* 24 WM. & MARY L. REV. 169, 173 (1983), 12.

Williams, Robert F., *Foreword: The Importance of an Independent State Constitutional Equality Doctrine in School Finance Cases and Beyond,* 24 CONN. L. REV. 675 (1992), 30.

Williams, Robert F., *The State Constitutions of the Founding Decade: Pennsylvania's Radical 1776 Constitution and its Influences On American Constitutionalism,* 62 TEMP. L. REV. 541 (1989), 14.

Williams, Robert F., *The New Jersey State Constitution: A Reference Guide* (Wesptport, Conn.: Greenwood Press, 1990), 13-16, 64.

Wisdom, John M., *Foreword: The Ever-Whirling Wheels of American Federalism,* 59 NOTRE DAME L. REV. 1063 (1984), 62.

Wood, Gordon S., *State Constitution-Making in the American Revolution,* 24 RUTGERS L.J. 911, 921 (1993), 19.

Wood, Gordon S., The Creation of the American Republic 1776-1787 (1969), 7.

Young, Alfred F., *The Democratic Republicans of New York: The Origins 1763-1797,* 20-21 (1967), 24.

Constitutions

Alaska Const. art. VIII, § 15, 5.

Ark. Const. art. II, § 24, 524.

Cal. Const. art. I, § 4, 545.

Cal. Const. art. IX, § 5, 583.

Conn. Const. Ordinance of 1776, art. I, *reprinted in* 2 *Sources and Documents of United State Constitutions* 143-44 (William F. Swindler ed., 1973-1979) [hereinafter State Constitutions], 19.

1776 Constitution of the State of Delaware, art. 26, 19

Del. Const. of 1792, art. 2 §§ 8, 9; N.Y. Const. of 1777, § XV; Pa. Const. of 1776, §§ 13, 14, 19.

Declaration of Rights and Fundamental Rules of the Delaware State of 1776, § 1, 18.

Del. Declaration of Rights of 1776, reprinted in 2 State Constitutions, 19.

Fla. Const. art. I, § 3, 546.

Haw. Const. art I, § 4, xxi.

Ill. Const. art. I, § 3, 524.

Ind. Const. art. 8, § 1, 583.

Md. Const. of 1776, Declaration of Rights art. XX and XXXVIII, 19

Md. Const. art. VIII, § 1, 583.

Md. Declaration of Rights of 1776, reprinted in 4 State Constitutions, 19.

Mass. Const. art. 46, § 1, 523.

Mass. Const. of 1780, pt. I, *reprinted in* 5 State Constitutions, 19.

Minn. Const. art. I, § 16, 524, 536.

Mont. Const. art. X, § 1, cl. 3, 583.

Neb. Const. art. I, § 4, 524.

Neb. Const. art. VII, § 1, 583.

N.H. Const. of 1784, pt. 1, *reprinted in* 6 State Constitutions, 19.

N.J. Const. art. I, § 4, 546.

Other Sources

Letter from John Adams to William Hooper (ante Mar. 27, 1776), *in* 4 *Papers of John Adams* 73-78 (Robert J. Taylor ed., 1979), 21.

Letter from William Hooper to Fifth Provincial Congress (Oct. 26, 1776), *in* 10 *The Colonial Records of North Carolina* 862-70 (William L. Saunders ed., Raleigh, Josephus Daniels, Printer to the State, 1890), 21.

Letter from Philip Livingston, James Duane, and William Duer to Abraham TenBroeck (Apr. 19, 1777), *reprinted in* 6 LETTERS FROM THE DELEGATES TO CONGRESS, *supra* note 130, at 686-87, 23.

Letters of Benjamin Rush 1761-1792, at 114-15 (L. Butterfield ed. 1941), *quoted in* J, 18.

The Constitutional Status of Tort Law: Due Process and the Right to a Law for the Redress of Wrongs, 115 YALE L.J. 524 (2005), 665.

The Federal and State Constitutions, Colonial Charters, and Other Organic Laws of the States, Territories, and Colonies Now or Heretofore Forming the United States of America, ed. Francis N. Thorpe (Washington, D.C.: U.S. Government Printing Office, 1909), 2:961, 29.

The Federalist No. 83, ed. Jacob E. Cooke (Middletown, Conn.: Wesleyan University Press, 1961) p. 582, 61.

The Federalist No. 1, ed. Jacob E. Cooke (Middletown, Conn.: Wesleyan University Press, 1961) p. 3, 15.

U.S. Congress, Senate, *Globe*, 39th Cong., 1st Sess. (1865-66), 2765, quoted in Richard C. Cortner, *The Supreme Court and the Second Bill of Rights: The Fourteenth Amendment and the Nationalization of Civil Liberties* (Madison: University of Wisconsin Press, 1981), 5, 50.

EXPLANATORY NOTE

The case book is designed to present a wide variety of materials in an accessible and interesting way. To that end, we have edited the opinions to remove unnecessary discussions, to eliminate unilluminating citations and to omit unhelpful footnotes. Our practice has been to use ellipses only when we have removed language from the opinion in the middle of a paragraph. Otherwise, whenever we have removed paragraphs, citations and footnotes, or even when we have omitted discussions at the beginning or end of a paragraph, we have not used ellipses. As to the (few) footnotes that remain, we have numbered them sequentially within each chapter and, where appropriate, have identified the original number of the footnote in an adjacent bracket. Through it all, the critical point is that we have created these abridged opinions to facilitate teaching an important subject, not to make legal research easier and above all not for the purpose of using the opinions as citations or quotations in legal pleadings. Before citing any of these materials, the lawyer should consult the original opinion or article.

ACKNOWLEDGEMENTS

Special thanks go to Michele Rutledge, who took on the herculean task of pulling the draft chapters together, of creating a uniform document and of putting up with a seemingly endless stream of edits. We also would like to thank several individuals who provided valuable research assistance to this project: Nathan Colvin, John Lillig, Mary K. Pritchett, Hyatt Shirkey, Chris Stocki, Stephen Tanner and Marjorie Yano.

PERMISSION TO REPRINT

The authors and publishers gratefully acknowledge permission to use excerpts from the following:

Mark Edward DeForrest, *An Overview and Evaluation of State Blaine Amendments: Origins, Scope, and First Amendment Concerns*, 26 Harv. J. L. & Pub. Pol'y. 551 (2003);

Martha Dragich, *State Constitutional Restriction on Legislative Procedure: Rethinking the Analysis of Original Purpose, Single Subject, and Clear Title Challenges*, 38 Harv. J. Legis. 103 (2001);

Peter J. Galie and Christopher Bopst, *The Constitutional Commission in New York: A Worthy Tradition*, 64 Alb. L. Rev. 1285 (2001);

Judith L. Maute, *Selecting Justice in State Courts: The Ballot Box or the Backroom?* 40 S. Tex. L. Rev. 1197 (2000);

Anne Permaloff, *Altering State Constitutions*, 33 Cumb. L. Rev. 217 (2003);

Shannon M. Roesler, *The Kansas Remedy By Due Course Of Law Provision: Defining A Right To A Remedy*, 47 Kan. L. Rev. 655 (1999);

Jeffrey M. Shaman, EQUALITY AND LIBERTY IN THE GOLDEN AGE OF STATE CONSTITUTIONAL LAW (Oxford University Press 2008);

Jeffrey S. Sutton, *Why Teach—and Why Study—State Constitutional Law*, 34 Okla. City Univ. L. Rev. 165 (2009);

Jeffrey S. Sutton, San Antonio Independent School District v. Rodriguez *and Its Aftermath*, 94 Va. L. Rev. 1963 (2008).

STATE CONSTITUTIONAL LAW
THE MODERN EXPERIENCE

CHAPTER I

INTRODUCTION

All law schools in this country offer a course called "Constitutional Law," and virtually all of these courses (and textbooks) teach just half of the story. They teach the course from the perspective of the Federal Constitution, infrequently mentioning, much less developing, the role of the State Constitutions in our system of government and laws. In one sense, that is quite understandable; it is difficult enough to teach all of *federal* constitutional law in a full-year course. In another sense, it is a missed opportunity, as too many students never learn the full story.

When the Framers "split the atom of sovereignty," *U.S. Term Limits, Inc. v. Thornton*, 514 U.S. 779, 838 (1995) (Kennedy, J., concurring), they created a dual system of government, one with two sets of sovereigns for every corner of the country, not just one. It is a singularly American innovation, the one idea that the Framers could have patented because no other government had tried it and no political philosopher had ever proposed it. The American experiment launched a governmental structure with horizontal separation of powers (dividing the executive, legislative and judicial branches at the national level) *and* vertical separation of powers (dividing the national and the state governments).

In this country, we thus have 51 Constitutions—51 charters of government that simultaneously empower and constrain: that give two sets of sovereigns in any one location in the country the power to regulate most areas of American life and that limit those regulations through individual-liberty guarantees and other limitations on the legislative and executive branches. American constitutional law is not the study of *federal* constitutional law, and it is not the study of *state* constitutional law. A full understanding of the one cannot be understood without an appreciation of the other. To think otherwise about the matter is akin to taking a course on civil procedure without learning that there are state court procedures as well as federal ones.

While it is not the objective of this textbook to cover *all* of Constitutional Law—to cover the subject from the perspective of all of its federal and state counterparts—it is our mission to correct the imbalance. Our focus is on the 50 State Constitutions, yet our method of presentation emphasizes the interrelation of the two sets of constitutions, frequently explaining how the U.S. Constitution deals with an issue before explaining how the State Constitutions handle it or in some instances explaining how the State Constitutions contain provisions that have no parallel in the U.S. Constitution.

Like most torts, property and contracts textbooks, this case book uses decisions from courts throughout the country. It does not focus on the constitutions or cases from any one State but surveys the most interesting and thoughtful cases from all of the States.

The book covers three distinct topics. The first chapter is historical. It explains the framing of the State Constitutions, discussing the pre-1789 Constitutions and showing how they influenced each other and how they eventually laid the foundation for many components of the U.S. Constitution. It then addresses the later State Constitutions and the waves of amendments to all State Constitutions through various eras in American history. The middle part of the case book makes up the overwhelming majority of it. Here we address a variety of civil and criminal individual-liberty guarantees of the State Constitutions. Some, as we show, have exact counterparts in the U.S. Constitution and often were the models for the first eight provisions of the federal Bill of Rights. Others have similarities to their federal cousins. And still others have no counterparts in the U.S. Constitution. The last two chapters address the branches of state government. They consider the grants of authority to the three divisions of state government and the structural limitations placed on that power. They then consider the amendment process for State Constitutions, which generally require just a majority vote. It might be said that the U.S. Constitution is too difficult to amend, and the State Constitutions are too easy to amend, and we will consider the impact of the amendment procedure on the development of state constitutional law.

Why take a class in state constitutional law? A lawyer's duty to a client is a good place to start. Our 51 constitutions place two sets of constitutional limitations on the validity of (nearly) every state and local law. Lawyers are problem solvers, and when a state or local law stands in the way of a client's objective, it generally will matter little to the client whether the lawyer manages to strike down the law on federal or state grounds. A constitutional claimant needs to win just once. No State permits a law invalidated under its constitution to be enforced; and the Supremacy Clause of the United States Constitution prohibits any State from enforcing laws invalidated under the Federal Constitution. A necessary consequence of a system of dual sovereignty is that it permits serial, or at least dual, claims of unconstitutionality. The first reason for studying state constitutional law, then, is simple: Lawyers are paid to solve problems for their clients, and one way to do that is to win cases. Lawyers paid to help a client win a case will have some explaining to do if they fail to consider taking two shots, rather than just one, at invalidating a state or local law.

State constitutional law not only gives the client two chances to win, but in some settings it may give the client a *better* chance to win. The

United States Supreme Court is at a considerable disadvantage relative to the state courts when it comes to defining constitutional rights and crafting constitutional remedies in many areas of the law. Because the Supreme Court must announce rights and remedies for fifty States, one National Government and over 300 million people, it is more constrained than a state supreme court addressing a difficult problem for one State and, say, fifteen million people. That reality begins to explain why, as you will read in Chapter XI, the United States Supreme Court might reject a constitutional challenge to Texas's system for funding public education, but the Texas Supreme Court later would grant relief in a similar challenge filed under the Texas Constitution. *Compare San Antonio Indep. Sch. Dist. v. Rodriguez*, 411 U.S. 1 (1973), *with Edgewood Indep. Sch. Dist. v. Kirby*, 777 S.W.2d 391 (Tex. 1989). In some settings, the challenge of imposing a constitutional solution on the whole country at once will increase the likelihood that federal constitutional law will be under enforced or that a "federalism discount" will be applied to the right. State courts face no such problem in construing their own constitutions.

State courts also have a freer hand in doing something the Supreme Court cannot: allowing local conditions and traditions to affect their interpretation of a constitutional guarantee and the remedies imposed to implement that guarantee. The Alaska Supreme Court might gauge privacy issues differently from other States or for that matter the United States Supreme Court. The Montana Supreme Court might gauge property rights differently from other States or the United States Supreme Court. Or the Utah and Rhode Island Supreme Courts might gauge free-exercise rights differently from other state courts. State constitutional law respects—and embraces—differences between and among the States by allowing fifty constitutions to be interpreted differently to account for these differences in culture, geography and history. In state constitutional law, as in state legislation, the States may be "laboratories of experimentation." *New State Ice Co. v. Liebmann*, 285 U.S. 262, 311 (1932) (Brandeis, J., dissenting).

State constitutional law also holds promise as a way to facilitate the development of *federal* constitutional law. For too long, we have lived in a top-down constitutional world, in which the United States Supreme Court announces a ruling, and the state supreme courts move in lockstep in construing the counterpart guarantees of their own constitutions. Why not do the reverse? That is the way other areas of the law traditionally have developed, be it tort, property or contract law. In these settings, the state courts are the vanguard—the first ones to decide whether to embrace or reject innovative legal claims. Over time, the market of common law decisions identifies winners and losers. An opinion by a Cardozo or a Traynor might become the benchmark, after which other state courts opt to follow that view or variations on it. Or the state courts might go their separate ways. In either event, the federal courts profit from the experience, as they can choose whether to federalize the issue *after* learning the strengths and weaknesses of the competing ways of addressing the problem.

Once the student learns that State Constitutions are documents of independent force—that the meaning of state guarantees is a matter for the state courts, not the U.S. Supreme Court, to resolve—it opens up a new way of thinking about constitutional law. By the second or third year of law school, most students come to appreciate that many constitutional issues do not lend themselves to one-size-fits-all solutions. It is one thing to apply the requirement that the President be thirty-five years of age, Art. II, §1, cl. 5, U.S. Const., or a requirement that the Governor of a State be thirty years of age, Ala. Const. Art. V, §117. Miss. Const. Art. V, § 117. But it is quite another to decipher what the more-generalized individual-liberty guarantees—say, due process or free speech—mean when they appear in the State and Federal Constitutions.

As to these vexing areas of the law, the state courts may adopt their own interpretations of parallel (or somewhat parallel) guarantees found in their own constitutions. When difficult areas of constitutional litigation arise, why assume that the United States Supreme Court is the only supreme court in the country capable of offering an insightful solution to a difficult problem? Three distinct levels of scrutiny—rational basis, intermediate or strict—may be the best way to assess equal-protection claims, but they are hardly the self-ordained way. Rational-basis review may be the best way to assess free-exercise challenges to neutral, generally applicable laws as a matter of national constitutional law, *see Employment Div., Dep't of Human Res. of Or. v. Smith*, 494 U.S. 872 (1990), but the same may not be true for each state constitution, *see Humphrey v. Lane*, 728 N.E.2d 1039, 1043 (Ohio 2000). A modest standard for enforcing the Takings Clause may work for national taking-of-property claims, *see Kelo v. City of New London*, 545 U.S. 469, 483 (2005), but it is by no means clear that every State should embrace the same approach in addressing similar challenges under its own constitution, *see Bd. of County Comm'rs of Muskogee County v. Lowery*, 136 P.3d 639, 652 (Okla. 2006). The more difficult the constitutional question, as these cases show, the more indeterminate the answer may be. In these settings, it may be appropriate to have fifty-one imperfect solutions rather than one imperfect solution—particularly when imperfection may be something we invariably will have to live with in a given area.

In some cases, the *only* way a lawyer can win a case is through the state constitution because it is the only constitution with a provision on point. State constitutions have a variety of clauses found nowhere in the

United States Constitution: right-to-remedy clauses, single-subject clauses, uniform-law clauses, to name a few. And some state constitutions have exotic clauses found in few, if any, other state constitutions. The Ohio Constitution, for example, bars the taxation of food sold for human consumption, *see* Ohio Const. art. XII, § 13, and the Alaska Constitution generally forbids the creation of any "exclusive right or special privilege of fishery" within Alaskan waters, Alaska Const. art. VIII, § 15.

If ever there were a propitious time for thinking twice about the meaning of "constitutional law"—its federal and state components—now may be it. Many of the most ground-breaking constitutional disputes of the day are being waged in the state courts under the state constitutions. Whether it is school funding, property rights, the definition of marriage or other modern rights disputes, the state courts in recent years have gone from being civil-rights followers to leaders. There is, indeed, a softer side to federalism: A loss in the United States Supreme Court no longer inevitably foreshadows a loss in the state courts when the claim is premised on a state constitutional counterpart. And, as many of these debates confirm, state constitutional litigation can proceed without waiting for, or worrying about, the shadow of federal constitutional law.

In the twenty-first century, no lawyer worth his or her salt can be a good advocate without appreciating the possibility—the value—of raising state constitutional claims when representing a client. Ask many students why they went to law school, and you will find a common answer among many of them: the opportunity to make a difference in the great issues of the day. No lawyer can take advantage of these opportunities without understanding state constitutional law. *See generally* Jeffrey S. Sutton, *"Why Teach – and Why Study – State Constitutional Law,"* 34 Okla. City Univ. L. Rev. 165 (Summer 2009).

CHAPTER II[1]

THE FRAMING OF STATE CONSTITUTIONS AND THEIR HISTORY

PREFACE

State frameworks of government are the foundation of American constitutional law. The purpose and function of a state constitution has evolved. A knowledge of the origins and history of state constitutions is essential to understanding federalism in the United States.[2] One eminent historian, James Bryce, has said:

> The State Constitutions are the oldest things in the political history of America, for they are continuations and representatives of the royal colonial charters, whereby the earliest English settlements in America were created ...

> They are full of interest; and he [or she] who would understand the changes that have passed over American Democracy will find far more instruction in the study of the state government than of the Federal Constitution. ...

> Their interest is all the greater, because the succession of Constitutions and amendments to Constitutions from 1776 till today enables the annals of legislation and political sentiment to be read in these documents more easily and succinctly than in any similar series of laws in any other country. They are a mine of instruction for the natural history of democratic communities.[3]

A. STATE CONSTITUTIONS' NASCENCY

Colonial Interregnum Concerns

The armed conflict between the American colonies and England began on April 19, 1775 at the Battle of Lexington and Concord in Massachusetts. The Second Continental Congress[4] was scheduled to meet

---

1 This chapter is taken from the thesis written by Randy J. Holland for a Master of Law in the Judicial Process at the University of Virginia School of Law.

[2] See generally A.E. Dick Howard, The Road From Runnymede: Magna Carta and Constitutionalism in America 203-15 (1968); Gordon S. Wood, The Creation of the American Republic 1776-1787 (1969); Brevard Crihfield & Frank Smothers, The States in the Federal System, 34 N.Y.U. L. REV. 1018 (1959); Frank P. Grad, The State Constitution: Its Function and Form for Our Time, 54 VA. L. REV. 928 (1968); Thomas C. Grey, Origins of the Unwritten Constitution: Fundamental Law in American Revolutionary Thought, 30 STAN. L. REV. 843 (1978); William F. Swindler, "Rights of Englishmen" Since 1776: Some Anglo-American Notes, 124 U. PA. L. REV. 1083 (1976); Herbert Wechsler, The Political Safeguards of Federalism: The Role of the States in the Composition and Selection of the National Government, 54 COLUM. L. REV. 543 (1954).

[3] James Bryce, 1 *The American Commonwealth* 434 2d rev., ed. (New York: Macmillan 1981).

[4]The First Continental Congress adjourned in October 1774.

on May 10, 1775. John Adams, a Massachusetts delegate urged the Continental Congress to do six things: first, recommend that each colony arrest and detain all officers of the King until Boston was free from British martial law; second, recommend that each colony immediately form "Governments for themselves, under their own Authority;" third, declare that the colonies were free and or independent sovereign states; fourth, communicate to the King that the colonies were desirous of resolving all differences; fifth, threaten to ally with France, Spain, and other European powers; sixth, appoint a general to command the army outside of Boston and recognize it as the "Continental Army."[5] Adams' six-part action plan for all of the American colonies made no immediate progress in the Continental Congress.

On June 2, 1775, the provincial Congress of Massachusetts requested that the Continental Congress advise it about exercising the "powers of civil government."[6] The inquiry suggested that Massachusetts contemplated two choices: "it could either accept a constitution drafted by the Continental Congress for all the colonies, or it could draw up its own constitution."[7] Although John Adams spoke in favor of forming new governments for each colony and creating a "Confederacy of States," such ideas were "strange and terrible Doctrines" to a majority of the delegates.[8]

The Continental Congress considered the request from Massachusetts for one week. Its two-part reply was carefully formulated to accommodate those delegates who still hoped for a reconciliation with Britain.[9] First, the Continental Congress declared Parliament's violation of the Massachusetts Charter of 1691 unconstitutional.[10] Second, it advised Massachusetts to hold new elections and to consider the officers of governor and lieutenant governor vacant until the King appointed successors who would adhere to the provisions of the Massachusetts Charter.[11] Those recommendations were acted upon immediately.

---

[5]Willi Paul Adams, The First American Constitutions: Republican Ideology and the Making of the State Constitutions in the Revolutionary Era 51-52 (1980).

[6]*Id.* at 53.

[7]*Id.* (citing 2 JOURNALS OF THE CONTINENTAL CONGRESS, 1774-1789, 76-78 (Worthington C. Ford et al. eds., 1904-1937).

[8] *Id.* at 53; 3 Diary and Autobiography of John Adams 351-52 (L.H. Butterfield et al. eds., 1961); 1 Letters of Members of the Continental Congress 106-09 (Edmund C. Burnett ed., 1921-1936).

[9] Willi Paul Adams, The First American Constitutions: Republican Ideology and the Making of the State Constitutions in the Revolutionary Era 54 (1980).

[10] *Id.*

[11] Willi Paul Adams, The First American Constitutions: Republican Ideology and the Making of the State Constitutions in the Revolutionary Era 54 (1980).

On October 18, 1775, New Hampshire asked the same question that Massachusetts had promulgated to the Continental Congress in May: "How could the administration of justice and other badly neglected governmental functions best be reorganized?"[12] Although the question seemed innocuous, it was intended to be rhetorical by those "who had given up hope for reconciliation with crown and Parliament."[13] As such, it was an effort to force the Continental Congress to squarely confront the issue of independence.

As long as the majority of the delegates in the Congress were not prepared to pursue independence openly, the answers that were sent to the provincial capitals had to be reconcilable with British constitutional law; an unguarded recommendation to draft new constitutions would rightly have been considered as equivalent to declaring independence.[14]

An assemblage of delegates from throughout New Hampshire was convened during the close of 1775 in violation of British law.[15] The colony of New Hampshire adopted a constitution on January 6, 1776.[16] This was the first constitution that had ever been written without approval from the reigning English monarch or Parliament.[17]

Anticipating Independence

In early 1776, a break with England was so inevitable that the American colonies all began to anticipate and debate the parameters of self-governance. A period of interregnum began following the Battle of Lexington and Concord. The remaining vestiges of royal authority were destined to be ephemeral.

On January 9, 1776, a pamphlet entitled *Common Sense* was published in Philadelphia by Thomas Paine, a recently immigrated English tradesman. According to Paine, the proper foundation for successful self-governance was political egalitarianism. Paine urged each colony to form simple republican governments operated by unicameral legislatures and chosen by an expanded electoral franchise.

---

[12] 3 Journals of the Continental Congress, 1774-1789, 298 (Worthington C. Ford et al. eds., 1904-1937).

[13] Willi Paul Adams, The First American Constitutions: Republican Ideology and the Making of the State Constitutions in the Revolutionary Era 56 (1980).

[14] *Id.*

[15] *Id.*

[16] Willi Paul Adams, The First American Constitutions: Republican Ideology and the Making of the State Constitutions in the Revolutionary Era 5 (1980).

[17] *Id.*

Paine described the process of setting forth principles of popular sovereignty in written charters or constitutions as America's coronation of the rule of law. Thomas Paine made the following analogy:

> Let a day be solemnly set apart for proclaiming the charter; let it be brought forth placed on the divine law, the Word of God; let a crown be placed thereon, by which the world may know, that so far as we approve of monarchy, that in America the law is king. For as in absolute governments the king is law, so in free countries the law ought to be king; and there ought to be no other. But lest any ill use should afterwards arise, let the crown at the conclusion of the ceremony be demolished, and scattered among the people whose right it is. [18]

The unique opportunity for self-determination that history had afforded the American colonies was characterized by Thomas Paine as the beginning of a new world:

> The present time, likewise, is that peculiar time which never happens to a nation but once, viz. the time of forming itself into a government. Most nations have let slip the opportunity, and by that means have been compelled to receive laws from their conquerors, instead of making laws for themselves. First, they had a king, and then a form of government;...but from the errors of other nations let us learn wisdom, and lay hold of the present opportunity.... We have every opportunity and every encouragement before us, to form the noblest, purest constitution on the face of the earth. We have it in our power to begin the world over again.[19]

John Adams, like Paine, also described the American colonies' prospect of formulating an ideal political structure in epoch terms:

> You and I, my dear friend, have been sent into life at a time when the greatest lawgivers of antiquity would have wished to live. How few of the human race have ever enjoyed an opportunity of making an election of government...for themselves or their children! When, before the present epocha, had three millions of people full power and a fair opportunity to form and establish the wisest and happiest government that human wisdom can contrive?[20]

Adams responded to Paine's *Common Sense* with an alternative framework for new colonial governments. Adams' pamphlet, *Thoughts on Government*, advocated a system for self-governance that distributed power between a bicameral legislature and a carefully restrained executive. Although Adams contemplated that the paramount power would be vested in a popularly elected lower legislative body, Adams proposed to limit the holding of public office and the exercise of voting rights to landowners.

---

[18] Common Sense, in 1 The Complete Writings of Thomas Paine 29 (Philip S. Foner ed., 1945).

[19] *Id.* at 36-37, 45 (Philip S. Foner ed., 1945).

[20] John Adams, Thoughts on Government, in 4 The Works of John Adams 200 (Charles Francis Adams ed., 1850-1856).

Thus, in early 1776, Thomas Paine and John Adams identified the theories and framed the issues of state constitutional debates for the next ten years. How would the new governments be structured? Who would participate in the new governments, directly as office holders, and indirectly as voters?

The situation extant in most of the American colonies during the spring of 1776 is depicted in the memoirs of William Moultrie about South Carolina.

> The affairs of the province became too unwieldly for the management of [the provincial] Congress, and the council of safety or general committee: Everything was running into confusion, and although our criminal laws were still of force, yet they were virtually repealed for want of proper officers to execute them, all those under the royal authority being suspended from office, it was therefore thought absolutely necessary to frame a constitution for the purpose of forming a regular system of government, and for appointing public officers for the different departments to put the laws into execution.[21]

On March 26, 1776, a provincial congress inspired by New Hampshire's leadership, as well as by Adams' and Paine's writing, adopted a temporary constitution for the "colony" of South Carolina.

State Constitutions Authorized

As the collective estrangement between the American colonies and the British monarch mounted, the need for stabilizing each colony's internal affairs intensified. In May of 1776, all hope of reconciliation was abandoned. The Second Continental Congress advised the colonies to form new governments.[22] Its resolutions of May 10, 1776,[23] recommended to the respective assemblies and conventions of the "United Colonies":

> where no government sufficient to the exigencies of their affairs, have been hitherto established to adopt such Government as shall, in the Opinion of the Representatives of the People, best conduce to the Happiness and Safety of their Constituents in particular and America in general.[24]

The American colonies were in agreement that the *sine qua non* of government was consent. There was widespread disagreement, however,

---

[21] William Moultrie, 1 Memoirs of the American Revolution, So Far as It Related to the States of North and South Carolina, and Georgia 125 (1802).

[22] Gordon S. Wood, The Creation of the American Republic 1776-1787, 131-32 (1969).

[23] The resolution was adopted May 10, 1776. A preamble was added on May 15, 1776. Willi Paul Adams, The First American Constitutions: Republican Ideology and the Making of the State Constitutions in the Revolutionary Era 61 (1980). John Adams served with Edward Rutledge of South Carolina and Richard Henry Lee of Virginia on the committee that drafted the resolution. See Gordon S. Wood, The Creation of the American Republic 1776-1787, 131-32 (1969)..

[24] Willi Paul Adams, The First American Constitutions: Republican Ideology and the Making of the State Constitutions in the Revolutionary Era 61 (1980).

about "(1) who is to give consent, (2) to whom is consent given, (3) what act or acts constitute giving consent, and (4) over what range of issues must consent be permanently withheld?"[25]

The Continental Congress considered, but eventually declined to recommend any model format of governance for the states to adopt.[26] It had been impossible to reach an agreement on the format for a model state constitution.[27] The Continental Congress did recommend, however, that the new state constitutions be based on "the authority of the people."[28]

On May 11, 1776, the provincial congress of North Carolina passed several resolutions that comprised "a temporary Civil Constitution."[29] In essence, that "constitution" established a safety council for all of North Carolina. The thirteen member council was charged with exercising all powers of government, consistent with prior legislative enactments, until the provincial congress reconvened.[30]

A Virginia convention gathered at Williamsburg in May of 1776. It adopted a two-fold resolution on May 15, 1776. First, Virginia's delegates in Philadelphia were instructed to move for independence.[31] Second, the Virginia delegates in Williamsburg were directed to appoint a committee "to prepare a DECLARATION OF RIGHTS, and such a plan of government as will be most likely to maintain peace and order in this colony, and secure substantial and equal liberty to the people."[32] In examining these actions by the Virginians gathered in Williamsburg, Professor Howard aptly observed:

> Those members of the 1776 convention steeped in Lockean notions of the social contract might well have considered themselves in a "state of nature" upon the

---

[25] Donald S. Lutz, Popular Consent and Popular Control: Whig Political Theory in the Early State Constitutions 1-2, 45 (1980).

[26] Robert F. Williams, State Constitutional Law Processes, 24 WM. & MARY L. REV. 169, 173 (1983).

[27] Willi Paul Adams, The First American Constitutions: Republican Ideology and the Making of the State Constitutions in the Revolutionary Era 56 (1980).

[28] Willi Paul Adams, The First American Constitutions: Republican Ideology and the Making of the State Constitutions in the Revolutionary Era 100 (1980).

[29] Willi Paul Adams, The First American Constitutions: Republican Ideology and the Making of the State Constitutions in the Revolutionary Era 81 (1980).

[30] Id.

[31] A.E. Dick Howard, The Road From Runnymede: Magna Carta and Constitutionalism in America, 54 U.VA.L.REV. 816, 820 (1968).

[32] 1 Jefferson Papers 290-91 (Boyd ed.) cited by A.E. Dick Howard, The Road From Runnymede: Magna Carta and Constitutionalism in America, 54 U. VA. L. REV. 816, 820 (1968).

dissolution of the bond with Great Britain. Thus, to declare man's natural rights was a logical step en route to forming a new social compact.[33]

On May 26, 1776, John Adams articulated the proposition and then posed a question to which there was no uniform response: "It is certain, in theory, that the only moral foundation of government is, the consent of the people. But to what extent shall we carry this principle?"[34] On June 3, 1776, John Adams wrote to Patrick Henry that the "natural course and order of things [should be] for every colony to institute a government; for all the colonies to confederate, and define the limits of the continental Constitution; then to declare the colonies a sovereign state, or a number of confederated sovereign states; and last of all, to form treaties with foreign powers."[35] Adams' letter continued, however, with a recognition that there was not enough time for such a logical and orderly progression: "But I fear we cannot proceed systematically, and that we shall be obliged to declare ourselves independent States, before we confederate, and indeed before all the colonies have established their governments."[36]

The provincial congress of New Jersey convened on June 10, 1776. According to its journal entries, a resolution was passed on June 21 to follow the May 15 recommendation of the Continental Congress and to draft a constitution. New Jersey's first constitution was passed like a legislative act and became effective immediately on July 2, 1776.[37]

On June 12, 1776, the provincial congress of Virginia adopted the first declaration of rights that was separate from the text of a state constitution. The Virginia Constitution was ratified on June 29, 1776. Virginia's bifurcated format was frequently replicated in charters that were subsequently adopted by other states. The Virginia Declaration of Rights rejected the British monarchy as a basis for government and instead asserted that "all power is vested in and consequently derived from the people..." Nevertheless, the Virginia Declaration of Rights also included "restatement of English principles—the principles of the Magna Charta, the Petition of Right, the Commonwealth Parliament, and the Revolution of 1688."[38]

---

[33] A.E. Dick Howard, The Road From Runnymede: Magna Carta and Constitutionalism in America 820 (1968).

[34] John Adams to James Sullivan, May 26, 1776, in 9 The Works of John Adams 375 (Charles Francis Adams ed., 1850-1856).

[35] Correspondence from John Adams to Patrick Henry, June 3, 1776, in 1 Letters of Members of the Continental Congress 47 (Edmund C. Burnett ed., 1921-1936).

[36] Id.

[37] Charles R. Erdman, The New Jersey Constitution of 1776 (Princeton, N.J. 1929).

[38] A.E. Dick Howard, The Road From Runnymede: Magna Carta and Constitutionalism in America, 54 U.VA.L.REV. 823 (1968).

The state constitutions of New Hampshire, South Carolina, New Jersey, and Virginia, were enacted prior to the Declaration of Independence and were all intended to be provisional until the future of the American colonies' relationship with England had been resolved.

B. FIRST STATE CONSTITUTIONAL FORAYS

One noted constitutional scholar, Benjamin Wright, has stated that 1776 must "rank with 1787 as one of the two most significant years in the history of modern constitution-making."[39] The first forays into state constitution-making, after the Declaration of Independence, were completed within six months: Delaware (September 11, 1776); Pennsylvania (September 28, 1776); Maryland (November 8, 1776); North Carolina (December 14, 1776); Georgia (February 4, 1777).[40] Thus, by the end of 1776, eight state constitutions had been adopted and two more had been modified.[41]

Frameworks

Before the substantive content of those state constitutions could be debated, however, it was necessary to establish a process for drafting and adopting the proposed charters of government. The majority of the initial state constitutions were written by state legislatures.[42]

Although the initial state constitutions introduced concepts of representative democracy, they also carried over many provisions from each new state's prior colonial charter or propriety grant. The first state constitutions also perpetuated the individual liberties and property rights that had been afforded to American colonists by the English common law. In lieu of formally adopting state constitutions, however, Connecticut and Rhode Island simply modified their colonial charters. In fact, those states functioned under their old charters, with modifications, until 1819 and 1842, respectively.

Two of the most prominent features of the initial state constitutions were written Declarations of Rights and the exaltation of legislative

---

[39] George A. Billias, American Constitutionalism and Europe, 1776-1848, in American Constitutionalism Abroad 13-14, 19-23 (George A. Billias ed. 1990).

[40] Robert F. Williams, The State Constitutions of the Founding Decade: Pennsylvania's Radical 1776 Constitution and its Influences On American Constitutionalism, 62 TEMP. L. REV. 541 (1989). See also Willi Paul Adams, The First American Constitutions: Republican Ideology and the Making of the State Constitutions in the Revolutionary Era 5 (1980). John A. Munroe, History of Delaware, 2d ed. (Newark: University of Delaware Press, 1984), 69-70.

[41] George A. Billias, American Constitutionalism and Europe, 1776-1848, in American Constitutionalism Abroad 13-14, 19-23 (George A. Billias ed. 1990).

[42] *Id.*

power. With the exception of the unicameral legislature provided for by the first Pennsylvania and Georgia constitutions, the initial state constitutions divided legislative power between upper and lower houses of elected representatives.[43] Membership in the lower houses was expanded through reapportionment, by broadening the base for suffrage eligibility, and by opening the qualifications for office holding.[44] The antecedent models for the upper houses in the first state constitutions were the colonial governor's councils. Therefore, the first state constitutions often authorized the upper house to perform both executive and legislative functions.[45]

The office of governor was profoundly transformed in the first state constitutions. As an instrument for implementing British policy during the colonial period, governors had been vested with prerogative powers that included an absolute veto of legislative acts. In reaction to England's colonial gubanatorial system, the first state constitutions frequently subordinated the executive to the legislature by denying the governor any veto and often providing for the governor to be appointed by the upper house.[46] Thus, the initial state constitutions changed the office of governor to a position that was almost entirely dependent upon and dominated by the newly constituted state legislatures.

Religion and Education

There was a consensus in the American colonies that moral virtue was desirable in public officials and integral to good citizenship. Nevertheless, the first state constitutions reflected diverse approaches to the relationship of church and state, although most included some form of religious test for office holders.[47] The Maryland Constitution of 1776 empowered the legislature with the discretionary authority "to lay a general and equal tax,

---

[43] The Federalist No. 1, ed. Jacob E. Cooke (Middletown, Conn.: Wesleyan University Press, 1961) p. 3.

[44] See Donald L. Lutz, Political Participation in Eighteenth Century America Toward a Usable Past: Liberty Under State Constitutions, edited by Paul Finkelman and Stephen E. Gottleib, University of Georgia Pres (1991).

[45] Robert F. Williams, *The State Constitutions of the Founding Decade: Pennsylvania's Radical 1776 Constitution and its Influences On American Constitutionalism*, 62 TEMP. L. REV. 541 (1989).

[46] *Id.*

[47] For a summary of religion provisions in early state constitutions see Morton Borden, *Jews, Turks, and Infidels* (Chapel Hill: University of North Carolina Press, 1984), 11-15. Stephen Botein, "*Religious Dimensions of the Early American State,*" in *Beyond Confederation: Origins of the Constitution and American National Identity*, ed. Richard Beeman, Sephen Botein, and Edward C. Carter II (Chapel Hill: University of North Carolina Press, 1987).

for the support of the Christian religion."[48] The New Jersey Constitution of 1776 provided that "there shall be no establishment of any one religious sect in this Province, in preference to another."[49] The North Carolina Constitution of 1776 restricted office holding to Protestant Christians, by precluding anyone "who shall hold religious principles incompatible with the freedom and safety of the state."[50] The New York Constitution of 1777 provided for the free exercise of religion to guard against "the bigotry and ambition of weak and wicked priests and princes [who] have scourged mankind."[51]

Several of the initial state constitutions included provisions that provided for the support or establishment of public schools. In the early part of 1776, John Adams had urged the states to provide for public education in their new constitutions.[52] According to Adams, a democratic republic could only be sustained over time by an educated electorate. The North Carolina Constitution of 1776 called for the establishment of "a school or schools."[53] The 1776 Pennsylvania Constitution contemplated the establishment of a public "school or schools" in each county and "one or more universities."[54]

Pennsylvania 1776

A convention to draft Pennsylvania's state constitution was convened at the State House in Philadelphia (Independence Hall) on July 15, 1776.[55] The Pennsylvania Convention adopted a Declaration of Rights on August 16, 1776. Pennsylvania's Declaration of Rights was patterned after Virginia's, but Pennsylvania's Article XII contained one of the broadest statements of speech and press freedom: "The People have a right to freedom of speech, and of writing, and publishing their sentiments; therefore the freedom of the press ought not to be restrained." Article XVI provided: "That the people have a right to assemble together, to consult for their common good, to instruct their representatives, and to apply to the legislature for redress of grievances, by address, petition or remonstrance."

Pennsylvania's Frame of Government also protected various rights. For example, Section 35 specified: "The printing presses shall be free to every

---

[48] Md. Const. (1776), Declaration of Rights, § 33.

[49] N.J. Const. (1776), § 19.

[50] N.C. Const. (1776), § 32.

[51] N.Y. Const. (1777), § 38.

[52] John Adams, *Thoughts on Government* (Boston, 1776), in *American Political Writing*, ed. Hyneman and Lutz, 1:407.

[53] N.C. Const. § 41, in *Federal and State Constitutions*, ed. Thorpe, 5:2794.

[54] Pa. Const. § 44, in *Federal and State Constitutions*, ed. Thorpe, 5:3091.

[55] *See* R. Brunhouse, *The Counter-Revolution in Philadelphia 1776-1790* at 13 (1942).

person who undertakes to examine the proceedings of the legislature, or any part of government. Thus, Pennsylvania's Declaration of Rights and the Frame of Government operated in tandem to not only guarantee individual rights but to preserve the particular form of republican government that had been established for that state.[56]

The Frame of Government proposed by the Pennsylvania Convention on September 5, 1776, was adopted on September 28, 1776.[57] Pennsylvania's "ultra democratic" 1776 constitution was written by some of Thomas Paine's closest friends; Dr. Thomas Young, Judge George Brigan, and James Cannon.[58] Accordingly, many of the themes advanced by Paine in *Common Sense* were implemented in the 1776 Pennsylvania Constitution.

The unicameral legislature set forth in Section 2 of its Pennsylvania's 1776 Frame of Government was intended to eliminate any element of "aristocracy."[59] It was defended as the logical extension of prior unicameral legislatures in Pennsylvania with origins dating from William Penn's 1701 Charter of Privileges.[60] The lack of restraint on the unicameral legislature in Pennsylvania's 1776 Constitution was an intentional decision to prevent any "undemocratic" restriction on the will of the people's elected representatives.

The commitment to popular sovereignty in the 1776 Pennsylvania Constitution is further illustrated by two other provisions. First, ordinary statutory legislation, as distinguished from constitutional amendments in other states, did not become operative unless approved by two consecutive legislative sessions. Second, the legislation that passed the first session had to be published between sessions for the benefit of the voting public.[61]

---

[56] Palmer, *Liberties as Constitutional Provisions, 1776-1791*, in W. Nelson & R. Palmer, *Liberty and Community: Constitution and Rights in the Early American Republic*, 64, 68 (1987).

[57] *See* A. Blaustein & J. Sigler, *Constitutions That Made History* 20 (1988).

[58] Robert F. Williams, *The State Constitutions of the Founding Decade: Pennsylvania's Radical 1776 Constitution and its Influences on American Constitutionalism*, 62 TEMP. L. REV. 541, 544 (1989). *See also* John Paul Selsam, *The Pennsylvania Constitution of 1776* (New York: Octagon Books, 1971).

[59] Robert F. Williams, *The State Constitutions of the Founding Decade: Pennsylvania's Radical 1776 Constitution and its Influences on American Constitutionalism*, 62 Temp. L. Rev. 541 (1989).

[60] Nix & Schweitzer, Pennsylvania's Contributions to the Writing and the Ratification of the Constitution, 112 PA. MAG. HIST. 7 BIOG. 3, 8-9 (1988).

[61] John Paul Selsam, The Pennsylvania Constitution of 1776 (New York: Octagon Books, 1971).

Pennsylvania's 1776 Constitution, with its unicameral legislature, provided a national focal point for the competing arguments on many of the initial key state constitutional issues. John Adams was especially critical of the Pennsylvania Frame of Government. As Benjamin Rush recalled:

> So great was [Adams'] disapprobation of a government composed of a single legislature, that he said to me upon reading the first constitution of Pennsylvania "The people of your state will sooner or later fall upon their knees to the King of Great Britain to take them again under his protection, in order to deliver them from the tyranny of their own government."[62]

Rush wrote to Adams: "From you I learned to discover the danger of the Constitution of Pennsylvania."[63] One of North Carolina's delegates to the Continental Congress, also a member of the provincial congress working on the North Carolina Constitution, wrote to Samuel Johnson:

> You have seen the constitution of Pennsylvania - the motley mixture of limited monarchy and an execrable democracy - a beast without a head.[64]

Delaware 1776

The constitutional convention was an American innovation and was based on the concept of "the people as a constitutional power."[65] Delaware's 1776 Constitution was the first to be drafted by a convention elected expressly for that purpose.[66] The preamble to Delaware's 1776 Declaration of Rights and Fundamental Rules provided that "all government of right originates from the people, is founded in compact only, and instituted solely for the good of the whole."[67] The initial

---

[62] G. Corner at 142. See also D. Hawke, In the Midst of a Revolution 178 (discussion of Adams's dislike for the Pennsylvania Constitution).

[63] Letters of Benjamin Rush 1761-1792, at 114-15 (L. Butterfield ed. 1941), quoted in J. Coleman, Thomas McKean: Forgotten Leader of the Revolution, at 203 n. 56.

[64] Douglass, Thomas Burke, Disillusioned Democrat, 26 N.C. HIST. REV. 150, 157 (1950).

[65] R.R. Palmer, The Age of Democratic Revolution: The Challenge (Princeton: Princeton University Press, 1959), p. 215. See also Gordon S. Wood, The Creation of the American Republic 1776-1787 (New York: W. W. Norton, 1969), pp. 259-343.

[66] Donald S. Lutz, Popular Consent and Popular Control: Whig Political Theory in the Early State C Constitutions 1-2 (1980). John A. Munroe, History of Delaware, 2d ed. (Newark: University of Delaware Press, 1984), 69-70.

[67] Declaration of Rights and Fundamental Rules of the Delaware State of 1776, § 1. Many of the first state constitutions included "common good" clauses as "the guiding value for the exercise of legitimate government." Willi Paul Adams, The First American Constitutions: Republican Ideology and the Making of the State Constitutions in the Revolutionary Era 222 (1980). The state constitution adopted by North Carolina in 1776 also was accompanied by a declaration of rights. It began with the proclamation that: "[A]ll political power is vested in and derived from the people only." N.C. CONST. of 1776, reprinted in 5 F. Thorpe, American Charters, Constitutions and Organic Laws:

Constitutions of Georgia, Maryland, and North Carolina were also drafted by conventions. Each of those constitutional conventions, however, also discharged legislative functions.[68]

Delaware's initial constitution was typical of the first state constitutions by differing from the colonial charter it replaced in two important respects: it provided for more legislative and less executive power; and, it was preceded by a Declaration of Rights.[69] The 1776 Delaware Constitution was unique, however, in prohibiting the future importation of slaves.[70] The first constitutions of Delaware, Pennsylvania, and New York had provisions that mandated legislative meetings to be open to the public. Those same state constitutions also required that proceedings of the legislature be published.[71]

Declarations of Rights

A majority of the original thirteen states enacted separate declarations of rights along with their first state constitutions.[72] Some rights were also included within the next state constitutions. The initial separate declarations of rights were frequently written as statements of broad principles rather than legal codes. They were often articulated in an admonitory fashion, with words like "ought" and "should" rather than "shall" and "will."[73] Examples of such hortatory draftsmanship are: "no

---

1492-1908, at 2787 (1909). See also MD. CONST. of 1776, Declaration of Rights art. II; PA. CONST. of 1776, Declaration of Rights art. IV.

[68] Don E. Fehrenbacher, *Sectional Crisis and Southern Constitutionalism*, 84, LOUISIANA STATE UNIVERSITY PRESS (1995).

[69] The Declaration of Rights and Fundamental Rules of the State of Delaware was adopted by the convention on September 11, 1776. Shortly thereafter, the first Constitution of the State of Delaware was enacted on September 20, 1776. *See* Gordon S. Wood, *State Constitution-Making in the American Revolution*, 24 RUTGERS L.J. 911, 921 (1993).

[70] 1776 Constitution of the State of Delaware, art. 26.

[71] Del. Const. of 1792, art. 2 §§ 8, 9; N.Y. Const. of 1777, §XV; Pa. Const. of 1776, §§ 13, 14.

[72] *See* Conn. Const. Ordinance of 1776, art. I, *reprinted in* 2 *Sources and Documents of United State Constitutions* 143-44 (William F. Swindler ed., 1973-1979) [hereinafter State Constitutions]; *Del. Declaration of Rights of 1776, reprinted in* 2 State Constitutions, *supra*, at 197-99; *Md. Declaration of Rights of 1776, reprinted in* 4 State Constitutions, *supra*, 372-75; *Mass. Const. of 1780*, pt. I, *reprinted in* 5 State Constitutions, *supra*, at 93-96; *N. H. Const. of 1784*, pt. 1, *reprinted in* 6 State Constitutions, *supra*, at 344-47; *N.C. Const. of 1776, Declaration of Rights, reprinted in* 7 State Constitutions, *supra*, at 402-04; *Pa. Const. of 1776, Declaration of Rights, reprinted in* 8 State Constitutions, *supra*, at 278-79; *Va. Declaration of Rights of 1776, reprinted in* 10 State Constitutions, *supra*, at 48-50.

[73] *See* Donald S. Lutz, *Popular Consent and Popular Control: Whig Political Theory in the Early State Constitutions* 67 (Baton Rouge: Louisiana State University Press 1980). (table on the use of shall and ought in state declarations of rights).

man ought to be compelled to give evidence against himself" and "the liberty of the press ought to be inviolably preserved."[74]

Other rights, such as the right to a jury trial, were phrased unequivocally. The English common law form of trial by jury had been transported to the American Colonies through the influence of the common law writers such as Coke, Hale and Blackstone. The American colonies resented royal interference with the right to trial by jury.[75] On October 14, 1774, the First Continental Congress declared:

> That the respective colonies are entitled to the common law of England, and more especially to the great and inestimable privilege of being tried by their peers of the vicinage, according to the course of that law.[76]

The Declaration of Independence stated solemn objections to the King's "depriving us in many cases, of the benefits of Trial by Jury ..."[77] The right to trial by jury was perpetuated as a fundamental component of the judicial system in every new sovereign state. In 1776, ten states allowed juries to decide both the facts and the law.[78] That right was often inserted into the first state constitutions.[79]

Maryland 1776

On July 3, 1776, Maryland's provincial congress acted upon the Constitutional Congress's recommendation of May 15. It decided to elect a new congress "for the express purpose of forming a new Government by the authority of the People only, and enacting and ordering all things for the preservation, safety, and general weal of this Colony."[80]

The members elected to serve in Maryland's convention met during the second week of August in 1776. They sought advice from John Dickinson of Pennsylvania about how to avoid ending up with a constitution like Pennsylvania's.[81] A declaration of rights was passed on November 3, 1776. The convention enacted a constitution for Maryland on November 8,

---

[74] Md. Const. of 1776, Declaration of Rights art. XX and XXXVIII.

[75] *Duncan v. Louisiana*, 391 U.S. 145, 152 (1968).

[76] *Duncan v. Louisiana*, 391 U.S. 145, 152 (1968). *See* 2 J. Kent, *Commentaries on American Law* 13 (13th ed. 1884).

[77] *Duncan v. Louisiana*, 391 U. S. 145, 152 (1968). *See also* Vol. 1, *Del.C.* p. 13.

[78] Lloyd E. Moore, *The Jury: Tool of Kings, Palladium of Liberty* (Cincinnati: W. H. Anderson,, 1973), 112 *See, e.g.,* Ga. Const. of 1777, art. XLI, in *Sources and Documents*, ed. Swindler, 2:448 ("jury shall be judges of law as well as of fact").

[79] *See, e.g.*, Ga. Const. of 1777, art. XLI, in *Sources and Documents,,* ed. Swindler, 2:448 ("jury shall be judges of law as well as of fact").

[80] Willi Paul Adams, *The First American Constitutions: Republican Ideology and the Making of the State Constitutions in the Revolutionary Era* 80 (1980).

[81] R. Hoffman, *A Spirit of Dissention: Economics, Politics and the Revolution in Maryland* 170-183, 269 (1973).

1776. It became effective immediately.[82] As early as 1776, the first constitutions of both Maryland and Delaware provided for amendments pursuant to the approval of two successive legislatures.

North Carolina 1776

In August 1776, the safety council of North Carolina scheduled elections for October 15, 1776. The elected representatives at that time would have not only legislative responsibility but would draft a constitution. North Carolina's new legislature convened on November 12, 1776.

On November 13, 1776, the Fifth Provincial Congress of North Carolina appointed a committee to draft a declaration of rights and a constitution.[83] The committee had the benefit of reviewing John Adam's *Thoughts on Government* and also received copies of constitutions and declarations of rights that had been recently adopted in other states.[84] Those documents, along with two letters of advice from John Adams, had been sent to the committee by William Hooper, North Carolina's delegate to the Continental Congress.[85]

Hooper also wrote a letter of his own to the North Carolina convention. Hooper provided his assessment of the constitutions of Pennsylvania, Delaware, South Carolina and New Jersey. Hooper recommended against a unicameral legislature like Pennsylvania's and against the election of judges, as had been provided for in Rhode Island's Constitution.[86]

After some modifications to the committee's drafts, the North Carolina Congress passed the Declaration of Rights on December 17, 1776, and the Constitution on December 18, 1776.[87] The framers of North Carolina's

---

[82] Willi Paul Adams, *The First American Constitutions: Republican Ideology and the Making of the State Constitutions in the Revolutionary Era* 81 (1980).

[83] John V. Orth, Symposium: "The Law of the Land": The North Carolina Constitution and State Constitutional Law: North Carolina Constitutional History, 70 N.C. L. REV. 1759, 1760 (1992).

[84] John Adams, Thoughts on Government (Boston, 1776), in American Political Writing, ed. Hyneman and Lutz, 1:407.

[85] Letter from William Hooper to Fifth Provincial Congress (Oct. 26, 1776), in 10 The Colonial Records of North Carolina 862-70 (William L. Saunders ed., Raleigh, Josephus Daniels, Printer to the State, 1890); Letter from John Adams to William Hooper (ante Mar. 27, 1776), in 4 Papers of John Adams 73-78 (Robert J. Taylor ed., 1979).

[86] Fletcher Green, Constitutional Development in the South Atlantic States, 1776-1860, p. 67 (1930).

[87] John V. Orth, Symposium: "The Law of the Land": The North Carolina Constitution and State Constitutional Law: North Carolina Constitutional History, 70 N.C. L. REV. 1759, 1761 (1992).

first constitution had drawn selectively upon the constitutional acumen of their contemporaries in other states. In language almost identical to the Maryland Declaration of Rights, North Carolina's Declaration of Rights provided that "the Legislative, Executive, and Supreme Judicial Powers of government ought to be forever separate and distinct from each other."[88] The provisions in the North Carolina Declaration of Rights acknowledging the sovereignty of the people and freedom of religion were patterned after similar provisions in the rights' declarations of Virginia and Pennsylvania, respectively.[89] Similarly, the Georgia and North Carolina constitutions mandated that the legislature establish public schools, was modeled upon an identical provision in the Pennsylvania Constitution.[90] The first constitution of North Carolina also prohibited incarceration for debt after all property of a debtor had been relinquished for the benefit of all creditors.

Unlike Pennsylvania, which had opted for a concentration of power in a unicameral legislature, almost all of the other states concluded that a balance of power between the branches of government was a preferable constitutional framework.[91] Georgia was the only state other than Pennsylvania, and the area known as Vermont, to adopt a unicameral legislature.[92]

Georgia 1777

Georgia adopted a constitution in February of 1777. The form and content of Georgia's Constitution was influenced by Button Gwinnett, one of Georgia's delegates to the Second Constitutional Congress. In 1776, while in Philadelphia, Gwinnett had been exposed to the wide range of the extant state constitutional drafts, pamphlets, and arguments. Benjamin Rush noted that Gwinnet had taken the Pennsylvania Constitution back to Georgia.[93] After the Georgia Constitution of 1777 was adopted, the legislature declared "that all laws of England, statute as well as common,

---

[88] N.C. Const. of 1776, Declaration of Rights, § 4. See MD. CONST. of 1776, Declaration of Rights, § 6.

[89] John V. Orth, Symposium: "The Law of the Land": The North Carolina Constitution and State Constitutional Law: North Carolina Constitutional History, 70 N.C. L. REV. 1759, 1765 (1992).

[90] John V. Orth, Symposium: "The Law of the Land": The North Carolina Constitution and State Constitutional Law: North Carolina Constitutional History, 70 N.C. L. REV. 1759, 1766-67 (1992).

[91] Robert F. Williams, The State Constitutions of the Founding Decade: Pennsylvania's Radical 1776 Constitution and its Influences on American Constitutionalism 62 TEMP. L. REV., 541 (1989).

[92] Adams, First American Constitutions, 300, 307; James Dealey, Growth of American State Constitutions (1915; rpt. New York: Da Capo Press, 1972), 37-39.

[93] B. Rush, The Autobiography of Benjamin Rush 113-14 at 153 (G. Corner ed. 1948).

and all laws passed by the general assembly should be in full force and effect as the law of the land."[94]

New York 1777

State constitutional activity continued from the adoption of New York's Constitution later in 1777 until the enactment of New Hampshire's Constitution in 1784. The extended forays into state constitution-making reflected an evolutionary pattern of transition from legislative dominance toward an expanded role for both the executive and judicial branches. The evolution in the adoption of the first state constitutions was also characterized by an introduction of structural changes designed to check and balance the initial state constitutions' tendency to amalgamate power within the legislature.

In early 1777, New York's delegates to the Continental Congress in Philadelphia wrote home about the controversy among Pennsylvanians regarding their Constitution of 1776:

> The unhappy Dispute about their constitution is the fatal Rock on which they have split, and which threatens them with Destruction. We ardently wish that in our own State the utmost Caution may be used to avoid a like calamity. Every wise Man here wishes that the establishment of new Forms of Government had been deferred. ...[95]

New York's 1777 Constitution provided a model based on a blending of governmental powers that appealed to many of those who opposed the Pennsylvania Constitution. Alfred Young described the polar positions that led to what he described as the "middle of the road" New York Constitution of 1777. It is illustrative of the general divergence of opinion concerning state constitutions during the founding decade:

> The [New York] constitution of 1777 retained many "aristocratic" features.... At the same time the constitution made several democratic departures from provincial precedent.... Had extreme conservatives had their way, they would have gotten elections at four-year intervals by voice voting, an upper house indirectly chosen, a governor elected by an upper house, and a governor with more of the powers of his royal predecessors. Had the most democratic elements had their way, there would have been taxpayer suffrage, a secret ballot for all elections...annual election of all state officials, and popular election of country and local officials; furthermore the appointive power would have been vested

---

[94] Fletcher Green, Constitutional Development in the South Atlantic States, 1776-1860, p. 67 (1930).

[95] Letter from Philip Livingston, James Duane, and William Duer to Abraham TenBroeck (Apr. 19, 1777), reprinted in 6 LETTERS FROM THE DELEGATES TO CONGRESS, supra note 130, at 686-87.

exclusively in the assembly and the governor's veto power would have been eliminated.[96]

The veto provision in the New York Constitution of 1777 subsequently served as a model for the presidential veto in the United States Constitution.[97] The New York Constitution of 1777 did not, however, include a separate declaration of rights.

Vermont 1777

Vermont addressed the issue of drafting a state constitution in 1777, even though it was not yet recognized as an independent sovereign entity. Already estranged from New York, Vermont concluded that the recently enacted New York Constitution of 1777 was a "horrible example." The drafters of the 1776 Pennsylvania Constitution sent copies to representatives of Vermont, who had traveled to Philadelphia to lobby the Second Continental Congress to recognize it as a separate state. A constitution modeled closely after Pennsylvania's was proposed for the geographic area known as Vermont at that time.

South Carolina 1778

The South Carolina Constitution was revised in 1778. The word "State" replaced "colony" and the name of the chief executive became governor rather than president. A bicameral legislature was established. Public offices were established on a rotating basis. And the governor's veto power was eliminated. Popular suffrage was expanded by a reduction in the property requirement, but then contracted by the addition of a religious qualification.[98] The 1778 South Carolina Constitution provided that it could only be amended by a majority vote of both houses following ninety days' notice.

Massachusetts 1780

The 1780 Massachusetts constitution was not only written by a special convention but was submitted for popular ratification.[99] In 1778, the proposed Massachusetts Constitution was defeated by a popular referendum, in part, because it had been drafted by the legislature rather

---

[96] Alfred F. Young, The Democratic Republicans of New York: The Origins 1763-1797, 20-21 (1967).

[97] C. Thach, Jr., The Creation of the Presidency, 1775-1789, at 110-16; E. Douglass, (1955) at 65.

[98] Fletcher Green, Constitutional Development in the South Atlantic States, 1776-1860, p. 67 (1930)

[99] For a discussion of the process leading to the 1780 Massachusetts Constitution, see generally Cella, *The People of Massachusetts, A New Republic, and the Constitution of 1780: The Evolution of Principles of Popular Control of Political Authority, 1774-1780*, 14 SUFFOLK U.L. REV.975 (1980).

than a constitutional convention of the people.[100] The 1780 Massachusetts Constitution has been described by Donald Lutz as:

> the most important one written between 1776 and 1789 because it embodied the Whig theory of republican government, which came to dominate state level politics; the 1776 Pennsylvania Constitution was the second most important because it embodied the strongest alternative. The Massachusetts document represented radical Whiggism, moderated somewhat by the form of mixed government if not the actual substance. Pennsylvania Whigs wrote the most radical constitution of the era, one lacking even a bow in the direction of mixed government.[101]

Massachusetts has held several constitutional conventions since 1780 but has never adopted a completely revised constitution. Thus, the 1780 Massachusetts Constitution is still operative today and, as such, is the world's oldest written framework of government.[102] By the close of the Revolutionary War in 1783, every state except Connecticut and Rhode Island had written a new constitution.[103] Prior to the Declaration of Independence, the colonies of Rhode Island and Connecticut were operating as republics, pursuant to their corporate charters. Therefore, those two states "simply confined themselves to the elimination of all mention of royal authority in their existing charters."[104]

C. NEW NATION BEGINS

STATE CONSTITUTIONS REWRITTEN

Following the ratification of the United States Constitution, some of the original thirteen states began to rewrite their constitutions almost immediately.[105] Fifteen existing states re-wrote their constitutions prior to the Civil War. In exercising their residual sovereign powers, states adopted constitutions that continued to adhere to the same basic principles

---

[100] E. Morgan, *The Birth of the Republic* 89-90 (1977).

[101] Robert F. Williams, The State Constitutions of the Founding Decade: Pennsylvania's Radical 1776 Constitution and its Influences On American Constitutionalism, 62 TEMP. L. REV. 541, 549 (1989) (citing D. Lutz, Popular Consent and Popular Control: Whig Political Theory in The Early State Constitutions 1 (1980). See also Alfred Young, The Democratic-Republicans of New York: Their Origins 1763-1797, 20-21 (1967) (quoting Donald S. Lutz).

[102] Paul C. Reardon, "The Massachusetts Constitution Marks a Milestone," Publius: The Journal of Federalism 12 (Winter 1982): 45-55.

[103] Delaware v. Van Arsdall, 475 U.S. 673 (1986) (Justice Stevens, dissenting).

[104] Gordon S. Wood, State Constitution-Making in the American Revolution, 24 RUTGERS L.J. 133 (1993).

[105] See, e.g., Del. Const. of 1792; see generally Claudio v. State, 585 A.2d 1278 (Del. 1991).

of republican democracy, but from their own unique perspectives.[106] These documents, for example, reaffirmed each state's commitment to its own declaration of rights and common law traditions.

Georgia 1788

On January 30, 1788, the Georgia legislature decided to call a state constitutional convention after nine states had ratified the proposed Constitution of the United States:

> That they would proceed to name three fit and discreet persons from each county to be convened at Augusta, by the executive, as soon as may be after official information is received that nine states have accepted the federal constitution; and a majority of them shall proceed to take under their consideration the alterations and amendments that are necessary to be made in the constitution of this state, and to arrange, digest and alter the same, in such manner as, in their judgment will be most consistent with the interest and safety, and best secure the rights and liberties to the citizens thereof.[107]

Georgia adopted a new constitution in May 1789. There were several changes in all three branches of government. A bicameral legislature was created to replace the former unicameral house of assembly. Provisions were included for the governor to be elected by the legislature for a term of two years. The 1789 Constitution of Georgia was the first state constitution that required candidates for legislative office to have resided longer in the United States than in the State of Georgia:

> Senators were to be twenty-eight years of age, inhabitants of the United States nine years, citizens of the state three years and of the county six months, and possessed of 250 acres of land or other property worth L250. Members of the lower house of the legislature were to be twenty-one years of age, citizens of the United States seven years, inhabitants of the state two years and of the county three months, and possessed of 250 acres of land or other property worth L150.[108]

South Carolina 1790

On March 13, 1789, the legislature of South Carolina passed an act that called for a state constitutional convention to convene at Columbia in May 1790.[109] The new constitution provided for the capital to be moved from Charleston to Columbia. The qualifications for office-holding were changed by reducing the property requirement and eliminating the necessity "of being of the Protestant religion." There were also revisions to

---

[106] See, e.g., Del. Const. of 1792; see generally Claudio v. State, 585 A.2d 1278 (Del. 1991).

[107] Stevens, History of Georgia, II, 388 quoted in Fletcher M. Green, Constitutional Development in the South Atlantic States, 1776-1860, p. 127 (1930).

[108] Fletcher Green, Constitutional Development in the South Atlantic States, 1776-1860, p. 130 (1930).

[109] *Id.* at p. 150.

the suffrage requirements: a three shilling tax was provided for as an alternative to owning fifty acres of land; and, the religious qualification was deleted.[110] The new South Carolina Constitution also adjusted the powers in each of its three branches of government, provided for freedom of religion, and importuned the legislature to "pass laws for the abolition of the rights of primogeniture, and for giving an equitable distribution of the real estate of interstates."[111] Finally, the new constitution of South Carolina provided for future amendments by: supermajority votes of both houses; a popular vote; and additional supermajority votes of both houses, after an intervening popular election.[112]

D. STATEHOOD ADMISSION REQUIREMENTS

The United States Constitution assigned the process of admitting new states to Congress:

New states may be admitted by the Congress into this Union; but no new State shall be formed or erected within the Jurisdiction of any other State; nor any State be formed by the Junction of two or more States, or Parts of States, without the Consent of the Legislatures of the States concerned as well as of the Congress.[113]

Twenty new states were admitted to the Union prior to the Civil War. The provision in the United States Constitution for admitting new states was initially invoked by Vermont. Vermont became a state in 1791.[114] Vermont's Constitution was the first to eliminate the requirement that a man either own property or pay taxes to be permitted to vote.[115] It enfranchised all free males older than twenty-one who would take the Freeman's Oath. On June 1, 1792, Kentucky was the second state to be admitted to the Union. The Congressional acts admitting Kentucky and Vermont contained no terms or conditions. Each act provided for admission "as a new and entire member of the United States of America."[116]

When Tennessee was admitted as the third new State, it was declared to be "one of the United States of America," "on an equal footing with the

---

[110] Fletcher Green, Constitutional Development in the South Atlantic States, 1776-1860, p. 122 (1930).

[111] *Id.* at p. 124.

[112] *Id.*

[113] U.S. Const. art. IV, § 3.

[114] Act of Feb. 18, 1791, ch. VII, 1 State. 191 (1791).

[115] Vt. Const. of 1793, ch. II, § 21, in *Sources and Documents*, ed., Swindler, 9:507, 512.

[116] *Coyle v. Smith*, 221 U.S. 559 (1911).

original States in all respects whatsoever."[117] That language has remained substantially the same in all subsequent admission acts.[118]

Enabling Statute Concept

When the first independent territorial requests for statehood were being contemplated, it was a thought that an enabling statute from Congress was a necessary condition precedent to calling for a state constitutional convention.[119] This precedent was established in 1802, when Ohio petitioned Congress for such authorization. That practice was followed by Alabama, Illinois, Indiana, Louisiana, Mississippi and Missouri. The procedure changed between 1836 and 1848.[120] Wisconsin was admitted following the passage of an enabling act. Arkansas, Florida, Iowa, and Michigan were all admitted to statehood, however, without any prior authorization from Congress to assemble a state constitutional convention. Thereafter, the procedure was not uniform, e.g., California, Kansas, and Oregon organized without the authorization of an enabling act; but Nebraska, Nevada, and Minnesota all received Congressional approval to proceed.[121] Each new state had to have a "Republican form of Government."[122] This requirement had at least two direct affects on the future of constitutions drafted in contemplation of admission to statehood. First, to achieve a "Republican form of Government" the constitutions proposed by many new states were simply adaptations or combinations of provisions in the constitutions of existing states.[123] Second, Congress assumed that public education was "an essential feature of a republican government based upon the will of the people."[124] Therefore, as a condition for admission to the Union, Congress frequently insisted that proposed state constitutions include provisions that guaranteed public education.[125] This latter phenomena was simply a perpetuation of the recognition of the need for an educated electorate that began with the Northwest Ordinance of 1787, to wit: "Religion, morality and knowledge,

---

[117] *Coyle v. Smith*, 221 U.S. 559 (1911).

[118] *Id.*

[119] Donald C. Colson, *Idaho's Constitution: The Tie That Binds* 1, 4-6, 220-23 (University of Idaho 1991).

[120] *Id.*

[121] *Id.*

[122] U.S. Const. art. IV § 4.

[123] James Willard Hurst, *The Growth of American Law: The Law Makers* (Boston: Little, Brown, 1950), 336.

[124] David Tyack, Thomas James, and Aaron Benavot, *Law and the Shaping of Public Education*, 1785-1954 (Madison: University of Wisconsin Press, 1987), 20.

[125] *Id.* at p. 20-42.

being necessary to good government and the happiness of mankind, schools and the means of education shall be forever encouraged."[126]

One related issue that confronted the writers of state constitutions after 1787 was the propriety of including religion as a component of public education.[127] To varying degrees, the states concluded that moral virtue was a necessary foundation for the institutions of government in a democratic society.[128] Consequently, the articles on public education in many state constitutions often began with preambles or mission statements regarding both civil and moral aims.[129] Throughout the nineteenth century, those aims were often linked inexorably in state constitutions.

Enabling Acts Evolve

The enabling act passed at the close of the nineteenth century for North Dakota, South Dakota, Montana, and Washington is illustrative of how the public school mandate was retained even after sectarian controls were prohibited:

> An act to provide for the division of Dakota into two States and to enable the people of North Dakota, South Dakota, Montana, and Washington to form constitutions and State governments and to be admitted into the Union on an equal footing with the original States, and to make donations of public lands to such States.
>
> ...whereupon the said conventions shall be, and are hereby, authorized to form constitutions and States governments for said proposed States, respectively. The constitutions shall be republican in form ...
>
> And said conventions shall provide, by ordinances irrevocable without the consent of the United States and the people of said States; ...
>
> Fourth. That provision shall be made for the establishment and maintenance of systems of public schools, which shall be open to all the children of said States, and free from sectarian control.[130]

---

[126] *The Federal and State Constitutions, Colonial Charters, and Other Organic Laws of the States, Territories, and Colonies Now or Heretofore Forming the United States of America*, ed. Francis N. Thorpe (Washington, D.C.: U.S. Government Printing Office, 1909), 2:961.

[127] *See Pfeiffer v. Board of Education*, 118 Mich. 560, 565 (1898).

[128] Benjamin Rush, "Thoughts upon the Mode of Education Proper in a Republic," in *Essays on Education in the Early Republic*, ed. Frederick Rudolph (Cambridge, Mass.: Harvard University Press, 1965), 3-23.

[129] David Tyack and Thomas James, "State Government and American Public Education: Exploring the 'Primeval Forest,'" *History of Education Quarterly* 26 (1986): 39-69.

[130] Robert F. Williams, *State Constitutional Law: Cases and Materials* 76-77 (2d ed. 1993) *citing* Chapter 180, *Fiftieth Congress*, Second Session 1889.

E. STRUCTURES OF GOVERNMENT

State constitutional law, like its federal counterpart, is not limited to issues involving the common law or individual rights. Numerous other areas of law involve the application of state constitutions. The structure and power of state and local governments,[131] the state judicial system,[132] taxation, public finance,[133] and public education[134] are all affected by a state's constitution and its interpretation.

Beginning with several state constitutions that were adopted in the 1790s, e.g., Delaware, Kentucky, and Tennessee, provisions were made "for the legislature to submit the question of calling a Constitutional convention to a vote of the people."[135] If the populace voted in favor of calling a constitutional convention, delegates were elected to that body. Some state constitutional conventions could take definitive action while others were required to submit proposals to amend or replace a constitution to another vote of the electorate.[136]

Revising State Constitutions

There were originally two general methods of writing or amending a state constitution: by convention[137] and by legislative action.[138]

---

[131] John Devlin, Toward a State Constitutional Analysis of Allocation of Powers: Legislators and Legislative Appointees Performing Administrative Functions, 66 TEMP. L. REV. 1205 (1993); James E. Herget, The Missing Power of Local Governments: A Divergence Between Text and Practice in Our Early State Constitution, 62 VA. L. REV. 999, 1001 (1976); Michael E. Libonati, Intergovernmental Relations in State Constitutional Law: A Historical Overview, 496 ANNALS AM. ACAD. POL. & SOC. SCI. 107 (1988).

[132] Jonathan Feldman, Separation of Powers and Judicial Review of Positive Rights Claims: The Role of State Courts in an Era of Positive Government, 24 RUTGERS L.J. 1057 (1993).

[133] Robert F. Williams, Foreword: The Importance of an Independent State Constitutional Equality Doctrine in School Finance Cases and Beyond, 24 CONN. L. REV. 675 (1992).

[134] William E. Thro, Note, To Render Them Safe: The Analysis of State Constitutional Provisions in Public School Finance Reform Litigation, 75 VA. L. REV. 1639, 1661-70 (1989); Allen W. Hubsch, The Emerging Right to Education Under State Constitutional Law, 65 TEMP. L. REV. 1325 (1992). State constitutions, except for Mississippi, provide for public education.

[135] Don E. Fehrenbacher, Sectional Crisis and Southern Constitutionalism, p. 87 LOUISIANA STATE UNIVERSITY PRESS (1995).

[136] Id.

[137] See Robert J. Martineau, The Mandatory Referendum on Calling a State Constitutional Convention: Enforcing the People's Right to Reform Their Government, 31 OHIO ST. L.J. 421 (1970); Robert F. Williams, Are State Constitutional Conventions Things of the Past? The Increasing Role of the Constitutional Commission in State Constitutional Change, 1 HOFSTRA L. & POLY'S SYMP. 1 (1996).

[138] See, e.g., Del. Const. art. XVI, § 1.

Amendment by popular initiative was a third method that began to appear in state constitutions, especially at the turn of the century.[139] The initiative has been challenged as a form of pure democracy that "is in contravention of a republican form of government guaranteed to each state by Article IV, Section 4 of the United States Constitution."[140] The United States Supreme Court held that the issue was a non-justiciable political question that was "embraced within the scope of powers conferred upon Congress."[141] The initiative remains operative in many states.

In a majority of states, either the legislature alone or the legislature and a popular referendum can call for a constitutional convention. Some state constitutions either permit a convention to be brought about by an initiative petition or require that the question of having a convention be submitted to the voters at specific periodic intervals.[142] When there is a referendum on the issue of having a constitutional convention, some state constitutions require it to be approved by a majority of those voting in the election, not just a majority of those voting on the question.[143]

State Constitutions More Lengthy

State constitutions are generally more detailed, and therefore, longer than the United States Constitution.[144] Over the years, state constitutions have been rewritten entirely or amended, in part, to include a great variety of specific matters that could have been enacted by statute.[145] Once a provision is part of a state constitution, it is beyond change by normal, statutory law-making processes.[146]

---

[139] James W. Hurst, The Growth of American Law: The Law Makers 199-204 (1950). See Thomas E. Cronin, Direct Democracy: The Politics of Initiative, Referendum, and Recall (1989); David B. Magleby, Direct Legislation: Voting on Ballot Propositions in the United States (1983); David B. Schmidt, Citizen Lawmakers: The Ballot Initiative Revolution (1989).

[140] Pacific States Telephone and Telegraph v. Oregon, 223 U.S. 188 (1912).

[141] *Id.*

[142] W. Brooke Graves, State Constitutional Law: A Twenty-Five Year Summary, 8 WM. & MARY L. REV. 1, 4 (1966).

[143] W. Brooke Graves, State Constitutional Law: A Twenty-Five Year Summary, p. 5, 8 WM. & MARY L. REV. 1 (1966).

[144] Frank P. Grad, *The State Constitution: Its Function and Form for Our Time*, 54 VA. L. REV. 928 (1968).

[145] Robert F. Williams, *State Constitutional Law Processes*, 24 WM. & MARY L. REV. 169, 202 (1983). *See* Strum, Albert L., *Methods of State Constitutional Reform*, University of Michigan Press, Ann Arbor (1954).

[146] Frank P. Grad, *The State Constitution: Its Function and Form for Our Time*, 54 VA. L. REV. 928, 928-29, 942-43, 945-47, 972-73 (1968). Janet Cornelius, *Constitution Making in Illinois 1818-1970* (Urbana: University of Illinois Press, 1972), p. 42.

Legislation enacted into state constitutions reflects the political and social feeling of the time.[147] Several of the recurring subjects addressed in state constitutions relate to suffrage, apportionment, property, economics, slavery, lotteries, banks, corporations, divorces, indebtedness, internal improvements, length of legislative sessions, sinking funds, public credit, and state regulation or performance of services, such as, health and education.[148] The original or amended substance of such provisions was often the product of political party or special-interest group conflicts.[149] "In short, state government performed many more of what we think of as the normal tasks of government, while the federal government, especially in the Jacksonian period and after, was more of a caretaker government with only a rudimentary bureaucracy."[150]

Georgia 1798

Georgia convened another constitutional convention in May of 1798. The constitution it adopted at that time was perceived to achieve a better balance of power between Georgia's three branches of government. Certain restrictions were placed upon the legislature, *e.g.*, quorum requirements and recording of votes.[151] The legislature was authorized to establish superior and inferior courts, with the judges of both courts to be elected by the legislature.[152] Several substantive rights provisions were included in the 1798 Georgia Constitution. Incarceration was prohibited for a debtor who had relinquished all property for the benefit of creditors. Several clauses promoted religious freedom. The importation of slaves was prohibited. And, dismembering or killing a slave was punishable as a crime on the same basis as such an act against anyone else[153]

---

[147] James W. Hurst, *The Growth of American Law: The Law Makers*, 237-38, 240-46 (1950). *See also* Fletcher Green, *Constitutional Development in the South Atlantic States, 1776-1860* (1930); Merrill D. Peterson, *Democracy, Liberty & Property: The State Constitutional Conventions of the 1820s* (1966).

[148] Michael Heise, *State Constitutions, School Finance Litigation, and the "Third Wave": From Equity to Adequacy*, 68 TEMP. L. REV. 1151 (1995).

[149] *Id.*

[150] Stephen M. Griffin, American Constitutionalism From Theory to Politics, p. 34 (Princeton University Press 1996).

[151] Fletcher Green, Constitutional Development in the South Atlantic States, 1776-1860, pp. 124-135 (1930).

[152] *Id.*

[153] *Id.*

F. NINETEENTH CENTURY DAWNS

STATE CONSTITUTIONS POPULARIZED

The election of President Thomas Jefferson in 1800 was a significant political change that was indicative of what was happening in many states. There was widespread support for implementing Jeffersonian democracy by invoking the principles of the Declaration of Independence and the Virginia Bill of Rights. The ascendency into power of Jeffersonian Republicans commenced several decades of efforts to amend or revise the provisions in state constitutions, in particular, with regard to suffrage and representation. Georgia, for example, passed a series of amendments to its state constitutions between 1808 and 1824 that provided for the direct popular election of public officials, including the governor, in lieu of legislative appointment.

Connecticut 1818

Connecticut adopted its first operative state constitution in 1818. Its structure of government provided for a traditional separation of powers between the legislature, an executive, and a judiciary. Since the Declaration of Independence, Connecticut had operated in an essentially parliamentary format. The Connecticut Constitution of 1818 also included a bill of rights. Many of the rights written into the 1818 Constitution had well-established common law antecedents in Connecticut.[154]

Jacksonian Influences

The state constitutions that were written or amended in this era characterized by the presidency of Andrew Jackson were frequently influenced by individuals who were interested in issues relating to popular sovereignty.[155] Thus, the state constitutions of that time were often rights-conscious documents.[156] For example, many state constitutions were revised or amended during this era to: expand the right to vote and hold office, by eliminating property requirements and religious tests; substitute popular elections for offices that had been appointed by either the legislature or a governor; and limit or restrict the legislature's right to act on a myriad of subjects.

---

[154] Ellen A. Peters, "State Constitutional Law: Federalism in the common Law Tradition," MICH. L. REV. 84 (1986). Ellen A. Peters *Common Law Antecedents of Constitutional Law in Connecticut*, in Paul Finkelman and Stephen E. Gottlieb, *Toward a Usable Past: Liberty Under State Constitutions*.

[155] James A. Henretta, *Foreward: Rethinking the State Constitutional Tradition*, 22 RUTGERS L.J. 819, 819-26, 836-39 (1991). *See also* Merrill D. Peterson, *Democracy, Liberty & Property: The State Constitutional Conventions of the 1820s* (1966).

[156] *Id.*

Nearly all Jacksonian-era state constitutions added or expanded declarations of rights and, as in Delaware's 1831 Constitution, placed them at the beginning of the document.[157] In construing this portion of Delaware's Constitution, one court noted: "Most of the matters mentioned in the first article, are merely declaratory of the doctrines of the common law on the same subjects, formerly affirmed by the [M]agna [C]harta, in the year 1215, and afterwards by the bill of rights, in 1688, as the undoubted rights and liberties of the people of [England]."[158] The corollary to expanding the rights of the populace was often an enlargement of the educational provisions in state constitutions, because of the continuing belief that an informed civil conscience was needed in a democracy to resist challenges of self-interest and demagoguery.[159]

Virginia 1830

Virginia held a state constitutional convention in Richmond from October 5, 1829 until January 15, 1830. Its members included a future President of the United States, John Tyler; two former Presidents, James Monroe and James Madison; and, the sitting Chief Justice of the United States, John Marshall. James Monroe was selected as the convention's president. The convention was called for the purpose of broadening the right of suffrage and providing for an equalization of representation.

The revised constitution provided for representation in both houses of the legislature from defined districts and for future reapportionment according to districts every ten years. Suffrage continued to be limited to white males who were at least 21 years of age and who also met various property requirements. The governor's term was increased to three years. A few changes were made to the legislative and judicial articles. The Virginia Bill of Rights was left intact. The revised Virginia Constitution of 1830 was ratified by a popular vote.[160]

Mississippi 1832

The Mississippi Constitution of 1832 provided for universal suffrage for white males. It also provided for the election of state officials and

---

[157] James A. Henretta, *Foreward: Rethinking the State Constitutional Tradition*, 22 RUTGERS L.J. 819, 819-26, 836-39 (1991).

[158] *Rice v. Foster*, 4 Harr. 479, 488 (Del. 1847).

[159] Daniel Walker Howe, *The Political Culture of the American Whigs* (Chicago: University of Chicago Press, 1979).

[160] Fletcher Green, Constitutional Development in the South Atlantic States, 1776-1860, p. 210-224 (1930).

judges. The purpose of these latter changes was to limit government and make it accountable.[161]

North Carolina 1835

Although many states re-wrote their constitutions completely during this era, it is noteworthy that during the 1835 Constitution Convention, North Carolina "chose to resolve their constitutional dispute by amending the existing document rather than by writing a new instrument."[162] In fact, the legislative act calling for the North Carolina Convention prohibited it initially from revising the bill of rights or any part of the Constitution not mentioned in the act.[163] An additional act was passed in 1834 that gave the convention discretionary power to consider additional subjects including: "the establishment of a tribunal for impeachment; the election of attorney-general for a term of years, the disqualification from office for conviction of crime; the removal of judges by two-thirds vote of the legislature; the limitation of the legislature in special legislation; and provision for future amendments of the constitution.[164]

The convention met at Raleigh on June 4, 1835. The leader of the Jeffersonian party in North Carolina, Nathaniel Macon, was selected as the convention's president. Ultimately, several important amendments were added to the North Carolina Constitution in 1835, for example: both houses of the legislature were limited in number and made more equal in representation; the sessions of the legislature were changed from annual to biennial; the governor would be elected by popular vote rather than by the legislature; and no private act could be introduced without thirty days notice.[165] In accordance with the democratic momentum of the times, another change to the North Carolina Constitution in 1835 expanded the concept of constitutional amendment by extraordinary legislative action to also include submission for popular ratification.[166] After an extended

---

[161] Kermit L. Hall, "Mostly Anchor and Little Sail," The Revolution of American and State Constitutions in Paul Finkelman and Stephen E. Gottlieb, eds., Toward a Usable Past: Liberty Under State Constitutions, p. 402.

[162] John V. Orth, Symposium: "The Law of the Land": The North Carolina Constitution and State Constitutional Law: North Carolina Constitutional History, 70 N.C. L. REV. 1759, 1770 (1992), citing North Carolina Constitutional Convention, Proceedings and Debates of the Convention of North Carolina, Called to Amend the Constitution of the State, which assembled at Raleigh, June 4, 1835 to which are Subjoined the Convention Act and the Amendments to the Constitution (J. Gales 1836).

[163] Acts of the General Assembly of North Carolina, Session of 1833-34, ch. I, pp. 5-6.

[164] Id. at pp. 5-7.

[165] Fletcher Green, Constitutional Development in the South Atlantic States, 1776-1860, p. 232 (1930).

[166] Don E. Fehrenbacher, Sectional Crisis and Southern Constitutionalism, p. 86 LOUISIANA STATE UNIVERSITY PRESS (1995).

debate, Article 32 of the North Carolina Constitution was amended to substitute the word "Christian" for the word "Protestant." It is interesting to note that the amendment to provide for the popular election of the governor was opposed at the North Carolina convention of 1835 based upon what the opponents viewed as its lack of success in Tennessee.[167]

Georgia 1830s

In 1839, Georgia enacted legislation calling for its second constitutional convention of the decade. Amendments proposed by an 1833 convention had been defeated at the polls. The act which called for the 1839 constitution convention in Georgia, like its predecessor, limited the conventions authority to two subjects: a reduction in the size of the legislature and an equalization of representation. The amendments proposed by the 1839 convention were also rejected by the voters of Georgia. In a letter transmitting that result to the legislature in December 1839, Governor Gilmer stated:

> The amendments to the constitution which were proposed to the people for ratification by the late convention, have been rejected by the most decided expression of public opinion. This is the second time that the people have refused to sanction the proceedings of conventions, held to reform the constitution; and in both instances have probably been induced to the course pursued, by the belief that the amendments offered for their approval, were intended for sectional or temporary party purposes.[168]

Notwithstanding Georgia's two unsuccessful efforts with constitutional conventions in the 1830s, several amendments were made to the Georgia Constitution during that decade by enactments passed in two successive legislative sessions: a limitation on legislative power to grant divorces, except with the concurrence of two special juries (1833); the elimination of property qualifications for legislative office (1834); and a reorganization of the judicial branch (1835).

Rhode Island's Dorr Rebellion

Although many states responded to popular demands for calling constitutional conventions in the 1830s, Rhode Island's legislature refused. In response to the legislature's resistance, an insurgent group held an extra-legal state constitutional convention in Rhode Island. Those citizens, who were frustrated by the sitting legislature's intransigence, not only drafted a new constitution but held elections pursuant to its terms. During 1831 and 1832, Rhode Island was in a state of turmoil. The competing claims to legitimacy, by what became two operating governments in Rhode Island, were resolved when vestiges of the Dorr Rebellion reached

---

[167] Fletcher Green, *Constitutional Development in the South Atlantic States, 1776-1860* (1930).

[168] *Georgia Journal*, December 5, 1839.

the United States Supreme Court.[169] That case was an action in trespass. It was an appeal from a Circuit Court of the United States.

The controversy arose from the efforts of the adherents of 'the government established by a voluntary convention' to overthrow the established charter government.[170] The defendants asserted that their actions were authorized by the charter government during a period of martial law. The plaintiffs denied the legitimacy of the charter government following the establishment of the voluntary government. The Courts of Rhode Island had decided in favor of the charter government.

Thomas W. Dorr was elected governor pursuant to the state constitution for Rhode Island adopted by those who opposed the charter government. According to Dorr, the charter government had lost is republican character and was subject to being divested of its authority with the adoption of a new constitution by the ultimate sovereign of Rhode Island—its people. The question presented to the United States Supreme Court was which Rhode Island Constitution provided its citizens with a republican form of government as guaranteed to the constituents of every state by the United States Constitution. The United States Supreme Court concluded that question was inherently political in character. It held that whether a state's government was republican in form was a matter that the United States Constitution had committed exclusively to the legislative branch and that the decision of the legislature in that regard was binding upon the judiciary:

> Moreover, the constitution of the United States, as far as it has provided for an emergency of this kind, and authorized the general government to interfere in the domestic concerns of a State, has treated the subject as political in its nature, and placed the power in the hands of that department.
>
> The fourth section of the fourth article of the Constitution of the United States provided that the United States shall guarantee to every State in the Union a republican form of government, and shall protect each of them against invasion; and on the application of the legislature or of the executive (when the legislature cannot be convened) against domestic violence.
>
> Under this article of the Constitution it rests with congress to decide what government is the established one in a State. For, as the United States guarantee to each State a republican government, Congress must necessarily decide what government is established in the State before it can determine whether it is republican or not. And when the senators and representatives of a State are admitted into the councils of the Union, the authority of the government under which they are appointed, as well as its republican character, is recognized by the proper constitutional authority. And its decision is binding on every other department of the government, and could not be questioned in a judicial tribunal. It is true that the contest in this case did not last long enough to bring the matter

---

[169] *Luther v. Borden*, 7 How. 1 (1849).

[170] Pacific States Telephone & Telegraph Co. v. Oregon, 233 U.S. 118 (1912).

to this issue; and as no senators or representatives were elected under the authority of the government of which Mr. Dorr was the head, congress was not called upon to decide the controversy. Yet the right to decide is placed there, and not in the courts.[171]

This holding would be of great significance following the Civil War. The official position of the Union during the Civil War had been that it was impossible for a state to secede. Therefore, when the conditions of re-admitting the Confederate states to the Union are described, it is more accurate to characterize the process, including the requirement of amending the state constitutions, as establishing conditions precedent to having the Senators and Representatives elected by the Confederate states seated in the United States Congress. In effect, Congress would not recognize the new constitutions of the former Confederate states, as providing a republican form of government, in the absence of compliance with the conditions that had been imposed.

G. ANTEBELLUM STATE CONSTITUTIONS

Special Privilege Limited

One of the recurring themes that influenced the writing or amending of state constitutions after 1840 was the desire to limit special privilege.[172] Efforts to ameliorate that concern resulted in either general or specific prohibitions on the enactment of "special" and "local" legislation.[173] A related fear, that special favors would be granted surreptitiously, was addressed in state constitutions by requirements that the title of every bill state its subject matter clearly and that every bill deal with only one subject.[174] These same concerns are assuaged in state constitutional requirements designed to insure full publicity and open deliberation regarding the merits of legislation, *e.g.*, three readings, reference to committee, and requirements for the recording of yea and nay votes.[175]

---

[171] Luther v. Borden, 7 HOW. 1 (1849).

[172] James W. Hurst, The Growth of American Law: The Law Makers 237-38, 240-46 (1950). See Michael F. Holt, The Political Crisis of the 1850s (1978).

[173] See generally Grace v. Howlett, 283 N.E.2d 474 (Ill. 1972); Vreeland v. Byrne, 370 A.2d 825 (N.J. 1977); Green, A Malapropian Provision of State Constitutions, 24 WASH. U. L.Q. 359 (1939); Horack, Special Legislation: Another Twilight Zone, 12 IND. L.J. 109 (1937); Sidney Z. Karasik, Equal Protection of the Law Under the Federal and Illinois Constitutions: A Contrast in Unequal Treatment, 30 DEPAUL L. REV. 263 (1981).

[174] See generally Turnbull v. Fink, Del. Supr., 668 A.2d 1370, 1381-91 (1995) (Holland, J. dissenting); Millard H. Ruud, No Law Shall Embrace More Than One Subject 42 MINN. L. REV. 389 (1958).

[175] James W. Hurst, The Growth of American Law: The Law Makers 237-38, 240-46 (1950).

Manifest Destiny

During the middle of the 1840s, the most compelling national issue became America's Manifest Destiny. In 1845, a New York newspaper editor wrote that it was America's "manifest destiny to overspread and possess the whole of the continent which Providence has given us for the great experiment of liberty and federated self-government entrusted to us."[176] This external national focus was accompanied simultaneously by an interest in revising the internal processes of governing in some of the states that were extant.

Between 1848 and 1852, New Hampshire, Maryland, Virginia, Ohio, Indiana, Michigan, Wisconsin, Kentucky, and Louisiana adopted new state constitutions.[177] Significant amendments were added to constitutions in many states where completely new constitutions were not adopted. Massachusetts and Delaware drafted new constitutions but they were both rejected at the polls in 1853.

Direct Democracy and Legislative Restriction

The state constitutions enacted during this era reflected the popular demand for more direct democracy. The new constitutions provided for the direct popular election of many state and local officials, *e.g.*, judges, auditors, justices of the peace, and sheriffs, who had previously been appointed by governors or legislators.[178] In fact, "by 1861, twenty-four of the thirty-four states selected judges by election rather than by appointment."[179]

The new state constitutions also often restricted the power of legislatures to act in the economic realm. Almost all of the new state constitutions replaced annual sessions of the legislature with biennial sessions. "They also mandated a substantial amount of legislation concerning courts and governmental operations that the ensuing session of the legislature would have to pass to put the constitution into operation."[180] For example, in Indiana, it was reported in early 1852 that

---

[176] Blum, Callon, Morgan, Schlecinger, Staupp and Woodward, The National Experience: A History of the United States (Harcourt, Brace & World, Inc. 1963) p. 261.

[177] Michael F. Holt, *The Political Crisis of the 1850s*, p. 106 (John Wiley & Sons, Inc. 1978).

[178] *Id.* at p. 107.

[179] G. Alan Tarr, *Constitutional Politics in the States, Contemporary Controversies and Historical Patterns*, p. 8 (Greenwood Press 1996).

[180] Michael F. Holt, *The Political Crisis of the 1850s*, p. 107 (John Wiley & Sons, Inc. 1978).

"[o]ur legislature is in session and are consuming much time remodeling the laws in unison with the new constitution."[181]

The new state constitutions of this era often imposed specific restrictions on the operations of banks chartered by the legislature. "Even before this period, the Louisiana Constitution of 1845 and the Arkansas Constitution of 1846 had banned the chartering of banks."[182] Accordingly, many of these constitutions resolved what had been major Jacksonian economic issues with regard to banking and currency.[183]

New York 1846

New York held a state constitutional convention in 1846.[184] The debates at that convention were a continuation of the rights-conscious dialogue that had dominated the state for almost two decades. The original 1777 Constitution of New York did not contain a bill of rights. The New York Constitution of 1821 had set forth a list of rights in Article VII. Article I of the 1846 New York Constitution, however, began by setting forth the rights of each "member of this State."[185] "The catalogue of rights in the New York Constitution of 1846 was so comprehensive that subsequent state conventions, in 1867, 1893, and 1915, incorporated it without significant change into the document they proposed for ratification. Only with the convention of 1938, which confronted problems created by the new society of the twentieth century, did New York's politically active classes begin to rethink this long-standing definition of citizens' rights."[186]

The 1846 convention in New York focused on the popular interest of the time in expanding suffrage rights. Ultimately, the concept of universal suffrage was not adopted by a majority of the convention's delegates. The right to vote was not extended to women.[187] The prior $250 property

---

[181] Michael F. Holt, *The Political Crisis of the 1850s*, p. 107 (John Wiley & Sons, Inc. 1978).

[182] *Id.* at p. 108.

[183] *Id.*

[184] William B. Bishop and William H. Attree, *Report of the Debates and Proceedings of the Convention for the Revision of the Constitution of New York, 1846,* (Albany: Evening Atlas, 1846).

[185] *Id.*

[186] James A. Henretta, *Foreward: Rethinking the State Constitutional Tradition*, 22 RUTGERS L.J. 819, 819-26, 836-39 (1991).

[187] William B. Bishop and William H. Attree, Report of the Debates and Proceedings of the Convention for the Revision of the Constitution of New York, 1846, (Albany: Evening Atlas, 1846).

qualification for black voters was retained.[188] Article II, Section 1 of the 1846 New York Constitution, however, gave the right to vote to every white male who had been "a citizen for ten days, and an inhabitant of this State for one year."

The 1846 constitutional convention in New York was also confronted with a dilemma that existed in every state at the time: how to reconcile a continuing commitment to popular sovereignty with the influence exercised by an emergence of disciplined political parties. The disproportionate amount of power that had been vested intentionally in the legislative branch of government by the New York Constitution of 1777 was tempered by placing additional checks and more balance in the state constitutional separation of powers.

The 1846 convention decided to retain the gubernatorial veto power that New York had pioneered. Restrictions were added in the state constitution, however, on the governor's age and residency. The convention also decided to attenuate what was perceived to be the influence of a political party caucus by providing for the election of judges.[189] The 1846 New York Constitution did not only reallocate the separation of powers that had previously existed. It extended the authority of the judiciary and restricted the authority of the executive:

> The Constitution of 1846 laid the foundation for judicial protection of private property rights. Article VIII, section 3, explicitly extended to corporations many of the legal rights of "natural persons," thus bringing them under the protection of the due process clause of Article I, section 6. Likewise, Article V, section 8, diminished some of the traditional "police powers" of state governments. It abolished all state offices for "inspecting any merchandise, produce, manufacture, or commodity whatever." This laissez-faire administrative policy was the work of Jacksonian Democrats. It implemented their vision of a negative state by reducing "the patronage of government...[by] 500 officers." It also revealed a new confidence in the market system and in the ability of individual Americans to govern themselves in economics as well as politics.[190]

---

[188] William B. Bishop and William H. Attree, Report of the Debates and Proceedings of the Convention for the Revision of the Constitution of New York, 1846, (Albany: Evening Atlas, 1846).

[189] N.Y. Const. of 1846, Art. VI, §§ 2, 4, 12, 14, 17. See Kermit L. Hall, "The Judiciary on Trial: State Constitutional Reform and the Rise of an Elected Judiciary, 1846-1860," Historian 44 (May 1983).

[190] James A. Henretta, "The Rise and Decline of "Democratic-Republicanism" Political Rights in New York and the Several States, 1800-1915 in Toward a Usable Past: Liberty Under State Constitutions, Paul Finkelman and Stephen E. Gottlieb, p. 77-78.

The 1846 Constitution also mandated the creation of a commission to codify the procedural law of New York. The result was "the origin of the Field codes that replaced common law pleading."[191]

The 1846 Constitution redressed the grievances of the so-called Rent Wars that had taken place during the late 1830s in the Helderberg Mountains. The farmers in that region south of Albany objected to the quitrents that they were required to pay to the descendants of the early Dutch patrons that had dominated land ownership in the Hudson and Mohawk valleys. The 1846 Constitution of New York abolished quitrents, prohibited long term agricultural leases, and provided for "fee simple tenure of allodial land."[192]

The 1846 convention also provided for state constitutional prohibitions on the legislature's authority to extend credit to private persons and limited the legislature's ability to incur public debt.[193] The 1846 New York Constitution also abolished legislative divorce, prohibited lotteries, restricted state indebtedness, and authorized general corporation acts, but prohibited special legislative charters except for banking corporations.[194]

California 1849

The California constitutional convention met in September 1849 at Monterey. The delegates were influenced by the constitutions of other states, in particular, the recently revised New York Constitution and the 1846 Iowa Constitution. Delegate William Gwin distributed copies of the Iowa Constitution and suggested that it be used as a "working standard." Some delegates recommended looking to other state constitutions for guidance, especially the 1846 New York Constitution.

The debates in the California convention, which preceded the final draft, involved a mix of parochial and national concerns: boundaries, suffrage, banking corporation, the rights of free Negroes, and the expansion of slavery.[195] In the final analysis, "the Iowa and New York Constitutions lay behind virtually every section of the Californians'

---

[191] William M. Wiecek, State Protection of Personal Liberty: Remembering the Future, in Toward a Usable Past: Liberty Under State Constitution, 371, 379-80 (University of Georgia Press 1991).

[192] *Id.*

[193] N.Y. Const. 1846, Art. VII.

[194] William M. Wiecek, State Protection of Personal Liberty: Remembering the Future, in Toward a Usable Past: Liberty Under State Constitutions 371, 379-80 (University of Georgia Press 1991).

[195] David Alan Johnson, Founding the Far West: California, Oregon, and Nevada, 1840-1890, at 101-04, 108, 120-21, 138-39, 140, 142, 189-90, 192-93 (University of California Press 1992).

document."[196] In fact, some sections of the Iowa Constitution were adopted verbatim.

Maryland 1850-1851

In 1850, Maryland enacted legislation calling for a state constitutional convention. The enabling legislation gave the convention complete power to revise the constitution with one exception: it was not permitted to change the extant state constitutional relationship between master and slave. The enabling legislation also required that the new constitution proposed by the convention had to be submitted to the voters of Maryland for ratification or rejection.[197]

The convention convened at Annapolis on November 4, 1850 and adjourned on May 15, 1851. The revised constitution was approved by Maryland's voters. The prior Maryland Constitution was virtually rewritten. A new Article 41 urged the legislature to encourage knowledge, virtue, literature, science, agriculture, manufacturing, and commerce.[198] The governor's term was increased to four years but his former appointment powers were changed by providing for those offices to be elected. Legislative sessions were limited to a period from January to March of each year. Legislative powers were eliminated or restricted on a diverse range of subjects: divorce, debts, lotteries, the power to charter banks and corporations, and the property rights of married women. The new Maryland Constitution provided for the election of judges and also created the elective office of comptroller.[199]

Virginia 1850-1851

In October 1850, the Virginia "Reform Convention of 1850-51" met in Richmond. It continued its work until August 1, 1851. One of the most important issues debated by the convention was the proper basis for representation.[200] At this time, Virginia was "one of the last two states in the Union to accept free white manhood suffrage."[201] The 1851 Constitution expanded suffrage by making age, residence, and white male citizenship the only requirements for voting. The legislature was

---

[196] David Alan Johnson, Founding the Far West: California, Oregon, and Nevada, 1840-1890, at 101-04, 108, 120-21, 138-39, 140, 142, 189-90, 192-93 (University of California Press 1992).

[197] Fletcher Green, Constitutional Development in the South Atlantic States, 1776-1860, p. 276 (1930).

[198] Id. at p. 284.

[199] Id. at p. 286.

[200] Id. at p. 290.

[201] Wythe Holt, Virginia's Constitutional Convention of 1901-1902, at 1-2, 24-25, 30-31, 104-05, 109, 254 (Garland Publishing, Inc. 1990).

reorganized and it was subjected to specific constitution obligations and restrictions, for example:

> It might restrict the emancipation of slaves, and any freed Negro who remained in the state longer than one year was to lose his freedom. Taxation was to be equal and uniform throughout the state, except that slaves were not to be taxed until 12 years of age, and then only at the rate of $300 per capita. A capitation tax might be laid on white males over 21 years of age equal to the tax on property valued at $200. An equal moiety of this was to be used for primary and free schools. The legislature might bar from office, by law, all persons who engaged in a duel. It could require registration for voting, the registration of births, deaths, and marriages, and the taking of a census five years after each national census. It could also levy taxes on income, salaries, or licenses. Among the prohibitions were the granting of divorces, establishment of lotteries, chartering of churches or religious denominations, pledging the faith or binding the state for the debt of corporations, or contracting any debt for a longer period than 34 years. Should it incur debts it was to set aside annually a sum equal to one per cent above the annual interest to add to the sinking fund. A sinking fund was to be created by setting aside seven per cent of the annual revenue of the state.[202]

With regard to the executive branch of government, the 1851 Virginia Constitution provided for the governor to be popularly elected, created the office of lieutenant governor, and also created a board of public works. The judicial branch was changed to provide terms of office rather than life tenure, selection of the judiciary by popular election, and removal by a concurrent majority of both houses in addition to the traditional impeachment process.[203]

Crime Control Concerns

The state constitutional debates of the 1850s continued to be concerned with traditional American concerns about "due process" protections against government oppression but also introduced what is now characterized as the competing theme of "crime control."[204] For example, Article VII section 17 in the Indiana Constitution of 1851 provided that "the General Assembly may modify or abolish the Grand Jury system." The debates about this proposal reflected a concern about whether faster criminal proceedings would deter crime and how much personal liberty might be affected if criminal proceedings were initiated more expeditiously by the filing of informations rather than indictments.[205]

---

[202] Fletcher Green, Constitutional Development in the South Atlantic States, 1776-1860, p. 295 (1930).

[203] Id. at p. 296.

[204] .Herbert Packer, The Limits of the Criminal Sanction (Stanford: Stanford University Press, 1968).

[205] .See David J. Bodenhamer, *The Pursuit of Justice: Crime and Law in Antebellum Indiana* (New York: Garland, 1986), chap. 3. *See also* Brent E. Dickson, *Lawyers and Judges as Framers of Indiana's 1851 Constitution*, 30 INDIANA L. REV. 397 (1997).

Many years later, a provision in the California Constitution that made the grand jury optional was upheld by the United States Supreme Court on the rationale that although the grand jury had once been a guard "against executive usurpation and tyranny" it should not be permitted to undermine or obstruct the "just and necessary discretion of legislative power.[206]

Bible Reading Challenged

The first state supreme court case to address Bible reading in public schools was decided by Maine in 1854.[207] In that case, a Catholic student relied upon the state constitution in refusing to read the King James Bible, as required by the public school's curriculum. The majority opinion affirmed the Catholic student's expulsion and held that the proper forum to resolve the issue was in the legislature rather than the state courts:

> The legislature establishes general rules for the guidance of its citizens. It does not necessarily follow that they are unconstitutional, nor that a citizen is to be legally absolved from obedience, because they may conflict with his conscientious views of religious duty or right. To allow this would be to subordinate the State to the individual conscience. A law is not unconstitutional, because it may prohibit what a citizen may conscientiously think right, or require what he may conscientiously think wrong. The State is governed by its own views of duty. The right or wrong of the State, is the right or wrong as declared by legislative Acts constitutionally passed.[208]

For many decades, thereafter, the religious values of the majority prevailed in most states. In the Cincinnati Bible case, the majoritarian approach resulted in the rejection of a religious challenge to a majority decision to prohibit Bible reading in public schools.[209] More frequently, however, state constitutions either encouraged or permitted religious instruction to promote civic morality and only prohibited "sectarian" uses of the Bible in public schools.[210]

Oregon 1857

Oregon held a state constitutional convention in 1857 at Salem. The Oregonian delegates were influenced most strongly by the Indiana

---

[206].*Hustado v. California*, 110 U.S. 516 (1884).

[207]*Donahoe v. Richards*, 38 Me. 376 (1854).

[208] *Id.* at pp. 376, 410.

[209] *Board of Education of Cincinnati v. Minor*, 23 Ohio St. 211 (1872). *See also Nessle v. Hum*, 1 Ohio N.P. 140 (1894).

[210] *See* Samuel W. Brown, *The Secularization of American Education as Shown by State Legislation, State Constitutional Provisions and State Supreme Court Decisions* (New York: Bureau of Publications, Teachers College, Columbia University, 1912).

Constitution. They also looked for guidance in the state constitutions of Ohio, Michigan, Iowa and Wisconsin.[211]

Nevada 1864

In 1864, Nevada delegates convened in Carson City to write a state constitution. At the time, not only was America in the middle of Civil War but Nevada miners were experiencing an economic crisis. From the outset, the Nevada delegates, "viewed the task before them narrowly, concerned with affirming loyalty to the Union and constructing a charter that would help resolve the economic crisis."[212]

H. ANTEBELLUM INDIVIDUAL RIGHTS

Although state constitutions afforded the primary protection of individual property rights and liberty interests in the antebellum years, the Supremacy Clause was periodically invoked by the United States Supreme Court to reconcile apparently conflicting and often competing interests involving contracts [213] and matters of interstate commerce.[214] There was one conspicuous area, however, in which state constitutions and statutes were consistently unsuccessful in the face of Federal Constitutional challenges, during the antebellum years. That was the effort of some states to provide individual liberty rights for slaves when their owners asserted federal property protections.[215] Conversely, limitations on the individual liberty of slaves in the constitutions of southern states were upheld. The nadir of this jurisprudence was reached in 1857 by the *Dred Scott* decision.[216]

In *Dred Scott*, the United States Supreme Court held that blacks had never been citizens of the United States. In reaction to that opinion, the Republican controlled legislature of New York proposed an equal suffrage amendment to the New York Constitution. The *New York Tribune* wrote that the proposed amendment would "carry back the State Constitutions to

---

[211] David Alan Johnson, *Founding the Far West: California, Oregon, and Nevada*, 1840-1890 (University of California Press 1992).

[212] *Id.*

[213] *Fletcher v. Peck*, 10 U.S. (6 Cranch) 87 (1810); and *Dartmouth College v. Woodard*, 17 U.S. (4 Wheat) 518 (1819). Nevertheless, certain economic interests were held to be subject to state law and state constitutions, e.g., *Charles River Bridge & Co. v. Warren Bridge Co.*, 36 U.S. (11 Pet.) 420 (1837).

[214] *Gibbons v. Ogden*, 22 U.S. (9 Wheat) 1 (1824) and *The Passanger Cases*, 48 U.S. (7 How.) 283 (1849).

[215] *Prigg v. Pennsylvania*, 41 U.S. (16 Pet.) 539 (1842).

[216] *Dred Scott v. Sandford*, 60 U.S. (19 How.) 393 (1857).

those principles upon which they were originally established."[217] Although a majority of New Yorkers voted to elect Abraham Lincoln President, a greater majority voted to defeat the proposed equal suffrage amendment to the New York Constitution.[218]

Nevertheless, in 1860, the highest court of New York declined to follow the *ratio decidendi* of *Dred Scott.*[219] The New Court of Appeals held that slaves, who were brought into the state voluntarily, became free. The United States Supreme Court was never called upon to review that New York decision.

With the advent of the Civil War, the slavery debate moved from the courtroom into the battlefields. Ultimately, the United States Supreme Court never had to reconsider *Dred Scott.* Following the Civil War, that holding was overruled by the Reconstruction Amendments to the United States Constitution.

I.   RECONSTRUCTION REVISIONS

CONFEDERATE STATES' CONSTITUTIONS

President Andrew Johnson announced his plans for Reconstruction in two proclamations that were issued on May 29, 1865. At the same time, he appointed William W. Holden as the provisional governor of North Carolina. President Johnson directed Governor Holden to "call a convention to amend the state's prewar constitution so as to create a 'republican form of government' that would entitle North Carolina to its right within the Union."[220] Any person who had not been pardoned by the President's first proclamation was prohibited from voting for delegates to the state constitutional convention. Similar edicts were issued subsequently for the other confederate states.   Constitutional conventions began to assemble in the summer of 1865. Mississippi's was the first to convene in mid-August. Initially, President Johnson only wanted the Confederate states to "acknowledge the abolition of slavery and repudiate secession."[221] In October, however, President Johnson also directed the seceding states to void debts they had incurred on behalf of the Confederacy. Texas wrote a constitution in 1866. It abolished slavery

---

[217] James A. Henretta *The Rise and Decline of "Democratic-Republicanism"* Political Rights in New York and the Several States, 1800-1915; Paul Finkelman and Stephen E. Gottlieb, *Toward a Usable Past: Liberty Under State Constitutions.*

[218] See Phyllis F. Field, The Politics of Race in New York: The Struggle for Black Suffrage in the Civil War Era (Ithaca: Cornell University Press, 1982).

[219] People v. Lemmon, 20 N.Y. 526 (1860).

[220] Eric Foner, Reconstruction: America's Unfinished Revolution, 1863-1877 (Harper Collins Publishers, Inc. 1988) p. 183.

[221] *Id.*

and nullified secession. In most other regards, it followed the 1845 Constitution that preceded it.

The Reconstruction Act of 1867 set forth the final and definitive requirements for recognition of a state's Congressional delegation after the Civil War.[222] With the exception of Tennessee, the eleven Confederate states were divided into five military districts. The Reconstruction Act provided that a state government could be created and recognized by writing a new state constitution that provided for: manhood suffrage and was approved by a majority of registered voters. The other condition precedent to Congressional recognition was ratification of the Fourteenth Amendment.

North Carolina 1868

North Carolina called for a constitutional convention in 1868 at the initiative of the United States Congress.[223] The federally mandated changes were incorporated in the draft of its new state constitution, *e.g.*, "Every citizen of this State owes paramount allegiance to the Constitution and government of the United States."[224] Following the ratification of that new state constitution and the Fourteenth Amendment to the United States Constitution, North Carolina's Senators and Representatives were seated in Congress.[225]

Virginia 1869

In 1868, a convention framed the new Virginia Constitution. It not only prohibited slavery but afforded equal civil and political rights to all citizens.[226] The new Virginia Constitution provided for state funding of a public school system.[227] The 1869 Virginia Constitution also enacted several provisions that were designed to enhance the democratic process, e.g., secret ballot; annual legislative sessions; expansion of the number of elective offices through the creation of townships; and, removal of

---

[222]*Id.* at p. 276-77.

[223] John V. Orth, Symposium: "The Law of the Land": The North Carolina Constitution and State Constitutional Law: North Carolina Constitutional History, 70 N.C. L. REV. 1759, 1776 (1992).

[224] N.C. Const., 1878, art. I, § 4, in Sources and Documents of United States Constitutions, ed. William Swindler (Dobbs Ferry, N.Y.: Oceana Publications, 1973-78), 7:415.

[225] John V. Orth, Symposium: "The Law of the Land": The North Carolina Constitution and State Constitutional Law: North Carolina Constitutional History, 70 N.C. L. REV. 1759, 1781 (1992).

[226] Wythe Holt, Virginia's Constitutional Convention of 1901-1902, at 1-2, 24-25, 30-31, 104-05, 109, 254 (Garland Publishing, Inc. 1990).

[227] *Id.*

legislative and executive functions from the county courts.[228] Many of the reforms in what has been characterized as the Virginia "carpetbagger Underwood Constitution" of 1869 have been attributed to the occupation of federal troops.[229]

Texas 1869

Texas wrote another state constitution in 1869. It provided for a centralized state government. It expanded the gubernatorial power of appointment. It introduced a state-financed public school system. It also maintained the bill of rights from the 1845 Texas Constitution, as it had done in 1866.[230]

J. FOURTEENTH AMENDMENT

AFFECTS STATE SOVEREIGNTY

The Fourteenth Amendment fundamentally altered the original balance of power in the United States Constitution, by expanding federal power at the expense of state autonomy.[231] The first section of the Fourteenth Amendment contains prohibitions expressly directed at the states.[232] "No State shall...deny to any person within its jurisdiction the equal protection of the laws."[233] The fifth section of that amendment provides that "The Congress shall have the power to enforce, by appropriate legislation, the provisions of this article."[234]

The Civil War was a cataclysmic alternative to a continuation of the philosophical debate about dual sovereignty and federalism within the United States.[235] That controversy had continued almost unabated since the Constitutional Convention of 1787. Extreme states rights theorists adhered to the Anti-Federalist view that sovereignty remained vested in

---

[228] *Id.*

[229] *Id.*

[230] John Walker Mauer, State Constitutions in a Time of Crisis: The Case of the Texas Constitution of 1876, 68 TEX. L. REV. 1615 (1990).

[231] City of Rome v. United States, 446 U.S. 156, 179 (1980); Fitzpatrick v. Bitzer, 427 U.S. 445, 455 (1976). See also William E. Nelson, The Fourteenth Amendment: From Political Principle to Judicial Doctrine (1988).

[232] City of Rome v. United States, 446 U.S. 156, 179 (1980).

[233] U.S. CONST. amend. XIV, § 1.

[234] U.S. CONST. amend. XIV § 5. See Fitzpatrick v. Bitzer, 427 U.S. 445, 453 (1976).

[235] See Phillip S. Paludan, "The American Civil War Considered as a Crisis in Law and Order," AMER. HIST. REV. 77 (1972): 1021.

the People of each state. For the Federalists, sovereignty resided with the People of the United States as a whole.[236]

Following the Civil War, the Reconstruction Amendments to the United States Constitution strengthened the Federalists' view of popular sovereignty and significantly influenced the operation of dual sovereignty in state constitutions. The states that had attempted to secede from the Union were required to amend their state constitutions in certain respects and to ratify the Fourteenth Amendment as a condition precedent to having their delegations seated in the United States House of Representatives and Senate.

According to Senator Jacob M. Howard of Michigan, the specific purpose of the Fourteenth Amendment was to protect "the personal rights guaranteed...by the first eight amendments of the [United States] Constitution.[237] Until the adoption of the Fourteenth Amendment in 1868, the federal Bill of Rights protected individual rights and liberties solely against encroachment by the federal government.[238] In the Slaughterhouse Cases and the Civil Rights Cases, the United States Supreme Court held that the Reconstruction Amendments were intended to protect former slaves and their decedents.[239] In 1884, however, the United States Supreme Court held that the Fourteenth Amendment did *not* require states to adhere to the provisions of the Bill of Rights.[240]

---

[236] A current majority of the United States Supreme Court appears to adhere to the view that "We the People" means ultimate sovereignty resides with a single national populace rather than with the people of the individual states. See U.S. Term Limits, Inc. v. Thornton, 115 S.Ct. 1842, 1875 (1995) (Kennedy, J. concurring). But see U.S. Term Limits, Inc. v. Thornton, 115 S. Ct. at 1875 (Thomas, J., dissenting, joined by Rehnquist, C.J., O'Connor, J., and Scalia, J.) ("The ultimate source of the Constitution's authority is the consent of the people of each individual State, not the consent of the undifferentiated people of the Nation as a whole."). See Akhil Reed Amar, Of Sovereignty and Federalism, 96 YALE L.J. 1425, 1429 (1987).

[237] U.S. Congress, Senate, Globe, 39th Cong., 1st Sess. (1865-66), 2765, quoted in Richard C. Cortner, The Supreme Court and the Second Bill of Rights: The Fourteenth Amendment and the Nationalization of Civil Liberties (Madison: University of Wisconsin Press, 1981), 5.

[238] Gerald Gunther, Constitutional Law 422-40 (11th ed. 1985). See Barron v. Baltimore, 32 U.S. (7 Pet.) 243 (1833); see also Shirley S. Abrahamson, Divided We Stand: State Constitutions in a More Perfect Union, 18 HASTINGS CONST. L.Q. 723, 727-28 (1991); Stanley Mosk, State Constitutionalism: Both Liberal and Conservative, 63 TEX. L. REV. 1081, 1081-82 (1985); Stewart G. Pollock, Adequate and Independent State Grounds as a Means of Balancing the Relationship Between State and Federal Courts, 63 TEX. L. REV. 977, 979 (1985).

[239] Slaughterhouse Cases, 83 U.S. (16 Wall.) 36 (1873), and Civil Rights Cases, 109 U.S. 3 (1883).

[240] Huratado v. California, 110 U.S. 516 (1884). The Court reaffirmed this idea in Maxwell v. Dow, 176 U.S. 581 (1900) and Twining v. New Jersey, 211 U.S. 78 (1908).

The major exceptions to the United States Supreme Court's general refusal to construe the Fourteenth Amendment as imposing national standards of rights or liberties on the states were in cases about private property and liberty of contract. In 1897, the United States Supreme Court held that under the Due Process clause of the Fourteenth Amendment the states could not take private property without just compensation.[241] In 1905, the United States Supreme Court further held that the Due Process clause of the Fourteenth Amendment could be applied to freedom of contract. That same term the Supreme Court reaffirmed its prior holding that the adoption of the Fourteenth Amendments did not make *all* of the Bill of Rights binding upon the States.[242] In 1908, however, the Supreme Court upheld a state law regulating the hours women could work, in the context of a Due Process challenge, as a reasonable restriction on contract rights.[243]

Between 1890 and 1910, a trilogy of cases from three different states relied upon equal protection principles in their state constitutions to invalidate Bible reading in public schools.[244] Those courts concluded that state constitutional principles of equal protection included the formation of a moral conscience. Those states rejected the argument that there should be a unified public conscience and that it should be Christian.[245] Most state supreme courts, however, continued to construe their state constitution as permitting the majority to control the issue of Bible reading in public schools.[246] In 1940, the United States Supreme Court held that the religion clauses of the First Amendment applied to the states by virtue of the incorporation doctrine and the Fourteenth Amendment's expanded protections.[247]

K. RECONSTRUCTION AND BEYOND

Following the Civil War, the Reconstruction era was marked by popular interest in governmental reform. There was widespread debate not only over the proper role of government in American life, but also its structure and operation. Between 1864 and 1879, thirty-seven new state

---

[241] Chicago, Burlington & Quincy Railroad Co. v. Chicago, 166 U.S. 226 (1897).

[242] Lochner v. New York, 198 U.S. 45 (1905).

[243] Muller v. Oregon, 208 U.S. 412 (1908).

[244] Weiss v. District Board, 76 Wis. 177 (1890); State ex rel. Freeman v. Scheve, 65 Neb. 853 (1902); People v Board of Educ., 245 Ill.334 (1910).

[245] *Id.*

[246] Alvin W. Johnson, The Legal Status of Church-State Relationships in the United States (Minneapolis: University of Minnesota Press, 1934).

[247] Cantwell v. Connecticut, 310 U.S. 296 (1940).

constitutions were written and ratified.[248] Within that same time period, however, the voters rejected new constitutions that were proposed in Michigan, Nebraska, New York and Ohio.[249] Delaware Republicans called unsuccessfully for a new constitution in 1874 "as a means of securing the reforms that are so much needed in the organic law of the State, and of keeping pace with the enlightened progress of the age, and with our sister States."[250]

Illinois 1870

The 1870 Illinois Constitution revised the judiciary, strengthened the executive branch, and included several specific prohibitions on the legislature's authority to act. The Illinois Constitution of 1870 also included specific provisions relating to the regulation of: grain elevators and warehouses; as well as freight and passenger railroad tariffs.[251] The rapid expansion of railroads in the three decades after the Civil War gave rise to many regulatory amendments in state constitutions to temper the results that had been yielded by the encouraging effect of earlier state constitutional provisions. With the adoption of a "damage clause," the 1870 Illinois Constitution also introduced an important change in the concept of eminent domain, e.g., compensation for damage, in addition to compensation for a "taking" and the right to have a jury determine the value of the private property owner's loss.[252]

North Carolina 1875

An effort to replace North Carolina's "carpetbagger" constitution of 1868 was defeated in 1870. In 1875, the legislature called for a state constitutional convention. Thirty amendments to the 1868 North Carolina Constitution were proposed and ratified by the voters in 1876. After those amendments were incorporated into the text, it became customary to refer to the amended 1868 constitution as the North Carolina Constitution of 1876.[253]

---

[248] Morton Keller, Affairs of State: Public Life in Late Nineteenth Century America 111 (1977).

[249] *Id.*

[250] Morton Keller, Affairs of State: Public Life in Late Nineteenth Century America 112 (1977).

[251] Kermit L. Hall, "Mostly Anchor and Little Sail," *The Revolution of American and State Constitutions* in Paul Finkelman and Stephen E. Gottlieb, eds., *Toward a Usable Past: Liberty Under State Constitutions* (Athens: University of Georgia Press, 1991) p. 404.

[252] *Id.*

[253] John V. Orth, *Symposium: "The Law of the Land": The North Carolina Constitution and State Constitutional Law: North Carolina Constitutional History*, 70 N.C. L. REV. 1759, 1782 (1992).

Segregation and Suffrage

Notwithstanding the enactment of the Reconstruction Amendments to the United States Constitution, provisions for mandatory racial segregation and other requirements that perpetuated racial discrimination were made a part of several state constitutions throughout the balance of the nineteenth century. The Tennessee Constitution of 1870, for example, provided that no school receiving state funds "shall allow white and negro children to be received as scholars together."[254] The "separate but equal" doctrine was approved by the United States Supreme Court in 1896.[255]

The corollary of mandatory segregation in state constitutions was often disfranchisement. Although the Reconstruction Amendments were successful in extending the right of suffrage to blacks, that expansion was frequently curtailed by provisions in state constitutions. In 1898, the United States Supreme Court upheld both the poll tax and the literacy provisions in the 1890 Mississippi Constitution.[256] In 1915, however, the United States Supreme Court decided that the grandfather clauses in several southern state constitutions violated the United States Constitution.[257] Those provisions had exempted the sons and grandsons of white voters during the Civil War from the subsequently enacted property and educational qualifications for voting.

Texas 1875

Texas assembled a state constitutional convention at Austin in August of 1875. The 1876 Texas Constitution was influenced by the agrarian reform movement. The *Grange*, in particular, had a dominant role at the convention.

The Texas convention was not only cognizant but also influenced by national trends in state constitution-making. Accordingly, many new sections were added in an effort to either restrict or limit legislation power. "Eleven of the 18 new sections of the Legislative Article were taken in whole or in part from the Missouri Constitution of 1875 and several others were copied almost verbatim from the Pennsylvania Constitution of 1873, including section 56 that enumerated 29 specific topics of special or local laws that the legislature was prohibited from passing."[258] The 1876 Texas Constitution also provided for the direct election of judges.

---

[254] Tenn. Const., 1879, art. XI, § 12, in *Sources and Documents*, ed. Swindler, 9:186.

[255] *Plessy v. Ferguson*, 163 U.S. 537 (1896).

[256] *Williams v. Mississippi*, 170 U.S. 213 (1898).

[257] *Guinn v. U.S.*, 238 U.S. 347 (1915).

[258] Janice C. May, *The Texas State Constitution: A Reference Guide*, p. 13 (Greenwood Press 1996).

Missouri 1876

The Missouri Constitution of 1876 introduced the concept of granting home rule to local municipalities.[259] Home rule authorized local communities to incorporate and operate autonomously within the parameters set by the state constitution. The trend of sharing power within each state between multiple political subdivisions continues today.

California 1879

The 1879 California Constitution was written by a convention that was dominated by Democrats and the Workingman's party.[260] That constitution provided for the regulation of railroads, banks, and mining companies. It also included several anti-Chinese provisions. State funding for public education was restricted to primary schools.[261]

Restricting Political Party Influence

State constitutions enacted during Reconstruction frequently restricted the power of party government within the state legislatures. This was accomplished by giving veto powers to the executive; mandating limits on state debts; requiring budgets to be balanced; regulating the legislative process to deter log-rolling; limiting state interference with local government, *e.g.*, with "ripper clauses,"[262] or home rule charters; giving local government "options" in limited areas, *e.g.*, the sale of alcohol; and as in Delaware's 1897 Constitution, by requiring political balance within the judiciary.[263] Consequently, by the end of the nineteenth century, a generation of state constitutional revisions had circumscribed the authority of the state government in a variety of procedural and substantive ways.

Omnibus Act 1889

In 1889, four states were admitted to the Union: North Dakota, South Dakota, Montana, and Washington. In February 1889, Congress had authorized each of their state constitutional conventions in an Omnibus Act. Each of these new states' constitutions included sections that not only framed the structure of government but also provided for its administration, primarily by placing limitations on the legislature; the

---

[259] William Swindler, "Missouri Constitutions: History, Theory and Practice," 23 MISSOURI L. REV. 35-37 (January 1958).

[260] Morton Keller, *Affairs of State: Public Life in Late Nineteenth Century America* 111-14 (The Belknap Press of Harvard University 1977).

[261] Morton Keller, *Affairs of State: Public Life in Late Nineteenth Century America* 111-14 (The Belknap Press of Harvard University 1977).

[262] David O. Porter, *The Ripper Clause In State Constitutional Law: An Early Urban Experiment - Part I*, 1969 UTAH L. REV. 287, 306-11 (1969).

[263] Del. Const. art. IV, § 3.

executive, and the judiciary. Each legislature was restricted with regard to special legislation, private legislation, corporations, and public credit. The governors' powers were restricted, e.g., the power of appointment. Each of these four state constitutions modified the jury system and other traditional provisions in the judicial articles of the constitutions in other states. These four constitutions also provided for the election of administrative officers.

Idaho 1889

On July 4, 1889, delegates from the territory of Idaho convened in Boise City to write a state constitution. The Idaho Territory had originally been severed from the Washington territory in 1863 to keep the capital of Washington in Olympia. The Idaho Territory was later divided to create the Montana Territory and the Wyoming Territory. The impetus for statehood in the remaining Idaho Territory was a proposal to subdivide it further by annexing the northern portion to either Washington or Montana and southern Idaho to Nevada. In fact, Congress agreed to annex northern Idaho to Washington in 1887, but the bill was pocket vetoed by President Cleveland.[264]

The Idaho constitutional convention was called by its Territorial Governor Edward A. Stevenson without either an enabling act from Congress or any authorizing action by the territorial legislature.[265] Although there was only limited precedent for such action, there was a sense of urgency in proceeding. The Idaho Constitution has been characterized as "extraordinarily important because it is a charter for the framework of decision."[266] Idaho's Constitution established institutional procedures for reaching decisions within the process of state government. One measure of that success is its continuous operation for more than a century later.[267]

L. PROGRESSIVE ERA POTPOURRI

TWENTIETH CENTURY BEGINS

As the nineteenth century was drawing to a close, one commentator, James Bryce, noted that state constitutions included many provisions that did not relate to the structure of state governments e.g., "minute provisions regarding the management and liabilities of banking companies, or

---

[264] Dennis C. Colson, *Idaho's Constitution: The Tie That Binds* 1, 4-6, 220-23 (University of Idaho 1991).

[265] *Id.*

[266] *Id.*

[267] *Id.*

railways, or corporations generally.[268] Bryce also remarked on an escalation in the trend to disregard any distinction between those provisions which were properly of constitutional dimensions and those subjects which were better addressed by statutes. "Following the Civil War, Bryce detected a transformation in which not only did state constitutions gradually lose the power to mold conclusively the course of public policies in [internal] areas they one exclusively dominated, but their prestige in relation to the [United States] Constitution also plummeted."[269]

Alabama 1901

"The Alabama Constitution Convention of 1901 was part of a movement that swept the post-Reconstruction South to disenfranchise blacks."[270] John B. Knox was president of the all-white convention. In his opening address to the delegates, he stated: "And what is it that we want to do? Why it is within the limits imposed by the Federal Constitution to establish white supremacy in this State."[271]

Article VIII, Section 182 of the Alabama Constitution of 1901 provided for the disenfranchisement of anyone convicted of certain enumerated crimes and 'any crime…involving moral turpitude." In 1985, the United States Supreme Court was called upon to decide 'the constitutionality of Article VIII, Section 182 of the Alabama Constitution of 1901" in the context of an allegation that the neutrally written state law produced disproportionate effects along racial lines.[272] The United States Supreme Court held:

> Without deciding whether sec. 182 would be valid if enacted today without any impermissible motivation, we simply observe that its original enactment was motivated by a desire to discriminate against blacks on account of race and the section continues to this day to have that effect. As such, it violates equal protection …

The record on appeal included "the proceedings before the convention, several historical studies, and the testimony of two expert historians."[273]

---

[268] James Bryce, *The American Commonwealth*, ed. Louis Hacker (New York: Capricorn Books, G.P. Putnam's Sons, 1959), 1:116.

[269] Kermit L. Hall, *"Mostly Anchor and Little Sail," The Revolution of American and State Constitutions* in Paul Finkelman and Stephen E. Gottlieb, eds., *Toward a Usable Past: Liberty Under State Constitutions* (Athens: University of Georgia Press, 1991) p. 403.

[270] *Hunter v. Underwood*, 471 U.S. 222 (1985).

[271] 1 *Official Proceedings of the Constitution Convention of the State of Alabama*, May 21st, 1901 to September 3d 1901, p. 8 (1940).

[272] *Hunter v. Underwood*, 471 U.S. 222 (1985).

[273] *Id.*

Initiative

Thirteen states changed their constitutions between 1898 and 1913 to provide for popular initiatives.[274] Such provision permitted voters to propose state constitution amendments.[275] State constitutional provisions for initiatives were enacted during the same period that nineteen states were authorizing legislation by initiatives and twenty-two states were permitted the electorate to accept or reject specific laws by popular referendum.[276]

Enabling Act Incursions

Congressional efforts to control the provisions of state constitutions as a prerequisite to approval for admission to the Union continued in the twentieth century. For example, on June 20, 1910, Congress passed an Enabling Act that authorized the Territory of New Mexico to form a constitution. When New Mexico subsequently applied for admission to the Union, however, the constitution that it had adopted was not acceptable. The Congress of the United States passed a joint resolution on August 21, 1911, that required the electors of New Mexico to amend its proposed state constitution as a condition precedent to admission. On January 6, 1912, President William Howard Taft issued a Proclamation that:

> in accordance with the provisions of the Act of Congress and the joint resolution of Congress herein named, declare and proclaim the fact that the fundamental conditions imposed by Congress on the State of New Mexico to entitle that State to admission have been ratified and accepted, and that the admission of the State into the Union on an equal footing with the other States is now complete.[277]

In 1911, at about the same time that Congress of directing that the proposed constitution for New Mexico had to be amended, the United States Supreme Court upheld a challenge to Oklahoma's refusal to adhere to a provision in its Enabling Act subsequent to Oklahoma's admission to the Union.[278] The Oklahoma Enabling Act provided, in part:

> The capital of said State shall temporarily be at the city of Guthrie, and shall not be changed therefrom previous to Anno Domini Nineteen Hundred and Thirteen, but said capital shall after said year be located by the electors of said State at an election to be provided for by the legislature; provided, however, that the legislature of said State, except as shall be necessary for the convenient transaction of the public business of said State at said capital, shall not

---

[274] G. Alan Tarr, *Constitutional Politics in the States, Contemporary Controversies and Historical Patterns*, p. 11 (Greenwood Press 1996).

[275] *Id.*

[276] *Id.*

[277] Reprinted in Robert F. Williams, *State Constitution Law, Cases and Materials* 79-80 (2d ed. Michie 1993).

[278] *Coyle v. Smith*, 221 U.S. 559 (1911).

appropriate any public moneys of the State for the erection of buildings for capital purposes during said period.[279]

Oklahoma was admitted to statehood on November 16, 1907. On December 29, 1910, its legislature passed an act that provided for the immediate removal of the capital from Guthrie to Oklahoma City. That statute was upheld by the Supreme Court of Oklahoma. Upon appeal to the United States Supreme Court, the question before it for review was framed as: "whether the provision of the enabling act was a valid limitation upon the power of the State after its admission, which overrides any subsequent state legislation repugnant thereto."[280] The United States Supreme Court then noted:

> The power to locate its own seat of government and to determine when and how it shall be changed from one place to another, and to appropriate its own public funds for that purpose, are essentially and peculiarly state powers. That one of the original thirteen States could now be shorn of such powers by an act of Congress would not be for a moment entertained. The question then comes to this: Can a State be placed upon a plane of inequality with its sister States in the Union if the Congress chooses to impose conditions which so operate, at the time of its admission?[281]

In analyzing the issue presented, the United States Supreme Court determined that America was "a union of States equal in power, dignity, and authority, each competent to exist that residum of sovereignty not delegated to the United States by the Constitution itself.[282] This premise led it to hold:

> …when a new State is admitted into the Union, it is so admitted with all of the powers of sovereignty and jurisdiction which pertain to the original States, and that such powers may not be constitutionally diminished, impaired or shorn away by any conditions, compacts or stipulations embraced in the act under which the new State came into the Union, which would not be valid and effectual if the subject of congressional legislation after admission.[283]

Therefore, the United States Supreme Court held that 'by virtue of her jurisdictional sovereignty as a State," Oklahoma was entitled to "determine for her own people the proper location of the local seat of government.[284]

---

[279] *Coyle v. Smith*, 221 U.S. 559 (1911).

[280] *Id.*

[281] *Id.*

[282] *Id.*

[283] *Id.*

[284] *Id.*

Arizona

President Taft visited the territory of Arizona in October 1909. During speeches in Phoenix and Prescott, he advised its citizens not to model their state constitution after that of Oklahoma, which he apparently described as a "zoological garden of cranks."[285] President Taft encouraged the people of Arizona to make their state constitution a simple framework of fundamental principles. He also urged them implicitly to eschew such progressive spirited features as the initiative and referendum.[286]

The Arizona Enabling Act was signed by President Taft on June 20, 1910. It included several provisions that were intended to be mandatory for inclusion in the Arizona Constitution "by an ordinance irrevocable without the consent of the United States and the people of said State."[287] These mandatory requirements covered a broad range of subjects: religious freedom, polygamy, Indian lands, and the location of the state capital.[288] The Arizona Enabling Act further provided that these provisions in the state constitution could not be amended without the consent of Congress. These mandates became article XX of the Arizona Constitution. Over time, some of these provisions have been ignored or abrogated by the Arizona legislature, while others have been changed by state constitutional amendments that Congress has approved.[289]

Voting Rights

Another aspect of the Oklahoma Constitution was before the United States Supreme Court in 1915.[290] At issue was the grandfather clause for voting in Art. 3 section 4A. That section was held to be a violation of the suffrage rights guaranteed by the United States Constitution.[291]

Local Governments

During the twentieth century, there have been significant substantive changes in many state constitutions with regard to local governments. Examples of those amendments include state constitutional provisions for county and municipal home rule. Political subdivisions within a state have also been authorized to levy taxes and issue bonds. The New Jersey

---

[285] John D. Leshy, *The Making of the Arizona Constitution*, 20 ARIZ. ST. L.J. 1, 31 (1988).

[286] *Id.*

[287] John D. Leshy, *The Making of the Arizona Constitution*, 20 ARIZ. ST. L.J. 1, 5-11, 13, 16-19,21-25 (1988).

[288] John D. Leshy, *The Making of the Arizona Constitution*, 20 ARIZ. ST. L.J. 1, 5-11, 13, 16-19,21-25 (1988).

[289] *Id.*

[290] *Guinn v. United States*, 238 U.S. 347 (1915).

[291] *Id.*

Constitution contains some of the more far-reaching language concerning county and municipal governments:

> The provisions of this Constitution and of any law concerning municipal corporations formed for local government or concerning counties, shall be liberally construed in their favor. The powers of counties and such municipal corporations shall include not only those granted in express terms but also those of necessary or fair implication, or incident to the powers expressly conferred, or essential thereto, and not inconsistent with or prohibited by this Constitution or by law.[292]

Other noteworthy provisions affecting the operation of local governments have appeared in the state constitutions of: Missouri (joint performance of certain governmental functions and authorizing contractual arrangements for others); Georgia (county consolidation); and, Oregon (county manager government).[293]

Constitutional Commissions and Limited Conventions

During this century, two methods of amending state constitutions became increasingly popular. First, many states created state constitutional commissions. Those commissions were often comprised of political leaders, legal scholars, and distinguished citizens.[294] One purpose of those commissions has been "to dismantle the archaic institutional remains of participational democracy."[295] A state constitutional commission's final recommendations are submitted to the legislature and/or the public for approval. Second, limited constitutional conventions were called by several states to address or avoid addressing specific issues. The limited state constitutional convention has also been used to "deal with special situations, more or less of an emergency character."[296]

M. INCORPORATION DOCTRINE'S IMPACT

In 1925, there was a paradigm shift in the operation of America's state and federal jurisprudence. The United States Supreme Court began applying the Bill of Rights to the states by incorporating it into the Fourteenth Amendment through the Due Process Clause. In upholding New York's criminal anarchy statute the United States Supreme Court

---

[292] W. Brooke Graves, *State Constitutional Law: A Twenty-Five Year Summary*, 8 WM. & MARY L. REV. 1, 31 (1966). New Jersey Constitution art. IV, Section 7, Paragraph 11.

[293] *Id.*

[294] *See* Sturm, Albert L. and Craig, James B. Jr., *State Constitutional Commissions: Fifteen Years of Increasing Use.* 39 STATE GOVERNANCE pp. 56-63 (Winter 1966).

[295] Harvey Wheeler, *The Rise and Fall of Political Democracy*, p. 16, Center for the Study of Democratic Institutions, Santa Barbara (1966).

[296] W. Brooke Graves, *State Constitutional Law: A Twenty-Five Year Summary*, 8 WM. & MARY L. REV. 1, 8-9 (1966), *e.g.* New Jersey (1947); Virginia (1945-46); Tennessee (1952-53 and 1959).

said: "For present purposes we may and do assume that freedom of speech and of the press - which are protected by the First Amendment from abridgment by Congress - are among the fundamental personal rights and 'liberties' protected by the due process clause of the Fourteenth Amendment from impairment by the States."[297]

Thereafter, the United States Supreme Court continued to hold that other selected provisions of the federal Bill of Rights also afforded protection against state action by virtue of the Due Process clause of the Fourteenth Amendment.[298] This process is known as the incorporation doctrine.[299] The right to a jury trial is illustrative of the selective incorporation process.

The right to trial by jury has been described as "the morning star of liberty which…revolutionized America and a valuable safeguard to liberty or the very palladium of a free government."[300] The constitutions adopted the original States and "the constitution of every State entering the Union thereafter, in one form or another," have protected the right to trial by jury in criminal cases.[301] "The guarantees of jury trial in the Federal and State Constitutions reflect a *profound judgment* about the *way* in which law should be enforced and justice administered."[302]

---

[297] *Gitlow v. New York*, 268 U.S. 652, 665-66 (1925).

[298] See Michael Kent Curtis, No State Shall Abridge: The Fourteenth Amendment and the Bill of Rights (Durham: Duke University Press, 1986), and Richard Cortner, The Supreme Court and the Second Bill of Rights: The Fourteenth Amendment and the Nationalization of Civil Liberties (Madison: University of Wisconsin Press, 1981).

[299] For discussions regarding the incorporation of the federal Bill of Rights into the Due Process Clause of the Fourteenth Amendment, thereby making them applicable to the states, see Louis Henkin, "Selective Incorporation" in the Fourteenth Amendment, 73 YALE L.J. 74 (1963). See Richard C. Cortner, The Supreme Court and the Second Bill of Rights: The Fourteenth Amendment and the Nationalization of Civil Liberties (1981); Akhil Reed Amar, The Bill of Rights and the Fourteenth Amendment, 101 YALE L.J. 1193 (1992); Michael K. Curtis, The Fourteenth Amendment and the Bill of Rights, 14 CONN. L. REV. 237 (1982); Charles Fairman, Does the Fourteenth Amendment Incorporate The Bill of Rights? 2 STAN. L. REV. 5 (1949).

[300] The Federalist No. 83, ed. Jacob E. Cooke (Middletown, Conn.: Wesleyan University Press, 1961) p. 582.

[301] Duncan v. State of Louisiana, 391 U.S. 145, 153 (1968).

[302] Duncan v. State of Louisiana, 391 U.S. 145, 155 (1968) (emphasis added). A number of states, for example, now authorize juries of a size less than the common law number of twelve. Maxwell v. Dow, 176 U.S. 581 (1900). Several states do not adhere to the common law requirement for unanimous verdict. Jordan v. Commonwealth, 225 U.S. 167 (1912); and Fay v. NY, 332 U.S. 261 (1947). see, e.g., Note, Trial by Jury in Criminal Cases, 69 COLUMBIA L. REV. 419, 430 (1969); and Williams v. Florida, 399 U.S. 78 (1970).

The right to trial by jury is guaranteed by the Sixth and Seventh amendments to the Federal Constitution. Following the adoption of the Fourteenth Amendment to the United States Constitution, the Sixth Amendment right to trial by jury in *criminal* proceedings has been deemed to have been incorporated by the Due Process clause.[303] Accordingly, that Sixth Amendment right now provides protection against state action also. The United States Supreme Court has not yet, however, held that the Seventh Amendment's guarantee of jury trials in *civil* proceedings was made applicable to the states by the adoption of the Fourteenth Amendment.[304] Accordingly, the right to a jury trial in civil proceedings has always been and remains exclusively protected by provisions in the state constitutions.[305] Forty-nine states have state constitutional provisions similar to the Seventh Amendment.[306] Only Louisiana does not have a constitutional provision granting the right to trial by jury.

Federal Constitutional standards, however, set only a minimum level of protection.[307] The declaration of rights or substantive provisions in a state's constitution may, and often do, provide for broader or additional rights.[308] The expansion beyond federally guaranteed individual liberties by a state constitution is attributable to a variety of reasons: differences in textual language, legislative history, pre-existing state law, structural differences, matters of particular concern, and state traditions.[309]

N. NEW DEAL CHALLENGES

By the time of the Great Depression, many state constitutions had become "super" statutory codes because of multiple amendments over an

---

[303] Duncan v. Louisiana, 391 U.S. 145 (1968).

[304] Minneapolis v. St. Louis R.R. v. Bombolis, 241 U.S. 211 (1916); Walker v. Sauvinet, 92 U.S. 90 (1876).

[305] McCool v. Gehret, 657 A.2d 269, 281 (Del. 1995); Richard S. Arnold, Trial by Jury: The Constitutional Right to a Jury of Twelve in Civil Trials, 22 HOFSTRA L. REV. 1 (1993).

[306] J. Kendall Few, In Defense of Trial by Jury, 469-76 (1993).

[307] *See also* William J. Brennan, Jr., *The Bill of Rights and the States: The Revival of State Constitutions as Guardians of Individual Rights*, 61 N.Y.U. L. REV. 535 (1986); William J. Brennan, Jr., *State Constitutions and the Protection of Individual Rights*, 90 HARV. L. REV. 489 (1977).

[308] Phyllis W. Beck, *Foreword: Stepping Over the Procedural Threshold in the Presentation of State Constitutional Claims*, 68 TEMP. L. REV. 1035 (1995); Hans A. Linde, *First Things First: Rediscovering the States' Bills of Rights*, 9 U. BALT. L. REV. 379, 381 (1980); *see also* Stanley Mosk, *State Constitutionalism: Both Liberal and Conservative*, 63 TEX. L. REV. 1081, 1081-82 (1985); John M. Wisdom, *Foreword: The Ever-Whirling Wheels of American Federalism*, 59 NOTRE DAME L. REV. 1063 (1984).

[309] *State v. Williams*, 459 A.2d 641 (N.J. 1983); *State v. Gunwall*, 720 P.2d 808, 811-13 (Wash. 1986). *Commonwealth v. Edmunds*, 586 A.2d 887 (Pa. 1991).

extended period of time. Ironically, many of the popularly enacted social and economic provisions in state constitutions restricted the states' ability to enact timely statutory solutions to any rapidly developing crisis.[310] Consequently, the federal government was called upon to solve the nation's collective problems. The New Deal legislation, that eventually passed Federal Constitutional muster, responded to the nation's economic distress and caused another paradigm shift in the concept of state sovereignty.[311] The enactment of federal legislation that impacts upon the internal operations of each state and its citizenry has continued unabated since the New Deal era.[312] The provisions in many state constitutions now often compete or conflict with federally created or subsidized programs. It has been noted "that many states which bemoan their loss of power to the Federal Government still cling to constitutional limitations which cripple their own legislatures."[313] In fact, one critic of state constitution-making in the twentieth century has written:

> Changes in state constitutions still are largely directed toward the goals of the Efficiency and Economy movement of two generations ago, concentrating upon professionalization of all branches of government rather than upon improving the responsiveness of state government to widespread popular demands and the major contemporary issues in society.[314]

This is because the so-called modernization of state constitutions has been tempered by the normal processes of majoritarian partisan politics. Notwithstanding their laudatory intentions, the revisors of many state constitutions have been unable to overcome the temptation "to predetermine decisions with respect of policies and services...by writing specific prohibitions, mandates, or prescriptions into state constitutions."[315] Consequently, many state constitutions continued to be filled with legislative and administrative obstacles that were impervious to statutory solutions.

---

[310] See Kermit L. Hall, "*Mostly Anchor and Little Sail*," in Finkelman and Gottlieb, eds., *Toward a Usable Past* (Athens: University of Georgia Press, 1991) p. 408.

[311] Tribe, *American Constitutional Law*, p. 386. *See also* Bruce Ackerman, *We The People Foundations (Cambridge: Harvard University Press (1991)*.

[312] *See United States v. Lopez*, 115 S. Ct. 1624, 1628 (1995).

[313] W. Brooke Graves, *State Constitutional Law: A Twenty-Five Year Summary*, 8 WM. & MARY L. REV. 1, 25 (1966). *See also* W. Brooke Graves, 14 LA. L. REV. 749-763 (1954).

[314] Adrian, *Trends in State Constitutions*, 5 HARV. J. LEGIS. 311, 341 (1968) quoted in William F. Swindler, *State Constitutions for the 20th Century*, 50 NEB. L. REV. 577, 577-78 (1971).

[315] William F. Swindler, *State Constitutions for the 20th Century*, 50 NEB. L. REV. 577, 578 (1971).

O. COLD WAR REVISIONS

There was a "wave" of state constitutional revisions between 1945 and 1970. The recurring theme of those revisions was often an effort to modernize the operation of a state's framework of government. These efforts frequently realigned the structure and allocation of power between the political sub-divisions within a state. The focal points were usually related to taxation, public finance, and a shared responsibility for the rendition of intra-state constituent services.

Several state constitutions provided for representation in either one or both houses of its legislature without regard to population.[316] The 1897 Delaware Constitution, for example, not only provided for malapportionment by describing legislative districts with particularity, but also included no mechanism for reappointment.[317] A similar provision in the New Jersey Constitution prevented any state constitutional reform for three decades in this century, until an agreement was reached to exclude reappointment from the agenda of the constitutional convention.[318] In 1964, the United States Supreme Court held that the Fourteenth Amendment's equal protection clause mandated that both houses of bicameral state legislatures had to be apportioned by population.[319]

The constitutions of at least thirteen states were revised between 1963 and 1976.[320] There was a great deal of interest in rewriting state constitutions as the decade of the 1960s drew to a close. North Carolina adopted a new (third) constitution in 1971 that was primarily the product of its State Constitution Study Commission. "The text of the new frame of government was that of the 1868 constitution as amended, subjected to rigorous editorial revision," along with some revisions and clarifications.[321] The amendment process was deemed to be most advisable for fundamental reforms.[322]

---

[316] *See* Robert G. Dixon, *Democratic Representation: Reapportionment in Law and Politics* (New York: Oxford University Press, 1968), 62-63, chart I.

[317] *See* James Q. Dealey, *Growth of American State Constitutions* 97 (New York: Da Capo Press, 1972).

[318] Robert F. Williams, *The New Jersey State Constitution: A Reference Guide* (Wesptport, Conn.: Greenwood Press, 1990), 13-16.

[319] *Reynolds v. Sims*, 377 U.S. 533 (1964).

[320] .James A. Henretta, *Foreword: Rethinking the State Constitutional Tradition*, 22 RUTGERS L.J. 836-39 (1991).

[321] John V. Orth, Symposium: "The Law of the Land": The North Carolina Constitution and State Constitutional Law: North Carolina Constitutional History, 70 N.C. L. REV. 1759, 1791 (1992).

[322] *Id.* at 1792-96 (1992).

P. PATTERNS AND MODELS

According to Daniel J. Elazar, there has been a tendency to perpetuate the basic political and cultural values of the majority by reflecting them in state constitutional provisions.[323] Six patterns of state constitutions have been identified and summarized by Elazar in what G. Alan Tarr characterizes as a political-cultural model.[324] The features and characteristics of Elazar's six political-cultural patterns of state constitutions will be described seriatim.[325]

Commonwealth Pattern

According to Elazar, the commonwealth pattern emerged from the state constitutions in and around New England.[326] The philosophic nature of those frameworks of government is to provide definitive guidance for the operation of a civilized society under a republican form of government. The commonwealth pattern is the oldest form of state constitution. Originally characterized by their brevity, the underlying premise is a covenant. The format is to describe the elements of government, while at the same time guaranteeing the preservation of fundamental individual and property rights. The state constitutional commonwealth pattern has demonstrated a capacity for adaptation without the need for wholesale revision. According to Elazar, eight states outside of the New England region have state constitutions based upon the commonwealth pattern.

Commercial Republic Pattern

The commercial republic pattern of constitution described by Elazar became prevalent in states situated to the south and west of New England.[327] This type of state constitution evolved from a series of compromises. In each state where this pattern emerged, there was a history of commercial development and urbanization, in combination with a citizenry increasingly buoyed by migrants with diverse ethnic heritages. The competition between commercial interests and ethnic ideals resulted in frequent and expansive revisions to the framework of government. The length of the provisions the commercial republic pattern is attributable to

---

[323] Daniel J. Elazar, The Principles and Traditions Underlying State Constitutions, 12 Publius: the Journal of Federalism 11, 18-22 (1982).

[324] G. Alan Tarr, Constitutional Politics in the States, Contemporary Controversies and Historical Patterns, p. 4 (Greenwood Press 1996).

[325] Daniel J. Elazar, The Principles and Traditions Underlying State Constitutions, 12 Publius: The Journal of Federalism 11, 18-22 (1982).

[326] *Id.*

[327] Daniel J. Elazar, The Principles and Traditions Underlying State Constitutions, 12 Publius: The Journal of Federalism 11, 18-22 (1982).

the explicit and detailed nature of the solutions to areas of earlier disagreement. The Illinois Constitution is illustrative of the commercial republic pattern.

Southern Contractual Pattern

The southern contractual pattern of state constitution is evidenced, according to Elazar, by frequent changes that are directly attributable to paradigm shifts in social, political, and economic policies.[328] These state constitutions often contained provisions that were normally the subject matter of ordinary legislation. The state constitutional experience of Texas is illustrative: in 1836, a constitution was adopted for the Republic of Texas; in 1845, Texas adopted a new constitution for admission to statehood; it adopted another constitution in 1861, when Texas joined the Confederacy; a fourth constitution was needed before Texas could rejoin the Union in 1866; the fifth Texas Constitution was adopted in 1869, through the efforts of Republican Reconstructionalists; and the sixth Texas Constitution was adopted in 1876. The electorate defeated a proposal and substantially revised constitution for Texas in 1975.

Civil Code Pattern

The civil code pattern described by Elazar is attributed only to the state constitutions of Louisiana.[329] Drawing upon its French legal background, the Louisiana constitutions have resembled the long and detailed civil codes of Europe. Between 1812 and 1982, Louisiana had eleven constitutions. The tenth constitution was adopted in 1921 and had been amended 439 times by 1965. A revised and abbreviated state constitution was adopted for Louisiana in 1974.

Frame of Government Pattern

The frame of government pattern is found by Elazar in the state constitutions of the Far West.[330] The primary focus of these documents is to establish a framework of state government. The emphasis in each was upon limited government except for a few specific subjects involving economic development.

Managerial Model

Finally, Elazar depicts the constitutions of Hawaii and Alaska as most approximating the managerial model designed by constitutional reformers in this century.[331] These constitutions provide for broad grants of power to

---

[328] *Id.*

[329] Daniel J. Elazar, The Principles and Traditions Underlying State Constitutions, 12 Publius: The Journal of Federalism 11, 18-22 (1982).

[330] *Id.*

[331] *Id.*

the executive branch and few restrictions on the legislature. They also include provisions that address social legislation, natural resource presentation, and relationships with local political subdivisions. These state constitutions have been analogized to the Hamiltonian managerial model.

Model State Constitution

The National Municipal League published its first Model State Constitution in 1921. During the next fifty years, that Model State Constitution was revised many times and appeared in six editions. The Model State Constitution sets forth both a framework of government and an enumeration of fundamental rights. It has been drawn upon selectively by some states for guidance. This is the "model" that Elazar refers to in his analysis of the constitutions adopted by Alaska and Hawaii.

Historical-Movement Model

Some scholars, other than Elazar, have identified what G. Alan Tarr characterizes as an "historical-movement model" in state constitutions.[332] Unlike Elazar, who looked at the unique aspects of the intra-state politics and culture, those scholars contend that state constitutions reflect the political forces that were prevalent nationally at the time of their adoption.[333] Thus, proponents of the historical movements model in state constitutional-making submit that state constitutional revisions inculcated the epic national themes of their time, e.g., Jacksonian democracy, Antebellum concerns, Reconstruction problems, the Progressive movement in the early twentieth century, etc.

Ordinary Politics Model

Another theory of state constitution-making is what Tarr describes as the ordinary-politics model.[334] According to that theory, provisions inserted into state constitutions reflect the ordinary political fluctuations within a state that are an inevitable consequence when the majority in power shifts between parties, regions, or other affiliated interests. To the extent that a group with particular perspectives has the ability to amend

---

[332] G. Alan Tarr, Constitutional Politics in the States, Contemporary Controversies and Historical Patterns, p. 4 (Greenwood Press 1996).

[333] See Albert L. Sturm, "The Development of American State Constitutions," Publius: The Journal of Federalism 12 (Winger 1982): 57-98; and Kermit L. Hall, "Mostly Anchor and Little Sail: The Evolution of American State Constitutions," in Toward a Usable Past: Liberty Under State Constitutions, ed. Paul Finkelman and Stephen E. Gottleib (Athens: University of Georgia Press, 1991), 388-417.

[334] See Elmer E. Cornwell, Jr., Jay S. Goodman, and Wayne R. Swanson, State Constitutional Conventions (New York: Praeger, 1975); and Charles Press, "Assessing Policy and Operational Implications of State Constitutional Change," Publius: The Journal of Federalism 12 (Winter 1982): 99-111.

the state's constitution, it can enhance the institutionalization of its view more effectively than it could with a statute. Consequently, this model is used to explain why the design of many state constitutions may appear to resemble a patchwork quilt more than a mosaic.

CONCLUSION[335]

The United States Constitution "created a legal system unprecedented in form and design, establishing two orders of government, each with its own direct relationship, its own privity, its own set of mutual rights and obligations to the people who sustain it and are governed by it." State governments became subject to a superior regime of law, established by the people, through a specific delegation of their sovereign power to a national government that was paramount within its delegated sphere. Chief Justice Marshall described the national and state governments as "each sovereign, with respect to the objects committed to it, and neither sovereign with respect to the objects committed to the other."

"From the inception of the American republic, federal and state constitutional traditions have been distinct." The United States Constitution has retained its original character as a document which fixed the basic structure of government and allocated power among its three branches. State constitution-making and amending has been a recurring process within the broader political, social, economic, and historical contexts of time and place.

The goal of American federalism, in the words of the Preamble to the United States Constitution, was to form a "more perfect Union," by providing for a division of sovereign power at two levels. In structuring federalism to unite the country, the United States Constitution simultaneously provided for the recognition of the pre-existing format of state governments and strengthened the national government, without concentrating all sovereign power at that level. The result is a deterrence of tyranny, the dual protection of individual liberty, and a division of governmental responsibility in addressing social and economic issues.

The 1787 United States Constitution, as amended, and the succession of state constitutions from 1776 until today, as amended, reflect the history of how democracy has operated within America and each of its United States.

---

[335] Taken from Randy J. Holland, State Constitutions: Purpose and Function, 69 Temple L. Rev 989, 1006 (1996).

CHAPTER III

DUAL SOVEREIGNTY: THE INTERRELATION OF THE STATE AND FEDERAL CONSTITUTIONS

A. INTRODUCTION

States operate as true sovereigns within the system created by the federal Constitution. The concept of "federalism", however, is nowhere explicitly written into or defined by the U.S. Constitution. Instead, it is a uniquely American contribution to political theory that is inherent in numerous constitutional provisions. Federalism is a large topic in its own right, one that could easily fill its own casebook. This casebook, with its focus on state constitutional law, is not the proper forum for a lengthy examination of federalism principles.

Instead, this chapter focuses only on some provisions in the U.S. Constitution that tend to bear most directly on state constitutional law, though in some very different ways. The chapter is divided into two major sections: (1) federal provisions that limit or influence the content of state constitutions; and (2) the distribution of federal and state powers under the U.S. Constitution. The first section focuses on Articles IV and VI of the U.S. Constitution. Article IV directly addresses a number of matters central to the States' sovereignty and their role in the federal system. Article VI contains the all important Supremacy Clause which makes clear that federal law preempts contrary state law, including state constitutional law. The second section examines the relationship between state and federal governmental powers, with attention to the powers exclusive to the federal government, the powers exclusive to the States, and the overlapping powers that the two sovereigns share.

B. FEDERAL PROVISIONS THAT LIMIT OR INFLUENCE THE CONTENT OF STATE CONSTITUTIONS

Article IV of the U.S. Constitution contains a number of provisions directly relevant to the States and their role in the federal system. In particular, Article IV contains the Full Faith and Credit Clause, the Privileges and Immunities Clause, and the Extradition Clause, all of which essentially require the States to respect other States. (Article IV also includes the Fugitive Slave Clause; a provision superseded and rendered a nullity by the Thirteenth Amendment, which abolished slavery.) Article IV also gives Congress the power to admit new States into the union and includes a provision known as the Guarantee Clause. All of these provisions are addressed in more detail below, using a handful of illustrative cases. Coverage here is intended to introduce the student to some of the important connections between federal constitutional provisions and the States, but the treatment is not intended to be comprehensive.

1. Article IV

a. Full Faith and Credit

Section 1 of Article IV provides that "Full Faith and Credit shall be given in each State to the public Acts, Records, and judicial Proceedings of every other State." Complex and difficult questions can and do arise about what judgments of one State must be accorded legal recognition by another State. A common example of applying full faith and credit would be enforcing a civil tort judgment of State A in the courts of State B. A much more controversial example would be an effort to compel State A, which allows only heterosexual marriages, to recognize a same sex marriage authorized by and entered into in State B. See Chapter VI.D.

b. Privileges and Immunities

Section 2 of Article IV declares that the "Citizens of each State shall be entitled to all Privileges and Immunities of Citizens in the several States." This Privileges and Immunities Clause (to be distinguished from the Privileges or Immunities Clause of the Fourteenth Amendment) is essentially a non-discrimination principle. An illustrative case follows.

SUPREME COURT OF NEW HAMPSHIRE v. PIPER
470 U.S. 274 (1985)

POWELL, J., delivered the opinion of the Court.

The Rules of the Supreme Court of New Hampshire limit bar admission to state residents. We here consider whether this restriction violates the Privileges and Immunities Clause of the United States Constitution, Art. IV, § 2.

I

A

Kathryn Piper lives in Lower Waterford, Vermont, about 400 yards from the New Hampshire border. In 1979, she applied to take the February 1980 New Hampshire bar examination. Piper submitted with her application a statement of intent to become a New Hampshire resident. Following an investigation, the Board of Bar Examiners found that Piper was of good moral character and met the other requirements for admission. She was allowed to take, and passed, the examination. Piper was informed by the Board that she would have to establish a home address in New Hampshire prior to being sworn in.

On May 7, 1980, Piper requested from the Clerk of the New Hampshire Supreme Court a dispensation from the residency requirement. Although she had a "possible job" with a lawyer in Littleton, New Hampshire, Piper stated that becoming a resident of New Hampshire would be inconvenient. Her house in Vermont was secured by a mortgage with a favorable interest rate, and she and her husband recently had become parents.

[Piper's request was denied. Piper] then formally petitioned the New Hampshire Supreme Court for permission to become a member of the bar. The Supreme Court denied Piper's request.

B

Piper filed this action [and]…alleged that Rule 42 of the New Hampshire Supreme Court, that excludes nonresidents from the bar, violates the Privileges and Immunities Clause of Art. IV, § 2, of the United States Constitution.

II

A

Article IV, § 2, of the Constitution provides that the "Citizens of each State shall be entitled to all Privileges and Immunities of Citizens in the several States." This Clause was intended to "fuse into one Nation a collection of independent, sovereign States." Recognizing this purpose, we have held that it is "[o]nly with respect to those 'privileges' and 'immunities' bearing on the vitality of the Nation as a single entity" that a State must accord residents and nonresidents equal treatment. *Baldwin Montana Fish & Game Com'n*, 436 U.S 371, 383 (1978). In *Baldwin,* for example, we concluded that a State may charge a nonresident more than it charges a resident for the same elk-hunting license. Because elk hunting is "recreation" rather than a "means of a livelihood," we found that the right to a hunting license was not "fundamental" to the promotion of interstate harmony.

Derived, like the Commerce Clause, from the fourth of the Articles of Confederation, the Privileges and Immunities Clause was intended to create a national economic union. It is therefore not surprising that this Court repeatedly has found that "one of the privileges which the Clause guarantees to citizens of State A is that of doing business in State B on terms of substantial equality with the citizens of that State." In *Ward v. Maryland,* 12 Wall. 418 (1871), the Court invalidated a statute under which nonresidents were required to pay $300 per year for a license to trade in goods not manufactured in Maryland, while resident traders paid a fee varying from $12 to $150. Similarly...the Court [has] held that nonresident fishermen could not be required to pay a license fee of $2,500 for each shrimp boat owned when residents were charged only $25 per boat. Finally, in *Hicklin v. Orbeck,* 437 U.S. 518 (1978), we found violative of the Privileges and Immunities Clause a statute containing a resident hiring preference for all employment related to the development of the State's oil and gas resources.

There is nothing in [our cases] suggesting that the practice of law should not be viewed as a "privilege" under Art. IV, § 2. Like the occupations considered in our earlier cases, the practice of law is important to the national economy.

B

Appellant asserts that the Privileges and Immunities Clause should be held inapplicable to the practice of law because a lawyer's activities are "bound up with the exercise of judicial power and the administration of justice." Its contention is based on the premise that the lawyer is an "officer of the court," who "exercises state power on a daily basis." Appellant concludes that if the State cannot exclude nonresidents from the bar, its ability to function as a sovereign political body will be threatened.

Lawyers do enjoy a "broad monopoly...to do things other citizens may not lawfully do." We do not believe, however, that the practice of law involves an "exercise of state power" justifying New Hampshire's residency requirement. In *In re Griffiths*, 413 U.S. 717 (1973), we held that the State could not exclude an alien from the bar on the ground that a lawyer is an "'officer of the Court who'...is entrusted with the 'exercise of actual governmental power.'" We concluded that a lawyer is not an "officer" within the ordinary meaning of that word. He "'makes his own decisions, follows his own best judgment, collects his own fees and runs his own business.'" Moreover, we held that the state powers entrusted to lawyers do not "involve matters of state policy or acts of such unique responsibility as to entrust them only to citizens." We therefore conclude that the right to practice law is protected by the Privileges and Immunities Clause.

III

The conclusion that Rule 42 deprives nonresidents of a protected privilege does not end our inquiry. The Court has stated that "[l]ike many other constitutional provisions, the privileges and immunities clause is not an absolute." The Clause does not preclude discrimination against nonresidents where (i) there is a substantial reason for the difference in treatment; and (ii) the discrimination practiced against nonresidents bears a substantial relationship to the State's objective.

The Supreme Court of New Hampshire offers several justifications for its refusal to admit nonresidents to the bar. It asserts that nonresident members would be less likely (i) to become, and remain, familiar with local rules and procedures; (ii) to behave ethically; (iii) to be available for court proceedings; and (iv) to do *pro bono* and other volunteer work in the State. We find that none of these reasons meets the test of "substantiality," and that the means chosen do not bear the necessary relationship to the State's objectives.

There is no evidence to support appellant's claim that nonresidents might be less likely to keep abreast of local rules and procedures. Nor may we assume that a nonresident lawyer-any more than a resident-would disserve his clients by failing to familiarize himself with the rules. As a practical matter, we think that unless a lawyer has, or anticipates, a considerable practice in the New Hampshire courts, he would be unlikely to take the bar examination and pay the annual dues of $125.

We also find the appellant's second justification to be without merit, for there is no reason to believe that a nonresident lawyer will conduct his practice in a dishonest manner. The nonresident lawyer's professional duty and interest in his reputation should provide the same incentive to maintain high ethical standards as they do for resident lawyers. Furthermore,...[t]he Supreme Court of New Hampshire has the authority to discipline all members of the bar, regardless of where they reside.

There is more merit to the appellant's assertion that a nonresident member of the bar at times would be unavailable for court proceedings. Even the most conscientious lawyer residing in a distant State may find himself unable to appear in court for an unscheduled hearing or proceeding. Nevertheless, we do not believe that this type of problem justifies the exclusion of nonresidents from the state bar. One may assume that a high percentage of nonresident lawyers willing to take the state bar examination and pay the annual dues will reside in places reasonably convenient to New Hampshire. Furthermore, in those cases where the nonresident counsel will be unavailable on short notice, the State can protect its interests through less restrictive means. The trial court, by rule or as an exercise of discretion, may require any lawyer who resides at a great distance to retain a local attorney who will be available for unscheduled meetings and hearings.

The final reason advanced by appellant is that nonresident members of the state bar would be disinclined to do their share of *pro bono* and volunteer work. Perhaps this is true to a limited extent, particularly where the member resides in a distant location. We think it is reasonable to believe, however, that most lawyers who become members of a state bar will endeavor to perform their share of these services.

In summary, appellant neither advances a "substantial reason" for its discrimination against nonresident applicants to the bar, nor demonstrates that the discrimination practiced bears a close relationship to its proffered objectives.

c. Extradition

Article IV, section 2 also provides that a fugitive "who shall flee from Justice, and be found in another State, shall on Demand of the executive Authority of the State from which he fled, be delivered up, to be removed to the State having Jurisdiction of the Crime." The Extradition Clause was the subject of a fascinating Supreme Court decision on the eve of the Civil War, resulting in the courts playing a limited role in enforcing the clause for over 125 years until the Supreme Court eventually overruled the earlier case and expanded the courts' ability to require extradition.

KENTUCKY v. DENNISON
65 U.S. (24 How.) 66 (1861)

[A grand jury in the Commonwealth of Kentucky issued the following indictment: "WOODFORD CIRCUIT COURT. *The Commonwealth of Kentucky* against *Willis Lago, free man of color.* The grand jury of Woodford county, in the name and by the authority of the Commonwealth of Kentucky, accuse Willis Lago, free man of color, of the crime of assisting a slave to escape, &c., committed as follows, namely: the said Willis Lago, free man of color, on the fourth day of October 1859, in the county aforesaid, not having lawful claim, and not having any color of claim thereto, did seduce and entice Charlotte, a slave, the property of C. W. Nuckols, to leave her owner and possessor, and did aid and assist said slave in an attempt to make her escape from her said owner and possessor, against the peace and dignity of the Commonwealth of Kentucky."

Lago, a resident of Ohio, was in Ohio when the indictment was issued. Governor Magoffin of Kentucky requested that the Governor of Ohio, William Dennison, turn Lago over to Kentucky for prosecution. Governor Dennison, an ardent abolitionist, refused to do so. Kentucky then brought a mandamus action under the Supreme Court's original jurisdiction, seeking to compel Governor Dennison to deliver Lago to Kentucky.]

TANEY, C. J., delivered the opinion of the court.

The court is sensible of the importance of this case, and of the great interest and gravity of the questions involved in it, and which have been raised and fully argued at the bar. [After addressing various jurisdictional issues and concluding that the Court had jurisdiction over the matter, The Chief Justice proceeded to the Extradition Clause.]

This brings us to the examination of the clause of the Constitution which has given rise to this controversy. It is in the following words:

> A person charged in any State with treason, felony, or other crime, who shall flee from justice, and be found in another State, shall, on demand of the Executive authority of the State from which he fled, be delivered up, to be removed to the State having jurisdiction of the crime.

Looking to the language of the clause, it is difficult to comprehend how any doubt could have arisen as to its meaning and construction. The words, 'treason, felony, or other crime,' in their plain and obvious import, as well as in their legal and technical sense, embrace every act forbidden and made punishable to a law of the State. The word 'crime' of itself includes every offence, from the highest to the lowest in the grade of offences, and includes what are called 'misdemeanors,' as well as treason and felony.

The argument on behalf of the Governor of Ohio, which insists upon excluding from this clause new offences created by a statute of the State, and growing out of its local institutions, and which are not admitted to be offences in the State where the fugitive is found, nor so regarded by the general usage of civilized nations, would render the clause useless for any practical purpose. For where can the line of division be drawn with anything like certainty? Who is to mark it? The Governor of the demanding State would probably draw one line, and the Governor of the other State another. And, if they differed, who is to decide between them? Under such a vague and indefinite construction, the article would not be a bond of peace and union, but a constant source of controversy and irritating discussion. It would have been far better to omit it altogether, and to have left it to the comity of the States, and their own sense of their respective interests, than to have inserted it so conferring a right, and yet defining that right so loosely as to make it a never-failing subject of dispute and ill-will.

Looking, therefore, to the words of the Constitution-to the obvious policy and necessity of this provision to preserve harmony between States, and order and law within their respective borders, and to its early adoption by the colonies, and then by the Confederated States, whose mutual interest it was to give each other aid and support whenever it was needed-the conclusion is irresistible, that this compact engrafted in the Constitution included, and was intended to include, every offence made punishable by the law of the State in which it was committed, and that it gives the right to the Executive authority of the State to demand the fugitive from the Executive authority of the State in which he is found; that the right given to 'demand' implies that it is an absolute right; and it follows that there must be a correlative obligation to deliver, without any reference to the character of the crime charged, or to the policy or laws of the State to which the fugitive has fled.

This is evidently the construction put upon this article in the act of Congress of 1793, under which the proceedings now before us are instituted. It is therefore the construction put upon it almost contemporaneously with the commencement of the Government itself, and when Washington was still at its head, and many of those who had assisted in framing it were members of the Congress which enacted the law.

Congress passed the act of 1793, February 12th, which, as far as relates to this subject, is in the following words:

> Section 1. That whenever the Executive authority of any State in the Union, or of either of the Territories northwest or south of the river Ohio, shall demand any person as a fugitive from justice of the Executive authority of any such State or Territory to which such person shall have fled, and shall, moreover, produce the copy of an indictment found, or an affidavit made before a magistrate of any State or Territory as aforesaid, charging the person so demanded with having committed treason, felony, or other crime, certified as authentic by the Governor or chief Magistrate of the State or Territory from whence the person so charged fled, it shall be the duty of the Executive authority of the State or Territory to which such person shall have fled to cause him or her to be arrested and secured, and notice of the arrest to be given to the Executive authority making such demand...and to cause the fugitive to be delivered....

The question which remains to be examined is a grave and important one. When the demand was made, the proofs required by the act of 1793 to support it were exhibited to the Governor of Ohio, duly certified and authenticated; and the objection made to the validity of the indictment is altogether untenable. [W]hether the charge against Lago is legally and sufficiently laid in this indictment according to the laws of Kentucky, is a judicial question to be decided by the courts of the State, and not by the Executive authority of the State of Ohio.

The demand being thus made, the act of Congress declares, that 'it shall be the duty of the Executive authority of the State' to cause the fugitive to be arrested and secured, and delivered to the agent of the demanding State. The words, 'it shall be the duty,' in ordinary legislation, imply the assertion of the power to command and to coerce obedience. But looking to the subject-matter of this law, and the relations which the United States and the several States bear to each other, the court is of opinion, the words 'it shall be the duty' were not used as mandatory and compulsory, but as declaratory of the moral duty which this compact created, when Congress had provided the mode of carrying it into execution. The act does not provide any means to compel the execution of this duty, nor inflict any punishment for neglect or refusal on the part of the Executive of the State; nor is there any clause or provision in the Constitution which arms the Government of the United States with this power. Indeed, such a power would place every State under the control and dominion of the General Government, even in the administration of its internal concerns and reserved rights. And we think it clear, that the Federal Government, under the Constitution, has no power to impose on a State officer, as such, any duty whatever, and compel him to perform it; for if it possessed this power, it might overload the officer with duties which would fill up all his time, and disable him from performing his obligations to the State, and might impose on him duties of a character incompatible with the rank and dignity to which he was elevated by the State.

And it would seem that when the Constitution was framed, and when this law was passed, it was confidently believed that a sense of justice and of mutual interest would insure a faithful execution of this constitutional provision by the Executive of every State, for every State had an equal interest in the execution of a compact absolutely essential to their peace and well being in their internal concerns, as well as members of the Union. Hence, the use of the words ordinarily employed when an undoubted obligation is required to be performed, 'it shall be his duty.'

But if the Governor of Ohio refuses to discharge this duty, there is no power delegated to the General Government, either through the Judicial Department or any other department, to use any coercive means to compel him.

And upon this ground the motion for the mandamus must be overruled.

PUERTO RICO v. BRANSTAD
483 U.S. 219 (1987)

MARSHALL, J., delivered the opinion of the Court.

This case requires that we reconsider the holding of *Kentucky v. Dennison,* 24 How. 66 (1861), that federal courts have no power to order the Governor of a State to fulfill the State's obligation under the Extradition Clause of the Constitution, Art. IV, § 2, to deliver up fugitives from justice.

I

[R]espondent Ronald Calder, then a civilian air traffic controller employed by the Federal Aviation Administration in San Juan, Puerto Rico, struck two people with his automobile. One of the victims, Antonio de Jesus Gonzalez, was injured; his wife, Army Villalba, was killed. Villalba was eight months pregnant; her unborn child did not survive. The incident occurred in the parking lot of a grocery store in Aguadilla, Puerto Rico, after what was apparently an altercation between Calder and de Jesus Gonzalez. According to two sworn statements taken by police, after striking the couple Calder backed his car two or three times over...Villalba.

On the basis of these statements, Calder was arrested, charged with homicide, arraigned before a municipal judge, and released on $5,000 bail. Calder failed to appear at a preliminary hearing...and bail was increased to $50,000. Despite representations by counsel that Calder would appear at a [rescheduled] preliminary hearing, he did not do so. At that time Calder was declared a fugitive from justice, and bail was increased to $300,000. The Puerto Rican police, having reason to believe that Calder had left Puerto Rico and returned to his family's home in Iowa, notified local authorities in Iowa that Calder was a fugitive wanted in Puerto Rico on murder charges. [Eventually], Calder surrendered to local authorities in Polk County, Iowa, posted...[a] bond set [in] Iowa, and was released.

[T]he Governor of Puerto Rico submitted to the Governor of Iowa a request for Calder's extradition. Counsel for Calder requested that the Governor of Iowa hold an extradition hearing, which was conducted by the Governor's counsel. This hearing was only partially transcribed, but the record does show that one of Calder's counsel was permitted to testify to his belief that "a white American man ... could not receive a fair trial in the Commonwealth of Puerto Rico," while Calder himself testified...that "on numerous occasions" witnesses in Puerto Rican courts had been "bought."

After the extradition hearing in Iowa, discussions...were held, apparently with a view to negotiating a reduction of the charges lodged against Calder. These discussions were unavailing, and...Iowa's Governor formally notified the Governor of Puerto Rico that in the absence of a "change to a more realistic charge," the request for extradition was denied. A subsequent extradition request made to [the Iowa] Governor's successor in office, respondent Terry Branstad, was also denied.

[The] Commonwealth of Puerto Rico filed a complaint in the United States District Court for the Southern District of Iowa...seeking a declaration that failure to deliver Calder upon presentation of proper extradition papers violated the Extradition Clause and the Extradition Act, 18 U.S.C. § 3182 (Act). The complaint further requested the issuance of a writ of mandamus directing respondent Branstad to perform the "ministerial duty" of extradition. Respondents stipulated before the District Court that the extradition papers fully complied with the requirements of the Act. The District Court dismissed the complaint, agreeing with respondents that...*Kentucky v. Dennison,* 24 How. 66 (1861), absolutely barred any attempt to invoke federal judicial authority to compel compliance with the Clause or the Act. The Court of Appeals "[r]eluctantly" affirmed.

II

A

Kentucky v. Dennison was an action brought under this Court's original jurisdiction to compel by writ of mandamus the extradition of a fugitive felon. The defendant was a resident of Ohio, and papers requesting his extradition were served upon William Dennison, the Governor of that State. Dennison secured an opinion from Ohio's Attorney General, who took the view that the Extradition Clause covered only those acts which were crimes under the law of the asylum State, or which were "regarded as *malum in se* by the general judgment and conscience of civilized nations." On this basis Dennison refused extradition, and Kentucky brought its mandamus action in this Court.

The case was heard in February 1861, and decided on March 14. On that date secession was a fact, and civil war a threatening possibility. The Representatives of the States of the Deep South had withdrawn from the Congress. Justice Campbell was reputedly engaged in mediation efforts between the seceding States and the Lincoln administration, but his resignation from the Court and departure from Washington were imminent; he resigned on April 30, 1861. It was in these circumstances, with the practical power of the Federal Government at its lowest ebb since the adoption of the Constitution, that Chief Justice Taney delivered the opinion of the Court.

B

Thus, for over 125 years, *Kentucky v. Dennison* has stood for two propositions: first, that the Extradition Clause creates a mandatory duty to deliver up fugitives upon proper demand; and second, that the federal courts have no authority under the Constitution to compel performance of this ministerial duty of delivery. As to the first of these, the passage of time has revealed no occasion for doubt. The language of the Clause is "clear and explicit."

The second, and dispositive, holding of *Kentucky v. Dennison* rests upon a foundation with which time and the currents of constitutional change have dealt much less favorably. If it seemed clear to the Court in 1861, facing the looming shadow of a Civil War, that "the Federal Government, under the Constitution, has no power to impose on a State officer, as such, any duty whatever, and compel him to perform it," basic constitutional principles now point as clearly the other way. Within 15 years of the decision in *Dennison* it was said that "when a plain official duty, requiring no exercise of discretion, is to be performed, and performance is refused, any person who will sustain personal injury by such refusal may have a *mandamus* to compel its performance," and it was no objection that such an order might be sought in the federal courts against a state officer. It has long been a settled principle that federal courts may enjoin unconstitutional action by state officials. See *Ex parte Young,* 209 U.S. 123 (1908). It would be superfluous to restate all the occasions on which this Court has imposed upon state officials a duty to obey the requirements of the Constitution, or compelled the performance of such duties; it may suffice to refer to *Brown v. Bd of Educ.,* 349 U.S. 294 (1955), and *Cooper v. Aaron,* 358 U.S. 1 (1958). The fundamental premise of...*Dennison*-"that the States and the Federal Government in all circumstances must be viewed as coequal sovereigns-is not representative of the law today." *FERC v. Mississippi,* 456 U.S. 742, 761 (1982).

Yet, with respect to extradition, the law has remained as it was more than a century ago. Considered *de novo,* there is no justification for distinguishing the duty to deliver fugitives from the many other species of constitutional duty enforceable in the federal courts. Because the duty is directly imposed upon the States by the Constitution itself, there can be no need to weigh the performance of the federal obligation against the powers reserved to the States under the Tenth Amendment.

III

Kentucky v. Dennison is the product of another time. The conception of the relation between the States and the Federal Government there announced is fundamentally incompatible with more than a century of constitutional development. Yet this decision has stood while the world of which it was a part has passed away. We conclude that it may stand no longer.

d. Congressional Power To Admit New States

An important Article IV provision that has at times very directly and significantly affected the substantive content of state constitutions is the first clause of Section 3, which provides that "New States may be admitted by the Congress into this Union." This provision has been understood to mean that Congress may impose substantive conditions on new States that require the inclusion, for example, of particular provisions or prohibitions in a State's constitution as a condition for admission to the Union.

ROMER v. EVANS
517 U.S. 620, 648-649 (1996)

SCALIA, J., dissenting.

The Constitutions of the States of Arizona, Idaho, New Mexico, Oklahoma, and Utah...contain provisions stating that polygamy is "forever prohibited." See Ariz. Const., Art. XX, par. 2; Idaho Const., Art. I, § 4; N.M. Const., Art. XXI, § 1; Okla. Const., Art. I, § 2; Utah Const., Art. III, § 1. The United States Congress...*required* the inclusion of these antipolygamy provisions in the Constitutions of Arizona, New Mexico,

Oklahoma, and Utah, as a condition of their admission to statehood. See Arizona Enabling Act, 36 Stat. 569; New Mexico Enabling Act, 36 Stat. 558; Oklahoma Enabling Act, 34 Stat. 269; Utah Enabling Act, 28 Stat. 108. (For Arizona, New Mexico, and Utah, moreover, the Enabling Acts required that the antipolygamy provisions be "irrevocable without the consent of the United States and the people of said State".)

COYLE v. SMITH
221 U.S. 559 (1911)

LURTON, J., delivered the opinion of the court.

This is a writ of error to the supreme court of Oklahoma to review the judgment of that court upholding a legislative act of the state, providing for the removal of its capital from Guthrie to Oklahoma City....

The question reviewable under this writ of error, if any there be, arises under the claim set up by the petitioner, and decided against him, that the Oklahoma act of December 29, 1910, providing for the immediate location of the capital of the state at Oklahoma City, was void as repugnant to the enabling act of Congress of June 16, 1906, under which the state was admitted to the Union. The 2d section is lengthy and deals with the organization of a constitutional convention, and concludes in these words: 'The capital of said state shall temporarily be at the city of Guthrie...and shall not be changed therefrom previous to Anno Domini nineteen hundred and thirteen; but said capital shall, after said year, be located by the electors of said state at an election to be provided for by the legislature....' The 22d and last section, applicable to Oklahoma, reads thus: 'That the constitutional convention provided for herein shall by ordinance irrevocably accept the terms and conditions of this act.'

The [Oklahoma] Constitution as framed contains nothing as to the location of the state capital; but the convention which framed it adopted a separate ordinance in these words:

> Enabling act accepted by ordinance irrevocable. Be it ordained by the constitutional convention for the proposed state of Oklahoma, that said constitutional convention do, by this ordinance irrevocable, accept the terms and conditions of an act of the Congress of the United States, entitled, 'An Act to Enable the People of Oklahoma and the Indian Territory to Form a Constitution and State Government, and be Admitted into the Union on an Equal Footing with the Original States....'

The only question for review by us is whether the provision of the enabling act was a valid limitation upon the power of the state after its admission, which overrides any subsequent state legislation repugnant thereto.

The power to locate its own seat of government, and to determine when and how it shall be changed from one place to another, and to appropriate its own public funds for that purpose, are essentially and peculiarly state powers. That one of the original thirteen states could now be shorn of such powers by an act of Congress would not be for a moment entertained. The question, then, comes to this: Can a state be placed upon a plane of inequality with its sister states in the Union if the Congress chooses to impose conditions which so operate, at the time of its admission? The argument is, that while Congress may not deprive a state of any power which it *possesses*, it may, as a condition to the admission of a new state, constitutionally restrict its authority, to the extent, at least, of suspending its powers for a definite time in respect to the location of its seat of government. This contention is predicated upon the constitutional power of admitting new states to this Union, and the constitutional duty of guaranteeing to 'every state in this Union a republican form of government.'

The power of Congress in respect to the admission of new states is found in the 3d section of the 4th article of the Constitution. That provision is that, 'new states may be admitted by the Congress into this Union.' The only expressed restriction upon this power is that no new state shall be formed within the jurisdiction of any other state, nor by the junction of two or more states, or parts of states, without the consent of such states, as well as of the Congress. But what is this power? It is not to admit political organizations which are less or greater, or different in dignity or power, from those political entities which constitute the Union.

The definition of 'a state' is found in the powers possessed by the original states which adopted the Constitution,-a definition emphasized by the terms employed in all subsequent acts of Congress admitting new states into the Union. The first two states admitted into the Union were the states of Vermont and Kentucky, one as of March 4, 1791, and the other as of June 1, 1792. No terms or conditions were exacted from either. Each act declares that the state is admitted 'as a new and *entire member* of the United States of America.' [E]ven stronger was the declaration upon the admission in 1796 of Tennessee as the third new state, it being declared to be 'one of the United States of America,' 'on an equal footing with the original states in all respects whatsoever,'-phraseology which has ever since been substantially followed in admission acts, concluding with the Oklahoma act, which declares that Oklahoma shall be admitted 'on an equal footing with the original states.'

The power is to admit 'new states into *this* Union.' 'This Union' was and is a union of states, equal in power, dignity, and authority, each competent to exert that residuum of sovereignty not delegated to the United States by the Constitution itself. To maintain otherwise would be to say that the Union, through the power of Congress to admit new states, might come to be a union of states unequal in power, as including states whose powers were restricted only by the Constitution, with others whose powers had been further restricted by an act of Congress accepted as a condition of admission.

The argument that Congress derives from the duty of 'guaranteeing to each state in this Union a republican form of government,' power to impose restrictions upon a new state which deprive it of equality with other members of the Union, has no merit. It may imply the duty of such new state to provide itself with such state government, and impose upon Congress the duty of seeing that such form is not changed to one anti-republican, but it obviously does not confer power to admit a new state which shall be any less a state than those which compose the Union.

We come now to the question as to whether there is anything in the decisions of this court which sanctions the claim that Congress may, by the imposition of conditions in an enabling act, deprive a new state of any of those attributes essential to its equality in dignity and power with other states.

As to requirements in such enabling acts as relate only to the contents of the Constitution for the proposed new state, little need[s] to be said. The constitutional provision concerning the admission of new states is not a mandate, but a power to be exercised with discretion. From this alone it would follow that Congress may require, under penalty of denying admission, that the organic law of a new state at the time of admission shall be such as to meet its approval. A Constitution thus supervised by Congress would, after all, be a Constitution of a state, and as such subject to alteration and amendment by the state after admission. Its force would be that of a state Constitution, and not that of an act of Congress.

So far as this court has found occasion to advert to the effect of enabling acts as affirmative legislation affecting the power of new states after admission, there is to be found no sanction for the contention that any state may be deprived of any of the power constitutionally possessed by other states, as states, by reason of the terms in which the acts admitting them to the Union have been framed.

The plain deduction from [the Court's] case[s] is that when a new state is admitted into the Union, it is so admitted with all of the powers of sovereignty and jurisdiction which pertain to the original states, and that such powers may not be constitutionally diminished, impaired, or shorn away by any conditions, compacts, or stipulations embraced in the act under which the new state came into the Union, which would not be valid and effectual if the subject of congressional legislation after admission.

It may well happen that Congress should embrace in an enactment introducing a new state into the Union legislation intended as a regulation of commerce among the states, or with Indian tribes situated within the limits of such new state, or regulations touching the sole care and disposition of the public lands or reservations therein, which might be upheld as legislation within the sphere of the plain power of Congress. But in every such case such legislation would derive its force not from any agreement or compact with the proposed new state, nor by reason of its acceptance of such enactment as a term of admission, but solely because the power of Congress extended to the subject, and therefore would not operate to restrict the state's legislative power in respect of any matter which was not plainly within the regulating power of Congress.

No such question is presented here. The legislation in the Oklahoma enabling act relating to the location of the capital of the state, if construed as forbidding a removal by the state after its admission as a state, is referable to no power granted to Congress over the subject, and if it is to be upheld at all, it must be implied from the power to admit new states. If power to impose such a restriction upon the general and undelegated power of a state be conceded as implied from the power to admit a new state, where is the line to be drawn against restrictions imposed upon new states?

Has Oklahoma been admitted upon an equal footing with the original states? If she has, she, by virtue of her jurisdictional sovereignty as such a state, may determine for her own people the proper location of the local seat of government. She is not equal in power to them if she cannot.

In *Lane County v. Oregon*, 7 Wall. 76 [74 U.S. 71, (1868)], [Chief Justice Chase] said:

> The people of the United States constitute one nation, under one government; and this government, within the scope of the powers with which it is invested, is supreme. On the other hand, the people of each state compose state, having its own government, and endowed with all the functions essential to separate and independent existence. The states disunited might continue to exist. Without the states in union there could be no such political body as the United States.

To this we may add that the constitutional equality of the states is essential to the harmonious operation of the scheme upon which the Republic was organized. When that equality disappears we may remain a free people, but the Union will not be the Union of the Constitution.

e. The Guarantee Clause

A final Article IV provision that could have had significant influence over the States and the state constitutions is the Guarantee Clause, a provision in Section 4 which declares that the "United States shall guarantee to every State in this Union a Republican Form of Government." As the following cases illustrate, however, the Supreme Court of the United States has never been inclined to give this provision substantive content and instead has tended to treat arguments that the

Clause has been violated as raising nonjusticiable, political questions that are not to be answered by the courts.

LUTHER v. BORDEN
48 U.S. (7 How.) 1 (1849)

TANEY, C. J., delivered the opinion of the court.

This case has arisen out of the unfortunate political differences which agitated the people of Rhode Island in 1841 and 1842. It is an action of trespass brought by Martin Luther, the plaintiff in error, against Luther M. Borden and others...for breaking and entering the plaintiff's house. The defendants justify upon the ground that large numbers of men were assembled in different parts of the State for the purpose of overthrowing the government by military force, and were actually levying war upon the State; that, in order to defend itself from this insurrection, the State was declared by competent authority to be under martial law; that the plaintiff was engaged in the insurrection; and that the defendants, being in the military service of the State, by command of their superior officer, broke and entered the house and searched the rooms for the plaintiff, who was supposed to be there concealed, in order to arrest him, doing as little damage as possible. The plaintiff replied that the trespass was committed by the defendants of their own proper wrong, and without any such cause.

The evidence offered by the plaintiff and the defendants...and the questions decided by the Circuit Court, and brought up by the writ of error, are not such as commonly arise in an action of trespass. The existence and authority of the government under which the defendants acted was called in question; and the plaintiff insists, that, before the acts complained of were committed, that government had been displaced and annulled by the people of Rhode Island, and that the plaintiff was engaged in supporting the lawful authority of the State, and the defendants themselves were in arms against it.

This is a new question in this court, and certainly a very grave one; and at the time when the trespass is alleged to have been committed it had produced a general and painful excitement in the State, and threatened to end in bloodshed and civil war.

The evidence shows that the defendants, in breaking into the plaintiff's house and endeavouring to arrest him, as stated in the pleadings, acted under the authority of the government which was established in Rhode Island at the time of the Declaration of Independence, and which is usually called the charter government. For when the separation from England took place, Rhode Island did not, like the other States, adopt a new constitution, but continued the form of government established by the charter of Charles the Second in 1663; making only such alterations, by acts of the legislature, as were necessary to adapt it to their condition and rights as an independent State. It was under this form of government that Rhode Island united with the other States in the Declaration of Independence, and afterwards ratified the Constitution of the United States and became a member of this Union; and it continued to be the established and unquestioned government of the State until the difficulties took place which have given rise to this action.

For some years previous to the disturbances of which we are now speaking, many of the citizens became dissatisfied with the charter government, and particularly with the restriction upon the right of suffrage. Memorials were addressed to the legislature upon this subject, urging the justice and necessity of a more liberal and extended rule. But they failed to produce the desired effect. And thereupon meetings were held and associations formed by those who were in favor of a more extended right of suffrage, which finally resulted in the election of a convention to form a new constitution to be submitted to the people for their adoption or rejection. This convention was not authorized by any law of the existing government. It was elected at voluntary meetings, and by those citizens only who favored this plan of reform; those who were opposed to it, or opposed to the manner in which it was proposed to be accomplished, taking no part in the proceedings. The persons chosen as above mentioned came together and framed a constitution, by which the right of suffrage was extended to every male citizen of twenty-one years of age, who had resided in the State for one year, and in the town in which he offered to vote, for six months, next preceding the election. The convention also prescribed the manner in which this constitution should be submitted to the decision of the people,-permitting every one to vote on that question who was an American citizen, twenty-one years old, and who had a permanent residence or home in the State.

Upon the return of the votes, the convention declared that the constitution was adopted and ratified by a majority of the people of the State.... The charter government did not, however, admit the validity of these proceedings, nor acquiesce in them. On the contrary, when this new constitution was communicated to the governor, and by him laid before the legislature, it passed resolutions declaring all acts done for the purpose of imposing that constitution upon the State to be an assumption of the powers of government, in violation of the rights of the existing government and of the people at large; and that it would maintain its authority and defend the legal and constitutional rights of the people.

But, notwithstanding the determination of the charter government, and of those who adhered to it, to maintain its authority, Thomas W. Dorr, who had been elected governor under the new constitution, prepared to assert the authority of that government by force, and many citizens assembled in arms to support him. The charter government thereupon passed an act declaring the State under martial law, and at the same time proceeded to call out the militia, to repel the threatened attack and to subdue those who were engaged in it. In this state of the contest, the house of the plaintiff, who was engaged in supporting the authority of the new government, was broken and entered in order to arrest him. The defendants were, at the time, in the military service of the old government, and in arms to support its authority.

The plaintiff contends that the charter government was displaced, and ceased to have any lawful power, after the organization, in May, 1842, of the government which he supported, and although that government never was able to exercise any authority in the State, nor to command obedience to its laws or to its officers, yet he insists that it was the lawful and established government, upon the ground that it was ratified by a large majority of the male people of the State of the age of twenty-one and upwards.

The Circuit Court…instructed the jury that the charter government and laws under which the defendants acted were, at the time the trespass is alleged to have been committed, in full force and effect as the form of government and paramount law of the State, and constituted a justification of the acts of the defendants.

Certainly, the question which the plaintiff proposed to raise by the testimony he offered has not heretofore been recognized as a judicial one in any of the State courts. Undoubtedly the courts of the United States have certain powers under the Constitution and laws of the United States which do not belong to the State courts. But the power of determining that a State government has been lawfully established, which the courts of the State disown and repudiate, is not one of them. Upon such a question the courts of the United States are bound to follow the decisions of the State tribunals, and must therefore regard the charter government as the lawful established government during the time of this contest.

Moreover, the Constitution of the United States, as far as it has provided for an emergency of this kind, and authorized the general government to interfere in the domestic concerns of a State, has treated the subject as political in its nature, and placed the power in the hands of that department. The fourth section of the fourth article of the Constitution of the United States provides that the United States shall guarantee to every State in the Union a republican form of government, and shall protect each of them against invasion; and on the application of the legislature or of the executive (when the legislature cannot be convened) against domestic violence.

Under this article of the Constitution it rests with Congress to decide what government is the established one in a State. For as the United States guarantee to each State a republican government, Congress must necessarily decide what government is established in the State before it can determine whether it is republican or not. And when the senators and representatives of a State are admitted into the councils of the Union, the authority of the government under which they are appointed, as well as its republican character, is recognized by the proper constitutional authority. And its decision is binding on every other department of the government, and could not be questioned in a judicial tribunal.

Congress...by the act of February 28, 1795, provided, that, 'in case of an insurrection in any State against the government thereof, it shall be lawful for the President of the United States, on application of the legislature of such State or of the executive (when the legislature cannot be convened), to call forth such number of the militia of any other State or States, as may be applied for, as he may judge sufficient to sufficient to suppress such insurrection.'

By this act, the power of deciding whether the exigency had arisen upon which the government of the United States is bound to interfere, is given to the President. He is to act upon the application of the legislature or of the executive, and consequently he must determine what body of men constitute the legislature, and who is the governor, before he can act. The fact that both parties claim the right to the government cannot alter the case, for both cannot be entitled to it. If there is an armed conflict, like the one of which we are speaking, it is a case of domestic violence, and one of the parties must be in insurrection against the lawful government. And the President must, of necessity, decide which is the government, and which party is unlawfully arrayed against it.

After the President has acted and called out the militia, is a Circuit Court of the United States authorized to inquire whether his decision was right? If the judicial power extends so far, the guarantee contained in the Constitution of the United States is a guarantee of anarchy, and not of order. No one, we believe, has ever doubted the proposition, that, according to the institutions of this country, the sovereignty in every State resides in the people of the State, and that they may alter and change their form of government at their own pleasure. But whether they have changed it or not by abolishing an old government, and establishing a new one in its place, is a question to be settled by the political power.

PACIFIC STATES TELEPHONE & TELEGRAPH CO. v.
OREGON
223 U.S. 118 (1912)

WHITE, C. J., delivered the opinion of the court.

We premise by saying that while the controversy which this record presents is of much importance, it is not novel. It is important, since it calls upon us to decide whether it is the duty of the courts or the province of Congress to determine when a state has ceased to be republican in form, and to enforce the guaranty of the Constitution on that subject. It is not novel, as that question has long since been determined by this court conformably to the practice of the government from the beginning to be political in character, and therefore not cognizable by the judicial power, but solely committed by the Constitution to the judgment of Congress.

The case is this: In 1902 Oregon amended its Constitution. This amendment, while retaining an existing clause vesting the exclusive legislative power in a general assembly consisting of a senate and a house of representatives, added to that provision the following: 'But the people reserve to themselves power to propose laws and amendments to the Constitution, and to enact or reject the same at the polls, independent of the legislative assembly, and also reserve power at their own option to approve or reject at the polls any act of the legislative assembly.' Specific means for the exercise of the power thus reserved was contained in further clauses authorizing both the amendment of the Constitution and the enactment of laws to be accomplished by the method known as the initiative and that commonly referred to as the referendum. In 1903 detailed provisions for the carrying into effect of this amendment were enacted by the legislature.

By resort to the initiative in 1906, a law taxing certain classes of corporations was submitted, voted on, and promulgated by the governor in 1907 as having been duly adopted. By this law telephone and telegraph companies were taxed, by what was qualified as an annual license, 2 per centum upon their gross revenue derived from business done within the state. Penalties were provided for nonpayment, and methods were created for enforcing payment in case of delinquency.

The Pacific States Telephone & Telegraph Company, an Oregon corporation engaged in business in that state, made a return of its gross receipts, as required by the statute, and was accordingly assessed 2 per cent upon the amount of such return. The suit which is now before us was commenced by the state to enforce payment of this assessment and the statutory penalties for delinquency. [The company challenged the tax assessment, lost, and appealed to the Supreme Court.]

The assignments of error...are numerous. The entire matters covered by each and all of them in the argument, however, are reduced to six propositions, which really amount to but one.... In other words, the propositions [of alleged error] each and all proceed alone upon the theory that the adoption of the initiative and referendum destroyed all government republican in form in Oregon. Before immediately considering the text of § 4 of article 4, in order to uncover and give emphasis to the anomalous and destructive effects upon both the state and national governments which the adoption of the proposition implies,...let us briefly fix the inconceivable expansion of the judicial power and the ruinous destruction of legislative authority in matters purely political which would necessarily be occasioned by giving sanction to the doctrine which underlies and would be necessarily involved in sustaining the propositions contended for.

We shall not stop to consider the text [of Article IV, § 4] to point out how absolutely barren it is of support for the contentions sought to be based upon it, since the repugnancy of those contentions to the letter and spirit of that text is so conclusively established by prior decisions of this court as to cause the matter to be absolutely foreclosed. In view of the importance of the subject, the apparent misapprehension on one side and seeming misconception on the other, suggested by the argument as to the full significance of the previous doctrine, we do not content ourselves with a mere citation of the cases, but state more at length than we otherwise would the issues and the doctrine expounded in the leading and absolutely controlling case, *Luther v. Borden*, 7 How. 1 [1849]. [The Court then examines and quotes at length from *Luther*.]

The fundamental doctrines thus so lucidly and cogently announced by the court, speaking through Mr. Chief Justice Taney in [*Luther*], have never been doubted or questioned since, and have afforded the light guiding the orderly development of our constitutional system from the day of the deliverance of that decision up to the present time. It is indeed a singular misconception of the nature and character of our constitutional system of government to suggest that the settled distinction...between judicial authority over justiciable controversies and legislative power as to purely political questions tends to destroy the duty of the judiciary in proper cases to enforce the Constitution. The suggestion but results from failing to distinguish between things which are widely different; that is, the legislative duty to determine the political questions involved in deciding whether a state government republican in form exists, and the judicial power and ever-present duty whenever it becomes necessary, in a controversy properly submitted, to enforce and uphold the applicable provisions of the Constitution as to each and every exercise of governmental power.

How better can the broad lines which distinguish these two subjects be pointed out than by considering the character of the defense in this very case? The defendant company does not contend here that it could not have been required to pay a license tax. It does not assert that it was denied an opportunity to be heard as to the amount for which it was taxed, or that there was anything inhering in the tax or involved intrinsically in the law which violated any of its constitutional rights. If such questions had been raised, they would have been justiciable, and therefore would have required the calling into operation of judicial power. Instead, however, of doing any of these things, the attack on the statute here made is of a wholly different character. Its essentially political nature is at once made manifest by understanding that the assault which the contention here advanced makes is not on the tax as a tax, but on the state as a state. It is addressed to the framework and political character of the government by which the statute levying the tax was passed. It is the government, the political entity, which (reducing the case to its essence) is called to the bar of this court, not for the purpose of testing judicially some exercise of power, assailed on the ground that its exertion has injuriously affected the rights of an individual because of repugnancy to some constitutional limitation, but to demand of the state that it establish its right to exist as a state, republican in form.

As the issues presented, in their very essence, are, and have long since by this court been, definitely determined to be political and governmental, and embraced within the scope of the powers conferred upon Congress, and not, therefore, within the reach of judicial power, it follows that the case presented is not within our jurisdiction, and the writ of error must therefore be, and it is, dismissed for want of jurisdiction.

2. Article VI

Article VI may contain the most important provision of all for the States with respect to the effect of federal law on the States. The Supremacy Clause declares that "This Constitution, and the Laws of the United States which shall be made in pursuance thereof; and all Treaties made, or which shall be made, under the Authority of the United States, shall be the supreme Law of the Land; and the Judges in every State shall be bound thereby, any Thing in the Constitution or Laws of any State to the Contrary notwithstanding." The Supremacy Clause is further bolstered by Article VI's provision that "the Members of the several State Legislatures, and all executive and judicial Officers, both of the United States and of the several States, shall be bound by Oath or Affirmation, to support this Constitution."

These two clauses make clear – in explicit terms – that federal law has primacy over state law, including state constitutions, when there is a conflict between any federal law (constitutional, statutory, or even regulatory) and state law. Although that general principle is quite clear and explicit, the devil is in the details of applying the principle to the innumerable contexts in which claims have arisen that state law is preempted by federal law. Federal preemption doctrine is a complex and intricate area of the law, with outcomes often turning on the specifics of the federal and state laws implicated in a particular case. Thus, the following cases are simply illustrations of situations in which federal law was alleged to preempt state constitutional provisions. In other words, these cases are not offered for the federal substantive principles on which they may be based, such as equal protection, but rather to demonstrate that federal law—both constitutional and statutory—may preempt state constitutional provisions.

Note also that in the latter two of these preemption cases the parties may invoke and the Court may discuss the Tenth Amendment—part of the Bill of Rights—which declares that "[t]he powers not delegated to the United States by the Constitution, nor prohibited by it to the States, are reserved to the States respectively, or to the people." Sometimes resolving preemption questions under Article VI implicates the residual powers of the States, as the argument may be that federal law cannot preempt what has been reserved exclusively to the States. For the most part, however, the Supreme Court has not given the Tenth Amendment substantive meaning, but tended to treat it as a "truism" stating what is essentially fundamental under the federalism the Constitution creates: If the federal government has the power to take certain action, then it necessarily may preempt contrary state law by virtue of the Supremacy Clause, but if the federal government lacks such power, then the power necessarily resides solely in the States.

ROMER v. EVANS
517 U.S. 620 (1996)

KENNEDY, J., delivered the opinion of the Court.

I

The enactment challenged in this case is an amendment to the Constitution of the State of Colorado, adopted in a 1992 statewide referendum. The parties and the state courts refer to it as "Amendment 2." The impetus for the amendment and the contentious campaign that preceded its adoption came in large part from ordinances that had been passed in various Colorado municipalities. For example, the cities of Aspen and Boulder and the city and County of Denver each had enacted ordinances which banned discrimination in many transactions and activities, including housing, employment, education, public accommodations, and health and welfare services. What gave rise to the statewide controversy was the protection the ordinances afforded to persons discriminated against by reason of their sexual orientation. Amendment 2 repeals these ordinances to the extent they prohibit discrimination on the basis of "homosexual, lesbian or bisexual orientation, conduct, practices or relationships."

Yet Amendment 2, in explicit terms, does more than repeal or rescind these provisions. It prohibits all legislative, executive or judicial action at any level of state or local government designed to protect the named class, a class we shall refer to as homosexual persons or gays and lesbians. The amendment reads:

> No Protected Status Based on Homosexual, Lesbian or Bisexual Orientation. Neither the State of Colorado, through any of its branches or departments, nor any of its agencies, political subdivisions, municipalities or school districts, shall enact, adopt or enforce any statute, regulation, ordinance or policy whereby homosexual, lesbian or bisexual orientation, conduct, practices or relationships shall constitute or otherwise be the basis of or entitle any person or class of persons to have or claim any minority status, quota preferences, protected status or claim of discrimination. This Section of the Constitution shall be in all respects self-executing.

Soon after Amendment 2 was adopted, this litigation to declare its invalidity and enjoin its enforcement was commenced in the District Court for the City and County of Denver. Among the plaintiffs (respondents here) were homosexual persons, some of them government employees. They alleged that enforcement of Amendment 2 would subject them to immediate and substantial risk of discrimination on the basis of their sexual orientation. Other plaintiffs (also respondents here) included the three municipalities whose ordinances we have cited and certain other governmental entities which had acted earlier to protect homosexuals from discrimination but would be prevented by Amendment 2 from continuing to do so.

[The Colorado courts declared Amendment 2 unconstitutional under federal law.]

II

The State's principal argument in defense of Amendment 2 is that it puts gays and lesbians in the same position as all other persons. So, the State says, the measure does no more than deny homosexuals special rights. This reading of the amendment's language is implausible. We rely not upon our own interpretation of the amendment but upon the authoritative construction of Colorado's Supreme Court. The state court, deeming it unnecessary to determine the full extent of the amendment's reach, found it invalid even on a modest reading of its implications.

Sweeping and comprehensive is the change in legal status effected by this law. So much is evident from the ordinances the Colorado Supreme

Court declared would be void by operation of Amendment 2. Homosexuals, by state decree, are put in a solitary class with respect to transactions and relations in both the private and governmental spheres. The amendment withdraws from homosexuals, but no others, specific legal protection from the injuries caused by discrimination, and it forbids reinstatement of these laws and policies.

III

The Fourteenth Amendment's promise that no person shall be denied the equal protection of the laws must coexist with the practical necessity that most legislation classifies for one purpose or another, with resulting disadvantage to various groups or persons. We have attempted to reconcile the principle with the reality by stating that, if a law neither burdens a fundamental right nor targets a suspect class, we will uphold the legislative classification so long as it bears a rational relation to some legitimate end.

Amendment 2 fails, indeed defies, even this conventional inquiry. First, the amendment has the peculiar property of imposing a broad and undifferentiated disability on a single named group, an exceptional and, as we shall explain, invalid form of legislation. Second, its sheer breadth is so discontinuous with the reasons offered for it that the amendment seems inexplicable by anything but animus toward the class it affects; it lacks a rational relationship to legitimate state interests.

A second and related point is that laws of the kind now before us raise the inevitable inference that the disadvantage imposed is born of animosity toward the class of persons affected. Amendment 2,...in making a general announcement that gays and lesbians shall not have any particular protections from the law, inflicts on them immediate, continuing, and real injuries that outrun and belie any legitimate justifications that may be claimed for it. We conclude that, in addition to the far-reaching deficiencies of Amendment 2 that we have noted, the principles it offends, in another sense, are conventional and venerable; a law must bear a rational relationship to a legitimate governmental purpose, and Amendment 2 does not.

The primary rationale the State offers for Amendment 2 is respect for other citizens' freedom of association, and in particular the liberties of landlords or employers who have personal or religious objections to homosexuality. Colorado also cites its interest in conserving resources to fight discrimination against other groups. The breadth of the amendment is so far removed from these particular justifications that we find it impossible to credit them. We cannot say that Amendment 2 is directed to any identifiable legitimate purpose or discrete objective. It is a status-based enactment divorced from any factual context from which we could discern a relationship to legitimate state interests; it is a classification of persons undertaken for its own sake, something the Equal Protection Clause does not permit. Amendment 2 classifies homosexuals not to further a proper legislative end but to make them unequal to everyone else. This Colorado cannot do. A State cannot so deem a class of persons a stranger to its laws.

US TERM LIMITS, INC. v. THORNTON
514 U.S. 779 (1995)

STEVENS, J., delivered the opinion of the Court.

The Constitution sets forth qualifications for membership in the Congress of the United States. Article I, § 2, cl. 2, which applies to the House of Representatives, provides: "No Person shall be a Representative who shall not have attained to the Age of twenty five Years, and been seven Years a Citizen of the United States, and who shall not, when elected, be an Inhabitant of that State in which he shall be chosen."

Article I, § 3, cl. 3, which applies to the Senate, similarly provides: "No Person shall be a Senator who shall not have attained to the Age of thirty Years, and been nine Years a Citizen of the United States, and who shall not, when elected, be an Inhabitant of that State for which he shall be chosen."

Today's cases present a challenge to an amendment to the Arkansas State Constitution that prohibits the name of an otherwise-eligible candidate for Congress from appearing on the general election ballot if that candidate has already served three terms in the House of Representatives or two terms in the Senate. The Arkansas Supreme Court held that the amendment violates the Federal Constitution. We agree with that holding. Such a state-imposed restriction is contrary to the "fundamental principle of our representative democracy," embodied in the Constitution, that "the people should choose whom they please to govern them." Allowing individual States to adopt their own qualifications for congressional service would be inconsistent with the Framers' vision of a uniform National Legislature representing the people of the United States. If the qualifications set forth in the text of the Constitution are to be changed, that text must be amended.

I

At the general election on November 3, 1992, the voters of Arkansas adopted Amendment 73 to their State Constitution. Proposed as a "Term Limitation Amendment," its preamble stated:

> The people of Arkansas find and declare that elected officials who remain in office too long become preoccupied with reelection and ignore their duties as representatives of the people. Entrenched incumbency has reduced voter participation and has led to an electoral system that is less free, less competitive,

and less representative than the system established by the Founding Fathers. Therefore, the people of Arkansas, exercising their reserved powers, herein limit the terms of elected officials.

The limitations in Amendment 73 apply to three categories of elected officials. Section 3, the provision at issue in these cases, applies to the Arkansas Congressional Delegation. It provides:

> (a) Any person having been elected to three or more terms as a member of the United States House of Representatives from Arkansas shall not be certified as a candidate and shall not be eligible to have his/her name placed on the ballot for election to the United States House of Representatives from Arkansas.

> (b) Any person having been elected to two or more terms as a member of the United States Senate from Arkansas shall not be certified as a candidate and shall not be eligible to have his/her name placed on the ballot for election to the United States Senate from Arkansas.

Amendment 73 states that it is self-executing and shall apply to all persons seeking election after January 1, 1993.

On November 13, 1992, respondent Bobbie Hill, on behalf of herself, similarly situated Arkansas "citizens, residents, taxpayers and registered voters," and the League of Women Voters of Arkansas, filed a complaint in the Circuit Court for Pulaski County, Arkansas, seeking a declaratory judgment that § 3 of Amendment 73 is "unconstitutional and void." The State of Arkansas, through its Attorney General, intervened as a party defendant in support of the amendment. Several proponents of the amendment also intervened, including petitioner U.S. Term Limits, Inc.

[Ultimately, the Arkansas Supreme Court held Section 3 to be unconstitutional].

II

As the opinions of the Arkansas Supreme Court suggest, the constitutionality of Amendment 73 depends critically on the resolution of two distinct issues. The first is whether the Constitution forbids States to add to or alter the qualifications specifically enumerated in the Constitution. The second is, if the Constitution does so forbid, whether the fact that Amendment 73 is formulated as a ballot access restriction rather than as an outright disqualification is of constitutional significance.

III

Petitioners argue that the Constitution contains no express prohibition against state-added qualifications, and that Amendment 73 is therefore an appropriate exercise of a State's reserved power to place additional restrictions on the choices that its own voters may make. We disagree for two independent reasons. First, we conclude that the power to add qualifications is not within the "original powers" of the States, and thus is not reserved to the States by the Tenth Amendment. Second, even if States possessed some original power in this area, we conclude that the Framers intended the Constitution to be the exclusive source of qualifications for Members of Congress, and that the Framers thereby "divested" States of any power to add qualifications.

The "plan of the convention" as illuminated by the historical materials, our opinions, and the text of the Tenth Amendment draws a basic distinction between the powers of the newly created Federal Government and the powers retained by the...States.

In short, as the Framers recognized, electing representatives to the National Legislature was a new right, arising from the Constitution itself. The Tenth Amendment thus provides no basis for concluding that the States possess reserved power to add qualifications to those that are fixed in the Constitution. Instead, any state power to set the qualifications for membership in Congress must derive not from the reserved powers of state sovereignty, but rather from the delegated powers of national sovereignty. In the absence of any constitutional delegation to the States of power to add qualifications to those enumerated in the Constitution, such a power does not exist.

Even if we believed that States possessed as part of their original powers some control over congressional qualifications, the text and structure of the Constitution, the relevant historical materials, and, most importantly, the "basic principles of our democratic system" all demonstrate that the Qualifications Clauses were intended to preclude the States from exercising any such power and to fix as exclusive the qualifications in the Constitution. In light of the Framers' evident concern that States would try to undermine the National Government, they could not have intended States to have the power to set qualifications.

Similarly, we believe that state-imposed qualifications, as much as congressionally imposed qualifications, would undermine the second critical idea recognized in [a previous case], that an aspect of sovereignty is the right of the people to vote for whom they wish. Again, the source of the qualification is of little moment in assessing the qualification's restrictive impact.

Finally, state-imposed restrictions...violate a third idea central to this basic principle: that the right to choose representatives belongs not to the States, but to the people. From the start, the Framers recognized that the "great and radical vice" of the Articles of Confederation was "the principle of LEGISLATION for STATES or GOVERNMENTS, in their CORPORATE or COLLECTIVE CAPACITIES, and as contradistinguished from the INDIVIDUALS of whom they consist." The Federalist No. 15, at 108 (Hamilton). Thus the Framers, in perhaps their most important contribution, conceived of a Federal Government directly responsible to the people, possessed of direct power over the people, and chosen directly, not by States, but by the people. The Framers implemented this ideal most clearly in the provision, extant from the beginning of the Republic, that calls for the Members of the House of Representatives to be "chosen every second Year by the People of the several States." Art. I, § 2, cl. 1. Following the adoption of the Seventeenth Amendment in 1913, this ideal was extended to elections for the Senate. The Congress of the United States, therefore, is not a confederation of nations in which separate sovereigns are represented by appointed delegates, but is instead a body composed of representatives of the people.

IV

Petitioners argue that, even if States may not add qualifications, Amendment 73 is constitutional because it is not such a qualification, and because Amendment 73 is a permissible exercise of state power to regulate the "Times, Places and Manner of holding Elections." [Article I, § 4, cl. 1] We reject these contentions.

Unlike §§ 1 and 2 of Amendment 73, which create absolute bars to service for long-term incumbents running for state office, § 3 merely provides that certain Senators and Representatives shall not be certified as candidates and shall not have their names appear on the ballot. They may run as write-in candidates and, if elected, they may serve. Petitioners contend that only a legal bar to service creates an impermissible qualification, and that Amendment 73 is therefore consistent with the Constitution.

In our view, Amendment 73 is an indirect attempt to accomplish what the Constitution prohibits Arkansas from accomplishing directly. As the plurality opinion of the Arkansas Supreme Court recognized, Amendment 73 is an "effort to dress eligibility to stand for Congress in ballot access clothing," because the "intent and the effect of Amendment 73 are to disqualify congressional incumbents from further service." We must, of course, accept the state court's view of the purpose of its own law: We are thus authoritatively informed that the sole purpose of § 3 of Amendment 73 was to attempt to achieve a result that is forbidden by the Federal Constitution. Indeed, it cannot be seriously contended that the intent behind Amendment 73 is other than to prevent the election of incumbents.

Petitioners make the related argument that Amendment 73 merely regulates the "Manner" of elections, and that the amendment is therefore a permissible exercise of state power under Article I, § 4, cl. 1 (the Elections Clause), to regulate the "Times, Places and Manner" of elections. We cannot agree.

A necessary consequence of petitioners' argument is that Congress itself would have the power to "make or alter" a measure such as Amendment 73. That the Framers would have approved of such a result is unfathomable. As our...discussion above make[s] clear, the Framers were particularly concerned that a grant to Congress of the authority to set its own qualifications would lead inevitably to congressional self-aggrandizement and the upsetting of the delicate constitutional balance. Petitioners would have us believe, however, that even as the Framers carefully circumscribed congressional power to set qualifications, they intended to allow Congress to achieve the same result by simply formulating the regulation as a ballot access restriction under the Elections Clause. We refuse to adopt an interpretation of the Elections Clause that would so cavalierly disregard what the Framers intended to be a fundamental constitutional safeguard.

V

The merits of term limits, or "rotation," have been the subject of debate since the formation of our Constitution, when the Framers unanimously rejected a proposal to add such limits to the Constitution. The cogent arguments on both sides of the question that were articulated during the process of ratification largely retain their force today. Over half the States have adopted measures that impose such limits on some offices either directly or indirectly, and the Nation as a whole, notably by constitutional amendment, has imposed a limit on the number of terms that the President may serve. Term limits, like any other qualification for office, unquestionably restrict the ability of voters to vote for whom they wish. On the other hand, such limits may provide for the infusion of fresh ideas and new perspectives, and may decrease the likelihood that representatives will lose touch with their constituents. It is not our province to resolve this longstanding debate.

We are, however, firmly convinced that allowing the several States to adopt term limits for congressional service would effect a fundamental change in the constitutional framework. Any such change must come not by legislation adopted either by Congress or by an individual State, but rather-as have other important changes in the electoral process-through the amendment procedures set forth in Article V. The Framers decided that the qualifications for service in the Congress of the United States be fixed in the Constitution and be uniform throughout the Nation. That decision reflects the Framers' understanding that Members of Congress are chosen by separate constituencies, but that they become, when elected, servants of the people of the United States. They are not merely delegates appointed by separate, sovereign States; they occupy offices that are integral and essential components of a single National Government. In the absence of a properly passed constitutional amendment, allowing individual States to craft their own qualifications for Congress would thus erode the structure envisioned by the Framers, a structure that was designed, in the words of the Preamble to our Constitution, to form a "more perfect Union."

GREGORY v. ASHCROFT
501 U.S. 452 (1991)

O'CONNOR, J., delivered the opinion of the Court.

Article V, § 26, of the Missouri Constitution provides that "[a]ll judges other than municipal judges shall retire at the age of seventy years." We consider whether this mandatory retirement provision violates the federal Age Discrimination in Employment Act of 1967 (ADEA or Act), 29 U.S.C. §§ 621-634, and whether it comports with the federal constitutional prescription of equal protection of the laws.

I

Petitioners are Missouri state judges. Judge Ellis Gregory, Jr., is an associate circuit judge for the Twenty-first Judicial Circuit. Judge Anthony P. Nugent, Jr., is a judge of the Missouri Court of Appeals, Western District. Both are subject to the § 26 mandatory retirement provision.

Petitioners and two other state judges filed suit against John D. Ashcroft, the Governor of Missouri...challenging the validity of the mandatory retirement provision. The judges alleged that the provision violated both the ADEA and the Equal Protection Clause of the Fourteenth Amendment to the United States Constitution. The Governor filed a motion to dismiss.

The District Court granted the motion, holding that Missouri's appointed judges are not protected by the ADEA because they are "appointees ... 'on a policymaking level' " and therefore are excluded from the Act's definition of "employee." The court held also that the mandatory retirement provision does not violate the Equal Protection Clause because there is a rational basis for the distinction between judges and other state officials to whom no mandatory retirement age applies.

The United States Court of Appeals for the Eighth Circuit affirmed.

II

The ADEA makes it unlawful for an "employer" "to discharge any individual" who is at least 40 years old "because of such individual's age." 29 U.S.C. §§ 623(a), 631(a). The term "employer" is defined to include "a State or political subdivision of a State." § 630(b)(2). Petitioners work for the State of Missouri. They contend that the Missouri mandatory retirement requirement for judges violates the ADEA.

A

As every schoolchild learns, our Constitution establishes a system of dual sovereignty between the States and the Federal Government. This Court also has recognized this fundamental principle. The Constitution created a Federal Government of limited powers. "The powers not delegated to the United States by the Constitution, nor prohibited by it to the States, are reserved to the States respectively, or to the people." U.S. Const., Amdt. 10. The States thus retain substantial sovereign authority under our constitutional system. The Federal Government holds a decided advantage in this delicate balance: the Supremacy Clause. U.S. Const., Art. VI, cl. 2. As long as it is acting within the powers granted it under the Constitution, Congress may impose its will on the States. Congress may legislate in areas traditionally regulated by the States. This is an extraordinary power in a federalist system. It is a power that we must assume Congress does not exercise lightly.

The present case concerns a state constitutional provision through which the people of Missouri establish a qualification for those who sit as their judges. This provision goes beyond an area traditionally regulated by the States; it is a decision of the most fundamental sort for a sovereign entity. Through the structure of its government, and the character of those who exercise government authority, a State defines itself as a sovereign. "It is obviously essential to the independence of the States, and to their peace and tranquility, that their power to prescribe the qualifications of their own officers...should be exclusive, and free from external interference, except so far as plainly provided by the Constitution...."

Congressional interference with this decision of the people of Missouri...would upset the usual constitutional balance of federal and state powers. For this reason, "it is incumbent upon the federal courts to be certain of Congress' intent before finding that federal law overrides" this balance. We explained recently:

> [I]f Congress intends to alter the 'usual constitutional balance between the States and the Federal Government,' it must make its intention to do so 'unmistakably clear in the language of the statute.' Congress should make its intention 'clear and manifest' if it intends to pre-empt the historic powers of the States....

Will v. Mich. Dept. of State Police, 491 U.S. 58, 65 (1989). This plain statement rule is nothing more than an acknowledgment that the States retain substantial sovereign powers under our constitutional scheme, powers with which Congress does not readily interfere.

These cases stand in recognition of the authority of the people of the States to determine the qualifications of their most important government officials. It is an authority that lies at "the heart of representative government." It is a power reserved to the States under the Tenth Amendment and guaranteed them by that provision of the Constitution under which the United States "guarantee[s] to every State in this Union a Republican Form of Government." U.S. Const., Art. IV, § 4.

B

In 1974, Congress extended the substantive provisions of the ADEA to include the States as employers. At the same time, Congress amended the definition of "employee" to exclude all elected and most high-ranking government officials.

Governor Ashcroft contends that the exclusion of certain public officials also excludes judges, like petitioners, who are appointed to office by the Governor and are then subject to retention election. Governor Ashcroft relies on the plain language of the statute: It exempts persons appointed "at the policymaking level." The Governor argues that state judges, in fashioning and applying the common law, make policy. Missouri is a common law state. The common law, unlike a constitution or statute, provides no definitive text; it is to be derived from the interstices of prior opinions and a well-considered judgment of what is best for the community.

The statute refers to appointees "on the policymaking level," not to appointees "who make policy." It may be sufficient that the appointee is in a position requiring the exercise of discretion concerning issues of public importance. This certainly describes the bench, regardless of whether judges might be considered policymakers in the same sense as the executive or legislature.

Nonetheless, "appointee at the policymaking level," particularly in the context of the other exceptions that surround it, is an odd way for Congress to exclude judges; a plain statement that judges are not "employees" would seem the most efficient phrasing. But in this case we are not looking for a plain statement that judges are excluded. We will not read the ADEA to cover state judges unless Congress has made it clear that judges are *included.* This does not mean that the Act must mention judges explicitly, though it does not. Rather, it must be plain to anyone reading the Act that it covers judges. In the context of a statute that plainly excludes most important state public officials, "appointee on the policymaking level" is sufficiently broad that we cannot conclude that the statute plainly covers appointed state judges. Therefore, it does not.

III

Petitioners argue that, even if they are not covered by the ADEA, the Missouri Constitution's mandatory retirement provision for judges violates the Equal Protection Clause of the Fourteenth Amendment to the United States Constitution. Petitioners contend that there is no rational basis for the decision of the people of Missouri to preclude those aged 70 and over from serving as their judges. They claim that the mandatory retirement provision makes two irrational distinctions: between judges who have reached age 70 and younger judges, and between judges 70 and over and other state employees of the same age who are not subject to mandatory retirement.

Petitioners are correct to assert their challenge at the level of rational basis. This Court has said repeatedly that age is not a suspect classification under the Equal Protection Clause. Nor do petitioners claim that they have a fundamental interest in serving as judges. The State need therefore assert only a rational basis for its age classification. In this case, we are dealing not merely with government action, but with a state constitutional provision approved by the people of Missouri as a whole. This constitutional provision reflects both the considered judgment of the state legislature that proposed it and that of the citizens of Missouri who voted for it. "[W]e will not overturn such a [law] unless the varying treatment of different groups or persons is so unrelated to the achievement of any combination of legitimate purposes that we can only conclude that the [people's] actions were irrational."

The people of Missouri have a legitimate, indeed compelling, interest in maintaining a judiciary fully capable of performing the demanding tasks that judges must perform. It is an unfortunate fact of life that physical and mental capacity sometimes diminish with age. The people may therefore wish to replace some older judges. Voluntary retirement will not always be sufficient. Nor may impeachment-with its public humiliation and elaborate procedural machinery-serve acceptably the goal of a fully functioning judiciary.

The election process may also be inadequate. Whereas the electorate would be expected to discover if their governor or state legislator were not performing adequately and vote the official out of office, the same may not be true of judges. Most voters never observe state judges in action, nor read judicial opinions. State judges also serve longer terms of office than other public officials, making them-deliberately-less dependent on the will of the people. Most of these judges do not run in ordinary elections. The people of Missouri rationally could conclude that retention elections-in which state judges run unopposed at relatively long intervals-do not serve as an adequate check on judges whose performance is deficient. Mandatory retirement is a reasonable response to this dilemma.

The Missouri mandatory retirement provision, like all legal classifications, is founded on a generalization. It is far from true that all judges suffer significant deterioration in performance at age 70. It is probably not true that most do. It may not be true at all. But... [t]he people of Missouri rationally could conclude that the threat of deterioration at age 70 is sufficiently great, and the alternatives for removal sufficiently inadequate, that they will require all judges to step aside at age 70.

IV

The people of Missouri have established a qualification for those who would be their judges. It is their prerogative as citizens of a sovereign State to do so. Neither the ADEA nor the Equal Protection Clause prohibits the choice they have made.

C. THE DISTRIBUTION OF GOVERNMENTAL POWERS

1. Exclusive Federal Powers

a. Article I, § 8

Article I, § 8 of the federal Constitution enumerates the majority of Congress's powers, many of which are exclusive in nature. Such exclusive powers include the power to establish rules of naturalization and immigration, regulate bankruptcy, coin money, establish post offices, protect intellectual property through patent, copyright, and trademark laws, constitute the lower federal courts, regulate and punish piracy, declare war, raise and support an army and a navy, and govern federal territories.

Some Article I powers are theoretically exclusive, but in practice end up intertwined and often overlapping with traditional state police powers, a prime example being Congress's Article I power to regulate commerce "among the several states." In theory, the power to regulate interstate commerce belongs to Congress alone, even to the point of the Supreme Court developing a "Dormant" or "Negative" commerce doctrine which the Court has used to find implied preemption of state police power regulations that, in the Court's view, unduly intrude into matters of interstate commerce. The Court invokes this doctrine in the absence of any Act of Congress either expressly or implicitly requiring such federal preemption. As a practical matter, the dormant commerce power has proven extremely important federal limitation on the States' efforts to regulate a variety of matters.

Thus, the reality is that the federal commerce power in particular has proven particularly difficult to separate from traditional state police powers, even though it is in theory an exclusive federal power. The Supreme Court has at times also attempted to draw lines regarding Congress's affirmative use of this power, in other words when Congress has passed a statute pursuant to its commerce power, though the lines are generally anything but clear. Further, in some contexts, the Court has altogether abandoned any effort to limit Congress's power over interstate commerce insofar as a law is challenged as improperly intruding into the States' sovereignty and government activities. *See, e.g., Garcia v. San Antonio Metropolitan Transit Auth.*, 469 U.S. 528 (1985). A few examples of Supreme Court cases applying the "Dormant" commerce power doctrine follow, and Section III.C.3. below presents an example of the Court's efforts to define the limits of Congress's affirmative use of the commerce power in the context of enacting federal criminal laws.

DEPARTMENT OF REVENUE OF KENTUCKY v. DAVIS
553 U.S. ___, 128 S. Ct. 1801 (2008)

SOUTER, J., delivered the opinion of the Court.

II

The Commerce Clause empowers Congress "[t]o regulate Commerce ... among the several States," Art. I, § 8, cl. 3, and although its terms do not expressly restrain "the several States" in any way, we have sensed a negative implication in the provision since the early days, see, *e.g., Cooley v. Board of Wardens of Port of Philadelphia ex rel. Soc. for Relief of Distressed Pilots,* 12 How. 299, 318-319 (1852); cf. *Gibbons v. Ogden,* 9 Wheat. 1, 209 (1824) (Marshall, C.J.) (dictum). The modern law of what has come to be called the dormant Commerce Clause is driven by concern about "economic protectionism-that is, regulatory measures designed to benefit in-state economic interests by burdening out-of-state competitors." The point is to "effectuat[e] the Framers' purpose to 'prevent a State from retreating into [the] economic isolation'" "that had plagued relations among the Colonies and later among the States under the Articles of Confederation."

The law has had to respect a cross purpose as well, for the Framers' distrust of economic Balkanization was limited by their federalism favoring a degree of local autonomy. Compare The Federalist Nos. 7 (A. Hamilton), 11 (A. Hamilton), and 42 (J. Madison), with The Federalist No. 51 (J. Madison); see also *Garcia v. San Antonio Metropolitan Transit Authority,* 469 U.S. 528, 546 (1985) ("The essence of our federal system is that within the realm of authority left open to them under the Constitution, the States must be equally free to engage in any activity that their citizens choose for the common weal").

Under the resulting protocol for dormant Commerce Clause analysis, we ask whether a challenged law discriminates against interstate commerce. A discriminatory law is "virtually *per se* invalid," and will survive only if it "advances a legitimate local purpose that cannot be adequately served by reasonable nondiscriminatory alternatives." Absent discrimination for the forbidden purpose, however, the law "will be upheld unless the burden imposed on [interstate] commerce is clearly excessive in relation to the putative local benefits." *Pike v. Bruce Church, Inc.,* 397 U.S. 137, 142 (1970). State laws frequently survive this *Pike* scrutiny, though not always, as in *Pike* itself.

Some cases run a different course, however, and an exception covers States that go beyond regulation and themselves "participat[e] in the market" so as to "exercis[e] the right to favor [their] own citizens over others." This "market-participant" exception reflects a "basic distinction...between States as market participants and States as market regulators," "[t]here [being] no indication of a constitutional plan to limit the ability of the States themselves to operate freely in the free market." Thus,...[the Court] accepted South Dakota's policy of giving in-state customers first dibs on cement produced by a state-owned plant, and...held that a Boston executive order requiring half the workers on city-financed construction projects to be city residents passed muster.

[The Court also has] upheld a "flow control" ordinance requiring trash haulers to deliver solid waste to a processing plant owned and operated by a public authority.... We found "[c]ompelling reasons" for "treating [the ordinance] differently from laws favoring particular private businesses over their competitors." State and local governments that provide public goods and services on their own, unlike private businesses, are "vested with the responsibility of protecting the health, safety, and welfare of [their] citizens," and laws favoring such States and their subdivisions may "be directed toward any number of legitimate goals unrelated to protectionism." And if more had been needed to show that New York's object was consequently different from forbidden protectionism, we pointed out that "the most palpable harm imposed by the ordinances-more expensive trash removal-[was] likely to fall upon the very people who voted for the laws," rather than out-of-state interests.

WYOMING v. OKLAHOMA
502 U.S. 437 (1992)

WHITE, J., delivered the opinion of the Court.

[Although Wyoming is a major coal-producing State, the government of Wyoming does not itself does sell coal, and thus Wyoming is not directly participating in the market for coal. Wyoming law does, however, impose a severance tax on those who extract coal in Wyoming. From 1981 to 1986, four Oklahoma electric utilities purchased virtually 100% of their coal from Wyoming sources, and the Wyoming sellers consequently paid severance taxes on that coal to the State of Wyoming. The Oklahoma Legislature then passed an Act requiring coal-fired electric utilities in Oklahoma to burn a mixture containing at least 10% Oklahoma-mined coal, with the results that the Oklahoma-based utilities reduced their purchases of Wyoming coal in favor of Oklahoma coal and Wyoming's severance tax revenues declined. Wyoming brought an original action in the Supreme Court, alleging that the Oklahoma law violated dormant commerce principles. After deciding both that Wyoming had standing to bring the suit, and that the Supreme Court itself had original jurisdiction over the matter, the Court addressed the merits of the commerce claim.]

III

The Commerce Clause of the United States Constitution provides that "[t]he Congress shall have Power...[t]o regulate Commerce...among the several States...." It is long established that, while a literal reading evinces a grant of power to Congress, the Commerce Clause also directly limits the power of the States to discriminate against interstate commerce. "This 'negative' aspect of the Commerce Clause prohibits economic protectionism-that is, regulatory measures designed to benefit in-state economic interests by burdening out-of-state competitors." When a state statute clearly discriminates against interstate commerce, it will be struck down, unless the discrimination is demonstrably justified by a valid factor unrelated to economic protectionism. Indeed, when the state statute amounts to simple economic protectionism, a "virtually *per se* rule of invalidity" has applied.

The Special Master correctly found that the [Oklahoma] Act, on its face and in practical effect, discriminates against interstate commerce. [T]he Act expressly reserves a segment of the Oklahoma coal market for Oklahoma-mined coal, to the exclusion of coal mined in other States. Such a preference for coal from domestic sources cannot be characterized as anything other than protectionist and discriminatory, for the Act purports to exclude coal mined in other States based solely on its origin. The stipulated facts confirm that from 1981 to 1986 Wyoming provided virtually 100% of the coal purchased by Oklahoma utilities. In 1987 and 1988, following the effective date of the Act, the utilities purchased Oklahoma coal in amounts ranging from 3.4% to 7.4% of their annual needs, with a necessarily corresponding reduction in purchases of Wyoming coal.

Oklahoma attempts to discount this evidence by emphasizing that the Act sets aside only a "small portion" of the Oklahoma coal market, without placing an "overall burden" on out-of-state coal producers doing business in Oklahoma. The volume of commerce affected measures only the *extent* of the discrimination; it is of no relevance to the determination whether a State has discriminated against interstate commerce.

Because the Act discriminates both on its face and in practical effect, the burden falls on Oklahoma "'to justify it both in terms of the local benefits flowing from the statute and the unavailability of nondiscriminatory alternatives adequate to preserve the local interests at stake.'" "At a minimum such facial discrimination invokes the strictest scrutiny of any purported legitimate local purpose and of the absence of nondiscriminatory alternatives." Oklahoma has not met its burden in this respect. In this Court, Oklahoma argues quite briefly that the Act's discrimination against out-of-state coal is justified because sustaining the Oklahoma coal-mining industry lessens the State's reliance on a single source of coal delivered over a single rail line. This justification...is foreclosed by the Court's reasoning in [prior] cases that the State's brief ignores. We have often examined a "presumably legitimate goal," only to find that the State attempted to achieve it by "the illegitimate means of isolating the State from the national economy."

WEST LYNN CREAMERY, INC. v. HEALY
512 U.S. 186 (1994)

STEVENS, J., delivered the opinion of the Court.

[A Massachusetts pricing order subjected all milk sold by dealers to Massachusetts retailers to an assessment. Although most of the milk subject to the assessment was produced outside of Massachusetts, the entire amount collected was then redistributed solely to Massachusetts dairy farmers. Licensed milk dealers who purchased milk produced by out-of-state farmers and sold it in Massachusetts sued, arguing that the assessment and subsidy scheme violated the Commerce Clause. The Supreme Court of Massachusetts rejected the challenge, concluding that the pricing order (1) was not facially discriminatory and (2) applied evenhandedly to all milk producers, with only an incidental burden on interstate commerce, a burden outweighed by the "local benefits" to the dairy industry.]

II

The Commerce Clause vests Congress with ample power to enact legislation providing for the regulation of prices paid to farmers for their products. An affirmative exercise of that power led to the promulgation of [a] federal order setting minimum milk prices. The Commerce Clause also limits the power of the Commonwealth of Massachusetts to adopt regulations that discriminate against interstate commerce. "This 'negative' aspect of the Commerce Clause prohibits economic protectionism-that is, regulatory measures designed to benefit in-state economic interests by burdening out-of-state competitors.... Thus, state statutes that clearly discriminate against interstate commerce are routinely struck down...unless the discrimination is demonstrably justified by a valid factor unrelated to economic protectionism."

The paradigmatic example of a law discriminating against interstate commerce is the protective tariff or customs duty, which taxes goods imported from other States, but does not tax similar products produced in State. A tariff is an attractive measure because it simultaneously raises revenue and benefits local producers by burdening their out-of-state competitors. Nevertheless, it violates the principle of the unitary national market by handicapping out-of-state competitors, thus artificially encouraging in-state production even when the same goods could be produced at lower cost in other States.

Because of their distorting effects on the geography of production, tariffs have long been recognized as violative of the Commerce Clause. In fact, tariffs against the products of other States are so patently unconstitutional that our cases reveal not a single attempt by any State to enact one. Instead, the cases are filled with state laws that aspire to reap some of the benefits of tariffs by other means. In *Baldwin v. G.A.F. Seelig, Inc.,* 294 U.S. 511 (1935), the State of New York attempted to protect its dairy farmers from the adverse effects of Vermont competition by establishing a single minimum price for all milk, whether produced in New York or elsewhere. This Court did not hesitate, however, to strike it down...because the minimum price regulation had the same effect as a tariff or customs duty-neutralizing the advantage possessed by lower cost out-of-state producers-it was held unconstitutional. Similarly, in *Bacchus Imports, Ltd. v. Dias,* 468 U.S. 263 (1984), this Court invalidated a law which advantaged local production by granting a tax exemption to certain liquors produced in Hawaii. Other cases of this kind are legion.

Under these cases, Massachusetts' pricing order is clearly unconstitutional. Its avowed purpose and its undisputed effect are to enable higher cost Massachusetts dairy farmers to compete with lower cost dairy farmers in other States. The "premium payments" are effectively a tax which makes milk produced out of State more expensive. Although the tax also applies to milk produced in Massachusetts, its effect on Massachusetts producers is entirely (indeed more than) offset by the subsidy provided exclusively to Massachusetts dairy farmers. Like an ordinary tariff, the tax is thus effectively imposed only on out-of-state products. The pricing order thus allows Massachusetts dairy farmers who produce at higher cost to sell at or below the price charged by lower cost out-of-state producers.

III

Respondent advances [several] arguments against the conclusion that its pricing order imposes an unconstitutional burden on interstate commerce. We discuss each of these arguments in turn.

A

Respondent's principal argument is that, because "the milk order achieves its goals through lawful means," the order as a whole is constitutional. He argues that the payments to Massachusetts dairy farmers from the Dairy Equalization Fund are valid, because subsidies are constitutional exercises of state power, and that the order premium which provides money for the fund is valid, because it is a nondiscriminatory tax. Therefore the pricing order is constitutional, because it is merely the combination of two independently lawful regulations. In effect, respondent argues, if the State may impose a valid tax on dealers, it is free to use the proceeds of the tax as it chooses; and if it may independently subsidize its farmers, it is free to finance the subsidy by means of any legitimate tax.

Even granting respondent's assertion that both components of the pricing order would be constitutional standing alone, the pricing order nevertheless must fall. A pure subsidy funded out of general revenue ordinarily imposes no burden on interstate commerce, but merely assists local business. The pricing order in this case, however, is funded principally from taxes on the sale of milk produced in other States. By so funding the subsidy, respondent not only assists local farmers, but burdens interstate commerce. The pricing order thus violates the cardinal principle that a State may not "benefit in-state economic interests by burdening out-of-state competitors."

More fundamentally, respondent errs in assuming that the constitutionality of the pricing order follows logically from the constitutionality of its component parts. By conjoining a tax and a subsidy, Massachusetts has created a program more dangerous to interstate commerce than either part alone. Nondiscriminatory measures, like the evenhanded tax at issue here, are generally upheld, in spite of any adverse effects on interstate commerce, in part because "[t]he existence of major in-state interests adversely affected...is a powerful safeguard against legislative abuse." However, when a nondiscriminatory tax is coupled with a subsidy to one of the groups hurt by the tax, a State's political processes can no longer be relied upon to prevent legislative abuse, because one of the in-state interests which would otherwise lobby against the tax has been mollified by the subsidy. So, in this case, one would ordinarily have expected at least three groups to lobby against the order premium, which, as a tax, raises the price (and hence lowers demand) for milk: dairy farmers, milk dealers, and consumers. But because the tax was coupled with a subsidy, one of the most powerful of these groups, Massachusetts dairy farmers, instead of exerting their influence against the tax, were in fact its primary supporters.

Our Commerce Clause jurisprudence is not so rigid as to be controlled by the form by which a State erects barriers to commerce. Rather our cases have eschewed formalism for a sensitive, case-by-case analysis of purposes and effects. As the Court declared over 50 years ago: "The commerce clause forbids discrimination, whether forthright or ingenious. In each case it is our duty to determine whether the statute under attack, whatever its name may be, will in its practical operation work discrimination against interstate commerce."

D

Finally, respondent argues that any incidental burden on interstate commerce "is outweighed by the 'local benefits' of preserving the

Massachusetts dairy industry." In a closely related argument, respondent urges that "the purpose of the order, to save an industry from collapse, is not protectionist." If we were to accept these arguments, we would make a virtue of the vice that the rule against discrimination condemns. Preservation of local industry by protecting it from the rigors of interstate competition is the hallmark of the economic protectionism that the Commerce Clause prohibits. [W]e have explicitly rejected any distinction "between thriving and struggling enterprises." Whether a State is attempting to "'enhance thriving and substantial business enterprises'" or to "'subsidize…financially troubled'" ones is irrelevant to Commerce Clause analysis. With his characteristic eloquence, Justice Cardozo responded to an argument that respondent echoes today:

> The argument is pressed upon us, however, that the end to be served by the Milk Control Act is something more than the economic welfare of the farmers or of any other class or classes. The end to be served is the maintenance of a regular and adequate supply of pure and wholesome milk, the supply being put in jeopardy when the farmers of the state are unable to earn a living income. Let such an exception be admitted, and all that a state will have to do in times of stress and strain is to say that its farmers and merchants and workmen must be protected against competition from without, lest they go upon the poor relief lists or perish altogether. To give entrance to that excuse would be to invite a speedy end of our national solidarity. The Constitution was framed under the dominion of a political philosophy less parochial in range. It was framed upon the theory that the peoples of the several states must sink or swim together, and that in the long run prosperity and salvation are in union and not division.

SPORHASE v. NEBRASKA, EX REL. DOUGLAS
458 U.S. 941 (1982)

STEVENS, J., delivered the opinion of the Court.

[A Nebraska statute provides that any person who intends to withdraw ground water from any well located in the State and transport it for use in an adjoining State must obtain a permit from the Nebraska Department of Water Resources. If the Director of Water Resources finds that such withdrawal is reasonable, not contrary to the conservation and use of ground water, and not otherwise detrimental to the public welfare, he will grant the permit if the State in which the water is to be used grants reciprocal rights to withdraw and transport ground water from that State for use in Nebraska. Appellants jointly own contiguous tracts of land in Nebraska and Colorado, on which a well on the Nebraska tract pumps ground water for irrigation of both the Nebraska and Colorado tracts, but they never applied for the permit required by the statute. Appellee [the State] brought an action in a Nebraska state court to enjoin appellants [the landowners] from transferring the water across the border without a permit. Rejecting the defense that the statute imposed an undue burden on interstate commerce, the trial court granted the injunction. The Nebraska Supreme Court affirmed.]

Appellants challenge the constitutionality of a Nebraska statutory restriction on the withdrawal of ground water from any well within Nebraska intended for use in an adjoining State. The challenge presents three questions under the Commerce Clause: (1) whether ground water is an article of commerce....; (2) whether the Nebraska restriction on the interstate transfer of ground water imposes an impermissible burden on commerce; and (3) whether Congress has granted the States permission to engage in ground water regulation that otherwise would be impermissible.

I

[The Court held that ground water is an article of commerce.]

II

Our conclusion that water is an article of commerce raises, but does not answer, the question whether the Nebraska statute is unconstitutional. For the existence of unexercised federal regulatory power does not foreclose state regulation of its water resources, of the uses of water within the State, or indeed, of interstate commerce in water. Determining the validity of state statutes affecting interstate commerce requires a more careful inquiry:

> Where the statute regulates evenhandedly to effectuate a legitimate local public interest, and its effects on interstate commerce are only incidental, it will be upheld unless the burden imposed on such commerce is clearly excessive in relation to the putative local benefits. If a legitimate local purpose is found, then the question becomes one of degree. And the extent of the burden that will be tolerated will of course depend on the nature of the local interest involved, and on whether it could be promoted as well with a lesser impact on interstate activities." *Pike v. Bruce Church, Inc.*, 397 U.S. 137, 142 (1970).

The only purpose that appellee advances for [the Nebraska law] is to conserve and preserve diminishing sources of ground water. The purpose is unquestionably legitimate and highly important, and the other aspects of Nebraska's ground water regulation demonstrate that it is genuine. The State's interest in conservation and preservation of ground water is advanced by the first three conditions in [the statute] for the withdrawal of water for an interstate transfer. Those requirements are "that the withdrawal of the ground water requested is reasonable, is not contrary to the conservation and use of ground water, and is not otherwise detrimental to the public welfare." Although Commerce Clause concerns are implicated by the fact that [the law] applies to interstate transfers but not to intrastate transfers, there are legitimate reasons for the special treatment accorded requests to transport ground water across state lines. Obviously, a State that imposes severe withdrawal and use restrictions on its own citizens is not discriminating against interstate commerce when it seeks to prevent the uncontrolled transfer of water out of the State. An exemption for interstate transfers would be inconsistent with the ideal of evenhandedness in regulation.

Appellants, however, do challenge the requirement that "the state in which the water is to be used grants reciprocal rights to withdraw and transport ground water from that state for use in the State of Nebraska"-the reciprocity provision.... Because Colorado forbids the exportation of its ground water, the reciprocity provision operates as an explicit barrier to commerce between the two States. The State therefore bears the initial burden of demonstrating a close fit between the reciprocity requirement and its asserted local purpose.

The reciprocity requirement fails to clear this initial hurdle. For there is no evidence that this restriction is narrowly tailored to the conservation and preservation rationale. Even though the supply of water in a particular well may be abundant, or perhaps even excessive, and even though the most beneficial use of that water might be in another State, such water may not be shipped into a neighboring State that does not permit its water to be used in Nebraska. If it could be shown that the State as a whole suffers a water shortage, that the intrastate transportation of water from areas of abundance to areas of shortage is feasible regardless of distance, and that the importation of water from adjoining States would roughly compensate for any exportation to those States, then the conservation and preservation purpose might be credibly advanced for the reciprocity provision. A demonstrably arid State conceivably might be able to marshal evidence to establish a close means-end relationship between even a total ban on the exportation of water and a purpose to conserve and preserve water. Appellee, however, does not claim that such evidence exists. We therefore are not persuaded that the reciprocity requirement-when superimposed on the first three restrictions in the statute-significantly advances the State's legitimate conservation and preservation interest; it surely is not narrowly tailored to serve that purpose. The reciprocity requirement does not survive the "strictest scrutiny" reserved for facially discriminatory legislation.

b. Article I, §10, cl. 1

Article I, §10, cl. 1, of the federal constitution essentially repeats and emphasizes the exclusive nature of a handful of Congress's powers set forth in Article I, § 8. It does so by declaring such powers off limits to the States, emphatically stating that "No State shall" enter into treaties or confederations, coin money, or emit bills of credit. Article I, § 10, cl. 2 and cl. 3, make clear that the States may exercise certain powers only with the concurrence and consent of Congress. For example, the second clause declares that States may not lay imposts or duties on imports or exports without the "Consent of the Congress." Similarly, the third clause makes clear that no State may lay any duty of tonnage, keep troops or ships of war in peace time, or enter into any agreement with another state or a foreign nation, again unless the State has the "Consent of Congress."

2. Exclusive State Powers

a. Organization of State Government – See Chapter XV.

Nothing in the federal Constitution or Supreme Court decisions purports to limit or direct the organization of state governments, other than the Article IV promise that the United States shall guarantee to every state in the union a "Republican Form" of government, a provision addressed above and which the Supreme Court has left entirely to the Congress and the President to enforce, if it is to be enforced at all. Also, the Supreme Court has declined to require that state governments follow federal separation of powers principles. Thus, as explored more fully in Chapter XV, the States may choose, for example, a unicameral rather than bicameral legislature (Nebraska), give their Governors a variety of powers, including some the President of the United States is not permitted, (such as a line item veto), and generally may structure their state court systems as they wish, including the use of elections to select judges. Thus, the organization of state government and the powers accorded the various branches and officials of state government, are a subject about which the federal Constitution has virtually nothing to say and plays essentially no role.

b. Traditional Police Powers

The States, unlike the federal government, are the repository of traditional police powers, understood as a general authority for enacting any and all laws relating to the public health, safety, welfare and morals. Thus, with the States, the constitutional question generally is not whether they have the authority to pass a particular law but, rather, whether there is any constitutional prohibition on the passing of such a law. This is the opposite of the presumption that applies to Congress, which must point to some enumerated power in the federal Constitution giving Congress the authority to affirmatively legislate on a particular matter.

The result is that the vast majority of criminal law, domestic relations law, tort law, property law, contract law, commercial law, and a host of other traditional areas of the law are dominated by state rather than federal law. Expansion of the understanding of Congress's commerce power has resulted in some regulation by the federal government in areas once exclusively the provinces of the States, but even where that is true (*e.g.*, in the criminal law), the bulk of all criminal law in this country is state law and the vast majority of criminal prosecutions remain state prosecutions.

c. The "Anti-commandeering" Principle

PRINTZ v. UNITED STATES
521 U.S. 898 (1997)

SCALIA, J., delivered the opinion of the Court.

The question presented in these cases is whether certain interim provisions of the Brady Handgun Violence Prevention Act, commanding state and local law enforcement officers to conduct background checks on prospective handgun purchasers and to perform certain related tasks, violate the Constitution.

I

The Gun Control Act of 1968 (GCA), establishes a detailed federal scheme governing the distribution of firearms. It prohibits firearms dealers from transferring handguns to any person under 21, not resident in the dealer's State, or prohibited by state or local law from purchasing or possessing firearms. It also forbids possession of a firearm by, and transfer of a firearm to, convicted felons, fugitives from justice, unlawful users of controlled substances, persons adjudicated as mentally defective or committed to mental institutions, aliens unlawfully present in the United States, persons dishonorably discharged from the Armed Forces, persons who have renounced their citizenship, and persons who have been subjected to certain restraining orders or been convicted of a misdemeanor offense involving domestic violence.

In 1993, Congress amended the GCA by enacting the Brady Act. The Act requires the Attorney General to establish a national instant background-check system by November 30, 1998, and immediately puts in place certain interim provisions until that system becomes operative. Under the interim provisions, a firearms dealer who proposes to transfer a handgun must first: (1) receive from the transferee a statement (the Brady Form), containing the name, address, and date of birth of the proposed transferee along with a sworn statement that the transferee is not among any of the classes of prohibited purchasers; (2) verify the identity of the transferee by examining an identification document; and (3) provide the "chief law enforcement officer" (CLEO) of the transferee's residence with notice of the contents (and a copy) of the Brady Form. With some exceptions, the dealer must then wait five business days before consummating the sale, unless the CLEO earlier notifies the dealer that he has no reason to believe the transfer would be illegal.

The Brady Act creates two significant alternatives to the foregoing scheme. A dealer may sell a handgun immediately if the purchaser possesses a state handgun permit issued after a background check, or if state law provides for an instant background check. In States that have not rendered one of these alternatives applicable to all gun purchasers, CLEOs are required to perform certain duties. When a CLEO receives the required notice of a proposed transfer from the firearms dealer, the CLEO must "make a reasonable effort to ascertain within 5 business days whether receipt or possession would be in violation of the law, including research in whatever State and local recordkeeping systems are available and in a national system designated by the Attorney General." The Act does not require the CLEO to take any particular action if he determines that a pending transaction would be unlawful; he may notify the firearms dealer to that effect, but is not required to do so. If, however, the CLEO notifies a gun dealer that a prospective purchaser is ineligible to receive a handgun, he must, upon request, provide the would-be purchaser with a written statement of the reasons for that determination. Moreover, if the CLEO does not discover any basis for objecting to the sale, he must destroy any records in his possession relating to the transfer, including his copy of the Brady Form. Under a separate provision of the GCA, any person who "knowingly violates [the section of the GCA amended by the Brady Act] shall be fined under this title, imprisoned for not more than 1 year, or both."

Petitioners Jay Printz and Richard Mack, the CLEOs for Ravalli County, Montana, and Graham County, Arizona, respectively, filed separate actions challenging the constitutionality of the Brady Act's interim provisions. In each case, the District Court held that the provision requiring CLEOs to perform background checks was unconstitutional, but concluded that that provision was severable from the remainder of the Act, effectively leaving a voluntary background-check system in place. A divided panel of the Court of Appeals for the Ninth Circuit reversed, finding none of the Brady Act's interim provisions to be unconstitutional.

II

From the description set forth above, it is apparent that the Brady Act purports to direct state law enforcement officers to participate, albeit only temporarily, in the administration of a federally enacted regulatory scheme. Petitioners here object to being pressed into federal service, and contend that congressional action compelling state officers to execute federal laws is unconstitutional. Because there is no constitutional text speaking to this precise question, the answer to the CLEOs' challenge must be sought in historical understanding and practice, in the structure of the Constitution, and in the jurisprudence of this Court. We treat those three sources, in that order, in this and the next two sections of this opinion.

The Government observes that statutes enacted by the first Congresses required state courts to record applications for citizenship, to transmit abstracts of citizenship applications and other naturalization records to the

Secretary of State, and to register aliens seeking naturalization and issue certificates of registry. Other statutes of that era apparently or at least arguably required state courts to perform functions…such as resolving controversies between a captain and the crew of his ship concerning the seaworthiness of the vessel, hearing the claims of slave owners who had apprehended fugitive slaves and issuing certificates authorizing the slave's forced removal to the State from which he had fled, taking proof of the claims of Canadian refugees who had assisted the United States during the Revolutionary War, and ordering the deportation of alien enemies in times of war.

These early laws establish, at most, that the Constitution was originally understood to permit imposition of an obligation on state *judges* to enforce federal prescriptions, insofar as those prescriptions related to matters appropriate for the judicial power. That assumption was perhaps implicit in one of the provisions of the Constitution, and was explicit in another. In accord with the so-called Madisonian Compromise, Article III, § 1, established only a Supreme Court, and made the creation of lower federal courts optional with the Congress-even though it was obvious that the Supreme Court alone could not hear all federal cases throughout the United States. And the Supremacy Clause, Art. VI, cl. 2, announced that "the Laws of the United States ... shall be the supreme Law of the Land; and the Judges in every State shall be bound thereby." It is understandable why courts should have been viewed distinctively in this regard; unlike legislatures and executives, they applied the law of other sovereigns all the time. The principle underlying so-called "transitory" causes of action was that laws which operated elsewhere created obligations in justice that courts of the forum State would enforce. The Constitution itself, in the Full Faith and Credit Clause, Art. IV, § 1, generally required such enforcement with respect to obligations arising in other States.

For these reasons, we do not think the early statutes imposing obligations on state courts imply a power of Congress to impress the state executive into its service. Indeed, it can be argued that the numerousness of these statutes, contrasted with the utter lack of statutes imposing obligations on the States' executive (notwithstanding the attractiveness of that course to Congress), suggests an assumed *absence* of such power.

III

A

It is incontestible that the Constitution established a system of "dual sovereignty." *Gregory v. Ashcroft,* 501 U.S. 452, 457 (1991). Although the States surrendered many of their powers to the new Federal Government, they retained "a residuary and inviolable sovereignty," The Federalist No. 39, at 245 (J. Madison). This is reflected throughout the Constitution's text, including (to mention only a few examples) the prohibition on any involuntary reduction or combination of a State's territory, Art. IV, § 3; the Judicial Power Clause, Art. III, § 2, and the Privileges and Immunities Clause, Art. IV, § 2, which speak of the "Citizens" of the States; the amendment provision, Article V, which requires the votes of three-fourths of the States to amend the Constitution; and the Guarantee Clause, Art. IV, § 4, which "presupposes the continued existence of the states and ... those means and instrumentalities which are the creation of their sovereign and reserved rights." Residual state sovereignty was also implicit, of course, in the Constitution's conferral upon Congress of not all governmental powers, but only discrete, enumerated ones, Art. I, § 8, which implication was rendered express by the Tenth Amendment's assertion that "[t]he powers not delegated to the United States by the Constitution, nor prohibited by it to the States, are reserved to the States respectively, or to the people."

This separation of the two spheres is one of the Constitution's structural protections of liberty. The power of the Federal Government would be augmented immeasurably if it were able to impress into its service-and at no cost to itself-the police officers of the 50 States.

B

The dissent perceives a simple answer in that portion of Article VI which requires that "all executive and judicial Officers, both of the United States and of the several States, shall be bound by Oath or Affirmation, to support this Constitution," arguing that by virtue of the Supremacy Clause this makes "not only the Constitution, but every law enacted by Congress as well," binding on state officers, including laws requiring state-officer enforcement. The Supremacy Clause, however, makes "Law of the Land" only "Laws of the United States which shall be made in Pursuance [of the Constitution]," Art. VI, cl. 2, so the Supremacy Clause merely brings us back to the question discussed earlier, whether laws conscripting state officers violate state sovereignty and are thus not in accord with the Constitution.

IV

Finally, and most conclusively in the present litigation, we turn to the prior jurisprudence of this Court. When we were at last confronted squarely with a federal statute that unambiguously required the States to enact or administer a federal regulatory program, our decision should have come as no surprise. At issue in *New York v. United States,* 505 U.S. 144 (1992), were the so-called "take title" provisions of the Low-Level Radioactive Waste Policy Amendments Act of 1985, which required States either to enact legislation providing for the disposal of radioactive waste generated within their borders, or to take title to, and possession of, the waste-effectively requiring the States either to legislate pursuant to Congress's directions, or to implement an administrative solution. We concluded that Congress could constitutionally require the States to do neither. "The Federal Government," we held, "may not compel the States to enact or administer a federal regulatory program."

The Government contends that *New York* is distinguishable on the following ground: Unlike the "take title" provisions invalidated there, the background-check provision of the Brady Act does not require state legislative or executive officials to make policy, but instead issues a final directive to state CLEOs. The Government purports to find support for its proffered distinction of *New York* in our decisions in *Testa v. Katt,* 330 U.S. 386 (1947), and *FERC v. Mississippi,* 456 U.S. 742 (1982). We find neither case relevant. *Testa* stands for the proposition that state courts cannot refuse to apply federal law-a conclusion mandated by the terms of the Supremacy Clause ("the Judges in every State shall be bound [by federal law]"). As we have suggested earlier, that says nothing about whether state executive officers must administer federal law. As for *FERC,* it stated (as we have described earlier) that "this Court never has sanctioned explicitly a federal command to the States to promulgate and enforce laws and regulations," and upheld the statutory provisions at issue precisely because they did *not* commandeer state government, but merely imposed preconditions to continued state regulation of an otherwise pre-empted field....

The dissent makes no attempt to defend the Government's basis for distinguishing *New York,* but instead advances what seems to us an even more implausible theory. The Brady Act, the dissent asserts, is different from the "take title" provisions invalidated in *New York* because the former is addressed to individuals-namely, CLEOs-while the latter were directed to the State itself. That is certainly a difference, but it cannot be a constitutionally significant one. While the Brady Act is directed to "individuals," it is directed to them in their official capacities as state officers; it controls their actions, not as private citizens, but as the agents of the State. To say that the Federal Government cannot control the State, but can control all of its officers, is to say nothing of significance. By resorting to this, the dissent not so much distinguishes *New York* as disembowels it.

We held in *New York* that Congress cannot compel the States to enact or enforce a federal regulatory program. Today we hold that Congress cannot circumvent that prohibition by conscripting the State's officers directly. The Federal Government may neither issue directives requiring the States to address particular problems, nor command the States' officers, or those of their political subdivisions, to administer or enforce a federal regulatory program. It matters not whether policymaking is involved, and no case-by-case weighing of the burdens or benefits is necessary; such commands are fundamentally incompatible with our constitutional system of dual sovereignty.

d. Immunity from Suits under Federal Law

The Eleventh Amendment provides that "[t]he Judicial power of the United States shall not be construed to extend to any suit in law or equity, commenced or prosecuted against one of the United States by Citizens of another State, or by Citizens or Subjects of any Foreign State." Although there is general agreement that this amendment was a reaction to the Supreme Court's decision in *Chisholm v. Georgia*, 2 U.S. 419 (1793), permitting a suit by a citizen of South Carolina to proceed in federal court over Georgia's objections, there is much disagreement about the scope of the constitutional immunity the Eleventh Amendment recognizes.

Importantly, the Supreme Court long ago decided that the immunity is not limited to the diversity jurisdiction-depriving literal terms of the amendment, and instead protects the States more broadly. *Hans v. Louisiana*, 134 U.S. 1 (1890) (holding that the immunity also bars a citizen of a State from suing her own state, even though the literal text does not bar such a suit). Further, the Court in recent years has held that the immunity is from suit under federal law, no matter where the suit is brought, so even a suit in the State's own courts is barred. *Alden v. Maine*, 527 U.S. 706 (1999). This area of the law has been actively litigated the past fifteen years, and many of the cases have produced 5 – 4 decisions by the Supreme Court. The case below is offered simply to illustrate the questions raised and the nature of the constitutional immunity that the Supreme Court recognizes. Extensive treatment of the States' constitutional immunity must be left to other courses.

**FEDERAL MARITIME COM'N v.
SOUTH CAROLINA STATE PORTS AUTH.**
535 U.S. 743 (2002)

THOMAS, J., delivered the opinion of the Court.

This case presents the question whether state sovereign immunity precludes petitioner Federal Maritime Commission (FMC or Commission) from adjudicating a private party's complaint that a state-run port has violated the Shipping Act of 1984. We hold that state sovereign immunity bars such an adjudicative proceeding.

I

On five occasions, South Carolina Maritime Services, Inc. (Maritime Services), asked respondent South Carolina State Ports Authority (SCSPA) for permission to berth a cruise ship, the M/V *Tropic Sea,* at the SCSPA's port facilities in Charleston, South Carolina. Maritime Services intended to offer cruises on the M/V *Tropic Sea* originating from the Port of Charleston. Some of these cruises would stop in the Bahamas while others would merely travel in international waters before returning to Charleston with no intervening ports of call. On all of these trips, passengers would be permitted to participate in gambling activities while on board.

The SCSPA repeatedly denied Maritime Services' requests, contending that it had an established policy of denying berths in the Port of Charleston to vessels whose primary purpose was gambling. As a result, Maritime Services filed a complaint with the FMC, contending that the SCSPA's refusal to provide berthing space to the M/V *Tropic Sea* violated the Shipping Act. Maritime Services alleged in its complaint that the SCSPA had implemented its antigambling policy in a discriminatory fashion by providing berthing space in Charleston to two Carnival Cruise Lines vessels even though Carnival offered gambling activities on these ships. Maritime Services therefore complained that the SCSPA had unduly and unreasonably preferred Carnival over Maritime Services in violation of 46 U.S.C.App. § 1709(d)(4), and unreasonably refused to deal or negotiate with Maritime Services in violation of § 1709(b)(10). It further alleged that the SCSPA's unlawful actions had inflicted upon Maritime Services a "loss of profits, loss of earnings, loss of sales, and loss of business opportunities."

To remedy its injuries, Maritime Services prayed that the FMC: (1) seek a temporary restraining order and preliminary injunction in the United States District Court for the District of South Carolina "enjoining [the SCSPA] from utilizing its discriminatory practice to refuse to provide berthing space and passenger services to Maritime Services;" (2) direct the SCSPA to pay reparations to Maritime Services as well as interest and reasonable attorneys' fees; (3) issue an order commanding, among other things, the SCSPA to cease and desist from violating the Shipping Act; and (4) award Maritime Services "such other and further relief as is just and proper."

Consistent with the FMC's Rules of Practice and Procedure, Maritime Services' complaint was referred to an Administrative Law Judge (ALJ). The SCSPA then filed an answer, maintaining, *inter alia,* that it had adhered to its antigambling policy in a nondiscriminatory manner. It also filed a motion to dismiss, asserting, as relevant, that the SCSPA, as an arm of the State of South Carolina, was "entitled to Eleventh Amendment immunity" from Maritime Services' suit. The SCSPA argued that "the Constitution prohibits Congress from passing a statute authorizing Maritime Services to file [this] Complaint before the Commission and, thereby, sue the State of South Carolina for damages and injunctive relief."

The ALJ agreed, concluding that recent decisions of this Court "interpreting the 11th Amendment and State sovereign immunity from *private* suits ... require [d] that [Maritime Services'] complaint be dismissed." While Maritime Services did not appeal the ALJ's dismissal of its complaint, the FMC on its own motion decided to review the ALJ's ruling to consider whether state sovereign immunity from private suits extends to proceedings before the Commission. It concluded that "[t]he doctrine of state sovereign immunity...is meant to cover proceedings before judicial tribunals, whether Federal or state, not executive branch administrative agencies like the Commission." As a result, the FMC held that sovereign immunity did not bar the Commission from adjudicating private complaints against state-run ports and reversed the ALJ's decision dismissing Maritime Services' complaint. The SCSPA filed a petition for review, and the United States Court of Appeals for the Fourth Circuit reversed.

II

Dual sovereignty is a defining feature of our Nation's constitutional blueprint. See *Gregory v. Ashcroft,* 501 U.S. 452, 457 (1991). States, upon ratification of the Constitution, did not consent to become mere appendages of the Federal Government. Rather, they entered the Union "with their sovereignty intact." An integral component of that "residuary and inviolable sovereignty," The Federalist No. 39, p. 245 (C. Rossiter ed. 1961) (J. Madison), retained by the States is their immunity from private suits.

States, in ratifying the Constitution, did surrender a portion of their inherent immunity by consenting to suits brought by sister States or by the Federal Government. Nevertheless, the Convention did not disturb States' immunity from private suits, thus firmly enshrining this principle in our constitutional framework.

III

We now consider whether the sovereign immunity enjoyed by States as part of our constitutional framework applies to adjudications conducted by the FMC. Petitioner FMC and respondent United States initially maintain that the Court of Appeals erred because sovereign immunity only shields States from exercises of "judicial power" and FMC adjudications are not judicial proceedings. As support for their position, they point to the text of the Eleventh Amendment and contend that "[t]he Amendment's reference to 'judicial Power' and to 'any suit in law or equity' clearly mark it as an immunity from judicial process." Brief for United States 15.

For purposes of this case, we will assume, *arguendo,* that in adjudicating complaints filed by private parties under the Shipping Act, the FMC does not exercise the judicial power of the United States. Such an assumption, however, does not end our inquiry as this Court has repeatedly held that the sovereign immunity enjoyed by the States extends beyond the literal text of the Eleventh Amendment. Adhering to that well-reasoned precedent, we must determine whether the sovereign immunity embedded in our constitutional structure and retained by the States when they joined the Union extends to FMC adjudicative proceedings.

A

"[L]ook[ing] first to evidence of the original understanding of the Constitution," as well as early congressional practice, we find a relatively barren historical record, from which the parties draw radically different conclusions. In truth, the relevant history does not provide direct guidance for our inquiry. The Framers, who envisioned a limited Federal Government, could not have anticipated the vast growth of the administrative state. Because formalized administrative adjudications were all but unheard of in the late 18th century and early 19th century, the dearth of specific evidence indicating whether the Framers believed that the States' sovereign immunity would apply in such proceedings is unsurprising.

This Court, however, has applied a presumption…that the Constitution was not intended to "rais[e] up" any proceedings against the States that were "anomalous and unheard of when the Constitution was adopted." We therefore attribute great significance to the fact that States were not subject to private suits in administrative adjudications at the time of the founding or for many years thereafter. For instance, while the United States asserts that "state entities have long been subject to similar administrative enforcement proceedings," the earliest example it provides did not occur until 1918.

B

To decide whether the…presumption applies here, however, we must examine FMC adjudications to determine whether they are the type of proceedings from which the Framers would have thought the States possessed immunity when they agreed to enter the Union. Turning to FMC adjudications specifically, neither the Commission nor the United States disputes the Court of Appeals' characterization below that such a proceeding "walks, talks, and squawks very much like a lawsuit." Nor do they deny that the similarities identified in [a previous case] between administrative adjudications and trial court proceedings are present here.

A review of the FMC's Rules of Practice and Procedure confirms that FMC administrative proceedings bear a remarkably strong resemblance to civil litigation in federal courts. Likewise, discovery in FMC adjudications largely mirrors discovery in federal civil litigation. Not only are discovery procedures virtually indistinguishable, but the role of the ALJ, the impartial officer designated to hear a case, is similar to that of an Article

III judge. In short, the similarities between FMC proceedings and civil litigation are overwhelming. In fact, to the extent that situations arise in the course of FMC adjudications "which are not covered by a specific Commission rule," the FMC's own Rules of Practice and Procedure specifically provide that "the Federal Rules of Civil Procedure will be followed to the extent that they are consistent with sound administrative practice."

C

The preeminent purpose of state sovereign immunity is to accord States the dignity that is consistent with their status as sovereign entities. Given both this interest in protecting States' dignity and the strong similarities between FMC proceedings and civil litigation, we hold that state sovereign immunity bars the FMC from adjudicating complaints filed by a private party against a nonconsenting State. Simply put, if the Framers thought it an impermissible affront to a State's dignity to be required to answer the complaints of private parties in federal courts, we cannot imagine that they would have found it acceptable to compel a State to do exactly the same thing before the administrative tribunal of an agency, such as the FMC. The affront to a State's dignity does not lessen when an adjudication takes place in an administrative tribunal as opposed to an Article III court. In both instances, a State is required to defend itself in an adversarial proceeding against a private party before an impartial federal officer.

IV

Two final arguments raised by the FMC and the United States remain to be addressed.

A

The FMC maintains that sovereign immunity should not bar the Commission from adjudicating Maritime Services' complaint because "[t]he constitutional necessity of uniformity in the regulation of maritime commerce limits the States' sovereignty with respect to the Federal Government's authority to regulate that commerce." Although the Federal Government undoubtedly possesses an important interest in regulating maritime commerce, see U.S. Const., Art. I, § 8, cl. 3, we [have] noted...that "the background principle of state sovereign immunity embodied in the Eleventh Amendment is not so ephemeral as to dissipate when the subject of the suit is an area...that is under the exclusive control of the Federal Government." Thus, "[e]ven when the Constitution vests in Congress complete lawmaking authority over a particular area, the Eleventh Amendment prevents congressional authorization of suits by private parties against unconsenting States."

B

Finally, the United States maintains that even if sovereign immunity were to bar the FMC from adjudicating a private party's complaint against a state-run port for purposes of issuing a reparation order, the FMC should not be precluded from considering a private party's request for other forms of relief, such as a cease-and-desist order. As we have previously noted, however, the primary function of sovereign immunity is not to protect state treasuries, but to afford the States the dignity and respect due sovereign entities. As a result,..." the relief sought by a plaintiff suing a State is irrelevant to the question whether the suit is barred by the Eleventh Amendment."

While some might complain that our system of dual sovereignty is not a model of administrative convenience, that is not its purpose. By guarding against encroachments by the Federal Government on fundamental aspects of state sovereignty, such as sovereign immunity, we strive to maintain the balance of power embodied in our Constitution and thus to "reduce the risk of tyranny and abuse from either front." *Gregory v. Ashcroft,* 501 U.S., at 458. Although the Framers likely did not envision the intrusion on state sovereignty at issue in today's case, we are nonetheless confident that it is contrary to their constitutional design....

3. Overlapping or Shared Powers

a. Individual Liberties

With respect to individual liberties, the federal and state constitutions have considerable overlap, though students should not forget that state constitutional liberties predated the federal Constitution's Bill of Rights and the Fourteenth Amendment. Indeed, several revolutionary era state constitutions served as models for the Bill of Rights which James Madison introduced in the first session of Congress.

Not infrequently, state supreme courts have declared that state provisions which are identical or directly analogous to federal provisions are to be interpreted as the Supreme Court of the United States interprets the federal provision (*e.g.,* defining what is an "unreasonable search or seizure under the Fourth Amendment). But in other instances, the States have adopted their own interpretations of such identical or similar provisions. Moreover, there are many state provisions that simply do not have a federal counterpart.

Another important factor in this regard is the federal "incorporation" doctrine which relies on the Due Process Clause of the Fourteenth Amendment and its prohibition on State conduct violative of that provision to "incorporate" against the States most of the individual liberties protected by the federal Bill of Rights. Long ago, the Supreme

Court held that the Bill of Rights by their terms only restricts the federal government. *Barron v. Mayor and City Council of Baltimore*, 32 U.S. 243 (1833). But following the Civil War, Reconstruction, and the adoption of the Fourteenth Amendment, the argument was made that "due process of law" necessarily should include the protections of the Bill of Rights, for example liberties such as freedom of speech and religion, the right to bear arms, freedom from unreasonable searches and seizures, the privilege against self-incrimination, the right to counsel and to a jury trial in criminal cases, and freedom from cruel and unusual punishment. Over the course of time, the Supreme Court has held that virtually all of the Bill of Rights protections apply to the States, with the exception of the right to indictment by a grand jury for felonies and the right to a jury trial in civil cases. Another open question is whether the Second Amendment's right to keep and bear arms applies to the States, but the Supreme Court appears poised to answer that question soon in *McDonald v. City of Chicago*, No. 08-1521, *cert. granted* Sept. 30, 2009.

Two aspects of the incorporation doctrine are important for purposes of studying state constitutional law. First, if a Bill of Rights protection is incorporated against the States and thus part of the requirement of "due process of law," federal preemption means that the States cannot give such liberties *less* protection than the federal provision requires. Second, the States do have choices, however, in interpreting their own constitutional provisions that may be analogous or identical to federal provisions and certainly can choose to provide *more* protection of such liberties under their own constitutions than the federal provision requires. A recent example of this would be a North Carolina Supreme Court's decision holding that even if the Second Amendment right to keep and bear arms does not apply to the States, the North Carolina Constitution's counterpart provision provides significant protection of this right to North Carolina citizens. See Chapter XIII.D. Another example is the response of some state supreme courts to a recent Takings Clause decision of the Supreme Court of the United States. See Chapter IX.B.

Another possibility, and one that is not uncommon, is that state supreme courts declare that provisions in their own constitutions will be interpreted to have the same meaning as the Supreme Court of the United States gives to the identical or similar federal provisions. This, of course, results in symmetry in state and federal constitutional law and permits state courts to rely on the decisions of the Supreme Court, both of which may be attractive to state courts. Symmetry may be extremely helpful, for example, in providing law enforcement officials with one clear set of rules to follow, rather than two different sets of rules, one federal and one state. Also, because the Supreme Court decides so many Fourth Amendment cases, for example, there is a wealth of precedent on which to draw in deciding such questions, something that frequently is not the case with respect to decisions interpreting state constitutional provisions in a single state. Of course, there is an argument that too much deference by state courts to the Supreme Court of the United States' decisions abdicates the state courts' duty and responsibility to interpret state constitutions independently of their federal counterpart. *See, e.g.*, Stephen R. McAllister, Comment, *Interpreting the State Constitution: A Survey and Assessment of Current Methodology*, 35 Kan. L. Rev. 593 (1987).

b. Interstate Compacts – Article I, § 10, cl. 3

An interesting example of overlapping federal and state powers is found in Article I, § 10, cl. 3, which declares that "No State shall, without the Consent of Congress...enter into any Agreement or Compact with another State...." States, of course, do enter into agreements with each other, and sometimes such agreements are essential, for example in resolving a boundary dispute, or allocating water rights in interstate rivers. That said, Congress must give its blessing to such agreements and thus has some leverage to influence the nature and substance of such agreements. Below is an example of an interstate compact that resulted in litigation and what the Supreme Court had to say about the overlapping powers in this context.

VIRGINIA v. WEST VIRGINIA
78 U.S. 39 (1870)

MILLER, J., delivered the opinion of the court.

[The case involved a dispute between Virginia and West Virginia over the boundary between them, West Virginia having been created from the original boundaries of Virginia, with the consent of the Virginia Legislature. The dispute was over certain counties along the border and whether they belonged to West Virginia or to Virginia.]

As there seems to be no question, then, that the State of West Virginia, from the time she first proposed, in the constitution under which she became a State, to receive these counties, has ever since adhered to, and continued her assent to that proposition, [these] questions remain to be considered.

1. Did the State of Virginia...consent to this proposition....?

The first step in this matter was taken by the organic convention of the State of Virginia, which in 1861 reorganized that State.... The convention...assembled in Wheeling, November 26, 1861. It does not appear that either Berkeley or Jefferson [County] was represented, but it framed a constitution which, after naming the counties composing the new

State...provided...that if a majority of the votes cast at an election to be held for that purpose in the district composed of the counties of Berkeley, Jefferson, and Frederick, should be in favor of adopting the constitution, they should form a part of the State of West Virginia. That constitution also provided for representation of these counties in the Senate and House of Delegates if they elected to become a part of the new State.... A distinct section also declares, in general terms, that additional territory may be admitted into and become part of the State with the consent of the legislature.

The schedule of this constitution arranged for its submission to a vote of the people on the first Thursday in April, 1862. This vote was taken and the constitution ratified by the people; but it does not appear that either of the three counties of Jefferson, Berkeley, and Frederick, took any vote at that time.

[T]he act of the Virginia legislature of May 13, 1862, passed shortly after the vote above...gives the consent of the State of Virginia to the formation of the State of West Virginia out of certain counties named under the provisions set forth in its constitution, and by its second section it is declared that the consent of the legislature of Virginia is also given that the counties of Berkeley, Jefferson, and Frederick, shall be included in said State '*whenever* the voters of said counties shall ratify and assent to said constitution, at an election held for that purpose, at such time and under such regulations as the commissioners named in the said schedule may prescribe.'

This act was...sent to the senators and representatives of Virginia in Congress, with instructions to obtain the consent of Congress to the admission of the State of West Virginia into the Union. Accordingly on the 31st of December, 1862, Congress acted on these matters, and reciting the proceedings of the Convention of West Virginia, and that both that convention and the legislature of the State of Virginia had requested that the new State should be admitted into the Union, it passed an act for the admission of said State....

Let us pause a moment and consider what is the fair and reasonable inference to be drawn from the actions of the State of Virginia, the Convention of West Virginia, and the Congress of the United States in regard to these counties. It seems to us that here was an agreement between the old State and the new that these counties should become part of the latter, subject to [the approval election] condition alone.

2. But did Congress consent to this agreement?

Unless it can be shown that the consent of Congress, under that clause of the Constitution which forbids agreements between States without it, can only be given in the form of an express and formal statement of every proposition of the agreement, and of its consent thereto, we must hold that the consent of that body was given to this agreement.

The attention of Congress was called to the subject by the very short statute of the State of Virginia requesting the admission of the new State into the Union, consisting of but three sections, one of which was entirely devoted to giving consent that these two counties and the county of Frederick might accompany the others, if they desired to do so. The constitution of the new State was literally cumbered with the various provisions for receiving these counties if they chose to come, and in two or three forms express consent is there given to this addition to the State. The subject of the relation of these counties to the others...must have received the attentive consideration of Congress. To hold otherwise is to suppose that the act for the admission of the new State passed without any due or serious consideration.

It is, therefore, an inference clear and satisfactory that Congress by that statute, intended to consent to the admission of the State with the contingent boundaries provided for in its constitution and in the statute of Virginia, which prayed for its admission on those terms, and that in so doing it necessarily consented to the agreement of those States on that subject. There was then a valid agreement between the two States consented to by Congress, which agreement made the accession of these counties dependent on the result of a popular vote in favor of that proposition.

DAVIS, J., with whom concurred CLIFFORD and FIELD, dissenting.

There is no difference of opinion between us in relation to the construction of the provision of the Constitution which affects the question at issue. We all agree that until the consent of Congress is given, there can be no valid compact or agreement between States. And that, although the point of time when Congress may give its consent is not material, yet, when it is given, there must be a reciprocal and concurrent consent of the three parties to the contract. Without this, it is not a completed compact. If, therefore, Virginia withdrew its assent before the consent of Congress was given, there was no compact within the meaning of the Constitution.

To my mind nothing is clearer, than that Congress never did undertake to give its consent to the transfer of Berkeley and Jefferson counties to the State of West Virginia until March 2, 1866. If so, the consent came too late, because the legislature of Virginia had, on the fifth day of December, 1865, withdrawn its assent to the proposed cession of these two counties. This withdrawal was in ample time, as it was before the proposal of the State had become operative as a concluded compact, and the bill (in my judgment) shows that Virginia had sufficient reasons for recalling its proposition to part with the territory embraced within these counties.

c. Criminal Law

The States need no justification for enacting criminal laws other than that such laws serve the general health, welfare, safety and morals of their citizens. Indeed, enacting and enforcing the criminal laws is a core aspect of the States' traditional police powers. The federal government, in contrast, is not given any general power to enact criminal laws. Instead, it must point to powers in Article I, § 8 or elsewhere, that justify the creation of federal crimes, or that in combination with the Necessary and Proper Clause will support such enactments. Perhaps the most frequently invoked federal power to justify the enactment of criminal laws is the power of Congress to regulate commerce "among the Several states." Expansive federal use of this power has caused some controversy and resulted in some important Supreme Court decisions in recent years. An important example follows.

UNITED STATES v. LOPEZ
514 U.S. 549 (1995)

REHNQUIST, C. J., delivered the opinion of the Court.

In the Gun-Free School Zones Act of 1990, Congress made it a federal offense "for any individual knowingly to possess a firearm at a place that the individual knows, or has reasonable cause to believe, is a school zone." The Act neither regulates a commercial activity nor contains a requirement that the possession be connected in any way to interstate commerce. We hold that the Act exceeds the authority of Congress "[t]o regulate Commerce ... among the several States...."

On March 10, 1992, respondent, who was then a 12th-grade student, arrived at Edison High School in San Antonio, Texas, carrying a concealed .38-caliber handgun and five bullets. Acting upon an anonymous tip, school authorities confronted respondent, who admitted that he was carrying the weapon. He was arrested and charged under Texas law with firearm possession on school premises. The next day, the state charges were dismissed after federal agents charged respondent by complaint with violating the Gun-Free School Zones Act of 1990.

A federal grand jury indicted respondent on one count of knowing possession of a firearm at a school zone, in violation of § 922(q). Respondent moved to dismiss his federal indictment on the ground that § 922(q) "is unconstitutional as it is beyond the power of Congress to legislate control over our public schools." The District Court denied the motion, concluding that § 922(q) "is a constitutional exercise of Congress' well-defined power to regulate activities in and affecting commerce, and the 'business' of elementary, middle and high schools...affects interstate commerce." The District Court found [Lopez] guilty of violating § 922(q), and sentenced him to six months' imprisonment and two years' supervised release. The Court of Appeals...reversed respondent's conviction... [holding that the statute] is invalid as beyond the power of Congress under the Commerce Clause."

We start with first principles. The Constitution creates a Federal Government of enumerated powers. As James Madison wrote: "The powers delegated by the proposed Constitution to the federal government are few and defined. Those which are to remain in the State governments are numerous and indefinite." The Federalist No. 45, pp. 292-293 (C. Rossiter ed. 1961). This constitutionally mandated division of authority "was adopted by the Framers to ensure protection of our fundamental liberties." The commerce power "is the power to regulate; that is, to prescribe the rule by which commerce is to be governed. This power, like all others vested in congress, is complete in itself, may be exercised to its utmost extent, and acknowledges no limitations, other than are prescribed in the constitution." The *Gibbons* Court, however, acknowledged that limitations on the commerce power are inherent in the very language of the Commerce Clause.

[E]ven [the Court's] modern-era precedents which have expanded congressional power under the Commerce Clause confirm that this power is subject to outer limits. [W]e have identified three broad categories of activity that Congress may regulate under its commerce power. First, Congress may regulate the use of the channels of interstate commerce. Second, Congress is empowered to regulate and protect the instrumentalities of interstate commerce, or persons or things in interstate commerce, even though the threat may come only from intrastate activities. Finally, Congress' commerce authority includes the power to regulate those activities having a substantial relation to interstate commerce, *i.e.,* those activities that substantially affect interstate commerce.

We now turn to consider the power of Congress, in the light of this framework, to enact § 922(q). The first two categories of authority may be quickly disposed of: § 922(q) is not a regulation of the use of the channels of interstate commerce, nor is it an attempt to prohibit the interstate transportation of a commodity through the channels of commerce; nor can § 922(q) be justified as a regulation by which Congress has sought to protect an instrumentality of interstate commerce or a thing in interstate commerce. Thus, if § 922(q) is to be sustained, it must be under the third category as a regulation of an activity that substantially affects interstate commerce.

[First,] Section 922(q) is a criminal statute that by its terms has nothing to do with "commerce" or any sort of economic enterprise, however broadly one might define those terms.[1] Section 922(q) is not an essential part of a larger regulation of economic activity, in which the regulatory scheme could be undercut unless the intrastate activity were regulated. It cannot, therefore, be sustained under our cases upholding regulations of activities that arise out of or are connected with a commercial transaction, which viewed in the aggregate, substantially affects interstate commerce.

Second, § 922(q) contains no jurisdictional element which would ensure, through case-by-case inquiry, that the firearm possession in question affects interstate commerce.

[Third,] [a]lthough as part of our independent evaluation of constitutionality under the Commerce Clause we of course consider legislative findings, and indeed even congressional committee findings, regarding effect on interstate commerce, the Government concedes that "[n]either the statute nor its legislative history contain[s] express congressional findings regarding the effects upon interstate commerce of gun possession in a school zone." We agree with the Government that Congress normally is not required to make formal findings as to the substantial burdens that an activity has on interstate commerce. But to the extent that congressional findings would enable us to evaluate the legislative judgment that the activity in question substantially affected interstate commerce, even though no such substantial effect was visible to the naked eye, they are lacking here.

The Government's essential contention, *in fine,* is that we may determine here that § 922(q) is valid because possession of a firearm in a local school zone does indeed substantially affect interstate commerce. The Government argues that possession of a firearm in a school zone may result in violent crime and that violent crime can be expected to affect the functioning of the national economy in two ways. First, the costs of violent crime are substantial, and, through the mechanism of insurance, those costs are spread throughout the population. Second, violent crime reduces the willingness of individuals to travel to areas within the country that are perceived to be unsafe. The Government also argues that the presence of guns in schools poses a substantial threat to the educational process by threatening the learning environment. A handicapped educational process, in turn, will result in a less productive citizenry. That, in turn, would have an adverse effect on the Nation's economic well-being.

We pause to consider the implications of the Government's arguments. The Government admits, under its "costs of crime" reasoning, that

---

[1] [3] Under our federal system, the "'States possess primary authority for defining and enforcing the criminal law.'" The Government acknowledges that § 922(q) "displace[s] state policy choices in...that its prohibitions apply even in States that have chosen not to outlaw the conduct in question."

Congress could regulate not only all violent crime, but all activities that might lead to violent crime, regardless of how tenuously they relate to interstate commerce. Similarly, under the Government's "national productivity" reasoning, Congress could regulate any activity that it found was related to the economic productivity of individual citizens: family law (including marriage, divorce, and child custody), for example. Under the theories that the Government presents...it is difficult to perceive any limitation on federal power, even in areas such as criminal law enforcement or education where States historically have been sovereign. Thus, if we were to accept the Government's arguments, we are hard pressed to posit any activity by an individual that Congress is without power to regulate.

Although Justice BREYER argues that acceptance of the Government's rationales would not authorize a general federal police power, he is unable to identify any activity that the States may regulate but Congress may not. Justice BREYER posits that there might be some limitations on Congress' commerce power, such as family law or certain aspects of education. These suggested limitations, when viewed in light of the dissent's expansive analysis, are devoid of substance.

For instance, if Congress can, pursuant to its Commerce Clause power, regulate activities that adversely affect the learning environment, then, *a fortiori,* it also can regulate the educational process directly. Congress could determine that a school's curriculum has a "significant" effect on the extent of classroom learning. As a result, Congress could mandate a federal curriculum for local elementary and secondary schools because what is taught in local schools has a significant "effect on classroom learning," and that, in turn, has a substantial effect on interstate commerce.

Admittedly, a determination whether an intrastate activity is commercial or noncommercial may in some cases result in legal uncertainty. But...so long as [Congress's] powers are interpreted as having judicially enforceable outer limits,...legislation under the Commerce Clause always will engender "legal uncertainty."

These are not precise formulations, and in the nature of things they cannot be. But we think they point the way to a correct decision of this case. The possession of a gun in a local school zone is in no sense an economic activity that might, through repetition elsewhere, substantially affect any sort of interstate commerce. Respondent was a local student at a local school; there is no indication that he had recently moved in interstate commerce, and there is no requirement that his possession of the firearm have any concrete tie to interstate commerce.

To uphold the Government's contentions here, we would have to pile inference upon inference in a manner that would bid fair to convert congressional authority under the Commerce Clause to a general police power of the sort retained by the States. Admittedly, some of our prior cases have taken long steps down that road, giving great deference to congressional action. The broad language in these opinions has suggested the possibility of additional expansion, but we decline here to proceed any further. To do so would require us to conclude that the Constitution's enumeration of powers does not presuppose something not enumerated, and that there never will be a distinction between what is truly national and what is truly local. This we are unwilling to do.

NOTE

The Supreme Court has continued to wrestle with drawing lines between federal and state power in this context. In *United States v. Morrison*, 529 U.S. 598 (2000), the Court held that provisions of federal law that created a civil cause of action for those who are victims of domestic violence exceeded Congress's commerce power, in part because the activity at issue was not economic in nature and in part because matters of domestic violence are well within the States' traditional police powers. However, in *Gonzales v. Raich*, 545 U.S. 1 (2005), the Court held that the federal government could criminalize the growing of marijuana for purely personal medicinal use, even though state law expressly allowed such activity, because the cumulative effect of individuals growing marijuana, with the potential for it to enter interstate markets, provided a sufficient connection to interstate commerce to justify federal regulation.

d. A Close Case?

Some cases may be particularly close or difficult, because the assertion of federal power may be in an area in which the federal government traditionally has not regulated and the area lies at the core of the States' traditional police powers. In *United States v. Comstock*, No. 08-1224 (*cert. granted*), the Supreme Court will consider the following questions: "Whether Congress has the constitutional authority to enact 18 U.S.C. § 4248, which authorizes court-ordered civil commitment by the federal government of (1) "sexually dangerous" persons who are already in the custody of the Bureau of Prisons, but who are coming to the end of their federal prison sentences, and (2) "sexually dangerous" persons who are in the custody of the Attorney General because they have been found mentally incompetent to stand trial."

The Fourth Circuit in *Comstock* held that providing for the civil commitment of dangerous offenders in federal custody exceeded any Article I power of Congress, including the commerce power. 551 F.3d 274 (4th Cir. 2009). The Fourth Circuit emphasized that civil commitment traditionally has been exercised as a State police power and there is no explicit constitutional basis which authorizes a federal civil commitment statute. The court also held that the Necessary and Proper Clause could not justify the federal sex offender civil commitment program because the court would have to pile "inference upon inference" in order to justify the federal law.

The Eighth Circuit, however, reached the opposite conclusion in *United States v. Tom*, 565 F.3d 497 (8th Cir. 2009). The Eighth Circuit held that the federal sex offender commitment statute is justified under the Necessary and Proper Clause because a number of federal sex crimes are properly enacted pursuant to the commerce power and, thus, dealing with sex offenders who violate such federal laws is a necessary and proper exercise of congressional authority. Further, the Eighth Circuit relied on the fact that those subject to the civil commitment law are by definition in federal custody, making it both necessary and proper for Congress to provide for their care and treatment prior to releasing them from custody, if they pose a threat to the public.

Can you make arguments, based on the cases in the chapter, for or against the constitutionality of the federal statute challenged in *United States v. Comstock*?

CHAPTER IV

THEORIES BY WHICH STATE COURTS MAY CONSTRUE STATE CONSTITUTIONS DIFFERENTLY FROM THEIR FEDERAL COUNTERPARTS

In this chapter, we develop one of the main themes of the textbook: the reasons why state courts might choose to construe a guarantee in their own constitutions differently from a related guarantee in the U.S. Constitution. Before discussing what state courts might do in this respect, it is worth remembering why they may do it. The Supremacy Clause of the U.S. Constitution says that the "Constitution...of the United States...shall be the supreme Law of the Land" and makes "the Judges in every State...bound thereby," notwithstanding any "Thing in the Constitution...of any State to the Contrary." Art. VI, U.S. Const. The Clause amounts to a conflict-of-laws provision: Much as the U.S. Constitution governs when it conflicts with a federal law, *see Marbury v. Madison*, 5 U.S. 137 (1803), so the Supremacy Clause establishes that federal law governs when it conflicts with a state law or state constitution. In establishing that federal law trumps contrary state law, however, the Supremacy Clause does nothing to limit the force of state law in the absence of a relevant federal provision or decision. That means the state supreme courts not only have the final say over the meaning of their own constitutions, they also have the final say over the "constitutional" limitations in the State to the extent those limitations exceed any floor set by the U.S. Constitution.

Another way to think about it is this: A litigant challenging the validity of a state or local law may seek relief under the federal or the relevant state constitution. When "[t]he Framers split the atom of sovereignty," *U.S. Term Limits, Inc. v. Thornton*, 514 U.S. 779, 838 (1995) (Kennedy, J., concurring), they established a government that features two sets of sovereigns over any given part of the country, that produced fifty-one constitutions and that in the end places two constitutional limitations on the validity of most state and local laws. The constitutional claimant needs to win just once, and a victory under the one invalidates a local law no less than a victory under the other. One upshot of a federal system of dual sovereignty is that it permits dual claims of unconstitutionality.

To say that a state supreme court *may* invalidate a law under its constitution, however, is not to say that it *should*. The key point of this chapter is to offer reasons why state courts in some areas have charted different paths from the U.S. Supreme Court in construing identical or related constitutional guarantees. The chapter breaks down into three parts. The first considers what may be a counter-intuitive concept to many law students: the reasons why a state court might choose to construe an identically worded guarantee in its own constitution differently from a parallel provision in the U.S. Constitution. The second part considers the state courts' treatment of uniquely worded guarantees. And the third part considers two related topics: (1) why a state court might choose not to chart a separate path from the federal constitutional baseline and (2) how one determines whether a state court has relied on an independent and adequate state law ground and thereby insulated its ruling from review by the U.S. Supreme Court. The chapter is prelude to the next several chapters of the casebook, which develop these themes in the context of specific areas of constitutional law, such as equal protection, due process, property rights, criminal procedure and several others.

A. SIMILARLY WORDED GUARANTEES

Why might a state supreme court construe an individual-rights guarantee of its state constitution differently from one found in the U.S. Constitution and do so even when the guarantees parallel each other word for word? There are several reasons.

Scope of jurisdiction. The U.S. Supreme Court, in the first place, faces geographical and jurisdictional challenges that the state courts do not. Because the Supreme Court must announce rights and remedies for fifty States, one National Government and over 300 million people, it is far more constrained than a state supreme court addressing a difficult problem for one State and, say, ten million people. All U.S. Supreme Court Justices, no matter the president who appointed them or the world view they embrace, are sensitive to the risks of issuing rulings that prevent the democratic processes from working in fifty-one different jurisdictions.

New constitutional rights not only require the articulation of a new constitutional theory, they also require the management of a new constitutional right. All judges worry about the next case when they identify a new constitutional right. But U.S. Supreme Court Justices have more to worry about than state court judges in view of the breadth of their jurisdiction and the wider variety of circumstances that each new right will confront. In some settings, the challenge of imposing a constitutional solution on the whole country at once will increase the likelihood that federal constitutional law will be underenforced or that a "federalism discount" will be applied to the right. Jeffrey S. Sutton, *San Antonio Independent School District v. Rodriguez and Its Aftermath*, 94 Va. L. Rev. 1963, 1979 (2008). State courts face no such problem in construing their own constitutions.

A mistaken or an ill-conceived constitutional decision is also easier to correct at the state level than it is at the federal level. Not only do the state courts have a narrower jurisdiction and smaller populations that their decisions will affect, but the people at the state level have other remedies at their disposal: an easier constitutional amendment process and, for better or worse, judicial elections. In some settings, these considerations will give state courts more room to innovate—to be the familiar "laboratories of experimentation" that Justice Brandeis envisioned.

Local conditions and traditions. State courts also have a freer hand to do something the Supreme Court cannot: to allow local conditions and traditions to affect their interpretation of a constitutional guarantee and the remedies imposed to implement that guarantee. In one State, the right to privacy may warrant greater protection than in another. In a rural State, individual property rights and the right to bear arms may warrant greater protection than in a State with large suburban and urban populations. Free exercise concerns may resonate differently in some States than in others. And the right to equal protection, and its application to the definition of marriage, may be viewed differently in some States than in others. State constitutional law respects these distinct traditions by allowing the fifty constitutions to be interpreted differently to account for these differences in culture, geography and history. Through it all, the counterpart guarantees of the U.S. Constitution provide a potential floor in each of these areas.

Indeterminate questions. Another reason why the state courts might not follow the federal courts in construing identical constitutional guarantees is that the legal and equitable complexities of many issues do not lend themselves to one-size-fits-all solutions. Some constitutional issues do not readily submit to a clear answer, and indeterminate legal questions often lead to indeterminate legal answers. The federal courts might apply a balancing test in construing a liberty guarantee, while the state courts might apply a bright-line rule or might adopt a balancing test but balance the competing interests differently. The federal courts might adopt an originalist approach in construing a guarantee, while the state courts might embrace a living constitutionalist approach to the same language. Another protection might be construed in a pragmatic way in the federal courts but construed in a formalistic way in a state court. The more indeterminate the answer to a legal question the more one should expect federal and state court judges of good will, faced with distinct geographical limitations on their power, to construe similar language differently.

Disagreement with the U.S. Supreme Court. In some cases, the state court's analysis comes to nothing more than an analytical or policy-based objection to the federal precedent. While these cases may be influenced by the above factors, the theme that dominates the state court's ruling is a fundamental disagreement with the National Court's interpretation of similar language. A system of dual sovereignty contemplates, tolerates and ultimately embraces state and federal differences of opinion.

In the cases that follow, and in the chapters that follow, ask yourself why the state courts chose to construe the guarantees of their constitutions differently from the similarly worded guarantees of the U.S. Constitution.

SITZ v. DEPARTMENT OF STATE POLICE
506 N.W.2d 209 (Mich. 1993)

BOYLE, J.

The case before us concerns a challenge to the use of sobriety checkpoints by the Michigan State Police. The United States Supreme Court held that the checkpoint scheme does not constitute a violation of the Fourth Amendment of the United States Constitution. *Michigan Dep't of State Police v. Sitz*, 496 U.S. 444 (1990). On remand from that Court, a two-judge majority of the Michigan Court of Appeals determined that sobriety checkpoints violate art. 1, § 11 of the Michigan Constitution. Because there is no support in the constitutional history of Michigan for the proposition that the police may engage in warrantless and suspicionless seizures of automobiles for the purpose of enforcing the criminal law, we hold that sobriety check points violate art. 1, § 11 of the Michigan Constitution.

The first sobriety checkpoint operation was conducted at Dixie Highway and Gretchen Road in Saginaw County on May 17 and 18, 1986. The Saginaw County Sheriff's Department cooperated in the operation which lasted from about 11:45 p.m. to 1:00 a.m. One hundred twenty-six vehicles passed though the checkpoint in that time, with an average delay to motorists of twenty-five seconds or less. Two drivers were retained for sobriety field tests; one was arrested for driving while under the influence of alcohol. A third driver drove through the checkpoint without stopping, was pulled over by an officer in an observation vehicle, and was arrested for driving under the influence.

[The U.S. Supreme Court held] that the Michigan sobriety checkpoint program did not violate the Fourth Amendment of the United States Constitution: "In sum, the balance of the State's interest in preventing drunken driving, the extent to which this system can reasonably be said to advance that interest, and the degree of intrusion upon individual motorists who are briefly stopped, weighs in favor of the state program. We therefore hold that it is consistent with the Fourth Amendment...." *Sitz*, 496 U.S. at 455.

During the decade of United States Supreme Court jurisprudence "commonly characterized as the 'criminal law revolution of the Warren Court,'" the Supreme Court "rapidly extend[ed] the reach of various constitutional provisions applicable to the criminal justice process...." 1 LaFave & Israel, Criminal Procedure, § 2.1, p. 56 and n. 1. Subsequent decisions of the Burger Court were characterized by some commentators as pulling back from, suspending, or weakening the scope of constitutional protections, including the specific guarantees of the Bill of Rights.

Awakened to the potential for a reappraisal of claims based on state constitutional grounds, members of the Michigan bar joined their colleagues across the country in pressing claims seeking interpretations of state law that provided more expansive criminal procedure protections than those recognized under federal law. By 1983, the number of rights-expansive claims based on state law had proliferated to the point that guidance from this Court was deemed both appropriate and necessary.

Thus, in *People v. Nash*, 418 Mich. 196, 341 N.W.2d 439 (1983), the Court conducted the first modern-day comprehensive survey of the circumstances surrounding the creation of Const.1963, art. 1, § 11 to determine whether our constitution required a higher level of search and seizure protection than the Fourth Amendment of the United States Constitution. Our conclusion in Nash, that "[t]he history of Const.1963, art. 1, § 11, and its plain import, ... suggest that its further expansion ... should occur only when there is a compelling reason to do so," *id.* at 214, 341 N.W.2d 439, was intended to clarify for the bench and bar that claims that art. 1, § 11 should be interpreted more expansively than the Fourth Amendment must rest on more than a disagreement with the United States Supreme Court.

Our analysis in *Nash* began by noting that the federal and state constitutional provisions that forbid unreasonable searches and seizures are nearly identical.[1]

---

[1]U.S. Const., Am. IV provides:

The right of the people to be secure in their persons, houses, papers, and effects, against unreasonable searches and seizures, shall not be violated, and no Warrants shall issue, but upon probable cause, supported by Oath or affirmation, and particularly describing the place to be searched, and the persons or things to be seized.

Const.1963, art. 1, § 11 provides:

The person, houses, papers and possessions of every person shall be secure from unreasonable searches and seizures. No warrant to search any place or to seize any person or things shall issue without describing them, nor without probable cause, supported by oath or affirmation. The provisions of this section shall not be construed to bar from evidence in any criminal proceeding any narcotic drug, firearm, bomb, explosive or any other dangerous weapon, seized by a peace officer outside the curtilage of any dwelling house in this state....

The judiciary of this state is not free to simply engraft onto art. 1, § 11 more "enlightened" rights than the framers intended. By the same token, we may not disregard the guarantees that our constitution confers on Michigan citizens merely because the United States Supreme Court has withdrawn or not extended such protection .

The Michigan Declaration of Rights, like the federal Bill of Rights, is "drawn to restrict governmental conduct and to provide protection from governmental infringement and excesses...." *Woodland v. Citizens Lobby*, 423 Mich. 188, 204, 378 N.W.2d 337 (1985). When there is a clash of competing rights under the state and federal constitutions, the Supremacy Clause, art. VI, cl. 2, dictates that the federal right prevails. Where a right is given to a citizen under federal law, it does not follow that the organic instrument of state government must be interpreted as conferring the identical right. Nor does it follow that where a right given by the federal constitution is not given by a state constitution, the state constitution offends the federal constitution. It is only where the organic instrument of government purports to deprive a citizen of a right granted by the federal constitution that the instrument can be said to violate the constitution.

Thus, appropriate analysis of our constitution does not begin from the conclusive premise of a federal floor. Indeed, the fragile foundation of the federal floor as a bulwark against arbitrary action is clearly revealed when, as here, the federal floor falls below minimum state protection. As a matter of simple logic, because the texts were written at different times by different people, the protections afforded may be greater, lesser, or the same.

As long ago as 1889, the justices of this Court stated:

> Personal liberty, which is guaranteed to every citizen under our Constitution and laws, consists of the right of locomotion-to go where one pleases, and when, and to do that which may lead to one's business or pleasure, only so far restrained as the rights of others may make it necessary for the welfare of all other citizens. One may travel along the public highways or in public places; and while conducting themselves in a decent and orderly manner, disturbing no other, and interfering with the rights of no other citizens, there, they will be protected under the law, not only in their persons, but in their safe conduct. The Constitution and the laws are framed for the public good, and the protection of all citizens, from the highest to the lowest; and no one may be restrained of his liberty, unless he has transgressed some law. [*Pinkerton v. Verberg*, 78 Mich. 573, 584, 44 N.W. 579 (1889).]

 Our commitment to the protection of liberty was further demonstrated when the Supreme Court of Michigan adopted an exclusionary rule in 1919, forty-two years before it was mandated by federal law. *People v. Marxhausen*, 204 Mich. 559, 171 N.W. 557 (1919). Moreover, as the cases discussed in part IV demonstrate, this Court's "historical general power ... to construe the constitutional provision relating to searches and seizures," *Nash*, *supra*, 418 Mich. at 214, 341 N.W.2d 439, has been extended to the seizure and search of vehicles.

The history of our jurisprudence conclusively demonstrates that, in the context of automobile seizures, we have extended more expansive protection to our citizens than that extended in *Sitz*. This Court has never recognized the right of the state, without any level of suspicion whatsoever, to detain members of the population at large for criminal investigatory purposes. Nor has Michigan completely acquiesced to the judgment of "politically accountable officials" when determining reasonableness in such a context. *Sitz*, 496 U.S. at 453. In these circumstances, the Michigan Constitution offers more protection than the United States Supreme Court's interpretation of the Fourth Amendment.

In *Roache*, *supra*, 237 Mich. at 222, this Court showed a marked hostility toward the use of a license check as a pretext to investigate criminal activity. In *Lansing Municipal Judge*, *supra*, 327 Mich. at 432, we stressed:

> It will be said that no legislature would go so far as to dry up the entire stream of constitutional immunity. But it is not the genius of our system that the constitutional rights of persons shall depend for their efficacy upon legislative benevolence. Rather, the courts are charged with the solemn obligation of erecting around those rights, in adjudicated cases, a barrier against legislative or executive invasion.

The Michigan Constitution has historically treated searches and seizures for criminal investigatory purposes differently than those for regulatory or administrative purposes. These administrative or regulatory searches and seizures have traditionally been regarded as "reasonable" in a constitutional sense. However, seizures with the primary goal of enforcing the criminal law have generally required some level of suspicion, even if that level has fluctuated over the years.

We do not suggest that in a different context we might not reach a similar result under the balancing test of reasonableness employed in *Sitz*. Indeed, our precedent regarding automobiles implicitly incorporates a balancing test that is inherent in assessing the reasonableness of warrantless searches and seizures. We hold only that the protection afforded to the seizures of vehicles for criminal investigatory purposes has both an historical foundation and a contemporary justification that is not outweighed by the necessity advanced. Suspicionless criminal investigatory seizures, and extreme deference to the judgments of politically accountable officials is, in this context, contrary to Michigan constitutional precedent.

NOTE

Consider the following excerpts from the U.S. Supreme Court's decision in *Sitz* remanding the case to the Michigan Supreme Court:

Conversely, the weight bearing on the other scale—the measure of the intrusion on motorists stopped briefly at sobriety checkpoints—is slight. We reached a similar conclusion as to the intrusion on motorists subjected to a brief stop at a highway checkpoint for detecting illegal aliens. We see virtually no difference between the levels of intrusion on law-abiding motorists from the brief stops necessary to the effectuation of these two types of checkpoints, which to the average motorist would seem identical save for the nature of the questions the checkpoint officers might ask. The trial court and the Court of Appeals, thus, accurately gauged the "objective" intrusion, measured by the duration of the seizure and the intensity of the investigation, as minimal.

[T]he balance of the State's interest in preventing drunken driving, the extent to which this system can reasonably be said to advance that interest, and the degree of intrusion upon individual motorists who are briefly stopped, weighs in favor of the state program. We therefore hold that it is consistent with the Fourth Amendment.

Michigan Dept. of State Police v. Sitz, 496 U.S. 444, 451-52, 455 (1990).

Did the state court simply balance these interests differently? Did it rely on traditions unique to Michigan? Did it simply disagree with the U.S. Supreme Court?

STATE v. HEMPELE
576 A.2d 793 (N.J. 1990)

CLIFFORD, J.

The issue in these appeals, argued together, is the constitutionality of warrantless seizures and searches of garbage bags left on the curb for collection.

In *State v. Hempele* a confidential source informed the state police that defendants, Conrad D. Hempele and Sharon Hempele, were distributing illicit drugs from their home at 303 Mill Street in Belvidere. The informant claimed to have seen fifty pounds of marijuana in Conrad's bedroom.

On the basis of that information, a trooper seized the trash sitting in front of 303 Mill Street six months later. 303 Mill Street is one of about ten attached row houses, each with its own front entrance. A short stairway runs from each row house to an eight-foot-wide sidewalk abutting the street. The seized trash was next to the flight of stairs leading to 303 Mill Street. Two weeks later the trooper again seized the garbage in front of the Hempeles' home. On both occasions the trooper removed white plastic trash bags from a plastic garbage can and took the bags to the State Police Tri-Man Unit, where, without a warrant, he opened them and analyzed their contents. He discovered traces of marijuana, cocaine, and methamphetamine in the trash.

A search warrant for defendants' home issued on the basis of the informant's tip and the evidence found in the garbage. When the subsequent search turned up controlled substances and drug paraphernalia, the Hempeles were indicted for drug offenses.

We consider first whether the garbage searches in these two cases violated the United States Constitution.

In *California v. Greenwood*, 486 U.S. 35 (1988), the United States Supreme Court held that the fourth amendment does not prohibit unreasonable searches and seizures of garbage left for collection in an area accessible to the public.... The Supreme Court held that the warrantless searches of Greenwood's garbage "would violate the Fourth Amendment only if respondents [had] manifested a subjective expectation of privacy in their garbage that society accepts as objectively reasonable." Ruling that a privacy expectation in garbage is not reasonable, the Court rejected the defendants' argument.

The Court decided that people lose any reasonable expectation of privacy in their trash by leaving it in bags alongside the street, because such garbage is vulnerable to an unscrupulous person or scavenging animal. Furthermore, garbage is placed on the curb for the specific purpose of having a third party remove it. The defendants should have realized that the trash collector might look through the garbage or allow another person to do so. The Court added that the fourth amendment does not protect what a person knowingly exposes to the public because "the police cannot reasonably be expected to avert their eyes from evidence of criminal activity that could have been observed by any member of the public."

Having decided that an expectation of privacy in trash left for collection in an area accessible to the public is unreasonable, the Court found it unnecessary to determine whether the defendants had manifested a subjective expectation of privacy. The warrantless garbage searches did not violate the fourth amendment.

Under *Greenwood* the issue is whether the garbage was left at a location "accessible to the public."... The Hempeles left their garbage at a location accessible to the public. They cannot escape the force of *Greenwood*.

We now determine whether the New Jersey Constitution protects curbside garbage from unreasonable searches and seizures. Despite the similarity between the text of article I, paragraph 7 of the New Jersey Constitution and the text of the fourth amendment, we have found on several occasions that the former "affords our citizens greater protection against unreasonable searches and seizures than does the fourth amendment."

For most of our country's history, the primary source of protection of individual rights has been state constitutions, not the federal Bill of Rights. The genius of federalism is that the fundamental rights of citizens are protected not only by the United States Constitution but also by the laws of each of the states. The system may be untidy on occasion, but that untidiness invests it with "a vibrant diversity." "As tempting as it may be to harmonize results under the state and federal constitutions, federalism contemplated that state courts may grant greater protection to individual rights if they choose."

Cognizant of the diversity of laws, customs, and mores within its jurisdiction, the United States Supreme Court is necessarily "hesitant to impose on a national level far-reaching constitutional rules binding on each and every state." That Court establishes no more than the floor of constitutional protection. The Supreme Court must be especially cautious in fourth-amendment cases. When determining whether a search warrant is necessary in a specific circumstance, the Court must take note of the disparity in warrant-application procedures among the several states, and must consider whether a warrant requirement in that situation might overload the procedure in any one state. In contrast, we are fortunate to have in New Jersey a procedure that allows for the speedy and reliable issuance of search warrants based on probable cause. A warrant requirement is not so great a burden in New Jersey as it might be in other states.

The Supreme Court itself has implied that garbage searches are an appropriate issue on which state courts may rise above "the lowest common denominator." In holding that the fourth amendment does not protect garbage, the Court suggested that "[i]ndividual States may surely construe their own constitutions as imposing more stringent constraints on police conduct than does the Federal Constitution." *California v. Greenwood*, 486 U.S. at 43.

In determining the reasonableness of an expectation of privacy in curbside garbage left for collection, we start from the premise that "[e]xpectations of privacy are established by general social norms." The "ultimate question" is whether, if garbage searches are "permitted to go unregulated by constitutional restraints, the amount of privacy and freedom remaining to citizens would be diminished to a compass inconsistent with the aims of a free and open society." With that question in mind, we first examine whether it is reasonable for a person to want to keep the contents of his or her garbage private.

Clues to people's most private traits and affairs can be found in their garbage. "[A]lmost every human activity ultimately manifests itself in waste products and...any individual may understandably wish to maintain the confidentiality of his refuse." A plethora of personal information can be culled from garbage:

> A single bag of trash testifies eloquently to the eating, reading, and recreational habits of the person who produced it. A search of trash, like a search of the bedroom, can relate intimate details about sexual practices, health, and personal hygiene. Like rifling through desk drawers or intercepting phone calls, rummaging through trash can divulge the target's financial and professional status, political affiliations and inclinations, private thoughts, personal relationships, and romantic interests.

[*California v. Greenwood*, 486 U.S. at 50 (Brennan, J., dissenting].

Most people seem to have an interest in keeping such matters private; few publicize them voluntarily. Undoubtedly many would be upset to see a neighbor or stranger sifting through their garbage, perusing their discarded mail, reading their bank statements, looking at their empty pharmaceutical bottles, and checking receipts to see what videotapes they rent. The California Supreme Court commented that it could "readily ascribe many reasons why residents would not want their castaway clothing, letters, medicine bottles or other telltale refuse and trash to be examined by neighbors or others.... Half truths leading to rumor and gossip may readily flow from an attempt to 'read' the contents of another's trash." *People v. Edwards*, 71 Cal.2d 1096, 1104 (1969) (garbage left inside curtilage is constitutionally protected).

Like the fourth amendment, article I, paragraph 7 "provides protection to the owner of every container that conceals its contents from plain view."...There is no "constitutional distinction between 'worthy' and 'unworthy' containers...." "[P]aper bags, locked trunks, lunch buckets, and orange crates" all receive the same treatment. A privacy expectation does not depend on the value or quality of the container.

The critical issue is whether the container conceals its contents from plain view. Because ordinary opaque garbage bags conceal their contents from plain view, the presumption is that an expectation of privacy in the contents is reasonable.

The New Jersey Constitution "requires the approval of an impartial judicial officer based on probable cause before most searches may be undertaken." "Any warrantless search is *prima facie* invalid." Those principles certainly apply to opaque containers.

Once the protections of article I, paragraph 7 apply, a lower expectation of privacy is not a sufficient basis on which to carve out an exception to the warrant and probable-cause requirement. We can dispense with that requirement "[o]nly in those exceptional circumstances in which special needs, beyond the normal need for law enforcement, make the warrant and probable cause requirement impracticable...." If a "special need" does exist, we can then make an exception to the requirement only after we "balance the nature and quality of the intrusion on the individual's [article I, paragraph 7] interests against the importance of the governmental interests alleged to justify the intrusion."

Thus, even if garbage searches are only "minimally intrusive" of a person's privacy, the warrant and probable-cause requirement for garbage searches can be scrapped only if a special government interest significantly outweighs those privacy interests.

Because we find no special state interest that makes the warrant requirement impracticable, we hold that the State must secure a warrant based on probable cause in order to search garbage bags left on the curb for collection.

In summary, article I, paragraph 7 applies to the search but not to the seizure of a garbage bag left on the curb for collection. Law-enforcement officials need no cause to seize the bag, but they must have a warrant based on probable cause to search it.

Our decision today does not follow the course set by the Supreme Court because "we are persuaded that the equities so strongly favor protection of a person's privacy interest that we should apply our own standard rather than defer to the federal provision." We are aware that our ruling conflicts not only with *California v. Greenwood* but also with the holdings of virtually every other court that has considered this issue.... Although the weight of the cited authority is impressive, our thorough consideration of the issue leads us to record our respectful disagreement with those courts that have reached a result contrary to ours.

We do concur, however, in the observation that there is no "unique New Jersey state attitude about garbage." Our differences with the cited authority rest on other grounds. As the trial court in *Pasanen* so eloquently put it, "the trouble with those cases is that they are flatly and simply wrong as the matter of the way people think about garbage." Garbage can reveal much that is personal. We do not find it unreasonable for people to want their garbage to remain private and to expect that it will remain private from the meddling of the State.

Article I, paragraph 7 confers "as against the government, the right to be let alone-the most comprehensive of rights and the right most valued by civilized men." *Olmstead v. United States*, 277 *U.S.* 438, 478 (1927) (Brandeis, J., dissenting). Permitting the police to pick and poke their way through garbage bags to peruse without cause the vestiges of a person's most private affairs would be repugnant to that ideal. A free and civilized society should comport itself with more decency.

BLUM, v. MERRELL DOW PHARMACEUTICALS, INC.
626 A.2d 537 (PA 1993)

NIX, C.J.

The issue before this Court is whether Article I, Section 6 of the Pennsylvania Constitution entitles a party who demands a twelve person jury to a verdict from a jury of twelve persons. For the reasons that follow, we affirm the Superior Court Order and hold that Section 6 of Article I of the Pennsylvania Constitution entitles a party who properly demands a twelve person jury to a verdict from a jury of twelve persons.

Our starting point must be the decision of the United States Supreme Court in *Williams v. Florida,* 399 *U.S.* 78 (1970). In *Williams,* the Supreme Court departed from a long history of requiring a twelve person jury as a necessary ingredient of the Sixth Amendment guarantee of trial by jury in all criminal cases. The Supreme Court in *Williams* concluded that the "twelve man panel is not a necessary ingredient of 'trial by jury,' and that [Florida's] refusal to impanel more than six members provided for by Florida law did not violate [Williams'] Sixth Amendment rights as applied to the states through the Fourteenth [Amendment]."... We must now determine whether the *Williams, Colgrove* and *Ballew* trilogy, which allows trial by less than twelve member juries in civil cases, is properly part of the jurisprudence of this Commonwealth, by virtue of Section 6 of Article I of the Pennsylvania Constitution.

This Court has emphasized that, in interpreting a provision of the Pennsylvania Constitution, we are not bound by the decisions of the United States Supreme Court which interpret similar federal constitutional provisions. *Commonwealth v. Edmunds,* 526 Pa. 374, 388 (1991).... In *Edmunds,* Mr. Justice Cappy, writing for the majority of the Court, established the following four part framework which we consider in analyzing our State Constitution:

[L]itigants [must] brief and analyze at least the following four factors:

1) text of the Pennsylvania Constitutional provision;

2) history of the provision, including Pennsylvania case law;

3) related case law from other states;

4) policy considerations, including unique issues of state and local concern, and applicability within modern Pennsylvania jurisprudence.

A. Text

The text of Section 6 of Article I of the Pennsylvania Constitution provides as follows:

Trial by Jury

Section 6. Trial by jury shall be as heretofore and the right thereof remain inviolate. The General Assembly may provide, however, by law, that a verdict may be rendered by not less than five-sixths of the jury in any civil case.

On its face, Article I, Section 6 preserves the following two things: the right to trial by jury shall be as heretofore; and the right to trial by jury remains inviolate. The Seventh Amendment to the United States Constitution, although worded differently, is similar to the Pennsylvania provision. On its face, the Seventh Amendment provides the right to trial by jury is preserved and no fact tried by a jury shall be otherwise reexamined other than according to the rules of common law. Although worded differently, both provisions retain the right to trial by jury in civil cases where it existed at common law. Therefore, we must undertake an examination of the history of Section 6 of Article I of our Constitution to determine the meaning of that provision and to decide whether our constitutional scheme is the same as the Federal Constitution or requires a verdict from a twelve member jury in a civil case when a demand for a twelve member jury is properly made.

B. The History of the Provision

Before discussing any case law, however, we must give an overview of the concept of juries of twelve members throughout this Commonwealth's history. The Superior Court in this case gave an excellent overview of the twelve member jury concept in this Commonwealth. The Superior Court stated:

> [T]he concept of juries of twelve in this Commonwealth ... has its origin in a document introduced and adopted in Pennsylvania in 1682 by William Penn and known as "Laws Agreed Upon in England." Comment, *The Jury Size Question In Pennsylvania: Six Of One And A Dozen Of The Other*, 53 Temple L.Q. 89, 100 (1980).

> Penn's other writings discussed the evolution of the jury and his belief that it was a "fundamental" part of the government and important to a free society. However, "nowhere did he endeavor to explain why a jury required *twelve* members to fulfill its purpose." *Id.* at 103.

One commentator has observed:

> Penn's own writings and deeds appear to show that his commitment to twelve-member juries was not based on any reasoned notion that twelve was required to assure fairness, but instead stemming from his adherence to traditional common law principles that required twelve member juries.

> *Id.* at 104-105 (footnote omitted). Likewise, there is little information available that casts any light on the intent of the framers of the Pennsylvania Constitution of 1776 regarding the size of juries. *Id.* at 106. The same can be said with regard to the Constitutional Conventions of 1790 and 1838. As for the 1873 Convention, discussion was had on the deletion of the unanimity requirement and the elimination of the term "heretofore." Some saw no problem with this since they *equated a trial by jury with a jury of twelve men*, whereas others believed excising the word "heretofore" would pave the way for a jury of "'three

or five or seven ... [or less than twelve] as a constitutional jury...."' *Id.* at 112-113. The proposal was defeated without explanation.

The framers at Pennsylvania's 1968 Convention did not consider the jury provision at all, believing that it was beyond their jurisdiction to affect that right. Even so, our first Constitution of 1776 contained verbiage which has survived and appears in the present-day Article I, § 6. E.g., the 1776 Constitution declared that "trials by jury shall be as *heretofore.*" The Constitution of 1790, and the amended ones of 1838, 1873 and 1968, adopted substantially the same provision. Their language was "trial by jury shall be as *heretofore,* the right thereof remain inviolate."

As the Superior Court stated, all of our Constitutions have had the identical language, that being "trial by jury shall be as heretofore." The following language was added to Section 6 of Article I of our Constitution by amendment on May 18, 1971:

> The General Assembly may provide, however, by law, that a verdict may be rendered by not less than five-sixths of the jury in a civil case.

Every Constitution of this Commonwealth has guaranteed to the parties a verdict from a jury of twelve persons where the parties would have had that right at common law. The Constitution, beginning in 1776, has always provided that "trial by jury shall be as heretofore." As stated above, our history and our case law evidence that that language, "trial by jury shall be as heretofore," was understood to guarantee a jury of twelve persons. Thus, Appellants' statement that there is no rationale in 1991 for following *Smith* and the other cases which commented upon the "heretofore" language in our earlier Constitutions is incorrect.

Appellants also argue, assuming *arguendo* that a right to a twelve person jury exists, the 1971 Pennsylvania Constitution and the subsequently enacted five-sixths rule, 42 Pa.C.S. § 5104(b), allow that a decision by ten of twelve jurors constitutes "the verdict of the jury" and it "shall have the same effect as a unanimous verdict of the jury." Therefore, Appellants aver that the decision of ten jurors is always constitutionally sufficient and no constitutional right in this appeal could have been violated where eleven of eleven jurors agree on a verdict.

When the people of this Commonwealth amended Section 6 of Article I of our Constitution in 1971, authorizing the General Assembly to provide for a verdict by not less than five-sixths of the jury in any civil case, they reaffirmed the constitutional right to a jury of twelve persons. A provision of the Constitution will be interpreted, not in a strained or technical manner, but as understood by the people who adopted it. As previously discussed, in this Commonwealth "trial by jury shall be as heretofore" has always required a jury of twelve persons. When the people of this Commonwealth approved the May 18, 1971 amendment to Section 6 of Article I, they understood the reference to "the jury in any civil case" to be to a jury of twelve persons. Thus, the people of this Commonwealth amended only the unanimity feature and reaffirmed that a jury is made up of twelve persons.

C. Related Case Law from Other States

The third element we will analyze is the case law from other jurisdictions. Subsequent to the United States Supreme Court decisions, a number of states other than Pennsylvania confronted the issue of whether their state constitutions require a twelve person jury.

Most significantly, after the United States Supreme Court decision in *Williams*, the Supreme Court of Rhode Island, in an advisory opinion to the Senate, held that the jury referred to in Section 15 of Article I of the Rhode Island Constitution requires a panel of twelve. After a thorough analysis of Rhode Island's constitutional history, that court reasoned:

> Although the Supreme Court in *Williams* described the common-law requirement that a petit jury be composed of precisely twelve people as an "historical accident," the Court obviously could not share this observation made in June 1970 with the framers and adopters of the Rhode Island Constitution. Accident or not, it is our firm belief that in 1842 when the draftsmen and the voters said that the right to a jury trial was to remain inviolate, they were extending to an accused, or any litigant who might be entitled to a jury trial, the immutable right to have his case considered in the courts of this state by petit jury composed of exactly twelve persons.

Thus, the Rhode Island Supreme Court, after analyzing its case law and constitutional history, went above the minimum standards set forth by the United States Supreme Court in *Williams* and determined that, under the Rhode Island Constitution, a jury is composed of twelve members.

We similarly conclude that, because of Pennsylvania's history and case law, a jury must be composed of twelve persons where that right existed at common law and the demand for a twelve person jury is properly made. If this Court changed a right that had been understood and guaranteed to the people of this Commonwealth for over 200 years, we would be breaching our duty to speak the will of the people of this Commonwealth. We refuse to breach that duty by allowing a jury to be composed of less than twelve jurors. Only the people of this Commonwealth, by constitutional amendment, may make such a change.

D. Policy Considerations

The last prong of the *Edmunds* test is an examination of policy considerations and their applicability within modern Pennsylvania jurisprudence. One policy consideration Appellants request us to consider is the financial burden a jury of twelve persons presents for this Commonwealth.

We find that the most substantial policy consideration is that the people of this Commonwealth have understood since our first Constitution was adopted in 1776 that a "trial by jury" meant a jury composed of twelve persons. Given that understanding of the constitutional right, it is not for the legislative, executive, or judicial branch to change that right; rather, it is exclusively left to the people of this Commonwealth to amend the twelve member jury requirement if they desire that change.

Conclusion

Our constitutional history and case law mandate that we refrain from adopting the United States Supreme Court analysis in *Williams*, *Colgrove*, and *Ballew*, which held that verdicts from juries of less than twelve did not violate the Federal Constitution. This Court is under a duty to guarantee that the intent of the people of this Commonwealth in adopting the Pennsylvania Constitution is carried forward. We are convinced that, when Pennsylvania adopted its first Constitution in 1776, the framers assumed that a jury meant twelve persons. This Court has repeatedly adopted that view. Therefore, even though Section 6 of Article I of the Pennsylvania Constitution does not explicitly state that a jury is constituted of twelve members, our constitutional history and case law make it apparent that "trial by jury" means a jury of twelve persons.

NOTE

The Pennsylvania and U.S. Constitutions both preserve the right to "trial by jury." Why does the state court take a different tack in interpreting this language? Does the state court embrace any aspects of the relevant federal decisions? '

B. DIFFERENTLY WORDED PROVISIONS

When the language of the state constitutional guarantee differs materially from its federal counterpart, the state courts have an additional reason for construing their constitutions differently. That, however, does not diminish the force of the earlier considerations: the scope of jurisdiction of the two courts; the effect of local history (including the history and purpose of the state constitutional provision), local traditions and local customs; the difficulty of answering some constitutional questions; and disagreement between the two courts. In the following cases, consider the impact of the difference in language between the state and federal guarantees on the courts' decisions relative to the role of these other considerations.

RACING ASS'N OF CENTRAL IOWA v. FITZGERALD
675 N.W.2d 1 (Iowa 2004)

TERNUS, J.

When this case was initially before our court, we held that a statute taxing gross gambling receipts generated at racetracks at a rate nearly twice the rate imposed on gross gambling receipts generated on riverboats violated the United States Constitution and the Iowa Constitution. On certiorari to the United States Supreme Court, that part of our decision holding the statute violated the Equal Protection Clause of the United States Constitution was reversed. The Supreme Court then remanded the case "for further proceedings not inconsistent with [its] opinion." Although this court's ruling that the statute also violated the equality provision contained in the Iowa Constitution was not reviewed by the Supreme Court, we take the opportunity on remand to reconsider our prior decision on the state constitution claim in light of the Court's ruling on the federal constitution issue.

After giving due consideration to the Court's analysis and decision, we find no basis to change our earlier opinion that the differential tax violates article I, section 6 of the Iowa Constitution. Therefore, we reverse the trial court's contrary ruling and remand this case for a determination of the appropriate relief.

I. *Review of Pertinent Background Facts and Proceedings.*

This action was commenced by the appellant, Racing Association of Central Iowa (RACI), to enjoin the collection of that portion of taxes it was required to pay on adjusted gross receipts from gambling in excess of the tax charged to "excursion boats" on such receipts. *See generally* 1989 Iowa Acts ch. 67 (authorizing gambling on "excursion boats"). RACI claimed the tax was unconstitutional under the Equal Protection Clauses of the United States and Iowa Constitutions.

The tax statute challenged by these parties is Iowa Code section 99F.11 (1999), which imposes a tax "on the adjusted gross receipts received annually from gambling games." The maximum rate is twenty percent. The statute has an exception, however, for the "adjusted gross receipts ... from gambling games at racetrack enclosures." *Id.* The tax rate on racetrack gambling receipts began at twenty-two percent in 1997, and has automatically increased by two percent each year to a maximum rate of thirty-six percent in 2004.

In our first consideration of this case, we held this differential tax violated the Equal Protection Clause of the United States Constitution and article I, section 6 of the Iowa Constitution.[2]

II. *Import of Supreme Court's Decision that Statute Did Not Violate the Equal Protection Clause of the United States Constitution.*

It is this court's constitutional obligation as the highest court of this sovereign state to determine whether the challenged classification violates Iowa's constitutional equality provision. While the Supreme Court's judgment on the constitutionality of Iowa's disparate tax rates under the federal Equal Protection Clause is persuasive, it is not binding on this court as we evaluate this law under the Iowa Constitution.

III. *Governing Legal Principles.*

The Supreme Court has stated that the Equal Protection Clause "is essentially a direction that all persons similarly situated should be treated alike." Whether this ideal has been met in the context of economic legislation is determined through application of the rational basis test. In its consideration of the case at hand, the Court described the rational basis test as follows:

> "[T]he Equal Protection Clause is satisfied so long as there is a plausible policy reason for the classification, the legislative facts on which the classification is apparently based rationally may have been considered to be true by the governmental decisionmaker, and the relationship of the classification to its goal is not so attenuated as to render the distinction arbitrary or irrational."

The Court has in the past more succinctly stated this standard as "whether the classifications drawn in a statute are reasonable in light of its purpose." It was this enunciation of the rational basis test that our court said in Bierkamp was appropriate for analyzing a claim based on the Iowa equality provision found in article I, section 6 of the Iowa Constitution.

Based on these principles, this court must first determine whether the Iowa legislature had a valid reason to treat racetracks differently from riverboats when taxing the gambling revenue of these businesses. Moreover, the claimed state interest must be "*realistically conceivable.*" Our court must then decide whether this reason has a basis in fact. Finally, we must consider whether the relationship between the classification, i.e., the differences between racetracks and excursion boats, and the purpose of the classification is so weak that the classification must be viewed as arbitrary.

---

[2]The United States Constitution provides that no state shall "deny to any person within its jurisdiction the equal protection of the laws." U.S. Const. amend. 14. In contrast, article I, section 6 of the Iowa Constitution states: "All laws of a general nature shall have a uniform operation; the general assembly shall not grant to any citizen, or class of citizens, privileges or immunities, which, upon the same terms shall not equally belong to all citizens."

Our examination of this statute must also be guided by the general legal principles that control a court's review of the constitutionality of a legislative enactment. These tenets are well established. "Statutes are cloaked with a strong presumption of constitutionality." Therefore, a person challenging a statute shoulders a heavy burden of rebutting this presumption. This burden includes the task of negating every reasonable basis that might support the disparate treatment. These rigorous standards have not, however, prevented this court from finding economic and social legislation in violation of equal protection provisions. Our prior cases illustrate that, although the rational basis standard of review is admittedly deferential to legislative judgment, "'it is not a toothless one'" in Iowa. Indeed, this court's meaningful review of social and economic legislation is mandated by our constitutional obligation to safeguard constitutional values by ensuring all legislation complies with those values.

IV. *Discussion.*

Although the State has advanced several reasons for the legislative classification challenged in this case, we focus our discussion primarily on those found satisfactory by the Supreme Court, as that is the reason for our reconsideration of the state constitutional claim. The Supreme Court viewed the issue as whether there was "rational support for the 20 percent/36 percent differential." It then concluded "[t]hat difference" was helpful to the riverboats because it (1) "encourage[d] the economic development of river communities [and] promote[d] riverboat history"; (2) "protect[ed] the reliance interests of riverboat operators" who were accustomed to a twenty percent tax rate; and (3) "aid[ed] the financial position of the riverboats." We will address each suggested purpose separately.

Our court does not accept the economic development of river communities and the promotion of riverboat history as a rational basis for the legislature's distinction between excursion boats and racetracks. Although these are laudable legislative goals, "the legislative facts on which the classification is apparently based [cannot] rationally [be] considered to be true by the governmental decisionmaker," as required by the Court's articulation of the rational basis test. We note initially that excursion boat gambling was never anticipated as solely a "river" activity so as to promote "river communities." When the legislature authorized gambling on "excursion boats" in 1989, it was envisioned that these boats would be located on inland waters, such as lakes and reservoirs, as well as on the Mississippi River and Missouri River, the historical location of riverboats. Moreover, there is nothing peculiar about racetracks that prevents their location in river cities. In fact, two of the three communities in which racetracks are located-Dubuque and Council Bluffs-are river communities. The Dubuque racetrack is actually on an island in the

Mississippi River. On the other hand, the excursion boat docked near Osceola, Iowa, is moored on a lake, not a river, and is certainly not located in a river community. In addition, one river community-Council Bluffs-has both a racetrack and an excursion boat, only blocks apart. So, to justify the differential tax treatment of these enterprises on the supposed connection of excursion boats to river communities and riverboat history and the absence of such a connection by racetracks is illogical.

We acknowledge "the overinclusive-underinclusive dichotomy is usually applied only as part of a strict scrutiny analysis." But our court has stated, in holding legislation violative of the state constitution under the rational basis test, "that as a classification involves extreme degrees of overinclusion and underinclusion in relation to any particular goal, it cannot be said to reasonably further that goal." That is precisely the case here insofar as the differential tax is based on the promotion of river communities and riverboat history. Thus, this legislative purpose cannot withstand review under the rational basis standard.

Even if this court were to take a more expansive view of potential legislative purposes and assume the general assembly sought to promote economic development in general, the taxing scheme still suffers from an irrational classification. There is nothing in the record, nor is it a matter of common knowledge, that excursion boats are a superior economic development tool as compared to racetracks. To the contrary, it appears that both types of gambling enterprises have the potential to enhance the economic climate of the communities in which they are located. If we presume the legislature thought the promotion of gambling was in the economic interests of the general public, then we find no rational basis for distinguishing between gambling that takes place on a floating casino and gambling that occurs at a land-based casino. Regardless of the relative number of such establishments or the size of the city in which they are to be found, excursion boats and racetracks contribute in the same manner to the economy of the local area: they are both gambling enterprises generating gambling receipts that are indistinguishable in terms of the economic benefits to the local community.

Our decision today is a difficult one because we have great respect for the legislature. Notwithstanding our preference to defer to its judgment, we declare the differential tax at issue here invalid under the Iowa Constitution because we are convinced the classifications made in section 99F.11 lack a rational basis in the constitutional sense. Because we are keenly aware of the legislature's constitutional role to make decisions of a policy and political nature, we have not lightly undertaken today's decision. Nonetheless, "[o]ur obligation not to interfere with the legislature's right to pass laws is no higher than our obligation to protect the citizens from discriminatory class legislation violative of the constitutional guaranty of equality of all before the law." Consequently, we decline the opportunity to alter our prior decision that the statutory exception to the twenty percent tax rate on gambling receipts violates article I, section 6 of the Iowa Constitution. We reverse the decision of the district court upholding the higher tax rate on racetracks under the Iowa Constitution and remand for further proceedings.

NOTES

1. Does the Iowa Supreme Court apply the same equal protection test as the U.S. Supreme Court or a different test?

2. Do you think the U.S. Supreme Court would find the Iowa Supreme Court's most recent decision convincing? Might the Iowa Supreme Court's recent explanation alter the U.S. Supreme Court's analysis under federal law?

MANUFACTURED HOUSING COMMUNITIES OF WASHINGTON v. STATE
13 P.3d 183 (Wash. 2000)

IRELAND, J.

Manufactured Housing Communities of Washington challenges the constitutionality of chapter 59.23 RCW, the mobile home parks-resident ownership act, which gives qualified tenants a right of first refusal to purchase a mobile home park. Finding an unconstitutional taking of private property for private use in violation of amended article I, section 16 of the Washington State Constitution, we reverse the Court of Appeals.

In 1995, Manufactured Housing Communities of Washington (Park Owners), an association of mobile home park owners, commenced this declaratory judgment action. The Park Owners argued that the mobile home parks-resident ownership act (the Act) creates an unconstitutional taking of property in violation of amended article I, section 16 of the Washington State Constitution, as well as the Fifth Amendment of the United States Constitution.

In 1993, the Washington State Legislature, concerned with the availability of mobile home park housing, adopted chapter 59.23 RCW, the Act. This Act gives mobile home park tenants a right of first refusal when the park owner decides to sell a mobile home park.

To exercise a right of first refusal, the tenants must organize into a "qualified tenant organization" and give the park owner written notice of "a present and continuing desire to purchase the mobile home park." Once the park owner has received such notice, the park owner must notify the tenants of any agreement to sell the park to a third party, as well as disclose the agreement's terms. If the park owner fails to properly notify the qualified tenant organization, a pending third party sale is voidable.

The Park Owners contend chapter 59.23 RCW eviscerates fundamentally important ownership rights. Specifically, the Park Owners believe the Act's mere existence destroys the right to (1) freely dispose of their property, (2) exclude others, and (3) immediately close the sale of a mobile home park. The Park Owners claim that if a park owner decides to sell, chapter 59.23 RCW allows the State to delay the sale and forcibly substitute the owner's chosen buyer with a buyer selected by the State. According to the Park Owners, taking the right of first refusal and then granting this right to private mobile home park tenants, solely for the tenants' private use, violates amended article I, section 16 of the Washington State Constitution, which expressly provides "Private property shall not be taken for private use...." The Park Owners believe invalidation of chapter 59.23 RCW is the only appropriate remedy.

Under existing Washington and federal law, a police power measure can violate amended article I, section 16 of the Washington State Constitution or the Fifth Amendment of the United States Constitution and thus be subject to a categorical "facial" taking challenge when: (1) a regulation effects a total taking of all economically viable use of one's property; or (2) the regulation has resulted in an actual physical invasion upon one's property; or (3) a regulation destroys one or more of the fundamental attributes of ownership (the right to possess, exclude other and to dispose of property); or (4) the regulations were employed to enhance the value of publicly held property.

We must determine, based upon a *Gunwall* analysis, whether a regulatory taking rather than lawful use of police power has occurred under the Washington State Constitution. This undertaking requires us first to examine six nonexclusive neutral criteria to determine whether the Washington State Constitution extends broader rights to its citizens than does the United States Constitution."

The first two *Gunwall* factors are: (1) the textual language of the state constitutional provision at issue and (2) differences in the parallel texts of the federal and state constitutions.

Amended article I, section 16 of the Washington State Constitution provides:

> § 16 EMINENT DOMAIN. Private property shall not be taken for private use, except for private ways of necessity, and for drains, flumes, or ditches on or across the lands of others for agricultural, domestic, or sanitary purposes. No private property shall be taken or damaged for public or private use without just compensation having been first made, or paid into court for the owner, and no right-of-way shall be appropriated to the use of any corporation other than municipal until full compensation therefor be first made in money, or ascertained and paid into court for the owner, irrespective of any benefit from

any improvement proposed by such corporation, which compensation shall be ascertained by a jury, unless a jury be waived, as in other civil cases in courts of record, in the manner prescribed by law. Whenever an attempt is made to take private property for a use alleged to be public, the question whether the contemplated use be really public shall be a judicial question, and determined as such, without regard to any legislative assertion that the use is public: *Provided*, That the taking of private property by the state for land reclamation and settlement purposes is hereby declared to be for public use.

On the other hand, the takings clause of the Fifth Amendment states simply: "nor shall private property be taken for public use, without just compensation." A striking textual difference between these two constitutions is the sheer detail of article I, section 16. A second significant difference is the addition of the word damaged in the state version and the requirement that compensation must *first* be made. Neither of these differences, however, are key to this analysis. What is key is article I, section 16's absolute prohibition against taking private property for private use. The Fifth Amendment only provides similar protections by inference. Moreover, unlike the Fifth Amendment, article I, section 16 expressly renders the question of public versus private a judicial question: "Whenever an attempt is made to take private property for a use alleged to be public, the question whether the contemplated use be really public shall be a judicial question, and determined as such, without regard to any legislative assertion that the use is public...." Const. art I, § 16 (amend.9).

The key differences between the Fifth Amendment and article I, section 16 are significant and support a literal interpretation of "private use" as employed in the Washington State Constitution.

The third *Gunwall* factor requires an examination of Washington constitutional and common law history. The Park Owners contend that because the federal constitution predates the state constitution, the state drafters presumably knew the contents of the federal document and deliberately chose to make the state constitutional provision more detailed, providing greater protection for the property owner.

During the Washington State Constitutional Convention in 1889, concern was publicly voiced over the taking of private property for private enterprise. Moreover, certain constitutional delegates were strongly opposed to various exceptions to the absolute prohibition against taking private property for private use.

The fourth *Gunwall* factor addresses preexisting state law. The State of Washington has a long history of extending greater protections against governmental takings of private property by literally defining what constitutes "private use." Before examining preexisting Washington law concerning private versus public use, we first compare the use of terms in relevant federal case law. While Washington case law concerns "private/public use" the federal cases concern "private/public purposes." Case law demonstrates these terms are not synonymous.

The United States Supreme Court has repeatedly stated "one person's property may not be taken for the benefit of another private person without justifying public purpose, even though compensation be paid." However, if the legislature's purpose is legitimate and its means not irrational, a legislative taking can and will withstand a public use challenge provided just compensation is paid.

Washington courts, on the other hand, have provided a more restrictive interpretation of public use. In fact, this court has consistently held that a "beneficial use is not necessarily a public use." Accordingly, preexisting state law provides a literal definition of "private use." Washington state courts thus provide Washington citizens with enhanced protections against taking private property for private use.

The fifth *Gunwall* factor, structural differences between the federal and state constitutions[,] also favors enhanced protections to Washington citizens by maintaining a literal interpretation of "private use." As previously noted, there are marked differences between the two relevant provisions. But, because the United States Constitution is a grant of enumerated powers to the federal government and the Washington State Constitution serves to limit the otherwise plenary powers of the state government, the state constitution can be looked at as a source of great protections directly reserved in the people. Thus, the structural differences allow Washington courts to forbid the taking of private property for private use even in cases where the Fifth Amendment may permit such takings.

The sixth and last *Gunwall* factor asks whether the clause deals with matters of particular state or local concern. It suffices to say that taking private property for private use is clearly a matter of local concern consistently recognized by Washington courts.

Having concluded on the basis of the foregoing analysis that "private use" under amended article I, section 16 is defined more literally than under the Fifth Amendment, and that Washington's interpretation of "public use" has been more restrictive, we next apply these terms to the present case.

Chapter 59.23 RCW authorizes the State to take from the park owner the right to sell to anyone of choice, at any time, and gives tenants a right to preempt the owner's sale to another and to substitute themselves as buyers. This is apparent from RCW 59.23.015, which says that if a qualified tenant organization expresses a "desire" to purchase, "the park may then be sold only according to this chapter." Moreover, RCW 59.23.025 provides that, if the tenant organization tenders two percent of the price plus a purchase and sale agreement comparable to the third party's offer, "the mobile home park owner must sell the mobile home park to the qualified tenant organization." Therefore, the legislature takes from the park owner the right to freely dispose of his or her property and gives to tenants a right of first refusal to acquire the property by blocking the owner's sale to the third party and substituting themselves as buyers. The result is that the Legislature has authorized the taking of private property from the owner for the tenants' private use in direct violation of the first sentence of article I, section 16.

The eminent domain provision of the Washington State Constitution provides a complete restriction against taking private property for private use: "Private property shall not be taken for private use...." Const. art. I, § 16 (amend.9). This absolute language is further strengthened by the enumeration of specific, but here inapplicable, exceptions "for private ways of necessity, and for drains, flumes, or ditches on or across the lands of others for agricultural, domestic, or sanitary purposes." Const. art. I, § 16 (amend.9). These specific exceptions are incorporated into an otherwise absolute prohibition precluding taking private property for private use. This prohibition is not conditioned on payment of compensation. *Whether or not a tenant organization might ultimately pay the owner the same price he or she is to receive from a third party buyer is irrelevant*. Hence, this absolute prohibition against taking private property for private use bars any additional inquiry about compensation and requires invalidation of Chapter 59.23 RCW.

We conclude that a right of first refusal in the hands of the Park Owners is a fundamental attribute of ownership and a valuable property right, and that the forced transfer of this right under chapter 59.23 RCW constitutes a taking. We next consider whether the proposed use of the property is constitutionally permitted.

Both the state and federal constitutions give citizens the guarantee that private property shall not be taken for "public use" without just compensation. U.S. Const. amend. V; Wash. Const. art. I, § 16 (amend.9). "The Fifth Amendment's guarantee that private property shall not be taken for public use without just compensation was designed to bar Government from forcing some people alone to bear public burdens which, in all fairness and justice, should be borne by the public as a whole." While the eminent domain provision of the Washington State Constitution similarly recognizes the requirement of just compensation when private property is taken for a public use, this constitutional provision also expressly provides that "Private property shall not be taken for private use...." Const. art I, § 16 (amend.9). Thus, unless a private use falls within article I, section 16's specifically articulated exceptions, the Washington State Constitution explicitly prohibits taking private property solely for a private use-with or without compensation.

Chapter 59.23 RCW authorizes the State to take from the park owner the right to sell to anyone of choice, at any time, and gives tenants a right to preempt the owner's sale to another and to substitute themselves as buyers. Then, after a mobile home park has been forcibly sold to a "qualified tenant organization," no member of the public can use the park. In fact, only the park tenants can freely use it. Although preserving dwindling housing stocks for a particularly vulnerable segment of society provides a "public benefit," this public benefit does not constitute a public use.

We have found that the statutory grant of a right of first refusal to tenants of mobile home parks, amounts to a taking and transfer of private property without a judicial determination of public necessity and without just compensation having been first paid as required by amended article I, section 16. Moreover, the transfer is legislatively granted to the tenants who are private persons, not the public. Giving the provision in article I, section 16 that "Private property shall not be taken for private use ..." its deserved effect, chapter 59.23 RCW must be invalidated. The state constitution's absolute prohibition against taking private property solely for a private use is not conditioned on payment of compensation. Whether or not a tenant organization might ultimately pay the owner the same price he or she is to receive from a third party is irrelevant. Hence, this absolute prohibition against taking private property for private use bars any additional inquiry about compensation and requires invalidation of chapter 59.23 RCW.

Here, the well-intentioned effort of the Legislature to encourage the conversion of mobile home parks to resident ownership conflicts with Washington State's constitutional prohibition against taking private property solely for a private use.

STATE v. JORDEN
156 P.3d 893 (Wash. 2007)

BRIDGE, J.

Timothy Jorden appeals his conviction for unlawful possession of cocaine. On March 15, 2003, a Pierce County deputy sheriff conducted a random warrant check of the Golden Lion Motel's guests via the guest registry and discovered Jorden's presence at the Lakewood motel as well as the fact of two outstanding warrants for Jorden's arrest. Deputy sheriffs then entered Jorden's motel room in order to arrest him for the outstanding warrants. Upon entering the room, officers saw cocaine in plain view. Jorden contends that the random check of the motel registry revealing his whereabouts constitutes a violation of his privacy rights under article I, section 7 of the Washington State Constitution.

The Pierce County Sheriff's Department takes part in the "Lakewood Crime-Free Hotel Motel Program." 1 Verbatim Report of Proceedings (VRP) at 11. The program offers assistance to motels and hotels that have a history of significant criminal activity, providing training on methods of crime reduction. The program also encourages officers to review the guest registries of hotels and motels on a random basis and without individualized or particularized suspicion. Officers often conduct random criminal checks of the names in guest registries at motels with reputations for frequent criminal activity. When checking into a participating motel, guests are advised that a valid identification is required for check-in and that the identification information is kept on file, but the guests are not told of the possibility for random, suspicionless searches of the registry by law enforcement.

Article I, section 7 of the Washington Constitution provides that "[n]o person shall be disturbed in his private affairs, or his home invaded, without authority of law." "[I]t is well established that article I, section 7 qualitatively differs from the Fourth Amendment and in some areas provides greater protections than does the federal constitution." We must therefore determine "whether article I, section 7 affords enhanced protection in the particular context." Accordingly, we must determine whether that heightened protection is available in these circumstances to Jorden.

Article I, section 7 protects against warrantless searches of a citizen's private affairs. Therefore, a warrantless search is per se unreasonable unless it falls under one of Washington's recognized exceptions. Here, the State does not argue the motel registry review falls into one of the exceptions, but argues that the information in the registry is not a private affair and thus there was no search triggering article I, section 7 protection.

Private affairs are those "'interests which citizens of this state have held, and should be entitled to hold, safe from government trespass.'" In determining whether a certain interest is a private affair deserving article I, section 7 protection, a central consideration is the *nature* of the information sought—that is, whether the information obtained via the governmental trespass reveals intimate or discrete details of a person's life.

In addition, this court has also considered whether there are historical protections afforded to the perceived interest. *McKinney*, 148 Wash.2d at 27. And, where the perceived interest involves the gathering of personal information by the government, this court has also considered the purpose for which the information sought is kept, and by whom it is kept.

Our most important inquiry then becomes whether a random and suspicionless search of a guest registry reveals intimate details of one's life. We first consider that here there is more information at stake than simply a guest's registration information: an individual's very presence in a motel or hotel may in itself be a sensitive piece of information. There are a variety of lawful reasons why an individual may not wish to reveal his or her presence at a motel. As the amicus American Civil Liberties Union (ACLU) points out, couples engaging in extramarital affairs may not wish to share their presence at the hotel with others, just as a closeted same-sex couple forced to meet at the motel also would not. The desire for privacy may extend to business people engaged in confidential negotiations or celebrities seeking respite from life in the public eye. One could also imagine a scenario, as Jorden's trial attorney pointed out during the motion to suppress, where a domestic violence victim flees to a hotel in hopes of remaining hidden from an abuser.

Additionally, we note the sensitivity of the registry information in and of itself. Not only does it reveal one's presence at the motel, it may also reveal co-guests in the room, divulging yet another person's personal or business associates. Thus, it appears that the information gleaned from random, suspicionless searches of a guest registry may indeed provide "intimate details about a person's activities and associations."

Therefore, the information contained in a motel registry-including one's whereabouts at the motel-is a private affair under our state constitution, and a government trespass into such information is a search. We hesitate to allow a search of a citizen's private affairs where the government cannot express at least an individualized or particularized suspicion about the search subject or present a valid exception to a warrantless search. A random, suspicionless search is a fishing expedition, and we have indicated displeasure with such practices on many occasions.

Consequently, we hold that the practice of checking the names in a motel registry for outstanding warrants without individualized or particularized suspicion violated the defendant's article I, section 7 rights.

We are not insensitive to the difficulties facing law enforcement in ensuring our motels and hotels remain relatively crime-free, but as a practical matter our holding does not unduly restrict the investigative powers of the police. Random, suspicionless registry checks are but one part of the Lakewood Crime-Free Hotel Motel Program. Law enforcement may continue to randomly run checks of the license plates of cars parked at the motels, provide training to motel owners, and encourage motel owners to be watchful of behavior evincing criminal activity. Reports of such observations may engender the requisite individualized suspicion that is notably missing from current program techniques.

Information contained in a motel registry constitutes a private affair under article I, section 7 of the Washington State Constitution because it reveals sensitive, discrete, and private information about the motel's guest. Absent a valid exception to the prohibition against warrantless searches, random viewing of a motel registry violates article I, section 7 of the Washington State Constitution. The evidence obtained from the registry of the Golden Lion Motel, which led officers to Jorden's room, was obtained through unlawful means and should have been excluded.

C. INDEPENDENT AND ADEQUATE STATE GROUNDS: STATE COURT RULINGS THAT ADDRESS FEDERAL AND STATE BASES FOR DECISION

Given the reality that the state courts may construe a constitutional guarantee in their own constitutions more broadly than one found in the U.S. Constitution, lawyers often will raise both grounds in challenging the validity of a state or local law or practice. When that happens, at least two issues arise: Will the state court rely on just one constitutional guarantee or both of them? And, if it relies on both of them or at least precedents from both jurisdictions, how will a reviewing court—the U.S. Supreme Court—know whether the state court has relied on an independent and adequate state ground, which is insulated from review, or on a federal ground, which is open to review? The answers to both questions have strategic consequences. The losing litigant, for example, will want to show that the state court decision turns on federal law, so that it may seek review in the U.S. Supreme Court. Otherwise, the case is over—unless the litigant can convince the people of the State to amend the state constitution.

In *Michigan v. Long*, 463 U.S. 1032 (1983), the Court provided some guidance on these issues. It created a clear-statement rule to the effect that, unless the state court expressly says otherwise, the U.S. Supreme Court would presume that a state court decision dealing with federal and state law issues was based on federal law. Here is how the Court put it:

> Accordingly, when, as in this case, a state court decision fairly appears to rest primarily on federal law, or to be interwoven with the federal law, and when the adequacy and independence of any possible state law ground is not clear from the face of the opinion, we will accept as the most reasonable explanation that the state court decided the case the way it did because it believed that federal law required it to do so. If a state court chooses merely to rely on federal precedents as it would on the precedents of all other jurisdictions, then it need only make clear by a plain statement in its judgment or opinion that the federal cases are being used only for the purpose of guidance, and do not themselves compel the result that the court has reached. In this way, both justice and judicial administration will be greatly improved. If the state court decision indicates clearly and expressly that it is alternatively based on bona fide separate, adequate, and independent grounds, we, of course, will not undertake to review the decision.

Despite the guidance provided by *Michigan v. Long*, state court cases continue to arise in which the ground of decision remains unclear. The next set of decisions presents a case study of this problem—by examining three decisions concerning the same traffic stop, two by the Ohio Supreme Court and one by the U.S. Supreme Court. *Ohio v. Robinette* also considers the other half of the issue this chapter introduces: Why state courts sometimes *resist* relying on independent and adequate state law grounds, even when they have the authority to do so and even when they are expressly told in a given case that they have that authority.

In *Robinette*, the courts dealt with a traffic stop governed by the Fourth Amendment and a virtually identical state guarantee. Section 14 of Article I of the Ohio Constitution provides: "The right of the people to be secure in their persons, houses, papers, and possessions, against unreasonable searches and seizures shall not be violated; and no warrant shall issue, but upon probable cause, supported by oath or affirmation, particularly describing the place to be searched, and the person and things to be seized." The Fourth Amendment, similarly, provides: "The right of the people to be secure in their persons, houses, papers, and effects, against unreasonable searches and seizures, shall not be violated, and no Warrants shall issue, but upon probable cause, supported by oath or affirmation, and particularly describing the place to be searched, and the persons or things to be seized."

OHIO v. ROBINETTE
653 N.E.2d 695 (Ohio 1995)

PFEIFER, J.

The issue in this case is whether the evidence used against Robinette was obtained through a valid search. We find that the search was invalid since it was the product of an unlawful seizure. We also use this case to establish a bright-line test, requiring police officers to inform motorists that their legal detention has concluded before the police officer may engage in any consensual interrogation.

In order to justify any investigative stop, a police officer "must be able to point to specific and articulable facts which, taken together with the rational inferences from those facts, reasonably warrant that intrusion." Absent any additional articulable facts arising after the stop is made, the police officer must tailor his detention of the driver to the original purpose of the stop.

In this case, Newsome certainly had cause to pull over Robinette for speeding. The question is when the validity of that stop ceased. Newsome testified that from the outset he never intended to ticket Robinette for speeding. When Newsome returned to Robinette's car after checking Robinette's license, every aspect of the speeding violation had been investigated and resolved. All Newsome had to do was to issue his warning and return Robinette's driver's license.

Instead, for no reason related to the speeding violation, and based on no articulable facts, Newsome extended his detention of Robinette by ordering him out of the vehicle. Newsome retained Robinette's driver's license and told Robinette to stand in front of the cruiser. Newsome then returned to the cruiser and activated the video camera in order to record his questioning of Robinette regarding whether he was carrying any contraband in the vehicle.

When the motivation behind a police officer's continued detention of a person stopped for a traffic violation is not related to the purpose of the original, constitutional stop, and when that continued detention is not based on any articulable facts giving rise to a suspicion of some separate illegal activity justifying an extension of the detention, the continued detention constitutes an illegal seizure.

The entire chain of events, starting when Newsome had Robinette exit the car and stand within the field of the video camera, was related to the questioning of Robinette about carrying contraband. Newsome asked Robinette to step out of his car for the sole purpose of conducting a line of questioning that was not related to the initial speeding stop and that was not based on any specific or articulable facts that would provide probable cause for the extension of the scope of the seizure of Robinette, his passenger and his car. Therefore the detention of Robinette ceased being legal when Newsome asked him to leave his vehicle.

However, this case contains a [unique] feature...: Robinette consented to the search of his vehicle during the illegal seizure. Because Robinette's consent was obtained during an illegal detention, his consent is invalid unless the state proves that the consent was not the product of the illegal detention but the result of an independent act of free will. The burden is on the state to prove that the consent to search was voluntarily given. The factors used in consideration of whether the consent is sufficiently removed from the taint of the illegal seizure include the length of time between the illegal seizure and the subsequent search, the presence of intervening circumstances, and the purpose and flagrancy of the circumstances.

In this case there was no time lapse between the illegal detention and the request to search, nor were there any circumstances that might have served to break or weaken the connection between one and the other. The sole purpose of the continued detention was to illegally broaden the scope of the original detention. Robinette's consent clearly was the result of his illegal detention, and was not the result of an act of will on his part. Given the circumstances, Robinette felt that he had no choice but to comply.

This case demonstrates the need for this court to draw a bright line between the conclusion of a valid seizure and the beginning of a consensual exchange. A person has been seized for the purposes of the Fourth Amendment when a law enforcement officer, by means of physical force or show of authority, has in some way restrained his liberty such that a reasonable person would not feel free to walk away.

The transition between detention and a consensual exchange can be so seamless that the untrained eye may not notice that it has occurred. The undetectability of that transition may be used by police officers to coerce citizens into answering questions that they need not answer, or to allow a search of a vehicle that they are not legally obligated to allow.

The present case offers an example of the blurring between a legal detention and an attempt at consensual interaction. Even assuming that Newsome's detention of Robinette was legal through the time when Newsome handed back Robinette's driver's license, Newsome then said, "One question *before you get gone*: are you carrying any illegal contraband in your car?" (Emphasis added.) Newsome tells Robinette that before he leaves Newsome wants to know whether Robinette is carrying any contraband. Newsome does not ask if he may ask a question, he simply asks it, implying that Robinette must respond before he may leave. The interrogation then continues. Robinette is never told that he is free to go or that he may answer the question at his option.

Most people believe that they are validly in a police officer's custody as long as the officer continues to interrogate them. The police officer retains the upper hand and the accouterments of authority. That the officer lacks legal license to continue to detain them is unknown to most citizens, and a reasonable person would not feel free to walk away as the officer continues to address him.

We are aware that consensual encounters between police and citizens are an important, and constitutional, investigative tool. However, citizens who have not been detained immediately prior to being encountered and questioned by police are more apt to realize that they need not respond to a police officer's questions. A "consensual encounter" immediately following a detention is likely to be imbued with the authoritative aura of the detention. Without a clear break from the detention, the succeeding encounter is not consensual at all.

Therefore, we are convinced that the right, guaranteed by the federal and Ohio Constitutions, to be secure in one's person and property requires that citizens stopped for traffic offenses be clearly informed by the detaining officer when they are free to go after a valid detention, before an officer attempts to engage in a consensual interrogation. Any attempt at consensual interrogation must be preceded by the phrase "At this time you legally are free to go" or by words of similar import.

While the legality of consensual encounters between police and citizens should be preserved, we do not believe that this legality should be used by police officers to turn a routine traffic stop into a fishing expedition for unrelated criminal activity. The Fourth Amendment to the federal Constitution and Section 14, Article I of the Ohio Constitution exist to protect citizens against such an unreasonable interference with their liberty.

OHIO v. ROBINETTE
519 U.S. 33 (1996)

REHNQUIST, C.J.

We are here presented with the question whether the Fourth Amendment requires that a lawfully seized defendant must be advised that he is "free to go" before his consent to search will be recognized as voluntary. We hold that it does not.

We have long held that the "touchstone of the Fourth Amendment is reasonableness." Reasonableness, in turn, is measured in objective terms by examining the totality of the circumstances.

In applying this test we have consistently eschewed bright-line rules, instead emphasizing the fact-specific nature of the reasonableness inquiry. Thus, in *Florida v. Royer*, 460 U.S. 491 (1983), we expressly disavowed any "litmus-paper test" or single "sentence or ... paragraph ... rule," in recognition of the "endless variations in the facts and circumstances" implicating the Fourth Amendment. Then, in *Michigan v. Chesternut*, 486 U.S. 567 (1988), when both parties urged "bright-line rule[s] applicable to all investigatory pursuits," we rejected both proposed rules as contrary to our "traditional contextual approach." And again, in *Florida v. Bostick*, 501 U.S. 429 (1991), when the Florida Supreme Court adopted a *per se* rule that questioning aboard a bus always constitutes a seizure, we reversed, reiterating that the proper inquiry necessitates a consideration of "all the circumstances surrounding the encounter."

We have previously rejected a *per se* rule very similar to that adopted by the Supreme Court of Ohio in determining the validity of a consent to search. In *Schneckloth v. Bustamonte*, 412 U.S. 218 (1973), it was argued that such a consent could not be valid unless the defendant knew that he had a right to refuse the request. We rejected this argument: "While knowledge of the right to refuse consent is one factor to be taken into account, the government need not establish such knowledge as the *sine qua non* of an effective consent." And just as it "would be thoroughly impractical to impose on the normal consent search the detailed requirements of an effective warning," so too would it be unrealistic to require police officers to always inform detainees that they are free to go before a consent to search may be deemed voluntary.

The Fourth Amendment test for a valid consent to search is that the consent be voluntary, and "[v]oluntariness is a question of fact to be determined from all the circumstances." The Supreme Court of Ohio having held otherwise, its judgment is reversed, and the case is remanded for further proceedings not inconsistent with this opinion.

GINSBURG, J., concurring in the judgment.

I write separately...because it seems to me improbable that the Ohio Supreme Court understood its first-tell-then-ask rule to be the Federal Constitution's mandate for the Nation as a whole. "[A] State is free *as a matter of its own law* to impose greater restrictions on police activity than those this Court holds to be necessary upon federal constitutional standards." But ordinarily, when a state high court grounds a rule of criminal procedure in the Federal Constitution, the court thereby signals its view that the Nation's Constitution would require the rule in all 50 States. Given this Court's decisions in consent-to-search cases such as *Schneckloth v. Bustamonte* and *Florida v. Bostick*, however, I suspect that the Ohio Supreme Court may not have homed in on the implication ordinarily to be drawn from a state court's reliance on the Federal Constitution. In other words, I question whether the Ohio court thought of the strict rule it announced as a rule for the governance of police conduct not only in Miami County, Ohio, but also in Miami, Florida.

Formerly, the Ohio Supreme Court was "reluctant to use the Ohio Constitution to extend greater protection to the rights and civil liberties of Ohio citizens" and had usually not taken advantage of opportunities to "us[e] the Ohio Constitution as an independent source of constitutional rights." Recently, however, the state high court declared: "The Ohio Constitution is a document of independent force.... As long as state courts provide at least as much protection as the United States Supreme Court has provided in its interpretation of the federal Bill of Rights, state courts are unrestricted in according greater civil liberties and protections to individuals and groups."

The first-tell-then-ask rule seems to be a prophylactic measure not so much extracted from the text of any constitutional provision as crafted by the Ohio Supreme Court to reduce the number of violations of textually guaranteed rights. In *Miranda v. Arizona*, 384 U.S. 436 (1966), this Court announced a similarly motivated rule as a minimal national requirement without suggesting that the text of the Federal Constitution required the precise measures the Court's opinion set forth. Although all parts of the United States fall within this Court's domain, the Ohio Supreme Court is not similarly situated. That court can declare prophylactic rules governing the conduct of officials in Ohio, but it cannot command the police forces of sister States. The very ease with which the Court today disposes of the federal leg of the Ohio Supreme Court's decision strengthens my impression that the Ohio Supreme Court saw its rule as a measure made for Ohio, designed to reinforce in that State the right of the people to be secure against unreasonable searches and seizures.

The Ohio Supreme Court's syllabus and opinion, however, were ambiguous. Under *Long*, the existence of ambiguity regarding the federal- or state-law basis of a state-court decision will trigger this Court's jurisdiction. *Long* governs even when, all things considered, the more plausible reading of the state court's decision may be that the state court did not regard the Federal Constitution alone as a sufficient basis for its ruling.

It is incumbent on a state court, therefore, when it determines that its State's laws call for protection more complete than the Federal Constitution demands, to be clear about its ultimate reliance on state law. Similarly, a state court announcing a new legal rule arguably derived from both federal and state law can definitively render state law an adequate and independent ground for its decision by a simple declaration to that effect. A recent Montana Supreme Court opinion on the scope of an individual's privilege against self-incrimination includes such a declaration:

> "While we have devoted considerable time to a lengthy discussion of the application of the Fifth Amendment to the United States Constitution, it is to be noted that this holding is also based separately and independently on [the defendant's] right to remain silent pursuant to Article II, Section 25 of the Montana Constitution." *State v. Fuller*, 276 Mont. 155, 167, 915 P.2d 809, 816, cert. denied, 519 U.S. 930 (1996).

An explanation of this order meets the Court's instruction in *Long* that "[i]f the state court decision indicates clearly and expressly that it is alternatively based on bona fide separate, adequate, and independent grounds, [this Court] will not undertake to review the decision."

On remand, the Ohio Supreme Court may choose to clarify that its instructions to law enforcement officers in Ohio find adequate and independent support in state law, and that in issuing these instructions, the court endeavored to state dispositively only the law applicable in Ohio. To avoid misunderstanding, the Ohio Supreme Court must itself speak with the clarity it sought to require of its State's police officers. The efficacy of its endeavor to safeguard the liberties of Ohioans without disarming the State's police can then be tested in the precise way Our Federalism was designed to work.

OHIO v. ROBINETTE
685 N.E.2d 762 (Ohio 1997)

LUNDBERG STRATTON, J.

The first issue that we must determine is whether this court's prior holding should be reaffirmed under the adequate and independent ground of the Constitution of the state of Ohio.

When the United States Supreme Court incorporated the federal Bill of Rights into the Fourteenth Amendment, the United States Constitution became the primary mechanism to safeguard an individual's rights. As a result, state court litigation of constitutional issues was based primarily upon the authority of the United States Constitution.

However, more recently, there has been a trend for state courts to rely on their own constitutions to provide broader protection for individual rights, independent of protections afforded by the United States Constitution. A state may impose greater restrictions on police activity pursuant to its own state constitution than is required by federal constitutional standards. This movement toward enforcing state constitutions independently has been called the "New Federalism."

Despite this wave of New Federalism, where the provisions are similar and no persuasive reason for a differing interpretation is presented, this court has determined that protections afforded by Ohio's Constitution are coextensive with those provided by the United States Constitution.

The language of Section 14, Article I of the Ohio Constitution and the Fourth Amendment is virtually identical. Accordingly, this court has interpreted Section 14, Article I of the Ohio Constitution as affording the same protection as the Fourth Amendment. In *Nicholas v. Cleveland* (1932), 125 Ohio St. 474, 484, 182 N.E. 26, 30, [the Court,] in comparing the Fourth Amendment and Section 14, Article I of the Ohio Constitution, stated:

> "While we are not bound by federal decisions upon this feature of the case, since the Bill of Rights in the Constitution of the United States is in almost the exact language of that found in our own, the reasoning of the United States court upon this aspect of the case should be very persuasive. The state courts, however, with practical unanimity, have adopted the same principle as the federal courts."

Thus, case law indicates that, consistent with *Robinette II*, we should harmonize our interpretation of Section 14, Article I of the Ohio Constitution with the Fourth Amendment, unless there are persuasive reasons to find otherwise.

We will first determine whether Robinette's stop and continued detention were justified. It is undisputed that Officer Newsome's act of stopping Robinette was justified because Robinette was speeding. We also find that Newsome's instruction for Robinette to exit the vehicle was also justified because it was a traffic stop. Once Newsome administered the warning for speeding to Robinette, the reason for the stop ended.

However, Newsome continued to detain Robinette pursuant to a drug interdiction policy. The drug interdiction policy required police officers to ask persons detained during a traffic stop whether they had any contraband and then to ask to search the vehicle.

Royer and *Brown* set out a standard whereby police officers, under certain circumstances, may briefly detain an individual without reasonably articulable facts giving rise to suspicion of criminal activity, if the detention promotes a legitimate public concern, *e.g.*, removing drunk drivers from public roadways or reducing drug trade.

In the case at bar, we find that, pursuant to *Royer* and *Brown*, Officer Newsome was justified in briefly detaining Robinette in order to ask him whether he was carrying any illegal drugs or weapons pursuant to the drug interdiction policy, because such a policy promotes the public interest in quelling the drug trade.

The next issue for our determination is whether the continued detention of Robinette after this point was lawful.

If during the initial detention to ask the contraband question, the officer ascertained reasonably articulable facts giving rise to a suspicion of criminal activity, the officer may then further detain and implement a more in-depth investigation of the individual. For example, at a sobriety checkpoint an officer who detects slurred speech would be justified in detaining the individual to perform a field test.

In the case at bar, Newsome did not have any reasonably articulable facts or individualized suspicion to justify Robinette's further detention in order to ask to search his car. Accordingly, Newsome was not justified in detaining Robinette in order to ask for and execute an intrusive search.

Even though we have determined that Newsome unlawfully detained Robinette to ask for permission to search his car, our analysis is not complete. Voluntary consent, determined under the totality of the circumstances, may validate an otherwise illegal detention and search.

Robinette argues that retention of *Robinette I 's* "free to go" rule would provide predictability in determining whether an individual consented to a search. We find that Robinette's conclusion is based on an oversimplified approach to the issue of consent.

In sum, every search situation is unique unto itself and no set of fixed rules will be sufficient to cover every situation. For that reason, *Bustamonte* utilized the totality-of-the-circumstances test to determine when consent is voluntary. Such a test serves both interests of allowing police to legitimately investigate under varying circumstances while protecting individuals from unreasonable searches and seizures.

In the case at bar, Officer Newsome stopped Robinette for driving sixty-nine miles per hour in a forty-five-mile-per-hour construction zone. Officer Newsome asked Robinette to step to the rear of his (Robinette's) car, which was in front of the patrol car. Newsome returned to his patrol car and turned on a video camera. Newsome gave Robinette a verbal warning *and advised Robinette that he was letting him off with only a verbal warning. But without any break in the conversation* and still in front of the camera, Newsome then asked Robinette, "One question before you get gone: are you carrying any illegal contraband in your car? Any weapons of any kind, drugs, anything like that?" Robinette denied having any contraband in the car. Newsome then immediately asked Robinette if he could search the car. Robinette hesitated, looked at his car, then back at the officer, then nodded his head. Newsome commenced a lengthy search of Robinette's car. During the search Newsome recovered some marijuana and a pill. Robinette was charged with drug abuse.

At the suppression hearing, Robinette provided the following testimony pertaining to the search:

"Q And did he [Newsome] indicate to you that at that time [when he returned from activating the video camera] that he was giving you a warning and that you were free to go?

"A Yes, he did.

"Q And then at that time, I think, as the tape will reflect, the officer asked you some questions about did you have any weapons of any kind, drugs, anything like that. Do you recall that question?

"A Yes.

" * * *

"Q Did you in fact feel that you were free to leave at that point?

"A I thought I was.

" * * *

"Q The officer then asked if he could search your vehicle. What went through your mind at that point in time?

"A Uhm, I was still sort of shocked and I-I thought-I just automatically said yes.

"Q Did-did you feel that you could refuse the officer?

"A No."

Newsome's words did not give Robinette any indication that he was free to go, but rather implied just the opposite-that Robinette was *not free* to go until he answered Newsome's additional questions. The timing of Newsome's immediate transition from giving Robinette the warning for speeding into questioning regarding contraband and the request to search is troubling. As the majority stated in *Robinette I*:

When these factors are combined with a police officer's superior position of authority, any reasonable person would have felt compelled to submit to the officer's questioning. While Newsome's questioning was not expressly coercive, the circumstances surrounding the request to search made the questioning impliedly coercive. Even the state conceded, at an oral argument before the United States Supreme Court, that an officer has discretion to issue a ticket rather than a warning to a motorist if the motorist becomes uncooperative. From the totality of the circumstances, it appears that Robinette merely submitted to "a claim of lawful authority" rather than consenting as a voluntary act of free will. Under *Royer*, this is not sufficient to prove voluntary compliance.

We are very mindful that police officers face the enormous and difficult task of fighting crime. Furthermore, we explicitly continue to recognize that officers may conduct checkpoint-type questioning and consensual searches, and may progress to further detention and investigation when individualized suspicion of criminal activity arises during questioning based on reasonably articulable facts. But allowing police officers to do their jobs must be balanced against an individual's right to be free from unreasonable searches. At some point, individual rights must prevail. This is just such a case.

Accordingly, we find that Section 14, Article I of the Ohio Constitution affords protections that are coextensive with those provided by the Fourth Amendment and, therefore, the Ohio Constitution does not require a police officer to inform an individual, stopped for a traffic violation, that he or she is free to go before the officer may attempt to engage in a consensual interrogation. Further, under Section 14, Article I of the Ohio Constitution, we find that the totality-of-the circumstances test is controlling in an unlawful detention to determine whether permission to search a vehicle is voluntary. Once an individual has been unlawfully detained by law enforcement, for his or her consent to be considered an independent act of free will, the totality of the circumstances must clearly demonstrate that a reasonable person would believe that he or she had the freedom to refuse to answer further questions and could in fact leave.

Therefore, pursuant to the totality of the circumstances, we find that Robinette did not voluntarily consent to allow Newsome to search his automobile. As a result, the evidence collected in that search is inadmissible.

NOTES

1. Did the second Ohio Supreme Court decision satisfy *Michigan v. Long*? In other words, does it establish an adequate and independent state law ground? If not, why not?

2. As for the merits, why did the Ohio Supreme Court choose to align the interpretation of its "unreasonable searches and seizures" protection with the similarly worded federal guarantee? Was the initial bright-line rule indefensible as a matter of state law? How was it different from the U.S. Supreme Court's bright-line rule for applying the Fifth Amendment under *Miranda*? What explains the state supreme court's second decision?

CHAPTER V

EQUALITY

A. INTRODUCTION

Jeffrey M. Shaman, EQUALITY AND LIBERTY IN THE GOLDEN AGE OF STATE CONSTITUTIONAL LAW (2008) 1-5

Equality is a principle that enjoys a long history in state constitutional law. Some of the earliest state constitutions, which are the oldest political documents in America, proclaimed: "All men are born equally free and independent, and have certain inherent and indefeasible rights."[1] Today, that sentiment can still be found in a number of state constitutions, but is more likely to be expressed as: "All people are created equal and are entitled to equal rights and opportunity under the law."[2] A number of the early state constitutions also contained provisions prohibiting the granting of unequal privileges or immunities. These provisions, too, along with their close counterparts banning special entitlements, can be found in many state constitutions today. After the Civil War and the enactment in the Federal Constitution of the Fourteenth Amendment guaranteeing equal protection of the laws to all persons, some states were moved to follow suit by adding equal protection clauses to their constitutions when the opportunity arose. The civil rights movement of the 1950s and 60s inspired some states to add provisions to their constitutions prohibiting discrimination against persons in the exercise of their civil rights. And after the Equal Rights Amendment (ERA) prohibiting discrimination on the basis of sex failed to gain passage at the federal level, some states adopted their own versions of the ERA. It is worthy of note that long before the conception of the ERA, both Utah and Wyoming enacted state constitutional provisions guaranteeing equal civil, political, and religious rights and privileges for "male and female citizens."

Furthermore, in a number of state constitutions there are provisions that grant specialized protection for various kinds of equality. For instance, a few state constitutions provide for "free and equal elections." There are provisions in three state constitutions that expressly bar segregation. The Alaska constitution states that "No exclusive right or special privilege of fishery shall be created or authorized in the natural waters of the State." Some state constitutions expressly prohibit certain forms of discrimination in the private sector as well as the public one.

---

[1] Pa. Const. art. I, §1 (1776). *See also* Va. Const. Bill of Rights, §1 (1776) ("All men are by nature equally free and independent....").

[2] Wis. Const. art. I, §1 (1982).

Other state constitutions contain so-called "uniformity clauses" that call for taxes to be uniformly levied within the same class of subjects. (See Chapter XIV, sect. E.)

It is important to mention that a number of state constitutions contain a combination of equality provisions. In some cases, the combination of provisions included in a state constitution amounts to a comprehensive mandate for equal treatment under the law. Perhaps the Connecticut constitution contains the most comprehensive protection of equality by declaring that:

> All men when they form a social compact, are equal in rights; and no man or set of men are entitled to exclusive public emoluments or privileges from the community...No person shall be denied the equal protection of the law nor be subjected to segregation or discrimination in the exercise or enjoyment of his or her civil or political rights because of religion, race, color, ancestry, national origin, sex or physical or mental disability.

At the opposite end of the spectrum, there are some state constitutions that contain no language expressly addressing equality or that only briefly refer to it. Nevertheless, other language in those constitutions may be interpreted to encompass a guarantee of equality. The Maryland Court of Appeals, for example, has ruled that although the Maryland Declaration of Rights does not contain an express equal protection clause, the concept of equal protection is embodied in the due process article of the Declaration of Rights. Similarly, the West Virginia Supreme Court of Appeals has held that although the phrase "equal protection" is not found in the state constitution, the principle of equality is an integral part of the state's constitutional law, inherent in the due process clause of the West Virginia Bill of Rights. And the Minnesota Supreme Court has recognized that the law of the land provision in the Minnesota Bill of Rights embraces principles of equality synonymous with the Equal Protection Clause of the Fourteenth Amendment to the Federal Constitution.

The state constitutions, then, are a rich source of protection for equality.

B. RACIAL CLASSIFICATIONS

SHEFF V. O'NEILL
678 A.2d 1267 (Conn. 1996)

PETERS, C.J.

The public elementary and high school students in Hartford suffer daily from the devastating effects that racial and ethnic isolation, as well as poverty, have had on their education. Federal constitutional law provides no remedy for their plight. The principal issue in this appeal is whether, under the unique provisions of our state constitution, the state, which already plays an active role in managing public schools, must take further measures to relieve the severe handicaps that burden these children's education. The issue is as controversial as the stakes are high. We hold today that the needy schoolchildren of Hartford have waited long enough. The constitutional imperatives contained in article eighth, § 1,[3] and article first, §§ 1 and 20,[4] of our state constitution entitle the plaintiffs to relief. At the same time, the constitutional imperative of separation of powers persuades us to afford the legislature, with the assistance of the executive branch, the opportunity, in the first instance, to fashion the remedy that will most appropriately respond to the constitutional violations that we have identified. The judgment of the trial court must, accordingly, be reversed.

The stipulation of the parties and the trial court's findings establish the following relevant facts. Statewide, in the 1991-92 school year, children from minority groups constituted 25.7 percent of the public school population. In the Hartford public school system in that same period, 92.4 percent of the students were members of minority groups, including, predominantly, students who were either African-American or Latino. Fourteen of Hartford's twenty-five elementary schools had a white student enrollment of less than 2 percent. The Hartford public school system currently enrolls the highest percentage of minority students in the state. In the future, if current conditions continue, the percentage of minority students in the Hartford public school system is likely to increase rather than decrease. Although enrollment of African-American students in the twenty-one surrounding suburban towns has increased by more than 60 percent from 1980 to 1992, only seven of these school districts had a minority student enrollment in excess of 10 percent in 1992. Because of the negative consequences of racial and ethnic isolation, a more integrated public school system would likely be beneficial to all schoolchildren.

A majority of the children who constitute the public school population in Hartford come from homes that are economically disadvantaged, that are headed by a single parent and in which a language other than English

---

[3] [1] The constitution of Connecticut, article eighth, § 1, provides: "There shall always be free public elementary and secondary schools in the state. The general assembly shall implement this principle by appropriate legislation."

[4] [2] The constitution of Connecticut, article first, § 1, provides: "All men when they form a social compact, are equal in rights; and no man or set of men are entitled to exclusive public emoluments or privileges from the community."

The constitution of Connecticut, article first, § 20, as amended by articles five and twenty-one of the amendments, provides: "No person shall be denied the equal protection of the law nor be subjected to segregation or discrimination in the exercise or enjoyment of his or her civil or political rights because of religion, race, color, ancestry, national origin, sex or physical or mental disability."

is spoken. The percentage of Hartford schoolchildren at the elementary level who return to the same school that they attended the previous year is the lowest such percentage in the state. Such socioeconomic factors impair a child's orientation toward and skill in learning and adversely affect a child's performance on standardized tests. The gap in the socioeconomic status between Hartford schoolchildren and schoolchildren from the surrounding twenty-one suburban towns has been increasing. The performance of Hartford schoolchildren on standardized tests falls significantly below that of schoolchildren from the twenty-one surrounding suburban towns.

The state has not intentionally segregated racial and ethnic minorities in the Hartford public school system. Except for a brief period in 1868, no students in Connecticut have intentionally been assigned to a public school or to a public school district on the basis of race or ethnicity. There has never been any other manifestation of de jure segregation either at the state or the local level. In addition to various civil rights initiatives undertaken by the legislature from 1905 to 1961 to combat racial discrimination, the state board of education was reorganized, during the 1980s, to concentrate on the needs of urban schoolchildren and to promote diversity in the public schools. Since 1970, the state has supported and encouraged voluntary plans for increasing interdistrict diversity.

The state has nonetheless played a significant role in the present concentration of racial and ethnic minorities in the Hartford public school system. Although intended to improve the quality of education and not racially or ethnically motivated, the districting statute that the legislature enacted in 1909, now codified at § 10-240, is the single most important factor contributing to the present concentration of racial and ethnic minorities in the Hartford public school system. The districting statute and the resultant school district boundaries have remained virtually unchanged since 1909. The districting statute is of critical importance because it establishes town boundaries as the dividing line between all school districts in the state.

The defendants maintain that...the plaintiffs are not entitled to judicial relief because the educational disparities of which they complain do not result from the requisite state action. The plaintiffs claim that the state bears responsibility to correct the constitutional violations alleged in their complaint because of the state's failure to "take corrective measures to [e]nsure that its Hartford public schoolchildren receive an equal educational opportunity." That failure is actionable, according to the plaintiffs, because of the state's knowledge of the racial and ethnic isolation in the Hartford schools, combined with the state's extensive involvement in the operations of Connecticut's public schools and the impact of state statutes mandating school attendance within statutorily defined school districts. The defendants maintain, to the contrary, that the state's constitutional duty to provide for the elementary and secondary education of Connecticut schoolchildren is triggered only by state action that is alleged to be intentional state misconduct.

The defendants' argument, derived largely from principles of federal constitutional law, founders on the fact that article eighth, § 1, and article first, §§ 1 and 20, impose on the legislature an affirmative constitutional obligation to provide schoolchildren throughout the state with a substantially equal educational opportunity. It follows that, if the legislature fails, for whatever reason, to take action to remedy substantial inequalities in the educational opportunities that such children are being afforded, its actions and its omissions constitute state action.

The affirmative constitutional obligation that we recognized in *Horton I* and *Horton III*, and reaffirmed recently in *Moore v. Ganim*, 660 A.2d 742 (1995), was not premised on a showing that the legislature had played an active role in creating the inequalities that the constitution requires it to redress. In *Horton I*, we determined that the state's educational financing scheme was unconstitutional even though it was facially nondiscriminatory and even though the disparities resulting therefrom had not been created intentionally by the legislature. These constitutionally unacceptable disparities developed, instead, "from the circumstance that over the years there [had] arisen a great disparity in the ability of local communities to finance local education," and from the legislature's failure to consider "the financial capability of [each] municipality...." In declaring this statutory scheme unconstitutional in *Horton I*, and in requiring further remedial action in *Horton III*, we necessarily determined that the state's failure adequately to address school funding inequalities constituted the state action that is the constitutional prerequisite for affording judicial relief.

The claims now before us likewise implicate the legislature's affirmative constitutional obligation to provide a substantially equal educational opportunity to all of the state's schoolchildren. The plaintiffs document the existence of an extensive statutory system developed in response to the legislature's plenary authority over state public elementary and secondary schools. As a general matter, the plaintiffs challenge the failure of the legislature to address continuing unconstitutional inequities resulting, de facto, from that scheme. The failure adequately to address the racial and ethnic disparities that exist among the state's public school districts is not different in kind from the legislature's failure adequately to address the "great disparity in the ability of local communities to finance local education" that made the statutory scheme at issue in *Horton I* unconstitutional in its application.

The defendants urge us to follow federal precedents that concededly require, as a matter of federal constitutional law, that claimants seeking judicial relief for educational disparities pursuant to the equal protection clause of the fourteenth amendment to the United States constitution must prove intentional governmental discrimination against a suspect class. According to the defendants, because the plaintiffs raise claims of unconstitutional disparities in educational opportunities on the basis of severe racial and ethnic imbalances among school districts, the plaintiffs, too, must prove intentional state action.

For two reasons, we are not persuaded that we should adopt these precedents as a matter of state constitutional law. First and foremost, the federal cases start from the premise that there is no right to education under the United States constitution. Our Connecticut constitution, by contrast, contains a fundamental right to education and a corresponding affirmative state obligation to implement and maintain that right. Second, the federal cases are guided by principles of federalism as "a foremost consideration in interpreting any of the pertinent constitutional provisions under which [a court] examines state action." As the United States Supreme Court noted, "it would be difficult to imagine a case having a greater potential impact on our federal system than the one now before us, in which we are urged to abrogate systems of financing public education presently in existence in virtually every State." Principles of federalism, however, do not restrict our constitutional authority to enforce the constitutional mandates contained in article eighth, § 1, and article first, §§ 1 and 20.

In summary, under our law, which imposes an affirmative constitutional obligation on the legislature to provide a substantially equal educational opportunity for all public schoolchildren, the state action doctrine is not a defense to the plaintiffs' claims of constitutional deprivation. The state had ample notice of ongoing trends toward racial and ethnic isolation in its public schools, and indeed undertook a number of laudable remedial efforts that unfortunately have not achieved their desired end. The fact that the legislature did not affirmatively create or intend to create the conditions that have led to the racial and ethnic isolation in the Hartford public school system does not, in and of itself, relieve the defendants of their affirmative obligation to provide the plaintiffs with a more effective remedy for their constitutional grievances.

Since *Horton I*, it is common ground that the state has an affirmative constitutional obligation to provide all public schoolchildren with a substantially equal educational opportunity. Any infringement of that right must be strictly scrutinized….The issue presented by this case is whether the state has fully satisfied its affirmative constitutional obligation to provide a substantially equal educational opportunity if the state demonstrates that it has substantially equalized school funding and resources. For the purposes of the present litigation, we decide only that the scope of the constitutional obligation expressly imposed on the state by article eighth, § 1, is informed by the constitutional prohibition against segregation contained in article first, § 20. Reading these constitutional provisions conjointly, we conclude that the existence of extreme racial and ethnic isolation in the public school system deprives schoolchildren of a substantially equal educational opportunity and requires the state to take further remedial measures.

Two factors persuade us that it is appropriate to undertake a conjoint reading of these provisions of our state constitution. One is the special nature of the affirmative constitutional right embodied in article eighth, § 1. The other is the explicit prohibition of segregation contained in article first, § 20.

The affirmative constitutional obligation of the state to provide a substantially equal educational opportunity, which is embodied in article eighth, § 1, differs in kind from most constitutional obligations. Organic documents only rarely contain provisions that explicitly require the state to act rather than to refrain from acting. Nothing in the description of the relevant legal landscape in any of our cases suggests that the constitutional right that we articulated in *Horton I* was limited to school financing.

For Connecticut schoolchildren, the scope of the state's constitutional obligation to provide a substantially equal educational opportunity is informed and amplified by the highly unusual[5] provision in article first, § 20, that prohibits segregation not only indirectly, by forbidding discrimination, but directly, by the use of the term "segregation." The section provides in relevant part: "No person shall be denied the equal protection of the law nor be subjected to segregation or discrimination ... because of ... race [or] ... ancestry...."

The express inclusion of the term "segregation" in article first, § 20, has independent constitutional significance. The addition of this term to the text of our equal protection clause distinguishes this case from others in which we have found a substantial equivalence between our equal protection clause and that contained in the United States constitution. Fundamental principles of constitutional interpretation require that "[e]ffect must be given to every part of and each word in our constitution...." In other cases, we have held that, insofar as article first, § 20, differs textually from its federal counterpart, its judicial construction must reflect such a textual distinction.

---

[5] [29] The only other constitutions that explicitly prohibit segregation are those of Hawaii and New Jersey.

The issue before us, therefore, is what specific meaning to attach to the protection against segregation contained in article first, § 20, in a case in which that protection is invoked as part of the plaintiff school-children's fundamental affirmative right to a substantially equal educational opportunity under article eighth, § 1. In concrete terms, this issue devolves into the question of whether the state has a constitutional duty to remedy the educational impairment that results from segregation in the Hartford public schools, even though the conditions of segregation that contribute to such impairment neither were caused nor are perpetuated by invidious intentional conduct on the part of the state.

Linguistically, the term "segregation" in article first, § 20, which denotes "separation," is neutral about segregative intent. The section prohibits segregation that occurs "because of religion, race, color, ancestry, national origin, sex or physical or mental disability," without specifying the manner in which such a causal relationship must be established.

Whatever this language may portend in other contexts, we are persuaded that, in the context of public education, in which the state has an affirmative obligation to monitor and to equalize educational opportunity, the state's awareness of existing and increasing severe racial and ethnic isolation imposes upon the state the responsibility to remedy "segregation ... because of race [or] ... ancestry...." We therefore hold that, textually, article eighth, § 1, as informed by article first, § 20, requires the legislature to take affirmative responsibility to remedy segregation in our public schools, regardless of whether that segregation has occurred de jure or de facto.

The history of the promulgation of article eighth, § 1, and article first, § 20, supports our conclusion that these constitutional provisions include protection from de facto segregation, at least in public schools. That history includes not only the contemporaneous addition, in 1965, of these two provisions to our constitution, but also the strong commitment to ending discrimination and segregation that is evident in the remarks of the delegates to the 1965 constitutional convention.

Sound principles of public policy support our conclusion that the legislature's affirmative constitutional responsibility for the education of all public schoolchildren encompasses responsibility for segregation to which the legislature has contributed, even unintentionally. The parties agree, as the trial court expressly found, that racial and ethnic segregation is harmful, and that integration would likely have positive benefits for all children and for society as a whole. Further, as the trial court also expressly found, the racial and ethnic isolation of children in the Hartford schools is likely to worsen in the future.

Racial and ethnic segregation has a pervasive and invidious impact on schools, whether the segregation results from intentional conduct or from unorchestrated demographic factors. "[S]chools are an important socializing institution, imparting those shared values through which social order and stability are maintained." *Plyler v. Doe*, 457 U.S. 202, 222 n. 20 (1982). Schools bear central responsibility for "inculcating [the] fundamental values necessary to the maintenance of a democratic political system...." *Ambach v. Norwick*, 441 U.S. 68, 77 (1979). When children attend racially and ethnically isolated schools, these "shared values" are jeopardized: "If children of different races and economic and social groups have no opportunity to know each other and to live together in school, they cannot be expected to gain the understanding and mutual respect necessary for the cohesion of our society." *Jenkins v. Township of Morris School District*, 58 N.J. 483, 498 (1971). "[T]he elimination of racial isolation in the schools promotes the attainment of equal educational opportunity and is beneficial to all students, both black and white." *Lee v. Nyquist*, 318 F. Supp 710, 714 (W.D.N.Y. 1970), aff'd without opinion, 402 U.S. 935 (1971). Our state constitution, as amended in 1965, imposes on the state an affirmative obligation to respond to such segregation.

It is crucial for a democratic society to provide all of its schoolchildren with fair access to an unsegregated education. As the United States Supreme Court has eloquently observed, a sound education "is the very foundation of good citizenship. Today it is a principal instrument in awakening the child to cultural values, in preparing him for later professional training, and in helping him to adjust normally to his environment. In these days, it is doubtful that any child may reasonably be expected to succeed in life if he is denied the opportunity of an education. Such an opportunity, where the state has undertaken to provide it, is a right which must be made available to all on equal terms." *Brown v. Board of Education*, 347 U.S. at 493. "The American people have always regarded education and [the] acquisition of knowledge as matters of supreme importance.... We have recognized the public schools as a most vital civic institution for the preservation of a democratic system of government ... and as the primary vehicle for transmitting the values on which our society rests.... And these historic perceptions of the public schools as inculcating fundamental values necessary to the maintenance of a democratic political system have been confirmed by the observations of social scientists.... [E]ducation provides the basic tools by which individuals might lead economically productive lives to the benefit of us all. In sum, education has a fundamental role in maintaining the fabric of our society. We cannot ignore the significant social costs borne by our Nation when select groups are denied the means to absorb the values and skills upon which our social order rests." *Plyler v. Doe*, 457 U.S. at 221.

Our decision to reverse the judgment of the trial court, and to direct that judgment be rendered on behalf of the plaintiffs on the merits of their constitutional claims in the first and second counts of their complaint, requires us to consider what relief may properly be afforded to the plaintiffs.... We have decided...to employ the methodology used in *Horton I*. In that case, the trial court, after having found for the plaintiffs, limited its judgment by granting only declaratory relief but retained jurisdiction to grant consequential relief, if needed, at some future time. *Horton I*. In light of the complexities of developing a legislative program that would respond to the constitutional deprivation that the plaintiffs had established, we concluded, in *Horton I*, that further judicial intervention should be stayed "to afford the General Assembly an opportunity to take appropriate legislative action." Prudence and sensitivity to the constitutional authority of coordinate branches of government counsel the same caution in this case.

In staying our hand, we do not wish to be misunderstood about the urgency of finding an appropriate remedy for the plight of Hartford's public schoolchildren. Every passing day denies these children their constitutional right to a substantially equal educational opportunity. Every passing day shortchanges these children in their ability to learn to contribute to their own well-being and to that of this state and nation. We direct the legislature and the executive branch to put the search for appropriate remedial measures at the top of their respective agendas. We are confident that with energy and good will, appropriate remedies can be found and implemented in time to make a difference before another generation of children suffers the consequences of a segregated public school education.

BERDON, J., concurring.

I join the Chief Justice in her well reasoned majority opinion that concludes that the racial and ethnic segregation that exists in our public school system deprives schoolchildren of their state constitutional right to a "substantially equal educational opportunity." I write separately because, in my view and as the record reflects, a racially and ethnically segregated educational environment also deprives schoolchildren of an adequate education as required by the state constitution.

In order to provide an adequate or "proper" education, our children must be educated in a nonsegregated environment. The trial court found, "[e]ducation in its fullest sense for both white and minority school children involves interracial and multiethnic exposure to each other and interaction between them, because racial and ethnic isolation [have] negative effects on both groups." Indeed, a study commissioned by the state department of education in 1989, concluded that "desegregation has had some positive effect on the reading skills of black youngsters....

[T]here is some evidence that desegregation may help to break what can be thought of as a generational cycle of segregation and racial isolation." The study further concluded that "there are indications that desegregated schooling can provide students with valuable behavioral experience which prepares them to function in a pluralistic society.... [T]here is some evidence that school desegregation may have long-term positive consequences on adult social relationships, housing patterns, and the like."

The poor academic achievement of Hartford's students is insightful into the devastating effects of racial isolation on the students' education. For example, in 1991-92, 94 percent of the sixth graders in Hartford's public schools failed to meet the state's goal for mathematics; 80 percent failed to achieve the state's goal for reading; and 97 percent failed to obtain the state's goal for writing. Equally disturbing is the knowledge that, in that same year, 62 percent of Hartford's sixth graders failed to achieve even the state's remedial standards for reading.

Scholastic achievement scores, are but one effect of segregation on education. Children of every race and ethnic background suffer when an educational system is administered on a segregated basis. Education entails not only the teaching of reading, writing and arithmetic, but today, in our multicultural world, it also includes the development of social understanding and racial tolerance. If the mission of education is to prepare our children to survive and succeed in today's world, then they must be taught how to live together as one people. Anything less will surely result in a segregated society with one racial and ethnic community pitted against another. Instead of fostering social division, we must build an integrated society, commencing with educating our children in a nonsegregated environment.

BORDEN, J., dissenting.

The majority has reached a result driven conclusion based on a theory of constitutional liability that was never presented to the trial court or to this court, is ungrounded in the text and history of Connecticut's constitutional provisions regarding the rights to public education and equal protection of the laws and is wholly at odds with the factual record in this case.... In its zeal to reach a result that, it envisions, will eliminate racial and ethnic concentration in the public school districts of this state, the majority has "[renounced] this Court's historical commitment to a conception of the judiciary as a source of impersonal and reasoned judgments ...."

In addition, the majority sends to the legislature and the executive branch a mandate to fashion a remedy for de facto racial and ethnic concentration in our public schools, a task that those branches of government will inevitably find to be extraordinarily difficult or perhaps even impossible, because the majority articulates no principle upon which to structure such a remedy. The necessary implication of the majority's reasoning is that virtually every school district in the state is now either unconstitutional or constitutionally suspect. Without explicitly saying so, the majority has effectively struck down, not just for the greater Hartford area but for the entire state, the municipality based school system that has been in effect in this state since 1909.

I...agree that racial and ethnic isolation in our public schools is harmful-both to those races and ethnic groups that are so isolated and to the other races and ethnic groups from whom they are isolated. I also agree with the majority's statement, based upon the trial court's finding, that the racial and ethnic isolation of Hartford's schoolchildren is likely to worsen in the future. I agree, furthermore, that racial and ethnic integration of our public schools would be beneficial for all children and society in general. These points of agreement rest on the notions that, as the majority recognizes, schools are important socializing institutions that bear a central responsibility for imparting our shared democratic values to our children, and that the opportunity for children of different races, ethnic backgrounds, economic levels and social groups to get to know each other in school is important if they are to understand and respect each other. Finally, I agree with the majority that the health of the economy of our state requires an educated workforce, which includes "the urban poor as an integral part of our future economic strength." Thus, I agree with the majority on the importance in our state-indeed, in our nation-of finding a way to cross the racial divide.

The majority, however, has transformed a laudable educational philosophy into a constitutional mandate. Thus, the majority has used this court's power to interpret the constitution in order to mandate a vast and unprecedented social experiment.

The majority somehow concludes that "segregation" means de facto, as well as de jure, segregation, on the basis of the text of article first, § 20, and the history in the 1965 constitutional convention of the adoption of article eighth, § 1, and article first, § 20. The text provides no support for the majority's conclusion, and the history of the 1965 convention squarely contradicts it.

The constitution of Connecticut, article first, § 20, as amended by articles fifth and twenty-first of the amendments, provides: "No person shall be denied the equal protection of the law nor be subjected to segregation or discrimination in the exercise or enjoyment of his or her civil or political rights because of religion, race, color, ancestry, national origin, sex or physical or mental disability."... Critical to the majority's analysis is its conclusion that the phrase "because of" and the term "segregation" do not require a showing of an intent by the state to segregate or discriminate when those terms are applied to the right to public education guaranteed under article eighth, § 1. Thus, the major, albeit unstated, premise of the majority opinion is that, although "because of" and "segregation" may require a showing of an intent by the state to segregate when applied to all other "civil or political rights" covered by article first, § 20, that same language does not require such an intent when applied to public education under article eighth, § 1.

Despite the majority's futile attempt to avoid the necessary implications of its rationale, it is clear that one such necessary implication is that the language at issue either does or does not require a segregative intent when applied in other contexts. Thus, I can read this passage from the majority opinion in only two possible ways: (1) "because of" and "segregation" do not require a state intent to segregate, irrespective of the particular legal context; or (2) "because of" and "segregation" do require a state intent to segregate when applied to other legal contexts, but not when applied to public education.

The majority cannot mean that these terms do not require such an intent irrespective of the legal context. That would necessarily mean that, with respect to the exercise of all civil and political rights, the state would be required to take affirmative steps to assure that these rights are not exercised by racially or ethnically concentrated groups, regardless of any state intent to segregate. This would mean, in turn, that any electoral district that is religiously, racially or ethnically concentrated is unconstitutional and has been such since 1965, and that such was the intent of the delegates to that convention. It would also mean that presently existing public housing projects in Hartford and other cities whose tenants are racially or ethnically concentrated, not by design but as a result of demographic and economic factors over which the state has no control, are unconstitutional and have been such because the 1965 convention delegates meant them to be. It is not hyperbole to say that the delegates would be astonished to have such an intent attributed to them. Nor is it hyperbole to say that such an interpretation would be so bizarre and unworkable as to be ludicrous.

Although I disagree with the majority, I am not willing to attribute that meaning to it. It must be, therefore, that the majority means to say that, although segregative intent is required when "because of" and "segregation" are applied to other civil and political rights, it is not required when applied to public education. This, of course also necessarily means that the same language has opposite meanings when applied to different rights-an interpretation that, in my view, is also utterly implausible. Under the majority's view, therefore, the phrase "because of" and the term "segregation" have one meaning when applied to public elementary and secondary education, namely, that racial concentration need not be intentional on the part of the state, and the opposite meaning when applied to all other political and civil rights, namely, that racial concentration must be intentional.

This tortures the text of article first, § 20, and turns the process of constitutional adjudication upside down. I acknowledge that it is an accepted, necessary and appropriate part of the judicial process to stretch the meaning of language in order to render a statutory scheme constitutional. That does not justify, however, as the majority would have it, breaking constitutional language in two so that the same words in the same sentence have two opposite meanings when applied to different sets of rights, in order to render a statutory scheme unconstitutional.

The history of the term "segregation" in article first, § 20, in the 1965 convention makes even clearer than its text that the members of the convention did not intend it to mean de facto racial or ethnic concentration. It is inconceivable-except that the majority conceives it-and it is untenable to hold-except that the majority holds it-that the delegates to the 1965 constitutional convention intended the term "segregation" in that article to include de facto racial and ethnic concentration in the public schools irrespective of any state intent to bring about or to perpetuate such concentration. This question is not even close.

The trial court found that "the 1965 constitutional convention was a very conservative body that made only those changes that had to be made in order to comply with the legislative reapportionment mandates of the federal courts and it was extremely reluctant to change anything that did not have to be changed."... One cannot square this unchallenged characterization of the 1965 convention with the notion that, when in the course of accomplishing its principal objective of legislative apportionment it also adopted article first, § 20, this "very conservative" convention also intended to accomplish results that would at that time have rendered unconstitutional-or, at the very least, would have called into serious constitutional question-many school districts and general assembly districts in the state. Yet, despite what the majority may say, these are the necessary implications of its decision and rationale.

My view of the intent of the convention delegates is buttressed by the fact that, as even the plaintiffs emphasized in their posttrial brief to the trial court and in their appellate brief to this court, "[t]he documentation of racial and economic isolation in Connecticut schools in the 1960s was thorough and comprehensive." In constitutionalizing the right of Connecticut's children to a free public education, however, the politically seasoned delegates to the 1965 convention uttered not one word even suggesting that this well documented problem would be addressed by the constitutional amendments that they had gathered to draft.

If the majority's startling textual and historical conclusions are correct, it is curious that no one at the time understood what the convention had done, not even the delegates themselves.

It is a bedrock principle of our system of government that the legislative branch is the source of the fundamental public policy of the state, and that the courts may invalidate such a policy only where it is established beyond a reasonable doubt that it violates a constitutional right. Not only does the majority fail even to give lip service to this principle, the majority violates it.

Although the majority may disagree with the legislature's choices and initiatives, it cannot be maintained that reasonable people may not differ regarding the best way to reach the goal of diversity in our public schools. Indeed, in states and communities across the nation people of goodwill of all races and ethnic groups are struggling to find acceptable and feasible ways to reach and maintain that goal and, at the same time, to reach the twin goal of improving the quality of their children's education. This case, in which there are such disagreements and in which the defendants are engaged in a good faith effort to reach those goals, is the quintessential case for deference to the policy choice of the legislative branch.

NOTE

In *Brown v. Board of Education*, 347 U.S. 483 (1954), the Supreme Court of the United States ruled that racial segregation in public schools violated the Equal Protection Clause of the United States Constitution. In that momentous decision and others adhering to its principles, the Supreme Court rendered classifications based on race constitutionally suspect and subject to strict judicial scrutiny. Since then, litigation concerning racial discrimination has occurred primarily in the federal courts and has been predominantly a matter of federal constitutional law. As illustrated by *Sheff v. O'Neill*, however, in some instances state constitutional provisions may be interpreted to provide more extensive protection for equality than the Federal Constitution provides.

Some years after *Brown*, the Supreme Court drew a distinction between *de jure* and *de facto* racial segregation, ruling that the latter amounted to a violation of the Equal Protection Clause only when proven to be the result of intentional racial discrimination. In California, the state supreme court ruled otherwise, holding in a series of cases that the California equal protection clause prohibited *de facto* as well as *de jure* racial segregation in public schools and that state officials had an affirmative obligation to eradicate all forms of racial segregation in public schools. *Jackson v. Pasadena City School District*, 382 P.2d 878 (Cal. 1963); *San Francisco Unified School District v. Johnson*, 479 P.2d 669 (Cal. 1971); *Crawford v. Board of Education*, 551 P.2d 28 (Cal. 1976). In these cases, the California high court took the position that even in the absence of intentional discriminatory conduct the state constitution required the elimination of racial segregation in public schools. The force of these rulings, though, subsequently was nullified by a ballot initiative amending the state constitution. In contrast, no action has been taken to overrule *Sheff v. O'Neill*, and that decision still stands.

MALABED v. NORTH SLOPE BOROUGH
70 P.3d 416 (Alaska 2003)

BRYNER, J.

In 1997 the North Slope Borough enacted an ordinance that creates a mandatory preference for hiring, promoting, transferring, and reinstating Native Americans in borough government employment. The current version of the preference extends to all Native American applicants who are minimally qualified or meet most minimum job requirements and can meet the remaining requirements during their probationary period of employment; for purposes of the preference, "Native American" is defined to include any person belonging to an Indian tribe under federal law.

The borough enacted this preference after a study of economic conditions showed that the Native American population within the borough, specifically the resident Inupiat Eskimos, was both underemployed and earning substantially less money per capita than borough residents of other races.

Article I, section 1, of the Alaska Constitution guarantees equal protection, providing that "all persons are equal and entitled to equal rights, opportunities, and protection under the law." In addition, Article I, section 3, of the Alaska Constitution categorically prohibits discrimination based on race or national origin: "No person is to be denied the enjoyment of any civil or political right because of race, color, creed, sex, or national origin." The legislature implemented these provisions in part by enacting the Alaska Human Rights Act, which prohibits employment discrimination based on race or national origin, and AS 29.20.630, which specifically prohibits Alaska's municipalities-including home rule municipalities like the North Slope Borough-from engaging in racial and national origin discrimination. In recognition of these requirements, the borough's charter itself prohibits these forms of discrimination: "No person may be discriminated against in any borough employment because of race, age, color, political or religious affiliation, or [national] origin."

Relying on these provisions, Malabed argues that the borough's hiring preference adopts a racial classification or, alternatively, a *classification* based on national origin, in violation of the Alaska Constitution. The borough responds by denying that its preference uses a race-conscious classification; instead, the borough insists, the preference adopts a well-accepted and constitutionally permissible political classification based on membership in federally recognized tribes. In advancing this argument, the borough relies chiefly on *Morton v. Mancari* 417 U.S. 535 (1974).

In *Mancari* the Supreme Court upheld a Bureau of Indian Affairs employment preference for hiring and promoting Native Americans within the BIA. Several non-Native American employees challenged the preference, arguing that the 1972 Equal Employment Opportunity Act had repealed the BIA's statutory authority to grant hiring preferences to Native Americans and that the preference amounted to invidious racial discrimination in violation of their Fifth Amendment due process rights. But the Court found that Congress had not repealed the BIA's authority to prefer Native Americans in hiring. And after analyzing the unique historical relationship between the federal government and Native Americans, the Court concluded that the preference was not only not invidious racial discrimination but was not based on race at all.

The Court pointed out that the disputed BIA preference applied only to members of federally recognized tribes and thus excluded many individuals who were racially Native American. Noting the "unique legal status of Indian tribes under federal law" and the BIA's special interest in furthering Native American self-government, the Court held that the hiring preference was "reasonably and directly related to a legitimate, nonracially based goal."

Assuming for present purposes that the borough's ordinance reflects this kind of political classification and does not discriminate on the basis of race, the ordinance might avoid problems with the Alaska Constitution's bar against racial discrimination. But the political nature of the classification would not necessarily insulate the ordinance from Malabed's equal protection challenge. For the borough, unlike the BIA in *Mancari*, has no obvious governmental interest, as a borough, in furthering Native American self-government; and Native Americans have no explicitly established "unique legal status" under borough law, as *Mancari* found them to have under federal law. Given these disparities between federal and local law, the legitimacy of the borough's hiring preference as a political classification is less apparent than the legitimacy of the BIA's hiring preference in *Mancari*. We must therefore consider whether the ordinance's ostensibly political lines discriminate in a way that offends the Alaska Constitution's guarantee of equal protection.

We have long recognized that the Alaska Constitution's equal protection clause affords greater protection to individual rights than the United States Constitution's Fourteenth Amendment. To implement Alaska's more stringent equal protection standard, we have adopted a three-step, sliding-scale test that places a progressively greater or lesser burden on the state, depending on the importance of the individual right affected by the disputed classification and the nature of the governmental interests at stake: first, we determine the weight of the individual interest impaired by the classification; second, we examine the importance of the purposes underlying the government's action; and third, we evaluate the means employed to further those goals to determine the closeness of the means-to-end fit.

To determine how the borough's hiring preference fares under this standard, we begin by considering the importance of the individual interests implicated by the preference. Here, the borough's hiring preference impairs Malabed's right to seek and obtain employment in his profession. Under similar circumstances, we have declared the right to employment to be an important right. In *State, Departments of Transportation & Labor v. Enserch Alaska Construction, Inc.*, 787 P.2d 624 (Alaska 1989), we reviewed an equal protection challenge to an Alaska statute that provided hiring preferences to residents of economically distressed zones for employment on public works projects. A contractor building a road for the state challenged the preference as a violation of Alaska equal protection. Addressing the first step of Alaska's three-step analysis, we held that the "right to engage in an economic endeavor within a particular industry is an 'important' right for state equal protection purposes."

In the second part of the equal protection analysis we consider the borough's interests, asking whether it had important and legitimate reasons to adopt the hiring preference. The borough offers several reasons supporting its ordinance: reducing unemployment of the largest group of unemployed borough residents-Inupiat Eskimos; strengthening the borough's economy; and training its workforce. But we found comparable governmental interests insufficient in *Enserch*. There the state tried to establish an important and legitimate governmental interest by arguing that the challenged hiring preference reduced unemployment, remedied social harms resulting from chronic unemployment, and assisted economically disadvantaged residents. Though acknowledging these interests as important, we found them to be illegitimate because they favored one class of Alaskans over another:

> While these goals are important, they conceal the underlying objective of economically assisting one class over another. We have held that this objective is illegitimate. In *Lynden Transport, Inc. v. State*, 532 P.2d 700 (Alaska 1975), we ruled that "discrimination between residents and nonresidents based solely on the object of assisting the one class over the other economically cannot be upheld under the equal protection clause." While that case involved discrimination between state residents and nonresidents, the principle is equally applicable to discrimination among state residents. We conclude that the disparate treatment of unemployed workers in one region in order to confer an economic benefit on similarly-situated workers in another region is not a legitimate legislative goal.

Here, as in *Enserch*, it might seem that "[t]his conclusion essentially ends our inquiry." But the borough nevertheless claims a special interest in preferring to hire Native Americans (an interest not present in *Enserch*).

We reject the notion that the Alaska Constitution radiates implied guardianship powers allowing the state or its boroughs to treat Alaska Natives as if they were wards. To be sure, the United States Supreme Court has recognized implied powers in the United States Constitution that allow Congress broad latitude to legislate on behalf of Native Americans. The borough reasons that the Alaska Constitution must implicitly grant parallel powers to state and municipal governments. But the federal government's implied powers spring directly from the express powers granted to Congress in the United States Constitution's Indian Commerce and Treaty clauses.

In contrast to the federal constitution's provisions dealing with Indian tribes, the Alaska Constitution includes no provisions authorizing state action regarding Alaska Natives and so grants no express powers from which implied powers could arise. To the extent that the Alaska Constitution implies anything concerning the state's relations with Alaska Natives, then, it mirrors the constitutional drafters' well-recognized desire to treat Alaska Natives like all other Alaska citizens. The Alaska Constitution thus implies nothing that would give the borough a legitimate interest in enacting the disputed preference.

We by no means suggest that boroughs are categorically barred from adopting hiring preferences. Nor do we suggest that all state or local legislation pertaining to Alaska Natives or tribal governments should be assumed to establish suspect classifications presumptively barred by equal protection. Our focus is considerably narrower: we simply hold, in keeping with *Enserch*, that the borough has no legitimate basis to claim a general governmental interest in enacting hiring preferences favoring one class of citizens over others; and we find that the borough has failed to identify any source of a legitimate, case-specific governmental interest in the preference it actually adopted-a hiring preference favoring Native Americans. Because the borough is a political subdivision of Alaska, its legitimate sphere of municipal interest lies in governing for all of its people; preferring the economic interests of one class of its citizens at the expense of others is not a legitimate municipal interest, regardless of whether we view its ordinance as drawing distinctions founded on political status or race.

The last step of equal protection analysis under the Alaska Constitution examines the nexus between the state's asserted interests and the means selected to implement those interests. As previously mentioned, even when the state acts for important and legitimate reasons, its action must bear a close connection to those interests to justify impairing an important individual right. Here, of course, because we have found no legitimate borough interest supporting the challenged preference, we need not dwell on the closeness of its means-to-end fit. But a brief comment on the issue is nevertheless important to establish an alternative basis for our equal protection ruling.

For even assuming that the borough had legitimate and important interests in enacting a hiring preference favoring Native Americans, its preference is not closely related to attaining those interests. Addressing a similar situation in *Enserch,* we found a hiring preference in favor of residents of economically distressed areas unconstitutional under Alaska's equal protection guarantee in part because the fit between the preference and its objective was not sufficiently close. We noted that the preference failed to "prioritize relief for those areas most affected by nonresident employment" and that it set no meaningful limits on the state's power to declare any part of Alaska economically distressed at any time.

Here, the nexus between the borough's preference and its stated goals is insufficiently close for comparable reasons. The primary interest asserted by the borough lies in reducing Native American unemployment. But when viewed in light of this purpose, the borough's hiring preference is stunningly broad: it extends borough-wide and to all aspects of borough employment; is potentially limitless in duration; covers not only hiring but also promotions, transfers, and reinstatements; and applies absolutely-even to the extent of requiring Native American applicants without minimum qualifications to be hired over qualified non-Native applicants. Because the borough advances no particular reasons to justify these sweeping provisions, it fails to establish a close fit between its goals and its actions.

We conclude that the borough's hiring preference violates the Alaska Constitution's guarantee of equal protection because the borough lacks a legitimate governmental interest to enact a hiring preference favoring one class of citizens at the expense of others and because the preference it enacted is not closely tailored to meet its goals.

MATTHEWS, J., concurring.

I agree with the opinion of the court that the borough hiring preference violates the equal rights clause of the Alaska Constitution and with much of the court's reasoning. But I prefer to address directly the question whether the ordinance discriminates on the basis of race. I believe that it does, for the reasons that follow.

Inupiat Eskimos are a racial rather than a tribal group. The ordinance frankly acknowledges that its goal is to benefit them. In a prefatory clause the ordinance states "that its purpose in establishing an employment preference for Native Americans is to employ and train its Inupiat Eskimo residents in permanent, full-time positions...." Another clause sounds the same theme: "Whereas, to increase the employment of Inupiat Eskimos, the North Slope Borough would like to give an employment preference to Native Americans...." Similarly, the implementation plan for the ordinance expressly states that its purpose is to employ Inupiat Eskimo residents. Further, at oral argument counsel for the borough explained that one reason the term "Native American" was defined in terms of tribal membership was that it served to distinguish eligible Native Americans from others who are not eligible for benefits under the preference ordinance even though they may have some Native American ancestors. Tribal membership was thus used as a convenient mechanism to describe bona fide Native Americans.

Based on the above we can say with confidence that the purpose of the ordinance was to discriminate on the basis of race. Because by the express terms of the civil rights clause of the Alaska Constitution race is a suspect category, the ordinance must be subjected to strict scrutiny in order to determine whether it is permissible under the equal rights and civil rights clauses. But even if there were no clear indicators of an intent to discriminate on the basis of race, I believe that strict scrutiny would still be required because tribal membership is not only a political category but a racial one.

I reach the conclusion that state or municipal laws that grant individual benefits differentially based on tribal membership should be subject to strict scrutiny for a number of reasons. As noted, this is how we treat all race-based classifications. Further, strict scrutiny is well designed to ensure that laws remain race-neutral, as contemplated by the framers of the Alaska Constitution. This case illustrates that tribal membership readily lends itself to use as a proxy for a racial classification and as a pretext for racial discrimination. An effective tool is necessary to prevent these abuses. In addition, strict scrutiny is the approach taken by some federal courts in tribal classification cases when construing the equal protection clause of the Fourteenth Amendment to the federal constitution. Since the federal constitution contains provisions authorizing legislation on behalf of Native Americans, while the Alaska Constitution presumptively prohibits such legislation, it follows that stronger reasons exist for using the strict scrutiny method for state constitutional questions than for those arising under the federal constitution.

Although strict scrutiny review presents a high barrier, it is a barrier that may be overcome in deserving cases. It is impossible to categorize the kinds of cases that might pass strict scrutiny review. But a federal law calling on the state to give preferential treatment to tribal members would almost certainly present a compelling justification for state legislation. On balance, I believe that strict scrutiny properly accommodates the state's strong interest in preventing discrimination on the basis of race and its relatively rare and limited need to act adjunctively with the federal government in programs that favor tribal members over other state citizens.

The present ordinance does not survive strict scrutiny review. As the opinion of the court establishes, the borough had no legitimate interest, much less a compelling one, in adopting the preference. I believe therefore that the ordinance is prohibited by article I, sections 1 and 3 of the Alaska Constitution.

NOTE

In *Brackett v. Civil Service Commission*, 850 N.E.2d 533 (Mass. 2006), the Supreme Court of Massachusetts upheld an affirmative action program designed to increase the hiring and promotion of women and minorities in the state civil service. In upholding the program, the Court took the position that the standard for equal protection analysis under the Massachusetts Declaration of Rights was the same as the standard under the Federal Constitution. Following the federal standard, the court ruled that the program was justified as a means of remedying the continuing effects of past racial and gender discrimination, and therefore did not violate either the Massachusetts or Federal Constitution.

In recent years, three states--California, Michigan, and Washington-- have amended their constitutions to prohibit affirmative action programs. The California Constitution, for example, now provides that:

> The state shall not discriminate against, or grant preferential treatment to, any individual   or group on the basis of race, sex, color, ethnicity, or national origin in the operation of public employment, public education, or public contracting.

After enactment of the above provision, the Supreme Court of California found that it was contravened by an outreach program that required contractors bidding on city projects to employ a specified percentage of minority and female subcontractors. *Hi Voltage Wire Works, Inc. v. San Jose*, 12 P.3d 1068 (Cal. 2000).

C. CLASSIFICATIONS BASED ON GENDER

COMMONWEALTH v. PENNSYLVANIA INTERSCHOLASTIC ATHLETIC ASSOCIATION
334 A.2d 839 (Pa. 1975)

BLATT, J.

On November 13, 1973 the Commonwealth of Pennsylvania, acting through its Attorney General initiated suit against the Pennsylvania Interscholastic Athletic Association (PIAA) by filing a complaint in equity in this Court. The PIAA is a voluntary unincorporated association whose members include every public senior high school in this Commonwealth, except for those in Philadelphia. It also includes some public junior high schools as well as some private schools. The PIAA regulates interscholastic competition among its members in the following sports: football, cross-country, basketball, wrestling, soccer, baseball, field hockey, lacrosse, gymnastics, swimming, volleyball, golf, tennis, track, softball, archery and badminton.

The complaint here specifically challenges the constitutionality of Article XIX, Section 3B of the PIAA By-Laws which states: "Girls shall not compete or practice against boys in any athletic contest." The Commonwealth asserts that this provision violates both the equal protection clause of the Fourteenth Amendment to the United States Constitution and also Article I, Section 28 of the Pennsylvania Constitution, the so-called Equal Rights Amendment (ERA), in that it denies to female student athletes the same opportunities which are available to males to practice for and compete in interscholastic sports.

Article I, Section 28 of the Pennsylvania Constitution provides:

> Prohibition against denial or abridgment of equality of rights because of sex.

> Equality of rights under the law shall not be denied or abridged in the Commonwealth of Pennsylvania because of the sex of the individual.

Since the adoption of the ERA in the Commonwealth of Pennsylvania, the courts of this state have unfailingly rejected statutory provisions as well as case law principles which discriminate against one sex or the other. In *Conway v. Dana*, 318 A.2d 324 (1974) the court cast aside the presumption which had previously existed to the effect that the father, because of his sex, must accept the principal burden of financial support of minor children. The court there indicated that support is the equal responsibility of both parents and that, in light of the ERA, the courts must now consider the property, income, and earning capacity of both in order to determine their respective obligations.

In *Hopkins v. Blanco*, 320 A.2d 139 (1974) the court extended to the wife the right to recover damages for loss of consortium, a right previously available only to the husband. The court there stated: 'The obvious purpose of the Amendment was to put a stop to the invalid discrimination which was based on the sex of the person. The Amendment gave legal recognition to what society had long recognized, that men and women must have equal status in today's world.'

Most recently in *Henderson v. Henderson*, 327 A2d 60 (1974) the section of the Divorce Law which permitted only the wife to receive alimony pendente lite, counsel fees and expenses was ruled unconstitutional. The court in broad terms proclaimed:

> The thrust of the Equal Rights Amendment is to insure equality of rights under the law and to eliminate sex as a basis for distinction. The sex of citizens of this Commonwealth is no longer a permissible factor in the determination of their legal rights and legal responsibilities. The law will not impose different benefits

or different burdens upon the members of a society based on the fact that they may be man or woman.

Commonwealth v. Butler, 328 A.2d 851 (1974), filed on the same day as Henderson, held unconstitutional the provision of the Muncy Act which prevented trial courts from imposing a minimum sentence on women convicted of a crime. Only male criminals were subject to the minimum sentence provision.

The PIAA seeks to justify the challenged By-Law on the basis that men generally possess a higher degree of athletic ability in the traditional sports offered by most schools and that because of this, girls are given greater opportunities for participation if they compete exclusively with members of their own sex. This attempted justification can obviously have no validity with respect to those sports for which only one team exists in a school and that team's membership is limited exclusively to boys. Presently a girl who wants to compete interscholastically in that sport is given absolutely no opportunity to do so under the challenged By-Law. Although she might be sufficiently skilled to earn a position on the team, she is presently denied that position solely because of her sex. Moreover, even where separate teams are offered for boys and girls in the same sport, the most talented girls still may be denied the right to play at that level of competition which their ability might otherwise permit them. For a girl in that position, who has been relegated to the "girls' team", solely because of her sex, equality under the law has been denied.

The notion that girls as a whole are weaker and thus more injury-prone, if they compete with boys, especially in contact sports, cannot justify the By-Law in light of the ERA. Nor can we consider the argument that boys are generally more skilled. The existence of certain characteristics to a greater degree in one sex does not justify classification by sex rather than by the particular characteristic. If any individual girl is too weak, injury-prone, or unskilled, she may, of course, be excluded from competition on that basis but she cannot be excluded solely because of her sex without regard to her relevant qualifications. We believe that this is what our Supreme Court meant when it said in *Butler*, *supra*, that 'sex may no longer be accepted as an exclusive classifying tool.'

Although the Commonwealth in its complaint seeks no relief from discrimination against female athletes who may wish to participate in football and wrestling, it is apparent that there can be no valid reason for excepting those two sports from our order in this case.

For the foregoing reasons, therefore, we issue the following

ORDER

Now, the 19th day of March --, 1975, the motion of the Commonwealth for summary judgment is granted to the extent that Article XIX, Section 3B of the Pennsylvania Interscholastic Athletic Association is hereby declared unconstitutional, and the Pennsylvania Interscholastic Athletic Association is hereby ordered to permit girls to practice and compete with boys in interscholastic athletics, this order to be effective for the school year beginning in the fall of 1975 and thereafter.

BOWMAN, P.J. (dissenting).

The Supreme Court decisions cited and quoted by the majority not only bind me but have my full support and approbation. In my view, however, they do not lend the controlling support attributed to them by the majority as each of said decisions was concerned with either a statute or a previously judicially declared right or duty applicable to one sex to the exclusion of the other. There remains the question of whether the constitutional provision in question is absolute or subject to the concept of rational classification in general contexts excluding or including the role of "state action" as a controlling or influencing factor.

In deciding this case on a motion for summary judgment, the majority, in my view, has acted too soon and gone too far. I would deny plaintiff's motion for summary judgment.

NOTE

In the 1970s the Equal Rights Amendment (ERA), which would prohibit the denial or abridgement of rights on account of sex, failed to gain passage as an amendment to the Federal Constitution. However, between 1970 and 1978 fifteen states adopted constitutional amendments modeled on the ERA. They joined three other states—California, Utah, and Wyoming—whose constitutions have contained provisions expressly banning sexual discrimination since the late 1800's. By now, twenty state constitutions include equality provisions that expressly prohibit discrimination on the basis of sex.

In most states whose constitutions contain a provision expressly proscribing discrimination on the basis of sex, the courts take a strong stance against gender discrimination. The Supreme Court of Washington has taken an especially forceful stance regarding the ERA in declaring that:

> The ERA absolutely prohibits discrimination on the basis of sex and is not subject to even the narrow exceptions permitted under traditional "strict scrutiny"....The ERA mandates equality in the strongest of terms and absolutely prohibits the sacrifice of equality for any state interest, no matter how compelling. *Southwest Washington Chapter, National Electric Contractors Association v. Pierce County*, 667 P.2d 1092, 1102 (Wash. 1983).

A few courts in other states take a nearly absolutist approach to the ERA by ruling that classifications based on gender are prohibited except when necessitated by physical differences between the sexes. Most states that have adopted the ERA, however, take the position that the ERA elevates gender to a suspect classification calling for strict judicial scrutiny of any law that classifies persons on the basis of sex. In one or two states that have adopted a version of the ERA, the courts use an intermediate level of scrutiny to assess gender classifications.

In states whose constitutions do not contain a provision expressly barring sex discrimination, the courts tend to follow the federal approach of using intermediate scrutiny to review classifications based on gender. Some of these states have found that intermediate scrutiny can be an effective means to combat sexual discrimination. For example, in West Virginia, which has not adopted the ERA, the state supreme court used intermediate scrutiny in ruling that the state due process clause, which encompasses an equal protection principle, was violated by a regulation barring girls from playing on high school baseball teams. *Israel v. West Virginia Secondary Schools Activities Commission*, 388 S.E.2d 480 (1989). In striking down the regulation, the court stated that the purpose of the equal protection principle was "to avoid this type of artificial distinction based solely on gender."

Intermediate scrutiny, though, has its limits, and occasionally is used to uphold gender classifications that might be struck down under strict scrutiny. For instance, in *O'Connor v. Board of Education of School Dist. No. 23*, 645 F.2d 578 (7th Cir. 1981), the court employed intermediate scrutiny in upholding a junior high school regulation barring girls from playing on the boys' interscholastic basketball team. Although there was a separate girls' basketball team, it functioned at a lower level of competition than the boys' team and therefore did not offer an equivalent opportunity for the development of athletic skills. Given the substantial disparity between the girls' and boys' teams, it is questionable whether the regulation could have survived strict scrutiny.

GRIFFIN v. CRANE
716 A.2d 1029 (Md. 1998)

BELL, C.J.

James M. Giffin, the petitioner, and Donna L. (Valtri) Crane, the respondent, the parents of two daughters... separated in May, 1992, after more than 12 years of marriage. At separation, the petitioner and the parties' two daughters remained in the marital home, while the respondent lived nearby and maintained regular visitation with the children. A year later, the respondent moved to Louisville, Kentucky.... Both parties sought to obtain a divorce. The petitioner and the respondent both asked for custody of the two children... The custody and visitation issues were resolved by the parties when they entered into...a written agreement... (providing that the petitioner shall have sole physical custody of the children.) The agreement contemplated the possibility of annual reviews of the residential status of the children.

(In 1995, the respondent requested a review of the children's residential status.) A hearing was held on the respondent's motion, during which the court, over a span of six days, received testimony from more than twenty witnesses and viewed a number of exhibits, including private investigators' reports and a videotape. At that hearing, the interests of the children were represented by an attorney appointed by the court. The court granted the respondent's Petition for Modification of Residential Custody, thus modifying the custody agreement by transferring custody of the children from their father to their mother.

The petitioner appealed the judgment to the Court of Special Appeals. He argued in that court that the trial court erred by considering the sex of the parents as a factor in its determination of custody. In an unreported opinion, the intermediate appellate court held, inter alia, that "[t]he consideration of gender was a valid consideration in determining residential custody in this case." In response, the petitioner filed a petition for a writ of certiorari, which this Court granted.

The question that we must decide is whether, in a child custody proceeding, the sex of either parent is a legitimate and proper consideration in determining which of them is the appropriate residential custodian. It is an issue in this case because of some of the language the trial court used to explain its custody decision. As we have seen, the court opined:

> [T]he Court gleans from ... the testimony from at least one expert in this case relative to a girl child having particular need for her mother has seemed to come to the fore and is a necessary factor in my determinations in this case ... The Court feels that the best interests of the children ... as exemplified by the reaching an age where Emily at the very least exemplifies a need for a female hand, causes the Court to come to the conclusion that the children should reside with their mother.

When one considers the trial court's explanation of its decision, it is clear, unambiguously so, that the court was relying on the respondent's gender as the decisive basis for modifying the custody order.

Maryland's Equal Rights Amendment, Article 46 of the Maryland Declaration of Rights, provides: "Equality of rights under the law shall not be abridged or denied because of sex." The words of the Equal Rights Amendment are clear, unambiguous and unequivocal; the Amendment "mandated equality of rights under the law and rendered state-sanctioned sex-based classifications suspect." *State v. Burning Tree Club, Inc.*, 554 A.2d 366, 374 (Md. 1989).

The basic principle of the Maryland Equal Rights Amendment, thus, is that sex is not a permissible factor in determining the legal rights of women, or men, so that the treatment of any person by the law may not be based upon the circumstance that such person is of one sex or the other.... (T)his constitutional provision drastically altered traditional views of the validity of sex-based classifications imposed under the law, and was cogent evidence that the people of Maryland were fully committed to equal rights for men and women. (T)he equality between the sexes demanded by the Maryland Equal Rights Amendment focuses on "rights" of individuals "under the law," which encompasses all forms of privileges, immunities, benefits and responsibilities of citizens. As to these, the Maryland E.R.A. absolutely forbids the determination of such "rights," as may be accorded by law, solely on the basis of one's sex, i.e., sex is an impermissible factor in making any such determination. It is clear, therefore, that the Equal Rights Amendment flatly prohibits gender-based classifications, absent substantial justification, whether contained in legislative enactments, governmental policies, or by application of common law rules.

Although this Court has not had the occasion to address the issue this case presents, our cases since the adoption of the Equal Rights Amendment and the Legislature's action in enacting the Family Law Article make clear what the proper result should be. As we have seen, this Court has interpreted the Amendment's "broad, sweeping mandatory language" as the expression of Maryland's commitment to equal rights for men and women and the statement of its intention to alter traditional attitudes with respect to such rights.

At issue in *Rand v. Rand*, 374 A.2d 900, 904-05 (Md. 1977), was the validity, in light of the Maryland Equal Rights Amendment, of the common law rule that placed the primary liability for the support of minor children on the father. Holding the rule irreconcilable with the E.R.A., we concluded that the "parental obligation for child support is not primarily an obligation of the father, but is one shared by both parents." Another common law rule was at issue in *Kline v. Ansell*, 414 A.2d 929, 933 (Md. 1980), that only men could sue or be sued for criminal conversation. We held that the rule violated the Equal Rights Amendment, explaining that it "provides different benefits for and imposes different burdens upon its citizens based solely upon their sex." In *Condore v. Prince George's Co.*, 425 A.2d 1011 (Md. 1981), we held that the common law doctrine of necessaries, which obligated the husband, but not the wife, to pay for his spouse's necessaries, violated the Equal Rights Amendment. Noting the Court's consistent holdings "that a law that imposes different benefits and different burdens upon persons based solely upon their sex violates the Maryland E.R.A.," this Court, in *Turner v. State*, 474 A.2d 1297, 1302 (Md. 1984), invalidated a criminal statute which prohibited the employment by taverns of so-called female sitters to solicit customers to purchase drinks. We pointed out that, under the statute, a man could be employed as a sitter but a woman could not.

This Court's custody decision in *Elza v. Elza*, 475 A.2d 1180 (Md. 1984), is also instructive, as is the Legislature's recodification, as a part of Code Revision, of former Article 72A § 1. The issue in Elza was the validity of the maternal preference presumption and whether the trial court in a child custody proceeding erred in basing its award of custody to the mother solely on it. Stating that the 1974 amendment to Art. 72A, § 1, by providing, clearly and unambiguously, that "neither parent shall be given preference solely because of his or her sex," expressed the intent of the General Assembly to eradicate sex as a factor in child custody proceedings, this Court abolished the maternal preference doctrine in this State because it permitted custody to be awarded solely on the basis of the mother's sex.

The Pennsylvania Supreme Court, in *Commonwealth ex rel. Spriggs v. Carson*, 368 A.2d 635 (Pa. 1977), held that the "tender years" doctrine, which is Pennsylvania's equivalent of Maryland's maternal preference doctrine, was abolished by that State's E.R.A. The "tender years" doctrine, in essence, maintains that, in a child custody dispute, where a child is of tender years, the mother is presumed to be the more fit parent. The court in *Spriggs* struck down that presumption, stating:

> We ... question the legitimacy of a doctrine that is predicated upon traditional or stereotypic roles of men and women in a marital union. Whether the tender years doctrine is employed to create a presumption which requires the male parent to overcome its effect by presenting compelling contrary evidence of a particular nature, or merely as a makeshift where the scales are relatively balanced, such a view is offensive to the concept of the equality of the sexes which we have embraced as a constitutional principle within this jurisdiction. Courts should be wary of deciding matters as sensitive as questions of custody by the invocation of 'presumptions'. Instead, we believe that our courts should inquire into the circumstances and relationships of all the parties involved and reach a determination based solely upon the facts of the case then before the Court."

The trial court erred, as a matter of law, in the instant case; it assumed that the respondent necessarily would be a better custodian solely because she has a female hand, and that a girl child of a certain age has a particular and specific need to be with her same sex parent. In so doing, the trial court applied an invalid legal principle. A review of the record of the hearing reveals that, but for the trial court's perception of the need for a female hand for a girl child of Emily's age, that it believed each parent would be a proper and fit custodian. Indeed, that sex-based reason for the custody award to the respondent was the only reason given for the court's decision. Therefore, we will remand the case to the circuit court for further proceedings in that court.... The trial court will be required, of course, on remand once again to consider the best interest of the children in deciding their custody and it must fully set forth and explain the reasons for its decision, consistent with this opinion.

McAULIFFE, J., dissenting.

I cannot agree that the record in this case discloses an impermissible use of gender by the chancellor in the determination of this custody dispute. I would agree that the oral opinion of the chancellor, delivered from the bench after six days of trial, is perhaps inelegant and lacking in as complete a discussion of the rationale for the decision as may have been desired, but viewed in the context of the testimony and of prior statements of the chancellor, it is clear to me that the references to gender related to appropriate considerations.

What is important to understand in this case is that the witnesses were not saying that an adolescent daughter is always better able to communicate with her mother than father, or that there is always an emotional need of a daughter to be with her mother. What was said was in the context of this mother and this daughter, and not some stereotypical figures. In discussing the particular need that existed in this case, the witnesses simply noted that the situation was hardly atypical, and often occurred between a child and the same-sex parent. This is a far cry from establishing a preference or presumption based on gender.

Judges should be precluded from concluding that a special relationship, bonding, or ability to communicate between a parent and a child exists solely on the basis that the parent and child are of the same sex; judges should not be precluded from finding the existence of such a relationship from the facts of the case, even though that relationship may have resulted in part from the reality that the parent and child are of the same sex.

In addition to my disagreement with the interpretation the majority gives to the chancellor's remarks, I dissent because I am concerned that the tone of the majority's opinion may cause trial judges to shy away from perfectly valid and important case-specific findings merely because those findings reflect relationships and needs that are consistent with a particular parent and child being of the same sex.

STATE v. RIVERA
612 P.2d 526 (Haw. 1980)

OGATA, J.

Appellant was convicted of first degree rape under HRS s 707-730 (1976). The applicable statute was amended as of June 26, 1979 and as we understand appellant he would have no equal protection challenge to the new statute. The purpose of the amendment was to restate the statutory provisions in gender-neutral terms.... Appellant challenges the constitutionality of HRS s 707-730 prior to its amendment, and claims that, by its terms, it denied him the equal protection of the law by punishing only men and no women, and protecting only women and no men, thus violating the equal protection guarantees of the Fourteenth Amendment of the United States Constitution and Article I, Section 4 of the Hawaii State Constitution and the equal rights amendment, Article I, Section 21, of the Hawaii State Constitution (ERA).

To withstand judicial scrutiny under the equal protection clause, a sex-based distinction must serve governmental objectives and must be substantially related to achievement of those objectives. Under this principle, the question is whether the sex-based classification in the former rape law served an important governmental objective and was substantially related to achievement of that objective. We find that it plainly met the test.

Although the statute sets up a gender-based classification by defining rape as an offense which can be committed only by a male, it reflects a legislative judgment as to the degree of harm posed to potential victims of nonconsensual intercourse. "While we recognize that it is possible for females to commit a sex offense which might be deemed rape, the fact remains that historically and generally rape is a crime committed by males against females." *Moore v. Cowan*, 560 F.2d 1298, 1303 (6th Cir. 1977). The legislature chose to selectively deal with the act of forced intercourse by men upon women as a more significant societal problem where the need for proscription was clearest. Protecting women from nonconsensual intercourse is an important legislative objective. And a law which punishes males for nonconsensual intercourse with women against their will is substantially related to that objective. Appellant's contentions might be more persuasive if he had provided us with empirical data tending to show that female rapes of males presented a social problem. In *West Coast Hotel Co. v. Parrish*, 300 U.S. 379 (1937), the United States Supreme Court restated the principle that "(i)f 'the law presumably hits the evil where it is most felt, it is not to be overthrown because there are other instances to which it might have been applied.'" We are dealing with a criminal sex offense statute. We are not dealing with an overbroad generalization based on sex which is entirely irrelevant to any difference between men and women or which demeans the ability or status of the affected class. The courts have been reluctant in striking down criminal sex laws and all have upheld rape statutes against constitutional challenges.

Appellant claims that because Article I, Section 4, now Article I, Section 5, of the Hawaii State Constitution specifically enumerates sex along with race, religion and ancestry, this specific enumeration requires a more stringent test than that required by the Fourteenth Amendment. Moreover, the ERA, which, by its terms forbids classifications based on sex, is said to necessitate a judicial standard of review at least as high as the "strict scrutiny" standard under equal protection analysis.

Not even the ERA, however, forbids all classifications. "The fundamental legal principle underlying the ERA…is that the law must deal with particular attributes of individuals ...." A classification based on a physical characteristic unique to one sex is not an impermissive under- or over-inclusive classification because the differentiation is based on the unique presence of a physical characteristic in one sex and not based on an averaging of a trait or characteristic which exists in both sexes. Two frequently-cited examples are laws relating to wet nurses, which would apply to all or some women but no men; or laws regulating sperm donation which would apply to all or some men, but no women.

Rape was defined in HRS s 707-730 (1976) as a male engaging in "sexual intercourse, by forcible compulsion, with a female." A sex-based distinction existed in the former rape statute but the differentiation in treatment was based upon unique physical characteristics of men and women and the unique characteristics justified the classification. Insofar as rape was defined as forced intercourse by a male with a female, it was based on a physiological characteristic unique to males. Furthermore, as the court stated in *Finley v. State*, 527 S.W.2d at 556 "(h)ymen and uterine injury to female rape victims, the possibility of pregnancy, and the physiological difficulty of a woman forcing a man to have sexual intercourse with her all suggest a justification for the sexual distinction." It has also been said that "(s)o long as the law deals only with a characteristic found in all (or some) women but no men, or in all (or some) men but no women, it does not ignore individual characteristics found in both sexes ...." As such, the statute neither denied equal rights to men nor did it violate the ERA.

D. CLASSIFICATIONS BASED ON AGE

O'NEILL v. BANE
568 S.W.2d 761 (Mo. 1978)

SIMEONE, J.

This is an appeal from a judgment of the Circuit Court of St. Louis County entered on May 4, 1978, holding that s 476.458, RSMo 1976 Supp., requiring mandatory retirement for magistrate and probate judges at age seventy, is unconstitutional as violative of equal protection and due process. Amend. XIV, U.S.Const., Art. I, ss 2 and 10, Mo. Const.... For reasons hereinafter stated, we hold that the statute is not unconstitutional and does not violate equal protection or due process and reverse the judgment of the trial court.

The sole question for our determination is the constitutionality of the mandatory retirement statute relating to magistrate and probate judges embodied in s 476.458 adopted in 1976. In passing, we note that Judge O'Neil has rendered many years of faithful and competent service to the citizens of this state, and especially to the citizens of St. Louis County. He continues to do so. We are aware that although the passage of time has added years to Judge O'Neil's age, it has not lessened his legal abilities. We recognize, as did the several witnesses at the hearing that Judge O'Neil is competent both physically and mentally, that his health is generally good, that he is very competent and that he desires to continue to serve the public.

But those factors do not control the issue. The constitutionality of legislation cannot be determined on an individual basis. The facts are that Judge O'Neil became seventy years of age on November 5, 1977, and has served more than twelve years, and will, on December 31, 1978, complete his term.

In recent years, compulsory retirement systems have come under constitutional attack. Equal protection and due process challenges have been made in a great number of decisions and in a great variety of contexts. In *Massachusetts Bd. of Retirement v. Murgia*, 427 U.S. 307 (1976), the Supreme Court of the United States upheld a Massachusetts compulsory retirement statute relating to a state police officer, which required state police officers to retire at age 50. The Court held (1) that the proper standard of judicial review of the equal protection claim was not "strict scrutiny" but the traditional rational basis test wherein classifications are constitutional if they bear a rational relationship to a permissible state interest; and (2) that the compulsory retirement provision involved satisfied the rational basis standard.... The standard which we must utilize in the instant case is therefore the rational basis test.

Mandatory retirement provisions are recognized by private industry, by state governments and by the federal system under recent legislative amendments. Mandatory retirement systems perform beneficial societal functions. The justification most commonly offered for mandatory retirement schemes is that there is a reasonable connection between increased age and declining job capabilities so that mandatory retirement is a convenient method of insuring an effective and productive work force.

Because there are rational bases for the statute, we hold that s 476.458 is not violative of equal protection or due process.... Several rational bases related to the furtherance of a legitimate state interest are implied in the statute and are clearly recognizable.

First, s 476.458, "marks a stage" in life at which judges must end their regular, daily judicial duties. Judges serve in a sensitive position. Judges' decisions affect many aspects of peoples' lives and property. Judges must be able to adapt to changes in the law and in society. Judges are held to the highest possible standards.

Our citizens are entitled to a judicial system of the highest caliber and to judges with the highest possible mental and physical qualifications. Mandatory judicial retirement is an attempt by the General Assembly to insure the fitness of the judiciary as a whole and to insure the continued competency of the system. The General Assembly in adopting the statute dealt in probabilities. That is all humans can do. There are certain ages in life, learned from experience, at which there is a lessening in mental, physical abilities. If mandatory retirement is invalid at age 70, then at what age 80, 90, or 100? To paraphrase Holmes, in life, one must make choices. That is what the General Assembly did. The statute draws a line at a certain age which attempts to uphold the high competency for judicial posts and which fulfills a societal demand for the highest caliber of judges in the system. The statute is an attempt to insure that, on the whole, only those judges who have the vigor, health and vitality will carry out the public's work in administering justice. The function of mandatory retirement is to permit the withdrawal from the bench that group of judges in which disabilities related to aging are most likely to occur.

Second, the statute which is presumptively valid draws a legitimate line to avoid the tedious and often perplexing decisions to determine which judges after a certain age are physically and mentally qualified and those who are not. A mandatory provision avoids these traumatic and often lengthy hearings.

Third, mandatory retirement increases the opportunity for qualified persons men and women alike to share in the judiciary and permits an orderly attrition through retirement.

Such a provision not only achieves the maximum in qualified judicial personnel, but equally important widens the opportunities for qualified younger members of the Bar to seek a judicial post.... (A) state might prescribe a mandatory retirement for judges in order to "open up" judicial opportunities for younger lawyers and to bring young persons with fresh ideas and techniques into the system.

Fourth, such a mandatory provision also assures predictability and ease in establishing and administering judge's pension plans. The General Assembly, having the constitutional power to do so, has established a comprehensive retirement plan for judges based on retirement at age 70. As a corollary, the General Assembly must be able to plan and determine the amount of appropriations necessary to fulfill the statutory benefits provided for the retirement of judges.

Furthermore, we know that age seventy is an age a time of life which is recognized by society as being "about" the time when the physical and mental processes weaken among many men and women. That recognition is embodied in statutes, in private retirement systems and in the policy of the Congress. All of this, and more, is embodied in the policy of s 476.458.

In sum, we conclude that compulsory retirement of magistrate and probate judges at age seventy embodied in the statute is rationally related to the fulfillment of several legitimate state objectives and hence the statute does not violate equal protection.... (W)e hold that s 476.458 is not violative of the equal protection or due process clauses of the Federal or Missouri Constitutions and hence is constitutional.

In reaching this conclusion we are aware of the substantial contributions that our elderly citizens make to society and "we do not make light of the substantial economic and psychological effects...compulsory retirement can have on an individual...." Retirement can well be a time of life of many useful pursuits. In short "age is not a cage" but a time of life when many new things can be accomplished. But in determining the provisions for mandatory retirement embodied in s 476.458., the General Assembly has weighed these personal considerations against the social goals which compulsory retirement furthers. In this instance we will not intrude into the legislative prerogative and strike down a legislative choice.

NOTE

In *Maddux v. Blagojevich*, 911 N.E.2d 979 (Ill. 2009), the Supreme Court of Illinois struck down a state statute mandating the retirement of judges at age 75. Although the state constitution contained a provision authorizing the General Assembly to provide by law for the retirement of judges at a prescribed age, the court nonetheless found that the statute in question violated the constitutional requirement of equal protection of the laws. In striking down the statute, the court noted that it mandated retirement of judges at 75 while other persons 75 and older could run for and hold judicial office:

> Consider the situation of a 76-year-old citizen who has never held judicial office. If that person runs for judicial office and wins, he would *never* face the prospect of compulsory retirement because, under the Act's operation, automatic retirement occurs "at the expiration of the term in which the judge attains the age of 75." There would never be a "term in which" such a judge would "attain the age of 75." (The same would, of course, be true for a judge who left judicial office before turning 75, who then ran for election after turning 76.) The successful candidate in this scenario would fall outside the statute's language and would be eligible for retention at the conclusion of the term. Mandatory retirement would exist for some, but not all, judges because there would exist a class of judges who would be immune from the mandatory retirement envisioned under the Act.

The Act, therefore, does nothing to advance the goal of insuring a "more vigorous judiciary" since it would allow for people older than 75 years to serve terms of 6 and possibly 10 years. More importantly, the Act creates an irrational classification that could not, in terms of equal protection, withstand scrutiny under our state constitution. Equal protection requires that similarly situated individuals will be treated similarly unless the government can demonstrate an appropriate reason to do otherwise. In cases like this one, where the statutory classification at issue does not involve fundamental rights, courts employ "rational basis scrutiny" to determine whether the classification bears a rational relation to a legitimate purpose.

There is no rational basis upon which the legislature can prevent 75-year-old or older *former judges* from running in an election, but not citizens 75 years old or older *who were never judges* when the disqualifying characteristic is age. If the legitimate state interest is to insure a "vigorous judiciary," the classification we describe above cannot be deemed rationally related to that purpose. We stress again that if age defines ability (and both the constitutional and legislative history indicate that it was believed that it does), either *all* those 75 years of age or older are unfit or they are not. No presumption of constitutionality could save legislation like this that so blatantly violates equal protection.

Legislation is presumed constitutional and must be construed as not offending the constitution, provided, of course, that the construction is reasonable. This presumption, however, is only the starting point in constitutional analysis; it is not outcome determinative. Thus, notwithstanding a statute's presumption of constitutionality, this court has acknowledged its "power to strike down" legislation when it is "violative of the clear requirements of the constitution."

As we have explained, the judicial article allows for the General Assembly to enact mandatory judicial retirement legislation; however, the plain language of the specific legislation that has been enacted pursuant to the constitution violates equal protection. Moreover, as it is written, it allows certain judges to avoid mandatory retirement. This court is mindful that restraint is called for when presented with challenges to the constitutionality of legislation enacted pursuant to a specific grant of constitutional authority. But we cannot be reluctant to invalidate legislation that either goes beyond the specific grant of authority or is otherwise inconsistent with our constitution....

We have determined that the Act as written is unconstitutional. It is, of course, the General Assembly's prerogative, to attempt to reenact mandatory judicial retirement legislation. Our holding today recognizes this authority. It is also fair to acknowledge, however, the difficulty in exercising that discretion where retirement is linked to age absent a corresponding constitutional age ceiling...which would disqualify a person from running for judicial office.

ARNESON v. STATE
864 P.2d 1245 (Mont. 1993)

R.C. McDONOUGH, J.

This is an appeal from the decision of the District Court of the First Judicial District, Lewis and Clark County, concluding that § 19-20-711, MCA) is unconstitutional to the extent that it employed an unreasonable classification in violation of the equal protection clause of the Montana Constitution, Article II, Section 4. We affirm.

In 1989 the legislature passed Chapter 115 Session Laws of 1989 which, for its purpose, provided for a post-retirement adjustment increase in the pensions of the beneficiaries of the Teachers' Retirement System. The law provided that to be eligible for the adjustment, retirees or their beneficiaries must be 55 years of age or older; or, irrespective of age, all those receiving disability or survivorship benefits.

The respondent's benefit was derived from her mother, who was a member of the Teachers' Retirement System, and who had reached retirement age and retired. The mother selected the retirement option that would permit benefits to be paid to her for her lifetime and upon her death continue through the life of her beneficiary (respondent). The mother died shortly after her retirement and the respondent began receiving the benefits. The respondent is 31 years of age.... Being under 55 years of age she did not receive the adjustment. However, if her mother had continued to work and died while working the respondent would be considered a survivor and would receive the adjustment even though she was 31 years of age.

This statute, under the equal protection question, does not come under the strict scrutiny test because strict scrutiny of a legislative classification is required only when the classification impermissibly interferes with the exercise of a fundamental right or operates to a peculiar disadvantage of a suspect class. Here the respondent is not a member of a suspect class nor is a fundamental right involved.

The respondent urges us to adopt the middle-level scrutiny test.... The middle-level scrutiny test has been recently applied by the U.S. Supreme Court in discussing cases involving such things as gender, alienage and illegitimacy, but the court has specifically refused to invoke it involving age and has applied the rational test thereto.... We have previously declined to apply the middle tier scrutiny test to an "age plus" classification, absent a constitutionally based benefit. We also decline to apply it here.... The District Court applied the lowest level of scrutiny, the rational basis test, which determines whether the classification is rationally related to furthering a legitimate state purpose.... We will also apply the rational basis test.

The purpose of this law is to grant to the Retirement System beneficiaries, retirees' survivors, and disabled, an amount to alleviate the eroding effect of inflation on their pension. Both the survivor of an employee and the beneficiary of an employee who has retired, are subject to the effect of inflation. But the classification as to who is to receive the post-retirement adjustment does not include the respondent who is the beneficiary of a former employee who had retired. As a result, this legislation is "under inclusive." This differentiation does not create a reasonable classification between such ultimate adult survivor and adult beneficiary. They are both similarly situated with respect to the purpose of this law.

The respondent states that there is no possible purpose which can be conceived to justify such a classification considering the overall purpose of the legislation of post-retirement adjustment to compensate for inflation. The respondent contends no distinction should be made between a beneficiary of a retired employee and the beneficiary of an employee who died while working when the beneficiaries are both under the age of 55. We agree.

We are unable to find any rational relationship to the purpose of the legislation for the establishment of such a classification. It is wholly arbitrary and an example of the legislature picking and choosing who will receive benefits. Such a classification must distinguish one class from another taking into consideration the purpose of the statute.

The granting of a post-retirement adjustment does not come within the approach of considering whether the enactment is experimental or piecemeal, and therefore applying the legislation to one phase of the problem and not affecting others. As we stated above, the legislature cannot arbitrarily pick and choose. The appellant has made such an argument on a money saving basis, but even if the governmental purpose is to save money, it cannot be done on a wholly arbitrary basis. The classification must have some rational relationship to the purpose of the legislation. There is nothing in the record or by conjecture which would justify the differentiation here.

There is no reasonable basis to the classification which permits an adult beneficiary of a disabled or deceased member to receive the adjustment regardless of age, and deny the adult beneficiary of a deceased service retiree who retired under voluntary or involuntary circumstances the adjustment because the beneficiary is under 55 years of age. The constitutional defect of the statute as applied to respondent is revealed when it is reviewed in light of its practical application. We conclude that its application to this respondent whereby the classification excludes her from receiving the post-retirement adjustment, is unconstitutional and in violation of Article II, Section 4 of the Montana Constitution.

TRIEWEILER, J., concurring.

I rejoice at the majority's re-discovery of the rights provided for in the Equal Protection Clause of Article II, Section 4, of Montana's Constitution. However, I find it peculiar that nowhere in the majority's opinion is any mention made of the majority's decision in *Stratemeyer v. MACO Workers' Compensation Trust* (Mont.1993), 855 P.2d 506. Perhaps that is because the result in this case cannot be reconciled with the majority's decision in *Stratemeyer*. That is because under *Stratemeyer* there is no legislative classification which won't satisfy the toothless rational basis test.

This same majority held in *Stratemeyer* that even where no rational basis for a legislative classification is established by the Legislature or proven in district court, this Court can speculate about why the Legislature acted as it did, and that speculation can serve as the basis for overcoming a constitutional challenge. This Court went on to add that even when the State offers no evidence to justify a legislative classification, a person challenging the legislation has the burden of proving that there is no rational basis. In other words, under the *Stratemeyer* decision, a citizen victimized by legislative discrimination has to, first of all, imagine every conceivable basis for that discrimination about which this Court might speculate and then somehow disprove it. This Court then went on in *Stratemeyer* to conclude that a justification for the classification at issue in that case could have been the Legislature's intention to save money, even though there was no evidence in the record that the classification would save money. This Court held that:

> The exclusion of mental claims rationally relates to the *possible goal* of reducing costs and having a viable program for the State and the enrolled employers and employees in the workers' compensation field. [Emphasis added]. *Stratemeyer*, 855 P.2d at 511.

Certainly, by that standard the classification in this case passes any rational basis test. Who can dispute that discriminating against beneficiaries under a certain age "relates to the possible goal of reducing costs" for the teachers' retirement system?

I, of course, have no regard for the *Stratemeyer* decision. I would not follow it and will urge its early demise at every opportunity.... The majority, however, has neither followed it, distinguished it, nor overruled it. Therefore, its decision in this case is both legally and intellectually inconsistent.

I believe that the right to be free from discrimination based on age is a significant enough right that classifications based on age warrant middle-tier scrutiny.... A need exists to develop a meaningful middle-tier analysis. Equal protection of law is an essential underpinning of this free society. The old rational basis test allows government to discriminate among classes of people for the most whimsical reasons.

According to the laws of Montana, age is a "sensitive" if not "suspect" basis for classification. To hold otherwise would be to ignore the import of the Montana Human Rights Act which provides that "[t]he right to be free from discrimination because of ... age ... is recognized as and declared to be a civil right." Accordingly, I would hold that statutory classifications based upon age involve a sensitive basis for classification and warrant a middle-tier test for determining whether they violate the Equal Protection Clause of Montana's Constitution.

D.P. v STATE
705 So.2d 593 (Fla. 1997)

COPE, J.

Dade County passed a comprehensive anti-graffiti ordinance, which forbids the sale to minors of spray paint cans and broadtipped markers ("jumbo markers"). The ordinance provides that minors can possess spray paint or jumbo markers on public property only if accompanied by a responsible adult. On private property, the minor must have the consent of the property owner, but need not be accompanied by an adult. It is a misdemeanor for a minor to possess spray paint or a jumbo marker without the required supervision or consent. D.P. challenges the facial constitutionality of the provisions of the anti-graffiti ordinance that restrict minors' possession of spray paint or jumbo markers. We conclude that the ordinance is constitutional and affirm the adjudication of delinquency.

D.P. argues that the ordinance violates the due process clauses of the state and federal constitutions because the ordinance imposes a criminal penalty for a minor's possession of spray paint or jumbo markers without the State being required to show that the minor had any criminal intent. D.P. reasons that spray paint and jumbo markers are ordinary household items that have legitimate uses. D.P. urges that it is impermissible for the County to criminalize simple possession of ordinary household objects.

D.P. suggests that in its attack on graffiti, the County has two viable alternatives. First, the County can impose a criminal penalty for possession of spray paint or jumbo markers with intent to make graffiti. The anti-graffiti ordinance already does this. Alternatively, D.P. states that the County could constitutionally place a total ban on possession and sale of spray paint and jumbo markers by anyone, adult or minor. This is an approach that was taken in the City of Chicago and was held constitutional. *See National Paint & Coating Association v. City of Chicago*, 45 F.3d 1124, 1126 (7th Cir. 1995). D.P. reasons that if spray paint and jumbo markers cannot legally be purchased or possessed by anyone, then there would be no such thing as innocent possession of spray paint or jumbo markers. It would follow, therefore, that a criminal penalty could be imposed for possession of the forbidden objects. D.P. reasons, however, that so long as spray paint and jumbo markers are available in households in Dade County (because spray paint and jumbo markers can be lawfully purchased by adults), it follows that the County cannot impose a criminal penalty on minors for possession of the same household objects.

In our view, the anti-graffiti ordinance passes constitutional muster. In the first place, this ordinance does not place an outright ban on possession of spray paint or jumbo markers by minors. The ordinance allows a minor to possess these items on public property, so long as the minor is accompanied by a responsible adult. Possession is allowed on private property so long as the minor has the consent of the owner. Rather than imposing an outright ban, the ordinance simply requires that possession be with supervision.

D.P. concedes that the County could constitutionally pass an ordinance that totally banned all spray paint and jumbo markers. Under this approach, which was taken in Chicago, no one (adult or minor) could buy or possess spray paint or jumbo markers anywhere in Dade County. If a total ban is permissible, then surely it is permissible to take the less extreme measure of prohibiting sales to minors and allowing possession only with supervision.[6]

D.P. suggests that it is impermissible to treat minors differently than adults. That suggestion is clearly incorrect. There are many activities that are legal for adults but prohibited to minors: drinking, and driving under legal age, being the most obvious examples. Some supervisory requirements apply to minors that do not apply to adults, such as compulsory school attendance and the curfew ordinance. In the trial court order holding the ordinance to be constitutional, the Judge Petersen said:

> Having considered the cases and authorities cited by the Juvenile, this Court finds that the analysis under the due process and equal protection provisions of the Florida Constitution do not differ in a manner that changes the result of this case from the analysis under ... the United States constitution. Indeed, the cases cited by the Juvenile referred interchangeably to Florida and Federal due process and equal protection provisions.

No fundamental right is implicated in the possession of spray paint and jumbo markers. Nor is youth a suspect classification. *White Egret Condominium, Inc. v. Franklin,* 379 So.2d 346, 351 (Fla.1979) ("The law is now clear that restriction of individual rights on the basis of age need not pass the strict scrutiny test, and therefore age is not a suspect class."); Metropolitan Dade County v. Pred, 665 So.2d 252 (Fla. 3d DCA 1995)[, review denied, 676 So.2d 413 (Fla.1996)]. ("[U]nder both the Florida and United States Constitution, children, due to their special nature and vulnerabilities, do not enjoy the same quantum or quality of rights as adults.").

The Court's review is therefore limited to the rational basis test. The rational basis test does not turn on whether this Court agrees or disagrees with the legislation at issue, and this Court will not attempt to impose on a

---

[6] [1] The trial court noted that based on anecdotal evidence, the graffiti problem appeared to be concentrated in the fifteen-, sixteen-, and possibly seventeen-year-old age group.

duly-elected legislative body his reservations about the wisdom of the subject ordinance. Instead, the rational basis test focuses narrowly on whether a legislative body could rationally believe that the legislation could achieve a legitimate government end. The end of controlling the blight of graffiti is obviously legitimate and the Juvenile does not challenge this fact.

In addition, a legislative body could rationally conclude that the subject prohibition of possession by minors of spray paint and jumbo markers without supervision on public property or permission of the private-property owner would serve to control and limit incidences of graffiti. Indeed, the prohibition at issue is less restrictive than the prohibitions on spray paint and jumbo markers upheld in *National Paint.* The Court notes that juveniles can avoid the restrictions at issue by using markers less than one-half inch in [writing surface] or markers that contain water-soluble ink.

For the above reasons, the Court finds that the challenged graffiti ordinance does not offend the due process or equal protection provisions of either the Florida or Federal Constitutions. Accordingly, the Juvenile's Motion to Dismiss is denied.

GREEN, J., dissenting.

Respectfully, I believe that sections 21-30.01(e)(2) and (3) of the Dade County Graffiti Ordinance are facially unconstitutional in that they are violative of the due process clause of both the state and federal constitutions.

I do not believe that it can be realistically maintained, as the state attempts to do on this appeal, that sections 21-30.01(e)(2) and (e)(3) of the graffiti ordinance were enacted for the protection of the public's health, safety, welfare or morals. They were clearly enacted solely for the protection of property within the county. Moreover, the act of criminalizing the possession of spray paint and/or jumbo markers by all unsupervised minors, regardless of their intent, is wholly unreasonable, arbitrary, and capricious and is not reasonably related to the county's legitimate objective in protecting property from graffiti.

We are...confronted in this case with two inherently innocuous items (i.e., spray paint and jumbo markers) that are widely utilized both privately and commercially by minors and adults alike for a variety of innocent purposes as well as to make graffiti. It is true, as a general proposition, that the "[r]egulation of items that have some lawful as well as unlawful uses is not an irrational means of discouraging [criminal behavior]." Although the regulation of such items is not per se irrational, the legislature still has constitutional constraints when enacting a blanket or conditional prohibition on the possession or use of such items. Our state supreme court has said that any prohibition against the possession of objects having a common and widespread lawful use must be "reasonably required as incidental to the accomplishment of the primary purpose of the Act. To be sure, sections 21-30.01(e)(2) and (e)(3) will simplify the state's burden of enforcing the graffiti ordinance against minors, who are deemed to be the primary makers of graffiti. "Expediency, however, is not the test...." I therefore cannot agree that the county can constitutionally criminalize all possession of spray paint and jumbo markers by unsupervised minors on public property, regardless of the circumstances, in the hopes of ensnaring the actual graffiti artists.

The challenged subsections of the graffiti ordinance are virtually indistinguishable from the statutes and ordinances repeatedly struck down under the "innocent acts doctrine" with one exception; the challenged subsections under the graffiti ordinance pertain solely to minors. For this reason, I believe that the central issue in this case is whether minors possess diminished substantive due process rights when it comes to statutes or ordinances that seek to criminalize the possession of inherently innocent items which can be used in criminal endeavors. Neither our state nor the federal supreme court appears to have squarely addressed this issue, but I do not believe that existing law supports the notion that the substantive due process rights of minors are not co-equal to those of adults under the "innocent acts doctrine."

The majority points out that it is not constitutionally impermissible to treat minors differently from adults. While that is certainly true, it is true only in some delineated areas.... The central rationale for finding diminished constitutional rights of minors, in limited circumstances, appears to be for the personal protection of the child or the personal protection of others from the acts of minors. For example, in *T.M. v. State,* 689 So.2d 443 (Fla. 3d DCA 1997), we found section 790.22(9)(a), Florida Statutes, which mandates the imposition of a five day detention period on any juvenile who commits any offense involving the use or possession of a firearm, to be constitutional notwithstanding the fact that an adult who similarly commits any such offense is not subject to the same mandatory incarceration period. The statute in *T.M.,* unlike the graffiti subsections in this case, was attempting to regulate a minor's possession and/or use of an inherently dangerous item. In *Metropolitan Dade County v. Pred,* 665 So.2d 252, 253 (Fla. 3d DCA 1995), we similarly upheld the power of the county to impose a curfew for minors, for the personal well-being of minors. Likewise, the laws which prohibit minors from drinking and driving under the legal age limit are constitutionally permissible because they are for the purpose of protecting minors from inherently dangerous activities.

Thus, although the constitutional rights of minors are not co-equal with those of adults under certain circumstances, I must conclude that those factors which generally tend to support a reduction of the rights of minors are simply not present in this case. The purpose of the challenged subsections of the graffiti ordinance is wholly unrelated to the personal protection of minors or others. The county's sole aim is to protect property from graffiti artists. While that is certainly a legitimate and laudable objective, I do not believe that it can be pursued by the county at the expense and deprivation of fundamental due process rights which both adults and minors share. Because I conclude that minors do not have diminished substantive due process rights under the "innocent acts" doctrine, the challenged subsections of this ordinance are no different than the statutes which have been repeatedly struck down by our supreme court under the "innocent acts" doctrine. For that reason, I believe that the challenged subsections of the graffiti ordinance must suffer the same fate.

E. CLASSIFICATIONS BASED ON SEXUAL ORIENTION

TANNER v. OREGON HEALTH SCIENCES UNIVERSITY
971 P.2d 435 (Or. Ct. App. 1998)

LANDAU, P.J.

At issue in this case is the lawfulness of Oregon Health Science University's (OHSU) denial of health and life insurance benefits to the unmarried domestic partners of its homosexual employees. Plaintiffs...initiated this action for judicial review of State Employees' Benefits Board (SEBB) orders affirming the lawfulness of the denial.... Plaintiffs contend that OHSU's actions violate...Article I, section 20, of the Oregon Constitution, which prohibits granting privileges or immunities not equally belonging to all citizens.... Before this controversy arose, OHSU provided group health insurance benefits to its employees. In accordance with SEBB eligibility criteria, OHSU permitted employees to purchase insurance coverage for "family members." Under the SEBB criteria, unmarried domestic partners of employees were not "family members" who were entitled to insurance coverage.

Plaintiffs are three lesbian nursing professionals employed by OHSU and their unmarried domestic partners. Each of the couples has enjoyed a long-term and committed relationship, which each wishes to continue for life. Each of the couples would be married if Oregon law permitted homosexual couples to marry.... All three OHSU employees applied for medical and dental insurance benefits for their domestic partners. The OHSU benefits manager refused to process the applications on the ground that the domestic partners of the employees did not meet the SEBB eligibility criteria.

Article I, section 20, prohibits granting privileges or immunities to one citizen or class of citizens that are not equally available to all citizens. That generally is understood to express two separate prohibitions. As the Supreme Court explained in its seminal opinion, *State v. Clark*, 630 P.2d 810 (1981), the clause "forbids inequality of privileges or immunities not available upon the same terms, first, to any citizen, and second, to any class of citizens." In this case, plaintiffs contend that they are members of a class of citizens, homosexual couples, to whom certain privileges, insurance benefits, are not made available.

As used in the Article I, section 20, case law, the term "class" takes on special meaning; only laws that disparately treat a "true class" may violate that section of the constitution. In attempting to describe precisely what is meant by a "true class," the cases draw a distinction between classes that are created by the challenged law or government action itself and classes that are defined in terms of characteristics that are shared apart from the challenged law or action.... The standard example of a nontrue class, drawn from the Supreme Court's decision in Clark, is the classification created by a statute that imposes a filing deadline for filing a petition for review. Such legislation creates two classes of persons: (1) those who timely file petitions for review, and (2) those who do not. Both are "classes" of persons, at least in the colloquial sense of groups having something in common. But in the absence of the statute, they have no identity at all. Legislation that disparately affects such "classes" does not violate Article I, section 20, because of the essentially circular nature of the argument: The legislation cannot disparately affect a class that the legislation itself creates.

In contrast, Article I, section 20, does protect against disparate treatment of true classes, those that have identity apart from the challenged law itself. Various formulations have been used to describe in some affirmative way what a true class is, as opposed to merely what it is not in reference to classes created by the challenged legislation. The cases refer to classification by "ad hominem characteristic," by "personal characteristic," and by "antecedent personal or social characteristics or societal status." Examples of true classes include gender, ethnic background, legitimacy, past or present residency, and military service.

To say that disparately treated true classes are protected by Article I, section 20, does not end the matter. Depending on what type of true class is involved, the legislation or governmental action may or may not be upheld in spite of the disparity. In that regard, the cases draw a distinction between "suspect" classes and other true classes. The former classes are subject to a more demanding level of scrutiny, and legislation or government action disparately treating such classes is much more likely to run afoul of Article I, section 20, than is legislation or government action that disparately treats a nonsuspect class.

The leading opinion on suspect classes is *Hewitt v. SAIF*, 653 P.2d 970 (1982). In that case, the plaintiff, a man, challenged the constitutionality of a statute that permitted an unmarried woman to collect death benefits upon the death of an unmarried man with whom she cohabited for over one year. He contended that the statute, which made no provision for death benefits to an unmarried man who had cohabited with an unmarried woman for the required period, violated Article I, section 20, of the Oregon Constitution. The court held that, under Article I, section 20, disparate treatment of classes that may be regarded as "suspect" is subject to particularly exacting scrutiny. The court did not define precisely what it meant by "suspect" class. It did say that a class is suspect when it is defined in terms of "immutable" characteristics and "can be suspected of reflecting 'invidious' social or political premises, that is to say prejudice or stereotyped prejudgments." The court held that gender constitutes such a class. It then held that the denial of benefits to the plaintiff, a member of the suspect class defined by his male gender, was "inherently suspect." That suspicion, the court held, could be overcome only by evidence that the denial of benefits to him is justified on the basis of "biological differences" between those who are entitled to the benefits under the statute and those who are not. Finding no such justification in the record, the court declared that the statute violated Article I, section 20.

Although the court in *Hewitt* referred to "immutable" characteristics as being sufficient for defining a suspect class under Article I, section 20, subsequent cases make clear that immutability-in the sense of inability to alter or change-is not necessary. The court has since explained that, in addition to gender, such classes as alienage, religious affiliation, race and religion are suspect classes. Both alienage and religious affiliation may be changed almost at will. For that matter, given modern medical technology, so also may gender. We therefore understand from the cases that the focus of suspect class definition is not necessarily the immutability of the common, class-defining characteristics, but instead the fact that such characteristics are historically regarded as defining distinct, socially-recognized groups that have been the subject of adverse social or political stereotyping or prejudice. If a law or government action fails to offer privileges and immunities to members of such a class on equal terms, the law or action is inherently suspect and, as the court made clear in *Hewitt*, may be upheld only if the failure to make the privileges or immunities available to that class can be justified by genuine differences between the disparately treated class and those to whom the privileges and immunities are granted.

Turning to the facts of this case, there is no question but that plaintiffs are members of a true class. That class-unmarried homosexual couples-is not defined by any statute nor by the practices that are the subject of plaintiffs' challenges. Moreover, the class clearly is defined in terms of ad hominem, personal and social characteristics. The question then is whether plaintiffs are members of a suspect class. Here, too, we have no difficulty concluding that plaintiffs are members of a suspect class. Sexual orientation, like gender, race, alienage, and religious affiliation is widely regarded as defining a distinct, socially recognized group of citizens, and certainly it is beyond dispute that homosexuals in our society have been and continue to be the subject of adverse social and political stereotyping and prejudice.

Because plaintiffs are members of a suspect class to which certain privileges and immunities are not made available, we must determine whether the fact that the privileges and immunities are not available to that class may be justified by genuine differences between the class and those to whom the privileges and immunities are made available. Stated perhaps more plainly, we must determine whether the fact that the domestic partners of homosexual OHSU employees cannot obtain insurance benefits can be justified by their homosexuality. The parties have suggested no such justification, and we can envision none.

OHSU's defense is that it determined eligibility for insurance benefits on the basis of marital status, not sexual orientation. According to OHSU, the fact that such a facially neutral classification has the unintended side effect of discriminating against homosexual couples who cannot marry is not actionable under Article I, section 20. We are not persuaded by the asserted defense. Article I, section 20, does not prohibit only intentional discrimination. On point in that regard is the Supreme Court's decision in *Zockert v. Fanning*, 800 P.2d 773 (1990). In that case, the plaintiff parent challenged the constitutionality of a statutory scheme that provided indigent parents court-appointed counsel in parental termination proceedings but did not provide for court-appointed counsel in adoption proceedings that have the effect of terminating parental rights. After concluding that the plaintiff was a member of a true class…it observed that the legislature apparently was unaware of the disparity between the parental termination and adoption proceeding statutes and did not make a conscious policy to treat indigent parents in the two similar proceedings unequally. The court nevertheless concluded that the unintended side effect of providing counsel in termination proceedings was to treat a true class of citizens disparately in violation of Article I, section 20. Intentional conduct, the court held, is not required for discrimination to be actionable under that section of the constitution.

So also in this case, OHSU has taken action with no apparent intention to treat disparately members of any true class of citizens. Nevertheless, its actions have the undeniable effect of doing just that. As in *Zockert*, OHSU's intentions in this case are not relevant. What is relevant is the extent to which privileges or immunities are not made available to all citizens on equal terms.

OHSU insists that in this case privileges and immunities are available to all on equal terms: All married employees-heterosexual and homosexual alike-are permitted to acquire insurance benefits for their spouses. That reasoning misses the point, however. Homosexual couples may not marry. Accordingly, the benefits are not made available on equal terms. They are made available on terms that, for gay and lesbian couples, are a legal impossibility.

We conclude that OHSU's denial of insurance benefits to the unmarried domestic partners of its homosexual employees violated Article I, section 20, of the Oregon Constitution and that the trial court correctly entered judgment in favor of plaintiffs on that ground.

NOTE

Several state courts have addressed the question of whether classifications based on sexual orientation should be considered suspect and therefore reviewed with heightened judicial scrutiny. The results of these cases have been mixed; some courts, like the Oregon Court of Appeals in *Tanner*, have concluded that classifications based on sexual orientation should be reviewed with heightened scrutiny, while other courts have concluded that classifications based on sexual orientation should be reviewed with only minimal scrutiny. E.g., *Singer v. O'Hara*, 522 P.2d 1187 (Wash. Ct. App. 1974).

In *Tanner*, the court ruled that facially neutral laws that have a disparate impact against gay and lesbian persons amount to unconstitutional discrimination on the basis of sexual orientation. Some courts have declined to take this position. For instance, in upholding a rule limiting health insurance coverage to married couples, the Supreme Court of Wisconsin stated, "The challenged rule distinguishes between married and unmarried employees, not between homosexual and heterosexual employees." *Phillips v. Wisconsin Personnel Commission*, 482 N.W.2d 121, 127 (Wis. 1992). Other courts, though, have sided with *Tanner* by striking down laws that deny benefits to same-sex couples that are available to married opposite-sex couples.

In *Baker v. State*, 744 A.2d 864 (Vt. 1999), the Supreme Court of Vermont ruled that by excluding same-sex couples from the legal benefits of marriage, the state marriage laws violated the common benefits clause of the Vermont Constitution, which reads:

That government is, or ought to be, instituted for the common benefit, protection, and security of the people, nation, or community, and not for the particular emolument or advantage of any single person, family, or set of persons, who are a part only of that community.

The court's opinion stated that:

Assuming that the marriage statutes preclude their eligibility for a marriage license, plaintiffs contend that the exclusion violates their right to the common benefit and protection of the law guaranteed by Chapter I, Article 7 of the Vermont Constitution. They note that in denying them access to a civil marriage license, the law effectively excludes them from a broad array of legal benefits and protections incident to the marital relation, including access to a spouse's medical, life, and disability insurance, hospital visitation and other medical decisionmaking privileges, spousal support, intestate succession, homestead protections, and many other statutory protections.

In considering this issue, it is important to emphasize at the outset that it is the Common Benefits Clause of the Vermont Constitution we are construing, rather than its counterpart, the Equal Protection Clause of the Fourteenth Amendment to the United States Constitution. It is altogether fitting and proper that we do so. Vermont's constitutional commitment to equal rights was the product of the successful effort to create an independent republic and a fundamental charter of government, the Constitution of 1777, both of which preceded the adoption of the Fourteenth Amendment by nearly a century. As we explained in *State v. Badger,* 450 A.2d 336, 347 (Vt. 1982), "our constitution is not a mere reflection of the federal charter. Historically and textually, it differs from the United States Constitution. It predates the federal counterpart, as it extends back to Vermont's days as an independent republic. It is an independent authority, and Vermont's fundamental law."

The first point to be observed about the text is the affirmative and unequivocal mandate of the first section, providing that government is established for the common benefit of the people and community as a whole....The words of the Common Benefits Clause are revealing. While they do not, to be sure, set forth a fully-formed standard of analysis for determining the constitutionality of a given statute, they do express broad principles which usefully inform that analysis. Chief among these is the principle of inclusion. As explained more fully in the discussion that follows, the specific proscription against governmental favoritism toward not only groups or "set[s] of men," but also toward any particular "family" or "single man," underscores the framers' resentment of political preference of any kind. The affirmative right to the "common benefits and protections" of government and the corollary proscription of favoritism in the distribution of public "emoluments and advantages" reflect the framers' overarching objective "not only that everyone enjoy equality before the law or have an equal voice in government but also that everyone have *an equal share in the fruits of the common enterprise.*" W. Adams, *The First American Constitutions* 188 (1980) (emphasis added). Thus, at its core the Common Benefits Clause expressed a vision of government that afforded every Vermonter its benefit and protection and provided no Vermonter particular advantage.

The legal benefits and protections flowing from a marriage license are of such significance that any statutory exclusion must necessarily be grounded on public concerns of sufficient weight, cogency, and authority that the justice of the deprivation cannot seriously be questioned. Considered in light of the extreme logical disjunction between the classification and the stated purposes of the law-protecting children and "furthering the link between procreation and child rearing"-the exclusion falls substantially short of this standard. The laudable governmental goal of promoting a commitment between married couples to promote the security of their children and the community as a whole provides no reasonable basis for denying the legal benefits and protections of marriage to same-sex couples, who are no differently situated with respect to *this goal* than their opposite-sex counterparts. Promoting a link between procreation and childrearing similarly fails to support the exclusion….Thus, viewed in the light of history, logic, and experience, we conclude that none of the interests asserted by the State provides a reasonable and just basis for the continued exclusion of same-sex couples from the benefits incident to a civil marriage license under Vermont law.

While holding that same-sex couples were entitled to the same legal benefits afforded to married opposite-sex couples, the court decided to leave it to the legislature to resolve exactly how those benefits should be extended to same-sex couples. This gave the legislature several options, one of which was to enact a statute to establish an alternative legal status to marriage for same-sex couples. In response, the Vermont legislature enacted a civil union law providing comprehensive legal benefits (akin to marriage rights) for same sex couples. For further consideration of *Baker*, see Chapter VI.

The decision in *Baker* extends the legal benefits of marriage, but not the right to marry itself, to same-sex couples. In 2003, the Supreme Court of Massachusetts went a dramatic step further by ruling, in *Goodridge v. Department of Public Health*, 798 N.E.2d 941 (Mass. 2003), that under the Massachusetts constitution, the commonwealth could not deny persons of the same sex the right to marry. *Goodridge* was a momentous decision that provoked an intense reaction across the nation, arousing strong sentiments both for and against it. Since *Goodridge*, a number of courts in other states have confronted the issue of same-sex marriage. The results in these cases have been mixed; some courts have agreed with *Goodridge* that laws precluding same-sex marriage are unconstitutional, while others have disagreed and found nothing unconstitutional about such laws. For further consideration of *Goodridge*, see Chapter VI.

F. ECONOMIC RIGHTS

NOTE

The use of heightened judicial review in cases involving business or economic regulations raises concerns about the revival of "Lochnerism." This refers to the practice, most prominently of the United States Supreme Court in the early part of the 20th Century, of adopting extreme laissez faire economic policy as constitutional doctrine to invalidate remedial statutes regulating wages, prices, or working conditions. The term derives from *Lochner v. New York*, 198 U.S. 45 (1905), in which the Supreme Court ruled that a state statute setting maximum hours of work was a violation of the Due Process Clause of the Fourteenth Amendment. *Lochner* has come to symbolize an era of excessive judicial intervention, during which the Supreme Court combined constitutional doctrine and questionable economic policy to strike down a number of progressive laws regulating business and working conditions.

In the federal court system, minimal judicial scrutiny was devised to counteract Lochnerism by restraining judicial review in economic cases. Since the 1940's, the Supreme Court has consistently used the most minimal form of judicial review in economic cases, granting great deference to the legislature and rarely, if ever, striking down economic legislation.

Many states, also wary of Lochnerism, follow the federal example of applying minimal scrutiny in reviewing economic regulations. In states that adhere to the federal approach, judicial review in cases involving economic matters is extremely reserved, allowing the legislature considerable latitude to regulate economic affairs. Within the confines of minimal judicial scrutiny, economic laws are usually found to be constitutional. While minimal scrutiny of economic legislation represents the norm in state court systems, there are a number of exceptions to this practice. In certain instances, state courts have adopted a less restrained form of scrutiny to assess economic legislation. Using an enhanced variety of judicial review, some state courts have struck economic legislation on the ground that it runs afoul of an equality provision in the state constitution. The cases that follow in this section illustrate both the deferential approach and the enhanced approach to reviewing economic legislation.

BENSON v. NORTH DAKOTA WORKMEN'S COMPENSATION BUREAU
283 N.W.2d 96 (N.D. 1979)

PEDERSON, J.

The district court of Stark County has twice held in this case that the statute which excludes agricultural service from the mandatory provisions of the Workmen's Compensation Act violates both the Constitution of North Dakota and the Constitution of the United States. When the first holding was appealed to this court, we remanded because of procedural deficiencies and made suggestions as to procedure and issues. On this appeal, we will address the merits of the constitutionality of the agricultural exclusion under the Workmen's Compensation Act.

The record reveals that Benson's scope of employment as an agricultural employee was extremely broad, and included: milking, livestock feeding, equipment operation, cleaning cattle, cleaning barn, hauling silage and grain, assisting in calving, repairing machinery, welding tuning motors, changing oil and greasing machinery, repairing fences and corrals, operating augers, carpentry, driving tractors, trucks and swathers, chopping corn, operating a power saw, painting, and "about anything you could name."

Although North Dakota's Workmen's Compensation Act has been often amended, the stated purpose of the Act has remained essentially as enacted in 1919. The title to the Act clearly discloses that this is an act creating a fund for the benefit of employees injured, and the dependents of employees killed in hazardous employment.

There was no contention by anyone in this case that agricultural employment is not hazardous. By the very nature and scope of tasks required of a general agricultural service employee, such as Benson in the instant case, a jack-of-all-trades develops who may be the master-of-none. While operating a power saw a few minutes during a week, we would not expect Benson to be as proficient or careful as a carpenter helper who operates a power saw forty hours a week. The composite activities of a farmhand are obviously more hazardous than the total of the individual activities when performed full time.

Courts from Montana and Michigan have been the most recent to have considered at least some of the aspects of an agricultural exclusion from workmen's compensation statutes. Both courts expressed some general principles with which we agree.... In *Gutierrez v. Glaser Crandell Company*, 202 N.W.2d 786 (Mich. 1972), out of the seven Michigan justices, four concluded that:

> There is no basis for distinguishing the work of a laborer who drives a truck at a factory from a laborer who drives one on the farm or for any one of numerous other labor activities 'on the farm' as distinguished from the same activity in industry, wholesaling, retailing, or building.... (T)he argument that Section 115(e) is especially tailored to meet the problems of the small farmer and his occasional employees fails to account for the need for similar treatment as to the small businessman grocer, clothier, butcher or as to the small contractor plumber, carpenter, roofer or as to numerous other categories of small employers and their employees who are not accorded this treatment.

Although this court desires to portray an image of intellectual vitality and to display its capacity to identify and evaluate each analytically distinct ingredient of the contending interests, we have a legacy of judicial restraint which we should not cavalierly abandon. Use of judicial restraint, however, does not permit a court to ignore its responsibility. If taken too literally, the rule that a court will not substitute its judgment for that of the legislature could result in the abdication by the court of any authority to review the constitutionality of legislation. The ultimate result would be a destruction of the constitution as a limitation on legislative action. The pendulum could likewise swing too far the other way and the court could become so aggressively creative that the judge's notions as to what is good or bad or necessary or unnecessary could improperly restrict policy-making functions of the legislative branch.

Government could not function without making classifications. The discriminatory effects of classification ordinarily do not violate equal protection as long as there is a basis for disparate treatment that naturally inheres in the subject matter. Any classification can be challenged as denying equal protection; it then becomes the duty of the court to determine the statute's validity and to uphold the classification if it includes all, and only those, persons who are similarly situated with respect to the purpose of the law. Generally, when the legislature has expressed the Purpose of the law, courts need only examine the statute itself in determining whether or not: (1) a particular classification bears some rational relationship to the expressed purpose; (2) the classification is based upon a permissible distinction (that is, are similar things treated similarly); and (3) the classification is clearly arbitrary or unreasonable.

The North Dakota Legislature explicitly expressed the purpose of the Act but the exclusion of agricultural services has no correspondence to that expressed purpose. The legislature made no attempt to express any purpose for the exclusion.... There are four possible purposes for excluding agricultural employees from the benefits offered other employees by the Workmen's Compensation Act:

> (1) The purpose of excluding agricultural employees was to overcome political opposition to passage of a workmen's compensation act by a farm-oriented legislature.... (T)his purpose, if we can call it that, only supports a conclusion that agricultural employees had little influence in legislative matters, but supplies no justification for the exclusion in a constitutional sense.

> (2) Farm employees should be excluded because their work is not as hazardous as other employment and compulsory coverage for them is not needed. "Least convincing of all is the assertion that farm laborers do not need this kind of protection. Whatever the compensation acts may say, agriculture is one of the most hazardous of all occupations. In 1964, of 4,761,000 agricultural workers, 3,000 were fatally injured, while of 17,259,000 manufacturing employees, the number of fatalities was 2,000." 1B Larson, Workmen's Compensation Law, Farm Labor, s 53:20, p. 9-109.... A conclusion that modern-day farming is nonhazardous defies reality and provides no explanation for the exclusion of agricultural employees from coverage under the Act. It is readily acknowledged that driving cattle on horseback has not become more dangerous than it was in 1919, yet riders employed at sales rings and stockyards have always benefited from coverage while riders employed by farmers and ranchers have not.

> (3) Farm employees should be excluded because the "family farm" is a closely knit community of relatives and friends who care for each other's needs and injuries and no other protection is needed.... In this case, Benson's employer,

Decker, testified in effect that he thought that he had private insurance that would have taken care of any employee accident. He did carry farm liability coverage which included $2,000 no-fault medical benefits, and these were, in fact, paid to Benson. Decker asserted that he discovered, after the accident, that the coverage he thought he had is not even available from commercial insurance carriers and that it would be "too costly" to carry voluntary workmen's compensation coverage. There may be farmers even more beneficent than Decker but there undoubtedly are many migrant, temporary, part-time employees who have no reason whatsoever to expect to be cared for, if injured, out of any beneficence of their farmer-employer.

(4) Farm employees should be excluded because farm employers cannot afford to pay the premium. We accord this justification considerable weight and perceive more than an element of truth in it. Any addition to the overhead costs of operating a farm threatens the chances of a profitable operation. The latest edition of 1B Larson, Workmen's Compensation Law, s 53:10, indicates that not more than seventeen states have mandatory workmen's compensation coverage for agricultural workers. All other things being equal, there is a recognizable, competitive edge for a farmer who is freed from any item of overhead cost.

We cannot ignore the effect of the exemption upon agricultural employees. When we look at the effect of the agricultural service exclusion, we must focus upon both employer and employee and, although some inequality is permissible, we must balance the benefits against the burdens imposed on each class.... We find unacceptable the suggestion by the attorney general that by excluding farm workers from workmen's compensation coverage, the legislature has, in effect, spread the burden of injured farm workers to the widest possible base to the taxpayers in general because injured farm workers who are poor can receive welfare. The burden still rests entirely upon the injured farm employee, if not economically, surely in the loss of dignity.

We agree with the trial court's conclusion that the exclusion of agricultural employees from the benefits of the Workmen's Compensation Act is unreasonable and contrary to the expressed purpose of the Act. Because of the exclusion, the Act withholds from agricultural employees the sure and certain relief awarded to other wage earners. There is no correspondence between the purpose of the Act and the agricultural classification. There are no proper and justifiable distinctions between agricultural employees and nonagricultural employees in relation to the risk of injury from employment. We hold that the agricultural exemption in the Workmen's Compensation Act violates s 20, Article I, North Dakota Constitution.[*]

---

[*] ADDENDUM Since the concurrence of four members of this (five-person) Court is required to declare a statute unconstitutional (Section 88, North Dakota Constitution), and only three member of the Court concur in this opinion, the agricultural exclusion from the Workmen's Compensation coverage is not declared unconstitutional by a sufficient majority.

SAND, J., dissenting.

The principal issue is whether or not subdivision (1), the agricultural exemption, is constitutional. In every instance where this question was presented to a court it was upheld. However, in *Gutierrez v. Glaser Crandell Company*, 202 N.W.2d 786 (Mich.1972), the court held invalid a classification within a classification relating to employees engaged in agricultural activities. Numerous court decisions concerned with this topic and the case law, together with the legal rationale, as well as the cases cited in support of the decision overwhelmingly support the validity of the agricultural service exclusion from the Workmen's Compensation Act.

The exclusion of farming and ranching from the Workmen's Compensation Act was challenged in *State of Montana ex rel. Hammond v. Hager*, 503 P.2d 52 (Mont. 1972). In ruling that the exclusion was not arbitrary and unreasonable, the Montana Supreme Court (said):

> Our legislature might have concluded to exclude farming operations because they were hazardous enough that the cost of coverage to the farmer would be an unnecessary and unreasonable burden, particularly since the legislature may not have believed that conditions of farm employment generally were similar to those of the industries the Act did cover. Speculating further, one could as well conclude that the legislature excluded coverage of farmers on the basis, for example, that a great majority of Montana farmers employ too few people to justify the cost and administrative expense required to comply with the Act; that most farm employees are too seasonal or casual to require coverage; or, that Montana's farmers should not be put at a competitive disadvantage since most other states also exclude agriculture.

I believe it is common knowledge, or at least well established, that a farmer is not able to pass on the costs to the purchaser or consumer, as is the situation in other commercial enterprises and business. The farmer is required to absorb any additional costs himself. To this should be added that it is common knowledge for farmers to exchange help, particularly with the family farm. Added to this is the further knowledge that minor members of the family, as distinguished from other businesses, perform work as part of the "growing up process" without any given salary, and also exchange services with other family farms. While other businesses also have members of the family working, in most instances they are adults and not minors, as the situation is on the farm.

The majority opinion has not pointed to one single factor why the act is invidiously discriminatory. It simply states so without any support whatsoever. The exclusion does not fall within the suspect class, therefore the need to support the act is not present but it is up to the challengers to clearly illustrate and demonstrate that the act amounts to an invidious discrimination. This has not been done.

COLLINS v. DAY
644 N.E.2d 72 (Ind. 1994)

DICKSON, J.

This case presents a state constitutional challenge to the exclusion of agricultural workers from the coverage of the Indiana Worker's Compensation Statute. The parties have stipulated to the facts. On February 11, 1989, plaintiff-appellant Eugene Collins sustained a broken right leg in an accident in the course of his employment as an agricultural employee of defendant-appellee Glen Day. The defendant denies that any compensable accident occurred under the provisions of the Act and has not paid the plaintiff any worker's compensation benefits. In the plaintiff's application for such benefits, he claims medical expenses of $12,000.00 and average weekly earnings at the time of the accident of $140.00 per week, in addition to the value of the use of a residence.

The full Worker's Compensation Board affirmed the single Hearing Judge's order granting the defendant's Motion to Dismiss, which generally raised the statutory agricultural exemption to the Indiana Worker's Compensation Act, which provides in part that the Act "shall not apply to casual labor ... nor to farm or to agricultural employees, nor to domestic servants, nor to the employers of such persons." The plaintiff appealed, contending that the agricultural exemption violated Article I, Section 23 of the Indiana Constitution (hereafter "Section 23"), which provides:

> The General Assembly shall not grant to any citizen, or class of citizens, privileges or immunities which, upon the same terms, shall not equally belong to all citizens.

In this appeal, the plaintiff argues that the worker's compensation agricultural exemption violates Section 23 because it extends to a special class of employers, an immunity denied to the general class of employers. He further contends that the statutory grant to agricultural employers of the option to elect either to be covered by or to be exempt from the Indiana Worker's Compensation Act is a privilege both denied to a comparable class of agricultural employees and denied to the general class of Indiana employers.

Initially, we must determine whether settled Indiana law forecloses consideration of plaintiff's contention that federal Fourteenth Amendment jurisprudence does not necessarily apply to a claim brought under Section 23 of the Indiana Constitution. During the 143 years since the ratification of Section 23, this Court has assumed various postures with respect to the applicability of federal Fourteenth Amendment standards to Section 23 questions. One such approach suggests that a distinction ought to be drawn between Section 23 and the Fourteenth Amendment. There are striking textual differences between the two provisions. The Fourteenth

Amendment prohibits laws which "abridge" privileges or immunities, whereas Section 23 prohibits laws which "grant" unequal privileges or immunities. Many Indiana cases have considered and applied Section 23 separately from the Fourteenth Amendment. For example, in *Graffty v. City of Rushville*, 8 N.E. 609 (Ind. 1886) we noted that Section 23 considerations were to be analyzed independently from the "provisions of the National Constitution." In at least one case, a statute was found to comply with the federal Privileges and Immunities Clause but nevertheless to violate the parallel provision in Indiana's Section 23. *Sperry & Hutchinson Co. v. State*, 122 N.E. 584 (Ind. 1919). Several decisions of this Court have expressly acknowledged that Section 23 "is the antithesis of the 14th amendment to the federal Constitution." Similarly suggesting the distinction between Section 23 and the Fourteenth Amendment, numerous other cases have undertaken the analysis of constitutional claims under first one of the provisions and then the other.

A contrasting line of cases has maintained that Section 23 and the Fourteenth Amendment share substantially the same considerations. In *Dortch v. Lugar*, 266 N.E.2d 25 (Ind. 1971) our opinion noted that Section 23 and the Fourteenth Amendment "concerning the abridging of privileges and immunities of citizens protect substantially identical rights." Other cases have considered the two provisions essentially synonymous. Numerous cases have treated the two provisions simultaneously, without any explicit statement as to equivalence or separateness.

Notwithstanding that the privileges and immunities cases brought under Section 23 have often assimilated federal equal protection analysis, we are under no obligation to follow Fourteenth Amendment jurisprudence in resolving a Section 23 issue. An analogous issue was encountered in *Miller v. State*, 517 N.E.2d 64 (Ind. 1987), where we observed that Indiana courts had often relied upon federal case law addressing the Sixth Amendment to the United States Constitution in reviewing claims invoking the right of confrontation arising from Article 1, Section 13, of the Indiana Constitution. Nevertheless, we there declared that such precedents do not preclude us from forming an independent standard for analyzing state constitutional claims.

We conclude that there is no settled body of Indiana law that compels application of a federal equal protection analytical methodology to claims alleging special privileges or immunities under Indiana Section 23 and that Section 23 should be given independent interpretation and application... Excluding the line of cases which have applied federal equal protection methodology to state Section 23 issues, there exists a considerable body of case law reviewing the state constitutional question, from which a substantially uniform, though still evolving, analytical standard has emerged. Our review discloses several recurrent themes which we now distill into two general factors.

The considerations embodied in the first of the two factors focus upon the nature of the classifications of citizens upon which the legislature is basing its disparate treatment. Numerous cases have stated that the basis of such classification must "inhere in the subject matter." In *Heckler v. Conter*, 187 N.E. 878 (Ind. 1933), we stated that legislative classification must be "based upon substantial distinctions germane to the subject matter and the object to be attained." The distinctions must involve something more than mere characteristics which will serve to divide or identify the class. There must be inherent differences in situation related to the subject-matter of the legislation which require, necessitate, or make expedient different or exclusive legislation with respect to the members of the class.

The significant common theme shared by such formulations is the requirement that, where the legislature singles out one person or class of persons to receive a privilege or immunity not equally provided to others, such classification must be based upon distinctive, inherent characteristics which rationally distinguish the unequally treated class, and the disparate treatment accorded by the legislation must be reasonably related to such distinguishing characteristics. We believe that this requirement incorporates and satisfies the often expressed concerns that such legislative classifications be "just," "natural," "reasonable," "substantial," "not artificial," "not capricious," and "not arbitrary." This requirement, then, comprises the first prong of the two-part Section 23 standard we articulate today.

The second of the two factors embraces concerns, frequently expressed in Section 23 cases, regarding the need for uniformity and equal availability of the preferential treatment for all persons similarly situated. In *Dixon v. Poe*, 65 N.E. 518 (Ind. 1902), an enactment was invalidated because it failed to "embrace all of the class to which it is naturally related." Section 23 was found to be violated when a law "creates a preference, and establishes an inequality among a class of citizens all of whom are equally meritorious" or which "applies to persons in certain situations, and excludes from effect other persons who are not dissimilar in these respects." Similar considerations are emphasized in numerous cases reviewing Section 23 issues. For example, in *McErlain v. Taylor*, 192 N.E. 260 (Ind. 1934), this Court stated:

> But, if there are other general classes situate[d] in all respects like the class benefitted by the statute, with the same inherent needs and qualities which indicate the necessity or expediency of protection for the favored class, and legislation....withholds the same protection from, the other class or classes in like situation, it cannot stand.

It is important to note that, in applying the two-part standard we articulate today to claims asserted under Section 23, the courts must accord considerable deference to the manner in which the legislature has balanced the competing interests involved. Presuming the statute to be constitutional, courts place the burden upon the challenger "to negative every conceivable basis which might have supported the classification." The question of classification under Section 23 is primarily a legislative question. *Chaffin v. Nicosia*, 310 N.E. 2d 867 (Ind. 1974). As this Court has stated:

> Legislative classification becomes a judicial question only where the lines drawn appear arbitrary or manifestly unreasonable. So long as the classification is based upon substantial distinctions with reference to the subject matter, we will not substitute our judgment for that of the legislature; nor will we inquire into the legislative motives prompting such classification. *Id.* at 869.

In *Sperry & Hutchinson Co.*, 122 N.E. at 587, we said that "[i]f any state of facts within the fair range of probability can be reasonably supposed, which would supply an adequate reason on which to base the classification made, such state of facts will be assumed to have existed when the law was enacted."

To summarize, we hold that Article 1, Section 23 of the Indiana Constitution imposes two requirements upon statutes that grant unequal privileges or immunities to differing classes of persons. First, the disparate treatment accorded by the legislation must be reasonably related to inherent characteristics which distinguish the unequally treated classes. Second, the preferential treatment must be uniformly applicable and equally available to all persons similarly situated. Finally, in determining whether a statute complies with or violates Section 23, courts must exercise substantial deference to legislative discretion.

The resolution of Section 23 claims does not require an analytical framework applying varying degrees of scrutiny for different protected interests. The protections assured by Section 23 apply fully, equally, and without diminution to prohibit any and all improper grants of unequal privileges or immunities, including not only those grants involving suspect classes or impinging upon fundamental rights but other such grants as well. For example, this Court has applied Section 23 to invalidate grants of privilege which were improperly gender-based without using a heightened level of scrutiny. The multiple-level system remains, of course, an integral aspect of the test of a statute's constitutionality under federal Fourteenth Amendment jurisprudence. This Court anticipates that our independent state privileges and immunities jurisprudence will evolve in future cases facing Indiana courts to assure and extend protection to all Indiana citizens in addition to that provided by the federal Fourteenth Amendment.

The plaintiff contends that the exclusion of agricultural employers from the compulsory scope of coverage and the creation of an exclusive privilege for such employers to waive this exclusion each violates Section 23. He contends that the exemption of employers is an immunity extended to one class of employers which is denied to the general class of employers, and that the right to elect coverage is a privilege denied to both agricultural employees and the general class of employers.

We first address whether the treatment of agricultural employers separately from agricultural employees and from the general class of employers is a classification based upon distinctive, inherent characteristics and, if so, whether the unequal treatment is reasonably related to such distinguishing characteristics.

Applying the required deferential standard of review, we find that there are inherent distinctions between these classifications that are reasonably related to the exemption. The legislative classification may have been based upon various features reasonably distinguishing Indiana agricultural employers from other employers, among which are: the prevalence of sole proprietorships and small employment units, including numerous family operations; the distinctive nature of farm work, its attendant risks, and the typical level of worker training and experience; the traditional informality of the agricultural employment relationship and the frequent absence of formal ancillary employee benefit programs; and the peculiar difficulties agricultural employers experience in passing along the additional cost of worker's compensation insurance coverage to the ultimate consumer. Furthermore, we find that within the classification of agricultural employers, the exemption from worker's compensation coverage for employees is uniformly applicable and equally available to all persons who are or may become agricultural employers.

The amicus curiae, Legal Services Organization of Indiana, Inc., through its Migrant Farmworker Project, has submitted a forceful, thorough, and well-documented brief to support its contention that "the nature of agricultural work and the structure of agriculture in 1974 and today is so radically different than in 1915, that the continued exclusion of farmworkers from worker's compensation coverage does not comply with legislat[ive] intent." We do not deny that preferential legislative treatment for a classification which was proper when enacted may later cease to satisfy the requirements of Section 23 because of intervening changes in social or economic conditions. In the present case, however, because we find the plaintiff has failed to carry the burden placed upon the challenger to negative every reasonable basis for the classification, we are not persuaded that the agricultural exemption has become inconsistent with the requirements of Section 23.

We therefore conclude that the statutory agricultural exemption to the Indiana Worker's Compensation Act, Ind.Code § 22-3-2-9(a), does not presently constitute a special immunity in violation of the Indiana Privileges and Immunities Clause, Article I, Section 23 of the Indiana Constitution.

SULLIVAN, J., dissenting without opinion, would deny transfer because he believes the analysis of the Court of Appeals in this case was correct.

FOLEY v. DEPARTMENT OF FISHERIES
837 P.2d 14 (Wash. 1992)

JOHNSON, J.

Sea urchins are spiny invertebrates resembling rolled-up porcupines. Young urchins must hide beneath the spines of larger urchins for survival. Sea urchins are commercially harvested by divers working from fishing vessels. Divers are required to observe minimum and maximum size limitations when harvesting urchins. These size limits ensure enough oversized urchins exist to protect the young urchins, and undersized urchins are allowed to spawn at least once before being harvested. The urchin harvesting season generally runs from October 1 to March 31.

The sea urchin fishery remained relatively small throughout the 1970's and the first half of the 1980's. Only 12 vessels harvested urchins in the 1985-86 season. The fishery began to experience dramatic growth in the 1986-87 season when 39 vessels harvested urchins. In spite of this growth, no shortage or overharvesting of urchins occurred during this season, and divers generally complied with the size limit regulations.

Overharvesting problems first began to occur, however, during the 1987-88 urchin season in which 97 vessels landed urchins. Divers found it increasingly difficult to find any urchins of legal harvesting size. Consequently, some divers violated the size limit regulations, and the Department of Fisheries (Fisheries) cited numerous vessels for oversized urchins.

This situation worsened in the 1988-89 urchin season when almost 200 vessels competed to harvest urchins. Poaching violations occurred, as well as size limit violations. Virtually no urchins of *any* size remained in certain areas after harvesting by divers had occurred. One harvesting area had to be closed midseason because of overharvesting. Many inexperienced and insufficiently trained divers entered the fishery at this time. Too many people were trying to harvest sea urchins, and this problem threatened the economic viability of the urchin fishery.

The Legislature enacted RCW 75.30.210 in an effort to address this problem, and the statute's requirements became effective on October 1, 1989. RCW 75.30.210 places limits on the number of people who can harvest urchins. Under this statute, it is unlawful to commercially harvest sea urchins from a vessel that lacks a sea urchin endorsement to a shellfish diver license. A sea urchin endorsement will only be issued to vessel owners who:

(a) Held a commercial shellfish diver license ... between January 1, 1988, and December 31, 1988, or had transferred to the vessel such a license;

(b) Have not transferred the license to another vessel; and

(c) Can establish, by means of dated shellfish receiving documents issued by the [Department of Fisheries], that twenty thousand pounds of sea urchins were caught and landed under the license during the period of April 1, 1986, through March 31, 1988.

The statute provides for a 2-year qualifying period, from April 1, 1986 through March 31, 1988, for meeting the landing requirement. The 17 respondents in this case are vessel owners who did not make the 20,000-pound landing requirement during the qualifying period. Most of them did not purchase their vessels until 1988, and none made significant urchin landings until after the end of the qualifying period. Each applied for a sea urchin endorsement, and Fisheries denied each of these requests.

The superior court ruled that RCW 75.30.210 violates both the equal protection clause contained in the federal constitution and article 1, section 12 of the Washington Constitution...(which) provides that:

No law shall be passed granting to any citizen [or] class of citizens ... privileges or immunities which upon the same terms shall not equally belong to all citizens.

The court has treated claims under these two constitutional provisions as presenting one equal protection challenge to the governmental classification at issue. The court has at times recognized, however, that article 1, section 12 may provide broader protections than those provided under the federal equal protection clause. The respondents do not argue that article 1, section 12 of the state constitution should be construed independently from the federal equal protection clause. We accordingly analyze this case as presenting one equal protection challenge to the sea urchin endorsement statute.

The first step in analyzing an equal protection claim is determining the standard of review. The parties agree that the statute at issue is an economic regulation that does not involve either a suspect classification, such as race, or a fundamental right. It is well established that legislative bodies have broad discretion in enacting economic legislation that does not employ suspect classifications or burden fundamental rights. *New Orleans v. Dukes,* 427 U.S. 297 (1976). Such statutes are accordingly subject only to minimum scrutiny. *Omega Nat'l Ins. Co.,* 799 P.2d 235 (Wash. 1990).

The court will apply the rational basis test in cases involving minimum scrutiny review. Under this test, a statutory classification violates the equal protection clause only if it fails to rationally further a legitimate state interest. A legislative classification will be upheld so long as "the relationship of the classification to its [legislative purpose] is not so attenuated as to render the distinction arbitrary or irrational." The challenging party has the burden of showing that the classification contained in the statute is purely arbitrary.

We first identify the interest the Legislature sought to further in applying the rational basis test to the sea urchin endorsement statute. The sea urchin resource showed serious signs of depletion prior to the legislation. In enacting RCW 75.30.210, the Legislature determined:

> increased regulation of commercial sea urchin fishing is necessary to preserve and efficiently manage the commercial sea urchin fishery in the waters of the state.

The legislative purpose behind RCW 75.30.210 is thus to protect and efficiently regulate the sea urchin fishery. The Legislature may enact fish and game regulations pursuant to its police power, and it has done so since territorial days. The State has a legitimate interest in protecting and regulating its sea urchin fishery. The Legislature thus sought to further a legitimate state interest in enacting RCW 75.30.210.

We must now determine whether the classification contained in RCW 75.30.210 rationally furthers the State's legitimate interest in protecting and regulating its sea urchin fishery. The statute creates a limited class of vessel owners eligible to harvest sea urchins. Under the statute, vessel owners who evidenced substantial participation in the urchin fishery during the 2-year qualifying period fall within this class. The 20,000-pound landing requirement distinguishes those vessel owners who made substantial landings from those who made only isolated, sporadic landings during the 2-year qualifying period. Those who made substantial landings during this period could reasonably have a greater financial dependence on continued participation in the urchin fishery than those who did not. The statute thus rationally furthers the State's legitimate interest in preserving and regulating the urchin fishery by limiting the number of vessel owners harvesting urchins, and the criteria contained in the statute for limiting this number are not arbitrary or irrational. The sea urchin endorsement statute thus meets the rational basis test.

Prior case law supports this conclusion. In *Weikal v. Department of Fisheries,* 679 P.2d 956 (Wash. 1984), the Court of Appeals held that former RCW 75.28.275, the crab endorsement statute, did not violate the equal protection clause. Former RCW 75.28.275 limited the number of people who could participate in the crab fishery by means of a crab endorsement requirement. The statute provided that crab endorsements would only be issued to vessels which: (1) held a commercial shellfish pot license during a 5-year qualifying period; and (2) landed 1,000 pounds of crab under the license during any 1-year period. In upholding the statute, the Court of Appeals reasoned that:

> Limiting the number of those who may participate in [a] fishery is rationally related to the goal of protecting the resource and regulating the industry. With fewer participating, those holding licenses will be able to harvest sufficient quantities to be financially solvent without seriously depleting the crop.

As in *Weikal,* the fishery in this case became overcrowded, and limits were required to preserve the fishery's economic viability. The statute upheld in *Weikal* does not differ materially from the sea urchin endorsement statute for the purposes of our minimum scrutiny review. We accordingly conclude that RCW 75.30.210, like the crab endorsement statute, does not violate the equal protection clause.

The respondents argue the urchin statute is unconstitutional because the Legislature chose not to include the 1988-89 urchin season in the qualifying period. Many of the respondents landed urchins during this season. They argue the statute is entirely arbitrary and irrational because those vessel owners who did not make substantial urchin landings until the 1988-89 season could conceivably have as much interest in remaining in the fishery as those who *do* qualify for urchin endorsements under the statute.

We must reject this argument. The Legislature evidently concluded it could not effectively address the overharvesting problem if the qualifying period extended to the 1988-89 urchin season. Sixty-two vessels each landed at least 20,000 pounds of urchins during the statute's 2-year qualifying period. Almost 100 *additional* vessel owners entered the urchin fishery during the 1988-89 season. Of these additional vessel owners, approximately 44 landed over 20,000 pounds of urchins and would have thus qualified for urchin endorsements if the qualifying period included the 1988-89 season. If the 1988-89 season had been included in the qualifying period, a total of over 100 vessel owners would have qualified for endorsements. The sea urchin resource showed the first signs of depletion in the 1987-88 season when almost 100 vessels participated in the fishery. By the 1988-89 season, the economic viability of the urchin fishery was in danger because of overharvesting. The Legislature could thus logically conclude that it needed to limit the number of vessels below the number that had participated in the 1987-88 season. Its decision to exclude the 1988-89 season from the qualifying period was thus neither arbitrary nor irrational. *See New Orleans v. Dukes,* 427 U.S. 297, (1976) (ordinance excluding pushcart vendors who had operated less than 8 years in the city's French Quarter from continued operations in the Quarter was not arbitrary or irrational under the rational basis test).

The trial court in this case relied on *State ex rel. Bacich v. Huse,* 59 P.2d 1101 (Wash. 1936) in ruling the urchin endorsement law is unconstitutional. In *Bacich,* a statute restricted the issuance of gill net salmon fishing licenses to people who held such licenses in either 1932 or 1933. Under the statute, people who obtained licenses during these 2 years were the only ones ever eligible to have and renew such licenses. The court in *Bacich* concluded the statute violated the equal protection clause because it created an entirely arbitrary class of people eligible to have and renew the licenses.

The sea urchin endorsement statute does not suffer from the same flaws as the statute in *Bacich.* The statute in this case restricts eligibility for urchin endorsements to those vessel owners who demonstrated substantial participation in the fishery by means of the 20,000-pound landing requirement. The statute in *Bacich* did not impose any landing requirement.... The sea urchin endorsement statute does not create an arbitrary class of persons, and this case is accordingly distinguishable from *Bacich.*

The superior court ruling that RCW 75.30.210 is unconstitutional is reversed.

CHURCH v. STATE
646 N.E.2d 572 (Ill. 1995)

BILANDIC, C.J.

On April 4, 1988, the plaintiff purchased a private alarm contracting business and began operating the business on a part-time basis. The plaintiff worked approximately 1,000 hours a year leasing, selling and servicing alarm systems. On May 8, 1991, the plaintiff learned that the Private Detective, Private Alarm and Private Security Act of 1983 (Act) required him to obtain a license from the Department before engaging in the private alarm contracting business.

On May 31, 1991, the plaintiff submitted an application for a private alarm contractor's license to the Department. The plaintiff characterized his application as one to obtain a license without examination. As part of his application, the plaintiff informed the Board that he was currently employed as a patrolman for the Petersburg police department, and had been employed in that capacity since 1984, working approximately 1,200 hours a year. The plaintiff also informed the Board that he had 18 years of experience as a police officer. During such period of time, the plaintiff had investigated or assisted in investigating 50 different thefts or burglaries. The plaintiff also informed the Board that his police training included classes and seminars in field sobriety testing, mandatory firearms training, shooting decisions training, police traffic radar certification, use of force/civil liability, legal aspects of deadly force and night firearms, operation scams, domestic violence, criminal law, law for police, interview and interrogation, and an in-service refresher.

On September 12, 1991, the Private Detective, Private Alarm, and Private Security Board (Board) held a meeting where the plaintiff's application was considered. The Board recommended that the application be denied. The Director of the Department approved the Board's recommendation and notified the plaintiff that his application was denied "due to the fact that [his] experience does not meet statutory requirements" under the Act.... At issue in this appeal are the experience requirements set forth in section 14(c)(11)(B) of the Act. That section provides:

> (A)ll persons applying for licensure...shall have a minimum of 3 years experience out of the 5 years immediately preceding his application as a full-time supervisor, manager or administrator or an agency licensed in the State of Illinois as a private alarm contractor agency.

We must now consider the plaintiff's claim that section 14(c)(11)(C), as interpreted by the Department, is unconstitutional because it requires an applicant to have three years of employment with a private alarm contractor as a precondition to licensure. The plaintiff argues that the statute thereby grants members of the private alarm contracting industry an unregulated monopoly over entrance into the private alarm contracting trade. (T)he Department argues that the State, pursuant to its inherent police powers, may regulate businesses for the protection of public health, safety and welfare. The Department notes that the legislature has expressly declared that private alarm contracting is a practice affecting the public health, safety and welfare, and therefore, is subject to regulation.

The fact that the legislature has invoked its police power to regulate a particular trade, however, is not conclusive that such power was lawfully exercised. The means of regulation which the legislature adopts by statute must have a definite and reasonable relationship to the end of protecting the public health, safety and welfare. Here, we must determine whether those portions of the Act relating to the licensing of private alarm contractors bear a reasonable relationship to the legislature's goal of protecting the public from the hazards of incompetent private alarm contractors.

In *People v. Brown*, 95 N.E.2d 888 (Ill. 1950), the court invalidated the 1935 plumbing license statute, which provided that a person could not take the examination to become a licensed master plumber until he had spent five years in the employment of a master plumber as an apprentice and then, spent an additional five years in the employment of a master as a journeyman plumber. The court found the statute unconstitutional, in part, because it gave master plumbers monopolistic control over the avenues of entry into the plumbing business. The court found that no matter how well qualified a person might be by instruction or training, that person could never become a certified registered plumber's apprentice, a journeyman plumber or a master plumber, unless a licensed master plumber so willed. By limiting the manner in which a person could learn the plumbing trade to apprenticeship with a master plumber, when many schools could offer similar instruction, the statute conferred on master plumbers an exclusive monopoly on instruction. The court concluded:

> The legislature conferred a special privilege upon master plumbers, as a class, when it gave them the arbitrary and exclusive right to determine who shall, or shall not, engage in the vocation of learning the trade of journeyman plumber, coupled with their having the sole right, with the uncontrolled exercise thereof, to instruct plumbers' apprentices in that trade.

In *People v. Johnson*, 369 N.E.2d 898 (Ill. 1977) the court invalidated yet another version of the plumbing licensing statute…. The *Johnson* court acknowledged that the legislature may reasonably require an applicant to have practical experience, such as an apprenticeship, as a prerequisite to licensure. The court established a two-part test to determine whether an apprenticeship provision is constitutionally valid: "(1) [the provision] must not have the effect, when implemented, of conferring on members of the trade a monopolistic right to instruct, *and* (2) [it] must be structured in such a way that the apprenticeship it requires is calculated to enhance the…expertise of prospective licensees." (Emphasis added.)

Viewing the instant Act in light of the two-part test established in *Johnson*, we conclude that the licensing scheme for private alarm contractors is unconstitutional. The Act violates the first part of the *Johnson* two-part test, because it grants members of the private alarm contracting trade monopolistic control over individuals who wish to gain entrance into the field. Under the Act, as implemented by the Department, applicants without private alarm contractor experience do not qualify for licensure under the Act. An applicant can gain such experience only by being employed full-time for a licensed private alarm contractor agency or for an entity within the industry for three years in a supervisory or managerial capacity. No matter how well qualified a person may be by instruction, training or prior experience, he or she can never of his or her own free will become a licensed private alarm contractor unless a member of the regulated industry is willing to hire him or her on a full-time basis for the requisite time period in a particular capacity. The Act does not require private alarm contractors to employ a person who wishes to enter the field, nor does the refusal to employ such a person need to be based upon any valid reason. As in *Brown, Schroeder* and *Johnson,* it may be predicated upon an understanding between members of the private alarm contracting industry to limit the number of potential competitors allowed into the trade. In effect, the experience provisions within the Act, as implemented by the Department, give members of the private alarm industry an unregulated and monopolistic right to control entrance to the private alarm business.

The two decisions which the Department cites as authority for the proposition that the Act is constitutional are distinguishable. In *People ex rel. Chicago Dental Society v. A.A.A. Dental Laboratories, Inc.,* 134 N.E.2d 285 (Ill. 1956), the court upheld a portion of the Dental Practice Act that prohibited dental laboratory technician from constructing or repairing dentures, bridges or other replacements for teeth, except when employed to do so by a dentist. The court distinguished the statute from the plumbing license laws invalidated in *Brown, Schroeder* and *Johnson.* The court noted that "[t]here is in the present case no prescribed economic hierarchy, with access to each successive stage controlled by the dominant interest. Any person is free to become a dental laboratory technician. The statute places no artificial restraint upon him." The statute at issue in *A.A.A. Dental Laboratories* did not prohibit access to the industry, but merely prohibited dental technicians from performing certain tasks within the industry unless they were performed under the guidance of a licensed dentist.

The Department's reliance upon *Illinois Polygraph Society v. Pellicano,* 414 N.E.2d 458 (Ill. 1980), is likewise misplaced. In that case, the court upheld a statute which required polygraph examiners to complete a six-month course of study prescribed by the Department of Registration and Education as a prerequisite for licensure. The court rejected an argument that the statute, like the plumbing licensing laws at issue in *Brown, Schroeder* and *Johnson,* was unconstitutional. In upholding the validity of the statute, the *Pellicano* court relied upon several factors that do not exist under the instant statute. The court noted that the statute simply required a certain amount of course study as a prerequisite to licensure and did not require employment for a period of years before an applicant qualified for a license. The *Pellicano* court also noted that any person could obtain an internship license under the statute simply by applying and paying the required fee, and that the courses required by statute were not necessarily taught by licensed examiners. Thus, the court concluded that licensed examiners did not possess a monopolistic right to instruct prospective licensees.

The instant Act also violates the second part of the test set forth in *Johnson,* because there is nothing to suggest that the nature and duration of employment required under the statute are calculated to enhance the expertise of prospective licensees. Section 27 of the Act specifies that employees of a private alarm contractor agency who respond to alarm systems must complete at least 20 hours of classroom training on subject matters related to private security, such as: the law of arrest, search and seizure; civil and criminal liability; the use of force; arrest and control techniques; elements of offenses under the Criminal Code; the law on private police; fire prevention and safety; service of process and report writing; and human and public relations. An agency may, but need not, provide any additional training to employees who respond to alarm systems. Employees who do not respond to alarm systems and employees of other entities within the private alarm field are not required by statute to receive *any* particular training.

Even a cursory review of the plaintiff's application for licensure demonstrates that the plaintiff received training in almost every subject matter listed in section 27 while employed as a police officer. Thus, it appears that the training the plaintiff received outside the private alarm contracting field is at least equal to, if not more extensive than, the limited training statutorily required of employees within the private alarm contracting industry. The Department's brief suggests that the plaintiff lacked sufficient electrical experience to qualify for licensure under the Act. Yet, under the Department's interpretation of the Act, an applicant with the plaintiff's experience and extensive electrical experience would still not qualify for licensure unless he or she was employed full-time for three years in a supervisory capacity within the private alarm contracting field. While the legislature and the Department may have rationally believed that practical experience is necessary to assure competence in the private alarm contracting trade, there is nothing to suggest that the duration and type of experience required under the Act is necessary to enhance the expertise of prospective licensees. There is nothing in the record to suggest that the expertise needed to be a competent private alarm contractor can be provided only by full-time employment as a private alarm contractor for three years in a supervisory capacity. Accordingly, we conclude that the Act, as interpreted by the Department, violates the second prong of the *Johnson* test.

Although we agree with the plaintiff's argument that the experience requirements for private alarm contractors under the Act are invalid, we reject his claim that the circuit court properly ordered the Department to issue him a license. Nothing in the statute or the record before us supports the circuit court's conclusion that the plaintiff is *automatically* entitled to a license.... (S)ection 14(c)(12) of the Act specifically states that the Department "*may* conduct an examination which shall include subjects reasonably related to the activities licensed so as to provide for the protection of the health and safety of the public." (Emphasis added.) Here, the Department determined that the plaintiff was not qualified to sit for the examination, because his experience did not meet statutory requirements. Our conclusion that the statutory experience requirements are invalid does not *ipso facto* lead to the conclusion that the plaintiff is entitled to a license. Rather, we simply reverse the Department's finding that the plaintiff is not qualified to take the licensure examination. For the foregoing reasons, we set aside the decision of the Department, and remand this cause to the Department with directions that the plaintiff shall be allowed to sit for the licensing examination.

G. THE RIGHT TO VOTE

LEAGUE OF WOMEN VOTERS OF INDIANA, INC. v. ROKITA
915 N.E.2d 151 (Ind. App. 2009)

RILEY, J.

Appellant-Plaintiff, League of Women Voters of Indiana, Inc. and League of Women Voters of Indianapolis, Inc. (collectively the League), appeal the trial court's dismissal of their Amended Complaint for Declaratory Judgment seeking a judicial declaration that Indiana's Voter I.D. Law violates the Indiana Constitution. We reverse and remand with instructions.

In 2005, the Indiana General Assembly passed a law requiring "citizens voting in person on election day or casting a ballot in person at the office of the circuit court clerk prior to election day to present photo identification issued by the government." *Crawford v. Marion County Election Bd.*, 128 S.Ct. 1610, 1613 (2008). The Voter I.D. Law applies to voting in both primary and general elections. It does not apply, however, to voters casting absentee ballots by mail or those who happen to reside at a state licensed care facility where a precinct polling place is located. To be an acceptable identification card, it must have been issued by the State of Indiana or the United States of America and must contain an expiration date which has not expired as of the time when the voter casts her ballot, or if it has, it did so after the most recent general election. The Voter ID Law additionally made free identification cards available to individuals who do not have a valid Indiana driver's license and who will be at least eighteen at the next election.

If a voter fails to present acceptable proof of identification, the voter can cast a provisional ballot and execute a challenged voter affidavit. If the voter wishes her provisional ballot to be counted she must appear before the circuit court clerk or the county election board before noon ten days following the election. Upon appearing, the voter can either, (1) provide proof of identification and execute an affidavit that she was the person who cast the provisional ballot on election day; or (2) file an affidavit attesting to her religious objection to being photographed or averring that she is indigent and cannot obtain proof of identification without payment of a fee. Once a voter has taken one of these two steps, the county election board shall count the voter's ballot as long as no other challenge to the provisional ballot exists.

The League contends that the Voter I.D. law violates Article 1, Section 23 (Section 23) of the Indiana Constitution, otherwise known as the Equal Privileges and Immunities Clause, which provides: "The General Assembly shall not grant to any citizen, or class of citizens, privileges or immunities which, upon the same terms, shall not equally belong to all citizens." The analytical process for determining whether a statute which treats certain citizens differently than others passes muster under the Equal Privileges and Immunities Clause was summarized in *Collins v. Day*, 644 N.E.2d 72, 80 (Ind.1994), as follows:

> First, the disparate treatment accorded by the legislation must be reasonably related to inherent characteristics which distinguish the unequally treated classes. Second, the preferential treatment must be uniformly applicable and equally available to all persons similarly situated. Finally, in determining whether a statute complies with or violates Section 23, courts must exercise substantial deference to legislative discretion.

"Legislative classification becomes a judicial question only where the lines drawn appear arbitrary or manifestly unreasonable, and the challenger must negate every reasonable basis for the classification." *W.C.B. v. State*, 855 N.E.2d 1057, 1063 (Ind.Ct.App.2006), trans. denied. Furthermore, Section 23 differs from analysis under the equal protection clause of the Fourteenth Amendment of the federal constitution. Specifically, it does not "require an analytical framework applying varying degrees of scrutiny for different protected interests." *Id.*

The League contends that three aspects of the Voter I.D. Law violates Section 23:(1) the disparate treatment between mail-in absentee voters and in-person voters; (2) the disparate treatment between voters who reside at state licensed care facilities that by happenstance are polling places and elderly and disabled voters who do not reside at state licensed care facilities that also happen to be polling places; and (3) the requirements that an identification contain an expiration date and photograph is not reasonably related to the purpose of the statute.

A. Mail-in Voters versus In-Person Voters

Indiana Code section 3-11-10-1.2 provides: "An absentee voter is not required to provide proof of identification when: (1) mailing, delivering, or transmitting an absentee ballot under section 1 of this chapter; or (2) voting before an absentee board under section 25 of this chapter." The League first contends, relevant to the disparate treatment between mail-in and in-person voters, that "the claimed distinctions between" these groups "do not support the claimed purpose of the" Voter I.D. Law. The crux of the League's contention is that mail-in voters are not required by law to execute an affidavit regarding their identity, but in-person voters are required to produce a government issued photo identification card which contains an expiration date. The League directs our attention to our supreme court's decision in *Horseman v. Keller*, 841 N.E.2d 164 (Ind.2006). In *Horseman*, the trial court declared Indiana Code section 3-12-1-13 unconstitutional because it did not allow mailed-in absentee ballots lacking two sets of clerks' initials to be counted in a recount although ballots cast in-person, but lacking two sets of clerks' initials, could be counted in the recount. Our supreme court declared to the contrary that the statute was constitutional, because inherent differences make mailed-in ballots more susceptible to improper influences or fraud, and, therefore, "it is reasonable that the legislature believed it in the interest of Indiana voters to more stringently govern absentee balloting." *Id.* at 173. Because of this conclusion, the League contends that it is irrational for our legislature to require identification of in-person voters but not require an affidavit affirming the identity of mail-in voters. We agree.

If it is reasonable to "more stringently govern absentee balloting," then it follows that a statute that imposes a less stringent requirement for absentee voters than for those voting in person would not be reasonable. This is what the Voter I.D. law does.

B. Voters Not Residing at a State Licensed Care Facility versus Those Who Do

Indiana Code sections 3-10-1-7.2 and 3-11-8-25.1 provide that "[a] voter who votes in person at a precinct polling place that is located at a state licensed care facility where the voter resides is not required to provide proof of identification before voting in" a primary election or in an election. The League contends that this preferential treatment violates both prongs of Section 23 analysis.

We first notice when reviewing the arguments of the parties with respect to the second prong they propose different definitions of those similarly situated. The State contends that those similarly situated is just what the statute says-persons who reside at a state licensed care facility which also happens to be a polling place. However, the League would have us more broadly define those similarly situated by acknowledging that persons who reside at health care facilities are the disabled and elderly, thereby framing the interpretation so that it becomes apparent when the second prong analysis is performed that the disabled and elderly are treated unequally under the Voter I.D. law. It seems that these differing positions stem from different views of what are the inherent and natural characteristics of the class, which is not surprising considering the overlap amongst the concepts of "classification" and "similarly situated."

As we stated above the "classifications must be 'just,' 'natural,' 'reasonable,' 'substantial,' 'not artificial,' 'not capricious,' and 'not arbitrary.'" *Collins*, at 79. Moreover, the basis of the classification must "inhere in the subject matter." *Id.* at 78. In *Heckler v. Confer*, 206 Ind. 376, 187 N.E. 878 (1933), one of the cases relied upon by the Collins court to articulate the first prong of our analysis, it was said regarding classes:

> The distinctions must involve something more than mere characteristics which will serve to divide or identify the class. There must be inherent differences in situation related to the subject matter of the legislation which require, necessitate, or make expedient different or exclusive legislation with respect to the members of the class. The classification must embrace all who possess the attributes or characteristics which are the basis of the classification, and their differences from those excluded must be substantial and related to the purpose of the legislation. *Id.* at 381, 187 N.E. 879-880.

So, is a class of persons who reside at a state licensed care facility that by happenstance serves as a polling place a classification that passes muster under the Equal Privileges and Immunities Clause? The State contends that by conferring the privilege to be free of the identification requirement upon those who reside at state licensed care facilities:

> The General Assembly was simply acknowledging and accommodating a few basic self-evident realities: (1) regardless of where they live, all seniors and disabled voters can vote absentee and need not provide photo identification in doing so; (2) seniors and the disabled living in licensed care facilities that are not polling places may be likely to vote absentee in order to avoid the travel required for voting; (3) seniors and the disabled who live in care facilities that are polling places may be more likely to vote in person because they will not have to travel to do so; (4) seniors and the disabled who live in care facilities would likely have particular difficulty traveling to obtain photo identification; and (5) seniors and the disabled who vote in person in the facilities where they live are likely to be identifiable as residents by election officials and unlikely to commit fraud by intentionally misidentifying themselves. (Appellee's Br. pp. 32-33) (emphasis supplied).

First, we note that the way in which the State describes the "realities" conveys that they accept that old age or disability is a natural, inherent characteristic of the classification. Each proposed "reality" refers to "seniors and the disabled." Thus, the question that remains is whether residing at a state licensed care facility which also happens to be a polling place is a natural or inherent characteristic.

The enumerated contentions by the State do not support a conclusion that either the class created by the Indiana Code sections 3-10-1-7.2 and 3-11-8-25.1 is based on natural or inherent characteristics, or that it treats all similarly situated uniformly. Moreover, the first enumerated "reality" contended by the State calls into question the "requirement," "necessity," or "expediency" of the privilege conferred upon those who reside at state health care facilities that are polling places. If these voters can vote without identification by mailing their vote just as any other elderly or disabled person, then why would the privilege be required, necessary, or expedient as required by Heckler?

As for the second and third "realities" contended by the State, they are nothing more than an acknowledgment that certain persons will take advantage of the privileges afforded them. As for the fourth "reality" contended by the State, the difficulty of obtaining an identification is shared by all elderly and disabled, so acknowledging this reality supports a conclusion that similarly situated persons are not being treated uniformly as required by the second prong of Section 23 analysis. And, as for the fifth "reality" proposed by the State, in many communities voters will be recognized by election officials. Further, the State contends that residents of state licensed care facilities which happen to be polling places will be easily "identifiable as residents." (Appellant's Br. p. 33). This would not prevent a resident from assuming the identity of another resident who may choose not to vote or be unable to vote for one reason or another.

In *Collins*, our supreme court relied, in part, upon *Dixon v. Poe*, 159 Ind. 492, 65 N.E. 518 (1902), to craft the second prong of Section 23 analysis. The statute at issue in *Dixon* prohibited "merchants" from paying coal miners with tickets or tokens which could be exchanged for merchandise. Our supreme court found the act to be a violation of the Equal Privileges and Immunities Clause.

> The mechanic, the farmer, the professional man, the banker or broker may lawfully take an assignment of the wages of the coal miner, and, in consideration of such transfer, may issue to the miner a check, ticket, or token payable only in merchandise, work, produce, professional services, or depreciated notes or currency.

> Laborers and employ'es engaged in a particular industry, who are no less intelligent and no less competent to care for their own interests than laborers and employ'es pursuing other occupations, are by the statute singled out and authorized to avoid their express agreements, when, under like circumstances, such other laborers and employ'es enjoy no such privilege. The law does not embrace all of the class to which it is naturally related. It creates a preference, and establishes an inequality among a class of citizens all of who are qually meritorious. It applies to persons in certain situations, and excludes from its effect other persons who are not dissimilar in these respects. Leaving the miner and the merchant free to deal with all other citizens, the act disqualifies them from contracting with each other. *Dixon*, 159 Ind. at 495-496, 65 N.E. at 519.

Another precedent relied upon by the *Collins* court was *State Board of Barber Examiners v. Cloud*, 220 Ind. 552, 44 N.E.2d 972 (1942). In Cloud, our supreme court found a Huntington County Ordinance which set minimum prices and hours of operation for barber shops to be unconstitutional. The *Cloud* court acknowledged that the nature of barber shops made them subject to certain regulations to promote sanitation, "[b]ut the right to regulate for some purposes and in some ways does not include the right to regulate for all purposes in all ways." *Id.* at 561, 44 N.E. at 976.

Using the precedents of *Dixon* and *Cloud*, we conclude that the class created by Indiana Code sections 3-10-1-7.2 and 3-11-8-25.1 is based in part upon an arbitrary or unnatural characteristic which grants an unequal privilege or immunity to residents of state licensed care facilities which also happen to be polling places and fails to treat persons similarly situated uniformly. The nature of state licensed care facilities and the inherent natural characteristics of the residents who reside in them may make them subject to certain directed legislation, but the Voter I.D.'s grant of immunity from the identification requirement for in-person voters is not appropriately related to those characteristics. Moreover, the privilege or immunity granted those persons in the class is unnecessary when it is acknowledged that those residing at state licensed care facilities already have an opportunity to vote absentee without showing identification. Therefore, we conclude that Indiana Code sections 3-10-1-7.2 and 3-11-8-25.1 violate the Equal Privileges and Immunities Clause.

It seems that the inconsistent and impartial treatment favoring voters who reside at state care facilities which also happen to be polling places could be excised from the Voter I.D. Law without destroying the primary objectives of the Law. However, the same cannot be said for the inconsistent and partial treatment favoring absentee voters who choose to mail their votes without destroying the opportunity for mailing votes. There may be different ways in which the inconsistent and partial treatment of the Voter I.D. Law could be cured, but it is not our task to form suggestions for legislation. Therefore, we must reverse and remand, with instructions to the trial court that it enter an order declaring the Voter I.D. Law void.

CONCLUSION

Based on the foregoing, we conclude that the Voter I.D. law violates Indiana Constitution Article 1, Section 23, and must be declared void because it regulates voters in a manner that is not uniform and impartial.

NOTES

1. A year before the decision of the Indiana Court of Appeals in *League of Women Voters of Indiana, Inc. v. Rokita*, the Supreme Court of the United States considered a challenge to the same Indiana Voter ID Law under the Federal Equal Protection Clause. *Crawford v. Marion County Election Board*, 128 S.Ct. 1610 (2008). The high Court upheld the law by a vote of 6-3, finding no violation of the Equal Protection Clause. Justice Stevens' plurality opinion in *Crawford* concluded that the Indiana Voter ID law served the important state interest of preventing voter fraud while imposing only a limited burden on the right to vote. Although his opinion

described the Indiana law as a "nondiscriminatory law...supported by valid neutral justifications," it did not consider the possibly discriminatory aspects of the law in depth. Whereas the Supreme Court decision focused on weighing the state's interest in preventing voter fraud as compared to the burden the law placed on the right to vote, the decision of the Indiana Court of Appeals focused on the discriminatory aspects of the Voter ID law, which, of course, it found to violate the Indiana Equal Privileges and Immunities Clause. The decision of the Court of Appeals in *League of Women Voters* has been appealed to the Supreme Court of Indiana.

2. A few state constitutions contain provisions expressly guaranteeing "free and equal elections." For example, the Constitution of Delaware states: "All Elections shall be free and equal." Del. Const. art. I, §3 (1897). *See also*, Wyo. Const. art. I, §27.

CHAPTER VI

DUE PROCESS OF LAW

A. INTRODUCTION

Conferred by King John on the meadow of Runnymede in the year 1215, the Magna Carta proclaimed:

> No Free man shall be taken or imprisoned, or be disseised of his Freehold, or Liberties, or free Customs, or be outlawed, or exiled, or any other wise destroyed; nor will we not pass upon him, nor condemn him, but by lawful judgment of his Peers, or by the Law of the land. We will sell to no man, we will not deny or defer to any man either Justice or Right.

The Magna Carta served as a model for the American colonies, many of which adopted laws based upon the great charter. Shortly after achieving independence, most of the new states enacted constitutional provisions prohibiting the deprivation of life, liberty, or property except by the "law of the land." In time, some states used a somewhat different phraseology, prohibiting the deprivation of life, liberty, or property without "due process of law." Eventually, all of the states enacted either law of the land clauses or due process clauses as part of their state constitutions. According to Thomas Cooley, an eminent constitutional scholar of the late nineteenth century, whichever phrase was used, "the meaning (was) the same in every case." Thomas M. Cooley, A TREATISE ON THE CONSTITUTIONAL LIMITATIONS WHICH REST UPON THE LEGISLATIVE POWER OF THE STATES OF THE AMERICAN UNION 353 (1868).

There are those who argue that the phrase "due process of law" was meant only to refer to the procedures required before a person may be deprived of life, liberty or property, and did not comprehend judicial authority to invalidate legislation on substantive grounds. Others disagree and believe that due process of law encompassed a substantive component. Beginning in the 1790's an increasing number of state courts gave a substantive content to due process of law in striking down statutes found to arbitrarily divest persons of property rights. By the end of the nineteenth century, an evolving body of law existed that recognized a substantive element to due process of law. See Jeffrey M. Shaman, *On the 100th Anniversary of Lochner v. New York*, 72 Tenn. L. R. 455, 476-88 (2005).

Some state constitutions also contain other provisions directed to safeguarding life, liberty, or property. The Kentucky Constitution, for example, states: "Absolute and arbitrary power over the lives, liberty and property of freemen exists nowhere in a republic, not even in the largest majority."[1] In other states, protection for life, liberty, or property has been found implicit in constitutional provisions declaring that "All persons are by nature free and independent, and have certain natural and inalienable rights"[2] or stating that "The enumeration in this Constitution of certain rights shall not be construed to deny, impair, or disparage others retained by, the people."[3]

As constitutional doctrine evolved, the right of privacy was recognized as a fundamental element of liberty. State constitutional conceptions of the right of privacy first emerged in the early twentieth century, but then fell into quiescence for decades, before being revived for further development. In the meantime, the United States Supreme Court took the lead in formulating a constitutional right of privacy under the Due Process Clause of the Fourteenth Amendment. First, the high Court ruled that the Due Process Clause protects a fundamental right of privacy that encompasses the right to reproductive autonomy. In subsequent decisions, the Court expanded the federal right of privacy to encompass certain family rights and, eventually, a right of intimate association. Yet the Court has placed definitive limits on family and reproductive rights and also has refused to extend the right of privacy to other areas. Over time, the Supreme Court's commitment to the right of privacy has vacillated considerably, leaving the scope of the right of privacy under the Federal Constitution far from certain.

Building on federal doctrine, a number of states have gone on to strengthen the right of privacy by turning to provisions in their state constitutions. Five states—Alaska, California, Florida, Hawaii, and Montana—have amended their constitutions to expressly protect the right of privacy. These express provisions offer a sound textual basis for the expansion of privacy rights. In some states that have no express constitutional protection for privacy, the courts have used more generally worded provisions, such as a due process clause, to recognize and eventually enlarge the right of privacy. Not all states have been willing to join this movement; some state courts have thought it best to recognize no constitutional privacy rights other than those required by the Federal Constitution. But a number of state courts have used their state constitutions to enhance the right of privacy beyond federal dictates.

The guarantee of due process of law mandates that the government follow fair procedures before depriving anyone of life, liberty, or property. The principle of procedural due process applies to all government proceedings, both civil and criminal. At its core, the principle of

---

[1] Ky. Const., Bill of Rights, §2,

[2] N.J. Const., art I, § 1.

[3] Ok. Const., art. II, § 33.

procedural due process requires notice and an opportunity to be heard in a fair proceeding. In some instances, the scope of protection afforded by procedural due process under a state constitution has been extended beyond that provided by the Federal Constitution.

B. REPRODUCTIVE AUTONOMY

DAVIS v. DAVIS
842 S.W.2d 588 (Tenn. 1992)

DAUGHTREY, J.

This appeal presents a question of first impression, involving the disposition of the cryogenically-preserved product of in vitro fertilization (IVF), commonly referred to in the popular press and the legal journals as "frozen embryos." The case began as a divorce action, filed by the appellee, Junior Lewis Davis, against his then wife, appellant Mary Sue Davis. The parties were able to agree upon all terms of dissolution, except one: who was to have "custody" of the seven "frozen embryos" stored in a Knoxville fertility clinic that had attempted to assist the Davises in achieving a much-wanted pregnancy during a happier period in their relationship.

Mary Sue Davis originally asked for control of the "frozen embryos" with the intent to have them transferred to her own uterus, in a post-divorce effort to become pregnant. Junior Davis objected, saying that he preferred to leave the embryos in their frozen state until he decided whether or not he wanted to become a parent outside the bounds of marriage.... We note, in this latter regard, that their positions have already shifted: both have remarried and Mary Sue Davis (now Mary Sue Stowe) has moved out of state. She no longer wishes to utilize the "frozen embryos" herself, but wants authority to donate them to a childless couple. Junior Davis is adamantly opposed to such donation and would prefer to see the "frozen embryos" discarded.

At the outset, it is important to note the absence of two critical factors that might otherwise influence or control the result of this litigation: When the Davises signed up for the IVF program at the Knoxville clinic, they did not execute a written agreement specifying what disposition should be made of any unused embryos that might result from the cryopreservation process. Moreover, there was at that time no Tennessee statute governing such disposition, nor has one been enacted in the meantime. In addition, because of the uniqueness of the question before us, we have no case law to guide us to a decision in this case.

The Right of Procreational Autonomy

The essential dispute here is…whether the parties will become parents. The Court of Appeals held in effect that they will become parents if they both agree to become parents. The Court did not say what will happen if they fail to agree. We conclude that the answer to this dilemma turns on the parties' exercise of their constitutional right to privacy.

The right to privacy is not specifically mentioned in either the federal or the Tennessee state constitution, and yet there can be little doubt about its grounding in the concept of liberty reflected in those two documents…. [I]n the Tennessee Constitution, the concept of liberty plays a central role. Article I, Section 8 provides:

> That no man shall be taken or imprisoned, or disseized of his freehold, liberties or privileges, or outlawed, or exiled, or in any manner destroyed or deprived of his life, liberty or property, but by the judgment of his peers or the law of the land.

Indeed, the notion of individual liberty is so deeply embedded in the Tennessee Constitution that it, alone among American constitutions, gives the people, in the face of governmental oppression and interference with liberty, the right to resist that oppression even to the extent of overthrowing the government. The relevant provisions establishing this distinctive political autonomy appear in the first two sections of Article I of the Tennessee Constitution, its Declaration of Rights:

> Section 1. All power inherent in the people-Government under their control.

> That all power is inherent in the people, and all free governments are founded on their authority, and instituted for their peace, safety, and happiness; for the advancement of those ends they have at all times, an inalienable and indefeasible right to alter, reform, or abolish the government in such manner as they may think proper.

> Section 2. Doctrine of nonresistance condemned.

> That government being instituted for the common benefit, the doctrine of non-resistance against arbitrary power and oppression is absurd, slavish, and destructive of the good and happiness of mankind.

Obviously, the drafters of the Tennessee Constitution of 1796 could not have anticipated the need to construe the liberty clauses of that document in terms of the choices flowing from in vitro fertilization procedures. But there can be little doubt that they foresaw the need to protect individuals from unwarranted governmental intrusion into matters such as the one now before us, involving intimate questions of personal and family concern. Based on both the language and the development of our state constitution, we have no hesitation in drawing the conclusion that there is a right of individual privacy guaranteed under and protected by the liberty clauses of the Tennessee Declaration of Rights.

Undoubtedly, that right to privacy incorporates some of the attributes of the federal constitutional right to privacy and, in any given fact situation, may also share some of its contours. As with other state constitutional rights having counterparts in the federal bill of rights, however, there is no reason to assume that there is a complete congruency. Here, the specific individual freedom in dispute is the right to procreate. In terms of the Tennessee state constitution, we hold that the right of procreation is a vital part of an individual's right to privacy. Federal law is to the same effect.

In construing the reach of the federal constitution, the United States Supreme Court has addressed the affirmative right to procreate in only two cases. In *Buck v. Bell*, 274 U.S. 200 (1927), the Court upheld the sterilization of a "feebleminded white woman." However, in *Skinner v. Oklahoma*, 316 U.S. 535 (1942), the Supreme Court struck down a statute that authorized the sterilization of certain categories of criminals. The Court described the right to procreate as "one of the basic civil rights of man [sic]," and stated that "[m]arriage and procreation are fundamental to the very existence and survival of the race." In the same vein, the United States Supreme Court has said:

> If the right of privacy means anything, it is the right of the *individual*, married or single, to be free from unwarranted governmental intrusion into matters so fundamentally affecting a person as the decision whether to bear or beget a child. *Eisenstadt v. Baird*, 405 U.S. 438 (1972) (emphasis in original).

That a right to procreational autonomy is inherent in our most basic concepts of liberty is also indicated by the reproductive freedom cases, see, e.g., *Griswold v. Connecticut*, 381 U.S. 479 (1965); and *Roe v. Wade*, 410 U.S. 113 (1973), and by cases concerning parental rights and responsibilities with respect to children. See, e.g., *Wisconsin v. Yoder*, 406 U.S. 205 (1972); *Prince v. Massachusetts*, 321 U.S. 158 (1944); *Cleveland Board of Education v. LaFleur*, 414 U.S. 632 (1974); *Pierce v. Society of the Sisters of the Holy Names of Jesus and Mary*, 268 U.S. 510 (1925); and *Bellotti v. Baird*, 443 U.S. 622 (1979). In fact, in *Bellotti v. Baird*, the Supreme Court noted that parental autonomy is basic to the structure of our society because the family is "the institution by which we inculcate and pass down many of our most cherished values, moral and cultural."

The United States Supreme Court has never addressed the issue of procreation in the context of in vitro fertilization. Moreover, the extent to which procreational autonomy is protected by the United States Constitution is no longer entirely clear. For the purposes of this litigation it is sufficient to note that, whatever its ultimate constitutional boundaries, the right of procreational autonomy is composed of two rights of equal significance-the right to procreate and the right to avoid procreation. Undoubtedly, both are subject to protections and limitations.

The equivalence of and inherent tension between these two interests are nowhere more evident than in the context of in vitro fertilization. None of the concerns about a woman's bodily integrity that have previously precluded men from controlling abortion decisions is applicable here. We are not unmindful of the fact that the trauma (including both emotional stress and physical discomfort) to which women are subjected in the IVF process is more severe than is the impact of the procedure on men. In this sense, it is fair to say that women contribute more to the IVF process than men. Their experience, however, must be viewed in light of the joys of parenthood that is desired or the relative anguish of a lifetime of unwanted parenthood. As they stand on the brink of potential parenthood, Mary Sue Davis and Junior Lewis Davis must be seen as entirely equivalent gamete-providers.

It is further evident that, however far the protection of procreational autonomy extends, the existence of the right itself dictates that decisional authority rests in the gamete-providers alone, at least to the extent that their decisions have an impact upon their individual reproductive status.... [N]o other person or entity has an interest sufficient to permit interference with the gamete-providers' decision to continue or terminate the IVF process, because no one else bears the consequences of these decisions in the way that the gamete-providers do.

Further, at least with respect to Tennessee's public policy and its constitutional right of privacy, the state's interest in potential human life is insufficient to justify an infringement on the gamete-providers' procreational autonomy. The United States Supreme Court has indicated in *Webster*, and even in *Roe*, that the state's interest in potential human life may justify statutes or regulations that have an impact upon a person's exercise of procreational autonomy. This potential for sufficiently weighty state's interests is not, however, at issue here, because Tennessee's statutes contain no statement of public policy which reveals an interest that could justify infringing on gamete-providers' decisional authority over the preembryos to which they have contributed.

Tennessee's abortion statute reveals a public policy decision weighing the interests of living persons against the state's interest in potential life. At least during certain stages of a pregnancy, the personal interests of the pregnant woman outweigh the state's interests and the pregnancy may be terminated. Taken collectively, our statutes reflect the policy decision that, at least in some circumstances, the interest of living individuals in avoiding procreation is sufficient to justify taking steps to terminate the procreational process, despite the state's interest in potential life.

Certainly, if the state's interests do not become sufficiently compelling in the abortion context until the end of the first trimester, after very significant developmental stages have passed, then surely there is no state interest in these preembryos which could suffice to overcome the interests of the gamete-providers. The abortion statute reveals that the increase in the state's interest is marked by each successive developmental stage such that, toward the end of a pregnancy, this interest is so compelling that abortion is almost strictly forbidden. This scheme supports the conclusion that the state's interest in the potential life embodied by these four- to eight-cell preembryos (which may or may not be able to achieve implantation in a uterine wall and which, if implanted, may or may not begin to develop into fetuses, subject to possible miscarriage) is at best slight. When weighed against the interests of the individuals and the burdens inherent in parenthood, the state's interest in the potential life of these preembryos is not sufficient to justify any infringement upon the freedom of these individuals to make their own decisions as to whether to allow a process to continue that may result in such a dramatic change in their lives as becoming parents.

The unique nature of this case requires us to note that the interests of these parties in parenthood are different in scope than the parental interest considered in other cases. Previously, courts have dealt with the child-bearing and child-rearing aspects of parenthood. Abortion cases have dealt with gestational parenthood. In this case, the Court must deal with the question of genetic parenthood. We conclude, moreover, that an interest in avoiding genetic parenthood can be significant enough to trigger the protections afforded to all other aspects of parenthood. The technological fact that someone unknown to these parties could gestate these preembryos does not alter the fact that these parties, the gamete-providers, would become parents in that event, at least in the genetic sense. The profound impact this would have on them supports their right to sole decisional authority as to whether the process of attempting to gestate these preembryos should continue. This brings us directly to the question of how to resolve the dispute that arises when one party wishes to continue the IVF process and the other does not.

Balancing the Parties' Interests

Resolving disputes over conflicting interests of constitutional import is a task familiar to the courts. In this case, the issue centers on the two aspects of procreational autonomy-the right to procreate and the right to avoid procreation. Beginning with the burden imposed on Junior Davis, we note that the consequences are obvious. Any disposition which results in the gestation of the preembryos would impose unwanted parenthood on him, with all of its possible financial and psychological consequences. The impact that this unwanted parenthood would have on Junior Davis can only be understood by considering his particular circumstances, as revealed in the record.

Junior Davis testified that he was the fifth youngest of six children. When he was five years old, his parents divorced, his mother had a nervous break-down, and he and three of his brothers went to live at a home for boys run by the Lutheran Church. Another brother was taken in by an aunt, and his sister stayed with their mother. From that day forward, he had monthly visits with his mother but saw his father only three more times before he died in 1976. Junior Davis testified that, as a boy, he had severe problems caused by separation from his parents. He said that it was especially hard to leave his mother after each monthly visit. He clearly feels that he has suffered because of his lack of opportunity to establish a relationship with his parents and particularly because of the absence of his father.

In light of his boyhood experiences, Junior Davis is vehemently opposed to fathering a child that would not live with both parents. Regardless of whether he or Mary Sue had custody, he feels that the child's bond with the non-custodial parent would not be satisfactory. He testified very clearly that his concern was for the psychological obstacles a child in such a situation would face, as well as the burdens it would impose on him. Likewise, he is opposed to donation because the recipient couple might divorce, leaving the child (which he definitely would consider his own) in a single-parent setting.

Balanced against Junior Davis's interest in avoiding parenthood is Mary Sue Davis's interest in donating the preembryos to another couple for implantation. Refusal to permit donation of the preembryos would impose on her the burden of knowing that the lengthy IVF procedures she underwent were futile, and that the preembryos to which she contributed genetic material would never become children. While this is not an insubstantial emotional burden, we can only conclude that Mary Sue Davis's interest in donation is not as significant as the interest Junior Davis has in avoiding parenthood. If she were allowed to donate these preembryos, he would face a lifetime of either wondering about his parental status or knowing about his parental status but having no control over it. He testified quite clearly that if these preembryos were brought to term he would fight for custody of his child or children. Donation, if a child came of it, would rob him twice-his procreational autonomy would be defeated and his relationship with his offspring would be prohibited.

The case would be closer if Mary Sue Davis were seeking to use the preembryos herself, but only if she could not achieve parenthood by any other reasonable means. We recognize the trauma that Mary Sue has already experienced and the additional discomfort to which she would be subjected if she opts to attempt IVF again. Still, she would have a reasonable opportunity, through IVF, to try once again to achieve parenthood in all its aspects-genetic, gestational, bearing, and rearing.

Further, we note that if Mary Sue Davis were unable to undergo another round of IVF, or opted not to try, she could still achieve the child-rearing aspects of parenthood through adoption. The fact that she and

Junior Davis pursued adoption indicates that, at least at one time, she was willing to forego genetic parenthood and would have been satisfied by the child-rearing aspects of parenthood alone.

Conclusion

In summary, we hold that disputes involving the disposition of preembryos produced by in vitro fertilization should be resolved, first, by looking to the preferences of the progenitors. If their wishes cannot be ascertained, or if there is dispute, then their prior agreement concerning disposition should be carried out. If no prior agreement exists, then the relative interests of the parties in using or not using the preembryos must be weighed. Ordinarily, the party wishing to avoid procreation should prevail, assuming that the other party has a reasonable possibility of achieving parenthood by means other than use of the preembryos in question. If no other reasonable alternatives exist, then the argument in favor of using the preembryos to achieve pregnancy should be considered. However, if the party seeking control of the preembryos intends merely to donate them to another couple, the objecting party obviously has the greater interest and should prevail.

But the rule does not contemplate the creation of an automatic veto, and in affirming the judgment of the Court of Appeals, we would not wish to be interpreted as so holding. For the reasons set out above, the judgment of the Court of Appeals is affirmed, in the appellee's favor. This ruling means that the Knoxville Fertility Clinic is free to follow its normal procedure in dealing with unused preembryos, as long as that procedure is not in conflict with this opinion. Costs on appeal will be taxed to the appellant.

NOTE

In re Roberto D.B., 923 A.2d 115 (Md. 2007), presented the question of whether a woman who carried and gave birth to twins, but was genetically unrelated to them, must be listed on the birth certificate as the mother of the twins. The twins were conceived through in vitro fertilization when Roberto D. B., who was unmarried, provided his sperm to fertilize eggs from a donor. The fertilized eggs were then implanted in another woman to gestate in her womb. Eight months later, the woman gave birth to twins at a hospital in Silver Spring, Maryland. As required by law, the hospital provides information regarding births to the Maryland Division of Vital Records (MDVR), which issues birth certificates. Unless a court orders otherwise, the hospital will report the gestational carrier as the "mother" of a child to the MDVR. The hospital followed this procedure. Roberto D.B. and the gestational carrier petitioned a circuit court to issue a birth certificate that did not list the gestational carrier as the children's mother. In the petition, they asked the court to declare that Roberto D.B. was the father of the children, and to authorize the hospital to report only the name of the father to the MDVR. Both parties averred that they never intended the gestational carrier to exercise any parental rights over the children and that they agreed that her role in the lives of the children would end upon their birth. The circuit court refused to grant the petition, and an appeal was taken to the Maryland Supreme Court, which ruled that the petition should be granted, allowing the gestational carrier's name to be deleted from the birth certificate.

The court's decision resulted from its construction of a state paternity statute that, as written, provided an opportunity for genetically unrelated males to avoid parentage, while genetically unrelated females did not have the same option. Because the state Equal Rights Amendment prohibited the granting of more rights to one sex than to the other, the court ruled that the paternity statute must be construed to allow genetically unrelated females to have the same right as genetically unrelated males to avoid parentage.

IN RE T.W.
551 So.2d 1186 (Fla. 1989)

SHAW, J.

We have on appeal *In re T.W.*, 543 So.2d 837 (Fla. 5th DCA 1989), which declared unconstitutional section 390.001(4)(a), Florida Statutes (Supp.1988), the parental consent statute. We approve the opinion of the district court and hold the statute invalid under the Florida Constitution.

The procedure that a minor must follow to obtain an abortion in Florida is set out in the parental consent statute and related rules. Prior to undergoing an abortion, a minor must obtain parental consent or, alternatively, must convince a court that she is sufficiently mature to make the decision herself or that, if she is immature, the abortion nevertheless is in her best interests. Pursuant to this procedure, T.W., a pregnant, unmarried, fifteen-year-old, petitioned for a waiver of parental consent under the judicial bypass provision on the alternative grounds that (1) she was sufficiently mature to give an informed consent to the abortion, (2) she had a justified fear of physical or emotional abuse if her parents were requested to consent, and (3) her mother was seriously ill and informing her of the pregnancy would be an added burden. The trial court, after appointing counsel for T.W. and separate counsel as guardian ad litem for the fetus, conducted a hearing within twenty-four hours of the filing of the petition.

The relevant portions of the hearing consisted of T.W.'s uncontroverted testimony that she was a high-school student, participated in band and flag corps, worked twenty hours a week, baby-sat for her mother and neighbors, planned on finishing high school and attending vocational school or community college, had observed an instructional film on abortion, had taken a sex education course at school, would not put her child up for adoption, and had discussed her plans with the child's father and obtained his approval. She informed the court that due to her mother's illness, she had assumed extra duties at home caring for her sibling and that if she told her mother about the abortion, "it would kill her." Evidence was introduced showing that the pregnancy was in the first trimester.

The seminal case in United States abortion law is *Roe v. Wade*, 410 U.S. 113, (1973). There, the Court ruled that a right to privacy implicit in the fourteenth amendment embraces a woman's decision concerning abortion. Autonomy to make this decision constitutes a fundamental right and states may impose restrictions only when narrowly drawn to serve a compelling state interest. The Court recognized two important state interests, protecting the health of the mother and the potentiality of life in the fetus, and ruled that these interests become compelling at the completion of the first trimester of pregnancy and upon viability of the fetus (approximately at the end of the second trimester), respectively. Thus, during the first trimester, states must leave the abortion decision to the woman and her doctor; during the second trimester, states may impose measures to protect the mother's health; and during the period following viability, states may possibly forbid abortions altogether. Subsequent to *Roe*, the Court issued several decisions dealing directly with the matter of parental consent for minors seeking abortions. See *Planned Parenthood Ass'n v. Ashcroft*, 462 U.S. 476 (1983); *City of Akron v. Akron Center for Reproductive Health Inc.*, 462 U.S. 416 (1983); *Bellotti v. Baird*, 443 U.S. 622 (1979) (plurality opinion); *Planned Parenthood v. Danforth*, 428 U.S. 52 (1976).

To be held constitutional, the instant statute must pass muster under both the federal and state constitutions. Were we to examine it solely under the federal Constitution, our analysis necessarily would track the decisions noted above. However, Florida is unusual in that it is one of at least four states having its own express constitutional provision guaranteeing an independent right to privacy, and we opt to examine the statute first under the Florida Constitution. If it fails here, then no further analysis under federal law is required.

As we noted in *Winfield v. Division of Pari-Mutuel Wagering*, 477 So.2d 544 (Fla.1985), the essential concept of privacy is deeply rooted in our nation's political and philosophical heritage. Pursuant to this principle, the United States Supreme Court has recognized a privacy right that shields an individual's autonomy in deciding matters concerning marriage, procreation, contraception, family relationships, and child rearing and education. The Court, however, has made it clear that the states, not the federal government, are the final guarantors of personal privacy: "But the protection of a person's *general* right to privacy-his right to be let alone by other people-is, like the protection of his property and of his very life, left largely to the law of the individual States." *Katz v. United States*, 389 U.S. 347, 350-51, (1967) (emphasis in original). While the federal Constitution traditionally shields enumerated and implied individual liberties from encroachment by state or federal government, the federal Court has long held that state constitutions may provide even greater protection. See, e.g., *Pruneyard Shopping Center v. Robins*, 447 U.S. 74 (1980).

In 1980, Florida voters by general election amended our state constitution to provide:

> Right of privacy.-Every natural person has the right to be let alone and free from governmental intrusion into his private life except as otherwise provided herein. This section shall not be construed to limit the public's right of access to public records and meetings as provided by law. Art. I, §23, Fla. Const.

This Court in *Winfield v. Division of Pari-Mutuel Wagering*, 477 So.2d 544 (Fla. 1985). described the far-reaching impact of the Florida amendment:

> The citizens of Florida opted for more protection from governmental intrusion when they approved article I, section 23, of the Florida Constitution. This amendment is an independent, freestanding constitutional provision which declares the fundamental right to privacy. Article I, section 23, was intentionally phrased in strong terms. The drafters of the amendment rejected the use of the words "unreasonable" or "unwarranted" before the phrase "governmental intrusion" in order to make the privacy right as strong as possible. Since the people of this state exercised their prerogative and enacted an amendment to the Florida Constitution which expressly and succinctly provides for a strong right of privacy not found in the United States Constitution, it can only be concluded that the right is much broader in scope than that of the Federal Constitution. *Winfield*, 477 So.2d at 548.

Consistent with this analysis, we have said that the amendment provides "an explicit textual foundation for those privacy interests inherent in the concept of liberty which may not otherwise be protected by specific constitutional provisions." *Rasmussen v. South Fla. Blood Serv.*, 500 So.2d 533, 536 (Fla.1987). We have found the right implicated in a wide range of activities dealing with the public disclosure of personal matters. See *Barron v. Florida Freedom Newspapers*, 531 So.2d 113 (Fla.1988) (closure of court proceedings and records); *Rasmussen* (confidential donor information concerning AIDS-tainted blood supply); *Winfield* (banking records); *Florida Bd. of Bar Examiners re: Applicant*, 443 So.2d 71 (Fla.1983) (bar application questions concerning disclosure of psychiatric counselling). Florida courts have also found the right involved in a number of cases dealing with personal decisionmaking. See *Public Health Trust v. Wons*, 541 So.2d 96 (Fla.1989) (refusal of blood transfusion that is necessary to sustain life); *Corbett v. D'Alessandro*, 487 So.2d 368 (Fla. 2d

DCA), (removal of nasogastric feeding tube from adult in permanent vegetative state); *In re Guardianship of Barry*, 445 So.2d 365 (Fla. 2d DCA 1984) (removal of life support system from brain-dead infant); see also *Satz v. Perlmutter*, 379 So.2d 359 (Fla.1980) (removal of respirator from competent adult, decided prior to passage of privacy amendment under general right of privacy).

The privacy section contains no express standard of review for evaluating the lawfulness of a government intrusion into one's private life, and this Court when called upon, adopted the following standard:

> Since the privacy section as adopted contains no textual standard of review, it is important for us to identify an explicit standard to be applied in order to give proper force and effect to the amendment. The right of privacy is a fundamental right which we believe demands the compelling state interest standard. This test shifts the burden of proof to the state to justify an intrusion on privacy. The burden can be met by demonstrating that the challenged regulation serves a compelling state interest and accomplishes its goal through the use of the least intrusive means. *Winfield*, 477 So.2d at 547.

Florida's privacy provision is clearly implicated in a woman's decision of whether or not to continue her pregnancy. We can conceive of few more personal or private decisions concerning one's body that one can make in the course of a lifetime, except perhaps the decision of the terminally ill in their choice of whether to discontinue necessary medical treatment.

> Of all decisions a person makes about his or her body, the most profound and intimate relate to two sets of ultimate questions: first, whether, when, and how one's body is to become the vehicle for another human being's creation; second, when and how-this time there is no question of "whether"-one's body is to terminate its organic life. L. Tribe, *American Constitutional Law* 1337-38 (2d ed. 1988).

The decision whether to obtain an abortion is fraught with specific physical, psychological, and economic implications of a uniquely personal nature for each woman. The Florida Constitution embodies the principle that "[f]ew decisions are more personal and intimate, more properly private, or more basic to individual dignity and autonomy, than a woman's decision ... whether to end her pregnancy. A woman's right to make that choice freely is fundamental." *Thornburgh v. American College of Obstetricians and Gynecologists*, 476 U.S. 747 (1986).

The next question to be addressed is whether this freedom of choice concerning abortion extends to minors. We conclude that it does, based on the unambiguous language of the amendment: The right of privacy extends to "[e]very natural person." Minors are natural persons in the eyes of the law and "[c]onstitutional rights do not mature and come into being magically only when one attains the state-defined age of majority. Minors, as well as adults...possess constitutional rights." *Danforth*, 428 U.S. at 74.

See also *Ashcroft*; *City of Akron*; *H.L. v. Matheson*, 450 U.S. 398 (1981); and *Bellotti*.

Common sense dictates that a minor's rights are not absolute; in order to overcome these constitutional rights, a statute must survive the stringent test announced in Winfield: The state must prove that the statute furthers a compelling state interest through the least intrusive means.

The challenged statute fails because it intrudes upon the privacy of the pregnant minor from conception to birth. Such a substantial invasion of a pregnant female's privacy by the state for the full term of the pregnancy is not necessary for the preservation of maternal health or the potentiality of life. However, where parental rights over a minor child are concerned, society has recognized additional state interests-protection of the immature minor and preservation of the family unit. For reasons set out below, we find that neither of these interests is sufficiently compelling under Florida law to override Florida's privacy amendment.

In evaluating the validity of parental consent and notice statutes, the federal Court has taken into consideration the state's interests in the well-being of the immature minor, see *Ashcroft*; *City of Akron*; *Matheson*; *Bellotti*; *Danforth*, and in the integrity of the family, see *Matheson*; *Bellotti*. In *Bellotti*, the Court set forth three reasons justifying the conclusion that states can impose more restrictions on the right of minors to obtain abortions than they can impose on the right of adults: "[T]he peculiar vulnerability of children; their inability to make critical decisions in an informed, mature manner; and the importance of the parental role in child rearing." *Bellotti*, 443 U.S. at 634. The Court pointed out that "during the formative years of childhood and adolescence, minors often lack the experience, perspective, and judgment to recognize and avoid choices that could be detrimental to them," and that the role of parents in "teaching, guiding, and inspiring by precept and example is essential to the growth of young people into mature, socially responsible citizens." In assessing the validity of parental consent statutes, the federal Court applied a relaxed standard; the state interest need only be "significant," not "compelling," to support the intrusion.

We agree that the state's interests in protecting minors and in preserving family unity are worthy objectives. Unlike the federal Constitution, however, which allows intrusion based on a "significant" state interest, the Florida Constitution requires a "compelling" state interest in all cases where the right to privacy is implicated. We note that Florida does not recognize these two interests as being sufficiently compelling to justify a parental consent requirement where procedures other than abortion are concerned. Section 743.065, Florida Statutes (1987), provides:

Unwed pregnant minor or minor mother; consent to medical services for minor or minor's child valid.-

(1) An unwed pregnant minor may consent to the performance of medical or surgical care or services relating to her pregnancy by a hospital or clinic or by a physician licensed under chapter 458 or chapter 459, and such consent is valid and binding as if she had achieved her majority.

(2) An unwed minor mother may consent to the performance of medical or surgical care or services for her child by a hospital or clinic or by a physician licensed under chapter 458 or chapter 459, and such consent is valid and binding as if she had achieved her majority.

(3) Nothing in this act shall affect the provisions of s. 390.001 [the abortion statute].

Under this statute, a minor may consent, without parental approval, to any medical procedure involving her pregnancy or her existing child-no matter how dire the possible consequences-except abortion. Under *In re Guardianship of Barry,* 445 So.2d 365 (Fla. 2d DCA 1984) (parents permitted to authorize removal of life support system from infant in permanent coma), this could include authority in certain circumstances to order life support discontinued for a comatose child. In light of this wide authority that the state grants an unwed minor to make life-or-death decisions concerning herself or an existing child without parental consent, we are unable to discern a special compelling interest on the part of the state under Florida law in protecting the minor only where abortion is concerned. We fail to see the qualitative difference in terms of impact on the well-being of the minor between allowing the life of an existing child to come to an end and terminating a pregnancy, or between undergoing a highly dangerous medical procedure on oneself and undergoing a far less dangerous procedure to end one's pregnancy. If any qualitative difference exists, it certainly is insufficient in terms of state interest. Although the state does have an interest in protecting minors, "the selective approach employed by the legislature evidences the limited nature of the ... interest being furthered by these provisions." We note that the state's adoption act similarly contains no requirement that a minor obtain parental consent prior to placing a child up for adoption, even though this decision clearly is fraught with intense emotional and societal consequences.

Based on the foregoing analysis of our state law, we hold that section 390.001(4)(a), violates the Florida Constitution. Accordingly, no further analysis under federal law is required. We expressly decide this case on state law grounds and cite federal precedent only to the extent that it illuminates Florida law. We approve the district court's decision.

GRIMES, J., concurring in part, dissenting in part.

In 1980, the Florida Constitution was amended to specifically guarantee persons the right to privacy. As a consequence, it was thereafter unnecessary to read a right of privacy into the due process provision of Florida's equivalent to the fourteenth amendment. However, this did not mean that Florida voters had elected to create more privacy rights concerning abortion than those already guaranteed by the United States Supreme Court. By 1980, abortion rights were well established under the federal Constitution, and I believe the privacy amendment had the practical effect of guaranteeing these same rights under the Florida Constitution. If the United States Supreme Court were to subsequently recede from *Roe v. Wade*, this would not diminish the abortion rights now provided by the privacy amendment of the Florida Constitution. Consequently, I agree with the analysis contained in parts I and II of the majority opinion, which I read as adopting, for purposes of the Florida Constitution, the qualified right to have an abortion established in *Roe v. Wade*.

In part III, however, the majority opinion interprets the Florida Constitution differently than the United States Supreme Court has interpreted the federal Constitution with respect to a minor's right to an abortion.... [T]he United States Supreme Court has consistently recognized that a state statute requiring parental consent to a minor's abortion is constitutional if it provides a judicial alternative in which the consent is obviated if the court finds that the minor is mature enough to make the abortion decision or, in the absence of the requisite maturity, the abortion is in the minor's best interest.

While purporting to acknowledge the state's interest in protecting minors and in preserving family unity, the majority reaches the conclusion that these interests as reflected in the instant statute must fall in the face of its broad interpretation of the privacy amendment. In effect, the Court has said that the state's interest in regulating abortions is no different with respect to minors than it is with adults. Under this ruling, even immature minors may decide to have an abortion without parental consent. I do not agree with either the majority's broad interpretation of the privacy amendment or its limited view of the state's interest concerning the conduct of minors.

Moreover, I cannot accept the majority's conclusion that section 743.065, which permits an unwed pregnant minor to consent to the performance of medical or surgical care except with respect to abortions, somehow makes the statute under consideration in the instant case unconstitutional. Section 743.065 was designed to permit doctors to avoid liability for providing medical services to minors without parental consent and to ensure that emergency treatment would be available. The decision to have an abortion is clearly different than the decision to undergo other medical or surgical care with respect to pregnancy, and the legislature has a right to determine that different criteria should be followed with respect to consenting to an abortion.

It is this Court's duty to uphold the constitutionality of statutes whenever this can be done consistent with sound legal principles. Clearly, this statute is valid under our federal Constitution as interpreted by the United States Supreme Court. Admittedly, this Court has the authority to give the Florida Constitution a broader interpretation, but there should be a compelling reason for taking such a step.

Here, the legislature has concluded that it is ordinarily desirable that a minor should have the advice and consent of her parents before having an abortion. However, by providing a judicial alternative which is simple, speedy, and confidential, the legislature has also ensured that an abortion will be denied to a minor only when she is too immature to make the decision and when it is against her best interest. Section 390.001(4)(a)(1) reflects a legitimate state concern over the welfare of children and impinges upon the minor's right to privacy in the least intrusive manner. I would uphold the constitutionality of the statute.

NOTE

In 1999, the Florida legislature enacted a statute requiring parental notification (rather than parental consent) before a minor could undergo an abortion. The statute provided for a judicial bypass in lieu of parental notification. Relying on its previous decision in *T.W.*, the Florida Supreme Court ruled that the statute was unconstitutional. *North Florida Women's Health and Counseling Services, Inc. v. State*, 866 So.2d 612 (Fla. 2003). In response, the state legislature proposed a constitutional amendment, adopted by the voters of the state, that counteracted the decision in *North Florida Women's Health and Counseling Services* by specifically authorizing the legislature to require parental notification before a minor has an abortion so long as the legislature also establishes a procedure for judicial bypass of the notification requirement. Fla. Const. art. X, § 22. The amendment did not address parental consent and accordingly had no effect on the ruling in *T.W.*

PLANNED PARENTHOOD v. SUNDQUIST
38 S.W.3d 1 (Tenn. 2000)

ANDERSON, C.J.

This is an appeal from the Circuit Court for Davidson County, which applied an undue burden standard and struck down as unconstitutional the provisions of Tennessee's criminal abortion statutes requiring that physicians inform their patients that "abortion in a considerable number of cases constitutes a major surgical procedure," Tenn. Code Ann. § 39-15-

202(b)(4) (1997), and mandating a two-day waiting period requirement, Tenn. Code Ann. § 39-15-202(d)(1). The trial court upheld the second trimester hospitalization requirement, Tenn. Code Ann. § 39-15-201(c)(2), the remaining informed consent requirements, Tenn. Code Ann. § 39-15-202(b)(1)-(3), (b)(5)-(c), and the medical emergency exceptions, Tenn. Code Ann. § 39-15-202(d)(3), (g). The Court of Appeals reversed the judgment of the trial court in part and affirmed in part. The Court of Appeals upheld the following provisions as not imposing an undue burden: the waiting period requirement, based upon the facts of this case; the second trimester hospitalization requirement; and, except for the "major surgical procedure" provision, the remaining informed consent requirements. We granted application for permission to appeal those issues of first impression. We specifically hold that a woman's right to terminate her pregnancy is a vital part of the right to privacy guaranteed by the Tennessee Constitution. We further hold that the right is inherent in the concept of ordered liberty embodied in our constitution and is therefore fundamental. Accordingly, the statutes regulating this fundamental right must be subjected to strict scrutiny analysis. When reviewed under the correct standard, we conclude that none of the statutory provisions at issue withstand such scrutiny. The Court of Appeals' judgment is therefore affirmed in part and reversed in part.

The initial issue which this Court must decide is whether the right of privacy implicated in this case as guaranteed by the Tennessee Constitution is broader than the right as guaranteed by the federal constitution and as construed by the United States Supreme Court. Implicit in this determination is whether the statutes at issue are to be judged under the less demanding undue burden standard, or the more stringent strict scrutiny standard. Planned Parenthood argues that the state right to procreational autonomy is broader than the federal right and that the appropriate standard to apply is strict scrutiny. The State, on the other hand, asserts that the Court of Appeals correctly concluded that the appropriate standard to apply under the Tennessee Constitution is the "undue burden" standard adopted by the United States Supreme Court in *Casey*.

United States Supreme Court Cases

In 1973, the United States Supreme Court first recognized a woman's right to terminate her pregnancy in *Roe v. Wade*, 410 U.S. 113, 153 (1973). *Roe* involved a challenge to a Texas criminal abortion statute that criminalized all abortions except those necessary to preserve the life of the mother. In a plurality opinion, the Court concluded that the constitutional right of privacy encompassed a "woman's decision whether or not to terminate her pregnancy." The Court also recognized that the State has "important interests in safeguarding health, in maintaining medical standards, and in protecting potential life" and that, "[a]t some point in pregnancy, these respective interests become sufficiently compelling to sustain regulation." Accordingly, the Court concluded that a woman's right to choose abortion is not absolute and "must be considered against important state interests in regulation."

Nineteen years after deciding *Roe,* the Court modified *Roe* in *Planned Parenthood v. Casey,* 505 U.S. 833 (1992). A majority of the Court reaffirmed *Roe*'s holding that the Constitution protects a woman's right to terminate her pregnancy before viability without undue interference from the State. After viability, the state has the power to restrict abortions "if the law contains exceptions for pregnancies which endanger the woman's life or health."

Three justices concluded that the "undue burden standard is the appropriate means of reconciling the State's interest with the woman's constitutionally protected liberty." *Id.* at 876 (joint opinion of O'Connor, Kennedy and Souter, JJ.). Four justices, concurring in part and dissenting in part, criticized the undue burden test. The justices noted that the undue burden approach has no recognized basis in constitutional law. *Id.* at 964 (Rehnquist, C.J., joined by White, Scalia, and Thomas, JJ., concurring in part and dissenting in part).

Most recently, in *Stenberg v. Carhart,* 530 U.S. 914 (2000), a majority of the Court reaffirmed the "undue burden" standard. The Court struck down a statute banning partial birth abortions because it had no exception for the health of the mother and applied to dilation and evacuation abortions as well as to dilation and extraction abortions, thereby constituting an undue burden on the woman's ability to choose an abortion.

Although the United States Supreme Court has now replaced the strict scrutiny standard in the abortion context with the less exacting undue burden standard, this action does not determine the standard which this Court must apply under the Tennessee Constitution. We now turn to the issue of the appropriate standard to apply under our state constitution.

Tennessee Cases

Though we have never before had the abortion issue squarely before us, we have considered the related issue of procreational autonomy. In *Davis v. Davis,* 842 S.W.2d 588 (Tenn. 1992), we first recognized a right to privacy under the Tennessee Constitution. *Davis* involved a divorce dispute over the disposition of seven frozen preembryos the parties had created during their marriage. The husband did not want to become a father outside of the marital relationship and therefore wanted the preembryos destroyed. The wife wanted to donate the preembryos to a childless couple. Our analysis of whether the parties would "become parents" turned on the exercise of the parties' constitutional right to privacy.

After observing that the right to privacy is not specifically mentioned in either the federal or the Tennessee constitutions, we initially reviewed the development of the federal right to privacy for guidance in interpreting our state constitution. We noted that the United States Supreme Court has recognized a federal constitutional right of privacy despite the absence of specific language mentioning such a right in the United States Constitution. We reasoned that, likewise, the "right to privacy, or personal autonomy..., while not mentioned explicitly in our state constitution, is nevertheless reflected in several sections of the Tennessee Declaration of Rights." We further reasoned that the drafters of the Tennessee Constitution surely "foresaw the need to protect individuals from unwarranted governmental intrusion into matters...involving intimate questions of personal and family concern." We thus concluded that the Tennessee Constitution protects the individual's right to privacy and explained that:

> the specific individual freedom in dispute is the right to procreate. *In terms of the Tennessee state constitution,* we hold that the right of procreation is a vital part of an individual's right to privacy.

Davis, 842 S.W.2d at 600 (emphasis added). Accordingly, we explicitly relied on the Tennessee Constitution in *Davis* to extend protection to the husband's right to procreational autonomy.

Since the *Davis* decision, we have identified privacy rights in other contexts. We have held that a parent's right to the custody of his or her child implicates a fundamental right of privacy and may not be abridged absent a compelling state interest. The Court of Appeals has relied upon *Davis* to find a privacy interest in consensual adult homosexuality. There is no exhaustive list of activities that fall under the protection of the right to privacy, at either the federal or the state level. However, it is clear that such activities must be of the utmost personal and intimate concern.

We hold that a woman's right to obtain a legal termination of her pregnancy is sufficiently similar in character to those personal and private decisions and activities identified in state and federal precedent to implicate a cognizable privacy interest.

Protections Afforded the Right to Privacy

Determining whether an asserted interest is fundamental is essential because fundamental rights receive special protection under both federal and state constitutions. Federal case law uniformly holds the government regulation of the exercise of fundamental rights is unconstitutional unless the regulations both serve a compelling governmental interest and are narrowly tailored to serve that interest. Tennessee courts have adopted this "strict scrutiny" approach in regard to fundamental rights without exception.

In *Davis,* we found the right to procreational autonomy to be "inherent in our most basic concepts of liberty." That test was essentially a restatement of the fundamental rights approach of *Roe.* Because a woman's right to terminate her pregnancy and an individual's right to procreational autonomy are similar in nature, we find the *Davis* test to be most appropriate here. Thus, a woman's right to terminate her pregnancy is fundamental if it can be said to be inherent in the concept of ordered liberty embodied in the Tennessee Constitution.

Without question, the protections afforded Tennessee citizens by the Tennessee Constitution's Declaration of Rights share the contours of the protections afforded by the United States Constitution's Bill of Rights. This is due, in large part, to affinity of purpose. Both documents were written with the intent to reserve to the people various liberties and to protect the free exercise of those liberties from governmental intrusion.

Therefore, Tennessee courts are rightfully reluctant to find greater protection from the text of the state constitution where the protections of the federal constitution suffice. As a result, more interpretive case law is generated in regard to the federal constitution. Therefore, analysis of case law interpreting the federal constitution is often a first step in interpreting provisions of our own constitution that are similar in wording, intent or purpose.

It is equally without question, however, that the provisions of our Tennessee Declaration of Rights from which the right to privacy emanates differ from the federal Bill of Rights in marked respects. In *Davis,* we found that the right to privacy guaranteed by the Tennessee Constitution sprang from the express grants of rights in article I, sections 3, 7, 19 and 27, and also from the grants of liberty in article I, sections 1, 2 and 8.

These protections contained in our Declaration of Rights are more particularly stated than those stated in the federal Bill of Rights. For example, the explicit guarantee of freedom of worship found under the United States Constitution occupies but sixteen words in an amendment generally guaranteeing freedom of worship, freedom of speech, freedom of the press, the right to assemble, and the right to petition the government for redress of grievances.

In contrast, the guarantee of worship under the Tennessee Constitution exists in its own paragraph constituting eighty-one words. It characterizes mankind's right to worship as "a natural and indefeasible right" and declares "that no human authority can, in any case whatever, control or interfere with the rights of conscience." Tenn. Const. art I, § 3. This Court has said that the language of this section, when compared to the guarantee of religious freedom contained in the federal constitution, is a stronger guarantee of religious freedom. *See Carden v. Bland*, 288 S.W.2d 718, 721 (Tenn. 1956).

Tennessee's guarantees of free speech and free press are similarly more descriptive than the federal grant. The verbal expression of these basic freedoms in our constitution is infused with a strong sense of individuality and personal liberty: "The free communication of thoughts and opinions, is one of the invaluable rights of man, and every citizen may freely speak, write and print on any subject, being responsible for the abuse of that liberty." Tenn. Const. art. I, § 19.

This Court is not free to discount the fact that the framers of our state constitution used language different from that used by the framers of the United States Constitution. No words in our constitution can properly be said to be surplusage and differences in expressions of right are particularly relevant to determining the "concept of liberty" embodied in our constitution.

Today, we remain opposed to any assertion that previous decisions suggesting that synonymity or identity of portions of our constitution and the federal constitution requires *this* Court to interpret our constitution as coextensive to the United States Constitution. "Tennessee constitutional standards are not destined to walk in lock step with the uncertain and fluctuating federal standards and do not relegate Tennessee citizens to the lowest levels of constitutional protection, those guaranteed by the national constitution." We have said time and again that:

> The concept of ordered liberty embodied in our constitution requires our finding that a woman's right to legally terminate her pregnancy is fundamental. The provisions of the Tennessee Constitution imply protection of an individual's right to make inherently personal decisions, and to act on those decisions, without government interference. A woman's termination of her pregnancy is just such an inherently intimate and personal enterprise. This privacy interest is closely aligned with matters of marriage, child rearing, and other procreational interests that have previously been held to be fundamental. To distinguish it as somehow non-fundamental would require this Court to ignore the obvious corollary.

The Appropriate Standard

It is well settled that where a fundamental right is at issue, in order for a state regulation which interferes with that right to be upheld, the regulation must withstand strict scrutiny. The State's interest must be sufficiently compelling in order to overcome the fundamental nature of the right.

Other jurisdictions have applied heightened scrutiny of governmental regulation of abortion since *Casey* was decided. Our rejection of the *Casey* standard is similar to the action taken by those state courts. In *Women of the State of Minn. v. Gomez*, 542 N.W.2d 17 (Minn. 1995), the Minnesota Supreme Court considered a complaint for declaratory and injunctive relief challenging the constitutionality of statutes restricting the use of public medical assistance and general assistance funds for abortions. The Court determined that the Minnesota Constitution guaranteed a right of privacy rooted in several provisions of the constitution, including a due process provision, a "law of the land" provision, and a provision protecting against unreasonable searches and seizures. *Id.* at 27 n.10. The Court held that the right of privacy includes a woman's right to choose to have an abortion. Stating that it could think of few decisions more intimate, personal and profound than a woman's decision between childbirth and abortion, it held that the case was one of those limited circumstances in which it would interpret the Minnesota Constitution to provide more protection than that afforded under the federal constitution. It subjected the regulations to strict scrutiny because the right of privacy is fundamental. *See also Planned Parenthood League of Massachusetts, Inc. v. Attorney General*, 677 N.E.2d 101, 104 (Mass. 1997) (holding that the state constitution's Declaration of Rights afforded a greater degree of protection to the right asserted than did the federal constitution as interpreted by the United States Supreme Court).

The application of the strict scrutiny approach is entirely consistent with our jurisprudence considering laws which impose upon or restrict fundamental rights. While the joint opinion in *Casey* adopted the "undue burden" approach, Justice Scalia in a separate dissent and concurrence criticized the so-called standard as being "ultimately standardless." He noted that the undue burden standard was "created largely out of whole cloth" and essentially had no recognized basis in constitutional law.

We agree that the undue burden approach is essentially no standard at all, and, in effect, allows judges to impose their own subjective views of the propriety of the legislation in question. The dissent has criticized the majority for "convert[ing] itself into a roving constitutional convention which is free to strike down the duly enacted laws of the legislature for no other reason than the Court feels they are burdensome and unwise." In fact, that is exactly what the undue burden approach allows. Under that test, the Court is free to determine, under the justices' own subjective opinions as to the wisdom of the legislation, whether the legislation creates an undue burden upon a woman's right to terminate her pregnancy. Application of strict scrutiny, a recognized principle of constitutional law, on the other hand, requires the Court to apply a standard that has been applied repeatedly over the years, and the Court may draw upon that precedent in determining whether the legislation passes muster.

The subjective nature of the undue burden analysis is aptly illustrated by the fact that the majority and the dissent reach diametrically opposed results when applying the analysis. The majority would find each of the challenged abortion statutes to be unconstitutional under *Casey*, while the dissent, applying exactly the same analysis, would reach the opposite result as to each statute, save one.

The undue burden test requires a judge to consider only the effect of the governmental regulation. It fails, however, to offer an objective standard by which the effect should be judged. Accordingly, a regulation held to be an undue burden by one judge could just as easily be found to be reasonable by another judge because the gauge for what is an undue burden necessarily varies from person to person.

Thus, the *Casey* test offers our judges no real guidance and engenders no expectation among the citizenry that governmental regulation of abortion will be objective, evenhanded or well-reasoned. This Court finds no justification for exchanging the long-established constitutional doctrine of strict scrutiny for a test, not yet ten years old and applicable to a single, narrow area of the law, that would relegate a fundamental right of the citizens of Tennessee to the personal caprice of an individual judge.

It may be appropriate in some areas of our law to provide judges individual, and necessarily subjective, discretion. Subjective judicial opinion has no place, however, in determining the constitutionality of the exercise of fundamental rights. Accordingly, we conclude that strict scrutiny is the appropriate standard to apply in this case.

In summary, we hold that a woman's right to terminate her pregnancy is a vital part of the right to privacy guaranteed by the Tennessee Constitution. That right is inherent in the concept of ordered liberty embodied in the Tennessee Constitution and is similar to other privacy interests that have previously been held to be fundamental. We therefore conclude that this specific privacy interest is fundamental. Therefore, the statutory provisions regulating abortion must be subjected to strict scrutiny analysis. After our review of the record and applicable authorities, we conclude that under the Tennessee Constitution, the statutes at issue, Tenn. Code Ann. §§ 39-15-201(c)(2) (the second trimester hospitalization requirement), 39-15-202(b), (c) (the informed consent and physician-only counseling requirements), 39-15-202(d)(1) (the mandatory waiting period requirement), and 39-15-202(d)(3) and (g) (the medical emergency exceptions), are unconstitutional because the statutes are not narrowly tailored to further compelling state interests.

REPRODUCTIVE HEALTH SERVICE OF PLANNED PARENTHOOD OF ST. LOUIS REGION, INC. v. NIXON
185 S.W. 3d 685 (Mo. 2006)

PER CURIAM

Section 188.039, RSMo Supp.2003, creates an informed consent requirement including a 24-hour waiting period before elective abortions may be performed in Missouri. Planned Parenthood argues that...the 24-hour waiting provision violates rights of liberty and privacy under the Missouri Constitution. All of Planned Parenthood's federal claims have been reserved for adjudication in federal court. This case only concerns Planned Parenthood's facial claims under the Missouri Constitution.

Section 188.039 states:

1. For purposes of this section, "medical emergency" means a condition which, on the basis of the physician's good faith clinical judgment, so complicates the medical condition of a pregnant woman as to necessitate the immediate abortion of her pregnancy to avert her death or for which a delay will create a serious risk of substantial and irreversible impairment of a major bodily function.

2. Except in the case of medical emergency, no person shall perform or induce an abortion unless at least twenty-four hours prior thereto a treating physician has conferred with the patient and discussed with her the indicators and contraindicators, and risk factors including any physical, psychological, or situational factors for the proposed procedure and the use of medications, including but not limited to mifepristone, in light of her medical history and medical condition. For an abortion performed or an abortion induced by a drug or drugs, such conference shall take place at least twenty-four hours prior to the writing or communication of the first prescription for such drug or drugs in connection with inducing an abortion. Only one such conference shall be required for each abortion.

3. The patient shall be evaluated by a treating physician during the conference for indicators and contraindicators, risk factors including any physical, psychological, or situational factors which would predispose the patient to or increase the risk of experiencing one or more adverse physical, emotional, or other health reactions to the proposed procedure or drug or drugs in either the short or long term as compared with women who do not possess such risk factors.

4. At the end of the conference, and if the woman chooses to proceed with the abortion, a treating physician shall sign and shall cause the patient to sign a written statement that the woman gave her informed consent freely and without coercion after the physician had discussed with her the indicators and contraindicators, and risk factors, including any physical, psychological, or situational factors. All such executed statements shall be maintained as part of the patient's medical file, subject to the confidentiality laws and rules of this state.

Planned Parenthood...argues that the 24-hour waiting provision violates the Missouri Constitution. The Supreme Court of the United States held in *Planned Parenthood v. Casey,* that a 24-hour waiting period does not violate the federal constitution. 505 U.S. 833, 887 (1992). That opinion stated:

[W]e are not convinced that the 24-hour waiting period constitutes an undue burden.... [T]he right protected by *Roe* is a right to decide to terminate a pregnancy free of undue interference by the State. Because the informed consent requirement facilitates the wise exercise of that right, it cannot be classified as an interference with the right *Roe* protects. The informed consent requirement is not an undue burden on that right.

Despite *Casey*, Planned Parenthood argues that the Missouri constitution should be construed more broadly than the United States constitution.

> The federal due process clause states, in part: "[N]or shall any State deprive any person of life, liberty, or property, without due process of law...." U.S. Const. amend. XIV, sec. 1. The Missouri constitution contains two related clauses. Missouri's due process clause states: "That no person shall be deprived of life, liberty or property without due process of law." Mo. Const. art. I, sec. 10.

Article I, section 2 of the Missouri constitution also states:

> That all constitutional government is intended to promote the general welfare of the people; that all persons have a natural right to life, liberty, the pursuit of happiness and the enjoyment of the gains of their own industry; that all persons are created equal and are entitled to equal rights and opportunity under the law; that to give security to these things is the principal office of government, and that when government does not confer this security, it fails in its chief design.

There is no reason, within the context of this case, to construe this language from the Missouri constitution more broadly than the language used in the United States constitution. *See State v. Walsh,* 713 S.W.2d 508, 513 (Mo. banc 1986); *see generally State ex rel. Danforth v. Cason,* 507 S.W.2d 405, 408-09 (Mo. banc 1973).

C. THE RIGHT OF INTIMATE ASSOCIATION

STATE v. SAUNDERS
381 A.2d 333 (N.J. 1977)

PASHMAN, J.

Defendant Charles Saunders was indicted along with Bernard Busby on charges of rape, assault with intent to rape and armed robbery. At trial both admitted to having had sexual intercourse with the two complainants, but insisted that the women had participated willingly in exchange for a promise that they would receive "reefers" (marijuana cigarettes) in return. The trial judge, on his own initiative, charged the jury that the defendants could be convicted of the "lesser included offense" of fornication (N.J.S.A. 2A:110-1) if they were found not guilty on the other counts. The jury acquitted the defendants of the charges in the indictment and convicted them of fornication. In charging the jury, the judge defined the crime of fornication as "an act of illicit sexual intercourse by a man, married or single, with an unmarried woman."

Defendant asserts that the instant statute, N.J.S.A. 2A:110-1, is unconstitutional on its face since it generally seeks to outlaw conduct which the State has no power to prohibit.... The right of privacy, upon which defendant bases his attack, is not explicitly mentioned in either the New Jersey or United States Constitutions. However, both documents have been construed to include such a right. On the federal level, the right was first recognized as being of constitutional stature by a majority of the Court in *Griswold v. Connecticut*, 381 U.S. 479 (1965). Subsequent Supreme Court decisions have firmly established the constitutional nature of the right of privacy. In *Roe v. Wade*, 410 U.S. 113 (1973), the Court found that the right of privacy encompassed a woman's decision whether or not to terminate a pregnancy. More recently the right has been recognized in the Court's decisions in *Carey v. Population Services International*, 431 U.S. 678 (1977); *Whalen v. Roe*, 429 U.S. 589 (1977); and *Paul v. Davis*, 424 U.S. 693 (1976).

However, the precise scope of the interests protected by the right of privacy are not easily defined. As the Court noted in *Carey v. Population Services International, supra*, the interests which have been held to fall within the protections of the right have been "personal" ones; they have included those "relating to marriage, *Loving v. Virginia*, 388 U.S. 1 (1967); procreation, *Skinner v. Oklahoma*, 316 U.S. 535 (1942); contraception, *Eisenstadt v. Baird*, 405 U.S. 438 (1972);   family relationships, *Prince v. Massachusetts*, 321 U.S. 158, 166 (1944); and child rearing and education, *Pierce v. Society of Sisters*, 268 U.S. 510 (1925);" *Meyer v. Nebraska*, 262 U.S. 390 (1923); *Carey, supra*.

Although the Court in *Carey* observed that the "decision whether or not to beget or bear a child is at the very heart of this cluster of constitutionally protected choices," we believe that the right of privacy is not confined to the private situations involved in each of these decisions. Indeed, the Court's references in *Roe v. Wade* to cases having nothing to do with such decisions should effectively dispel any such notion. While *Carey* certainly emphasizes the importance of a person's choice regarding whether or not to have children, it indicates that the constitutional basis for the protection of such decisions is their relationship to individual autonomy. Mr. Justice Brennan observed that such personal choices concern "the most intimate of human activities and relationships," adding that "decisions whether to accomplish or to prevent conception are among the most private and sensitive." 431 U.S. at 685.

This view of the right of privacy is consistent with the approach taken by this Court in our recent decision in *In re Quinlan*, 355 A.2d 647 (N.J. 1976). There we held, as a matter of State constitutional law, that this important right was broad enough to encompass the freedom to make a personal choice as to the continuance of artificial life-support mechanisms. Though Chief Justice Hughes noted for the Court that the right of privacy had theretofore been primarily associated with decisions involving contraception and family life, he also found that its underlying concern was with the protection of personal decisions, and that it might be included within "the class of what have been called rights of 'personality.'" Our *Quinlan* decision could not have been predicated on privacy grounds if the class of cognizable privacy interests was limited to personal decisions concerning procreative matters.

Any discussion of the right of privacy must focus on the ultimate interest (by) which protection the Constitution seeks to ensure the freedom of personal development. Whether one defines that concept as a "right to 'intimacy' and a freedom to do intimate things," or "a right to the 'integrity' of one's 'personality,'" the crux of the matter is that governmental regulation of private personal behavior under the police power is sharply limited. As Mr. Justice Brandeis stated so eloquently in his dissent in *Olmstead v. United States*, 277 U.S. 438 (1928):

> The makers of our Constitution undertook to secure conditions favorable to the pursuit of happiness. They recognized the significance of man's spiritual nature, of his feelings and of his intellect. They knew that only a part of the pain, pleasure and satisfactions of life are found in material things. They sought to protect Americans in their beliefs, their thoughts, their emotions and their sensations. They conferred, as against the government, the right to be let alone the most valued by civilized men. (277 U.S. at 478.)

We conclude that the conduct statutorily defined as fornication involves, by its very nature, a fundamental personal choice. Thus, the statute infringes upon the right of privacy. Although persons may differ as to the propriety and morality of such conduct and while we certainly do not condone its particular manifestations in this case, such a decision is necessarily encompassed in the concept of personal autonomy which our Constitution seeks to safeguard.

We recognize that the conduct prohibited by this statute has never been explicitly treated by the Supreme Court as falling within the right of privacy. In fact, we note that this question has been specifically reserved by the Court. Nevertheless, our decision today is consistent with the tenor and thrust of the Court's more recent decisions. As we stated earlier, the Court in *Carey* and *Wade* underscored the inherently private nature of a person's decision to bear or beget children. It would be rather anomalous if such a decision could be constitutionally protected while the more fundamental decision as to whether to engage in the conduct which is a necessary prerequisite to child-bearing could be constitutionally prohibited. Surely, such a choice involves considerations which are at least as intimate and personal as those which are involved in choosing whether to use contraceptives. We therefore join with other courts which have held that such sexual activities between adults are protected by the right of privacy. See *State v. Pilcher*, 242 N.W.2d 348 (Iowa 1976).

Finally, we note that our doubts as to the constitutionality of the fornication statute are also impelled by this Court's development of a constitutionally mandated "zone" of privacy protecting individuals from unwarranted governmental intrusion into matters of intimate personal and family concern. It is now settled that the right of privacy guaranteed under the Fourteenth Amendment has an analogue in our State Constitution, *In re Quinlan*, supra, 355 A.2d 647. Although the scope of this State right is not necessarily broader in all respects, the lack of constraints imposed by considerations of federalism permits this Court to demand stronger and more persuasive showings of a public interest in allowing the State to prohibit sexual practices than would be required by the United States Supreme Court.

Yet our inquiry cannot end here. Having found that the statute impinges upon the fundamental right of privacy, we must go on to consider whether that impingement can be justified by some compelling state interest. In an attempt to justify the statute's infringement of protected rights, the State cites its interests in preventing venereal disease and an increase in the number of illegitimate children, and in protecting the marital relationship and public morals by preventing illicit sex.

Perhaps the strongest reason favoring the law is its supposed relationship to the furtherance of the State's salutary goal of preventing venereal disease. We do not question the State's compelling interest in preventing the spread of such diseases. Nor do we dispute the power of the State to regulate activities which may adversely affect the public health. However, we do not believe that the instant enactment is properly designed with that end in mind. First, while we recognize that the statute would substantially eliminate venereal diseases if it could successfully deter people from engaging in the prohibited activity, we doubt its ability to achieve that result. The risk of contracting venereal disease is surely as great a deterrent to illicit sex as the maximum penalty under this act: a fine of $50 and/or imprisonment in jail for six months. As the Court found in *Carey*, absent highly coercive measures, it is extremely doubtful that people will be deterred from engaging in such natural activities. The Court there rejected the assertion that the threat of an unwanted pregnancy would deter persons from engaging in extramarital sexual activities. We conclude that the same is true for the possibility of being prosecuted under the fornication statute.

Furthermore, if the State's interest in the instant statute is that it is helpful in preventing venereal disease, we conclude that it is counter-productive. To the extent that any successful program to combat venereal disease must depend upon affected persons coming forward for treatment, the present statute operates as a deterrent to such voluntary participation. The fear of being prosecuted for the "crime" of fornication can only deter people from seeking such necessary treatment.

We similarly fail to comprehend how the State's interest in preventing the propagation of illegitimate children will be measurably advanced by the instant law. If the unavailability of contraceptives is not likely to deter people from engaging in illicit sexual activities, it follows that the fear of unwanted pregnancies will be equally ineffective. See *Carey*, supra.

The last two reasons offered by the State as compelling justifications for the enactment that it protects the marital relationship and the public morals by preventing illicit sex offer little additional support for the law. Whether or not abstention is likely to induce persons to marry, this statute can in no way be considered a permissible means of fostering what may otherwise be a socially beneficial institution. If we were to hold that the State could attempt to coerce people into marriage, we would undermine the very independent choice which lies at the core of the right of privacy. We do not doubt the beneficent qualities of marriage, both for individuals as well as for society as a whole. Yet, we can only reiterate that decisions such as whether to marry are of a highly personal nature; they neither lend themselves to official coercion or sanction, nor fall within the regulatory power of those who are elected to govern.

This is not to suggest that the State may not regulate, in an appropriate manner, activities which are designed to further public morality. Our conclusion today extends no further than to strike down a measure which has as its objective the regulation of private morality. To the extent that N.J.S.A. 2A:110-1 serves as an official sanction of certain conceptions of desirable lifestyles, social mores or individualized beliefs, it is not an appropriate exercise of the police power.

Fornication may be abhorrent to the morals and deeply held beliefs of many persons. But any appropriate "remedy" for such conduct cannot come from legislative fiat. Private personal acts between two consenting adults are not to be lightly meddled with by the State. The right of personal autonomy is fundamental to a free society. Persons who view fornication as opprobrious conduct may seek strenuously to dissuade people from engaging in it. However, they may not inhibit such conduct through the coercive power of the criminal law. As aptly stated by Sir Francis Bacon, "(t)he sum of behavior is to retain a man's own dignity without intruding on the liberty of others." The fornication statute mocks the dignity of both offenders and enforcers. Surely police have more pressing duties than to search out adults who live a so-called "wayward" life. Surely the dignity of the law is undermined when an intimate personal activity between consenting adults can be dragged into court and "exposed." More importantly, the liberty which is the birthright of every individual suffers dearly when the State can so grossly intrude on personal autonomy.

SCHREIBER, J., concurring.

I concur in the result reached by the Court but for different reasons. The majority relies heavily on recent United States Supreme Court decisions involving the right of privacy for its conclusion that the State cannot interfere with the conduct proscribed by the New Jersey fornication statute. I believe they have misgauged the scope of those decisions. For the reasons developed below, I would rest the invalidity of this statute squarely on the ground that it conflicts with Article I, par. 1 of the New Jersey Constitution:

> All persons are by nature free and independent, and have certain natural and unalienable rights, among which are those of enjoying and defending life and liberty and of pursuing and obtaining safety and happiness.

The rights of two adults to make personal decisions are inherent in their freedom of thought. Implementation of those decisions in pursuit of their concept of happiness manifests an exercise of human liberty. Whatever else may be said of happiness, it is best obtained in a climate of free decision where each individual has the choice of consenting or not to acts or events which may affect him. Different persons have differing spiritual and moral views and so long as their personal conduct does not affect others, individuals have freedom to think, decide and act as they see fit. This freedom is an aspect of their right of privacy. Private consensual sexual conduct represents an exercise of that right.

Unlike the United States Constitution, the New Jersey Constitution is not a grant of enumerated powers, but rather a limitation of the sovereign powers of the State vested in the Legislature. That legislative authority is circumscribed by constitutional provisions, including those expressed in Article I, par. 1. Although the Legislature, in exercising its powers, may incidentally affect the natural and unalienable rights of individuals to liberty and the pursuit of happiness which have been recognized in Article I, the validity of any statute directly limiting those rights should be carefully scrutinized in light of its legislative purposes.

At common law fornication was not a crime. As explained by Blackstone:

> In the year 1650, when the ruling power found it for their interest to put on the semblance of a very extraordinary strictness and purity of morals, not only incest and wilful adultery were made capital crimes; but also the repeated act of keeping a brothel, or committing fornication, were (upon a second conviction) made felony without benefit of clergy. But at the restoration, when men, from an abhorrence of the hypocrisy of the late times, fell into a contrary extreme of licentiousness, it was not thought proper to renew a law of such unfashionable rigor. And these offences have been ever since left to the feeble coercion of the spiritual court, according to the rules of the canon law. (W. Blackstone Commentaries, Book IV, Ch. IV, *64-65)

The State rationalizes that the fornication statute is justifiable as a means of preventing the spread of venereal disease and the birth of illegitimate children. As the majority indicates, these grounds are not persuasive. More importantly, there is no evidence that this statute was intended as anything but an attempt to regulate private morality.

The Legislature cannot infringe on the rights of individuals who in private and without affecting others adopt and live by standards which differ from those of society.... It is only when the public interest would be substantially adversely affected by some exercise of the right of privacy or when the public interest would be otherwise substantially promoted by legislation that the Legislature may infringe upon that right.

CLIFFORD, J., dissenting.

I hold to the view (and as I read the other opinions, so do all the other members of this Court) that absent a compelling state interest the State may not regulate a person's private decisions which have merely incidental effects on others. In application that principle leads to the conclusion that if two people freely determine that they wish to have sexual relations in a setting inoffensive to and only incidentally affecting others, the State is without authority to interfere through the criminal process with that decision, despite the fact that such decision may be in violation of conventional community standards of morality. And that includes the grubby little exercise in self-gratification involved here.

But I think we need not, and I would not, get to the constitutional issue, at least not at this point. Rather I would call for the submission of briefs and further argument of counsel on the question whether fornication is a lesser included offense with respect to rape. For several reasons this is the desirable course.

First, there is the sound, oft-expressed principle that constitutional questions should not be reached and resolved unless absolutely imperative in the disposition of the litigation. Inasmuch as there may be another, non-constitutional basis for decision, we should heed that admonition and defer addressing the constitutional question here.

Additionally, the interests of the parties will be amply served by a decision on the narrower "lesser included offense" ground. If fornication is not included in rape, then defendant goes free; certainly Mr. Saunders' interests are fully vindicated, it being neither apparent nor even likely that he has any burning curiosity about, or yearning for resolution of, the constitutional dimensions of the controversy in which he finds himself embroiled. If fornication is a lesser included offense of the crime of rape, then that issue (not heretofore directly presented or authoritatively determined in this State) will have been put to rest, thereby clarifying the law. We would then proceed in the instant case to the constitutional question.

NOTE

In *Commonwealth v. Bonadio*, 415 A.2d 47 (Pa. 1980), the Supreme Court of Pennsylvania struck down a statute that criminalized "deviate sexual intercourse" (defined as oral or anal sex) between persons who were not husband and wife. In the course of its opinion, the court explained that:

> The threshold question in determining whether the statute in question is a valid exercise of the police power is to decide whether it benefits the public generally. The state clearly has a proper role to perform in protecting the public from inadvertent offensive displays of sexual behavior, in preventing people from being forced against their will to submit to sexual contact, in protecting minors from being sexually used by adults, and in eliminating cruelty to animals. To assure these protections, a broad range of criminal statutes constitute valid police power exercises, including proscriptions of indecent exposure, open lewdness, rape, involuntary deviate sexual intercourse, indecent assault, statutory rape, corruption of minors, and cruelty to animals. The statute in question serves none of the foregoing purposes and it is nugatory to suggest that it promotes a state interest in the institution of marriage. The Voluntary Deviate Sexual Intercourse Statute has only one possible purpose: to regulate the private conduct of consenting adults. Such a purpose, we believe, exceeds the valid bounds of the police power while infringing the right to equal protection of the laws guaranteed by the Constitution of the United States and of this Commonwealth.

> With respect to regulation of morals, the police power should properly be exercised to protect each individual's right to be free from interference in defining and pursuing his own morality but not to enforce a majority morality on persons whose conduct does not harm others. "No harm to the secular interests of the community is involved in atypical sex practice in private between consenting adult partners." MODEL PENAL CODE s 207.5 Sodomy & Related Offenses. Comment (Tent. Draft No. 4, 1955). Many issues that are considered to be matters of morals are subject to debate, and no sufficient state interest justifies legislation of norms simply because a particular belief is followed by a number of people, or even a majority. Indeed, what is considered to be "moral" changes with the times and is dependent upon societal background. Spiritual leadership, not the government, has the responsibility for striving to improve the morality of individuals. Enactment of the Voluntary Deviate Sexual Intercourse Statute, despite the fact that it provides punishment for what many believe to be abhorrent crimes against nature and perceived sins against God, is not properly in the realm of the temporal police power.

> The concepts underlying our view of the police power in the case before us were once summarized as follows by the great philosopher, John Stuart Mill, in his eminent and apposite work, *On Liberty* (1859):

> > (T)he sole end for which mankind are warranted, individually or collectively, in interfering with the liberty of action of any of their number, is self-protection.... (T)he only purpose for which power can be rightfully exercised over any member of a civilised community, against his will, is to prevent harm to others. His own good, either physical or moral is not a sufficient warrant. He cannot rightfully be compelled to do or forbear because it will be better for him to do so, because it will make him happier, because, in the opinions of others, to do so would be wise, or even right. These are good reasons for remonstrating with him, or reasoning with him, or persuading him, or entreating him, but not for compelling him, or visiting him with any evil in case he do otherwise. To justify that, the conduct from which it

is desired to deter him must be calculated to produce evil to some one else. The only part of the conduct of any one, for which he is amenable to society, is that which concerns others. In the part which merely concerns himself, his independence is, of right, absolute. Over himself, over his own body and mind, the individual is sovereign.

COMMONWEALTH v. WASSON
842 S.W.2d 487 (Ky. 1992)

LEIBSON, J.

Appellee, Jeffrey Wasson, is charged with having solicited an undercover Lexington policeman to engage in deviate sexual intercourse. KRS 510.100 punishes "deviate sexual intercourse with another person of the same sex" as a criminal offense, and specifies "consent of the other person shall not be a defense." Nor does it matter that the act is private and involves a caring relationship rather than a commercial one. It is classified as a Class A misdemeanor.

The charges were brought in the Fayette District Court where appellee moved to dismiss the charge on grounds that a statute criminalizing deviate sexual intercourse between consenting adults of the same sex, even if the act is committed in the privacy of a home, violates the Kentucky Constitution as: (1) an invasion of a constitutionally protected right of privacy; and (2) invidious discrimination in violation of constitutionally protected rights to equal treatment.

The Fayette District Judge held the statute violated appellee's right of privacy, and dismissed the charge. The Commonwealth appealed to Fayette Circuit Court which affirmed, and further held this statute infringed upon equal protection guarantees found in the Kentucky Constitution. Once more the Commonwealth appealed, and, because of the constitutional issues involved, this Court granted transfer.

Both courts below decided the issues solely on state constitutional law grounds, and our decision today, affirming the judgments of the lower courts, is likewise so limited. Federal constitutional protection under the Equal Protection Clause was not an issue reached in the lower courts and we need not address it. *Bowers v. Hardwick*, 478 U.S. 186 (1986) held federal constitutional protection of the right of privacy was not implicated in laws penalizing homosexual sodomy. We discuss *Bowers* in particular, and federal cases in general, not in the process of construing the United States Constitution or federal law, but only where their reasoning is relevant to discussing questions of state law.

I. RIGHTS OF PRIVACY

No language specifying "rights of privacy," as such, appears in either the Federal or State Constitution. The Commonwealth recognizes such rights exist, but takes the position that, since they are implicit rather than explicit, our Court should march in lock step with the United States Supreme Court in declaring when such rights exist. Such is not the formulation of federalism. On the contrary, under our system of dual sovereignty, it is our responsibility to interpret and apply our state constitution independently. We are not bound by decisions of the United States Supreme Court when deciding whether a state statute impermissibly infringes upon individual rights guaranteed in the State Constitution so long as state constitutional protection does not fall below the federal floor, meaning the minimum guarantee of individual rights under the United States Constitution as interpreted by the United States Supreme Court.

Contrary to popular belief, the Bill of Rights in the United States Constitution represents neither the primary source nor the maximum guarantee of state constitutional liberty. Our own constitutional guarantees against the intrusive power of the state do not derive from the Federal Constitution. The adoption of the Federal Constitution in 1791 was preceded by state constitutions developed over the preceding 15 years, and, while there is, of course, overlap between state and federal constitutional guarantees of individual rights, they are by no means identical. State constitutional law documents and the writings on liberty were more the source of federal law than the child of federal law.... Thus, while we respect the decisions of the United States Supreme Court on protection of individual liberty, and on occasion we have deferred to its reasoning, certainly we are not bound to do so, and we should not do so when valid reasons lead to a different conclusion.

We are persuaded that we should not do so here for several significant reasons. First, there are both textual and structural differences between the United States Bill of Rights and our own, which suggest a different conclusion from that reached by the United States Supreme Court is more appropriate. More significantly, Kentucky has a rich and compelling tradition of recognizing and protecting individual rights from state intrusion in cases similar in nature, found in the Debates of the Kentucky Constitutional Convention of 1890 and cases from the same era when that Constitution was adopted. The judges recognizing that tradition in their opinions wrote with a direct, firsthand knowledge of the mind set of the constitutional fathers, upholding the right of privacy against the intrusive police power of the state.

Kentucky cases recognized a legally protected right of privacy based on our own constitution and common law tradition long before the United States Supreme Court first took notice of whether there were any rights of privacy inherent in the Federal Bill of Rights.... The United States Supreme Court, defining the reach of the zone of privacy in terms of federal due process analysis, limits rights of privacy to "liberties that are 'deeply rooted in this Nation's history and tradition.'" Sodomy is not one of them. *Bowers v. Hardwick* decides that rights protected by the Due Process Clauses in the Fifth and Fourteenth Amendments to the United States Constitution do not "extend a fundamental right to homosexuals to engage in acts of consensual sodomy." See 478 U.S. at 192.

Bowers decides nothing beyond this. But state constitutional jurisprudence in this area is not limited by the constraints inherent in federal due process analysis. Deviate sexual intercourse conducted in private by consenting adults is not beyond the protections of the guarantees of individual liberty in our Kentucky Constitution simply because "proscriptions against that conduct have ancient roots." 478 U.S. at 192. Kentucky constitutional guarantees against government intrusion address substantive rights. The only reference to individual liberties in the Federal Constitution is the statement in the Preamble that one of the purposes in writing in the Constitution is to "secure the Blessings of Liberty to ourselves and our Posterity." Similarly, the Kentucky Constitution has a Preamble:

> We, the people of the Commonwealth of Kentucky, grateful to Almighty God for the civil, political and religious liberties we enjoy, and invoking the continuance of these blessings, do ordain and establish this Constitution.

But the Kentucky Constitution of 1891 does not limit the broadly stated guarantee of individual liberty to a statement in the Preamble. It amplifies the meaning of this statement of gratitude and purpose with a Bill of Rights in 26 sections, the first of which states:

> § 1. All men are, by nature, free and equal, and have certain inherent and inalienable rights, among which may be reckoned:
>
> > First: The right of enjoying and defending their lives and liberties....
>
> > Third: The right of seeking and pursuing their safety and happiness....
>
> § 2. Absolute and arbitrary power over the lives, liberty and property of freemen exists nowhere in a republic, not even in the largest majority.

The leading case on this subject is *Commonwealth v. Campbell*, 117 S.W. 383 (Ky. 1909). At issue was an ordinance that criminalized possession of intoxicating liquor, even for "private use." Our Court held that the Bill of Rights in the 1891 Constitution prohibited state action thus intruding upon the "inalienable rights possessed by the citizens" of Kentucky. Our Court interpreted the Kentucky Bill of Rights as defining a right of privacy, even though the constitution did not say so in that terminology:

> Man in his natural state has the right to do whatever he chooses and has the power to do. When he becomes a member of organized society, under

governmental regulation, he surrenders, of necessity, all of his natural right the exercise of which is, or may be, injurious to his fellow citizens. This is the price that he pays for governmental protection, but it is not within the competency of a free government to invade the sanctity of the absolute rights of the citizen any further than the direct protection of society requires…. It is not within the competency of government to invade the privacy of a citizen's life and to regulate his conduct in matters in which he alone is concerned, or to prohibit him any liberty the exercise of which will not directly injure society…. [L]et a man therefore be ever so abandoned in his principles, or vicious in his practice, provided he keeps his wickedness to himself, and does not offend against the rules of public decency, he is out of the reach of human laws.

The Court concludes, at p. 387:

The theory of our government is to allow the largest liberty to the individual commensurate with the public safety, or, as it has been otherwise expressed, that government is best which governs least. Under our institutions there is no room for that inquisitorial and protective spirit which seeks to regulate the conduct of men in matters in themselves indifferent, and to make them conform to a standard, not of their own choosing, but the choosing of the lawgiver.

The right of privacy has been recognized as an integral part of the guarantee of liberty in our 1891 Kentucky Constitution since its inception. The *Campbell* case is overwhelming affirmation of this proposition:

[W]e are of the opinion that it never has been within the competency of the Legislature to so restrict the liberty of this citizen, and certainly not since the adoption of the present [1891] Constitution. The Bill of Rights, which declares that among the inalienable rights possessed by the citizens is that of seeking and pursuing their safety and happiness, and that the absolute and arbitrary power over the lives, liberty, and property of freeman exists nowhere in a republic, not even in the largest majority, would be but an empty sound if the Legislature could prohibit the citizen the right of owning or drinking liquor, when in so doing he did not offend the laws of decency by being intoxicated in public…."

At the time Campbell was decided, the use of alcohol was as much an incendiary moral issue as deviate sexual behavior in private between consenting adults is today. Prohibition was the great moral issue of its time.

Nor is the Campbell case an aberration. Subsequent cases cited and followed Campbell. In *Commonwealth v. Smith*, 173 S.W. 340 (Ky. 1915), citing *Campbell*, the Court declared a statute unconstitutional that had led to Smith being arrested for drinking beer in the backroom of an office:

The power of the state to regulate and control the conduct of a private individual is confined to those cases where his conduct injuriously affects others. With his faults or weaknesses, which he keeps to himself, and which do not operate to the detriment of others, the state as such has no concern.

The holding in Smith is that "the police power may be called into play [only] when it is reasonably necessary to protect the public health, or public morals, or public safety." The clear implication is that immorality in private which does "not operate to the detriment of others," is placed beyond the reach of state action by the guarantees of liberty in the Kentucky Constitution.

In *Hershberg v. City of Barbourville*, 133 S.W. 985 (Ky. 1911), also citing *Campbell*, the Court declared an ordinance which purported to regulate cigarette smoking in such broad terms that it could be applied to persons who smoked in the privacy of their own home "unreasonably interfere[ed] with the right of the citizen to determine for himself such personal matters."

In the area of civil law, Kentucky has been in the forefront in recognizing the right of privacy. In 1909, our Court stepped outside traditional libel law and recognized invasion of privacy as a tort in *Foster-Milburn Co. v. Chinn*, 120 S.W. 364. Then in 1927, in *Brents v. Morgan* 299 S.W. 967, our Court defined this emerging right as "the right to be left alone, that is, the right of a person to be free from unwarranted publicity, or the right to live without unwarranted interference by the public about matters with which the public is not necessarily concerned."

> The right of privacy is incident to the person and not to property.... It is considered as a natural and an absolute or pure right springing from the instincts of nature. It is of that class of rights which every human being has in his natural state and which he did not surrender by becoming a member of organized society. The fundamental rights of personal security and personal liberty include the right of privacy, the right to be left alone.... The right to enjoy life [Ky. Const., § 1, first subpart] in the way most agreeable and pleasant, and the right of privacy is nothing more than a right to live in a particular way. *Id.* at 971, quoting 21 RCL parg. 3, p. 1197.

In the *Campbell* case our Court quoted at length from the "great work" On Liberty of the 19th century English philosopher and economist, John Stuart Mill. We repeat the quote in part:

> The only part of the conduct of anyone, for which he is amenable to society, is that which concerns others. In the part which merely concerns himself, his independence is, of right, absolute.... The principle requires liberty of taste and pursuits; of framing the plan of our life to suit our own character; of doing as we like, subject to such consequences as may follow; without impediment from our fellow creatures, so long as what we do does not harm them, even though they should think our conduct foolish, perverse, or wrong.

Mill's premise is that "physical force in the form of legal penalties," i.e., criminal sanctions, should not be used as a means to improve the citizen. The majority has no moral right to dictate how everyone else should live. Public indignation, while given due weight, should be subject to the overriding test of rational and critical analysis, drawing the line at harmful consequences to others. Modern legal philosophers who follow Mill temper this test with an enlightened paternalism, permitting the law to intervene to stop self-inflicted harm such as the result of drug taking, or failure to use seat belts or crash helmets, not to enforce majoritarian or conventional morality, but because the victim of such self-inflicted harm becomes a burden on society.

Based on the *Campbell* opinion, and on the Comments of the 1891 Convention Delegates, there is little doubt but that the views of John Stuart Mill, which were then held in high esteem, provided the philosophical underpinnings for the reworking and broadening of protection of individual rights that occurs throughout the 1891 Constitution.

We have recognized protection of individual rights greater than the federal floor in a number of cases, most recently: *Ingram v. Commonwealth*, 801 S.W.2d 321 (Ky. 1990), involving protection against double jeopardy and *Dean v. Commonwealth*, 777 S.W.2d 900 (Ky. 1989), involving the right of confrontation. Perhaps the most dramatic recent example of protection of individual rights under the state Constitution where the United States Supreme Court had refused to afford protection under the Federal Constitution, is *Rose v. Council for Better Educ., Inc.*, 790 S.W.2d 186 (Ky. 1989). In *Rose,* our Court recognized our Kentucky Constitution afforded individual school children from property poor districts a fundamental right to an adequate education such as provided in wealthier school districts, even though 16 years earlier the United States Supreme Court held the Federal Constitution provided no such protection in *San Antonio Independent School District v. Rodriguez*, 411 U.S. 1 (1973). The United States Supreme Court found there was no constitutional, or fundamental, right to a particular quality of education which justified invoking the Equal Protection Clause of the Fourteenth Amendment. Our Court found a duty in the Kentucky constitutional requirement that the General Assembly "provide an efficient system of common schools." Ky. Const. Sec. 183.

In *Fannin v. Williams*, 655 S.W.2d 480 (Ky. 1983), we held unconstitutional a statute that would permit the state librarian to supply textbooks to children in the state's non-public schools, even though in *Bd. of Education v. Allen*, 392 U.S. 236 (1968), the United States Supreme Court had held a statute accomplishing a similar purpose did not violate the "establishment of religion" clause in the United States Constitution. We stated:

> The problem in this case is not whether the challenged statute passes muster under the federal constitution as interpreted by the United States Supreme Court, but whether it satisfies the much more detailed and explicit proscriptions of the Kentucky Constitution. It does not.

We view the United States Supreme Court decision in *Bowers v. Hardwick* as a misdirected application of the theory of original intent. To illustrate: as a theory of majoritarian morality, miscegenation was an offense with ancient roots. It is highly unlikely that protecting the rights of persons of different races to copulate was one of the considerations behind the Fourteenth Amendment. Nevertheless, in *Loving v. Virginia*, 388 U.S. 1 (1967), the United States Supreme Court recognized that a contemporary, enlightened interpretation of the liberty interest involved in the sexual act made its punishment constitutionally impermissible.

II. EQUAL PROTECTION

Certainly, the practice of deviate sexual intercourse violates traditional morality. But so does the same act between heterosexuals, which activity is decriminalized. Going one step further, all sexual activity between consenting adults outside of marriage violates our traditional morality. The issue here is not whether sexual activity traditionally viewed as immoral can be punished by society, but whether it can be punished solely on the basis of sexual preference.

We do not speculate on how the United States Supreme Court as presently constituted will decide whether the sexual preference of homosexuals is entitled to protection under the Equal Protection Clause of the Federal constitution. We need not speculate as to whether male and/or female homosexuals will be allowed status as a protected class if and when the United States Supreme Court confronts this issue. They are a separate and identifiable class for Kentucky constitutional law analysis because no class of persons can be discriminated against under the Kentucky Constitution. All are entitled to equal treatment, unless there is a substantial governmental interest, a rational basis, for different treatment. The statute before us is in violation of Kentucky constitutional protection in Section Three that "all men (persons), when they form a social compact, are equal," and in Section Two that "absolute and arbitrary power over the lives, liberty and property of free men (persons) exist nowhere in a republic, not even in the largest majority." We have concluded that it is "arbitrary" for the majority to criminalize sexual activity solely on the basis of majoritarian sexual preference, and that it denied "equal" treatment under the law when there is no rational basis, as this term is used and applied in our Kentucky cases.

The Commonwealth has tried hard to demonstrate a legitimate governmental interest justifying a distinction, but has failed. Many of the claimed justifications are simply outrageous: that "homosexuals are more promiscuous than heterosexuals, that homosexuals enjoy the company of children, and that homosexuals are more prone to engage in sex acts in public." The only proffered justification with superficial validity is that "infectious diseases are more readily transmitted by anal sodomy than by other forms of sexual copulation." But this statute is not limited to anal copulation, and this reasoning would apply to male-female anal intercourse the same as it applies to male-male intercourse. The growing number of females to whom AIDS (Acquired Immune Deficiency Syndrome) has been transmitted is stark evidence that AIDS is not only a male homosexual disease. The only medical evidence in the record before us rules out any distinction between male-male and male-female anal intercourse as a method of preventing AIDS. The act of sexual contact is not implicated, per se, whether the contact is homosexual or heterosexual. In any event, this statute was enacted in 1974 before the AIDS nightmare was upon us. It was 1982 or 1983 before AIDS was a recognized diagnostic entity.

In the final analysis we can attribute no legislative purpose to this statute except to single out homosexuals for different treatment for indulging their sexual preference by engaging in the same activity heterosexuals are now at liberty to perform. By 1974 there had already been a sea change in societal values insofar as attaching criminal penalties to extramarital sex. The question is whether a society that no longer criminalizes adultery, fornication, or deviate sexual intercourse between heterosexuals, has a rational basis to single out homosexual acts for different treatment. Is there a rational basis for declaring this one type of sexual immorality so destructive of family values as to merit criminal punishment whereas other acts of sexual immorality which were likewise forbidden by the same religious and traditional heritage of Western civilization are now decriminalized? If there is a rational basis for different treatment it has yet to be demonstrated in this case. We need not sympathize, agree with, or even understand the sexual preference of homosexuals in order to recognize their right to equal treatment before the bar of criminal justice.

To be treated equally by the law is a broader constitutional value than due process of law as discussed in the *Bowers* case. We recognize it as such under the Kentucky Constitution, without regard to whether the United States Supreme Court continues to do so in federal constitutional jurisprudence. "Equal Justice Under Law" inscribed above the entrance to the United States Supreme Court, expresses the unique goal to which all humanity aspires. In Kentucky it is more than a mere aspiration. It is part of the "inherent and inalienable" rights protected by our Kentucky Constitution. Our protection against exercise of "arbitrary power over the...liberty...of freemen" by the General Assembly (Section Two) and our guarantee that all persons are entitled to "equal" treatment (in Section Three) forbid a special act punishing the sexual preference of homosexuals. It matters not that the same act committed by persons of the same sex is more offensive to the majority because Section Two states such "power...exists nowhere in a republic, not even in the largest majority."

The purpose of the present statute is not to protect the marital relationship against sexual activity outside of marriage, but only to punish one aspect of it while other activities similarly destructive of the marital relationship, if not more so, go unpunished. Sexual preference and not the act committed, determine criminality, and is being punished. Simply because the majority, speaking through the General Assembly, finds one type of extramarital intercourse more offensive than another, does not provide a rational basis for criminalizing the sexual preference of homosexuals.

LAMBERT, J., dissenting.

The issue here is not whether private homosexual conduct should be allowed or prohibited. The only question properly before this Court is whether the Constitution of Kentucky denies the legislative branch a right to prohibit such conduct. Nothing in the majority opinion demonstrates such a limitation on legislative prerogative.

To justify its view that private homosexual conduct is protected by the Constitution of Kentucky, the majority has found it necessary to disregard virtually all of recorded history, the teachings of the religions most influential on Western Civilization, the debates of the delegates to the Constitutional Convention, and the text of the Constitution itself. Rather than amounting to a decision based upon precedent as is suggested, this decision reflects the value judgment of the majority and its view that public law has no right to prohibit the conduct at issue here.... The history and traditions of this Commonwealth are fully in accord with the Biblical, historical and common law view. Since at least 1860, sodomy has been a criminal offense in Kentucky and this fact was well known to the delegates at the time of the 1890 Constitutional Convention.

Embracing "state constitutionalism," a practice in vogue among many state courts as a means of rejecting the leadership of the Supreme Court of the United States, the majority has declared its independence from even the influence of this nation's highest court. The majority cannot, however, escape the logic and scholarship of *Bowers* which reached the conclusion that nothing in the Due Process Clause of the United States Constitution prevented a state from punishing sodomy as a crime. While I do not advocate the view that state courts should march in lock step with the Supreme Court of the United States, on those occasions when state courts depart from that Court's reasoned interpretations, it should be for compelling reasons, usually text or tradition, and only in clearly distinguishable circumstances, none of which are present here.

Perhaps the greatest mischief to be found in the majority opinion is in its discovery of a constitutional right which lacks any textual support. The majority has referred generally to the twenty-six sections in the Bill of Rights of the Kentucky Constitution and quoted § 1 First and Third and §

2. None of the sections cited or quoted contain an inkling of reference to rights of privacy or sexual freedom of any kind. This is conceded by the majority as follows: "No language specifying 'rights of privacy,' as such, appears in either the Federal or State Constitution." The majority opinion is a departure from the accepted methodology of constitutional analysis which requires that text be the beginning point. The majority reasons that differences between the text of the Kentucky Constitution and the United States Constitution free this Court from federal influence, but it fails to explain its discovery of the rights announced here in the absence of any textual basis. This is a dangerous practice. When judges free themselves of constitutional text, their values and notions of morality are given free rein and they, not the Constitution, become the supreme law.

As has been demonstrated, a right of privacy protecting homosexual sodomy between or among consenting adults has no basis in the history and traditions of Western culture or in this nation or state. Likewise, the constitutional debates contain only the most oblique references to any right of privacy and Kentucky constitutional text is totally silent. As such, the majority must and does rest its entire case on a line of decisions rendered by this Court in the early twentieth century in which a right of privacy was held to exist with respect to the consumption of alcoholic beverages and the use of tobacco products. The leading decision of this genre is *Commonwealth v. Campbell*, 117 S.W. 383 (Ky. 1909), in which a statute which criminalized the possession of intoxicating liquor for private use was held unconstitutional and which, with rhetorical flourish declared the broadest possible right of privacy.

The fact that this Court broadly declared a right of privacy prior to World War I in cases which one suspects were influenced by local economic forces does not mean that such a doctrine should be applied in the extreme nearly a century later to a moral question not remotely considered by the *Campbell* court.

The major premise in the majority opinion is that the Constitution forbids any legal restriction upon the private conduct of adults unless it can be shown that such conduct is harmful to another. This view represents the essence of the philosophy of John Stuart Mill in his essay *On Liberty*. While espousing such a view, however, Mill recognized the difficulty of distinguishing that part of a person's life which affected only himself from that which affected others. He recognized that one who by deleterious vices harmed himself indirectly harmed others and that society suffered indirect harm by the mere knowledge of immoral conduct. Nevertheless, Mill clung to his philosophy by insisting that society was without *power* to punish gambling or drunkenness. He made a ringing defense of the right of persons so disposed to practice polygamy.

While the philosophy of John Stuart Mill as adopted by this Court in *Campbell v. Commonwealth* exalts individuality in the extreme, it has, nevertheless, a superficial appeal. It rejects majoritarian morality as a basis for law and imposes legal limits on the conduct of man only insofar as it may harm others. Unfortunately for the purposes of the majority, the philosophy of Mill and the views contained in the Campbell case, if logically applied, would necessarily result in the eradication of numerous other criminal statutes. For example, if majoritarian morality is without a role in the formulation of criminal law and the only standard is harm to another, all laws proscribing the possession and use of dangerous or narcotic drugs would fall. Likewise, incest statutes which proscribe sexual intercourse between persons of close kinship regardless of age or consent would be rendered invalid. Laws prohibiting cruelty to animals, the abuse of dead human bodies, suicide and polygamy would be held unconstitutional. Despite the majority's disingenuous departure from Mill based on "an enlightened paternalism" to prevent self-inflicted harm, many prevailing criminal statutes would nevertheless fail the "harm to another" test. While the majority of this Court manifestly sees the proposition otherwise, the Supreme Court of the United States has addressed the role of morality as a rationale to support criminal law and found no impediment.

> The law, however, is constantly based on notions of morality, and if all laws representing essentially moral choices are to be invalidated under the Due Process Clause, the courts will be very busy indeed. *Bowers*, 478 U.S. at 196.

From my study of this case, I have concluded that the privacy right found in the Constitution of Kentucky does not apply to claimed rights not remotely envisioned by the delegates to the Constitutional Convention or reasonably emerging from our history and traditions. As such, the right to determine whether sodomy should be a criminal offense belongs to the people through their elected representatives. We should not deprive the people of that right. As the majority has observed, many states have already decriminalized consensual sodomy. Appellee should take his case to the Kentucky General Assembly and let that branch of government say whether the crime shall remain or be abolished.

To resolve the equal protection issue, one must first review the statute, KRS 510.100. This Act is not limited in its application to persons who consider themselves homosexual nor is it limited to the male or female gender. Any person who engages in deviate sexual intercourse with another person of the same sex is in violation. The statute prohibits conduct and says nothing of the sexual preference or gender of the violator....There is nothing in the statute by which persons are classified and certainly nothing which accords unequal treatment to persons comprising a recognizable class on factors such as race, gender or ethnic origin.

The heart of the majority contention is that unequal treatment results when the same conduct is deemed criminal if committed by persons of the same sex, but not if the actors are of different sexes. It correctly observes that in former times all sexual contact between unmarried persons was viewed as immoral. From this the majority concludes the statute must be invalidated.

In *Plyler v. Doe*, 457 U.S. 202, (1982), The Supreme Court addressed this contention:

> A legislature must have substantial latitude to establish classifications that roughly approximate the nature of the problem perceived, that accommodate competing concerns both public and private, and that account for limitations on the practical ability of the State to remedy every ill. In applying the Equal Protection Clause to most forms of state action, we thus seek only the assurance that the classification at issue bears some fair relationship to a legitimate public purpose.

As persons who engage in homosexual sodomy have never been held to constitute a suspect classification, to be upheld, the statute at issue need only satisfy the lowest level of judicial scrutiny and demonstrate that it bears a rational relationship to a legitimate legislative objective. Protection of public "health, safety and morality" was held to be such an objective in *Bosworth v. City of Lexington*, 125 S.W.2d 995, (Ky. 1930). This objective found new vitality with the emergence of the AIDS epidemic which indisputably originated in this country in the homosexual community. Moreover, *Bowers v. Hardwick* held forthrightly that the rational basis standard was satisfied by majority sentiments as to the immorality of homosexuality.

I conclude with the view that this Court has strayed from its role of interpreting the Constitution and undertaken to make social policy. This decision is a vast extension of judicial power by which four Justices of this Court have overridden the will of the Legislative and Executive branches of Kentucky State Government and denied the people any say in this important social issue. No decision cited by the majority has ever gone so far and certainly none comes to mind. Where this slippery slope may lead is anybody's guess, but the ramifications of this decision will surely be profound.

NOTE

The majority opinion in *Wasson* discusses and rejects *Bowers v. Hardwick*, 478 U.S. 186 (1986), in which the United States Supreme Court upheld the constitutionality of a Georgia criminal law prohibiting sodomy and ruled that the Due Process Clause of the Federal Constitution does not protect the right of a consenting adult to engage in homosexual conduct. *Bowers* was decided by a 5-4 vote and was overruled seventeen years later in *Lawrence v. Texas*, 539 U.S. 558 (2003). In the seventeen year interim between the two cases, courts in five states—one of which was Georgia—rejected both the reasoning and result of *Bowers* in ruling that criminal laws prohibiting adult consensual homosexual activity violated state constitutional provisions protecting the right of privacy. The first decision of a state supreme court to do so was *Wasson*. The five state decisions rejecting *Bowers* were acknowledged by the Supreme Court in *Lawrence* and apparently played some part in convincing the high Court to overrule *Bowers*. *See* Jeffrey M. Shaman, EQUALITY AND LIBERTY IN THE GOLDEN AGE OF STATE CONSTITUTIONAL LAW 215-22 (2008).

D. CIVIL UNION AND MARRIAGE

BAKER v. STATE
744 A.2d 864 (Vt. 1999)

AMESTOY, C.J.

May the State of Vermont exclude same-sex couples from the benefits and protections that its laws provide to opposite-sex married couples? That is the fundamental question we address in this appeal, a question that the Court well knows arouses deeply-felt religious, moral, and political beliefs. Our constitutional responsibility to consider the legal merits of issues properly before us provides no exception for the controversial case. The issue before the Court, moreover, does not turn on the religious or moral debate over intimate same-sex relationships, but rather on the statutory and constitutional basis for the exclusion of same-sex couples from the secular benefits and protections offered married couples.

We conclude that under the Common Benefits Clause of the Vermont Constitution, which, in pertinent part, reads,

> That government is, or ought to be, instituted for the common benefit, protection, and security of the people, nation, or community, and not for the particular emolument or advantage of any single person, family, or set of persons, who are a part only of that community....

Vt. Const., ch. I, art 7., plaintiffs may not be deprived of the statutory benefits and protections afforded persons of the opposite sex who choose to marry. We hold that the State is constitutionally required to extend to same-sex couples the common benefits and protections that flow from marriage under Vermont law. Whether this ultimately takes the form of inclusion within the marriage laws themselves or a parallel "domestic partnership" system or some equivalent statutory alternative, rests with the Legislature. Whatever system is chosen, however, must conform with the constitutional imperative to afford all Vermonters the common benefit, protection, and security of the law.

Plaintiffs are three same-sex couples who have lived together in committed relationships for periods ranging from four to twenty-five years. Two of the couples have raised children together. Each couple applied for a marriage license from their respective town clerk, and each was refused a license as ineligible under the applicable state marriage laws.

Assuming that the marriage statutes preclude their eligibility for a marriage license, plaintiffs contend that the exclusion violates their right to the common benefit and protection of the law guaranteed by Chapter I, Article 7 of the Vermont Constitution. They note that in denying them access to a civil marriage license, the law effectively excludes them from a broad array of legal benefits and protections incident to the marital relation, including access to a spouse's medical, life, and disability insurance, hospital visitation and other medical decisionmaking privileges, spousal support, intestate succession, homestead protections, and many other statutory protections.

In considering this issue, it is important to emphasize at the outset that it is the Common Benefits Clause of the Vermont Constitution we are construing, rather than its counterpart, the Equal Protection Clause of the Fourteenth Amendment to the United States Constitution. It is altogether fitting and proper that we do so. Vermont's constitutional commitment to equal rights was the product of the successful effort to create an independent republic and a fundamental charter of government, the Constitution of 1777, both of which preceded the adoption of the Fourteenth Amendment by nearly a century. As we explained in *State v. Badger*, 450 A.2d 336, 347 (Vt. 1982), "our constitution is not a mere reflection of the federal charter. Historically and textually, it differs from the United States Constitution. It predates the federal counterpart, as it extends back to Vermont's days as an independent republic. It is an independent authority, and Vermont's fundamental law."

The words of the Common Benefits Clause are revealing. While they do not, to be sure, set forth a fully-formed standard of analysis for determining the constitutionality of a given statute, they do express broad principles which usefully inform that analysis. Chief among these is the principle of inclusion. As explained more fully in the discussion that follows, the specific proscription against governmental favoritism toward not only groups or "set[s] of men," but also toward any particular "family" or "single man," underscores the framers' resentment of political preference of any kind. The affirmative right to the "common benefits and protections" of government and the corollary proscription of favoritism in the distribution of public "emoluments and advantages" reflect the framers' overarching objective "not only that everyone enjoy equality before the law or have an equal voice in government but also that everyone have *an equal share in the fruits of the common enterprise.*" W. Adams, *The First American Constitutions* 188 (1980) (emphasis added). Thus, at its core the Common Benefits Clause expressed a vision of government that afforded every Vermonter its benefit and protection and provided no Vermonter particular advantage.

We must ultimately ascertain whether the omission of a part of the community from the benefit, protection and security of the challenged law bears a reasonable and just relation to the governmental purpose. Consistent with the core presumption of inclusion, factors to be considered in this determination may include: (1) the significance of the benefits and protections of the challenged law; (2) whether the omission of members of the community from the benefits and protections of the challenged law promotes the government's stated goals; and (3) whether the classification is significantly underinclusive or overinclusive.

The principal purpose the State advances in support of excluding same-sex couples from the legal benefits of marriage is the government's interest in "furthering the link between procreation and child rearing." The State has a strong interest, it argues, in promoting a permanent commitment between couples who have children to ensure that their offspring are considered legitimate and receive ongoing parental support. The State contends, further, that the Legislature could reasonably believe that sanctioning same-sex unions "would diminish society's perception of the link between procreation and child rearing...[and] advance the notion that fathers or mothers...are mere surplusage to the functions of procreation and child rearing." The State argues that since same-sex couples cannot conceive a child on their own, state-sanctioned same-sex unions "could be seen by the Legislature to separate further the connection between procreation and parental responsibilities for raising children." Hence, the Legislature is justified, the State concludes, "in using the marriage statutes to send a public message that procreation and child rearing are intertwined."

Do these concerns represent valid public interests that are reasonably furthered by the exclusion of same-sex couples from the benefits and protections that flow from the marital relation? It is beyond dispute that the State has a legitimate and long-standing interest in promoting a permanent commitment between couples for the security of their children. It is equally undeniable that the State's interest has been advanced by extending formal public sanction and protection to the union, or marriage, of those couples considered capable of having children, i.e., men and women. And there is no doubt that the overwhelming majority of births today continue to result from natural conception between one man and one woman.

It is equally undisputed that many opposite-sex couples marry for reasons unrelated to procreation, that some of these couples never intend to have children, and that others are incapable of having children. Therefore, if the purpose of the statutory exclusion of same-sex couples is to "further [ ] the link between procreation and child rearing," it is significantly underinclusive. The law extends the benefits and protections of marriage to many persons with no logical connection to the stated governmental goal.

Furthermore, while accurate statistics are difficult to obtain, there is no dispute that a significant number of children today are actually being raised by same-sex parents, and that increasing numbers of children are being conceived by such parents through a variety of assisted-reproductive techniques. See D. Flaks, et al., Lesbians Choosing Motherhood: A Comparative Study of Lesbian and Heterosexual Parents and Their Children, 31 Dev. Psychol. 105, 105 (1995) (citing estimates that between 1.5 and 5 million lesbian mothers resided with their children in United States between 1989 and 1990, and that thousands of lesbian mothers have chosen motherhood through donor insemination or adoption); G. Green & F. Bozett, Lesbian Mothers and Gay Fathers, in Homosexuality: Research Implications for Public Policy 197, 198 (J. Gonsiorek et al. eds., 1991) (estimating that numbers of children of either gay fathers or lesbian mothers range between six and fourteen million); C. Patterson, Children of the Lesbian Baby Boom: Behavioral Adjustment, Self-Concepts, and Sex Role Identity, in Lesbian and Gay Psychology (B. Greene et al. eds., 1994) (observing that although precise estimates are difficult, number of families with lesbian mothers is growing); E. Shapiro & L. Schultz, Single-Sex Families: The Impact of Birth Innovations Upon Traditional Family Notions, 24 J. Fam. L. 271, 281 (1985) ("[I]t is a fact that children are being born to single-sex families on a biological basis, and that they are being so born in considerable numbers.").

Thus, with or without the marriage sanction, the reality today is that increasing numbers of same-sex couples are employing increasingly efficient assisted-reproductive techniques to conceive and raise children. The Vermont Legislature has not only recognized this reality, but has acted affirmatively to remove legal barriers so that same-sex couples may legally adopt and rear the children conceived through such efforts. See 15A V.S.A. § 1-102(b) (allowing partner of biological parent to adopt if in child's best interest without reference to sex). The state has also acted to expand the domestic relations laws to safeguard the interests of same-sex parents and their children when such couples terminate their domestic relationship. See 15A V.S.A. § 1-112 (vesting family court with jurisdiction over parental rights and responsibilities, parent-child contact, and child support when unmarried persons who have adopted minor child "terminate their domestic relationship").

Therefore, to the extent that the state's purpose in licensing civil marriage was, and is, to legitimize children and provide for their security, the statutes plainly exclude many same-sex couples who are no different from opposite-sex couples with respect to these objectives. If anything, the exclusion of same-sex couples from the legal protections incident to marriage exposes their children to the precise risks that the State argues the marriage laws are designed to secure against. In short, the marital exclusion treats persons who are similarly situated for purposes of the law, differently.

The State also argues that because same-sex couples cannot conceive a child on their own, their exclusion promotes a "perception of the link between procreation and child rearing," and that to discard it would "advance the notion that mothers and fathers…are mere surplusage to the functions of procreation and child rearing" Apart from the bare assertion, the State offers no persuasive reasoning to support these claims. Indeed, it is undisputed that most of those who utilize nontraditional means of conception are infertile married couples, and that many assisted-reproductive techniques involve only one of the married partner's genetic material, the other being supplied by a third party through sperm, egg, or embryo donation. The State does not suggest that the use of these technologies undermines a married couple's sense of parental responsibility, or fosters the perception that they are "mere surplusage" to the conception and parenting of the child so conceived. Nor does it even remotely suggest that access to such techniques ought to be restricted as a matter of public policy to "send a public message that procreation and child rearing are intertwined." Accordingly, there is no reasonable basis to conclude that a same-sex couple's use of the same technologies would undermine the bonds of parenthood, or society's perception of parenthood.

The question thus becomes whether the exclusion of a relatively small but significant number of otherwise qualified same-sex couples from the same legal benefits and protections afforded their opposite-sex counterparts contravenes the mandates of Article 7. We turn, accordingly, from the principal justifications advanced by the State to the interests asserted by plaintiffs.

As noted, in determining whether a statutory exclusion reasonably relates to the governmental purpose it is appropriate to consider the history and significance of the benefits denied. What do these considerations reveal about the benefits and protections at issue here? In *Loving v. Virginia*, 388 U.S. 1, 12 (1967), the United States Supreme Court, striking down Virginia's anti-miscegenation law, observed that "[t]he freedom to marry has long been recognized as one of the vital personal rights." The Court's point was clear; access to a civil marriage license and the multitude of legal benefits, protections, and obligations that flow from it significantly enhance the quality of life in our society.

The Supreme Court's observations in *Loving* merely acknowledged what many states, including Vermont, had long recognized. One hundred thirty-seven years before *Loving*, this Court characterized the reciprocal rights and responsibilities flowing from the marriage laws as "the natural rights of human nature." See *Overseers of the Poor*, 2 Vt. 159. Decisions in other New England states noted the unique legal and economic ramifications flowing from the marriage relation. See, e.g., *Adams v. Palmer*, 51 Me. 480, 485 (1863) ("it establishes fundamental and most important domestic relations"). Early decisions recognized that a marriage contract, although similar to other civil agreements, represents much more because once formed, the law imposes a variety of obligations, protections, and benefits. As the Maine Supreme Judicial Court observed, the rights and obligations of marriage rest not upon contract, "but upon the general law of the State, statutory or common, which defines and prescribes those rights, duties and obligations. They are of law, not of contract." See id. at 483; see also *Ditson v. Ditson*, 4 R.I. 87, 105 (1856) (marriage transcends contract because "it gives rights, and imposes duties and restrictions upon the parties to it"). In short, the marriage laws transform a private agreement into a source of significant public benefits and protections.

While the laws relating to marriage have undergone many changes during the last century, largely toward the goal of equalizing the status of husbands and wives, the benefits of marriage have not diminished in value. On the contrary, the benefits and protections incident to a marriage license under Vermont law have never been greater. They include, for example, the right to receive a portion of the estate of a spouse who dies intestate and protection against disinheritance through elective share provisions, under 14 V.S.A. §§ 401-404, 551; preference in being appointed as the personal representative of a spouse who dies intestate, under 14 V.S.A. § 903; the right to bring a lawsuit for the wrongful death of a spouse, under 14 V.S.A. § 1492; the right to bring an action for loss of consortium, under 12 V.S.A. § 5431; the right to workers' compensation survivor benefits under 21 V.S.A. § 632; the right to spousal benefits statutorily guaranteed to public employees, including health, life, disability, and accident insurance, under 3 V.S.A. § 631; the opportunity to be covered as a spouse under group life insurance policies issued to an employee, under 8 V.S.A. § 3811; the opportunity to be covered as the insured's spouse under an individual health insurance policy, under 8 V.S.A. § 4063; the right to claim an evidentiary privilege for marital communications, under V.R.E. 504; homestead rights and protections, under 27 V.S.A. §§ 105-108, 141-142; the presumption of joint ownership of property and the concomitant right of survivorship, under 27 V.S.A. § 2; hospital visitation and other rights incident to the medical treatment of a family member, under 18 V.S.A. § 1852; and the right to receive, and the obligation to provide, spousal support, maintenance, and property division in the event of separation or divorce, under 15 V.S.A. §§ 751-752.

While other statutes could be added to this list, the point is clear. The legal benefits and protections flowing from a marriage license are of such significance that any statutory exclusion must necessarily be grounded on public concerns of sufficient weight, cogency, and authority that the justice of the deprivation cannot seriously be questioned. Considered in light of the extreme logical disjunction between the classification and the stated purposes of the law-protecting children and "furthering the link between procreation and child rearing"-the exclusion falls substantially short of this standard. The laudable governmental goal of promoting a commitment between married couples to promote the security of their children and the community as a whole provides no reasonable basis for denying the legal benefits and protections of marriage to same-sex couples, who are no differently situated with respect to this goal than their opposite-sex counterparts. Promoting a link between procreation and childrearing similarly fails to support the exclusion. We turn, accordingly, to the remaining interests identified by the State in support of the statutory exclusion.

The State asserts that a number of additional rationales could support a legislative decision to exclude same-sex partners from the statutory benefits and protections of marriage. The most substantive of the State's remaining claims relates to the issue of childrearing. It is conceivable that the Legislature could conclude that opposite-sex partners offer advantages in this area, although we note that child-development experts disagree and the answer is decidedly uncertain. The argument, however, contains a more fundamental flaw, and that is the Legislature's endorsement of a policy diametrically at odds with the State's claim. In 1996, the Vermont General Assembly enacted, and the Governor signed, a law removing all prior legal barriers to the adoption of children by same-sex couples. At the same time, the Legislature provided additional legal protections in the form of court-ordered child support and parent-child contact in the event that same-sex parents dissolved their "domestic relationship." In light of these express policy choices, the State's arguments that Vermont public policy favors opposite-sex over same-sex parents or disfavors the use of artificial reproductive technologies are patently without substance.

Finally, it is suggested that the long history of official intolerance of intimate same-sex relationships cannot be reconciled with an interpretation of Article 7 that would give state-sanctioned benefits and protection to individuals of the same sex who commit to a permanent domestic relationship. We find the argument to be unpersuasive for several reasons. First, to the extent that state action historically has been motivated by an animus against a class, that history cannot provide a legitimate basis for continued unequal application of the law. See *MacCallum*, 165 Vt. at 459-60, 686 A.2d at 939 (holding that although adopted persons had "historically been a target of discrimination," social prejudices failed to support their continued exclusion from intestacy law). As we observed recently in *Brigham*, 166 Vt. at 267, 692 A.2d at 396, "equal protection of the laws cannot be limited by eighteenth-century standards." Second, whatever claim may be made in light of the undeniable fact that federal and state statutes-including those in Vermont-have historically disfavored same-sex relationships, more recent legislation plainly undermines the contention. See, e.g., Laws of Vermont, 1977, No. 51, §§ 2, 3 (repealing former § 2603 of Title 13, which criminalized fellatio). In 1992, Vermont was one of the first states to enact statewide legislation prohibiting discrimination in employment, housing, and other services based on sexual orientation. See 21 V.S.A. § 495 (employment); 9 V.S.A. § 4503 (housing); 8 V.S.A. § 4724 (insurance); 9 V.S.A. § 4502 (public accommodations). Sexual orientation is among the categories specifically protected against hate-motivated crimes in Vermont. See 13 V.S.A. § 1455. Furthermore, as noted earlier, recent enactments of the General Assembly have removed barriers to adoption by same-sex couples, and have extended legal rights and protections to such couples who dissolve their "domestic relationship." See 15A V.S.A. §§ 1-102, 1-112.

Thus, viewed in the light of history, logic, and experience, we conclude that none of the interests asserted by the State provides a reasonable and just basis for the continued exclusion of same-sex couples from the benefits incident to a civil marriage license under Vermont law. Accordingly, in the faith that a case beyond the imagining of the framers of our Constitution may, nevertheless, be safely anchored in the values that infused it, we find a constitutional obligation to extend to plaintiffs the common benefit, protection, and security that Vermont law provides opposite-sex married couples. It remains only to determine the appropriate means and scope of relief compelled by this constitutional mandate.

We hold only that plaintiffs are entitled under Chapter I, Article 7, of the Vermont Constitution to obtain the same benefits and protections afforded by Vermont law to married opposite-sex couples. We do not purport to infringe upon the prerogatives of the Legislature to craft an appropriate means of addressing this constitutional mandate, other than to note that the record here refers to a number of potentially constitutional statutory schemes from other jurisdictions. These include what are typically referred to as "domestic partnership" or "registered partnership" acts, which generally establish an alternative legal status to marriage for same-sex couples, impose similar formal requirements and limitations, create a parallel licensing or registration scheme, and extend all or most of the same rights and obligations provided by the law to married partners. We do not intend specifically to endorse any one or all of the referenced acts, particularly in view of the significant benefits omitted from several of the laws.

Further, while the State's prediction of "destabilization" cannot be a ground for denying relief, it is not altogether irrelevant. A sudden change in the marriage laws or the statutory benefits traditionally incidental to marriage may have disruptive and unforeseen consequences. Absent legislative guidelines defining the status and rights of same-sex couples, consistent with constitutional requirements, uncertainty and confusion could result. Therefore, we hold that the current statutory scheme shall remain in effect for a reasonable period of time to enable the Legislature to consider and enact implementing legislation in an orderly and expeditious fashion.

The judgment of the superior court upholding the constitutionality of the Vermont marriage statutes under Chapter I, Article 7 of the Vermont Constitution is reversed. The effect of the Court's decision is suspended, and jurisdiction is retained in this Court, to permit the Legislature to consider and enact legislation consistent with the constitutional mandate described herein.

JOHNSON, J., concurring in part and dissenting in part.

I concur with the majority's holding, but I respectfully dissent from its novel and truncated remedy, which in my view abdicates this Court's constitutional duty to redress violations of constitutional rights. I would grant the requested relief and enjoin defendants from denying plaintiffs a marriage license based solely on the sex of the applicants.

In 1948, when the California Supreme Court struck down a state law prohibiting the issuance of a license authorizing interracial marriages, the court did not suspend its judgment to allow the legislature an opportunity to enact a separate licensing scheme for interracial marriages. See *Perez v. Lippold*, 198 P.2d 17, 29 (Calif. 1948) (granting writ of mandamus compelling county clerk to issue certificate of registry). Indeed, such a mandate in that context would be unfathomable to us today. Here, as in *Perez*, we have held that the State has unconstitutionally discriminated against plaintiffs, thereby depriving them of civil rights to which they are entitled. Like the Hawaii Circuit Court in *Baehr v. Miike*, No. 1996 WL 694235, (Haw.Cir.Ct., Dec. 3, 1996), which rejected the State's reasons for excluding same-sex couples from marriage, we should simply enjoin the State from denying marriage licenses to plaintiffs based on sex or sexual orientation. That remedy would provide prompt and complete relief to plaintiffs and create reliable expectations that would stabilize the legal rights and duties of all couples.

During the civil rights movement of the 1960's, state and local governments defended segregation or gradual desegregation on the grounds that mixing the races would lead to interracial disturbances. The Supreme Court's "compelling answer" to that contention was "that constitutional rights may not be denied simply because of hostility to their assertion or exercise." See *Watson*, 373 U.S. at 535. Here, too, we should not relinquish our duty to redress the unconstitutional discrimination that we have found merely because of "personal speculations" or "vague disquietudes." Id. at 536. While the laudatory goals of preserving institutional credibility and public confidence in our government may require elected bodies to wait for changing attitudes concerning public morals, those same goals require courts to act independently and decisively to protect civil rights guaranteed by our Constitution.

In our system of government, civil rights violations are remedied by courts, not because we issue "Holy Writ" or because we are "the only repository of wisdom." It is because the courts "must ultimately define and defend individual rights against government in terms independent of consensus or majority will." L. Tribe, *American Constitutional Law* § 15.3, at 896 (1978). Today's decision, which is little more than a declaration of rights, abdicates that responsibility....

This case is undoubtedly one of the most controversial ever to come before this Court. Newspaper, radio and television media have disclosed widespread public interest in its outcome, as well as the full spectrum of opinion as to what that outcome should be and what its ramifications may be for our society as a whole. One line of opinion contends that this is an issue that ought to be decided only by the most broadly democratic of our governmental institutions, the Legislature, and that the small group of men and women comprising this Court has no business deciding an issue of such enormous moment. For better or for worse, however, this is simply not so. This case came before us because citizens of the state invoked their constitutional right to seek redress through the judicial process of a perceived deprivation under state law. The Vermont Constitution does not permit the courts to decline to adjudicate a matter because its subject is controversial, or because the outcome may be deeply offensive to the strongly held beliefs of many of our citizens. We do not have, as does the Supreme Court of the United States, certiorari jurisdiction, which allows that Court, in its sole discretion, to decline to hear almost any case. To the contrary, if a case has been brought before us, and if the established procedures have been followed, as they were here, we must hear and decide it.

Moreover, we must decide the case on legal grounds. However much history, sociology, religious belief, personal experience or other considerations may inform our individual or collective deliberations, we must decide this case, and all cases, on the basis of our understanding of the law, and the law alone. This must be the true and constant effort of every member of the judiciary. That effort, needless to say, is not a guarantee of infallibility, nor even an assurance of wisdom. It is, however, the fulfillment of our pledge of office.

NOTES

1. In response to the decision in *Baker*, the legislature of Vermont enacted a statute authorizing civil unions for persons of the same sex. Vt. Stat., title 15, ch. 23. The statute provides that:

> Parties to a civil union shall have all the same benefits, protections and responsibilities under law, whether they derive from statute, administrative or court rule, policy, common law or any other source of civil law, as are granted to spouses in a marriage.

Subsequently, a number of states, following the lead of Vermont, enacted laws authorizing same-sex civil unions.

2. The opinion in *Baker* mentions *Baehr v. Miike*, No. 1996 WL 694235, (Haw.Cir.Ct., Dec. 3, 1996), a lower court decision ruling that a law limiting marriage to opposite-sex couples violated the Hawaii equal protection clause. Prior to that ruling, the Supreme Court of Hawaii had held that the law in question was presumptively unconstitutional unless the state could show that it was supported by a compelling state interest. *Baehr v. Lewin*, 852 P.2d 44 (Haw. 1993). Upon remand, the circuit court concluded that the law was not supported by a compelling state interest and therefore was unconstitutional. However, that ruling was superseded by an amendment to the Hawaii Constitution providing that the legislature shall have the power to reserve marriage to opposite-sex couples. Haw. Const. art. I, §23.

GOODRIDGE v. DEPARTMENT OF PUBLIC HEALTH
798 N.E.2d 941 (Mass. 2003)

MARSHALL, C.J.

Marriage is a vital social institution. The exclusive commitment of two individuals to each other nurtures love and mutual support; it brings stability to our society. For those who choose to marry, and for their children, marriage provides an abundance of legal, financial, and social benefits. In return it imposes weighty legal, financial, and social obligations. The question before us is whether, consistent with the Massachusetts Constitution, the Commonwealth may deny the protections, benefits, and obligations conferred by civil marriage to two individuals of the same sex who wish to marry. We conclude that it may not. The Massachusetts Constitution affirms the dignity and equality of all individuals. It forbids the creation of second-class citizens. In reaching our conclusion we have given full deference to the arguments made by the Commonwealth. But it has failed to identify any constitutionally adequate reason for denying civil marriage to same-sex couples.

We are mindful that our decision marks a change in the history of our marriage law. Many people hold deep-seated religious, moral, and ethical convictions that marriage should be limited to the union of one man and one woman, and that homosexual conduct is immoral. Many hold equally strong religious, moral, and ethical convictions that same-sex couples are entitled to be married, and that homosexual persons should be treated no differently than their heterosexual neighbors. Neither view answers the question before us. Our concern is with the Massachusetts Constitution as a charter of governance for every person properly within its reach. "Our obligation is to define the liberty of all, not to mandate our own moral code." *Lawrence v. Texas,* 123 S.Ct. 2472, 2480 (2003) quoting *Planned Parenthood of Southeastern Pa. v. Casey,* 505 U.S. 833, 850, (1992).

Whether the Commonwealth may use its formidable regulatory authority to bar same-sex couples from civil marriage is a question not previously addressed by a Massachusetts appellate court. It is a question the United States Supreme Court left open as a matter of Federal law in *Lawrence,* where it was not an issue. There, the Court affirmed that the core concept of common human dignity protected by the Fourteenth Amendment to the United States Constitution precludes government intrusion into the deeply personal realms of consensual adult expressions of intimacy and one's choice of an intimate partner. The Court also reaffirmed the central role that decisions whether to marry or have children bear in shaping one's identity. *Id.* at 2481. The Massachusetts Constitution is, if anything, more protective of individual liberty and equality than the Federal Constitution; it may demand broader protection for fundamental rights; and it is less tolerant of government intrusion into the protected spheres of private life.

Barred access to the protections, benefits, and obligations of civil marriage, a person who enters into an intimate, exclusive union with another of the same sex is arbitrarily deprived of membership in one of our community's most rewarding and cherished institutions. That exclusion is incompatible with the constitutional principles of respect for individual autonomy and equality under law.

The plaintiffs are fourteen individuals from five Massachusetts counties. As of April 11, 2001, the date they filed their complaint, the plaintiffs Gloria Bailey, sixty years old, and Linda Davies, fifty-five years old, had been in a committed relationship for thirty years; the plaintiffs Maureen Brodoff, forty-nine years old, and Ellen Wade, fifty-two years old, had been in a committed relationship for twenty years and lived with their twelve year old daughter; the plaintiffs Hillary Goodridge, forty-four years old, and Julie Goodridge, forty-three years old, had been in a committed relationship for thirteen years and lived with their five year old daughter; the plaintiffs Gary Chalmers, thirty-five years old, and Richard Linnell, thirty-seven years old, had been in a committed relationship for thirteen years and lived with their eight year old daughter and Richard's mother; the plaintiffs Heidi Norton, thirty-six years old, and Gina Smith, thirty-six years old, had been in a committed relationship for eleven years and lived with their two sons, ages five years and one year; the plaintiffs Michael Horgan, forty-one years old, and Edward Balmelli, forty-one years old, had been in a committed relationship for seven years; and the plaintiffs David Wilson, fifty-seven years old, and Robert Compton, fifty-one years old, had been in a committed relationship for four years and had cared for David's mother in their home after a serious illness until she died. The plaintiffs include business executives, lawyers, an investment banker, educators, therapists, and a computer engineer. Many are active in church, community, and school groups.

The plaintiffs alleged violation of the laws of the Commonwealth, including but not limited to their rights under arts. 1, 6, 7, 10, 12, and 16, and Part II, c. 1, ' 1, art. 4, of the Massachusetts Constitution.[4] The

---

[4] [7] Article 1, as amended by art. 106 of the Amendments to the Massachusetts Constitution, provides: "All people are born free and equal and have certain natural, essential and unalienable rights; among which may be reckoned the right of enjoying and defending their lives and liberties; that of acquiring, possessing and protecting property; in fine, that of seeking and obtaining their safety and happiness. Equality under the law shall not be denied or abridged because of sex, race, color, creed or national origin."

Article 6 provides: "No man, nor corporation, or association of men, have any other title to obtain advantages, or particular and exclusive privileges, distinct from those of the community, than what arises from the consideration of services rendered to the public...."

Article 7 provides: "Government is instituted for the common good; for the protection, safety, prosperity, and happiness of the people; and not for the profit, honor, or private interest of any one man, family or class of men: Therefore the people alone have an incontestable, unalienable, and indefeasible right to institute government; and to reform, alter, or totally change the same, when their protection, safety, prosperity and happiness require it."

Article 10 provides, in relevant part: "Each individual of the society has a right to be protected by it in the enjoyment of his life, liberty and property, according to standing laws...."

Article 12 provides, in relevant part: "[N]o subject shall be...deprived of his property, immunities, or privileges, put out of the protection of the law...or deprived of his life, liberty, or estate, but by the judgment of his peers, or the law of the land."

Article 16, as amended by art. 77 of the Amendments, provides, in relevant part: "The right of free speech shall not be abridged." Part II, c. 1, § 1, art. 4, as amended by art.

plaintiffs' claim that the marriage restriction violates the Massachusetts Constitution can be analyzed in two ways. Does it offend the Constitution's guarantees of equality before the law? Or do the liberty and due process provisions of the Massachusetts Constitution secure the plaintiffs' right to marry their chosen partner? In matters implicating marriage, family life, and the upbringing of children, the two constitutional concepts frequently overlap, as they do here. See, e.g., *M.L.B. v. S.L.J.,* 519 U.S. 102 (1996) (noting convergence of due process and equal protection principles in cases concerning parent-child relationships); *Perez v. Sharp,* 198 P.2d 17 (Cal. 1948) (analyzing statutory ban on interracial marriage as equal protection violation concerning regulation of fundamental right). Much of what we say concerning one standard applies to the other.

We begin by considering the nature of civil marriage itself. Simply put, the government creates civil marriage. In Massachusetts, civil marriage is, and since pre-Colonial days has been, precisely what its name implies: a wholly secular institution. See *Commonwealth v. Munson,* 127 Mass. 459, 460-466 (1879) (noting that "[i]n Massachusetts, from very early times, the requisites of a valid marriage have been regulated by statutes of the Colony, Province, and Commonwealth," and surveying marriage statutes from 1639 through 1834). No religious ceremony has ever been required to validate a Massachusetts marriage. *Id.*

Without question, civil marriage enhances the "welfare of the community." It is a "social institution of the highest importance." Civil marriage anchors an ordered society by encouraging stable relationships over transient ones. It is central to the way the Commonwealth identifies individuals, provides for the orderly distribution of property, ensures that children and adults are cared for and supported whenever possible from private rather than public funds, and tracks important epidemiological and demographic data.

Marriage also bestows enormous private and social advantages on those who choose to marry. Civil marriage is at once a deeply personal commitment to another human being and a highly public celebration of the ideals of mutuality, companionship, intimacy, fidelity, and family. "It is an association that promotes a way of life, not causes; a harmony in living, not political faiths; a bilateral loyalty, not commercial or social projects." *Griswold v. Connecticut,* 381 U.S. 479 (1965). Because it fulfils yearnings

---

112, provides, in pertinent part, that "full power and authority are hereby given and granted to the said general court, from time to time, to make, ordain, and establish all manner of wholesome and reasonable orders, laws, statutes, and ordinances, directions and instructions, either with penalties or without; so as the same be not repugnant or contrary to this constitution, as they shall judge to be for the good and welfare of this Commonwealth."

for security, safe haven, and connection that express our common humanity, civil marriage is an esteemed institution and the decision whether and whom to marry is among life's momentous acts of self-definition.

Tangible as well as intangible benefits flow from marriage. The marriage license grants valuable property rights to those who meet the entry requirements, and who agree to what might otherwise be a burdensome degree of government regulation of their activities. The benefits accessible only by way of a marriage license are enormous, touching nearly every aspect of life and death. The department states that "hundreds of statutes" are related to marriage and to marital benefits. With no attempt to be comprehensive, we note that some of the statutory benefits conferred by the Legislature on those who enter into civil marriage include, as to property: joint Massachusetts income tax filing; tenancy by the entirety (a form of ownership that provides certain protections against creditors and allows for the automatic descent of property to the surviving spouse without probate); extension of the benefit of the homestead protection (securing up to $300,000 in equity from creditors) to one's spouse and children; automatic rights to inherit the property of a deceased spouse who does not leave a will; the rights of elective share and of dower (which allow surviving spouses certain property rights where the decedent spouse has not made adequate provision for the survivor in a will); entitlement to wages owed to a deceased employee; eligibility to continue certain businesses of a deceased spouse; the right to share the medical policy of one's spouse; thirty-nine week continuation of health coverage for the spouse of a person who is laid off or dies; preferential options under the Commonwealth's pension system; preferential benefits in the Commonwealth's medical program, MassHealth; access to veterans' spousal benefits and preferences; financial protections for spouses of certain Commonwealth employees (fire fighters, police officers, and prosecutors, among others) killed in the performance of duty; the equitable division of marital property on divorce; temporary and permanent alimony rights; the right to separate support on separation of the parties that does not result in divorce; and the right to bring claims for wrongful death and loss of consortium, and for funeral and burial expenses and punitive damages resulting from tort actions.

Exclusive marital benefits that are not directly tied to property rights include the presumptions of legitimacy and parentage of children born to a married couple; and evidentiary rights, such as the prohibition against spouses testifying against one another about their private conversations, applicable in both civil and criminal cases. Other statutory benefits of a personal nature available only to married individuals include qualification for bereavement or medical leave to care for individuals related by blood or marriage; an automatic "family member" preference to make medical decisions for an incompetent or disabled spouse who does not have a contrary health care proxy; the application of predictable rules of child custody, visitation, support, and removal out-of-State when married parents divorce; priority rights to administer the estate of a deceased spouse who dies without a will, and the requirement that a surviving spouse must consent to the appointment of any other person as administrator; and the right to interment in the lot or tomb owned by one's deceased spouse.

Where a married couple has children, their children are also directly or indirectly, but no less auspiciously, the recipients of the special legal and economic protections obtained by civil marriage. Notwithstanding the Commonwealth's strong public policy to abolish legal distinctions between marital and nonmarital children in providing for the support and care of minors, the fact remains that marital children reap a measure of family stability and economic security based on their parents' legally privileged status that is largely inaccessible, or not as readily accessible, to nonmarital children. Some of these benefits are social, such as the enhanced approval that still attends the status of being a marital child. Others are material, such as the greater ease of access to family-based State and Federal benefits that attend the presumptions of one's parentage.

It is undoubtedly for these concrete reasons, as well as for its intimately personal significance, that civil marriage has long been termed a "civil right." See, e.g., *Loving v. Virginia,* 388 U.S. 1 (1967) ("Marriage is one of the 'basic civil rights of man,' fundamental to our very existence and survival"), quoting *Skinner v. Oklahoma,* 316 U.S. 535, 541 (1942. The United States Supreme Court has described the right to marry as "of fundamental importance for all individuals" and as "part of the fundamental 'right of privacy' implicit in the Fourteenth Amendment's Due Process Clause." *Zablocki v. Redhail,* 434 U.S. 374 (1978). See *Loving v. Virginia, supra* ("The freedom to marry has long been recognized as one of the vital personal rights essential to the orderly pursuit of happiness by free men").

Without the right to marry--or more properly, the right to choose to marry--one is excluded from the full range of human experience and denied full protection of the laws for one's "avowed commitment to an intimate and lasting human relationship." *Baker v. State,* 744 A.2d 864 (Vt. 1999). Because civil marriage is central to the lives of individuals and the welfare of the community, our laws assiduously protect the individual's right to marry against undue government incursion. Laws may not "interfere directly and substantially with the right to marry." *Zablocki v. Redhail, supra* at 387. See *Perez v. Sharp,* 32 Cal.2d 711, 714 (1948)

("There can be no prohibition of marriage except for an important social objective and reasonable means").

For decades, indeed centuries, in much of this country (including Massachusetts) no lawful marriage was possible between white and black Americans. That long history availed not when the Supreme Court of California held in 1948 that a legislative prohibition against interracial marriage violated the due process and equality guarantees of the Fourteenth Amendment, *Perez v. Sharp,* 198 P.2d 17 (Cal. 1948), or when, nineteen years later, the United States Supreme Court also held that a statutory bar to interracial marriage violated the Fourteenth Amendment, *Loving v. Virginia,* 388 U.S. 1 (1967). As both *Perez* and *Loving* make clear, the right to marry means little if it does not include the right to marry the person of one's choice, subject to appropriate government restrictions in the interests of public health, safety, and welfare. See *Perez v. Sharp, supra* ("the essence of the right to marry is freedom to join in marriage with the person of one's choice"). In this case, as in *Perez* and *Loving,* a statute deprives individuals of access to an institution of fundamental legal, personal, and social significance--the institution of marriage--because of a single trait: skin color in *Perez* and *Loving,* sexual orientation here. As it did in *Perez* and *Loving,* history must yield to a more fully developed understanding of the invidious quality of the discrimination.[5]

The Massachusetts Constitution protects matters of personal liberty against government incursion as zealously and often more so, than does the Federal Constitution, even where both Constitutions employ essentially the same language. That the Massachusetts Constitution is in some instances more protective of individual liberty interests than is the Federal Constitution is not surprising. Fundamental to the vigor of our Federal system of government is that "state courts are absolutely free to interpret state constitutional provisions to accord greater protection to individual rights than do similar provisions of the United States Constitution." *Arizona v. Evans,* 514 U.S. 1 (1995).

The individual liberty and equality safeguards of the Massachusetts Constitution protect both "freedom from" unwarranted government intrusion into protected spheres of life and "freedom to" partake in benefits created by the State for the common good. Both freedoms are involved here. Whether and whom to marry, how to express sexual

---

[5] [17] Recently, the United States Supreme Court has reaffirmed that the Constitution prohibits a State from wielding its formidable power to regulate conduct in a manner that demeans basic human dignity, even though that statutory discrimination may enjoy broad public support. The Court struck down a statute criminalizing sodomy. See *Lawrence, supra* at 2478 ("The liberty protected by the Constitution allows homosexual persons the right to make this choice").

intimacy, and whether and how to establish a family--these are among the most basic of every individual's liberty and due process rights. See, e.g., *Lawrence, supra* at 2481; *Planned Parenthood of Southeastern Pa. v. Casey,* 505 U.S. 833, 851 (1992); *Zablocki v. Redhail,* 434 U.S. 374 (1978); *Roe v. Wade,* 410 U.S. 113, 152-153 (1973); *Eisenstadt v. Baird,* 405 U.S. 438, 453 (1972); *Loving v. Virginia, supra.* And central to personal freedom and security is the assurance that the laws will apply equally to persons in similar situations. "Absolute equality before the law is a fundamental principle of our own Constitution." *Opinion of the Justices,* 98 N.E. 337 (Mass. 1912). The liberty interest in choosing whether and whom to marry would be hollow if the Commonwealth could, without sufficient justification, foreclose an individual from freely choosing the person with whom to share an exclusive commitment in the unique institution of civil marriage.

The Massachusetts Constitution requires, at a minimum, that the exercise of the State's regulatory authority not be "arbitrary or capricious." Under both the equality and liberty guarantees, regulatory authority must, at very least, serve "a legitimate purpose in a rational way"; a statute must "bear a reasonable relation to a permissible legislative objective." Any law failing to satisfy the basic standards of rationality is void.

The plaintiffs challenge the marriage statute on both equal protection and due process grounds. With respect to each such claim, we must first determine the appropriate standard of review. Where a statute implicates a fundamental right or uses a suspect classification, we employ "strict judicial scrutiny." For all other statutes, we employ the "'rational basis' test." For due process claims, rational basis analysis requires that statutes "bear[ ] a real and substantial relation to the public health, safety, morals, or some other phase of the general welfare." For equal protection challenges, the rational basis test requires that "an impartial lawmaker could logically believe that the classification would serve a legitimate public purpose that transcends the harm to the members of the disadvantaged class."

The department argues that no fundamental right or "suspect" class is at issue here, and rational basis is the appropriate standard of review. For the reasons we explain below, we conclude that the marriage ban does not meet the rational basis test for either due process or equal protection. Because the statute does not survive rational basis review, we do not consider the plaintiffs' arguments that this case merits strict judicial scrutiny.

The department posits three legislative rationales for prohibiting same-sex couples from marrying: (1) providing a "favorable setting for procreation"; (2) ensuring the optimal setting for child rearing, which the department defines as "a two-parent family with one parent of each sex";

and (3) preserving scarce State and private financial resources. We consider each in turn.

The judge in the Superior Court endorsed the first rationale, holding that "the state's interest in regulating marriage is based on the traditional concept that marriage's primary purpose is procreation." This is incorrect. Our laws of civil marriage do not privilege procreative heterosexual intercourse between married people above every other form of adult intimacy and every other means of creating a family. General Laws c. 207 contains no requirement that the applicants for a marriage license attest to their ability or intention to conceive children by coitus. Fertility is not a condition of marriage, nor is it grounds for divorce. People who have never consummated their marriage, and never plan to, may be and stay married. See *Franklin v. Franklin,* 28 N.E. 681 (Mass. 1891) ("The consummation of a marriage by coition is not necessary to its validity"). People who cannot stir from their deathbed may marry. While it is certainly true that many, perhaps most, married couples have children together (assisted or unassisted), it is the exclusive and permanent commitment of the marriage partners to one another, not the begetting of children, that is the sine qua non of civil marriage.

Moreover, the Commonwealth affirmatively facilitates bringing children into a family regardless of whether the intended parent is married or unmarried, whether the child is adopted or born into a family, whether assistive technology was used to conceive the child, and whether the parent or her partner is heterosexual, homosexual, or bisexual. If procreation were a necessary component of civil marriage, our statutes would draw a tighter circle around the permissible bounds of nonmarital child bearing and the creation of families by noncoital means. The attempt to isolate procreation as "the source of a fundamental right to marry," 440 Mass. at 370 (Cordy, J., dissenting), overlooks the integrated way in which courts have examined the complex and overlapping realms of personal autonomy, marriage, family life, and child rearing. Our jurisprudence recognizes that, in these nuanced and fundamentally private areas of life, such a narrow focus is inappropriate.

The "marriage is procreation" argument singles out the one unbridgeable difference between same-sex and opposite-sex couples, and transforms that difference into the essence of legal marriage. Like "Amendment 2" to the Constitution of Colorado, which effectively denied homosexual persons equality under the law and full access to the political process, the marriage restriction impermissibly "identifies persons by a single trait and then denies them protection across the board." *Romer v. Evans,* 517 U.S. 620, 633, (1996). In so doing, the State's action confers an official stamp of approval on the destructive stereotype that same-sex relationships are inherently unstable and inferior to opposite-sex relationships and are not worthy of respect.

The department's first stated rationale, equating marriage with unassisted heterosexual procreation, shades imperceptibly into its second: that confining marriage to opposite-sex couples ensures that children are raised in the "optimal" setting. Protecting the welfare of children is a paramount State policy. Restricting marriage to opposite-sex couples, however, cannot plausibly further this policy. "The demographic changes of the past century make it difficult to speak of an average American family. The composition of families varies greatly from household to household." *Troxel v. Granville,* 530 U.S. 57, 63 (2000). Massachusetts has responded supportively to "the changing realities of the American family," *id.* at 64, and has moved vigorously to strengthen the modern family in its many variations. See, e.g., G.L. c. 209C (paternity statute); G.L. c. 119, ' 39D (grandparent visitation statute); *Blixt v. Blixt,* 774 N.E.2d 1052 (Mass. 2002) (same); *E.N.O. v. L.M.M.,* 711 N.E.2d 886 (Mass. 1999) (de facto parent); *Youmans v. Ramos* 711 N.E.2d 165 (Mass. 1999) (same); and *Adoption of Tammy,* 619 N.E.2d 315 (Mass. 1993) (coparent adoption). Moreover, we have repudiated the common-law power of the State to provide varying levels of protection to children based on the circumstances of birth. See G.L. c. 209C (paternity statute); *Powers v. Wilkinson,* 506 N.E.2d 842 (Mass. 1987) ("Ours is an era in which logic and compassion have impelled the law toward unburdening children from the stigma and the disadvantages heretofore attendant upon the status of illegitimacy"). The "best interests of the child" standard does not turn on a parent's sexual orientation or marital status. See e.g., *Doe v. Doe,* 452 N.E.2d 293 (Mass. App. Ct. 1983) (parent's sexual orientation insufficient ground to deny custody of child in divorce action). See also *E.N.O. v. L.M.M.,* 711 N.E.2d 886 (best interests of child determined by considering child's relationship with biological and de facto same-sex parents); *Silvia v. Silvia,* 400 N.E.2d 1330 (Mass. App. Ct. 1980) (collecting support and custody statutes containing no gender distinction).

The department has offered no evidence that forbidding marriage to people of the same sex will increase the number of couples choosing to enter into opposite-sex marriages in order to have and raise children. There is thus no rational relationship between the marriage statute and the Commonwealth's proffered goal of protecting the "optimal" child rearing unit. Moreover, the department readily concedes that people in same-sex couples may be "excellent" parents. These couples (including four of the plaintiff couples) have children for the reasons others do--to love them, to care for them, to nurture them. But the task of child rearing for same-sex couples is made infinitely harder by their status as outliers to the marriage laws. While establishing the parentage of children as soon as possible is crucial to the safety and welfare of children, same-sex couples must undergo the sometimes lengthy and intrusive process of second-parent adoption to establish their joint parentage. While the enhanced income provided by marital benefits is an important source of security and stability for married couples and their children, those benefits are denied to families headed by same-sex couples. While the laws of divorce provide clear and reasonably predictable guidelines for child support, child custody, and property division on dissolution of a marriage, same-sex couples who dissolve their relationships find themselves and their children in the highly unpredictable terrain of equity jurisdiction. Given the wide range of public benefits reserved only for married couples, we do not credit the department's contention that the absence of access to civil marriage amounts to little more than an inconvenience to same-sex couples and their children. Excluding same-sex couples from civil marriage will not make children of opposite-sex marriages more secure, but it does prevent children of same-sex couples from enjoying the immeasurable advantages that flow from the assurance of "a stable family structure in which children will be reared, educated, and socialized." 440 Mass. at 381 (Cordy, J., dissenting).

No one disputes that the plaintiff couples are families, that many are parents, and that the children they are raising, like all children, need and should have the fullest opportunity to grow up in a secure, protected family unit. Similarly, no one disputes that, under the rubric of marriage, the State provides a cornucopia of substantial benefits to married parents and their children. The preferential treatment of civil marriage reflects the Legislature's conclusion that marriage "is the foremost setting for the education and socialization of children" precisely because it "encourages parents to remain committed to each other and to their children as they grow." 440 Mass. at 383, 798 N.E.2d at 996 (Cordy, J., dissenting).... It cannot be rational under our laws, and indeed it is not permitted, to penalize children by depriving them of State benefits because the State disapproves of their parents' sexual orientation.

The third rationale advanced by the department is that limiting marriage to opposite-sex couples furthers the Legislature's interest in conserving scarce State and private financial resources. The marriage restriction is rational, it argues, because the General Court logically could assume that same-sex couples are more financially independent than married couples and thus less needy of public marital benefits, such as tax advantages, or private marital benefits, such as employer-financed health plans that include spouses in their coverage.

An absolute statutory ban on same-sex marriage bears no rational relationship to the goal of economy. First, the department's conclusory generalization--that same-sex couples are less financially dependent on each other than opposite-sex couples--ignores that many same-sex couples, such as many of the plaintiffs in this case, have children and other dependents (here, aged parents) in their care. The department does not contend, nor could it, that these dependents are less needy or deserving than the dependents of married couples. Second, Massachusetts marriage laws do not condition receipt of public and private financial benefits to married individuals on a demonstration of financial dependence on each other; the benefits are available to married couples regardless of whether they mingle their finances or actually depend on each other for support.

The department suggests additional rationales for prohibiting same-sex couples from marrying, which are developed by some amici. It argues that broadening civil marriage to include same-sex couples will trivialize or destroy the institution of marriage as it has historically been fashioned. Certainly our decision today marks a significant change in the definition of marriage as it has been inherited from the common law, and understood by many societies for centuries. But it does not disturb the fundamental value of marriage in our society.

Here, the plaintiffs seek only to be married, not to undermine the institution of civil marriage. They do not want marriage abolished. They do not attack the binary nature of marriage, the consanguinity provisions, or any of the other gate-keeping provisions of the marriage licensing law. Recognizing the right of an individual to marry a person of the same sex will not diminish the validity or dignity of opposite-sex marriage, any more than recognizing the right of an individual to marry a person of a different race devalues the marriage of a person who marries someone of her own race. If anything, extending civil marriage to same-sex couples reinforces the importance of marriage to individuals and communities. That same-sex couples are willing to embrace marriage's solemn obligations of exclusivity, mutual support, and commitment to one another is a testament to the enduring place of marriage in our laws and in the human spirit.

We also reject the argument suggested by the department, and elaborated by some amici, that expanding the institution of civil marriage in Massachusetts to include same-sex couples will lead to interstate conflict. We would not presume to dictate how another State should respond to today's decision. But neither should considerations of comity prevent us from according Massachusetts residents the full measure of protection available under the Massachusetts Constitution. The genius of our Federal system is that each State's Constitution has vitality specific to its own traditions, and that, subject to the minimum requirements of the Fourteenth Amendment, each State is free to address difficult issues of individual liberty in the manner its own Constitution demands.

Several amici suggest that prohibiting marriage by same-sex couples reflects community consensus that homosexual conduct is immoral. Yet Massachusetts has a strong affirmative policy of preventing discrimination on the basis of sexual orientation. See G.L. c. 151B (employment, housing, credit, services); G.L. c. 265,'39 (hate crimes); G.L. c. 272,'98 (public accommodation); G.L. c. 76,'5 (public education). See also, e.g., *Commonwealth v. Balthazar,* 366 Mass. 298, 318 N.E.2d 478 (1974) (decriminalization of private consensual adult conduct); *Doe v. Doe,* 452 N.E.2d 293 (Mass. App. Ct. 1983) (custody to homosexual parent not per se prohibited).

The department has had more than ample opportunity to articulate a constitutionally adequate justification for limiting civil marriage to opposite-sex unions. It has failed to do so. The department has offered purported justifications for the civil marriage restriction that are starkly at odds with the comprehensive network of vigorous, gender-neutral laws promoting stable families and the best interests of children. It has failed to identify any relevant characteristic that would justify shutting the door to civil marriage to a person who wishes to marry someone of the same sex.

The marriage ban works a deep and scarring hardship on a very real segment of the community for no rational reason. The absence of any reasonable relationship between, on the one hand, an absolute disqualification of same-sex couples who wish to enter into civil marriage and, on the other, protection of public health, safety, or general welfare, suggests that the marriage restriction is rooted in persistent prejudices against persons who are (or who are believed to be) homosexual. "The Constitution cannot control such prejudices but neither can it tolerate them. Private biases may be outside the reach of the law, but the law cannot, directly or indirectly, give them effect." *Palmore v. Sidoti,* 466 U.S. 429, 433 (1984) (construing Fourteenth Amendment). Limiting the protections, benefits, and obligations of civil marriage to opposite-sex couples violates the basic premises of individual liberty and equality under law protected by the Massachusetts Constitution.

We consider next the plaintiffs' request for relief. We preserve as much of the statute as may be preserved in the face of the successful constitutional challenge…. Here, no one argues that striking down the marriage laws is an appropriate form of relief. Eliminating civil marriage would be wholly inconsistent with the Legislature's deep commitment to fostering stable families and would dismantle a vital organizing principle of our society. We face a problem similar to one that recently confronted the Court of Appeal for Ontario, the highest court of that Canadian province, when it considered the constitutionality of the same-sex marriage ban under Canada's Federal Constitution, the Charter of Rights and Freedoms (Charter). See *Halpern v. Toronto (City),* 172 O.A.C. 276

(2003). Canada, like the United States, adopted the common law of England that civil marriage is "the voluntary union for life of one man and one woman, to the exclusion of all others." *Id.* at par. (36), quoting *Hyde v. Hyde,* [1861-1873] All E.R. 175 (1866). In holding that the limitation of civil marriage to opposite-sex couples violated the Charter, the Court of Appeal refined the common-law meaning of marriage. We concur with this remedy, which is entirely consonant with established principles of jurisprudence empowering a court to refine a common-law principle in light of evolving constitutional standards.

We construe civil marriage to mean the voluntary union of two persons as spouses, to the exclusion of all others. This reformulation redresses the plaintiffs' constitutional injury and furthers the aim of marriage to promote stable, exclusive relationships. It advances the two legitimate State interests the department has identified: providing a stable setting for child rearing and conserving State resources. It leaves intact the Legislature's broad discretion to regulate marriage....We declare that barring an individual from the protections, benefits, and obligations of civil marriage solely because that person would marry a person of the same sex violates the Massachusetts Constitution.

GREANEY, J. concurring.

The right to marry is not a privilege conferred by the State, but a fundamental right that is protected against unwarranted State interference. See *Zablocki v. Redhail,* 434 U.S. 374, 384 (1978) ("the right to marry is of fundamental importance for all individuals"); *Loving v. Virginia,* 388 U.S. 1, 12, (1967) (freedom to marry is "one of the vital personal rights essential to the orderly pursuit of happiness by free men" under due process clause of Fourteenth Amendment); *Skinner v. Oklahoma,* 316 U.S. 535, 541 (1942) (marriage is one of "basic civil rights of man"). This right is essentially vitiated if one is denied the right to marry a person of one's choice. See *Zablocki v. Redhail, supra* at 384 (all recent decisions of United States Supreme Court place "the decision to marry as among the personal decisions protected by the right of privacy").

A comment is in order with respect to the insistence of some that marriage is, as a matter of definition, the legal union of a man and a woman. To define the institution of marriage by the characteristics of those to whom it always has been accessible, in order to justify the exclusion of those to whom it never has been accessible, is conclusory and bypasses the core question we are asked to decide. This case calls for a higher level of legal analysis. Precisely, the case requires that we confront ingrained assumptions with respect to historically accepted roles of men and women within the institution of marriage and requires that we reexamine these assumptions in light of the unequivocal language of art. 1, in order to ensure that the governmental conduct challenged here conforms to the supreme charter of our Commonwealth.... I do not doubt the sincerity of deeply held moral or religious beliefs that make inconceivable to some the notion that any change in the common-law definition of what constitutes a legal civil marriage is now, or ever would be, warranted. But, as a matter of constitutional law, neither the mantra of tradition, nor individual conviction, can justify the perpetuation of a hierarchy in which couples of the same sex and their families are deemed less worthy of social and legal recognition than couples of the opposite sex and their families.

I am hopeful that our decision will be accepted by those thoughtful citizens who believe that same-sex unions should not be approved by the State. I am not referring here to acceptance in the sense of grudging acknowledgment of the court's authority to adjudicate the matter. My hope is more liberating. The plaintiffs are members of our community, our neighbors, our coworkers, our friends. As pointed out by the court, their professions include investment advisor, computer engineer, teacher, therapist, and lawyer. The plaintiffs volunteer in our schools, worship beside us in our religious houses, and have children who play with our children, to mention just a few ordinary daily contacts. We share a common humanity and participate together in the social contract that is the foundation of our Commonwealth. Simple principles of decency dictate that we extend to the plaintiffs, and to their new status, full acceptance, tolerance, and respect. We should do so because it is the right thing to do.

SPINA, J., dissenting.

What is at stake in this case is not the unequal treatment of individuals or whether individual rights have been impermissibly burdened, but the power of the Legislature to effectuate social change without interference from the courts.... The power to regulate marriage lies with the Legislature, not with the judiciary. Today, the court has transformed its role as protector of individual rights into the role of creator of rights, and I respectfully dissent.

The marriage statutes do not impermissibly burden a right protected by our constitutional guarantee of due process implicit in art. 10 of our Declaration of Rights. There is no restriction on the right of any plaintiff to enter into marriage. Each is free to marry a willing person of the opposite sex. Substantive due process protects individual rights against unwarranted government intrusion.... [T]oday the court does not fashion a remedy that affords greater protection of a right. Instead, using the rubric of due process, it has redefined marriage.

Although this court did not state that same-sex marriage is a fundamental right worthy of strict scrutiny protection, it nonetheless deemed it a constitutionally protected right by applying rational basis review. Before applying any level of constitutional analysis there must be a recognized right at stake. Same-sex marriage, or the "right to marry the person of one's choice" as the court today defines that right, does not fall within the fundamental right to marry. Same-sex marriage is not "deeply rooted in this Nation's history," and the court does not suggest that it is. Except for the occasional isolated decision in recent years, see, e.g., *Baker v. State,* 170 Vt. 194, 744 A.2d 864 (1999), same-sex marriage is not a right, fundamental or otherwise, recognized in this country. In this Commonwealth and in this country, the roots of the institution of marriage are deeply set in history as a civil union between a single man and a single woman. There is no basis for the court to recognize same-sex marriage as a constitutionally protected right.

The remedy that the court has fashioned both in the name of equal protection and due process exceeds the bounds of judicial restraint mandated by art. 30. The remedy that construes gender-specific language as gender-neutral amounts to a statutory revision that replaces the intent of the Legislature with that of the court. Article 30 permits the court...to modify statutory language only if legislative intent is preserved. Here, the alteration of the gender-specific language alters precisely what the Legislature unambiguously intended to preserve, the marital rights of single men and women. Such a dramatic change in social institutions must remain at the behest of the people through the democratic process.

SOSMAN, J., dissenting.

Based on our own philosophy of child rearing, and on our observations of the children being raised by same-sex couples to whom we are personally close, we may be of the view that what matters to children is not the gender, or sexual orientation, or even the number of the adults who raise them, but rather whether those adults provide the children with a nurturing, stable, safe, consistent, and supportive environment in which to mature. Same-sex couples can provide their children with the requisite nurturing, stable, safe, consistent, and supportive environment in which to mature, just as opposite-sex couples do. It is therefore understandable that the court might view the traditional definition of marriage as an unnecessary anachronism, rooted in historical prejudices that modern society has in large measure rejected and biological limitations that modern science has overcome.

It is not, however, our assessment that matters. Conspicuously absent from the court's opinion today is any acknowledgment that the attempts at scientific study of the ramifications of raising children in same-sex couple households are themselves in their infancy and have so far produced inconclusive and conflicting results. Notwithstanding our belief that gender and sexual orientation of parents should not matter to the success of the child rearing venture, studies to date reveal that there are still some observable differences between children raised by opposite-sex couples and children raised by same-sex couples. Interpretation of the data gathered by those studies then becomes clouded by the personal and political beliefs of the investigators, both as to whether the differences identified are positive or negative, and as to the untested explanations of what might account for those differences. (This is hardly the first time in history that the ostensible steel of the scientific method has melted and buckled under the intense heat of political and religious passions.) Even in the absence of bias or political agenda behind the various studies of children raised by same-sex couples, the most neutral and strict application of scientific principles to this field would be constrained by the limited period of observation that has been available. Gay and lesbian couples living together openly, and official recognition of them as their children's sole parents, comprise a very recent phenomenon, and the recency of that phenomenon has not yet permitted any study of how those children fare as adults and at best minimal study of how they fare during their adolescent years. The Legislature can rationally view the state of the scientific evidence as unsettled on the critical question it now faces: are families headed by same-sex parents equally successful in rearing children from infancy to adulthood as families headed by parents of opposite sexes? Our belief that children raised by same-sex couples *should* fare the same as children raised in traditional families is just that: a passionately held but utterly untested belief. The Legislature is not required to share that belief but may, as the creator of the institution of civil marriage, wish to see the proof before making a fundamental alteration to that institution.

As a matter of social history, today's opinion may represent a great turning point that many will hail as a tremendous step toward a more just society. As a matter of constitutional jurisprudence, however, the case stands as an aberration. To reach the result it does, the court has tortured the rational basis test beyond recognition.

CORDY, J., dissenting.

The plaintiffs ground their contention that they have a fundamental right to marry a person of the same sex in a long line of Supreme Court decisions…that discuss the importance of marriage. In context, all of these decisions and their discussions are about the "fundamental" nature of the institution of marriage as it has existed and been understood in this country, not as the court has redefined it today. Even in that context, its "fundamental" nature is derivative of the nature of the interests that underlie or are associated with it. An examination of those interests reveals that they are either not shared by same-sex couples or not implicated by the marriage statutes.

Supreme Court cases that have described marriage or the right to marry as "fundamental" have focused primarily on the underlying interest of every individual in procreation, which, historically, could only legally occur within the construct of marriage because sexual intercourse outside of marriage was a criminal act.... Because same-sex couples are unable to procreate on their own, any right to marriage they may possess cannot be based on their interest in procreation, which has been essential to the Supreme Court's denomination of the right to marry as fundamental.

Supreme Court cases recognizing a right to privacy in intimate decision- making...have also focused primarily on sexual relations and the decision whether or not to procreate, and have refused to recognize an "unlimited right" to privacy.... Although some of the privacy cases also speak in terms of personal autonomy, no court has ever recognized such an open-ended right. "That many of the rights and liberties protected by the Due Process Clause sound in personal autonomy does not warrant the sweeping conclusion that any and all important, intimate, and personal decisions are so protected...." *Washington v. Glucksberg,* 521 U.S. 702, 727 (1997). Such decisions are protected not because they are important, intimate, and personal, but because the right or liberty at stake is "so deeply rooted in our history and traditions, or so fundamental to our concept of constitutionally ordered liberty" that it is protected by due process. *Id.* Accordingly, the Supreme Court has concluded that while the decision to refuse unwanted medical treatment is fundamental, *Cruzan v. Director, Mo. Dep't of Health,* 497 U.S. 261, 278, (1990), because it is deeply rooted in our nation's history and tradition, the equally personal and profound decision to commit suicide is not because of the absence of such roots. *Washington v. Glucksberg, supra.*

While the institution of marriage is deeply rooted in the history and traditions of our country and our State, the right to marry someone of the same sex is not.... Unlike opposite-sex marriages, which have deep historic roots...same-sex relationships, although becoming more accepted, are certainly not so "deeply rooted in this Nation's history and tradition" as to warrant such enhanced constitutional protection.

The burden of demonstrating that a statute does not satisfy the rational basis standard rests on the plaintiffs. It is a weighty one. "[A] reviewing court will presume a statute's validity, and make all rational inferences in favor of it.... The Legislature is not required to justify its classifications, nor provide a record or finding in support of them." The statute "only need[s to] be supported by a conceivable rational basis...."

It is difficult to imagine a State purpose more important and legitimate than ensuring, promoting, and supporting an optimal social structure within which to bear and raise children. At the very least, the marriage statute continues to serve this important State purpose.

The question we must turn to next is whether the statute, construed as limiting marriage to couples of the opposite sex, remains a rational way to further that purpose. Stated differently, we ask whether a conceivable rational basis exists on which the Legislature could conclude that continuing to limit the institution of civil marriage to members of the opposite sex furthers the legitimate purpose of ensuring, promoting, and supporting an optimal social structure for the bearing and raising of children. In considering whether such a rational basis exists, we defer to the decision-making process of the Legislature, and must make deferential assumptions about the information that it might consider and on which it may rely. We must assume that the Legislature (1) might conclude that the institution of civil marriage has successfully and continually provided this structure over several centuries; (2) might consider and credit studies that document negative consequences that too often follow children either born outside of marriage or raised in households lacking either a father or a mother figure, and scholarly commentary contending that children and families develop best when mothers and fathers are partners in their parenting; and (3) would be familiar with many recent studies that variously support the proposition that children raised in intact families headed by same-sex couples fare as well on many measures as children raised in similar families headed by opposite-sex couples; support the proposition that children of same-sex couples fare worse on some measures; or reveal notable differences between the two groups of children that warrant further study.

We must also assume that the Legislature would be aware of the critiques of the methodologies used in virtually all of the comparative studies of children raised in these different environments, cautioning that the sampling populations are not representative, that the observation periods are too limited in time, that the empirical data are unreliable, and that the hypotheses are too infused with political or agenda driven bias.

Taking all of this available information into account, the Legislature could rationally conclude that a family environment with married opposite-sex parents remains the optimal social structure in which to bear children, and that the raising of children by same-sex couples, who by definition cannot be the two sole biological parents of a child and cannot provide children with a parental authority figure of each gender, presents an alternative structure for child rearing that has not yet proved itself beyond reasonable scientific dispute to be as optimal as the biologically based marriage norm. Working from the assumption that recognition of same-sex marriages will increase the number of children experiencing this alternative, the Legislature could conceivably conclude that declining to recognize same-sex marriages remains prudent until empirical questions about its impact on the upbringing of children are resolved.

The fact that the Commonwealth currently allows same-sex couples to adopt, does not affect the rationality of this conclusion. The eligibility of a child for adoption presupposes that at least one of the child's biological parents is unable or unwilling, for some reason, to participate in raising the child. In that sense, society has "lost" the optimal setting in which to raise that child--it is simply not available. In these circumstances, the principal and overriding consideration is the "best interests of the child," considering his or her unique circumstances and the options that are available for that child. The objective is an individualized determination of the best environment for a particular child, where the normative social structure--a home with both the child's biological father and mother--is not an option. That such a focused determination may lead to the approval of a same-sex couple's adoption of a child does not mean that it would be irrational for a legislator, in fashioning statutory laws that cannot make such individualized determinations, to conclude generally that being raised by a same-sex couple has not yet been shown to be the absolute equivalent of being raised by one's married biological parents.

That the State does not preclude different types of families from raising children does not mean that it must view them all as equally optimal and equally deserving of State endorsement and support. For example, single persons are allowed to adopt children, but the fact that the Legislature permits single-parent adoption does not mean that it has endorsed single parenthood as an optimal setting in which to raise children or views it as the equivalent of being raised by both of one's biological parents. The same holds true with respect to same-sex couples--the fact that they may adopt children means only that the Legislature has concluded that they may provide an acceptable setting in which to raise children who cannot be raised by both of their biological parents. The Legislature may rationally permit adoption by same-sex couples yet harbor reservations as to whether parenthood by same-sex couples should be affirmatively encouraged to the same extent as parenthood by the heterosexual couple whose union produced the child.

There is no question that many same-sex couples are capable of being good parents, and should be (and are) permitted to be so. The policy question that a legislator must resolve is a different one, and turns on an assessment of whether the marriage structure proposed by the plaintiffs will, over time, if endorsed and supported by the State, prove to be as stable and successful a model as the one that has formed a cornerstone of our society since colonial times, or prove to be less than optimal, and result in consequences, perhaps now unforeseen, adverse to the State's legitimate interest in promoting and supporting the best possible social structure in which children should be born and raised. Given the critical importance of civil marriage as an organizing and stabilizing institution of society, it is eminently rational for the Legislature to postpone making fundamental changes to it until such time as there is unanimous scientific evidence, or popular consensus, or both, that such changes can safely be made.

While "[t]he Massachusetts Constitution protects matters of personal liberty against government incursion as zealously, and often more so, than does the Federal Constitution," this case is not about government intrusions into matters of personal liberty. It is not about the rights of same-sex couples to choose to live together, or to be intimate with each other, or to adopt and raise children together. It is about whether the State must endorse and support their choices by changing the institution of civil marriage to make its benefits, obligations, and responsibilities applicable to them. While the courageous efforts of many have resulted in increased dignity, rights, and respect for gay and lesbian members of our community, the issue presented here is a profound one, deeply rooted in social policy, that must, for now, be the subject of legislative not judicial action.

NOTES

1. After the decision in *Goodridge*, the Massachusetts Senate requested an advisory opinion from the Massachusetts Supreme Court concerning the constitutionality of a bill pending before the legislature that would prohibit same-sex couples from entering into marriage but allow them to form civil unions with all of the benefits, protections, rights and responsibilities of marriage.[6] In response to the request, the court issued an opinion declaring that civil union was not an adequate substitute for marriage and that to continue to disallow same-sex marriage would be a violation of the state constitution. *Opinion of the Justices to the Senate*, 802 N.E.2d 565 (2004). Excerpts from the court's opinion:

> The same defects of rationality evident in the marriage ban considered in *Goodridge* are evident in, if not exaggerated by, Senate No. 2175. Segregating same-sex unions from opposite-sex unions cannot possibly be held rationally to advance or "preserve" what we stated in *Goodridge* were the Commonwealth's legitimate interests in procreation, child rearing, and the conservation of resources. Because the proposed law by its express terms forbids same-sex couples entry into civil marriage, it continues to relegate same-sex couples to a different status. The holding in *Goodridge*, by which we are bound, is that group classifications based on unsupportable distinctions, such as that embodied in the proposed bill, are invalid under the Massachusetts Constitution. The history of our nation has demonstrated that separate is seldom, if ever, equal.

> The bill's absolute prohibition of the use of the word "marriage" by "spouses" who are the same sex is more than semantic. The dissimilitude between the terms "civil marriage" and "civil union" is not innocuous; it is a considered choice of language that reflects a demonstrable assigning of same-sex, largely

---

[6] The Massachusetts Constitution authorizes the Supreme Court to issue advisory opinions on important questions of law upon the request of either branch of the legislature, the governor, or the executive council. Mass. Const. Part II, c. 3, art. 2

homosexual, couples to second-class status. The denomination of this difference by the separate opinion of Justice Sosman (separate opinion) as merely a "squabble over the name to be used" so clearly misses the point that further discussion appears to be useless. If, as the separate opinion posits, the proponents of the bill believe that no message is conveyed by eschewing the word "marriage" and replacing it with "civil union" for same-sex "spouses," we doubt that the attempt to circumvent the court's decision in *Goodridge* would be so purposeful. For no rational reason the marriage laws of the Commonwealth discriminate against a defined class; no amount of tinkering with language will eradicate that stain. The bill would have the effect of maintaining and fostering a stigma of exclusion that the Constitution prohibits. It would deny to same-sex "spouses" only a status that is specially recognized in society and has significant social and other advantages. The Massachusetts Constitution, as was explained in the *Goodridge* opinion, does not permit such invidious discrimination, no matter how well intentioned.

We recognize that the pending bill palliates some of the financial and other concrete manifestations of the discrimination at issue in *Goodridge*. But the question the court considered in *Goodridge* was not only whether it was proper to withhold tangible benefits from same-sex couples, but also whether it was constitutional to create a separate class of citizens by status discrimination, and withhold from that class the right to participate in the institution of civil marriage, along with its concomitant tangible and intangible · protections, benefits, rights, and responsibilities. Maintaining a second-class citizen status for same-sex couples by excluding them from the institution of civil marriage is the constitutional infirmity at issue.We are of the opinion that Senate No. 2175 violates the equal protection and due process requirements of the Constitution of the Commonwealth and the Massachusetts Declaration of Rights....The bill maintains an unconstitutional, inferior, and discriminatory status for same-sex couples, and the bill's remaining provisions are too entwined with this purpose to stand independently.

2. In May of 2004, same-sex couples began to marry in Massachusetts. In 2007, the Massachusetts legislature initially voted to amend the state constitution to define marriage as a union between a man and a woman. However, to be effective, constitutional amendments in Massachusetts must be re-approved a second time by the legislature and then submitted to the electorate for a statewide vote. After the initial vote on the amendment, the legislature had a change of heart and voted against the amendment, thereby allowing the continuation of same-sex marriage in the Commonwealth. *See* Jeffrey M. Shaman, EQUALITY AND LIBERTY IN THE GOLDEN AGE OF STATE CONSTITUTIONAL LAW 207 (2008).

3. Since *Goodridge*, several other state high courts have addressed the issue of same-sex marriage, with varying results. Some state high courts, in disagreement with *Goodridge*, have found nothing unconstitutional about laws limiting marriage to opposite-sex couples. Others, in agreement with *Goodridge*, have struck down laws precluding same-sex marriage. *See* Jennifer Friesen, STATE CONSTITUTIONAL LAW— LITIGATING INDIVIDUAL RIGHTS, CLAIMS AND DEFENSES 2-106 (4TH ed. 2006), 2009 SUPPLEMENT, 23-5. In California, the state

supreme court ruled that state laws precluding same-sex marriage violated the equal protection clause of the California Constitution, *In re Marriages Cases*, 183 P.3d 384 (Cal. 2008), but that decision was nullified by a constitutional amendment adopted by the electorate stating that only marriage between a man and a woman is valid or recognized in California. Cal. Const. art. I, § 7.5.

4. The decision in *Goodridge* focused renewed attention on the Defense of Marriage Act (DOMA), adopted by Congress in 1996, in reaction to the Hawaii Supreme Court's decision in *Baehr v. Lewin, supra,* opening the door to same-sex marriage in that state until the state constitution was amended to bar same-sex marriage. DOMA defines marriage for purposes of federal law as the union of a man and a woman, and also authorizes a state to refuse to give effect to same-sex marriages from other states. As of 2007, 41 states have adopted their own version of DOMA, similarly defining marriage as the union of a man and a woman. Jennifer Friesen, 2009 SUPPLEMENT, *id,* at 22-3. Some states have enacted DOMA as amendments to their state constitutions, thereby blocking the courts in those states from finding the preclusion of same-sex marriage to be unconstitutional. *Id.* At the same time, an increasing number of states have enacted laws authorizing civil unions or domestic partnerships for same-sex couples. And in 2009, Vermont became the first state to legalize same-sex marriage by the legislature rather than the courts.

E. THE RIGHT OF BODILY INTEGRITY

MATTER OF FARRELL
529 A.2d 404 (N.J. 1987)

GARIBALDI, J.

Although we stated the general principle that competent informed patients have the right to decline life-sustaining treatment in both *In re Quinlan*, 355 A.2d 647 (N.J. 1976) and *In re Conroy*, 486 A.2d 1209 (N.J. 1985), each of those cases involved an incompetent institutionalized patient. In this case we deal for the first time with the right of a competent, terminally-ill adult patient living at home to withdraw a life-sustaining respirator.

Kathleen married Francis Farrell in 1969. They had two children. Prior to her illness, Mrs. Farrell worked as a keypunch operator. In November 1982, she began to experience symptoms associated with ALS, a disorder of the nervous system that results in degeneration of the victim's muscles. Although it eventually renders a patient incapable of movement, ALS does not impair the patient's mental faculties. The cause of the disease is unknown and there is no available treatment or cure. At the time of diagnosis, a victim's life expectancy even with life-sustaining treatment is usually one to three years.

After she became ill, Mrs. Farrell was admitted to a Philadelphia hospital where she underwent a tracheotomy and was connected to a respirator. In the autumn of 1983, she was released from the hospital because it could provide no further help for her condition. She returned home to live with her husband and their two teenage sons. Thereafter Mrs. Farrell was paralyzed and confined to bed in need of around-the-clock nursing care. Insurance covered all the expenses of this care.

In November 1985, after an experimental program that her husband characterized as "their last hope" had failed, Mrs. Farrell told him that she wanted to be disconnected from the respirator that sustained her breathing. Mr. Farrell told her doctor, John Pino, of her decision. The doctor advised Mrs. Farrell that she would die if her respirator were removed. Dr. Pino arranged for a psychologist, Dr. Jean Orost, to interview Mrs. Farrell. Dr. Orost determined that Mrs. Farrell was not clinically depressed and needed no psychiatric treatment. She concluded that Mrs. Farrell had made an informed, voluntary, and competent decision to remove the respirator. Dr. Orost continued to see Mrs. Farrell on a weekly basis from the time of their first interview in January 1986 until her death the following June.

On June 13, 1986, Francis Farrell filed a Chancery Division complaint seeking his appointment as Special Medical Guardian for his wife with specific authority to disconnect her respirator. He also sought a declaratory judgment that he and anyone who assisted him in disconnecting her respirator would incur no civil or criminal liability.... Part of the trial was conducted at the Farrells' home in order to enable Mrs. Farrell to testify. The court described Mrs. Farrell's medical condition at the time of the trial as follows:

> Mrs. Farrell presently appears to be a very fragile woman, weighing less than 100 pounds. In December 1982 she weighed 161 pounds. She has no control over her hands, arms, feet or legs, is incontinent as to bowel, and has difficulty with bladder function. She has difficulty in swallowing and is fed liquids, such as fruit juices, with a syringe by nurses who attend to her needs 24 hours a day. She is incapable of taking any solid foods by mouth. She is able to open and close her eyes and can see but has difficulty in talking. During her testimony, a court reporter took down what she said, and her husband at times repeated her answers to questions. Her answers were generally limited to yes or no, and at times an alphabet board was used to be certain her answer was understood. Her mouth tended to fill up with saliva and made her answers difficult to understand at times. When her children and better days were discussed with Mrs. Farrell, her eyes filled with tears and her husband assisted her in blowing her nose. She is incapable of moving her head, neck, or any other part of her body. On occasion she is put in a reclining chair and can watch television although she stated she usually falls asleep. She has pain in her arms and back, but medication does relieve it to some extent.

At the trial, Mrs. Farrell testified that she had discussed her decision to withdraw the respirator with her husband, their two sons, her parents, her sister, and her psychologist, Dr. Orost. These discussions had been upsetting, but resulted in open and full communication among all the parties. Mrs. Farrell had also discussed the consequences of her decision with a respiratory specialist, Dr. Sollami. When Mrs. Farrell was asked why she had decided to disconnect her respirator and to let nature take its course, she responded, "I'm tired of suffering."

After closing arguments on June 23, 1986, the trial court granted all the relief that Mr. Farrell had requested, but stayed his order pending appellate review. On June 29, 1986, Mrs. Farrell died while still connected to the respirator. Despite her death, both the guardian ad litem and Mr. Farrell have urged us to address her case and formulate guidelines that might aid future patients, their loved ones, and their physicians in dealing with similar situations. Because of the extreme importance of the issue and the inevitability of cases like this one arising in the future, we agree to render a decision on the merits.

In resolving this case, as well as the two other cases we decide today, we build on the principles established in *Quinlan* and *Conroy*. Hence, we start by reaffirming the well-recognized common-law right of self-determination that "[e]very human being of adult years and sound mind has a right to determine what shall be done with his own body...." *Schloendorff v. Society of New York Hosp.*, 105 N.E. 92, 93 (N.Y. 1914) (Cardozo, J.). In *Conroy*, we stated that "[t]he right of a person to control his own body is a basic societal concept, long recognized in the common law." We explained that the doctrine of "informed consent" was developed to protect the right to self-determination in matters of medical treatment. This doctrine prescribes the "duty of a physician to disclose to a patient information that will enable him to evaluate knowledgeably the options available and the risks attendant upon each before subjecting that patient to a course of treatment."

As medical technology has been advancing, the doctrine of informed consent has been developing. Thus, in *Conroy* we recognized the patient's right to give an informed refusal to medical treatment as the logical correlative of the right to give informed consent. We stated that "a competent adult person generally has the right to decline to have any medical treatment initiated or continued."

While we held that a patient's right to refuse medical treatment even at the risk of personal injury or death is primarily protected by the common law, we recognized that it is also protected by the federal and state constitutional right of privacy. Numerous other courts have upheld the right of a competent patient to refuse medical treatment even if that decision will hasten his or her death.

Nevertheless, the right to refuse life-sustaining medical treatment is not absolute. The state has at least four potentially countervailing interests in sustaining a person's life:

> preserving life, preventing suicide, safeguarding the integrity of the medical profession and protecting innocent third parties. When a party declines life-sustaining medical treatment, we balance the patient's common-law and constitutional rights against these four state interests. In this case, none of these interests, as we interpreted them in *Conroy*, nor their concert, outweighs Kathleen Farrell's rights to privacy and self-determination.

The state's interest in preserving life embraces "an interest in preserving the life of the particular patient, and an interest in preserving the sanctity of all life." Neither of those interests is compelling in this case. In *Conroy*, we decided that the value of life is desecrated not by a decision to refuse medical treatment but "by the failure to allow a competent human being the right of choice." Thus, "[i]n cases that do not involve the protection of the actual or potential life of someone other than the decisionmaker, the state's indirect and abstract interest in preserving the life of the competent patient generally gives way to the patient's much stronger personal interest in directing the course of his own life."

The next two state interests that we consider in rejection-of-treatment cases, i.e., preventing suicide and safeguarding the integrity of the medical profession, are not threatened by Mrs. Farrell's decision. In *Conroy*, we determined that the State's interest in preventing suicide is "motivated by, if not encompassed within," its interest in preserving life. We explained that declining life sustaining medical treatment may not properly be viewed as an attempt to commit suicide. Refusing medical intervention merely allows the disease to take its natural course; if death were to eventually occur, it would be the result, primarily of the underlying disease, and not the result of a self-inflicted injury.

Courts in other jurisdictions have consistently agreed that refusal of life-supporting treatment does not amount to an attempt to commit suicide. Similarly, medical ethics create no tension in this case. Our review of well-established medical authorities finds them in unanimous support of the right of a competent and informed patient such as Mrs. Farrell to decline medical treatment.... Health care standards are not undermined by the medical authorities that support the right to self-determination that we recognize today. Even as patients enjoy control over their medical treatment, health-care professionals remain bound to act in consonance with specific ethical criteria. We realize that these criteria may conflict with some concepts of self-determination. In the case of such a conflict, a patient has no right to compel a health-care provider to violate generally accepted professional standards.

When courts refuse to allow a competent patient to decline life-sustaining treatment, it is almost always because of the state's interest in protecting innocent third parties who would be harmed by the patient's decision. "[F]or example, courts have required competent adults to undergo medical procedures against their will if necessary to protect the public health,…or to prevent the emotional and financial abandonment of the patient's minor children."

Although Mrs. Farrell left behind two teenage sons, her case is manifestly distinguishable from those in which a parent could be forced to accept treatment because his or her prospect for recovery was good and the parent's death threatened the security of a child or children. Mrs. Farrell did not disregard her children's interest when she decided to withdraw the respirator. In fact, she based her decision in part on her recognition that her medical condition had already put them under extreme stress. Moreover, Mr. Farrell's capacity to care for them in her absence is unquestioned. Therefore the state's interest in protecting innocent third parties does not militate against Mrs. Farrell's decision.

The guardian ad litem appointed by the Court to protect the children concluded that they would not be harmed if the court granted relief. His position was based on personal meetings with the children and on a report he received from a psychiatrist who had interviewed them. However, we need not rely on his testimony. Where the evidence reveals a close, loving family like the Farrells, we presume that when the parents make medical decisions, they are concerned about and will protect their children's interests. A guardian ad litem for the children is, therefore, unnecessary in the case of a family like the Farrells.

In light of all of the foregoing, we hold that the state's interests did not outweigh Mrs. Farrell's right to withdraw her respirator. Accordingly, we affirm the judgment of the trial court.

KRISCHER v. McIVER
697 So.2d 97 (Fla. 1997)

GRIMES, J.

Charles E. Hall and his physician, Cecil McIver, M.D., filed suit for a declaratory judgment that section 782.08, Florida Statutes (1995), which prohibits assisted suicide, violated the Privacy Clause of the Florida Constitution and the Due Process and Equal Protection Clauses of the Fourteenth Amendment to the United States Constitution. They sought an injunction against the state attorney from prosecuting the physician for giving deliberate assistance to Mr. Hall in committing suicide. Mr. Hall is thirty-five years old and suffers from acquired immune deficiency syndrome (AIDS) which he contracted from a blood transfusion. The court found that Mr. Hall was mentally competent and that he was in obviously deteriorating health, clearly suffering, and terminally ill.

At the outset, we note that the United States Supreme Court recently issued two decisions on the subject of whether there is a right to assisted suicide under the United States Constitution. In *Washington v. Glucksberg*, 521 U.S. 702 (1997), the Court reversed a decision of the Ninth Circuit Court of Appeals which had held that the State of Washington's prohibition against assisted suicide violated the Due Process Clause.... [T]he Court reasoned that the asserted "right" to assistance in committing suicide was not a fundamental liberty interest protected by the Due Process Clause. In the second decision, the Court upheld New York's prohibition on assisted suicide against the claim that it violated the Equal Protection Clause. *Vacco v. Quill*, 521 U.S. 793 (1997).... [T]he Court held that there was a logical and recognized distinction between the right to refuse medical treatment and assisted suicide and concluded that there were valid and important public interests which easily satisfied the requirement that a legislative classification bear a rational relation to some legitimate end.

The remaining issue is whether Mr. Hall has the right to have Dr. McIver assist him in committing suicide under Florida's guarantee of privacy contained in our constitution's declaration of rights. Art. I, § 23, Fla. Const. Florida has no law against committing suicide. However, Florida imposes criminal responsibility on those who assist others in committing suicide. Section 782.08, which was first enacted in 1868, provides in pertinent part that "every person deliberately assisting another in the commission of self murder shall be guilty of manslaughter." See also §§ 765.309, 458.326(4). Thus, it is clear that the public policy of this state as expressed by the legislature is opposed to assisted suicide.

Florida's position is not unique. Forty-five states that recognize the right to refuse treatment or unwanted life support have expressed disapproval of assisted suicide. As of 1994, thirty-four jurisdictions had statutes which criminalized such conduct. Since that date, at least seventeen state legislatures have rejected proposals to legalize assisted suicide.

In 1984, Governor Mario Cuomo convened the New York State Task Force on Life and the Law, a blue ribbon commission composed of doctors, ethicists, lawyers, religious leaders, and interested laypersons, with a mandate to develop public policy on a number of issues arising from medical advances. With respect to assisted suicide and euthanasia, the task force concluded as follows:

> In this report, we unanimously recommend that New York laws prohibiting assisted suicide and euthanasia should not be changed. In essence, we propose a clear line for public policies and medical practice between forgoing medical interventions and assistance to commit suicide or euthanasia. Decisions to forgo treatment are an integral part of medical practice; the use of many treatments would be inconceivable without the ability to withhold or to stop the treatments

in appropriate cases. We have identified the wishes and interests of patients as the primary guideposts for those decisions.

> Assisted suicide and euthanasia would carry us into new terrain. American society has never sanctioned assisted suicide or mercy killing. We believe that the practices would be profoundly dangerous for large segments of the population, especially in light of the widespread failure of American medicine to treat pain adequately or to diagnose and treat depression in many cases. The risks would extend to all individuals who are ill. They would be most severe for those whose autonomy and well-being are already compromised by poverty, lack of access to good medical care, or membership in a stigmatized social group. The risks of legalizing assisted suicide and euthanasia for these individuals, in a health care system and society that cannot effectively protect against the impact of inadequate resources and ingrained social disadvantage, are likely to be extraordinary.

The Advocacy Center for Persons with Disability, Inc., opposes the legalization of assisted suicide, either by judicial decision negating its prohibition or by legislative enactment. If assisted suicide is permitted in Florida, Floridians will be put on the so-called slippery slope of determining the relative value of life. Floridians with severe physical and mental disabilities, who are particularly vulnerable to being devalued as burdens of society, would be at grave risk.

This Court has also rendered several prior decisions declaring in various contexts that there is a constitutional privacy right to refuse medical treatment. Those cases recognized the state's legitimate interest in (1) the preservation of life, (2) the protection of innocent third parties, (3) the prevention of suicide, and (4) the maintenance of the ethical integrity of the medical profession. However, we held that these interests were not sufficiently compelling to override the patient's right of self-determination to forego life-sustaining medical treatment.

We cannot agree that there is no distinction between the right to refuse medical treatment and the right to commit physician-assisted suicide through self-administration of a lethal dose of medication. The assistance sought here is not treatment in the traditional sense of that term. It is an affirmative act designed to cause death-no matter how well-grounded the reasoning behind it. Each of our earlier decisions involved the decision to refuse medical treatment and thus allow the natural course of events to occur. *In re Dubreuil*, 629 So.2d 819 (Fla.1993) (due to religious beliefs, individual wanted to refuse blood transfusion); *In re Guardianship of Browning*, 568 So.2d 4 (Fla.1990) (surrogate asserted right of woman who was vegetative but not terminally ill to remove nasogastric feeding tube); *Satz v. Perlmutter*, 379 So.2d 359 (Fla.1980) (individual suffering from Lou Gehrig's disease sought to remove artificial respirator needed to keep him alive).

In the instant case, Mr. Hall seeks affirmative medical intervention that will end his life on his timetable and not in the natural course of events.

There is a significant difference between these two situations. As explained by the American Medical Association:

> When a life-sustaining treatment is declined, the patient dies primarily because of an underlying disease. The illness is simply allowed to take its natural course. With assisted suicide, however, death is hastened by the taking of a lethal drug or other agent. Although a physician cannot force a patient to accept a treatment against the patient's will, even if the treatment is life-sustaining, it does not follow that a physician ought to provide a lethal agent to the patient. The inability of physicians to prevent death does not imply that physicians are free to help cause death. AMA Council on Ethical and Judicial Affairs, Report I-93-8, at 2.

Measured by the criteria employed in our cases addressing the right to refuse medical treatment, three of the four recognized state interests are so compelling as to clearly outweigh Mr. Hall's desire for assistance in committing suicide. First, the state has an unqualified interest in the preservation of life. The state also has a compelling interest in preventing suicide. Finally, the state also has a compelling interest in maintaining the integrity of the medical profession.

We do not hold that a carefully crafted statute authorizing assisted suicide would be unconstitutional. Nor do we discount the sincerity and strength of the respondents' convictions. However, we have concluded that this case should not be decided on the basis of this Court's own assessment of the weight of the competing moral arguments. By broadly construing the privacy amendment to include the right to assisted suicide, we would run the risk of arrogating to ourselves those powers to make social policy that as a constitutional matter belong only to the legislature.

KOGAN, C.J., dissenting.

The notion of "dying by natural causes" contrasts neatly with the word "suicide," suggesting two categories readily distinguishable from one another. How nice it would be if today's reality were so simple. No doubt there once was a time when, for all practical purposes, the distinction was clear enough to all. But that was a time before today, before technology had crept into medicine, when dying was a far more inexorable process. Medicine now has pulled the aperture separating life and death far enough apart to expose a limbo unthinkable fifty years ago, for which the law has no easy description. Dying no longer falls into the neat categories our ancestors knew. In today's world, we demean the hard reality of terminal illness to say otherwise.

The ability of medicine to intrude so profoundly into the act of dying has prompted a rising emphasis on the right of privacy, with its deep concern with self-determination. Since being added to the state Constitution in 1980, Florida's privacy right unquestionably has subtracted certain death-inducing actions from the category of "suicide" as defined at common law. Thus, in *Satz v. Perlmutter*, 379 So.2d 359 (Fla.1980), we upheld the decision of an individual suffering Lou Gehrig's disease to cease artificial respiration needed to keep him alive. In *Public Health Trust v. Wons*, 541 So.2d 96 (Fla.1989), we upheld an individual's right to refuse a blood transfusion needed to save her life even though she had children, where refusal was based on religious beliefs. On similar facts, we reached the same conclusion *In re Dubreuil*, 629 So.2d 819, (Fla.1993), where the State failed to establish the unfitness of the other parent to assume custody of the children. *In re Guardianship of Browning*, 568 So.2d 4 (Fla.1990), we found that the right to refuse treatment could be asserted by a surrogate on behalf of a woman who was vegetative but not terminally ill, but who previously had indicated she wanted life support removed in such circumstances. All of these acts would have been suicide at common law, and the assistance provided by physicians would have been homicide. Today they are not.

Once Florida had set itself adrift from the common law definition, the problem that immediately arose-that has vexed our courts ever since-is where to draw the new dividing line between improper "suicide" and the emerging "right of self-determination" without simultaneously authorizing involuntary euthanasia. This is no simple task. The majority tries to fix the mark through scrutinizing the means by which dying occurs: Suicide thus is "active" death caused by a "death producing agent," whereas Floridians have a right to choose "passive" death through "natural causes." While language in our prior opinions can be read to support this view, I am not convinced this language can be stretched beyond the differing facts we previously faced.

The issue is different here. In cases of this type, we simply cannot focus on the means by which death occurs, but on the fact that the patient at the time in question has reached the death bed. That is the fact unique in this case that was not present in the earlier cases, and it is the reason why we must use a different analysis. A means-based test works well in the context of refusing medical treatment where life otherwise will continue. It does not work where there is no question death must occur, and must occur painfully.

To my mind, the right of privacy attaches with unusual force at the death bed. This conclusion arises in part from the privacy our society traditionally has afforded the death bed, but also from the very core of the right of privacy-the right of self-determination even in the face of majoritarian disapproval. What possible interest does society have in saving life when there is nothing of life to save but a final convulsion of agony? The state has no business in this arena. Terminal illness is not a portrait in blacks and whites, but unending shades of gray, involving the most profound of personal, moral, and religious questions. Many people can and do disagree over these questions, but the fact remains that it is the dying person who must resolve them in the particular case. And while we certainly cannot ignore the slippery-slope problem, we previously have established fully adequate standards to police the exercise of privacy rights in this context to ensure against abuse.

Finally, I cannot ignore the majority's statement that the issues in this case must be left to the legislature. Such a statement ignores fundamental tenets of our law. Constitutional rights must be enforced by courts even against the legislature's powers, and privacy in particular must be enforced even against majoritarian sentiment. Indeed, the overarching purpose of the Florida Declaration of Rights along with its privacy provision is to "protect each individual within our borders from the unjust encroachment of state authority-from whatever official source-into his or her life.

RAVIN v. STATE
537 P.2d 494 (Alaska 1975)

RABINOWITZ, C. J.

The constitutionality of Alaska's statute prohibiting possession of marijuana is put in issue in this case.... We first address petitioner's contentions that his constitutionally protected right to privacy compels the conclusion that the State of Alaska is prohibited from penalizing the private possession and use of marijuana. Ravin's basic thesis is that there exists under the federal and Alaska constitutions a fundamental right to privacy, the scope of which is sufficiently broad to encompass and protect the possession of marijuana for personal use. Given this fundamental constitutional right, the State would then have the burden of demonstrating a compelling state interest in prohibiting possession of marijuana.

In Alaska this court has dealt with the concept of privacy on only a few occasions. One of the most significant decisions in this area is *Breese v. Smith*, 501 P.2d 159 (Alaska 1972), where we considered the applicability of the guarantee of 'life, liberty, the pursuit of happiness' found in the Alaska Constitution, to a school hairlength regulation. Noting that hairstyles are a highly personal matter in which the individual is traditionally autonomous, we concluded that governmental control of personal appearance would be antithetical to the concept of personal liberty under Alaska's constitution. Subsequent to our decision in *Breese*, a right to privacy amendment was added to the Alaska Constitution. Article I, section 22 reads:

> The right of the people to privacy is recognized and shall not be infringed. The legislature shall implement this section.

The effect of this amendment is to place privacy among the specifically enumerated rights in Alaska's constitution. But this fact alone does not, in and of itself, yield answers concerning what scope should be accorded to this right of privacy. We have suggested that the right to privacy may afford less than absolute protection to "the ingestion of food, beverages or other substances." For any such protection must be limited by the legitimate needs of the State to protect the health and welfare of its citizens.

[I]n our view, the right to privacy amendment to the Alaska Constitution cannot be read so as to make the possession or ingestion of marijuana itself a fundamental right. Nor can we conclude that such a fundamental right is shown by virtue of the analysis we employed in *Breese*. In that case, the student's traditional liberty pertaining to autonomy in personal appearance was threatened in such a way that his constitutionally guaranteed right to an education was jeopardized. Hairstyle, as emphasized in *Breese*, is a highly personal matter involving the individual and his body. Few would believe they have been deprived of something of critical importance if deprived of marijuana, though they would if stripped of control over their personal appearance. Therefore, if we were employing our former test, we would hold that there is no fundamental right, either under the Alaska or federal constitutions, either to possess or ingest marijuana.

The foregoing does not complete our analysis of the right to privacy issues.... Ravin's right to privacy contentions are not susceptible to disposition solely in terms of answering the question whether there is a general fundamental constitutional right to possess or smoke marijuana. This leads us to a more detailed examination of the right to privacy and the relevancy of where the right is exercised. If there is any area of human activity to which a right to privacy pertains more than any other, it is the home. The importance of the home has been amply demonstrated in constitutional law. Among the enumerated rights in the federal Bill of Rights are the guarantee against quartering of troops in a private house in peacetime (Third Amendment) and the right to be "secure in their...houses...against unreasonable searches and seizures..." (Fourth Amendment). The First Amendment has been held to protect the right to "privacy and freedom of association in the home." The Fifth Amendment has been described as providing protection against all governmental invasions "of the sanctity of a man's home and the privacies of life." The protection of the right to receive birth control information in *Griswold v. Connecticut*, 381 U.S. 479 (1965), was predicated on the sanctity of the marriage relationship and the harm to this fundamental area of privacy if police were allowed to "search the sacred precincts of marital bedrooms." And in *Stanley v. Georgia*, 394 U.S. 557 (1969), the Court emphasized the home as the situs of protected "private activities." The right to receive information and ideas was found in *Stanley* to take on an added dimension precisely because it was a prosecution for possession in the home. In a later case, the Supreme Court noted that *Stanley* was not based on the notion that the obscene matter was itself protected by a constitutional penumbra of privacy, but rather was a "reaffirmation that 'a man's home is his castle.'" At the same time the Court noted, "the Constitution extends special safeguards to the privacy of the home, just as it protects other special privacy rights such as those of marriage, procreation, motherhood, child rearing, and education." And as the Supreme Court pointed out, there exists a 'myriad' of activities which may be lawfully conducted within the privacy and confines of the home, but may be prohibited in public.

In Alaska we have also recognized the distinctive nature of the home as a place where the individual's privacy receives special protection. This court has consistently recognized that the home is constitutionally protected from unreasonable searches and seizures, reasoning that the home itself retains a protected status under the Fourth Amendment and Alaska's constitution distinct from that of the occupant's person. The privacy amendment to the Alaska Constitution was intended to give recognition and protection to the home. Such a reading is consonant with the character of life in Alaska. Our territory and now state has traditionally been the home of people who prize their individuality and who have chosen to settle or to continue living here in order to achieve a measure of control over their own lifestyles which is now virtually unattainable in many of our sister states.

The home, then, carries with it associations and meanings which make it particularly important as the situs of privacy. Privacy in the home is a fundamental right, under both the federal and Alaska constitutions. We do not mean by this that a person may do anything at anytime as long as the activity takes place within a person's home. There are two important limitations on this facet of the right to privacy. First, we agree with the Supreme Court of the United States, which has strictly limited the *Stanley* guarantee to possession for purely private, noncommercial use in the home. And secondly, we think this right must yield when it interferes in a serious manner with the health, safety, rights and privileges of others or with the public welfare. No one has an absolute right to do things in the privacy of his own home which will affect himself or others adversely. Indeed, one aspect of a private matter is that it is private, that is, that it does not adversely affect persons beyond the actor, and hence is none of their business. When a matter does affect the public, directly or indirectly, it loses its wholly private character, and can be made to yield when an appropriate public need is demonstrated.

Thus, we conclude that citizens of the State of Alaska have a basic right to privacy in their homes under Alaska's constitution. This right to privacy would encompass the possession and ingestion of substances such as marijuana in a purely personal, non-commercial context in the home unless the state can meet its substantial burden and show that proscription of possession of marijuana in the home is supportable by achievement of a legitimate state interest.

The evidence which was presented at the hearing before the district court consisted primarily of several expert witnesses familiar with various medical and social aspects of marijuana use. Numerous written reports and books were also introduced into evidence. The justifications offered by the State to uphold AS 17.12.010 are generally that marijuana is a psychoactive drug; that it is not a harmless substance; that heavy use has concomitant risk; that it is capable of precipitating a psychotic reaction in at least individuals who are predisposed towards such reaction; and that its use adversely affects the user's ability to operate an automobile. The State relies upon a number of medical researchers who have raised questions as to the substance's effect on the body's immune system, on chromosomal structure, and on the functioning of the brain. On the other hand, in almost every instance of reports of potential danger arising from marijuana use, reports can be found reaching contradictory results. It appears that there is no firm evidence that marijuana, as presently used in this country, is generally a danger to the user or to others. But neither is there conclusive evidence to the effect that it is harmless. The one significant risk in use of marijuana which we do find established to a reasonable degree of certainty is the effect of marijuana intoxication on driving.

Given the evidence of the effect of marijuana on driving, an individual's right to possess or ingest marijuana while driving would be subject to the prohibition provided for in AS 17.12.010. However, given the relative insignificance of marijuana consumption as a health problem in our society at present, we do not believe that the potential harm generated by drivers under the influence of marijuana, standing alone, creates a close and substantial relationship between the public welfare and control of ingestion of marijuana or possession of it in the home for personal use. Thus we conclude that no adequate justification for the state's intrusion into the citizen's right to privacy by its prohibition of possession of marijuana by an adult for personal consumption in the home has been shown. The privacy of the individual's home cannot be breached absent a persuasive showing of a close and substantial relationship of the intrusion to a legitimate governmental interest. Here, mere scientific doubts will not suffice. The state must demonstrate a need based on proof that the public health or welfare will in fact suffer if the controls are not applied.

The state has a legitimate concern with avoiding the spread of marijuana use to adolescents who may not be equipped with the maturity to handle the experience prudently, as well as a legitimate concern with the problem of driving under the influence of marijuana. Yet these interests are insufficient to justify intrusions into the rights of adults in the privacy of their own homes. Further, neither the federal or Alaska constitution affords protection for the buying or selling of marijuana, nor absolute protection for its use or possession in public. Possession at home of amounts of marijuana indicative of intent to sell rather than possession for personal use is likewise unprotected.

In view of our holding that possession of marijuana by adults at home for personal use is constitutionally protected, we wish to make clear that we do not mean to condone the use of marijuana. The experts who testified below, including petitioner's witnesses, were unanimously opposed to the use of any psychoactive drugs. We agree completely. It is the responsibility of every individual to consider carefully the ramifications for himself and for those around him of using such substances. With the freedom which our society offers to each of us to order our lives as we see fit goes the duty to live responsibly, for our own sakes and for society's. This result can best be achieved, we believe, without the use of psychoactive substances.

NOTES

1. A few years after *Ravin*, the Alaska Supreme Court upheld the constitutionality of a criminal law prohibiting the use and possession of cocaine. *State v. Erickson*, 574 P.2d 1 (Alaska 1978). In upholding the law, the court ruled that the personal use and possession of cocaine in the home was not encompassed within the right of privacy. The court distinguished *Ravin* on the ground that cocaine, unlike marijuana, was shown by scientific evidence to be a serious hazard to health and welfare.

2. Courts in other states have declined to follow *Ravin*. The Supreme Court of Hawaii, for example, refused to allow a right to smoke marijuana, even in the home, notwithstanding that Hawaii's Constitution, like Alaska's, contains a provision expressly protecting the right of privacy. *State v. Mallan*, 950 P.2d 178 (Haw. 1998). The Hawaii high court repudiated *Ravin*, commenting that it was based, at least partially, on social and cultural factors unique to Alaska. Aside from Alaska, no other state has recognized a constitutional right to smoke marijuana.

3. In *Seeley v. State*, 940 P.2d 604 (Wash. 1997), the Supreme Court of Washington refused to approve a right for a terminally ill cancer patient to smoke marijuana for medicinal purposes. The patient averred that marijuana offered the most effective relief from the nausea and vomiting he suffered as a result of chemotherapy. Although the patient claimed only a limited right to smoke marijuana for medical treatment, the court rejected his claim:

> This court has held that "[t]he right to smoke marijuana is not fundamental to the American scheme of justice, it is not necessary to ordered liberty, and it is not within a zone of privacy." *State v. Smith*, 610 P.2d 869 (Wash. 1980). Other

federal and state courts have agreed that possession of marijuana is not a fundamental right guaranteed by the United States Constitution. However, Respondent contends the right infringed is not a general right to smoke marijuana but, rather, a right to have marijuana prescribed as his preferred medical treatment for the nausea and vomiting associated with chemotherapy.

Here, Respondent asserts a constitutionally protected interest in having his physician prescribe marijuana, an unapproved drug which is regulated as a Schedule I controlled substance, for medical treatment.... (S)cientifically reliable evidence showed that currently available therapies are more effective and do not carry with them the same risks which are attributable to marijuana.... This court and other federal and state courts have reviewed evidence similar to that which has been submitted in this case and have all upheld the constitutionality of marijuana's classification.

The challenged legislation involves conclusions concerning a myriad of complicated medical, psychological and moral issues of considerable controversy. We are not prepared on this limited record to conclude that the legislature could not reasonably conclude that marijuana should be placed in schedule I of controlled substances. It is clear not only from the record in this case but also from the long history of marijuana's treatment under the law that disagreement persists concerning the health effects of marijuana use and its effectiveness as a medicinal drug. The evidence presented by the Respondent is insufficient to convince this court that it should interfere with the broad judicially recognized prerogative of the legislature. Respondent has not shown that the legislative treatment of marijuana is "so unrelated" to the achievement of the legitimate purposes of the legislature or that "the facts have so far changed as to render the classification arbitrary and obsolete." See *Smith*, 610 P.2d 869.

F. PROCEDURAL DUE PROCESS

STATE v. VEALE
972 A.2d 1009 (N.H. 2009)

HICKS, J.

The defendant, Scott W. Veale, appeals orders of the Superior Court relating to its finding that he is incompetent to stand trial. We affirm. The relevant facts are as follows. The defendant is a real estate broker who has been involved in various land and logging disputes for many years. He was indicted in June 2003 for one count of timber trespass and one count of theft by unauthorized taking, after a property owner alleged that he cut and removed oak timber from the owner's property. The court appointed a public defender to represent the defendant. A second public defender entered an appearance to assist in the defense because of his familiarity with real estate issues.

The attorney-client relationship deteriorated over the following months. The defendant believed that he owned the timber and the property. He also believed that local and State authorities prosecuted him as part of an ongoing conspiracy to deprive him of property rights. The public defender conferred with two real estate attorneys to determine whether the defendant's claim had merit. Both concluded that it did not. The defendant, however, continued to insist that the public defenders seek funds for a property survey. Eventually, the defendant accused the public defenders of being part of the conspiracy against him and his family. This severely impaired communication and the public defenders concluded that he was unable to assist in his defense. In July 2004, defense counsel filed a motion to determine competency. Dr. James Adams, a psychiatrist, examined the defendant in November 2004 and ultimately determined that, although the defendant suffered from a paranoid disorder, he was competent to stand trial. Defense counsel moved for, and were granted funds for, a second opinion. Dr. Philip Kinsler, a clinical and forensic psychologist, examined the defendant in March 2005 and concluded that he suffered from a delusional disorder and was incompetent. The defendant filed a *pro se* motion in July 2005 summarizing the breakdown of communication with his appointed counsel, outlining their disagreement over "the need for a mental evaluation," requesting a finding that such evaluation was unnecessary, and requesting new counsel. The clerk refused these pleadings "under Superior Rule 5 for non-compliance with Rule 15."

The Superior Court (*Barry*, J.) held a competency hearing in September 2005, receiving testimony from each doctor. The State conducted the direct examination of Dr. Adams and cross-examination of Dr. Kinsler. The public defender conducted the direct examination of Dr. Kinsler and cross-examination of Dr. Adams. The court also made limited inquiry. The defendant was present at the hearing but did not testify. The court ultimately found the defendant incompetent to stand trial and ruled that he could not be restored to competency. The court later held a hearing on dangerousness, ruled that the defendant was not dangerous and granted the defendant's motion to dismiss the criminal charges.

The defendant filed a *pro se* notice of appeal raising several issues. We appointed the appellate defender to represent him on appeal. The appellate defender moved to withdraw, citing a conflict of interest due to an ineffective assistance of counsel claim alleged against the public defenders. On remand, the trial court appointed the defendant's current counsel. Counsel filed an amended ineffective assistance claim and a motion to vacate the competency finding. The motion alleged a denial of procedural due process. After a hearing, the Trial Court ruled against the defendant on the ineffective assistance of counsel claim and denied his motion to vacate the finding of incompetence. The court noted that defense counsel was ethically bound to raise the competency issue and that such action did not deprive the defendant of procedural due process.

We appointed the defendant's trial counsel to represent him on appeal and granted the appellate defender's motion to withdraw. The defendant appeals only the denial of his motion to vacate, arguing that he was denied due process in the competency determination. He cites the Due Process Clauses of the Fourteenth Amendment to the Federal Constitution and Part I, Article 15 of the State Constitution. We first address this argument under the State Constitution and cite federal opinions for guidance only.

Part I, Article 15 of the State Constitution provides, in relevant part: "No subject shall be...deprived of his property, immunities, or privileges, put out of the protection of the law, exiled or deprived of his life, liberty, or estate, but by the judgment of his peers, or the law of the land...." Law of the land in this article means due process of law. Our threshold determination in a procedural due process claim is "whether the challenged procedures concern a legally protected interest." Undoubtedly, the state constitutional right to due process protects defendants from standing trial if they are legally incompetent. The defendant's due process challenge, however, does not implicate this right. Indeed, the competency proceedings below resulted in a dismissal of the two indictments, and resulted in no confinement because the defendant was found not to be dangerous. The defendant grounds his due process challenge on the stigma attached to his reputation by virtue of the incompetency finding. He argues that, while the competency proceedings may have protected his right not to be tried if incompetent, they erroneously imposed upon him an "indelible stigma" affecting the exercise of various civil rights. It is through this lens that we consider his procedural due process challenge. The State contends that the defendant's asserted reputational interest fails to trigger a due process analysis because he simply "speculates about a number of potential consequences that 'may' or 'can' flow from a finding of incompetence," rendering each "too speculative and remote to constitute the kind of liberty or property interest contemplated by the constitution."

The State would have a stronger argument if we had adopted the analysis in *Paul v. Davis*, 424 U.S. 693 (1976), under our State Constitution. In *Paul*, the Supreme Court coined what would later be known as the "stigma plus" test. The Court noted that "[t]he words 'liberty' and 'property' as used in the Fourteenth Amendment do not in terms single out reputation as a candidate for special protection...." It narrowed its prior holding in *Wisconsin v. Constantineau*, 400 U.S. 433 (1971), by concluding that defamation alone could not constitute an interest triggering due process protection. Instead, the Court read *Wisconsin* as recognizing a cognizable right warranting due process protection where reputational stigma exists in addition to state action altering or extinguishing "a right or status previously recognized by state law." In *Siegert v. Gilley*, 500 U.S. 226 (1991), the Court extended the doctrine by requiring, in addition to the stigma, a contemporaneous tangible loss. We, however, have never adopted the stigma-plus test as the touchstone for procedural due process under the State Constitution. Although other cases have approached the issue, they have merely assumed that state constitutional due process attaches to a reputational right. Accordingly, the issue remains open under the State Constitution.

Although we do not necessarily agree with all of the scholarly criticism of the stigma-plus doctrine, we are mindful that constitutional scholars have not received the doctrine well. By requiring that a separate liberty or property interest accompany the reputational injury, the decision in *Paul* marked a drastic narrowing of its predecessors. In our view, *Paul* effectively relegates the reputational interest to insignificance because the separate injury would, itself, often invoke the Due Process Clause.

Although in interpreting the New Hampshire Constitution we have often followed and agreed with the federal treatment of parallel provisions of the federal document, we never have considered ourselves bound to adopt the federal interpretations." In *Clark v. Manchester*, 305 A.2d 668 (N.H.1973), we concluded that a probationary employee was not entitled to due process, in part, because he failed to show "that the governmental conduct likely will...seriously damage his standing and associations in the community...[or] impose a stigma upon the employee that will foreclose future opportunities to practice his chosen profession." In *Petition of Bagley*, 513 A.2d 331 (N.H. 1986), we stated that "[t]he general rule is that a person's liberty may be impaired when governmental action seriously damages his standing and associations in the community." We also "recognized that the stigmatization that attends certain governmental determinations may amount to a deprivation of constitutionally protected liberty." *Bagley*, 128 N.H. at 284. Thus, we find ample support in our jurisprudence for the proposition that reputational stigma can, by itself, constitute a deprivation of liberty deserving due process.

Accordingly, we hold that competency determinations sufficiently implicate reputational interests to warrant the protection afforded by the State Due Process Clause. Guaranteeing some minimal process guards against the difficulty of undoing harm once visited upon a person's good name. *Cf. Goldberg v. Kelly*, 397 U.S. 254 (1970). In instances such as the present one, a person may not immediately suffer the more tangible effects of such a determination. We have long recognized that some forms of reputational harm can safely be assumed.

Having concluded that competency determinations can potentially damage the protected interest in reputation, we consider what process is required to protect that interest. In so doing, we balance three factors: First, the private interest that will be affected by the official action; second, the risk of an erroneous deprivation of such interest through the procedures used, and the probable value, if any, of additional or substitute procedural safeguards; and finally, the Government's interest, including the function involved and the fiscal and administrative burdens that the additional or substitute procedural requirement would entail.

After balancing the private interest here at issue; the risk of an erroneous deprivation of that interest through the procedures used, and the probable value of additional procedural safeguards; and the Government's interest, we conclude that due process does not require additional process under the State Constitution.

M.E.K. v. R.L.K.
921 So.2d 787 (Fla. App. 2006)

PLEUS, C.J.

The sole issue in this appeal is whether an indigent mother facing involuntary termination of parental rights in an adoption proceeding has a constitutional right to appointment of trial and appellate counsel. We believe she does and therefore reverse the order denying her counsel.

J.L.K. was born in September 2004. A month later, the Department of Children and Families sheltered J.L.K. with his maternal grandmother and initiated dependency proceedings based on allegations that his mother was unable to care for him. Prior to the adjudicatory hearing, J.L.K.'s grandmother moved to dismiss the dependency proceeding on the ground that she would file a separate adoption proceeding pursuant to Chapter 63 and would seek to have the mother's parental rights terminated as part of the adoption. The dependency court abated the dependency proceeding to allow the adoption to proceed.

In March 2005, the grandmother filed a petition for termination of parental rights pending adoption pursuant to Chapter 63 of the Florida Statutes. The lower court terminated the mother's parental rights by default after the mother failed to file a responsive pleading. She was incarcerated at the time. Subsequently, the mother's attorney in the dependency action filed a notice of appearance in the adoption action. He also filed an affidavit of indigency, motion to appoint counsel and motion to vacate the final judgment and set aside default. The mother's appellate attorney appealed the final judgment terminating her parental rights and also filed a motion in the lower court to appoint appellate counsel. The court denied the motions to appoint trial and appellate counsel in the adoption proceeding. The mother appealed this order as well. We consolidated these appeals and temporarily relinquished jurisdiction, after which the lower court approved the parties' stipulation to set aside the final judgment and reinstate the dependency proceedings. Based on this development, we acknowledged dismissal of appeal of the final judgment but agreed to proceed with the appeal of the order denying appointed counsel.

In a 1980 appeal of an order terminating parental rights under Chapter 39, the Florida Supreme Court held that an indigent parent has a right, under both the Florida and United States Constitutions, to appointed counsel in "proceedings involving the permanent termination of parental rights to a child." *In the Interest of D.B.*, 385 So.2d 83 (Fla.1980).

A year later, in *Lassiter v. Dep't of Social Serv. of Durham County, N.C.*, 452 U.S. 18 (1981), the U.S. Supreme Court held that the federal due process clause does not require appointed counsel in every state-initiated termination of parental rights proceeding. Instead, it required trial courts to evaluate the need for counsel on a case-by-case basis. The court noted that it was only determining the minimum due process standard under the federal constitution and that many states have higher standards based on wise public policy. In *O.A.H. v. R.L.A.*, 712 So.2d 4 (Fla. 2d DCA 1998), the second district held that an indigent parent has a constitutional right to appointed counsel in a Chapter 63 involuntary adoption proceeding. It recently reaffirmed that holding in *In the Interest of M.C.*, 899 So.2d 486 (Fla. 2d DCA 2005). Both *O.A.H.* and *M.C.* are similar to the instant case in that they involved indigent parents who did not attend the final hearing in which their parental rights were terminated because they were incarcerated at the time.

In denying the mother's requests for appointed counsel, the lower court declined to follow *O.A.H.* or *M.C.*, stating:

> Ordinarily, the Court would be bound by precedent from another District Court of Appeal in the absence of contrary authority from the Fifth District Court of Appeal. However, the Court in this matter is bound by the U.S. Supreme Court decision in *Lassiter v. Department of Social Services of Durham County, N.C.*

We disagree with this reasoning.... *Lassiter* addressed only the minimum due process requirements under the federal due process clause. The citizens of Florida are also protected by the due process clause in Article 1, section 9 of the Florida Constitution. In our federal system of jurisprudence, the United States Constitution establishes the minimum level of due process protections for all people, but state constitutions and laws may provide additional due process protections.

In the area of termination of parental rights, the Florida due process clause provides higher due process standards than the federal due process clause. Under the federal provision, *Lassiter* does not require appointment of counsel in every case. It only requires a case-by-case determination. But under the state due process clause, *D.B.* requires appointment of counsel in "proceedings involving the permanent termination of parental rights to a child." *D.B.*, 385 So.2d at 90. *O.A.H.* noted that:

> In the years following *Lassiter*, Florida's supreme court has continued to confirm that *D.B.* stands for the proposition that a constitutional right to appointed counsel arises when the proceeding can result in a permanent loss of parental rights.

For these reasons, the lower court should have followed *O.A.H.* and *M.C.* rather than *Lassiter.*

Alternatively, the grandmother argues that even if the trial court was obligated to follow *O.A.H.*, this Court is free to disagree with it. She urges us to reject *O.A.H.*, claiming that it disregards the underlying reasons for appointing counsel and because its broad interpretation of state action creates a slippery slope that will obligate the state to provide counsel in many other types of civil cases. The grandmother is wrong on both counts. In *M.L.B.*, the United States Supreme Court rejected a similar slippery slope argument. *M.L.B.* involved the right of an indigent parent to have the state pay for a transcript of the hearing in an appeal of a private termination of parental rights case. Justice Thomas argued in dissent that extending due process protections found in criminal cases involving the loss of one's liberty to a civil case involving termination of parental rights would create a dangerous precedent used to extend such protections to other civil cases.

The majority rejected this argument, noting that termination of parental rights work "unique kind of deprivation" involving the "awesome authority of the State" to permanently destroy legal recognition of the parental relationship. Therefore, finding certain due process protections applicable in termination of parental rights cases could not be used as precedent to extend such protections to other civil cases. The same analysis is true in the instant case. Finding a right to counsel in a civil termination of parental rights case does not create a dangerous precedent for finding such a right in other civil cases because other civil cases do not involve the same unique deprivation of a fundamental right by the State.

The grandmother also argues that *O.A.H.* ignores the underlying reasons for appointing counsel. She instead urges us to apply the factors found in *Mathews v. Eldridge, 424 U.S. 319, (1976)*, for determining whether a right to counsel exists. However, *D.B.* makes clear that in the context of determining whether a right to appointed counsel exists in a case involving the parent-child relationship, Florida courts must weigh the factors enunciated in *Potvin v. Keller,* 313 So.2d 703 (Fla.1975), not *Mathews.* Those factors include: (1) the potential length of parent-child separation, (2) the degree of parental restrictions on visitation, (3) the presence or absence of parental consent, (4) the presence or absence of disputed facts, and (5) the complexity of the proceeding in terms of witnesses and documents. The *D.B.* court further stated that in applying these factors, "counsel will always be required where permanent termination of custody might result, but where there is no threat of permanent termination of parental custody, the test should be applied on a case-by-case basis."

We also note that the first district recently reached the same conclusion in *G.C. v. W.J.,* 917 So.2d 998 (Fla. 1st DCA 2005). G.C. followed *D.B.* and *O.A.H.* in holding that there is a constitutional right to appointed counsel in a Chapter 63 termination of parental rights proceeding.

We therefore hold, as our sister courts have, that article 1, section 9 of the Florida Constitution mandates that counsel be appointed to an indigent parent in an involuntary termination of parental rights proceeding under Chapter 63. Accordingly, we reverse the order denying appointed counsel and remand directing the trial court to enter an order appointing trial and appellate counsel *nunc pro tunc* to the date of the mother's motion to appoint counsel.

PEOPLE v. WASHINGTON
665 N.E.2d 1330 (Ill. 1996)

FREEMAN, J.

The question in this case is whether due process is implicated in a claim of innocence based upon new evidence so as to permit the claim to be raised in a petition under the Post-Conviction Hearing Act. We hold that it is.

In 1982, Kurtis Washington was sentenced to 25 years in prison for murdering Tony Hightie. Hightie had been murdered outside his home in Chicago shortly after 9 p.m. on May 9, 1980. Washington was implicated in the crime by Donna McClure, Hightie's girlfriend, and Ronald Tapes. McClure and Tapes witnessed the murder. At trial, they said that they had been sitting in a parked car near Hightie's home when they were approached by a man. The man said that he was looking for someone named Will. When McClure and Tapes proved no help, the man approached Hightie just as he left his home. Hightie had been wearing a jacket and hat that belonged to Tapes' brother who was named William. McClure and Tapes said that after a few words with Hightie, the man shot him. The man, McClure and Tapes said, was Washington.

Washington's defense was that he had been at a grocery store at the time of Hightie's murder. The store cashier, a person who had accompanied Washington and Washington's mother all testified to that fact.

The appellate court affirmed the conviction and sentence on direct review. In 1990, Washington filed a post-conviction petition, alleging nine grounds of error, six of which asserted ineffective assistance of trial counsel. One of the grounds was that Washington's trial counsel, a private attorney who also served as Washington's appellate counsel, failed to investigate evidence that someone other than Washington murdered

Hightie. The claim was supported with an affidavit of Jacqueline Martin dated March 3, 1990. Evidence was permitted on that as well as the other ineffective-assistance claims.

The trial judge held an in camera hearing in which he considered Martin's testimony. Martin told how Hightie had been shot after having been mistaken for someone else. Martin, who was 16 years old at the time, told how she had been present when Marcus Halsey, then her boyfriend, and Frank Caston had left Halsey's house to revenge an earlier beating of Halsey's brother. She, Halsey, Caston, and Caston's girlfriend drove in a car to an alley in a neighborhood in Chicago. She later learned that it happened to be the neighborhood where Hightie lived. Martin told how, after Halsey and Caston left the car, she had heard two gunshots, and, when the two returned, she had heard Halsey say "it was the wrong guy." Halsey and Caston later changed clothes, discarding in another alley what they had earlier worn. Martin said that they drove to the home of one of Halsey's sisters, where she stayed the rest of the night.

Halsey was questioned by police the next morning. Martin accompanied him to the police station, as did Caston's girlfriend. At the station, Martin found in her pocket bullets that Halsey had handed to her the night before. She said that she threw the bullets away.

Martin said that after the police questioning, Halsey had threatened to kill her if she told anyone what had happened. Halsey's threats continued, Martin said, and so she eventually stopped going to Halsey's house. Some months later, Halsey's brother confronted her as she was walking near a park and forcibly took her to Halsey. She said that she was kept against her will at Halsey's house for three weeks to a month. She eventually escaped with the help of an unnamed acquaintance whom she happened to see while looking out a window. Martin said that she went immediately to her mother's house. That same day she left for Mississippi. She stayed there for six years. Martin told how at the time of the hearing she still feared Halsey.

In view of Martin's in camera testimony, Washington successfully sought to amend his post-conviction petition to add a tenth claim based upon the newly discovered evidence. The trial judge denied relief under the first nine claims Washington asserted, including the ineffectiveness claim which was supported by Martin's affidavit and testimony. Regarding that claim, the judge referred to testimony given by Washington's defense counsel that, in preparation for trial, he had tried to contact Martin. Counsel had also testified that he believed Washington had a strong alibi defense and his strategy was to focus on that rather than to try to prove that someone other than Washington murdered Hightie. However, the trial judge granted a new trial on the ground that Martin's testimony was new evidence which, if believed, would have "had some significant impact" upon the jury. The appellate court affirmed the grant of relief as to the newly discovered evidence claim....

The claim Washington raised is a "free-standing" claim of innocence; unlike the ineffective-assistance claim supported by Martin's testimony, the newly discovered evidence is not being used to supplement an assertion of a constitutional violation with respect to his trial. The issue is not whether the evidence at trial was insufficient to convict Washington beyond a reasonable doubt. The appellate court rejected that challenge on direct appeal. The issue is whether Washington's claim of newly discovered evidence can be raised in a petition under the Post-Conviction Hearing Act to entitle Washington to a new trial. Post-conviction relief is Washington's remaining hope for a judicial remedy, the time limitations of other avenues offering relief for such a claim having lapsed.

To decide the issue, we must see if either a federal or Illinois constitutional right is implicated in such a freestanding claim of innocence, since Post-Conviction Hearing Act relief is limited to constitutional claims. Washington argues that his claim implicates due process protections. The beginning point for addressing that argument is *Herrera v. Collins*, 506 U.S. 390 (1993), where the Supreme Court rejected the contention as a federal constitutional matter. In light of our own constitution's due process guaranty, we must also assess Washington's argument as a matter of Illinois constitutional jurisprudence.

Federal Due Process

The issue in *Herrera* was whether a freestanding claim of innocence following a Texas capital conviction could be raised in a habeas corpus petition in view of either the eighth amendment protection against cruel and unusual punishment or the fourteenth amendment due process clause. Ten years after his conviction, *Herrera* claimed that his brother, who had since died, committed the crimes. The claim was supported by two affidavits. The Court said that the claim implicated neither the eighth nor the fourteenth amendment but also offered that, even if that were not the case, the claim was unpersuasive anyway.

It is no criticism to read *Herrera* as a conflicted decision. As Justice O'Connor said, claims of innocence-even those in noncapital cases-present troubling issues. We are, of course, bound by the Supreme Court's interpretation of the United States Constitution. Conflicted or not, at least for noncapital cases, *Herrera* clearly states, as the Court did in *Townsend v. Sain*, that a freestanding claim of innocence is not cognizable as a fourteenth amendment due process claim. And so Washington's effort to state a federal constitutional due process claim under the Post-Conviction Hearing Act must fail.

Due Process Under the Illinois Constitution

The possibility remains that Washington's claim may be cognizable under the Illinois Constitution's due process protection. That protection is stated as it is in the fourteenth amendment: no person "shall be deprived of life, liberty or property without due process of law." Ill. Const. 1970, art. I, § 2; see U.S. Const., amend. V. The Record of Proceedings of the Constitutional Convention does not reveal anything as to what the drafters intended for the Illinois protection different from the federal counterpart.

Nevertheless, in *People v. McCauley*, 645 N.E.2d 923 (Ill. 1994), we noted that we labor under no self-imposed constraint to follow federal precedent in "lockstep" in defining Illinois' due process protection. In *McCauley*, we looked primarily to how the protection had been interpreted with respect to the issue there presented: police interference with a suspect's right to legal assistance. We found historical support to say that, as a state matter, due process should protect against deliberate attempts to deny legal counsel.

As for Washington's claim here, there are decisions in which this court has perfunctorily evaluated new evidence claims in cases brought under the Post-Conviction Hearing Act. But neither this court nor the appellate court has ever expressly identified the constitutional right implicated in a freestanding claim of innocence based upon new evidence. Again, Post-Conviction Hearing Act relief is impossible if no constitutional right is implicated in the claim asserted. Essentially, then, the issue is the time relativeness of due process as a matter of this State's constitutional jurisprudence; that is, should additional process be afforded in Illinois when newly discovered evidence indicates that a convicted person is actually innocent?

We believe so as a matter of both procedural and substantive due process. In terms of procedural due process, we believe that to ignore such a claim would be fundamentally unfair. Imprisonment of the innocent would also be so conscience shocking as to trigger operation of substantive due process. The conflicted analysis in *Herrera* is some proof of that. Though the Court rejected the application of substantive due process principles as grounds in *Herrera*, the Court nevertheless conceded that "a truly persuasive demonstration of 'actual innocence'" would make a conviction unconstitutional.

We have no difficulty seeing why substantive due process as a matter of Illinois constitutional law offers the grounds for such a conclusion. The Supreme Court rejected substantive due process as means to recognize freestanding innocence claims because of the idea that a person convicted in a constitutionally fair trial must be viewed as guilty. That made it impossible for such a person to claim that he, an innocent person, was unfairly convicted.

We think that the Court overlooked that a "truly persuasive demonstration of innocence" would, in hindsight, undermine the legal construct precluding a substantive due process analysis. The stronger the claim-the more likely it is that a convicted person is actually innocent-the weaker is the legal construct dictating that the person be viewed as guilty. A "truly persuasive demonstration of innocence" would effectively reduce the idea to legal fiction. At the point where the construct falls apart, application of substantive due process principles, as Justice Blackmun favored, is invited. *Herrera*, 506 U.S. at 436, (Blackmun, J., dissenting, joined by Stevens and Souter, JJ.)

We believe that no person convicted of a crime should be deprived of life or liberty given compelling evidence of actual innocence. Given the limited avenues that our legislature has so far seen fit to provide for raising freestanding claims of innocence, that idea-but for the possibility of executive clemency-would go ignored in cases like this one. We therefore hold as a matter of Illinois constitutional jurisprudence that a claim of newly discovered evidence showing a defendant to be actually innocent of the crime for which he was convicted is cognizable as a matter of due process. That holding aligns Illinois with other jurisdictions likewise recognizing, primarily as a matter of state habeas corpus jurisprudence, a basis to raise such claims under the rubric of due process.

That only means, of course, that there is footing in the Illinois Constitution for asserting freestanding innocence claims based upon newly discovered evidence under the Post-Conviction Hearing Act. Procedurally, such claims should be resolved as any other brought under the Act. Substantively, relief has been held to require that the supporting evidence be new, material, noncumulative and, most importantly, "of such conclusive character" as would "probably change the result on retrial."

As for this case, we find neither reason to disagree with the appellate court that those concerns were satisfied nor need to elaborate upon that conclusion.

The judgment of the appellate court is affirmed.

CHAPTER VII

CRIMINAL PROCEDURE

A. RIGHT TO JURY TRIAL

One of the foundations of the American legal system is the common law right to a trial by jury that existed in England prior to the Declaration of Independence. Traditionally, a jury consisted of twelve jurors who had to reach a unanimous verdict. That is no longer the standard provided for in the United States Constitution or the constitutions of many states.

CLAUDIO v. STATE
MAYMI v. STATE
585 A.2d 1278 (Del. 1991)

HOLLAND, J.

The defendants' claim of error presents a novel question in this jurisdiction. The defendants contend that the trial judge improperly substituted an alternate juror for a regular juror after the jury's deliberations had begun. Before the twelve jurors retired to deliberate on the guilt/innocence phase of the trial, the trial judge read his instructions to the twelve regular jurors and the three alternates. When the jury had not reached a verdict at 5:00 p.m., it was sequestered separately as required by title 11, section 4209(b) of the Delaware Code.

The jury began its deliberations at approximately 10:30 a.m. on December 1, 1987. During the first day of deliberations, the jury requested a view of the face of the defendant, Claudio. The trial judge acceded to this request. The twelve jurors and the three alternates were brought back into the courtroom to view Claudio. When the jury had not reached a verdict at 5:00 p.m., it was sequestered for the night.

During the night, one of the regular jurors became ill. The next morning, December 2, he was excused by the trial judge. The trial judge decided to replace the ill juror with one of the alternates, who had been separately sequestered during the first day of deliberations. Defense counsel moved for a mistrial. That motion was denied.

The judge asked the three alternates if they had discussed the case among themselves during their sequestration. The alternates stated they had not discussed the case. The trial judge then permitted the first alternate to become a member of the regular jury in place of the incapacitated juror. Thereafter, the trial judge gave a special instruction to the reconstituted jury. In particular, he instructed the jury to begin its deliberations anew and emphasized the importance of the alternate familiarizing herself with the views of the other eleven jurors.

The reconstituted jury began its deliberations at approximately 9:30 a.m. It deliberated until approximately 5:00 that evening, breaking only for lunch. The jury reconvened at approximately 10:00 a.m. on December 3. It deliberated until it took a break for lunch at noon. The jury continued deliberating after lunch. At approximately 2:00 p.m., the jury indicated that it had arrived at verdicts on all charges. Thus, the jury deliberated six-and-one-half hours prior to the substitution of the alternate juror and the reconstituted jury deliberated "anew" for approximately nine-and-one-half hours.

Claudio and Maymi also contend that the substitution of an alternate juror during the deliberative process violates their right to trial by jury, as it is guaranteed by the Delaware Constitution. The constitutions adopted by the original States and "the constitution of every State entering the Union thereafter, in one form or another," have protected the right to trial by jury in criminal cases. *Duncan v. Louisiana,* 391 U.S. 145, 153 (1968). "The guarantees of jury trial in the Federal and State Constitutions reflect a *profound judgment* about the *way* in which law should be enforced and justice administered."

The Delaware Constitution is not a mirror image of the United States Constitution. The right to a trial by jury in the Delaware Constitution is not phrased identically to its corollary in the original federal Constitution or the federal Bill of Rights. Del. Const. art. I, §§ 4 and 7; U.S. Const. art. III and amend. 6. A review of the history and origin of the right to trial by jury in the Delaware Constitution, *vis-a-vis* the history and origins of that right in the United States Constitution, reveals that the differences in phraseology between the Delaware and the federal right to trial by jury are not merely stylistic. There is, in fact, a significant substantive difference in that historic right, as it has been preserved for Delaware's citizens.

Delaware History of Jury Trials

The right to trial by jury which is provided for in the Delaware Constitution has a long and distinguished historical origin. "Jury trial came to America with English colonists and received strong support from them." *Duncan v. Louisiana,* 391 U.S. at 152. The legal heritage from England was followed in the Delaware courts. It is probable that a jury was empaneled in Delaware as early as 1669. By 1675, trial by jury had become a fixed institution in Delaware.

The American colonies resented royal interference with the right to trial by jury. On October 14, 1774, the First Continental Congress declared:

> That the respective colonies are entitled to the common law of England, and
> more especially to the great and inestimable privilege of being tried by their
> peers of the vicinage, according to the course of that law.

The Declaration of Independence stated solemn objections to the King's "depriving us in many cases, of the benefits of Trial by Jury. . . ." *Duncan v. Louisiana,* 391 U.S. at 152.

Following the signing of the Declaration of Independence on July 4, 1776, several states adopted their own constitutions, which included their own "bills of rights." A convention met in Delaware at New Castle on August 27, 1776, to draft a Constitution for Delaware. One of the delegates to that convention was Richard Bassett. The importance of Richard Bassett's participation in framing Delaware's original Constitution, for the purpose of this case, will become apparent.

The Declaration of Rights and Fundamental Rules of the State of Delaware was adopted by the convention on September 11, 1776. Section 13 of that declaration provided: "That trial by jury of facts where they arise is one of the greatest securities of the lives, liberties, and estates of the people."

Shortly thereafter, the first Constitution of the State of Delaware was enacted on September 20, 1776. Article 25 of that first Delaware Constitution stated:

> *The common law of England,* as well as so much of the statute law as have been
> heretofore adopted in practice in this state, *shall remain in force,* unless they
> shall be altered by a future law of the Legislature; such parts only excepted as
> are repugnant to the rights and privileges contained in this constitution and the
> declaration of rights, & c. agreed to by this convention. (emphasis added).

Thus, Delaware commenced its existence as an independent State with an unambiguous expression of its intention to perpetuate the right to trial by jury, as it had existed at common law, for its citizens.

During the Revolutionary War, the states governed themselves with virtual autonomy. After securing their freedom from England, the states were reluctant to subject themselves to any other central government, particularly one with substantial powers. Consequently, when the several independent states united following the American Revolutionary War, pursuant to the Articles of Confederation, each state's own sovereignty was made paramount to the national sovereignty. Moreover, since "the Articles of Confederation asserted no authority over individuals," it also afforded no individual protections. Therefore, Delaware's citizens continued to be protected by the Declaration of Fundamental Rights and the Constitution which had been adopted by Delaware in 1776.

Delaware and Debates on the Federal Right to Trial by Jury

When the Constitution of the United States was being considered for ratification in other states, one of the overriding concerns expressed by many was the effect that the presence of a strong central government and the absence of a federal Bill of Rights would have on fundamental rights which had existed at common law, e.g., trial by jury. Article III of the proposed federal Constitution provided that "[t]he Trial of all Crimes…shall be by Jury; and such Trial shall be held in the State where the said Crimes shall have been committed." "The 'very scanty history of this provision in the records of the Constitutional Convention' sheds little light either way on the intended correlation between Article III's 'jury' and the features of the jury at common law." However, in John Dickinson's view, the provision in Article III perpetuated the right to trial by jury as it had existed at common law.

In stating that view in 1788 and urging other states to follow Delaware's lead in ratifying the federal Constitution, John Dickinson described several aspects of the common law right to trial by jury in detail. Dickinson's understanding of Article III and the common law right to trial by jury is particularly instructive in this case.

> It seems highly probable, that those who would reject this labour of public love [the proposed Constitution], would also have rejected the Heaven-taught institution of trial by jury, had they been consulted upon its establishment. Would they not have cried out, that there never was framed so detestable, so paltry, and so tyrannical a device for extinguishing freedom, and throwing unbounded domination into the hands of the king and barons, under a contemptible pretence of preserving it? "What!…Why then is it insisted on; but because the fabricators of it know that it will, and intend that it shall reduce the people to slavery? Away with it—Freemen will never be enthralled by so insolent, so execrable, so pitiful a contrivance."
>
> Happily for us our ancestors thought otherwise. They were not so over-nice and curious, as to refuse blessing, because, they might possibly be abused….
>
> Trial by Jury is our birth-right; and tempted to his own ruin, by some seducing spirit, must be the man, who in opposition to the genius of United American, shall dare to attempt its subversion….
>
> In the proposed confederation, it is preserved inviolable in criminal cases, and cannot be altered in other respects, but when United America demands it.

Despite the assurances from John Dickinson and other Federalist writers, fears had continued to be expressed that Article III's provision failed to preserve *all of the common-law rights* to trial by jury, *e.g.*, the right to be tried by a "jury of the vicinage." That concern, as well as the desire "to preserve the right to jury in civil as well as criminal cases, furnished part of the impetus for introducing amendments to the Constitution that ultimately resulted in the jury trial provisions of the Sixth and Seventh Amendments."

When President George Washington gave his first annual message to Congress in 1789, he noted that demands for amendments to the United States Constitution were widespread. On June 8, 1789, not long after

President Washington's first annual message to Congress, James Madison addressed the House of Representatives. The proposed amendments to the United States Constitution, which were described by Madison in that address, covered all of the provisions which eventually became the federal Bill of Rights.

The amendment relating to jury trial in criminal cases, as introduced by James Madison in the House, would have provided that: "The trial of all crimes...shall be by an impartial jury of freeholders of the vicinage, with the requisite of unanimity for conviction, of the right of challenge, and other accustomed requisites." That Amendment passed the House in substantially the same form in which it was submitted. For the purpose of this case, it is important to note the common law form in which the right to trial by jury originally passed in the United States House of Representatives, since John Vining of Delaware was the Chairman of the House Committee Select which had studied Madison's proposals.

After more than a week of debate in the Senate, Madison's proposed amendment with regard to trial by jury was returned to the House in a considerably altered form. "The version that finally emerged from the Committee was the version that ultimately became the Sixth Amendment, ensuring an accused: the right to a speedy and public trial, by an impartial jury of the State and district wherein the crime shall have been committed, which district shall have been previously ascertained by law." The provisions spelling out such *common-law features* of the jury as "unanimity," or "the accustomed requisites" *were gone.* The "vicinage" requirement had been replaced by wording that reflected a compromise between broad and narrow definitions of that term. Thus, it was left to Congress to determine the actual size of the "vicinage" through the establishment of judicial districts. Significantly, one of Delaware's first two United States Senators during the time of this debate was Richard Bassett. Senator Bassett voted in favor of the common law right to trial by jury, as originally proposed by Madison and recommended by the House Committee Select, chaired by John Vining.

The United States Supreme Court has concluded that three significant features may be observed in the history of the enactment of the United States Constitution's jury trial provisions.

> First, even though the vicinage requirement was as much a feature of the common-law jury as was the twelve-man requirement, the mere reference to "trial by jury" in Article III was not interpreted to include that feature....Second, provisions that would have explicitly tied the "jury" concept to the "accustomed requisites" of the time were eliminated....Finally, contemporary legislative and constitutional provisions indicate that where Congress wanted to leave no doubt that it was incorporating existing common-law features of the jury system, it knew how to use express language to that effect. *Williams v. Florida,* 399 U.S. 78, 96 (1970).

Consequently, the United States Supreme Court has concluded that it is not "able to divine precisely what the word 'jury' imported to the Framers, the First Congress, or the States in 1789....But there is absolutely no indication in 'the intent of the Framers' of an explicit decision to equate the [United States] constitutional and common-law characteristics of the jury."

The debates about Madison's proposed amendments to the United States Constitution ended in 1791 with the adoption of the federal Bill of Rights. When the debates about the federal Bill of Rights were over, John Dickinson's interpretation of the phrase "trial by jury" in Article III, as preserving the common law right to trial by jury, had been proven incorrect. Moreover, despite the original urging of James Madison, the subsequent endorsement of that recommendation by the House Committee Select, chaired by Delaware's Congressman John Vining and the support of Senators, such as Delaware's Richard Bassett, the effort to preserve *all* of the common law rights to trial by jury in the federal Bill of Rights had not prevailed. Congress had made an express decision not to preserve all of the features of the common law right to trial by jury, when it could have done so in the Sixth and Seventh Amendments to the United States Constitution.

On September 8, 1791, the Delaware General Assembly called for a state constitutional convention. The Delaware Constitutional Convention "assembled at Dover, on Tuesday, November 29, 1791, and elected John Dickinson, president." Delaware's United States Senator, Richard Bassett, who had been a delegate to the state constitutional convention in 1776 was also a delegate to the Delaware Constitutional Convention in 1791.

John Dickinson's involvement in the debates about the right to trial by jury in Article III, during the ratification process of the United States Constitution in 1788, as well as Congressman John Vining's and Senator Richard Bassett's involvement with the debates on that subject, preceding the enactment of the federal Bill of Rights in 1791, provide important historical insight into what happened in 1791, when Delaware decided to amend its own Constitution. After the debates about the meaning of the term "trial by jury" in Article III and the provisions on that subject to be included in the federal Bill of Rights were finished, Delawareans, especially John Dickinson and Richard Bassett, were acutely aware of the need to set forth an intention to perpetuate fundamental rights, as they had existed at common law, in unambiguous language.

When the amendments to the United States Constitution, which had been proposed by Madison, were being discussed by the House of Representatives Committee Select, John Vining had urged "a plainness and simplicity of style on this and every other occasion, which should be easily understood." John Vining's advice was followed by Dickinson, Bassett, and the other delegates to the 1791 Delaware Constitutional

Convention. When the convention concluded its work on December 31, 1791, its draft of the proposed Delaware Constitution provided that "trial by jury shall be as heretofore," i.e., the provision in the 1776 Delaware Constitution perpetuating the guarantee of trial by jury as it existed at common law.

Thus, Delaware's unambiguous commitment to the preservation of the common law right to trial by jury was evidenced with a "simplicity of style." The draft was signed by the members of the Delaware Constitutional Convention on January 12, 1792. The signatures of the long-time champions of the common law right to trial by jury, John Dickinson and Richard Bassett, signify their satisfaction and approval of the provision that "trial by jury shall be as heretofore" in the December 31, 1791, draft. That draft was adopted, without change, as Delaware's Constitution later in 1792.

Delaware's constitutional commitment to continue to guarantee the right to trial by jury for its citizens, as it existed at common law, was expressly recognized in the arguments presented in the earliest reported decision to construe the phrase "trial by jury shall be as heretofore" in the Delaware Constitution of 1792:

> The [Delaware] Constitution is express that "trial by jury shall be as heretofore," plainly intending to secure both the form and the substance, the trial and the constitution of the jury.
>
> The framers of the [Delaware] Constitution of 1776 were aware of that importance, when they declared it to be a fundamental rule "that trial by jury of facts where they arise is one of the greatest securities of the lives, liberties and estates of the people." The provision in the present Constitution is stronger and more positive, "Trials by jury shall be as heretofore."
>
> A comparison of the [Delaware] Constitution or System of Government and Declaration of Rights of 1776 with the present Constitution will convince any one, if a doubt exists on the subject, that the Convention of 1792 had the old Constitution before them and made it in fact the groundwork of their labors; for many of its most important provisions are inserted in the present Constitution without the slightest variation even of the expressions, while other principles of the old system are adopted in language differing but little in its terms, and bearing precisely the same purport. The fourteenth section of the Declaration of Rights is made the seventh section of first article of the present [Delaware] Constitution, with this important exception, that it is not provided in the latter, as in the former, that no person shall be found guilty without the unanimous consent of an impartial jury. But are we therefore to suppose that it was intended to vest the legislature with the power of enacting that a person accused of a criminal offense might be convicted upon the finding of a majority of a jury? By no means. It was considered that this principle was secured by the fourth section, which says that "trial by jury shall be as heretofore," and a repetition of it was deemed unnecessary. *Wilson v. Oldfield*, Clayton 169, 1 Delaware Cases 622, 624-27 (1818).

The teaching of *Oldfield* was ratified and reaffirmed by this Court one hundred and fifty years later:

> It is of course fundamental under our law that the verdict of a jury must be unanimous. This follows from article I, section 4 of the Delaware Constitution, providing that, "The right to trial by jury shall be as heretofore." This provision of our Constitution guarantees the right to trial by jury as it existed at common law....Unanimity of the jurors is therefore required to reach a verdict since such was the common law rule. *Fountain v. State*, 275 A.2d 251 (Del. 1971).

One year earlier, in 1970, the Delaware Constitution Revision Commission had written in its study commentary:

> Article I, section 4, of the present constitution deals with three distinct subjects: (1) Right of trial by jury in civil cases; (2) right of trial by jury in criminal cases; and (3) requirement, composition, and conduct of the grand jury. Since the three types of juries, including special juries, existed at common law, the 1792 Constitution's adoption of the right of trial by jury "as heretofore," and its carryover in successive constitutions to date, brings forward to the present day reliance on the common law as to right of the petit jury in civil and criminal actions, the special jury in civil actions, and the grand jury. Because of this situation, reference must always be made to common law to properly interpret the meaning of the present constitution.

Article I, section 4 of the Delaware Constitution still provides that "[t]rial by jury shall be as heretofore." This language has appeared in article I, section 4 of three successive Delaware constitutions—1792, 1831 and 1897. This language was left unchanged when article I, section 4 was amended as recently as 1984. This Court and the other courts of Delaware have always construed that provision in the Delaware Constitution as "guaranteeing the right to trial by jury as it existed at common law."

In *Williams v. Florida,* when examining the federal Constitutional right to a jury trial, the United States Supreme Court stated:

> While "the intent of the Framers" is often an elusive quarry, the relevant constitutional history casts considerable doubt on the easy assumption in our past decisions that if a given feature existed in a jury at common law in 1789, then it was necessarily preserved in the Constitution.

After an extensive review of the history leading to the actual wording of the right to trial by jury in the federal Bill of Rights, the United States Supreme Court concluded:

> [T]here is absolutely no indication in "the intent of the Framers" of an explicit decision to equate the constitutional and common-law characteristics of the jury.

Accordingly, the United States Supreme Court has turned to other than purely historical considerations to determine which features of the jury system, as it existed at common law, were preserved in the United States Constitution.

Conversely, it is untenable to conclude that the right to trial by jury in the Delaware Constitution means exactly the same thing as that right in the

United States Constitution. The history of the right to trial by jury "as heretofore," which has remained unchanged in the Delaware Constitution since 1792, demonstrates an unambiguous intention to equate Delaware's constitutional right to trial by jury with the common law characteristics of that right. Consequently, all of the fundamental features of the jury system, as they existed at common law, have been preserved for Delaware's citizens. Therefore, the proper focus of any analysis of the right to trial by jury, as it is guaranteed in the Delaware Constitution, requires an examination of the common law.

At common law, when a member of a jury became ill or died during the trial, the jury was discharged. The other eleven members of the jury were then recalled along with another juror to complete the twelve. The parties were given their full complement of challenges and afforded the opportunity to use them against the reconstituted panel. Once a new jury was selected and sworn, the trial began anew. This was obviously a costly and time consuming process.

This Court and others have recognized the validity of implementing procedures which improve the operation of the jury system, as it existed at common law, *without* changing the fundamental common law features of right to trial by jury. For example, in an effort to save scarce judicial resources, statutes and court rules have been enacted which permit the selection of alternate jurors at the beginning of the trial when the regular jurors are selected. Delaware adopted a rule analogous to that used in the federal system. Superior Court Criminal Rule 24(c) permits the selection of up to four alternates along with the regular jury, to "replace jurors who, prior to the time the jury retires to consider its verdict, become or are found to be unable or disqualified to perform their duties."

The present procedure in the Superior Court, which provides for the simultaneous selection of regular and alternate jurors and allows alternate jurors to be substituted prior to the commencement of the jury's deliberations, is the functional equivalent of the common law system. The jurors and the alternates are assiduously instructed not to discuss the case until it has been submitted to them for deliberation.

The present practice preserves the common law system of submitting the case to twelve persons, who deliberate for the first time, only after all of the evidence has been presented. As one court has stated:

> There is no question that the provision for the substitution of alternate jurors prior to the submission of the case to the jury is constitutional. During the course of the trial the 12 regular jurors and the alternate jurors are treated similarly in all respects. And since the jurors are not permitted to discuss the case among themselves until it is submitted to them, there is no way in which the defendants' rights could be prejudiced if 1 or more of the 12 jurors are replaced by an alternate juror. Twelve jurors who hear the evidence and are in all respects treated as jurors participate in the deliberations and render a verdict.

In fact, the present procedure, pursuant to Superior Court Criminal Rule 24, which provides for the use of alternate jurors and their substitution prior to the commencement of the jury's deliberations has been upheld under the Delaware Constitution by this Court.

Although the substitution of an alternate juror prior to the commencement of the jury's deliberations is the functional equivalent of the practice at common law, the substitution of an alternate juror during the jury's deliberations is the antithesis of the practice at common law. At common law, the commencement of the jury's deliberative process marked a unique and inviolate stage of the trial proceeding. As one commentator notes:

> In 1354, we find among the Parliament Rolls a striking petition,…"that hereafter when any people are at issue and the inquest is charged and sworn, all evidence which is to be said (*totes evidences que sont a dire*) be openly said at the bar, so that after the inquest departs with its charge, no justice or other person have conference (*parlance*) with them to move or procure the said inquest, but that they say the fact upon their own peril and oath." This petition was granted.

In the 18th century, Blackstone wrote:

> Our law has therefore wisely placed this strong and two-fold barrier, of a presentment and a trial by jury, between the liberties of the people, and the prerogative of the crown....[T]he founders of the English law have with excellent forecast contrived, that…the truth of every accusation, whether preferred in the shape of indictment, information, or appeal, should afterwards be confirmed by the unanimous suffrage of twelve of his equals and neighbours, indifferently chosen and superior to all suspicion.

Blackstone described the jury's deliberative process as follows:

> The jury, after the proofs are summed up, unless the case be very clear, withdraw from the bar to consider of their verdict: and, in order to avoid intemperance and causeless delay, are to be kept without meat, drink, fire, or candle, unless by the permission of the judge, till they are all unanimously agreed.

Thus, at common law, once it retired to consider its verdict, "the jury" was irrevocably constituted. The deliberative process was required to continue inviolate by those twelve persons "until they are all unanimously agreed."

All of the fundamental features of the right to trial by jury, as they existed at common law, have been preserved by the Delaware Constitution. This Court has expressly held that under the Delaware Constitution, unanimity of the jurors is required to reach a verdict since such was the common law rule. It has also been expressly recognized that the Delaware Constitution guarantees the common law right to a trial by a jury of twelve persons in a criminal proceeding. Similarly, the right to trial by jury at common law required a unanimous verdict by the same twelve jurors who retired to deliberate. Thus, that common law characteristic of the right to trial by jury in a criminal proceeding is guaranteed by the Delaware Constitution.

At common law, the rule was "[i]f a juror becomes unable to serve after the jury retires to deliberate, a mistrial must be declared if one or both parties refuse to stipulate to a verdict delivered by a jury of less than twelve members." In this case, the substitution of an alternate juror during the deliberative process was in derogation of the common law. Consequently, it was contrary to defendants' right to trial by jury "as heretofore," which has been guaranteed by the Delaware Constitution since 1792.

NOTES

1. The unanimity requirement of the Delaware Constitution applies to the jury's determination of a statutory aggravating circumstance in the penalty phase of a capital case. *Capano v. State*, 889 A.2d 968 (Del. 2006).

2. In criminal cases, the Pennsylvania Constitution provides the prosecution "shall have the same right to trial by jury as does the accused." Pa. Const. art. I, § 6; *Commonwealth v. White*, 910 A.2d 648 (Pa. 2006) (prosecution asserted the right).

3. The Montana Constitution requires the state's consent to waive a jury trial in a criminal case. Mont. Const. art. II, § 26.

4. The Delaware Constitution provides that "judges shall not charge juries with respect to matters of fact, but may state the questions of fact in issue and declare the law." Del. Const. art. IV, § 19; *Herring v. State*, 805 A.2d 872, 876 (Del. 2002).

5. Some state constitutions not only specify the number of jurors required in a criminal proceeding but distinguish between the number of jurors needed when the charged offense is either a felony or misdemeanor. Article I, section 16 of the California Constitution provides:

> In criminal actions in which a felony is charged, the jury shall consist of 12 persons. In criminal actions in which a misdemeanor is charged, the jury shall consist of 12 persons or a lesser number agreed on by the parties in open court.

6. Article I, section 18(a) of the New York Constitution provides:

> The Legislature may provide that in any court of original jurisdiction a jury shall be composed of six or twelve persons . . ., provided, however, that crimes prosecuted by indictment shall be tried by a jury composed of twelve persons, unless a jury trial has been waived.

7. The Utah Constitution requires "jury unanimity" as to a specific crime and as to each element of the crime. *State v. Saunders*, 992 P.2d 951 (Utah 1999).

8. The elimination of jury trial for offenses punishable by less than six months in jail violated the New Hampshire Constitution because the

framers intended to guarantee jury trial to all facing the possibility of incarceration. *Opinion of the Justices*, 608 A.2d 202 (N.H. 1992).

B. SELF-INCRIMINATION

The federal Fifth Amendment provides in part: "No person...shall be compelled in any criminal case to be a witness against himself." Textual differences in about twenty state constitutions broaden the scope of the privilege beyond compelled testimonial evidence by providing that: "No person shall be compelled to give evidence against himself." *See* Conn. Const. art. I, § 8; *see also* Pa. Const. art. I, § 9 ("In all criminal prosecutions the accused...cannot be compelled to give evidence against himself. . . ."). The origin of this wording was probably the Virginia provision, *see* Va. Const. art. I, § 8 (The accused "shall not...be compelled in any criminal proceeding to give evidence against himself") or the Massachusetts provision. *See* Mass. Const. pt. I, art. XII ("No subject shall be...compelled to accuse, or furnish evidence against himself."). Other states adopted those models rather than the federal one. *See* Miss. Const. art. III, § 26 ("In all criminal prosecutions the accused...shall not be compelled to give evidence against himself."); Tex. Const. art. I, § 19 ("In all criminal prosecutions the accused...shall not be compelled to give evidence against himself.").

STATE v. ARMSTEAD
262 S.E.2d 233 (Ga. Ct. App. 1979)

SHULMAN, Judge.

This is an interlocutory appeal from the trial court's denial of the state's motion to compel defendant to produce handwriting exemplars. We affirm.

In considering whether the state may compel an individual to produce handwriting exemplars, the following constitutional and statutory law is relevant. Article I, section I, paragraph XIII of the Georgia Constitution of 1976 states: "No person shall be compelled to give testimony tending in any manner to criminate himself." Section 38-416 of the Georgia Code provides: "No person, who shall be charged in any criminal proceeding with the commission of any indictable offense or any offense punishable on summary conviction, shall be compellable to give evidence for or against himself." Ga. Code Ann. § 38-416 (1962).

In *Creamer v. State*, 192 S.E.2d 350 (Ga. 1972), our Supreme Court, in considering these provisions, held that although evidence may be compulsorily adduced from an accused, it is constitutionally impermissible to compel an accused to perform an act which results in the production of incriminating evidence. The distinction is between forcing an accused to do an act against his will and requiring an accused to submit to an act. While the latter "takes evidence from the defendant," and is constitutionally acceptable, the former compels the defendant, in essence, to give evidence which violates an individual's right not to incriminate himself.

Thus, even though one's handwriting may be identifying physical indicia, forcing a defendant to produce such handwriting is not sanctioned by our Constitution. To compel a handwriting exemplar is to compel the defendant to do an act, not to submit to an act.

The fact that the United States Supreme Court has held that handwriting exemplars can be compelled—which compulsion does not violate the Fifth Amendment privilege against self-incrimination, *see Gilbert v. California*, 388 U.S. 263 (1967)—does not require a different result in the present case.

"Georgia has long granted more protection to its citizens than has the United States and…while the States cannot grant less protection (they) can grant more."

"While the language in the United States Constitution has long been construed to be limited to 'testimony,' the Georgia Constitution has been construed to limit the State from forcing the individual to present Evidence, oral or real." It is clear that the "evidence" contemplated in the Code is not limited to that which is deemed testimonial. An accused cannot be compelled to produce evidence, oral or real, regardless of whether or not it is "testimonial." To force the defendant, then, to produce samples of his handwriting potentially incriminating evidence which may be used as evidence in the defendant's prosecution would violate constitutional sanctions against self-incrimination.

Neither *Bradford v. State*, 164 S.E.2d 264 (Ga. Ct. App. 1968), nor *Reeves v. State*, 228 S.E.2d 201 (Ga. Ct. App. 1976), necessitates a contrary result.

In *Bradford*, this court held that a person could be compelled by the state to give a voice exemplar—that the mere use of the defendant's voice as an identifying physical characteristic did not involve or abridge rights of the defendant under the Fifth Amendment. Since *Bradford* does not involve a claim that rights afforded under Georgia law and the Georgia Constitution were abridged, *Bradford* is not dispositive of the issue before us.

The issue presented in *Reeves* was the scope of Fourth Amendment protection in regard to one's handwriting. In holding that the defendant had no reasonable expectation of privacy in his handwriting so as to invoke Fourth Amendment protection, the court did not address the issue presented here, i.e., the issue of compulsory production of one's handwriting. *Cf. Hyde v. State*, 26 S.E.2d 744 (Ga. 1943), recognizing the distinction between the right to be free from unreasonable searches and seizures and the right not to incriminate oneself. *Reeves*, therefore, is not controlling authority for the state's position.

Since we have determined that to compel handwriting exemplars of the defendant would compel him to produce criminating evidence in violation of rights afforded under Georgia law, the judgment of the trial court must be affirmed.

C. RIGHT TO COUNSEL

BRYAN v. STATE
571 A.2d 170 (Del. 1990)

MOORE, J.

Ransford H. Bryan, III, was convicted by a jury of murder in the first degree, possession of a deadly weapon during the commission of a felony, and theft of over $500 by false pretenses. Bryan contends that the trial court erred in denying his motion to suppress a confession made to police during a custodial interrogation despite his attorney's repeated admonitions not to question the defendant in the absence of counsel. Moreover, the interrogation of Bryan commenced despite the fact that counsel for Bryan had contacted the police investigators following Bryan's arrest and had specifically warned the police not to question the suspect in his absence.

Bryan raises several issues on appeal, but we address only one: Whether a knowing waiver of the right to counsel, guaranteed in Delaware by article I, section 7 of the Constitution of 1897, can occur when the State prevents counsel, whom the State knows has been designated and retained to represent the defendant, from rendering effective legal assistance to his client during a custodial interrogation. In our opinion such police conduct is thoroughly incompatible with fundamental principles of the Delaware Constitution. Accordingly, we reverse.

The defendant was an 18-year-old youth who had had no previous dealings with the criminal justice system. He had just graduated from high school and was living with a friend, Douglas Brockway, Jr.

On October 13, 1987, Brockway told his mother that he believed someone had been stealing money from his bank account using his Money Access Card (MAC). She advised him to contact his bank. The next day, October 14, Brockway went to the bank with his father and signed an affidavit of forgery alleging that money had been withdrawn from his account without his permission on four separate occasions, totaling $810. Later that day, Bryan's mother observed Brockway holding Bryan against a wall and threatening him. He said, "If I find out that you are—that you did this, it is going to be between you and me."

The following day, October 15, Bryan and Brockway told Brockway's mother that they intended to go squirrel hunting. The boys took a twenty-gauge shotgun with them. There is a dispute as to how the gun was removed from the house. Bryan claims that Brockway's gun was passed through the bedroom window, however, Brockway's mother claims that she saw Brockway carrying Bryan's shotgun with shells in hand out of the front door. In any event, the boys left the house together at approximately 6:30 p.m. About 45 minutes later Bryan returned home, alone.

Immediately upon returning Bryan told Brockway's mother that her son had a drug habit and owed $2,000 to a drug dealer. He also stated that he had made the withdrawals from Brockway's account as part of a conspiracy between Brockway and himself to defraud the bank in order to obtain money to pay off the drug debt. He said that Brockway intended to go to the bank and complain about the theft, get reimbursed, and use the proceeds to pay off the drug debt. He further claimed that Brockway had solicited his help to make the withdrawals in an effort not to alert Brockway's mother. During this discussion Bryan also stated that he and Brockway had not gone squirrel hunting, but had instead gone to a shopping center where Brockway, carrying $1,200, met a Mexican drug dealer. Bryan claimed that Brockway talked to the drug dealer, and then told Bryan that he was leaving with him. Bryan said that he saw Brockway drive off with the drug dealer in a red Pontiac.

Detective Warrington of the Delaware State Police began an investigation into the disappearance of Brockway on October 19. He interviewed the victim's mother, father and Bryan at the victim's house. Bryan participated in this interview voluntarily. During the interview Bryan related the Mexican-drug-dealer story. The interviews left Detective Warrington with some suspicions. Specifically, he was concerned first about the inconsistency concerning the removal of the shotgun from the house. Second, he wondered why Bryan related the drug story to the victim's mother and recanted the squirrel hunting story if the purpose of the squirrel hunting story was to cover up the alleged drug involvement. Third, he was concerned about Bryan's denial of knowledge of the $300 of Sussex Trust MAC money found in his wallet.

The following day, October 20, Detective Warrington re-interviewed Bryan and Brockway's family, inquiring into the particular inconsistencies in the defendant's story. Detective Warrington also asked Bryan directly at this time if he knew where Brockway was or had any more information regarding his whereabouts. Bryan denied any such knowledge. However, about this time the police received photographs from Brockway's bank showing Bryan withdrawing money from its MAC machine. The last photo showed defendant withdrawing $300 on October 13. Detective Warrington attempted to get Bryan to take a polygraph test, but his mother stated that retained counsel had advised against it, and that Bryan would not take the test.

On October 21, Bryan's retained counsel, Jack Rubin, a Baltimore lawyer, called Detective Warrington and told him that Bryan would not submit to a polygraph, and that he was not to interrogate Bryan unless there was a warrant for his arrest. Both Bryan and his mother were in Rubin's office during the call. Detective Warrington then told Rubin that he did in fact have a warrant for Bryan's arrest on charges of theft. Rubin then arranged for Bryan to turn himself in the following day and clearly stated to Detective Warrington that he was not to question Bryan and was to deal with the defendant only through counsel.

The following day, October 22, Bryan turned himself in on the theft warrant and was arraigned by a Justice of the Peace. Bryan was accompanied by a local Delaware attorney, who was co-counsel with Rubin. Detective Warrington did not request to question Bryan on this occasion. However, some time later, Detective Warrington telephoned Bryan's Delaware attorney and stated that, as a part of his investigation into Brockway's disappearance, he wanted more information from Bryan. Bryan's Delaware attorney advised Detective Warrington to contact Rubin concerning that request.

Thereafter, Detective Warrington spoke to Rubin, stressing his need for more information. Rubin stated that he would speak with Bryan. On October 27, Detective Warrington called Rubin to see if he had obtained any additional information concerning the whereabouts of Brockway. During that telephone call, Rubin and Detective Warrington scheduled a meeting in Delaware, at the State Police barracks near Lewes, for the following day. At the meeting, Rubin again informed Detective Warrington that the police were not to question Bryan and that all contact between the police and Bryan was to be through Rubin.

In the meantime, a preliminary hearing on the theft charge had been scheduled for October 29. Rubin was becoming concerned that the theft charge and arrest were being used to coerce Bryan into giving a statement regarding the disappearance of Brockway. On October 29, Bryan, accompanied by his Delaware attorney and Rubin, appeared and waived his right to a preliminary hearing. Following Bryan's waiver of a preliminary hearing, Rubin confronted Warrington with his concern. Warrington acknowledged that the theft charge and investigation into Brockway's disappearance were "all interrelated." Consequently, while they were still in the Sussex County Courthouse, Rubin again told Warrington, in Bryan's presence, that Bryan had asserted his right to remain silent and wished to deal with the police only through counsel.

On November 6, two deer hunters found a body in a wooded area near Route 277. The body was clad in a green and white tee shirt matching the description of the tee shirt Brockway was wearing at the time of his disappearance. There were holes in the upper torso of the body consistent with multiple shotgun wounds.

Later that afternoon, Detective Warrington and another police officer went to the defendant's father's residence and informed him that Brockway's body had been found and that they intended to arrest Bryan for murder. Bryan's father was asked to come with them. The reason for this is unclear, however, Detective Warrington testified that Bryan's father agreed to go, and he felt that the father's presence might help "the truth come out." Detective Warrington also testified that they "needed to get the truth out and know exactly what happened that day." When Bryan's father asked Warrington to call Bryan's mother, who had been responsible for hiring Bryan's attorney earlier in the investigation, Warrington indicated that this could be done at the police station.

The police and Bryan's father went to the construction site where Bryan was working. There Bryan was arrested for first degree murder. At the police station Bryan and his father were permitted to talk alone for approximately 30 minutes. During that time the police called Bryan's mother, told her of the arrest, and informed her that Bryan's father was currently talking to her son. Several minutes later Rubin called Detective Warrington and told him again that "you know not to talk to him."

When Bryan's father emerged from the interrogation room he exclaimed, "He says he didn't do it." Two detectives, one of whom was Detective Warrington, immediately entered the room. Bryan was read his *Miranda* warnings but nothing was said to him of Rubin's call. Bryan did not ask for a lawyer and an interrogation ensued, culminating in Bryan making a statement that he accidentally shot Brockway. Bryan then took Detective Warrington to the location where he left the guns and some of the victim's clothing. He acknowledged that his gun inflicted the fatal wounds.

On May 23, 1988, Bryan moved to suppress the statements he made and the tainted evidence flowing from those statements on grounds that the statements were obtained in violation of his rights under the Fourth, Fifth and Sixth amendments to the United States Constitution, and under sections 6 and 7 of the Delaware Constitution of 1897. The motion was denied by the trial court.

Miranda v. Arizona, 384 U.S. 436 (1966), requires that police advise those whom they subject to custodial interrogation of their constitutional rights. Before police may interrogate a suspect in custody, they must obtain a waiver by that suspect of his rights. To be effective, a waiver of rights must be voluntary, knowing and intelligent.

Our decision today examines the prerequisites for a voluntary, knowing and intelligent waiver of the right to counsel in Delaware. Our most recent examination of the issue was in *Weber*.

There, relying in part on article I, section 7 of the Delaware Constitution, we held that:

> To...effectuate the protection given to the accused by *Miranda,* and ensure that a suspect knowingly and intelligently waives his rights, we establish the following rule for the guidance of the trial court: if prior to or during custodial interrogation, and unknown to the suspect, a specifically retained or properly designated lawyer is actually present at the police station seeking an opportunity to render legal advice or assistance to the suspect, and the police intentionally or negligently fail to inform the suspect of that fact, then any statement obtained after the police themselves know of the attorney's efforts to assist the suspect, or any evidence derived from any such statement, is not admissible on any theory that the suspect intelligently and knowingly waived his right to remain silent and his right to counsel as established by *Miranda.*

Weber was decided in the context of a lawyer being present at a police station and attempting to render legal advice to his client.

For purposes of the protections afforded by the Delaware Constitution, there is no distinction between an in-person request by retained counsel to render assistance to his client and a telephonic request by that lawyer. The relevant inquiry is not whether counsel is physically present at the interrogation site, but simply whether specifically retained counsel has made a reasonable, diligent and timely attempt to consult with his client or otherwise render legal services.

The denial of the assistance of counsel is a violation of the due process of law guaranteed by article I, section 7 of the Delaware Constitution. Accordingly, the procedural protections afforded by the Delaware Constitution demand that an accused be afforded the unqualified opportunity to consult with counsel prior to custodial interrogation, provided that (i) the lawyer has clearly made a reasonable, diligent and timely attempt to render legal advice or otherwise perform legal services on behalf of his client, the accused, and (ii) the lawyer has been specifically retained or designated to represent the accused.

Furthermore, when counsel has been specifically designated and retained to represent a suspect and the suspect has clearly made police aware of his desire to deal with police only through his counsel during the investigation leading to the arrest, we impose a heavy presumption against waiver if the lawyer is present and denied access to his client, or, as here, has repeatedly advised the police that no interrogations of the defendant were to occur. We adopt this presumption because an abrupt decision by a suspect to waive his right to counsel without counsel being present, after previously expressing a desire to have his lawyer present, undermines any notion of a knowing, voluntary and intelligent waiver. The Supreme Court has expressed a similar concern: "[T]he accused having expressed his own view that he is not competent to deal with the authorities without legal advice, a later decision at the authorities' insistence to make a statement without counsel's presence may properly be viewed with skepticism."

Although this presumption bears some resemblance to the New York rule, under which a suspect may never waive his right to counsel in the absence of his attorney, we specifically decline to adopt that principle, and reaffirm our decision in *Weber* to that effect. The presumption does not alter the principle that a suspect may knowingly, intelligently and voluntarily waive his right to counsel, even without consulting with his counsel, after first being informed of counsel's efforts. The presumption reflects the additional weight accorded the "factor" or "circumstance" of a consistent prior course of dealing with police under a totality of circumstances analysis, required before a waiver will be considered knowing, voluntary and intelligent. As we have previously held, "the totality of the circumstances include[s] the behavior of the interrogators, the conduct of the defendant, his age, his intellect, his experience, and all other pertinent factors."

In evaluating the totality of the circumstances, a court makes a two-part inquiry. First, the waiver must have been voluntary—it must have been "the product of a free and deliberate choice rather than intimidation, coercion, or deception." Second, the waiver must have been made upon "a full awareness of both the nature of the right being abandoned and the consequences of the decision to abandon it." However, a purported waiver can never satisfy a totality of the circumstances analysis when police do not even inform a suspect that his attorney seeks to render legal advice.

We recognize that a defendant's right to have counsel present during questioning is his own; the decision whether to waive his right can only be made by the defendant and he need not follow the advice of his lawyer. Our holding simply recognizes that to knowingly, voluntarily and intelligently waive this right, a defendant must be informed that his counsel has attempted or is attempting to render legal advice or perform legal services on his behalf. To hold otherwise would be to condone "affirmative police interference in a communication between an attorney and suspect."

In reaching our decision we clarify the confusion in the trial court as to the difference in the protections afforded by article I, section 7 of the Delaware Constitution and by the Fifth Amendment to the United States Constitution. In *Moran v. Burbine,* the United States Supreme Court held that events occurring outside the presence of a suspect have no bearing on his ability to knowingly, voluntarily and intelligently waive his right to counsel under the Fifth Amendment of the United States Constitution. Accordingly, the Supreme Court refused to adopt a rule requiring police to inform a suspect of an attorney's efforts to reach him. Nonetheless, *Moran* invited the States to adopt a more stringent rule under their own constitutions. We do so here on independent State grounds.

Thus, in *Weber* we concluded that "a suspect, who is indifferent to the usual abstract offer of counsel, recited as part of the warnings required by *Miranda*," will not disdain an opportunity to consult with counsel he has specifically retained. It is undisputed that the Delaware Constitution may provide broader protections than the United States Constitution. This principle was expressly recognized in *Moran*: "Nothing we say today disables the States from adopting different requirements for the conduct of its employees and officials as a matter of state law." Accordingly, we decide this issue solely under article I, section 7 of the Delaware Constitution. This is in accord with the holdings of the highest courts of other states when presented with a situation analogous to that in *Moran*.

This brings us to an application of the foregoing legal principles. The trial court's findings of fact reveal deliberate, intentional and willful police conduct intended to subvert the protections afforded by the Delaware Constitution. Under the circumstances, the requirement of a knowing and voluntary waiver of counsel is of paramount importance to any inquiry.

The defendant made police aware of his desire to deal with them only through retained counsel on at least five occasions during the investigation and prior to his arrest. In that period, virtually all of the contact between the investigating officers and the defendant occurred in the presence of counsel. After the defendant's arrest Rubin contacted police and advised them again that they were not to interrogate the defendant in his absence.

Instead, the police disregarded these assertions of the defendant's rights and purportedly obtained a waiver of those rights without informing the defendant of his lawyer's latest attempt to render services on his behalf. The police then immediately interrogated the defendant and obtained a confession. Under such circumstances the defendant could not waive his right to counsel without first being informed that his lawyer was on the phone and was attempting to render legal advice. At a minimum, the defendant had an absolute right to know these facts, and any statement obtained from him violative of this right cannot pass muster under article I, section 7 of the Delaware Constitution.

Accordingly, the use of the confession against Bryan at trial, and evidence derived from it, constituted error. We therefore reverse and order a new trial.

NOTES

1. The Connecticut Constitution requires, as a matter of due process pursuant to article I, section 8, that police promptly inform a suspect of

timely efforts by retained counsel to render assistance. *State v. Stoddard*, 537 A.2d 446 (Conn. 1988).

2. The privilege against compelled self-incrimination in the Massachusetts and New Hampshire Constitutions required the rejection of *Moran. State v. Roache*, 803 A.2d 572 (N.H. 2002); *Commonwealth v. Mavredakis*, 725 N.E.2d 169 (Mass. 2000). Other states that have declined to follow *Moran* include Illinois, Kentucky, Michigan, Indiana, and New Jersey.

D. CONFRONTATION – FACE TO FACE

COMMONWEALTH v. LUDWIG
594 A.2d 281 (Pa. 1991)

ZAPPALA, J.

We granted review in this case to determine whether the use of closed circuit television testimony by an alleged child victim violates the confrontation clauses of the United States and Pennsylvania Constitutions. We hold that the confrontation clause of the Pennsylvania Constitution does not permit such infringement of a defendant's constitutional right to meet a witness face to face. The use of closed circuit television to transmit the testimony of the witness in this case violates the constitutional protection given to the defendant under article I, section 9 of the Pennsylvania Constitution. Consequently, we reverse the Order of the Superior Court upholding appellant's conviction and sentence.

On August 9, 1984, appellant was charged with rape, involuntary deviate sexual intercourse, incest, indecent assault, corrupting the morals of a minor, and endangering the welfare of children. The alleged victim of these crimes was appellant's five-year-old daughter. At the preliminary hearing, the victim testified that she did not remember what happened with appellant. The victim was unresponsive to further questioning, and the Commonwealth requested a continuance so that it could prepare a petition to the court seeking to use videotaped testimony at the preliminary hearing. The petition was filed by the Commonwealth, and a hearing held. At the hearing, the Commonwealth presented testimony of a psychologist to the effect that the victim had undergone "emotional freezing" at the preliminary hearing and that the condition could occur again. The psychologist also testified that the victim had become withdrawn following the incident, but was now making psychological progress. The psychologist was concerned that the progress might be impaired if the child was forced to testify in court in the physical presence of her father.

The court granted the Commonwealth's petition to the extent that it allowed the child to testify by way of closed circuit television. At the second preliminary hearing, the alleged victim did testify on closed circuit television and the evidence was deemed sufficient to hold the appellant for trial. Notwithstanding appellant's objection, the trial court allowed the same closed circuit television procedures to be employed during the trial itself.

A jury trial began on March 7, 1985. The child testified at the trial via closed circuit television from another room. The child's foster mother was permitted to sit next to the child while the child testified. Also in the room where the child was located was the video camera operator. The courtroom where the judge, prosecutor, defense counsel, appellant and jury were located was linked to the child by microphone. Although the child could not see the people in the courtroom, she could hear them and respond to their questions.

Article I, section 9 of our state constitution guarantees an accused the right to meet his accusers:

> In all criminal prosecutions the accused hath a right to be heard by himself and his counsel, to demand the nature and cause of the accusations against him, to meet the witnesses *face to face*...(emphasis added).

This language is unlike its federal counter-part, the Sixth Amendment, which provides that a defendant in a criminal case "shall enjoy the right...to be confronted with the witnesses against him."

In *Maryland v. Craig*, 497 U.S. 836 (1990), the United States Supreme Court was presented with a challenge to a Maryland statute which permitted closed circuit testimony if a judge determined that the child victim's testimony in the courtroom would result in serious emotional distress and the child's inability to communicate. The trial court rejected the defendant's objection to the procedure as violative of the confrontation clause of the Sixth Amendment to the United States Constitution. The Maryland Court of Appeals reversed, holding that the State did not present sufficient evidence to meet the requirements set forth in *Coy v. Iowa,* 487 U.S. 1012 (1988). The United States Supreme Court reversed in a five to four decision.

Writing for the majority, Justice O'Connor held that in *Coy v. Iowa*, the Court did construe the confrontation clause as guaranteeing the defendant a face to face meeting with witnesses. Since there had been no finding that the particular child witness needed special protection, no reason existed for disallowing face to face confrontation. However, the Court specifically reserved the issue of whether the confrontation clause guarantees an *absolute* right to a face to face meeting.

Reviewing federal case law, the majority held that the purpose of the confrontation clause was to insure that witnesses give testimony under oath, submit to cross-examination and permit observations of witness's demeanor to assist in the assessment of credibility. Thus, federal case law reflects a *preference* for face to face confrontation, not an absolute guarantee. However, a face to face confrontation may only be dispensed of where denial is necessary to further an important public policy and where the reliability of the testimony is otherwise assured. The Court concluded that a state's interest in the physical and psychological well being of child abuse victims may be sufficiently important to outweigh face to face confrontation.

In a stinging dissent, Justice Scalia, joined in by Justices Brennan, Marshall and Stevens, chastised the majority for applying an interest balancing analysis when the text of the Constitution does not permit it. The Defendant was not requesting an expansive interpretation of the scope of the Sixth Amendment but rather a strict adherence to its words. When a Constitutional guarantee is clear and explicit, as in this instance, an interest balancing analysis is the wrong approach. The confrontation clause does not guarantee reliable evidence but rather it guarantees specific trial procedures that were thought to assure reliable evidence. In effect, the majority subordinated an explicit constitutional protection to "current favored public policy."

Unlike the Sixth Amendment to the United States Constitution, article 1, section 9 of the Pennsylvania Constitution specifically provides for a "face to face" confrontation. We have long held that in interpreting our Constitution we are not bound by the United States Supreme Court's interpretation of similar federal constitutional provisions.

In *Commonwealth v. Sell*, we embraced the admonitions of Justice Brennan of the United States Supreme Court:

> [T]he decisions of the Court are not, and should not be, dispositive of questions regarding rights guaranteed by counter-part provisions of State Law. Accordingly, such decisions are not mechanical applicable to state law issues, and state court judges and the members of the bar seriously err if they so treat them. Rather, state court judges, and also practitioners, do well to scrutinize constitutional decisions by federal courts, for only if they are found to be logically persuasive and well-reasoned, paying due regard to precedent and the policies underlying specific constitutional guarantees, may they properly claim persuasive weight as guide posts when interpreting counter-part state guarantees.

We then refused to adopt the United States Supreme Court's abolition of "automatic standing" under the Fourth Amendment of the United States Constitution reaffirming our holding in *Commonwealth v. Tate* that the:

> State may provide through its constitution a basis for the rights and liberties of its citizens independent from that provided by the federal constitution, and that the rights so guaranteed may be more expansive than their federal counter-parts.

Most recently, in *Commonwealth v. Edmunds*, this Court was again requested to blindly adopt federal jurisprudence to support a "good faith" exception to the exclusionary rule as articulated by the United States Supreme Court in *United States v. Leon,* 468 U.S. 897 (1984). There, after an extensive review of the history of article 1, section 8, our precedents and policy considerations, we determined that adoption of federal jurisprudence was unwarranted.

Unlike its federal counter-part, article 1, section 9 of the Pennsylvania Constitution does not reflect a "preference" but clearly, emphatically and unambiguously requires a "face to face" confrontation. This distinction alone would require that we decline to adopt the United States Supreme Court's analysis and reasoning in *Maryland v. Craig.* However, in addition, we have our own case law which mandates a "face to face" confrontation.

In *Commonwealth v. Russo*, we addressed the "face to face" requirement of article I, section 9 of our Constitution, stating:

> Many people possess the trait of being loose tongued or willing to say something behind a person's back that they dare not or cannot truthfully say to his face or under oath in a courtroom. It was probably for this reason, as well as to give the accused the right to cross-examine his accusers and thereby enable the jury to better determine the credibility of the Commonwealth's witnesses and the strength and truth of its case, that this important added protection was given to every person accused of crime. We have no right to disregard or (unintentionally) erode or distort any provision of the constitution, especially where, as here, its plain and simple language make its meaning unmistakably clear; indeed, because of the times in which we live we have a higher duty than ever before to zealously protect and safeguard the constitution.

Although we were quite emphatic about the importance of this right, no right is absolute. Indeed, the right to confront an accuser is not without exception. In *Commonwealth v. Rodgers*, we permitted the prosecution to use preliminary hearing testimony of a witness at trial when that witness was unavailable. In *Commonwealth v. Stasko*, the prosecutor was permitted to use a videotape deposition of a witness unavailable for trial. In both instances, the original testimony was given in the presence of the defendant with the defendant having the opportunity to face and cross-examine his accuser. However, in each instance, the witnesses' subjective reactions to testifying in the presence of the accused were not a consideration.

Although we have recognized exceptions to the right to confront a witness, the policy reasons underlying those decisions are absent in this case. The witness in this case was neither unavailable nor subjected to cross-examination during prior testimony given in the presence of the accused. In fact, the trial judge instructed the jury that the victim was totally unaware of the existence of the trial itself: "We want [the child] to be as relaxed and casual and normal as possible and she doesn't really know that you are here in this setting. She doesn't really understand that this is all actually a trial. It probably has little significance to her."

Having diluted the significance of her testimony to that extent, it is questionable whether the victim would be testifying under the proper aura.

While we have recognized exceptions to the constitutional right of confrontation, we have done so only in those instances in which the accused has already had the opportunity to confront the witnesses against him face to face. We were satisfied that in those limited instances, the constitutional right to confront the witness had been afforded to the accused. Those decisions cannot be interpreted to permit restrictions on face to face confrontation where the right to confront the witness has *never* been afforded to the accused.

We are cognizant of society's interest in protecting victims of sexual abuse. However, that interest cannot be preeminent over the accused's constitutional right to confront the witnesses against him face to face. The record in this case does not disclose any conduct by the appellant during the proceedings that would give rise to the need to isolate the witness. The subjective fears of the witness, without more, are insufficient to restrict this important constitutional right. Since the trial court relied exclusively upon these fears, its actions cannot be affirmed. The appellant is entitled to face his accusers and the failure to protect that right was error. The appellant is therefore entitled to a new trial during which time the victim must testify in the courtroom before the judge, jury and appellant.

The Order of the Superior Court affirming the Order of the Court of Common Pleas of Monroe County is reversed.

NOTES

1. Following the holding of the Supreme Court of Pennsylvania in *Commonwealth v. Ludwig*, article I, section 9 of the Pennsylvania Constitution was amended.

2. Other states that have rejected as unconstitutional efforts to admit child testimony that was given outside the physical presence of the accused include Hawaii, Illinois, Indiana, New Hampshire, Utah, Texas, and Massachusetts.

3. The constitutions of Idaho, Nevada and North Dakota do not contain a clause that guarantees the right to confrontation.

E. DUTY TO PRESERVE EVIDENCE

HAMMOND v. STATE
569 A.2d 81 (Del. 1989)

HOLLAND, J.

The defendant-appellant, George M. Hammond, III, was convicted on June 2, 1988, following a jury trial, of two counts of Vehicular Homicide in the First Degree. Hammond was sentenced on August 17, 1988. Hammond filed this appeal on August 18, 1988.

In this appeal, Hammond argues that: the police negligently failed to gather and preserve evidence material to the preparation of his defense.

We find no reversible error. Therefore, the judgments of the Superior Court are affirmed.

Facts

On July 25, 1986, at about 5:00 a.m., Hammond, then age eighteen, Keith Douglas Moore, and Leon Buddy Carter, were involved in a single car accident. They were all occupants in an automobile which left the roadway and came to rest partially imbedded in the foundation of a townhouse that was under construction. The accident resulted in the deaths of Moore and Carter.

Officer William Wayne Walls of the City of Dover Police Department was one of the first persons to reach the accident scene. Walls testified as to what he saw when he arrived. Hammond was in the driver's seat of the vehicle, with his left shoulder against the left door, and his right shoulder against the driver's seat. Hammond's right leg, which was in a cast, was entangled between the accelerator and the brake pedal. Moore was also in the front seat area. Moore's head was on Hammond's chest and his feet were in the passenger's footwell. Carter was slumped over in the left rear seat.

Hammond testified in his own defense. His memory had been "hypnotically refreshed." Hammond stated that he graduated from high school on July 24, 1986, after completing summer courses. Following the graduation ceremony, Hammond and several friends celebrated at Scott William Kisters' apartment. Hammond, Carter, and Moore left Kister's apartment in the early morning hours of July 25, 1986, just prior to the accident. Hammond testified that they had all been drinking and that none of them were in "very good shape." He told the jury that Moore was driving Kisters' car at the time of the accident. According to Hammond's testimony, the force of the collision must have moved him and Moore about within the crash vehicle.

In support of his defense, Hammond presented testimony by Dr. George C. Govatos, a consulting engineer who was qualified as an accident reconstruction expert. Dr. Govatos testified about the kinematics of occupants in a crash vehicle, who are not wearing seatbelts. Dr. Govatos showed the jury a video tape of a test he had performed. The video tape depicted how the impact of a collision could cause the driver and the passenger to be thrown about and come to rest in each other's original seat. Dr. Govatos testified that an examination of the actual vehicle involved in the collision would have been important to his analysis because of the possibility of evidence in the interior of the vehicle that might have been left by the people as they were moved about by the collision, *e.g.*, hair, blood, pieces of clothing, or other physical evidence. Dr. Govatos testified that the existence of such evidence would have helped him to substantiate his opinion on the movement of Hammond and Moore within the crash vehicle. Dr. Govatos also testified that he would have needed the vehicle in order to determine whether mechanical failure could have caused or partially caused the collision.

The crash vehicle was not available to Dr. Govatos because the Dover police no longer had it in their possession when Hammond's attorney filed a discovery request on October 14, 1986. Although the crash vehicle had been towed from the scene and impounded, it was released by the Dover police on August 8, 1986. No evidence was collected from the vehicle by the Dover police before it was released. Hammond moved for a judgment of acquittal, or for a special instruction to the jury, as a result of the State's failure to preserve or to test the crash vehicle. The Superior Court denied both motions.

Right of Access to Evidence

The first issue raised by Hammond on appeal is that the failure of the Dover police to preserve the crash vehicle itself or to gather evidence of blood, clothing, tissue, and fingerprints, from inside of the crash vehicle, violated his constitutionally guaranteed right of access to evidence. This Court has recognized that the "obligation to preserve evidence is rooted in the due process provisions of the Fourteenth Amendment to the United States Constitution and the Delaware Constitution, article I, section 7." *Deberry v. State,* 457 A.2d 744, 751-52 (Del. 1983). The independent and alternative constitutional bases for our holding in *Deberry* is particularly significant in view of the subsequent development of the "access to evidence" doctrine in this Court and the United States Supreme Court. A review of the evolution of these precedents is not only instructive but necessary for a proper evaluation of Hammond's claim.

In *Deberry,* the question presented was "what relief is appropriate when the State had or should have had the requested evidence, but the evidence does not exist when the defense seeks its production?" In answering that inquiry, we held that claims of this type must be examined according to the following paradigm:

   1) Would the requested material, if extant in the possession of the State at the time of the defense request, have been subject to disclosure under Criminal Rule 16 or *Brady?*

   2) If so, did the government have a duty to preserve the material?

   3) If there was a duty to preserve, was the duty breached, and what consequences should flow from a breach?

The consequences which should flow from a breach of the duty to preserve evidence are determined in accordance with a separate three-part analysis which considers:

1) the degree of negligence or bad faith involved;

2) the importance of the missing evidence considering the probative value and reliability of secondary or substitute evidence that remains available; and

3) the sufficiency of the other evidence produced at the trial to sustain the conviction.

Bailey v. State, 521 A.2d 1069, 1091 (Del. 1987) (citing *Deberry v. State,* 457 A.2d at 752).

In *Deberry,* we concluded "[a] claim that *potentially* exculpatory evidence was lost or destroyed by the State can only be decided after each element of the above analysis has been considered." In *Deberry,* we also noted, for future guidance, the "agencies that create rules for evidence preservation should broadly define discoverable evidence to include any material that *could* be favorable to the defendant."

The year following our decision in *Deberry,* the United States Supreme Court decided *California v. Trombetta,* 467 U.S. 479 (1984). It held:

Whatever duty the Constitution imposes on the States to preserve evidence, that duty must be limited to evidence that might be expected to play a significant role in the suspect's defense. To meet this standard of constitutional materiality, evidence must both possess an exculpatory value that was apparent before the evidence was destroyed, and be of such a nature that the defendant would be unable to obtain comparable evidence by other reasonably available means.

This Court has examined the "access to evidence" doctrine following *Trombetta.* In doing so, we have not limited our inquiry to *Trombetta's* construction under the United States Constitution. Instead, we have held that "[w]hen a defendant claims that the State has failed to preserve evidence, by losing it after it has been gathered, the analysis which a [Delaware] Court must follow is set forth in *Deberry." Bailey v. State,* 521 A.2d at 1090; *see* Del. Const. art I, § 7.

Following our decision in *Bailey,* the United States Supreme Court decided *Arizona v. Youngblood,* 488 U.S. 51 (1988). It held:

The Due Process Clause of the Fourteenth Amendment, as interpreted in *Brady,* makes the good or bad faith of the State irrelevant when the State fails to disclose to the defendant material exculpatory evidence. But we think the Due Process Clause requires a different result when we deal with the failure of the State to preserve evidentiary material of which no more can be said than that it could have been subjected to tests, the results of which might have exonerated defendant....We therefore hold that unless a criminal defendant can show bad faith on the part of the police, failure to preserve potentially useful evidence does not constitute a denial of due process of law.

It appears that, as a matter of federal Constitutional law, the United States Supreme Court has developed a *hybrid approach* when a claim of denial of access to evidence is asserted. The principles of *Trombetta* are applicable to claims relating to a denial of access to *Brady* types of evidence. The "good faith" principles of *Youngblood* are applicable to allegations of a denial of access to potentially favorable types of evidence. However, in *Deberry,* in the event that *either* claim was made, this Court adopted a *unitary* approach.

In Hammond's case, the State has asked this Court to reconsider its decision in *Deberry,* in view of the holding in *Youngblood.* In *Deberry,* the conduct of the State was only one of three factors to be considered when potentially exculpatory evidence had not been preserved. The State argues that *Youngblood* has now established a *single* bright-line "good faith" test which should be applied by this Court in lieu of the *Deberry three-part analysis,* whenever a denial of access is asserted with respect to evidence that *could* be favorable to the defendant.

We remain convinced that fundamental fairness, as an element of due process, requires the State's failure to preserve evidence that could be favorable to the defendant "[to] be evaluated in the context of the entire record." When evidence has not been preserved, the conduct of the State's agents is a relevant consideration, but it is not determinative. Equally relevant is a consideration of the importance of the missing evidence, the availability of secondary evidence, and the sufficiency of the other evidence presented at trial. "[T]here may well be cases which the defendant is unable to prove that the State acted in bad faith but in which the loss or destruction of evidence is nonetheless so critical to the defense as to make a criminal trial fundamentally unfair." *Arizona v. Youngblood,* 488 U.S. at 61.

"Rules concerning [the] preservation of evidence are generally matters of state, not federal constitutional law." *California v. Trombetta,* 467 U.S. at 491. We reaffirm our prior holdings, pursuant to the "due process" requirements of the Delaware Constitution. When the State has failed to preserve evidence that could be favorable to the defendant, the analysis which a court must follow is set forth in *Deberry* and *Bailey.* That analysis draws a balance between the nature of the State's conduct and the degree of prejudice to the accused. In general terms, if the duty to preserve evidence has been breached, a Delaware court must consider: "1) the degree of negligence or bad faith involved; 2) the importance of the missing evidence, considering the probative value and reliability of secondary or substitute evidence that remains available; and 3) the sufficiency of the other evidence used at trial to sustain conviction." We will examine Hammond's contentions in accordance with these principles.

The first step in a *Deberry* evaluation is to determine whether the crash vehicle, if extant in the possession of the State, would have been subject to disclosure under Superior Court Criminal Rule 16 or *Brady*? As we noted in *Deberry,* determining whether the crash vehicle would have been discoverable under *Brady* would be an artificial exercise, since it is no longer available for examination or testing. Therefore, we begin with the provisions of Rule 16.

"[U]nder Superior Court Criminal Rule 16(b), a defendant need only show that an item 'may be material to the preparation of his defense' to be discoverable." This Court has held in another homicide case, that the car which the defendants were using, when the victim was shot and killed, was clearly material to the defense and discoverable under Rule 16. A fortiori, the crash vehicle may clearly be material to the preparation of the defense of a person, such as Hammond, charged with vehicular homicide. Therefore, if the crash vehicle were in the possession of the State, it would have been discoverable under Superior Court Criminal Rule 16.

The second step in a *Deberry* evaluation requires an examination of the State's duty to preserve discoverable evidence. This Court has declined to prescribe the exact procedures that are necessary for the various law enforcement agencies in this State to follow, in order to fulfill their duties to preserve evidence. However, this Court has held that in fulfilling these duties, agencies should create rules for gathering and preserving evidence that are broad enough to include any material that could be favorable to a defendant. In *Deberry*, we observed:

> It is most consistent with the purposes of those safeguards to hold that the duty of disclosure attaches in some form once the Government has first gathered and taken possession of the evidence in question. Otherwise, disclosure might be avoided by destroying vital evidence before prosecution begins or before defendants hear of its existence....Only if evidence is carefully preserved during the early stages of investigation will disclosure be possible later.

We find that the police had a duty to gather and to preserve a crash vehicle which they knew was involved in a fatal accident, when criminal charges were pending and a criminal investigation was continuing.

The record reflects that the crash vehicle was "gathered." It was towed from the scene of the crime and impounded, at the direction of the Dover Police Department, on July 25, 1986. However, the crash vehicle was not preserved. It was released on August 8, 1986. Although Hammond was arrested shortly after the accident, he was not indicted until September 3, 1986. Consequently, when Hammond's attorney filed a discovery request on October 14, 1986, pursuant to Criminal Rule 16, the Dover police no longer had possession of the crash vehicle. The record reflects that the duty to preserve the crash vehicle, at least until the defendant had a reasonable opportunity to inspect it, was breached in Hammond's case.

The final step in a *Deberry* evaluation requires a three-part analysis to determine the consequences which should flow from a breach of the duty to preserve evidence. The first factor to be considered is "the degree of negligence or bad faith involved." Hammond does not contend that the Dover police department released the crash vehicle in bad faith. Hammond does argue that the police were negligent.

The State argues that the police were not negligent in releasing the crash vehicle. When the police arrived, they found the bodies of the accident victims inside of the crash vehicle, in positions which indicated Hammond was the driver. At the hospital, Hammond told one of the investigating police officers that he was the driver. Under these conditions, the State argues that the police had no basis to believe that Hammond would deny being the driver or that the crash vehicle could be material to the preparation of his defense.

The State's argument is addressed to the good faith of the Dover police in releasing the crash vehicle. However, Hammond does not argue that the Dover police acted in bad faith. Hammond's position is that the police were negligent in not preserving the crash vehicle when he was charged with vehicular homicide, since the crash vehicle was the instrumentality of that crime. The Superior Court expressed concern "why a major piece of evidence [the crash vehicle] would not be held at least a little bit longer to give the defendant a chance to look at it." We conclude that the Dover police should have preserved the crash vehicle, for a reasonable time, to permit its inspection by Hammond.

The second factor to be considered in this portion of a *Deberry/Bailey* evaluation is the importance of the missing evidence and the reliability of the secondary or substitute evidence that remains available. Hammond argues that the crash vehicle was important to his case for two separate reasons. First, because evidence of fingerprints, blood, hair, or torn clothing in the interior of the crash vehicle might have established that he was not the driver. Alternatively, because the crash vehicle could have been examined for mechanical failure as a cause of the accident, rather than driver negligence.

The secondary evidence which the State provided to Hammond consisted primarily of photographs of the crash vehicle. The maintenance records of the crash vehicle's owner were also available. Hammond contends that the secondary evidence, especially as it related to his ability to identify the driver, was not a satisfactory substitute. Hammond admits that his expert was able to prepare a video tape of a test, which supported his theory of the hypothetical movement of Hammond and Moore in the vehicle upon impact. However, Hammond argues that without either access to scientific test results or the opportunity to test the interior of the crash vehicle, he was unable to confirm his expert's opinion.

The police found no evidentiary value in the crash vehicle or its contents. In this case, once again, we decline to establish specific procedures which are necessary for law enforcement agencies in this State to fulfill the duty to gather and to preserve evidence. Nevertheless, assuming *arguendo* that there was no duty to gather and test evidence of the interior of the crash vehicle, the crash vehicle in a vehicular homicide should have been preserved. If the crash vehicle itself had been preserved, it would have been available to Hammond for testing. There was little, if any, probative value in the secondary evidence of the crash vehicle's interior that was made available to Hammond, *i.e.*, a single photograph.

The evidence obtained from the interior of the car included the following: torn pieces of clothing found in the car; pieces of car seat fabric; the brake and clutch pads; the steering wheel; test results from blood stains found in the car; test results from arm and head hairs found in the car; and numerous photographs taken from various angles at the scene and at the autobody shop.

The final factor in determining what consequences should flow from the State's breach of the duty to preserve evidence in a *Deberry* evaluation, requires an examination of the sufficiency of the other evidence, which the State presented at trial. In Hammond's case, the State presented eyewitness testimony from another driver, who saw the crash vehicle pass him at a high rate of speed immediately prior to the collision. The record also reflects that the crash vehicle did not turn over and that all of its occupants remained inside. The crash vehicle became lodged in the foundation of a townhouse. Several persons reached the scene of the accident, almost immediately after it occurred. All of them testified that they saw Hammond in the driver's seat. Rescue workers testified that Hammond's leg was in a cast, which was wedged between the accelerator and the brake. The ambulance attendant testified that Hammond told him that he was driving, and that the accident occurred when the cast on his leg caused his foot to slip off of the brake pedal.

The question which must now be answered is what consequences should flow from the failure to preserve the crash vehicle. In the Superior Court, Hammond moved for dismissal or an instruction to the jury that the lost evidence, if available would be exculpatory in nature. In ruling on Hammond's motions, the Superior Court stated it is "clear that the occupants were moved around in the car after the collision." Nevertheless, the Superior Court denied both of Hammond's motions because he had not shown that the evidence, which was not available, would have been conclusively exculpatory to the defendant.

The "conclusively exculpatory" standard, which was applied by the Superior Court, is obviously inconsistent with our holding in *Deberry*. Nevertheless, we find that the State's case against Hammond was strong.

Hammond's trial for vehicular homicide, even in the absence of the crash vehicle, was not so fundamentally unfair that his prosecution should have been barred as a denial of due process. Del. Const. art I, § 7. The Superior Court properly denied Hammond's motion to dismiss the State's case.

However, since the State must bear responsibility for the loss of evidence, Hammond was entitled to the inference that the crash vehicle, if available, would have been exculpatory. "Due process" required an appropriate instruction to the jury in a prosecution for vehicular homicide, in the absence of the preservation of the crash vehicle or of secondary evidence having a significant probative value. *See Deberry v. State,* 457 A.2d at 754; Del. Const. art. I, § 7. Such an instruction was given in *Arizona v. Youngblood,* even though no federal Constitutional right was found to have been violated.

More significantly, the trial judge instructed the jury: "If you find that the State has...allowed to be destroyed or lost any evidence whose content or quality are in issue, you may infer that the true fact is against the State's interest." As a result, the uncertainty as to what the evidence might have proved was turned to the defendant's advantage. *Arizona v. Youngblood,* 488 U.S. at 59-60.

We must now determine the effect of the Superior Court's failure to give such an instruction. Hammond's expert witness was able to prepare a video tape of a test supporting Hammond's theory of the hypothetical movement of the crash vehicle's occupants. Although Hammond's request for a jury instruction was denied, the Superior Court permitted Hammond's attorney to make "factual arguments" to the jury about the absence of the crash vehicle or any tests of its interior, and he did so forcefully. Given the strength of the State's case against Hammond, we are convinced beyond a reasonable doubt, that the Superior Court's failure to give a specific instruction was harmless error.

F. DOUBLE JEOPARDY

RICHARDSON v. STATE
717 N.E.2d 32 (Ind. 1999)

DICKSON, J.

With today's decision, we address the application of the Indiana Double Jeopardy Clause in article I, section 14 of the Indiana Constitution as distinct from its federal counterpart in the Fifth Amendment to the United States Constitution.

Prohibitions against double jeopardy protect the integrity of jury acquittals and the finality interest of defendants, shield against excessive and oppressive prosecutions, and ensure that defendants will not undergo the anxiety and expense of repeated prosecution and the increased probability of conviction upon re-prosecution. While double jeopardy provisions are found in both the United States Constitution and the Indiana Constitution, the defendant in this case does not allege any violation of the federal Double Jeopardy Clause. Rather, he claims the protection of the Indiana Double Jeopardy Clause.

Commentators note that double jeopardy provisions, which appear straightforward and simple, are often extremely difficult to apply and the underlying jurisprudence enormously challenging and complex. Recently, in a series of decisions, this Court acknowledged that some of our decisions during the past twenty years misapplied federal double jeopardy jurisprudence. We did not, however, address whether the Double Jeopardy Clause of the Indiana Constitution provides identical or different protections than its federal counterpart. Today, with our opinions in this case and its companion cases, we address this issue.

The Double Jeopardy Clause of the Indiana Constitution

Questions arising under the Indiana Constitution are to be resolved by "examining the language of the text in the context of the history surrounding its drafting and ratification, the purpose and structure of our constitution, and case law interpreting the specific provisions." In construing the Constitution, "a court should look to the history of the times, and examine the state of things existing when the constitution or any part thereof was framed and adopted, to ascertain the old law, the mischief, and the remedy." Because the "intent of the framers of the Constitution is paramount in determining the meaning of a provision," this Court will consider "the purpose which induced the adoption," "in order that we may ascertain what the particular constitutional provision was designed to prevent."

When this State was founded in 1816, the framers and ratifiers adopted a double jeopardy provision which provided that, "in all criminal prosecutions, the accused...shall not...be twice put in jeopardy for the same offence." Ind. Const. art 1, § 13 (1816). However, our ability to discern the framers' intentions is limited because the journal of the 1816 Constitutional Convention does not report the delegates' remarks or disclose procedural matters informative to the issue.

When the present version of our Constitution was adopted in 1851, the original double jeopardy provision was only slightly modified. Article I, section 14 provides in part: "No person shall be put in jeopardy twice for the same offense." The provision was adopted with no debate and has not been modified to date. The "cardinal principle of constitutional construction [is] that words are to be considered as used in their ordinary sense." Contemporaneous with the adoption of the 1851 Constitution, "offense" was defined as a "crime" or "transgression of law." This definition of "offense," however, does not explain the meaning of "same offense," which has become a term of art. It is not surprising that "[f]or decades, commentators and judges have attempted to define which offenses are the same, and the problem continues to be the focus of much of the contemporary scholarly criticism of double jeopardy doctrine."

Despite the lack of discussion at the 1850-51 Convention regarding Indiana's Double Jeopardy Clause, this Court has recognized that the intent of the framers and ratifiers derived from English common law double jeopardy principles. In *State v. Elder* we explained: "That no person shall be put in jeopardy twice for the same offence is a common-law principle, which, we believe, is incorporated into the constitution of each of the States which compose the United States." With the understanding that the constitutional protection against double jeopardy is one of the "least understood" and "most frequently litigated provisions of the Bill of Rights," "[i]t has always been an accepted judicial technique to have resort to the common law in order to ascertain the true meaning of the double jeopardy clause." Thus, understanding our Double Jeopardy Clause requires that we go beyond its text. The common law is helpful in determining the framers' understanding of the term "same offense."

Scholars trace double jeopardy principles back to ancient Greek, Roman and biblical sources. While some historians trace double jeopardy protections in England to the dispute between King Henry II and Archbishop Thomas à Becket in 1176, the earliest treatise on the English common law, published in the late twelfth century, did not directly mention double jeopardy protections. In the English case reporters between 1290 and 1535, "the word 'jeopardy' occurs only eleven times in reports involving criminal cases, and in only three of these instances was it used in the statement that a man's life shall not be twice 'put in jeopardy' for the same offense."

During the 1600s and 1700s, double jeopardy protections were further examined by Lord Edward Coke and William Blackstone. Lord Coke only found double jeopardy protections in the three pleas of *autrefois acquit* (former acquittal), *autrefois convict* (former conviction), and former pardon. By the late 1700s, a fourth plea of *autrefois attaint* was also recognized. Writing 100 years after Coke, Blackstone began using the phrase "jeopardy" more often, noting that "the plea of *autrefois acquit,* or a former acquittal, is grounded on this universal maxim of the common law of England that no man is to be brought into jeopardy of his life, more than once, for the same offence."

As a further indicator of the framers' understanding of the common law of double jeopardy, we note that the early American colonies departed in some respects from English common law, recognizing broader double jeopardy protections. For example, the bar against double jeopardy for

Lord Coke depended on the reasons for the prior acquittal, whereas early American double jeopardy law barred retrial for *any* prior acquittal. Blackstone described double jeopardy protections as applying only to criminal *felony* prosecutions, whereas early American double jeopardy protections applied to *all* criminal prosecutions. Under English common law, jeopardy did not attach until a verdict or acquittal was actually rendered, thus allowing retrials following hung juries or mistrials, whereas early American double jeopardy law barred re-prosecution in certain hung jury or mistrial circumstances. Further, early English double jeopardy protections were developed in the context of criminal law practice and procedure different from that which existed and continues to exist in this country. When Coke formulated the double jeopardy prohibition against second prosecutions for the same offense, there did not exist the same number of closely related offenses as we have today. As one commentator has noted, "the law distinguished among rape, arson, and murder, but not between 'intimidating any person from voting' and 'interfering with his right to vote.'" "At the time of Henry III there were only eleven felonies. In Coke's time the number had risen to thirty." By the time the United States Constitution was ratified, England had 160 different felonies.

Also, early American colonies and states embodied double jeopardy principles in statutory and organic laws, unlike England. In 1641, the Bay Colony of Massachusetts drafted the Body of Liberties, which led to the adoption of the Massachusetts Code of 1648. "The fact that the Bay Colony reduced double jeopardy protection to a written form and expanded it beyond the common law guarantee demonstrates that the colonists regarded the concept to be fundamental." Although New Hampshire was the first (and only) state to include double jeopardy protections in its state constitution *prior* to the ratification of the United States Constitution, almost every state has now included some type of protection against double jeopardy in its state constitution.

As states developed and applied their respective double jeopardy principles, two divergent analyses appeared for determining whether the offenses are the same: (1) the behavioral approach; and (2) the evidentiary approach. The "behavioral approach focuses on the defendant's conduct rather than on the prosecutor's evidence. Courts which use this approach adopt an act, transaction, or intent test." This behavioral approach (also referred to as the same transaction or same conduct approach) was explicitly rejected early by the Indiana Supreme Court. The *Elder* Court noted that two lines of Double Jeopardy Clause interpretation appeared throughout the nation. One line held that state double jeopardy clauses provide "a more liberal rule...in favor of the accused." This more liberal rule was the same transaction/conduct test, which prohibited multiple prosecutions arising out of the "same state of facts, although they may include several offences." Under the other line of interpretation, the evidentiary approach, state double jeopardy clauses "mean no more than the common-law principle." After reviewing Indiana court decisions and the decisions from other state and federal courts, the *Elder* Court rejected the more liberal test, stating that it could "not adopt the rule held in some States, that the accused can not, in any case, be convicted but once upon the same facts when they constitute different offences."

The evidentiary approach (also referred to as the same evidence test) is apparent in the English common law case of *The King v. Vandercomb & Abbot,* 2 Leach 708, 168 Eng. 455 (1796). That court explained the test as follows:

> if crimes are so distinct that evidence of the one will not support the other, it is as inconsistent with reason, as it is repugnant to the rules of law, to say that they are so far the same that an acquittal of the one shall be a bar to a prosecution for the other.

However, American jurisprudence in the last two centuries provides no single, generally accepted articulation of the same evidence test. Rather, the test has assumed three separate formulations: a "required evidence test," an "alleged evidence test," and an "actual evidence test."

In discerning the approach required by the Indiana Constitution, we first note that "[e]arly decisions of this Court interpreting our Constitution...have been accorded strong and superseding precedential value." In seeking the proper interpretation of our Double Jeopardy Clause, we draw from cases involving subsequent prosecutions because double jeopardy claims in multiple punishments cases did not emerge until after 1930, and because this Court has not distinguished between double jeopardy protections in multiple punishment cases and those in subsequent prosecution cases. Our double jeopardy case law appears to fall into five different subsequent prosecution categories—those following a conviction; a mistrial or the discharge of the jury or defendant; a successful appeal; an acquittal; and a civil action.

Our earliest jurisprudence demonstrates that this Court did not limit itself to any single formulation of the evidence test, such as an "actual evidence test," a "required evidence test," or an "alleged evidence test," in determining whether the offenses were the same. In the cases most contemporaneous (1859 to 1884) with the adoption of the 1851 Constitution, this Court did not identify a singular test or restrict the double jeopardy inquiry to the statutory elements or charging instruments, but instead considered all of the circumstances and evidence available to the reviewing court to determine whether the offenses were the same.

After the ratification of our Constitution in 1851, the Indiana Supreme Court considered whether the convictions were the "same offense" in *Wininger v. State.* In *Wininger,* the defendant was first convicted of assault and battery and then tried for the crime of riot, each arising out of the same event. Noting "conflict in the decisions of some of the sister states," the *Wininger* Court considered whether double jeopardy was violated, holding that "the true rule, in prosecutions for offenses of this character, is, that where the gravamen of the riot consists in the commission of an assault and battery, then, a conviction for that assault, & c., would be a bar to a prosecution for a riot." However, "where the commission of an assault and battery was merely incidental to the riot, then a conviction for the one would not bar a prosecution for the other." Thus, "[t]he question would be, is the one act included in the other?" Looking to the evidence introduced at trial, the Court reversed the second conviction, finding that the Double Jeopardy Clause was violated because "the gravamen of the riot was the assault and battery."

In 1978, the analysis under the Indiana Constitution was merged with the federal constitutional test in *Elmore v. State*: "Now that we are bound by the federal Double Jeopardy Clause, it is more necessary than ever that we be in line with federal standards." Although the *Elmore* Court erroneously concluded that the federal Supremacy Clause required that the federal test govern all Indiana claims, it is clear that this Court, by 1978, considered *both* the Indiana Double Jeopardy Clause and the federal Double Jeopardy Clause to require the same test—a statutory "identity of offense" or "same evidence" test. During the twenty years following *Elmore,* this Court frequently decided double jeopardy issues by looking to the offenses as charged, believing that this approach was required by federal double jeopardy jurisprudence, and often referring in passing to the Indiana Constitution. We have recently recognized that this methodology is an inaccurate statement of federal double jeopardy law as established by *Blockburger v. United States*, 284 U.S. 299 (1932). Considering *Elmore's* merger of Indiana double jeopardy law into federal constitutional analysis and its declaration that our state's double jeopardy jurisprudence must "be in line with federal standards," it is not surprising that we did not separately evaluate the Indiana Constitution as an additional, independent source of double jeopardy protection. Instead, we generally addressed double jeopardy claims by applying the prevailing understanding of federal jurisprudence and merely referred to the Indiana Double Jeopardy Clause. This Court today recognizes that these post-*Elmore,* pre-*Games* cases do not constitute precedent regarding the application of the Indiana Double Jeopardy Clause. Our action today should be understood to supercede these cases.

From our review of the constitutional text, the history and circumstances surrounding its adoption, and the earliest cases interpreting and applying the provision, we conclude that Indiana's Double Jeopardy Clause was intended to prevent the State from being able to proceed against a person twice for the same criminal transgression. While none of the early cases presented a comprehensive analysis, a generally articulated test, or a standard of review for double jeopardy claims, the holdings in these decisions do reflect a common theme. A criminal transgression was a person's conduct that violated a statutorily defined crime. In seeking to determine whether two criminal transgressions were the same, this Court in its earliest decisions did not restrict its review only to a comparison of statutory elements of the crime or to an analysis of the language in the charging instruments. Rather, this Court also reviewed the actual evidence presented at trial when available.

Synthesizing these considerations, we therefore conclude and hold that two or more offenses are the "same offense" in violation of article I, section 14 of the Indiana Constitution, if, with respect to *either* the statutory elements of the challenged crimes *or* the actual evidence used to convict, the essential elements of one challenged offense also establish the essential elements of another challenged offense. Both of these considerations, the statutory elements test and the actual evidence test, are components of the double jeopardy "same offense" analysis under the Indiana Constitution.

Because the defendant's convictions for both robbery and battery as a class A misdemeanor, under the circumstances presented, violate the Double Jeopardy Clause of the Indiana Constitution, we vacate the conviction and sentence for battery as a class A misdemeanor. This cause is remanded to the trial court for disposition consistent with this opinion.

G. PROPORTIONALITY

Nine state constitutions provide that punishment, penalties or fines be determined or "proportioned" according to the nature of the crime. Ill. Const. art. I, § 11 ("All penalties shall be determined...according to the seriousness of the offense."); Ind. Const. art I, § 16 ("All penalties shall be proportioned to the nature of the offense."); Me. Const. art I, § 9 ("all penalties and punishments shall be proportioned to the offense"); Neb. Const. art. I, § 15 (same); N.H. Const. pt. I, art. 18 ("All penalties ought to be proportioned to the nature of the offense."); Or. Const. art I, § 16 (same as Maine and Nebraska provisions); R.I. Const. art. I, § 8 ("all punishments ought to be proportioned to the offense"); Vt. Const. ch. II, § 39 ("all fines shall be proportioned to the offences"); W. Va. Const. art. III, § 5 ("Penalties shall by proportioned to the character and degree of the offence."). There is no federal counterpart to these provisions.

The provision in the Vermont Constitution—"All fines shall be proportioned to the offences"—is said to derive from Chapter 14 of the Magna Carta. The word "fines" in Vermont denotes all forms of punishment, whether by fine, imprisonment, forfeiture, or disqualification. *State v. Burlington Drug Co.*, 78 A. 882, 884-85 (Vt. 1911).

STATE v. WHEELER
175 P.3d 438 (Or. 2007)

BALMER, J.

The issue in this criminal case is whether the life sentences that the trial court imposed on defendant violate the proportionality clause of article I, section 16 of the Oregon Constitution, which provides that "all penalties shall be proportioned to the offense." A jury convicted defendant of 18 criminal charges, including sexual abuse, sodomy, and using a child in a display of sexually explicit conduct, based on conduct involving three boys between the ages of nine and 15. Defendant previously had been convicted of two felony sex crimes. Based on the convictions in this case and defendant's prior convictions, and acting pursuant to a recidivism statute for felony sex offenders, the trial court imposed a sentence of life imprisonment without possibility of parole on each of the 18 charges, with the sentences to run consecutively. Defendant appealed, arguing that the sentences were disproportionate to the offenses of which he was convicted. The Court of Appeals affirmed without opinion. We allowed defendant's petition for review and now affirm.

In construing the Oregon Constitution, we seek to determine the meaning of the constitutional text by examining the wording of the constitutional provision at issue, the case law surrounding it, and the historical circumstances leading to its adoption.

> The purpose of our inquiry under the *Priest* methodology is "to understand the wording [of the constitutional provision] in the light of the way that the wording would have been understood and used by those who created the provision...and to apply faithfully the principles embodied in the Oregon Constitution to modern circumstances as those circumstances arise."

We begin with the text of article I, section 16 of the Oregon Constitution. That section provides:

> Excessive bail shall not be required, nor excessive fines imposed. Cruel and unusual punishments shall not be inflicted, but *all penalties shall be proportioned to the offense.*—In all criminal cases whatever, the jury shall have the right to determine the law, and the facts under the direction of the Court as to the law, and the right of new trial, as in civil cases. (emphasis added).

Before turning to the specific wording, "all penalties shall be proportioned to the offense," we briefly examine the context of that wording. The issue in this case turns on the relationship between crimes and punishment, and the provisions in article I, section 16, regarding excessive bail and the respective powers of the court and jury in a criminal trial have little bearing on that relationship. The reference to "excessive fines," however, adds some context to the proportionality requirement. Although this case involves imprisonment, rather than a fine, the use of the term "excessive" (rather than the term "proportional") in relation to fines raises the question whether requiring proportionality differs from prohibiting excessiveness. If the Oregon Constitutional Convention had wanted to prevent only *excessive* penalties, it could have indicated as much. Instead, it indicated that penalties should be *proportioned,* and we turn to a consideration of the meaning of that requirement.

The term "proportion" indicates a comparative relationship between at least two things. Here, the two things being related are "penalties" and "the offense," and the provision requires that the penalties for each particular offense be "proportioned"—that is, comparatively related—to that offense. The strong implication of that requirement is that a greater or more severe penalty should be imposed for a greater or more severe offense, and, conversely, that a less severe penalty should be imposed for a less severe offense. Additionally, by using the article "the" and the word "offense" in the singular, rather than the plural, the text focuses on the "proportion" between a specific offense and the penalties for that offense, rather than on the proportion between the penalty for one offense (*e.g.,* murder) and the penalty for another offense (*e.g.,* theft). However, the constitutional text does not suggest the precise nature of the relationship that is required between the offense and the penalties, nor does it indicate how the severity of an offense is to be measured.

It also is unclear, based solely on examining the text, what relationship the second half of the sentence in question ("but all penalties shall be proportioned to the offense") bears to the first half of the sentence ("cruel and unusual punishments shall not be inflicted"). The two phrases could be independent constitutional commands, or the second half of the sentence could modify the first half of the sentence. Specifically, the presence of the conjunction "but" may suggest an exception or some kind of contrast, or it may simply be serving its ordinary function as a conjunction, *viz.,* joining the two clauses into a single sentence without purporting to define the particular relationship between them—whatever it may be. Because "proportionality" and the prohibition of "cruel and unusual punishments" are different concepts, each of which could stand alone as a constitutional requirement, the text of the second sentence of article I, section 16 suggests that each should be interpreted independently, although the interpretation of one may inform the interpretation of the other. The text, however, does not provide a more specific understanding of the meaning of the proportionality clause, and we therefore turn to the historical background of the clause to seek a fuller understanding of that provision.

This court has interpreted article I, section 16 in a number of decisions, which we discuss below. However, we never have reviewed in any detail the origins of the proportionality requirement in an effort to determine what the framers of the Oregon Constitution were concerned about, and therefore intended, when they adopted it, and we take the opportunity to do so now.

When the drafters of the Oregon Constitution took the proportionality requirement from the Indiana Constitution of 1851, they did not discuss the meaning of that provision or their reasons for using it. However, the proportionality requirement, in one form or another, has an ancient lineage, dating back to Magna Carta, and the legal requirement that the penalty for a crime be proportional to the offense can be traced from those early sources to the American colonial experience and then to state constitutions adopted in the nineteenth century, including Oregon's. Accordingly, we begin with a brief review of that history.

Concerns about both proportionality and severity in criminal sentencing in English law may be found as early as Magna Carta of 1215 and in the English Bill of Rights of 1689. The concerns expressed in those documents did not address imprisonment, however, but rather fines or "amercements," perhaps because, when those documents were written, fines were a far more common form of punishment than imprisonment. Magna Carta provided that fines should be set according to the "magnitude" or "degree" of the crime—concepts similar to proportionality—and according to the legal status of the offender.

The English Bill of Rights added the prohibition on "excessive fines" and the different concept of "cruel and unusual punishment." The latter provision did not apply to capital punishment or even many forms of corporal punishment, but rather to forms of torture that were illegal or at least not customary.

The world of Magna Carta and the English Bill of Rights (and the words used in those documents) was so divorced from nineteenth century reality that we would hesitate to rely too heavily on those sources, if they stood alone. Happily, they do not, because William Blackstone and the early American state constitution writers—far more accessible and readable sources—provide a link between the older sources and the text used in the Oregon Constitution. In reviewing the common law of crimes in England in the middle of the eighteenth century, Blackstone maintained that punishment should be proportional to the offense in question and to the social aims of criminal punishment generally. "The method...of inflicting punishment ought always to be proportioned to the particular purpose it is meant to serve, and by no means exceed it." 4 William Blackstone, *Commentaries on the Laws of England* 12 (1769). Of course, in Blackstone's time, many crimes still were punishable by death, and this was particularly so if the defendant had committed previous crimes.

Blackstone thus advocated penalties "proportioned" to the purpose of the punishment, whether that be the "amendment" of a particular defendant's disposition to commit crime or the deterrence of "future offenses." He also suggested that the elimination or isolation of dangerous or repeat offenders, in the interest of protecting the greater public, represented one of the important purposes of punishment. We should bear in mind, however, that in mid-eighteenth century England, lengthy imprisonment still was not the most common punishment, and it did not become widespread until the advent of the criminal reformation movements of the early nineteenth century. Until then, death, corporal punishment and transportation were common punishments for many serious offenses. Blackstone described what he called the "melancholy truth" that English law prescribed the death penalty for no fewer than 160 different crimes.

Blackstone emphasized the legislative role in selecting punishments. Indeed, there being no constitutional standards by which an English judge could overrule a legislative choice, his remarks necessarily were directed to legislators and would-be legislators. Regarding the applicability of the death penalty, he wrote: "I would not be understood to *deny* the right of the legislature in any country to enforce its own laws by [requiring] the death of the transgressor...but only to suggest a few hints for the consideration of such as are, or may hereafter become, legislators." In that spirit, Blackstone made certain recommendations with the hope that Parliament would reconsider what he believed to be disproportionately severe penalties, including the death penalty, for many crimes.

Although Blackstone suggested that fine distinctions in ranges of punishment may be difficult to make and are best left to legislative judgment, he set out a number of principles, at least some of them inspired by his reading of Cesare Beccaria's contemporary treatise on criminal law and punishment, *On Crimes and Punishments* (1764; first English trans 1767). Blackstone, following Beccaria, emphasized rationality in the imposition of punishments, rather than the indiscriminate application of harsh punishments such as the death penalty. Punishment, in Blackstone's view (as influenced by Beccaria), should take into account the manifold complexities of aggravating and extenuating circumstances, including a weighing of the effectiveness of a particular penalty in preventing future crimes.

In particular, Blackstone agreed both with Beccaria's observation that the certainty of punishment is more important than severity in preventing future crimes and with Montesquieu's view that the "excessive severity of laws...hinders their execution," particularly when jurors withhold conviction if they perceive that the likely punishment will be unjust. He concluded that "punishments of *unreasonable* severity, especially when indiscriminately inflicted, have less effect in preventing crimes, and amending the manners of a people, than such as are more merciful in general, yet properly intermixed with due distinctions of severity."

Blackstone also criticized the use of brutal punishments, which he referred to as "sanguinary laws," as "a bad symptom of the distemper of any state." He was especially critical of the arbitrary and indiscriminate use of such laws, particularly the death penalty.

Blackstone's *Commentaries* were an important influence on reformers, including early state constitution writers, and provisions in a number of state constitutions written in the late eighteenth century reflect Blackstone's concern with proportionality in sentencing. The first American constitution to adopt a clause requiring proportionality in sentencing appears to have been the Pennsylvania Constitution of 1776. That constitution stated that "[t]he penal laws as heretofore used shall be reformed by the legislature of this state, as soon as may be, and punishments made in some cases less sanguinary, and in general more proportionate to the crimes." Pa. Const. of 1776, § 38; *see also* § 39 (prisons should be constructed "to make sanguinary punishments less necessary"). Similarly, South Carolina's 1778 constitution indicated that "the penal laws, as heretofore used, shall be reformed, and punishments made in some cases less sanguinary, and in general more proportionate to the crime." S.C. Const. of 1778, art. XL. The reference to "sanguinary" laws echoes Blackstone's criticisms of disproportionately harsh punishments in English law, which the framers of the colonial constitutions saw as applicable to colonial criminal sentences.

Of all the state constitutions from that period, we think the New Hampshire Constitution of 1784 provided the most lucid explanation of the rationale for its provision requiring proportional sentencing:

> All penalties ought to be proportioned to the nature of the offense. No wise legislature will affix the same punishment to the crimes of theft, forgery and the like, which they do to those of murder and treason; where the same undistinguishing severity is exerted against all offences[,] the people are led to forget the real distinction in the crimes themselves, and to commit the most flagrant with as little compunction as they do those of the lightest dye: For the same reason a multitude of sanguinary laws is both impolitic and unjust. The true design of all punishments being to reform, not to exterminate, mankind.

N.H. Const. of 1784, pt. I, art. XVIII. The foregoing provision seems to be a summary of Blackstone's discussion of proportionality in punishment. In later years, the Illinois Constitution condensed the New Hampshire text: "All penalties shall be proportioned to the nature of the offence, the true design of all punishment being to reform, not to exterminate, mankind." Ill Const. art. VIII, § 14 (1818).

Notably, many states that included proportionality clauses in their original state constitutions abandoned them in subsequent revisions. In 1790, Pennsylvania and South Carolina abandoned their proportionality clauses in favor of formulations that followed the Eighth Amendment to the United States Constitution, prohibiting excessive fines and cruel and unusual punishments. Like Pennsylvania and South Carolina, Ohio adopted a proportionality clause only to abandon it later.

The cause for abandonment is not difficult to find. In many states, legislative projects were undertaken to divide significant crimes into degrees (*e.g.,* first-degree murder, second-degree murder), reserving the most severe punishments for crimes committed "in the first degree," and to limit the death penalty generally. Thus, in light of criminal sentencing reforms in the early nineteenth century, it is likely that proportionality was no longer widely perceived in those states as a pressing issue that required constitutional guidance.

We turn to the Indiana Constitution, which draws our attention in part because many provisions of the Oregon Constitution were taken from it. The 1816 Indiana Constitution provided: "All penalties shall be proportioned to the nature of the offence." In the 1816 constitution, that provision was contained in a separate section from the provision that instructed that "[e]xcessive bail shall not be required; excessive fines shall not be imposed; nor cruel and unusual punishments inflicted." Ind. Const. of 1816, art. I, § 15. In the revised Indiana Constitution of 1851, however, those two provisions were merged to read: "Excessive bail shall not be required. Excessive fines shall not be imposed. Cruel and unusual punishments shall not be inflicted. All penalties shall be proportioned to the nature of the offence." Ind. Const., Art. I, § 16 (1851). Unfortunately, the debates on the Indiana Constitution shed little light on the contemporary meaning of the clause.

Obviously, the framers of the Oregon Constitution borrowed the two sentences of article I, section 16, with which we are concerned here, from the Indiana Constitution of 1851. The framers combined the cruel and unusual punishment provision and the proportionality provision—each of which appears in a short, separate sentence in the Indiana Constitution—into a single sentence, connected by the conjunction "but." As we have described above, those provisions have distinct histories and purposes—the proportionality provision has origins in Magna Carta and in Blackstone's argument in favor of punishments that were reasonably related to the severity of particular offenses, while the prohibition on cruel and unusual punishments was first articulated in the English Bill of Rights and focuses on prohibited methods of punishment. Those differences suggest that, when the drafters of the Oregon Constitution combined the two provisions with the word "but" in article I, section 16, they did not intend the proportionality provision to be an exception or qualification to the bar on cruel and unusual punishments. In other words, the prohibition on cruel and unusual punishment and the requirement of proportionality appear to be independent constitutional commands, joined in one sentence because they both concern appropriate punishment for crimes.

The framers of the Oregon proportionality provision made one other change in the text of the Indiana provision, omitting the words "nature of," and thus requiring that penalties be "proportioned to the offense," rather than "proportioned to the *nature of* the offense." Although the framers left no record indicating why they made that change, the text of the Oregon provision at least suggests that the framers intended the proportionality inquiry to focus on the specific criminal "offense" at issue, rather than on a potentially more open-ended inquiry into the "nature" of the offense. Indeed, the Indiana courts have emphasized that the reference in the Indiana proportionality requirement to the "nature of the offense" indicates that the courts should look behind the legislative classification of the offense and consider the "nature" and "gravity" of the offense of conviction and, in the case of a repeat offender, the "nature" of the prior offenses. Although it is not clear how application of the Indiana provision would differ in practice from that of the Oregon provision, article I, section 16 plainly directs us to consider only "the" offense and whether "the" penalties are "proportioned" to that offense.

The Oregon provision has not changed since 1857: "Excessive bail shall not be required, nor excessive fines imposed. Cruel and unusual punishments shall not be inflicted, but all penalties shall be proportioned to the offense." Or. Const. art. I, § 16. Other than suggesting the likelihood that the provenance of the provision was the 1851 Indiana Constitution, the records of the Oregon Constitutional Convention shed no light on the changes or the meaning of the constitutional text. Recent research shows that the sentence in question, taken from the Indiana Constitution, remained the same throughout the convention, although the section disappeared at one point before reappearing in the final version of the draft constitution.

Nothing in the records of the constitutional convention indicates that, when the framers of the Oregon Constitution adopted the proportionality requirement, they had any different concerns than those which had led Blackstone and later the framers of state constitutions from Pennsylvania to Indiana to emphasize the need for proportionality in sentencing. We therefore assume that those same concerns animated the Oregon framers. Those concerns, in turn, inform our interpretation of the Oregon provision. At the most basic level, the framers' concern was that the penalty imposed on a criminal defendant be "proportioned" to the specific offense for which the defendant was convicted—that it bear the appropriate "comparative relation" to the severity of that crime.

We turn to this court's previous cases interpreting article I, section 16. This court first articulated the test for determining whether a sentence violates the proportionality provision of article I, section 16 in *Sustar v. County Court of Marion Co.,* 201 P. 445 (Or. 1921). The defendant there had been sentenced to six months in jail and fined $500, the maximum permitted under the applicable statute, for possessing two quarts of "moonshine." The court stated that the trial court "went to the verge by inflicting the extreme penalty, nevertheless, the sentence was within the law." As to the defendant's claim that his sentence nevertheless violated the proportionality requirement, the court quoted a United States Supreme Court case interpreting the cruel and unusual punishment provision of the Eighth Amendment, *Weems v. United States,* 217 U.S. 349, 367 (1910), for the proposition that "[i]t is a precept of justice that punishment for crime should be graduated and proportioned to offense." This court then stated: "In order to justify the court in declaring punishment cruel and unusual with reference to its *duration,* the punishment most be so proportioned to the offense committed as to *shock the moral sense* of all reasonable men as to what is right and proper under the circumstances."

To summarize, this court's cases do not provide a comprehensive understanding of the scope of article I, section 16, but they do provide some perspective on certain aspects of the proportionality requirement. The court has used the test of whether the penalty was so disproportioned to the offense as to "shock the moral sense of reasonable people" and ordinarily has deferred to legislative judgments in assigning penalties for particular crimes, requiring only that the legislature's judgments be reasonable. The cases permit the legislature to impose enhanced sentences on recidivists, even if those sentences would be disproportionate when applied to a defendant without prior convictions. Finally, the proportionality provision bars the legislature from punishing a lesser-included offense (such as an attempt) more severely than the greater-inclusive offense (such as completion of the attempted crime).

With the foregoing understanding of the proportionality requirement of article I, section 16, we turn to defendant's specific arguments that the sentences imposed on him are unconstitutional. Defendant's arguments include both a facial and an as-applied challenge. To the extent that defendant argues that the criminal statutes that were the basis for his prior convictions and the recidivism statute under which he was sentenced in this case, *see* Ore. Rev. Stat. § 1·37.719(1), permit a sentence that is disproportionate to sentences imposed under other sentencing statutes, his challenge appears to be a facial one. To the extent that defendant focuses on what he characterizes as the limited harm to his victims (in the earlier crimes and in the crimes in this case) in weighing proportionality, the challenge appears to be an as-applied one.

Defendant makes two arguments that section 137.719(1) of the Oregon Code is facially unconstitutional. He argues that had he committed "the more serious felony of murder," the presumptive sentence would have been life with a 25-year minimum term. That argument, of course, ignores the fact that section 137.719(1) is a recidivism statute that applies to defendant only because he has two prior felony convictions for sex crimes. The fact that the presumptive sentence for a murder committed by a defendant with *no prior convictions* is less severe than the presumptive sentence for a felony sex crime committed by a defendant who has been convicted of two prior felony sex crimes does not, in our view, "shock the moral sense of reasonable people." As *Smith* and *Jensen* made clear many years ago, the legislature may protect society from those who cannot or will not conform their behavior to criminal statutes by imposing more severe sentences on repeat offenders. That is what the legislature did by enacting section 137.719(1).

Defendant also argues that section 137.719(1) is disproportionate compared to other recidivism statutes, asserting that a person with prior convictions of assault, who is again convicted of assault, is likely to receive a sentence less severe than the sentence imposed on defendant here. The legislature, however, has set the presumptive penalty for a felony sex crime, when committed by a person with two prior convictions for such crimes, to be life imprisonment without possibility of parole (unless the trial court decides to impose a lesser sentence). The question is whether that penalty is "proportioned to the offense." We cannot say that it is not. The legislature evidently considered the repeated sex crimes at issue here—whether because sex crime victims often are young and vulnerable to adult coercion, because of the possibility of recidivism by sex offenders, or because of the severity of the impact of such crimes on the victims—to be deserving of a greater presumptive penalty than assault, even an assault by a person with a previous assault conviction. As we noted in *Isom,* even if defendant's opinion of the relative "seriousness" of an assault compared to a sex felony made sense—a proposition that we need not decide—the legislature had a different opinion. The legislature chose to impose a more serious penalty on the serial sex offender. We cannot say that the legislature was unreasonable in doing so, or that the penalty it established would shock the moral sense of reasonable people.

Defendant's "as applied" challenge also fails. Defendant argues that the life sentences without possibility of parole imposed on him under section 137.719(1), when compared to the ordinary guidelines sentence of over 111 years that he otherwise would have faced, would "shock" anyone's moral sense. As described above, this court's previous cases have permitted lengthy sentences, including life imprisonment, as a response to recidivism. Defendant also argues that the life sentences imposed on him are unconstitutionally disproportionate because "[t]he felonies did not involve a physical assault and did not involve a permanent physical injury." Sex crimes may or may not result in permanent physical injury, but the legislature is entitled to presume that they are a serious matter in light of the potential for both physical and psychological injury and that lengthy sentences are necessary to protect the public from further harm by recidivists. *See* Or. Const. art. I, § 15 (protection of society is an appropriate goal of criminal punishment).

We therefore hold that, under the test articulated above, defendant's sentences bear a sufficient relationship to the gravity of the crimes of which he was convicted and his prior felony convictions. The sentences do not violate the proportionality clause of article I, section 16 of the Oregon Constitution.

The decision of the Court of Appeals and the judgment of the circuit court are affirmed.

NOTES

1. A restitution award violates the excessive fines clause of the Montana Constitution if the award is grossly disproportionate to the gravity of the crime for which a defendant has been convicted. Mont. Const. art. II, § 22; *State v. Kuykendall*, 136 P.3d 983 (Mont. 2006).

2. In death penalty cases, the Florida Supreme Court performs "a proportionality review to prevent the imposition of 'unusual' punishments contrary to article I, section 17 of the Florida Constitution." *Hunter v. State*, 8 So.3d 1052 (Fla. 2008).

3. The Hawaii Supreme Court held that a sentence of five consecutive terms of ten-years imprisonment for five first-degree theft convictions was not disproportionate to the crimes. Haw. Const. art I, § 12; *State v. Kahapea*, 141 P.3d 440 (Haw. 2006).

4. The proportionate penalties clause in the Illinois Constitution has been interpreted to be "coextensive" with the Cruel and Unusual Punishment Clause in the Eighth Amendment of the United States Constitution. *People v. Rodney H.*, 861 N.E.2d 623, 628 (Ill. 2006). In fact, the Illinois Constitution is generally construed to be in "lock step" with the United States Constitution. *See People v. Moss*, 842 N.E.2d 699 (Ill. 2005).

H. CRUEL AND UNUSUAL PUNISHMENT

PEOPLE v. BULLOCK
485 N.W.2d 866 (Mich. 1992)

CAVANAGH, C. J.

We address in these consolidated cases the question whether Michigan's mandatory penalty of life in prison without possibility of parole, for possession of 650 grams or more of any mixture containing cocaine, is "cruel or unusual" under our state constitution.

On February 24, 1988, defendant Hasson traveled by air from Los Angeles to Lansing's Capital City Airport. He had a return ticket to Los Angeles on a flight scheduled to leave less than four hours after his arrival, yet he had checked two large suitcases. Acting on a tip from airline agents relayed through the Los Angeles police, the Michigan State Police met Hasson's flight. Before Hasson claimed his luggage, a police dog alerted officers to the presence of illegal drugs in both suitcases. The police observed Hasson deplane, retrieve his luggage, make a call from a public phone, and walk outside to the public driveway. After about thirty minutes, Hasson flagged down a car driven and owned by defendant Bullock. Bullock's seventeen-year-old grandson was a passenger in the car. Hasson placed his luggage in the trunk and got in the car, which began to pull away.

At that point, the police stopped the car and arrested all three occupants. The police, without attempting to obtain a warrant, then proceeded to search the entire car. They examined the glove compartment, Bullock's purse which she left in the car, and the luggage Hasson had placed in the trunk. They found traces of cocaine in the glove compartment and Bullock's purse, and over fifteen kilograms of cocaine in Hasson's luggage. The police also found two burnt marijuana cigarettes and assorted drug paraphernalia in the passenger compartment, and several thousand dollars in cash in Bullock's purse.

The cocaine was admitted as evidence at trial over Hasson's and Bullock's objections, and both were convicted, in separate jury trials, of knowingly possessing 650 grams or more of cocaine violation of section 333.7403(2)(a)(i) of the Michigan Compiled Laws. As mandated by that statute, in conjunction with section 791.234(4), both defendants were sentenced to life in prison without any possibility of parole.

We granted leave to appeal and subsequently agreed to consider whether the mandatory penalty of life in prison without possibility of parole was invalid under either the federal or state constitutions. Following oral argument, we ordered reargument to address the effect of the United States Supreme Court's intervening decision dealing with the penalty issue in *Harmelin v. Michigan,* 501 U.S. 957 (1991).

The Applicability of article 1, section 16 of the Michigan Constitution

The United States Supreme Court, in *Harmelin v. Michigan,* rejected a challenge, brought under the "cruel and unusual punishments" clause of the Eighth Amendment of the United States Constitution, to Michigan's mandatory penalty of life in prison without possibility of parole for possession of 650 grams or more of a mixture containing cocaine. We address here a challenge to that penalty on the basis of article 1, section 16 of the Michigan Constitution of 1963, which is worded differently from, and was ratified more than 171 years after, the Eighth Amendment. The Eighth Amendment of the United States Constitution provides: "Excessive bail shall not be required, nor excessive fines imposed, nor cruel *and* unusual punishments inflicted." Article 1, section 16 of the Michigan Constitution provides: "Excessive bail shall not be required; excessive fines shall not be imposed; cruel *or* unusual punishment shall not be inflicted; nor shall witnesses be unreasonably detained."

While *Harmelin* is binding and authoritative for purposes of applying the United States Constitution, it is only persuasive authority for purposes of this Court's interpretation and application of the Michigan Constitution. This Court alone is the ultimate authority with regard to the meaning and application of Michigan law. In the case of a divided United States Supreme Court decision, we may in some cases find more persuasive, and choose to rely upon, the reasoning of the dissenting justices of that Court, and not the majority, for purposes of interpreting our own Michigan Constitution.

To note that we have the authority to interpret the Michigan Constitution more expansively than the United States Constitution does not, of course, lead to the conclusion that we should or will choose to exercise that authority in any particular area. It is entirely possible, in a given case or area, that our independent judgment will lead to our agreeing with the reasoning of the United States Supreme Court. For example, in the area of search and seizure law, governed by the Fourth Amendment of the United States Constitution and article 1, section 11 of the Michigan Constitution, this Court has held, on the basis of a careful examination of the text and history of the latter clause, and the understanding of the voters who adopted it, that it should not be interpreted to afford any greater protection than the parallel federal clause, absent a "compelling reason" for doing so.

The application of the "compelling reason" standard remains an issue on which jurists of reason may differ, as they have differed in the past. We have no need, however, to further explore this broad issue in these cases. We find that regardless of whether it is or should be necessary to adduce a "compelling reason" to interpret article 1, section 16 of the Constitution of 1963 more broadly than the United States Supreme Court interprets the Eighth Amendment, at least three compelling reasons do, in fact, exist to interpret our state constitutional provision more broadly in these cases than the United States Supreme Court interpreted the Eighth Amendment in *Harmelin.* We set forth these reasons below. Furthermore, we find that a proper interpretation of article 1, section 16, in accordance with this Court's longstanding precedent in this area, requires us to strike down the penalty at issue as unjustifiably disproportionate to the crime for which it is imposed, and therefore "cruel or unusual."

Textual Differences

First, as we have already noted, the Michigan provision prohibits "cruel *or* unusual" punishments, while the Eighth Amendment bars only punishments that are both "cruel *and* unusual." This textual difference does not appear to be accidental or inadvertent. Language providing that "no cruel or unusual punishments shall be inflicted" was included in Article II of the Northwest Ordinance of 1787. Michigan's first Constitution, adopted in 1835, provided that "cruel *and unjust* punishments shall not be inflicted." Mich. Const. of 1835, art. 1, § 18. The Constitution of 1850 provided that "cruel *or* unusual punishment shall not be inflicted." Mich. Const. of 1850, art. 6, § 31. Identical language was adopted as part of the 1908 and 1963 Constitutions. *See* Mich. Const. of 1908, art. 2, § 15; Mich. Const. of 1963, art. 1, § 16.

This Court, in *People v. Lorentzen,* 194 N.W.2d 827 (Mich. 1972), took specific note of this difference in phraseology and suggested that it might well lead to different results with regard to allegedly disproportionate prison terms. "The prohibition of punishment that is unusual but not necessarily cruel carries an implication that unusually excessive imprisonment is included in that prohibition." *Cf. Harmelin* (conceding that "[s]evere, mandatory penalties may be cruel," but maintaining that "they are not unusual in the constitutional sense").

As this Court has noted, a "significant textual difference [ ] between parallel provisions of the state and federal constitutions" may constitute a "compelling reason" for a different and broader interpretation of the state provision.

Historical Factors

Second, while two members of the *Harmelin* majority maintained that the historical circumstances and background of the adoption of the Eighth Amendment preclude the notion that the federal clause contains a "proportionality principle," such a conclusion cannot be reached with regard to the framing and adoption of the Michigan Constitution of 1963. Whatever the legal terms "cruel" and "unusual" were understood to mean in 1791 when the Eighth Amendment was ratified—or in 1689 when its antecedent, the English Bill of Rights, was adopted—by 1963 those words had been interpreted and understood by the United States Supreme Court *and by this Court* for more than half a century to include a prohibition on grossly disproportionate sentences.

This would constitute another "compelling reason" for a broader view of state constitutional protection, in that "history provide[s] reason to believe that those who framed and adopted the state provision had a different purpose in mind"—different, at any rate, from the historical understanding asserted by Justice Scalia.

Longstanding Michigan Precedent

Finally, this Court, in interpreting article 1, section 16 of the Constitution of 1963, has long followed an approach more consistent with the reasoning of the *Harmelin* dissenters than with that of the *Harmelin* majority. Twenty years ago, in *People v. Lorentzen*, we struck down, under both the Eighth Amendment of the United States Constitution and article 1 section 16 of the Michigan Constitution of 1963, a mandatory minimum sentence of twenty years in prison (reducible to approximately ten years by earning "good time") for selling any amount of marijuana.

Our analysis in *Lorentzen* foreshadowed in a striking manner the three-pronged test later adopted by the United States Supreme Court in *Solem v. Helm,* 463 U.S. 277, 290-291 (1983). Thus, *Lorentzen* noted the severity of the sentence imposed and the fact that it would apply to a marijuana sale by "a first offender high school student." *Lorentzen* then compared the penalty to those imposed for numerous other crimes in Michigan. *Lorentzen* further compared Michigan's penalty for selling marijuana to the penalties imposed for that offense by other states. Finally, *Lorentzen* applied a fourth criterion rooted in Michigan's legal traditions, and reflected in the provision for "indeterminate sentences" of article 4, section 45 of the Michigan Constitution of 1963 (the goal of rehabilitation).

It is unclear, in the wake of Harmelin, whether *Lorentzen's* or *Solem's* analysis survives as a matter of federal constitutional law, and that need not concern us in any event. Lorentzen's analysis, although relying in the alternative on the Eighth Amendment, was firmly and sufficiently rooted in article 1, section 16. Indeed, we preceded our proportionality analysis in *Lorentzen* with a lengthy review of Michigan case law dating back to 1879. We believe the precedential weight of *Lorentzen* and its antecedents, as a matter of Michigan law, constitutes a very compelling reason not to reflexively follow the latest turn in the United States Supreme Court's Eighth Amendment analysis. We therefore continue to adhere, on the basis of the Michigan Constitution, to the analysis set forth in *Lorentzen* and later adopted in *Solem.*

Application

Applying the *Lorentzen-Solem* analysis to these cases, we conclude, largely for the reasons stated by Justice White in his dissenting opinion in *Harmelin,* that the penalty at issue here is so grossly disproportionate as to be "cruel or unusual." The penalty is imposed for mere possession of cocaine, without any proof of intent to sell or distribute. The penalty would apply to a teenage first offender who acted merely as a courier. Indeed, on the basis of the information before this Court, it appears that prior to the offense giving rise to this case, defendant Bullock, a forty-eight-year-old grandmother, had never been convicted of any serious crime and had held a steady job as an autoworker for sixteen years.

It is true, as Justice Kennedy noted in *Harmelin,* that the collateral effects flowing even from mere possession of cocaine are terrible indeed. But conviction of the crime involved here does not require any proof that the defendant committed, aided, intended, or even contemplated any loss of life or other violent crime, or even any crime against property. As Justice White correctly noted in *Harmelin,* "[t]o be constitutionally proportionate, punishment must be tailored to a defendant's personal responsibility and moral guilt." While we emphatically do not minimize the gravity and reprehensibility of defendants' crime, it would be profoundly unfair to impute full personal responsibility and moral guilt to defendants for any and all collateral acts, unintended by them, which might have been later committed by others in connection with the seized cocaine. Persons who independently commit violent and other crimes in connection with illegal drugs can and should be held individually responsible by our criminal justice system.

Thus, even under Justice Kennedy's restrictive view of *Solem,* it is clear that an application of *Solem*'s first prong "leads to an inference of gross disproportionality." Application of the second and third prongs of the *Lorentzen-Solem* analysis strongly reinforces that inference. As Justice White noted in *Harmelin,* aside from manufacture, delivery, possession with intent to deliver, and possession of 650 grams or more of a substance containing cocaine or illegal narcotics, only first-degree murder—that is, "wilful, deliberate, and premeditated" murder, or murder committed in the course of certain serious felonies—is punishable in Michigan by mandatory life imprisonment without possibility of parole. The defendants in this case have been punished more severely than they could have been for second-degree murder, rape, mutilation, armed robbery, or other exceptionally grave and violent crimes.

Furthermore, as Justice White also noted, no other state in the nation imposes a penalty even remotely as severe as Michigan's for mere possession of 650 grams or more of cocaine. "Of the remaining 49 states, only Alabama provides for a mandatory sentence of life imprisonment without possibility of parole for a first-time drug offender, and then only when a defendant possesses ten kilograms or more of cocaine."

In sum, the only fair conclusion that can be reached regarding the penalty at issue is that it constitutes an unduly disproportionate response to the serious problems posed by drugs in our society. However understandable such a response may be, it is not consistent with our constitutional prohibition of "cruel or unusual punishment." The penalty is therefore unconstitutional on its face.

The proportionality principle inherent in article 1, section 16, is not a simple, "bright-line" test, and the application of that test may, concededly, be analytically difficult and politically unpopular, especially where application of that principle requires us to override a democratically expressed judgment of the Legislature. The fact is, however, the people of Michigan, speaking through their constitution, have forbidden the imposition of cruel or unusual punishments, and we are duty-bound to devise a principled test by which to enforce that prohibition, and to apply that test to the cases that are brought before us. The very purpose of a constitution is to subject the passing judgments of temporary legislative or political majorities to the deeper, more profound judgment of the people reflected in the constitution, the enforcement of which is entrusted to our judgment.

For the reasons stated, we strike down the sentences imposed on both defendants as "cruel or unusual" under article 1, section 16 of the Michigan Constitution of 1963.

NOTES

1. Some states, like the United States Constitution, prohibit "cruel and unusual punishments": Alaska Const. art. I, § 12; Ariz. Const. art. II, § 15; Colo. Const. art. II, § 20; Ga. Const. art. I, § 1, ¶ 17; Idaho Const. art. I, § 6; Ind. Const. art. I, § 16; Iowa Const. art. I, § 17; Md. Decl. of Rights, art. 16; Mos. Const. art. I, § 21; Neb. Const. art. I, § 9; N.J. Const. art. I, ¶ 12; N.M. Const. art. II, § 13; N.Y. Const. art. I, § 5; Ohio Const. art. I, § 9; Or. Const. art. I, § 16; Tenn. Const. art. I, § 16; Utah Const. art. I, § 9; Va. Const. art. I, § 9; W. Va. Const. art. III, § 5; Wis. Const. art. I, § 6.

2. Other states prohibit "cruel or unusual punishments": Ala. Const. art. I, § 15; Ark. Const. art. II, § 9; Cal. Const. art. I, § 17; Fla. Const. art. I, § 17; Haw. Const. art. I, § 12; Kan. Bill of Rights, § 9; La. Const. art. I, § 20 (cruel, excessive, or unusual punishments); Me. Const. art. I, § 9; Md. Decl. of Rights, art. 25; Mont. Const. art. II, § 22; Nev. Const. art. I, § 6; N.C. Const. art. I, § 27; N.D. Const. art. I, § 11; Okla. Const. art. II, § 9; S.C. Const. art. I, § 15; Tex. Const. art. I, § 13; Wyo. Const. art. I, § 14.

3. Maryland's Declaration of Rights uses both the conjunctive (article 16) and disjunctive (article 25) forms of the ban.

4.   A few states prohibit only cruel punishments. Del. Const. art. I, § 11; Ky. Bill of Rights, § 17; Pa. Const. art. I, § 13; R.I. Const. art. I, § 8; S.D. Const. art. IV, § 23; Wash. Const. art. I, § 14.

5.   The highest courts in California and Massachusetts declared that the death penalty is, *per se*, a cruel or unusual punishment forbidden by the state constitution for any crime. In both states, that result was subsequently overturned by constitutional amendment.

6. Connecticut has no provision regarding punishment in its constitutional bill of rights.

CHAPTER VIII

SEARCH AND SEIZURE

A. INTRODUCTION

The prohibition on unreasonable searches and seizures in many state constitutions is almost identical to the Fourth Amendment of the United States Constitution. However, some state constitutions have textual differences that can be outcome determinative. *See, e.g.*, Haw. Const. art. I, § 7; N.Y. Const. art I, § 12; La. Const. art I, § 5. Under the Fourth Amendment, warrantless searches are *per se* unreasonable unless they fall within an exception to the warrant requirement. Some of the exceptions to the Fourth Amendment's warrant requirement are: frisks, inventory searches, searches incident to arrest, consensual searches, automobile searches and searches under exigent circumstances. These and other exceptions are not always permitted in whole or in part by state constitutions.

State constitutions also have been construed to have standards that differ from the Fourth Amendment to determine probable cause and standing. The purpose, policy and operation of the exclusionary rule under state constitutions are frequently different from the federal exclusionary rule.

B. PROBABLE CAUSE

PEOPLE v. GRIMINGER
524 N.E.2d 409 (N.Y. 1988)

TITONE, J.

The primary issue presented is whether the *Aguilar-Spinelli* two-prong test, or the *Gates* totality-of-the-circumstances test, should be employed in determining the sufficiency of an affidavit submitted in support of a search warrant application. *See Illinois v. Gates,* 462 U.S. 213 (1983); *Spinelli v. United States,* 393 U.S. 410 (1969); *Aguilar v. Texas,* 378 U.S. 108 (1964). We conclude that, as a matter of State law, our courts should apply the *Aguilar-Spinelli* test.

Special agents of the United States Secret Service arrested a counterfeiting suspect, and, in the course of interrogation, he signed a detailed statement accusing defendant of keeping large quantities of marihuana and cocaine in his bedroom and adjacent attic. Consequently, one of the agents prepared an affidavit for a warrant to search defendant's home. According to the affidavit, a confidential informant known as source "A" observed substantial quantities of marihuana and quantities of cocaine in defendant's bedroom and attic on numerous occasions, saw defendant sell drugs on numerous occasions, and, as recently as seven days ago, "A" observed 150 to 200 pounds of marihuana in defendant's bedroom and adjacent attic. The affidavit further stated that, pursuant to a consent search, approximately four pounds of marihuana were found in a garbage can at defendant's residence.

Although the agent did not personally know the counterfeiting suspect, his affidavit said that the undisclosed informant was "a person known to your deponent." The agent also omitted the fact that the informant was under arrest when he provided this information. Based solely upon this affidavit, a Federal Magistrate issued the search warrant. On August 26, 1983, the warrant was executed by 2 Federal agents and 6 or 7 Nassau County policemen. The search produced 10 ounces of marijuana, over $6,000 in cash and drug-related paraphernalia. Additionally, the Federal agents turned over the marijuana discovered during the consent search referred to in the warrant to Nassau County law enforcement officials.

Defendant was charged with two counts of criminal possession of marihuana, as well as with criminal sale of marihuana arising out of an unrelated May 1984 incident. Defendant sought to suppress the evidence obtained as a result of the August 26 search, but County Court denied the motion. Although the court found that the agent's affidavit failed to satisfy the "reliability" prong of the *Aguilar-Spinelli* test, it concluded that the *Gates* test should be applied in assessing the sufficiency of a search warrant. Under that test, the court determined that there was probable cause to issue the warrant.

Prior to *Illinois v. Gates,* Federal courts applied the two-pronged *Aguilar-Spinelli* test in probable cause determinations when evaluating hearsay information from an undisclosed informant. Under this test, the application for a search warrant must demonstrate to the issuing Magistrate (i) the veracity or reliability of the source of the information, and (ii) the basis of the informant's knowledge. We adopted this standard as a matter of State constitutional law. In *Illinois v. Gates,* the United States Supreme Court altered its position and adopted the seemingly more relaxed "totality-of-the- circumstances approach."

In *People v. Johnson,* 488 N.E.2d 439 (N.Y. 1985), this court expressly rejected the *Gates* approach for evaluating warrantless arrests. In *People v. Bigelow,* 488 N.E.2d 451 (N.Y. 1985), although the People urged us to adopt the *Gates* test in the search warrant context, we found it unnecessary to decide the question, since "the People's evidence [did] not meet minimum standards of probable cause even if *Gates* was applied." This appeal squarely presents the issue left undecided in *Bigelow.* We are not persuaded, however, that the *Gates* approach provides a sufficient measure of protection, and we now hold that, as a matter of State constitutional law, the *Aguilar-Spinelli* two- prong test should be applied in determining whether there is a sufficient factual predicate upon which to issue a search warrant.

We reaffirm today that in evaluating hearsay information the Magistrate must find some minimum, reasonable showing that the informant was reliable and had a basis of knowledge. Our courts should not "blithely accept as true the accusations of an informant unless some good reason for doing so has been established." The *Aguilar-Spinelli* two-pronged inquiry has proven a satisfactory method of providing reasonable assurance that probable cause determinations are based on information derived from a credible source with firsthand information, and we are not convinced that the *Gates* test offers a satisfactory alternative.

The reasons advanced by the People in support of the *Gates* test are similar to those enunciated by the Supreme Court itself in *Illinois v. Gates*. They contend that the less stringent *Gates* test will encourage the use of warrants, a highly desirable goal. They assert that the *Aguilar-Spinelli* test has been applied in a rigid, inflexible manner to the detriment of law enforcement. The commonsense approach of *Gates,* posit the People, is a more reasonable rule of law, since the hypertechnical two-prong test places an unnecessary burden on law enforcement officers who are not lawyers, but rather public officials "acting under stress and often within the context of a volatile situation."

Although we agree with the People that the use of warrants should be encouraged, there is no reason to believe that police will refrain from obtaining a warrant merely because this State continues to apply the *Aguilar-Spinelli* test. With limited exceptions, carefully circumscribed by our courts, it is always incumbent upon the police to obtain a warrant before conducting a search. Furthermore, whether there was probable cause will generally be raised by the defendant at a suppression hearing. If a Magistrate has already determined that probable cause existed, great deference will be accorded that finding, resulting in far fewer suppression problems. This, in turn, results in a more efficient use of police resources; it is indeed wasteful to make an arrest or conduct a search without a warrant only to have those efforts invalidated by a suppression court.

Nor is the *Aguilar-Spinelli* test a hypertechnical approach to evaluating hearsay information. As we stated in *People v. Hanlon*, "in the real world, we are confronted with search warrant applications which are generally not composed by lawyers in the quiet of a law library but rather by law enforcement officers who are acting under stress and often within the context of a volatile situation. Consequently such search warrant applications should not be read in a hypertechnical manner as if they were entries in an essay contest. On the contrary, they must be considered in the clear light of everyday experience and accorded all reasonable inferences."

In *People v. Johnson*, we recognized that the more structured "bright line" *Aguilar-Spinelli* test better served the highly desirable "aims of predictability and precision in judicial review of search and seizure cases," and that "the protection of the individual rights of our citizens are best promoted by applying State constitutional standards." We find this reasoning equally persuasive in cases involving search warrants. Given the deference paid to the Magistrate's probable cause finding, and given the somewhat subjective nature of the probable cause inquiry, the aims of predictability and precision are again well served by providing the Magistrate with *Aguilar-Spinelli's* concrete, structured guidelines. More importantly, this will also prevent the disturbance of the rights of privacy and liberty upon the word of an unreliable hearsay informant, a danger we perceive under the *Gates* totality-of-the-circumstances test.

The unreliability of the hearsay informant was established by County Court and affirmed by the Appellate Division. We have no basis upon which to review or disturb that finding. The reliability prong of *Aguilar-Spinelli* having not been satisfied, we therefore affirm the Appellate Division order finding the warrant invalid and suppressing the fruits of the search.

COMMONWEALTH v. GRAY
503 A.2d 921 (Pa. 1985)

HUTCHINSON, J.

This case requires us to determine whether the United States Supreme Court's decision in *Illinois v. Gates,* 462 U.S. 213 (1983), adopting a "totality of the circumstances" standard under the federal constitution in analyzing probable cause for search warrants based on information received from confidential informants, also meets the requirements of article I, section 8 of our Pennsylvania Constitution. Appellant was convicted of possession of marijuana with intent to deliver. Superior Court affirmed the conviction and we granted appellant's petition for allowance of appeal.

Several confidential informants told police that appellant and his girlfriend had approximately twenty pounds of marijuana at their residence. On January 27, 1981, the police obtained a search warrant for the premises and two vehicles, one of which was at the home. The probable cause allegations in the accompanying affidavit are the only source of controversy in this case. Because of the importance of this issue we set out those allegations in full:

On 27 January 1981 a confidential informant related the following information to your affiant:

Between 23 January 1981 and 27 January 1981 the confidential informant # 1 was at the residence of Ronald Gray, specifically described above. At the time the informant was present the informant personally saw approximately 20 pounds of marijuana. The informant further related that he had seen marijuana in the automobiles described above.

Your affiant believes the confidential informant to be reliable for the following reasons: Two other confidential informants gave confirming information. In addition Trp. Thomas R. Scales confirmed information.

On 16 January 1981 your affiant spoke with confidential informant # 2. At this time informant # 2 related that RONALD GRAY is one of the major drug distributors in Lycoming County. Informant # 2 is believed to be reliable because he has given information relating to Laughlin Jennings who is presently under criminal charges; Regina Webster and Curtis Missien who are presently under criminal charges; and David Fryday who is presently under criminal charges (the information relating to Fryday confirmed in a statement by Gina Brown who related that she purchased her drugs from Fryday). The informant # 2 stated that Fryday would be found in Wellsboro, Pa. as Fryday had left Williamsport. On 27 January 1981 Fryday was arrested in Wellsboro.

On 18 January 1981 Mr. Brown and Trp. Monahan spoke with confidential informant # 3. At this time confidential informant # 3 related that RONALD GRAY is one of the largest drug dealers in Lycoming County. Informant # 3 related that he had some contact relative to the purchase of drugs with Gray.

On 27 January 1981 Trp. Thomas R. Scales related the following to your affiant:

During the fall of 1978 Trp. Scales had set up a transaction with Gray to purchase (2) cases of morphine from RONALD GRAY. During the course of the transaction, which took place in a cabin off Leg.Rte. 41028, a phone call came stating that there were police in the area. Gray then refused to complete the transaction at that time. This information is contained in P.S.P. reports.

On 27 January 1981 when confidential informant # 1 related the information he was under oath.

On 27 January 1981 Trp. Carey in the presence of Ptl. Mark McCracken (South Williamsport Police) and confidential informant # 1 went to the residence of RONALD GRAY. At that time Trp. Carey located the above described home and the vehicles. The vehicles were present at the location described by the confidential informant.

On 27 January confidential informant # 1 further related that he had contacted Gray concerning the marijuana between 25 January 1981 and 27 January 1981. At this time the informant # 1 stated that Gray said he still had marijuana.

Search Warrant and Affidavit dated January 27, 1981.

The police attempted to obtain appellant's consent to the search by asking him to accompany them while they executed the warrant. After appellant refused, the police went to appellant's home, served the search warrant, and began their search. They uncovered a total of nineteen plastic bags with about one pound of marijuana in each. Drug paraphernalia was found inside the house. The search of the second car produced no evidence used at trial.

Appellant filed an omnibus pre-trial motion in which he asserted that the evidence from this search should have been suppressed because the warrant was defective under the current state of the law. The court denied this portion of the motion, finding that the allegation of probable cause was sufficiently reliable. Appellant was tried and convicted of possession with intent to deliver.

Superior Court affirmed appellant's conviction. It stated that because the allegation of probable cause was sufficient under the relaxed standard of *Illinois v. Gates*, the motion to suppress was properly denied. This appeal followed.

Until 1983, the generally accepted standard for reviewing affidavits of probable cause supporting a search warrant based on information provided by confidential informants came from the United States Supreme Court cases *Aguilar v. Texas* and *Spinelli v. United States*. Those cases required a warrant to pass two specific tests, under which the issuing authority had to be able to see, on the face of the affidavit of probable cause, both the informant's basis for his knowledge and independent facts showing the reliability of the informant.

The warrant in this case fails the *Aguilar-Spinelli* tests because no one of the parts which make up its whole meets both the basis of knowledge test and the test of the particular informant's reliability. The information from Informant No. One satisfies the basis of knowledge test since the affidavit states that this informant "personally saw" marijuana in the cars described in the search warrant. This information was not stale as the drugs were seen during the four-day period immediately preceding the application for the warrant. *See Commonwealth v. Stamps*, 427 A.2d 141 (Pa. 1981) (evidence of possession of large quantities of drugs within fourteen days is not stale).

However, the affidavit does not satisfy the *Aguilar-Spinelli* standards of demonstrating the reliability of this particular informant. It states only that two other confidential informants gave similar information, and that a named trooper confirmed it. Thus, there is no independent demonstration of the reliability of Informant No. One. His reliability is wholly dependent on that of the other informants.

Conversely, Informant No. Two's statement that appellant was a major distributor of drugs in the area does not independently satisfy the basis of knowledge prong of the two-part test. There is no indication that the informant knew about the drugs in appellant's car, and, although he had given credible information regarding other current prosecutions, there is nothing to show any specific information about appellant's current activity. His past reliability is insufficient, by itself, to establish probable cause. Therefore, this informant's statement that appellant is a drug distributor does not independently support a finding of probable cause and does not confirm the other information the affidavit sets out under the *Aguilar-Spinelli* analysis tests, as contrasted with the *Gates* test of synthesis.

Similarly, Informant No. Three does not bolster the credibility of Informant No. One. The application for the warrant states that No. Three knows appellant is a drug distributor, and that he had "some contact relative to the purchase of drugs with [appellant]." This may provide a sufficient basis of knowledge, but it does not demonstrate this third informant's reliability. Consequently, application of the two-pronged *Aguilar-Spinelli* analytical approach to the various pieces of information in the affidavit leaves us without a basis to believe that appellant currently possessed drugs in his car.

Finally, the trooper's statement that he arranged to buy drugs from appellant over two years before does not independently demonstrate the first informant's reliability. These allegations establish only that appellant was a known drug dealer. Only Informant No. One, whose reliability is not independently shown, had direct knowledge of the current possession, and the confirming information by informants whose reliability does appear was as to appellant's status as a drug dealer. That status, standing alone, is insufficient to justify this search.

We therefore turn to the propriety of adopting the standards of *Illinois v. Gates* as sufficient under article I, section 8 of the Pennsylvania Constitution. In *Gates,* the United States Supreme Court decided that its prior holdings creating "tests" for determining whether or not probable cause existed ran contrary to the notion of probable cause as based on "the factual and practical considerations of everyday life on which reasonable and prudent men, not legal technicians, act." The Court also noted that:

> the direction taken by decisions following *Spinelli* poorly serves "the most basic function of any government": "to provide for the security of the individual and of his property." *Miranda v. Arizona,* 384 U.S. 436, 539 (1966). The strictures that inevitably accompany the "two-pronged test" cannot avoid seriously impeding the task of law enforcement....If,...that test must be rigorously applied in every case, anonymous tips would be of greatly diminished value in police work. Ordinary citizens, like ordinary witnesses, *see* Federal Rules of Evidence 701, Advisory Committee Note (1976), generally do not provide extensive recitations of the basis of their everyday observations. Likewise,...the veracity of persons supplying anonymous tips is by hypothesis largely unknown, and unknowable. As a result, anonymous tips seldom could survive a rigorous application of either of the *Spinelli* prongs. Yet, such tips, particularly when supplemented by independent police investigation, frequently contribute to the solution of otherwise "perfect crimes." While a conscientious assessment of the basis for crediting such tips is required by the Fourth Amendment, a standard that leaves virtually no place for anonymous citizen informants is not.

The Court stated its new test for analyzing warrants:

> The task of the issuing magistrate is simply to make a practical, common-sense decision whether, given all the circumstances set forth in the affidavit before him, including the "veracity" and "basis of knowledge" of persons supplying hearsay information, there is a fair probability that contraband or evidence of a crime will be found in a particular place. And the duty of a reviewing court is simply to ensure that the magistrate had a "substantial basis for...conclud[ing] that probable cause existed."

We have looked at this test before, and have called it "more practical." In addition, we have always held that probable cause determinations must be based on common sense non-technical analysis. Heretofore we have not been presented with a factual background requiring us to determine whether we should reject the *Aguilar-Spinelli* standards. In this case, however, the warrant fails these tests and we must reach the *Gates* issue in order to decide it. This Court is no longer bound by *Aguilar-Spinelli* as a matter of federal constitutional law. Therefore, our prior decisions, based on their two-pronged test, are no longer authoritative. While we can interpret our own constitution to afford defendants greater protections than the federal constitution does, there should be a compelling reason to do so. In *Chandler*, we already noted that the *Gates* analysis appears more practical. That this is so is even more plain on this record. Besides, there is no substantial textual difference between the Fourth Amendment to the United States Constitution and article I, section 8 of the Pennsylvania Constitution that would require us to expand the protections afforded under the federal document.

We do not find persuasive the reasoning applied by other states in rejecting *Gates* and adopting *Aguilar-Spinelli* under state constitutions. *See, e.g., State v. Kimbro,* 496 A.2d 498 (Conn. 1985); *Commonwealth v. Upton,* 476 N.E.2d 548 (Mass. 1985) (on remand from the United States Supreme Court); *State v. Jackson,* 688 P.2d 136 (Wash. 1984). Those cases rejected *Gates* as too amorphous, claiming it was practically equivalent to no standard at all. We, however, believe that a totality of the circumstances approach is as workable here as in those other areas of criminal procedure where a common-sense, practical approach is indicated. Thus, we adopt the *Gates* standard under the Pennsylvania Constitution.

Under the *Gates* totality of the circumstances approach, the warrant in this case is valid. Informant No. One states specifically that he saw a substantial quantity of marijuana in appellant's car within the four-day period preceding the application for the warrant. Although the affidavit does not show on its face that this informant is especially credible or reliable, the whole affidavit contains facts consistent with it. Their total effect confirms it with the ring of truth which is sufficient for men of common sense to conclude that a search is reasonable and justified by probable cause. Three people—one police officer and two confidential informants—have stated that appellant is a known drug dealer. A third confidential informant says he saw twenty pounds of marijuana and that appellant carried this quantity in his car. Viewed together, these allegations raise a fair inference that appellant was in possession of a substantial quantity of a controlled substance. Thus, there was probable cause for the issuance of the search warrant under *Gates*.

Because we hold that article I, section 8 of the Pennsylvania Constitution is satisfied by the *Gates* standard, and because we hold that the warrant in this case satisfied the *Gates* standard, we must affirm appellant's judgment of sentence.

NOTES

1. States that retain, as a matter of state law, the *Aguilar-Spinlelli* test or a state variant thereof include: Alaska, Hawaii, Massachusetts, New Jersey, New Mexico, New York, Oregon, Tennessee, and Washington.

2. States that have adopted the *Gates* test are: Colorado, Delaware, Georgia, Iowa, Maine, Michigan, Minnesota, Montana, Nevada, New Hampshire, North Dakota, Pennsylvania, Utah, Texas, and Wyoming.

3. Article I, section 7 of the Tennessee Constitution has been construed to distinguish between information provided by citizen or bystander informants and by an informant from a "criminal milieu." Information from the former is "presumed to be reliable" while information from the latter must be examined by a two-part inquiry adopted in *State v. Jacumin*, 778 S.W.2d 430 (Tenn. 1989), *i.e.*, the affidavit supporting a search warrant must show: (1) the basis for the informant's knowledge and (2) the reliability of the informant or the information. *Accord State v. Williams*, 193 S.W.3d 502 (Tenn. 2006).

C. GOOD FAITH EXCEPTION TO WARRANT REQUIREMENT

COMMONWEALTH v. EDMUNDS
586 A.2d 887 (Pa. 1991)

CAPPY, J.

HISTORY OF THE CASE

The issue presented to this court is whether Pennsylvania should adopt the "good faith" exception to the exclusionary rule as articulated by the United States Supreme Court in the case of *United States v. Leon,* 468 U.S. 897 (1984). We conclude that a "good faith" exception to the exclusionary rule would frustrate the guarantees embodied in article I, section 8 of the Pennsylvania Constitution. Accordingly, the decision of the Superior Court is reversed.

The defendant in the instant case was found guilty after a non-jury trial on August 18, 1987, of criminal conspiracy, simple possession, possession with intent to deliver, possession with intent to manufacture and manufacture of a controlled substance. The conviction was premised upon the admission into evidence of marijuana seized at the defendant's property pursuant to a search warrant, after information was received from two anonymous informants.

The trial court held that the search warrant failed to establish probable cause that the marijuana would be at the location to be searched on the date it was issued. The trial court found that the warrant failed to set forth with specificity the date upon which the anonymous informants observed the marijuana. However, the trial court went on to deny the defendant's motion to suppress the marijuana. Applying the rationale of *Leon,* the trial court looked beyond the four corners of the affidavit, in order to establish that the officers executing the warrant acted in "good faith" in relying upon the warrant to conduct the search. In reaching this conclusion the trial court also decided that *Leon* permitted the court to undercut the language of Pennsylvania Rule of Criminal Procedure 2003, which prohibits oral testimony outside the four corners of the written affidavit to supplement the finding of probable cause.

Rule 2003 provides in relevant part:

(a) No search warrant shall issue but upon probable cause supported by one or more affidavits sworn to before the issuing authority. The issuing authority, in determining whether probable cause has been established, may not consider any evidence outside the affidavits.

(b) At any hearing on a motion for the return or suppression of evidence, or for the suppression of the fruits of the evidence obtained pursuant to a search warrant, no evidence shall be admissible to establish probable cause other than the affidavits provided for in paragraph (a).

The Superior Court in a divided panel decision affirmed the judgment of the trial court, specifically relying upon the decision of the United States Supreme Court in *Leon.* Allocatur was granted by this Court.

The pertinent facts can be briefly summarized as follows. On August 5, 1985, State Police Trooper Michael Deise obtained a warrant from a district magistrate to search a white corrugated building and curtilage on the property of the defendant. As the affidavit of probable cause is central to our decision, we will set it forth in full:

On the date of August 4, 1985, this affiant Michael D. Deise, Penna. State Police, was in contact by telephone with two anonymous Males who were and are members of the community where Louis R. Edmunds resides. Both anonymous males advised the affiant that while checking out familiar hunting areas off Rte. 31, east of Jones Mills and along the south side of Rte. 31. (sic) These men observed growing marijuana near a white corrugated building approximately 20 x 40 feet in a cleared off area. These men looked into the building and observed several plants that appeared to be marijuana. This affiant questioned both of these men as to their knowledge of marijuana. This affiant learned that one of these men saw growing marijuana numerous times while he was stationed in Viet Nam. The other male saw growing marijuana while at a police station. This affiant described a growing marijuana plant and its characteristics and they agreed that what they had viewed agreed with the description and also that it appeared to them to be marijuana as fully described by the affiant. The two males wish to remain anonymous for fear of retaliation or bodily harm. An anonymous male advised this affiant that Louis R. Edmunds lived there. Edmund's description being that of a white male in his middle thirties and he lived at the aforementioned location.

On the 5th of August, 1985, this affiant with the use of a State Police helicopter, flew over the described location and observed the white corrugated building in the mountain area and located as described by the two males. Also on this date this affiant drove past the Rte. 31 entrance and observed a mail box with "Edmunds 228" printed on it.

After obtaining the warrant from the local magistrate, Trooper Deise, accompanied by three other troopers, served the warrant upon the defendant at his residence. Though he did not place the defendant under arrest at this time, the trooper did advise him of his Miranda rights, and had him read the warrant. The trooper also explained to the defendant that the warrant was not for his residence, although the warrant itself included the residence. Rather, the trooper stated that the warrant was meant to relate to the white corrugated building, and that they were searching for marijuana in that building.

After producing the lease which indicated that the white corrugated building was in fact leased to Thomas Beacon, the defendant accompanied the troopers to the building, which was approximately one-quarter of a mile away, up a steep mountainous terrain, on a separate parcel of property owned by Edmunds. The record is devoid of evidence that there was marijuana growing outside the corrugated building. The defendant unlocked the door of the white building and entered with the troopers. Inside the building the troopers discovered seventeen growing marijuana plants, along with gardening implements, high-wattage lights, and a watering system. The marijuana was seized and the charges as recited above were brought against the defendant.

As a preliminary matter, we concur with the inevitable conclusion of the trial court and the Superior Court, that probable cause did not exist on the face of the warrant. In *Conner,* this Court made clear that a search warrant is defective if it is issued without reference to the time when the informant obtained his or her information. Coupled with Rule 2003, which mandates that courts in Pennsylvania shall not consider oral testimony outside the four corners of the written affidavit to supplement the finding of probable cause for a search warrant, we are compelled to conclude that the affidavit of probable cause and warrant were facially invalid. As the Superior Court candidly stated, the affidavit in question "did not contain facts from which the date of the hunters' observations could be determined."

The sole question in this case, therefore, is whether the Constitution of Pennsylvania incorporates a "good faith" exception to the exclusionary rule, which permits the introduction of evidence seized where probable cause is lacking on the face of the warrant.

Put in other terms, the question is whether the federal *Leon* test circumvents the acknowledged deficiencies under Pennsylvania law, and prevents the suppression of evidence seized pursuant to an *invalid search warrant.* For the reasons that follow, we conclude that it does not.

Our starting point must be the decision of the United States Supreme Court in *Leon.* In *Leon,* the Supreme Court in 1984 departed from a long history of exclusionary rule jurisprudence dating back to *Weeks v. United States,* 232 U.S. 383 (1914), and *Mapp v. Ohio,* 367 U.S. 643 (1961). The Court in *Leon* concluded that the Fourth Amendment does not mandate suppression of illegally seized evidence obtained pursuant to a constitutionally defective warrant, so long as the police officer acted in good faith reliance upon the warrant issued by a neutral and detached magistrate.

We must now determine whether the good-faith exception to the exclusionary rule is properly part of the jurisprudence of this Commonwealth, by virtue of article 1, section 8 of the Pennsylvania Constitution. In concluding that it is not, we set forth a methodology to be followed in analyzing future state constitutional issues which arise under our own Constitution.

FACTORS TO CONSIDER IN UNDERTAKING PENNSYLVANIA CONSTITUTIONAL ANALYSIS

This Court has long emphasized that, in interpreting a provision of the Pennsylvania Constitution, we are not bound by the decisions of the United States Supreme Court which interpret similar (yet distinct) federal constitutional provisions.

As Mr. Chief Justice Nix aptly stated in *Sell,* the federal constitution establishes certain minimum levels which are "equally applicable to the [analogous] state constitutional provision." However, each state has the power to provide broader standards, and go beyond the minimum floor which is established by the federal Constitution.

The United States Supreme Court has repeatedly affirmed that the states are not only free to, but also encouraged to engage in independent analysis in drawing meaning from their own state constitutions. Indeed, this is a positive expression of the jurisprudence which has existed in the United States since the founding of the nation. Alexander Hamilton, lobbying for the ratification of the United States Constitution in the

Federalist Papers over two hundred years ago, made clear that the Supremacy Clause of the Federal Constitution was never designed to overshadow the states, or prevent them from maintaining their own pockets of autonomy. *See* The Federalist No. 33 (A. Hamilton), in *The Federalist Papers* (The New American Library ed.) 204.

Here in Pennsylvania, we have stated with increasing frequency that it is both important and necessary that we undertake an independent analysis of the Pennsylvania Constitution, each time a provision of that fundamental document is implicated. Although we may accord weight to federal decisions where they "are found to be logically persuasive and well reasoned, paying due regard to precedent and the policies underlying specific constitutional guarantees," we are free to reject the conclusions of the United States Supreme Court so long as we remain faithful to the minimum guarantees established by the United States Constitution.

The recent focus on the "New Federalism" has emphasized the importance of state constitutions with respect to individual rights and criminal procedure. As such, we find it important to set forth certain factors to be briefed and analyzed by litigants in each case hereafter implicating a provision of the Pennsylvania constitution. The decision of the United States Supreme Court in *Michigan v. Long,* 463 U.S. 1032 (1983), now requires us to make a "plain statement" of the adequate and independent state grounds upon which we rely, in order to avoid any doubt that we have rested our decision squarely upon Pennsylvania jurisprudence. Accordingly, as a general rule, it is important that litigants brief and analyze at least the following four factors:

> 1) text of the Pennsylvania constitutional provision;
>
> 2) history of the provision, including Pennsylvania case-law;
>
> 3) related case-law from other states;
>
> 4) policy considerations, including unique issues of state and local concern, and applicability within modern Pennsylvania jurisprudence.

Depending upon the particular issue presented, an examination of related federal precedent may be useful as part of the state constitutional analysis, not as binding authority, but as one form of guidance. However, it is essential that courts in Pennsylvania undertake an independent analysis under the Pennsylvania Constitution. Utilizing the above four factors, and having reviewed *Leon,* we conclude that a "good faith" exception to the exclusionary rule would frustrate the guarantees embodied in article I, section 8 of our Commonwealth's constitution.

ANALYSIS

A. *Text*

The text of article 1, section 8 of the Pennsylvania Constitution provides as follows:

Security from Searches and Seizures

Section 8. The people shall be secure in their persons, houses, papers and possessions from unreasonable searches and seizures, and no warrant to search any place or to seize any person or things shall issue without describing them as nearly as may be, nor without probable cause, supported by oath or affirmation subscribed to by the affiant.

Although the wording of the Pennsylvania Constitution is similar in language to the Fourth Amendment of the United States Constitution, we are not bound to interpret the two provisions as if they were mirror images, even where the text is similar or identical. Thus, we must next examine the history of article I, section 8, in order to draw meaning from that provision and consider the appropriateness of a "good faith" exception to the exclusionary rule in the Pennsylvania constitutional scheme.

B. *History*

We have made reference, on repeated occasions, to the unique history of article 1, section 8, as well as other provisions of the Pennsylvania Constitution. As we noted in *Sell:* "constitutional protection against unreasonable searches and seizures existed in Pennsylvania more than a decade before the adoption of the federal Constitution, and fifteen years prior to the promulgation of the Fourth Amendment."

Perhaps the extent of the untapped history of the Pennsylvania Constitution should be underscored. Pennsylvania's Constitution was adopted on September 28, 1776, a full ten years prior to the ratification of the United States Constitution. Like the constitutions of Virginia, New Jersey, Maryland, and most of the original 13 Colonies, Pennsylvania's Constitution was drafted in the midst of the American Revolution, as the first overt expression of independence from the British Crown. *See* W. Adams, *The First American Constitutions* at 61 (1980). The Pennsylvania Constitution was therefore meant to reduce to writing a deep history of unwritten legal and moral codes which had guided the colonists from the beginning of William Penn's charter in 1681. *See* White, *Commentaries on the Constitution of Pennsylvania* (1907). Unlike the Bill of Rights of the United States Constitution which emerged as a later addendum in 1791, the Declaration of Rights in the Pennsylvania Constitution was an organic part of the state's original constitution of 1776, and appeared (not coincidentally) first in that document.

Thus, contrary to the popular misconception that state constitutions are somehow patterned after the United States Constitution, the reverse is true.

The federal Bill of Rights borrowed heavily from the Declarations of Rights contained in the constitutions of Pennsylvania and other colonies. For instance, the Pennsylvania Declaration of Rights was the "direct precursor" of the freedom of speech and press. The Delaware Declaration of Rights prohibited quartering of soldiers and ex-post facto laws. North Carolina's Declaration of Rights provided a number of protections to the criminally accused—the right to trial by jury, the privilege against self-incrimination, and others—which later appeared in the United States Constitution.

With respect to article 1, section 8 of the present Pennsylvania Constitution, which relates to freedom from unreasonable searches and seizures, that provision had its origin prior to the Fourth Amendment, in Clause 10 of the original Constitution of 1776. Specifically, the original version of the search and seizure provision reads as follows:

> The people have a right to hold themselves, their houses, papers and possessions free from search and seizure, and therefore warrants without oaths or affirmations first made, affording sufficient foundation for them, and whereby any officer or messenger may be commanded or required to search suspected places, or to seize any person or persons, his or their property, not particularly described, are contrary to that right and ought not be granted.

The above provision was reworded at the time the Pennsylvania Constitution was revised extensively in 1790, and reappeared as article 1, section 8. The modern version of that provision has remained untouched for two hundred years, with the exception of the words "subscribed to by the affiant," which were added by the Constitutional Convention of 1873.

The requirement of probable cause in this Commonwealth thus traces its origin to its original Constitution of 1776, drafted by the first convention of delegates chaired by Benjamin Franklin. The primary purpose of the warrant requirement was to abolish "general warrants," which had been used by the British to conduct sweeping searches of residences and businesses, based upon generalized suspicions. Therefore, at the time the Pennsylvania Constitution was drafted in 1776, the issue of searches and seizures unsupported by probable cause was of utmost concern to the constitutional draftsmen.

Moreover, as this Court has stated repeatedly in interpreting article 1, section 8, that provision is meant to embody a strong notion of privacy, carefully safeguarded in this Commonwealth for the past two centuries. As we stated in *Sell:* "the survival of the language now employed in article 1, section 8 through over 200 years of profound change in other areas demonstrates that the paramount concern for privacy first adopted as part of our organic law in 1776 continues to enjoy the mandate of the people of this Commonwealth."

The history of article I, section 8, thus indicates that the purpose underlying the exclusionary rule in this Commonwealth is quite distinct from the purpose underlying the exclusionary rule under the Fourth Amendment, as articulated by the majority in *Leon.*

The United States Supreme Court in *Leon* made clear that, in its view, the *sole purpose* for the exclusionary rule under the Fourth Amendment was to deter police misconduct. The *Leon* majority also made clear that, under the Federal Constitution, the exclusionary rule operated as "a judicially created remedy designed to safeguard Fourth Amendment rights generally through its deterrent effect, rather than a personal constitutional right of the party aggrieved."

This reinterpretation differs from the way the exclusionary rule has evolved in Pennsylvania since the decision of *Mapp v. Ohio* in 1961 and represents a shift in judicial philosophy from the decisions of the United States Supreme Court dating back to *Weeks v. United States.*

Like many of its sister states, Pennsylvania did not adopt an exclusionary rule until the United States Supreme Court's decision in *Mapp* required it to do so. However, at the time the exclusionary rule was embraced in Pennsylvania, we clearly viewed it as a constitutional mandate. This interpretation was in keeping with a long line of federal cases, beginning with *Weeks* in 1914, which viewed the exclusionary rule as a necessary corollary to the prohibition against unreasonable searches and seizures.

As one commentator noted in piecing together the history of the exclusionary rule: "'Deterrence', now claimed to be the primary ground for exclusion, seems to have had no substantial place in any of these conceptions of the practice."

During the first decade after *Mapp,* our decisions in Pennsylvania tended to parallel the cases interpreting the Fourth Amendment. However, beginning in 1973, our case-law began to reflect a clear divergence from federal precedent. The United States Supreme Court at this time began moving toward a metamorphosed view, suggesting that the purpose of the exclusionary rule "is not to redress the injury to the privacy of the search victim (but, rather) to deter future unlawful police conduct." At the same time this Court began to forge its own path under article I, section 8 of the Pennsylvania Constitution, declaring with increasing frequency that article I, section 8 of the Pennsylvania Constitution embodied a strong notion of privacy, notwithstanding federal cases to the contrary. In *Commonwealth v. Platou* and *Commonwealth v. DeJohn,* we made explicit that "the right to be free from unreasonable searches and seizures contained in article I, section 8 of the Pennsylvania Constitution is tied into the implicit right to privacy in this Commonwealth." In *DeJohn,* we specifically refused to follow the United States Supreme Court's decision in *United States v.*

Miller, 425 U.S. 435 (1976), which had held that a citizen had no standing to object to the seizure of his or her bank records.

From *DeJohn* forward, a steady line of case-law has evolved under the Pennsylvania Constitution, making clear that article I, section 8 is unshakably linked to a right of privacy in this Commonwealth.

As Mr. Justice Flaherty noted in *Denoncourt v. Commonwealth,* in echoing the wisdom of Justice Brandeis over 60 years ago: "The makers of our Constitution undertook to secure conditions favorable to the pursuit of happiness....They conferred, as against the government, the right to be let alone—the most comprehensive of rights and the right most valued by civilized men."

Most recently, in *Melilli,* this Court cited with approval the decision of the Superior Court in *Commonwealth v. Beauford,* holding that article I, section 8 of the Pennsylvania Constitution was offended by the installation of a pen register device without probable cause. Mr. Justice Papadakos, in rejecting the holding of the United States Supreme Court in *Smith v. Maryland,* 442 U.S. 735 (1979), emphasized that "article I, section 8 of the Pennsylvania Constitution...may be employed to guard *individual privacy* rights against unreasonable searches and seizures more zealously than the federal government does under the Constitution of the United States by serving as an independent source of supplemental rights." Mr. Justice Papadakos went on to conclude that, because a pen register "is the equivalent of a search warrant in its operative effect where the intrusion involves a violation of a privacy interest," the affidavit and order "must comply with the requirements of probable cause required under Pa. Rules of Criminal Procedure Chapter 2000, Search Warrants."

Thus, the exclusionary rule in Pennsylvania has consistently served to bolster the twin aims of article I, section 8; to-wit, the safeguarding of privacy and the fundamental requirement that warrants shall only be issued upon probable cause. As this Court explained in *Commonwealth v. Miller*:

> The linch-pin that has been developed to determine whether it is appropriate to issue a search warrant is the test of probable cause. It is designed to protect us from unwarranted and even vindictive incursions upon our privacy. It insulates from dictatorial and tyrannical rule by the state, and preserves the concept of democracy that assures the freedom of its citizens. This concept is second to none in its importance in delineating the dignity of the individual living in a free society.

Whether the United States Supreme Court has determined that the exclusionary rule does not advance the Fourth Amendment purpose of deterring police conduct is irrelevant. Indeed, we disagree with that Court's suggestion in *Leon* that we in Pennsylvania have been employing the exclusionary rule all these years to deter police corruption. We flatly reject this notion. We have no reason to believe that police officers or district justices in the Commonwealth of Pennsylvania do not engage in "good faith" in carrying out their duties. What is significant, however, is that our Constitution has historically been interpreted to incorporate a strong right of privacy, and an equally strong adherence to the requirement of probable cause under article 1, section 8. Citizens in this Commonwealth possess such rights, even where a police officer in "good faith" carrying out his or her duties inadvertently invades the privacy or circumvents the strictures of probable cause. To adopt a "good faith" exception to the exclusionary rule, we believe, would virtually emasculate those clear safeguards which have been carefully developed under the Pennsylvania Constitution over the past 200 years.

C. *Related Case-Law From Other States*

A number of states other than Pennsylvania have confronted the issue of whether to apply a "good faith" exception to the exclusionary rule, under their own constitutions, in the wake of *Leon.*

The highest courts of at least two states—Arkansas and Missouri— have seemingly embraced the good faith exception under their own constitutions. *See Jackson v. State,* 722 S.W.2d 831 (Ark. 1987); *State v. Brown,* 708 S.W.2d 140 (Mo. 1986) (en banc). Intermediary appellate courts in at least four other states—Indiana, Kansas, Maryland and Louisiana—have indicated their acceptance of the "good faith" exception. *See Mers v. State,* 482 N.E.2d 778 (Ind. Ct. App. 1985); *State v. Huber,* 704 P.2d 1004 (Kan. Ct. App. 1985); *Howell v. State,* 483 A.2d 780 (Md. Ct. Spec. App. 1984); *State v. Martin,* 487 So.2d 1295 (La. Ct. App.), *writ denied,* 491 So.2d 25 (La. 1986). In virtually all of those states embracing the "good-faith" exception under their own constitutions, however, the reasoning is a simple affirmation of the logic of *Leon,* with little additional state constitutional analysis.

On the other hand, the highest courts of at least four states—New Jersey, New York, North Carolina and Connecticut—have chosen to reject the "good-faith" exception under their own constitutions, with more detailed analysis of state constitutional principles. *See State v. Marsala,* 579 A.2d 58 (Conn. 1990); *State v. Novembrino,* 519 A.2d 820 (N.J. 1987); *People v. Bigelow,* 488 N.E.2d 451 (N.Y. 1985); *State v. Carter,* 370 S.E.2d 553 (N.C. 1988). *See also Mason v. State,* 534 A.2d 242 (Del. 1987) (rejecting good-faith exception as statutory matter); *Commonwealth v. Upton,* 476 N.E.2d 548 (Mass. 1985) (same). The intermediate appellate courts of at least four additional states—Tennessee, Wisconsin, Michigan, and Minnesota—have likewise eschewed the logic of *Leon* under their own state constitutions. *See State v. Taylor,* 763 S.W.2d 756 (Tenn. Crim. App. 1987); *State v. Grawein,* 367 N.W.2d 816 (Wis. Ct. App. 1985);

People v. Sundling, 395 N.W.2d 308 (Mich. Ct. App. 1986); *State v. Herbst,* 395 N.W.2d 399, 404 (Minn. Ct. App. 1986).

A mere scorecard of those states which have accepted and rejected *Leon* is certainly not dispositive of the issue in Pennsylvania. However, the logic of certain of those opinions bears upon our analysis under the Pennsylvania Constitution, particularly given the unique history of article 1, section 8.

In this respect, we draw support from other states which have declined to adopt a "good faith" exception, particularly New Jersey, Connecticut and North Carolina. In *State v. Novembrino,* the New Jersey Supreme Court found that the "good faith" exception to the exclusionary rule was inconsistent with the New Jersey Constitution, because it would undermine the requirement of probable cause. Although New Jersey, like Pennsylvania, had no exclusionary rule in place prior to *Mapp v. Ohio* in 1961, the New Jersey Court found that it had become "imbedded" in the jurisprudence under that state's constitution. As the New Jersey court wrote in *Novembrino*:

> The exclusionary rule, by virtue of its consistent application over the past twenty-five years, has become an integral element of our state-constitutional guarantee that search warrants will not issue without probable cause. Its function is not merely to deter police misconduct. The rule also serves as the indispensable mechanism for vindicating the constitutional right to be free from unreasonable searches.

Similarly, the Connecticut Supreme Court—which most recently rejected the good faith exception on August 7, 1990—concluded that the purpose of the exclusionary rule under article I, section 7 of the Connecticut Constitution, was to "preserve the integrity of the warrant issuing process as a whole." Thus, when evidence was suppressed under this provision due to a defective warrant, "the issuing authority...is not being 'punished' for a mistake, but is, rather, being informed that a constitutional violation has taken place and is also being instructed in how to avoid such violations in the future."

More directly on point, the North Carolina Supreme Court in *State v. Carter* rejected the "good faith" exception to the exclusionary rule, noting the importance of the *privacy rights* flowing from the search and seizure provision in the North Carolina Constitution. The court in *Carter* emphasized the need to preserve the integrity of the judiciary in North Carolina, in excluding illegally seized evidence when such important rights of the citizenry were at stake. Wrote the North Carolina Supreme Court:

> The exclusionary sanction is indispensable to give effect to the constitutional principles prohibiting unreasonable search and seizure. We are persuaded that the exclusionary rule is the only effective bulwark against governmental disregard for constitutionally protected privacy rights. Equally of importance in

our reasoning, we adhere to the rule for the sake of maintaining the integrity of the judicial branch of government.

We similarly conclude that, given the strong right of privacy which inheres in article 1, section 8, as well as the clear prohibition against the issuance of warrants without probable cause, or based upon defective warrants, the good faith exception to the exclusionary rule would directly clash with those rights of citizens as developed in our Commonwealth over the past 200 years. To allow the judicial branch to participate, directly or indirectly, in the use of the fruits of illegal searches would only serve to undermine the integrity of the judiciary in this Commonwealth. From the perspective of the citizen whose rights are at stake, an invasion of privacy, in good faith or bad, is equally as intrusive. This is true whether it occurs through the actions of the legislative, executive or the judicial branch of government.

D. *Policy Considerations*

We recognize that, in analyzing any state constitutional provision, it is necessary to go beyond the bare text and history of that provision as it was drafted 200 years ago, and consider its application within the modern scheme of Pennsylvania jurisprudence. An assessment of various policy considerations, however, only supports our conclusion that the good faith exception to the exclusionary rule would be inconsistent with the jurisprudence surrounding article 1, section 8.

First, such a rule would effectively negate the judicially created mandate reflected in the Pennsylvania Rules of Criminal Procedure, in Rules 2003, 2005 and 2006. Specifically, Rule 2003 relates to the requirements for the issuance of a warrant, and provides in relevant part:

> (a) No search warrant shall issue but upon probable cause supported by one or more affidavits sworn to before the issuing authority. The issuing authority, in determining whether probable cause has been established, may not consider any evidence outside the affidavits.

> (b) At any hearing on a motion for the return or suppression of evidence, or for suppression of the fruits of evidence, obtained pursuant to a search warrant, no evidence shall be admissible to establish probable cause other than the affidavits provided for in paragraph (a).

Rule 2003 serves to underscore the incongruity of adopting a good faith exception to the exclusionary rule in Pennsylvania. Although Rule 2003 is not constitutionally mandated by article 1, section 8, as *Milliken* correctly explains, it reflects yet another expression of this Court's unwavering insistence that probable cause exist before a warrant is issued, and only those facts memorialized in the written affidavit may be considered in establishing probable cause, in order to eliminate any chance of incomplete or reconstructed hindsight. It is true, as *Milliken* summarizes, that the history of article 1, section 8 does not itself prohibit the use of oral testimony to establish probable cause, outside the four corners of the warrant. Nonetheless, we have chosen to adopt that Rule as an administrative matter, and that Rule has now stood in Pennsylvania for 17 years.

In the instant case, probable cause—as defined under Pennsylvania law—is lacking. Two lower courts have so held; we concur. Applying the federal *Leon* test would not only frustrate the procedural safeguards embodied in Rule 2003, but would permit the admission of illegally seized evidence in a variety of contexts where probable cause is lacking, so long as the police officer acted in "good faith." In *Leon* itself probable cause was absent entirely, yet illegally seized evidence was admitted into evidence.

We cannot countenance such a wide departure from the text and history of article 1, section 8, nor can we permit the use of a "good faith" exception to effectively nullify Pennsylvania Rule of Criminal Procedure 2003. Our Constitution requires that warrants shall not be issued except upon probable cause. We have specifically adopted Rule 2003 for the purpose of confining the probable cause inquiry to the written affidavit and warrant, in order to avoid any doubt as to the basis for probable cause. We decline to undermine the clear mandate of these provisions by slavishly adhering to federal precedent where it diverges from two hundred years of our own constitutional jurisprudence.

A second policy consideration which bolsters our conclusion is that the underlying premise of *Leon* is still open to serious debate. Although it is clear that the exclusionary rule presents some cost to society, in allowing "some guilty defendants (to)…go free," the extent of the costs are far from clear. A number of recent studies have indicated that the exclusion of illegally seized evidence has had a marginal effect in allowing guilty criminals to avoid successful prosecution. Indeed, the *Leon* decision itself indicates relatively low statistics with respect to the impact of the exclusionary rule in thwarting legitimate prosecutions. Equally as important, the alternative to the exclusionary rule most commonly advanced—*i.e.*, allowing victims of improper searches to sue police officers directly—has raised serious concern among police officers.

A third policy consideration which compels our decisions is that, given the recent decision of the United States Supreme Court in *United States v. Gates* adopting a "totality of the circumstances test" in assessing probable cause, there is far less reason to adopt a "good faith" exception to the exclusionary rule. We have adopted *Gates* as a matter of Pennsylvania law in the recent case of *Commonwealth v. Gray*. As a number of jurists have pointed out, the flexible *Gates* standard now eliminates much of the prior concern which existed with respect to an overly rigid application of the exclusionary rule.

Finally, the dangers of allowing magistrates to serve as "rubber stamps" and of fostering "magistrate-shopping," are evident under *Leon.* As the instant case illustrates, police officers and magistrates have historically worked closely together in this Commonwealth. Trooper Deise and District Justice Tlumac prepared the warrant and affidavit with Trooper Deise dictating the affidavit while the magistrate typed it verbatim.

There is no suggestion here that Trooper Deise and District Justice Tlumac acted other than in utmost "good faith" when preparing the warrant. Nevertheless, we are mindful of the fact that both state and federal interpretations of the Fourth Amendment require a warrant to be issued by a "neutral and detached magistrate," because as Mr. Justice Papadakos noted, there is a requirement of "an independent determination of probable cause." The reason for this requirement is evident. Would the District Justice act as nothing more than an adjunct of the police department, there would be no opportunity for *review* of the warrant prior to its issuance, and hence, a search warrant would be nothing more than the police's own determination of whether probable cause exists. We cannot countenance such a policy as it clearly runs afoul of our historically based system of government; which requires three *independent* branches.

It must be remembered that a District Justice is not a member of the executive branch—the police—but a member of the judiciary. By falling within the judicial branch of government, the District Justice is thus charged with the responsibility of being the *disinterested* arbiter of disputes and is charged further with acting as the bulwark between the police and the rights of citizens. Unless and until a magistrate independently determines there is probable cause, no warrant shall issue.

This is not to say that we distrust our police or district justices; far from it. We, in fact, have no doubt that police officers and district justices in Pennsylvania are intelligent, committed and independent enough to carry out their duties under the scheme which has evolved over the past thirty years, in order to safeguard the rights of our citizens.

However, requiring "neutral and detached magistrates" furthers the twin aims of safeguarding privacy and assuring that no warrant shall issue but upon probable cause. As such, we see no reason to eliminate this requirement, for if we did, we would eviscerate the purpose of requiring warrants prior to searches. As one member of the Mississippi Supreme Court noted in a similar vein: "If it ain't broke, don't fix it." *Stringer v. State,* 491 So.2d 837, 850 (Miss. 1986).

CONCLUSION

Thirty years ago, when the exclusionary rule was first introduced, police officers were perhaps plagued with ill-defined, unarticulated rules governing their conduct. However, the past thirty years have seen a gradual sharpening of the process, with police officers adapting well to the exclusionary rule.

The purpose of Rule 2003 is not to exclude *bona fide* evidence based upon technical errors and omissions by police officers or magistrates. Rather, Rule 2003 is meant to provide support for the probable cause requirement of article I, section 8 of the Pennsylvania Constitution by assuring that there is an objective method for determining when probable cause exists, and when it does not.

In the instant case, the evidence seized from defendant Edmunds was the product of a constitutionally defective search warrant. Article I, section 8 of the Pennsylvania Constitution does not incorporate a "good faith" exception to the exclusionary rule. Therefore, the marijuana seized from the white corrugated building, the marijuana seized from Edmund's home, and the written and oral statements obtained from Edmunds by the troopers, must be suppressed. We base our decision strictly upon the Pennsylvania Constitution; any reference to the United States Constitution is merely for guidance and does not compel our decision.

Justice Brandeis, in his eloquent dissent in *Olmstead v. United* States, minded us over a half-century ago:

> In a government of laws, existence of the government will be imperiled if it fails to observe the law scrupulously. Our government is the potent, the omnipresent teacher. For good or for ill, it teaches the whole people by its example. Crime is contagious. If the Government becomes a lawbreaker, it breeds contempt for law; it invites every man to become a law unto himself; it invites anarchy.

Although the exclusionary rule may place a duty of thoroughness and care upon police officers and district justices in this Commonwealth, in order to safeguard the rights of citizens under article I, section 8, that is a small price to pay, we believe, for a democracy.

NOTES

1. In *Leon*, the United States Supreme Court characterized the adoption of the federal exclusionary rule in *Calandra* as a prophylactic measure to deter police conduct and not as a holding that was required by the Fourth Amendment. *United States v. Calandra*, 414 U.S. 338 (1974). This construction permits the Court to recognize exceptions like the "good faith" exception in *Leon*.

2. The rationale in *Leon* has been rejected by the majority of state courts in construing state constitutions, including: Connecticut, Delaware, Georgia, Idaho, Iowa, Massachusetts, Michigan, Minnesota, New Hampshire, New Jersey, New Mexico, New York, North Carolina, Oklahoma, Pennsylvania, South Carolina, Texas, Vermont, and Washington. States that have adopted the *Leon* good faith exception are: Arkansas, Kentucky, Mississippi, Missouri, Nebraska, and South Dakota.

3. In rejecting the good faith exception under article I, section 17 of the Idaho Constitution, the Supreme Court of Idaho conducted an extensive analysis and concluded that the policy behind the Idaho exclusionary rule was incompatible with the good faith exception in *Leon* and *Calandra*. *See State v. Guzman*, 842 P.2d 660 (Idaho 1992).

4. The California and Florida Constitutions have been amended to prohibit any state constitutional exclusionary rule, beyond what is required for violations of the Fourth Amendment. *See* Cal. Const. art. I, § 28(d); Fla. Const. art. I, § 12. Therefore, the California and Florida Constitutions required the adoption of *Leon* because the search and seizure provisions in both constitutions must be construed in lockstep with the Fourth Amendment.

D. AUTOMATIC STANDING

STATE v. BULLOCK
901 P.2d 61 (Mont. 1995)

TRIEWEILER, J.

The defendants, Eddie Peterson and Bill Bullock, were charged in Jefferson County Justice Court with unlawfully killing a game animal and possession of an unlawfully killed animal. The Justice Court suppressed all of the State's evidence pertaining to Peterson, and dismissed the charges against Bullock. The State appealed to the District Court for a trial *de novo*. On appeal, the District Court denied the defendants' motions to dismiss and to suppress evidence. Peterson then pled guilty to unlawfully killing a game animal; Bullock pled guilty to unlawfully possessing a game animal; and both defendants reserved their right to appeal the District Court's order denying their motions to dismiss and suppress evidence. Following two orders by this Court which remanded this case to the District Court for further proceedings, we affirm the District Court's order which denied the defendants' motion to dismiss, and reverse the District Court's order which denied the defendants' motion to suppress evidence.

FACTUAL BACKGROUND

At about 6:30 a.m. on October 31, 1991, while returning home from work, Chuck Wing observed what he estimated was a large six or seven point antlered bull elk on Boulder Hill near Boulder, Montana. He recognized that the elk was in Hunting District 380 where hunters were allowed to shoot only "spikes" unless they had a special permit. As Wing observed the elk, he heard a gunshot, saw the elk fall, and observed two men and a boy standing near a pickup truck in the vicinity of the fallen elk. He believed the pickup belonged to defendant Eddie J. Peterson. He then observed the three people drag the elk to the truck and load it without field-dressing it. Wing reported the incident to Jefferson County Sheriff Tom Dawson, who, in turn, relayed the information to Game Warden Chris Anderson, an employee of the Montana Department of Fish, Wildlife, and Parks. Anderson traveled from Helena to Boulder that morning to investigate the incident.

Anderson first interviewed Wing who related the above information. He then drove to Peterson's home in Boulder, but Peterson was not at home. Anderson returned to the sheriff's office where he learned that Peterson had a cabin in Basin Creek. Rather than try to give directions, Dawson agreed to accompany him to the cabin. To reach Peterson's cabin, it is necessary to travel approximately seven miles on a one-lane forest service road which is bounded by forest on both sides. At least one sign along that road indicates that the road is bordered by private property and advises the public to remain on the road.

Peterson's property is separated from the road by a fence. There is a gate which provides access to his property from the forest service road. "No Trespassing" signs are posted on trees on each side of the gate. His cabin is located at the end of a private road 334 feet from the forest service road. Between the forest service road and Peterson's cabin, the terrain is slightly elevated in a way that conceals Peterson's cabin and the other structures on his property. He moved his cabin beyond the hill at an earlier time so that it would not be evident to passersby.

When Anderson and Dawson reached Peterson's property, the gate was open. They entered the property through the gate and drove approximately 180 feet down Peterson's private road. As they descended the crest of the hill between his cabin and the forest service road, they first observed a large bull elk hanging from a tree in an area about 126 feet from Peterson's cabin. The elk could not be seen from the public road, nor was there evidence that it could be seen from any other public location. Peterson testified that the elk was hanging between his cabin, several vehicles, and a guest sleeping cabin.

The parties agreed that, in the past, anyone who wished to enter Peterson's property or drive on his private road had called to ask permission. In fact, the Jefferson County Sheriff's Office had done so a few days earlier prior to conducting a search for lost hunters. On the date in question, neither Dawson nor Anderson asked or received permission to be on Peterson's property. Neither had they secured a search warrant, in spite of the fact that Anderson testified in Justice Court that he believed there was probable cause that a crime had been committed, that Peterson was involved, and that Peterson still possessed evidence of that crime.

At the hearing held in the District Court pursuant to the defendants' motion to suppress, there was disagreement about exactly what Anderson and Dawson did after observing the elk hanging near Peterson's cabin. However, in stipulations filed with the court earlier, the parties agreed that after observing the elk, Anderson and Dawson went over to examine it. After conducting the examination, Anderson then requested that Peterson take him and Dawson to the place where the elk was killed. Peterson did so, but at the site where the law enforcement officers were taken, there were no elk tracks—only a pile of the elk's entrails. It was apparent to Anderson that the elk had not been killed at that location.

Anderson then confronted Peterson with the information he had received from Wing. Peterson provided him with an explanation that ultimately was found to be inaccurate. Bullock was then questioned, provided responses consistent with Peterson's, and declined the State's offer of immunity in exchange for testimony that would incriminate Peterson.

The following day, Anderson returned to Peterson's cabin and confiscated the elk carcass.

On November 8, 1991, Peterson was charged in Jefferson County Justice Court with unlawfully killing a game animal. Bullock was charged with possession of an unlawfully killed animal. Both defendants pled not guilty to those charges.

Did defendant Bullock have standing to challenge the State's entry upon and search of land owned by Peterson?

The State contends that Bullock has no standing to challenge the legality of the State's entry onto and search of Peterson's land because he had no ownership interest in that land. It contends that pursuant to this Court's recent decisions in *State v. Gonzales* 751 P.2d 1063 (Mont. 1988), and *State v. Powers*, 758 P.2d 761 (Mont. 1988), a party must have some interest in the property searched before he or she can contest the admissibility of evidence gathered during the search.

Bullock responds that he was charged with possessing the elk carcass seized from Peterson's property, and that under our prior decisions, that possessory interest was sufficient to establish standing.

We agree that the State construes our prior decisions regarding standing too narrowly.

Even after the United States Supreme Court retreated from its "automatic standing" rule in cases where a defendant is charged with illegal possession of some item, in *United States v. Salvucci*, 448 U.S. 83 (1980), we held that ownership of the property searched is not necessary to establish standing to object to the legality of a search. *State v. Isom* 641 P.2d 417 (Mont. 1982). We stated:

> Notwithstanding the limitations placed on *Jones* [*v. United States*, 362 U.S. 257 (1960)], the Court in *Rakas* [*v. Illinois*, 439 U.S. 128 (1978)], and again in

Salvucci, emphasized that ownership is not a key element in determining standing. The test for standing is not to be based on distinctions out of property and tort law: "In defining the scope of that interest, we adhere to the view expressed in *Jones* and echoed in later cases that arcane distinctions in property and tort law between guests, licensees, invitees, and the like ought not to control." The controlling view, then, seems to be that expressed in *Mancusi v. DeForte,* 392 U.S. 364 (1968), in which the Court said that the *Katz* test of "'legitimate expectation of privacy' makes it clear that capacity to claim the protection of the Fourth Amendment depends not upon a property right in the invaded place, but upon whether the area was one in which there was a reasonable expectation of freedom from governmental intrusion."

Following this rationale, we concluded in *Isom* that a defendant who was a guest in his uncle's home at the time that it was searched had standing to object to the government search of that home, even though he had no ownership interest in the premises.

We have since held in both *Gonzales* and *Powers* that a possessory interest in either the premises searched *or the property seized* is sufficient to establish standing. However, we have never modified nor reversed our position in *Isom.*

Other states which have held that a possessory interest in the items seized is sufficient to establish standing to challenge the legality of a search or the property's seizure, have adopted automatic standing rules on independent state grounds where the defendant is charged with unlawfully possessing that item.

For example, in *State v. Alston,* 440 A.2d 1311 (N.J. 1981), the defendants were passengers in a vehicle from which weapons were seized during a search of the vehicle. They were later charged with unlawful possession of the weapons. Pursuant to the defendants' motion, the evidence was suppressed by the trial court, based on the illegality of the police search. On appeal, the state contended that the defendant passengers had no standing to challenge the legality of the search of the vehicle, despite their possessory interest in the weapons which had been seized.

After reviewing the United States Supreme Court's decisions on standing, including *Salvucci,* that court noted an inconsistency in the federal law which appeared to allow prosecutors to assert contradictory positions: "[T]hat the defendant possessed the contraband property for the purposes of proving criminal liability, but that he had insufficient possessory interest in the property for the purposes of defending the legality of the search and seizure." The court pointed out that a basic principle of American federalism confers on state courts the power to afford citizens of each state greater protection against unreasonable searches and seizures than may be required by the Supreme Court's interpretation of the Fourth Amendment, and on that basis, concluded that the *Salvucci* decision afforded inadequate protection against unreasonable searches and seizures.

Finally, the New Jersey Supreme Court concluded that based on its rule of standing which provided that "a criminal defendant is entitled to bring a motion to suppress evidence obtained in an unlawful search and seizure if he has a proprietary, possessory or participatory interest in either the place searched or the property seized," it would retain the automatic standing rule where a defendant is charged with an offense in which possession of the seized evidence at the time of the contested search is an essential element of guilt. It adopted reasoning from former Justice Thurgood Marshall that:

> [t]he automatic standing rule is a salutary one which protects the rights of defendants and eliminates the wasteful requirement of making a preliminary showing of standing in pretrial proceedings involving possessory offenses, where the charge itself alleges an interest sufficient to support a Fourth Amendment claim.

Other states have also adopted the rule of automatic standing for crimes of possession. *See State v. White*, 574 P.2d 840 (Ariz. Ct. App. 1978); *State v. Alosa*, 623 A.2d 218 (N.H. 1993).

We agree with the reasoning in *Alston*. Based on independent state grounds pursuant to article II, section 11 of the Montana Constitution, we hold that when the charge against the defendant includes an allegation of a possessory interest in the property which is seized, the defendant has standing to object to the prosecutorial use of that evidence based on either the unlawful search of the location where it was found, or its unlawful seizure.

Since Bullock was accused by the State of unlawfully possessing the elk carcass which was found on Peterson's property, we conclude, based on our prior decisions and the logical application of those decisions as set forth above, that he had standing to object to the State's search of Peterson's property and seizure of that carcass.

NOTE

In *United States v. Salvucci*, 448 U.S. 83 (1980), the United States Supreme Court abolished the automatic standing rule for purposes of the Fourth Amendment. As in Montana, a minority of state constitutions are still construed to provide automatic standing for defendants charged with possession of an item seized, without requiring the defendant to assert an ownership or possessory interest. *See, e.g., Commonwealth v. Armendola*, 550 N.E.2d 121 (Mass. 1990); *State v. Evans*, 150 P.3d 105 (Wash. 2007).

E. WARRANT REQUIREMENT

STATE v. BRYANT
950 A.2d 467 (Vt. 2008)

SKOGLUND, J.

The issue on this appeal from a conviction for cultivation of marijuana is whether the warrantless aerial scrutiny of defendant's yard, for the purpose of detecting criminal activity by the occupant of the property, violated privacy rights secured by the Vermont Constitution. We hold that Vermont citizens have a constitutional right to privacy that ascends into the airspace above their homes and property. The warrantless aerial surveillance in this case violated that constitutionally protected privacy right. Accordingly, we reverse.

Defendant was charged with felony possession and cultivation of marijuana. He moved to suppress from evidence the marijuana plants discovered growing by his house, alleging a violation of chapter I, article 11 of the Vermont Constitution. The trial court denied the motion. A jury convicted defendant on the cultivation charge, but not on the possession charge. Defendant appeals from the trial court's denial of his motion to suppress. We reverse.

Defendant argues that an unconstitutional aerial surveillance of his property resulted in the issuance of a search warrant that led to the discovery of defendant's marijuana cultivation. At a hearing on the motion to dismiss, the following facts were found by the court or were uncontested. Defendant lives in a remote area on a wooded hill in the town of Goshen, in Addison County. The property is accessible by a locked gate on a Forest Service road to which only defendant, his partner, and the Forest Service have keys. Beyond the gate, the dirt road passes defendant's homestead and continues a short distance into the National Forest, where the road dead-ends. Where the road cuts across defendant's property, the Forest Service has a restricted right-of-way. Defendant has posted prominent no-trespassing signs around his property. Prior to the aerial surveillance, defendant told a local forest official that he did not want the Forest Service or anyone else trespassing on his land.

The local forest official suspected that defendant was responsible for marijuana plants that were reportedly growing in the National Forest (not on defendant's property) because he found defendant's insistence on privacy to be "paranoid." The forest official suggested to the State Police that a Marijuana Eradication Team (MERT) flight over defendant's property might be a good idea. MERT is an anti-drug program, and MERT flights are executed by the Vermont State Police in cooperation with the Army National Guard. A state trooper, scheduled to do a MERT flight, was given the information identifying the defendant's residence as a good target. On August 7, 2003, the state trooper and an Army National Guard pilot flew in a National Guard helicopter to the Goshen area. Having previously located the site on a map, the trooper directed the pilot to defendant's property, where two plots of marijuana were observed growing about 100 feet from the house.

Defendant introduced testimony of several people who witnessed the flight. One witness, who was working outside at the time of the flyover, described the helicopter as being at twice the height of her house, or approximately 100 feet above ground level. She testified that the noise was "deafening." She observed the helicopter spend "a good half-hour" in the area of defendant's residence, where it circled "very low down to the trees." After the flight, the state trooper prepared an application for a search warrant based solely on his observation during the aerial surveillance of what he believed to be marijuana plants. In the application, the trooper characterized the surveillance as having been from "an aircraft at least 500 feet above the ground." The warrant was issued and executed, and three marijuana plots were discovered by defendant's home.

Based on the evidence presented at the suppression hearing, the court found that the helicopter circled defendant's property for approximately fifteen to thirty minutes, well below 500 feet in altitude, and at times as low as 100 feet above the ground. Although both the trooper and the pilot testified that the helicopter remained at least 500 feet off the ground at all times, the court did not find their testimony to be credible. The court further found that pilots doing MERT flights in Vermont are told to stay at least 500 feet above the ground and that, according to a National Guard pilot who testified for the State, the reason MERT pilots are so directed is to avoid invasions of privacy.

The court, however, denied defendant's motion, holding that defendant had no reasonable expectation of privacy from the sky. The court reasoned that, while helicopter flights over one's property in rural Vermont might be infrequent, a reasonable person would still assume that such flights will happen. The court concluded that the police surveillance was not so intrusive as to violate the Vermont Constitution. We disagree and reverse.

Article 11 of the Vermont Constitution protects the people's right to be free "from unreasonable government intrusions into legitimate expectations of privacy." When government conducts a warrantless search, the law presumes that the intrusion is unreasonable. The aerial surveillance at issue in this case was warrantless, and therefore presumptively unreasonable. Thus, the sole issue in this case is whether the aerial surveillance constitutes a search under article 11 of Vermont's Constitution.

An article 11 search occurs when the government intrudes into "areas or activities" that are the subject of "'legitimate expectations of privacy.'" Under article 11, the question of whether an individual has a legitimate expectation of privacy "'hinges on the essence of underlying constitutional values—including respect for both private, subjective expectations and public norms.'" Therefore, in order to invoke article 11 protection, a person must "exhibit [] an actual (subjective) expectation of privacy…that society is prepared to recognize as reasonable." In other words, article 11 requires an individual to have "conveyed an expectation of privacy in such a way that a reasonable person would conclude that he sought to exclude the public." "Whether the steps taken are adequate for this purpose will depend on the specific facts of each case."

We have often noted the "significance of the home as a repository of heightened privacy expectations," and have deemed those heightened expectations legitimate. Therefore, although we have disagreed amongst ourselves about the extent to which circumstances may alter the general rule, government intrusions into the home are searches for purposes of article 11 even if an individual fails to take affirmative steps to convey his expectation of privacy.

A home's curtilage—the "area outside the physical confines of a house into which the 'privacies of life' may extend"—merits "the same constitutional protection from unreasonable searches and seizures as the home itself." *State v. Rogers,* 638 A.2d 569, 572 (Vt. 1993) (quoting *Oliver v. United States,* 466 U.S. 170, 180 (1984)). However, relying on the principle that there is no invasion of privacy—and therefore no search when government observes that which is willingly exposed to the public, we have consistently held that an individual must take affirmative steps to protect his privacy in his curtilage and his "open fields"—the real property beyond his curtilage. Government does conduct a search when it intrudes onto open fields that a reasonable person would expect to be private. Fences, gates, and no-trespassing signs generally suffice to apprise a person that the area is private.

In this case, we consider whether surveillance from an Army helicopter, circling at 100 feet over defendant's home and garden for fifteen to thirty minutes for the purpose of detecting contraband, violated his legitimate expectations of privacy. Whether and when aerial surveillance constitutes a search are questions that we have not squarely confronted before. We decide this case solely on Vermont Constitutional grounds, but may be guided by decisions of our sister states and the United States Supreme Court on similar questions. We begin our analysis with a survey of those decisions.

The United States Supreme Court has decided three aerial-surveillance cases; the Court ruled in each that the surveillance at issue was not a search within the meaning of the Fourth Amendment. *Florida v. Riley,* 488 U.S. 445, 448 (1989); *Dow Chem. Co. v. United States,* 476 U.S. 227, 239 (1986); *California v. Ciraolo,* 476 U.S. 207, 214 (1986). For the reasons explained below, we find minimal guidance in these decisions.

In *Dow Chemical,* the Court held that enhanced aerial photography of an industrial complex from an aircraft lawfully operating at altitudes of 12,000 feet, 3,000 feet and 1,200 feet was not a search. In *Dow,* the Court likened an industrial complex to an open field, and reasoned that "as such it is open to the view and observation of persons in aircraft lawfully in the public airspace immediately above or sufficiently near the area for the reach of cameras." The Court also found it "important that this is *not* an area immediately adjacent to a private home, where privacy expectations are most heightened." In light of our rejection of the federal open-fields doctrine, and the fact that the aerial surveillance in this case took place over defendant's curtilage, we find *Dow Chemical* unpersuasive for purposes of our article 11 analysis.

In *Ciraolo,* the Court examined "whether naked-eye observation of the [defendant's] curtilage by police from an aircraft lawfully operating at an altitude of 1,000 feet violates an expectation of privacy that is reasonable." The Court found that the defendant's construction of tall fences around his yard "[c]learly...met the test of manifesting his own subjective intent and desire to maintain privacy," but found that the defendant could not reasonably have expected that his garden was protected from public or official inspection from the air. The Court likened the public airways to public highways, and wrote that "Fourth Amendment protection...has never been extended to require...officers to shield their eyes when passing by a home on public thoroughfares." Further, the Court reasoned that "the mere fact that an individual has taken measures to restrict some views of his activities" does not "preclude an officer's observations from a public vantage point where he has a right to be and which renders the activities clearly visible."

We are not persuaded that the facts of *Ciraolo* make it analogous to this case. In *Ciraolo,* the five-member majority relied heavily on likening airplane travel above the defendant's suburban house at 1,000 feet to "passing by a home on public thoroughfares," reasoning that "[i]n an age where private and commercial flight in the public airways is routine, it is unreasonable for [the defendant] to expect that his marijuana plants were constitutionally protected from being observed...from an altitude of 1,000 feet." We find the air travel in this case—fifteen to thirty minutes of hovering over defendant's property at altitudes as low as 100 feet—to be distinctly unlike "passing by a home on public thoroughfares."

In addition, we find the Court's analysis in *Ciraolo* to lack the consideration for the significance of the home and its curtilage as "repositor[ies] of heightened privacy expectations" that our article 11 jurisprudence demands. The *Ciraolo* Court gave no weight to the fact that the aerial surveillance targeted a home and its curtilage. This omission is glaring, especially in light of the Court's acknowledgment in *Dow Chemical,* issued on the same day, that "privacy expectations are most heightened" in areas immediately adjacent to homes.

In *Riley,* the Court evaluated an aerial surveillance more analogous to the one at issue in this case; the surveillance was conducted in a helicopter being operated closer to the ground. The defendant lived in a mobile home on five acres of rural property with a greenhouse located ten to twenty feet behind the home. A wire fence surrounded the home and greenhouse, and the property was posted with a "DO NOT ENTER" sign. Based on an anonymous tip that marijuana was being grown on the defendant's property, sheriff's department officers circled twice over the property in a helicopter at an elevation of 400 feet. At the time of the flyover, the greenhouse had two roof panels missing and was open on two sides. Based on what an officer saw from the helicopter, he obtained a warrant, and subsequently found marijuana growing in the greenhouse. The Florida Supreme Court held that the flyover constituted a search under the Fourth Amendment for which a warrant was required.

The United States Supreme Court ruled that *Ciraolo* controlled, and reversed. Justice White's opinion for a plurality of four Justices opined that, while the defendant's precautions evinced a subjective expectation of privacy, he "could not reasonably have expected that his greenhouse was protected from public or official observation from a helicopter." Justice White cautioned that "it is of obvious importance that the helicopter in this case was not violating the law," as it was within navigable airspace. "We would have a different case," the plurality reasoned, "if flying at [400 feet] had been contrary to law or regulation." Cautioning that "not...[every] inspection of the curtilage of a house from an aircraft will always pass muster...simply because the plane is within the navigable airspace specified by law," the plurality also found relevant the fact that the surveillance was relatively nonintrusive. "Neither is there any intimation here," it reasoned, "that the helicopter interfered with [the defendant's] normal use of...the curtilage...[or that] intimate details connected with the use of the home or curtilage were observed and there was no undue noise, no wind, dust, or threat of injury."

Since the rulings in *Dow Chemical, Ciraolo* and *Riley,* and despite the fact that all the *Riley* opinions engaged in a multi-factored analysis, some state courts have relied solely on the legality of a helicopter's position in public airspace to determine whether the aerial surveillance at issue was a search. *See, e.g., State v. Ainsworth,* 801 P.2d 749, 750-52 (Or. 1990) (upholding surveillance from helicopter solely on basis of lawfulness of officer's vantage point, where testimony as to altitude ranged from fifteen feet above the tree line to "pretty close to four or five hundred feet"). Because FAA regulations allow helicopters to fly at any altitude "if the operation is conducted without hazard to persons or property on the surface," 14 C.F.R. § 91.119 (emphasis added), the inevitable result of this reasoning—in the absence of more restrictive state aviation laws—is that the *dangerousness* of police surveillance may become the yardstick by which constitutional privacy protection is measured. As a case on point, in *Commonwealth v. Oglialoro,* the Supreme Court of Pennsylvania reasoned that by using a transparent or translucent roof on a pole barn located within the curtilage of the defendant's house, the defendant "knowingly exposed his [marijuana plants] to persons lawfully operating aircraft over his property who might decide to take a look." 579 A.2d 1288, 1292 (Pa. 1990). The court thus rejected the suggestion that any expectation of privacy attached in such situations. However, the court held that the police-surveillance flight, which involved a helicopter hovering fifty feet above the barn for fifteen seconds, had violated FAA regulations and thus the Fourth Amendment because it "represented a hazard to persons and property on the ground."

Other state courts have developed a more nuanced approach to privacy protection. Some courts adopt the reasoning of Justice White's plurality in *Riley* and consider the legality and intrusiveness of the surveillance flight. *See Henderson v. People,* 879 P.2d 383, 389-90 (Colo. 1994) (upholding a surveillance where a helicopter made five passes above the defendant's home over the course of several minutes at or above 500 feet, where there was little evidence of noise, wind, dust, threat of injury or interference with the defendant's use of his curtilage, and where there was no indication that the defendant's neighbors felt compelled to exit their houses to observe the commotion); *Rowell v. State,* 544 So.2d 1089, 1093 (Fla. Dist. Ct. App. 1989) (upholding a surveillance where an airplane was operating at unknown altitude but where there was no evidence of illegality or "obtrusive[ness]"); *State v. Rodal,* 985 P.2d 863, 867 (Or. Ct. App. 1999) (upholding a surveillance where a military helicopter made two passes over the defendant's home at an altitude of 600 feet because the helicopter was being operated in a lawful and unintrusive manner); *State v. Wilson,* 988 P.2d 463, 465-66 (Wash. Ct. App. 1999) (upholding a surveillance where an airplane was operating at 500 feet over the defendant's rural residence and where no evidence that "visual enhancement equipment" made the method of viewing intrusive).

Still other state courts attempt to give effect to all of the *Riley* opinions by evaluating legality, intrusiveness, and the frequency of flight at the altitude at which the surveillance took place. In *People v. Pollock,* for example, the court acknowledged the legality of a helicopter's position at the altitude of 200 feet, but struck down the aerial surveillance based on the infrequency of helicopter flights at 200 feet and the intrusiveness of the "excessive noise" it created as it circled the targeted area. 796 P.2d 63, 64 (Colo. Ct. App. 1990). In *People v. McKim,* the court upheld surveillance conducted from a helicopter operating at 400 feet where there was "no evidence...that the helicopter surveillance over [the] defendant's residence interfered with [the] defendant's use of his property, or revealed intimate details connected with the use of his home or curtilage, or created any undue noise, wind, dust, or threat of injury." 263 Cal. Rptr. 21, 25 (Cal. Ct. App. 1989).

A remaining group of state courts rely on a multitude of factors of their own articulation. *See, e.g., Commonwealth v. One 1985 Ford Thunderbird Auto.,* 624 N.E.2d 547, 550-51 (Mass. 1993) (upholding surveillance where helicopter was operating at altitudes of 700 feet and above after considering (1) "whether the police had a lawful right to be where they were," (2) "whether the public had access to, or might be expected to be in, the area from which the surveillance was undertaken," (3) "the nature of the intrusion," and (4) "the character of the area (or object) which was the subject of the surveillance"). And, in the view of at least one state court, the legality of the surveillance can depend, in part, on whether the aerial observation was "part of [an] investigative operation" or was instead "wholly fortuitous." *State v. Vogel,* 428 N.W.2d 272, 274 (S.D. 1988).

It is our opinion that many of the factors relied on by our sister states and the Supreme Court in *Riley* are relevant to evaluating the legitimacy of privacy expectations under article 11 in the context of the aerial surveillance at issue in this case. The legitimacy of an individual's expectation of privacy is a broad question of "'private, subjective expectations and public norms.'" When we declined to adopt the federal open-fields doctrine in *Kirchoff,* we recognized that Vermonters normally expect their property to remain private when posted as such. We have also recognized that Vermonters normally have high expectations of privacy in and around their homes. Therefore, we think it is also likely that Vermonters expect—at least at a private, rural residence on posted land— that they will be free from intrusions that interrupt their use of their property, expose their intimate activities, or create undue noise, wind, or dust.

We are also persuaded that the legality of the altitude at which aerial surveillance takes place can be relevant to the determination of whether an individual has a legitimate expectation of privacy in his real property. Indeed, the citizens of Vermont likely expect that law enforcement personnel as well as other air travelers will abide by safety rules and other applicable laws and regulations when flying over their homes. However, it simply does not follow that whether a member of the public is abiding by the law in occupying a particular spot in the public airspace is an adequate test of whether government surveillance from that same spot is constitutional. Therefore, we disagree with those courts that would use the legality of an aircraft's position alone to evaluate the constitutionality of the surveillance conducted aboard it.

In any event, at least on the facts of this case, no one factor need act as a litmus test of constitutionality, because the surveillance at issue here was a patent violation of defendant's legitimate expectations of privacy. We understand that our abstention from drawing a bright line that makes the legality or frequency of flights at certain altitudes a quick index to the constitutionality of aerial surveillance gives limited guidance to trial courts and law enforcement personnel in the context of other cases. But we are not presented with other cases; we are presented only with this case. In this case, defendant has demonstrated that he has a subjective expectation of privacy in his back yard. He has taken precautions to exclude others from his back yard by posting his land and by communicating to a local forest official that he did not want people trespassing on his land.

The overriding function of article 11 is to protect personal privacy and dignity against unwarranted intrusion by the state. It requires that the state temper its efforts to apprehend criminals with a concern for the impact of its methods on our fundamental liberties. Principles established in cases such as this delineate the extent to which official intrusion into the privacy of any citizen will be constitutionally permissible.

In *Johnson v. United States,* the Supreme Court wrote that the Fourth Amendment reflects a choice that our society should be one in which citizens "dwell in reasonable security and freedom from surveillance." 333 U.S. 10, 14 (1948). With technological advances in surveillance techniques, the privacy-protection question is no longer whether police have physically invaded a constitutionally protected area. Rather, the inquiry is whether the surveillance invaded a constitutionally protected legitimate expectation of privacy. In this case, the targeted, low-level helicopter surveillance by the police of activities in an enclosed backyard is not consistent with that expectation—not without a warrant.

It may be easy to forget, especially in view of current concerns over drug abuse in our society, that the scope of article 11's protection "does not turn on whether the activity disclosed by a search is illegal or innocuous." The interest protected by article 11, like the Fourth Amendment, "is the expectation of the ordinary citizen, who has never engaged in illegal conduct in his life." In his dissent in *White,* Justice Harlan reasoned that the scope of constitutional protection must reflect "the impact of a practice on the sense of security that is the true concern of the [constitution's] protection of privacy." We agree. We protect defendant's marijuana plots against such surveillance so that law-abiding citizens may relax in their backyards, enjoying a sense of security that they are free from unreasonable surveillance.

The aerial surveillance in this case was a warrantless search forbidden by the Vermont Constitution. The warrant authorizing the subsequent search of defendant's premises for marijuana plants was obtained solely on the basis of the aerial observations. The evidence seized upon executing the warrant should therefore have been excluded from defendant's trial. Since the error was clearly prejudicial, his conviction must be overturned.

NOTES

1. The Vermont Constitution has been construed consistently as having a strong preference for warrants, *i.e.*, "one of the essential checks on unrestrained government determined by the framers…to be necessary to the preservation of individual freed." *State v. Bauder*, 924 A.2d 38 (Vt. 2007). Under article 11 of the Vermont Constitution, police must get a search warrant before searching a closed container unless "exceptional" circumstances—risk of undue delay, destruction of evidence or danger to officers—make getting a warrant impracticable. *State v. Neil*, 958 A.2d 1173 (Vt. 2008). Interestingly, article I, section 9 of the Texas Constitution "contains no requirement that a seizure or search be authorized by a warrant, and that a search or seizure that is otherwise reasonable will not be found to be in violation of that section because it was not authorized by a warrant." *Hulit v. State*, 982 S.W.2d 431 (Tex. Crim. App. 1998).

2. The United States Supreme Court has held that there is no reasonable expectation of privacy in garbage left in a public place with intent to disregard it. Thus, there was no Fourth Amendment search when police officers inspected the contents of opaque plastic bags left out for garbage collection. *California v. Greenwood*, 486 U.S. 35 (1988). Although most state constitutions have been construed to permit a warrantless search of trash that has been left out for collection, some state constitutions require a warrant. *See State v. Goss*, 834 A.2d 316 (N.H. 2003). *Greenwood* was also rejected on the basis of the greater privacy protection provided by the text in article I, section 7 of the Washington Constitution. *State v. Boland*, 800 P.2d 1112 (Wash. 1990). *See also* Chapter IV.

F. PHYSICAL SEIZURE OF INDIVIDUAL BY POLICE

STATE v. BEAUCHESNE
868 A.2d 972 (N.H. 2005)

DUGGAN, J.

Following a bench trial on stipulated facts, the defendant, John Beauchesne, was convicted of possession of cocaine, possession of marijuana, and resisting detention. On appeal, he challenges his convictions for possession of cocaine and marijuana, arguing that the Superior Court erroneously denied his motion to suppress the cocaine and marijuana. The defendant does not challenge his conviction for resisting detention. We reverse and remand.

On September 27, 2002, Detective Peter Morelli of the Derry Police Department was on duty patrolling downtown Derry. Detective Morelli was in an unmarked cruiser, wearing street clothes and "on the lookout for 'drug crime.'" Although Detective Morelli testified that he previously had investigated drug transactions in the area he was patrolling, he also testified that a drug transaction was no more likely to occur there than any other area in Derry.

At approximately 6:30 p.m., Detective Morelli observed two men standing in an alley off Railroad Avenue. One man was straddling a bike. The defendant was facing the man on the bike. Detective Morelli saw the defendant hand something small and "unidentifiable" to the man straddling the bike, then turn and walk toward the street.

Believing that he had just witnessed a drug transaction, Detective Morelli stopped and exited his cruiser, made eye contact with the defendant and motioned for the defendant to approach him. The defendant did not respond and walked away. Detective Morelli then yelled to the defendant, identifying himself as a police officer and ordering the defendant to stop. The defendant again did not respond and continued walking away.

Detective Morelli followed the defendant on foot. When he saw that the defendant was running away, Detective Morelli again yelled that he was a police officer and ordered the defendant to stop. The defendant continued to run and Detective Morelli followed him. Detective Morelli eventually caught up with the defendant and attempted to grab him. The defendant, however, fell to the ground. During his fall, the defendant either dropped or threw a plastic bag containing a green vegetative matter, which Detective Morelli was able to identify immediately as marijuana. Detective Morelli then fell over the defendant.

Detective Morelli arrested the defendant for resisting detention and possessing marijuana. Detective Morelli subsequently searched the defendant's person and discovered a quantity of cocaine.

The defendant moved to suppress the cocaine and marijuana obtained as a result of the seizure because Detective Morelli lacked reasonable, articulable suspicion when he first ordered the defendant to stop. The trial court denied the motion, ruling that under *California v. Hodari D.*, 499 U.S. 621, 626 (1991), the defendant was not seized until he "fell and thus submitted to the detective's show of authority," at which time Detective Morelli had reasonable, articulable suspicion that the defendant had committed a crime.

On appeal, the defendant argues that the trial court erred in ruling that, under part I, article 19 of the State Constitution, the defendant was not seized until he submitted to Detective Morelli's show of authority. To that end, the defendant argues that we should not adopt the holding in *Hodari D.*, which requires submission to a show of authority, for determining when a seizure occurs under the State Constitution. In addition, the defendant argues that because he was seized for State constitutional purposes when Detective Morelli ordered him to stop, the trial court erred in denying his motion to suppress the cocaine and marijuana because the detective lacked reasonable, articulable suspicion at the time of the seizure.

Seizure

The defendant argues that he was subject to an unlawful seizure because Detective Morelli lacked reasonable suspicion when he first ordered the defendant to stop. Accordingly, the defendant argues that the trial court erred in denying his motion to suppress the cocaine and marijuana as fruits of the unlawful seizure.

It is well settled that "[i]n order for a police officer to undertake an investigatory stop, the officer must have a reasonable suspicion—based on specific, articulable facts taken together with rational inferences from those facts—that the particular person stopped has been, is, or is about to be, engaged in criminal activity." An investigatory stop is a very limited seizure. Thus, in deciding whether Detective Morelli conducted a lawful investigatory stop, we must conduct a two-step inquiry. First, we must determine when the defendant was seized. Second, we must determine whether, at that time, Detective Morelli possessed a reasonable suspicion that the defendant was, had been or was about to be engaged in criminal activity.

The crux of this appeal is the determination of when, under part I, article 19 of the State Constitution, the defendant was seized. The defendant argues that, for State constitutional purposes, he was seized when Detective Morelli first ordered him to stop. The State, relying upon the holding in *Hodari D.*, argues that the defendant was seized when he fell and submitted to Detective Morelli's show of authority.

Not all interactions between the police and citizens involve a seizure of the person. "[A] seizure does not occur simply because a police officer approaches an individual and asks a few questions." *Florida v. Bostick,* 501 U.S. 429 (1991). This is true "[s]o long as a reasonable person would feel free to disregard the police and go about his business." Indeed, the police may request to examine the individual's identification or for consent to search the individual or his belongings. The person stopped, however, is not obliged to answer and the police may not convey a message that compliance with their request is required. Moreover, unless the police officer has reasonable suspicion, the person approached may not be detained.

An interaction between a police officer and a citizen becomes a seizure, however, when a reasonable person believes he or she is not free to leave. *United States v. Mendenhall,* 446 U.S. 544 (1980); *Riley,* 490 A.2d 1362 (adopting the *Mendenhall* definition of seizure). This occurs when an officer, by means of physical force or show of authority, has in some way restrained the liberty of the person. Circumstances indicating a "show of authority" might include the threatening presence of several officers, the display of a weapon by an officer, some physical touching of the person, or the use of language or tone of voice indicating that compliance with the officer's request might be compelled. The analysis is an objective one, requiring a determination of whether the defendant's freedom of movement was sufficiently curtailed by considering how a reasonable person in the defendant's position would have understood his situation.

In *Hodari D.,* the United States Supreme Court addressed the "narrow question...whether, with respect to a show of authority...a seizure occurs even though the subject does not yield." In that case, two police officers on patrol in a high-crime area observed four or five youths, including the defendant, huddled around a car parked at the curb. When the youths saw the police car approach, they ran. One of the officers exited the car and pursued the defendant on foot. As the officer neared, the defendant tossed away what was later determined to be crack cocaine. The Court concluded that the defendant was not seized when the police officer was pursuing him and, thus, the cocaine was admissible because he had not yet been seized when he discarded it. Rather, relying primarily upon the dictionary definition of seizure and the common law of arrest, the Court held that:

> The word "seizure" readily bears the meaning of a laying on of hands or application of physical force to restrain movement, even when it is ultimately unsuccessful. ("She seized the purse-snatcher, but he broke out of her grasp.") It does not remotely apply, however, to the prospect of a policeman yelling "Stop, in the name of the law!" at a fleeing form that continues to flee. That is no seizure.

Accordingly, the Court held that a seizure "requires either physical force...or, where that is absent, submission to the assertion of authority."

Several States have considered whether to adopt the holding in *Hodari D.* for determining when a seizure occurs under their respective state constitutions. Numerous state courts have rejected *Hodari D.* on state constitutional grounds. The Supreme Court of Tennessee summarized the "extensive criticisms" of *Hodari D.* as follows:

> First, the majority's analysis in *Hodari D.* represents a marked departure from the standard the Supreme Court adopted in *United States v. Mendenhall, i.e.,* that a seizure occurs when "in view of all of the circumstances surrounding the incident, a reasonable person would have believed he was not free to leave." Second, the majority's analysis fails to apply common law principles under which an arrest would not be distinguished from an attempted arrest in determining whether a person has been seized. Third, the majority's analysis is flawed for practical reasons and is subject to potential abuse by officers who pursue a subject without reasonable suspicion and use a flight or refusal to submit to authority as reason to execute an arrest or search.

State v. Randolph, 74 S.W.3d 330, 336 (Tenn. 2002); *see also State v. Oquendo,* 613 A.2d 1300, 1310 (Conn. 1992); *Jones v. State,* 745 A.2d 856, 864-66 (Del. 1999) (noting that *Hodari D.* is inconsistent with the State's historic commitment to protecting the privacy of citizens because it "would allow a police officer lacking reasonable suspicion to create that suspicion through an unjustified attempted detention"); *Commonwealth v. Stoute,* 665 N.E.2d 93, 97 (Mass. 1996) (noting that pursuit is no less intrusive on a person's freedom of movement than a stop); *State v. Clayton,* 45 P.3d 30, 33-34 (Mont. 2002) (noting that *Hodari D.* imposes "a subjective element to the traditionally objective test of whether a seizure has occurred" and that utilizing an objective test "allows the police to determine in advance whether the conduct contemplated will implicate [the state constitution] and does not shift the focus of the inquiry to a person's subjective reaction to police conduct"); *State v. Tucker,* 642 A.2d 401, 405 (N.J. 1994) (noting that the Supreme Court's reliance on dictionary definitions of seizure "may be misplaced" because although "[t]he Court correctly states that the officer's chase was not a common-law arrest, [it] fails to point out that this conduct amounted to an attempted arrest, which was also unlawful at common law" (quotation omitted)); *Commonwealth v. Matos,* 672 A.2d 769, 775 (Pa. 1996) (rejecting *Hodari D.* because it is inconsistent with Pennsylvania's recognition that "our citizens enjoy a strong right of privacy, and that our citizens are therefore entitled to broader protection in certain circumstances under our state constitution").

Of the States that have adopted *Hodari D.* under their state constitutions, many do so noting that they do not have a history of providing greater privacy protection to their citizens than the Federal

Constitution. *See, e.g., Perez v. State,* 620 So.2d 1256, 1258 (Fla. 1993) (noting that the Florida Constitution specifically prohibits a court from interpreting the Florida Constitution as providing greater protection than the Fourth Amendment to the United States Constitution); *State v. Cronin,* 509 N.W.2d 673, 676 (Neb. 1993) ("Nebraska has neither an explicit constitutional right of privacy nor a history of affording individuals greater rights than are afforded by the federal Constitution.").

In contrast, we have recognized that our State Constitution incorporates a strong right of privacy and provides greater protection for individual rights than the Federal Constitution. *See State v. Canelo,* 653 A.2d 1097 (N.H. 1995). Accordingly, we are persuaded by the reasoning of those States that have declined to adopt the holding in *Hodari D.* for determining when a seizure occurs as a matter of State constitutional law.

We have held that part I, article 19, provides greater protection for individual rights than does the Fourth Amendment. Indeed, we have recognized that "[o]ur Constitution has historically been interpreted to incorporate a strong right of privacy." In *Canelo,* for instance, we adopted the exclusionary rule under the State Constitution because it served to deter police misconduct and "to redress the injury to the privacy of the search victim." We also declined to adopt a good faith exception to the exclusionary rule because it was "incompatible with and detrimental to our citizens' strong right of privacy inherent in part I, article 19."

Likewise, the *Hodari D.* rule is incompatible with the guarantees of part I, article 19. As the Massachusetts Supreme Judicial Court aptly noted:

> [S]tops provoke constitutional scrutiny because they encumber a person's freedom of movement. Pursuit that appears designed to effect a stop is no less intrusive than a stop itself. Framed slightly differently, a pursuit, which, objectively considered, indicates to a person that he would not be free to leave the area (or to remain there) without first responding to a police officer's inquiry, is the functional equivalent of a seizure, in the sense that the person being pursued is plainly the object of an official assertion of authority, which does not intend to be denied, and which infringes considerably on the person's freedom of action.

Commonwealth v. Stoute, 665 N.E.2d 93, 97 (Mass. 1996). Because of the intrusiveness of a police officer's assertion of authority, requiring police officers to possess reasonable suspicion prior to asserting their authority is necessary to adequately protect individual rights under the State Constitution. Thus, under part I, article 19 of the State Constitution, a police officer must possess reasonable suspicion before taking an action that would communicate to a reasonable person that he or she is not free to leave.

Our holding today is supported by sound practical and policy reasons. First, focusing the definition of seizure on the police officer's conduct, and not the individual's conduct, results in the same State constitutional implications for similar police conduct. In this case, for example, Detective Morelli's conduct of identifying himself as a police officer and ordering the defendant to stop is the same, whether or not the defendant submitted to the officer's show of authority. It would be an anomaly to hold that the officer's conduct was a seizure had the defendant submitted, but because the defendant did not submit, the same conduct by the officer was not a seizure. If the officer's attempt to detain the defendant lacks reasonable suspicion, it is unlawful whether or not the defendant submits to the show of authority. Thus, by defining the moment a seizure occurs by the police officer's conduct, "the police [can] determine in advance whether the conduct contemplated will implicate [the state constitution]."

Second, constitutional protections become "meaningful only when it is assured that at some point the conduct of those charged with enforcing the laws can be subjected to the more detached, neutral scrutiny of a judge who must evaluate the reasonableness of a particular search or seizure." *Terry*, 392 U.S. at 21. The *Mendenhall* test achieves this goal by providing an objective standard for judicial review of the seizure. *See Mendenhall*, 446 U.S. at 554. Thus, our holding allows courts to continue to objectively evaluate the reasonableness of the police officer's actions, not the defendant's reaction. Third, we do not write on a blank slate for defining when a seizure occurs. An analysis that focuses exclusively on the conduct of the police is, as several state courts have pointed out, consistent with the well-settled definition of seizure in *Mendenhall*. In *Quezada*, a police officer called to the defendant, "Hey, you, stop," and after the defendant did not respond, called out again, "Hey, I want to speak to you." One of the key factors in our analysis of whether a seizure occurred was that the officer used "language indicating that compliance was not optional." We thus concluded that, "[g]iven the late hour, the absence of other citizens in the vicinity, the presence of two uniformed police officers, and the language of [the officer's] requests, no reasonable person would have believed he was free to ignore the officer and simply walk away." In holding that there was a sufficient "show of authority" to effect a seizure, our analysis focused upon the officer's actions and the other surrounding circumstances. The defendant's reaction was not a part of our seizure analysis.

Finally, our holding serves to effectuate the goal of the exclusionary rule to deter police misconduct. Indeed, one of the primary criticisms of the holding in *Hodari D.* is that it is subject to potential abuse. *See, e.g.*, *Stoute*, 665 N.E.2d at 97-98 (noting that the holding in *Hodari D.* would allow "the police [to] turn a hunch into a reasonable suspicion by inducing the conduct...justifying the suspicion" (quotation omitted)). Thus, because the police are not required to possess reasonable suspicion prior to asserting their authority under *Hodari D.*, that rule "will encourage unlawful displays of force that will frighten countless innocent citizens into surrendering whatever privacy rights they may still have."

Having determined when a seizure occurs under part I, article 19, we must now determine when the defendant was seized. As stated above, a seizure occurs only when a reasonable person believes he is not free to leave because the officer, by means of physical force or show of authority, has in some way restrained the liberty of the person. The analysis is an objective one, requiring a determination of whether the defendant's freedom of movement was sufficiently curtailed by considering how a reasonable person in the defendant's position would have understood his situation.

In this case, although Detective Morelli was in an unmarked cruiser and wearing street clothes, he yelled to the defendant, identified himself as a police officer and ordered the defendant to stop. Detective Morelli then pursued the defendant on foot, again identifying himself as a police officer and ordering the defendant to stop. In view of all the circumstances, the encounter transcended a mere request to communicate. Given Detective Morelli's repeated identification of himself as a police officer and his orders to stop, no reasonable person would have believed he was free to ignore the officer and simply walk away. Thus, the defendant was seized when Detective Morelli first identified himself as a police officer and ordered the defendant to stop.

JONES v. STATE
745 A.2d 856 (Del. 1999)

VEASEY, C. J.

In this criminal appeal, we reverse the judgment and sentence of the Superior Court because evidence was invalidly seized from the defendant. The seizure resulted from an encounter with a police officer in which the officer, based only on an anonymous 911 call that there was a "suspicious black male wearing a blue coat" in a particular vicinity, ordered the defendant to stop and remove his hands from his pockets. As a result of this stop, cocaine was seized. To stop and detain an individual pursuant to the Delaware detention statute and the Delaware Constitution, a peace officer must have a reasonable and articulable suspicion of criminal activity. The information possessed by the officer in this case did not rise to that level. As a consequence, the search was invalid and the evidence inadmissible.

Facts

Shortly before 10:00 p.m. on February 11, 1997, the New Castle County Police Department received a 911 call reporting that a "suspicious black male wearing a blue coat" had been standing for some time in front of 98 Karlyn Drive in the Garfield Park area of New Castle County. The caller provided no other information, and the 911 operator failed to record the name of the caller. At approximately 9:53 p.m., Patrolman Clay Echevarria of the New Castle County Police Department was in uniform on routine car patrol of the Garfield Park area with his partner when he received a radio dispatch relaying the 911 complaint and no other information. Within three minutes of receiving the dispatch, Patrolman Echevarria and his partner arrived in the vicinity of the address referred to in the 911 call. The officers did not notice anyone in front of, or near, 98 Karlyn Drive. After circling the block, the officers drove past the area again. This time they noticed two black males standing on the sidewalk in front of 85 Karlyn Drive, approximately four houses from 98 Karlyn Drive. One of them (the defendant Joseph Jones) was wearing a blue coat and had his hands in his coat pockets.

Patrolman Echevarria testified that he did not see either individual engaging in suspicious activity. He also testified that he was very familiar with Garfield Park and its reputation as a high crime, high drug area. Although he knew many of the "regular" drug-dealers in the area, he testified that he did not recognize Jones as a person known to be involved in illegal activity.

Patrolman Echevarria parked his patrol car, exited the vehicle and approached Jones. He did not first ask Jones to state his name, address, business abroad or destination as required by the detention statute, 11 *Del. C.* § 1902. As we interpret the record developed at the suppression hearing in the Superior Court, the officer ordered Jones to stop and remove his hands from his coat pockets. Jones did not comply with the order. He turned and began walking away from the officers. After ordering Jones three times, without effect, to remove his hands from his coat pockets, Patrolman Echevarria grabbed Jones' hands in an attempt to remove them from the coat pockets, at which time Jones threw an object over the officer's head. A struggle then ensued. After subduing and handcuffing Jones, the officers recovered the thrown object, a small bag containing a substance later determined to be cocaine. A further search of Jones' person and the vicinity of 85 Karlyn Drive resulted in the seizure of more cocaine and paraphernalia (a scale) commonly used in illicit drug transactions.

The Analytical Framework

A trial court's determination whether a peace officer possessed reasonable and articulable suspicion to detain an individual is an issue of law and fact. Here, there are no disputed issues of fact. Therefore, this

Court reviews *de novo* the Superior Court's alleged errors in formulating and applying the law.

An individual's right to be free of unlawful searches and seizures in Delaware is secured by two independent, though correlative sources. The Fourth Amendment to the United States Constitution guarantees to individuals the right to be "secure in their persons, houses, papers, and effects, against unreasonable searches and seizures." In similar language, Article I, § 6 of the Delaware Constitution guarantees that the people of the State of Delaware "shall be secure in their persons, houses, papers and possessions, from unreasonable searches and seizures." This Court has never decided whether, and in what situations, Article I, § 6 of the Delaware Constitution should be interpreted to provide protections that are greater than the rights accorded citizens by the Fourteenth Amendment as it has been interpreted by the United States Supreme Court. The defendant here contends that federal and state constitutional guarantees as well as the officer's failure to comply with 11 *Del. C.* § 1902 constitute separate and independent grounds supporting reversal of his conviction.

In *Terry v. Ohio,* the United States Supreme Court held that a police officer may detain an individual for investigatory purposes for a limited scope and duration, but only if such detention is supported by a reasonable and articulable suspicion of criminal activity. We have defined reasonable and articulable suspicion as an "officer's ability to 'point to specific and articulable facts which, taken together with rational inferences from those facts, reasonably warrant th[e] intrusion.'" A determination of reasonable suspicion must be evaluated in the context of the totality of the circumstances as viewed through the eyes of a reasonable, trained police officer in the same or similar circumstances, combining objective facts with such an officer's subjective interpretation of those facts. Delaware has codified this standard for investigatory stops and detentions in 11 *Del. C.* § 1902. For the purpose of this analysis, "reasonable ground" as used in Section 1902(a) has the same meaning as reasonable and articulable suspicion.

When the Stop Occurred

The question of when a seizure has occurred is perhaps the most critical issue. The State contends that Jones' failure to stop and remove his hands from his coat is an independent factor supporting the seizure, based on the fact that Jones started walking away and ignored the Officer's orders before he was seized. We assume arguendo, but need not decide, that if a person attempts to flee before being seized, the court may consider the attempt to flee, and any information derived therefrom, as one factor in deciding whether a police officer had an articulable basis for effecting the seizure. But, in our view, if the seizure preceded the attempt to flee, that attempt or any information derived therefrom, is not a proper factor in assessing the validity of a seizure.

In *Terry,* the United States Supreme Court held that a seizure occurs "when the officer, by means of physical force or show of authority, has in some way restrained the liberty" of the individual. In *INS v. Delgado,* the Court refined this standard to mean that a seizure has occurred only "'if, in view of all the circumstances surrounding the incident, a reasonable person would have believed that he was not free to leave.'" The Court further refined this standard in *Michigan v. Chesternut* by focusing not on whether a reasonable person would feel free to leave but on whether the officer's conduct would "have communicated to a reasonable person that he was not at liberty to ignore the police presence and go about his business."

In 1991, however, the United States Supreme Court carved out a controversial exception to the *Chesternut* standard in its interpretation of the rights guaranteed by the Fourth Amendment. In *California v. Hodari D.,* the United States Supreme Court held that, even when an officer has manifested a "show of authority," a seizure within the meaning of the Fourth Amendment further "requires *either* physical force ... *or,* where that is absent, *submission* to the assertion of authority." The majority in *Hodari D.* found that the *Chesternut* standard states only "a *necessary,* but not a *sufficient,* condition for seizure ... effected through a 'show of authority.'" Thus, the majority in *Hodari D.* found that a show of authority by itself, even if it would cause a reasonable person to believe that he or she was not free to leave, is not alone sufficient for a seizure giving rise to the protections provided by the Fourth Amendment.

The case now before us presents a different situation. By ordering Jones to stop and remove his hands from his coat, Patrolman Echevarria engaged in conduct that would communicate to a reasonable person that he or she was not free to ignore the police presence. The reasonableness of Patrolman Echevarria's suspicion must rest on the facts known to him at the time he ordered Jones to stop. He had no reasonable and articulable ground to suspect that Jones was committing, had committed or was about to commit a crime. In *Hodari D.,* the officers had not seized the defendant before the defendant's flight. Even assuming that flight (combined with other articulable factors and when not provoked by an unwarranted police seizure) may provide sufficient reasonable and articulable suspicion to justify a seizure, that did not occur here, and therefore this case is distinguishable from *Hodari D.*

The State relies on *Hodari D.* for the proposition that seizure does not occur until the officer uses physical force or the defendant submits to the authority of the officer. *Hodari D.* is binding precedent for this Court insofar as it interprets the Fourth Amendment to the United States

Constitution because the almost two hundred year old doctrine of judicial review established the United States Supreme Court as the final arbiter of the United States Constitution.

But in this case, our holding rests not on the Fourth Amendment but on the Delaware detention statute, 11 *Del. C.* § 1902, and Article I, § 6 of the Delaware Constitution. The Delaware Constitution, like the constitutions of certain other states, may provide individuals with greater rights than those afforded by the United States Constitution. For example, we have held that the Delaware Constitution provides greater rights than the United States Constitution in the preservation of evidence used against a defendant, the right of confrontation, the right to counsel, and the right to trial by jury. *Hodari D.* is not consistent with our view of when a person is "seized" within the meaning of Article I, § 6 of the Delaware Constitution in that *Hodari D.* would allow a police officer lacking reasonable suspicion to create that suspicion through an unjustified attempted detention. A number of states have likewise interpreted *Hodari D.* as inconsistent with the protections provided by their state constitutions.

The issue in the present case is whether the search and seizure language in the Delaware Constitution means the same thing as the United States Supreme Court's construction of *similar* language in the United States Constitution. To answer that question requires this Court to apply a logical, deductive analytical process. Our comprehensive historical analysis of the right to trial by jury in *Claudio* demonstrates that the guarantees in the Delaware Constitution for trial by jury were originally intended to be greater than those in the United States Constitution and remain that way.

Several other states have developed useful criteria for determining whether a provision in the United States Constitution has a meaning identical to a similar provision on the same subject in a state's constitution. The following is a partial list of those non-exclusive criteria from other states as marshalled by Justice Handler of the New Jersey Supreme Court in his 1982 concurrence in *State v. Hunt:*

> (1) Textual Language-A state constitution's language may itself provide a basis for reaching a result different from that which could be obtained under federal law. Textual language can be relevant in either of two contexts. First, distinctive provisions of our State charter may recognize rights not identified in the federal constitution....
>
> Second, the phrasing of a particular provision in our charter may be so significantly different from the language used to address the same subject in the federal Constitution that we can feel free to interpret our provision on an independent basis ....

(2) Legislative History-Whether or not the textual language of a given provision is different from that found in the federal Constitution, legislative history may reveal an intention that will support reading the provision independently of federal law....

(3) Preexisting State Law-Previously established bodies of state law may also suggest distinctive state constitutional rights. State law is often responsive to concerns long before they are addressed by constitutional claims. Such preexisting law can help to define the scope of the constitutional right later established.

(4) Structural Differences-Differences in structure between the federal and state constitutions might also provide a basis for rejecting the constraints of federal doctrine at the state level. The United States Constitution is a grant of enumerated powers to the federal government. Our State Constitution, on the other hand, serves only to limit the sovereign power which inheres directly in the people and indirectly in their elected representatives. Hence, the explicit affirmation of fundamental rights in our Constitution can be seen as a guarantee of those rights and not as a restriction upon them.

(5) Matters of Particular State Interest or Local Concern-A state constitution may also be employed to address matters of peculiar state interest or local concern. When particular questions are local in character and do not appear to require a uniform national policy, they are ripe for decision under state law. Moreover, some matters are uniquely appropriate for independent state action....

(6) State Traditions-A state's history and traditions may also provide a basis for the independent application of its constitution ....

(7) Public Attitudes-Distinctive attitudes of a state's citizenry may also furnish grounds to expand constitutional rights under state charters. While we have never cited this criterion in our decisions, courts in other jurisdictions have pointed to public attitudes as a relevant factor in their deliberations.

"The enumerated criteria, which are synthesized from a burgeoning body of authority, are essentially illustrative, rather than exhaustive. They share a common thread-that distinctive and identifiable attributes of a state government, its laws and its people justify recourse to the state constitution as an independent source for recognizing and protecting individual rights."

As noted earlier, the search and seizure provision in the Delaware Constitution preceded the adoption of the Fourth Amendment and was originally like a similar provision in the Pennsylvania Constitution. When the Delaware Constitution was amended in 1792 after the Fourth Amendment had already been adopted, Delaware continued to follow the search and seizure language from the Pennsylvania Constitution rather than the language in the Fourth Amendment.

Delaware adopted the first search and seizure protections for its citizens in September of 1776 as part of the Declaration of Rights and Fundamental Rules of the Delaware State, which read as follows:

> Sect. 17. That all warrants without oath to search suspected places, or to seize any person or his property, are grievous and oppressive; and all general warrants to search suspected places, or to apprehend all persons suspected, without naming or describing the place or any person in special, are illegal and ought not to be granted.

Delaware's Declaration of Rights was based upon a similar provision in the Pennsylvania Declaration of Rights. The chairman of the committee that drafted Delaware's Declaration of Rights was George Read. On September 17, 1776, Read wrote that "the Declaration of Rights ... has been completed somedays past but there being nothing particularly in it-I did not think it an object of much curiosity, it is made out of the Pensilvania [sic] & Maryland Draughts."

Delaware ratified the Bill of Rights to the United States Constitution on January 28, 1790. Pennsylvania adopted a new state constitution in 1791. Delaware adopted a new constitution in 1792.

The Delaware Constitution of 1792 "resembled in some ways the federal constitution because of the presence of John Dickinson and Richard Bassett, who had served as members of the Philadelphia Convention, and because the members were familiar with the federal constitution." Article I in the 1792 Delaware Constitution "contained a [B]ill of [R]ights of nineteen provisions, which was mostly a rewriting of the Declaration of Rights of the Delaware [C]onstitution of 1776. Some portions showed that the members were familiar with the [1791] [C]onstitution of Pennsylvania." The search and seizure provision in the 1792 Delaware Constitution exemplifies that familiarity because it tracks a similar provision in the 1791 Pennsylvania Constitution.

In a 1991 case, *Commonwealth v. Edmunds,* the Pennsylvania Supreme Court undertook a comprehensive historical review of the search and seizure provision in the Pennsylvania Constitution. The *Edmunds* Court concluded that the history of that provision reflected *different* and *broader* protections than those guaranteed by the Fourth Amendment. In a 1996 case, *Commonwealth v. Matos,* the Pennsylvania Supreme Court concluded that the construction of the United States Constitution in *Hodari D.* by the United States Supreme Court was "inconsistent with the constitutional protections afforded under Article I, Section 8 of the Pennsylvania Constitution." That conclusion was based on the fact that "the survival of the language now employed in Article I, Section 8 through over 200 years of profound change in other areas demonstrates that the paramount concern for privacy first adopted as part of our organic law in 1776 continues to enjoy the mandate of the people of this Commonwealth."

We reach the same conclusion with regard to the search and seizure provision in the Delaware Constitution based upon its historical convergence for more than two hundred years with the same provision in the Pennsylvania Constitution. The history of search and seizure in Delaware reflects the same commitment to protecting the privacy of its citizens. As we have previously noted, that commitment is illustrated by Delaware's nighttime search warrant statute which, even in its original version adopted by the Delaware General Assembly almost 150 years ago, required a stricter standard than probable cause before a court could issue a nighttime search warrant.

The United States Constitution establishes a system of dual sovereignty: a federal government and state governments. That system has horizontal and vertical aspects. Vertical federalism binds the states to the will of the federal sovereign government with regard to the enumerated powers that have been surrendered. Horizontal federalism permits the states to look to the jurisprudence of sister states in defining the sovereign powers that have been reserved for state governments.

In our view, the question presented by Jones of when a seizure has occurred under Article I, § 6 of the Delaware Constitution requires focusing upon the police officer's actions to determine when a reasonable person would have believed he or she was not free to ignore the police presence. Under that analysis, Jones was seized within the meaning of Section 1902 and Article I, § 6 when Patrolman Echevarria first ordered him to stop and remove his hands from his pockets. If that seizure was not based upon reasonable and articulable suspicion, anything recovered as a result of that seizure is inadmissible at trial. We conclude that Jones' actions in walking away from Patrolman Echevarria and his refusal to obey or submit to the officer's commands to stop and remove his hands from his pockets did not furnish grounds for reasonable and articulable suspicion to effect the seizure.

Our finding that the 911 complaint alone did not suffice to establish reasonable and articulable suspicion requires us to search the record for any other evidence the police might have possessed to support a finding of reasonable and articulable suspicion sufficient to detain Jones. The record fails to reveal any such evidence. As the United States Supreme Court noted in *White*, "if a tip has a relatively low degree of reliability, more information will be required to establish the requisite quantum of suspicion than would be required if the tip were more reliable." Here, the question is whether the evidence remaining once the tip is removed suffices to establish that Patrolman Echevarria held a reasonable and articulable suspicion of criminal activity prior to seizing Jones. Without the benefit of the 911 complaint, the first and fourth bases enumerated by the Superior Court cannot aid in establishing reasonable suspicion. The fact that Patrolman Echevarria found Jones wearing a blue coat near 98 Karlyn Drive, by itself, indicates nothing to suggest any criminal activity.

Second and third bases enumerated by the Superior Court (that the events took place at night in a high crime/high drug area) do not depend on the 911 complaint. In *Brown v. Texas,* the United States Supreme Court held that a defendant's presence in a high crime area, by itself, will not establish reasonable suspicion. In our opinion, the fact that a defendant's presence in such a neighborhood took place at ten o'clock at night does not suggest a result different from that reached in *Brown.* Courts generally use factors such as nighttime and the negative reputation of a neighborhood as additional support to bolster a finding of reasonable suspicion, not as the sole bases on that finding. Reasonable and articulable suspicion cannot be based on a defendant's presence in a particular neighborhood at a particular time of day with no independent evidence that the defendant has committed, is committing or is about to commit a crime. It is reasonable to assume that the framers of our constitutional protections against unreasonable searches and seizures were aware that law-abiding citizens who found themselves inadvertently in similar circumstances during colonial times were challenged by British soldiers.

The facts presented by the State are not "specific and articulable facts which, taken together with rational inferences from those facts, reasonably warrant th[e] intrusion." Therefore, under our interpretation of 11 *Del. C.* § 1902 and Article I, § 6 of the Delaware Constitution, we find that Patrolman Echevarria did not possess a reasonable and articulable suspicion to stop Jones.

Conclusion

The law concerning unreasonable searches and seizures reflects differing standards between federal and state constitutions and a labyrinth of factual situations. It is important, however, that Delaware courts be clear. If an officer attempts to seize someone before possessing reasonable and articulable suspicion, that person's actions stemming from the attempted seizure may not be used to manufacture the suspicion the police lacked initially.

The courts cannot naively turn a blind eye to the realities of society's war against drugs and the experience of police officers in combating drug traffic in our cities, towns and rural areas. This case, however, turns on the constitutional rights provided to all citizens by the framers of our Delaware Constitution to be free of unreasonable searches and seizures. The judicial branch of government is obliged to enforce these rights for the protection of all citizens.

The Framers of the United States Constitution adopted a " 'constitutionally mandated balance of power' between the States and the Federal Government ... to ensure the protection of 'our fundamental liberties.'" The preservation of diversity in the legal and governmental systems of each state was expressly contemplated when the United States Constitution was framed and adopted.

We hold that the Superior Court erred as a matter of Delaware statutory and Delaware constitutional law in denying Jones' motion to suppress evidence seized on the night of January 11, 1997. Accordingly, the judgment of the Superior Court is reversed.

NOTES

1. Under the New Hampshire Constitution "a seizure occurs when an officer, by means of physical force or show of authority, has in some way restrained the liberty of the person." *State v. Beauchesne*, 868 A.2d 972 (N.H. 2005).

2. The Tennessee Supreme Court held that a defendant was seized, for purposes of the state constitution, "at the moment when the officer pulled up behind the defendant's stopped vehicle and activated his blue emergency lights." *State v. Williams*, 185 S.W.3d 311 (Tenn. 2006).

3. A seizure does not occur under article I, section 6 of the Delaware Constitution when uniformed officers follow a walking pedestrian and request to speak to him, without doing anything more. *Ross v. State*, 925 A.2d 489 (Del. 2007).

4. The rationale of *Hodari D.* was held to be contrary to the unique language in article I, section 8 of the Washington Constitution that restricts police invasions of privacy: "No person shall be disturbed in his private affairs, or his home invaded, without authority of law." *State v. Young*, 957 P.2d 681 (Wash. 1998).

G. WARRANTLESS AUTOMOBILE SEARCH INCIDENT TO ARREST

STATE v. ECKEL
888 A.2d 1266 (N.J. 2006)

LONG, J., delivered the opinion of the Court.

The issue raised in this appeal is whether the police may conduct a warrantless search of an automobile as incident to an arrest after the occupants have been removed from the vehicle and are secured in police custody. Because the search incident to arrest exception to the warrant requirement was limned for two specific purposes—the protection of the police and the preservation of evidence—and because neither purpose can be advanced by searching the vehicle of a person who effectively is incapacitated, we hold that such a search is incompatible with article I, paragraph 7 of the New Jersey Constitution. To the extent *New York v. Belton,* 453 U.S. 454 (1981), has concluded otherwise in interpreting the Federal Constitution, we respectfully part company with the United States Supreme Court.

On June 30, 2002, at around 3:20 p.m., while on routine patrol, Officer Douglas Whitten received a report of a stolen vehicle, described as a green Mercury Cougar bearing the license plate FTY1380. Earlier in the day, the owners of the vehicle, Mr. and Mrs. Sanfillipo, reported that the car had been stolen by their daughter, Dana, and that Dana's boyfriend, defendant William B. Eckel, also might be in the car. At the time, Officer Whitten knew that there was a warrant issued by Upper Township for Eckel's arrest based on failure to appear for municipal court dates.

Officer Whitten waited across the street from defendant's residence on Seashore Road and observed the green Mercury Cougar pulling out of the driveway. A young woman, later identified as Dana Sanfillipo, was at the wheel and defendant was in the front passenger seat. A male juvenile was sitting in the rear passenger seat. Officer Whitten stopped the vehicle with the assistance of Sergeant Jack Beers.

When Officer Whitten approached the driver's side of the vehicle and asked Dana Sanfillipo for her license, registration and insurance documents, Sergeant Beers approached the passenger side and asked defendant to exit the car. Sergeant Beers informed defendant that he was under arrest on an outstanding warrant, placed him in handcuffs and put him in the rear seat of the patrol car, which was parked behind the Sanfillipo vehicle. Officer Whitten estimated that it took only "a couple of minutes" for Sergeant Beers to arrest defendant and place him in the back of the patrol car.

Officer Whitten then asked Dana Sanfillipo to exit the vehicle and step to the rear, off to the side of the road. During a subsequent conversation with Officer Whitten, Dana asked permission to kiss defendant goodbye and give him the clothing he had left in the car. Officer Whitten told Dana to stay where she was and that he would retrieve the clothing. He testified that he would not let Dana go to the vehicle to retrieve defendant's clothes because it could have jeopardized the officers' safety.

Officer Whitten went to the front passenger side of the vehicle, where the door was open, and began picking up the clothing from the floor by the passenger seat. Underneath the clothing, Officer Whitten observed a phone book with some "green vegetation and stems" lying on top that he believed to be marijuana. The officer also observed an open box of "Philly

Blunt" cigars behind the passenger seat, which contributed to his belief that the vegetation was marijuana.

Officer Whitten then retrieved a pair of blue denim shorts from behind the passenger seat. The officer found a softball-sized baggie rolled up in the shorts and opened it. Inside, there was an additional baggie, inside of which were several different items, including a clear plastic baggie containing a white powdery substance, an electronic scale with white residue on the tray, and several different types of small glassine bags. Officer Whitten suspected the white powder to be cocaine. He asked the juvenile to step out of the back seat of the car, and continued to search the passenger compartment. In between the rear seat and the door, Officer Whitten found a larger baggie containing green vegetation that he believed to be marijuana.

When questioned, the occupants all denied ownership of the suspected marijuana and cocaine found in the vehicle. Dana Sanfillipo indicated that the shorts might belong to her brother who also used the car.

Defendant and Dana Sanfillipo were charged with third-degree possession of a controlled dangerous substance (cocaine), third-degree possession of a controlled dangerous substance (cocaine) with intent to distribute, and fourth-degree possession of a controlled dangerous substance (marijuana) with intent to distribute. There were no charges relating to the stolen vehicle because, at the scene, Mr. and Mrs. Sanfillipo indicated that they did not wish to press charges.

Defendant moved to suppress the evidence against him. The trial judge credited Officer Whitten's testimony that he entered the vehicle in response to a request by Dana Sanfillipo. The court concluded that, under the circumstances, Officer Whitten's entry into the car was reasonable and that his observations at that point, along with the fluid nature of what was transpiring, constituted probable cause and exigent circumstances to search.

In *Belton*, after a New York State trooper stopped a vehicle for speeding, he smelled the odor of burned marijuana and observed an envelope marked "Supergold" on the floor of the car that he suspected contained marijuana. He ordered the occupants out of the car and placed them under arrest for possession of marijuana. He patted them down, directed them to stand in separate areas and opened the envelope. Finding marijuana, the trooper searched the occupants and the passenger compartment of the vehicle where he discovered cocaine in the zipped pocket of the defendant's jacket. Defendant was indicted and later moved to suppress the cocaine. The New York Court of Appeals invalidated the search, concluding that: "[a] warrantless search of the zippered pockets of an unaccessible jacket may not be upheld as a search incident to a lawful arrest where there is no longer any danger that the arrestee or a confederate might gain access to the article.

The Supreme Court reversed. Although stressing its re-affirmation of the fundamental principles of *Chimel,* the Court nevertheless accepted the notion that articles "inside the relatively narrow compass of the passenger compartment of an automobile are in fact generally, even if not inevitably, within 'the area into which an arrestee might reach in order to grab a weapon or evidentiary ite[m].'" Over the dissents of Justices Brennan and Marshall, who declared that the opinion was not a reaffirmation but a rejection of *Chimel,* the Court broadly held:

> [W]hen a policeman has made a lawful custodial arrest of the occupant of an automobile, he may, as a contemporaneous incident of that arrest, search the passenger compartment of that automobile [and] ... may also examine the contents of any containers found within the passenger compartment, for if the passenger compartment is within reach of the arrestee, so also will containers in it be within his reach.

In *Thornton v. United States,* 541 U.S. 615 (2004), the Supreme Court revisited *Belton.* There, an officer discovered that the defendant's license plates belonged to another car. Before he had a chance to pull the car over, the defendant "drove into a parking lot, parked, and got out of the vehicle." The officer approached, patted down, and questioned the defendant, who admitted to having narcotics, pulled out a bag of marijuana and crack cocaine, and handed it to the officer. The officer arrested the defendant, handcuffed him, and placed him in his patrol car and then proceeded to search the defendant's vehicle, uncovering a handgun. In denying the defendant's motion to suppress, the trial judge found the search valid pursuant to *Belton.* The Fourth Circuit affirmed.

The Supreme Court in *Thornton* upheld the vehicle search under *Belton,* affirming

> [t]he need for a clear rule, readily understood by police officers and not depending on differing estimates of what items were or were not within reach of an arrestee at any particular moment, justifies the sort of generalization which *Belton* enunciated. Once an officer determines that there is probable cause to make an arrest, it is reasonable to allow officers to ensure their safety and to preserve evidence by searching the entire passenger compartment.

Applying that rule, the Court stated, "[s]o long as an arrestee is the sort of 'recent occupant' of a vehicle such as petitioner was here, officers may search that vehicle incident to the arrest." Several Justices pronounced their reservations regarding that application of *Belton.* Justice O'Connor concurred, expressing her "dissatisfaction with the state of the law in this area," declaring that "lower court decisions seem to treat the ability to search a vehicle incident to the arrest of a recent occupant as a police entitlement rather than as an exception justified by the twin rationales of *Chimel v. California.* That erosion is a direct consequence of *Belton's* shaky foundation." Justice Scalia, urging a return to *Harris-Rabinowitz*, also concurred, joined by Justice Ginsburg:

> When petitioner's car was searched in this case, he was neither in, nor anywhere near, the passenger compartment of his vehicle. Rather, he was handcuffed and secured in the back of the officer's squad car. The risk that he would nevertheless "grab a weapon or evidentiary ite[m]" from his car was remote in the extreme. The Court's effort to apply our current doctrine to this search stretches it beyond its breaking point, and for that reason I cannot join the Court's opinion.

Those criticisms of *Belton* have been widely recapitulated in scholarly writings. In *Pierce,* we cited a number of them. Since *Pierce*, the drumbeat of scholarly opposition to *Belton* has remained constant. *See* 3 Wayne R. LaFave, *Search and Seizure* § 7.1(c) at 527 (4th ed. 2004) (stating that "[o]n balance…there is good reason to be critical of the Court's work in *Belton* ").

Some states have simply followed *Belton*. However, a number have declined to do so based upon their own constitutional provisions. That is the backdrop for our inquiry.

New Jersey's traditional approach to the search incident to arrest exception parallels *Chimel*. In *Welsh*, a case decided less than one year before *Belton,* this Court applied a *Chimel* analysis to decide the validity of a search incident to arrest in the motor vehicle context under the Federal Constitution. There, we ruled that "once the occupant has been removed from the vehicle, placed under custodial arrest and seated in a police car, there is no danger that the arrestee might reach into his own vehicle to gain possession of a weapon or destructible evidence," thus obviating resort to the search incident to arrest exception to the warrant requirement.

Alston, decided several months after *Belton,* did not require us to reach the *Belton* question because the automobile search at issue was valid under the automobile exception. We acknowledged, however, that *Welsh* would have been decided differently under *Belton* and expressly reserved decision on *Belton,* stating, "we leave to future consideration the question of the continued viability of our analysis of the scope of the *Chimel* exception as expressed in *Welsh*."

We later considered the applicability of *Belton* under the New Jersey constitution in *Pierce*. There, the driver of a motor vehicle was pulled over and subsequently arrested, handcuffed, and placed in the patrol car for driving while his license was suspended. Additionally, both passengers were removed from the car, patted down, and secured behind the vehicle by "back-up officers." The arresting officer then searched the interior of the vehicle and found a stolen revolver and cocaine. The trial judge found the search to be valid and citing *Belton,* the Appellate Division affirmed.

We granted certification. In ruling that *Belton* does not apply to warrantless arrests for motor-vehicle offenses, we observed in *Pierce* that the two *Chimel* justifications for a search incident to arrest (officer safety and avoidance of the destruction of evidence) have little relevance when the arrest is for a routine motor vehicle violation. We further acknowledged that "motorists arrested for traffic offenses almost invariably are removed from the vehicle and secured," and "[w]hen an arrestee…has been handcuffed and placed in the patrol car…the officer's justification for searching the vehicle and the passenger's clothing and containers is minimal." Therefore, we held that "in the context of arrests for motor-vehicle violations, the bright-line *Belton* holding extends the *Chimel* rule beyond the logical limits of its principle.…We reject not the rationale of *Chimel,* but *Belton's* automatic application of *Chimel* to authorize vehicular searches following all arrests for motor-vehicle offenses."

We acknowledged:

> the virtue of simple, straightforward rules to guide police officers in applying Fourth Amendment doctrine. Nevertheless, we are convinced that automatic application of the *Belton* bright-line rule to authorize vehicular searches incident to all traffic arrests poses too great a threat to rights guaranteed to New Jersey's citizens by their State Constitution, and that that threat to fundamental rights outweighs any incidental benefit that might accrue to law enforcement because of the simplicity and predictability of the *Belton* rule.

We saved for another day the question whether *Belton* or *Chimel,* as adopted in *Welsh,* applies to arrests other than those occurring as a result of minor motor vehicle offenses.

We now determine that issue. Article I, paragraph 7 of the New Jersey Constitution provides:

> The right of the people to be secure in their persons, houses, papers, and effects, against unreasonable searches and seizures, shall not be violated; and no warrant shall issue except upon probable cause, supported by oath or affirmation, and particularly describing the place to be searched and the papers and things to be seized.

Although that paragraph is almost identical to the text of the Fourth Amendment to the Federal Constitution, we have not hesitated in the past to afford our citizens greater protection against unreasonable searches and seizures under article I, paragraph 7 that would be the case under its federal counterpart.

Moreover, as we have said, the United States Supreme Court interpretations of the Federal Constitution establish not the ceiling but only "the floor of minimum constitutional protection."

Our conclusion regarding whether to tether ourselves to federal jurisprudence in this matter is influenced simultaneously by a number of considerations. Initially, we return to the text of our constitution: "The right of the people to be secure in their persons, houses, papers, and effects, against unreasonable searches and seizures, shall not be violated." N.J. Const. art. I, ¶ 7. It is against that clear recognition of the privacy interests of our citizens that a specific warrantless search is to be judged. Clearly, the search of an automobile is an invasion of privacy, and the fact of an arrest does not render that invasion less substantial. Without doubt, we have acknowledged that there is a somewhat lesser expectation of privacy in an automobile than in a home or office, thus allowing for distinct analyses of searches in those settings. However, we have never agreed that the word "automobile" is a "talisman in whose presence the Fourth Amendment fades away and disappears." *Coolidge v. New Hampshire,* 403 U.S. 443 (1971). Thus, a warrantless search of an automobile will violate our constitution unless it falls squarely within a known exception to the warrant requirement.

In this matter our concern is the search incident to arrest exception. As we have indicated, both our prior case law and federal case law have recognized the specific contours of that exception: it is invocable to ensure police safety or to avoid the destruction of evidence.

However, in *Belton,* and later in *Thornton,* the Supreme Court altered *Chimel,* establishing a bright-line rule that essentially validates every automobile search upon the occupant's arrest, regardless of whether the occupant has the capacity to injure the police or destroy evidence. In concluding as it did, *Belton* detached itself from the theoretical underpinnings that initially animated the search incident to arrest exception. Unmoored as it is from *Chimel* and established Fourth Amendment jurisprudence, all that is left in *Belton* is the benefit to police of a so-called bright line rule. Without question, along with protecting privacy and "regulat[ing] the distribution of power between the people and the government," guiding the police is one distinct level on which the Fourth Amendment operates. However, it cannot, standing alone, support an exception to the warrant requirement. By focusing solely on procedure and writing out of the exception the two *Chimel* justifications, the Supreme Court in *Belton* reached a result that is detached from established Fourth Amendment jurisprudence.

We decline to adopt *Belton* and its progeny because to do so would require us to accept a theoretically rootless doctrine that would erode the rights guaranteed to our own citizens by article I, paragraph 7 of our constitution—the right to be free from unreasonable searches and seizures. To us, a warrantless search of an automobile based not on probable cause but solely on the arrest of a person unable to endanger the police or destroy evidence cannot be justified under any exception to the warrant requirement and is unreasonable.

We do not view article I, paragraph 7 as a procedural matter but as a reaffirmation of the privacy rights guaranteed to our citizens and of our duty as judges to secure them. So viewed, the *Belton* rationale simply does not pass muster. That is not to suggest that bright lines are not salutary, only that they cannot be the sole justification for a warrantless search. Indeed, a bright-line that remains true to an exception's roots is a worthy consideration. In that connection, one scholar has observed:

> If any bright line rule had been necessary to resolve the issue in *Belton,* it would have been the opposite of the rule that the Court announced....[O]ccupants almost invariably are removed before an automobile is searched; and once they have been removed, there is no longer much chance that they can secure weapons from the automobile or destroy evidence there. Albert W. Alschuler, *Bright Line Fever and the Fourth Amendment,* 45 U. Pitt. L. Rev. 227, 274 (1984).

That is the line we draw here. Once the occupant of a vehicle has been arrested, removed and secured elsewhere, the considerations informing the search incident to arrest exception are absent and the exception is inapplicable. We thus return to *Chimel* and to *Welsh* and declare their reasoning to be the critical path to the application of the search incident to arrest exception under article I, paragraph 7 of our constitution. That, in turn, answers the open issue in *Pierce.*

Obviously, where a defendant has been arrested but has not been removed and secured, the court will be required to determine, on a case-by-case basis whether he or she was in a position to compromise police safety or to carry out the destruction of evidence, thus justifying resort to the search incident to arrest exception.

One final note, we emphasize that we do not diverge lightly from federal constitutional interpretation. However, as Justice Clifford so eloquently put our relationship with our federal counterpart:

> although that Court may be a polestar that guides us as we navigate the New Jersey Constitution, we bear ultimate responsibility for the safe passage of our ship. Our eyes must not be so fixed on that star that we risk the welfare of our passengers on the shoals of constitutional doctrine. In interpreting the New Jersey Constitution, we must look in front of us as well as above us.

In charting a course distinct from *Belton,* that is what we have done.

NOTES

1. In *Arizona v. Grant,* 556 U.S. (2009), the United States Supreme Court limited *Belton* in part and overruled it in part.

2. Under the Nevada Constitution, "there must exist both probable cause and exigent circumstances for police to conduct a warrantless search of an automobile incident to a lawful custodial arrest." *Camacho v. State,* 75 P.3d 370, 373-74 (Nev. 2003).

3.   Under the Wyoming Constitution, a warrantless non-consensual search of a vehicle incident to the defendant's arrest was unreasonable when the operator was arrested for driving with a suspended license and was handcuffed outside the vehicle. *Pierce v. State*, 171 P.3d 525 (Wyo. 2007).

4.   Under the Vermont Constitution, the police may not search a vehicle without a warrant after the driver has been arrested, handcuffed and placed in a police car, unless there is a reasonable need to preserve evidence of a crime or protect the police officer's safety. *State v. Bauder*, 924 A.2d 38 (Vt. 2007).

H. MIRANDA   VIOLATION   –   PHYSICAL   EVIDENCE EXCLUDED

The United States Supreme Court held that physical evidence uncovered as a result of *Miranda* violations need not be suppressed. *United States v. Patane*, 542 U.S. 630 (2004). A contrary result has been reached under some state constitutions.

STATE v. PETERSON
923 A.2d 585 (Vt. 2007)

DOOLEY, J.

The issue in this case is the scope of the exclusionary rule in criminal cases, specifically, whether physical evidence obtained as a result of a violation of defendant's *Miranda* rights must be excluded at trial. We conclude that under chapter I, article 10 of the Vermont Constitution and the Vermont exclusionary rule, physical evidence obtained in violation of *Miranda* rights must be suppressed. We reverse in part and remand.

Defendant James Peterson appeals the denial of two suppression motions. Both involve a core set of undisputed facts. Defendant was looking for his girlfriend and drove his car next to a police vehicle so that he and the officer could speak out of their windows. Upon speaking to defendant, the officer smelled marijuana through the vehicle window. During the conversation, defendant admitted that he had been convicted of a drug offense and that he had a marijuana "roach" in his vehicle. The officer then asked defendant to exit the vehicle, which he did.

The officer patted defendant down; he found no weapons, but smelled the odor of marijuana emanating from the front pocket of defendant's sweatshirt. The officer patted the pocket and, feeling nothing, used his flashlight to look inside the pocket, where he saw green flakes of marijuana plant. When asked, defendant admitted he had picked the marijuana earlier that day from a plant or two he had at home for personal use. The officer then asked defendant for consent to search both his vehicle and his home; defendant consented to these searches both verbally and in writing. The written consent form identified defendant's residence to be searched as "3141 Jersey St. & property" in Panton, Vermont.

After searching defendant's vehicle and finding a burned marijuana cigarette as well as a blanket smelling of marijuana, the officer and a state police trooper proceeded to defendant's residence. Defendant was placed in handcuffs for protection of the police, but was advised by the officer that he was not under arrest. The handcuffs were removed upon arrival at defendant's residence and were intermittently taken on and off while the officers conducted the home search. During the home search, the officer located a garbage bag containing a significant amount of marijuana and marijuana paraphernalia. Defendant led the officers to one marijuana plant growing behind his house.

Upon completion of the home search, the officer informed defendant that they would proceed to the Vergennes Police Department for processing. He placed defendant in handcuffs and instructed him to walk in front of the officer. During the walk, the officer expressed that he doubted so much marijuana came from just one plant, and asked defendant whether he had other marijuana plants. He did not inform defendant of his *Miranda* rights. Defendant eventually admitted to the existence of other plants. The officer asked defendant to show him the other plants, and the two men walked through a wooded area with high brush to a plot where twenty-seven growing plants were located. The plot where the twenty-seven plants were growing is not on, nor visible from, defendant's property.

As a result of the search, the police charged defendant with felony possession of more than twenty-five plants of marijuana and felony possession of marijuana consisting of an aggregate weight of one pound or more. Defendant moved to suppress "all evidence obtained by Vermont Law Enforcement Officials subsequent to his being taken into custody," asserting the officers in question violated his rights to be free from self-incrimination and unlawful search and seizure under both the Vermont and United States Constitutions. Defendant's primary argument was that the police had engaged in custodial interrogation, but failed to give defendant the required warnings under *Miranda v. Arizona,* 384 U.S. 436 (1966), and that the finding of the twenty-seven marijuana plants was the result of the unwarned interrogation. The State responded primarily that the search was pursuant to defendant's consent.

Following the testimony and argument on the motion, the court *sua sponte* requested that the parties brief the impact of *United States v. Patane,* 542 U.S. 630 (2004). After receiving the additional briefing, the court denied defendant's motion to suppress, basing its denial on *Patane.* The court concluded that defendant was in custody at the time he was questioned about possible additional marijuana plants, and as such was entitled to *Miranda* warnings at that time prior to further interrogation. Since it was undisputed that the police did not give defendant *Miranda* warnings, the court held that any statements made after defendant was in custody were made in response to interrogation that violated *Miranda.* The court denied the motion to suppress the twenty-seven plants, however, under *Patane,* which held that physical evidence uncovered as a result of a *Miranda* violation need not be suppressed. The court rejected defendant's additional argument that *Patane* is not good law under the Vermont Constitution.

Following the decision, defendant entered into a conditional plea of guilty allowing him to appeal the denial of his motion to suppress. The issue defendant raises on appeal is whether the twenty-seven marijuana plants must be suppressed.

We, therefore, consider the legality of the use of the twenty-seven marijuana plants as evidence and whether we will follow *United States v. Patane* under the Vermont Constitution.

Patane involved an arrest of a convicted felon for violating an abuse prevention order. Without completing *Miranda* warnings, the arresting officer asked the defendant whether he had a gun because gun possession was illegal for a felon, and there was a report that the defendant had a gun. Under persistent questioning, the defendant told the officer that he had a gun in his bedroom and gave permission to retrieve it. When the defendant was charged with illegally possessing a firearm, he moved to suppress the gun as the fruit of a confession given as a result of a custodial interrogation without *Miranda* warnings.

A majority of the United States Supreme Court concluded that the gun was admissible, but it did so in two separate opinions that differed in part. The plurality opinion written by Justice Thomas and joined by Chief Justice Rehnquist and Justice Scalia held:

> [T]he *Miranda* rule is a prophylactic employed to protect against violations of the Self-Incrimination Clause. The Self-Incrimination Clause, however, is not implicated by the admission into evidence of the physical fruit of a voluntary statement. Accordingly, there is no justification for extending the *Miranda* rule to this context. And just as the Self-Incrimination Clause primarily focuses on the criminal trial, so too does the *Miranda* rule. The *Miranda* rule is not a code of police conduct, and police do not violate the Constitution (or even the *Miranda* rule, for that matter) by mere failures to warn. For this reason, the exclusionary rule articulated in cases such as *Wong Sun* does not apply.

The plurality went on to explain that because prophylactic rules "sweep beyond the actual protections of the Self-Incrimination Clause, any further extension of these rules must be justified by its necessity for the protection of the actual right against compelled self-incrimination." It concluded that a "blanket suppression rule could not be justified by reference to the Fifth

Amendment goal of assuring trustworthy evidence or by any deterrence rationale," and that such a rule would therefore violate the Court's requirement that it maintain "the closest possible fit...between the Self-Incrimination Clause and any rule designed to protect it."

The concurring opinion of Justices Kennedy and O'Connor accepted part of the plurality's rationale. They concluded that admission of the gun did "not run the risk of admitting into trial an accused's coerced incriminating statements against himself" and went on to state:

> In light of the important probative value of reliable physical evidence, it is doubtful that exclusion can be justified by a deterrence rationale sensitive to both law enforcement interests and a suspect's rights during an in-custody interrogation.

Three of the dissenters, Justices Souter, Stevens and Ginsburg, defined the issue as "whether courts should apply the fruit of the poisonous tree doctrine lest we create an incentive for the police to omit *Miranda* warnings before custodial interrogation." They concluded that the majority decision created an "unjustifiable invitation to law enforcement officers to flout *Miranda* when there may be physical evidence to be gained." Justice Breyer joined the dissent except where the failure to give *Miranda* warnings "was in good faith."

In examining whether we should follow *Patane* under the Vermont Constitution, we start with the context of our decision. The right against self-incrimination is guaranteed in the Fifth Amendment to the United States Constitution, which prohibits compelling a criminal defendant to "be a witness against himself." U.S. Const. amend. V. Equivalently, article 10 of the Vermont Constitution prohibits compelling a person "to give evidence against oneself." Vt. Const. ch. I, art. 10. We have held, with respect to adults, that "the article 10 privilege against self-incrimination and that contained in the Fifth Amendment are synonymous." Consistent with this view, we have held that evidence gathered in violation of the prophylactic rules established in *Miranda* is also a violation of article 10. We have not, however, gone beyond *Miranda* and found a violation of the principles of that decision where the United States Supreme Court has not done so.

If this case involved the substance of *Miranda,* for example, the nature of the warnings or the circumstances under which they must be given, the State would have a strong argument that our precedents require that we not go beyond the limits in the decisions of the United States Supreme Court. This, however, is a case in which the district court found a violation of *Miranda* under accepted principles and defendant made a confession to an additional crime under custodial interrogation, a confession that is inadmissible under *Miranda*. The issue is the scope of the remedy for the

Miranda violation, and on this point our precedents take a different view from that of the United States Supreme Court.

A starting point for examination of this question is *State v. Brunelle*, 534 A.2d 198, 200 (Vt. 1987), where we addressed whether we would follow the decisions in *Harris v. New York*, 401 U.S. 222 (1971), and *United States v. Havens*, 446 U.S. 620 (1980). These decisions allowed the prosecution to impeach a criminal defendant who testifies with statements taken in violation of *Miranda*. We rejected these decisions under the Vermont Constitution because they are inconsistent with the right under article 10 of a defendant "to be heard by himself and his counsel." We held instead that the prosecution can impeach with the suppressed evidence only where "a defendant has testified on direct examination to facts contradicted by previously suppressed evidence bearing directly on the crime charged." Although *Brunelle* is based primarily on a defendant's right to testify, the decision explained its relationship to the right against self-incrimination and *Miranda*. As discussed above, it held that a violation of *Miranda* was also a violation of the article 10 right against self-incrimination. Accordingly, the Court described *Brunelle* as "a limited exception to *State v. Badger*, 450 A.2d 336, 349 (Vt. 1982), which held that '[e]vidence obtained in violation of the Vermont Constitution, or as a result of a violation, cannot be admitted at trial as a matter of state law.'" *Brunelle* necessarily holds that the broad exclusionary rule of *Badger* applies to *Miranda* violations.

Badger is itself an important precedent because it applied a locally-created exclusionary rule to *Miranda* violations to suppress physical evidence, there the defendant's clothing. *Badger* found a violation of article 10 based in part on a failure to give *Miranda* warnings and an invalid waiver under *Miranda*, although it did not explicitly hold that a violation of *Miranda* was a violation of article 10. It went on to develop the broad exclusionary rule for such a violation, because:

> Introduction of such evidence at trial eviscerates our most sacred rights, impinges on individual privacy, perverts our judicial process, distorts any notion of fairness, and encourages official misconduct.

With respect to the clothing at issue, it held that "the seizure of the clothing is too directly connected to the illegal confession to allow" its admission.

Defendant argues with considerable force that *Badger* is directly on point and rejects the *Patane* holding that the exclusionary rule does not extend to physical evidence acquired as a result of a *Miranda* violation. The holding in *Badger* is reinforced by *Brunelle*, and *Brunelle* is independently important because it rejects *Harris* and *Havens* both significant building blocks of the limited exclusionary rule set forth in *Patane* and demonstrates that our adherence to *Miranda* under article 10 does not include adherence to the federal exclusionary rule for *Miranda* violations.

We note that the three state supreme courts that have analyzed *Patane* under their state constitutions have concluded that they cannot adopt it because it undercuts the enforcement of *Miranda*. In *Commonwealth v. Martin,* 827 N.E.2d 198 (Mass. 2005), the Massachusetts Supreme Judicial Court refused to follow *Patane* in enforcing *Miranda* rights through article 12 of the Declaration of Rights of the Massachusetts Constitution. The court agreed with the observation of Justice Souter, dissenting in *Patane,* that the decision added "'an important inducement for interrogators to ignore the [*Miranda*] rule'" and created "'an unjustifiable invitation to law enforcement officers to flout *Miranda* when there may be physical evidence to be gained.'" It concluded: "To apply the *Patane* analysis to the broader rights embodied in article 12 would have a corrosive effect on them, undermine the respect we have accorded them, and demean their importance to a system of justice chosen by the citizens of Massachusetts in 1780." Thus, it followed earlier decisions in which it had rejected United States Supreme Court rulings weakening the applicability of *Miranda*.

In *State v. Knapp,* 700 N.W.2d 899 (Wis. 2005), the Wisconsin Supreme Court reached the same conclusion under article I, section 8 of the Wisconsin Constitution in a case where the evidence showed that the police had intentionally violated *Miranda*. It relied on the loss of deterrence, the discouragement of police misconduct, and the need to preserve judicial integrity, in deciding to reject *Patane*.

The decisions in *Martin* and *Knapp* were followed under section 10, article I of the Ohio Constitution by the Ohio Supreme Court in *State v. Farris,* 849 N.E.2d 985 (Ohio 2006). Again, the main rationale is the reduction in deterrence of *Miranda* violations:

> We believe that to hold otherwise would encourage law-enforcement officers to withhold *Miranda* warnings and would thus weaken section 10, article I of the Ohio Constitution. In cases like this one, where possession is the basis for the crime and physical evidence is the keystone of the case, warning suspects of their rights can hinder the gathering of evidence. When physical evidence is central to a conviction and testimonial evidence is not, there can arise a virtual incentive to flout *Miranda*. We believe that the overall administration of justice in Ohio requires a law-enforcement environment in which evidence is gathered in conjunction with *Miranda,* not in defiance of it.

We agree with the analysis and result reached in each of these cases.

For the above reasons, we conclude that we will not follow *United States v. Patane* under article 10 of the Vermont Constitution and our exclusionary rule. Physical evidence gained from statements obtained under circumstances that violate *Miranda* is inadmissible in criminal proceedings as fruit of the poisonous tree. Since it is undisputed that the marijuana plants were such fruit in this case, the district court erred in failing to suppress them.

NOTES

1.   Under the self-incrimination clause in article I, section 10 of the Ohio Constitution, only evidence "obtained as the direct result of statements made in custody without the benefit of a *Miranda* warning should be excluded." *State v. Farris*, 849 N.E.2d 985 (Ohio 2006).

2.   The Massachusetts Supreme Court held that evidence received as the result of a defendant's pre-warning statement to police had to be suppressed as the "fruit" of the detective's unlawful questioning, to safeguard the Massachusetts Constitution's privilege against self-incrimination. *Commonwealth v. Martin*, 827 N.E.2d 198 (Mass. 2005).

CHAPTER **IX**

PROPERTY RIGHTS

A. INTRODUCTION

State constitutions and state law protect a variety of property rights. In fact, the U.S. Supreme Court has made clear that, in general, state law (not federal law) primarily determines what constitutes "property" protected by various constitutional provisions: "Because the Constitution protects rather than creates property interests, the existence of a property interest is determined by reference to 'existing rules or understandings that stem from an independent source such as state law.'" *Phillips v. Washington Legal Foundation*, 524 U.S. 156, 164 (1998).

The major section of this chapter focuses on one state constitutional provision that protects property rights and which has a direct federal counterpart. Most, if not all, state constitutions contain "takings clauses" which parallel the Takings Clause in the Fifth Amendment of the U.S. Constitution. With respect to takings law, this chapter covers an interesting story of dynamic federalism, with state courts and legislatures reacting negatively to a U.S. Supreme Court decision that interpreted the federal takings clause in favor of broad governmental power to take private property. Thus, although the state and federal takings clauses generally mirror each other in terms of language, the interpretation of some state takings provisions is significantly different from the U.S. Supreme Court's interpretation of the federal counterpart.

The chapter also includes a section on the importance of state law in the context of federal procedural due process. Because state law, rather than federal law, generally determines what "property" is protected by the Due Process Clause of the Fourteenth Amendment, state law often plays an important role in federal procedural due process cases. Though the determination of what procedures are constitutionally required is a matter of federal law in Fourteenth Amendment due process cases, state law generally determines the preliminary question whether protected "property" interests are at stake in the first place.

B. TAKINGS PROVISIONS AND THE POST-*KELO* STORY

Most state constitutions prohibit the government from taking private property for public use, unless just compensation is paid. The U.S. Constitution imposes a similar restraint, declaring "nor shall private property be taken for public use without just compensation." U.S. Const. Amend. V. In *Kelo v. City of New London*, 545 U.S. 469 (2005), the

Supreme Court rejected a takings challenge to a city's plan for transferring certain private property obtained through eminent domain to private developers, because the Court held that the plan served a public *purpose* (redeveloping blighted or less valuable property for more valuable uses) and thus satisfied the "public use" requirement.

The *Kelo* decision caused prompt responses in many states, with only a handful of states failing to take any action following *Kelo*. In most states, there was strong objection to the notion that taking private property for redevelopment—as opposed to doing so to build schools or public buildings or roads, for example—was constitutional. Some states responded with legislation, others with constitutional amendments, and a few with court decisions favorable to property owners. As one observer puts it,

> over the last several years, through state legislation, state constitutional amendments and state-court decisions, property-rights advocates have made considerable gains--perhaps obtaining as much as, if not more than, a favorable *Kelo* decision could have offered them. As of today, most States have enacted legislation addressing issues of public use and eminent domain. Seven States have limited the public purposes for which eminent domain is acceptable. Nine States have enacted laws expressly limiting the States' power to exercise eminent domain. Five others have adopted variations on these themes. Some States have sought to reduce the potential abuse of eminent domain by developing procedural changes, requiring state agencies to make stronger showings of public use, requiring agencies to create redevelopment plans, and setting notice and offer requirements to prevent "stealth" condemnation. In other States, court rulings prompted the changes. In 2006, the Ohio and Oklahoma Supreme Courts extended their state constitutional protections against eminent domain beyond the federal baseline by holding that economic benefit alone does not constitutionally justify the exercise of eminent domain. Only a handful of States have not enacted legislation in the wake of *Kelo*.

Jeffrey S. Sutton, *San Antonio Independent School District v. Rodriguez And Its Aftermath*, 94 Va. L. Rev., 1963, 1984–1985 (2008) (footnotes omitted).

Following are two state decisions rejecting the *Kelo* rule and providing property owners in their states with greater protection than the federal Constitution requires. In the last case, a New York court largely followed the *Kelo* approach under its own constitution.

CITY OF NORWOOD v. HORNEY
853 N.E.2d 1115 (Ohio 2006)

O'CONNOR, J.

We decide the constitutionality of a municipality's taking of an individual's property by eminent domain and transferring the property to a private entity for redevelopment. In doing so, we must balance two competing interests of great import in American democracy: the individual's rights in the possession and security of property and the sovereign's power to take private property for the benefit of the community.

Appropriation cases often represent more than a battle over a plot of cold sod in a farmland pasture or the plat of municipal land on which a building sits. For the individual property owner, the appropriation is not simply the seizure of a house. It is the taking of a home-the place where ancestors toiled, where families were raised, where memories were made. Fittingly, appropriations are scrutinized by the people and debated in their institutions.

In reviewing an appropriation similar to that at issue here, a sharply divided United States Supreme Court recently upheld the taking over a federal Fifth Amendment challenge mounted by individual property owners. *Kelo v. New London*, 545 U.S. 469 (2005). Although it determined that the Federal Constitution did not prohibit the takings, the court acknowledged that property owners might find redress in the states' courts and legislatures, which remain free to restrict such takings pursuant to state laws and constitutions.

In response to that invitation in *Kelo*, Ohio's General Assembly unanimously enacted 2005 Am.Sub.S.B. No. 167. The legislature expressly noted in the Act its belief that as a result of *Kelo*, "the interpretation and use of the state's eminent domain law could be expanded to allow the taking of private property that is not within a blighted area, ultimately resulting in ownership of that property being vested in another private person in violation of Sections 1 and 19 of Article I, Ohio Constitution."

The appellants' property was appropriated by the city of Norwood after the city determined that the appellants' neighborhood was a "deteriorating area," as that term is defined in the provisions governing appropriations in the Codified Ordinances of the City of Norwood ("Norwood Code"). Although, as we shall discuss below, we have held that a city may take a slum, blighted, or deteriorated property for redevelopment, and suggested that the taking is proper even when the city transfers the appropriated property to a private party for redevelopment, we have never been asked whether a city may appropriate property that the city determines is in an area that may deteriorate in the future.

We hold that although economic factors may be considered in determining whether private property may be appropriated, the fact that the appropriation would provide an economic benefit to the government and community, standing alone, does not satisfy the public-use requirement of Section 19, Article I of the Ohio Constitution.

I. RELEVANT BACKGROUND

A

Norwood and Its Denizens

The city of Norwood is a modern urban environment. Surrounded by the city of Cincinnati, Norwood was once home to several manufacturing plants and businesses that provided a substantial tax base for the municipality. Despite that industrial component, Norwood was, and for many remains, a desirable place to live. Norwood's neighborhoods were composed of traditional single-family houses and duplexes that provided homes to generations of families and many individuals.

Over the past 40 years, however, Norwood underwent many changes. Like many municipalities in Ohio, Norwood's industrial base eroded, taking with it tax dollars vital to the city. Municipal jobs and many services were eliminated, and the city is millions of dollars in debt. Though the financial outlook of Norwood has been altered greatly over the years, perhaps the most significant change for our purposes here is the physical nature of the city itself.

In the 1960s, property was appropriated from the appellants' neighborhood and used in the construction of a major highway-Interstate 71-through Cincinnati. In the neighborhoods affected, numerous homes were razed and front yards diminished in order to make way for the access roads and ramps to the highway. The streets became busier, creating safety problems for residents who had to back onto busy roadways from their driveways. Residential roads that once ran between major thoroughfares were bisected by the new highway, creating dead-end streets.

Over time, businesses arose in places where houses once stood. The neighborhood became less residential and more commercial. Other changes in the neighborhood's character followed. Traffic increased dramatically due to motorists seeking the highway and businesses in the area. Noise increased, and light pollution became more prevalent.

A private, limited-liability company, Rookwood Partners, Ltd. ("Rookwood"), entered discussions with Norwood about redeveloping the appellants' neighborhood. The preliminary plans for the development call for the construction of more than 200 apartments or condominiums and over 500,000 square feet of office and retail space (all of which would be owned by Rookwood), as well as two large public-parking facilities (which would be owned by Norwood) with spaces for more than 2,000 vehicles. The city expects the redeveloped area to result in nearly $2,000,000 in annual revenue for Norwood.

Norwood, operating with a deficit, was unable to fix the problems or redevelop the appellants' neighborhood on its own .... Discussions between

Norwood and Rookwood culminated in a redevelopment contract in which Rookwood agreed to reimburse the city for the expenses of the project, including the costs arising from any need to use eminent domain to appropriate the property necessary for the project.

Rookwood preferred that Norwood acquire the property needed for the project through eminent domain, but Norwood resisted. It encouraged Rookwood to purchase the property through voluntary sales of homes and businesses, without the city's intervention.

Rookwood was largely successful; it secured acquisition agreements from a substantial majority of the owners of the property necessary to complete the project. The appellants, however, refused to sell.

Because the appellants refused to sell their property, Rookwood asked Norwood to appropriate the appellants' properties and transfer them to Rookwood. Rookwood, in turn, agreed to raze the existing structures (including the appellants' homes), reconfigure the streets, and redevelop the area.

B

The Takings

Norwood used funds provided by Rookwood to retain a consulting firm, Kinzelman Kline Grossman ("KKG"), to prepare an urban-renewal study of the appellants' neighborhood. The study concluded that the construction of I-71 and ensuing conversion of residential and industrial properties to commercial use had led to significant, negative changes in Norwood. Despite acknowledging that many homes were in fair to good condition, KKG concluded that the neighborhood was a "deteriorating area" as that term is defined in the Norwood Code. KKG further determined that the neighborhood would continue to deteriorate and that there would be "continuing piecemeal conversion" of residences to businesses that could be detrimental to the area.

After public hearings and town meetings were held and the local planning commission recommended approval of the redevelopment plan, Norwood City Council passed a series of ordinances adopting the plan and authorizing the mayor to enter the redevelopment agreement with Rookwood and to appropriate the appellants' property. The city then filed complaints against the appellants to appropriate their properties.

At trial, Norwood relied on the testimony of KKG employees to support its conclusion that the appellants' neighborhood was deteriorating. [Ultimately, the trial] concluded ... that there was no showing that Norwood had abused its discretion in finding that the neighborhood was a "deteriorating area."

II. CONSTITUTIONAL CONSIDERATIONS

A

Individual Property Rights

The rights related to property, i.e., to acquire, use, enjoy, and dispose of property, are among the most revered in our law and traditions. Indeed, property rights are integral aspects of our theory of democracy and notions of liberty.

Believed to be derived fundamentally from a higher authority and natural law, property rights were so sacred that they could not be entrusted lightly to "the uncertain virtue of those who govern." As such, property rights were believed to supersede constitutional principles.

In light of [such] notions of property rights, it is not surprising that the founders of our state expressly incorporated individual property rights into the Ohio Constitution in terms that reinforced the sacrosanct nature of the individual's "inalienable" property rights, Section 1, Article I, which are to be held forever "inviolate." Section 19, Article I.

Ohio has always considered the right of property to be a fundamental right. There can be no doubt that the bundle of venerable rights associated with property is strongly protected in the Ohio Constitution and must be trod upon lightly, no matter how great the weight of other forces.

B

The State's Power of Eminent Domain

There is an inherent tension between the individual's right to possess and preserve property and the state's competing interests in taking it for the communal good. Mindful of that friction and the potential for misuse of the eminent-domain power, James Madison's proposed draft of the Takings Clause included two equitable limitations on its use that were eventually incorporated into the Fifth Amendment: the "public use" requirement and the "just compensation" rule. The amendment confirms the sovereign's authority to take, but conditions the exercise of that authority upon satisfaction of two conjunctive standards: that the taking is for a "public use" and that "just compensation" for the taking is given to the property owner.

Similarly, almost every state constitution eventually included provisions related to eminent-domain powers. Both the Northwest Ordinance and the Ohio Constitution recognized the state's right to take property from an individual, but conditioned the right to take on the equitable considerations of just compensation and public use. Section 19, Article I requires that the taking be necessary for the common welfare and, to "insure that principle of natural justice," that the persons deprived of their property will be compensated for "every injury resulting from this act," "every infringement on their [property] rights," and "every injurious interference with the control of their own property."

It is axiomatic that the federal and Ohio constitutions forbid the state to take private property for the sole benefit of a private individual, even when just compensation for the taking is provided. A sine qua non of eminent domain in Ohio is the understanding that the sovereign may use its appropriation powers only upon necessity for the common good.

However, the concept of public use has been malleable and elusive. While broad conceptualizations of public use evolved during the first decades of the 20th century, civic and government leaders became increasingly concerned with living conditions in urban areas and the array of social problems caused by the lack of adequate and safe, affordable housing in cities. The federal government eventually enacted sweeping legislation in an attempt to ameliorate some of those concerns. These modern urban-renewal and redevelopment efforts fostered the convergence of the public-health police power and eminent domain.

In this paradigm, the concept of public use was altered. Rather than furthering a public benefit by appropriating property to *create* something needed in a place where it did not exist before, the appropriations power was used to *destroy* a threat to the public's general welfare and well-being: slums and blighted or deteriorated property.

Historic notions equating physical, moral, and social illnesses with slums and blighted areas were reinforced. The term "blight" itself, borrowed from science and connoting an organism that promotes disease, became synonymous with urban decay, and courts were soon invoking the language of disease. Almost all courts, including this one, have consistently upheld takings that seized slums and blighted or deteriorated private property for redevelopment, even when the property was then transferred to a private entity, and continue to do so. These rulings properly employed an elastic public-use analysis to promote eminent domain as an answer to clear and present public-health concerns, permitting razing and "slum clearance."

Inherent in many decisions affirming pronouncements that economic development alone is sufficient to satisfy the public-use clause is an artificial judicial deference to the state's determination that there was sufficient public use.

Although there is merit in the notion that deference must be paid to a government's determination that there is sufficient evidence to support a taking in a case in which the taking is for a use that has previously been determined to be a public use, see *Kelo,* 545 U.S. at 490, (Kennedy, J., concurring), that deferential review is not satisfied by superficial scrutiny. To the contrary, it remains an essential and critical aspect in the analysis of any proposed taking.

There can be no doubt that our role-though limited-is a critical one that requires vigilance in reviewing state actions for the necessary restraint, including review to ensure that the state takes no more than that necessary to promote the public use, and that the state proceeds fairly and effectuates takings without bad faith, pretext, discrimination, or improper purpose. Thus, our precedent does not demand rote deference to legislative findings in eminent-domain proceedings, but rather, it preserves the courts' traditional role as guardian of constitutional rights and limits. Accordingly, "questions of public *purpose* aside, whether…proposed condemnations [are] consistent with the Constitution's 'public use' requirement [is] a constitutional question squarely within the Court's authority."

A court's independence is critical, particularly when the authority for the taking is delegated to another or the contemplated public use is dependent on a private entity. In such cases, the courts must ensure that the grant of authority is construed strictly and that any doubt over the propriety of the taking is resolved in favor of the property owner.

Similarly, when the state takes an individual's private property for transfer to another individual or to a private entity rather than for use by the state itself, the judicial review of the taking is paramount. A primordial purpose of the public-use clause is to prevent the legislature from permitting the state to take private property from one individual simply to give it to another.

Although we have permitted economic concerns to be considered in addition to other factors, such as slum clearance, when determining whether the public-use requirement is sufficient, we have never found economic benefits alone to be a sufficient public use for a valid taking. We decline to do so now.

We hold that an economic or financial benefit alone is insufficient to satisfy the public-use requirement of Section 19, Article I. In light of that holding, any taking based solely on financial gain is void as a matter of law, and the courts owe no deference to a legislative finding that the proposed taking will provide financial benefit to a community.

III. APPLICATION OF THE LAW TO THE FACTS

A

Norwood Code's Use of "Deteriorating Area" as a Standard for a Taking

The takings in the instant cases were based solely on a finding that the neighborhood was a deteriorating area. But what notice does the term "deteriorating area" give to an individual property owner?

As defined by the Norwood Code, a "deteriorating area" is not the same as a "slum or blighted or deteriorated area," the standard typically employed for a taking. And here, of course, there was no evidence to support a taking under that standard. To the contrary, the buildings in the neighborhood were generally in good condition and the owners were not delinquent in paying property taxes. There is no suggestion that the area was vermin-infested or subject to high crime rates or outbreaks of disease, or otherwise posed an impermissible risk to the larger community.

Some of the factors upon which the court relied, such as diversity of ownership, could apply to many neighborhoods. And although the term commonly appears in eminent-domain cases and regulations, it is susceptible of many meanings and to manipulation.

Moreover, diversity of ownership is a factor of questionable weight. As seems to have been the case here, diversity of ownership is typically considered to be a negative factor for a neighborhood because it purportedly impedes development. Yet Rookwood was able to secure virtually every property owner's assent to sale without any apparent difficulty. Thus, though diversity of ownership may be a factor to consider in determining whether an area is deteriorated, it is not a compelling one.

In essence, "deteriorating area" is a standardless standard. Rather than affording fair notice to the property owner, the Norwood Code merely recites a host of subjective factors that invite ad hoc and selective enforcement-a danger made more real by the malleable nature of the public-benefit requirement. We must be vigilant in ensuring that so great a power as eminent domain, which historically has been used in areas where the most marginalized groups live, is not abused.

As important, the standard for "deteriorating area" defined in the Norwood Code is satisfied not just upon a finding that a neighborhood *is* deteriorating or *will* deteriorate, but is also satisfied by a finding that it " *is in danger of* deteriorating into a blighted area." The statutory definition, therefore, incorporates not only the existing condition of a neighborhood, but also extends to what that neighborhood might become. But what it *might* become may be no more likely than what *might not* become. Such a speculative standard is inappropriate in the context of eminent domain, even under the modern, broad interpretation of "public use."

A fundamental determination that must be made before permitting the appropriation of a slum or a blighted or deteriorated property for redevelopment is that the property, because of its existing state of disrepair or dangerousness, poses a threat to the public's health, safety, or general welfare. Although we adhere to a broad construction of "public use," we hold that government does not have the authority to appropriate private property based on mere belief, supposition, or speculation that the property may pose such a threat in the future. To permit a taking of private property based solely on a finding that the property is deteriorating or in danger of deteriorating would grant an impermissible, unfettered power to the government to appropriate.

We therefore hold that ... the term "deteriorating area" cannot be used as a standard for a taking, because it inherently incorporates speculation as to the future condition of the property into the decision on whether a taking is proper rather than focusing that inquiry on the property's condition at the time of the proposed taking.

Because Norwood may not justify its taking of appellants' property on either the basis that the neighborhood was deteriorating or on the basis that the redeveloped area would bring economic value to the city, there is no showing that the taking was for public use. Our conclusion is not altered by the amount of compensation offered to the property owners in this case, even if it was in excess of the fair market value of their property. Though the questions of just compensation and public use are both critical in an eminent-domain analysis, they must be assessed and satisfied independently. Here, there is not an adequate showing that the takings were for a public use.

BD. OF COUNTY COMM'RS OF MUSKOGEE COUNTY v. LOWERY
136 P.3d 639 (Okl. 2006)

LAVENDER, J.

The issues in the present cause are as follows: (1) whether the County's exercise of eminent domain in the instant cases is for public use in accordance with Article 2, § 23 and Article 2, § 24 of the Oklahoma Constitution and (2) whether the County's taking for purposes of economic development of Muskogee County constitutes "public purposes" within the meaning of 27 O.S.2001 § 5 to support such a taking.

I

FACTS AND PROCEDURAL HISTORY

Plaintiff/Appellee County initiated condemnation proceedings against Defendant/Landowners for the purpose of acquiring temporary and permanent right-of-way easements for the installation of three water pipelines. Two of the proposed water pipelines (referred to by the parties and hereinafter collectively referred to as "the Eagle Pipeline") would solely serve Energetix, a privately owned electric generation plant, which was proposed for construction in Muskogee County. By way of the Eagle Pipeline, Energetix's proposed operations would require a maximum of 8,000,000 gallons of water daily for use in cooling towers associated with the operation of an 825 megawatt natural gas-fired power plant.

Energetix proposed to build the third water pipeline (hereinafter "the Water District Pipeline") on behalf of the Rural Water District No. 5 (hereinafter "Water District") pursuant to a contract...which expressly provided for Energetix's agreement to build this pipeline at no cost to the Water District "as part of the consideration to induce certain property owners to grant private easements for the Eagle Pipeline." The Water District Pipeline was intended to serve residents of the Water District who were not currently being served and to enhance current water service to residents of the Water District, who were receiving it.

Landowners filed an answer and counterclaim in each case seeking declaratory and injunctive relief on the basis that the County's proposed taking was an unlawful taking of private property for private use and private purpose of the private company, Energetix, in violation of 27 O.S.2001 § 5 and the eminent domain provisions contained within both the Oklahoma Constitution and the U.S. Constitution.

The Report of Commissioners was thereafter filed, which provided the takings were for a public purpose and established the amount of just compensation to be awarded to Landowners for their respective properties. Landowners filed their respective Exceptions to the Commissioners' Report, objecting primarily on the basis that the takings were not for a valid public purpose, but rather an unlawful taking of private property for private purpose.

The trial court ultimately agreed with the County and entered an Order confirming the takings in these cases. Landowners appealed, and the COCA reversed and remanded...[holding] that the takings in the instant cases were unlawful in that they were for the direct benefit of a private company and not for "public purposes" as required.

II

THE LAW APPLICABLE TO THIS CONDEMNATION PROCEEDING

The Oklahoma General Eminent Domain Statute and Constitutional Eminent Domain Provisions

The County sought to condemn Landowners' private property pursuant to its general eminent domain power granted by 27 O.S.2001 § 5, which provides as follows:

> Any county, city, town, township, school district, or board of education, or any board or official having charge of cemeteries created and existing under the laws of this state, shall have power to condemn lands in like manner as railroad companies, for highways, rights-of-way, building sites, cemeteries, public parks and *other public purposes.*

Additionally, we are guided by the applicable general federal constitutional and state constitutional eminent domain provisions, including and perhaps most notably our special provision concerning the taking of private property. Article 2, § 23 provides as follows:

> No private property shall be taken or damaged for private use, with or without compensation, unless by consent of the owner, except for private ways of necessity, or for drains and ditches across lands of others for agricultural, mining, or sanitary purposes, in such manner as may be prescribed by law.

Our Constitution further generally provides "private property shall not be taken or damaged for public use without just compensation." OKLA. CONST. art. 2, § 24. That constitutional provision additionally states "[in] all cases of condemnation of private property for public or private use, the determination of the character of the use shall be a judicial question." The law is clear that "[p]rivate property may not be taken or damaged by the condemning agency unless the taking or damage is necessary for the accomplishment of a lawful public purpose." [W]e have used the terms "public use" and "public purpose" interchangeably in our analysis of our state constitutional eminent domain provisions, and we therefore view these terms as synonymous.

The Constitutional Limitations and the Framers' Intent

It is settled law that the constitutional eminent domain provisions "are not grants of power, but limitations placed upon the exercise of government power." The framers of the Oklahoma Constitution ... recognized "that to protect both life and property is the first duty of government." In keeping with these principles, we have determined the government's power of eminent domain "lies dormant in the state until the Legislature by specific enactment designates the occasion, modes and agencies by which it may be placed in operation."

"Public Purpose" in the Context of Eminent Domain

As a general rule, we construe our state constitutional eminent domain provisions "strictly in favor of the owner and against the condemning party." Additionally, Oklahoma eminent domain statutes must conform to the restrictions placed on the exercise of such power by the Oklahoma constitutional eminent domain provisions. We adhere to the strict construction of eminent domain statutes in keeping with our precedent, mindful of the critical importance of the protection of individual private property rights as recognized by the framers of both the U.S. Constitution and the Oklahoma Constitution. If we were to construe "public purpose" so broadly as to include economic development within those terms, then we would effectively abandon a basic limitation on government power by "wash[ing] out any distinction between private and public use of property- and thereby effectively delet[ing] the words 'for public use' from [the constitutional provisions limiting governmental power of eminent domain.]" *Kelo*, 125 S.Ct. at 2671 (O'Connor, J., dissenting). In our view, the power of eminent domain should be exercised with restraint and we therefore construe the term "public purpose" narrowly specifically in this context.

III

AS A MATTER OF OKLAHOMA CONSTITUTIONAL AND STATUTORY LAW, ECONOMIC DEVELOPMENT ALONE IS NOT A PUBLIC PURPOSE TO JUSTIFY THE EXERCISE OF COUNTY'S POWER OF EMINENT DOMAIN.

The County's primary argument is that the general eminent domain statute ... authorizes its exercise of eminent domain for the sole purpose of economic development (i.e., increased taxes, jobs and public and private investment in the community) because economic development constitutes a "public purpose" within the meaning of the statute as well as the state constitutional eminent domain provisions.

We recognize the general rule that where legal relief is available on alternative, non-constitutional grounds, we avoid reaching a determination on the constitutional basis. However, the circumstances of this case lead us to the conclusion that it is necessary for us to reach a constitutional determination in addition to our statutory determination. Here, the two determinations are intertwined. The analysis under both the applicable eminent domain statute and under the state constitutional provisions turns on the identical determination of the meaning of the term "public purpose," which we have previously noted ... is synonymous with "public use" as provided in the Oklahoma Constitution.

Considering the fact that the proposed Eagle Pipeline would be solely dedicated to the purpose of serving a private entity to enable its construction and operation in energy production, it is clear that the County in this case urges a broad interpretation of "public purposes." While arguing the construction of the plant will serve a public purpose by significantly enhancing the economic development of Muskogee County through increased taxes, jobs and public and private investment, County urges our adoption of a rule, which has been applied in other jurisdictions that the exercise of eminent domain for purposes of economic development alone (in the absence of blight) satisfies the constitutional "public use" or "public purpose" requirement. We recognize that the U.S. Supreme Court recently upheld [in *Kelo*] a city's exercise of eminent domain power in furtherance of an economic development plan, holding that economic development satisfied the "public use" restriction in the Fifth Amendment's Takings Clause and finding the city's economic development plan served a "public purpose."

The U.S. Supreme Court expressly limited its holding in *Kelo* as follows: "[t]his Court's authority, however, extends only to determining whether the City's proposed condemnations are for a 'public use' within the meaning of the Fifth Amendment to the Federal Constitution." Notably, the Court in *Kelo* additionally expressly provided as follows:

> We emphasize that nothing in our opinion precludes any State from placing further restrictions on its exercise of the takings power. Indeed, many states already impose "public use" requirements that are stricter than the federal baseline. Some of these requirements have been established as a matter of state constitutional law, while others are expressed in state eminent domain statutes that carefully limit the grounds upon which takings may be exercised.

Contrary to the Connecticut statute applicable in *Kelo,* which expressly authorized eminent domain for the purpose of economic development, we note the absence of such express Oklahoma statutory authority for the exercise of eminent domain in furtherance of economic development in the absence of blight. The statute at issue in the instant cases is a general grant of power that permits condemnation "in like manner as railroad companies, for highways, rights-of-way, building sites, cemeteries, public parks and other public purposes." County here seeks a broad, expansive interpretation of the term "public purpose" to permit the exercise of eminent domain pursuant to the County's general statutory power of eminent domain. However, we have already rejected such a broad interpretation of "public purpose"...[and have held that] "a municipality is not possessed with an unfettered discretion to condemn property for economic redevelopment projects outside of the scope of statutory schemes that the Legislature has provided for removal of blighted property." Accordingly, we hold that economic development alone does not constitute a public purpose and therefore, does not constitutionally justify the County's exercise of eminent domain. Pursuant to our own narrow requirements in our constitutional eminent domain provisions, we view the transfer of property from one private party to another in furtherance of potential economic development or enhancement of a community in the absence of blight as a purpose, which must yield to our greater constitutional obligation to protect and preserve the individual fundamental interest of private property ownership.

To the extent that our determination may be interpreted as inconsistent with the U.S. Supreme Court's holding in *Kelo v. City of New London,* today's pronouncement is reached on the basis of Oklahoma's own special constitutional eminent domain provisions, which we conclude provide private property protection to Oklahoma citizens beyond that which is afforded them by the Fifth Amendment to the U.S. Constitution. In other words, we determine that our state constitutional eminent domain provisions place more stringent limitation on governmental eminent domain power than the limitations imposed by the Fifth Amendment of the U.S. Constitution. We join other jurisdictions including Arizona, Arkansas, Florida, Illinois, South Carolina, Michigan, and Maine, which have reached similar determinations on state constitutional grounds. Other states have similarly restricted the government's eminent domain power through state statute.

While the Takings Clause of the U.S. Constitution provides "nor shall private property be taken for public use without just compensation," the Oklahoma Constitution places further restrictions by expressly stating "[n]o private property shall be taken or damaged *for private use,* with or without compensation." That constitutional provision additionally expressly lists the exceptions for common law easements by necessity and drains for agricultural, mining and sanitary purposes. The proposed purpose of economic development, with its incidental enhancement of tax and employment benefits to the surrounding community, clearly does not fall within any of these categories of express constitutional exceptions to the general rule against the taking of private property for private use. To permit the inclusion of economic development alone in the category of "public use" or "public purpose" would blur the line between "public" and "private" so as to render our constitutional limitations on the power of eminent domain a nullity. If property ownership in Oklahoma is to remain what the framers of our Constitution intended it to be, this we must not do.

EDMONDSON, J., Dissenting and joined by WINCHESTER, V.C.J.

The Court's decision reflects an understandable sensitivity to the United States Supreme Court's recent approval in *Kelo v. City of New London* of a municipal exercise of eminent domain to take unblighted private residential property and deliver it to a private business in anticipation of public benefits to be derived solely from economic development.

In Oklahoma, our State Constitution extends greater protection to private property than does the Federal Constitution, as the majority opinion ably demonstrates. It also mandates that no private property be taken without just compensation.

However, I do not believe our greater measure of safety for private property was intended to deny non-riparian neighbors access to state water resources; particularly when the water is abundant, access can be achieved merely by taking an easement and is essential to the neighbor's survival, and the purpose is, as here, to expand electrical power resources in an economy in which energy is in critically short supply.

No one should be denied access to public water resources unless it is demonstrated that the access would impair the welfare of the public itself. New generation of electrical power is legislatively favored though it be by a private company and marketed directly to a private consumer, because it contributes to the national energy pool and to the ultimate benefit and security of the public.

GOLDSTEIN v. NEW YORK STATE URBAN DEV. CORP.
___ N.E.2d ___, 2009 N.Y. Slip Op. 08677, 2009 WL 4030939

LIPPMAN, C. J.

We are asked to determine whether respondent's exercise of its power of eminent domain to acquire petitioners' properties for purposes of the proposed land use improvement project, known as Atlantic Yards, would be in conformity with certain provisions of our State Constitution. We answer in the affirmative.

On December 8, 2006, respondent Empire State Development Corporation (ESDC) issued a determination pursuant to Eminent Domain Proceedings Law (EDPL) § 204, finding that it should use its eminent domain power to take certain privately owned properties located in downtown Brooklyn for inclusion in a 22-acre mixed-use development proposed, and to be undertaken, by private developer Bruce Ratner and the real estate entities of which he is a principal, collectively known as the Forest City Ratner Companies (FCRC).

The project is to involve, in its first phase, construction of a sports arena to house the NBA Nets franchise, as well as various infrastructure improvements-most notably reconfiguration and modernization of the Vanderbilt Yards rail facilities and access upgrades to the subway transportation hub already present at the site. The project will also involve construction of a platform spanning the rail yards and connecting portions of the neighborhood now separated by the rail cut. Atop this platform are to be situated, in a second phase of construction, numerous high rise buildings and some eight acres of open, publicly accessible landscaped space. The 16 towers planned for the project will serve both commercial and residential purposes. They are slated to contain between 5,325 and 6,430 dwelling units, more than a third of which are to be affordable either for low and or middle income families.

The project has been sponsored by respondent ESDC as a "land use improvement project" within the definition of Urban Development Corporation Act, upon findings that the area in which the project is to be situated is "substandard and insanitary" or, in more common parlance, blighted. It is not disputed that the project designation and supporting blight findings are appropriate with respect to more than half the project footprint, which lies within what has, since 1968, been designated by the City of New York as the Atlantic Terminal Urban Renewal Area (ATURA). To the south of ATURA, however, and immediately adjacent to the Vanderbilt Rail Yard cut, are two blocks and a fraction of a third which, although within the project footprint, have not previously been designated as blighted. FCRC has purchased many of the properties in this area, but there remain some that it has been unsuccessful in acquiring, whose transfer ESDC now seeks to compel in furtherance of the project, through condemnation. In support of its exercise of the condemnation power with respect to these properties, some of which are owned by petitioners, ESDC, based on studies conducted by a consulting firm retained by FCRC, has made findings that the blocks in which they are situated possess sufficient indicia of actual or impending blight to warrant their condemnation for clearance and redevelopment ... and that the proposed land use improvement project will, by removing blight and creating in its place the above-described mixed-use development, serve a "public use, benefit or purpose."

Petitioners' initial challenge to ESDC's determination authorizing condemnation of their properties was made in a timely federal court action. The gist of that action was that the disputed condemnation was not supported by a public use and thus violated the Fifth Amendment of the Federal Constitution. Petitioners' federal claims were rejected by the Federal District Court, and the ... judgment dismissing the complaint was affirmed by the Second Circuit. Within six months, petitioners commenced the present proceeding in the Appellate Division ... [and] alleged ... that the proposed taking was not for a "public use" but for the benefit of a private party and thus would be in violation of article I, § 7(a) of the New York State Constitution.

The Appellate Division ... found for respondent on the merits. It observed that, while the State Constitution, literally read and in its early construction, permitted the taking of property only for "public use," "public use" had since come to be understood as entailing no more than a dominant public purpose. The Court noted that it was well established that the eradication of blight was such a public purpose and found that ESDC's blight findings were supported by the area studies contained in the administrative record.

II

Turning now to the merits, petitioners first contend that the determination authorizing the condemnation of their properties for the Atlantic Yards project is unconstitutional because the condemnation is not for the purpose of putting their properties to "public use" within the meaning of article I, § 7(a) of the State Constitution-which provides that "[p]rivate property shall not be taken for public use without just compensation"-but rather to enable a private commercial entity to use their properties for private economic gain with, perhaps, some incidental public benefit. The argument reduces to this: that the State Constitution has from its inception, in recognition of the fundamental right to privately own property, strictly limited the availability of condemnation to situations in which the property to be condemned will actually be made available for public use, and that, with only limited exceptions prompted by emergent public necessity, the State Constitution's takings clause, unlike its federal counterpart, has been consistently understood literally, to permit a taking of private property only for "public use," and not simply to accomplish a public purpose.

Even if this gloss on this State's takings laws and jurisprudence were correct-and it is not-it is indisputable that the removal of urban blight is a proper, and, indeed, constitutionally sanctioned, predicate for the exercise of the power of eminent domain. It has been deemed a "public use" within the meaning of the State's takings clause at least since *Matter of New York City Housing Authority v. Muller* (270 N.Y. 333 [1936]) and is expressly recognized by the Constitution as a ground for condemnation. Article XVIII, § 1 of the State Constitution grants the Legislature the power to "provide in such manner, by such means and upon such terms and conditions as it may prescribe ... for the clearance, replanning, reconstruction and rehabilitation of substandard and insanitary areas," and section 2 of the same article provides "[f]or and in aid of such purposes, notwithstanding any provision in any other article of this constitution, ... the legislature may ... grant the power of eminent domain to any ... public corporation...." Pursuant to article XVIII, respondent ESDC has been vested with the condemnation power by the Legislature and has here sought to exercise the power for the constitutionally recognized public purpose or "use" of rehabilitating a blighted area.

Petitioners, of course, maintain that the blocks at issue are not, in fact, blighted and that the allegedly mild dilapidation and inutility of the property cannot support a finding that it is substandard and insanitary within the meaning of article XVIII. They are doubtless correct that the conditions cited in support of the blight finding at issue do not begin to approach in severity the dire circumstances of urban slum dwelling described by the *Muller* court in 1936, and which prompted the adoption of article XVIII at the State Constitutional Convention two years later. We, however, have never required that a finding of blight by a legislatively designated public benefit corporation be based upon conditions replicating those to which the Court and the Constitutional Convention responded in the midst of the Great Depression. To the contrary, in construing the reach of the terms "substandard and insanitary" as they are used in article XVIII-and were applied in the early 1950's to the Columbus Circle area upon which the New York Coliseum was proposed to be built-we observed:

> Of course, none of the buildings are as noisome or dilapidated as those described in Dickens' novels or Thomas Burke's 'Limehouse' stories of the London slums of other days, but there is ample in this record to justify the determination of the city planning commission that a substantial part of the area is 'substandard and insanitary' by modern tests. (*Kaskel v. Impellitteri*, 306 N.Y. 73, 78 [1953]).

And, subsequently, in *Yonkers Community Dev. Agency v. Morris* (37 N.Y.2d 478, 481-482 [1975]), in reviewing the evolution of the crucial terms' signification and permissible range of application, we noted:

> Historically, urban renewal began as an effort to remove 'substandard and insanitary' conditions which threatened the health and welfare of the public, in other words 'slums', whose eradication was in itself found to constitute a public purpose for which the condemnation powers of government might constitutionally be employed. Gradually, as the complexities of urban conditions became better understood, it has become clear that the areas eligible for such renewal are not limited to "slums" as that term was formerly applied, and that, among other things, economic underdevelopment and stagnation are also threats to the public sufficient to make their removal cognizable as a public purpose.

It is important to stress that lending precise content to these general terms has not been, and may not be, primarily a judicial exercise. Whether a matter should be the subject of a public undertaking-whether its pursuit will serve a public purpose or use-is ordinarily the province of the Legislature, not the Judiciary, and the actual specification of the uses identified by the Legislature as public has been largely left to quasi-legislative administrative agencies. It is only where there is no room for reasonable difference of opinion as to whether an area is blighted, that judges may substitute their views as to the adequacy with which the public purpose of blight removal has been made out for that of the legislatively designated agencies; where, as here, "those bodies have made their finding, not corruptly or irrationally or baselessly, there is nothing for the courts to do about it, unless every act and decision of other departments of government is subject to revision by the courts."

It is quite possible to differ with ESDC's findings that the blocks in question are affected by numerous conditions indicative of blight, but any such difference would not, on this record, in which the bases for the agency findings have been extensively documented photographically and otherwise on a lot-by-lot basis, amount to more than another reasonable view of the matter; such a difference could not, consonant with what we have recognized to be the structural limitations upon our review of what is essentially a legislative prerogative, furnish a ground to afford petitioners relief.

It may be that the bar has now been set too low-that what will now pass as "blight," as that expression has come to be understood and used by political appointees to public corporations relying upon studies paid for by developers, should not be permitted to constitute a predicate for the invasion of property rights and the razing of homes and businesses. But any such limitation upon the sovereign power of eminent domain as it has come to be defined in the urban renewal context is a matter for the Legislature, not the courts. Properly involved in redrawing the range of the sovereign prerogative would not be a simple return to the days when private property rights were viewed as virtually inviolable, even when they stood in the way of meeting compelling public needs, but a re-weighing of public as against private interests and a reassessment of the need for and public utility of what may now be out-moded approaches to the revivification of the urban landscape. These are not tasks courts are suited to perform. They are appropriately situated in the policy-making branches of government.

The dissenter, after thoughtful review of the evolution of the concept of public use-an evolution that even he acknowledges has sapped the concept of much of its limiting power-urges that there remains enough left in it to require that this case be decided differently. We cannot agree. The Constitution accords government broad power to take and clear substandard and insanitary areas for redevelopment. In so doing, it commensurately deprives the Judiciary of grounds to interfere with the exercise.

While there remains a hypothetical case in which we might intervene to prevent an urban redevelopment condemnation on public use grounds-where "the physical conditions of an area might be such that it would be irrational and baseless to call it substandard or insanitary"-this is not that case. The dissenter looks at the "Blight Study" contained in the administrative record and sees only a "normal and pleasant residential neighborhood," but others, it would appear not irrationally, have come to very different conclusions. This is not a record that affords the purchase necessary for judicial intrusion. The situation in the end is remarkably like ... *Kaskel* where ... the Court said:

> Plaintiff does not dispute with defendants as to the condition of these properties or of the whole area. He is simply opposing his opinion and his judgment to that of public officials, on a matter which must necessarily be one of opinion or judgment, that is, as to whether a specified area is so substandard or insanitary, or both, as to justify clearance and redevelopment under the law. It is not seriously contended by anyone that, for an area to be subject to those laws, every single building therein must be below civilized standards. The statute (and the Constitution), like other similar laws, contemplates that clearing and redevelopment will be of an entire area, not of a separate parcel, and, surely, such statutes would not be very useful if limited to areas where every single building is substandard.

Here too, all that is at issue is a reasonable difference of opinion as to whether the area in question is in fact substandard and insanitary. This is not a sufficient predicate for us to supplant respondent's determination.

SMITH, J., dissenting.

The good news from today's decision is that our Court has not followed the lead of the United States Supreme Court in rendering the "public use" restriction on the Eminent Domain Clause virtually meaningless. The bad news is that the majority is much too deferential to the self-serving determination by Empire State Development Corporation (ESDC) that petitioners live in a "blighted" area, and are accordingly subject to having their homes seized and turned over to a private developer. I do not think the record supports ESDC's determination, and I therefore dissent.

I

Article I, § 7(a) of the State Constitution says: "Private property shall not be taken for public use without just compensation ."

The words "public use" embody an important protection for property owners. They prevent the State from invoking its eminent domain power as a means of transferring property from one private owner to another who has found more favor with state officials, or who promises to use the land in a way more to the State's liking. They do not require that all takings result in public ownership of the property, but they do ordinarily require that, if the land is transferred to private hands, it be used after the taking in a way that benefits the public directly. A recognized exception permits the transfer of "blighted" land to private developers without so strict a limitation on its subsequent use, but that exception is applicable only in cases in which the use of the land by its original owner creates a danger to public health and safety.

These principles are established by two centuries of New York cases. A line of 19th century decisions made clear that the State could not use the eminent domain power to transfer property from one private owner to another, unless the use to which the second owner put the property would be "public" in some meaningful sense. In the 20th century, an era friendlier to government and less friendly to private property, this rule was diluted, but our cases do not justify the conclusion that the public use limitation was abandoned or rendered trivial. Rather, the 20th century cases created what may be called a "blight exception" to the public use limitation. The critical question on this appeal is whether that exception applies, a question that can be better understood after a more detailed description of the way our "public use" law has developed.

In the early 19th century, New York judges debated whether the eminent domain power could ever be used to transfer property from one private owner to another. Later cases make clear that this debate was settled in favor of the Chancellor's view that certain uses of property by private parties- *e.g.,* for "turnpike and other roads, railways, canals, ferries and bridges"-could be considered public, but that takings in which land was transferred to private hands would be strictly limited to situations in which the public nature of the use was clear. In *Matter of Niagara Falls & Whirlpool Ry. Co.* (108 N.Y. 375, 383 [1888]), we said: "The right of the state to authorize the condemnation of private property for the construction of railroads and to delegate the power to take proceedings for that purpose to railroad corporations, has become an accepted doctrine of constitutional law and is not open to debate." But we held that the proposed taking in the *Niagara* case, which was for a railroad that would serve "the sole purpose of furnishing sight-seers during about four months of the year, greater facilities than they now enjoy for seeing ... part of [the] Niagara river," was not for a public use.

Under the 19th century understanding of public use, the taking at issue in this case would certainly not be permitted. It might be possible to debate whether a sports stadium open to the public is a "public use" in the traditional sense, but the renting of commercial and residential space by a private developer clearly is not.

Our 20th century cases, while not all consistent and containing some confusing language, are best read as modifying, rather than nullifying or abandoning, the established public use limitation. A series of cases upheld takings for what was variously characterized as slum clearance, removal of blight, or correction of unsafe, unsanitary or substandard housing conditions. While these cases undoubtedly expanded the old understanding of public use, they did not establish the general proposition that property may be condemned and turned over to a private developer every time a state agency thinks that doing so would improve the neighborhood.

Muller approved a taking of property where "unsanitary and substandard housing conditions" were found to exist. We observed:

> The public evils, social and economic of such conditions, are unquestioned and unquestionable. Slum areas are the breeding places of disease which take toll not only from denizens, but, by spread, from the inhabitants of the entire city and State. Juvenile delinquency, crime and immorality are there born, find protection and flourish. Enormous economic loss results directly from the necessary expenditure of public funds to maintain health and hospital services for afflicted slum dwellers and to war against crime and immorality. Indirectly there is an equally heavy capital loss and a diminishing return in taxes because of the areas blighted by the existence of the slums.

Muller did not involve transfer to an ordinary private developer: the property in question was to be rented by the City, or by "limited dividend corporations," to people of low income. In *Muller,* we reiterated the essential principle of the public use limitation:

> Nothing is better settled than that the property of one individual cannot, without his consent, be devoted to the private use of another, even when there is an incidental or colorable benefit to the public. The facts here present no such case.... [T]he public is seeking to take the defendant's property and to administer it as part of a project conceived and to be carried out in its own interest and for its own protection.

Murray, unlike *Muller,* did involve a taking from which a purely private company "may ultimately reap a profit." The need to remedy "conditions in those blighted urban areas where slums exist," conditions that "affect the health, safety and welfare of the public," furnished the reason for upholding the taking.

Our later decision in *Yonkers Community Development* ... does seem to adopt a rather loose interpretation of "substandard" conditions that would justify a taking, but it also says that "courts are required to be more than rubber stamps in the determination of the existence of substandard conditions" and that "in order to utilize the public purpose attached to clearance of substandard land, such clearance must be the primary purpose of the taking, not some other public purpose, however laudable it might be." In *Yonkers,* we found that the agency had not provided factual support for its claim that the land to be taken was substandard, but held that the landowners had failed to raise this issue properly by their pleadings.

ESDC also relies on *Kaskel v. Impellitteri* (306 N.Y. 73 [1953]), which involved a very questionable "slum clearance" taking, but overlooks an important aspect of that case. The challenge to the governmental action there was brought not by a condemnee, but by a taxpayer suing under General Municipal Law § 51, and we emphasized that in such a case the plaintiff must show corruption, fraud or "a total lack of power ... under the law, to do the acts complained of." We implied that the case might be different if the "arbitrary and capricious" standard of an article 78 proceeding were applicable. Even on the stringent section 51 standard, Judges Van Voorhis and Fuld dissented and would have held plaintiff's claim sufficient to withstand summary judgment.

The most troubling cases cited by ESDC are *Cannata v. City of New York* (11 N.Y.2d 210 [1962]) and *Courtesy Sandwich Shop, Inc. v. Port of N.Y. Auth.* (12 N.Y.2d 379 [1963]), which can be read to support an interpretation of "public use" that would permit the transfer by eminent domain of almost anyone's property to a private entity if a state agency thinks the area would benefit from "redevelopment." These cases, however, must be understood in historical context. They were decided after the United States Supreme Court had adopted, in *Berman v. Parker* (348 U.S. 26, 33 [1954]), a "broad and inclusive" definition of public use, to include any "object ... within the authority of Congress." *Berman,* as later cases confirmed, eviscerated the "public use" limitation of the United States Constitution. And at the time of the *Cannata* and *Courtesy Sandwich Shop* decisions, our Court had not adopted the practice, which later became common, of interpreting our state Constitution to afford broader protection to individual rights and liberties than the federal Constitution does. I would view *Cannata* and *Courtesy Sandwich Shop* as mistakenly following *Berman's* lead, and would limit them to their facts or simply reject them.

II

The majority does not wholly reject what I have said in section I of this dissent. Indeed, the majority seems to accept the premise that the Eminent Domain Clause of the New York Constitution has independent vitality, and may offer more protection to property owners than its federal counterpart. I am pleased that the majority does not follow the Supreme Court's decisions in *Berman, Midkiff* and *Kelo,* which equate "public use" in the Constitution with public purpose, thus leaving governments free to accomplish by eminent domain any goal within their general power to act. Where I part company with the majority is in its conclusion that we must defer to ESDC's determination that the properties at issue here fall within the blight exception to the public use limitation.

It is clear to me from the record that the elimination of blight, in the sense of substandard and unsanitary conditions that present a danger to public safety, was never the bona fide purpose of the development at issue in this case. Indeed, blight removal or slum clearance, which were much in vogue among the urban planners of several decades ago, have waned in popularity .... It is more popular today to speak of an "urban landscape"- the words used by Bruce Ratner to describe his "vision" of the Atlantic Yards development in a public presentation in January 2004.

According to the petition in this case, when the project was originally announced in 2003 the public benefit claimed for it was economic development-job creation and the bringing of a professional basketball team to Brooklyn. Petitioners allege that nothing was said about "blight" by the sponsors of the project until 2005; ESDC has not identified any earlier use of the term. In 2005, ESDC retained a consultant to conduct a "blight study." In light of the special status accorded to blight in the New York law of eminent domain, the inference that it was a pretext, not the true motive for this development, seems compelling.

It is apparent from a review of ESDC's blight study that its authors faced a difficult problem. Only the northern part of the area on which Atlantic Yards is to be built can fairly be described as blighted. But the southern part of the project area, where petitioners live, has never been part of ATURA and appears, from the photographs and the descriptions contained in ESDC's blight study, to be a normal and pleasant residential community.

ESDC's consultants did their best. Proceeding lot by lot through the area in which petitioners live, they were able to find that a number of buildings were not in good condition; petitioners claim that this results in large part from the fact that Ratner's plan to acquire the properties and demolish the buildings had been public knowledge for years when the blight study was conducted. Choosing their words carefully, the consultants concluded that the area of the proposed Atlantic Yards development, taken as a whole, was "characterized by blighted conditions." They did not find, and it does not appear they could find, that the area where petitioners live is a blighted area or slum of the kind that prompted 20th century courts to relax the public use limitation on the eminent domain power.

The majority opinion acknowledges that the conditions ESDC relies on here "do not begin to approach in severity the dire circumstances of urban slum dwelling" contemplated by the cases that developed the blight exception. The majority concludes, however, that determining whether the area in question is really blighted is not "primarily a judicial exercise." In doing so, I think, the majority loses sight of the nature of the issue.

The determination of whether a proposed taking is truly for public use has always been a judicial exercise-as the cases cited in section I of this dissent, from *Bloodgood* in 1837 through *Yonkers Community Development* in 1975, demonstrate. The right not to have one's property taken for other than public use is a constitutional right like others. It is hard to imagine any court saying that a decision about whether an utterance is constitutionally protected speech, or whether a search was unreasonable, or whether a school district has been guilty of racial discrimination, is not primarily a judicial exercise. While no doubt some degree of deference is due to public agencies and to legislatures, to allow them to decide the facts on which constitutional rights depend is to render the constitutional protections impotent.

The whole point of the public use limitation is to prevent takings even when a state agency deems them desirable. To let the agency itself determine when the public use requirement is satisfied is to make the agency a judge in its own cause. I think that it is we who should perform the role of judges, and that we should do so by deciding that the proposed taking in this case is not for public use.

NOTES

1. Why might some state courts be more or less protective of property rights in the context of eminent domain? Could geography or population influence how a court reads a state constitutional takings provision?

2. Can you make arguments for and against a state court reading the state constitution's takings clause differently than the federal Takings Clause? Will different readings cause headaches for local governments and developers?

3. Should state courts interpret the state constitutions to restrict the power of eminent domain, or should that decision be left to each state's political

processes, whether the legislature or public referendum? Some state constitutions expressly provide that "the question whether the contemplated use be really public shall be a judicial question, and determined as such without regard to any legislative assertion that the use is public." Colo. Const. Art. II, § 15; *see also* Okla. Const. Art. II, § 24 ("In all cases of condemnation of private property for public or private use, the determination of the character of the use shall be a judicial question"); Wash. Const. Art. I, § 16 (same language as the Colorado provision quoted above). Does requiring judicial determination ensure greater protection of property rights?

4.   Are courts the only or even the best protectors of property rights? Some states responded to the concerns *Kelo* raised by adopting stricter *procedural requirements* for takings that were not for a traditional public use. *See, e.g.,* Fla. Const., Art. 10, § 6(c) ("Private property taken by eminent domain...on or after January 2, 2007, may not be conveyed to a natural person or private entity except as provided by general law passed by a three-fifths vote of the membership of each house of the Legislature.") Others adopted a flat prohibition that would appear to leave little, if any, room for court interpretation. *See, e.g.,* N.H. Const. Pt. 1, Art. 12-a ("No part of a person's property shall be taken by eminent domain and transferred, directly or indirectly, to another person if the taking is for the purpose of private development or other private use of the property.")

5.   What are the consequences of providing greater protection to property owners under the state constitutions than the federal Takings Clause provides?

C. TAKINGS AND THE IMPAIRMENT OF CONTRACTS

HAGELAND AVIATION SERVICES, INC. v. HARMS
210 P.3d 444 (Alaska 2009)

FABE, C. J.

I.   INTRODUCTION

Pilots of Hageland Aviation Services, Inc. filed a class action lawsuit in 2002 for unpaid overtime wages under the Alaska Wage and Hour Act. After the Alaska Legislature amended the Act in 2003 to exempt pilots from the Act's overtime compensation provision, Hageland moved to dismiss the lawsuit. The superior court held that the legislative change exempting pilots from the Act applied only from the amendment's effective date of July 16, 2003. The legislature again amended the Act in 2005 to make its 2003 amendment to the Act retroactive to 2000. Hageland moved for summary judgment based on the retroactive exemption, and the pilots cross-moved for summary judgment, arguing that the retroactive exemption violates numerous provisions of the state and federal constitutions. The superior court concluded that the 2005 amendment violates the takings and contract clauses of the Alaska Constitution. Hageland appeals. Because we agree with the superior court that the 2005 amendment is a violation of the takings and contract clauses, we affirm.

IV. DISCUSSION

Before us in this appeal are the questions whether Chapter 19's retroactive application of the statutory exemption of flight crews from the Act's overtime compensation provision violates the takings or contract clauses of the Alaska Constitution.

A. Chapter 19 Is an Unconstitutional Taking.

Article I, section 18 of the Alaska Constitution provides: "Private property shall not be taken or damaged for public use without just compensation." In analyzing whether a taking has occurred in this case, we address two questions. First, are the pilots' claims for unpaid compensation property interests protected by the takings clause? Second, if the claims are protected property interests, does Chapter 19 effect a taking of that property? The superior court answered both of these questions in the affirmative, reasoning that each pilot had a protected property interest in the wages owed by law at the end of each pay period and that under our multifactor test for takings violations an unconstitutional taking had occurred. We agree.

1. The pilots have vested property interests that are protected by the Alaska Constitution's takings clause.

We have recognized that "a cause of action for unpaid overtime accrues at the end of each pay period in which overtime is due." Applying this rule to the present case, the pilots' claims had already accrued when Chapter 19 was passed in 2005 because their claims were for unpaid overtime compensation for work performed between June 26, 2000, and July 16, 2003.

Although Hageland argues that the claims for unpaid overtime are not protected by the Alaska Constitution's takings clause before a final judgment has been entered, we have held "that a chose in action...is a form of property" that the claimant cannot be deprived of litigating without due process of law. Unlitigated causes of action become property when they accrue. Thus, a cause of action becomes a vested property interest that is protected by the takings clause as soon as it accrues and so has that status even before the issuance of a final judgment. Here, the pilots' property interests in their claims for unpaid overtime are protected by our constitution at the time their claims accrued; their claims need not have been reduced to final judgment to create vested property interests that are protected by the takings clause.

2.   Chapter 19 takes the pilots' vested property interests in violation of the Alaska Constitution's takings clause.

We consider three factors to determine whether a government action effects a taking: (1) the character of the government action, which includes consideration of the legitimacy of the interest advanced by the action; (2) its economic impact; and (3) its interference with reasonable investment-backed expectations.

Turning first to the character of the government action, Hageland argues that the legislature was exercising its police power by regulating employee wages when it passed Chapter 19 and that it did so for the common good, without "tak[ing] anything for its own use." Hageland's argument fails for two reasons. First, Hageland explores the character of the legislative decision to exempt pilots from the Act's overtime compensation provision rather than the government action at issue: the retroactivity provided in Chapter 19. When the legislature passed Chapter 11, it shifted future economic burdens once borne by air carriers to their flight crews. While this enactment may have been a legitimate exercise of the legislature's police power to regulate employment and wages, the broad purpose of Chapter 11's exclusion stands in stark contrast to the narrow purpose of Chapter 19's retroactivity. The avowed purpose of Chapter 19 was to eliminate the pilots' claims along with the claims of two other class actions against Alaska air carriers. The legislature enacted Chapter 19 to extinguish retroactively all claims for unpaid overtime compensation for "work performed on or after January 1, 2000" because, as the sponsor statement for Chapter 19's senate bill explained, Chapter 11 "failed to fully enact the legislative intent necessary to deflect court actions seeking recovery for periods dating back to the year 2000." In carrying out the legislature's narrow purpose to prevent litigation of these class actions, Chapter 19 effectively transferred money from the pockets of one private party to another.

Second, despite Hageland's focus on the fact that the State did not take the pilots' claims for its own use when it enacted Chapter 19, whether the State receives a benefit from the alleged taking is irrelevant to the takings analysis. We have recognized that "[t]he finding of a taking, finally, depends on whether someone has been deprived of the economic benefits of ownership, not whether the State captures any of those benefits."

Chapter 19's significant economic impact on the pilots is obvious. Although Hageland acknowledges that Chapter 19 eliminated the pilots' claims to unpaid overtime, it maintains that their claims were "inchoate," "speculative," and "uncertain." But the pilots' recovery was certain when Chapter 19 was enacted. Hageland had already been found liable for the pilots' unpaid overtime and the only unresolved issue before the superior court was the exact value of the judgment against Hageland, which was later stipulated by the parties to be $1,600,000-by no means a small sum of money. And even if there had not been a summary judgment ruling in favor of the pilots, they would still have suffered a substantial economic loss. They had already worked the overtime hours, and by law they were entitled to receive compensation for those hours of work at the end of each pay period.

With regard to the final factor, Hageland contends that the pilots did not have a reasonable investment-backed expectation of being paid overtime compensation because they did not have an actual expectation of being paid more than they had already received. But the test for reasonable expectations is an objective one, and the pilots reasonably expected that they would be paid according to the law for the work they had performed for Hageland. Regardless of whether the pilots knew the specifics of the law and whether it required payment of overtime wages under particular circumstances, they could reasonably expect that Hageland would comply with the existing wage and hour laws. Thus, the pilots had a reasonable investment-backed expectation protected by the takings clause and it was interfered with when Chapter 19 retroactively eliminated their claims for unpaid overtime.

B. Chapter 19 Is an Unconstitutional Impairment of Contracts.

Article I, section 15 of the Alaska Constitution provides: "No law impairing the obligation of contracts ... shall be passed." Because the language of the contract clause of the Alaska Constitution is nearly identical to that of the federal Contract Clause,[1] we apply the same two-part analysis to alleged violations of the Alaska and federal contract clauses. We first ask "whether the change in state law has operated as a substantial impairment of a contractual relationship." If there is a substantial impairment, we then examine "whether the impairment is reasonable and necessary to serve an important public purpose." The superior court determined that Chapter 19 substantially impaired the overtime compensation term of the parties' employment agreement. The superior court also determined that this impairment was not justified by a legitimate public purpose because "the legitimacy of targeting specific, ongoing lawsuits is questionable," and even if Chapter 19's public purpose was legitimate, it would not justify "[t]he retroactive removal of existing contract rights from one party in favor of another who clearly violated existing law."

1. Chapter 19 substantially impairs the parties' contractual relationship.

---

[1] [29] Article I, section 10 of the United States Constitution provides: "No State shall ... pass any ... Law impairing the Obligation of Contracts ...."

Under the first prong of the contract clause test, we consider: (1) whether there is a contractual relationship, (2) whether the law impairs the contractual relationship, and (3) whether the impairment is substantial. The parties do not deny there was a contractual relationship between Hageland and the pilots. It is also undisputed that under the parties' unwritten agreement the pilots would receive a daily rate for each day they were on duty.

As to whether Chapter 19 impairs the parties' contractual relationship, Hageland argues that the term of the contract alleged to be infringed-the payment of overtime compensation under AS 23.10.060-was not a part of the contract between Hageland and the pilots because the parties' contractual expectations did not include payment for overtime wages. Alaska Statute 23.10.060(c), however, expressly states that the Act's overtime compensation provision is "included in all contracts of employment."

By eliminating the pilots' claims to unpaid overtime, Chapter 19 substantially, and in fact completely, impaired Hageland's contractual obligation to pay overtime compensation as required by statute. Hageland disagrees with this conclusion, arguing that even if Chapter 19 impairs the parties' employment agreement, the impairment could not be substantial because the parties did not actually rely on the overtime compensation term of their agreement .... But the question whether the pilots expected to be paid more than they received from Hageland is separate from the question whether they actually relied on the overtime compensation provision because...the pilots had a reasonable belief that they would be compensated in accordance with the law.

Chapter 19 "totally eliminated" the pilots' important contractual right to overtime wages for work performed between June 26, 2000, and July 16, 2003. We agree ... that compensation for work performed according the parties' employment agreement is of great importance .... Hageland also argues that when the legislature abridges a right that it provided through an earlier act, the impairment is not substantial. But ... a legislature's impairment of a statutory right created through a prior enactment may be substantial .... For these reasons, Hageland's arguments are unavailing. Chapter 19 substantially impaired the overtime compensation provision of the parties' employment agreement when Chapter 19 "totally eliminated" the pilots' claims for unpaid overtime wages against Hageland.

2. Chapter 19's impairment of Hageland's obligation to pay the pilots overtime compensation for work already performed is not reasonable and necessary to serve an important public purpose.

Under the second prong of our contract clause analysis, we scrutinize whether Chapter 19 is reasonable and necessary to serve an important public purpose. "The severity of the impairment measures the height of the hurdle the state legislation must clear .... Severe impairment ... will push the inquiry to a careful examination of the nature and purpose of the state legislation." Here, Chapter 19's impairment of the pilots' contractual right to overtime compensation was severe in that it completely eliminated Hageland's obligation to pay the pilots the overtime wages that they were entitled to under the superior court's summary judgment orders on liability.

According to Hageland, the sponsor statement for Chapter 19's senate bill demonstrates the legislature's belief that Chapter 19 would serve the important public purpose of aiding the vulnerable air carrier industry in Alaska. The sponsor statement highlighted the burdens placed on the "critical yet fragile" air carrier industry threatened by "superfluous litigation."

We do not question that Chapter 11 serves an important public purpose by reallocating the financial burdens borne by air carriers and their employees in order to aid a struggling transportation industry that many Alaskans, especially those living in rural areas off the road system, depend upon to sustain their way of life. Yet it is difficult to discern how Chapter 19 serves this important public purpose by denying pilots employed by three air carriers the overtime they were entitled to under the existing law when they performed the work. Hageland cites the possibility that the pilots' suit, and others like it, would put Hageland and other air carriers out of business. But Chapter 19 only addresses the overtime wages of pilots employed by three of Alaska's more than sixty-five air carriers. As the superior court remarked, "[t]he retroactive removal of existing contract rights from one party in favor of another who clearly violated existing law is manifestly unfair." Thus, Chapter 19 is not reasonable and necessary to serve the important public purpose advanced by Hageland.

V. CONCLUSION

Because Chapter 19's retroactive application of the statutory exemption of flight crews to the Act's overtime compensation provision is an unconstitutional taking of the pilots' overtime wages and an unconstitutional impairment of the parties' employment agreement, we AFFIRM the superior court's holding that Chapter 19 violates the takings and contract clauses of the Alaska Constitution.

D. STATE PROPERTY RIGHTS AND FEDERAL DUE PROCESS

In *Bd. Of Regents v. Roth*, 408 U.S. 564, 577 (1972), a procedural due process case involving the non-renewal of an untenured teacher's contract, the Supreme Court of the United States declared as follows: "Property interests, of course, are not created by the Constitution. Rather they are created and their dimensions are defined by existing rules or understandings that stem from an independent source such as state law—rules or understandings that secure benefits and that support claims of entitlement to those benefits." Thus, state constitutions and state law generally create property interests, not federal law.

State-created "property," for federal due process purposes, includes a wide variety of interests. Important examples include state-issued licenses (such as driver's licenses, professional licenses, liqour licenses), public benefits, the right of children to attend public schools, and legal causes of action. To the extent state constitutions define or are interpreted to create property interests (*e.g.*, the right to a remedy provisions addressed in Chapter XII), they play a critical role in determining the preliminary question whether "property" interests are at stake in a particular federal procedural due process case. Thus, both state constitutions and the federal constitution may provide protection for state-created property interests.

Following are two Supreme Court decisions applying the principle that state law alone creates "property" interests for federal procedural due process purposes.

PERRY v. SINDERMAN
408 U.S. 593 (1972)

STEWART, J.

From 1959 to 1969 the respondent, Robert Sindermann, was a teacher in the state college system of the State of Texas. After teaching for two years at the University of Texas and for four years at San Antonio Junior College, he became a professor of Government and Social Science at Odessa Junior College in 1965. He was employed at the college for four successive years, under a series of one-year contracts.

During the 1968-1969 academic year, however, controversy arose between the respondent and the college administration. The respondent was elected president of the Texas Junior College Teachers Association. In this capacity, he left his teaching duties on several occasions to testify before committees of the Texas Legislature, and he became involved in public disagreements with the policies of the college's Board of Regents. In particular, he aligned himself with a group advocating the elevation of the college to four-year status-a change opposed by the Regents. And, on one occasion, a newspaper advertisement appeared over his name that was highly critical of the Regents.

Finally, in May 1969, the respondent's one-year employment contract terminated and the Board of Regents voted not to offer him a new contract for the next academic year. The Regents issued a press release setting forth allegations of the respondent's insubordination. But they provided him no official statement of the reasons for the nonrenewal of his contract. And they allowed him no opportunity for a hearing to challenge the basis of the nonrenewal.

The respondent then brought this action in Federal District Court. He alleged primarily that the Regents' decision not to rehire him was based on his public criticism of the policies of the college administration and thus infringed his right to freedom of speech. He also alleged that their failure to provide him an opportunity for a hearing violated the Fourteenth Amendment's guarantee of procedural due process. The petitioners-members of the Board of Regents and the president of the college-denied that their decision was made in retaliation for the respondent's public criticism and argued that they had no obligation to provide a hearing. [T]he District Court granted summary judgment for the petitioners. It concluded that the respondent had 'no cause of action against the (petitioners) since his contract of employment terminated May 31, 1969, and Odessa Junior College has not adopted the tenure system.'

The Court of Appeals reversed ... [holding] that, despite the respondent's lack of tenure, the failure to allow him an opportunity for a hearing would violate the constitutional guarantee of procedural due process if the respondent could show that he had an 'expectancy' of re-employment. It, therefore, ordered that this issue of fact also be aired upon remand.

I

[Omitted]

II

The respondent's lack of formal contractual or tenure security in continued employment at Odessa Junior College, though irrelevant to his free speech claim, is highly relevant to his procedural due process claim. But it may not be entirely dispositive.

We have held today in *Board of Regents v. Roth*, that the Constitution does not require opportunity for a hearing before the nonrenewal of a nontenured teacher's contract, unless he can show that the decision not to rehire him somehow deprived him of an interest in 'liberty' or that he had a 'property' interest in continued employment, despite the lack of tenure or a formal contract. In *Roth* the teacher had not made a showing on either point to justify summary judgment in his favor.

Similarly, the respondent here has yet to show that he has been deprived of an interest that could invoke procedural due process protection. As in *Roth*, the mere showing that he was not rehired in one particular job, without more, did not amount to a showing of a loss of liberty. Nor did it amount to a showing of a loss of property.

But the respondent's allegations-which we must construe most favorably to the respondent at this stage of the litigation-do raise a genuine issue as to his interest in continued employment at Odessa Junior College. He alleged that this interest, though not secured by a formal contractual tenure provision, was secured by a no less binding understanding fostered by the college administration. In particular, the respondent alleged that the college had a de facto tenure program, and that he had tenure under that program. He claimed that he and others legitimately relied upon an unusual provision that had been in the college's official Faculty Guide for many years:

> Teacher Tenure: Odessa College has no tenure system. The Administration of the College wishes the faculty member to feel that he has permanent tenure as long as his teaching services are satisfactory and as long as he displays a cooperative attitude toward his co-workers and his superiors, and as long as he is happy in his work.

We have made clear in *Roth* that 'property' interests subject to procedural due process protection are not limited by a few rigid, technical forms. Rather, 'property' denotes a broad range of interests that are secured by 'existing rules or understandings.' A person's interest in a benefit is a 'property' interest for due process purposes if there are such rules or mutually explicit understandings that support his claim of entitlement to the benefit and that he may invoke at a hearing.

A teacher, like the respondent, who has held his position for a number of years, might be able to show from the circumstances of this service-and from other relevant facts-that he has a legitimate claim of entitlement to job tenure. [T]here may be an unwritten 'common law' in a particular university that certain employees shall have the equivalent of tenure. This is particularly likely in a college or university, like Odessa Junior College, that has no explicit tenure system even for senior members of its faculty, but that nonetheless may have created such a system in practice.[2]

In this case, the respondent has alleged the existence of rules and understandings, promulgated and fostered by state officials, that may justify his legitimate claim of entitlement to continued employment absent 'sufficient cause.' We disagree with the Court of Appeals insofar as it held that a mere subjective 'expectancy' is protected by procedural due process, but we agree that the respondent must be given an opportunity to prove the legitimacy of his claim of such entitlement in light of 'the policies and practices of the institution.' Proof of such a property interest would not, of

---

[2] [7] We do not now hold that the respondent has any such legitimate claim of entitlement to job tenure. For '(p)roperty interests ... are not created by the Constitution. Rather, they are created and their dimensions are defined by existing rules or understandings that stem from an independent source such as state law ....' Board of Regents v. Roth, 408 U.S. at 577. If it is the law of Texas that a teacher in the respondent's position has no contractual or other claim to job tenure, the respondent's claim would be defeated.

course, entitle him to reinstatement. But such proof would obligate college officials to grant a hearing at his request, where he could be informed of the grounds for his nonretention and challenge their sufficiency.

CLEVELAND BD. OF EDUC. v. LOUDERMILL
470 U.S. 532 (1985)

WHITE, J.

In these cases we consider what pretermination process must be accorded a public employee who can be discharged only for cause.

I

In 1979 the Cleveland Board of Education hired respondent James Loudermill as a security guard. On his job application, Loudermill stated that he had never been convicted of a felony. Eleven months later, as part of a routine examination of his employment records, the Board discovered that in fact Loudermill had been convicted of grand larceny in 1968. By letter dated November 3, 1980, the Board's Business Manager informed Loudermill that he had been dismissed because of his dishonesty in filling out the employment application. Loudermill was not afforded an opportunity to respond to the charge of dishonesty or to challenge his dismissal. On November 13, the Board adopted a resolution officially approving the discharge.

Under Ohio law, Loudermill was a "classified civil servant." Such employees can be terminated only for cause, and may obtain administrative review if discharged. Pursuant to this provision, Loudermill filed an appeal with the Cleveland Civil Service Commission on November 12. The Commission appointed a referee, who held a hearing on January 29, 1981. Loudermill argued that he had thought that his 1968 larceny conviction was for a misdemeanor rather than a felony. The referee recommended reinstatement. On July 20, 1981, the full Commission heard argument and orally announced that it would uphold the dismissal.

Although the Commission's decision was subject to judicial review in the state courts, Loudermill instead brought the present suit in the Federal District Court for the Northern District of Ohio. The complaint alleged that the [Ohio statute] was unconstitutional on its face because it did not provide the employee an opportunity to respond to the charges against him prior to removal. As a result, discharged employees were deprived of liberty and property without due process.

The District Court dismissed for failure to state a claim on which relief could be granted, [holding] that because the very statute that created the property right in continued employment also specified the procedures for discharge, and because those procedures were followed, Loudermill was, by definition, afforded all the process due. The post-termination hearing also adequately protected Loudermill's liberty interests.

A divided panel of the Court of Appeals for the Sixth Circuit reversed in part and remanded. The Court of Appeals found that respondent had been deprived of due process. It disagreed with the District Court's original rationale. Instead, it concluded that the compelling private interest in retaining employment, combined with the value of presenting evidence prior to dismissal, outweighed the added administrative burden of a pretermination hearing.

II

Respondent's federal constitutional claim depends on [his] having had a property right in continued employment. Property interests are not created by the Constitution, "they are created and their dimensions are defined by existing rules or understandings that stem from an independent source such as state law...." The Ohio statute plainly creates such an interest. Respondent [was a] "classified civil service employee," entitled to retain [his] position "during good behavior and efficient service," who could not be dismissed "except ... for ... misfeasance, malfeasance, or nonfeasance in office." The statute plainly supports the conclusion, reached by both lower courts, that respondent possessed property rights in continued employment. Indeed, this question does not seem to have been disputed below.

The Board argues, however, that the property right is defined by, and conditioned on, the legislature's choice of procedures for its deprivation. The Board stresses that in addition to specifying the grounds for termination, the statute sets out procedures by which termination may take place. The procedures were adhered to in these cases. According to petitioner, "[t]o require additional procedures would in effect expand the scope of the property interest itself."

This argument, which was accepted by the District Court, has its genesis in the plurality opinion in *Arnett v. Kennedy,* 416 U.S. 134 (1974). *Arnett* involved a challenge by a former federal employee to the procedures by which he was dismissed. The plurality reasoned that where the legislation conferring the substantive right also sets out the procedural mechanism for enforcing that right, the two cannot be separated:

> The employee's statutorily defined right is not a guarantee against removal without cause in the abstract, but such a guarantee as enforced by the procedures which Congress has designated for the determination of cause. [W]here the grant of a substantive right is inextricably intertwined with the limitations on the procedures which are to be employed in determining that right, a litigant in the position of appellee must take the bitter with the sweet.

This view garnered three votes in *Arnett,* but was specifically rejected by the other six Justices. Since then, this theory has at times seemed to gather some additional support. More recently, however, the Court has clearly rejected it. In *Vitek v. Jones,* 445 U.S. 480, 491 (1980), we pointed out that "minimum [procedural] requirements [are] a matter of federal law, they are not diminished by the fact that the State may have specified its own procedures that it may deem adequate for determining the preconditions to adverse official action." This conclusion was reiterated in *Logan v. Zimmerman Brush Co.,* 455 U.S. 422, 432 (1982), where we reversed the lower court's holding that because the entitlement arose from a state statute, the legislature had the prerogative to define the procedures to be followed to protect that entitlement.

In light of these holdings, it is settled that the "bitter with the sweet" approach misconceives the constitutional guarantee. If a clearer holding is needed, we provide it today. The point is straightforward: the Due Process Clause provides that certain substantive rights-life, liberty, and property-cannot be deprived except pursuant to constitutionally adequate procedures. The categories of substance and procedure are distinct. Were the rule otherwise, the Clause would be reduced to a mere tautology. "Property" cannot be defined by the procedures provided for its deprivation any more than can life or liberty. The right to due process "is conferred, not by legislative grace, but by constitutional guarantee. While the legislature may elect not to confer a property interest in [public] employment, it may not constitutionally authorize the deprivation of such an interest, once conferred, without appropriate procedural safeguards."

REHNQUIST, J., dissenting.

In *Arnett v. Kennedy,* 416 U.S. 134 (1974), six Members of this Court agreed that a public employee could be dismissed for misconduct without a full hearing prior to termination. A plurality of Justices agreed that the employee was entitled to exactly what Congress gave him, and no more. The Chief Justice, Justice Stewart, and I said:

> Here appellee did have a statutory expectancy that he not be removed other than for 'such cause as will promote the efficiency of [the] service.' But the very section of the statute which granted him that right, a right which had previously existed only by virtue of administrative regulation, expressly provided also for the procedure by which 'cause' was to be determined, and expressly omitted the procedural guarantees which appellee insists are mandated by the Constitution. Only by bifurcating the very sentence of the Act of Congress which conferred upon appellee the right not to be removed save for cause could it be said that he had an expectancy of that substantive right without the procedural limitations which Congress attached to it. Congress was obviously intent on according a measure of statutory job security to governmental employees which they had not previously enjoyed, but was likewise intent on excluding more elaborate procedural requirements which it felt would make the operation of the new scheme unnecessarily burdensome in practice. Where the focus of legislation

was thus strongly on the procedural mechanism for enforcing the substantive right which was simultaneously conferred, we decline to conclude that the substantive right may be viewed wholly apart from the procedure provided for its enforcement. The employee's statutorily defined right is not a guarantee against removal without cause in the abstract, but such a guarantee as enforced by the procedures which Congress has designated for the determination of cause.

In [the case before us today], the relevant Ohio statute provides...that

> [t]he tenure of every officer or employee in the classified service of the state and the counties, civil service townships, cities, city health districts, general health districts, and city school districts thereof, holding a position under this chapter of the Revised Code, shall be during good behavior and efficient service and no such officer or employee shall be reduced in pay or position, suspended, or removed, except...for incompetency, inefficiency, dishonesty, drunkenness, immoral conduct, insubordination, discourteous treatment of the public, neglect of duty, violation of such sections or the rules of the director of administrative services or the commission, or any other failure of good behavior, or any other acts of misfeasance, malfeasance, or nonfeasance in office.

The very next paragraph of this section of the Ohio Revised Code provides that in the event of suspension of more than three days or removal the appointing authority shall furnish the employee with the stated reasons for his removal. The next paragraph provides that within 10 days following the receipt of such a statement, the employee may appeal in writing to the State Personnel Board of Review or the Commission, such appeal shall be heard within 30 days from the time of its filing, and the Board may affirm, disaffirm, or modify the judgment of the appointing authority.

Thus in one legislative breath Ohio has conferred upon civil service employees such as respondents in these cases a limited form of tenure during good behavior, and prescribed the procedures by which that tenure may be terminated. Here, as in *Arnett*, "[t]he employee's statutorily defined right is not a guarantee against removal without cause in the abstract, but such a guarantee as enforced by the procedures which [the Ohio Legislature] has designated for the determination of cause." We stated in *Board of Regents v. Roth*, 408 U.S. 564, 577 (1972):

> Property interests, of course, are not created by the Constitution. Rather, they are created and their dimensions are defined by existing rules or understandings that stem from an independent source such as state law-rules or understandings that secure certain benefits and that support claims of entitlement to those benefits.

We ought to recognize the totality of the State's definition of the property right in question, and not merely seize upon one of several paragraphs in a unitary statute to proclaim that in that paragraph the State has inexorably conferred upon a civil service employee something which it is powerless under the United States Constitution to qualify in the next paragraph of the statute. This practice ignores our duty under *Roth* to rely on state law as the source of property interests for purposes of applying the Due Process Clause of the Fourteenth Amendment. While it does not impose a federal definition of property, the Court departs from the full breadth of the holding in *Roth* by its selective choice from among the sentences the Ohio Legislature chooses to use in establishing and qualifying a right.

Because I believe that the Fourteenth Amendment of the United States Constitution does not support the conclusion that Ohio's effort to confer a limited form of tenure upon respondents resulted in the creation of a "property right" in their employment, I dissent.

NOTES

1. Can state constitutions or other state law create "conditional" property rights? In other words, can state law define the procedures required to deprive persons of any property interests that state law creates? Who has the better of the "bitter with the sweet" argument – Justice White or Justice Rehnquist?

2. Try to think of "property" interests that state law – constitutional or otherwise – creates. How important is it that federal due process principles apply to state-created "property" interests? Is there at least one such interest that may be of particular importance to law students?

3. Does the federal rule in this context create incentives or disincentives for the States in contexts such as public employment or public benefits?

CHAPTER X

RELIGION CLAUSES

The First Amendment to the United States Constitution says that "Congress shall make no law...respecting an establishment of religion, or prohibiting the free exercise thereof." Relying on the Due Process Clause of the Fourteenth Amendment and the selective-incorporation doctrine, the United States Supreme Court has extended the restrictions of the Free Exercise and Establishment Clauses to the States. *See Cantwell v. Connecticut*, 310 U.S. 296 (1940) (free exercise clause) and *Everson v. Bd. of Educ.*, 330 U.S. 1 (1947) (establishment clause).

Like the United States Constitution, most state constitutions contain religion clauses that prohibit governmental establishments of religion, *see* Jill Goldenziel, *Blaine's Name in Vain?: State Constitutions, School Choice, and Charitable Choice*, 83 Denv. U. L. Rev. 57, 63 (2005), and that provide protection for the free exercise of religious beliefs and practices, Mechthild Fritz, *Religion in a Federal System: Diversity versus Uniformity*, 38 Kan. L. Rev. 39, 49 (1989). Some of the state guarantees not only pre-date the Bill of Rights, but were the models for the federal Religion Clauses. *See* Michael W. McConnell, *The Origins and Historical Understanding of Free Exercise of Religion*, 103 Harv. L. Rev. 1409, 1455-58 (1990). We will first consider the state freedom of religion clauses, then turn to the state establishment clauses.

A. FREEDOM OF RELIGION

All fifty state constitutions contain provisions that safeguard the rights of their citizens to practice their faith.

Some state guarantees mirror the brief and general language of the national free exercise clause. *See, e.g.,* Mass. Const. art. 46, § 1 ("No law shall be passed prohibiting the free exercise of religion."); Pa. Const. of 1776, art. II, *reprinted in* 2 Federal and State Constitutions, Colonial Charters, and Other Organic Laws of the United States, 1328, 1450-1451 (B. Poore 2d ed. 1878) ("free exercise of religious worship") and Va. Bill of Rights of 1776, § 16 *reprinted in* 2 Federal and State Constitutions, Colonial Charters, and Other Organic Laws of the United States at 1908-1909 ("all men are equally entitled to the free exercise of religion").

But most of the state guarantees are more specific (and lengthy). The Ohio Constitution provides a good example:

> All men have a natural and indefeasible right to worship Almighty God according to the dictates of their own conscience. No person shall be compelled to attend, erect, or support any place of worship, or maintain any place of worship, against his consent; and no preference shall be given, by law, to any

religious society; nor shall any interference with the rights of conscience be permitted. No religious test shall be required, as a qualification for office, nor shall any person be incompetent to be a witness on account of his religious belief; but nothing herein shall be construed to dispense with oaths and affirmations. Religion, morality, and knowledge, however, being essential to good government, it shall be the duty of the general assembly to pass suitable laws to protect every religious denomination in the peaceable enjoyment of its own mode of public worship, and to encourage schools and the means of instruction.

Ohio Const. art. I, sec. 7. *See also* Minn. Const. art. I, sec. 16; Neb. Const. art. I, sec. 4; Tex. Const. art. I, sec. 6; Ark. Const. art. II, sec. 24; N.Y. Const. art. I, sec. 3 ("The free exercise and enjoyment of religious profession and worship, without discrimination or preference, shall forever be allowed in this state..."); Ill. Const. art. I, sec. 3; Va. Const. art. I, sec. 16 ("all men are equally entitled to the free exercise of religion..."). For background on the development and history of state free exercise clauses, see Angela C. Carmella, *State Constitutional Protection of Religious Exercise: An Emerging Post-Smith Jurisprudence,* 1993 B.Y.U. L. Rev. 277, 293-305 (1993).

The law in this area has developed considerably in the last few decades—as the state and federal courts and legislatures have reacted to each other through various decisions and legislation. Of particular interest in both court systems has been the vexing problem of regulating religious practices. It is one thing to ensure that citizens may believe whatever they wish. It is quite another to allow them to practice their religion in whatever way they wish. That distinction is at play in the following cases, which present a classic story of federalism, one that starts with a decision by the United States Supreme Court, that leads to a response from Congress, that leads to a second Supreme Court decision, and that ends (for now) with responses from the state supreme courts and the state legislatures.

EMPLOYMENT DIV., DEP'T OF HUMAN RES. OF OREGON v. SMITH
494 U.S. 872 (1990)

SCALIA, J.

This case requires us to decide whether the Free Exercise Clause of the First Amendment permits the State of Oregon to include religiously inspired peyote use within the reach of its general criminal prohibition on use of that drug, and thus permits the State to deny unemployment benefits to persons dismissed from their jobs because of such religiously inspired use.

Respondents Alfred Smith and Galen Black (hereinafter respondents) were fired from their jobs with a private drug rehabilitation organization because they ingested peyote for sacramental purposes at a ceremony of the Native American Church, of which both are members. When respondents applied to petitioner Employment Division (hereinafter petitioner) for unemployment compensation, they were determined to be ineligible for benefits because they had been discharged for work-related "misconduct." ...The Oregon Supreme Court held that respondents' religiously inspired use of peyote fell within the prohibition of the Oregon statute, which "makes no exception for the sacramental use" of the drug. It then considered whether that prohibition was valid under the Free Exercise Clause, and concluded that it was not.

The free exercise of religion means, first and foremost, the right to believe and profess whatever religious doctrine one desires. Thus, the First Amendment obviously excludes all "governmental regulation of religious *beliefs* as such." The government may not compel affirmation of religious belief, impose special disabilities on the basis of religious views, or lend its power to one or the other side in controversies over religious authority or dogma.

But the "exercise of religion" often involves not only belief and profession but the performance of (or abstention from) physical acts: assembling with others for a worship service, participating in sacramental use of bread and wine, proselytizing, abstaining from certain foods or certain modes of transportation. It would be true, we think...that a State would be "prohibiting the free exercise [of religion]" if it sought to ban such acts or abstentions only when they are engaged in for religious reasons, or only because of the religious belief that they display. It would doubtless be unconstitutional, for example, to ban the casting of "statues that are to be used for worship purposes," or to prohibit bowing down before a golden calf.

Respondents in the present case, however, seek to carry the meaning of "prohibiting the free exercise [of religion]" one large step further. They contend that their religious motivation for using peyote places them beyond the reach of a criminal law that is not specifically directed at their religious practice, and that is concededly constitutional as applied to those who use the drug for other reasons. They assert, in other words, that "prohibiting the free exercise [of religion]" includes requiring any individual to observe a generally applicable law that requires (or forbids) the performance of an act that his religious belief forbids (or requires).... We have never held that an individual's religious beliefs excuse him from compliance with an otherwise valid law prohibiting conduct that the State is free to regulate.

Subsequent decisions have consistently held that the right of free exercise does not relieve an individual of the obligation to comply with a "valid and neutral law of general applicability on the ground that the law proscribes (or prescribes) conduct that his religion prescribes (or proscribes)."

There being no contention that Oregon's drug law represents an attempt to regulate religious beliefs, the communication of religious beliefs, or the raising of one's children in those beliefs, the rule to which we have adhered ever since *Reynolds* plainly controls. "Our cases do not at their farthest reach support the proposition that a stance of conscientious opposition relieves an objector from any colliding duty fixed by a democratic government."

Values that are protected against government interference through enshrinement in the Bill of Rights are not thereby banished from the political process. Just as a society that believes in the negative protection accorded to the press by the First Amendment is likely to enact laws that affirmatively foster the dissemination of the printed word, so also a society that believes in the negative protection accorded to religious belief can be expected to be solicitous of that value in its legislation as well. It is therefore not surprising that a number of States have made an exception to their drug laws for sacramental peyote use. But to say that a nondiscriminatory religious-practice exemption is permitted, or even that it is desirable, is not to say that it is constitutionally required, and that the appropriate occasions for its creation can be discerned by the courts. It may fairly be said that leaving accommodation to the political process will place at a relative disadvantage those religious practices that are not widely engaged in; but that unavoidable consequence of democratic government must be preferred to a system in which each conscience is a law unto itself or in which judges weigh the social importance of all laws against the centrality of all religious beliefs.

NOTES

1. *Smith* limited the reach of *Sherbert v. Verner*, 374 U.S. 398 (1963), which involved a free exercise claim by a man who refused to work on Saturdays due to his religious beliefs and who claimed that the State could not deny him unemployment compensation based on his religious practices. Whereas *Smith* applied rational basis review to a neutral law of general applicability and rejected the free exercise claim, *Sherbert* applied strict scrutiny to the State's unemployment compensation system and granted relief to the religious objector. *Id.* at 406. In *Church of the Lukumi Babalu Aye, Inc. v. Hialeah*, 508 U.S. 520 (1993), the Court followed the *Smith* test, but it applied strict scrutiny because the city had targeted the religious practices of a local religious group for specific regulation.

2. Three years after *Smith,* Congress enacted the Religious Freedom Restoration Act (RFRA). Invoking its powers under section 5 of the Fourteenth Amendment, Congress sought to require courts to apply strict scrutiny to claims that state or federal laws burdened the practices of

sincere religious adherents. With RFRA, Congress sought to overrule *Smith* legislatively and in the process to extend the *Sherbert* rule to all free exercise claims. The next case shows the Supreme Court's response.

CITY OF BOERNE v. FLORES
521 U.S. 507 (1997)

KENNEDY, J.

A decision by local zoning authorities to deny a church a building permit was challenged under the Religious Freedom Restoration Act of 1993. The case calls into question the authority of Congress to enact RFRA.

RFRA prohibits "[g]overnment" from "substantially burden[ing]" a person's exercise of religion even if the burden results from a rule of general applicability unless the government can demonstrate the burden "(1) is in furtherance of a compelling governmental interest; and (2) is the least restrictive means of furthering that compelling governmental interest."

Congress relied on its Fourteenth Amendment enforcement power in enacting the most far-reaching and substantial of RFRA's provisions, those which impose its requirements on the States. The Fourteenth Amendment provides, in relevant part:

Section 5. The Congress shall have power to enforce, by appropriate legislation, the provisions of this article.

Congress' power under § 5...extends only to "enforc[ing]" the provisions of the Fourteenth Amendment.... The design of the Amendment and the text of § 5 are inconsistent with the suggestion that Congress has the power to decree the substance of the Fourteenth Amendment's restrictions on the States. Legislation which alters the meaning of the Free Exercise Clause cannot be said to be enforcing the Clause.

Respondent contends that RFRA is a proper exercise of Congress' remedial or preventive power. The Act, it is said, is a reasonable means of protecting the free exercise of religion as defined by Smith. It prevents and remedies laws which are enacted with the unconstitutional object of targeting religious beliefs and practices. To avoid the difficulty of proving such violations, it is said, Congress can simply invalidate any law which imposes a substantial burden on a religious practice unless it is justified by a compelling interest and is the least restrictive means of accomplishing that interest. If Congress can prohibit laws with discriminatory effects in order to prevent racial discrimination in violation of the Equal Protection Clause, then it can do the same, respondent argues, to promote religious liberty.

While preventive rules are sometimes appropriate remedial measures, there must be a congruence between the means used and the ends to be achieved. The appropriateness of remedial measures must be considered in light of the evil presented. Strong measures appropriate to address one harm may be an unwarranted response to another, lesser one.

Regardless of the state of the legislative record, RFRA cannot be considered remedial, preventive legislation, if those terms are to have any meaning.... It appears, instead, to attempt a substantive change in constitutional protections. Preventive measures prohibiting certain types of laws may be appropriate when there is reason to believe that many of the laws affected by the congressional enactment have a significant likelihood of being unconstitutional. Remedial legislation under § 5 "should be adapted to the mischief and wrong which the [Fourteenth] [A]mendment was intended to provide against."

The stringent test RFRA demands of state laws reflects a lack of proportionality or congruence between the means adopted and the legitimate end to be achieved. If an objector can show a substantial burden on his free exercise, the State must demonstrate a compelling governmental interest and show that the law is the least restrictive means of furthering its interest. Claims that a law substantially burdens someone's exercise of religion will often be difficult to contest. Requiring a State to demonstrate a compelling interest and show that it has adopted the least restrictive means of achieving that interest is the most demanding test known to constitutional law. If "'compelling interest' really means what it says ..., many laws will not meet the test.... [The test] would open the prospect of constitutionally required religious exemptions from civic obligations of almost every conceivable kind." Laws valid under Smith would fall under RFRA without regard to whether they had the object of stifling or punishing free exercise. We make these observations not to reargue the position of the majority in Smith but to illustrate the substantive alteration of its holding attempted by RFRA.... This is a considerable congressional intrusion into the States' traditional prerogatives and general authority to regulate for the health and welfare of their citizens.

NOTES

1. Although *City of Boerne* invalidated RFRA as applied to the States and local governments, it did not invalidate the law as applied to the National Government. In the aftermath of *City of Boerne*, Congress returned to the drawing board and enacted the Religious Land Use and Institutionalized Persons Act (RLUIPA) of 2000, which applies to the States and local governments. The new federal law, as its name suggests, applies only to land-use regulation and prison rules and regulations. RLUIPA, in contrast to RFRA, has withstood several constitutional

challenges. *See, e.g., Cutter v. Wilkinson*, 544 U.S. 709 (2005), (holding that RLUIPA does not violate the Establishment Clause); *Westchester Day Sch. v. Vill. of Mamaroneck*, 504 F.3d 338, 355-56 (2d Cir. 2007) (applying *Cutter v. Wilkinson* to the land use provisions of the RLUIPA in upholding the Act against an Establishment Clause challenge).

2. In a federal system, decisions of the United States Supreme Court not only may provoke responses from Congress, but they also may prompt action by the States. The state courts and legislatures have responded to *Smith* and *City of Boerne* in a variety of ways. Some state courts have declined to follow *Smith* as a matter of state constitutional law. And several state legislatures have enacted state RFRAs. The following cases explore these approaches.

HUMPHREY v. LANE
728 N.E.2d 1039 (Ohio 2000)

PFEIFER, J.

We hold that under Section 7, Article I of the Ohio Constitution, the standard for reviewing a generally applicable, religion-neutral state regulation that allegedly violates a person's right to free exercise of religion is whether the regulation serves a compelling state interest and is the least restrictive means of furthering that interest. We further hold that the [prison-guard] grooming policy in this case, while in furtherance of a compelling state interest, did not employ the least restrictive means of furthering that interest.

In employing our comparison [to the Free Exercise Clause of the First Amendment,] we are not doing a mere word count, but instead are looking for a qualitative difference. The Ohio Constitution does have an eleven-word phrase that distinguishes itself from the United States Constitution: "nor shall any interference with the rights of conscience be permitted." The United States Constitution states that Congress shall make no law "prohibiting the free exercise [of religion]." We find the phrase that brooks no "interference with the rights of conscience" to be broader than that which proscribes any law prohibiting free exercise of religion. The Ohio Constitution allows no law that even interferes with the rights of conscience. The federal Constitution concerns itself with laws that prohibit the free exercise of religion. By its nature the federal Constitution seems to target laws that specifically address the exercise of religion, i.e., not those laws that tangentially affect religion. Ohio's ban on any interference makes even those tangential effects potentially unconstitutional.

The United States Supreme Court's interpretation of the federal Constitution makes it clear that "the right of free exercise does not relieve an individual of the obligation to comply with a 'valid and neutral law of general applicability on the ground that the law proscribes (or prescribes) conduct that his religion prescribes (or proscribes).'" Under the standard enunciated by the court in Smith, the relevant issues are whether the regulation at issue is religion-neutral and whether it is generally applicable. If those elements are fulfilled, then the regulation does not violate the Free Exercise Clause.

We have made it clear that this court is not bound by federal court interpretations of the federal Constitution in interpreting our own Constitution. As this court held in Arnold v. Cleveland:

> "The Ohio Constitution is a document of independent force. In the areas of individual rights and civil liberties, the United States Constitution, where applicable to the states, provides a floor below which state court decisions may not fall. As long as state courts provide at least as much protection as the United States Supreme Court has provided in its interpretation of the federal Bill of Rights, state courts are unrestricted in according greater civil liberties and protections to individuals and groups."

As stated above, the Ohio Constitution's free exercise protection is broader, and we therefore vary from the federal test for religiously neutral, evenly applied government actions. We apply a different standard to a different constitutional protection. We adhere to the standard long held in Ohio regarding free exercise claims-that the state enactment must serve a compelling state interest and must be the least restrictive means of furthering that interest. That protection applies to direct and indirect encroachments upon religious freedom.

To state a prima facie free exercise claim, the plaintiff must show that his religious beliefs are truly held and that the governmental enactment has a coercive affect against him in the practice of his religion. There seems to be no dispute that Humphrey has successfully made those showings in this case.... Forcing Humphrey to cut his hair would certainly infringe upon the free exercise of his religion.

Since Humphrey has made his prima facie case, the burden shifts to the state to prove that the regulation furthers a compelling state interest. Once that aspect has been satisfied, the state must prove that its regulation is the least restrictive means available of furthering that state interest.

We are satisfied that the state does have a compelling interest in establishing a uniform and grooming policy for its guards. Maintenance of a prison system is a central role of government, an area it is uniquely suited for. It is an undertaking essential to justice and to the safety of the citizenry, but by its nature is fraught with danger and thus must be tightly controlled. A prison is a dangerous, potentially explosive environment.

The state has sufficiently established that there is a compelling state interest in establishing uniform and grooming policies for prison workers. The state must further prove, however, that the policy is the least restrictive means of furthering that interest…. We view the resolution of that issue to be a factual determination. The trial court found as a factual matter that the simple accommodation of allowing Humphrey to wear his hair pinned under his uniform cap was a less restrictive means of furthering ODRC's interest. The trial court saw Humphrey with his hair tucked beneath his cap and found that Humphrey presented the "professional and dignified image" required by the policy.

The trial judge also considered testimony concerning whether Humphrey's hair affected the attitudes of fellow guards, administrators, and inmates toward him, and viewed with his own eyes whether the accommodation was a practical one. The trial court found that a practical accommodation could be made. We defer to the trial court's factual finding.

Therefore, we hold that the ODRC can further its compelling interest of a uniform grooming policy through a less restrictive means than the policy it currently employs. We accordingly reverse the judgment of the court of appeals and reinstate the trial court's declaratory judgment and injunction.

ATTORNEY GENERAL v. DESILETS
636 N.E. 2d 233 (Mass. 1994)

WILKINS, J.

This case involves the tension between a statutory mandate that a landlord not discriminate against unmarried couples in renting accommodations and a landlord's sincerely held religious belief that he should not facilitate what he regards as sinful cohabitation.

The defendants have a policy of not leasing an apartment to any person who intends to engage in conduct that violates their religious principles. The defendants' sole reason for declining even to consider Lattanzi and Tarail as tenants was that religion-based policy. The defendants, who are Roman Catholics, believe that they should not facilitate sinful conduct, including fornication. Since developing the policy at least a decade earlier, the defendants have applied it ten or more times to deny tenancies to unmarried couples.

General Laws c. 151B, § 4(6)…provided, in part, that it shall be an unlawful practice for the owner of a multiple dwelling "to refuse to rent or lease…or otherwise to deny to or withhold from any person or group of persons such accommodations because of the race, religious creed, color, national origin, sex, age, ancestry or marital status of such person or persons." We shall conclude that the defendants violated the provisions of this statute and that, therefore, we must consider the defendants' argument that enforcement of the statute against them violates their rights under the State…Constitution[].

Despite the similarity of the [Federal and State[1]] constitutional provisions, this court should reach its own conclusions on the scope of the protections of art. 46, § 1, and should not necessarily follow the reasoning adopted by the Supreme Court of the United States under the First Amendment. Indeed, after the release of our Nissenbaum opinion, the Supreme Court substantially altered its standard for determining whether conduct was protected under the free exercise of religion clause by its decision in Employment Div.

In interpreting art. 46, § 1, we prefer to adhere to the standards of earlier First Amendment jurisprudence, such as we applied in Alberts v. Devine, Carroll v. Alberts, and Attorney Gen. v. Bailey. In each opinion, we used the balancing test that the Supreme Court had established under the free exercise of religion clause in Wisconsin v. Yoder, Sherbert v. Verner, and subsequent opinions. By applying the balancing test as we do, we extend protections to the defendants that are at least as great as those of the First Amendment. No further discussion of rights under the First Amendment is, therefore, necessary.

The next question is whether the prohibition against discrimination based on marital status substantially burdens the defendants' exercise of their religion…. We first consider whether there is any burden at all on the defendants' free exercise of religion. We have said that the government's failure to provide a child with subsidized transportation to a private sectarian school does not burden the child's free exercise of religion. Here, the situation differs because the government has placed a burden on the defendants that makes their exercise of religion more difficult and more costly. The statute affirmatively obliges the defendants to enter into a contract contrary to their religious beliefs and provides significant sanctions for its violation. Moreover, both their nonconformity to the law and any related publicity may stigmatize the defendants in the eyes of many and thus burden the exercise of the defendants' religion.

The fact that the defendants' free exercise of religion claim arises in a commercial context, although relevant when engaging in a balancing of interests, does not mean that their constitutional rights are not substantially burdened. This is not a case in which a claimant is seeking a financial advantage by asserting religious beliefs.

We must, therefore, consider whether the record establishes that the Commonwealth has or does not have an important governmental interest that is sufficiently compelling that the granting of an exemption to people

---

[1] Mass. Const. art. 46, § 1, states:."No law shall be passed prohibiting the free exercise of religion."

in the position of the defendants would unduly hinder that goal.... At the least, the Commonwealth must demonstrate that it has a compelling interest in the elimination of discrimination in housing against an unmarried man and an unmarried woman who have a sexual relationship and wish to rent accommodations to which § 4(6) applies.

Without supporting facts in the record or in legislative findings, we are unwilling to conclude that simple enactment of the prohibition against discrimination based on marital status establishes that the State has such a substantial interest in eliminating that form of housing discrimination that, on a balancing test, the substantial burden on the defendants' free exercise of religion must be disregarded.

We reject any argument that a general rule must be applied because of problems in determining whether religious beliefs sincerely underlie a landlord's refusal to lease. The sincerity of such action assertedly founded on religious beliefs is open to challenge in a free exercise of religion case. We would, moreover, not readily subscribe to a rule that justified the denial of constitutional rights simply because the protection of those rights required special effort. For similar reasons, in the absence of proof, we would not find a compelling State interest in this case simply because other individuals might assert the right to be exempt from this or some other law on religious grounds and in doing so would make enforcement of that law difficult. Yet the practical problems of administering a law with the exemption that the defendants seek may be shown to be such as to make the operation of such an exemption impractical. Finally, the compulsion of the State's interest appears somewhat weakened because the statute permits discrimination by a religious organization in certain respects if to do so promotes the principles for which the organization was established.

We are not persuaded on the record that the Commonwealth's interests in the availability of rental housing for cohabiting couples must always prevail over the religion-based practices that people such as the defendants wish to pursue. On the other hand, we cannot say that it is certain that the Commonwealth could not prove in this case that it has some specific compelling interest that justifies overriding the defendants' interests.

The Commonwealth has the task of establishing that it has a compelling interest in eliminating housing discrimination against cohabiting couples that is strong enough to justify the burden placed on the defendants' exercise of their religion. A task of this sort has been carried out successfully in some cases and not in others.

The summary judgment record does not establish that there is no disputed material fact bearing on the compelling State interest question. In that circumstance summary judgment is inappropriate. There are factual circumstances that bear on the question, both as to the existence of a general State interest in the elimination of discrimination in housing based on marital status and as to the existence of a particularized State interest in the Turners Falls area. Uniformity of enforcement of the statute may be shown to be the least restrictive means for the practical and efficient operation of the antidiscrimination law. It should be remembered that the task is to balance the State's interests against the nature of the burden on the defendants and that we are concerned here with the business of leasing apartments, not with participation in a formal religious activity.

NOTES

1. In *Abdul-Alazim v. Superintendent, Massachusetts Correctional Institution, Cedar Junction*, 778 N.E.2d 946 (Mass. 2002), a Massachusetts appeals court granted relief under *Desilets* to a claim filed by an inmate that prison officials had violated his state-law free exercise rights by prohibiting him from wearing a kufi, a prayer cap used by Muslims during religious worship.

2. In *Swanner v. Anchorage Equal Rights Commission*, 874 P.2d 274 (Alaska 1994), the Court declined to follow the *Smith* test in rejecting a landlord's claim that he had a constitutional right to refuse to rent to unmarried, cohabitating persons of the opposite sex.

In doing so, it reasoned as follows:

Swanner is correct in asserting that a state court may provide greater protection to the free exercise of religion under the state constitution than is now provided under the United States Constitution. Thus, even though the Free Exercise Clause of the Alaska Constitution is identical to the Free Exercise Clause of the United States Constitution, we are not required to adopt and apply the Smith test to religious exemption cases involving the Alaska Constitution merely because the United States Supreme Court adopted that test to determine the applicability of religious exemptions under the United States Constitution. We will apply Frank v. State, 604 P.2d 1068 (Alaska 1979), to determine whether the anti-discrimination laws violate Swanner's right to free exercise under the Alaska Constitution.

In Frank v. State, we adopted the Sherbert test to determine whether the Free Exercise Clause of the Alaska Constitution requires an exemption to a facially neutral law. We held that to invoke a religious exemption, three requirements must be met: (1) a religion is involved, (2) the conduct in question is religiously based, and (3) the claimant is sincere in his/her religious belief. Once these three requirements are met, "[r]eligiously impelled actions can be forbidden only 'where they pose some substantial threat to public safety, peace or order,' or where there are competing governmental interests 'of the highest order and ... [are] not otherwise served....' "

No one disputes that a religion is involved here (Christianity), or that Swanner is sincere in his religious belief that cohabitation is a sin and by renting to cohabitators, he is facilitating the sin.... [But] Swanner...made no showing of a religious belief which requires that he engage in the property-rental business.

HILL-MURRAY FEDERATION OF TEACHERS v. HILL-MURRAY HIGH SCHOOL
487 N.W.2d 857 (Minn. 1992)

KEITH, C.J.

The mission of Hill-Murray High School is "to provide a well-rounded quality education in a Christian context. The pursuit of excellence in all areas of learning and personal growth is integrated with a deepening faith in Christ's message for whole and effective living."... The vast majority (80%-85%) of students and teachers are Catholic although only teachers of religion are required to be Catholic. The school observes the Catholic seasons and holds at least one Mass per month which all students and teachers are expected to attend.... The religion teachers are certified by the Archdiocese and may be removed from employment by the Archbishop. The Archbishop reviews and oversees the church doctrine that is taught at the school.

Hill-Murray is accredited by the North Central Association Commission on Schools in compliance with the requirements of the State Board of Education. The school receives public aid on behalf of the students for textbook subsidies, counseling, guidance, health services, and transportation.

In 1989 the Hill-Murray Federation of Teachers petitioned the Bureau for determination of an appropriate unit and certification as exclusive representative of certain lay employees. The Bureau conducts elections pursuant to the MLRA to determine whether employees wish to be represented by a labor organization for the purposes of collective bargaining regarding rates of pay, wages, hours of employment and conditions of employment.... The bargaining unit was composed of teachers, counselors, and librarians, and excluded employees in supervisory positions, the teachers in the religion department, and the elementary school music teachers.... The Bureau certified the Minnesota Federation of Teachers as the exclusive representative. The Minnesota Federation of Teachers is a local union affiliated with the American Federation of Teachers and the AFL-CIO.

Hill-Murray raised constitutional objections to the Bureau's assertion of jurisdiction from the very beginning. The Bureau...appropriately declined to address the constitutional issues and specifically preserved them for consideration by the courts.

The Minnesota Constitution provides:

The right of every man to worship God according to the dictates of his conscience shall never be infringed; nor shall any man be compelled to attend, erect or support any place of worship, or to maintain any religious or ecclesiastical ministry, against his consent; nor shall any control of or interference with the rights of conscience be permitted, or any preference be given by law to any religious establishment or mode of worship; but the liberty of conscience hereby secured shall not be so construed as to excuse acts of licentiousness or justify practices inconsistent with the peace or safety of the state …. [Minn. Const. art. I, sec. 16].

We have construed this provision of our constitution to afford greater protection for religious liberties against governmental action than the first amendment of the federal constitution.

Because the Minnesota freedom of conscience clause provides more protection than the Federal Constitution, we will not follow the United States Supreme Court's limited analysis and will retain the compelling state interest balancing test. This test has four prongs: whether the objector's belief is sincerely held; whether the state regulation burdens the exercise of religious beliefs; whether the state interest in the regulation is overriding or compelling; and whether the state regulation uses the least restrictive means.

1. Sincerely Held Religious Belief

Because we believe judicial intervention into the determination and interpretation of religious beliefs warrants caution, we will recognize the presence of a sincerely held religious belief.

2. The Burden on the Exercise of Religious Beliefs

Hill-Murray argues that the application of the MLRA would result in significant interference with the school's religious autonomy that would compel the school to negotiate and compromise its doctrinal positions.

Hill-Murray asserts that negotiations about conditions of employment will lead to negotiations about religion. This assertion is remote and an insufficient basis to exempt Hill-Murray from the regulatory laws of the state.

We hold that matters of religious doctrine and practice at a religiously affiliated school are intrinsically inherent matters of managerial policy and therefore nonnegotiable. Terms and conditions of employment…specified in the Hill-Murray Faculty and Staff Handbook are not doctrinally related and are negotiable. Negotiations under the limits of the MLRA do not possess the tendency to undermine Hill-Murray's religious authority. Hill-Murray retains the power to hire employees who meet their religious expectations, to require compliance with religious doctrine, and to remove any person who fails to follow the religious standards set forth.

While Hill-Murray may have demonstrated that the application of the MLRA interferes with their authority as an employer, they have not established that this minimal interference excessively burdens their religious beliefs.

3. Compelling State Interests

We are conscious of the rationale inherent in labor relations acts and believe the legislature's intent was to institute a process that could resolve labor unrest in an orderly, efficient, and principled manner while protecting the interests of all parties involved, to the greatest extent possible. The process instituted by the state permits minimal state intervention; once the unit is certified, the parties are essentially left on their own.

We find that these goals are more than competing interests; they are overriding and compelling.... The state's interests in promoting the peace and safety of industrial relations, the recognition of the statutory guarantees of collective association and bargaining, and the first amendment protection of the right of association outweigh the minimal infringement of Hill-Murray's exercise of religious beliefs.

4.   Least Restrictive Alternatives

In the event it is possible to achieve these compelling interests through less restrictive, alternative means, article I, section 16 dictates the use of that alternative. Hill-Murray argues that the voluntary grievance procedure is a less restrictive alternative to mandatory good faith negotiations. The nature of the voluntary grievance procedure is just that-voluntary. The nature of collective bargaining is unique; other alternatives pale in comparison and remain unable to effectuate the strength of collective action. Collective bargaining allows the individual "David" to negotiate against the employer "Goliath."

We reiterate an earlier point that the valid subjects of negotiation are those purely secular conditions of employment such as those specified in...the Hill-Murray Faculty and Staff Handbook. Doctrinal and religious issues are matters of inherent managerial policy and are nonnegotiable. We believe that explicitly limiting the items of negotiations to those specifically enumerated conditions of employment is the best way to achieve the purpose and spirit of the Minnesota Constitution, the legislative intent behind the authorization of collective bargaining, and the rights of association.

While all of the employees of Hill-Murray possess a mutual goal of fostering the religious development of the students with whom they come into contact, a review of the record indicates that the Bureau's unit determination was an appropriate unit.

BARR v. CITY OF SINTON
295 S.W.2d 287 (Texas 2009)

HECHT, J.

The Texas Religious Freedom Restoration Act (TRFRA) provides that "a government agency may not substantially burden a person's free exercise of religion [unless it] demonstrates that the application of the burden to the person...is in furtherance of a compelling governmental interest [and] is the least restrictive means of furthering that interest." TRFRA does not immunize religious conduct from government regulation; it requires the government to tread carefully and lightly when its actions substantially burden religious exercise.

In this case, a city resident, as part of a religious ministry, offered men recently released from prison free housing and religious instruction in two homes he owned. In response, the city passed a zoning ordinance that not only precluded the use of the homes for that purpose but effectively banned the ministry from the city. The trial court found that the city had not violated TRFRA, and the court of appeals affirmed. We reverse and remand to the trial court for further proceedings.

In 1998, Pastor Richard Wayne Barr began a religious halfway house ministry through Philemon Restoration Homes, Inc., a nonprofit corporation he directed. The purpose of the ministry was to offer housing, biblical instruction, and counseling to low-level offenders released from prison on probation or parole in transition back into the community.... The guidelines emphasized to prospective residents that Philemon was "a biblical ministry, NOT a social service agency". Each morning began with group prayer and Bible study.

When Barr began his ministry, the City imposed no zoning or other restrictions on his use of the homes. In January 1999, Barr discussed his ministry with Sinton's mayor, city manager, and police chief, and a few weeks later he presented his ministry before the city council. In response to questions whether Philemon was in compliance with state law, Barr researched the matter and concluded that it was. In April, the city council held a public hearing at which a large number of people expressed both opposition to as well as support of Barr's ministry. A few days later, the city council passed Ordinance 1999-02, which added to the City Code a section that provided as follows:

> "A correctional or rehabilitation facility may not be located in the City of Sinton within 1000 feet of a residential area, a primary or secondary school, property designated as a public park or public recreation area by any governmental authority, or a church, synagogue, or other place of worship."

As the city manager later confirmed, Ordinance 1999-02 targeted Barr and Philemon. The halfway houses they operated were unquestionably within 1,000 feet of a church; indeed, they were across the street from the Grace Fellowship Church, which was helping to support the ministry. But the ordinance was broader, and was intended to be. Because Sinton is small, it would be difficult for a halfway house to be located anywhere within the city limits.

Smith's construction of the Free Exercise Clause does not preclude a state from requiring strict scrutiny of infringements on religious freedom, either by statute or under the state constitution, and many states have done just that, Texas among them. The Texas Legislature enacted TRFRA in 1999, which like RFRA provides in part, that government "may not substantially burden a person's free exercise of religion [unless it] demonstrates that the application of the burden to the person...is in furtherance of a compelling governmental interest; and... is the least restrictive means of furthering that interest." The Act states that "[t]he protection of religious freedom afforded by this chapter is in addition to the protections provided under federal law and the constitutions of this state and the United States."

Applying TRFRA to this case raises four questions, each succeeding question contingent on an affirmative answer to the one preceding:

• Does the City's Ordinance 1999-02 burden Barr's "free exercise of religion" as defined by TRFRA?

• Is the burden substantial?

• Does the ordinance further a compelling governmental interest?

• Is the ordinance the least restrictive means of furthering that interest?

A

The City argues that Barr's free exercise of religion is not involved because a halfway house need not be a religious operation. But the fact that a halfway house can be secular does not mean that it cannot be religious. TRFRA defines "free exercise of religion" as "an act or refusal to act that is substantially motivated by sincere religious belief", adding that "[i]n determining whether an act or refusal to act is substantially motivated by sincere religious belief under this chapter, it is not necessary to determine that the act or refusal to act is motivated by a central part or central requirement of the person's sincere religious belief." Not only is such a determination unnecessary, it is impossible for the judiciary.

The trial court appears to have been troubled that an operation which can be and often is conducted for purely secular purposes could be entitled to increased protection from government regulation if conducted for religious reasons. But TRFRA guarantees such protection. Just as a Bible study group and a book club are not treated the same, neither are a halfway house operated for religious purposes and one that is not.

The City does not dispute that the purpose of Barr's ministry was to provide convicts a biblically supported transition to civic life. Applicants were required to sign a statement of faith, agree to abide by stated biblical principles, and commit as a group to daily prayer and Bible study. They were specifically told that Barr's halfway house was "a biblical ministry, NOT a social service agency". Barr considered the halfway house a religious ministry, and it appears to have been supported by his church. The record easily establishes that Barr's ministry was "substantially motivated by sincere religious belief" for purposes of the TRFRA.

B

To determine whether a person's free exercise of religion has been substantially burdened, some courts have focused on the burden on the person's religious beliefs rather than the burden on his conduct. Under what have been referred to as the compulsion and centrality tests, the issue is whether the person's conduct that is being burdened is compelled by or central to his religion. The problems with these approaches are the same as those in determining whether conduct is religious. It may require a court to do what it cannot do: assess the demands of religion on its adherents and the importance of particular conduct to the religion. And it is inconsistent with the statutory directive that religious conduct be determined without regard for whether the actor's motivation is "a central part or central requirement of the person's sincere religious belief." These problems are avoided if the focus is on the degree to which a person's religious conduct is curtailed and the resulting impact on his religious expression. The burden must be measured, of course, from the person's perspective, not from the government's. Thus, the United States Court of Appeals for the Fifth Circuit, after surveying decisions by other courts, recently held that under RLUIPA, "a government action or regulation creates a 'substantial burden' on a religious exercise if it truly pressures the adherent to significantly modify his religious behavior and significantly violate his religious beliefs."

Ordinance 1999-02 prohibited Barr from operating his halfway house ministry in the two homes he owned adjacent to his supporting church, and the city manager testified that it was "a fair statement" that alternate locations were "probably... minimal" and "possibly" "pretty close to nonexistent". The court of appeals stated that "there is nothing in the ordinance that precludes Barr from providing his religious ministry to parolees and probationers, from providing instruction, counsel, and helpful assistance in other facilities in Sinton, or from housing these persons outside the City and providing his religious ministry to them there." But there is no evidence of any alternate location in the City of Sinton where the ordinance would have allowed Barr's ministry to operate, or of possible locations outside the city. Moreover, while evidence of alternatives is certainly relevant to the issue whether zoning restrictions substantially burden free religious exercise, evidence of some possible alternative, irrespective of the difficulties presented, does not, standing alone, disprove substantial burden. In a related context, the Supreme Court has observed that "one is not to have the exercise of his liberty of expression in appropriate places abridged on the plea that it may be exercised in some other place." As a practical matter, the ordinance ended Barr's ministry, as the City Council surely knew it would.... [A] burden on a person's religious exercise is not insubstantial simply because he could always choose to do something else.

C

"To say that a person's right to free exercise has been burdened, of course, does not mean that he has an absolute right to engage in the conduct." The government may regulate such conduct in furtherance of a compelling interest.

Although the government's interest in the public welfare in general, and in preserving a common character of land areas and use in particular, is certainly legitimate when properly motivated and appropriately directed, the assertion that zoning ordinances are per se superior to fundamental, constitutional rights, such as the free exercise of religion, must fairly be regarded as indefensible.

The Supreme Court held in Smith, not that the government's interest in neutral laws of general application is always compelling when compared to the people's interest in fundamental rights, but only that the United States Constitution does not require the two interests to be balanced every time they conflict. RFRA, RLUIPA, and TRFRA, as well as laws enacted in other states, now require that balance by statute when government action substantially burdens the free exercise of religion. The government's interest is compelling when the balance weighs in its favor-that is, when the government's interest justifies the substantial burden on religious exercise. Because religious exercise is a fundamental right, that justification can be found only in "interests of the highest order," to quote the Supreme Court in Yoder, and to quote Sherbert, only to avoid "'the gravest abuses, endangering paramount interest[s].'"

The Sinton City Council's recitation in Ordinance 1999-02-that "the requirements of this section are reasonably necessary to preserve the public safety, morals, and general welfare"-is the kind of "broadly formulated interest[ ]" that does not satisfy the scrutiny mandated by TRFRA. Likewise, the trial court's brief finding-that "[t]he ordinance was in furtherance of a compelling government interest"-falls short of the required scrutiny.

Although TRFRA places the burden of proving a substantial burden on the claimant, it places the burden of proving a compelling state interest on the government. The City argues that its compelling interest in Ordinance 1999-02 is established by statutes providing that correctional facility regulations presumptively meet strict scrutiny. As we have already explained, however, these statutes are inapplicable.

The City also asserts that Ordinance 1999-02 serves a compelling interest in advancing safety, preventing nuisance, and protecting children. But there is no evidence to support the City's assertion with respect to "the particular practice at issue"-Barr's ministry.

The City's failure to establish a compelling interest in this case in no way suggests that the government never has a compelling interest in zoning for religious use of property or in regulating halfway houses operated for religious purposes. TRFRA guarantees a process, not a result. The City's principal position in this case has been that it is exempt from TRFRA. We do not hold that the City could not have satisfied TRFRA; we hold only that it failed to do so.

D

Finally, TRFRA requires that even when the government acts in furtherance of a compelling interest, it must show that it used the least restrictive means of furthering that interest. The City has made no effort to show that it complied with this requirement. Ordinance 1999-02 is very broad. If as the city manager testified, locations in the City of Sinton more than 1,000 feet from a residential area, school, park, recreational area, or church are "pretty close to nonexistent", the ordinance effectively prohibits any private "residential facility...operated for the purpose of housing persons...convicted of misdemeanors...within one...year after having been released from confinement in any penal institution" inside the city limits. Read literally, this would prohibit a Sinton resident from leasing a room to someone within a year of his having been jailed for twice driving with an invalid license. Such restrictions are certainly not the least restrictive means of insuring that religiously operated halfway houses do not jeopardize children's safety and residents' well being.

We conclude, based on the record before us, that Ordinance 1999-02, as applied to Barr's ministry, violates TRFRA.

CATHOLIC CHARITIES OF THE DIOCESE OF ALBANY
v. SERIO
859 N.E.2d 459 (Ct. App. N.Y. 2006)

R.S. SMITH, J.

Plaintiffs challenge the validity of legislation requiring health insurance policies that provide coverage for prescription drugs to include coverage for contraception. Plaintiffs assert that the provisions they challenge violate their rights under the religion clauses of the federal and state constitutions. We hold that the legislation, as applied to these plaintiffs, is valid.

The Challenged Legislation

In 2002, the Legislature enacted what is known as the "Women's Health and Wellness Act" (WHWA), mandating expanded health insurance coverage for a variety of services needed by women, including mammography, cervical cytology and bone density screening. At issue here are provisions of the WHWA requiring that an employer health insurance contract "which provides coverage for prescription drugs shall include coverage for the cost of contraceptive drugs or devices."

At the heart of this case is the statute's exemption for "religious employers." Such an employer may request an insurance contract "without coverage for ... contraceptive methods that are contrary to the religious employer's religious tenets." Where a religious employer invokes the exemption, the insurer must offer coverage for contraception to individual employees, who may purchase it at their own expense "at the prevailing small group community rate."

Plaintiffs believe contraception to be sinful, and assert that the challenged provisions of the WHWA compel them to violate their religious tenets by financing conduct that they condemn. The sincerity of their beliefs, and the centrality of those beliefs to their faiths, are not in dispute.

Contending that they are constitutionally entitled to be exempt from the provisions of the WHWA providing for coverage of contraceptives, plaintiffs brought this action against the Superintendent of Insurance, seeking a declaration that these portions of the WHWA are invalid, and an injunction against their enforcement. The complaint asserts broadly that the challenged provisions are unconstitutional, but plaintiffs do not argue that they are unenforceable as to employers having no religious objections to contraception; in substance, plaintiffs challenge the legislation as applied to them.

Article I, § 3 of the New York Constitution provides:

"The free exercise and enjoyment of religious profession and worship, without discrimination or preference, shall forever be allowed in this state to all humankind; and no person shall be rendered incompetent to be a witness on account of his or her opinions on matters of religious belief; but the liberty of conscience hereby secured shall not be so construed as to excuse acts of licentiousness, or justify practices inconsistent with the peace or safety of this state."

In interpreting our Free Exercise Clause we have not applied, and we do not now adopt, the inflexible rule of Smith that no person may complain of a burden on religious exercise that is imposed by a generally applicable, neutral statute. Rather, we have held that when the State imposes "an incidental burden on the right to free exercise of religion" we must consider the interest advanced by the legislation that imposes the burden, and that "[t]he respective interests must be balanced to determine whether the incidental burdening is justified." We have never discussed, however, how the balancing is to be performed.... We now hold that substantial deference is due the Legislature, and that the party claiming an exemption bears the burden of showing that the challenged legislation, as applied to that party, is an unreasonable interference with religious freedom. This test, while more protective of religious exercise than the rule of Smith, is less so than the rule stated (though not always applied) in a number of other federal and state cases.

Since Smith, a number of state courts have interpreted their states' constitutions to call for the application of strict scrutiny. Often, however,...the courts rejected claims to religious exemptions, and it is questionable whether the scrutiny applied by those courts is really as strict as their statement of the rule implies.

The apparent reluctance of some courts to pay more than lip service to "strict scrutiny" may be an implicit recognition of what we now explicitly decide: Strict scrutiny is not the right approach to constitutionally-based claims for religious exemptions. Where the State has not set out to burden religious exercise, but seeks only to advance, in a neutral way, a legitimate object of legislation, we do not read the New York Free Exercise Clause to require the State to demonstrate a "compelling" interest in response to every claim by a religious believer to an exemption from the law; such a rule of constitutional law would give too little respect to legislative prerogatives, and would create too great an obstacle to efficient government. Rather, the principle stated by the United States Supreme Court in Smith-that citizens are not excused by the Free Exercise Clause from complying with generally applicable and neutral laws, even ones offensive to their religious tenets-should be the usual, though not the invariable, rule. The burden of showing that an interference with religious practice is unreasonable, and therefore requires an exemption from the statute, must be on the person claiming the exemption.

The burden the WHWA places on plaintiffs' religious practices is a serious one, but the WHWA does not literally compel them to purchase contraceptive coverage for their employees, in violation of their religious beliefs; it only requires that policies that provide prescription drug coverage include coverage for contraceptives. Plaintiffs are not required by law to purchase prescription drug coverage at all. They assert, unquestionably in good faith, that they feel obliged to do so because, as religious institutions, they must provide just wages and benefits to their employees. But it is surely not impossible, though it may be expensive or difficult, to compensate employees adequately without including prescription drugs in their group health care policies.

It is also important, in our view, that many of plaintiffs' employees do not share their religious beliefs. (Most of the plaintiffs allege that they hire many people of other faiths; no plaintiff has presented evidence that it does not do so.) The employment relationship is a frequent subject of legislation, and when a religious organization chooses to hire nonbelievers it must, at least to some degree, be prepared to accept neutral regulations imposed to protect those employees' legitimate interests in doing what their own beliefs permit. This would be a more difficult case if plaintiffs had chosen to hire only people who share their belief in the sinfulness of contraception.

Finally, we must weigh against plaintiffs' interest in adhering to the tenets of their faith the State's substantial interest in fostering equality between the sexes, and in providing women with better health care. The Legislature had extensive evidence before it that the absence of contraceptive coverage for many women was seriously interfering with both of these important goals. The Legislature decided that to grant the broad religious exemption that plaintiffs seek would leave too many women outside the statute, a decision entitled to deference from the courts. Of course, the Legislature might well have made another choice, but we cannot say the choice the Legislature made has been shown to be an unreasonable interference with plaintiffs' exercise of their religion. The Legislature's choice is therefore not unconstitutional.

B. ESTABLISHMENT OF RELIGION

1. Background

Just as some state freedom of religion clauses mirror their federal counterpart, some state establishment clauses closely resemble the First Amendment of the United States Constitution. All told, eleven States have establishment clauses similar to the First Amendment. Jennifer Friesen, State Constitutional Law: Litigating Individual Rights, Claims and Defenses 4-84 (2006); *see, e.g.,* Cal. Const. art. I, sec. 4 ("The Legislature shall make no law respecting an establishment of religion."); Haw. Const.

art I, sec. 4 ("No law shall be enacted respecting an establishment of religion."); Fla. Const. art. I, sec. 3 ("There shall be no law respecting the establishment of religion."). Thirty-two States have no-preference clauses. Friesen, Litigating Individual Rights, Claims and Defenses, 4-84; *see, e.g.,* N.J. Const. art. I, sec. 4 ("There shall be no establishment of one religious sect in preference to another."); Wis. Const. art. I, sec. 18 ("nor shall…any preference be given to any religious establishments or modes of worship"). And six States have neither an establishment nor a no-preference clause. Friesen, Litigating Individual Rights, Claims and Defenses, 4-84.

Unique to the state constitutions are clauses that expressly limit using public funds to aid religious organizations. Thirty-four States have provisions to this effect. Friesen, Litigating Individual Rights, Claims and Defenses, 4-86. As the following excerpt explains, these provisions, often called "Blaine Amendments," have a rich and controversial history.

Mark Edward DeForrest, An Overview and Evaluation of State Blaine Amendments: Origins, Scope, and First Amendment Concerns, 26 Harv. J. L. & Pub. Pol'y 551 (2003).

The original Blaine Amendment was a proposed amendment to the federal Constitution. The amendment took its name from its sponsor and originator, Representative James Blaine of Maine, who introduced the amendment on December 14, 1875. The text of his proposed amendment reads as follows:

> No State shall make any law respecting an establishment of religion or prohibiting the free exercise thereof; and no money raised by taxation in any State for the support of public schools, or derived from any public fund therefore, nor any public lands devoted thereto, shall ever be under the control of any religious sect, nor shall any money so raised or lands so devoted be divided between religious sects or denominations.

The overarching purpose to the Blaine Amendment, as its plain text demonstrates, was to control the development of government involvement in religious issues at the state level in two critical ways. First, it would have applied the religion clauses of the First Amendment directly to the states. Prior to the development of the incorporation doctrine by the Supreme Court in the twentieth century the provisions of the Bill of Rights (the first ten amendments to the United States Constitution) were not applied to the states by the courts. In Blaine's day, the states were yet to be restrained by the First Amendment; Blaine saw this as a deficiency and sought to remedy this situation by amending the Constitution to directly apply the religion clauses of the First Amendment to the states. The second effect of Blaine's amendment would have been to prohibit state governments from supporting private religious schools with funds from the public treasury.

The Blaine Amendment might have been expected to fade away into oblivion after its rejection by the Senate, but the opposite occurred. After its defeat on the national level, the Blaine Amendment took on new life in the states. Within a year of the defeat of Blaine's proposal, fourteen states had legislation on the books preventing state funds from being used in support of religious schools. By the 1890s, roughly thirty states would incorporate Blaine-style amendments into their constitutions. This trend continued into the twentieth century; even as late as the 1950s, Alaska and Hawaii would incorporate Blaine-style language into their state charters.

Blaine Amendments are found in roughly thirty state constitutions. The language and scope of the state Blaine provisions vary widely, however. Some states adopted Blaine-like provisions prior to the formal proposal of the national Blaine Amendment. Other states, both in the 19th and 20th centuries, willingly adopted Blaine provisions after the national Blaine Amendment failed. Still other states had Blaine provisions forced upon them as a condition of entering the Union. It should therefore come as no surprise that the Blaine provisions in the states evidence a considerable diversity in language and scope.

The first group of state Blaine provisions to be examined are those that place the narrowest restrictions on state government actions to provide some indirect assistance or aid to private religious or sectarian education. Examples of these kinds of Blaine Amendments can be seen in both New Jersey and Massachusetts. For the most part, these Blaine provisions demonstrate two basic concerns. First, they seek to ensure that primary and secondary public education remains free of sectarian instruction. Second, they usually make certain that public educational funds will not be used to directly support private religious schools. Outside of these two concerns, however, the states with less restrictive Blaine provisions allow some very limited government assistance either with basic transportation or higher education.

While the states discussed in the previous section have relatively liberal Blaine provisions in their state constitutions, other states have more stringent limitations on government aid to religious schools. While not as permissive as the less restrictive states and not as draconian as the most restrictive states, these states fall into a great middle ground regarding Blaine provisions. Most of these states' Blaine Amendments prohibit direct funding of religious institutions or schools, but leave open, at least within their constitutional texts, the question of whether or not indirect state funding, such as vouchers, are permissible. The language used in this intermediate tier of Blaine states varies considerably from state to state, as even brief examination of the state charters will demonstrate.

The Utah Constitution, which reflects church-state concerns unique to that state, contains two provisions dealing with public funding of religious education. The first, found at Article 1, Section 4 of the state charter, mandates that "[n]o public money or property shall be appropriated for or applied to any religious worship, exercise or instruction, or for the support of any ecclesiastical establishment." The second Utah Blaine provision, found at Article 10, Section 9, forbids any direct aid to all religious schools: "[n]either the state of Utah nor its political subdivisions may make any appropriation for the direct support of any school or educational institution controlled by any religious organization." Other states have Blaine-style provisions of similar effect, although the wording is different. Delaware, which in 1897 included a Blaine provision in its state constitution, has an extensive section in its fundamental charter prohibiting direct aid: "No portion of any fund now existing, or which may hereafter be appropriated, or raised by tax, for educational purposes, shall be appropriated to, or used by, or in aid of any sectarian, church or denominational school[.]"

Alabama, a state of the Old Confederacy, included a Blaine Amendment provision in its state constitution in 1901. This provision prohibits the use of state educational funds to support "any sectarian or denominational school." Kentucky includes a similar provision in its state constitution, but also includes additional language that prohibits the use of money from the state school fund for any purpose other than the "maintenance of the public schools."

The moderate Blaine language used by these states, while varied in expression, affirms the same fundamental principle: direct government aid for expressly sectarian education is prohibited, and for the most part, so is sectarian influence in public educational programs. The strength of this affirmation can be seen in the case of *Fiscal Court of Jefferson County v. Brady*. There, the Kentucky Supreme Court upheld a lower court ruling that struck down a state statute permitting county governments to establish programs to provide for the busing of students in religious or other private schools. Jefferson County had previously instituted a subsidy program that paid a direct sum to private schools to pay for the transportation of students. The private schools funded were overwhelmingly religious in character, and nearly half a million dollars was expended by the county through its subsidy program. The Kentucky Supreme Court found that the private schools involved in the subsidy program combined their own transportation funds with the county subsidy, providing the schools with control over government assets. The court noted specifically that the "financial aid is provided to the school rather than a transportation service to the child," and found that there was a constitutionally significant distinction between providing general transportation for all students and "providing direct payment to selected eligible schools."

The last group of state Blaine provisions to be examined uses language that places the broadest restrictions on government aid to religious schools and organizations. These Blaine provisions often go far beyond the prohibition of direct aid to schools by preventing indirect aid as well. In addition, many of the states include wording in their constitutions prohibiting aid not only to schools, but also to any religious or "sectarian" institution. Florida, for instance, combines a mandate that its state educational fund be used solely for "the support and maintenance of free public schools," with an absolute prohibition on the use of any state revenues "directly or indirectly in aid of any church, sect, or religious denomination or in aid of any sectarian institution." This sterner approach to direct or indirect government aid to religious schools or institutions is paralleled by several other states. Missouri's constitution prohibits the state from giving anything in aid to support:

> [A]ny religious creed, church or sectarian purpose, or to help to support or sustain any private or public school, academy, seminary, college, university, or other institution of learning controlled by any religious creed, church or sectarian denomination whatever; nor shall any grant or donation of personal property or real estate ever be made by the state, or any county, city, town, or other municipal corporation, for any religious creed, church, or sectarian purpose whatever.

Like Florida, Missouri teams an extensive prohibition on government aid to religious bodies and religious schools with another constitutional provision that mandates that the state educational fund be used only for the establishment and maintenance of "free public schools."

While some state Blaine provisions only target education, some go much further. Oklahoma's constitution includes not only the familiar prohibition on support for sectarian educational institutions, but also includes a prohibition on any government aid in support of any "sectarian institution as such." The Indiana Constitution, in a one sentence article, prevents the state from allocating any funds from the treasury "for the benefit of any religious or theological institution." The Georgia State Constitution includes a similar article, expressly mandating that the state refrain from direct or indirect funding "of any sectarian institution." Colorado's state charter, ratified in the same year that the national Blaine Amendment was voted on in the Senate, contains-along with the standard Blaine provisions prohibiting public funding of sectarian schools-a prohibition on state funding for any "charitable, industrial, educational or benevolent purposes" not controlled completely by the state, as well as any "denominational or sectarian institution or association." The Idaho Constitution, ratified in 1890 at the peak of the movement for inclusion of

Blaine language in state constitutions, includes a lengthy article banning the allocation of "anything in aid" to religious schools or to religiously-affiliated "literary or scientific institution[s]," while at the same time containing a caveat allowing the state to provide some assistance to non-profit "health facilities" operated by religious groups. Nevada's constitution simply states that the state government cannot provide "funds of any kind or character" for sectarian purposes. The language of all of these provisions extend the standard Blaine provision's prohibition on direct aid to private sectarian schools to include any type of aid to virtually every sort of religiously-controlled institution.

The narrowly-defeated push for a national Blaine Amendment has had a wide-ranging effect on most state constitutions. States, willingly or by command of the federal government, incorporated Blaine provisions into their charters. This move to include Blaine provisions in state constitutions extended into the twentieth century. The overall effect of these Blaine-style provisions, by their express wording or through later judicial interpretations, was usually to preclude both the direct or indirect transfer of state funds to religious or sectarian schools and institutions. The motivation behind the Blaine Amendment was two-fold. First, there was a high degree of hostility towards the teaching and practice of the Roman Catholic Church, and correspondingly there existed a strong desire to ensure that Catholics would be precluded from using the resources of the government to support their parochial schools and other religious institutions. Second, there was an almost imperative desire on the part of the proponents of the Blaine Amendment to protect generic Protestant religiosity in the common schools and the public square. State courts in the twentieth century, with a few exceptions already discussed, rigorously enforced Blaine language to preclude direct, and in many cases indirect, aid and assistance to religious schools or those who wish to attend such schools.

State Blaine provisions do not exist in a constitutional vacuum, however. And while there is no question that states are free to decline to provide money or other forms of aid to private non-governmental entities across the board, there is a significant question as to whether or not the First Amendment allows states to preclude both direct and indirect funding to private religious institutions if those institutions are simply seeking equal access to state funding programs that are open to other private institutions that are of a non-religious character.

2. Cases

Modern disputes about the role of these clauses have focused on governmental programs designed to provide parents (and students) choices outside of the public schools. The issue is whether the programs have the purpose or effect of providing aid to religious schools and other religious organizations on the one hand or of providing aid to the individuals who benefit from it on the other. We start by considering a decision of the United States Supreme Court, *Zelman v. Simmons-Harris*, 536 U.S. 639 (2002), which rejects a federal Establishment Clause challenge to a state voucher program. We then consider several state court decisions, one that predates *Zelman* and several that follow it.

ZELMAN v. SIMMONS-HARRIS
536 U.S. 639 (2002)

REHNQUIST, C. J.

The State of Ohio has established a pilot program designed to provide educational choices to families with children who reside in the Cleveland City School District. The question presented is whether this program offends the Establishment Clause of the United States Constitution. We hold that it does not.

There are more than 75,000 children enrolled in the Cleveland City School District. The majority of these children are from low-income and minority families. Few of these families enjoy the means to send their children to any school other than an inner-city public school.

The program provides two basic kinds of assistance to parents of children in a covered district. First, the program provides tuition aid for students in kindergarten through third grade, expanding each year through eighth grade, to attend a participating public or private school of their parent's choosing. Second, the program provides tutorial aid for students who choose to remain enrolled in public school.

The Establishment Clause of the First Amendment, applied to the States through the Fourteenth Amendment, prevents a State from enacting laws that have the "purpose" or "effect" of advancing or inhibiting religion. There is no dispute that the program challenged here was enacted for the valid secular purpose of providing educational assistance to poor children in a demonstrably failing public school system. Thus, the question presented is whether the Ohio program nonetheless has the forbidden "effect" of advancing or inhibiting religion.

To answer that question, our decisions have drawn a consistent distinction between government programs that provide aid directly to religious schools, and programs of true private choice, in which government aid reaches religious schools only as a result of the genuine and independent choices of private individuals. While our jurisprudence with respect to the constitutionality of direct aid programs has "changed significantly" over the past two decades, our jurisprudence with respect to true private choice programs has remained consistent and unbroken. Three times we have confronted Establishment Clause challenges to neutral government programs that provide aid directly to a broad class of individuals, who, in turn, direct the aid to religious schools or institutions of their own choosing. Three times we have rejected such challenges.

Mueller, Witters, and *Zobrest* thus make clear that where a government aid program is neutral with respect to religion, and provides assistance directly to a broad class of citizens who, in turn, direct government aid to religious schools wholly as a result of their own genuine and independent private choice, the program is not readily subject to challenge under the Establishment Clause. A program that shares these features permits government aid to reach religious institutions only by way of the deliberate choices of numerous individual recipients. The incidental advancement of a religious mission, or the perceived endorsement of a religious message, is reasonably attributable to the individual recipient, not to the government, whose role ends with the disbursement of benefits.

Respondents…claim that even if we do not focus on the number of participating schools that are religious schools, we should attach constitutional significance to the fact that 96% of scholarship recipients have enrolled in religious schools. They claim that this alone proves parents lack genuine choice, even if no parent has ever said so. We need not consider this argument in detail, since it was flatly rejected in *Mueller,* where we found it irrelevant that 96% of parents taking deductions for tuition expenses paid tuition at religious schools. Indeed, we have recently found it irrelevant even to the constitutionality of a direct aid program that a vast majority of program benefits went to religious schools. The constitutionality of a neutral educational aid program simply does not turn on whether and why, in a particular area, at a particular time, most private schools are run by religious organizations, or most recipients choose to use the aid at a religious school.

In sum, the Ohio program is entirely neutral with respect to religion. It provides benefits directly to a wide spectrum of individuals, defined only by financial need and residence in a particular school district. It permits such individuals to exercise genuine choice among options public and private, secular and religious. The program is therefore a program of true private choice. In keeping with an unbroken line of decisions rejecting challenges to similar programs, we hold that the program does not offend the Establishment Clause.

JACKSON v. BENSON
578 N.W.2d 602 (Wisc. 1998)

STEINMETZ, J.

The next question presented in this case is whether the amended MPCP, [a school voucher program,] violates art. I, § 18 of the Wisconsin Constitution. The Respondents argue, and the court of appeals concluded, that the amended MPCP violates both the "benefits clause" and the "compelled support clause" of art. I, § 18. Upon review, we conclude that the amended MPCP violates neither provision.

The "benefits clause" of art. I, § 18 provides: "nor shall any money be drawn from the treasury for the benefit of religious societies, or religious or theological seminaries." This is Wisconsin's equivalent of the Establishment Clause of the First Amendment. This court has remarked that the language of art. I, § 18, while "more specific than the terser" clauses of the First Amendment, carries the same import; both provisions "are intended and operate to serve the same dual purpose of prohibiting the 'establishment' of religion and protecting the 'free exercise' of religion." Although art. I, § 18 is not subsumed by the First Amendment, we interpret and apply the benefits clause of art. I, § 18 in light of the United States Supreme Court cases interpreting the Establishment Clause of the First Amendment.

Unlike the court of appeals, which focused on whether sectarian private schools were "religious seminaries" under art. I, § 18, we focus our inquiry on whether the aid provided by the amended MPCP is "for the benefit of" such religious institutions. We have explained that the language "for the benefit of" in art. I, § 18 "is not to be read as requiring that some shadow of incidental benefit to a church-related institution brings a state grant or contract to purchase within the prohibition of the section." Furthermore, we have stated that the language of art. I, § 18 cannot be read as being "so prohibitive as not to encompass the primary-effect test." The crucial question, under art. I, § 18, as under the Establishment Clause, is "not whether some benefit accrues to a religious institution as a consequence of the legislative program, but whether its principal or primary effect advances religion."

We find the Supreme Court's primary effect test, focusing on the neutrality and indirection of state aid, is well reasoned and provides the appropriate line of demarcation for considering the constitutionality of neutral educational assistance programs such as the amended MPCP. Since the amended MPCP does not transgress the primary effect test employed in Establishment Clause jurisprudence, we also conclude that the statute is constitutionally inviolate under the benefits clause of art. I, § 18.

This conclusion is not inconsistent with Wisconsin tradition or with past precedent of this court. Wisconsin has traditionally accorded parents the primary role in decisions regarding the education and upbringing of their children. This court has embraced this principle for nearly a century, recognizing that: "parents as the natural guardians of their children [are] the persons under natural conditions having the most effective motives and inclinations and being in the best position and under the strongest obligations to give to such children proper nurture, education, and training."

In this context, this court has held that public funds may be placed at the disposal of third parties so long as the program on its face is neutral between sectarian and nonsectarian alternatives and the transmission of funds is guided by the independent decisions of third parties, and that public funds generally may be provided to sectarian educational institutions so long as steps are taken not to subsidize religious functions.

In *Weiss,* the court held that reading of the King James version of the Bible by students attending public school violated the religious benefits clause of art. I, § 18. Although the court's reasoning in *Weiss* may have differed from ours, its holding is entirely consistent with the primary effects test the Supreme Court has developed and we apply today. Requiring public school students to read from the Bible is neither neutral nor indirect. The Edgerton schools reviewed in *Weiss* were directly supported by public funds, and the reading of the Bible was anything but religious-neutral. The program considered in *Weiss* is far different from the neutral and indirect aid provided under the amended MPCP. The holding in *Weiss,* therefore, does not control our inquiry in this case.

The Respondents additionally argue that the amended MPCP violates the "compelled support clause" of art. I, § 18. The compelled support clause provides "nor shall any person be compelled to attend, erect or support any place of worship, or to maintain any ministry without consent...." The Respondents assert that since public funds eventually flow to religious institutions under the amended MPCP, taxpayers are compelled to support places of worship against their consent. This argument is identical to the Respondents' argument under the benefits clause. We will not interpret the compelled support clause as prohibiting the same acts as those prohibited by the benefits clause. Rather we look for an interpretation of these two related provisions that avoids such redundancy.

The amended MPCP does not require a single student to attend class at a sectarian private school. A qualifying student only attends a sectarian private school under the program if the student's parent so chooses. Nor does the amended MPCP force participation in religious activities. On the contrary, the program prohibits a sectarian private school from requiring students attending under the program to participate in religious activities offered at such school. The choice to participate in religious activities is also left to the students' parents. Since the amended MPCP neither compels students to attend sectarian private schools nor requires them to participate in religious activities, the program does not violate the compelled support clause of art. I, § 18.

NOTE

In *Jackson*, the Wisconsin Supreme Court anticipated the U.S. Supreme Court's decision in *Zelman*, both as a matter of federal and state constitutional law. More frequently, state court individual rights decisions respond to United States Supreme Court decisions, either by following them in lockstep or by reacting against them. It is fair to ask whether constitutional law in general – state and federal – benefits from this top-down approach or whether we would benefit from a bottom-up approach in which the state courts initially wrestle with difficult constitutional issues before the Supreme Court announces the meaning of the relevant federal provision.

CAIN v. HORNE
202 P.3d 1178 (Ariz. 2009)

RYAN, J.

Article 2, Section 12, of the Arizona Constitution provides that "[n]o public money ... shall be appropriated to any religious worship, exercise, or instruction, or to the support of any religious establishment." Article 9, Section 10, of the Arizona Constitution states that "[n]o tax shall be laid or appropriation of public money made in aid of any church, or private or sectarian school, or any public service corporation." The issue before us is whether two state-funded programs violate these provisions of our constitution.

In 2006, the Legislature enacted two programs that, in part, appropriated state monies to allow students to attend a private school of their choice instead of the public school in the district in which they live.

The Arizona Scholarships for Pupils with Disabilities Program, codified at Arizona Revised Statutes, offers "pupils with disabilities...the option of attending any public school of the pupil's choice or receiving a scholarship to any qualified school of the pupil's choice." Under this program, a public-school student with a disability may transfer to a private primary or secondary school, with the State paying a scholarship up to the amount of basic state aid the student would generate for a public school district. A parent of a disabled student may apply for a scholarship if the pupil attended a public school during the prior school year, the parent "is dissatisfied with the pupil's progress," and "[t]he parent has obtained acceptance for admission of the pupil to a qualified school."

Arizona Displaced Pupils Choice Grant Program allows the State to pay $5,000 or the cost of tuition and fees, whichever is less, for children in foster care to attend the private primary or secondary school of their choice. The program is limited to 500 pupils. A grant school is "a nongovernmental primary school or secondary school or a preschool ... that does not discriminate on the basis of race, color, handicap, familial status or national origin, that maintains one or more grade levels from kindergarten through grade twelve...."

Sectarian and nonsectarian schools may participate in both programs; schools are not required to alter their "creed, practices or curriculum" in order to receive funding. Under both programs, (collectively "the voucher programs") parents or legal guardians select the private or sectarian school their child will attend. The State then disburses a check or warrant to the parent or guardian, who must "restrictively endorse" the instrument for payment to the selected school.

Horne and the intervenors argue that the Aid Clause should be interpreted just as the United States Supreme Court has interpreted the Establishment Clause of the United States Constitution, and that the parental choice involved in signing the state checks over to a private or sectarian school saves the voucher programs from unconstitutionality.

Contrary to Horne's assertion, *Kotterman* and *Jordan* do not compel us to interpret the Aid Clause as a mirror image of the Religion Clause or to interpret the Aid Clause as no broader than the federal Establishment Clause. More importantly, both the text and purpose of the Aid Clause support the conclusion that the clause requires a construction independent from that of the Religion Clause.

First, the text of the Aid Clause encompasses more than does the Religion Clause. The Aid Clause prohibits the use of public funds not only to aid *private* or sectarian schools, but to aid public corporations as well. Thus, under the Aid Clause, a statute granting funds to aid a public service corporation engaged exclusively in secular activities might be prohibited; such a statute would pose no difficulties under the Religion Clause, nor could it be readily analyzed under the Supreme Court's Establishment Clause jurisprudence. Likewise, the Religion Clause would prohibit an appropriation to pay for religious instruction in a public school, but the Aid Clause says nothing about such an appropriation, as public schools are not among the forbidden recipients of appropriations under the Aid Clause.

Second, although the two clauses overlap to some extent, they serve different purposes. The Religion Clause appears in Article 2, entitled "Declaration of Rights," and reinforces other provisions in the constitution "dealing with the separation of church and state." The Aid Clause is found in Article 9, entitled "Public Debt, Revenue, and Taxation," and "[u]nlike [Article 2, Section 12]...prohibits public aid to private nonsectarian schools and to public service corporations." The Aid Clause is thus primarily designed to protect the public fisc and to protect public schools.

Both the Aid and Religion Clauses prohibit certain appropriations of public money. In *Kotterman,* this Court addressed whether tax credits for contributions to organizations providing scholarships to students attending non-governmental schools violated the two clauses. We held that neither provision precluded the Legislature from granting a tuition tax credit, because the tax credit was not an appropriation. Because the funds in *Kotterman* were credits against tax liability, not withdrawals from the state treasury, the funds were never in the state's treasury; therefore, the credits did not constitute an appropriation.

Unlike the funds in *Kotterman,* the funds at issue here are withdrawn from the public treasury and earmarked for an identified purpose. Horne and the intervenors do not dispute that the vouchers therefore constitute appropriations of public funds. But ... they argue that the funds do not aid the schools; rather they characterize the funds as aid to students under a "true beneficiary" theory.

Under the true beneficiary theory, individuals benefitted by a government program, rather than the institution receiving the public funds, are characterized as the true beneficiaries of the aid. For example, in *Jordan,* we held that using state funds to partially reimburse the Salvation Army's expenses in providing emergency aid to those in need did not violate the Aid Clause. *Jordan* thus stands for the proposition that an entity covered by the Aid Clause may contract with the State to provide non-religious services to members of the public when such an entity "merely [acts as] a conduit and receives no financial aid or support therefrom."

The voucher programs, however, vary significantly from the program at issue in *Jordan.* In contrast to the program in *Jordan,* the voucher programs do not provide reimbursement for contracted services. In fact, they are designed in such a way that the State does not purchase anything; rather it is the parent or the guardian who exercises sole discretion to contract with the qualified school.

The Aid Clause flatly prohibits "appropriation of public money...in aid of any...private or sectarian school." No one doubts that the clause prohibits a direct appropriation of public funds to such recipients. For all intents and purposes, the voucher programs do precisely what the Aid Clause prohibits. These programs transfer state funds directly from the state treasury to private schools. That the checks or warrants first pass through the hands of parents is immaterial; once a pupil has been accepted into a qualified school under either program, the parents or guardians have no choice; they must endorse the check or warrant to the qualified school.

In sum, the language and purpose of the Aid Clause do not permit the appropriations these voucher programs provide; to rule otherwise would allow appropriations that would amount to "aid of...private or sectarian school[s]," and render the clause a nullity.

EMBRY v. O'BANNON
798 N.E.2d 157 (Ind. 2003)

DICKSON, J.

The taxpayers' lawsuit challenges the "dual-enrollment" process whereby the State provides public funds "which are used to pay teachers who teach classes in parochial schools and which are used to provide such things as internet services to parochial schools." The taxpayers contend that this practice violates Article 1, Section 6 of the Indiana Constitution, which states: "No money shall be drawn from the treasury, for the benefit of any religious or theological institution." Because this dual-enrollment process does not provide any substantial benefit to the participating parochial schools or directly fund activities of a religious nature, we hold that it does not violate Section 6, and we affirm the judgment of the trial court.

Under Indiana Law Code § 21-3-4.5-1, a portion of the public funding allocated to each Indiana public school corporation is directly proportional to that corporation's "average daily membership" or "ADM." Students enrolled in private schools may be counted in a public school corporation's ADM if the student also: 1) enrolls in the public school, 2) has legal settlement in the school corporation, and 3) receives instructional services from the school corporation. The Indiana Department of Education issued memoranda to all public school superintendents in 1993, 1997, and 1999 advising that it interpreted Indiana [law] to allow nonpublic school students enrolled in at least one specific class in the public school corporation to be counted in the corporation's ADM. Thereafter, many public school corporations entered into dual-enrollment agreements with private schools in which the public schools agreed to provide various secular instructional services to private school students, on the premises of the private school, in return for securing those students' enrollment in their respective public school corporations. Among the courses offered to the dual-enrolled students are fitness and health, art, foreign language, study skills, verbal skills, music, and computer technology (including internet services).

The plaintiffs challenge the dual-enrollment process, claiming that it results in money being drawn from the state treasury to benefit parochial schools. They argue that this violates the plain meaning of Section 6, and that their position is consistent with the history of the times surrounding the adoption of our 1851 constitution and with the limited case law interpreting Section 6.

The text of Section 6 is brief: "No money shall be drawn from the treasury, for the benefit of any religious or theological institution." This language did not appear in Indiana's 1816 constitution, but was a product of the 1850-51 constitutional convention and was included in our constitution of 1851 without any substantive discussion at the convention.

The determinative issue is whether the dual enrollment process challenged by the plaintiffs confers substantial benefits upon the participating parochial schools or directly funds activities of a religious nature. Neither the text of Section 6 nor the circumstances surrounding its adoption...provide guidance as to whether the phrase "for the benefit of" in Section 6 was intended to erect an absolute prohibition against any expenditure of public money that might confer merely pecuniary incidental benefit to a religious institution. Upon the issue of incidental benefits, we find guidance in prior Indiana case law.

In *State ex rel. Johnson v. Boyd,* 217 Ind. 348, 28 N.E.2d 256 (1940), this Court permitted the public school system in Vincennes to serve approximately 800 school children who had previously been attending Roman Catholic parochial schools prior to their closure by church authorities, by conducting public schools in the same parochial school buildings, and by employing as staff for the schools the "Sisters and Brothers [of] various Catholic orders." The Court focused on the total control of the schools by the public school system and found that they were no longer parochial schools. It observed, "[w]e see no valid reason why the said school trustees should not have leased the buildings and equipment furnished by the church authorities" and noted with approval cases from other jurisdictions that permitted religious buildings or facilities to be rented or used for the purpose of conducting public schools. Noting that the teachers, while members of religious orders, were nevertheless properly licensed, taught the course of education prescribed by the State Board of Education, and provided no sectarian instruction in the schools during school hours, the Court held that their salaries did not violate Section 6 as benefits for religious or theological institutions.

In *Center Township of Marion County v. Coe,* 572 N.E.2d 1350 (Ind.Ct.App.1991), the Trustee of Center Township provided emergency shelter assistance to the homeless under Indiana Code § 12-2-1-6 by entering into agreements with private religious mission shelters whereby the township paid the missions to feed and shelter a number of the township's homeless. The missions required attendance at religious services as a condition of receiving services, and some homeless persons complained that they were forced to attend the services against their will because no other shelters were available. In the resulting class action, the Court held that Section 6 was not offended by the mere fact that benefits accrued to the religious missions under the agreements, but ruled for the plaintiff class because the agreements themselves unconstitutionally conditioned access to publicly funded shelter on attendance at religious services.

While acknowledging that dual-enrollment programs do not provide any payment of public funds directly to religious institutions, the plaintiffs urge that the dual-enrollment agreements provide specific benefits to parochial schools because they make it unnecessary for the schools to hire and pay as many teachers, and because the schools may use the resources thus saved to expand curriculum and attract students. It is not disputed, however, that the dual-enrollment programs provide obvious significant educational benefits to the Indiana children for whom participation in a dual-enrollment program affords educational resources and training in subjects they would not otherwise receive. The programs likewise benefit the State by furthering its objective to encourage education for all Indiana students. In addition, the public school systems providing instructional services under a dual-enrollment plan benefit from increased public funding. Compared with the substantial educational benefits to children, the increased attainment of the State's objectives, and the additional funds made available to participating public school systems, we find any alleged "savings" to parochial schools and their resulting opportunities for curriculum expansion would be, at best, relatively minor and incidental benefits of the dual-enrollment programs.

In summary, while the text of Article 1, Section 6, in the context of history may be helpful in discerning whether its framers and ratifiers specifically intended it to apply to the funding of religious schools, the text and its historical context do not inform us whether the framers intended to prohibit all public funds from providing merely incidental benefits to religious and theological institutions. Indiana case law, however, has interpreted Section 6 to permit the State to contract with religious institutions for goods or services, notwithstanding possible incidental benefit to the institutions, and to prohibit the use of public funds only when directly used for such institutions' activities of a religious nature. Because the dual-enrollment programs permitted in Indiana do not confer substantial benefits upon any religious or theological institution, nor directly fund activities of a religious nature, such dual-enrollment programs do not violate Section 6.

CALIFORNIA STATEWIDE CMTY. DEV. AUTH. v. ALL PERS. INTERESTED IN THE MATTER OF THE VALIDITY OF A PURCHASE AGREEMENT
152 P.3d 1070 (Cal. 2007)

KENNARD, J.

Recognizing that an educated citizenry and workforce are vital to the preservation of the rights and liberties of the people of this state, California in 1879 included in its new Constitution a provision directing the state Legislature to encourage "by all suitable means the promotion of intellectual, scientific, moral, and agricultural improvement." Since 1879, our state Constitution has also included a provision prohibiting state and local governments from granting anything "in aid of any...sectarian purpose, or help[ing] to support or sustain any school, college, university, hospital, or other institution controlled by any...sectarian denomination whatever...."

Against that backdrop, this court in *California Educational Facilities Authority v. Priest* (1974) 526 P.2d 513, upheld a state bond program funding the construction of educational facilities at religiously affiliated colleges, which were expressly prohibited from using the bond proceeds (paid for by private purchasers of the bonds) for specified religious purposes. We concluded that neither the state nor the federal Constitution prohibited this form of indirect assistance to religiously affiliated colleges, a rule that for more than three decades has allowed California public entities to issue revenue bonds to raise private funds for campus improvements at religiously affiliated colleges. We declined in *Priest,* however, to decide whether that rule would also apply if a college were "pervasively sectarian," a term the United States Supreme Court had used in *Hunt v. McNair* (1973) 413 U.S. 734, to describe a religiously affiliated school that devotes a substantial portion of its functions to its religious mission.

This case involves bond financing agreements between a public entity and three religiously affiliated schools that, for purposes of this litigation, the parties have assumed to be pervasively sectarian. These schools are thus likely to include a religious perspective in their teachings. Each agreement expressly prohibits use of the bond proceeds for specified religious purposes. And, as in *Priest,* funds for the projects will not come from any government entity, but from private-sector purchasers of the bonds, and no public entity will have any obligation on the bonds in the event of default by the schools.

As explained below, in resolving the state constitutional issue we conclude that the pertinent inquiry should center on the substance of the education provided by these three schools, not on their religious character.

Therefore, whether the schools are pervasively sectarian (as the parties have assumed) is not a controlling factor in determining the validity of the bond funding program under our state Constitution. Rather, the program's validity turns on two questions: (1) Does each of the recipient schools offer a broad curriculum in secular subjects? (2) Do the schools' secular classes consist of information and coursework that is neutral with respect to religion? This test ensures that the state's interest in promoting the intellectual improvement of its residents is advanced through the teaching of secular information and coursework, and that the expression of a religious viewpoint in otherwise secular classes will provide a benefit to religion that is merely incidental to the bond program's primary purpose of promoting secular education.

[We apply] the following four-part test for determining whether the issuance of government bonds benefiting a religiously affiliated school violates the state constitutional provision in question: (1) The bond program must serve the public interest and provide no more than an incidental benefit to religion; (2) the program must be available to both secular and sectarian institutions on an equal basis; (3) the program must prohibit use of bond proceeds for "religious projects"; and (4) the program must not impose any financial burden on the government. Because the last three requirements can be easily disposed of in this case, we address them first.

It is undisputed that the Authority has issued tax exempt bonds to encourage private investment in a wide variety of private institutions, secular as well as sectarian. This satisfies *Priest's* second requirement - that the state bond program not discriminate between secular and sectarian institutions, treating both categories alike.

The bond agreements expressly prohibit each of the three schools from using the bond proceeds to construct or improve any facility for "religious projects," that is "sectarian instruction or as a place for religious worship or in connection with any part of the programs of any school or department of divinity for the useful life of the Project." This satisfies *Priest's* third requirement.

Because of the utilization of conduit or pass through financing, the capital for the construction projects at the three private schools is funded solely by private-sector purchasers of the bonds. The schools repay the advanced capital plus interest to an independent trustee, who then pays the private bondholders, who have no recourse for nonpayment against the Authority. All of the Authority's costs of issuing the bonds are reimbursed by the schools. Thus, the bond funding places no financial burden on the Authority or any other public entity. This satisfies *Priest's* fourth requirement, that the program not impose a financial burden on the government.

Having concluded that the second, third, and fourth requirements of *Priest* are satisfied, we still need to determine whether the bond program meets *Priest's* first requirement, that the program provide a public benefit and no more than incidentally benefit religion. *Priest* held that the state's issuance of revenue bonds for purchase by private investors to fund construction or improvements of facilities at religiously affiliated colleges benefited the public at large by "'encourag[ing] by all suitable means the promotion of intellectual...improvement'" in California, thus furthering the state constitutional mandate of article IX, section 1, and that it "[did] not have a substantial effect of supporting religious activities."

Here, the proposed state bond program would benefit three schools that the Authority throughout this litigation has described as "pervasively sectarian." Would that bond program satisfy *Priest's* first requirement, that the program serve the public interest and no more than incidentally benefit religion? To answer that question, we need to examine the bond program's purpose and effects. The program must have a "primary purpose...to advance legitimate public ends" and its effects may not include a benefit to religious activity that is other than "indirect, remote, [or] incidental" to the primary secular purpose. When a court attempts to determine how, if at all, a bond program would have the effect of supporting religious activity at schools, the characterization of the schools as "pervasively sectarian" does not provide a reliable or satisfactory answer. A more useful and effective approach, we conclude, is to examine the substance of the education that each of these religious schools offers its students.

The goal of the Authority's proposed issuance of revenue bonds here is to enhance the ability of private schools to improve their facilities through funding provided *exclusively by private investors.* By providing a tax exemption on interest earned on the bonds, the government makes the bonds more attractive to private investors and thereby enhances the ability of private institutions to expand their educational facilities. We pointed out in *Priest:* "The framers of [our state] Constitution recognized the importance of education in our social fabric, and imposed a constitutional duty on the Legislature to 'encourage by all suitable means the promotion of intellectual...improvement.'" In the circumstances of that case-a program available to sectarian and nonsectarian schools on an equal basis, in which all aid for religious projects was prohibited, and no financial burden was imposed upon the state-we concluded that the provision of tax exempt bond financing did not violate article XVI, section 5, because "its primary purpose [was] to advance legitimate public ends" and it "d[id] not have a substantial effect of supporting religious activities." Can the same be said of the proposed bond funding in this case with respect to a school that includes a religious perspective in its curriculum? The answer is yes, if certain requirements are met.

First, the school that is the subject of the revenue bond financing arrangement must provide a broad curriculum in secular subjects. When it does, the bond program assists the religious school in providing educational opportunities to California residents, enhancing their employment prospects and deepening their understanding of critical political, social, scientific, and cultural issues. This broad curriculum requirement excludes from the bond funding program religious schools that offer classes in only a few secular subjects, because to provide bond funding for such schools would not sufficiently advance the program's goal of expanding secular educational opportunities for Californians.

We are mindful of the concern that a school with a religious perspective may use the facilities built or improved with the revenue bond proceeds to substantially further its religious mission. Such use would provide more than an incidental benefit to religion, in violation of the principles we enunciated in *Priest.* To ensure that the classes in secular subjects promote the state's interest in secular education and no more than incidentally benefit religion, the religious school must meet a *second* requirement: the information and coursework used to teach secular subjects must be neutral with respect to religion. Of course, religion may be an object of study in classes such as history, social studies, and literature, just as in public schools, in a manner that neither promotes nor opposes any particular religion or religion in general. But a class that includes as part of the instruction information or coursework that promotes or opposes a particular religion or religious beliefs may not be taught in facilities financed through tax exempt bond financing. On remand, in determining religious neutrality, the straightforward assessment for the trial court to make is whether the academic content of a religious school's course in a secular subject such as math, chemistry, or Shakespeare's writings is typical of that provided in nonreligious schools. When a school establishes, through its course descriptions or otherwise, that the academic content of its secular classes is typical of comparable courses at public or other nonreligious schools, it is not necessary to scrutinize the school's day-to-day classroom communications. The circumstance that a teacher may, in addition to teaching a course's religiously neutral content, express an idea or viewpoint that may be characterized as "religious" does not result in a benefit to religion that is more than incidental to the state's primary purpose of enhancing secular education opportunities for California residents.

As we stated in *Priest* in addressing former section 24 of article XIII (the identically phrased predecessor of current section 5 of article XVI of the California Constitution), this "section has never been interpreted...to require governmental hostility to religion, nor to prohibit a religious institution from receiving an indirect, remote, and incidental benefit from a statute which has a secular primary purpose." *Priest* also observed: "'[M]any expenditures of public money give indirect and incidental benefit to denominational schools and institutions of higher learning. Sidewalks, streets, roads, highways, sewers are furnished for the use of all citizens regardless of religious belief.... Police and fire departments give the same protection to denominational institutions that they give to privately owned property and their expenses are paid from public funds.'" Here, we have *no* expenditure of public money, and application of the standards we have set out will ensure that any benefit to religion from the bond funding program is merely incidental.

NOTES

1. For an example of another case in which the state supreme court held that the state and federal Constitutions were coextensive, *see Anderson v. Town of Durham*, 895 A.2d 944 (Me. 2006), and for an example of a case in which the court held they were not, *see Simmons-Harris v. Goff*, 711 N.E.2d 203 (Ohio 1999) ("There is no reason to conclude that the Religion Clauses of the Ohio Constitution are coextensive with those in the United States Constitution").

2. For articles dealing with these issues in more depth, see Frank R. Kemerer, *The Constitutional Dimension of School Vouchers*, 3 Tex F. on C.L. & C.R. 137 (1998); Joseph P. Viteritti, *Blaine's Wake: School Choice, The First Amendment, and State Constitutional Law*, 22 Harv. J. L. & Pub. Pol'y 657 (1998).

CHAPTER **XI**

SCHOOL FUNDING LITIGATION

A. INTRODUCTION

In *Brown v. Board of Education*, 347 U.S. 483, 493 (1954), the Supreme Court observed that "education is perhaps the most important function of state and local governments" before holding that access to public schools "must be made available to all on equal terms." At the same time that *Brown* removed one impediment to equal educational opportunities, it left in place another: the disfiguring effects of wealth on the type of education that American children receive and the challenges that poverty poses for some public schools wishing to provide an education to their students "on equal terms" to the education offered by their wealthier counterparts.

In the late 1960s, while the federal courts faced lawsuits over the pace of the "all deliberate speed" mandate of *Brown II, Brown v. Board of Educ. of Topeka, Kan.*, 349 U.S. 294, 301 (1955), and related lawsuits premised on removing the vestiges of segregation by requiring school districts to use busing to create racially balanced schools, a new form of institutional litigation related to public education arose – one focused less on the racial makeup of primary and secondary schools and more on the disparities between the quality of education offered to students based on the property wealth of the school districts in which they lived. First in the California state courts, *see Serrano v. Priest*, 5 Cal. 3d 584 (Cal. 1971), and eventually in a federal court lawsuit filed in Texas, *see Rodriguez v. San Antonio Indep. Sch. Dist.*, 337 F. Supp. 280 (W.D. Tex. 1971), litigants argued that their respective state systems of funding a public education were unconstitutional because they primarily relied on local funding and local control, which permitted wide disparities in the quality of education that children within the State received based on little more than the property wealth of the school district in which their parents happened to live.

In *Serrano*, the California Supreme Court ruled in favor of the claimants. Relying on the State and Federal Constitutions, the Court made the following points: the "school financing system discriminates on the basis of wealth of a district and its residents," 5 Cal.3d 604; "the distinctive and priceless foundation of education in our society warrants, indeed compels, our treating it as a 'fundamental interest,'" *id.* at 608-609; the financing system is not necessary to accomplish a compelling state interest, *id.* at 604; and since the funding system "does not withstand 'strict scrutiny,' it denies to the plaintiffs and others similarly situated the equal protection of the laws," *id.* at 614-615.

In *Rodriguez*, the claimants sought to extend *Serrano*'s federal equal-protection holding from California to Texas and eventually to all other States in the country. They premised their lawsuit on two theories of unconstitutionality: that education is a fundamental right and that wealth is a suspect class. Both theories came to the same end, as each would have required Texas (and eventually each State) to satisfy the rigors of strict scrutiny in justifying its system of funding public schools – a test that would force a State to prove that it had done everything within its power to eliminate the marked disparities between the quality of a public education offered to children living in property-rich and property-poor school districts. A three-judge district court ruled for the plaintiffs. It invoked both grounds of unconstitutionality and held that the Equal Protection Clause guaranteed "fiscal neutrality" in Texas's creation and oversight of a school-funding system. 337 F. Supp. at 284, 286.

In a 5-4 decision, the United States Supreme Court reversed. In a decision written by Justice Powell, the Court rejected both claims of unconstitutionality. Education is not a fundamental right entitled to strict scrutiny, he wrote, because the Constitution nowhere mentions the topic, precluding fundamental-right status on that basis alone. 411 U.S. at 35. Nor, he added, do individuals have a fundamental right to governmental benefits merely because that benefit is significant or even essential. Otherwise, a State's allocation of all manner of public benefits – access to housing, food, health care, to name a few – would face strict scrutiny. *Id.* at 37. In rejecting the contention that wealth was a suspect classification, Justice Powell noted that Texas guaranteed all children a free public education regardless of wealth. It thus had not denied its residents a public benefit on the basis of wealth, but had merely created a system that tolerated a relatively worse public benefit to be provided to some citizens on the basis of wealth. *Id.* at 38-39.

Justice Marshall wrote the principal dissent. As the lead advocate for the plaintiffs in *Brown*, Justice Marshall surely understood the stakes of the *Rodriguez* litigation, "including the possibility that the promises of Brown would never be fulfilled unless the courts not only eliminated de jure segregation by race but also curbed the effects of de facto segregation by wealth." Jeffrey S. Sutton, *San Antonio Independent School District v. Rodriguez* and Its Aftermath, 94 Va. L. Rev. 1963, 1970 (2008). He concluded that the plain connection between a meaningful education and other constitutional guarantees made it essential to subject discrimination against a "powerless class[]" over this public benefit to strict scrutiny. *Id.* at 109 (Marshall, J., dissenting).

"For better, for worse or for more of the same, the majority in *Rodriguez* tolerated the continuation of a funding system that allowed serious disparities in the quality of the education a child received based solely on the wealth of the community in which his parents happened to live or could afford to live. Yet even after the Court gave the States the green light to continue relying on that system, they eventually demanded change – in some instances because the political processes prompted it and in other instances because the state courts required it." Sutton, *Rodriguez* and Its Aftermath, 94 Va. L. Rev. at 1971. Thus, although the Supreme Court in *Rodriguez* rejected the California Supreme Court's *federal* equal-protection analysis in *Serrano*, it did not overrule – indeed, it had no power to overrule – *Serrano*'s reliance on the California Constitution in ruling that the State's system of public education was unconstitutional or for that matter to prevent other States from doing the same under their own constitutions.

This chapter focuses on the aftermath of *Rodriguez*. The state-court litigation that followed *Rodriguez* provides a rich example of the independence of state constitutions (and state legislatures) as a source for protecting rights that the federal constitution (and national legislature) have not protected. In the several decades since the United States Supreme Court's decision in *Rodriguez*, the vast majority of state supreme courts have considered similar claims under their state constitutions, and an increasing majority of them have ruled in favor of the plaintiffs. The purpose of this chapter is to explore the state courts' resolution of these claims – first by considering state constitutional decisions premised on equality theories of unconstitutionality, then by considering state decisions premised on adequacy theories of unconstitutionality and finally by exploring remedial issues that have arisen in these cases.

B. EQUAL PROTECTION DECISIONS

The first wave of state-court decisions after *Rodriquez*, like the *Serrano* decision that preceded *Rodriguez*, principally addressed equal protection claims. As we saw in Chapter 5, many state constitutions (but by no means all of them) contain equal protection clauses. In the immediate aftermath of *Rodriquez*, particularly from 1973 to 1989, many school-finance plaintiffs premised their claims for relief on the equal protection clause, or a comparable reading of another clause, found in the State's constitution. As in *Rodriguez*, the claimants focused on the gap in funding between rich and poor school districts and the challenges faced by property-poor districts in closing the gap. While some of these claims succeeded, most did not. *See e.g., Dupree v. Alma Sch. Dist. No. 30,* 651 S.W.2d 90, 93 (Ark. 1983); *Horton v. Meskill,* 376 A.2d 359, 374 (Conn. 1977); *Pauley v. Kelly,* 255 S.E.2d 859, 878 (W. Va. 1979); *Washakie*

County Sch. Dist. No. One v. Herschler, 606 P.2d 310, 333-35 (Wyo. 1980); *see* Molly S. McUsic, The Future of Brown v. Board of Education: Economic Integration of The Public Schools, 117 Harv. L. Rev. 1334, 1344 (2004) ("Prior to 1989, virtually every school finance case made its equity claim under a state constitution's equal protection clause"). By 1988, the State defendants had prevailed in 15 of the 22 cases in which an equal protection theory of invalidity had been raised. Michael A. Rebell, "Educational Adequacy, Democracy, and the Courts," *in* National Research Council, Achieving High Educational Standards for All: Conference Summary 218, 226-27, n 47 (Timothy Ready et al. eds., 2002).

LEVITTOWN UNION FREE SCHOOL DIST. v. NYQUIST
439 N.E.2d 359 (N.Y. 1982)

JONES, J.

Succinctly stated, it is the gravamen of the complaint of the original plaintiffs (and the findings of the courts below provide factual support for their argument) that property-rich districts have an ability to raise greater local tax revenue enabling them to provide enriched educational programs beyond the fiscal ability of the property-poor districts.

We now modify the order of the Appellate Division and direct that judgment be entered declaring that the present admixture of statutory provisions for State aid to local school districts, considered in connection with the existing system for local financing, is constitutional…under both the equal protection clause and the education article of the State Constitution.

At the outset it is appropriate to comment briefly on the context in which the legal issues before us arise. Although New York State has long been acknowledged to be a leader in its provision of public elementary and secondary educational facilities and services, and notwithstanding that its per pupil expenditures for such purposes each year are very nearly the highest in the Nation, it must be recognized that there are nonetheless significant inequalities in the availability of financial support for local school districts, ranging from minor discrepancies to major differences, resulting in significant unevenness in the educational opportunities offered. These disparities may properly be ascribed in some respects to the wide variances between the property assessment bases on which local district taxes are imposed. Similarly, it may be accepted that the four major cities represented by the intervenors, by reason of the factors encompassed in metropolitan overburden, are forced to provide instructional services and facilities of a lesser quantity, variety, and quality than those provided in some other school districts. No claim is advanced in this case, however, by either the original plaintiffs or the intervenors that the educational facilities or services provided in the school districts that they represent fall below the State-wide minimum standard of educational quality and quantity fixed by the Board of Regents; their attack is directed at the existing disparities in financial resources which lead to educational unevenness above that minimum standard.

The determination of the amounts, sources, and objectives of expenditures of public moneys for educational purposes, especially at the State level, presents issues of enormous practical and political complexity, and resolution appropriately is largely left to the interplay of the interests and forces directly involved and indirectly affected, in the arenas of legislative and executive activity. This is of the very essence of our governmental and political polity. It would normally be inappropriate, therefore, for the courts to intrude upon such decision-making. With full recognition and respect, however, for the distribution of powers in educational matters among the legislative, executive and judicial branches, it is nevertheless the responsibility of the courts to adjudicate contentions that actions taken by the Legislature and the executive fail to conform to the mandates of the Constitutions which constrain the activities of all three branches. That because of limited capabilities and competences the courts might encounter great difficulty in fashioning and then enforcing particularized remedies appropriate to repair unconstitutional action on the part of the Legislature or the executive is neither to be ignored on the one hand nor on the other to dictate judicial abstention in every case. In the discharge of our judicial responsibility in this case, recognizing the existence of the very real disparities of financial support as found by the lower courts, we nonetheless conclude that such disparities do not establish that there has been a violation of [the] State Constitution.

The circumstance that public education is unquestionably high on the list of priorities of governmental concern and responsibility, involving the expenditures of enormous sums of State and local revenue, enlisting the most active attention of our citizenry and of our Legislature, and manifested by express articulation in our State Constitution, does not automatically entitle it to classification as a "fundamental constitutional right" triggering a higher standard of judicial review for purposes of equal protection analysis. Thus, in *Matter of Bernstein v. Toia*, where the concern was public assistance to the needy – clearly a matter of significant interest, provision for which is similarly included in our State Constitution – we employed the rational basis test as the proper standard for review. The more careful scrutiny standard has been applied when the challenged State action has resulted in intentional discrimination against a class of persons grouped together by reason of personal characteristics, the use of which called into question the propriety of the particular classifications.

No classification of persons is present in the case now before us....
The claim is of discrimination between property-poor and property-
wealthy school districts. No authority is cited to us, however, that
discrimination between units of local government calls for other than
rational basis scrutiny.

Our inquiry is therefore only whether there has been demonstrated the
absence of a rational basis for the present school financing system,
premised as it is on local taxation within individual school districts with
supplemental State aid allocated in accordance with legislatively approved
formulas and plans. Addressing the submissions of the original plaintiffs,
our conclusion is that there has not been such a showing, and that the
justification offered by the State – the preservation and promotion of local
control of education-is both a legitimate State interest and one to which
the present financing system is reasonably related.

Under the existing system the State is divided into more than 700 local
school districts, each of which varies from the others and, from time to
time, varies within itself, in greater or lesser degree, as to number of pupils
and value of assessable real property, as well as with respect to numerous
other characteristics, including personal wealth of its taxpayers. Outside
the cities in the State (in which school funding is a part of the total
municipal fiscal process), funds for the support of the education program
offered in the schools of a district are raised through the imposition of
local taxes following voter authorization based on approval of a budget
prepared and submitted by an elected board of education, reflecting the
instructional program (within standards fixed by the State) perceived by
the local board of education to be responsive to the needs and desires of
the community. By way of assuring that a basic education will be provided
and that a uniform, minimum expenditure per pupil will occur in each
district, the Legislature has long provided for payment of supplementing
State aid such that presently $1,885 per pupil (and, by a weighting
computation, larger amounts for particular types of pupils) is available for
education in each district. Throughout the State, voters, by their action on
school budgets, exercise a substantial control over the educational
opportunities made available in their districts; to the extent that an
authorized budget requires expenditures in excess of State aid, which will
be funded by local taxes, there is a direct correlation between the system
of local school financing and implementation of the desires of the
taxpayer.

It is the willingness of the taxpayers of many districts to pay for and to
provide enriched educational services and facilities beyond what the basic
per pupil expenditure figures will permit that creates differentials in
services and facilities.... Any legislative attempt to make uniform and
undeviating the educational opportunities offered by the several hundred

local school districts-whether by providing that revenue for local education shall come exclusively from State sources to be distributed on a uniform per pupil basis, by prohibiting expenditure by local districts of any sums in excess of a legislatively fixed per pupil expenditure, or by requiring every district to match the per pupil expenditure of the highest spending district by means of local taxation or by means of State aid (surely an economically unrealistic hypothesis)-would inevitably work the demise of the local control of education available to students in individual districts. The *amicus* brief filed on behalf of the 85 school districts puts it well: "For all of the nearly two centuries that New York has had public schools, it has utilized a statutory system whereby citizens at the local level, acting as part of school district units containing people with a community of interest and a tradition of acting together to govern themselves, have made the basic decisions on funding and operating their own schools. Through the years, the people of this State have remained true to the concept that the maximum support of the public schools and the most informed, intelligent and responsive decision-making as to the financing and operation of those schools is generated by giving citizens direct and meaningful control over the schools that their children attend."

HORNBECK v. SOMERSET COUNTY BD. OF EDUC.
458 A.2d 758 (Md. 1983)

MURPHY, C. J.

This case involves a challenge to the constitutionality of Maryland statutes which govern the system of financing public elementary and secondary schools in the State's twenty-four school districts, *i.e.,* in the twenty-three counties of Maryland and in Baltimore City. The litigation focuses upon the existence of wide disparities in taxable wealth among the various school districts, and the effect of those differences upon the fiscal capacity of the poorer districts to provide their students with educational offerings and resources comparable to those of the more affluent school districts.

The plaintiffs maintain that the lower court correctly held that the Maryland system of public school finance violates the equal protection guarantee of Art. 24 of the Maryland Declaration of Rights. They contend, as the trial judge held, that the right to education, even if it is not fundamental under the federal constitution, is nevertheless of fundamental caliber under the state constitutional provision because, within the formulation of *Rodriguez,* the right is explicitly guaranteed by the state constitution. Plaintiffs seek to buttress their position by referring to the provisions of § 52 of Art. III of the Maryland Constitution which direct in paragraph (4)(f) that the state budget include an "estimate of all appropriations...for the establishment and maintenance throughout the State of a thorough and efficient system of public schools in conformity with Article 8 of the Constitution and with the laws of the State." As paragraph (11) of § 52 directs the Governor to include such estimates for the public schools in the budget "without revision," and because paragraph (6) prohibits the General Assembly from amending the budget to affect the provisions made by the laws of the State for the public school system, the plaintiffs contend that public education is of such high status as to constitute a fundamental right in Maryland. Accordingly, the plaintiffs maintain that the lower court was right in concluding that the State's system of public school financing must be reviewed under the "strict scrutiny" standard, thereby requiring that the State demonstrate that the system promotes a compelling governmental interest-a test with which the Maryland system cannot comply.

While we have not considered the applicability of the *Rodriguez* test in determining whether a right is fundamental for purposes of equal protection review under Art. 24 of the Declaration of Rights, a number of states have considered, and rejected, that test in considering whether education is a fundamental right under state constitutional provisions similar to Art. VIII of the Maryland Constitution. These cases point out that state constitutions, unlike the federal constitution, are not of limited or delegated powers and are not restricted to provisions of fundamental import; consequently, whether a right is fundamental should not be predicated on its explicit or implicit inclusion in a state constitution.

These cases also point out that other public services, such as police, fire, welfare, health care and other social services, which benefit the entire population, are equally as important as education, even though they may not be mentioned in the state constitution. The observation has been made by one court that in terms of "fundamentality" there is little by way of essential difference between any of these vital areas of state concern, so that to apply a strict scrutiny analysis to legislation dealing with any of these "rights" is "to render automatically suspect every statutory classification made by state legislatures in dealing with matters which today occupy a substantial portion of their time and attention." In this regard, it must be noted that many, if not all, of these rights could, within the *Rodriguez* formulation of fundamental rights, be deemed implicitly guaranteed in most state constitutions, thereby requiring application of the strict scrutiny test-a result which the defendants say is certain to wreak havoc with the ability of state legislatures to deal effectively with such critical governmental services. To conclude that education is a right so fundamental as to require strict scrutiny analysis would, the defendants say, likely render unconstitutional a substantial portion of the statutes, bylaws and practices that regulate education in Maryland. The defendants advance the further suggestion that if there must be, as the trial judge held, a compelling State interest that would justify deviation from mathematically exact dollar per pupil equality among all of the school districts, intradistrict disparities between areas, schools and even classes within schools in the same county could not be sustained. Similarly, if the right to education is fundamental, it is suggested that the State would be required to show a compelling interest for maintaining any differences among the State's school districts, even if the differences were not financial.

We recognize, as do all the school finance cases, the vital role public education plays in our society. And we share the view expressed in *Lujan, supra,* that education "can be a major factor in an individual's chances for economic and social success as well as a unique influence on a child's development as a good citizen and on his future participation in political and community life." Nevertheless, we conclude that education is not a fundamental right for purposes of equal protection analysis under Art. 24 of the Declaration of Rights.

We decline to adopt the overly simplistic articulation of the fundamental rights test set forth in *Rodriguez, i.e.,* that the existence of a fundamental right is determined by whether it is explicitly or implicitly guaranteed in the constitution. Maryland's Constitution explicitly, not to mention implicitly, guarantees rights and interests which can in no way be considered "fundamental."

The directive contained in Article VIII of the Maryland Constitution for the establishment and maintenance of a thorough and efficient statewide system of free public schools is not alone sufficient to elevate education to fundamental status. Nor do the budgetary provisions of § 52 of Article III of the Constitution require that we declare that the right to education is fundamental. The right to an adequate education in Maryland is no more fundamental than the right to personal security, to fire protection, to welfare subsidies, to health care or like vital governmental services; accordingly, strict scrutiny is not the proper standard of review of the Maryland system of financing its public schools.

Plaintiffs next argue that "heightened review" is the appropriate standard for determining the constitutionality of Maryland's system of public school finance under Art. 24 of the Declaration of Rights because the system affects important personal rights to education and significantly interferes with or denies the exercise of such rights. Under this standard, as *Waldron* points out, a legislative classification must rest upon some ground of difference having a fair and substantial relationship to the object of the legislation. If this standard of review is applicable, it would, for reasons set forth hereinafter in considering the legislative purpose underlying the Maryland system of public school finance, satisfy the requirements of the "heightened review" test, *i.e.,* the means of financing the public school system do bear a fair and substantial relationship to the legitimate goal of providing an adequate education for all children, while at the same time maintaining the viability of local control. We hold, however, that the heightened review test is not applicable in this case because, as we have already observed, there has been no significant interference with, infringement upon, or deprivation of the underlying right to take advantage of a thorough and efficient education under Art. VIII of the Maryland Constitution.

Although the General Assembly has never explicitly stated the object of its public school financing system, it is readily apparent that a primary objective is to establish and maintain a substantial measure of local control over the local public school systems-control exercised at the local level through influencing the determination of how much money should be raised for the local schools and how that money should be spent. We think the legislative objective of preserving and promoting local control over education is both a legitimate state interest and one to which the present financing system is reasonably related. Utilizing property taxation to partly finance Maryland schools is, therefore, rationally related to effectuating local control over public schools. As the court stated in *Lujan*:

> "The use of local taxes affords a school district the freedom to devote more money toward educating its children than is otherwise available in the state-guaranteed minimum amount. It also enables the local citizenry greater influence and participation in the decision making process as to how these local tax dollars are spent. Some communities might place heavy emphasis on schools, while others may desire greater police or fire protection, or improved streets or public transportation. Finally, local control provides each district with the opportunity for experimentation, innovation, and a healthy competition for educational excellence."

HORTON v. MESKILL
376 A.2d 359 (Conn. 1977)

HOUSE, C. J.

As other courts have recognized, educational equalization cases are "in significant aspects sui generis" and not subject to analysis by accepted conventional tests or the application of mechanical standards. The wealth discrimination found among school districts differs materially from the usual equal protection case where a fairly defined indigent class suffers discrimination to its peculiar disadvantage. The discrimination is relative rather than absolute. Further, the children living in towns with relatively low assessable property values are afforded public education but, as the trial court found, the education they receive is to a substantial degree narrower and lower in quality than that which pupils receive in comparable towns with a larger tax base and greater ability to finance education. True, the state has mandated local provision for a basic educational program with local option for a program of higher quality but, as the trial court's finding indicates, that option to a town which lacks the resources to implement the higher quality educational program which it desires and which is available to property-richer towns is highly illusory. As Mr. Justice Marshall put it in his dissent in Rodriguez: "(T)his Court has never suggested that because some 'adequate' level of benefits is provided to all, discrimination in the provision of services is therefore constitutionally excusable. The Equal Protection Clause is not addressed to the minimal sufficiency but rather to the unjustifiable inequalities of state action. It mandates nothing less than that 'all persons similarly circumstanced shall be treated alike.'" With justification, the trial court found merit to the complaints of the plaintiffs about "the sheer irrationality" of the state's system of financing education in the state on the basis of property values, noting that their argument "'would be similar and no less tenable should the state make educational expenditures dependent upon some other irrelevant factor, such as the number of telephone poles in the district.'"

We find our thinking to be substantially in accord with the decisions of the New Jersey Supreme Court in Robinson v. Cahill and the California Supreme Court in Serrano v. Priest, (Serrano II), and whether we apply the "fundamentality" test adopted by Rodriguez or the pre-Rodriguez test under our state constitution (as the California Supreme Court did in Serrano II) or the "arbitrary" test applied by the New Jersey Supreme Court in Robinson v. Cahill, we must conclude that in Connecticut the right to education is so basic and fundamental that any infringement of that right must be strictly scrutinized.

"Connecticut has for centuries recognized it as her right and duty to provide for the proper education of the young." Education is so important that the state has made it compulsory through a requirement of attendance. The General Assembly has by word, if not by deed, recognized...that it is the concern of the state that "each child shall have...equal opportunity to receive a suitable program of educational experiences." Indeed the concept of equality is expressly embodied in the constitutional provision for distribution of the school fund in the provision (article eighth, s 4) that the fund "shall be inviolably appropriated to the support and encouragement of the public schools throughout the state, and for the equal benefit of all the people thereof."

The present-day problem arises from the circumstance that over the years there has arisen a great disparity in the ability of local communities to finance local education, which has given rise to a consequent significant disparity in the quality of education available to the youth of the state. It was well stated in the memorandum of decision of the trial court, which noted that the "present method (of financing education in the state) is the result of legislation in which the state delegates to municipalities of disparate financial capability the state's duty of raising funds for operating public schools within that municipality. That legislation gives no consideration to the financial capability of the municipality to raise funds sufficient to discharge another duty delegated to the municipality by the state, that of educating the children within that municipality. The evidence in this case is that, as a result of this duty-delegating to Canton without regard to Canton's financial capabilities, pupils in Canton receive an education that is in a substantial degree lower in both breadth and quality than that received by pupils in municipalities with a greater financial capability, even though there is no difference between the constitutional duty of the state to the children in Canton and the constitutional duty of the state to the children in other towns."

We conclude that without doubt the trial court correctly held that, in Connecticut, elementary and secondary education is a fundamental right, that pupils in the public schools are entitled to the equal enjoyment of that right, and that the state system of financing public elementary and secondary education as it presently exists and operates cannot pass the test of "strict judicial scrutiny" as to its constitutionality. These were the basic legal conclusions reached by the court.

While the development of an appropriate legislative plan is not without its complexities, the problem is not insoluble. Nor do we share the alarm expressed in the dissenting opinion at what it concludes are "the implications of the decision" as requiring total state financing of education, loss of local administrative control over educational decisions and the requirement that education in all towns "be brought up to the Darien standard" which, if it occurred, the trial court found would require an increase of $313,000,000 over the amounts being currently expended. To the contrary, as we have noted, the trial court expressly found that none of these consequences would of necessity follow the adoption by the state of a financing program designed to achieve a substantial degree of equality of educational opportunity and permit all towns to exercise a meaningful choice as to educational services to be offered to students, that the property tax is still a viable means of producing income for education, and that there is no reason why local control needs to be diminished in any degree merely because some system other than the one presently in effect is adopted. We find no reason to reject the validity of these findings. Obviously, absolute equality or precisely equal advantages are not required and cannot be attained except in the most relative sense. Logically, the state may recognize differences in educational costs based on relevant economic and educational factors and on course offerings of special interest in diverse communities. None of the basic alternative plans to equalize the ability of various towns to finance education requires that all towns spend the same amount for the education of each pupil. The very uncertainty of the extent of the nexus between dollar input and quality of educational opportunity requires allowance for variances as do individual and group disadvantages and local conditions.

VINCENT v. VOIGHT
614 N.W.2d 388 (Wis. 2000)

CROOKS, J.

A majority of this court holds that Wisconsin students have a fundamental right to an equal opportunity for a sound basic education. An equal opportunity for a sound basic education is one that will equip students for their roles as citizens and enable them to succeed economically and personally. The legislature has articulated a standard for equal opportunity for a sound basic education in Wis. Stat. §§ 118.30(lg)(a) and 121.02(L) (1997-98) as the opportunity for students to be proficient in mathematics, science, reading and writing, geography, and history, and to receive instruction in the arts and music, vocational training, social sciences, health, physical education and foreign language, in accordance with their age and aptitude. An equal opportunity for a sound basic education acknowledges that students and districts are not fungible and takes into account districts with disproportionate numbers of disabled students, economically disadvantaged students, and students with limited English language skills. So long as the legislature is providing sufficient resources so that school districts offer students the equal opportunity for a sound basic education as required by the constitution, the state school finance system will pass constitutional muster.

We conclude that the school finance system articulated in Wis. Stat. ch. 121 is constitutional under both art. X, § 3 and art. I, § 1 of the Wisconsin Constitution. The Petitioners have not shown beyond a reasonable doubt that the current school financing system violates either art. X, § 3, or art. I, § 1, and therefore, they have not made out a prima facie case in support of their motion for summary judgment.

ABRAHAMSON, C. J., concurring in part and dissenting in part.

The framers of the Wisconsin Constitution recognized the importance of education when they created article X governing the establishment and funding of public schools. Creating a system of free and uniform public schools was considered to be among the most essential of the framers' tasks. Throughout the 1846 and 1848 conventions, the framers expressed the desire that all of Wisconsin's students, rich and poor, would be educated together in the public schools. For example, the requirement in article X, § 4 that localities contribute to school funding was included "directly for the advantage of the poor," because it increased the commitment to local schools. Without local support "the common schools languished, and select schools rose on their ruins."

Article X read as a whole demonstrates that the framers intended to require the legislature to create and finance a school system that is equitable and uniform in character throughout the state and that provides equal educational opportunity for all students.

The constitution "virtually declares that public education is a state power and function, based upon the well-established principle that the whole state is interested in the education of the children of the state and that this function must be exercised by the people as a whole...." The framers believed that the creation of free and uniform public schools was "the only system on which we could depend for the preservation of our liberties." The legislature has recognized that "education is a state function" and that "the state must guarantee that a basic educational opportunity be available to each pupil."

The framers of the Wisconsin Constitution did not intend the school districts' boundaries to be uniform and therefore could not have envisioned the school districts' taxing and spending capacity to be uniform, since taxing and spending ability and school district boundaries are related. But the state school finance system must provide districts and schools with the funding needed to meet the constitutional mandate. The record, which is undisputed, shows that school districts vary widely in the amount spent per student (ranging from $13,534 to $5,301), in the ability to raise dollars for every mill levied, and in the actual levy rates.

The plaintiff-intervenors, the Wisconsin Education Association Council and a number of teachers and school administrators from school districts across the state, assert that the state school finance system is unconstitutional because it does not allow districts with significant numbers of high needs students to offer these students an adequate educational opportunity. High needs students include disabled children, economically disadvantaged children and children with limited skills in the English language. The State's brief concedes, as it must, that it probably costs more per child to educate high needs students.

A non-uniform education can result from treating similarly situated students and school districts differently, but it can also result from treating differently situated students and school districts in the same way. Consequently, to ensure that all students have an opportunity for a sound basic education, school districts with a disproportionate number of high needs students must be provided with extra financial resources to meet the standard that is constitutionally required.

Because the state school finance system fails to address the costs of educating high needs students, the plaintiff-intervenors argue that schools or school districts with a disproportionate number of such students are not able to provide anywhere near the educational opportunities of other schools or school districts. While the state school finance system especially fails property-poor school districts with disproportionate numbers of high needs students, the plaintiff-intervenors assert that even property-rich school districts that have disproportionate numbers of high needs students, such as Madison, are unable to offer educational opportunities that are uniform with the rest of the state. School districts with large numbers of high needs students may have to divert funds to pay for the higher costs associated with the high needs students, leaving the other students at a disadvantage.

Although I realize that equal dollars do not necessarily translate to equal educational opportunity, it is clear that substantial funding differences may significantly affect students' opportunities to learn. Money is not the only variable affecting educational opportunity, but it is one that the legislature can equalize.

Both the circuit court and court of appeals acknowledged that they were unable to adequately adjudicate this case because of the lack of a developed standard from this court regarding the requirements of article X, § 3. I would remand the cause to the circuit court for further proceedings in light of the standard the majority opinion sets forth in the present case to determine whether the defendants have met their constitutional obligation.

SYKES, J., concurring in part; dissenting in part.

I agree with the majority's conclusion that the state school finance system is not unconstitutional under Wis. Const. art. X, § 3, the uniformity clause of the education article, or Wis. Const. art. I, § 1, the Equal Protection Clause. Therefore, I join sections I and III of the opinion, as well as the decision to affirm. However, I cannot agree with sections II and V of the majority opinion, which announce an expansive new state constitutional right under art. X, § 3 to "an equal opportunity for a sound basic education," defined as an education "that will equip students for their roles as citizens and enable them to succeed economically and personally."

The petitioners allege that the current school finance formula violates the uniformity clause of the education article as well as the Equal Protection Clause of the Wisconsin Constitution by creating or failing to redress alleged educational disparities in so-called "property-poor" districts, districts with many high-needs children, and districts where charter schools and the school choice program decrease the enrollment in the public schools.

Any definition of education or standard for educational adequacy is inherently a political and policy question, not a justiciable one. The people of this state-through their elected representatives in the legislature, the governor's office and local school boards-decide what their schools will teach and how much education is adequate or desirable for their children. What constitutes an "adequate" or "sound" or even "basic" education is most emphatically not a question of constitutional law for this or any other court.

There is certainly nothing in the text of art. X, § 3 to support such a conclusion. Wisconsin Const. art. X, § 3 provides:

> The legislature shall provide by law for the establishment of district schools, which shall be as nearly uniform as practicable; and such schools shall be free and without charge for tuition to all children between the ages of 4 and 20 years.

The newly-minted constitutional right is as follows: "Wisconsin students have a fundamental right to an equal opportunity for a sound basic education. An equal opportunity for a sound basic education is one that will equip students for their roles as citizens and enable them to succeed economically and personally." The new right to education includes "the opportunity for students to be proficient in mathematics, science, reading and writing, geography, and history, and for them to receive instruction in the arts and music, vocational training, social sciences, health, physical education and foreign language, in accordance with their age and aptitude." There is more: "An equal opportunity for a sound basic education acknowledges that students and districts are not fungible and takes into account districts with disproportionate numbers of disabled students, economically disadvantaged students, and students with limited English language skills." And the legislature must henceforward provide "sufficient resources" to meet the new standard; otherwise, it will be in violation of art. X, § 3.

The problem with all of this is that there is no support for it anywhere in the text of the Wisconsin Constitution. It is entirely the product of judicial invention, despite efforts to tie some parts of the standard to particular statutory enactments. This may be fine education policy, and as a parent and a citizen I certainly support the educational aspirations and goals expressed by the new standard, as well as the requirement that schools include instruction in the specified curricular subject areas. But as a judge, I am compelled to say as forcefully as I can that the court's exercise in education clause standard-writing has nothing whatsoever to do with constitutional law.

My conclusion is based upon the text of art. X, § 3, the obvious lack of judicially discoverable or manageable standards for educational adequacy, and the impossibility of deciding the issue without undertaking an initial, clearly nonjudicial policy determination.

NOTE

Whether before 1989 or after, claimants who prevailed on state law equal protection grounds were the exception that proved the rule: Most of these claims failed. One problem with this theory of unconstitutionality, as with many federal and state equal protection claims, is the all-or-nothing-at-all nature of tiers of review. For many state courts, applying strict or intermediate review to all manner of educational policy decisions – including what subjects are offered, when classes are taught and what sports teams are available – was a bridge too far, establishing a level of scrutiny that was too difficult for States and local governments to satisfy. Yet at the same time, applying rational basis review created a level of scrutiny that was too easy for States to satisfy. Another problem, one to which we will return at the end of this chapter, concerned remedy. Even when the claimants managed to win under this theory, the courts struggled to identify meaningful and realistic remedies for closing the equity gap. Some remedies effectively required a statewide school-funding system that precluded local school districts from supplementing state aid. Others required a system that came to the same result, one that set a floor and a ceiling on educational spending. Still another obstacle to litigation success in these cases is that state legislatures after *Rodriguez* increasingly removed the most problematic disparity-causing features of their systems of funding public schools. In particular, they adopted school-funding equalization formulas that to one degree or another sought to ameliorate, though not eliminate, funding disparities.

C. ADEQUACY DECISIONS

Many of the obstacles faced by the equal protection cases prompted a second wave of state-court lawsuits. From 1989 to the present, claimants in this area frequently have seized on a different theory of unconstitutionality. Instead of focusing on equal protection and equity problems, as the claimants in *Rodriguez, Serrano* and the above cases did, these plaintiffs rely on unique state constitutional provisions that have no counterpart in the United States Constitution. Many States for example have provisions in their constitutions requiring the legislature to create a "thorough and efficient system of common schools." *See* Ohio Const. art. VI, §2; Md. Const. art. VIII, §1; W. Va Const. art. XII, §1; N.J. Const. art. VIII, §4, ¶ 1. Other state constitutions contain similar provisions, requiring the legislature to create a "uniform" system of public schools, Wis. Const. art. X, §3; N.D. Const. §148; N.C. Const. art. IX, §2; Ind. Const. art. 8, §1, a "quality" system of public schools, Mont. Const. art. X, §1, cl. 3; Va. Const. art. VIII, §1, a system of "free instruction," Neb. Const. art. VII, §1, or free "common schools," N.Y. Const. art. XI, §1, Cal. Const. art. IX, §5. While some of the equity decisions looked to these provisions in deciding whether the state recognized a fundamental right to education, they generally did not use the provisions to determine the adequacy of the state system. Relying on these provisions, recent school-funding claimants have placed less emphasis on the equity gap between property-poor and property-wealthy school districts, targeting instead the States' methods for determining the *adequacy* of the education they were guaranteeing to all children and families within their jurisdiction. At the core of these lawsuits is the contention that a State's legislative commitment to equalize educational opportunities by guaranteeing to fund a base level education, no matter how little revenue a local school district can raise on its own, came to little if the state-guaranteed funding level was too low. The objective of these lawsuits, then, was to rationalize and eventually to increase the state spending floor. In contrast to the first wave of litigation in this area, plaintiffs won nearly two-thirds of these lawsuits between 1989 and 2008. Rebell, at 228. As the following cases illustrate, the principal debate in this litigation turns on whether the States' education clauses amount to mere delegations of authority to the state legislatures or whether they also contain judicially enforceable limits on that authority.

EDGEWOOD INDEPENDENT SCHOOL DIST. v. KIRBY
777 S.W.2d 391 (Tex. 1989)

MAUZY, J.

There are approximately three million public school children in Texas. The legislature finances the education of these children through a combination of revenues supplied by the state itself and revenues supplied by local school districts which are governmental subdivisions of the state. Of total education costs, the state provides about forty-two percent, school districts provide about fifty percent, and the remainder comes from various other sources including federal funds. School districts derive revenues from local ad valorem property taxes, and the state raises funds from a variety of sources including the sales tax and various severance and excise taxes.

There are glaring disparities in the abilities of the various school districts to raise revenues from property taxes because taxable property wealth varies greatly from district to district. The wealthiest district has over $14,000,000 of property wealth per student, while the poorest has approximately $20,000; this disparity reflects a 700 to 1 ratio. The 300,000 students in the lowest-wealth schools have less than 3% of the state's property wealth to support their education while the 300,000 students in the highest-wealth schools have over 25% of the state's property wealth; thus the 300,000 students in the wealthiest districts have more than eight times the property value to support their education as the

300,000 students in the poorest districts. The average property wealth in the 100 wealthiest districts is more than twenty times greater than the average property wealth in the 100 poorest districts. Edgewood I.S.D. has $38,854 in property wealth per student; Alamo Heights I.S.D., in the same county, has $570,109 in property wealth per student.

The state has tried for many years to lessen the disparities through various efforts to supplement the poorer districts. Through the Foundation School Program, the state currently attempts to ensure that each district has sufficient funds to provide its students with at least a basic education. Under this program, state aid is distributed to the various districts according to a complex formula such that property-poor districts receive more state aid than do property-rich districts. However, the Foundation School Program does not cover even the cost of meeting the state-mandated minimum requirements. Most importantly, there are no Foundation School Program allotments for school facilities or for debt service. The basic allotment and the transportation allotment understate actual costs, and the career ladder salary supplement for teachers is underfunded. For these reasons and more, almost all school districts spend additional local funds. Low-wealth districts use a significantly greater proportion of their local funds to pay the debt service on construction bonds while high-wealth districts are able to use their funds to pay for a wide array of enrichment programs.

Because of the disparities in district property wealth, spending per student varies widely, ranging from $2,112 to $19,333. Under the existing system, an average of $2,000 more per year is spent on each of the 150,000 students in the wealthiest districts than is spent on the 150,000 students in the poorest districts.

The lower expenditures in the property-poor districts are not the result of lack of tax effort. Generally, the property-rich districts can tax low and spend high while the property-poor districts must tax high merely to spend low.

Property-poor districts are trapped in a cycle of poverty from which there is no opportunity to free themselves. Because of their inadequate tax base, they must tax at significantly higher rates in order to meet minimum requirements for accreditation; yet their educational programs are typically inferior. The location of new industry and development is strongly influenced by tax rates and the quality of local schools. Thus, the property-poor districts with their high tax rates and inferior schools are unable to attract new industry or development and so have little opportunity to improve their tax base.

The amount of money spent on a student's education has a real and meaningful impact on the educational opportunity offered that student. High-wealth districts are able to provide for their students broader educational experiences including more extensive curricula, more up-to-date technological equipment, better libraries and library personnel, teacher aides, counseling services, lower student-teacher ratios, better facilities, parental involvement programs, and drop-out prevention programs. They are also better able to attract and retain experienced teachers and administrators.

Article VII, section 1 of the Texas Constitution provides:

> A general diffusion of knowledge being essential to the preservation of the liberties and rights of the people, it shall be the duty of the Legislature of the State to establish and make suitable provision for the support and maintenance of an efficient system of public free schools.

This is not an area in which the Constitution vests exclusive discretion in the legislature; rather the language of article VII, section 1 imposes on the legislature an affirmative duty to establish and provide for the public free schools. This duty is not committed unconditionally to the legislature's discretion, but instead is accompanied by standards. By express constitutional mandate, the legislature must make "suitable" provision for an "efficient" system for the "essential" purpose of a "general diffusion of knowledge." While these are admittedly not precise terms, they do provide a standard by which this court must, when called upon to do so, measure the constitutionality of the legislature's actions.

There is no reason to think that "efficient" meant anything different in 1875 from what it now means. "Efficient" conveys the meaning of effective or productive of results and connotes the use of resources so as to produce results with little waste; this meaning does not appear to have changed over time.

If our state's population had grown at the same rate in each district and if the taxable wealth in each district had also grown at the same rate, efficiency could probably have been maintained within the structure of the present system. That did not happen. Wealth, in its many forms, has not appeared with geographic symmetry. The economic development of the state has not been uniform. Some cities have grown dramatically, while their sister communities have remained static or have shrunk. Formulas that once fit have been knocked askew. Although local conditions vary, the constitutionally imposed state responsibility for an efficient education system is the same for all citizens regardless of where they live.

We conclude that, in mandating "efficiency," the constitutional framers and ratifiers did not intend a system with such vast disparities as now exist. Instead, they stated clearly that the purpose of an efficient system was to provide for a "*general* diffusion of knowledge." (Emphasis added.) The present system, by contrast, provides not for a diffusion that is general, but for one that is limited and unbalanced. The resultant inequalities are thus directly contrary to the constitutional vision of efficiency.

The legislature's recent efforts have focused primarily on increasing the state's contributions. More money allocated under the present system would reduce some of the existing disparities between districts but would at best only postpone the reform that is necessary to make the system efficient. A band-aid will not suffice; the system itself must be changed.

We hold that the state's school financing system is neither financially efficient nor efficient in the sense of providing for a "general diffusion of knowledge" statewide, and therefore that it violates article VII, section 1 of the Texas Constitution. Efficiency does not require a per capita distribution, but it also does not allow concentrations of resources in property-rich school districts that are taxing low when property-poor districts that are taxing high cannot generate sufficient revenues to meet even minimum standards. There must be a direct and close correlation between a district's tax effort and the educational resources available to it; in other words, districts must have substantially equal access to similar revenues per pupil at similar levels of tax effort. Children who live in poor districts and children who live in rich districts must be afforded a substantially equal opportunity to have access to educational funds. Certainly, this much is required if the state is to educate its populace efficiently and provide for a general diffusion of knowledge statewide.

Although we have ruled the school financing system to be unconstitutional, we do not now instruct the legislature as to the specifics of the legislation it should enact; nor do we order it to raise taxes. The legislature has primary responsibility to decide how best to achieve an efficient system. We decide only the nature of the constitutional mandate and whether that mandate has been met. Because we hold that the mandate of efficiency has not been met, we reverse the judgment of the court of appeals. The legislature is duty-bound to provide for an efficient system of education, and only if the legislature fulfills that duty can we launch this great state into a strong economic future with educational opportunity for all.

DeROLPH v. STATE
677 N.E.2d 733 (Ohio 1997)

SWEENEY, J.

Section 2, Article VI of the Ohio Constitution requires the *state* to provide and fund a system of public education and includes an explicit directive to the General Assembly:

"The general assembly shall make such provisions, by taxation, or otherwise, as, with the income arising from the school trust fund, will secure a thorough and efficient system of common schools throughout the State ...."

The delegates to the 1850-1851 Constitutional Convention recognized that it was the *state's* duty to both present and future generations of Ohioans to establish a framework for a "full, complete and efficient system of public education." Thus, throughout their discussions, the delegates stressed the importance of education and reaffirmed the policy that education shall be afforded to every child in the state regardless of race or economic standing. Furthermore, the delegates were concerned that the education to be provided to our youth not be mediocre but be as perfect as could humanly be devised. These debates reveal the delegates' strong belief that it is the *state's* obligation, through the General Assembly, to provide for the full education of all children within the state.

In addition to deteriorating buildings and related conditions, it is clear from the record that many of the school districts throughout the state cannot provide the basic resources necessary to educate our youth. For instance, many of the appellant school districts have insufficient funds to purchase textbooks and must rely on old, outdated books. For some classes, there were no textbooks at all.

The accessibility of everyday supplies is also a problem, forcing schools to ration such necessities as paper, chalk, art supplies, paper clips, and even toilet paper. A system without basic instructional materials and supplies can hardly constitute a thorough and efficient system of common schools throughout the state as mandated by our Constitution.

Additionally, many districts lack sufficient funds to comply with the state law requiring a district-wide average of no more than twenty-five students for each classroom teacher. Indeed, some schools have more than thirty students per classroom teacher, with one school having as many as thirty-nine students in one sixth grade class. As the testimony of educators established, it is virtually impossible for students to receive an adequate education with a student-teacher ratio of this magnitude.

All the facts documented in the record lead to one inescapable conclusion – Ohio's elementary and secondary public schools are neither thorough nor efficient. The operation of the appellant school districts conflicts with the historical notion that the education of our youth is of utmost concern and that Ohio children should be educated adequately so that they are able to participate fully in society. Our state Constitution was drafted with the importance of education in mind. In contrast, education under the legislation being reviewed ranks miserably low in the state's priorities. In fact, the formula amount is established after the legislature determines the total dollars to be allocated to primary and secondary education in each biennial budget. Consequently, the present school financing system contravenes the clear wording of our Constitution and the framers' intent.

Furthermore, rather than following the constitutional dictate that it is the *state's* obligation to fund education (as this opinion has repeatedly underscored), the legislature has thrust the majority of responsibility upon local school districts. This, too, is contrary to the clear wording of our Constitution. The responsibility for maintaining a thorough and efficient school system falls upon the state. When a district falls short of the constitutional requirement that the system be thorough and efficient, it is the state's obligation to rectify it.

We also reject the notion that the wide disparities in educational opportunity are caused by the poorer school districts' failure to pass levies. The evidence reveals that the wide disparities are caused by the funding system's overreliance on the tax base of individual school districts. What this means is that the poor districts simply cannot raise as much money even with identical tax effort.

We recognize that disparities between school districts will always exist. By our decision today, we are not stating that a new financing system must provide equal educational opportunities for all. In a Utopian society, this lofty goal would be realized. We, however, appreciate the limitations imposed upon us. Nor do we advocate a "Robin Hood" approach to school financing reform. We are not suggesting that funds be diverted from wealthy districts and given to the less fortunate. There is no "leveling down" component in our decision today.

Moreover, in no way should our decision be construed as imposing spending ceilings on more affluent school districts. School districts are still free to augment their programs if they choose to do so. However, it is futile to lay the entire blame for the inadequacies of the present system on the taxpayers and the local boards of education. Although some districts have the luxury of deciding where to allocate extra dollars, many others have the burden of deciding which educational programs to cut or what financial institution to contact to obtain yet another emergency loan. Our state Constitution makes the state responsible for educating our youth. Thus, the state should not shirk its obligation by espousing cliches about "local control."

We recognize that money alone is not the panacea that will transform Ohio's school system into a model of excellence. Although a student's success depends upon numerous factors besides money, we must ensure that there is enough money that students have the chance to succeed because of the educational opportunity provided, not in spite of it. Such an opportunity requires, at the very least, that all of Ohio's children attend schools which are safe and conducive to learning. At the present, Ohio does not provide many of its students with even the most basic of educational needs.

MOYER, C.J., dissenting.

Only infrequently are the members of this court required to balance our appreciation for the principle of separation of powers among the three branches of government against our desire to use the considerable powers of this court to mandate action to improve the imperfect. The issue in this very important case is not whether education in Ohio should be better. All seven members of this court would agree that in an ideal school setting, all children would be taught in well-maintained school buildings by teachers with high salaries and would read from the latest-edition school books. Rather, the question presented is whether specific financing statutes adopted by the Ohio General Assembly violate the words and intent of the Ohio Constitution. By its words, the Constitution requires the General Assembly to "make such provisions, by taxation or otherwise, as...will secure a thorough and efficient system of common schools throughout the state." We find that the statutes withstand plaintiffs' constitutional challenge because, rather than abdicating its duty, the General Assembly has made provisions by the challenged statutes for funding a system of schools with minimum standards throughout the state. The issues of the level and method of funding, and thereby the quality of the system, are committed by the Constitution to the collective will of the people through the legislative branch.

One cannot disagree with the aspirations of the majority to provide a school system that enables children to "participate fully in society," that provides "high quality educational opportunities," and that "allows its citizens to fully develop their human potential." However, the majority relies upon the phrase "thorough and efficient" to declare Ohio's education financing system unconstitutional despite the fact that our Constitution commits the responsibility for ascribing meaning to the phrase "thorough and efficient" to the General Assembly and not to this court. The majority of this court, moreover, apparently interprets the Constitution as requiring that all schools be of the same undefined level of high quality without relying on any supporting text of the Constitution, and equates imperfect schools with an unconstitutional system of funding. We disagree with these conclusions.

We conclude that the question of what level of funding satisfies the constitutional standard of a "thorough and efficient" system of education is a question of quality that revolves around policy choices and value judgments constitutionally committed to the General Assembly. We conclude that defining a "thorough and efficient" system of education financing is a nonjusticiable question.

Such restraint should be exercised only after the court has decided a threshold justiciable issue, that is, whether the General Assembly has made provision by taxation or otherwise to secure a thorough and efficient system of schools. In view of the clear intention of the delegates to the Constitutional Convention of 1851, the words of the Constitution and the agreement among the parties to this case that all plaintiff school districts have met the minimum standards set by the State Department of Education, we conclude that the justiciable question has been answered in favor of the defendants.

Although we may personally favor it, it is not this court's place to order the General Assembly to give education "high priority" in its budget allocations, any more than it is our place to set policy or prioritize the allocation of funds to other state programs. Members of the legislative branch represent the collective will of the citizens of Ohio, and the manner in which public schools are funded in this state is a fundamental policy decision that is within the power of its citizens to change. Under our system of government, decisions such as imposing new taxes, allocating public revenues to competing uses, and formulating educational standards are not within the judiciary's authority.

In that determinations of educational funding adequacy and quality are inherently fluid, we believe that the majority's well-intentioned willingness to enter this fray today will only necessitate more comprehensive judicial involvement tomorrow as educational theories and goals evolve, conditions throughout the state change, and the General Assembly responds. The experiences of other states provide ample proof of the troubled history of litigation that ensues when the judiciary deems itself to be the ultimate authority in setting educational funding mechanisms and standards[.] [Many] cases from other states [confirm] the grim reality of a state supreme court involving itself in setting minimum educational standards, which has resulted in years of protracted litigation, ultimately placing the courts in the position of determining state taxation methods, budgetary priorities, and educational policy.

Plaintiffs stipulated in the trial court that they were all in compliance with state minimum standards on their most recent scheduled evaluations. In that "an Ohio Administrative Code section is a further arm, extension, or explanation of statutory intent implementing a statute passed by the General Assembly," it follows that those plaintiff schools met the standard of adequacy established by the General Assembly at that time. Plaintiffs did not prove that compliance with the minimum standards then in effect was insufficient to provide an adequate education. Plaintiffs did not attempt to prove that any graduate of any of the plaintiff school districts had been refused entrance to college because his or her diploma was unacceptable. No Ohio school was shown to have been denied accreditation. Plaintiffs did not prove that any Ohio child was without a school to attend.

In the absence of proof of a constitutional violation, the fact that hard problems require hard solutions does not justify judicial second-guessing of the educational funding system established by the General Assembly. Regardless of the appeal of plaintiffs' policy arguments before this court, their arguments are simply addressed to the wrong branch of government. Those who believe that the Education Clause should be changed have procedures available to them by which the Constitution can be amended.

Our dissent should not be viewed as an endorsement of the status quo. However, in the absence of a showing that the statutes in question violate the Constitution, responsibility for correcting the funding of Ohio's educational system does not rest with this court.

DeROLPH v. STATE
754 N.E.2d 1184 (Ohio 2001)

MOYER, C.J.

Since it was first docketed in this court in 1995, this dispute has produced from this court no fewer than three signed majority opinions, a *per curiam* opinion, eleven separate concurrences and dissents, and a number of rulings on motions filed by plaintiffs and defendants. Every justice of the court has expressed her and his views regarding the constitutional issue that once again is presented for our disposition nearly six years after the court exercised its discretionary jurisdiction to review the merits. The written opinions of the justices reflect deeply held beliefs regarding the responsibility of the court as an institution and the principles that define the framework by which each justice decides issues brought to the court. The informal and formal discussions among the justices regarding the jurisdictional and merit issues have been of an intensity and duration unmatched by any other case.

The range of the opinions that reflect the decisional process is broad …. Despite our differences, however, we all agree upon the fundamental importance of education to the children and citizens of this state. Educated, informed citizens sustain the vitality of our democratic institutions…. We agree regarding the goals of public education; we have vigorously disagreed with respect to whether the legislature or the judiciary has the ultimate authority to determine if the goals have been achieved.

The current plan for funding public primary and secondary education adopted by the General Assembly and signed by the Governor is probably not the plan that any one of us would have created were it our responsibility to do so. But that is not our burden, and it is not the test we apply in this decision. None of us is completely comfortable with the decision we announce in this opinion. But we have responded to a duty that is intrinsic to our position as justices on the highest court of the state. Drawing upon our own instincts and the wisdom of Thomas Jefferson, we have reached the point where, while continuing to hold our previously expressed opinions, the greater good requires us to recognize "the necessity of sacrificing our opinions sometimes to the opinions of others for the sake of harmony."

A climate of legal, financial, and political uncertainty concerning Ohio's school-funding system has prevailed at least since this court accepted jurisdiction of the case. We have concluded that no one is served by continued uncertainty and fractious debate. In that spirit, we have created the consensus that should terminate the role of this court in the dispute.

Despite the extensive efforts of the defendants to produce a plan that meets the requirements announced by this court, changes to the formula are required to make the new plan constitutional:

> Base Cost Formula: H.B. 94 recalculates the cost of providing an adequate education to be $4,814 per student in fiscal year 2002. The base cost formula uses one hundred twenty-seven model school districts as a basis for determining base cost support. That number of school districts is achieved by screening out districts in the top and bottom five percent of all Ohio districts based on income and property wealth from the state's pool of the one hundred seventy top-performing districts. Also included within this number are several districts that did not meet twenty of twenty-seven performance standards, but were included regardless because of a rounding procedure included within H.B. 94. R.C. 3317.012(B)(1), last paragraph. As the plaintiffs note, rounding and wealth screens include districts that should not be considered in the base cost formula and exclude districts that should be considered. Plaintiffs' arguments and our review of the record convince us that the formula must be modified to include the top five percent districts and the lower five percent districts, and by considering only those districts that *actually* meet twenty of twenty-seven performance standards without rounding. We make no determination regarding the time in which the state must calculate and implement actual changes in the amount of funds distributed to each district pursuant to today's order, but the new calculations must be applied retroactive to July 1, 2001, and to the subsequent years designated in R.C. 3317.012. Moreover, in determining future biennial budgets through fiscal year 2007, the rate of millage charged off as the local share of base cost funding under divisions (A)(1) and (2) of R.C. 3317.022 may not be changed from twenty-three mills, irrespective of the language of R.C. 3317.012(D)(4) suggesting such a methodology.

> The H.B. 94 model calculates its base cost amount using spending data for FY96, adjusted for inflation, or actual FY99 expenditure data, whichever is lower. The state uses the lower of the two figures to compensate for what it terms an "echo effect," or to adjust for districts that spent more than what was actually needed at the base level, due to line-item expenditures, other state funding outside of the foundation formula, and local enhancement revenues. The model districts subject to lowering of their base cost are those that the state

determined to be model districts in 1996. As the plaintiffs' experts observed, there has been insufficient evidence presented by the state to justify lowering the base cost amount to adjust for this supposed echo effect. Accordingly, we are persuaded by the plaintiffs that choosing the lower of FY96 expenditures or FY99 actual expenditures is unsupported by the evidence and should not be used to lower the base cost amount figure.

Parity Aid: The parity aid program is a salutary attempt to provide poorer districts with funds similar to those available to wealthier districts that are used to substantially enhance the educational experience of each student. The plan as adopted would fully fund the parity aid program by fiscal year 2006. We have concluded that the parity aid program must be fully funded no later than the beginning of fiscal year 2004.

To summarize, we observe that the state has chosen to retain a foundation program of funding primary and secondary public education. We find that, having so elected, it must, in order to meet the requirements of *DeRolph I* and *DeRolph II,* formulate the base cost of providing an adequate education by using all school districts meeting twenty of twenty-seven performance standards as set forth by the General Assembly in R.C. 3317.012(B)(1)(a) through (aa), without adjustments to exclude districts based on wealth screens, without rounding adjustments to include additional lower-spending districts, and without use of the "echo effect" adjustment, beginning effective July 1, 2001. In addition, the parity aid program established by the General Assembly must be fully funded no later than July 1, 2003.

With full implementation of these modifications to the funding plan adopted by the General Assembly the plan will meet the test for constitutionality created in *DeRolph I* and *DeRolph II*. While the changes will have a fiscal impact, they will not require structural changes to the school foundation program set forth in R.C. Chapter 3317.

One final observation is in order. Historically, the construction and maintenance of school facilities have been considered the responsibility of local school districts. By 1989, the General Assembly had begun addressing school facilities needs and committing funds to construction and repair of school buildings. We have described previously the substantial commitment of the state to the availability of adequate school buildings for every student enrolled in public education. However, the unmet needs are enormous and the time in which it is feasible to meet them is lengthy. We urge the General Assembly to review and consider alternative means of funding school buildings and related facilities.

The state is hereby ordered to implement the changes described above. Because we have no reason to doubt defendants' good faith, we have concluded that there is no reason to retain jurisdiction of the matter before us. If the order receives less than full compliance, interested parties have remedies available to them.

NOTE

In *State v. Lewis*, 99 Ohio St. 97 (2003), the *DeRolph* litigation came to a conclusion, when the Ohio Supreme Court granted a preemptory writ of prohibition to end the ongoing litigation in the trial court.

COLUMBIA FALLS ELEMENTARY SCHOOL DIST. NO. 6
v. STATE
109 P.3d 257 (Mont. 2005)

LEAPHART, J.

The State appeals from the District Court's order determining that the State of Montana's public school system violates Article X, Section 1(3), of the Montana Constitution.

Article X, Section 1(3), of the Montana Constitution mandates that "[t]he legislature shall provide a basic system of free quality public elementary and secondary schools.... It shall fund and distribute in an equitable manner to the school districts the state's share of the cost of the basic elementary and secondary school system." As we have just stated, the Legislature has made an initial policy determination regarding this language. It has created a public school system and a method of funding the system. Although Article X, Section 1(3), is textually committed to the Legislature in the first instance, once the Legislature acts we are not barred from reaching the question of whether the Legislature has fulfilled its constitutional obligation to "provide a basic system of free quality public elementary and secondary schools."

This funding system is not correlated with any understanding of what constitutes a "quality" education. The evidence for this is two-fold. First, as the State admitted at oral argument, in passing HB 667, the Legislature did not undertake a study of what the Public Schools Clause demands of it. That is, it did not seek to define "quality." As stated above, since the Legislature has not defined "quality" as that term is used in Article X, Section 1(3), we cannot conclude that the current funding system was designed to provide a quality education. Second, as found by the District Court, the Legislature, in creating the spending formula of HB 667, did not link the formula to any factors that might constitute a "quality" education.

The District Court found that the "major problems" with HB 667 were: it provided no mechanism to deal with inflation; it did not base its numbers on costs such as teacher pay, meeting accreditation standards, fixed costs, or costs of special education; increases in allowable spending were not tied to costs of increased accreditation standards or content and performance standards; relevant data was already two years old when the bill was passed; and no study was undertaken to justify the disparity in ANB dollars dispensed to high schools as compared to elementary schools. From these credible findings we must conclude that the Legislature did not endeavor to create a school funding system with quality in mind. Unless funding relates to needs such as academic standards, teacher pay, fixed costs, costs of special education, and performance standards, then the funding is not related to the cornerstones of a quality education.

The above analysis is essentially prospective in nature-that is, it states what the Constitution demands of the Legislature and what the Legislature must do to fashion a constitutional education system. Nonetheless, in order to address the Coalition's claims we have to address the *educational product* that the present school system provides, not just the *manner* in which the Legislature funds that school system. Even given the absence of a definition of "quality" education, the District Court's findings demonstrate that whatever legitimate definition of quality that the Legislature may devise, the educational product of the present school system is constitutionally deficient and that the Legislature currently fails to adequately fund Montana's public school system.

The evidence that the current system is constitutionally deficient includes the following unchallenged findings made by the District Court: school districts increasingly budgeting at or near their maximum budget authority; growing accreditation problems; many qualified educators leaving the state to take advantage of higher salaries and benefits offered elsewhere; the cutting of programs; the deterioration of school buildings and inadequate funds for building repair and for new construction; and increased competition for general fund dollars between special and general education.

The State counters by arguing that the District Court should have considered output measures, such as test scores, in determining whether the current system is constitutional, and that under such measures Montana compares very favorably with other states. Indeed, Montana's students often do perform quite well on standardized achievement tests. However, current test scores do not tell the whole story. First of all, a "system" of education includes more than high achievement on standardized tests. We have noted elsewhere, for example, that school districts have an interest in integrating their academic programs with extracurricular activities. Secondly, it may be that test scores are not attributable to the current educational system. The voluminous evidence presented at trial and summarized in the preceding paragraph established that although Montana's students are testing well when compared with students in similar states, there are serious concerns as to whether this level of achievement will continue. With the District Court's findings of fact in mind, it may be that the achievement registered by Montana's students is not *because* of the current educational system.

Therefore, because the Legislature has not defined what "quality" means we cannot conclude that the current system is designed to provide a "quality" education. Article X, Section 1(3), explicitly requires the Legislature to fund a "quality" educational system. Therefore we defer to the Legislature to provide a threshold definition of what the Public Schools Clause requires. We also conclude, however, that given the unchallenged findings made by the District Court, whatever definition the Legislature devises, the current funding system is not grounded in principles of quality, and cannot be deemed constitutionally sufficient.

ABBOTT v. BURKE
971 A.2d 989 (N.J. 2009)

LaVECCHIA, J.

One of the fundamental responsibilities of the State is to provide a public education for its children. The New Jersey Constitution requires that

> [t]he Legislature shall provide for the maintenance and support of a thorough and efficient system of free public schools for the instruction of all the children in the State between the ages of five and eighteen years.

Today we are almost a decade into the twenty-first century, and nearly twenty years have passed since this Court found that the State's system of support for public education was inadequate as applied to pupils in poorer urban districts. Finding that more severely disadvantaged pupils require more resources for their education, the Court held that the State must develop a funding formula that would provide all children, including disadvantaged children in poorer urban districts, with an equal educational opportunity as measured by the Constitution's thorough and efficient clause. A later decision added that the funding needed to be coupled to a set of educational program standards.

Today's decision marks the twentieth opinion or order issued in the course of the Abbott litigation. In the interim, much has changed. There have been significant demographic changes among school districts in terms of the distribution of at-risk pupils and changes in the level of State-provided education funding. The State now maintains that it has heeded our call to create a funding formula based on curriculum content standards and to demonstrate that the formula addresses the needs of disadvantaged students everywhere, thereby achieving constitutional compliance. Therefore, once again we assess the constitutionality of a State school funding system.

This matter is before us on the State's Motion for Review of the Constitutionality of the School Funding Reform Act of 2008 (SFRA), *L. 2007 c. 260 (N.J.S.A.* 18A:7F-43 to -63). The State's motion seeks a declaration that SFRA's funding formula satisfies the requirements of the thorough and efficient education clause of the New Jersey Constitution and that, therefore, the State is released from the Court's prior remedial orders concerning education funding for students in Abbott districts. Specifically, the State asks for elimination of the requirements that Abbott districts be provided parity aid and supplemental funding.

We have reviewed the record, the Special Master's findings and recommendations, and the arguments of the parties. We conclude that SFRA is constitutional, to the extent that this record permitted its review. We therefore hold that SFRA's funding formula may be applied in Abbott districts, with the following caveats. Our finding of constitutionality is premised on the expectation that the State will continue to provide school funding aid during this and the next two years at the levels required by SFRA's formula each year. Our holding further depends on the mandated review of the formula's weights and other operative parts after three years of implementation.

Our approval of SFRA under the State Constitution relies, as it must, on the information currently available. But a state funding formula's constitutionality is not an occurrence at a moment in time; it is a continuing obligation. Today's holding issues in the good faith anticipation of a continued commitment by the Legislature and Executive to address whatever adjustments are necessary to keep SFRA operating at its optimal level. The three year look-back, and the State's adjustments based on that review, will provide more information about the efficacy of this funding formula. There should be no doubt that we would require remediation of any deficiencies of a constitutional dimension, if such problems do emerge.

With that understanding, SFRA may be implemented as it was designed, as a state-wide unitary system of education funding. The State shall not be required to continue separate funding streams mandated under past remedial orders. During the two-year period until the look-back review occurs, we cannot ignore, as a practical matter, the substantial amount of additional funds that will be available from non-SFRA sources for pupils in Abbott districts. The availability of those funds further cushions the transition to SFRA's funding scheme. In sum, although no prediction is without some uncertainty, the record before us convincingly demonstrates that SFRA is designed to provide school districts in this state, including the Abbott school districts, with adequate resources to provide the necessary educational programs consistent with state standards.

For several decades, this Court has superintended the ongoing litigation that carries the name *Abbott v. Burke.*The Court's one goal has been to ensure that the constitutional guarantee of a thorough and efficient system of public education becomes a reality for those students who live in municipalities where there are concentrations of poverty and crime. Every child should have the opportunity for an unhindered start in life-an opportunity to become a productive and contributing citizen to our society.

The legislative and executive branches of government have enacted a funding formula that is designed to achieve a thorough and efficient education for every child, regardless of where he or she lives. On the basis of the record before us, we conclude that SFRA is a constitutionally adequate scheme. There is no absolute guarantee that SFRA will achieve the results desired by all. The political branches of government, however, are entitled to take reasoned steps, even if the outcome cannot be assured, to address the pressing social, economic, and educational challenges confronting our state. They should not be locked in a constitutional straitjacket. SFRA deserves the chance to prove in practice that, as designed, it satisfies the requirements of our constitution.

The State's motion, seeking declarations that SFRA satisfies the requirements of the thorough and efficient clause of Article VIII, section 4, paragraph 1 of the New Jersey Constitution and that the funding formula may be implemented in the Abbott districts, and further seeking an order relieving the State from this Court's prior remedial orders concerning funding to the Abbott districts, is granted. Plaintiffs' cross-motion seeking an order preserving and continuing the status quo concerning enforcement of this Court's prior remedial orders addressing funding to Abbott districts is denied.

NOTES

1. For other cases in which the courts found claims to be non-justiciable, see *Ex parte James*, 836 So.2d 813 (Ala. 2002); *Lewis E. v. Spagnolo*, 710 N.E.2d 798 (Ill. 1999); *Coalition for Adequacy & Fairness in School Funding, Inc. v. Chiles*, 680 So.2d 400 (Fla. 1996); *Nebraska Coalition for Educational Equity & Adequacy v. Heineman*, 731 N.W.2d 164 (Neb. 2007); *Oklahoma Education Ass'n v. State*, 158 P.3d 1058 (Okla. 2007).

2. For other cases in which the courts found claims to be justiciable, see *Brigham v. State*, 889 A.2d 715 (Vt. 2005); *Lake View School Dist. No. 25 of Phillips County v. Huckabee*, 220 S.W.3d 645 (Ark. 2005); *DeRolph v. State*, 677 N.E.2d 733 (Ohio 1997); *Idaho Schools for Equal Educational Opportunity, Inc. v. Evans*, 850 P.2d 724 (Idaho 1993); *Leandro v. State*, 488 S.E.2d 249 (N.C. 1997).

D. SCHOOL UNIFORMITY CLAUSES

In addition to containing "thorough and efficient" clauses, some state constitutions contain school "uniformity" clauses. The Florida Constitution, for example, provides: "Adequate provision shall be made by law for a *uniform*, efficient, safe, secure, and high quality system of free public schools." (Emphasis added). This next case illustrates how school-uniformity clauses can limit legislative initiatives in the education arena – in this instance, by invalidating a Florida school voucher program.

BUSH v. HOLMES
919 So.2d 392 (Fla. 2006)

PARIENTE, C.J.

Under the [Opportunity Scholarship Program (OSP)], a student from a public school that fails to meet certain minimum state standards has two options. The first is to move to another public school with a satisfactory record under the state standards. The second option is to receive funds from the public treasury, which would otherwise have gone to the student's school district, to pay the student's tuition at a private school. The narrow question we address is whether the second option violates a part of the Florida Constitution requiring the state to both provide for "the education of all children residing within its borders" and provide "by law for a uniform, efficient, safe, secure, and high quality system of free public schools that allows students to obtain a high quality education." Art. IX, § 1(a), Fla. Const.

As a general rule, courts may not reweigh the competing policy concerns underlying a legislative enactment. The arguments of public policy supporting both sides in this dispute have obvious merit, and the Legislature with the Governor's assent has resolved the ensuing debate in favor of the proponents of the program. In most cases, that would be the end of the matter. However, as is equally self-evident, the usual deference given to the Legislature's resolution of public policy issues is at all times circumscribed by the Constitution. Acting within its constitutional limits, the Legislature's power to resolve issues of civic debate receives great deference. Beyond those limits, the Constitution must prevail over any enactment contrary to it.

Our inquiry begins with the plain language of the second and third sentences of article IX, section 1(a) of the Constitution. The relevant words are these: "It is ... a paramount duty of the state to make adequate provision for the education of all children residing within its borders." Using the same term, "adequate provision," article IX, section 1(a) further states: "Adequate provision shall be made by law for a uniform, efficient, safe, secure, and high quality system of free public schools." For reasons expressed more fully below, we find that the OSP violates this language. It diverts public dollars into separate private systems parallel to and in competition with the free public schools that are the sole means set out in the Constitution for the state to provide for the education of Florida's children. This diversion not only reduces money available to the free schools, but also funds private schools that are not "uniform" when compared with each other or the public system. Many standards imposed by law on the public schools are inapplicable to the private schools receiving public monies. In sum, through the OSP the state is fostering plural, nonuniform systems of education in direct violation of the constitutional mandate for a uniform system of free public schools.

In 1998, in response in part to *Coalition for Adequacy & Fairness,* the Constitutional Revision Commission proposed and the citizens of this state approved an amendment to article IX, section 1 to make clear that education is a "fundamental value" and "a paramount duty of the state," and to provide standards by which to measure the adequacy of the public school education provided by the state:

> The education of children is a fundamental value of the people of the State of Florida. It is, therefore, a paramount duty of the state to make adequate provision for the education of all children residing within its borders. Adequate provision shall be made by law for a uniform, efficient, safe, secure, and high quality system of free public schools that allows students to obtain a high quality education and for the establishment, maintenance, and operation of institutions of higher learning and other public education programs that the needs of the people may require.

Art. IX, § 1(a), Fla. Const.

The provision (1) declares that the "education of children is a fundamental value of the people of the State of Florida," (2) sets forth an education mandate that provides that it is "a paramount duty of the state to make adequate provision for the education of all children residing within its borders," and (3) sets forth *how* the state is to carry out this education mandate, specifically, that "*[a]dequate* provision shall be made by law for a *uniform,* efficient, safe, secure, and *high quality system of free public schools.*"

Article IX, section 1(a) is a limitation on the Legislature's power because it provides both a mandate to provide for children's education and a restriction on the execution of that mandate.

The second sentence of article IX, section 1(a) provides that it is the "paramount duty of the state to make adequate provision for the education of all children residing within its borders." The third sentence of article IX, section 1(a) provides a restriction on the exercise of this mandate by specifying that the adequate provision required in the second sentence "shall be made by law for a uniform, efficient, safe, secure and high quality system of *free public schools.*" (Emphasis supplied.) The OSP violates this provision by devoting the state's resources to the education of children within our state through means other than a system of free public schools.

The Constitution prohibits the state from using public monies to fund a private alternative to the public school system, which is what the OSP does. Specifically, the OSP transfers tax money earmarked for public education to private schools that provide the same service-basic primary education. Thus, contrary to the defendants' arguments, the OSP does not supplement the public education system. Instead, the OSP diverts funds that would otherwise be provided to the system of free public schools that is the exclusive means set out in the Constitution for the Legislature to make adequate provision for the education of children.

Although opportunity scholarships are not now widely in use, if the dissent is correct as to their constitutionality, the potential scale of programs of this nature is unlimited. Under the dissent's view of the Legislature's authority in this area, the state could fund a private school system of indefinite size and scope as long as the state also continued to fund the public schools at a level that kept them "uniform, efficient, safe, secure, and high quality." However, because voucher payments reduce funding for the public education system, the OSP by its very nature undermines the system of "high quality" free public schools that are the sole authorized means of fulfilling the constitutional mandate to provide for the education of all children residing in Florida. The systematic diversion of public funds to private schools on either a small or large scale is incompatible with article IX, section 1(a).

In addition to specifying that a system of free public schools is the means for complying with the mandate to provide for the education of Florida's children, article IX, section 1(a) also requires that this system be "uniform." The OSP makes no provision to ensure that the private school alternative to the public school system meets the criterion of uniformity. In fact, in a provision directing the Department of Education to establish and maintain a database of private schools, the Legislature expressly states that it does not intend "to regulate, control, approve, or accredit private educational institutions."§ 1002.42(2)(h), Fla. Stat. (2005). This lack of oversight is also evident in section 1001.21, which creates the Office of Private Schools and Home Education Programs within the Department of Education but provides that this office "ha[s] no authority over the institutions or students served."§ 1001.21(1), Fla. Stat. (2005).

Further, although the parent of a student participating in the OSP must ensure that the student "takes all statewide assessments" required of a public school student, § 1002.38(5)(c), the private school's curriculum and teachers are not subject to the same standards as those in force in public schools. For example, only teachers possessing bachelor's degrees are eligible to teach at public schools, but private schools may hire teachers without bachelor's degrees if they have "at least 3 years of teaching experience in public or private schools, or have special skills, knowledge, or expertise that qualifies them to provide instruction in subjects taught."§ 1002.38(4)(g), Fla. Stat. (2005).

In addition, public school teachers must be certified by the state. See § 1012.55(1), Fla. Stat. (2005). To obtain this certification, teachers must meet certain requirements that include having "attained at least a 2.5 overall grade point average on a 4.0 scale in the applicant's major field of study" and having demonstrated a mastery of general knowledge, subject area knowledge, and professional preparation and education competence. See§ 1012.56(2)(c), (g)-(i), Fla. Stat. (2005).

Public teacher certification also requires the applicant to submit to a background screening. See § 1012.56(2)(d), Fla. Stat. (2005). Indeed, all school district personnel hired to fill positions that require direct contact with students must undergo a background check. See § 1012.32(2)(a), Fla. Stat. (2005). This screening is not required of private school employees. See § 1002.42(2)(c)(3), Fla. Stat. (2005) (providing that owners of private schools may require employees to file fingerprints with the Department of Law Enforcement).

Regarding curriculum, public education instruction is based on the "Sunshine State Standards" that have been "adopted by the State Board of Education and delineate the academic achievement of students, for which the state will hold schools accountable."§ 1003.41, Fla. Stat. (2005). Public schools are required to teach all basic subjects as well as a number of other diverse subjects, among them the contents of the Declaration of Independence, the essentials of the United States Constitution, the elements of civil government, Florida state history, African-American history, the history of the Holocaust, and the study of Hispanic and women's contributions to the United States. See § 1003.42(2)(a), Fla. Stat. (2005). Eligible private schools are not required to teach any of these subjects.

In addition to being "academically accountable to the parent," a private school participating in the OSP is subject only "to the...curriculum...criteria adopted by an appropriate nonpublic school accrediting body."§ 1002.38(4)(f), Fla. Stat. (2005). There are numerous nonpublic school accrediting bodies that have "widely variant quality standards and program requirements." Thus, curriculum standards of eligible private schools may vary greatly depending on the accrediting body, and these standards may not be equivalent to those required for Florida public schools.

In all these respects, the alternative system of private schools funded by the OSP cannot be deemed uniform in accordance with the mandate in article IX, section 1(a).

Reinforcing our determination that the state's use of public funds to support an alternative system of education is in violation of article IX, section 1(a) is the limitation of the use of monies from the State School Fund set forth in article IX, section 6. That provision states that income and interest from the State School Fund may be appropriated "only to the support and maintenance of free public schools." Art. IX, § 6, Fla. Const.

In sum, article IX, section 1(a) provides for the manner in which the state is to fulfill its mandate to make adequate provision for the education of Florida's children-through a system of public education. The OSP contravenes this constitutional provision because it allows some children to receive a publicly funded education through an alternative system of private schools that are not subject to the uniformity requirements of the public school system. The diversion of money not only reduces public funds for a public education but also uses public funds to provide an alternative education in private schools that are not subject to the "uniformity" requirements for public schools. Thus, in two significant respects, the OSP violates the mandate set forth in article IX, section 1(a).

We do not question the basic right of parents to educate their children as they see fit. We recognize that the proponents of vouchers have a strongly held view that students should have choices. Our decision does not deny parents recourse to either public or private school alternatives to a failing school. Only when the private school option depends upon public funding is choice limited. This limit is necessitated by the constitutional mandate in article IX, section 1(a), which sets out the state's responsibilities in a manner that does not allow the use of state monies to fund a private school education. As we recently explained, "[w]hat is in the Constitution always must prevail over emotion. Our oaths as judges require that this principle is our polestar, and it alone." *Bush v. Schiavo,* 885 So.2d 321, 336 (Fla.2004).

E. REMEDY

One of the most vexing issues for courts that grant constitutional relief in this area is the question of remedy. It is one thing for a court to recognize an enforceable state constitutional right in this area and even to say that a current school funding system is inadequate. It is quite another to identify what the legislature must do to make its funding system constitutional. Claimants frequently seek structural changes to the system and usually demand increased state funding in doing so. The courts have struggled to identify a rationale for deciding how much guaranteed state funding suffices – with some focusing on the cost of certain educational "inputs," some focusing on the costs of certain educational "outputs," and some looking to both.

HOKE COUNTY BD. OF EDUC. v. STATE
599 S.E.2d 365 (N.C. 2004)

ORR, J.

The Court now turns its attention to the substantive issues brought forward on appeal by the State. In its first question presented to this Court, the State contends that the trial court erred by applying the wrong standards for determining: (1) when a student has obtained a sound basic education; (2) causation (for a student's failure to obtain a sound basic education); and (3) the State's liability (for a student's failure to obtain a sound basic education). In further support of its initial argument, the State proffers three subarguments, which allege and target specific evidentiary lapses and flaws in the trial court's reasoning. In its argument labeled I(A), the State contends that the trial court erred by using standardized test scores as "the exclusive measure" of whether students were obtaining a sound basic education. In argument I(B), the State argues that the trial court erred by concluding that a denial of the right to a sound basic education could be inferred from the number of socio-economically disadvantaged ("at-risk") students scoring below Level III proficiency on standardized tests. And in argument I(C), the State contends that the trial court erred when it held the State responsible for administrative decisions made by local school boards.

In *Leandro,* this Court decreed that the children of the state enjoy the right to avail themselves of the opportunity for a sound basic education.... Ultimately, the Court defined a sound basic education as one that provides students with at least: (1) sufficient knowledge of fundamental mathematics and physical science to enable the student to function in a complex and rapidly changing society; (2) sufficient fundamental knowledge of geography, history, and basic economic and political systems to enable the student to make informed choices with regard to issues that affect the student personally or affect the student's community, state, and nation; (3) sufficient academic and vocational skills to enable the student to successfully engage in post-secondary education or vocational training; and (4) sufficient academic and vocational skills to enable the student to compete on an equal basis with others in formal education or gainful employment in contemporary society.

After declaring a child's constitutional right to the opportunity to receive a sound basic education and defining the elements of such an education, the Court concluded that some of the allegations in plaintiffs' complaint stated claims upon which relief may be granted and ordered the case remanded to the trial court to permit plaintiffs to proceed on such claims.

At trial, plaintiffs presented evidence that, in accordance with *Leandro,* can be categorized as follows: (1) comparative standardized test score data; (2) student graduation rates, employment potential, post-secondary education success (and/or lack thereof); (3) deficiencies pertaining to the educational offerings in Hoke County schools; and (4) deficiencies pertaining to the educational administration of Hoke County schools. The first two evidentiary categories fall under the umbrella of "outputs," a term used by educators that, in sum, measures student performance. The remaining two evidentiary categories fall under the umbrella of "inputs," a term used by educators that, in sum, describes what the State and local boards provide to students attending public schools. We examine each evidentiary category in turn.

In its brief, the State contends, at great length, that the trial court erred by using test scores "as the exclusive measure of a constitutionally adequate education." However, as we proceed in our analysis, the Court notes that the record reflects that the trial court considered "output" evidence beyond the realm of test scores, and that evidence such as graduation rates, dropout rates, post-secondary education performance, employment rates and prospects, comports with both this Court's definition of a sound basic education *and* the factors we provided the trial court to consider upon remand. Thus, we reject the State's contention that the trial court used test scores as the "exclusive measure" of a sound basic education.

In continuing our examination of the trial court's order, we move next to the trial court's conclusion that additional "output" evidence-*e.g.,* graduation rates, dropout rates, employment potential, and post-secondary education readiness-further demonstrates that an unacceptably high number of Hoke County students are failing to obtain a sound basic education. In considering evidence concerning dropout and graduation rates, the trial court found that in the mid-1990s only 41% of Hoke County freshmen went on to graduate-a retention rate that was 19% lower than the state average and was the worst retention rate in the state's 100 counties. The trial court went on to conclude that the evidence showed that the primary reason Hoke County's dropout rate was so high was that a great number of Hoke students are "not well prepared for high school" and that "students who do not do well in the early grades are more likely than other students to later drop out of school."

As for the effect of such a high dropout rate, the trial court concluded that the failure of large percentages of Hoke County students to complete high school "not only results in those children who leave having failed to obtain a sound basic education" but is also evidence "of a systematic weakness ... in meeting the needs of many of [Hoke County's] students."

As for those students who did graduate, the trial court's assessment was no less bleak. After considering evidence concerning the employment potential and post-secondary education potential for Hoke County graduates, the trial court concluded that many among the graduates had not obtained a sound basic education in that the evidence showed "they are poorly prepared to compete on an equal basis in gainful employment and further formal education in today's contemporary society." In support of its conclusion, the trial court cited to numerous examples of Hoke County graduates who pursued employment or who pursued further education at the college level.

In the realm of "outputs" evidence, we hold that the trial court properly concluded that the evidence demonstrates that over the past decade, an inordinate number of Hoke County students have consistently failed to match the academic performance of their statewide public school counterparts and that such failure, measured by their performance while attending Hoke County schools, their dropout rates, their graduation rates, their need for remedial help, their inability to compete in the job markets, and their inability to compete in collegiate ranks, constitute a clear showing that they have failed to obtain a *Leandro*-comporting education. As a consequence of so holding, we turn our attention to "inputs" evidence-evidence concerning what the State and its agents have provided for the education of Hoke County students-in an effort to determine the following two contingencies: (1) Does the evidence support the trial court's conclusion that the State's action and/or inaction has caused Hoke County students not to obtain a sound basic education and, if so; (2) Does such action and/or inaction by the State constitute a failure to meet its constitutional obligation to provide Hoke County students with the opportunity to obtain a sound basic education, as defined in *Leandro*?

It is one thing for plaintiffs to demonstrate that a large number of Hoke County students are failing to obtain a sound, basic public education. It is quite another for plaintiffs to show that such a failure is primarily the result of action and/or inaction of the State, which argues in this appeal that the trial court erred by concluding that a combination of State action and inaction resulted in the systematic poor performance of Hoke County students and graduates.

In defense of its educational offerings in Hoke County at trial, the State attempted to show that its combination of "inputs"-*i.e.,* expenditures, programs, teachers, administrators, etc.-added up to be an aggregate that met or exceeded this Court's definition of providing students with an opportunity for a sound basic education. In addition, both at trial and in this appeal, the State contended that the evidence showed the following:

(1) That the educational offerings it provides in Hoke County have improved significantly since the mid-nineties; (2) That such improvements are part and parcel of the State's own recognition of ongoing problems and the need to address them; (3) That if a cognizable group of students within Hoke County are failing to obtain a sound basic education, it is due to factors other than the educational offerings provided by the State; and, (4) That many of the deficiencies that may exist in the educational offerings of Hoke County are due to the administrative shortcomings of the semi-autonomous local school boards.

Plaintiffs, on the other hand, contend that the evidence at trial clearly showed that the State had consistently failed to provide Hoke County schools with the resources needed to provide students with the opportunity to obtain a sound basic education. In addition, plaintiffs argue that the evidence shows that Hoke County students have consistently failed to match the achievements of their statewide counterparts (*see* "outputs" discussion, above) because the State has failed to: (1) provide adequate teachers and/or administrators; (2) provide the funding necessary to offer each student the opportunity to obtain a sound basic education; (3) recognize the failings of Hoke County students as a whole; and (4) implement alternative educational offerings that have and/or would address and correct the problems that have placed and/or place Hoke County students *at risk* of academic failure.

Although the trial court explained that it was leaving the "nuts and bolts" of the educational resources assessment in Hoke County to the other branches of government, it ultimately provided general guidelines for a *Leandro*-compliant resource allocation system, including the requirements: (1) that "every classroom be staffed with a competent, certified, well-trained teacher"; (2) "that every school be led by a well-trained competent principal"; and (3) "that every school be provided, in the most cost effective manner, the resources necessary to support the effective instructional program within that school so that the educational needs of all children, including at-risk children, to have the equal opportunity to obtain a sound basic education, can be met." Finally, the trial court ordered the State to keep the court advised of its remedial actions through written reports filed with the trial court every ninety days.

In our view, the trial court conducted an appropriate and informative path of inquiry concerning the issue at hand. After determining that the evidence clearly showed that Hoke County students were failing, at an alarming rate, to obtain a sound basic education, the trial court in turn determined that the evidence presented also demonstrated that a combination of State action and inaction contributed significantly to the students' failings. Then, after concluding that the State's overall funding and resource provisions scheme was adequate on a statewide basis, the trial court determined that the evidence showed that the State's method of funding and providing for individual school districts such as Hoke County was such that it did not comply with *Leandro*'s mandate of ensuring that all children of the state be provided with the opportunity for a sound basic education. In particular, the trial court concluded the State's failing was essentially twofold in that the State: (1) failed to identify the inordinate number of "at-risk" students and provide a means for such students to avail themselves of the opportunity for a sound basic education; and (2) failed to oversee how educational funding and resources were being used and implemented in Hoke County schools.

In short, the trial court: (1) informed the State what was wrong with Hoke County schools; (2) directed the State to reassess its educational priorities for Hoke County; and (3) ordered the State to correct any and all education-related deficiencies that contribute to a student's inability to take advantage of his right to the opportunity to obtain a sound basic education. However, we note that the trial court also demonstrated admirable restraint by refusing to dictate how existing problems should be approached and resolved. Recognizing that education concerns were the shared province of the legislative and executive branches, the trial court instead afforded the two branches an unimpeded chance, "initially at least," to correct constitutional deficiencies revealed at trial. In our view, the trial court's approach to the issue was sound and its order reflects both findings of fact that were supported by the evidence and conclusions that were supported by ample and adequate findings of fact. As a consequence, we affirm those portions of the trial court's order that conclude that there has been a clear showing of a denial of the established right of Hoke County students to gain their opportunity for a sound basic education and those portions of the order that require the State to assess its education-related allocations to the county's schools so as to correct any deficiencies that presently prevent the county from offering its students the opportunity to obtain a *Leandro*-conforming education.

TENNESSEE SMALL SCHOOL SYSTEMS v. McWHERTER
91 S.W.3d 232 (Tenn. 2002)

ANDERSON, J.

This is the third appeal to this Court of the plaintiffs' suit challenging the constitutionality of the manner in which the State funds public education. In the first appeal, we held that the State was required by the Tennessee Constitution to maintain and support a system of public schools that affords substantially equal educational opportunities to all students, and we found that the State's school funding scheme unconstitutionally denied equal educational opportunities to all students. In the second appeal, we conditionally upheld a new funding plan allocating funds to school systems according to a formula based on the cost of forty-three components necessary for a basic education, known as the Basic Education Program ("BEP"), Tenn.Code Ann. §§ 49-3-351 to -360. We found, however, that the omission of a requirement for equalizing teachers' salaries was a significant defect in the Basic Education Program ("BEP"), which put the entire plan at risk both functionally and legally, and we concluded that "the plan must include equalization of teachers' salaries according to the BEP formula" in order for the plan to be constitutional.

In this third appeal, the question is whether the State's current method of funding salaries for teachers-the salary equity plan found in Tennessee Code Annotated § 49-3-366-equalizes teachers' salaries "according to the BEP formula" or whether it fails to do so and violates equal protection by denying students substantially equal educational opportunities. The trial court dismissed the case after finding that the State had met its constitutional obligation to equalize teachers' salaries under *Small Schools II*. The plaintiffs then filed a motion asking this Court to assume jurisdiction of the appeal, asserting that the State failed to comply with this Court's directive in *Small Schools II* to equalize teachers' salaries according to the BEP formula for funding public education. We granted the motion.

After careful consideration of the record and applicable authorities, we find that the salary equity plan embodied in Tennessee Code Annotated § 49-3-366 does not equalize teachers' salaries according to the BEP formula and contains no mechanism for cost determination or annual cost review of teachers' salaries, unlike the BEP conditionally approved in *Small Schools II*. We further find that no rational basis exists for structuring a basic education program consisting entirely of cost-driven components while omitting the cost of hiring teachers, the most important component of any education plan and a major part of every education budget. Therefore, the lack of teacher salary equalization in accordance with the BEP formula continues to be a significant constitutional defect in the current funding scheme. Accordingly, we hold that the salary equity plan fails to comply with the State's constitutional obligation to formulate and maintain a system of public education that affords a substantially equal educational opportunity to all students. The trial court's judgment dismissing the case is reversed and the case is remanded.

We can think of no rational basis, and the defendants have not suggested one, for structuring a basic education program where all of its components, including salaries for custodians, secretaries, nurses, librarians, social workers, principals and their assistants, assessment personnel, coordinators, supervisors, psychologists, and superintendents, are cost-driven, except for the largest and most important component of all, the cost of providing teachers. It seems to us, as we said in *Small Schools II,* that the rationale for cost determination and annual review of the BEP components applies with equal if not greater force to teachers' salaries, for it is undeniable that teachers are the most important component of any effective education plan, and that their salaries, a major item in every education budget, are a significant factor in determining where teachers choose to work.

The record supports the plaintiffs' argument that for the most part, the same disparities in teachers' salaries that existed when *Small Schools II* was decided still exist today. For example, in 1995, the City of Alcoa paid teachers an average of $40,672, while Jackson County paid teachers an average of $23,934, a difference of $16,738. In 1997, Oak Ridge paid its teachers an average of $42,268, while in Monroe County the figure was $28,025, a disparity of $14,243. In 1998-1999, the disparity between Oak Ridge and Monroe County grew to $14,554. Thus, wide disparities still exist, and it takes little imagination to see how such disparities can lead to experienced and more educated teachers leaving the poorer school districts to teach in wealthier ones where they receive higher salaries. In the end, the rural districts continue to suffer the same type of constitutional inequities that were present fourteen years ago when this litigation began.

In reaching the conclusion that the salary equity plan is constitutionally deficient, we are mindful that teachers' salaries will not be identical in every school district. We also stress that our opinion does not hinge upon the adequacy of the average salary relied upon by the legislature, *i.e.,* "$28,094," which the plaintiffs characterize variously as an "inadequate floor," "artificial," "erroneous," and "extremely outdated." It is not the business of the courts to decide how salaries are funded or at what level teachers should be compensated, for it is the legislature who "speaks for the people on matters of public policy" such as these. In addition, nothing in the law prevents a local school system from supplementing teachers' salaries from its own local non-BEP funds when such funds are in addition to its local BEP contribution. As such, some disparities in teachers' salaries from school district to school district will exist. In short, determining how to fund teachers' salaries and the appropriate level of those salaries are choices for the legislature to make, assuming of course that the legislature discharges its powers in a manner that comports with the Constitution.

As we recognized in *Small Schools I,* local spending on education will also vary due to differences in "geographical features, organizational structures, management principles and utilization of facilities," as well as other "factors that bear upon the quality and availability of educational opportunity [which] may not be subject to precise quantification in dollars." The critical point, however, is that the educational funding structure be geared toward achieving equality in educational opportunity for students, not necessarily "sameness" in teacher compensation. The objective of teacher salary equalization is to provide substantially equal opportunities for students, not teachers. While this case focuses largely on the methodology used to fund teachers' salaries, we realize that many elements, of which funding is but one, must come together in order for Tennessee schools to succeed and for children in this State to receive a substantially equal educational opportunity.

In our view, no rational basis exists for structuring a basic education funding system consisting entirely of cost-driven components except for teacher salaries. Thus, the lack of teacher salary equalization according to the BEP formula continues to be a significant constitutional defect in the current funding scheme. Accordingly, we hold that the salary equity plan fails to satisfy the State's constitutional obligation to formulate and maintain a system of public education that affords substantially equal educational opportunity to all students.

CLAREMONT SCHOOL DIST. v. GOVERNOR
794 A.2d 744 (N.H. 2002)

DUGGAN, J.

The issues before this court are: (1) whether the State's obligation to provide a constitutionally adequate public education requires it to include standards of accountability in the educational system; and, if so, (2) whether existing statutes, regulations and/or rules satisfy this obligation. We hold that accountability is an essential component of the State's duty and that the existing statutory scheme has deficiencies that are inconsistent with the State's duty to provide a constitutionally adequate education.

This litigation began in 1992 when the Claremont School District, along with four other "property poor" school districts, five school children and five taxpayers, filed a petition for declaratory relief in superior court alleging that the system by which the State financed education violated the New Hampshire Constitution. The trial court dismissed the lawsuit, ruling that the New Hampshire Constitution "imposes no qualitative standard of education which must be met" and "imposes no quantifiable financial duty regarding education." The plaintiffs appealed. After examining the meaning of the words used in the Encouragement of Literature Clause at the time the State Constitution was adopted in 1784, historical evidence of the significance of education to the constitutional framers and the interpretation given almost identical language in the Massachusetts Constitution by that State's highest court, this court concluded that Part II, Article 83 requires the State to "provide a constitutionally adequate education to every educable child in the public schools in New Hampshire and to guarantee adequate funding."

In *Claremont I*, we observed that the New Hampshire Constitution "expressly recognizes education as a cornerstone of our democratic system" and the Encouragement of Literature Clause "expressly recognizes that a free government is dependent for its survival on citizens who are able to participate intelligently in the political, economic, and social functions of our system." "Given the complexities of our society today, the State's constitutional duty extends beyond mere reading, writing and arithmetic. It also includes broad educational opportunities needed in today's society to prepare citizens for their role as participants and as potential competitors in today's marketplace of ideas."

This court specifically acknowledged that the task of defining the parameters of the education mandated by the constitution is in the first instance for the legislature and the Governor. That task includes the "responsibility ... to defin[e] the specifics of, and the appropriate means to provide through public education, the knowledge and learning essential to the preservation of a free government."

Regarding educational adequacy, the opinion underscored that

[m]ere competence in the basics-reading, writing, and arithmetic-is insufficient in the waning days of the twentieth century to insure that this State's public school students are fully integrated into the world around them. A broad exposure to the social, economic, scientific, technological, and political realities of today's society is essential for our students to compete, contribute, and flourish in the twenty-first century.

Claremont II also set forth "seven criteria...establishing general, aspirational guidelines for defining educational adequacy." This court deferred, however, in the first instance to the other branches of government to "promptly develop and adopt specific criteria implementing these guidelines."

After considering the pleadings and oral argument, this court decided to exercise its jurisdiction to resolve two specific legal questions:

(1) Whether the State's obligation to provide a constitutionally adequate public education under part II, article 83 of the New Hampshire Constitution requires the State to include standards of accountability in New Hampshire statutes, regulations and/or rules; and if so

(2) Whether existing statutes, regulations and/or rules satisfy this obligation.

Accountability is more than merely creating a system to deliver an adequate education. *Claremont I* did not simply hold that the State should deliver a constitutionally adequate education, but in fact held that it is the State's duty under the New Hampshire Constitution to do so. Accountability means that the State must provide a definition of a constitutionally adequate education, the definition must have standards, and the standards must be subject to meaningful application so that it is possible to determine whether, in delegating its obligation to provide a constitutionally adequate education, the State has fulfilled its duty. If the State cannot be held accountable for fulfilling its duty, the duty creates no obligation and is no longer a duty. We therefore conclude that the State's duty to provide a constitutionally adequate education includes accountability.

Having determined that standards of accountability are an essential component of the State's duty to provide a constitutionally adequate education, we must now determine whether the existing statutes, regulations and rules satisfy this obligation. The State argues that these existing laws, which include the definition of an adequate education in RSA 193-E:2; the State's minimum standards for education set forth in the department of education rules, *N.H. Admin. Rules*, Ed ch. 300; and the New Hampshire Education Improvement and Assessment Program (NHEIAP), RSA ch. 193-C (1999), together provide sufficient standards of accountability. According to the State, "it has given detailed curriculum instruction to schools and school boards, created a test to measure student performance, empowered State agencies to review and improve school performance, and enacted literally thousands of pages of other statutes, regulations, and rules to deliver an adequate education."

RSA 193-E:2 sets forth the criteria for an adequate education as follows:

> I. Skill in reading, writing, and speaking English to enable them to communicate effectively and think creatively and critically.
>
> II. Skill in mathematics and familiarity with methods of science to enable them to analyze information, solve problems, and make rational decisions.
>
> III. Knowledge of the biological, physical, and earth sciences to enable them to understand and appreciate the world around them.
>
> IV. Knowledge of civics and government, economics, geography, and history to enable them to participate in the democratic process and to make informed choices as responsible citizens.
>
> V. Grounding in the arts, languages, and literature to enable them to appreciate our cultural heritage and develop lifelong interests and involvement in these areas.
>
> VI. Sound wellness and environmental practices to enable them to enhance their own well-being, as well as that of others.
>
> VII. Skills for lifelong learning, including interpersonal and technological skills, to enable them to learn, work, and participate effectively in a changing society.

The State contends that a wide range of satisfactory methods can produce an effective system to deliver what it has defined as an adequate education. The State also asserts that it may choose from a wide array of tools to ensure that school districts are implementing the standards it sets out for the system it chooses. We agree that "there are many different ways that the Legislature could fashion an educational system while still meeting the mandates of the Constitution." The system the State currently has in place appears to use both standards based on what school districts provide (input-based standards) and results that school districts achieve (output-based standards). While minimum standards for school approval set forth what the schools, at the very least, must provide to students, NHEIAP uses curriculum frameworks and mandatory tests to assess what the school districts have achieved.

The State argues that as a central part of the system to deliver a constitutionally adequate education, it "dictates certain school approval standards that schools and school districts must meet. These input based standards are enforceable by the State and extend to virtually every aspect of education, from class size to teacher training to detailed curriculum requirements."

The board of education is required by statute to adopt rules relative to "[m]inimum curriculum and educational standards for all grades of the public schools." These rules are commonly referred to as the State's "minimum standards" or "school approval standards." The minimum standards contain a number of requirements imposed by the State on local school districts so that schools may be approved by the State. For example, the minimum standards set forth the number of days in a standard school year, staff qualifications, maximum class sizes, heating and ventilation requirements, the minimum number of credits required to be offered in certain courses, and the areas of specific substantive materials which must be taught.

The education that the individual schools provide is measured against these standards for approval. If a school does not meet these standards, it can lose its approval. There are four categories of approval: approved with distinction, approved, conditionally approved from one to three years, and unapproved. If a school is unapproved, the department of education is required to work with the local school board to "correct all deficiencies until such time as an unapproved school meets all applicable standards and is designated as an approved school." The purpose of these rules is to hold school districts accountable for providing an adequate education.

Excused noncompliance with the minimum standards for financial reasons alone directly conflicts with the constitutional command that the State must guarantee sufficient funding to ensure that school districts can provide a constitutionally adequate education. As we have repeatedly held, it is the State's duty to guarantee the funding necessary to provide a constitutionally adequate education to every educable child in the public schools in the State.

The responsibility for ensuring the provision of an adequate public education and an adequate level of resources for all students in New Hampshire lies with the State. While local governments may be required, in part, to support public schools, it is the responsibility of the State to take such steps as may be required in each instance effectively to devise a plan and sources of funds sufficient to meet the constitutional mandate.

As noted above, the State may not take the position that the minimum standards form an essential component of the delivery of a constitutionally adequate education and yet allow for the financial constraints of a school or school district to excuse compliance with those very standards. We hold, therefore, that to the extent the minimum standards for school approval excuse compliance solely based on financial conditions, it is facially insufficient because it is in clear conflict with the State's duty to provide a constitutionally adequate education.

NHEIAP, RSA chapter 193-C, is characterized by the State as "[a]nother important element of the State's system for delivering the opportunity for an adequate education." The goals of the program are to define what students should know and be able to do, develop and implement methods for assessing that learning and its application, report assessment results to all citizens of New Hampshire, help to provide accountability at all levels, and use the results, at both the State and local levels, to improve instruction and advance student learning. The department of education pamphlet describes NHEIAP as the "cornerstone of the state's initiatives to continuously improve education for all students."

The responsibility for administering NHEIAP lies with the department of education. The commissioner of education is charged with "develop[ing] and implement[ing] this program in conjunction with the state board of education and the legislative oversight committee." In fulfilling its duty pursuant to the statutory framework that makes up NHEIAP, the department of education is directed to develop a program that consists of three interlocking components. The first component is a set of educational standards, RSA 193-C:3, III(a), which the department of education has developed and implemented through curriculum frameworks. The second component is a statewide assessment program, which "shall be [a] valid and appropriate representation[ ] of the standards the students are expected to achieve." The final component is the "local education improvement and assessment plan which builds upon and complements the goals established for [NHEIAP]."

Under RSA 193-C:9, I, however, no school district is required to respond to the assessment results; rather "[e]ach school district in New Hampshire is *encouraged* to develop a local education improvement and assessment plan." This means that even if the assessment results show that all the students in a school are at novice level, neither the school district nor the department of education is required to do anything. Whether an individual school district is providing a constitutionally adequate education or not, it is merely encouraged to develop a local educational improvement plan, and if it opts to do so, the department of education is available to assist. Nothing more is required.

An output-based accountability system that merely encourages local school districts to meet educational standards does not fulfill the State's constitutional duty under Part II, Article 83. While the State may delegate its duty to provide a constitutionally adequate education, the State may not abdicate its duty in the process. The purpose of meaningful accountability is to ensure that those entrusted with the duty of delivering a constitutionally adequate education are fulfilling that duty. When the State chooses to use an output-based tool to measure whether school districts are providing a constitutionally adequate education, that tool must be meaningfully applied. The department of education cannot meaningfully apply the educational standards and assessment tests set out in RSA chapter 193-C when it cannot hold school districts accountable, but instead is limited to using the results to encourage school districts to develop a local education improvement and assessment plan. To the extent the State relies on RSA chapter 193-C to provide for accountability, it must do more than merely encourage school districts to meet the educational standards that are designed to indicate whether students are receiving a constitutionally adequate education.

The State suggests that "[a] student who receives an education of the quality described in [RSA] 193-E:2 and who acquires all of the various skills and types of knowledge expressed there would be well prepared as a citizen to participate in society." While we have no basis to disagree with this statement, the State has not provided a sufficient mechanism to require that school districts actually achieve this goal. We hold that because of deficiencies in the system as set out in this opinion, the State has not met its constitutional obligation to develop a system to ensure the delivery of a constitutionally adequate education.

As the State recognizes, "there are many different ways that the Legislature could fashion an educational system while still meeting the mandates of the Constitution." The development of meaningful standards of accountability is a task for which the legislative branch is uniquely suited. The policy choices to be made are complex, as there are several ways to address this issue. It is for the Governor and the legislature to choose how to measure or evaluate whether a constitutionally adequate education is being provided and what action to take if a school is determined to be deficient. The State's brief describes some of the issues involved:

Formulating a system for delivery might…require policy choices regarding what sort of standards should exist for teachers, students, schools, and school districts. For example, a delivery system might consist of detailed curriculum rules for each grade and subject area establishing the required substance of each lesson that students must be taught. Other delivery systems might make use of any number of other standards such as class size, graduation rate, college acceptance rate, test scores, or teacher qualifications.

…[D]evising a system to deliver educational services could also require decisions regarding how to implement the standards that are selected. If a school or school district is not meeting applicable standards, what will be the consequence? A system could rely on the Governor to ensure that local school districts are meeting statutory obligations through her power to enforce constitutional and statutory obligations. A different system might enforce standards by rewarding successful schools with increased funding. Alternatively, the system might impose penalties for not meeting standards, such as removing the principal, sending in a team of administrators to take control of the school, or any number of other consequences.

We agree with the State's contention that it may implement a variety of systems. However, when the State chooses a particular method to determine whether those it entrusts with the task are in fact providing a constitutionally adequate education, the State must include meaningful accountability to ensure that the State is fulfilling its constitutional duty.

We conclude that the State "needs to do more work" to fulfill its duty to provide a constitutionally adequate education and incorporate meaningful accountability in the education system. In light of the procedural history of this litigation, including efforts by the executive and legislative branches and their previous statements on this issue, and the application of settled law, this conclusion should be neither surprising nor unanticipated.

We remain mindful that "[w]hile the judiciary has the duty to construe and interpret the word 'education' by providing broad constitutional guidelines, the Legislature is obligated to give specific substantive content to the word and to the program it deems necessary to provide that 'education' within the broad guidelines." We recognize that we are not appointed to establish educational policy and have not done so today.

NEELEY v. WEST ORANGE-COVE CONSOL. INDEPENDENT SCHOOL DIST.
176 S.W.3d 746 (Tex. 2005)

HECHT, J.

Under article VII, section 1 of the Constitution of 1876, the accomplishment of "a general diffusion of knowledge" is the standard by which the adequacy of the public education system is to be judged. To achieve such a system, the Legislature has chosen to use local school districts. Borrowing from two statutory pronouncements, the district court concluded:

To fulfill the constitutional obligation to provide a general diffusion of knowledge, districts must provide "*all Texas children ... access* to a quality education that enables them to achieve their potential and fully participate now and in the future in the social, economic, and educational opportunities of our state and nation." Districts satisfy this constitutional obligation when they provide all of their students with a *meaningful opportunity* to acquire the essential knowledge and skills reflected in ... curriculum requirements ... such that upon graduation, students are prepared to "continue to learn in postsecondary educational, training, or employment settings."

We agree, with one caveat. The public education system need not operate perfectly; it is adequate if districts are *reasonably* able to provide their students the access and opportunity the district court described.

The system the Legislature has devised prescribes an education curriculum, and by means of accreditation standards, holds schools and districts accountable for teaching it. Schools and districts rated "academically acceptable" provide what we have referred to as an accredited education, and we have presumed, simply in deference to the Legislature, that such an education achieves a general diffusion of knowledge. The district court found that the plaintiffs and intervenors have rebutted this presumption. The court's principal reasons, set out in detailed findings and conclusions, may be summarized as follows:

- TAKS tests (and other such tests) cover only a small part of the prescribed curriculum;

- the cut scores and passing rates for TAKS tests (or other such tests) are too low and are set, not to reliably measure achievement, but to ensure a low rate of failure;

- completion and dropout rates are understated and unreliable, in fact fewer than 75% of all students and 70% of minority students complete high school, and this high attrition, worse in larger districts, is unacceptable;

- other important factors in determining whether a general diffusion of knowledge has been achieved, like college preparedness of graduates, for example, are not considered in rating schools and districts "academically acceptable" and reflect unfavorably on the system;

- the requirements for an "academically acceptable" rating are set to assure, not that there will be a general diffusion of knowledge, but that almost every district will meet them;

- the prescribed curriculum and TAKS testing have been made more demanding while funding to satisfy statutory requirements has not kept pace, producing budget pressures that have resulted in-

- a shortage of qualified teachers, an increase in teachers having to teach outside their fields, and high attrition and turnover rates;

• difficulty in providing special programs and remediation for students at risk of not completing their education;

• there has also been a lack of funding to meet increased federal requirements, like the No Child Left Behind Act;

• the changing demographics of the student population-with a majority being economically disadvantaged, 15% having limited proficiency in English, and both groups continuing to grow-have increased education costs while funding has lagged;

• the I/R econometric study correctly shows that the cost of an accredited education exceeds available per-student revenue.

The State defendants contend that the district court focused too much on "inputs" to the public education system-that is, available resources. They argue that whether a general diffusion of knowledge has been accomplished depends entirely on "outputs"-the results of the educational process measured in student achievement. We agree that the constitutional standard is plainly result-oriented. It creates no duty to fund public education at any level other than what is required to achieve a general diffusion of knowledge. While the end-product of public education is related to the resources available for its use, the relationship is neither simple nor direct; public education can and often does improve with greater resources, just as it struggles when resources are withheld, but more money does not guarantee better schools or more educated students. To determine whether the system as a whole is providing for a general diffusion of knowledge, it is useful to consider how funding levels and mechanisms relate to better-educated students. This, we think, is all the district court did.

In the extensive record before us, there is much evidence, which the district court credited, that many schools and districts are struggling to teach an increasingly demanding curriculum to a population with a growing number of disadvantaged students, yet without additional funding needed to meet these challenges. There are wide gaps in performance among student groups differentiated by race, proficiency in English, and economic advantage. Non-completion and dropout rates are high, and the loss of students who are struggling may make performance measures applied to those who continue appear better than they should. The rate of students meeting college preparedness standards is very low. There is also evidence of high attrition and turnover among teachers statewide, due to increasing demands and stagnant compensation. But the undisputed evidence is that standardized test scores have steadily improved over time, even while tests and curriculum have been made more difficult. By all admission, NAEP scores, which the district court did not mention, show that public education in Texas has improved relative to the other states. Having carefully reviewed the evidence and the district court's findings, we cannot conclude that the Legislature has acted arbitrarily in structuring and funding the public education system so that school districts are not reasonably able to afford all students the access to education and the educational opportunity to accomplish a general diffusion of knowledge.

NOTE

For more cases dealing with these vexing remedial issues, see *Campbell County School Dist. v. State*, 181 P.3d 43 (Wyo. 2008); *Paynter v. State*, 797 N.E.2d 1225 (N.Y. 2003); *Montoy v. State*, 112 P.3d 923 (Kan. 2005).

CHAPTER XII

THE RIGHT TO A REMEDY AND OPEN COURTS

A. INTRODUCTION AND HISTORICAL BACKGROUND

State constitutions protect a variety of rights. One important provision that most state constitutions include but that the federal constitution does not is often referred to as a "right to a remedy" clause or an "open courts" clause. Such provisions guarantee citizens the right to pursue legal remedies for deprivations of their interests, usually in terms indicating a right to a "remedy by due course of law" or that the courts of the state "shall be open." These provisions often also include language guaranteeing that justice shall be "without denial," "prompt," or "without delay."

The right to a remedy/open courts provisions may limit a state's authority to withdraw or modify existing legal remedies. A frequent area of litigation under these provisions is tort reform, with plaintiffs arguing that damages caps, statutes of repose, worker's compensation systems, and other limitations on various tort actions (*e.g.*, in the malpractice or governmental immunity contexts) violate these state constitutional provisions. There are an abundance of fascinating and challenging state cases interpreting these constitutional provisions, with courts applying various levels of scrutiny and a variety of tests, with a corresponding mix of outcomes regarding the constitutionality of various state statutes that affect legal remedies. This chapter provides several illustrative examples of these cases, but it is by no means exhaustive of this complex and important area of state constitutional law.

Right to a remedy, or open court, provisions have a long historical pedigree. In fact, they predate the U.S. Constitution by centuries, with their roots in the English Magna Carta. Furthermore, even though the right to a remedy principle is explicitly enshrined only in the State constitutions (and not the federal constitution), Chief Justice John Marshall recognized the principle's pedigree more than 200 years ago. In *Marbury v. Madison*, 5 U.S. (1 Cranch) 137, 162-63 (1803), he quoted Blackstone's *Commentaries* for the proposition that "'it is a general and indisputable rule, that where there is a legal right there is also a legal remedy by suit or action at law, whenever that right is invaded.'"

SHANNON M. ROESLER, THE KANSAS REMEDY BY DUE COURSE OF LAW PROVISION: DEFINING A RIGHT TO A REMEDY, 47 Kan. L. Rev. 655 (1999) (footnotes omitted)[1]

1. Introduction

The state constitutions of thirty-nine states…contain "remedy by due course of law" provisions. Historically, these provisions were intended as constitutional safeguards of an individual's right to a legal remedy. More than state equivalents of the federal Due Process Clause, these remedy provisions have resulted in a myriad of interpretations by state courts. Plaintiffs generally use state remedy provisions to challenge statutes restricting or eliminating previously established causes of action. In the last few decades, for example, injured parties have used state remedy provisions to challenge tort reform legislation, such as workers' compensation acts and statutory caps on medical malpractice damages.

2. Background

a.   The History of the Remedy Clause: The Magna Carta and Sir Edward Coke

Most states with remedy provisions adopted the provision from earlier state constitutions. In constructing the first state constitutions, the colonial and early American writers looked to English law and history, adopting Sir Edward Coke's interpretation of language in the Magna Carta. Like Coke, they sought to protect the judiciary from corruption and to ensure its independence.

The history of the remedy provision…begins with King John in the thirteenth century. King John's courts administered justice for a fee; those seeking access to the courts had to purchase writs, and the more costly writs guaranteed speedier and more successful claims. In response to the Crown's corrupting influence, Chapter 40 of the Magna Carta was written to restore the integrity of the courts by specifically prohibiting the selling of writs: "[t]o no one will we sell, to no one will we refuse or delay, right or justice."

Because the Magna Carta's purpose was to protect the courts from the Crown's corruption, it provided compelling authority for Sir Edward Coke as he battled King James and argued for the supremacy of the common law in the seventeenth century. As an absolutist monarch, King James exercised power over the courts, arguing judges were merely servants of the Crown. Coke, not only argued that the judiciary was independent from the Crown, but also that the King was subject to the common law. In his crusade to justify the judiciary's independence, Coke wrote the Second

---

Institute; the remedy provision first appears in this context as part of Coke's interpretation of the language in Chapter 40 of the Magna Carta.

Coke expounded on the language in the Magna Carta to fashion a remedy guarantee: "[E]very subject of this Realm, for injury done to him...may take his remedy by the course of the Law, and have justice and right for injury done him, freely without sale, fully without any denial, and speedily without delay." Although commentators have criticized Coke for misreading the Magna Carta, his intent in fashioning the provision, not his accuracy in translation, sheds light on the remedy provision and its historical development. Like the authors of the Magna Carta, he struggled to protect the English court from outside corruption and influence, thereby safeguarding its independence; he did not, however, seek to guarantee the creation of remedies for every injury. The remedy provision was not created, therefore, to address the relationship between the judiciary and the legislature, although this is its context today.

When the remedy provision appeared in...the Delaware Declaration of Rights, Coke's interpretation of Chapter 40 of the Magna Carta was the only textual authority for an independent judiciary. Although the English judiciary's independence was finally recognized in 1701, the colonial courts remained subject to the corrupt devices of the Crown. Thus, shortly before the American Revolution, grievances similar to those of Coke motivated colonists to seek language that would guarantee the integrity of the courts. Not surprisingly, five early bills of rights contain remedy provisions derived from Coke's Second Institute. Moreover, though the federal Bill of Rights does not contain a remedy provision, at least two states, Virginia and North Carolina, argued for the inclusion of remedy language.

b.   State Interpretations

The modern context of the remedy provision bears little resemblance to the provision's origins. Litigation involving the remedy provision often surfaces in response to fairly recent areas of law, such as workers' compensation, medical malpractice, and statutes of repose. Though the cases contain similar subject matter from state to state, interpretation of the remedy provision continues to be an area of rich diversity in state constitutional law.

Commentators have categorized the different state interpretations according to various schemes. Often classification schemes draw upon federal equal protection, distinguishing different courts' approaches by varying degrees of judicial scrutiny and by using federal language, such as "fundamental rights."...[One commentator] has divided the varied approaches into two large groups: one group consists of judicially created brightline, or per se, rules while the other group contains ad hoc balancing tests that focus on the particular costs and benefits of a challenged statute.

B. CASES DEFINING THE RIGHT

ARBINO v. JOHNSON & JOHNSON
880 N.E.2d 420 (Ohio 2007)

MOYER, C.J.

I. Introduction

Petitioner Melisa Arbino initiated a products-liability action against respondents Johnson & Johnson, Ortho-McNeil Pharmaceutical, Inc., and Johnson & Johnson Pharmaceutical Research & Development, L.L.C. (collectively, "Johnson & Johnson") in 2006. She alleges that she suffered blood clots and other serious medical side effects from using the Ortho Evra Birth Control Patch, a hormonal birth-control medication that Johnson & Johnson created.

The case was filed in the United States District Court for the Southern District of Ohio. Arbino's complaint contains challenges to the constitutionality of four tort-reform statutes...[The District Court] certified four questions of state law for review.

II. Tort Reform in Ohio and Stare Decisis

Before engaging in a specific analysis of these issues, it is necessary to briefly review the major tort-reform laws enacted by the General Assembly in recent history. Doing so provides the proper context for our decision and frames the necessary discussion of stare decisis.

Since 1975, the General Assembly has adopted several so-called tort-reform acts, which were inevitably reviewed by this court. In the course of this review, we have examined several specific provisions that are similar in language and purpose to those at issue here; all of these similar statutes have been declared unconstitutional.

The first reform provision we reviewed was former R.C. 2307.43, which was passed in the Ohio Medical Malpractice Act of 1975. This statute placed a $200,000 cap on general medical-malpractice damages not involving death, with no exceptions for those suffering severe injuries. The General Assembly passed this legislation to combat a perceived malpractice-insurance crisis. Although it took several years for a challenge to be raised, we ultimately held that R.C. 2307.43 violated the due-process protections of the Ohio Constitution.

The General Assembly's next major enactment was the Tort Reform Act of 1987, which sought to change civil-justice and insurance law to alleviate another "insurance crisis." In *Sorrell v. Thevenir* (1994), 69 Ohio

St.3d 415, 419-420, we examined one facet of this law, R.C. 2317.45, which placed a significant limitation on the collateral-source rule adopted in *Pryor v. Webber* (1970), 23 Ohio St.2d 104. The H.B. 1 version of R.C. 2317.45 required the trial court to subtract certain collateral benefits from a plaintiff's final award of compensatory damages. We held that this mandatory deduction of collateral benefits violated the right to a jury trial, due process, equal protection, and the right to a remedy.

In *Galayda v. Lake Hosp. Sys., Inc.* (1994), 71 Ohio St.3d 421, we reviewed…another tort-reform statute. This statute required trial courts to order awards of future damages in excess of $200,000 in medical-malpractice actions to be paid in a series of periodic payments upon the motion of any party. We deemed that statute unconstitutional as a violation of the right to a jury trial and of the Due Process Clause of the Ohio Constitution.

In *Zoppo v. Homestead Ins. Co.* (1994), 71 Ohio St.3d 552,…we examined [a] statute [that] required a trial judge to determine the amount of punitive damages to be awarded in a tort action, even when the trier of fact was a jury. We struck this section as a violation of the right to a jury trial in the Ohio Constitution.

Finally, the General Assembly passed substantial reforms in 1997. Among other things, it modified the collateral-source rule in tort actions to require the trier of fact to consider but not automatically set off collateral benefits, capped punitive damages and allowed the trier of fact to determine damages up to the cap in tort and products-liability claims, and capped noneconomic damages at different levels, with higher limits for permanent injuries.

The protracted interbranch tension on this subject establishes at least two key points. First, tort reform has been a major issue of concern in this state over the past several decades and remains one today. Ohio is hardly unique in this regard, as such reforms have been raised in nearly every state in the nation. State legislatures and judiciaries have differed widely in their responses to this issue, and a definite split in authority is clear. The federal judiciary has been drawn to the issue as well, with the United States Supreme Court offering guidance on several key issues over the past few years, most notably regarding punitive-damages awards.

A fundamental principle of the constitutional separation of powers among the three branches of government is that the legislative branch is "the ultimate arbiter of public policy." It necessarily follows that the legislature has the power to continually create and refine the laws to meet the needs of the citizens of Ohio. The fact that the General Assembly has repeatedly sought to reform some aspects of the civil tort system for over 30 years demonstrates the continuing prominence of this issue.

Second, even considering the numerous opinions by this court on this issue, the basic constitutionality of tort-reform statutes is hardly settled law. Our prior review has focused on certain unconstitutional facets of the prior tort-reform laws that can be addressed to create constitutionally valid legislation. We have not dismissed all tort reform as an unconstitutional concept.

III. Standard of Review

A. Limits on Noneconomic Damages in R.C. 2315.18

The first certified question concerns the constitutionality of R..C. 2315.18. The statute provides a basic procedure for the imposition of damages in certain tort actions. After a verdict has been reached for the plaintiff in one of the specified tort actions, the court (in a bench trial) will enter findings of fact or the jury (in a jury trial) will return a general verdict accompanied by answers to interrogatories. [T]hese findings or interrogatories will specify both the total compensatory damages recoverable by the plaintiff and the portions of those damages representing economic and noneconomic losses.

Thereafter, the court must enter judgment for the plaintiff for the amount of economic damages, without limitation. For noneconomic damages, the court must limit recovery to the greater of (1) $250,000 or (2) three times the economic damages up to a maximum of $350,000, or $500,000 per single occurrence. [T]hese limits on noneconomic damages do not apply if the plaintiff suffered "[p]ermanent and substantial physical deformity, loss of use of a limb, or loss of a bodily organ system," or "[p]ermanent physical functional injury that permanently prevents the injured person from being able to independently care for self and perform life-sustaining activities."

2.   Open Courts and Right to a Remedy

Arbino...argues that R.C. 2315.18 violates Ohio's "open courts" and "right to a remedy" provisions. The Constitution provides: "*All courts shall be open,* and every person, for an injury done him in his land, goods, person, or reputation, *shall have remedy* by due course of law, and shall have justice administered without denial or delay." (Emphasis added.) Section 16, Article I, Ohio Constitution.

The definition of these rights is well settled. "When the Constitution speaks of remedy and injury to person, property, or reputation, it requires an opportunity granted at a meaningful time and in a meaningful manner." We have interpreted this provision to prohibit statutes that effectively prevent individuals from pursuing relief for their injuries.

A statute need not "completely abolish the right to open courts" to run afoul of this section. Any enactment that eliminates an individual's right to a judgment or to a verdict properly rendered in a suit will also be unconstitutional. Thus, we struck down the statute in *Sorrell* under circumstances "where the collateral source benefits reduce *the entire jury award*." When an individual is wholly foreclosed from relief after a verdict is rendered in his or her favor, the rights to "a meaningful remedy and open courts become hollow rights hardly worth exercising."

Arbino states that R.C. 2315.18 violates this provision because it "denies *any* recovery for noneconomic damages for the increment of harm greater than $250,000." We disagree.

Although R.C. 2315.18 does limit certain types of noneconomic damages, those limits do not wholly deny persons a remedy for their injuries. Injured persons not suffering the catastrophic injuries (for which there are no damages limits) may still recover their full economic damages and up to $350,000 in noneconomic damages, as well as punitive damages. These available remedies are "meaningful" ones under the Constitution. While the statute prevents some plaintiffs from obtaining the same dollar figures they may have received prior to the effective date of the statute, it neither forecloses their ability to pursue a claim at all nor "completely obliterates the entire jury award." Therefore, R.C. 2315.18 does not violate the right to a remedy or the right to an open court under Section 16, Article I of the Ohio Constitution.

C. Punitive-Damages Limits in R.C. 2315.21

The third certified question concerns the constitutionality of R.C. 2315.21, which limits the recovery of punitive damages in certain tort actions. The S.B. 80 amendments to this section included a procedure for bifurcation of proceedings for compensatory and punitive damages and a limitation on the amount of punitive damages recoverable in tort actions. Arbino has not challenged the bifurcation process, instead focusing her attack on the punitive-damages limitations.

The statute limits punitive damages in tort actions to a maximum of two times the total amount of compensatory damages awarded to a plaintiff per defendant. However, these limitations do not apply if the defendant committed a felony in causing the injury, one of the elements of the felony is that it was committed purposely or knowingly, and the defendant was convicted of or pleaded guilty to the felony.

If the limitations do apply, punitive damages may be limited further if the defendant is a "small employer" or an individual. In that case, the punitive damages may not exceed "the lesser of two times the amount of the compensatory damages awarded to the plaintiff from the defendant or ten percent of the employer's or individual's net worth when the tort was committed, up to a maximum of three hundred fifty thousand dollars."

Additionally, punitive damages may not be awarded more than once against the same defendant for the same act or course of conduct once the maximum amount of damages has been reached. However, this restriction can be overcome if the plaintiff offers new and substantial evidence of previously undiscovered behaviors for which punitive damages are appropriate or the prior awards against the defendant were "totally insufficient" to punish the defendant.

2.   Right to a Remedy and Right to an Open Court

Arbino also argues that R.C. 2315.21 violates the right to a remedy in an open court. This right protects against laws that completely foreclose a cause of action for injured plaintiffs or otherwise eliminate the ability to receive a meaningful remedy.

Like the noneconomic-damages limits, the punitive-damages limits...do not deny plaintiffs the right to seek a remedy for their tort claims. Further, they do not eliminate the ability to seek a "meaningful" remedy for their injuries, primarily because punitive damages "are not compensation for injury. Instead, they are private fines levied by civil juries to punish reprehensible conduct and to deter its future occurrence."

Because punitive damages are separate and apart from any remedy for a plaintiff's injuries, and because [the statute] does not prevent potential plaintiffs from bringing a successful cause of action for their injuries, it does not violate Section 16, Article I of the Ohio Constitution.

IV. Conclusion

The decision in this case affirms the General Assembly's efforts over the last several decades to enact meaningful tort reforms. It also places Ohio firmly with the growing number of states that have found such reforms to be constitutional.[2] However, the issue remains a contentious one across the nation, with several states finding such statutes unconstitutional.[3]

We appreciate the policy concerns Arbino and her amici have raised. However, the General Assembly is responsible for weighing those concerns and making policy decisions; we are charged with evaluating the constitutionality of their choices. Issues such as the wisdom of damages limitations and whether the specific dollar amounts available under them best serve the public interest are not for us to decide.

McINTOSH v. MELROE CO.
729 N.E.2d 972 (Ind. 2000)

---

[2] [8] {¶ a} As of the date of this opinion, courts have upheld limits on noneconomic damages in at least 19 other jurisdictions. {¶ b} At least ten states have upheld limitations on punitive damages, including provisions requiring that a certain percentage of awards be allotted to a designated public fund.

[3] [9] Among those finding such attempts at reform unconstitutional are Illinois; New Hampshire; North Dakota; South Dakota; and Wisconsin.

BOEHM, J.

This case deals with the validity of the provision in the Product Liability Act that bars product liability claims for injuries sustained more than ten years after the product is delivered to its "initial user or consumer." The plaintiffs argue that this provision violates their constitutional right under Article I, Section 12 of the Indiana Constitution to a remedy by due course of law.

FACTUAL AND PROCEDURAL BACKGROUND

On June 9, 1993, James McIntosh was injured in an accident involving a Clark Bobcat skid steer loader manufactured by Melroe. McIntosh and his wife filed suit alleging that his injuries and her resulting loss of companionship were caused by a defect in the loader. Melroe responded with a motion for summary judgment based on the ten-year statute of repose, Indiana Code § 34-20-3-1(b). That section provides that "a product liability action must be commenced...within ten (10) years after the delivery of the product to the initial user or consumer." Melroe designated evidence establishing that the loader had been delivered to its initial user on September 9, 1980, almost thirteen years before the accident. The McIntoshes did not dispute this evidence, but replied that the statute of repose violated their rights under Article I, Sections 12...of the Indiana Constitution.

I. Article I, Section 12

Article I, Section 12 of the Indiana Constitution provides, in relevant part: "All courts shall be open; and every person, for injury done to him in his person, property, or reputation, shall have remedy by due course of law." The McIntoshes argue that the statute of repose violates Section 12 because it "abrogates all of the tort protections provided by common law," and these are claimed to be guaranteed by the "due course of law" provision of Section 12.

Melroe contends that this case is governed by our decision in *Dague v. Piper Aircraft Corp.*, 418 N.E.2d 207, 213 (Ind. 1981), which held that the statute of repose does not violate Section 12. The McIntoshes assert that *Dague* addressed only the provision in Section 12 that "all courts shall be open" and did not deal with the provision that "every person, for injury done to him in his person...shall have remedy by due course of law." Although *Dague* itself did not explicitly limit its holding to the "open courts" provision, at least two members of this Court suggested a decade ago that *Dague* did not fully address the constitutionality of the statute of repose under Section 12. *See Covalt v. Carey Canada, Inc.,* 543 N.E.2d 382, 387-90 (Ind. 1989) (dissenting opinions of Shepard, C.J., and Dickson, J.).

A. Methodology

We agree with the dissent that the various frequently invoked constitutional talismans-constitutional text, history of the times, intent of the framers, etc.-are proper keys to the interpretation of Article I, Section 12. But apart from the text itself, precedents of this Court, and precedents from other states with similar provisions, we find no relevant guideposts on this point. In particular, there appears to be no unique Indiana history surrounding the adoption of this Clause in 1816 or its redrafting in 1851.

B. The Branches of Federal Due Process and State Article I, Section 12 Doctrine

By 1986, this Court could correctly observe that there was a "substantial line of cases treating the 'due process' clause of the federal constitution and the 'due course' clause of the Indiana Constitution as interchangeable." *White v. State,* 497 N.E.2d 893, 897 n. 4 (Ind. 1986). The two constitutional provisions do share certain commonalities. Both prohibit state action that deprives a person of a protectable interest without a fair proceeding. Both also require, as a threshold matter, that the claimant have a "protectable interest."

This is not to say, however, that the "open courts" or "remedies" clause of Article I, Section 12 is in all applications to be equated with the due process provisions of the Fifth and Fourteenth Amendments. In broad brush, the federal provisions guarantee procedural and substantive due process rights. Procedural rights ensure, for example, that a party will be given "the opportunity to be heard 'at a meaningful time and in a meaningful manner.'" *Mathews v. Eldridge,* 424 U.S. 319, 333 (1976). Procedural rights are found in both the civil context, where due process imposes requirements of notice, a right to a hearing, etc., as well as the criminal context, where it is the source of an array of criminal procedural rights, either directly through the Due Process Clause of the Fifth Amendment or via the Due Process Clause of the Fourteenth Amendment.

The "substantive" due process strain declares some actions so outlandish that they cannot be accomplished by any procedure. In earlier times, this took the form of preservation of property and contractual rights. It reached a highwater mark in cases invalidating progressive era and New Deal legislation, most notably the now discredited *Lochner v. New York,* 198 U.S. 45 (1905), which struck down a state law limiting the work week to sixty hours. This doctrine remains today as a constitutional bar to actions that "shock the conscience," *see County of Sacramento v. Lewis,* 523 U.S. 833, 846 (1998), despite the recognition that "guideposts for responsible decisionmaking in this uncharted area are scarce and open-ended." *Collins v. City of Harker Heights,* 503 U.S. 115, 125 (1992).

Article I, Section 12 of our State Constitution also has multiple strains, but they are not the same as the federal pair. [T]he remedies clause prescribes procedural fairness. It guarantees a "remedy by due course of law" for injuries to "person, property, or reputation." Section 12 also differs from the due process clauses by providing that the courts "shall be open," a requirement that seems meaningful only to civil litigants.

In the context of a procedural right to "remedy by due course of law" in a civil proceeding, the Indiana Constitution has developed a body of law essentially identical to federal due process doctrine. [T]here also is a strain of Article I, Section 12 doctrine that is analogous to federal substantive due process. As elaborated below, in general this doctrine imposes the requirement that legislation interfering with a right bear a rational relationship to a legitimate legislative goal, but does not preserve any particular remedy from legislative repeal.

To presage and capsulize our conclusions under these differing lines of Section 12 doctrine, the Product Liability Act statute of repose is consistent with each. In terms of pure civil procedural due process analysis, there is no issue. The bar of the statute of repose in the Product Liability Act does not purport to regulate the procedure in the courts. Nor is the open courts requirement violated because, as *Dague* held, it remains the province of the General Assembly to identify legally cognizable claims for relief. If the law provides no remedy, denying a remedy is consistent with due course of law. Finally, there is no state constitutional "substantive" due course of law violation because this legislation has been held to be, and we again hold it to be, rationally related to a legitimate legislative objective. It is debatable whether the Product Liability Act eliminated a common law remedy, but even if it did, there is no substantive constitutional requirement that bars a statute from accomplishing that.

C. The Constitution Did Not Freeze the Common Law

The McIntoshes argue that they have a constitutional right to a remedy for their injuries because the framers of the 1851 Constitution "decided not to give the General Assembly broad powers to abolish the common law." From this they suggest that they have a protectable constitutional right to the remedy provided by the common law for product liability injuries. This amounts to a claim that common law remedies may not be abolished. It is fundamentally a claim that these remedies constitute a protected species similar to the rights thought embedded in the constitution by substantive due process. Although *Dague* did not address this contention in the context of upholding the Product Liability Act's statute of repose, precedent strongly rejects it. This Court has long recognized the ability of the General Assembly to modify or abrogate the common law. "Indiana courts have uniformly held that in cases involving injury to person or property, Article I, § 12 does not prevent the legislature from modifying or restricting common law rights and remedies." In sum, the courts of this

State, like those of most others, "generally agree that the constitutional assurance of a remedy for injury does not create any new substantive rights to recover for particular harms. Rather, the clause promises that, for injuries recognized elsewhere in the law, the courts will be open for meaningful redress." Jennifer Friesen, *State Constitutional Law* § 6-2(c) (2d ed. 1996).

Although there is a significant split in other states as to whether provisions similar to our "remedy by due course" provision permit the legislature to impose a statute of repose in product liability cases, we agree with the Supreme Court of Oregon that "[t]he legislature has the authority to determine what constitutes a legally cognizable injury." *Sealey v. Hicks*, 788 P.2d 435, 439 (Ore. 1990). Indeed, we believe that there is a very powerful reason that the General Assembly must have the authority to determine what injuries are legally cognizable, i.e., which injuries are wrongs for which there is a legal remedy. A contrary view implies a static common law that is inconsistent with the evolution of legal doctrine before and after 1851. Perhaps equally important, if we are to find some remedies chiseled in constitutional stone, we wander into the area of "scarce and open-ended" guideposts for identifying which remedies are of constitutional dimension, and which are not.

We have long held that the General Assembly has the authority to modify the common law and that there is no "fundamental right" to bring a particular cause of action to remedy an asserted wrong. Rather, because individuals have "no vested or property right in any rule of common law," the General Assembly can make substantial changes to the existing law without infringing on citizen rights. Because no citizen has a protectable interest in the state of product liability law as it existed before the Product Liability Act, the General Assembly's abrogation of the common law of product liability through the statute of repose does not run afoul of the "substantive" due course of law provision of Article I, Section 12.

D. If "Due Course of Law" Provides No Remedy, None Is Required by the Constitution

In this case, the General Assembly has determined that injuries occurring ten years after the product was delivered to a user are not legally cognizable claims for relief. Accordingly, the McIntoshes are not entitled to a "remedy" under Section 12. Thus, the statute of repose "'does not bar a cause of action; its effect, rather, is to prevent what might otherwise be a cause of action from ever arising.... The injured party literally has *no* cause of action. The harm that has been done is *damnum absque injuria*-a wrong for which the law affords no redress.'"

Although the state constitution requires courts to be open to provide remedy by due course of law, legislation by rational classification to abolish a remedy is consonant with due course of law. If the law provides no remedy, Section 12 does not require…one.

Finally, the dissent concludes that Article I, Section 12 guarantees to each citizen "a substantive right to remedy for injuries suffered." We think this confuses "injury" with "wrong." There is not and never has been a right to redress for every injury, as victims of natural disasters or faultless accidents can attest. Nor is there any constitutional right to any particular remedy. Indeed, as we have pointed out, some forms of "wrong" recognized at common law have long since been abolished by the legislature without conflict with the Indiana Constitution. Ironically, the wrong the dissent contends in this case to be preserved by the constitution against legislative interference, strict liability for product flaws, did not exist in 1851; it was adopted as part of the Product Liability Act in 1978. It is true, as the dissent notes, that the concept of strict liability did not originate with the Product Liability Act. Although strict liability did not exist in 1851, by the 1970s, it had become a recognized theory of recovery. This further underscores the point that the common law was not frozen in 1851 and is not chiseled in stone today.

E. The Statute Is A Rational Means of Achieving a Legitimate Legislative Goal

Although we reject the McIntoshes' [challenge], the legislature's authority is not without limits. Section 12 requires that legislation that deprives a person of a complete tort remedy must be a rational means to achieve a legitimate legislative goal. [W]e also [have held] that, as applied to the individual case, the limitation must not be an unreasonable impediment to the exercise of an otherwise valid claim.

The Product Liability Act meets both tests. The statute of repose represents a determination by the General Assembly that an injury occurring ten years after the product has been in use is not a legally cognizable "injury" that is to be remedied by the courts. This decision was based on its apparent conclusion that after a decade of use, product failures are "due to reasons not fairly laid at the manufacturer's door." The statute also serves the public policy concerns of reliability and availability of evidence after long periods of time, and the ability of manufacturers to plan their affairs without the potential for unknown liability. It provides certainty and finality with a bright line bar to liability ten years after a product's first use. It is also rationally related to the General Assembly's reasonable determination that, in the vast majority of cases, failure of products over ten years old is due to wear and tear or other causes not the fault of the manufacturer, and the substantial interests already identified warrant establishing a bright line after which no claim is created.

In sum, the McIntoshes do not have a vested interest in the state of the common law as it existed before the Product Liability Act was passed. The

General Assembly has made the permissible legislative choice to limit product liability actions to the first ten years of a product's use. Accordingly, the McIntoshes' injuries, which occurred after the ten-year statute of repose ended, were not legally cognizable injuries for which a remedy exists and the statute of repose does not violate Section 12.

DICKSON, J., dissenting.

This case presented us with an opportunity to restore to Indiana's jurisprudence important principles of our state constitution. By doing so, we could have vividly exemplified the Rule of Law notwithstanding the allure of pragmatic commercial interests. We should hold that the ten-year statute of repose provision in the Indiana Products Liability Act violates [] the Right to Remedy Clause[] of the Indiana Constitution.

Right to Remedy Clause

Within the Bill of Rights of the Indiana Constitution, Section 12 provides in relevant part: All courts shall be open; and every person, for injury done to him in his person, property, or reputation, shall have remedy by due course of law.[4] The majority today holds that the statute of repose in the Indiana Products Liability Act, which denies remedy to citizens injured by defective products that happen to be more than ten years old, does not violate this provision. Noting prior cases that have considered the Due Course of Law Clause of the Indiana Constitution analogous to the Due Process Clause of the U.S. Constitution, the majority correctly acknowledges that the two provisions are not synonymous, but nevertheless finds the statute of repose provision proper because it concludes that there is no constitutional right to remedy in Indiana. I disagree.

Indiana first adopted a "remedy by due course of law" provision as part of its original Constitution in 1816. This provision was retained with only slight modification (replacing "lands, goods" with "property") when our present Constitution was adopted in 1851. When Section 12 was adopted in 1851 (and when adopted in its initial form in 1816), the only source of federal due process protection was that provided in the Fifth Amendment, which did not contain a right to remedy clause and was not applicable to the states. From the time of the Declaration of Independence until after the Civil War, the rights and liberties of citizens were protected against government infringement only by the declarations of rights in the individual states. Justice Randy J. Holland, *State Constitutions: Purpose and Function,* 69 TEMPLE L.REV. 989, 998 (1996). The Fourteenth

---

[4] [1] The full provision states: "All courts shall be open; and every person, for injury done to him in his person, property, or reputation, shall have remedy by due course of law. Justice shall be administered freely, and without purchase; completely, and without denial; speedily, and without delay." IND. CONST. art. I, § 12.

Amendment to the U.S. Constitution, which includes the Due Process Clause that is applicable to the states, was not adopted until 1868, and thus could not have served as the model for Article I, Section 12 of Indiana's 1851 Constitution.

Thirty-seven other state constitutions also include a "remedies" provision. These provisions trace their roots to chapter 40 of the Magna Carta: "To no one will we sell, to no one will we deny, or delay right or justice." It is this assurance of access to justice that is embodied in our Right to Remedy Clause.

Applying our well-established methodology of constitutional interpretation, I conclude that Section 12 provides separate and distinct protections and is not coextensive with federal due process jurisprudence. I am also convinced that Section 12 ensures not only that procedures must comply with due course of law, but further that both the text and the history provide strong support for understanding Section 12 of Indiana's Bill of Rights to provide a substantive right to remedy for injuries suffered.

The legislature has the authority to modify or abrogate common law rights as long as such change does not interfere with constitutional rights. Although constitutional rights may be subjected to legislative restraints and burdens necessitated by the State's exercise of its police power to promote the peace, safety, and well-being of the public, this police power is not unlimited: "[T]here is within each provision of our Bill of Rights a cluster of essential values which the legislature may qualify but not alienate." *Price v. State,* 622 N.E.2d 954, 960 (Ind. 1993). "A right is impermissibly alienated when the State materially burdens one of the core values which it embodies." The right to remedy for injury is such a core value.

While legislative qualifications of this right may be enacted under the police power, the total abrogation of an injured person's right to remedy is an unacceptable material burden. The statute of repose provision in the Products Liability Act is no mere qualification. It does not merely limit the time within which to assert a remedy, nor does it merely modify the procedure for enforcing the remedy. Nor is it a narrow, limited immunity necessitated by police power. On the contrary, the repose provision completely bars the courthouse doors to all persons injured by products over ten years old, even for claims alleging negligence, and even where the products were designed, built, sold, and purchased with the expectation of decades of continued use. Although this provision denies all Indiana citizens access to justice ensured by the Right to Remedy Clause, it is especially pernicious to those economically disadvantaged citizens who must rely on older or used products rather than new ones.

I would find that the Products Liability Act repose provision violates our Right to Remedy Clause.

ROSE v. DOCTORS HOSPITAL
801 S.W.2d 841 (Tex. 1990)

COOK, J.

In this case, we once again consider the constitutionality of the damages provisions of the Medical Liability and Insurance Improvement Act, TEX.REV.CIV.STAT.ANN. art. 4590i, §§ 11.02 and 11.03 (Vernon Supp.1991) ("Medical Liability Act"), this time in the context of a wrongful death action. The court of appeals decided that the statutory damages limitations provisions are constitutional. We decided subsequently to the court of appeals opinion that statutory damages limitations are unconstitutional when applied to damages in common law medical malpractice actions. *Lucas v. United States,* 757 S.W.2d 687, 692 (Tex. 1988). Our holding in *Lucas,* however, did not extend to wrongful death actions. We now hold that the legislature may, through the Medical Liability Act, constitutionally curtail damages in wrongful death actions.

I.   FACTS

Rex Rose was admitted to Doctors Hospital and died there the next day. His widow, Lisa Beth, and his parents, Alton and Frances, brought a wrongful death action against the hospital, contending that Rex Rose had received a fatal dose of morphine while a patient at the hospital. The jury awarded $2,825,000 to Lisa Beth Rose and $815,000 each to Alton and Frances Rose, but the trial court rendered judgment notwithstanding the verdict.

The court of appeals reversed, holding that there was some evidence that the hospital caused Rex Rose's death. The court did, however, suggest remittiturs to reduce the damages awarded by the jury. Lisa Beth Rose's damages were reduced in accordance with § 11.02 of the Medical Liability Act. The court suggested a remittitur reducing Alton and Frances Rose's damages to the amount supported by the evidence.

The Roses responded by filing remittiturs within the time period prescribed by the court of appeals. However, the Roses expressly reserved the right to complain of the ruling requiring the remittiturs.

The Roses argue that the court of appeals was prohibited by the Texas Constitution and our decision in *Lucas* from reducing the damages awarded to Lisa Beth Rose.

II. STATUTORY VALIDITY

In *Lucas,* the United States Court of Appeals for the Fifth Circuit asked this court to decide whether the limitation on medical malpractice damages in the Medical Liability Act is consistent with the Texas Constitution. We looked to the open courts provision of our constitution to determine whether that provision thwarted application of the damages limitations. The provision [Tex. Const. art. I, § 13] states:

> All courts shall be open, and every person for an injury done him, in his lands, goods, person or reputation, shall have remedy by due course of law.

We noted that, in analyzing the litigant's right to redress under this provision, the litigant must satisfy two criteria. First, the litigant must have a cognizable common law cause of action that is being restricted. Second, the litigant must show that the restriction is unreasonable or arbitrary when balanced against the purpose and basis of the statute.

The court initially acknowledged that victims of medical negligence have a well-defined common law cause of action to sue for injuries. The court then concluded that the statutory damages limitations provisions at issue met the second criterion, that is, they were unreasonable and arbitrary when balanced against the purpose and basis of the statute. Having reached these conclusions, the court decided that the damages limitations provisions were unconstitutional "as applied to catastrophically damaged malpractice victims seeking a 'remedy by due course of law.'"

Notwithstanding the specific application of the *Lucas* holding to catastrophically damaged malpractice victims, the Roses argue that the holding voids the statute in all respects and for all applications. We disagree.

The application of §§ 11.02 and 11.03 to wrongful death claims remains complete in itself, capable of execution in accord with the legislature's intent, and independent of any application to common law claims. The statute, therefore, can be severed, leaving a valid law.

To reach any other conclusion would be to ignore not only the intent of the legislature and the specific holding in *Lucas,* but also our traditional distinction between common law personal injury and statutory wrongful death claims. We recognized this distinction in *Lucas,* restating the traditional rule that the open courts provision of our constitution applies only to common law claims. We relied upon this distinction to strike application of §§ 11.02 and 11.03 to common law medical malpractice claims. Had we faced a wrongful death claim in *Lucas,* we could not have reached the same conclusion, for the open courts provision does not apply to statutory claims. Can we now rely upon *Lucas* to do something we may not do under the law as delineated in *Lucas* itself, that is, declare the statute unconstitutional in the context of wrongful death claims? We think not. For this and all the other reasons discussed, we conclude that we are construing a statute which may be validly applied to all but common law claims.

III. CONSTITUTIONALITY   OF   STATUTORY   DAMAGES PROVISIONS

To determine whether the open courts provision prevents constitutional application of the Medical Liability Act in the case before us today, we are guided by the two-prong analysis in *Lucas*. We ask first whether the Roses' remedy is based upon a cognizable common law cause of action. If the remedy was so grounded, then the open courts provision prevents application of the Medical Liability Act in this case.

Like all actions based upon theories of negligence, the Roses' cause of action was a common law claim. It would have died with Rex Rose had it not been preserved by the legislature in the wrongful death statute. The Roses' remedy, therefore, was conferred by statute, not by the common law. Because the Roses do not seek a common law remedy, the open courts provision does not apply to their wrongful death claim. Accordingly, we hold that the open courts provision may not bar the application of the damages provisions of the Medical Liability Act in wrongful death cases.

In conclusion, we hold that the damages provisions of the Medical Liability Act are constitutional when applied to wrongful death actions.

IEROPOLI v. AC&S CORP.
842 A.2d 919 (Pa. 2004)

CAPPY, C. J.

In this appeal, we review the order of the court of common pleas granting summary judgment to Appellee Crown Cork & Seal Company, Inc. ("Crown Cork") pursuant to the newly enacted statute ("Statute") that limits the successor asbestos-related liabilities of certain Pennsylvania corporations. 15 Pa.C.S. § 1929.1. For all the reasons that follow, we hold that the Statute is unconstitutional as applied under Article I, Section 11 of the Pennsylvania Constitution.

On December 19, 2000, Appellants, Frank and Margaret Ieropoli, commenced a civil action, filing a complaint against Crown Cork and twenty-four other defendants. In their complaint, Appellants alleged that Frank Ieropoli was exposed to defendants' respective asbestos products while working as a machinist with General Electric from 1947 until 1979…Appellants asserted several causes of action against Crown Cork sounding in tort or contract. For the most part, Appellants asserted these same causes of action against Crown Cork's co-defendants. Appellants requested that a judgment for compensatory damages, punitive damages…be entered against Crown Cork and its co-defendants individually, and jointly and severally, where appropriate.

The Statute was passed by the General Assembly, signed into law on December 17, 2001, and made immediately effective. The Statute limits the asbestos-related liabilities of corporations incorporated in Pennsylvania before May 1, 2001 that arise out of mergers or consolidations. The Statute provides:

§ 1929.1. Limitations on asbestos-related liabilities relating to certain mergers or consolidations.-

(a) Limitation on successor asbestos-related liabilities.

(1) Except as further limited in paragraph (2) the cumulative successor asbestos-related liabilities of a domestic business corporation that was incorporated in this Commonwealth prior to May 1, 2001, shall be limited to the fair market value of the total assets of the transferor determined as of the time of the merger or consolidation, and such corporation shall have no responsibility for successor asbestos-related liabilities in excess of such limitation.

On February 7, 2002, Crown Cork filed a [motion for summary judgment]...requesting that judgment be entered in its favor in several hundred asbestos cases pending against it in the Court of Common Pleas in Philadelphia County. In its Motion, Crown Cork set forth the following undisputed, material facts of record: Crown Cork is a Pennsylvania business corporation and a manufacturer of beverage cans; Crown Cork purchased a majority of the stock of Mundet Cork Corporation ("Mundet Cork") in November 1963; Mundet Cork had a division that made, sold and installed asbestos insulation; Crown Cork never operated the insulation division; Crown Cork sold the insulation division 90 days after acquiring Mundet Cork's stock; Crown Cork acquired all of Mundet Cork's stock and merged with Mundet Cork on February 10, 1996; the value of Mundet Cork's assets at the time of the merger was in the range of $11 to $12 million; the value of Mundet Cork's assets at the time of the merger adjusted for inflation was in the range of $50 to $55 million; Crown Cork was reincorporated in Pennsylvania on March 30, 1996; Crown Cork was sued in asbestos-related cases solely as a successor to Mundet Cork; and Crown Cork has paid out $336 million on asbestos-related claims.

Based on these facts, Crown Cork asserted that because all of the cases that are the subject of its Motion come within the Statute's definition of "asbestos claims"; because it has already paid an amount in excess of the limit on liability created by the Statute; and because Appellants no longer have a damages remedy for the claims they asserted against it, the Statute required that its Motion be granted.

Appellants argued that application of the Statute in this case is unconstitutional under Article I, Section 11 of the Pennsylvania Constitution. More specifically, Appellants asserted that Article 1, Section 11 was violated because application of the Statute in this case serves to extinguish accrued causes of action. The trial court rejected Appellants' argument. While acknowledging that the Appellants' causes of action against Crown Cork accrued prior to the Statute's enactment, the trial court concluded that the Statute did not extinguish any cause of action.

We begin with a discussion of Article 1, Section 11 of the Pennsylvania Constitution. Article I, Section 11 has been in the Pennsylvania Constitution since 1790, and is part of the Constitution's Declaration of Rights. Article I, Section 11 states:

> § 11. Courts to be open; suits against the Commonwealth

> All courts shall be open; and every man for an injury done him in his lands, goods, person or reputation shall have remedy by due course of law, and right and justice administered without sale, denial or delay. Suits may be brought against the Commonwealth in such manner, in such courts and in such cases as the legislature may by law direct.

The constitutions of thirty-nine states contain a provision that is substantially similar to that part of Article 1, Section 11 that is highlighted. *See* David Schuman, *The Right to a Remedy,* 65 TEMP. L. REV.. 1197, 1201 (1992) ("The Schuman Article"). This provision, commonly referred to as the "open courts" or "remedies" clause, is derived from Magna Carta and Sir Edward Coke's Seventeenth Century commentary on the Great Charter, which was relied upon by the drafters of early American state constitutions. Jennifer Friesen, *State Constitutional Law: Litigating Individual Rights, Claims, and Defenses* § 6-2(a) (3d ed. 2000).

Turning to the respective arguments the parties have presented, Appellants assert that as a general proposition, Article 1, Section 11 does not prevent the General Assembly from enacting a statute that eliminates a cause of action that exists at common law. Appellants contend that what Article 1, Section 11 precludes is the elimination of accrued causes of action by newly-enacted legislation. According to Appellants, the application of the Statute to the causes of action they brought against Crown Cork violates this rule.

Crown Cork…contends that the Statute merely varies the remedy that was available to Appellants [and]…the fact that Appellants have collected settlement monies or will recover damages from its co-defendants shows that Article 1, Section 11 is not violated. Finally,…Crown Cork asserts that because the Statute only alters the allocation of damages among multiple defendants, Article 1, Section 11 is not implicated.

We begin our analysis of Appellant's constitutional challenge to the Statute by determining what the Statute's application in this case means for Crown Cork. This determination is a matter of statutory construction. Through the causes of action they brought against Crown Cork, Appellants seek a payment of damages from the company for the losses they allegedly sustained as a result of Frank Ieropoli's exposure to certain asbestos products that Crown Cork's merger partner manufactured and sold. Because Crown Cork has met § 1929.1(a)(1)'s limit, however, the Statute provides that Crown Cork "shall have no responsibility for cumulative successor asbestos-related liabilities...." Under § 1929.1(e)'s definition, "successor asbestos-related liabilities" are "[a]ny liabilities, whether known or unknown, asserted or unasserted, absolute or contingent, accrued or unaccrued, liquidated or unliquidated or due or to become due, related in any way to asbestos claims", and include payments made "in connection with settlements, judgments or other discharges in this Commonwealth or another jurisdiction." Under that same definition, an "asbestos claim" is "[a]ny claim, wherever or whenever made for damages, losses, indemnification, contribution or other relief arising out of, based on or in any way related to asbestos."

In our view, the Statute is clear and unambiguous as to the protection the General Assembly intended to give to Crown Cork. The words of the Statute state that a qualified corporation is not responsible for any liability that is related to any claim for relief related to asbestos. Thus, in the present case, the Statute protects Crown Cork from any liability to Appellants on the causes of action they brought against it.

It now remains to determine whether the protection from liability on Appellants' causes of action that the Statute gives to Crown Cork affects those causes of action in a way that Article 1, Section 11 prohibits. For this, we begin with the meaning of the phrase "cause of action". In this case, "cause of action" relates to remedy. It is the vehicle by which a person secures redress from another person for the consequences of an event that is a legal injury. Moreover, as we have seen, a cause of action that has accrued takes on an even greater meaning. It is a vested right, which under Article 1, Section 11, may not be eliminated by subsequent legislation.

In light of these principles, the violation of Article 1, Section 11 that the Statute's application occasions in this case is clear. Before the Statute's enactment, each cause of action that Appellants brought against Crown Cork was a remedy-it was the vehicle by which Appellants lawfully pursued redress, in the form of damages, from Crown Cork for an alleged legal injury. But under the Statute, Appellants cannot obligate Crown Cork to pay them damages on those causes of action. In this way, each cause of action has been stripped of its remedial significance, as it can no longer function as the means by which Appellants may secure redress from Crown Cork. As a remedy, each cause of action has been, in essence, extinguished. Under Article 1, Section 11, however, a statute may not extinguish a cause of action that has accrued.

By way of conclusion, we in the majority point out that we are as concerned with the heavy toll that asbestos litigation is visiting upon certain Commonwealth corporations as are our respected colleagues in the dissent. Nevertheless, any statutory effort aimed at reformation must not offend the Remedies Clause, if it is to pass constitutional muster. That Clause, which binds both the legislature and the courts, provides that an accrued cause of action is a vested right and as such, cannot be eliminated by subsequent legislation. This is the basic and undeniable principle that applies here. We know of no authority that supports the proposition that an accrued cause of action that is the subject of a merger does not receive the Remedies Clause's full protection. Likewise, we know of no authority (separate from the Statute) that would in these circumstances, override the general tenet of corporate law that states that the corporation that absorbs another corporation in a merger becomes legally responsible in every sense of the word for the latter's liabilities and debts.

Thus, for all of the foregoing reasons, we hold that the Statute as applied in this case is unconstitutional under Article 1, Section 11.

NEWMAN, J., dissenting.

The majority finds Section 1929.1 repugnant to Article I, Section 11 of the Pennsylvania Constitution, which states that "[a]ll courts shall be open; and every man for an injury done him in his lands, goods, person or reputation **shall have remedy by due course of law,** and right and justice administered without sale, denial or delay." (emphasis added). We have explained that this provision of our state Constitution ensures "that the Legislature may not extinguish a right of action which has already accrued to a claimant."

The problem in the instant case is the identification of the party legally responsible for the injuries suffered by the Ieropolis. The responsible party in the instant case is not Crown; rather it is Mundet Cork. My point in this regard is not intended to undo a century of successor liability law, but to acknowledge the artifice of deeming a successor corporation responsible for the injury. The cause of action in this case does not accrue against Crown; more accurately, it accrues against Mundet Cork and, pursuant to its status as successor, Crown steps into the shoes of Mundet Cork to ensure that, as between a blameless plaintiff and a corporation that has succeeded a corporation responsible for an injury, the successor corporation, not the blameless plaintiff, is responsible for the acts of the tortfeasor. Successor liability is an important tenet of our system of jurisprudence, but it is not one protected by Article I, Section 11 of the Pennsylvania Constitution. Causes of action in tort do not accrue in a vacuum-rather, they arise against an entity for a wrong done at the time an injury is incurred. Article I, Section 11 forecloses retroactive elimination or limitation of the liability of the tortfeasor.

Conceived of in this way, Section 1929.1 does not extinguish a vested right or an accrued cause of action. Neither does it eliminate a right to a remedy. Instead, Section 1929.1 limits the amount of liability that successor corporations can be made to be accountable for and, ultimately, limits the class of entities who can be made to bear the burden of that right. This is not to say that the legislature could constitutionally provide that all pending asbestos cases are summarily dismissed-this would extinguish vested causes of action against entities responsible for injuries. But the constitutional provision with which we are concerned, Article I, Section 11, does not estop the General Assembly from limiting (or eliminating) the effect of successor liability, even retroactively. Section 1929.1 does not retroactively limit or extinguish the liability because the successor corporation (in the case *sub judice,* Crown) is not the tortfeasor.

It is conceivable, although unlikely, that at some point in the future a plaintiff in a pending asbestos case could, by virtue of Section 1929.1, be denied any recovery. That would be an unfortunate result of my position in this case, but that potentiality should not enter into the consideration of a court of last resort charged with determining whether the statute passes constitutional muster.

SAYLOR, J., dissenting.

As indicated in the common pleas court's summary of the undisputed facts, Crown Cork is a Pennsylvania packaging manufacturing corporation that has never in its 110-year history made, distributed, or sold asbestos-its potential liability to plaintiffs in asbestos-related causes of action is predicated solely on the theory of successor liability based upon its brief, passive ownership of a company that once produced asbestos but did not do so while in Crown Cork's control. None of the cases presently cited by the majority involves a successor liability paradigm; rather, each concerns attempts to adjust interests and/or liabilities between parties with more direct involvement in the underlying affairs giving rise to the interests/liabilities at stake.

In my view, this attribute of the potential liabilities that the General Assembly has sought to address is due a greater role than the majority allows it in the assessment of the legislation's consonance with the Remedies Clause. Successor liability in the context of a merger represents an assumption of liabilities by operation of law which has the effect of exposing the successor's larger pool of assets to liability that, absent the merger, would not have attached. It is an issue of first impression whether the excess exposure created by the doctrine must share the same degree of vesting under Remedies Clause as would the tortfeasor's primary liability in the first instance. Where, as here, the General Assembly has attempted to reasonably limit such assumed, excess exposure, and particularly in a situation in which the successor corporation already has contributed toward payment of asbestos-related claims an amount several fold the value of the acquired entity's assets, I would not find that the statute, either facially or as applied, offends the Remedies Clause.

NOTES

1. What level of scrutiny do the courts apply when evaluating claims that a statutory enactment has violated the right to a remedy or open courts provisions? Does the standard resemble any standard applied in other state or federal contexts, e.g., in federal equal protection or due process analysis?

2. Is the "right to a remedy by due course of law" a procedural guarantee? A substantive protection? Or both?

3. Does it matter to the courts whether a challenged limitation affects only a common law claim? A statutory claim? Is there justification for treating statutory and common law claims differently?

LANEY v. FAIRVIEW CITY
57 P.3d 1007 (Utah 2002)

DURHAM, C. J.

This case addresses whether Utah Code Ann. § 63-30-2(4)(a) violates the "open courts" clause, of the Utah Constitution. The district court held that Fairview City (the City) is immune from suit for its alleged negligence under the Utah Governmental Immunity Act. We hold that the 1987 amendment, declaring all acts of municipalities to be governmental functions, is unconstitutional as applied to municipalities operating electrical power systems.

BACKGROUND

On September 16, 1991, John Laney was electrocuted and killed while moving irrigation pipe. The thirty-foot aluminum water irrigation pipe that Laney was carrying came into contact with, or within arcing distance of, high voltage power lines. The power lines were owned by the City.

Accordingly, Laney's wife and children brought a wrongful death action against the City claiming, inter alia, that the City was negligent for failing to maintain the power lines in a safe condition. The Laneys complain that the power lines did not meet minimum safety standards because they were too low to the ground. They also allege that the lines were unsafe because they were not insulated and did not contain warnings.

The City moved for summary judgment asserting that the decision whether or not to improve the power lines was a discretionary function entitled to immunity under Utah Code Ann. § 63-30-10(1) (1997). Discretionary function immunity is an exception to a waiver of sovereign immunity within the Utah Governmental Immunity Act. The Utah

Governmental Immunity Act declares that all governmental entities are immune from suit for any injury which results from the exercise of a "governmental function." The term governmental function is broadly defined in section 63-30-2(4)(a), and by virtue of that broad definition, the statute cloaks governmental entities with immunity for a wide range of activities. However, Utah Code Ann. § 63-30-10 waives sovereign immunity "for injury proximately caused by a negligent act or omission." Then, subsection (1) creates an exception to this waiver for negligence and immunizes governmental entities for "the exercise or performance or the failure to exercise or perform a discretionary function...."

The district court agreed that the City was entitled to immunity for its decision to not improve the power lines and granted the City's motion for summary judgment.

Plaintiffs appeal, claiming that Utah Code Ann. § 63-30-2(4)(a) is unconstitutional because it violates article I, section 11, the open courts clause, of the Utah Constitution.

ANALYSIS

II. CONSTITUTIONALITY OF UTAH CODE ANN. § 63-30-2(4)(a)

Because we find that the City's maintenance of the power lines constitutes a discretionary function within the meaning of the Governmental Immunity Act, we must address the plaintiffs' [constitutional] challenge. Article I, section 11 of the Utah Constitution provides:

> All courts shall be open, and every person, for an injury done to him in his person, property, or reputation, shall have remedy by due course of law, which shall be administered without denial or unnecessary delay; and no person shall be barred from prosecuting or defending before any tribunal in this state, by himself or counsel any civil cause to which he is a party.

Plaintiffs argue that the Act deprives them of their rights guaranteed by the open courts clause.

A. Berry v. Beech Aircraft Analysis

The State urges this court to abandon nearly a century of precedent, arguing for an interpretation that would virtually write article I, section 11 out of the Utah Constitution. Specifically, the State asks the court to overrule *Berry v. Beech Aircraft Corp.,* 717 P.2d 670 (Utah 1985), and the principles explained therein. As early as 1915, only twenty years after Utah's constitution was adopted, this court acknowledged that article I, section 11 placed "a limitation upon the Legislature to prevent that branch of the state government from closing the doors of the courts against any person who has a legal right which is enforceable in accordance with some known remedy."

1. Plain Meaning and Historical Purpose

In arguing for article I, section 11 to be treated solely as a procedural right, the State disregards the plain meaning and historical purpose of Utah's open courts provision. Throughout our state's history, this court has consistently recognized that the plain meaning of the guarantee "impose[s] some *substantive* limitation on the legislature to abolish judicial remedies in a capricious fashion."

[O]pen courts provisions in Utah and other states have served two principal purposes:

> First, they were intended to help establish an independent foundation for the judiciary as an institution. Second, open courts or remedies clauses were intended to grant individuals rights to a judicial remedy for the protection of their person, property, or reputation from abrogation and *unreasonable limitation by economic interests that could control state legislatures.*

Although some states with open courts provisions have construed them to guarantee only procedural rights and court access, such a construction has never been accepted in Utah. Article I, section 11's constitutional guarantee has been interpreted to protect substantive rights to remedies throughout our state's history. The open courts provision was adopted, as part of the original Constitution itself, at the end of the nineteenth century, during a period when abuse had generated concern and distrust of the legislative branch in numerous states. That abuse included misuse of political influence by railroads and other corporate interests, who convinced state legislators to favor private interests through legislative enactments insulating them from the general laws.

Focusing entirely on the "procedural" content of the language found in section 11, as the State does, is misleading. Constitutional language must be viewed in context, meaning that its history and purpose must be considered in determining its meaning. The language that a remedy shall be had by "due course of law" describes the law by which the remedy is secured, as well as the procedural guarantees also protected by this section. Article I, section 7 already contains a due process provision guaranteeing procedural rights. Thus, if the State's reading of section 11 is correct, section 11 is redundant and mere surplusage-it has no constitutional role or function that is not already performed by section 7. That view has never been embraced by any Utah decision.

B. Application of Berry to Subsection 63-30-2(4)(a)

We now turn to the analysis of the constitutionality of subsection 63-30-2(4)(a) using the test set forth in *Berry*. A legislative enactment that does not eliminate a remedy is not unconstitutional under the open courts provision. Therefore, we must first determine whether a cause of action has been abrogated by the legislative enactment. If no remedy was eliminated, there is no need to proceed with the *Berry* test.

1. Abrogation of Remedy

The State argues in this case that no remedy was abrogated because the 1987 amendment to the Governmental Immunity Act had been enacted four years before Mr. Laney was electrocuted in 1991. The issue under the open courts provision, however, is not whether a statute has already been enacted before a claim arises, but rather whether the statute abrogates a cause of action existing at the time of its enactment. Thus, the State's argument that there is no abrogation of a remedy if a statute is already in effect at the time a cause of action arises is inapplicable.

Plaintiffs assert that the 1987 amendment abrogated a remedy because the law in effect prior to the amendment provided individuals negligently injured by municipality-operated power lines with a cause of action against the municipality. Prior to the amendment, the scope of sovereign immunity depended on whether the governmental activity complained of was found to be a "governmental function" or a "proprietary function." Only those activities determined to be governmental functions were afforded immunity. The Act did not define what constituted a governmental function, therefore this court established a standard whereby a function could be considered a governmental function. This definition of governmental function was used to determine whether an activity was covered by the Act until the legislature redefined the term in 1987.

Plaintiffs argue that the City's operation and maintenance of a municipal electrical power system would not have been a governmental function under [this Court's] standard because maintaining power lines is not "of such a unique nature that it can only be performed by a governmental agency or that...is essential to the core of governmental immunity." We agree.

Prior to the 1987 amendment, the operation of an electrical power system was considered a proprietary function, which was not entitled to immunity under the Act. Under the 1987 amendment, however, a claim against a municipality for negligent maintenance of power lines can be barred by the scope of immunity protection afforded the City. Although the Act waives immunity for governmental functions if there is negligence involved, a plaintiff suing a municipality is now subject to the exceptions to the waiver of immunity. By defining a governmental function as *any* act of a governmental entity, whether or not the activity is characterized as governmental or proprietary, the 1987 amendment effectively grants immunity protection for some activities that...formerly...were not entitled to immunity. Therefore, we find that the 1987 amendment partially abrogated a remedy for a municipality's negligence. Because a remedy has been abrogated, we proceed with the *Berry* test to determine the constitutionality of the amendment under the open courts provision.

2. No Reasonable Alternative Remedy

Under the first prong of the *Berry* analysis, when a remedy has been abrogated, this court first determines whether the legislature has provided a "reasonable alternative remedy 'by due course of law' for vindication of [a plaintiff's] constitutional interest." In *Berry,* we held that the substitute benefit "must be substantially equal in value or other benefit to the remedy abrogated in providing essentially comparable substantive protection to one's person, property, or reputation, although the form of the substitute remedy may be different...." In the instant case, we find no indication that the legislature provided any substitute remedy, nor does the State make this argument. Therefore, we must turn to the second prong of the *Berry* test.

3. Elimination of Clear Social or Economic Evil

The State contends that even if a remedy was abrogated, the amendment is constitutional under the second prong of the *Berry* test, which provides that where no alternative remedy has been provided, "abrogation of the remedy or cause of action may be justified only if there is a clear social or economic evil to be eliminated and the elimination of an existing legal remedy is not an arbitrary or unreasonable means for achieving the objective."

Cases involving statutes of limitation and statutes of repose have come before this court with mixed results. In an early case, we held that article I, section 11, did not preclude the legislature from prescribing a one-year statute of limitations for the time within which to assail the regularity or organization of an irrigation district. In three cases, statutes of repose were struck down because they barred actions without regard to the occurrence of an injury and did not provide a reasonable amount of time to file a lawsuit. No effective and reasonable alternative was provided, and the abrogation of the remedy was held to be arbitrary and unreasonable.

In the only case that we have found which did *not* involve an act of the legislature, this court abolished the common law tort of criminal conversation and justified its abolition under the open courts provision on the ground that the cause of action was "unfair and bad policy," "serve[d]" no useful purpose, was subject to abuse, and protected interests that were already adequately served by the tort of alienation of affections.

Recently, in *Day v. State,* 980 P.2d 1171 (Utah 1999), we relied on the open courts provision to strike down a statute granting immunity for negligent operation of an emergency vehicle in circumstances where immunity had not previously existed. We declared the statute unconstitutional because the legislature was not acting to obviate a "clear social evil" in this state. The sponsor of the legislation had explained that the statute was necessary because of a rash of frivolous lawsuits, "especially in California." We noted that on its face, the sponsor's statement did not identify any social, economic, or any other evil in Utah.

With that backdrop ..., we turn to the instant case. The 1987 amendment eliminates the appellants' right to sue for Mr. Laney's wrongful death. The statutory amendment thus sharply limited instances where municipalities operating a power system could be held liable for their negligence.

According to the legislative history, the 1987 amendment [was proposed] in the "hope that passage of these bills will make it easier or cheaper for a government entity to obtain liability insurance." Thus the legislative objective appears to have been to make liability insurance more affordable for government entities by reducing liability risks. While that objective is worthy, the legislature swept too broadly when it severely curtailed negligence actions against municipalities operating power systems. The legislative concern about increased damage awards against governmental entities is stated in very general terms; no specifics are given. We do not know whether any municipality in this state operating an electrical system has sustained a large damage award. We do know that only a small fraction operate municipal power systems. The general nature of the legislative findings do not show that large damage awards have been made against municipalities in connection with their operation of an electrical power system, or that such operation has been affected in any way by potential liability.

The City generates an annual profit operating its electrical power system. It is not an operation subsidized by tax dollars. The cost of liability insurance, therefore, might not even be paid for by the taxpayers of the City, but rather by consumers of the electrical power, some of whom may live outside the City. If the City cannot afford to purchase reasonable amounts of liability insurance to meet its high standard of care, rate increases may be justified and necessary.

Equally disturbing is the broad sweep that the legislature took to meet its objective. In the instant case, the legislature has defined *all* activities of municipalities as governmental action, regardless of their nature. In its sweep, the operation of both a sewer system and a golf course is governmental, along with the operation of a municipal electrical power system, even though the potential for negligently causing death by the municipality is vastly greater in the latter activity.

If large verdicts are vexatious to cities, a reasonable approach might be to create very limited immunities to address specific problems, or to place "caps" on the amount of damages, as the legislature has done elsewhere in the Governmental Immunity Act. This court has, for example, upheld statutory caps on judgments for damages for personal injury against a governmental entity.

We therefore hold that the 1987 amendment is unconstitutional as it applies to municipalities operating electrical power systems. No clear social or economic evil has been specifically identified, and the broad sweep of the amendment is arbitrary and unreasonable when applied to the operation of a municipal electrical power system, where a high duty of care is imposed. We express no opinion on the constitutionality of the amendment as applied to other municipal activities since a lower standard of care may apply and different considerations may be relevant.

WILKINS, J., concurring and dissenting:

In my opinion, section 63-30-2(4)(a) of the Utah Governmental Immunity Act, does not violate article I, section 11 of the Utah Constitution, the Open Courts Clause. In my view, the Legislature acted within its constitutional authority in setting forth the current scheme of sovereign immunity in Utah. Under the statute, Fairview City should be entitled to immunity for its omissions, to not raise the height of, insulate, or provide further warnings on its power lines under section 63-30-10, a discretionary function within the discretionary function exception of the Utah Governmental Immunity Act.

In the recent past, the Open Courts Clause has been interpreted in such a way that it limits the legislature's ability to alter, modify, or eliminate the law by requiring legislation to meet this court's approval through the *Berry* test. In *Berry,* prior members of this court admittedly "broke new ground and read article I, section 11 ... as imposing a strong substantive limitation on the legislature's ability to limit or eliminate a cause of action for, or the remedies available for [personal injury]."

In my view, [the *Berry*] test permits a majority of this court to substitute its judgment of what constitutes good public policy for the judgment of the legislature, the branch of government that is not only best suited to determine and implement public policy under our system of government, but constitutionally obligated to do so. I am of the opinion that whether a substitute remedy is of "substantially equal value or other benefit to the remedy abrogated," and whether there is a clear social or economic evil to be eliminated, are two questions that should be answered by the legislature, not this court, and that we overstep our bounds in so doing. I agree that the Open Courts Clause limits legislative authority. Numerous constitutional provisions prevent the legislative branch from eliminating constitutional or inalienable rights. I do not think, however, that the Open Courts Clause guarantees one the right to a judicial remedy for every injury done to one's person, property, or reputation.

The first *Berry* assumption with which I disagree is the assumption that those who suffer because of legislation preventing recovery for personal injury are individuals who are somehow part of a minority that is not represented or underrepresented in the political process. [I]ndividuals who suffer injury to their person, property, or reputation are not a discreet and insular minority. All persons, regardless of ethnic background, economic background, gender, religious persuasion, or other affiliations, may suffer injury. Viewing an injured individual or group retrospectively, after they have suffered injury, they may very well be unable to rally the political process. Prospectively, however, all of us as citizens, regardless of status, are subject to legislation limiting our ability to recover for personal injury. No group is singled out by legislation that limits the ability to recover for personal injuries. All citizens face the possibility of personal injury, even those who are generally visible in society that belong to what we may think are privileged, identifiable groups. Those thwarted by the Utah Governmental Immunity Act, those who have suffered personal injuries at the hands of the government, may be any of us; they do not comprise a distinct and insular group whose voice may not be heard through the political process.

Second, *Berry* assumes that the Open Courts Clause contains language which should be interpreted to protect against majoritarian abuse. I disagree. Other provisions in our constitution are more suited to protecting against majoritarian abuse. They contain language which more specifically implies protection for political minorities, and these provisions have also been interpreted to protect groups and individuals that are isolated from the political process. [T]he language of the Open Courts Clause is ill-suited to protect against majoritarian abuse.

The real danger presented by the *Berry* test is that of majoritarian abuse by the members of this court. The risk, in my mind, lies in requiring that new legislation satisfy the policy predilections of a majority of the members of this court by providing, in the eyes of this court, an adequate alternative remedy; or by eliminating what is viewed as a clear social or economic evil by this court. The constitution vests power in the legislature to implement, as law, the will of the majority of the citizens of this State.

Third, the *Berry* interpretation assumes that each individual who suffers an injury to his or her person, property, or reputation, is constitutionally entitled to a remedy. The idea that a remedy can be fashioned for every injury is optimistic and well-intentioned, but, as a practical matter, impossible. The law cannot, and therefore does not, guarantee a remedy for every injury.

Individuals who have been injured in their persons, property, or reputation, are entitled to a remedy only when the law, statutory or common, recognizes an injury and permits a remedy. The Open Courts Clause should not be interpreted to provide a right to a remedy. It should be interpreted to guarantee *access* to seek a judicial determination as to whether the law grants a remedy for the injury suffered. The courts, through the common law, may create remedies when public policy dictates that certain interests are worthy of protection and the legislature has not spoken. Likewise, the legislature creates remedies when it determines, as a matter of public policy, that certain interests are worthy of protection. If the law provides for a remedy, then the Open Courts Clause guarantees the right to seek that permitted remedy through the courts.

The *Berry* test places this court in the position of sitting as a second legislature, re-weighing the social or economic policy, instead of analyzing, as other methods of constitutional analysis do, whether the law is rationally related to its avowed purpose. Substitution of the policy of three or more judges for the policy of the legislature, absent specific constitutional authority, is contrary to our system of government.

NOTES

1. Are right to a remedy/open courts provisions substantive, procedural, or both? What does "substantive" and "procedural" mean in this context?

2. How difficult is it for the courts to give content and meaning to right to a remedy/open courts provisions without usurping the legislative function? Are the separation of powers considerations in this context similar to or different from such concerns generally?

HOLT v. WESLEY MEDICAL CENTER
86 P.3d 1012 (Kan. 2004)

ALLEGRUCCI, J.

This medical malpractice action was filed by plaintiffs Kimberly R. Holt and Kenneth F. Holt, and their daughter, Kimberlyn D. Holt, by and through her parents in federal court. Defendants are Wesley Medical Center, LLC, d/b/a/ Wesley Medical Center, Wichita Center for Graduate Medical Education, Inc. (WCGME), and Doctors Benjamin J. Harris, Clifford S. Depew, James E. Delmore, and Travis W. Stembridge. Upon the application of plaintiffs, Judge Julie A. Robinson of the United States District Court for the District of Kansas ordered certification of a question of law to this court under K.S.A. 60-3201 *et seq.* The question arises from the legislature's retroactively including WCGME within the statutory definition of "health care provider," thus relieving it of vicarious liability pursuant to K.S.A.2001 Supp. 40-3403(h).

CERTIFIED QUESTION:

DOES THE RETROACTIVE APPLICATION, BY K.S.A.2001 SUPP. 40-3414(i)(1), OF L.2001, CH. 204 (S.B.366), AMENDING K.S.A. 40-3401(f) AND K.S.A. 40-3403(h) OF THE HEALTH CARE PROVIDER INSURANCE AVAILABILITY ACT, DEPRIVE PLAINTIFFS OF A VESTED PROPERTY RIGHT AND VIOLATE § 18 OF THE BILL OF RIGHTS OF THE KANSAS CONSTITUTION ...?

WCGME is comprised of the University of Kansas School of Medicine-Wichita, Wesley Medical Center (Wesley), and Via Christi Regional Medical Center. WCGME is a not-for-profit corporation that at all relevant times employed defendant Benjamin Harris as a resident physician. WCGME does not hold a license from the Kansas Board of Healing Arts, nor is WCGME licensed as a medical care facility. It is not a hospital, it maintains no medical supplies, and it does not advertise or solicit patients on its own or for the resident physicians it employs. Although WCGME does not engage in the practice of medicine, provide patient services, or provide medical services to the public, the resident physicians WCGME employs do.

The plaintiffs' claim is based upon the negligence of Dr. Harris as an employee and/or agent of WCGME based upon vicarious liability. Wesley contractually agreed to indemnify WCGME for the negligent acts of WCGME's physicians practicing at its facility. According to WCGME, Kimberlyn Holt was born at Wesley in Wichita, Kansas, on July 30, 1998. Since birth, she has had profound and permanent medical problems that plaintiffs attribute to negligence on the part of resident physicians, nurses, and other health care providers who participated in the labor and delivery. According to the Holts, the care and treatment of Kimberly Holt July 29-31 and October 22, 1998, resulted in her being unable to have other children and having bladder and urinary tract difficulties. The Holts also assert that they have sustained economic and noneconomic losses due to the continuing medical problems of mother and daughter.

The Holts contend that the retroactive provision of K.S.A.2001 Supp. 40-3414(i)(1) deprives them of a vested property right in violation of § 18 of the Bill of Rights of the Kansas Constitution. The constitutional provision provides that "[a]ll persons, for injuries suffered in person, reputation or property, shall have remedy by due course of law, and justice administered without delay." The statute provides:

> Subject to the provisions of paragraph (4), for the purposes of the health care provider insurance availability act, each nonprofit corporation organized to administer the graduate medical education programs of community hospitals or medical care facilities affiliated with the university of Kansas school of medicine shall be deemed to have been a health care provider as defined in K.S.A. 40-3401, and amendments thereto, from and after July 1, 1997.

The negligence alleged by the Holts occurred in 1998, and they filed suit on July 28, 2000. The challenged legislation was enacted in 2001.

There is no question that plaintiffs had an accrued cause of action against WCGME for derivative negligence at the time the challenged legislation was enacted. WCGME, however, argues that...the Holts'...derivative negligence cause of action was [not] a vested property right. It does not follow, however, that a cause of action for vicarious negligence would accrue only if there were a judgment against Dr. Harris for negligence. The cause of action for negligence against WCGME, like the cause of action for negligence against Dr. Harris, accrued when the alleged negligence occurred in 1998. The defendants have offered no convincing reason or authority why accrual of a tort cause of action based on vicarious liability for an injury would not also accrue when the elements of duty, breach, and resulting injury are present. The Holts' tort action for negligence against the defendants constituted a vested property right.

The Holts argue that the retroactive provision of K.S.A.2001 Supp. 40-3414(i)(1) violates their due process rights under § 18 of the Bill of Rights of the Kansas Constitution. WCGME argues that the challenged legislation in this case presents an exception to the general prohibition against retroactive legislation that impairs substantive rights. It is an exception, according to WCGME, because it was enacted to clarify ambiguities in existing law. The argument seems to be that no vested rights were impaired...because WCGME was a health care provider all along and the statute merely clarified the status quo.

The retroactive amendment at issue here was not part of a general revision or codification of the law concerning health care provider insurance. The amendment at issue instead was one of several provisions, all having to do with nonprofit corporations organized to administer graduate medical education programs that were inserted into the already existing Act concerning health care provider insurance. The effect of the amendments was to make the existing health care provider insurance scheme applicable to an additional category of providers rather than to alter the existing scheme. Under these circumstances, the presumption that when the legislature revises an existing law it intends to change the law is fairly strong. This court presumes that when the legislature revises an existing law, the legislature intended to change the law, and the presumption is fairly strong where, as here, the amendments were not adopted in a general revision of the law. In this case, WCGME has not offered an effective rebuttal of the presumption.

Thus, under the facts presented, the retroactive provision...deprives the Holts of a vested property right and violates their due process rights under § 18 of the Bill of Rights of the Kansas Constitution.

LEMUZ v. FIESER
933 P.2d 134 (Kan. 1997)

ABBOTT, J.

This case is before the court on a question certified by the United States District Court for the District of Kansas .... The facts...are as follows:

[T]his is essentially a medical malpractice action filed by the minor plaintiff and his parents against two medical doctors, Merle Fieser, M.D. and William King, M.D. and Central Kansas Medical Center. The action arises out of the birth of Layton Randall Lemuz at Central Kansas Medical Center (CKMC). Dr. Fieser was the treating physician during Sandra Lemuz's pregnancy and was the attending physician at delivery. Dr. King's role is not specified in the complaint. Plaintiffs allege that Dr. Fieser was negligent in her care and treatment of Sandra Lemuz and in the delivery and subsequent treatment of Layton Randall Lemuz. Plaintiffs allege negligence on the part of CKMC in granting obstetrical privileges to Dr. Fieser, when CKMC was aware of Dr. Fieser's alleged incompetence. Plaintiffs further allege negligence on the part of CKMC in its failure to order Dr. Fieser to transfer the minor plaintiff to a hospital with the personnel and facilities to care for a neurologically depressed newborn.

CKMC argues that it cannot be held liable for damages caused by Dr. Fieser's alleged negligence, since Dr. Fieser was not an employee of CKMC. CKMC's argument is based on K.S.A. 40-3403(h) and 65-442(b), and *McVay v. Rich,* 255 Kan. 371 (1994).

K.S.A. 40-3403(h) provides in pertinent part:

'A health care provider who is qualified for coverage under the [health care stabilization] fund shall have no vicarious liability or responsibility for any injury or death arising out of the rendering of or the failure to render professional services inside or outside this state by any other health care provider who is also qualified for coverage under the fund.'

K.S.A. 65-442(b) provides:

There shall be no liability on the part of and no action for damages shall arise against any licensed medical care facility because of the rendering of or failure to render professional services within such medical care facility by a person licensed to practice medicine and surgery if such person is not an employee or agent of such medical care facility.'

The parties are in agreement that Kansas law does not recognize the so-called 'corporate negligence' doctrine as it relates to hospitals-in other words, there is no cause of action against a hospital based upon a claim that the hospital negligently granted hospital privileges to a non-employee physician. Plaintiffs concede that the law, as presently interpreted, bars their claim for corporate negligence against CKMC. Plaintiffs argue that the statutes deprive plaintiffs of due process of law, in violation of section 18 of the Kansas Bill of Rights.

In *Bair v. Peck,* 811 P.2d 1176 (Kan. 1991), this court…found that the Health Care Provider Insurance Availability Act was an adequate quid pro quo or substitute remedy for the abrogation of the common-law remedy of vicarious liability against hospitals, even though this substitute remedy was not adopted simultaneously with the abrogation of the common-law remedy.

Section 18 of the Kansas Constitution Bill of Rights

The plaintiffs contend that K.S.A. 65-442(b) unconstitutionally violates § 18 of the Kansas Constitution Bill of Rights, which provides:

> "Justice without delay. All persons, for injuries suffered in person, reputation or property, shall have remedy by due course of law, and justice administered without delay."

The defendants assert that K.S.A. 65-442(b) does not violate § 18 because the statute does not implicate any interest protected by § 18. The defendants point out that the provisions of § 18 preserve the right to remedy by due course of law "only as to civil causes of action that were recognized as justiciable by the common law as it existed at the time our constitution was adopted." According to the defendants, the corporate negligence doctrine did not exist at the time the Kansas Constitution was adopted. Instead, the doctrine was first developed in 1965 in the case of *Darling v. Charleston Community Memorial Hospital,* 211 N.E.2d 253 (Ill. 1965). Since a cause of action for corporate negligence was not recognized at the time the Kansas Constitution was adopted, but is a judicial expansion of common-law negligence remedies, the defendants contend that the legislative preclusion of that cause of action by 65-442(b) does not implicate § 18. We disagree.

The plaintiffs' claim of corporate negligence against the hospital is based upon the basic principle of negligence, a common-law remedy which was recognized at the time the Kansas Constitution was adopted. In *McVay,* 874 P.2d 641, this court interpreted K.S.A. 65-442(b) to determine if it precluded corporate negligence lawsuits against hospitals. We noted that the theory of corporate negligence recognizes a "[hospital's] liability for negligently retaining or employing an independent contractor" because "'hospitals have an independent duty to ensure the health and safety of their patients,'" including "the duty to exercise reasonable care in granting, reviewing, and extending staff privileges." Once this new duty for hospitals is plugged into an old cause of action, negligence, the hospital's liability under the corporate negligence doctrine develops.

Thus, corporate negligence causes of action are not "new" causes of action but are simply different applications of the basic concepts of negligence which existed at common law when the Kansas Constitution was adopted. As such, corporate negligence causes of action are protected by § 18. If this were not the case, then any evolution of negligence law since the time the Kansas Constitution was adopted could be abrogated without implicating § 18.

Section 18 of the Kansas Constitution Bill of Rights is the section which provides due process protection. The standard in Kansas for reviewing § 18 due process challenges is:

> If a remedy protected by due process is abrogated or restricted by the legislature, 'such change is constitutional if "the change is reasonably necessary in the public interest to promote the general welfare of the people of the state," *Manzanares v. Bell,* 214 Kan. 589, 599 (1974), and the legislature provides an adequate substitute remedy' to replace the remedy which has been restricted." *Bonin v. Vannaman,* 261 Kan. 199, 217 (1996).

The plaintiffs assert that this is an inappropriate standard to use in reviewing § 18 challenges because § 18 does more than just protect against due process violations. The plaintiffs argue that they have a right to bodily integrity, including the right not to be exposed to an incompetent physician, [and]…that private law duties and remedies give substance to this fundamental right of bodily integrity. [T]he plaintiffs contend that § 18 is more than just the state's equivalent to federal due process protection…[and] assert that § 18 is a separate and distinct clause of the Kansas Constitution which is designed to protect fundamental rights of bodily integrity. Plaintiffs complain that…the rational basis test is not a strict enough standard to apply when evaluating possible § 18 violations.

Instead of using the rational basis test to evaluate § 18 challenges, the plaintiffs ask this court to draw from both the heightened scrutiny doctrine of equal protection and the compelling state interest test of substantive due process to determine that legislation will only be upheld under § 18 if it is narrowly tailored to substantially further a legitimate interest of the State.

This court does not use a [rational basis] standard for § 18 due process challenges. Instead, this court uses the quid pro quo test to review challenges under § 18. Under this test, Step 1 is similar to a rational basis test analysis. In referring to an analysis under Step 1 of the § 18 test, the court stated that "'[t]he test in determining the constitutionality of a statute under due process or equal protection weighs almost identical factors.'" However, this is not where the § 18 review stops. "[E]ven if the modification of a common-law remedy is consistent with public policy, this does not necessarily satisfy the due process concerns. In order to insure due process, the legislature is required to provide an adequate, substitute remedy when a common-law remedy, such as [a corporate negligence claim against a hospital] is modified or abolished."

This test is more stringent than the rational basis test because it requires a substantive quid pro quo to replace any common-law remedy that is…extinguished by statute. Thus, the plaintiffs' challenge of the "rational basis test" under § 18 has no merit. The real question in this case is whether, under the quid pro quo test, K.S.A. 65-442(b) violates § 18. The legislature enacted K.S.A. 65-442(b) to encourage hospitals to actively engage in the peer review of staff physicians, without the threat of liability from peer review. Peer review has the potential to lower malpractice incidents, thereby lowering malpractice insurance rates and encouraging doctors to practice in Kansas. Further, increased use of peer review should improve the overall quality of care provided in Kansas hospitals. Making sure that quality health care is available in the state is a valid legislative objective which promotes the general welfare of the people of the state. Thus, Step One of the § 18 test is satisfied.

Step Two of the § 18 test asks whether the legislature has provided an adequate substitute remedy or a quid pro quo for the abrogation of a common-law remedy. The plaintiffs contend that the quid pro quo requirement simply allows the legislature to shift the costs of the negligent activity of a tortfeasor from the tortfeasor to the most injured victims of the negligent activity. Thus, the plaintiffs assert that Step Two of the § 18 test, or the quid pro quo requirement, is unconstitutional in and of itself. This court has used the quid pro quo requirement for years in evaluating § 18 challenges. We see no reason to reverse the precedent now.

Under Step Two of the § 18 test, the question is whether the legislature provided an adequate substitute remedy or quid pro quo to replace the remedy which has been modified or abrogated. Under 65-442(b), the legislature abrogated the plaintiffs' remedy to bring suit against a hospital for corporate negligence. Did the legislature provide an adequate substitute to replace this lost remedy?

K.S.A. 65-442(b) was included in the legislature's medical malpractice crisis "package" in an effort to encourage hospitals to actively engage in peer review of staff physicians. The legislature thought that hospitals might be hesitant to engage in peer review because if the hospital became aware, through peer review, of some mistakes a staff physician had made, but the hospital did not immediately revoke the physician's staff privileges upon gaining knowledge of these mistakes, then this might open the hospital up to liability. To alleviate this fear, the legislature passed K.S.A. 65-442(b). With the threat of liability gone, the legislature hoped the use of peer review in hospitals would increase.

When the Act was adopted in 1976, it "required licensed health care providers to obtain primary malpractice insurance as a condition precedent to practicing their profession in Kansas," with "at least $100,000 per occurrence coverage and not less than $300,000 annual aggregate coverage for all claims of primary medical malpractice insurance." The Act also required physicians to purchase mandatory excess medical malpractice insurance through the Health Care Stabilization Fund (Fund). In 1976, "the Fund paid all judgments which were beyond the policy limits of the health care provider's primary coverage." In other words, the Fund had an unlimited liability limit and paid all malpractice awards beyond the health care provider's primary policy limit no matter how great. In 1976, the Act, the Plan, and the Fund guaranteed to all Kansas citizens that all health care providers in the state would have primary insurance coverage with at least a $100,000 policy limit plus unlimited excess malpractice insurance coverage. Thus, a medical malpractice victim was guaranteed to recover any judgment against a negligent health care provider. Without the Act, the Plan, and the Fund, victims of medical malpractice might not have received any recovery from a negligent health care provider if the provider was uninsured and judgment proof.

The plaintiffs seem to admit that in 1976, the Act, with its required medical malpractice insurance; the Plan, with its guaranteed availability of primary medical malpractice insurance; and the Fund, with its unlimited excess liability coverage, was an adequate quid pro quo for the abrogation of their remedy against the hospital. However, the plaintiffs contend that this adequate quid pro quo has become emasculated due to amendments to the Fund. For instance, in 1984, while a health care provider's primary malpractice insurance policy limits were required to increase to at least $200,000 per occurrence and not less than $600,000 per annual aggregate for all claims under K.S.A. 40-3402, the Fund's excess liability coverage was capped at $3 million, so that it could only pay $3 million "on any judgment above the health care provider's primary policy in any one case." The plaintiffs point out that the 1989 amendment to the Fund's excess insurance policy cap reduced their quid pro quo from $3.2 million required liability protection to $300,000 required liability protection in 1989.

Thus, the plaintiffs contend that the original quid pro quo provided in the Act, the Plan, and the Fund has been emasculated so much that it is no longer an adequate substitute remedy for the abrogation of the plaintiffs' remedy to sue a hospital for corporate negligence. The defendant argues that the amendments to the Act and the Fund were simply a necessary part of enacting complicated and comprehensive legislation and do not qualify as an emasculation of a once adequate quid pro quo for the abrogation of the plaintiffs' corporate negligence remedy against a hospital.

The defendants cite to *Bair,* [where the] question was whether a quid pro quo, enacted in the 1976 Act and Fund, could be an adequate substitute remedy for the abrogation of a common-law remedy which occurred in 1986. Here, the question is whether the quid pro quo provided in the 1976 Act and Fund, enacted at the same time that the remedy was abrogated, is still an adequate substitute remedy in light of the subsequent amendments the Act and Fund have undergone. *Bair* provided:

> We have long recognized, at least tacitly, that major statutory enactments establishing a broad, comprehensive statutory remedy or scheme of reparation in derogation of a previously existing common-law remedy may be subsequently amended or altered without each such subsequent change being supported by an independent and separate quid pro quo. Provisions of the original Workmen's Compensation Act adopted in 1911 and upheld as constitutional, have been repeatedly amended without the adoption of an additional quid pro quo each time an amendment operated to the detriment of the employee. The original quid pro quo providing recovery for injury regardless of fault or negligence has been

deemed sufficient to support dozens of amendments to the original act, many of which involved the abrogation of an existing common-law right.

The legislature has the right to modify and supplement a quid pro quo, especially in the area of a complicated, comprehensive statutory scheme. In summary, this court struggles with the bottom line figure as to how much a quid pro quo can be amended and still remain an adequate quid pro quo. Here, the legislature did *not* emasculate the quid pro quo…to a point where it was no longer an adequate substitute remedy, even when standing alone, without the supplemental quid pro quo provided in the risk management statutes. The public is benefitted by any insurance that is carried by that doctor. This is, and should be to some extent, a legislative call and we are unable to say that requiring $300,000 minimum to be available in every case is so inadequate that it is an inadequate quid pro quo. The plaintiffs herein will personally receive the benefit of the portion of the original quid pro quo that remains – required primary medical malpractice insurance and guaranteed excess medical malpractice insurance. Further, all plaintiffs will generally receive the benefit of the supplemental quid pro quo – risk management requirements that protect patients from incompetent doctors. Thus, the legislature has provided an adequate quid pro quo for the statutory abrogation of the plaintiffs' common-law remedy to sue a hospital for corporate negligence. The second step of the § 18 test has been satisfied.

MELLO v. BIG Y FOODS
826 A.2d 1117 (Conn. 2003)

BORDEN, J.

The two issues in this reservation are, first, whether the plaintiff's claim for permanent and significant scarring on her foot and ankle is barred by…the exclusive remedy provision of the Workers' Compensation Act (act), [and second, if] so, whether that bar violates article first, § 10, of the constitution of Connecticut. We answer the first question in the affirmative and the second question in the negative.

The plaintiff, Sharon Mello, filed a workers' compensation claim against the defendant, Big Y Foods, Inc., her employer, for scarring to her foot and ankle. The workers' compensation commissioner (commissioner) denied compensability. The plaintiff then filed this plenary negligence action against the defendant for compensation for that scarring. The trial court reserved two questions of law governing the case.

The parties stipulated to the following facts. The plaintiff was employed by the defendant. On July 3, 1998, during the course of and in the scope of her employment, the plaintiff sustained a compensable burn injury to her right foot and ankle, which later resulted in permanent and significant scarring. The plaintiff filed a claim pursuant to chapter 568 of the General Statutes seeking workers' compensation benefits, including a claim for benefits for permanent and significant scarring pursuant to General Statutes § 31-308(c). The defendant accepted the compensability of the plaintiff's underlying injury to her foot by way of voluntary agreement, and paid for medical treatment and indemnity benefits for missed work, and for a 3 percent permanent disability to her right foot. The defendant denied compensability, however, for the scarring to the plaintiff's foot and ankle. Thereafter, the commissioner found that there was no scarring to the plaintiff's face, head or neck, and that the scarring to her foot and ankle did not interfere with her ability to obtain or continue work. Accordingly, the commissioner denied the plaintiff's claim for scarring to her foot and ankle.

I

THE PLAINTIFF'S CLAIM IS BARRED BY THE ACT'S EXCLUSIVITY PROVISIONS

We begin by addressing the first reserved question: whether the plaintiff's claim is barred by the exclusivity provision of the act.

We conclude that the plaintiff's claim that her scarring should be actionable against her employer outside the workers' compensation system is inconsistent with the act. In place of the trade-offs provided by the act would be a situation in which employees could seek compensation for those aspects of their compensable injuries that are specifically enumerated in the act, while seeking damages in tort against their employers for those aspects of their injuries not specifically enumerated. Such a result would, in many cases, including the present action, expose employers to liability under both the act and the common law. The costs and the lack of predictability that would result from such a rule would be unreasonable in light of the legislature's endeavor to reduce the costs of the system and in light of the public policy behind the act, which seeks to afford remedies quickly and efficiently to injured employees.

II

THE EXCLUSIVITY BAR, AS APPLIED TO THE FACTS OF THIS CASE, DOES NOT VIOLATE ARTICLE FIRST, § 10, OF THE CONNECTICUT CONSTITUTION

Having answered the first question in the affirmative, we now turn to the second question: whether the exclusivity provision, as applied to the facts of this case, violates article first, § 10, of the constitution of Connecticut. That is, is the act's exclusivity provision unconstitutional, as applied to the facts of this case, because it precludes the plaintiff from exercising her preexisting common-law right to bring an action in negligence seeking damages for her scarring? We conclude that it is not.

Article first, § 10, of the constitution of Connecticut provides that "[a]ll courts shall be open, and every person, for an injury done to him in his person, property or reputation, shall have remedy by due course of law, and right and justice administered without sale, denial or delay." "This provision appears in the constitution of 1818 and in its several revisions and reenactments, and has been referred to as the right to redress." It is settled law that this provision restricts the power of the legislature to abolish a legal right existing at common law prior to 1818 without also establishing a "reasonable alternative to the enforcement of that right." In order to be reasonable, however, an alternative need not be the *exact* equivalent of the abolished common-law right or its remedy. "Thus for each remedy or item of damage existing under the prior fault system, it is not required that that item be duplicated under the [alternative] act but that the bulk of remedies under the act be of such significance that a court is justified in viewing this legislation on the whole as a substitute, the benefits from which are sufficient to tolerate the removal of the prior cause of action." In other words, in determining whether an alternative is reasonable, a court need only consider the aggregated benefits of the legislative alternative and assess whether those aggregated benefits reasonably approximate the rights formerly available under the common law.

We have concluded that the act is a reasonable alternative to claims in tort for damages that existed at common law as actions for trespass on the case. In *Daily,* the principal plaintiff claimed that the injury to his hand, sustained during routine maintenance of a precision machine, was actionable under a product liability theory, despite the fact that he was entitled to and had been receiving benefits under the act. We disagreed and concluded, instead, that through "the aggregate benefits associated with the workers' compensation laws...the legislature provided a 'reasonable alternative' to workers having product liability claims and that [it], as a result, did not enact legislation violative of article first, § 10, of the Connecticut constitution."

We conclude...that the act's rights and remedies provide a reasonable alternative to the plaintiff's common-law right to bring a negligence action for damages resulting from her scarring. The plaintiff has been compensated, through the act, for all compensable losses associated with the injury she sustained to her foot. This compensation included medical costs, lost wages and a permanent disability payment of 3 percent. Under the terms of the act, the plaintiff received these benefits without the delay of filing an action and the burden of proving negligence. This is the exchange offered by the act; workers forego certain damages and remedies available to them under common law, but they gain a predictable, reliable, speedy and inexpensive means of obtaining compensation. [T]he rights and remedies available under a legislative "'reasonable alternative'" need not equate, in every respect and detail, the superseded common-law rights and remedies. The aggregated benefits need only reasonably approximate the former right.

NOTES

1. Right to a remedy/open courts provisions have been litigated in a variety of contexts, as the cases illustrate. Should all contexts be treated the same for constitutional purposes? Or are there reasons to evaluate damages caps, repose periods, defenses, workers' compensation, or procedural limitations differently? Note that such cases might also arise in the criminal context. *See, e.g., Dorsey v. State*, 716 A.2d 807 (Del. 2000) (declaring right to a suppression remedy in the context of an unconstitutional search).

2. How do the standards the state courts use in evaluating right to a remedy/open courts provisions compare to federal due process and equal protection standards? Are they the same, similar, or distinctly different? Do right to a remedy provisions serve the same purposes as the Fourteenth Amendment's Due Process and Equal Protection Clauses?

3. For additional reading on state constitutional right to remedy/open courts provisions, see David Schuman, *The Right To A Remedy*, 65 Temple L. Rev. 1197 (1992); Jonathan M. Hoffman, *Questions Before Answers: The Ongoing Search to Understand the Origins of the Open Courts Clause*, 32 Rutgers L.J. 1005 (2001). *See also The Constitutional Status of Tort Law: Due Process and the Right to a Law for the Redress of Wrongs*, 115 Yale L.J. 524 (2005).

CHAPTER **XIII**

OTHER STATE INDIVIDUAL RIGHTS

A. PRIVACY

The right of privacy is a broad concept, used to refer to a variety of claims or entitlements. Professor Friesen notes that:

> The right of privacy under state constitutions potentially embraces at least three distinct types of interests: (1) the right to be free of unreasonable government (or, sometimes, private) surveillance; (2) the right to prevent the accumulation or dissemination of certain kinds of information (sometimes called "informational" privacy); and (3) the right to make important choices about personal or family life free of state coercion (sometimes called "autonomy" rights). Jennifer Friesen, 1 *State Constitutional Law: Litigating Individual Rights, Claims and Defenses* § 2.01 (4th ed. LexisNexis 2006).

The right of an individual to make personal decisions free from government control is covered in Chapter VI. At this point, the focus is on the right to be free from unreasonable governmental surveillance.

While the United States Constitution does not contain an express right of privacy, there is an explicit enumerated right to privacy in the state constitutions of Alaska, California, Florida, Hawaii, and Montana. Alaska Const. art. I, § 22; Cal. Const. art. I, § 1; Fla. Const. art. I, § 23; Haw. Const. art. I, § 6; Mont. Const. art. II, § 10. The privacy provision in the Florida Constitution states:

> Every natural person has the right to be let alone and free from governmental intrusion into the person's private life except as otherwise provided herein. This section shall not be construed to limit the public's right of access to public records and meetings as provided by law. Fla. Const. art I, § 23.

Six other state constitutions, although not having a separate right to privacy, protect forms of privacy through the "search and seizure" sections of the state constitution.

YORK v. WAHKIAKUM SCHOOL DISTRICT NO. 200
178 P.3d 995 (Wash. 2008) (*en banc*)

SANDERS, J.

The question before us is whether random and suspicionless drug testing of student athletes violates article I, section 7 of the Washington State Constitution.

The Wahkiakum School District ("school district") randomly drug tests all student athletes under the authority of Wahkiakum School Board

Policy No. 3515 ("policy 3515"). Aaron and Abraham York and Tristan Schneider played sports for Wahkiakum High School, agreed to the policy, and were tested. Their parents ("York and Schneider parents") sued the school district alleging its drug testing policy violated article I, section 7 of the Washington State Constitution. The school district claims random drug testing, without any individualized suspicion, is constitutional. The superior court agreed. We accepted direct review.

The school district asks us to adopt a "special needs" exception to the warrant requirement to allow random and suspicionless drug testing. But we do not recognize such an exception and hold warrantless random and suspicionless drug testing of student athletes violates the Washington State Constitution.

Wahkiakum requires its student athletes to refrain from using or possessing alcohol or illegal drugs. Beginning in 1994, the school district implemented myriad ways to combat drug and alcohol use among the student population. Nevertheless, drug and alcohol problems persisted. Acting independently of the school district, the Wahkiakum Community Network (community network) began surveying district students. From these surveys, the community network ranked teen substance abuse as the number one problem in Wahkiakum County. As reiterated by the trial court, the community network's surveys showed that in 1998, 40 percent of sophomores reported previously using illegal drugs and 19 percent of sophomores reported illegal drug use within the previous 30 days, while 42 percent of seniors reported previously using illegal drugs and 12.5 percent reported illegal drug use within the previous 30 days. In 2000, 50 percent of student athletes self-identified as drug and/or alcohol users.

As a result, the school district decided to implement random drug testing where all students may be tested initially and then subjected to random drug testing during the remainder of the season. The school district formed the Drug and Alcohol Advisory Committee (now the "Safe and Drug Free Schools Advisory Committee") to help deal with the student substance abuse problems. The committee evaluated the effectiveness of its previous programs, such as D.A.R.E. (Drug Abuse Resistance Education) and support groups, and contemplated adopting policy 3515, which would require random drug testing of student athletes. The trial court found:

> Based upon the evidence of substantial alcohol and drug use among students and pursuant to the School District's statutory authority and responsibility to maintain order and discipline in its schools, to protect the health and safety of its students, and to control, supervise and regulate interschool athletics, the Board of Directors adopted the policy.

As part of the policy, all student athletes must agree to be randomly drug tested as a condition of playing extracurricular sports. The drug testing is done by urinalysis, with the student in an enclosed bathroom stall and a health department employee outside. The sample is then mailed to Comprehensive Toxicology Services in Tacoma, Washington. If the results indicate illegal drug use, then the student is suspended from extracurricular athletic activities; the length of suspension depends on the number of infractions and whether the student tested positive for illegal drugs or alcohol. Also, the school district provides students with drug and alcohol counseling resources. The results are not sent to local law enforcement or included in the student's academic record. And the student is not suspended from school, only extracurricular sports.

During the 1999-2000 school year, Aaron York and Abraham York played sports and were tested under the policy. And Tristan Schneider was tested under the policy during the 2000-2001 year. The York and Schneider parents brought suit arguing the school district's policy violated the Washington State Constitution. Their motion for a preliminary injunction was denied by superior court Judge Penoyar, and the Court of Appeals dismissed the petition as moot. The trial court then held that while the school district's policy "approached the tolerance limit" of our constitution, the policy was nevertheless constitutional and narrowly tailored to reach a compelling government end.

The York and Schneider parents sought and obtained direct review in our court of a summary judgment order and ask us to determine whether the school district's policy 3515 is constitutional.

We are aware there are strong arguments, policies and opinions marshaled on both sides of this debate, but we are concerned only with the policy's constitutionality. And while we are loath to disturb the decisions of a local school board, we will not hesitate to intervene when constitutional protections are implicated. No matter the drawbacks or merits of the school district's random drug testing, we cannot let the policy stand if it offends our constitution. Students "do not 'shed their constitutional rights' at the schoolhouse door."

The question before us is narrow: Whether Wahkiakum School District's blanket policy requiring student athletes to submit to random drug testing is constitutional. The United States Supreme Court has held such activity does not violate the Fourth Amendment to the federal constitution. But we have never decided whether a suspicionless, random drug search of student athletes violates article I, section 7 of our state constitution. Therefore, we must decide whether our state constitution follows the federal standard or provides more protection to students in the state of Washington.

May Wahkiakum School District Perform Suspicionless, Random Drug Tests of Student Athletes?

a.   *Federal cases concerning public school searches*

The school district argues we should follow federal cases and allow suspicionless, random drug testing of its student athletes. Two federal cases are apposite to our consideration. These cases, while helpful, do not control how we interpret our state constitution. There are stark differences in the language of the two constitutional protections; unlike the Fourth Amendment, article I, section 7 is not based on a reasonableness standard.

The United States Supreme Court has held public school searches presented a "special need," which allowed a departure from the warrant and probable cause requirements. *New Jersey v. T.L.O.*, 469 U.S. 325 (1985). The *T.L.O.* Court held school teachers and administrators could search students without a warrant if: (1) there existed "reasonable grounds for suspecting that the search will turn up evidence that the student has violated or is violating either the law or the rules of the school," and (2) the search is "not excessively intrusive in light of the age and sex of the student and the nature of the infraction."

Next, in *Vernonia School District 47J v. Acton*, 515 U.S. 646 (1995), a public school district implemented a random drug testing of school athletes, similar to the one at issue here. Each student athlete was tested at the beginning of the season and then each week 10 percent were randomly selected for testing. Most critics of *Acton* are not persuaded the majority's analysis justifies a suspicionless search of the student athletes. But the *Acton* majority claimed individualized suspicion would unduly interfere with the government's goals and might actually make the situation worse. Its reasoning was based primarily on three rationales: (1) individualized suspicion would "transform[] the process into a badge of shame," where teachers could claim any troublesome student was abusing drugs; (2) teachers and student officials are neither trained nor equipped to spot drug use; and (3) individualized suspicion creates an unnecessary loss of resources in defending claims and lawsuits against arbitrary imposition, when students and parents will inevitably challenge whether reasonable suspicion did indeed exist.

But these arguments were unpersuasive several years earlier when the Court applied an individualized suspicion standard to public schools in *T.L.O.* The *Acton* majority never adequately explained why individual suspicion was needed in *T.L.O.* but not in *Acton*. Justice O'Connor spent much of her dissent taking issue with this standard:

> [N]owhere is it *less* clear that an individualized suspicion requirement would be ineffectual than in the school context. In most schools, the entire pool of

potential search targets—students—is under constant supervision by teachers and administrators and coaches, be it in classrooms, hallways, or locker rooms.

The great irony of this case is that most (though not all) of the evidence the District introduced to justify its suspicionless drug testing program consisted of first- or second-hand stories of particular, identifiable students acting in ways that plainly gave rise to reasonable suspicion of in-school drug use—and thus that would have justified a drug-related search under our *T.L.O.* decision.

The Wahkiakum School District modeled its policy after the one used by the Vernonia School District. But simply passing muster under the federal constitution does not ensure the survival of the school district's policy under our state constitution. The Fourth Amendment provides for "[t]he right of the people to be secure in their persons, houses, papers, and effects, against unreasonable searches and seizures." Therefore, a Fourth Amendment analysis hinges on whether a warrantless search is reasonable, and it is possible in some circumstances for a search to be reasonable without a warrant. But our state constitutional analysis hinges on whether a search has "authority of law" – in other words, a warrant. Wash. Const. art. I, § 7.

b.   Search and seizure analysis under article I, section 7

Our state constitution provides: "No person shall be disturbed in his private affairs, or his home invaded, without authority of law." Wash. Const. art. I, § 7. It is well established that in some areas, article I, section 7 provides greater protection than its federal counterpart – the Fourth Amendment. When determining whether article I, section 7 provides greater protection in a particular context, we focus on whether the unique characteristics of the constitutional provision and its prior interpretations compel a particular result. We look to the constitutional text, historical treatment of the interest at stake, relevant case law and statutes, and the current implications of recognizing or not recognizing an interest.

This requires a two-part analysis. First, we must determine whether the state action constitutes a disturbance of one's private affairs. Here that means asking whether requiring a student athlete to provide a urine sample intrudes upon the student's private affairs. Second, if a privacy interest has been disturbed, the second step in our analysis asks whether authority of law justifies the intrusion. The "authority of law" required by article I, section 7 is satisfied by a valid warrant, limited to a few jealously guarded exceptions. Because the Wahkiakum School District had no warrant, if we reach the second prong of the analysis we must decide whether the school district's activity fits within an exception to the warrant requirement. Relying on federal law, the school district claims there is a "special needs" exception to the warrant requirement that we should adopt. The York and

Schneider parents point out we have not adopted such an exception and urge us not to do so here.

Suspicionless, Random Drug Testing Disturbs a Student Athlete's Private Affairs.

When inquiring about private affairs, we look to "'those privacy interests which citizens of this state have held, and should be entitled to hold, safe from governmental trespass absent a warrant.'" This is an objective analysis.

The private affair we are concerned with today is the State's interference in a student athlete's bodily functions. Specifically, does it intrude upon a privacy interest to require a student athlete to go into a bathroom stall and provide a urine sample, even against that student's protest? Federal courts and our court both agree the answer is an unqualified yes, such action intrudes into one's reasonable expectation of privacy. Indeed, we offer heightened protection for bodily functions compared to the federal courts.

Because we determine that interfering with a student athlete's bodily functions disturbs one's private affairs, we must address the second prong of the article I, section 7 analysis: does the school district have the necessary authority of law to randomly drug test student athletes?

Under Article I, Section 7 There Is No Authority of Law That Allows a School District to Conduct Random Drug Tests.

We have long held a warrantless search is *per se* unreasonable, unless it fits within one of the "'jealously and carefully drawn exceptions.'" These exceptions include exigent circumstances, consent, searches incident to a valid arrest, inventory searches, the plain view doctrine, and *Terry* investigative stops. Any exceptions to the warrant requirement must be rooted in the common law. And it is always the government's burden to show its random drug testing fits within one of these narrow exceptions. Today the school district asks us to accept an analog to the federal special needs doctrine to justify its drug testing policy. The York and Schneider parents point out we have never formally adopted a special needs exception and therefore claim no exception to the warrant requirement exists here.

a. Federal special needs exception

Before addressing whether we have adopted or will adopt such a special needs exception, it is helpful to briefly examine the federal exception to understand both its requirements and its breadth. The United States Supreme Court has held there are certain circumstances when a search or seizure is directed toward "'special needs, beyond the normal need for law enforcement'" and "the warrant and probable-cause requirement [are] impracticable.'" For there to be a special need, not only must there be some interest beyond normal law enforcement but also any evidence garnered from the search or seizure should not be expected to be used in any criminal prosecution against the target of the search or seizure. The Court has applied such reasoning to administrative searches, border patrols, and prisoners and probationers.

The United States Supreme Court has also held drug testing presents a special need and may be done under certain circumstances without a warrant or individualized suspicion. In *Skinner v. Railway Labor Executives' Assoc.*, 489 U.S. 602, 634 (1989), the Court upheld warrantless and suspicionless blood and urine testing of railroad employees following major train accidents. The Court applied similar reasoning in *National Treasury Employees Union v. Von Raab*, 489 U.S. 656 (1989), when it held immigration officials may be subjected to random drug testing.

b.   Is there a Washington State special needs exception?

We have never adopted a special needs exception but have looked to federal special needs cases when dealing with similar issues. In cases concerning administrative searches, border patrols, and prisoners and probationers, our courts have departed from the warrant requirement in similar, but not always identical, ways.

We cannot countenance random searches of public school student athletes with our article I, section 7 jurisprudence. As stated earlier, we require a warrant except for rare occasions, which we jealously and narrowly guard. We decline to adopt a doctrine similar to the federal special needs exception in the context of randomly drug testing student athletes. In sum, no argument has been presented that would bring the random drug testing within any reasonable interpretation of the constitutionally required "authority of law."

Accordingly, we hold the school district's policy 3515 is unconstitutional and violates student athletes' rights secured by article I, section 7. Therefore we reverse the superior court. The York and Schneider parents shall recover their costs.

NOTE

The "special needs" rationale was adopted by the Supreme Court of New Jersey and led it to hold that the search and seizure protection in the state constitution did not prohibit a drug testing program in a public high school. The school's policy provided for the random, suspicionless drug and alcohol testing of all students who engaged in an extracurricular activity or who possessed a parking permit. *Joye v. Hunterdon Cent. Reg'l High Sch. Bd. of Educ.*, 826 A.2d 624 (N.J. 2003).

B. FREE SPEECH AND EXPRESSION

Although the texts of state constitutions regarding freedom of speech are quite similar to each other, they are different from the language in the First Amendment. The origins of the provisions in state constitutions can be traced to William Blackstone's Commentaries:

> Every freeman has an undoubted right to lay what sentiments he pleases before his public; to forbid this, is to destroy the freedom of the press: but if he publishes what is improper, mischievous, or illegal, he must take the consequences of his own temerity. William Blackstone, 4 Commentaries 152.

The first time that Blackstone's "abuse" qualification appeared in an American Constitution was the text of the Pennsylvania Constitution of 1790:

> The free communication of thoughts and opinions is one of the invaluable rights of man; and every citizen may freely speak, write, and print on any subject, being responsible for the abuse of that liberty. Pa. Const. of 1790, art. IX, § 7.

Today, protections for speech, expression and the press are found in more than forty state constitutions. The provision in the New York Constitution is typical:

> Every citizen may freely speak, write and publish his or her sentiments on all subjects, being responsible for the abuse of that right; and no law shall be passed to restrain or abridge the liberty of speech or of the press. N.Y. Const. art. I, § 8.

The free speech provisions in state constitutions generally have two components. The first part describes the protected right and the responsibility for the abuse of those rights. The second part prohibits laws that abridge the protected rights.

FASHION VALLEY MALL v. NATIONAL LABOR RELATIONS BOARD
172 P.3d 742 (Cal. 2007)

MORENO, J.

We granted the request of the United States Court of Appeals for the District of Columbia Circuit to decide whether, under California law, a shopping mall may enforce a rule prohibiting persons from urging customers to boycott a store in the mall. For the reasons that follow, we hold that the right to free speech granted by article I, section 2 of the California Constitution includes the right to urge customers in a shopping mall to boycott one of the stores in the mall.

On October 4, 1998, thirty to forty Union members had distributed leaflets to customers entering and leaving the Robinsons-May store at the Mall. The leaflets stated that Robinsons-May advertises in the Union-

Tribune, described several ways that the newspaper allegedly treated its employees unfairly, and urged customers who believed "that employers should treat employees fairly" to call the newspaper's "CEO," listing his name and telephone number. The administrative law judge concluded: "From all indications, the leafleters conducted their activity in a courteous and peaceful manner without a disruption of any kind and without hindrance to customers entering or leaving" the store.

Within fifteen or twenty minutes, Mall officials "arrived on the scene to stop the leafleting," notifying the Union members that they were trespassing because they had not obtained a permit from the Mall "to engage in expressive activity," and warning them that they "would be subject to civil litigation and/or arrest if they did not leave." A police officer appeared and, following a brief argument, the Union members moved to public property near the entrance to the Mall and continued distributing leaflets briefly before leaving the area.

The Mall has adopted rules requiring persons who desire to engage in expressive activity at the Mall to apply for a permit five business days in advance. The applicant "must agree to abide by" the Mall's rules, including rule 5.6.2, which prohibits "impeding, competing or interfering with the business of one or more of the stores or merchants in the shopping center by:....[u]rging, or encouraging in any manner, customers not to purchase the merchandise or services offered by any one or more of the stores or merchants in the shopping center."

The administrative law judge found that the Union "was attempting to engage in a lawful consumer boycott of Robinsons-May because Robinsons-May advertised in the Union-Tribune newspaper" and further found "that it would have been utterly futile for the Union to have followed [the Mall]'s enormously burdensome application-permit process because its rules contained express provisions barring the very kind of lawful conduct the Union sought to undertake at the Mall." The administrative law judge thus ordered the Mall to cease and desist prohibiting access to the Union's "leafleters for the purpose of engaging in peaceful consumer boycott handbilling."

Article I, section 2, subdivision (a) of the California Constitution declares: "Every person may freely speak, write and publish his or her sentiments on all subjects, being responsible for the abuse of this right. A law may not restrain or abridge liberty of speech or press." Nearly 30 years ago, in *Robins v. PruneYard Shopping Center,* 592 P.2d 341 (Cal. 1979)*, aff'd,* 447 U.S. 74 (1980), we held that this provision of our state Constitution grants broader rights to free expression than does the First Amendment to the United States Constitution by holding that a shopping mall is a public forum in which persons may exercise their right to free speech under the California Constitution. We stated that a shopping center "to which the public is invited can provide an essential and invaluable forum for exercising [free speech] rights." We noted that in many cities the public areas of the shopping mall are replacing the streets and sidewalks of the central business district which, "have immemorially been held in trust for the use of the public and, time out of mind, have been used for purposes of assembly, communicating thoughts between citizens, and discussing public questions." Because of the "growing importance of the shopping center[,]...to prohibit expressive activity in the centers would impinge on constitutional rights beyond speech rights," particularly the right to petition for redress of grievances. Accordingly, we held that the California Constitution "protect[s] speech and petitioning, reasonably exercised, in shopping centers even when the centers are privately owned." We added the caveat in *PruneYard* that "[b]y no means do we imply that those who wish to disseminate ideas have free rein," noting our previous "endorsement of time, place, and manner rules."

The Mall in the present case generally allows expressive activity, as mandated by the California Constitution, but requires persons wishing to engage in free speech in the Mall to obtain a permit. Under rule 5.6.2, the Mall will not issue a permit to engage in expressive activity unless the applicant promises to refrain from conduct "[u]rging, or encouraging in any manner, customers not to purchase the merchandise or services offered by any one or more of the stores or merchants in the shopping center." We must determine, therefore, whether a shopping center violates California law by banning from its premises speech urging the public to boycott one or more of the shopping center's businesses.

The idea that private property can constitute a public forum for free speech if it is open to the public in a manner similar to that of public streets and sidewalks long predates our decision in *PruneYard*. The United States Supreme Court recognized more than half a century ago that the right to free speech guaranteed by the First Amendment to the United States Constitution can apply even on privately owned land. In *Marsh v. Alabama*, 326 U.S. 501 (1946), the high court held that a Jehovah's Witness had the right to distribute religious literature on the sidewalk near the post office of a town owned by the Gulf Shipbuilding Corp., because the town had

> all the characteristics of any other American town.... In short, the town and its shopping district are accessible to and freely used by the public in general, and there is nothing to distinguish them from any other town and shopping center except the fact that the title to the property belongs to a private corporation.

The high court stated: "The more an owner, for his advantage, opens up his property for use by the public in general, the more do his rights become circumscribed by the statutory and constitutional rights of those who use it."

Our decision that the California Constitution protects the right to free speech in a shopping mall, even though the federal Constitution does not, stems from the differences between the First Amendment to the federal Constitution and article I, section 2 of the California Constitution. We observed in *Gerawan Farming, Inc. v. Lyons*, 12 P.3d 720 (Cal. 2000), that the free speech clause in article I of the California Constitution differs from its counterpart in the federal Constitution both in its language and its scope:

> It is beyond peradventure that article I's free speech clause enjoys existence and force independent of the First Amendment's. In section 24, article I states, in these very terms, that "[r]ights guaranteed by [the California] Constitution are not dependent on those guaranteed by the United States Constitution." This statement extends to all such rights, including article I's right to freedom of speech. For the California Constitution is now, and has always been, a "document of independent force and effect particularly in the area of individual liberties."

> As a general rule...article I's free speech clause and its right to freedom of speech are not only as broad and as great as the First Amendment's, they are even "broader" and "greater."

In *PruneYard*, high school students in the mall were prohibited from soliciting support for their opposition to a United Nations resolution against Zionism. We held that the mall could not prohibit the students' efforts despite the fact that this free speech activity was unrelated to the business of the center. In so holding, we relied upon our earlier decision in *Schwartz-Torrance,* which, we noted, "held that a labor union has the right to picket a bakery located in a shopping center." We cautioned, however, that we did not "imply that those who wish to disseminate ideas have free rein," noting our previous "endorsement of time, place, and manner rules." We also repeated Justice Mosk's observation in his dissent in *Diamond II* that compelling a shopping center to permit "[a] handful of additional orderly persons soliciting signatures and distributing handbills in connection therewith, under reasonable regulations adopted by defendant to assure that these activities do not interfere with normal business operations would not markedly dilute defendant's property rights."

The Mall argues that its rule banning speech that advocates a boycott is a "reasonable regulation" designed to assure that free expression activities "do not interfere with normal business operations" within the meaning of our decision in *PruneYard.* According to the Mall, it "has the right to prohibit speech that interferes with the intended purpose of the Mall," which is to promote "the sale of merchandise and services to the shopping public." We disagree.

It has been the law since we decided *Schwartz-Torrance* in 1964, and remains the law, that a privately owned shopping center must permit peaceful picketing of businesses in shopping centers, even though such picketing may harm the shopping center's business interests. Our decision in *Diamond* recognized that citizens have a strengthened interest, not a diminished interest, in speech that presents a grievance against a particular business in a privately owned shopping center, including speech that advocates a boycott.

The level of scrutiny with which we review a restriction of free speech activity depends upon whether it is a content-neutral regulation of the time, place, or manner of speech or restricts speech based upon its content. A content-neutral regulation of the time, place, or manner of speech is subjected to intermediate scrutiny to determine if it is "(i) narrowly tailored, (ii) serves a significant government interest, and (iii) leaves open ample alternative avenues of communication." A content-based restriction is subjected to strict scrutiny. "[D]ecisions applying the liberty of speech clause [of the California Constitution], like those applying the First Amendment, long have recognized that in order to qualify for intermediate scrutiny (*i.e.*, time, place, and manner) review, a regulation must be 'content neutral,' and that if a regulation is content based, it is subject to the more stringent strict scrutiny standard."

Prohibiting speech that advocates a boycott is not a time, place, or manner restriction because it is not content neutral. The Mall's rule prohibiting persons from urging a boycott is improper because it does not regulate the time, place, or manner of speech, but rather bans speech urging a boycott because of its content. Restrictions upon speech "that by their terms distinguish favored speech from disfavored speech on the basis of the ideas or views expressed are content based."

The Mall argues that its rule prohibiting speech that urges a boycott is "a 'content-neutral' restriction under California law because it applies to any and all requests for a consumer boycott of the Mall's merchants…regardless of the subject matter or viewpoint of the speaker advocating the boycott." The Mall is mistaken. The Mall's rule prohibiting all boycotts may be viewpoint neutral, because it treats all requests for a boycott the same way, but it is not content neutral, because it prohibits speech that urges a boycott while permitting speech that does not.

The rule at issue here prohibiting speech that advocates a boycott cannot similarly be justified by legitimate concerns that are unrelated to content. Peacefully urging a boycott in a mall does not by its nature cause congestion, nor does it promote fraud or duress. "[T]he boycott is a form of speech or conduct that is ordinarily entitled to protection under the First and Fourteenth Amendments." Our California Constitution provides greater, not lesser, protection for this traditional form of free speech. Unlike the ordinance in *Alliance,* the Mall's rule in the instant case is not concerned with the inherently intrusive nature of such speech, but rather with the impact such speech may have on its listeners. "Handbills…'depend entirely on the persuasive force of the idea.' The loss of customers because they read a handbill urging them not to patronize a business…is the result of mere persuasion." The Mall is concerned that the speech may be effective and persuade customers not to patronize a store. But "[l]isteners' reaction to speech is not a content-neutral basis for regulation." The Mall seeks to prohibit speech advocating a boycott solely because it disagrees with the message of such speech, which might persuade some potential customers not to patronize the stores in the Mall.

The Mall's rule prohibiting speech that advocates a boycott cannot withstand strict scrutiny. The Mall's purpose to maximize the profits of its merchants is not compelling compared to the Union's right to free expression. Urging customers to boycott a store lies at the core of the right to free speech. "The safeguarding of these rights to the ends that men may speak as they think on matters vital to them and that falsehoods may be exposed through the processes of education and discussion is essential to free government. Those who won our independence had confidence in the power of free and fearless reasoning and communication of ideas to discover and spread political and economic truth." The fact that speech may be convincing is not a proper basis for prohibiting it. The right to free speech "extends to more than abstract discussion, unrelated to action." The First Amendment is a charter for government, not for an institution of learning. "Free trade in ideas" means free trade in the opportunity to persuade to action, not merely to describe facts. The Mall cites no authority, and we are aware of none, that holds that a store has a compelling interest in prohibiting this traditional form of free speech.

A shopping mall is a public forum in which persons may reasonably exercise their right to free speech guaranteed by article I, section 2 of the California Constitution. Shopping malls may enact and enforce reasonable regulations of the time, place and manner of such free expression to assure that these activities do not interfere with the normal business operations of the mall, but they may not prohibit certain types of speech based upon its content, such as prohibiting speech that urges a boycott of one or more of the stores in the mall.

We hold that, under California law, Fashion Valley Mall may not maintain and enforce against the Union its rule 5.6.2, which prohibits "[u]rging, or encouraging in any manner, customers not to purchase the merchandise or services offered by any one or more of the stores or merchants in the shopping center."

NOTE

The United States Supreme Court decided one of the seminal cases involving state constitutional rights in *PruneYard Shopping Center v. Robins*, 447 U.S. 74 (1980). The issue before it was framed as "whether state constitutional provisions, which permit individuals to exercise free speech and petition rights on the property of a privately owned shopping center to which the public is invited, violate the shopping center owner's property rights under the Fifth and Fourteenth Amendments or his free speech rights under the First and Fourteenth Amendments." *Id.* at 76. The California Supreme Court held that article 1, sections 2 and 3 of the California Constitution "protects speech and petitioning, reasonably exercised, in shopping centers even when the centers are privately owned" and have a policy not to permit *any* publicly expressive activity, that is strictly enforced in a non-discriminatory fashion. *Robins v. PruneYard Shopping Center*, 592 P.2d 341, 347 (Cal. 1979).

In *Lloyd Corp. v. Tanner*, 407 U.S. 551 (1972), the United States Supreme Court had considered a similar issue in the context of First Amendment rights. In *Lloyd*, the court held that when a shopping center owner opens its private property to the public for the purpose of shopping, the First Amendment of the United States Constitution does not create individual rights in expression beyond those already existing under applicable law. *See PruneYard Shopping Center v. Robins*, 447 U.S. at 81. In *PruneYard*, the court's holding in *Lloyd* was distinguished on the basis that it did "not *ex proprio vigore* limit the authority of the State to exercise its police power or its sovereign right to adopt in its own Constitution individual liberties more expansive than those conferred by the Federal Constitution." *Id.*

The United States Supreme Court then pointed out that in *Lloyd*, unlike the situation presented in *PruneYard*, "there was no state constitutional or statutory provision that had been construed to create rights to the use of private property by strangers, comparable to those found to exist by the California Supreme Court." *Id.* The Supreme Court then addressed the argument that the rights conferred by the California Constitution, if exercised at the private shopping center, would constitute a taking of property without just compensation in violation of the Fifth and Fourteenth Amendments:

> It is true that one of the essential sticks in the bundle of property rights is the right to exclude others. And here there has literally been a "taking" of that right to the extent that the California Supreme Court has interpreted the State Constitution to entitle its citizens to exercise free expression and petition rights on shopping center property. But it is well established that "not every destruction or injury to property by governmental action has been held to be a 'taking' in the constitution sense."

> Here the requirement that appellants permit appellees to exercise state-protected rights of free expression and petition on shopping center property clearly does not amount to an unconstitutional infringement of appellants' property rights under the Taking Clause. There is nothing to suggest that preventing appellants from prohibiting this sort of activity will unreasonably impair the value or use of their property as a shopping center. The PruneYard is a large commercial complex that covers several city blocks, contains numerous separate business establishments, and is open to the public at large. The decision of the California Supreme Court makes it clear that PruneYard may restrict expressive activity by adopting time, place, and manner regulations that will minimize any interference with its commercial functions. Appellees were orderly, and they limited their activity to the common areas of the shopping center. In these circumstances, the fact that they may have "physically invaded" appellants' property cannot be viewed as determinative.

Id. at 82-84. Accordingly, the unique right of petition afforded by the California Constitution prevailed in *PruneYard* even though the assertion of a First Amendment right had not succeeded in *Lloyd,* despite an almost identical factual context.

The United States Constitution does not confer a general right to free speech in a privately owned shopping center. Most state constitutions have been construed the same way. The state constitutions of California, Oregon, Massachusetts, New Jersey and Colorado have been interpreted to confer certain rights of expression at privately owned shopping centers. Only California, however, has held that the free speech protection in its state constitution applies to both private and state action.

STATE v. STUMMER
194 P.3d 1043 (Ariz. 2008)

BERCH, V. C. J.

Petitioners Hubert August Stummer and Dennis Allen Lumm were charged with violating section 13-1422 of the Arizona Revised Statutes, which forbids adult bookstores from remaining open during certain early morning hours. We have been asked to determine whether the hours of operation provision of section 13-1422 violates the free speech provision of the Arizona Constitution.

Petitioners operate adult-oriented businesses in Phoenix that sell sexually explicit books and magazines. They were charged with violating section 13-1422(A), which requires adult bookstores to close for fifty-three hours each week: from 1 a.m. to 8 a.m., Monday through Saturday, and from 1 a.m. to noon on Sunday.

Petitioners moved to dismiss the charges, citing *Empress Adult Video & Bookstore v. City of Tucson,* 59 P.3d 814, 823-24 (Ariz. Ct. App. 2002), which held the hours of operation provision in section 13-1422(A) unconstitutional. Bound by *Empress*, the superior court granted the motion. The State appealed, arguing that *Empress* was wrongly decided.

Section 13-1422 limits the hours an adult bookstore may remain open:

> An adult arcade, adult bookstore or video store, adult cabaret, adult motion picture theater, adult theater, escort agency or nude model studio shall not remain open at any time between the hours of 1:00 a.m. and 8:00 a.m. on Monday through Saturday and between the hours of 1:00 a.m. and 12:00 noon on Sunday.

The Arizona Legislature enacted section 13-1422 in response to complaints from citizens and local businesses that "adult" businesses were causing negative effects, including increased prostitution and sexually oriented litter, in the surrounding communities. These negative effects were alleged to be more prevalent during the early morning hours and the proponents therefore urged the legislature to restrict the operating hours of these businesses to reduce the problems.

These negative effects are byproducts or "secondary effects" of speech. The legislature purportedly designed section 13-1422(A) to suppress these secondary effects, not to suppress the speech itself. Although such regulations necessarily affect speech, restrictions on secondary effects have received less exacting scrutiny under the Federal Constitution than have laws designed to directly curtail speech. We must decide what level of scrutiny Arizona courts should apply when determining the constitutionality, under article 2, section 6 of the Arizona Constitution, of content-based secondary effects regulations.

Analysis of Section 13-1422 Under the First Amendment

Under the First Amendment, regulations that target speech based on its content are typically subject to strict scrutiny. The federal courts, however, have carved out an exception to this rule: Certain time, place, and manner restrictions designed to address the secondary effects of speech are subject to intermediate scrutiny.

Finding such regulations justified by the goal of reducing secondary effects rather than suppressing speech, the Supreme Court initially characterized such regulations as content neutral. More recently, however, federal courts have begun to acknowledge that secondary effects laws directed exclusively at adult businesses are not truly content neutral.

Nonetheless, the federal courts continue to apply a form of intermediate scrutiny. Under the federal test, a "statute will be upheld if it is designed to serve a substantial government interest, is narrowly tailored to serve that interest, and does not unreasonably limit alternative avenues of communication."

Applying this test, several federal courts have upheld statutes imposing hours of operation restrictions on sexually oriented businesses against First Amendment challenges.

Soon after section 13-1422 became effective, a coalition of adult businesses challenged the statute in federal court, asserting that its hours provision violates the First Amendment. Applying the *Renton* test, the district court upheld section 13-1422 and denied injunctive relief. Affirming, the Ninth Circuit found the intermediate scrutiny test satisfied. It concluded that section 13-1422 serves a substantial government interest; is narrowly tailored because "Arizona's interest in ameliorating secondary effects 'would be achieved less effectively absent the regulation,'" and leaves open alternative channels for communication by allowing stores to remain open "seventeen hours per day Monday through Saturday, and thirteen hours on Sunday."

Interpreting Article 2, § 6 of the Arizona Constitution

The issue presented in this case is not...whether section 13-1422 violates the First Amendment to the United States Constitution, but rather whether it passes muster under article 2, section 6 of the Arizona Constitution. Both the First Amendment and article 2, section 6, protect speech from abridgment by the government. The First Amendment does so by restraining government interference with speech rights. It provides that "Congress shall make no law...abridging the freedom of speech, or of the press." U.S. Const. amend. I. Arizona's free speech provision, in contrast, guarantees each individual's right to speak freely. It states that "[e]very person may freely speak, write, and publish on all subjects, being responsible for the abuse of that right." Ariz. Const. art. 2, § 6.

The encompassing text of article 2, section 6 indicates the Arizona framers' intent to rigorously protect freedom of speech. In addressing censorship, we have said that the words of Arizona's free speech provision "are too plain for equivocation. The right of every person to freely speak, write and publish may not be limited."

Arizona courts have had few opportunities to develop Arizona's free speech jurisprudence. With regard to unprotected speech, Arizona courts construing article 2, section 6 have followed federal interpretations of the United States Constitution. For example, in being "responsible for the abuse" of the right to speak, write, and publish on "all subjects," one may be held liable for defamation, notwithstanding the right to "freely speak."

We have also stated that article 2, section 6 has "greater scope than the First Amendment." This is not a case, however, in which we need to determine the boundaries of Arizona's free speech provision. The State does not argue that the books and magazines in Petitioners' bookstores are obscene. Thus in selling those materials, Petitioners are engaging in protected speech under article 2, section 6. We need only decide whether and to what extent the State may curtail this protected speech in order to reduce secondary effects.

Our opinion in *Mountain States Telephone & Telegraph Co. v. Arizona Corporation Commission*, 773 P.2d 455 (Ariz. 1989), is the starting point for our analysis of this issue. That case involved the regulation of "ScoopLines": pay-per-call telephone numbers that provided customers with messages on a variety of topics, such as sports and weather. In response to consumer complaints, the Arizona Corporation Commission ordered Mountain States to block ScoopLines and "to propose a presubscription plan for the Commission's approval." Mountain States sought relief from this Court, arguing that the Commission's order violated article 2, section 6.

There, as here, the government argued that the regulation was intended to accomplish a goal unrelated to the suppression of protected speech and that any effect on speech rights was "incidental and permissible." Although we concluded that the Commission could impose content-neutral "time, place, and manner" regulations, we cautioned that, "given Arizona's constitutional protections, when dealing with regulations that affect speech, the [government] must regulate with narrow specificity so as to affect as little as possible the ability of the sender and receiver to communicate."

In *Empress,* the court of appeals interpreted *Mountain States'* "narrow specificity" language as requiring that the regulation "affect *as little as possible* the ability of the sender and receiver to communicate." The court of appeals thus effectively adopted a "least restrictive means" standard. Applying this standard, the court concluded that section 13-1422 violated the Arizona Constitution because closing adult businesses for at least seven hours a day was not the least restrictive means of addressing the secondary effects of adult businesses.

The booksellers here urge that we adopt the *Empress* standard. We conclude, however, that such a standard is not appropriate for judging the constitutionality of secondary effects regulations. When a regulation is content based, but directed at addressing the secondary effects of speech, the legislative choice is entitled to more deference than the strict scrutiny test permits. The government may have a substantial interest in addressing certain secondary effects of speech, and applying strict scrutiny may effectively preclude regulations designed to prohibit such effects.

The State urges us instead to apply the federal intermediate scrutiny standard articulated by the Supreme Court in *Renton* and *Alameda Books,* as did the Ninth Circuit in *Center for Fair Public Policy* and the court of appeals panel in this case. We decline to strictly apply the federal test because it is inconsistent with the broad protection of speech afforded by the Arizona Constitution. Because Arizona's speech provision safeguards the right to speak freely on all topics, our test must more closely scrutinize laws that single out speech for regulation based on its disfavored content. We thus turn to the question of the appropriate test for determining the constitutionality, under article 2, section 6, of secondary effects regulations.

The appropriate test for measuring the constitutionality of content-based secondary effects regulations must vindicate the constitutional right to free speech, yet accommodate the government's interest in protecting the public health, safety, and welfare. The test has two phases. First, to qualify for intermediate scrutiny, the State must demonstrate that a content-based regulation is directed at ameliorating secondary effects, not at suppressing protected speech. Second, to survive intermediate scrutiny, the State must show that, in addressing the secondary effects, the regulation does not sweep too broadly.

In the first phase, the challenger must demonstrate that the challenged provision interferes with the right to freely speak, write, or publish. Once the challenger has shown that a content-based or content-correlated regulation affects free expression, the State bears the burden of demonstrating that the enacting body had a reasonable basis for believing that the speech singled out for regulation created secondary effects different from or greater than the effects of speech generally, and that the challenged regulation was designed to suppress those secondary effects, not to suppress the speech itself.

The State may carry that burden by demonstrating to the court that, on the basis of the evidence before it, the enacting body might reasonably believe that the regulated speech created negative secondary effects greater than those created by speech generally and that the regulation would address those effects. If the State meets this burden of showing that the legislative body enacted the challenged regulation to respond to secondary effects rather than disfavored speech, we will address the challenged regulation under a form of intermediate scrutiny.

In the second phase of the inquiry for determining the constitutionality of a content-based secondary effects regulation, the court must examine whether the regulation protects substantial government interests and whether it significantly reduces secondary effects without unduly interfering with protected speech. The deference afforded at the first phase, in which the court determines whether intermediate scrutiny applies, does not extend to the second phase, in which the court assesses the effects of the challenged law. For the regulation to survive, its proponent must show that the government has a substantial interest, that the regulation significantly furthers that interest, and that the challenged regulation does not unduly burden speech. To establish or disprove these prongs, the challenger and the proponent of the regulation may bring forth pre- and post-enactment evidence.

In applying the phase-two test, the court must first assess the importance of the government's asserted interest. Regulations designed to reduce crime, protect children, or safeguard constitutional rights, for example, may justify some infringement on speech rights. Lesser concerns, such as the abatement of mere litter or governmental convenience, will not justify suppression of speech.

If the government advances a substantial interest, the court must then determine whether the regulation significantly furthers that interest. A court may find this prong satisfied if the regulation substantially reduces or has a significant ameliorative impact on secondary effects. In this analysis, the court must consider the likelihood that the regulation will achieve its intended result. For example, the court may consider how much sex-related crime occurs during the hours of forced closure. The answer to this inquiry may elucidate whether the regulation is designed to significantly reduce such negative secondary effects and thus whether it may achieve its intended result.

Finally, the third prong—whether the regulation unduly burdens speech—may be satisfied by establishing that the government's substantial interest would be less effectively achieved without the regulation and ample alternative means of communication exist. Although the test does not require the least restrictive means possible, the proponent must show a close fit or nexus between the ends sought and the means employed for achieving those ends.

In analyzing the facts of this case under the first phase of Arizona's secondary effects test, we conclude that the Petitioners have established that their protected speech is burdened by a content-based regulation. The State, in turn, has met its burden of demonstrating that the hours provision of section 13-1422 was designed to curb the secondary effects of speech, not to prohibit the speech itself. The State adduced evidence that the legislature reasonably believed that adult businesses encourage criminal activity and sexually oriented litter, that these effects were worse in the nighttime hours, and that the statute at issue would ameliorate those effects. We therefore turn to the second phase of the inquiry, application of the three-part test: whether the government's interests are substantial, whether the regulation significantly furthers those interests, and whether the regulation unduly burdens speech.

In the second phase, the court must first assess the significance of the government's interests. The existence of mere litter is not by itself sufficiently important to permit a substantial restriction on speech. As we stated in *New Times, Inc. v. Arizona Board of Regents*, 519 P.2d 169, 174 (Ariz. 1974), "minor matters of public inconvenience or annoyance cannot be transformed into substantive evils of sufficient weight to warrant the curtailment of liberty of expression." Combating criminal activity such as prostitution and public indecency, however, is a substantial governmental interest. We therefore move to the second and third prongs of the phase-two analysis.

As to the second prong, whether the statute significantly furthers the government's interest, the record is devoid of evidence that secondary effects are greater during the hours of forced closure. The record reflects only two pieces of evidence on this point. One was the testimony of a representative of the City of Phoenix who testified that the city could *not* show a relationship between the hours of operation and the incidence of crime. The other was a study from Glendale, Colorado, finding that *fewer* police calls or incidents arose from a particular adult business during the late night hours than during other times. Neither piece of evidence supports the assertion that the effects are greater during the hours of forced closure. Without such a showing, the State may have difficulty establishing that closure is an appropriate remedy—that is, that this statute significantly furthers the government's interest in reducing secondary effects. The government must establish that, during their early morning operation, adult bookstores disproportionately cause negative secondary effects and that these negative effects are or will be significantly lessened by closure during those hours.

Finally, regarding the third prong, the State has not shown that any substantial interests would be achieved less effectively without the bookstores' closure for fifty-three hours each week. The record also does not contain evidence regarding the availability of alternative channels of communication during the hours of closure.

In short, because this case was decided on a motion to dismiss, the record contains no evidence of the significance of the infringement on speech, the effectiveness of the statute in reducing negative secondary effects, the nexus between the ends sought and the means employed, or the availability of alternative measures.

Because no court below has had the opportunity to apply the test we formulate today for evaluating the constitutionality of content-based secondary effects regulations, we conclude that all parties should have the opportunity to present additional evidence supporting their positions, and the trial court should have the opportunity to apply the test for constitutionality detailed above. We therefore remand this case to the superior court for further proceedings consistent with this opinion.

We vacate the opinion of the court of appeals and remand this case to the trial court.

NOTE

The federal secondary effects standards have been adopted in construing the constitutions of some states. *See People v. Superior Court,* 774 P.2d 769 (Cal. 1989); *DiRaimo v. City of Providence,* 714 A.2d 554 (R.I. 1998).

STATE v. HENRY
732 P.2d 9 (Or. 1987)

JONES, J.

Shortly after defendant Earl Henry opened an adult bookstore in Redmond, Oregon, a search warrant was issued by a Deschutes County district judge which resulted in the seizure of almost the entire inventory of the store, including 73 magazines, 142 paperback books, seven newspapers, nine films, one film projector, six decks of playing cards, an additional six periodical magazines, and various business records. Defendant was charged with disseminating obscene material and possession of obscene material with the intent to disseminate under section 167.087 of the Oregon Code.

A jury found defendant guilty of dissemination of obscene material and possession of obscene material with the intent to disseminate. Judgment was entered on the two convictions and in each case defendant was fined $1,000 and sentenced to imprisonment for 30 days with the jail sentences to run consecutively. Execution of the sentences was stayed pending appeal.

We hold that section 167.087 contravenes article I, section 8 of the Oregon Constitution and cannot be justified as an "historical exception" from Oregon's constitutional guarantee of freedom of expression.

Article I, section 8 of the Oregon Constitution sets forth in plain words that:

> No law shall be passed restraining the free expression of opinion, or restricting the right to speak, write, or print freely on any subject whatever; but every person shall be responsible for the abuse of this right.

What does the expression "every person shall be responsible for the abuse of this right" mean? This court obliquely addressed that language in *State v. Jackson,* 356 P.2d 495 (Or. 1960). There Justice George Rossman related this final clause of the section to the statement in Blackstone's

Commentaries that the "liberty of the press" extended only to freedom from "previous restraints upon publications, and not in freedom from censure for criminal matter when published." But article I, section 8 does not in terms refer to "freedom of...the press" (as the First Amendment does), and Blackstone's narrow view of the extent of freedom of publication has long been rejected in this country as inadequate to the intended sweep of the American guarantees. Since *Jackson,* this court has related the clause holding every person "responsible for the abuse of" the right of free expression to civil responsibility for harm done thereby. If the "abuse" clause leaves one subject to criminal prosecution for publications, it could hardly be confined just to "obscene" publications. The clause does not affect the decision of the case before us.

We have recently said in *State v. Robertson,* 649 P.2d 569 (Or. 1982), and *In re Lasswell,* 673 P.2d 855 (Or. 1983), that the guarantee of freedom of expression of the Oregon Constitution forecloses the enactment of any prohibitory law backed by punitive sanctions that forbids speech or writing on any subject whatever, unless it can be shown that the prohibition falls within an original or modern version of an historically established exception to the protection afforded freedom of expression by article I, section 8, that this guarantee demonstrably was not intended to displace.

Section 167.087 as adopted by the legislature captured the obscenity test set forth by the Supreme Court of the United States in *Miller v. California,* 413 U.S. 15 (1973). Defendant concedes that the statute passes muster under the federal Court's current view of the First Amendment and therefore focuses his attack directly on the viability of the statute under article I, section 8, of the Oregon Constitution. We therefore address this issue as our own interpretation of the Oregon Constitution independent of any First Amendment analysis by the Supreme Court of the United States. We discuss the federal constitution and federal cases only when of assistance in the analysis of the Oregon Constitution.

We note that article I, section 8, separately precludes laws "restraining the free expression of opinion" as well as laws "restricting the right to speak, write, or print freely," whereas the First Amendment restrains "abridging the freedom of speech, or of the press." The text of article I, section 8, is broader and covers any expression of opinion, including verbal and nonverbal expressions contained in films, pictures, paintings, sculpture and the like. The Oregon constitutional provision also covers "any subject whatever" and does not contain any express exception for obscene communications.

The question remains whether "obscene" expressions fall within such historical exceptions as "perjury, solicitation or verbal assistance in crime, some forms of theft, forgery and fraud and their contemporary variants." *State v. Robertson,* 649 P.2d 569.

The first part of the *Robertson* test for determining whether a restriction on expression comes within an historical exception focuses on whether the restriction was well established when the early American guarantees of freedom of expression were adopted, *i.e.,* by the late eighteenth and mid-nineteenth centuries.

The United States Supreme Court addressed the history of obscenity laws in *Roth v. United States,* 354 U.S. 476 (1957). Justice Brennan, in his first year on the Supreme Court, wrote that "obscenity is not within the area of constitutionally protected speech or press," relying on an excerpt from *Chaplinsky v. New Hampshire,* 315 U.S. 568 (1942), which had excluded "the lewd and obscene [and] the profane" from the category of protected speech. Thus, for the first time the United States Supreme Court opined that "obscenity" was without First Amendment protection. The Court stated that "implicit in the history of the First Amendment is the rejection of obscenity as utterly without redeeming social importance."

From our review of the English and American cases and statutes, we conclude that restrictions on sexually explicit or obscene expressions were not well established at the time the early freedoms of expression were adopted. We disagree with the writers of the *Chaplinsky* and *Roth* opinions that sexually explicit expression was historically unprotected for that reason. The point of our historical review and the historical review relied upon by the United States Supreme Court in *Roth* is that while there may long have been a view that "obscene" materials were improper and not privileged, the pejorative label has not described any single type of impropriety. The term "obscene" simply functioned as a condemnatory term declaring words, pictures, ideas or conduct as improper by definition, whatever may, from time to time, be placed within the definition, *e.g.,* "blasphemous," "profane," "immoral," "depraved," "corrupt," "lewd," "lascivious," "impure" and "hard-core pornography."

We now turn to Oregon history to determine if there is any indication that legislation existing at or near the time of the adoption of Article I, section 8, of the Oregon Constitution demonstrates that "obscene" expressions should be included as an historical exception under the *Robertson* test.

In *Robertson* we said that article I, section 8,

> forecloses the enactment of any law written in terms directed to the substance of any 'opinion' or any 'subject' of communication, unless the scope of the restraint is wholly confined within some historical exception that was well established when the first American guarantees of freedom of expression were adopted *and that the guarantees then or in 1859 demonstrably were not intended to reach."*

We emphasize this last clause because the constitutional guarantee of free speech and press will not be overcome by the mere showing of some legal restraints on one or another form of speech or writing. The party opposing a claim of constitutional privilege must demonstrate that the guarantees of freedom of expression were not intended to replace the earlier restrictions. We were convinced that they were not so intended with regard to common law prosecutions for "perjury, solicitation or verbal assistance in crime, some forms of theft, forgery and fraud." But the state claims that "obscenity" would have been a conventional crime when Oregon's Bill of Rights was adopted in 1857. The state argues that

> in the Oregon Codes of 1853 and 1855, sale, distribution, and possession of obscene writings or pictures was punishable as a misdemeanor by fine and/or imprisonment. Thus, it is apparent that the same type of conduct prescribed under section 167.087, *i.e.*, dissemination of obscene writings and/or pictures, constituted a crime at least 5 years prior to adoption of the Oregon Bill of Rights. Therefore, such a crime falls within the historical exception delineated in *Robertson.*

As we cautioned in *State ex rel. Oregonian Pub. Co. v. Deiz,* 613 P.2d 23 (Or. 1980), "[c]ontemporaneous legislative actions should not necessarily be given much weight when construing constitutional principles. Constitutional draftsmen are concerned with broad principles of long-range significance." The only relevant Oregon territorial legislation enacted before article I, section 8, included prohibitions against the sale, distribution and possession of obscene writings or pictures which manifestly tended to corrupt the morals of youth. The territorial statute, which contained no definition of "obscene" and which was directed primarily to the protection of youth, certainly does not constitute any well-established historical exception to freedom of expression and that statute is in no way the equivalent of statutes punishing libel, perjury, forgery and the like.

In 1960, in *State v. Jackson,* a 4-3 decision in which the regular members of this Court divided equally, Justice Rossman, joined by Justices McAllister and Perry and Pro Tem Judge Millard, wrote:

> Neither party to this appeal argues that obscenity falls within the free speech guarantees of the federal or state constitutions. We think that the authorities marshalled by the majority opinion in *Roth v. United States,* supra, convincingly demonstrate that obscene speech enjoys no such immunity as a matter of history, and we reject an interpretation of our constitution which would protect it in Oregon.

We reject that language as historically unsound. Our approach in more recent cases is that stated in Justice O'Connell's dissenting opinion for three members of this court. He recognized that in interpreting article I, section 8, of our Oregon Constitution, the federal *Roth* case was of value only if the reasoning supporting that Court's interpretation of the federal constitution could be used as a guide in construing our own. The dissenting opinion in *Jackson* disagreed with the conclusion in *Roth* that "obscenity is not within the area of constitutionally protected speech or press." Justice O'Connell further commented that it is difficult to see how language or material dealing with love, lust and sex is any less entitled to First Amendment scrutiny when regulation is attempted than is the language or depiction of violence and revolution.

In *Roth,* Justice Douglas observed that the First Amendment was a product of a robust, not a prudish age. Likewise, although Oregon's pioneers brought with them a diversity of highly moral as well as irreverent views, we perceive that most members of the Constitutional Convention of 1857 were rugged and robust individuals dedicated to founding a free society unfettered by the governmental imposition of some people's views of morality on the free expression of others. We conclude as we did in reviewing English and American history that restrictions on sexually explicit and obscene expression between adults were not well established at the time of the adoption of Article I, section 8, of the Oregon Constitution. The history of restriction on undefined obscenity contrasts sharply with the Oregon and common law crimes involving expression such as perjury, theft, forgery and fraud that were well established by 1859. The very fact that "obscenity" originally was pursued and repressed for its "anti-establishment" irreverence rather than for its bawdiness elsewhere and only to protect the morals of youth in this state leads us to conclude that no broad or all-encompassing historical exception from the guarantees of free expression was ever intended. The restriction on sexually explicit expression embodied in section 167.087 does not satisfy the first part of the *Robertson* test.

We now turn to the issue whether section 167.087 censors free speech as guaranteed by the Oregon Constitution. As mentioned, this statute captured the obscenity test set forth by the 1973 Supreme Court of the United States in *Miller v. California, supra.* After *Roth,* the Supreme Court in numerous subsequent opinions for 15 years was unable to muster five votes for any theory of censorship of obscenity until *Miller* and *Paris Adult Theatre I v. Slaton,* 413 U.S. 49 (1973). By that time Justice Brennan had come to regret that he ever went for the idea of excluding "obscenity" from the First Amendment in the first place, and he dissented. He concluded that the *Roth/Miller/Paris Adult Theatre* approach is incompatible with a coherent theory of free expression under the First Amendment. We agree with Justice Brennan for the reasons previously expressed and conclude that it is equally incompatible with article I, section 8, of our state constitution.

In *Miller v. California, supra,* a five-Justice majority modified the *Roth* test and converted it to (1) whether the "average person, applying contemporary community standards" would find that the work, taken as a whole, appeals to the prurient interest, (b) whether the work depicts or describes, in a patently offensive way, sexual conduct specifically defined by the applicable state law, and (c) whether the work, taken as a whole, lacks serious literary, artistic, political, or scientific value. In *Paris Adult Theatre,* a case decided the same day as *Miller,* the Supreme Court rejected the argument that obscene films are constitutionally immune from state regulation simply because they are exhibited to consenting adults only. The Court previously had held, in *Stanley v. Georgia,* 394 U.S. 557 (1969), that mere private possession of obscene matter cannot be proscribed and the constitution protects the right to receive information and ideas and to be generally free from government intrusion into one's privacy. *Miller v. California* continues to represent the federal standard and the federal courts continue to exclude obscenity as defined in *Miller* from First Amendment protection.

Although the *Miller* test may pass federal constitutional muster and is recommended as a model for state legislatures by the Attorney General's Commission on Pornography, the test constitutes censorship forbidden by the Oregon Constitution. As Judge Tanzer aptly noted in *State v. Tidyman,* the problem with the United States Supreme Court's approach to obscene expression is that it permits government to decide what constitutes socially acceptable expression, which is precisely what Madison decried: "The difficulty [with the United States Supreme Court's approach] arises from the anomaly that the very purpose of the First Amendment is to protect expression which fails to conform to community standards."

We hold that characterizing expression as "obscenity" under any definition, be it *Roth, Miller* or otherwise, does not deprive it of protection under the Oregon Constitution. Obscene speech, writing or equivalent forms of communication are "speech" nonetheless. We emphasize that the prime reason that "obscene" expression cannot be restricted is that it is speech that does not fall within any historical exception to the plain wording of the Oregon Constitution that "no law shall be passed restraining the expression of [speech] freely on any subject whatsoever."

We do not hold that this form of expression, like others, may not be regulated in the interests of unwilling viewers, captive audiences, minors and beleaguered neighbors. No such issue is before us. But it may not be punished in the interest of a uniform vision on how human sexuality should be regarded or portrayed. We also do not rule out regulation, enforced by criminal prosecution, directed against conduct of producers or participants in the production of sexually explicit material, nor reasonable time, place and manner regulations of the nuisance aspect of such material or laws to protect the unwilling viewer or children. Again, no such issue is before us. However, no law can prohibit or censor the communication itself. In this state any person can write, print, read, say, show or sell anything to a consenting adult even though that expression may be generally or universally considered "obscene."

NOTE

The Tennessee Supreme Court held that a state obscenity statute, based upon the *Miller* test, did not violate the state constitution's guarantee in article I, section 19 of free communications of thoughts and opinions. *Tennessee v. Marshall*, 859 S.W.2d 289 (Tenn. 1993). The states of Maryland, Minnesota, Ohio, Texas and Washington have followed the First Amendment jurisprudence on obscenity even when there have been differences in the text of the state constitution.

C. CIVIL JURY TRIAL

Although the Sixth Amendment right to trial by jury in a criminal proceeding has been made binding upon the states by virtue of the Fourteenth Amendment, *Duncan v. Louisiana*, 391 U.S. 145, 156 (1968), the United States Supreme Court has thus far declined to hold that the Seventh Amendment right to trial by jury in a civil proceeding is binding upon the states. *See Minneapolis & St. Louis R.R. Co. v. Bombolis*, 241 U.S. 211 (1916). Accordingly, the right to a jury trial in civil proceedings has always been and remains exclusively protected by provisions in the constitution of each state.

SOFIE v. FIBREBOARD CORP.
771 P.2d 711 (Wash. 1989)

UTTER, J.

Austin and Marcia Sofie challenge the constitutionality of section 4.56.250 of the Washington Code. This statute, part of the 1986 tort reform act, places a limit on the noneconomic damages recoverable by a personal injury or wrongful death plaintiff. The Sofies brought a direct appeal to this court after the trial judge in their tort action, under the direction of the statute, reduced the jury's award of noneconomic damages. The respondents subsequently cross-appealed to the Court of Appeals, raising several issues of trial court error, issues we consider here.

The Sofies argue that section 4.56.250 violates their constitutional rights to trial by jury, equal protection, and due process. We find that the statute's damages limit interferes with the jury's traditional function to determine damages. Therefore, section 4.56.250 violates article 1, section 21 of the Washington Constitution, which protects as inviolate the right to a jury. Because the statute is unconstitutional on this basis, we do not consider its constitutionality under the latter two doctrines raised by appellants, although we briefly survey the equal protection issues. Respondents' arguments concerning trial court error are without merit.

The Washington Legislature passed section 4.56.250 in 1986 partly as a response to rising insurance premiums for liability coverage. The damages limit that the statute creates operates on a formula based upon the age of the plaintiff. As a result, the older a plaintiff is, the less he or she will be able to recover in noneconomic damages. The trial judge applies the limit to the damages found by the trier of fact. If the case is tried before a jury, the jury determines the amount of noneconomic damages without knowledge of the limit. The jury goes about its normal business and the judge reduces, according to the statute's formula and without notifying the jury, any damage verdicts that exceed the limit.

In September 1987, the Sofies sued Fibreboard Corp. and other asbestos manufacturers for the harm caused to Mr. Sofie by their asbestos products. Mr. Sofie, then aged 67, was suffering from a form of lung cancer—mesothelioma—caused by exposure to asbestos during his career as a pipefitter. At trial, Mr. Sofie's attorneys presented evidence of the extreme pain he experienced as a result of the disease. The testimony indicated that Mr. Sofie spent what remained of his life waiting for the next "morphine cocktail," for the next hot bath, for anything that would lessen his consuming physical agony.

At the end of the trial, the jury found the defendants at fault for Mr. Sofie's disease. They returned a verdict of $1,345,833 in favor of the Sofies. Of this amount, $1,154,592 went to compensate noneconomic damages: $477,200 for Mr. Sofie's pain and suffering and $677,392 for Mrs. Sofie's loss of consortium. While the trial judge specifically found the jury's finding of damages reasonable, he indicated he was compelled under the damages limit to reduce the noneconomic portion of the verdict to $125,136.45, resulting in a total judgment of $316,377.45.

The dispositive issue of this case is the right to a jury trial. This court has long approached the review of legislative enactments with great care. The wisdom of legislation is not justiciable; our only power is to determine the legislation's constitutional validity. In matters of economic legislation, we follow the rule giving every reasonable presumption in favor of the constitutionality of the law or ordinance. We employ this caution to avoid substituting our judgment for the judgment of the Legislature.

Other courts, faced with unconstitutional tort damage limits, have adhered to similar principles when reviewing those legislative actions. The Kansas Supreme Court put it well:

> This court is by the Constitution not made the critic of the legislature, but rather, the guardian of the Constitution. The constitutionality of a statute is presumed, and all doubts must be resolved in favor of its validity. Before a statute may be stricken down, it must clearly appear the statute violates the Constitution. Moreover, it is the court's duty to uphold the statute under attack, if possible, rather than defeat it, and if there is any reasonable way to construe the statute as constitutionally valid, that should be done. *Kansas Malpractice Victims Coalition v. Bell,* 757 P.2d 251, 256-57 (Kan. 1988).

To determine the extent of the right to trial by jury as it applies here, we must first identify the source of the constitutional protection. The seventh amendment to the United States Constitution does not apply through the Fourteenth Amendment to the states in civil trials. The right to jury trial in civil proceedings is protected solely by the Washington Constitution in article 1, section 21. Therefore, the relevant analysis must follow state doctrine; our result is based entirely on adequate and independent state grounds.

Article 1, section 21 states:

> The right of trial by jury shall remain inviolate, but the legislature may provide for a jury of any number less than twelve in courts not of record, and for a verdict by nine or more jurors in civil cases in any court of record, and for waiving of the jury in civil cases where the consent of the parties interested is given thereto.

Our basic rule in interpreting article 1, section 21 is to look to the right as it existed at the time of the constitution's adoption in 1889. We have used this historical standard to determine the scope of the right as well as the causes of action to which it applies. These two issues, scope and the applicable causes of action, merit separate discussion.

State ex rel. Mullen v. Doherty, 47 P. 958 (1897), being close in time to 1889, provides some contemporary insight on the scope issue. In *Mullen,* we cited section 248 of the Code of 1881, in force at the time of the constitution's passage, to determine the jury's role in the constitutional scheme: "either party shall have the right in an action at law, upon an issue of fact, to demand a trial by jury." Subsequent cases underscore the jury's fact finding province as the essence of the right's scope.

At issue in the present case is whether the measure of damages is a question of fact within the jury's province. Our past decisions show that it is indeed. The constitutional nature of the jury's damage-finding function is underscored by *Baker v. Prewitt,* 19 P. 149 (Wash. 1888). In that case, the territorial Supreme Court stated:

> Sections 204 and 289 of the [territorial] Code seem to require that in all actions for the assessment of damages the intervention of a jury must be had, save where a long account may authorize a referee, etc. This statute is mandatory, and we are satisfied that where the amount of damages is not fixed, agreed upon, or in some way liquidated, a jury must be called, unless expressly waived.

If our state constitution is to protect as inviolate the right to a jury trial at least to the extent as it existed in 1889, then *Baker's* holding provides clear evidence that the jury's fact-finding function included the determination of damages. This evidence can only lead to the conclusion that our constitution, in article 1, section 21, protects the jury's role to determine damages.

The present case is not the first time we have recognized the constitutional nature of the jury's damage-determining role. In *James v. Robeck,* 490 P.2d 878 (Wash. 1971), we stated: "To the jury is consigned under the constitution the ultimate power to weigh the evidence and determine the facts-and the amount of damages in a particular case is an ultimate fact."

The jury's role in determining noneconomic damages is perhaps even more essential. In *Bingaman v. Grays Harbor Comm'ty Hosp.,* 699 P.2d 1230 (Wash. 1985), the husband of a woman who died painfully 35 hours after giving birth, the result of medical malpractice, brought a wrongful death and survival action. The only issue before this court was whether the trial judge had properly reduced the jury's damage verdict of $412,000 for the woman's pain and suffering. In resolving the issue in the plaintiff's favor, we stated: "The determination of the amount of damages, *particularly in actions of this nature,* is primarily and peculiarly within the province of the jury, under proper instructions."

United States Supreme Court jurisprudence on the Seventh Amendment's scope in [federal] civil trials, while not binding on the states, also provides some insight. In *Dimick v. Schiedt,* 293 U.S. 474 (1935), the Court used historical analysis to determine whether the Seventh Amendment allowed additur. Citing cases and treatises dating from the time of the amendment's adoption, the Court found that determining damages, as an issue of fact, was very much within the jury's province and therefore protected by the Seventh Amendment. The Court also indicated that a judge should give more deference to a jury's verdict when the damages at issue concern a noneconomic loss. The Court quoted the English case of *Beardmore v. Carrington,* 2 Wils. 244, 248:

> There is great difference between cases of damages which [may] be certainly seen, and such as are ideal, as between assumpsit, trespass for goods where the sum and value may be measured, and actions of imprisonment, malicious prosecution, slander and other personal torts, where the damages are matter of opinion, speculation, ideal...

The Court clarified the implications of the difference between these two classes of actions by quoting from Mayne's Treatise on Damages, at 571: "'in cases where the amount of damages was uncertain their assessment was a matter so peculiarly within the province of the jury that the Court should not alter it.'"

A method of historical analysis used by the United States Supreme Court in *Tull v. United States,* provides further insight. The *Tull* Court looked for proceedings analogous to the enforcement action under the federal clean water act which were contemporary with the Seventh Amendment's adoption. Finding that the common law proceeding of debt, in which the litigants had a right to a jury, was analogous to the clean water act enforcement action, the Court applied the Seventh Amendment right to the modern action. Without stretching the analogy as far as the Supreme Court did, it is logical to apply the more recent tort theories by analogy to the common law tort actions that existed in 1889. We note again that we reach our result today on adequate and independent state grounds. The holding in *Tull,* like all United States Supreme Court precedent in the civil trial area of the Seventh Amendment, is not binding on the states and merely serves as an example to us. It does not compel the result we reach.

Ultimately, there is not even an issue whether the right to a jury attaches to the Sofies' case. While they asserted "newer" tort theories in their complaint, the heart of the appellants' cause of action centered on negligence and willful or wanton misconduct resulting in personal injury. These basic tort theories are the same as those that existed at common law in 1889. Subsequent cases and statutes have recognized newer theories of recovery within the framework of these basic tort actions, but the basic cause of action remains the same. Therefore, the right to trial by jury—with its scope as defined by historical analysis—remains attached here.

The potential impact of the constitution's language was not lost on the Legislature. During the floor debates on the Tort Reform Act, the legislators were warned of the possible constitutional problems with their new legislation. Senator Talmadge stated:

> The Constitution of this state in Article I, Section 21, talks about the right to trial by jury being inviolate, not being something that we can invade as members of the Legislature, and when you start to put limitations on what juries can do, you have, in fact, invaded the province of the jury and have not preserved the right to a trial by jury inviolate.

Senate Journal, 49th Legislature (1986), at 449.

It is highly persuasive that in Kansas, Texas, Ohio, and Florida, states that have found the damages limit unconstitutional, the operative language of the right to jury trial provisions in those states' constitutions is nearly identical to our own. *See* Kan. Const. Bill of Rights § 5 ("The right of trial by jury shall be inviolate"); Tex. Const. art. I, § 15 ("The right of trial by jury shall remain inviolate"); Ohio Const. art. I, § 5 ("The right of trial by jury shall be inviolate"); Fla. Const. art. I § 22 ("The right of trial by jury shall be secure to all and remain inviolate").

The weight of authority from other states, both numerically and persuasively, supports the conclusion that Washington's damages limit violates the right to trial by jury.

McCOOL v. GEHRET
657 A.2d 269 (Del. 1995)

HOLLAND, J.

This is an appeal from the Superior Court. In their original complaint, the plaintiffs-appellants, Paul and Tammera McCool (the "McCools") alleged medical negligence by the defendant-appellee, John Gehret, M.D. ("Dr. Gehret"), and certain other health care providers. The complaint was amended to allege tortious interference by Dr. Gehret with the plaintiffs' medical expert witness, Robert Dein, M.D. ("Dr. Dein"). Over the plaintiffs' objection, the Superior Court granted Dr. Gehret's motion to sever the trial of the McCools' claim for medical malpractice from the trial of their claim for tortious interference.

A jury trial was held on the medical malpractice claim only, beginning on January 18, 1994. The jury returned a verdict in favor of Dr. Gehret on January 26, 1994. On February 3, 1994, the plaintiffs filed a motion for a mistrial or, in the alternative, a new trial.

On April 20, 1994, a one-day bench trial was held regarding the tortious interference claim. This bench trial was held before a different Superior Court judge than the one who had presided at the malpractice trial.

The McCools contend that forcing them to proceed with a bench trial on their tortious interference claim, despite their objection, violated their Delaware Constitutional right to have a trial by jury in that civil proceeding. The historical origins of the right to trial by jury, which is provided for in the Delaware Constitution, was reviewed by this Court in *Claudio v. State*, 585 A.2d 1278 (Del. 1991). In *Claudio,* this Court noted that when Delaware adopted its Constitution in 1792, notwithstanding the ratification of the first ten amendments or federal Bill of Rights in 1791, it did not create "a mirror image of the United States Constitution" with regard to trial by jury.

When the Delaware Constitution of 1792 was adopted, the right to trial by jury set forth in the federal Bill of Rights as the Sixth and Seventh Amendments to the United States Constitution was only a protection against action by the federal government. Following the adoption of the Fourteenth Amendment to the United States Constitution, the Sixth Amendment right to trial by jury in *criminal* proceedings has been deemed to have been incorporated by the Due Process clause and now also provides protection against state action. Nevertheless, the United States Supreme Court has not held that the Seventh Amendment's guarantee of jury trials in *civil* proceedings was made applicable to the states by the incorporation doctrine with the adoption of the Fourteenth Amendment to the United States Constitution.

Accordingly, the right to a jury trial in civil proceedings has always been and remains exclusively protected by provisions in the Delaware Constitution. Delaware adopted its first Constitution in 1776, which provided, in pertinent part:

> The common law of England, as well as so much of the statute law as have been heretofore adopted in practice in this state, shall remain in force, unless they shall be altered by a future law of the Legislature; such parts only excepted as are repugnant to the rights and privileges contained in this constitution and the declaration of rights, & c. agreed to by this convention. Del. Const. of 1776, art. 25.

Delaware also adopted its own *Declaration of Rights* in 1776, which guaranteed the right to trial by jury to all citizens of the State of Delaware and included a statement "[t]hat trial by jury of facts where they arise is one of the greatest securities of the lives, liberties and estates of the people."

When Delaware adopted its next Constitution in 1792, its citizens were guaranteed the right to trial by jury "as heretofore." Consequently, since its inception in 1776, the Delaware Constitution has afforded its citizens the right to trial by jury in both criminal and civil proceedings. In doing so, the Delaware Constitution has expressly preserved all of the fundamental features of the jury system as they existed at common law.

A *sine qua non* of that common law jurisprudence is the principle that either party shall have the right to demand a jury trial upon an issue of fact in an action at law. As previously noted, the 1776 Delaware *Declaration of Rights,* which was preserved by the "heretofore" text in the 1792 Constitution, referred to the right to trial by jury regarding factual issues as "one of the greatest securities of the lives, liberties and estates of the people." Similarly, in a letter to Pierre S. DuPont, Thomas Jefferson described the fact finding function of jurors as:

> the very essence of a Republic.... We of the United States...think experience has proved it safer for the mass of individuals composing the society to reserve

to themselves personally the exercise of all rightful powers to which they are competent....

Hence, with us, the people...being competent to judge of the facts occurring in ordinary life,...have retained the functions of judges of facts under the name of jurors....

I believe...that action by the citizens, in person in affairs within their reach and competence, and in all others by representatives chosen immediately and removable by themselves, constitutes the essence of a Republic.

Letter from Thomas Jefferson to Pierre S. DuPont (April 4, 1816).

In 1855, the Delaware General Assembly enacted a statute that purportedly allowed judges to decide issues of fact without a jury in actions at law, with the agreement of all the parties. Nevertheless, because the Delaware Constitution preserved the right to trial by jury as "heretofore," Delaware judges took the position that, absent constitutional amendment, the General Assembly could not alter the right by statute. Therefore, notwithstanding the enactment of the 1855 statute by the General Assembly, Delaware judges remained reluctant to decide issues of fact in an action at law because they concluded that the Delaware Constitution required a jury to decide such questions.

When the present Delaware Constitution was rewritten in 1897, the General Assembly included several significant provisions regarding the right to trial by jury. Article I of the 1897 Delaware Constitution was denominated for the first time as the "Bill of Rights." Section 4 of that article provided for the right to trial by jury as "heretofore." Article IV, section 19 was a new addition in the 1897 Constitution and provided: "Judges shall not charge juries with respect to matters of fact, but may state the questions of fact in issue and declare the law." Del. Const. art. IV, § 19. The reason given during the Constitutional debates for the adoption of section 19 was to ensure "that Judges shall confine themselves to their business, which is to adjudge the law and leave juries to determine the facts."

In *Storey,* this Court characterized section 19 as perpetuating Delaware's commitment to trial by jury in civil actions at law with regard to issues of fact. In examining when a trial judge may set aside a jury verdict, this Court described Delaware's long history of commitment to trial by jury. We explained that section 19 reaffirmed Delaware's commitment to the common law principles regarding trial by jury:

> In the policy of the law of this state, declared by the courts in numberless decisions, the jury is the sole judge of the facts of a case, and so jealous is the law of this policy that by express provision of the Constitution the court is forbidden to touch upon the facts of the case in its charge to the jury.

In 1897, another new section was added to article IV of Delaware's Constitution. Article IV, section 20 provides that, "[i]n civil causes where matters of fact are at issue, if the parties agree, such matters of fact shall be tried by the court, and judgment rendered upon their decision thereon as upon a verdict by a jury." Del. Const. art. IV, § 20. According to the Constitutional debates, the purpose of the new section was to address the concerns of Delaware's jurists about the constitutionality of the 1855 statutory authorization for litigants to waive a trial by jury in an action at law on an issue of fact.

In this case the McCools specifically demanded a jury trial on their medical malpractice claim and their tortious interference claim. When the jury that heard their medical malpractice claim was discharged, the McCools agreed to waive their right to a jury trial regarding their tortious interference claim only because the original trial judge offered to decide the remaining claim as a bench trial. The record contains the following statement by the McCools' attorney to the second trial judge:

> For practical reasons, the [medical malpractice] trial went a bit longer than we expected. Because of the two-week period of the jury panel, [the original trial judge] explained to us that it did not appear we would be able to get the same jury.

> Discussing this in chambers as well as I think in the courtroom,...[the original trial judge] proposed [to personally hear] this count...[as] a bench trial, [the] benefit being, again, that even though we don't have the jury, at least we have a judge who did have the benefit of hearing all the testimony.

When the original trial judge subsequently declined to hear the tortious interference claim, the McCools objected to proceeding with a bench trial before another judge. Their attorney advised the second judge:

> Based on our understanding that the matter would be heard on the bench trial before [the original trial judge], my clients and I agreed to have it heard that way rather than [by] jury trial. [I] just want to go on record that is their position. They still are opposed to...the assignment of your honor.

Although a party has no right to insist on a bench trial before a particular judge, the record reflects that the McCools' waiver of their right to a jury trial was, in fact, permitted to be premised upon such a condition. The McCools only waived their right to a jury trial on the condition that the bench trial would be held before the original judge who had heard the medical malpractice claim and was familiar with much of the evidence relevant to the tortious interference claim. When the original trial judge, who had induced the McCools to waive their right to a jury trial, refused to hear their tortious interference claim, the condition upon which the McCools' waiver had been predicated ceased to exist.

This Court has recognized that the right to a trial by jury, as guaranteed by the Delaware Constitution, may be relinquished pursuant to a valid waiver. Under the circumstances presented in this case, however, the McCools could not be forced to proceed with a bench trial before a second judge, in the absence of an unconditional waiver of their fundamental right to a trial by jury. Consequently, the bench trial of the tortious interference claim that proceeded, without the McCools' express and unconditional waiver of a jury trial, violated article IV, section 20 and article I, section 4 of the Delaware Constitution.

NOTES

1.   Article I, section 13 the Illinois Constitution of 1970 states: "The right of trial by jury as heretofore enjoyed shall remain inviolate." Ill. Const. of 1970, art. I, § 13. The meaning of this provision has been explained as follows:

> The constitutional provision that "the right of trial by jury as heretofore enjoyed shall remain inviolate" means that the right to a jury trial shall continue in all cases where such right existed at common law at the time the Constitution was adopted, but that constitutional provision has never been held to prohibit the legislature from creating new rights unknown to the common law and provide for their determination without a jury.

Standidge v. Chicago Rys. Co., 98 N.E. 963 (Ill. 1912).

Therefore, the right to a jury trial under the Illinois Constitution is not guaranteed in any action that did not exist at common law, even if the action is legal in nature. However, the right to a jury trial continues in all civil cases where the right existed at common law at the time the federal Bill of Rights was adopted. In addition, it has been recognized that the Illinois General Assembly may create an action unknown at common law and provide a right to a trial by jury.

2.   In civil cases, the Kentucky Constitution has been construed as recognizing exceptions to the right to a jury trial, including causes of action at common law that would have been regarded as equitable.

3.   The Pennsylvania Constitution was amended to provide that a verdict may be rendered by not less than five-sixths of the jury in any civil case. Subject to that amendment, however, the right to trial by jury remained "as heretofore" and "inviolate." Pa. Const. art. I, § 6. In a civil case, twelve jurors retired to deliberate but one juror did not complete the deliberations. After the plaintiff-appellant's motion for a mistrial was denied, the eleven remaining jurors returned a unanimous verdict. The Pennsylvania Supreme Court reversed and held that the parties were entitled to a verdict of twelve jurors, notwithstanding the fact that the unanimous verdict of eleven jurors was greater than five-sixths of twelve. *See Blum v. Merrell Dow Pharmaceuticals, Inc.*, 626 A.2d 537 (Pa. 1993).

D. RIGHT TO BEAR ARMS

POSEY v. COMMONWEALTH
185 S.W.3d 170 (Ky. 2006)

GRAVES, J.

Appellant entered conditional guilty pleas to Trafficking in Marijuana (subsequent offense), Possession of a Firearm by a Convicted Felon, Misdemeanor Possession of a Controlled Substance, and Possession of Drug Paraphernalia in Jefferson Circuit Court. For these crimes, Appellant was sentenced to four years of probation with six months work release.

On January 6, 2002, two Louisville police officers attempted to serve an outstanding arrest warrant on an individual named James Powell. Powell's last known address was 1565 South Ninth Street. When the officers arrived at that address and knocked on the door, Appellant, Ricky L. Posey, appeared at the door. Appellant, who was standing immediately inside the threshold of the home, opened the door and began to talk with one of the officers. The other officer soon joined their conversation and as they were conversing with Appellant on the porch, they observed shotgun shells and individually wrapped packets of marijuana inside the home. They also smelled an odor of marijuana emanating from the home.

From these observations, the officers decided to step inside Appellant's home (through the open door) and arrest him for possession of a controlled substance. They immediately seized the marijuana and the shotgun shells in plain view and then proceeded to search the rest of the home. They found a gun lying on the floor in an adjoining room in plain view. In addition, they found a set of electronic scales and a bottle of codeine cough syrup.

Appellant was indicted for Trafficking in Marijuana (less than eight ounces) while in Possession of a Firearm (subsequent offense), Possession of a Firearm by a Convicted Felon, Misdemeanor Possession of a Controlled Substance, and Possession of Drug Paraphernalia. Appellant filed a pretrial motion to suppress all of the evidence seized during the search of his home. Appellant also filed a motion to dismiss the firearm possession charge, arguing that section 527.040 of the Kentucky Revised Statutes, Ky. Rev. Stat. Ann. § 527.040 (barring convicted felons from possessing handguns), was unconstitutional. The trial court denied both of Appellant's motions. Appellant subsequently entered conditional pleas of guilty for all charges, reserving for appeal the suppression issue and the constitutionality of section 527.040.

The Court of Appeals affirmed the trial court's rulings, holding that the officers' entry into the home for the purposes of arresting Appellant and seizing contraband in plain view did not violate the Fourth Amendment. The Court of Appeals further ruled section 527.040 constitutional, relying on this Court's decision in *Eary v. Commonwealth,* 659 S.W.2d 198 (Ky.1983). We accepted discretionary review and now affirm on both issues.

Constitutionality of Section 527.040

Appellant argues that section 527.040 is unconstitutional. Under section 527.040, it is a felony for convicted felons to possess, manufacture, or transport a firearm in the Commonwealth of Kentucky. Appellant contends that this law violates section 1(7) of the Kentucky Constitution which states:

> All men are, by nature, free and equal, and have certain inherent and inalienable rights, among which may be reckoned:...The right to bear arms in defense of themselves and of the State, subject to the power of the General Assembly to enact laws to prevent persons from carrying concealed weapons.

Appellant contends that the mandates of section 1(7) are clear and that its existence affirmatively operates to exempt the area of firearms possession from regulation by the General Assembly. Pursuant to section 26 of our constitution, Appellant argues that section 527.040 of the Kentucky Revised Statutes is essentially nullified by section 1(7) and should be declared invalid as an impermissible infringement upon the people's right to bear arms. For the reasons set forth herein, we disagree.

We begin by emphasizing that rights preserved to the people pursuant to sections 1 through 26 of our constitution cannot be usurped by legislative fiat. The Kentucky Bill of Rights has always been, and continues to be, recognized as the supreme law of this Commonwealth. Accordingly, we consider carefully and fully any possible infringements upon these rights by a governmental power.

Section 527.040 prohibits a specific class of individuals, namely convicted felons, from possessing firearms in the Commonwealth of Kentucky. Decades of decisions have taught us that a statute prohibiting a class of individuals from doing anything must, at a minimum, be based on some rational basis in order to satisfy constitutional standards. In this case, neither party disputes that regulation of firearms among convicted felons is supported by substantial and rational concerns.

Rather, Appellant contends that the constitution expressly protects the convicted felon's right to bear arms in spite of these substantial risks to public welfare and safety. He points to the plain language of section 1(7), and argues that when it is read in comparison to another right endowed by the constitution, there can be no doubt as to the meaning of the language.

We disagree, finding nothing in the constitution, either express or implied, which support Appellant's positions.

First, Appellant argues that the language of section 1(7) is plain and clear. It declares that all "men" have the right to bear arms in defense of themselves and of the Commonwealth subject only to "the power of the General Assembly to enact laws to prevent persons from carrying concealed weapons." He argues that use of the word "men" in the modern constitution rather than "citizens" (the word used in previous versions) implies that the right is meant to encompass all persons and not just those who were endowed with the rights and privileges which were commonly conferred on citizens.

While we agree that it may be reasonable to infer from this language change that the 1890 constitutional convention desired to expand the lot of persons entitled to possess firearms, we disagree that this expansion reasonably or necessarily included convicted felons. It is generally accepted that certain classes of persons are thought to lack the ability or the natural attributes to possess many of the rights which are recognized under our constitution. For example, none of the parties dispute the premise that children and insane or incompetent persons are likely not endowed with the natural right to bear arms. Historically, convicted felons were similarly accorded diminished status when it came to being endowed with certain natural rights.

Indeed, the view prevailing at the time our modern constitution was formulated was that felons were not endowed with the natural right to possess firearms. Thus, without further evidence to suggest that convicted felons were somehow accorded more status by the 1890 constitutional convention than was historically attributed to them, we cannot say that the use of the word "men" within our modern constitution was intended to necessarily encompass those men who were convicted felons.

Appellant similarly argues that the framers' intent to include convicted felons within the scope of section 1(7) of the Kentucky Constitution is illustrated by comparison to section 145 of the constitution. Section 145 describes, in detailed form, the types of "persons" who are entitled to vote in the Commonwealth of Kentucky. It states that these "persons" must be (1) at least eighteen years of age; and (2) be a citizen of the United States of America. It excludes, with specificity, the following "persons": (1) convicted felons; (2) people who are incarcerated at the time of election; and (3) idiots and insane persons. Ky Const. § 145.

Appellant contends that since section 145 excludes convicted felons with specificity, but section 1(7) does not, then it must be inferred that section 1(7) meant to include convicted felons among the class of persons who were entitled to possess firearms. This argument is also flawed. First, it is notable that the right of suffrage is not contained within the sections entitled "Kentucky's Bill of Rights." Rather, it is located within its own section entitled "Suffrage and Elections." Thus, Appellant's "consistency in form" argument is weak since the specimen provisions are found in two completely different sections of the constitution.

Moreover, the reason that voting rights exist within a completely different section of the constitution is because voting was not thought to be a natural, inalienable and inherent right of the people (like the right to bear arms) at the time that our modern constitution was drafted. Rather, voting was a privilege which was conferred to the people through the prudence and consent of the legislature. It is self-evident that a grant of power requires some specificity so as to prevent such power from being swallowed within those powers which have otherwise been limited or reserved. Such specificity is not particularly necessary or desired, however, when it comes to reserving (or perhaps, preserving) the people's natural and inherent rights. Accordingly, we also cannot infer a clear intent to endow convicted felons with the right to possess firearms by reference to language utilized in a different section of the constitution for a different purpose.

Finally, we find nothing to support Appellant's suggestion that the limiting language concerning "concealed weapons" utilized in section 1(7) (in conjunction with section 26) of the constitution somehow divests the legislature of power to reasonably regulate the area of firearms possession. The people's right to bear arms in defense of themselves and of the Commonwealth was first recognized and preserved by our constitution in 1792. Ky. Const. of 1792, art. 12, § 23 ("The rights of the citizens to bear arms in defense of themselves and the State shall not be questioned."). The language as we know it today was ratified in 1891. A review of the debates which accompany the modern formulation of section 1(7) indicate no intent on the part of the drafters to deem the right to bear arms in Kentucky absolute.

In fact, the concept of an individual right to bear arms sprung from classical republican ideology which required the individual holding that right to maintain a certain degree of civic virtue. This concept of civic virtue is similarly reflected in other provisions contained in section 1 of our Constitution, such as the rights of all persons to life, liberty, and the pursuit of happiness. Yet, neither party would claim that these rights are absolute or somehow immune from reasonable limitations in the interest of public safety and welfare.

Moreover, the text in section 1(7) does not support the notion that a person's right to bear arms is absolute since it plainly states that one may bear arms for the purpose of self-defense and defense of the State. Such language indicates that the right is conditioned on certain self-evident premises—that it be enjoyed lawfully and without undue interference with the rights of others. Thus, we reject Appellant's contention that our constitution somehow confers on all persons an absolute right to bear arms or that the area of firearms possession is completely exempt from legislative regulation.

In essence, Appellant's arguments boil down to mere presumptions or suggestions that could conceivably be inferred by the language present in our modern constitution. However, the mere possibility that language could be interpreted in a particular way is insufficient to invalidate the plain language of a statute. In balance, we defer to the reasonable interpretation of our legislature, finding that the constitution permits some reasonable regulation of the people's right to bear arms, but only to the extent that such regulation is enacted to ensure the liberties of all persons by maintaining the proper and responsible exercise of the general right contained in section 1(7). Under no circumstances may regulation by the legislature be enacted for an arbitrary or irrational purpose, nor may it unduly infringe upon the general exercise of this right as it was envisioned and preserved pursuant to section 1(7) of the Kentucky Constitution.

With this standard in mind, and considering that the vast majority of persons living in this Commonwealth are law-abiding and responsible individuals, we ultimately determine that the regulation contained within section 527.040 is not arbitrary or irrational and does not unduly infringe upon the right to bear arms which was reserved to the people through section 1(7) of our constitution. As previously stated by this Court, section 527.040 of the Kentucky Revised Statutes is "reasonable legislation in the interest of public safety." Since nothing in the constitution, either express or implied, undermines or prohibits such legislation, we find section 527.040 to be constitutional.

BRITT v. STATE
681 S.E.2nd 320 (N.C. 2009)

BRADY, J.

This case presents an as-applied challenge to the constitutionality of the 2004 amendment to N.C.G.S. § 14-415.1 that makes it "unlawful for any person who has been convicted of a felony to purchase, own, possess, or have in his custody, care, or control any firearm." We determine that N.C.G.S. § 14-415.1 is unconstitutional as applied to plaintiff and reverse the decision of the Court of Appeals.

FACTUAL AND PROCEDURAL BACKGROUND

In 1979 plaintiff Barney Britt pleaded guilty to felony possession with intent to sell and deliver the controlled substance methaqualone. Plaintiff's crime was nonviolent and did not involve the use of a firearm. Plaintiff was sentenced to two years in the North Carolina Department of Correction, with four months active imprisonment and the remainder suspended for two years, during which plaintiff was on supervised probation. He completed his probation in 1982, and in 1987 his civil rights were fully restored by operation of law, including his right to possess a firearm. At that time, N.C.G.S. § 14-415.1 only prohibited the possession of "any handgun or other firearm with a barrel length of less than 18 inches or an overall length of less than 26 inches" by persons convicted of certain felonies, mostly of a violent or rebellious nature, "within five years from the date of such conviction, or unconditional discharge from a correctional institution, or termination of a suspended sentence, probation, or parole upon such conviction, whichever is later."

Subsequently, in 1995 the General Assembly amended N.C.G.S. § 14-415.1 to prohibit the possession of such firearms by all persons convicted of any felony, without regard to the date of conviction or the completion of the defendant's sentence. The 1995 amendment did not change the previous provision in N.C.G.S. § 14-415.1 stating that "nothing [therein] would prohibit the right of any person to have possession of a firearm within his own house or on his lawful place of business." However, in 2004 the General Assembly amended N.C.G.S. § 14-415.1 to extend the prohibition on possession to all firearms by any person convicted of any felony, even within the convicted felon's own home and place of business.

Following passage of this amendment, plaintiff had a discussion with the Sheriff of Wake County, who concluded that possession of a firearm by plaintiff would violate the statute as amended in 2004. Plaintiff thereafter divested himself of all firearms, including his sporting rifles and shotguns that he used for game hunting on his own land. In the thirty years since plaintiff's conviction of a nonviolent crime he has not been charged with any other crime nor is there any evidence that he has misused a firearm in any way. Furthermore, no determination has been made by any agency or court that plaintiff is violent, potentially dangerous, or is more likely than the general public to commit a crime involving a firearm.

ANALYSIS

Article I, Section 30 of the North Carolina Constitution provides, in pertinent part: "A well regulated militia being necessary to the security of a free State, the right of the people to keep and bear arms shall not be infringed." This Court has held that regulation of the right to bear arms is a proper exercise of the General Assembly's police power, but that any regulation must be at least "reasonable and not prohibitive, and must bear a fair relation to the preservation of the public peace and safety." Accordingly, this Court must determine whether, as applied to plaintiff, N.C.G.S. § 14-415.1 is a reasonable regulation.

Plaintiff pleaded guilty to one felony count of possession with intent to sell and deliver a controlled substance in 1979. The State does not argue that any aspect of plaintiff's crime involved violence or the threat of violence. Plaintiff completed his sentence without incident in 1982. Plaintiff's right to possess firearms was restored in 1987. No evidence has been presented which would indicate that plaintiff is dangerous or has ever misused firearms, either before his crime or in the seventeen years between restoration of his rights and adoption of N.C.G.S. § 14-415.1's complete ban on any possession of a firearm by him. Plaintiff sought out advice from his local Sheriff following the amendment of N.C.G.S. § 14-415.1 and willingly gave up his weapons when informed that possession would presumably violate the statute. Plaintiff, through his uncontested lifelong nonviolence towards other citizens, his thirty years of law-abiding conduct since his crime, his seventeen years of responsible, lawful firearm possession between 1987 and 2004, and his assiduous and proactive compliance with the 2004 amendment, has affirmatively demonstrated that he is not among the class of citizens who pose a threat to public peace and safety. Moreover, the nature of the 2004 amendment is relevant. The statute functioned as a total and permanent prohibition on possession of any type of firearm in any location.

Based on the facts of plaintiff's crime, his long post-conviction history of respect for the law, the absence of any evidence of violence by plaintiff, and the lack of any exception or possible relief from the statute's operation, as applied to plaintiff, the 2004 version of N.C.G.S. § 14-451.1 is an unreasonable regulation, not fairly related to the preservation of public peace and safety. In particular, it is unreasonable to assert that a nonviolent citizen who has responsibly, safely, and legally owned and used firearms for seventeen years is in reality so dangerous that any possession at all of a firearm would pose a significant threat to public safety.

We conclude that N.C.G.S. § 14-415.1 is an unconstitutional violation of Article I, Section 30 of the North Carolina Constitution as applied to this plaintiff. As discussed above, pursuant to N.C.G.S. § 14-415.1, the State unreasonably divested plaintiff of his right to own a firearm. Such action violates plaintiff's right to keep and bear arms under Article I, Section 30 of the North Carolina Constitution. For that reason, we reverse the decision of the Court of Appeals to the extent that court determined N.C.G.S. § 14-415.1 can be constitutionally applied to plaintiff. This case is remanded to the Court of Appeals for further remand to the Superior Court, Wake County, for further proceedings not inconsistent with this opinion.

TIMMONS-GOODSON, J., dissenting.

Because the majority has crafted an individualized exception for a sympathetic plaintiff, thereby placing North Carolina in the unique position of being the first jurisdiction, either federal or state, to hold that the inherent police power of the State must yield to a convicted felon's right to own a firearm, I respectfully dissent. Plaintiff's right to possess a firearm is not absolute, but subject to regulation. The Felony Firearms Act at issue is a reasonable regulation of the right to bear arms, both facially and as applied to plaintiff.

The General Assembly's prohibition of firearm use by convicted felons is both reasonable and related to preserving public peace and safety. Felonies constitute our most serious offenses. One who has committed a felony has displayed a degree of lawlessness that makes it entirely reasonable for the legislature, concerned for the safety of the public it represents, to want to keep firearms out of the hands of such a person. As this Court stated in *State v. Jackson*, 546 S.E.2d 570 (2001):

> Just as there is heightened risk and public concern associated with firearms on educational property, which the legislature addressed through N.C.G.S. § 14-269.2, *there is also heightened risk and public concern associated with convicted felons possessing firearms,* which the legislature addressed through N.C.G.S. § 14-415.1. Both are exceptional situations, which have been addressed through dedicated statutory law.

The General Assembly, acting upon its compelling interest in the public welfare and safety, determined that, like the mentally insane, those convicted of felonies pose an unacceptable risk with regard to firearm possession. In so doing, the legislature has properly fulfilled its duty to reasonably regulate firearms: "'The preservation of the public peace, and the protection of the people against violence, are constitutional duties of the legislature, and the guarantee of the right to keep and bear arms is to be understood and construed in connection and in harmony, with these constitutional duties.'" Thus, because I conclude that N.C.G.S. § 14-415.1 is reasonable and related to preserving public peace and safety, both in general and to Mr. Britt in particular as a convicted drug offender, the Felony Firearms Act is constitutional on its face and as applied to Mr. Britt.

This case is difficult and poses a temptation for the Court to depart from established case law in order to accommodate Mr. Britt. However, as the Chief Justice of the United States Supreme Court recently articulated:

> Extreme cases often test the bounds of established legal principles. There is a cost to yielding to the desire to correct the extreme case, rather than adhering to the legal principle. That cost has been demonstrated so often that it is captured in a legal aphorism: "Hard cases make bad law."

Although Mr. Britt may be a sympathetic plaintiff, in that he made a huge mistake early in his life, he is nevertheless a convicted drug offender and a felon and as such, belongs to a class of persons deemed by the General Assembly and recognized by this Court to pose "heightened risk and public concern" with regard to firearm possession. Other state supreme courts have avoided the temptation to craft individualized exceptions for particular plaintiffs. *See State v. Smith,* 571 A.2d 279, 281 (1990) (holding that the state's felon-in-possession statute narrowly served a significant governmental interest in protecting the general public and was therefore constitutional under the New Hampshire Constitution, even though the New Hampshire Supreme Court recognized that some felons falling within the statute's reach were not potentially dangerous). Today's decision opens the floodgates wide before an inevitable wave of individual challenges to not only the Felony Firearms Act, but to our statutory provisions prohibiting firearm possession by incompetents and the mentally insane. The majority has not cited any direct authority from this Court or any other jurisdiction in support of its position that the legislature may not prohibit convicted felons like Mr. Britt from possessing firearms. Plaintiff does not cite any such case, and I have found none, all authority being to the contrary.

Although the majority stands up for Mr. Britt and other convicted felons who will now undoubtedly seek judicial exemption from N.C.G.S. § 14-415.1, this is a policy matter and determination best left to the executive or legislative branches. Mr. Britt may seek relief from the General Assembly through contact with individual legislators or from the Governor by way of a conditional or unconditional pardon. *See* N.C. Const. art. III, § 5, cl. 6; N.C.G.S. §§ 13-1 to 13-4. (2007). The majority resists judicial restraint in an effort to fashion an individual exception for Mr. Britt. I believe this Court should properly resist such temptation and affirm the decision of the Court of Appeals.

NOTES

1. The Second Amendment to the United States Constitution reads: "A well regulated militia being necessary to the security of a free State, the right of the people to keep and bear arms shall not be infringed." The United States Supreme Court recently construed that language in *District of Columbia v. Heller,* 128 S.Ct. 2783 (2008), holding that the amendment protects an *individual* right to bear arms.

2. In *Heller*, however, the Supreme Court declared that felon-in-possession statutes are permitted by the United States Constitution. In *Britt*, however, the North Carolina Supreme Court held that its state constitutional right to bear arms precluded the state from imposing a ban on a non-violent felon possessing a firearm. Thus, the North Carolina Constitution provides greater protection than the Second Amendment.

3. The Constitutions of forty-four states contain a provision that protects the right to bear arms. The texts of those state constitutional guarantees are often different from the Second Amendment. For example, the New Hampshire Constitution provides: "All persons have the right to keep and bear arms in defense of themselves, their families, their property and the state." N.H. Const. pt. 1, art. 2-a.

E.   EXCESSIVE FINES – PUNITIVE DAMAGES

COLONIAL PIPELINE CO. v. BROWN
365 S.E.2d 827 (Ga. 1988)

SMITH, J.

This appeal consolidates two related cases stemming from the destruction of a bulldozer after it hit and ruptured Colonial Pipeline's underground petroleum pipeline. The owner of the bulldozer, Wright Contracting Company, sued Colonial, Baxter Brown, the real estate developer who hired Wright to do grading work, and Malcolm Burnsed, the surveyor who did the grading plan.

Case No. 44926 is Colonial's appeal from a jury verdict awarding Wright $52,728.46 actual damages, $304.75 consequential damages and $5,000,000 punitive damages. We affirm in part and reverse in part case No. 44926—the punitive damages award is reversed.

Colonial purchased a right-of-way easement from Reese W. Cross and Eloise H. Cross in 1976. Colonial's pipeline was to be installed on part of their property that faced Westover Road, and it was to run parallel to the road. The property subject to the easement was higher than the road, and the easement required Colonial to bury the pipeline at least thirty inches below the grade of Westover Road.

Baxter Brown, an experienced real estate broker, purchased five acres of land out of a larger parcel owned by the Crosses. The five acres Mr. Brown purchased were subject to Colonial's recorded easement.

Mr. Brown hired Malcolm Burnsed, a registered land surveyor, to survey the property and prepare a boundary line survey and a grading plan.

Although a preliminary title opinion was prepared four days prior to the purchase of the property in December 1981, Mr. Brown asserted that he had not seen it prior to the date the pipeline was ruptured on June 15, 1982. Both the preliminary title opinion and the final title opinion contained identical language: "Right-of-way easement from REESE WILSON CROSS and ELOISE HUCKABEE CROSS to COLONIAL PIPELINE COMPANY, A DELAWARE CORPORATION, dated August 26, 1976, and recorded in Deed Book 568, pages 329-330, in the aforesaid Clerk's Office."

Neither the boundary line survey nor the grading plan prepared by Mr. Burnsed contained a hint of Colonial's easement. Mr. Burnsed found a warranty deed dated 1966 from L.W. Cross to R.W. Cross in the court records. Because the deed stated that it was "[s]ubject to easements of record," Mr. Burnsed used the grantor/grantee index to determine if there was an easement prior to 1966. He testified that he had looked at the property and did not see any physical evidence of a pipeline, therefore, he had no reason to check to see if an easement had been conveyed after 1966. Mr. Burnsed testified that he did not know that the pipeline was under the property he had surveyed until the pipeline was ruptured.

Mr. Burnsed testified that he did not obtain a copy of the title opinion in preparing his boundary line survey and admitted that the Rules of State Board of Registration for Professional Engineers and Land Surveyors, Section 180-7-.02 provides: "The surveyor prior to making [a boundary line survey] shall acquire all necessary data, including deeds, maps, *certificates of title.*" (emphasis supplied).

David James, the area manager for Wright Contracting Company, testified that he did not see any evidence of the pipeline on the property that Wright was hired to grade. He further testified that he did not see the Colonial Pipeline marker that was located 670 feet south of the property. He did indicate that he knew that the pipeline was in the area, but he did not know that it was under the property.

Mr. James stated that if he had known about the pipeline he would not have relied upon the terms of the easement, he would have called Colonial and they would have located the pipeline for him.

The Wright Contracting Company "Safety Rules Procedure" manual provides in part: "Construction Practices...*Excavating and Trenching* operations will include proper safeguards and inspections to *determine location and extent of underground utilities.*" (Emphasis supplied.)

An expert witness, Mr. John Sperry, testified that if he were going to cut a five acre tract out of a larger tract and provide a boundary line survey, he would look *forward* from the 1966 deed to see if any parcels or easements had been deeded out of the property. (If the surveyor had looked forward, he would have found the easement.) In answer to another question, Mr. Sperry testified that if he was hired to do a grade plan and topographical survey that he would ask for the title opinion. (If the surveyor had obtained the title opinion he would have found the easement.) Mr. Sperry indicated that there is no difficulty in securing a map from Colonial Pipeline that shows the location of the pipeline. He testified that the general standards by which one should conform as a surveyor are in Section 180-7-.02 of the Rules of State Board of Registration for Professional Engineers and Land Surveyors.

The bulldozer operator was grading between eight and nine inches below the level specified in the grading plan when the pipeline was ruptured.

Federal regulations require Colonial to conduct an aerial inspection of the entire pipeline every fourteen days to discover unusual activities. Colonial had contracted with a new aerial patrol contractor on May 1, 1982. He had difficulty finding the line from the air; as a result, only two partial inspections were conducted in the fourteen days preceding the occurrence. The red clay field where Wright was grading was observed by a Colonial employee on a June 11, 1982, flight, but he assumed the activity was farming and failed to report it.

The pipeline was installed approximately 48 inches below the surface of the land; however, it was approximately one and three-quarter inches above the center of Westover Road. Although a marker was located 1,120 feet south of the ruptured line and 670 feet south of the property line and another 2,245 feet north of the rupture at the intersection of Old Dawson Road and Westover Road, there were no markers on the property at the time of the rupture. The distance between the two markers was 3,358 feet. Federal law requires that "[e]ach operator shall place and maintain line markers over each buried line in accordance with the following: (1) Markers must be located at each public road crossing, at each railroad crossing and in sufficient number along the remainder of each buried line so that the location is accurately known."

There was also evidence that six years earlier another construction worker had hit a portion of the pipeline that was on property that was unmarked, but there were no damages.

The jury's verdict exonerated Mr. Brown and Mr. Burnsed and awarded Wright $52,728.46 actual damages, $304.75 consequential damages, and $5,000,000 punitive damages.

The appeal of the punitive damages award raises several issues. One is whether or not the complaint sounds in contract or tort. We hold that it sounds in tort, and inasmuch as we are reversing on the punitive damages phase of the case, we will not go into detail as to that point.

Colonial challenges the punitive damages element of this case on two grounds, due process and the Eighth Amendment prohibition against excessive fines contending that this prohibition applies to civil as well as criminal cases. Colonial then asserts that five million dollars in punitive damages violates this amendment. Because we are reversing this case under the excessive fines clause of the Georgia Constitution, article I, section I, paragraph XVII, we are not going to address the due process argument.

Ingraham v. Wright, 430 U.S. 651 (1977), has been relied upon to find that the Eighth Amendment does not apply to civil cases. But, *Ingraham* dealt only with the cruel and unusual punishment clause of the Eighth Amendment, it did not concern the excessive fines clause. It cannot be viewed as excluding punitive damages from scrutiny under the excessive fines clause of the Eighth Amendment. Moreover, even if *Ingraham* had held that the Eighth Amendment of the United States Constitution applied only to criminal cases, there would be nothing to prevent the application of the excessive fines clause of article I, section I, paragraph XVII of the 1983 Georgia Constitution to civil cases, thereby affording greater protection under state law.

Punitive damages "are private fines levied by civil juries to punish reprehensible conduct and to deter its future occurrence." In Georgia, when the tortious conduct amounts to "wilful misconduct, malice, fraud, wantonness, or oppression, or that entire want of care which would raise the presumption of a conscious indifference to consequences," punitive damages are allowed pursuant to section 51-12-5 of the Georgia Code to deter the wrongdoer from repeating his wrongful acts. Punitive damages cannot be imposed without a finding of some form of culpable conduct. Negligence, even gross negligence, is inadequate to support a punitive damage award. Punitive damages, although civil in nature, nonetheless serve the criminal law goal of deterrence rather than the traditional compensatory goal of civil law.

"The applicability of the Eighth Amendment always has turned on its original meaning, as demonstrated by its historical derivation." *Ingraham,* 430 U.S. at 670-71 n.39. A review of the history of the excessive fines clause of the Eighth Amendment indicates that it has an origin that was not limited to criminal cases.

Prior to 1215 a system developed whereby a monetary penalty was demanded from one who engaged in either criminal or civil misconduct. The penalty was called an "amercement." The amercement was not levied according to any fixed schedule but was imposed arbitrarily at the discretion of the court. Abuses in the use of "amercements" flourished.

The abuses were so pervasive that a great deal of space was devoted to them in the Magna Carta:

> Chapter 20 of the Great Charter, the king was made to concede that: A freeman shall not be amerced for a slight offense, except in accordance with the degree of the offense; and for a grave offense he shall be amerced in accordance with the gravity of the offense, yet saving always his "contenement;" and a merchant in the same way, saving his "merchandise;" and a villein shall be amerced in the same way, saving his "wainage"—if they have fallen into our mercy; and none of the aforesaid amercements shall be imposed except by the oath of honest men of the neighbourhood.

> From these three provisions of Magna Carta, two related protections emerge. First, there is a requirement of reasonableness, of proportionality, of sensible relation between punishment and offense. Second, the penalty inflicted should not, in any event, destroy the offender's means of making a living in his particular trade or calling. Magna Carta guaranteed not just bare survival, but continued productive economic viability.

The United States Constitution as originally submitted to the states was criticized for its failure to include a declaration of rights. "Magna Carta and the English Bill of Rights were invoked as models of what was required, and a tacit understanding was reached that some such provisions would be added by way of amendment." "The Eighth Amendment was based directly on Art. I, Sec. 9, of the Virginia Declaration of Rights (1776)...[which] in turn...adopted verbatim the language of the English Bill of Rights. There can be no doubt that the Declaration of Rights guaranteed at least the liberties and privileges of Englishmen."

We hold that the excessive fines clause of article I, section I, paragraph XVII of the Georgia Constitution applies to the imposition of punitive damages in civil cases because, "the purpose of the deprivation is among those ordinarily associated with punishment, such as retribution, rehabilitation, or deterrence," *Ingraham,* 430 U.S. at 687-88 (White, J., dissenting.), and because the Eighth Amendment excessive fines clause of the United States Constitution was intended as a protection from all excessive monetary penalties.

In order to decide what fines are excessive under the excessive fines clause of the Georgia Constitution, article I, section I, paragraph XVII, a look into the history of torts is necessary.

"Broadly speaking, a tort is a civil wrong, other than breach of contract, for which the court will provide a remedy in the form of an action for damages." W.L. Prosser and W.P. Keeton, *Prosser & Keeton, Handbook on the Law of Torts,* p. 2 (5th ed., 1984).

> In the early English law, after the Norman conquest, remedies for wrongs were dependent upon the issuance of writs to bring the defendant into court. In the course of the thirteenth century the principle was established that no one could bring an action in the King's common law courts without the King's writ. As a

result of the jealous insistence of the nobles and others upon the prerogatives of their local courts, the number of writs which the King could issue was limited, and their forms were strictly prescribed. There were, in other words, "forms of action," and unless the plaintiff's claim could be fitted into the form of some established and recognized writ, he was without a remedy in the King's courts. The result was a highly formalized system of procedure, which governed and controlled the law as to the substance of the wrongs which might be remedied.

The writs which were available for remedies that were purely tortious in character were two-the writ of trespass, and the writ of trespass on the case.

The form of action in trespass had originally a criminal character. It would lie only in cases of forcible breaches of the King's peace, and it was only on this basis that the royal courts assumed jurisdiction over the wrong. The purpose of the remedy was at first primarily that of punishment of the crime; but to this there was added later the satisfaction of the injured party's claim for redress. If the defendant was found guilty, damages were awarded to the successful plaintiff, and the defendant was imprisoned, and allowed to purchase his release by payment of a fine. What similarity remains between tort and crime is to be traced to this common beginning. *See* Woodbine, *The Origin of the Action of Trespass* 33 Yale L.J. 799 (1923), 34 Yale L.J. 343 (1934); Maitland, *The Forms of Action at Common Law* (1941) 65.

W.L. Prosser, *Cases and Materials on Torts,* p. 2 (6th ed., 1976).

Originally the two remedies [criminal and tort] were administered by the same court, and in the same action. Tort damages were at first awarded to the injured individual as an incident to an criminal prosecution; and as late as 1694 the defendant to a writ of trespass was still theoretically liable to a criminal fine and imprisonment. Because of this common origin, it is not unusual for a tort and a crime to bear the same name, such as "assault," "battery," "trespass," or "libel," and often enough such terms will refer to the same conduct. But tort and criminal law have developed along different lines, with different ends in view, and so it does not necessarily follow that the term has the same meaning in both. Thus it is entirely possible that an act may be a tort, but not a crime of the same name, or that it may amount to the crime and not the tort....

The idea of punishment, or of discouraging other offenses, usually does not enter into tort law, except in so far as it may lead the courts to weight the scales somewhat in favor of the plaintiff's interests in determining that a tort has been committed in the first place. In one rather anomalous respect, however, the ideas underlying the criminal law have invaded the field of torts. Where the defendant's wrongdoing has been intentional and deliberate, and has the character of outrage frequently associated with crime, all but a few courts have permitted the jury to award in the tort action "punitive" or "exemplary" damages, or what is sometimes called "smart money." Such damages are given to the plaintiff over and above the full compensation for the injuries, for the purpose of punishing the defendant, of teaching the defendant not to do it again, and of deterring others from following the defendant's example....

Something more than the mere commission of a tort is always required for punitive damages. There must be circumstances of aggravation or outrage, such as spite or "malice," or a fraudulent or evil motive on the part of the defendant, or such a conscious and deliberate disregard of the interests of others that the conduct may be called willful or wanton. There is general agreement that, because it lacks this element, mere negligence is not enough, even though it is so extreme in degree as to be characterized as "gross," a term of ill-defined content, which occasionally, in a few jurisdictions, has been stretched to include the element of conscious indifference to consequences, and so to justify punitive damages. Still less, of course, can such damages be charged against one who acts under an innocent mistake in engaging in conduct that nevertheless constitutes a tort.

Typical of the torts for which such damages may be awarded are assault and battery, libel and slander, deceit, seduction, alienation of affections, malicious prosecution, and intentional interferences with property such as trespass, private nuisance, and conversion. *But it is not so much the particular tort committed as the defendant's motives and conduct in committing it which will be important as the basis of the award.*

W.L. Prosser and W.P. Keeton, supra, pp. 8-11 (citations omitted) (emphasis supplied).

Thus it can be seen that the tort law grew out of the criminal law and as such retains some of the elements thereof, to-wit, punitive damages. The word punitive means to inflict punishment.

The statute in Georgia that allows an assessment of punitive damages is section 51-12-5. This statute authorizes a jury to award additional damages to "deter the wrongdoer from repeating the trespass"—the basis upon which the award was made in this case. The code section states that in every tort there may be aggravating circumstances, either in "the act or the intention" in which event additional or punitive damages may be awarded.

In a punitive damage case, the trier of fact must determine: First, was a personal injury or death involved or mere damage to property; and second, was the negligence active or passive. The next step in the determination as to whether punitive damages should be awarded is to decide if there was any evidence of wilful misconduct, malice, fraud, wantonness or oppression, or that entire want of care which would raise the presumption of a conscious indifference to consequences.

This case involved personal property damage only. The bulldozer was in an open field, not near any building or residence, and there was no bodily injury to this plaintiff. There was constructive notice to the landowner that Colonial's pipeline was under his property. The surveyor failed to discover the recorded easement, and the bulldozer operator was grading approximately eight or nine inches below the level specified in the grading plan when the pipeline was ruptured. The punitive damages awarded are approximately one hundred times the total of actual and consequential damages.

The trial court erred in denying the motion for new trial as to punitive damages. We, therefore, reverse the $5,000,000 award as being excessive because (1) any negligence present was passive; (2) there was no bodily injury to this plaintiff, and the award does not bear a rational relationship to the actual damages award; (3) there is no rational relationship between the offense and the punishment in that the punitive damage award was 100 times the property damage award.

NOTES

1. The United States Supreme Court held that awards of punitive damages in state private party civil cases are not covered by the Eighth Amendment's prohibition against "excessive fines." *Browning-Ferris Indus. v. Kelco Disposal, Inc.*, 492 U.S. 257 (1989).

2. The majority of state constitutions have been interpreted to apply excessive fine prohibitions only to penalties imposed for criminal offenses and not to an arguably excessive civil damage award.

3. In Ohio, a statute giving the judge, rather than the jury, authority to award punitive damages was held to violate the state constitutional guarantee to a jury trial. *Zoppo v. Homestead Ins. Co.*, 644 N.E.2d 397 (Ohio 1994). However, in Kansas, a statute that gave the judge power to set the amount of punitive damages, after the jury concluded punitive damages should be awarded, did not violate the state constitutional right to a jury trial. *Smith v. Printup*, 866 P.2d 985 (Kan. 1993).

4. In Montana, punitive damages were held to be civil actions under the "trial by jury" provision of the state constitution and, therefore, a two-thirds vote of the jury had the effect of unanimity. *Finstad v. W.R. Grace & Co.*, 8 P.3d 778 (Mont. 2000); Mont. const. art. II § 26.

F. CRIME VICTIMS' RIGHTS

SCHILLING v. CRIME VICTIMS RIGHTS BOARD
692 N.W.2d 623 (Wis. 2005)

ROGGENSACK, J.

The first sentence of article I, section 9m of the Wisconsin Constitution states: "This state shall treat crime victims, as defined by law, with fairness, dignity and respect for their privacy." We recognize that according crime victims fairness, dignity and respect is very important to a just enforcement of the criminal code of the State of Wisconsin. The legislature has recognized the importance of victims' rights as well, by enacting section 950.04 of the Wisconsin Statutes. However, because we conclude that this constitutional provision is a statement of purpose that describes the policies to be promoted by the State and does not provide an enforceable, self-executing right, we affirm the circuit court decision reversing the private reprimand of District Attorney Patrick Schilling issued by the Crime Victims Rights Board under section 950.09(2)(a).

BACKGROUND

Jennifer Hansen Marinko (Hansen) was murdered in Price County in October 1999. She was survived by her two children, her mother and nine siblings. Patrick Schilling, District Attorney for Price County, prosecuted Daniel Marinko (Marinko) in connection with her death, and on March 8, 2001, Marinko was convicted of both first-degree intentional homicide and armed burglary with a dangerous weapon.

At the sentencing hearing held on April 12, 2001, Schilling played part of the tape of the 911 telephone call that Hansen's son had made to the police after discovering his mother dead. While Schilling made sure that Hansen's children would not be present at the sentencing hearing, he did not inform other family members that he was going to play the tape or otherwise give them an opportunity to leave the courtroom before he played it. Schilling turned off the tape before it had finished playing because he recognized that it was having a dramatic effect on the family members.

In July 2001, five of Hansen's survivors (collectively "complainants") filed a complaint against Schilling with the Crime Victims Rights Board (Board). After determining that there was probable cause to believe that Schilling had violated the complainants' crime victims' rights, the Board held an evidentiary hearing on May 30 and 31, 2002.

In a written decision, the Board found that the tape of the 911 call was "highly upsetting" and that "Schilling knew of the tape's powerful emotional content...[which] was the reason for its presentation at the sentencing hearing." The Board further found that "Schilling intended to create an emotional event at the sentencing hearing for the purpose of influencing the sentencing decision, which, unfortunately, was at the expense of [Hansen's] family."

Citing article I, section 9m of the Wisconsin Constitution and section 950.01 of the Wisconsin Statutes for the principle that "[v]ictims of crime are entitled to be treated with fairness, dignity, respect, courtesy and sensitivity," the Board found that the complainants had "met their burden to prove by clear and convincing evidence that [] Schilling failed to treat them with fairness, dignity, respect, courtesy and sensitivity on April 12, 2001, when he played the 911 tape made on the day of [Hansen's] death at the sentencing hearing." Citing its authority under section 950.09(2)(a) of the Wisconsin Statutes, the Board ordered a private reprimand of Schilling "for violating the complainants' rights to be treated with fairness, dignity, respect and sensitivity in the playing of the 911 tape at the April 12, 2001, sentencing hearing."

Schilling sought judicial review of the Board's decision pursuant to sections 227.52, 227.53 and 227.57 of the Wisconsin Statutes in the circuit court for Dane County. The circuit court, the Honorable Michael N. Nowakowski presiding, reversed the Board's decision. The Board then appealed to the court of appeals, and we granted the court of appeals' certification.

DISCUSSION

Pursuant to section 950.09(2)(a) of the Wisconsin Statutes, the Board may "[i]ssue private and public reprimands of public officials, employees or agencies that violate the rights of crime victims provided under this chapter, ch. 938, and article I, section 9m, of the Wisconsin constitution." At issue in this case is whether the first sentence of article I, section 9m of the Wisconsin Constitution, which reads, "This state shall treat crime victims, as defined by law, with fairness, dignity and respect for their privacy," creates a "right" that the Board may enforce under section 950.09(2)(a) of the Wisconsin Statutes, or whether it is descriptive of policies to be furthered by the State.

The Board argues that the first sentence of article I, section 9m of the Wisconsin Constitution is self-executing and thereby provides crime victims an enforceable right to be treated with fairness, dignity and respect for their privacy. Schilling counters that the language in question instead serves to articulate general policies and does not create enforceable rights. We conclude that the constitutional language in question is a statement of purpose that describes the policies to be promoted by the State and does not create an enforceable, self-executing right.

Interpreting Article I, Section 9m of the Wisconsin Constitution

The Wisconsin Constitution was amended in 1993 to include article I, section 9m. We have explained that the purpose of construing a constitutional amendment is "to give effect to the intent of the framers and of the people who adopted it." The question presented in the present case is whether the first sentence of article I, section 9m of the Wisconsin Constitution was intended as a statement of purpose that articulates the importance of recognizing crime victim rights, or whether it was intended to provide crime victims with an enforceable right that is self-executing.

Like statutes, constitutional provisions may include statements of purpose that use broad language. As with a statute's statement of purpose, a constitutional section's statement of purpose does not provide for an independent, enforceable claim, as it is not in itself substantive. Such a statement of purpose is instead instructive of intent and guides implementation.

We have also explained that "[a] constitutional provision is self-executing if no legislation is necessary to give effect to it, and if there is nothing to be done by the legislature to put it in operation." However, a statement of purpose, policy or principle is not self-executing.

To ascertain whether the first sentence of article I, section 9m of the Wisconsin Constitution was intended to serve as a statement of purpose or was intended to provide an enforceable, self-executing right requires constitutional interpretation. We examine three sources in interpreting a constitutional provision: "the plain meaning of the words in the context used; the constitutional debates and the practices in existence at the time of the writing of the constitution; and the earliest interpretation of the provision by the legislature as manifested in the first law passed following adoption." We have broadly understood the second of these sources, the constitutional debates and practices in existence contemporaneous to the writing, to include the general history relating to a constitutional amendment.

Applying this analysis, we note first that the plain meaning of the first sentence of article I, section 9m of the Wisconsin Constitution in context indicates that it serves as a statement of purpose and does not create enforceable, self-executing rights. Article I, section 9m of the Wisconsin Constitution provides:

> This state shall treat crime victims, as defined by law, with fairness, dignity and respect for their privacy. This state shall ensure that crime victims have all of the following privileges and protections as provided by law: timely disposition of the case; the opportunity to attend court proceedings unless the trial court finds sequestration is necessary to a fair trial for the defendant; reasonable protection from the accused throughout the criminal justice process; notification of court proceedings; the opportunity to confer with the prosecution; the opportunity to make a statement to the court at disposition; restitution; compensation; and information about the outcome of the case and the release of the accused. The legislature shall provide remedies for the violation of this section. Nothing in this section, or in any statute enacted pursuant to this section, shall limit any right of the accused which may be provided by law.

The provision in question, "This state shall treat crime victims, as defined by law, with fairness, dignity and respect for their privacy," opens the section. It uses very broad terms to describe how the State must treat crime victims. The subsequent sentence requires the State to "ensure" that crime victims have a number of "privileges and protections," which are articulated in detail. This structure, opening the section with broad indications of how crime victims should be treated, followed by a detailed list of privileges and protections to which victims are entitled, shows that the first sentence was intended to serve as a general guide or statement of policy regarding victims' rights, whereas the second sentence was intended to provide an outline of the specific rights that the State shall afford crime victims.

Next, we examine the constitutional amendment's history. In an early attempt to secure the initial legislative approval needed to adopt a state constitutional victims' rights amendment, Senator Barbara Ulichny introduced 1989 Senate Joint Resolution 94. With her drafting request to the Legislative Reference Bureau (LRB), Senator Ulichny attached two articles written by other states' attorneys general as background material for the drafter that provide some evidence of the legislature's intent. *See* Don Siegelman & Courtney W. Tarver, *Victims' Rights in State Constitutions,* 1 Emerging Issues in St. Const. L. 163 (1988); Ken Eikenberry, *Victims of Crime/Victims of Justice,* 34 Wayne L. Rev. 29 (1987); Legislative Reference Bureau Drafting Record for 1989 S.J.R. 94.

From this background material, we learn that 1989 Senate Joint Resolution 94 was introduced in the midst of a larger, nationwide movement to recognize the rights of crime victims, particularly through the amendment of state constitutions. The materials note that crime victims were being treated insensitively and with a lack of consideration, even by well-meaning public agencies. Moreover, it was believed that rights of crime victims needed to be addressed both out of a sense of fundamental fairness and justice to victims, as well as to enhance the effectiveness of the criminal justice system, because the cooperation of crime victims and witnesses was understood to be central to law enforcement, Lois Haight Herrington, who chaired a presidential task force on victims of crime, explained that her task force concluded that:

> the treatment of crime victims in America was a national disgrace. Ignored, mistreated, or blamed, the innocent victims had been handled like photographs or fingerprints-mere evidence to be manipulated at the criminal justice system's convenience. By the end of the ordeal, many victims vowed that they would never again become embroiled in the system, and that they would tell their friends and loved ones to stay away from the courts. Just as a pebble dropped in a pool causes rippling all across the water, the mistreatment of victims spread resentment and distrust of the justice system throughout entire communities. *We saw that this insensitivity toward victims was not only unjust, it was unwise.* The criminal justice system is absolutely dependent upon the cooperation of crime

victims to report and testify. Without their help, the system cannot hold criminals accountable and stem the tide of future crime.

Eikenberry, *supra,* at 30 (emphasis added).

With this background established, we turn to the history of the actual language adopted. The legislature considered and rejected identical language for article I, section 9m of the Wisconsin Constitution in 1991 Assembly Joint Resolution 4 and 1989 Assembly Joint Resolution 138, both of which included a right to fairness and respect in a list of specifically enumerated rights:

> The rights of victims of crime shall be defined and protected by law and shall include: *the right to be treated with fairness and respect for their dignity and privacy throughout the criminal justice process;* the right to timely disposition of the case following arrest of the accused; the right to be reasonably protected from the accused throughout the criminal justice process; the right to notification of court proceedings; the right to attend trial and all other court proceedings that the accused has the right to attend; the right to confer with the prosecution; the right to make a statement to the court at sentencing; the right to restitution and compensation; and the right to information about the disposition of the case, including the conviction, sentence, imprisonment and release of the accused.

1991 A.J.R. 4 (emphasis added); 1989 A.J.R. 138 (emphasis added). The legislature rejected this language, deciding to remove the reference to fairness, dignity and respect from the list of enumerated rights and move it to a separate sentence. *See* Wis. Const. art. I, § 9m. We infer from that decision that the broad language of fairness, dignity and respect in the amendment's first sentence was intended to have a different significance than the language specifically articulating rights in the second sentence.

The statutory structure that was in place prior to the adoption of article I, section 9m of the Wisconsin Constitution provides evidence of the manner in which the amendment's first and second sentences were intended to differ in significance. The legislature had created Chapter 950, "Rights of victims and witnesses of crimes," in 1980. On its face, article I, section 9m of the Wisconsin Constitution appears to have adopted the structure of the pre-amendment codification of victims' rights. Section 950.01 of the Wisconsin Statutes of 1991-1992, entitled "Legislative intent," read in language very similar to the first sentence of article I, section 9m of the Wisconsin Constitution: "[T]he legislature declares its intent, in this chapter, to ensure that all victims...of crime are treated with dignity, respect, courtesy and sensitivity." Then, at section 950.04 of the Wisconsin Statutes of 1991-1992, entitled "Basic bill of rights for victims and witnesses," specific rights of victims and witnesses were enumerated in detail, as they are in the second sentence of article I, section 9m of the Wisconsin Constitution.

Not only is the structure of the constitutional amendment on its face parallel to the pre-existing codification, the Legislative Reference Bureau (LRB) has explained that the constitutional amendment was adopted with the Chapter 950 provisions in mind. A LRB publication regarding the amendment explained that advocates of the amendment believed it was "necessary to give weight to the statutory language" and included a rationale for the amendment given by Eau Claire County Supervisor Gerald L. Wilkie in 1990 that refers to the pre-existing codification of victim rights:

> Though we have a comprehensive set of victim rights, the real problem is that these laws carry little weight.... A constitutional amendment is important because it would permanently ensure the rights will be honored and it will give our courts a constitutional basis for recognizing the victim's interest.

As article I, section 9m of the Wisconsin Constitution was adopted to give weight to chapter 950 and parallels that statutory scheme's structure, our conclusion that the opening sentence of article I, section 9m of the Wisconsin Constitution was meant to be a statement of purpose, set apart from and then followed by the enumeration of the specific enforceable rights crime victims are afforded in the second sentence, is further reinforced.

We turn next to the legislature's earliest interpretation of article I, section 9m of the Wisconsin Constitution, as manifested in 1997 Wis. Act 181, the first significant law passed regarding the rights of crime victims following the amendment's adoption. With 1997 Wis. Act 181, the legislature retained the pre-amendment statutory structure of providing for rights in detail in a provision entitled "Basic bill of rights for victims and witnesses." Further, 1997 Wis. Act 181 created a subsection at section 950.04(1v) entitled "Rights of victims," which enumerated crime victim rights, none of which make reference to fairness, dignity or respect for privacy. Instead, the legislature retained the broad language referring to fairness and dignity in the provision entitled "Legislative intent" at section 950.01 of the Wisconsin Statutes.

Moreover, subsequent to the adoption of 1997 Wis. Act 181, the LRB explained that article I, section 9m of the Wisconsin Constitution "recognizes specified privileges and protections for crime victims and directs the legislature to provide remedies for violations of those rights." Thus, the amendment apparently was intended to require remedies, such as the private reprimand at issue in this case, only for violations of the "privileges and protections" enumerated in the second sentence of article I, section 9m of the Wisconsin Constitution. The LRB further noted that 1997 Wis. Act 181 lists "the rights of crime victims as protected by the Wisconsin Constitution and statutory law" in section 950.04(1v) of the

Wisconsin Statutes, which, because section 950.04(1v) does not list rights of fairness, dignity or respect for privacy, further supports our conclusion.

The LRB's analysis of Engrossed 1997 Assembly Bill 342, which created 1997 Wis. Act 181, also suggests that the legislature did not interpret article I, section 9m of the Wisconsin Constitution to provide a separate enforceable right to fairness, dignity and respect for privacy. The LRB's analysis lists the rights that the state constitution provides to crime victims, without including the right to fairness, dignity and respect for privacy in the list.

In sum, based on our examination of the plain meaning of article I, section 9m of the Wisconsin Constitution, which is affirmed by the history of and the legislature's earliest interpretation of that amendment, we conclude that the first sentence of article I, section 9m of the Wisconsin Constitution does not provide a self-executing right that the Board is empowered to enforce via private reprimand pursuant to section 950.09(2)(a) of the Wisconsin Statutes. However, we recognize that crime victims, by virtue of the crimes they suffer, experience profound tragedy before they encounter the criminal justice system. While every act of insensitivity towards a crime victim may not constitute a violation of a right enforceable under section 950.09(2)(a), we believe that justice requires that all who are engaged in the prosecution of crimes make every effort to minimize further suffering by crime victims. Accordingly, we encourage officials within the criminal justice system, including prosecuting attorneys and their staffs, to establish effective lines of communication and good rapport with crime victims to the furthest extent possible.

Moreover, this holding is not to be construed as rendering the first sentence of article I, section 9m of the Wisconsin Constitution without meaning or to minimize the importance of the rights of crime victims in this state. Rather, the first sentence of article I, section 9m of the Wisconsin Constitution is a constitutional mandate. It articulates this State's policy regarding the treatment of crime victims. It also functions to guide Wisconsin courts' interpretations of the state's constitutional and statutory provisions concerning the rights of crime victims.

CONCLUSION

The first sentence of article I, section 9m of the Wisconsin Constitution states: "This state shall treat crime victims, as defined by law, with fairness, dignity and respect for their privacy." We recognize that according crime victims fairness, dignity and respect is very important to a just enforcement of the criminal code of the State of Wisconsin. The legislature has recognized the importance of victims' rights as well, by enacting section 950.04 of the Wisconsin Statutes. However, because we conclude that this constitutional provision is a statement of purpose that describes the policies to be promoted by the State and does not provide an enforceable, self-executing right, we affirm the circuit court decision reversing the private reprimand of District Attorney Patrick Schilling issued by the Crime Victims Rights Board under section 950.09(2)(a) of the Wisconsin Statutes.

The decision of the circuit court is affirmed.

NOTES

1. In 1982, California was the first state to pass a victims' rights amendment to its constitution. *See Dying to Get Away with It: How the Abatement Doctrine Thwarts Justice—And What Should be Done Instead*, 75 Fordham L. Rev. 2193, 2207 (2007); *see also* Alice Kosklea, Comment, *Victim's Rights Amendments: An Irresistible Political Force Transforms the Criminal Justice System*, 34 Idaho L. Rev. 157, 165 (1997). The provision, approved by the California electorate, gave victims the right to "restitution, safe schools, consideration of public safety when setting bail, and an unrestricted admissibility of prior felony convictions," as well as "the absolute right to appear at sentencing and parole proceedings." Cal. Const. art. I, § 28. Florida and Michigan followed with voter-approved amendments in 1988. That same year, the states of Arizona and Washington attempted, but failed, to pass victims' rights amendments to their constitutions. Washington and Texas passed victims' rights amendments in 1990. By 1996, twenty-eight states had victims' rights constitutional amendments. Today, thirty-two states have victims' rights constitutional amendments.

2. The victims' rights amendments vary by state, but all seek to achieve one or more of the following objectives: (1) make the victim whole economically; (2) develop administrative sensitivity to the distress of the victim; (3) respect the victim's privacy; (4) provide protection against potential victim intimidation; (5) reduce the burdens on victims willing to assist with the prosecution of the defendant; (6) increase victim participation in the prosecution beyond simply appearing as a witness. *See* Jay M. Zitter, *Validity, Construction, and Application of State Constitutional or Statutory Victims' Bill of Rights*, 91 A.L.R.5th 343 § 2[a] (2008); LaFave *et al*, 1 Criminal Procedure § 1.4(k) (2d ed.).

3. Although Montana does not have a victims' rights amendment, in 1998, the voters approved a constitutional amendment that expanded the purpose of the criminal justice system to include restitution to crime victims. Mont. Const. art. II, § 28(1) ("Laws for the punishment of crime

shall be founded on the principles of prevention, reformation, public safety, and restitution for victims.").

4. A victims' right that has been the subject of case law in various states is the right to be present at trial. *See, e.g.,* Ariz. Const. art. II, § 2.1(A)(3) (giving victims of crimes the right "to be present at...all criminal proceedings where the defendant has the right to be present"); Utah Const. art. I, § 28 (stating that the victim has the right "to be present at...important criminal justice hearings related to the victim"). The victim's presence at trial has been argued to be prejudicial to the defendant because the victim hears the testimony of the other witnesses before testifying against the defendant. *See Gore v. State,* 599 So.2d 978 (Fla. 1992) (holding that the trial court's excusal of the murder victim's stepmother from the rule of witness sequestration because she was a relative of the victim and had the right to be present in the courtroom during trial did not prejudice the defendant). Some constitutional provisions try to balance the rights of the victim with the rights of the defendant by permitting the victim to be present at trial only where it does not interfere with the defendant's rights. Fla. Const. art. I, § 16(b) (giving victims of crimes "the right to...be present...at all crucial states of criminal proceedings, to the extent that these rights do not interfere with the constitutional rights of the accused").

CHAPTER XIV

STATE CONSTITUTIONAL PROVISIONS WITH NO FEDERAL COUNTERPARTS

A. INTRODUCTION

There is a wide variety of state constitutional provisions, some of which have no counterparts in the Federal Constitution. For example, while the Federal Constitution makes no mention of education, all state constitutions contain education articles that guarantee the right to a free public education. These constitutional guarantees of a free public education are discussed in Chapter XI. Many state constitutions contain provisions guaranteeing a right to a remedy or open courts; these provisions, which also have no federal counterparts, are covered in Chapter XII. A growing number of state constitutions contain provisions directing the legislature to protect the environment or guaranteeing public rights to a clean and healthy environment. See Barton H. Thompson, Jr., *The Environment and Natural Resources* (Chapter Ten) in G. Alan Tarr & Robert E. Williams (eds.) STATE CONSTITUTIONS IN THE 21st CENTURY (2006). A few state constitutions include provisions mandating aid for the needy. The Montana Constitution, for instance, states that: "The legislature shall provide such economic assistance and social and rehabilitative services as may be necessary for those inhabitants who, by reason of age, infirmities, or misfortune may have need for the aid of society." Montana Const. art. XII, § 3(3). Turning to another subject, the New Jersey Constitution guarantees employees in the private sector the right to "organize and bargain collectively." N.J. Const. art. I, § 19. As noted in the Introduction, some state constitutions have exotic provisions with no federal counterparts, such as article XII, § 13 of the Ohio Constitution, which bars the taxation of food sold for human consumption, or article VIII, § 15 of the Alaska Constitution, which forbids the creation of any "exclusive right or special privilege of fishery" within Alaskan waters.

In this Chapter, the focus is on state constitutional provisions with no federal counterparts that place limits on legislative authority. Three areas will be covered: single subject and clear title rules; public policy requirements, and uniformity clauses.

As their name suggests, single subject rules require that each bill considered by the legislature address but one subject. Clear title rules require that the subject of each bill be clearly expressed in its title. These types of provisions first began to appear around the end of the eighteenth century to counteract corruption and undue influence of special interest groups in state legislatures. See Millard H. Ruud, *No Law Shall Embrace More than One Subject*, 42 Minn.L.Rev. 389, 414-452 (1959). Today, they are included in the vast majority of state constitutions as a means to bring transparency, order, and fairness to the legislative process.

Some state constitutions include provisions requiring that public funds be spent only for public purposes. The Illinois Constitution, for example, states that "Public funds, property or credit shall be used only for public purposes." Ill. Const. art. VIII, §1 (1970). A public policy requirement also may be found underlying state constitutional provisions that prohibit the granting of special privileges or immunities. By banning special entitlements, state constitutions imply that legislation must be for the benefit of the public. See Jeffrey M. Shaman, EQUALITY AND LIBERTY IN THE GOLDEN AGE OF STATE CONSTITUTIONAL LAW 28-33 (2008). In other states, notwithstanding the absence of an express constitutional mandate, the courts have read a "public purpose doctrine" into their state constitutions. In Wisconsin, for instance, the public purpose doctrine is a well-established constitutional principle, even though it is not recited in any specific clause of the state constitution. *State* ex rel. *Warren v. Nusbaum*, 208 N.W.2d 780, 795 (Wis. 1973). Whether explicit or implicit, the tenet that public funds be spent only for public purposes is an important requirement of state constitutional law.

A number of state constitutions contain so-called "uniformity clauses" that require taxes to be uniformly levied upon the same class of subjects. Some uniformity clauses apply only to property taxes, while others apply to all taxes. In reviewing the constitutionality of tax laws under uniformity clauses, some state courts adopt a deferential stance that affords a fair degree of latitude that enables the legislature to make classifications for taxing purposes, so long as they are not unduly arbitrary or unreasonable. In other states, however, the courts are not so deferential to the legislature in reviewing tax laws under uniformity clauses. In these states, the courts apply more rigorous scrutiny to evaluate tax laws challenged as violating the constitutional requirement of uniformity.

B. SINGLE SUBJECT AND CLEAR TITLE RULES

Martha Dragich, STATE CONSTITUTIONAL RESTRICTION ON LEGISLATIVE PROCEDURE: RETHINKING THE ANALYSIS OF ORIGINAL PURPOSE, SINGLE SUBJECT, AND CLEAR TITLE CHALLENGES, 38 Harv. J. Legis. 103 (2001)

State constitutions contain a variety of provisions governing legislative procedures. Unlike substantive limits, procedural restrictions regulate only the process by which legislation is enacted. Common examples are original purpose, single subject, and clear title restrictions. Original purpose clauses prohibit the amendment of a bill so "as to change its original purpose." Single subject rules limit each bill to one subject. Clear title rules require that the subject of the bill be clearly expressed in the bill's title. These provisions are designed to eradicate perceived abuses in the legislative process, such as hasty, corrupt, or private interest legislation. They are intended to promote open, orderly, and deliberative legislative processes, and can be found in almost all state constitutions.

The genesis of state constitutional restrictions on legislative procedure has been recounted elsewhere. The clear title rule, for example, was first adopted in 1798 in Georgia and the single subject rule first appeared in 1818 in Illinois. Most other states followed suit in the mid-nineteenth century. Constitutional restrictions on legislative procedure have survived and have been re-adopted in modern constitutions despite criticism that they allow the invalidation of legislation on "technical" grounds.

State constitutional restrictions on legislative procedure, unlike legislative rules adopted by the two houses of Congress, provide an avenue for challenging statutes, and such litigation is fairly common. The large number of procedural challenge cases seems surprising since State courts consistently proclaim that statutes are presumed constitutional. The Missouri Supreme Court, for example, has long insisted that "[t]he use of these procedural limitations to attack the constitutionality of statutes is not favored. A statute has a presumption of constitutionality. We interpret procedural limitations liberally and will uphold the constitutionality of a statute against such an attack unless the act *clearly and undoubtedly* violates the constitutional limitation. The burden of establishing [a statute's] unconstitutionality rests upon the party questioning it."

Other states likewise favor a liberal construction of procedural restrictions. Courts have used a variety of phrases to express the high standard to be applied in these cases, stating that statutes will be held unconstitutional, for example, only if "clearly, plainly and palpably so," only if shown "beyond a reasonable doubt" to violate the constitution, or only in case of a "manifestly gross and fraudulent violation." As a result of these high standards, state courts uphold legislation against procedural challenges "more often than not." The Minnesota Supreme Court observed that from the late 1970s until 2000, it had decided five single subject/clear title cases, upholding the statute in every case. In 1984, a Missouri judge indicated that the Missouri Supreme Court had not sustained a procedural challenge in twenty years.

Why, then, do litigants continue to raise original purpose, single subject, and clear title claims? One explanation of this behavior is that "[s]uch challenges are easy to make because all that is necessary is reference to the face of the statute." Another explanation is that each of these cases, depending as it does on the specific text of a particular enactment, is sui generis. As such, there is always a chance that a court will sustain a challenge to one piece of legislation even though it has rejected challenges to many other statutes. A more cynical explanation is that procedural challenges offer litigants one last chance to attack legislation they were unable to defeat during the legislative process.

Whatever their motivations, these claims have begun to pay off. The Minnesota Supreme Court, for example, "sound[ed] an alarm that [it] would not hesitate to strike down" legislation violating single subject and clear title provisions. The Missouri Supreme Court has heard ten procedural challenge cases since 1994, finding violations in five of them. The Illinois Supreme Court sustained only one single subject challenge from 1970 to 1996, but it has sustained four challenges since 1997.

A recent Illinois decision led to a nationally publicized furor in the Illinois legislature. In *People v. Cervantes*, the Illinois Supreme Court struck down the Safe Neighborhoods Law for violation of the single subject restriction. The law had been in effect nearly five years at the time of the decision. The scope of the Illinois court's ruling-striking down the entire enactment-is important. The court found that the Safe Neighborhoods Law was intended to address neighborhood safety problems relating to "gangs, drugs, and guns." Two portions of the law were found to constitute separate subjects: provisions amending the WIC (Women, Infants, and Children nutrition program) Vendor Management Act, and provisions relating to the licensing of secure residential youth care facilities. The Illinois Supreme Court discerned "no natural and logical connection" between these provisions and neighborhood safety. The portion of the Safe Neighborhoods Law challenged in *Cervantes* related not to the WIC vendor management program or the licensing of residential youth care facilities, but to weapons. Because the entire act was ruled unconstitutional, however, the defendant's gunrunning charge was dismissed. In fact, prosecutors were "forced to dismiss" firearms charges against numerous defendants. Five years after initial passage of the Safe Neighborhoods Law, the Illinois legislature found itself sharply divided on the merits of reenacting the gun control provisions. The measure has not been reenacted even though the Governor called a special session of the legislature for that purpose.

The Safe Neighborhoods Law exemplifies one consistent thread among recent procedural challenge cases: major changes were introduced into the challenged bills very late in the legislative process. This type of legislative procedure runs directly counter to the open, rational, and deliberative model the constitutional restrictions contemplate. Bills enacted in a hasty, apparently deceptive, or ill-considered process thus seem to invite procedural challenges. To return to *Cervantes*, the original Senate bill, relating to community service sentencing, was amended in the House so as to replace its entire contents with new provisions, now described as the "Safe Neighborhoods Law." The Senate refused to concur with the House amendment. A conference committee was formed, and that body deleted the entire House amendment and substituted another entirely new bill, 157 pages long and containing three components. That version then passed the Senate and the House and was signed by the governor. Similarly, in a Missouri case, *St. Louis Health Care Network v. State*, a substitute bill was offered on the last day of the legislative session for a bill originally relating to the Missouri Family Trust. The substitute bill contained provisions relating to nonprofit corporations, charitable gift annuities, and same-sex marriages. In both cases, the timing and scope of the changes raised suspicion.

A court's description of the legislative procedure leading to passage of the bill at issue sometimes indicates that the court's willingness to overturn the law is based on a suspicion that the process was tainted. For example, the Maryland Court of Appeals described the "transmogrifi [cation]" of a one-page bill concerning a specific tax into "lengthy emergency legislation" extending to government ethics and county taxing authority. Similarly, the Supreme Court of Appeals of West Virginia explained how a bill on thoroughbred racing became "an omnibus bill which encompassed authorization for all agency rules considered that year."

1. Original Purpose

Missouri's original purpose provision is typical. It reads in pertinent part:

> No law shall be passed except by bill, and *no bill shall be so amended in its passage through either house as to change its original purpose*. Bills may originate in either house and be amended or rejected by the other. Every bill shall be read by title on three different days in each house.

By its text, section 21 not only establishes the original purpose rule, but also implies a limitation of the rule and hints at the rule's underlying rationale. The text makes clear that the original purpose rule does not prohibit amendments to a bill during the course of its consideration and passage. In fact, it explicitly permits either house to amend bills originating in the other house. The Missouri Supreme Court has indicated that "Article III, § 21 was not designed to inhibit the normal legislative processes, in which bills are combined and additions necessary to comply with the legislative intent are made." At least one other state agrees that the original purpose rule should not be applied in such a way as to "unduly hamper the legislature."

In essence, the original purpose rule is "designed to prevent the enactment of ... statutes in terms so blind that legislators themselves ... [would fail] to become apprised of the changes in the laws." The final sentence of section 21 supports this rationale. It provides for the reading by title of each bill on three different days in each house. The rule protects the legislative process by allowing bills to be read and monitored by title alone. That is, a legislator is entitled to read bills as originally introduced and to decide, on that basis, how extensively to monitor each bill's progress. Legislators are assured that the purpose of a bill will not have changed dramatically following its introduction. This same reasoning serves to provide adequate notice to members of the public who wish to monitor pending legislation.

The original purpose rule also reinforces the deadline for introduction of new bills by preventing legislators from disguising new bills as amendments to existing bills. Accordingly, the original purpose rule is concerned with *changes* in content of the bill. By aiding legislators in monitoring hundreds of bills introduced in each legislative session, the original purpose rule helps legislators to represent the desires of their constituents.

Though only a few of the recent cases involve original purpose claims, the outcomes are instructive. In *Barclay v. Melton*, a bill that "had as its sole purpose the creation of a tax credit for dependents" was amended by deleting all of the provisions contained in the introduced version and replacing them with new contents. As passed, the bill "assess[ed] a tax surcharge against ... residents of [certain] school districts." The Arkansas Supreme Court concluded that the change from a tax credit to a tax surcharge was a change in the bill's original purpose.

Changes less extreme than this about-face seem not to trigger invalidation on original purpose grounds. *Advisory Opinion No. 331* appears to be unusual in this regard. There, the Alabama Supreme Court ruled that a bill whose original purpose was "to make appropriations for the ordinary expenses of ... the government" was unconstitutionally altered so as to change its original purpose when provisions limiting the powers of government officials to make necessary expenditures were added. According to the court, the purpose of the bill changed "from one of making general appropriations ... to one of ... repealing and changing other provisions of law ...." This bill represents a more subtle change. As finally passed, it contained two contradictory elements: provisions authorizing expenditures and provisions limiting the same expenditures. This case adds credence to the notion that a change in direction is fundamental in establishing an original purpose violation.

1. Single Subject and Clear Title

In most states, the single subject and clear title rules are combined in one section of the constitution. The combined rule is commonly phrased: "[n]o bill shall contain more than *one subject*, which shall be *clearly expressed* in its title." In some states, a bill must embrace "one subject, and matters properly connected therewith." Exceptions are commonly made for certain types of bills, such as "general appropriation bills, which may embrace the various subjects and accounts for which moneys are appropriated," and bills revising or codifying the law. It is well-established that even when combined, the single subject/clear title provision sets forth two independent requirements-that a bill have only one subject, and that the bill's title clearly express that subject. The common phrasing of the rule suggests that clear title analysis cannot proceed until the subject of the bill has been determined and found to be "single."

a. Single Subject

Two reasons are thought to support the single subject requirement: the prevention of logrolling and the preservation of a meaningful role for the governor. Simply stated, the single subject rule exists "to secure to every distinct measure of legislation a separate consideration and decision, dependent solely upon its individual merits." One leading commentator observed, "limiting each bill to a single subject" allows legislators to "better grasp[] and more intelligently discuss[]" the issues presented by each bill. Without the rule, the danger is that "several minorities [may combine] their several proposals as different provisions of a single bill and thus consolidat[e] their votes so that a majority is obtained for the omnibus bill where perhaps no single proposal...could have obtained majority approval separately."

Furthermore, the single subject rule protects the governor's veto prerogative by "prevent[ing] the legislature from forcing the governor into a take-it-or-leave-it choice when a bill addresses one subject in an odious manner and another subject in a way the governor finds meritorious." The rule is "intended to prohibit [] anti-majoritarian tactic[s]." In a word, the single subject rule protects the *decision* of the legislators and governor on each individual legislative proposal.

Hammerschmidt v. Boone County is a classic case of a single subject violation. Two very narrow bills relating to the conduct of elections were combined, and thereafter provisions relating to the form of county governance were added. There was no "rational unity" between the provisions relating to election procedures and those relating to county governance, and no reason except "tactical convenience" for combining them in a single bill. Election procedures and county governance cannot be reconciled as parts of any single subject. No title could be written to express a single subject incorporating both of these elements.

Another good example is *People v. Cervantes*, an Illinois case. A bill originally relating to community service sentencing was amended several times during the course of its consideration. As passed, the bill expanded the offenses for which a minor can be tried as an adult, permitted longer sentences for felonies committed in furtherance of the activities of a gang, amended sentences for driving while intoxicated, adjusted sentences for drug offenses, and amended various other sentencing provisions. All of these provisions were found to be related to the amended bill's subject matter, neighborhood safety. Portions of the bill relating to the licensing of youth correctional facilities and welfare program vendor fraud, however, were held to relate to other subjects unconnected with neighborhood safety.

b. Clear Title

Two distinct purposes support the clear title requirement. Most importantly, the requirement "is designed to assure that the people are fairly apprised...of the subjects of legislation that are being considered in order that they have [an] opportunity of being heard thereon." Secondarily, by requiring the title to express the whole subject of the bill, the rule "defeats surprise within the legislative process" and prohibits a legislator from "surreptitiously inserting unrelated amendments into the body of a pending bill." These two purposes reflect a widespread concern with special interest legislation in the nineteenth century. The clear title rule, properly understood, safeguards openness and honesty in the legislative process and facilitates public participation.

There are two common variations of clear title violations: overly broad, "amorphous" titles and under-inclusive titles. *St. Louis Health Care Network v. State* is a paradigmatic case of an amorphous title so broad that it gave no notice of the contents of the bill. This Article classifies *St. Louis Health Care Network* as a clear title case rather than a single subject case precisely because the title is so vague that one cannot discern from it what the bill itself provides. Clear title is properly the basis on which this case was resolved.

National Solid Waste Management Ass'n v. Director, Department of Natural Resources is a paradigmatic case of an under-inclusive title. The title-"relating to solid waste management"-accurately described the subject of most of the bill's provisions, but failed to give any hint of its application to hazardous waste. As a result, the title failed to provide notice of a portion of the bill's subject. The court assumed that the bill's two aspects, solid waste and hazardous waste, could be reconciled as part of a broader subject, but because the title failed to express the full extent of the bill's subject, the court invalidated the law.

The preceding analysis demonstrates that the original purpose, single subject, and clear title provisions, though related, are distinct. The original purpose requirement allows legislators to monitor vast numbers of bills by reference to their titles, confident that each bill's original purpose will remain reasonably constant throughout the process of consideration. It also secures adequate time for the consideration of each proposal by preventing late amendments that drastically alter the bill. The single subject rule assures that legislators and the governor can make a choice based upon the merits of legislation on each subject by preventing them from having to swallow unrelated bitter provisions with the sweet. Finally, the clear title rule protects the right of the public to know the subjects of legislation being considered and to voice opinions on measures of concern to them, and protects against fraudulent or surreptitious legislation.

McINTIRE v. FORBES
909 P.2d 846 (Or. 1996)

GRABER, J.

Petitioners challenge the constitutionality of the light rail funding provisions of Senate Bill 1156 (SB 1156 or the Act), enacted by the Oregon legislature in special session in August 1995. They assert that sections 1 to 17 of the Act (the substantive provisions relating to light rail funding) are invalid for a number of reasons. We conclude that sections 1 to 17 of the Act are invalid because the legislative act in which they are contained violates the "one-subject" requirement of Article IV, section 20, of the Oregon Constitution.

Article IV, section 20, of the Oregon Constitution, provides in part:

"Every Act shall embrace but one subject, and matters properly connected therewith, which subject shall be expressed in the title. But if any subject shall be embraced in an Act which shall not be expressed in the title, such Act shall be void only as to so much thereof as shall not be expressed in the title.

At the outset, we will be mindful of this court's caution:

"The constitutional provision prohibiting a statute from containing more than one subject or object should not be technically, strictly, or narrowly, but reasonably, fairly, broadly, and liberally construed, with due regard to its purpose. It should not be so construed so as to hamper or cripple legislation, or render it oppressive or impracticable, by a strictness unnecessary to the accomplishment of the beneficial purpose for which it was adopted, or to make laws unnecessarily restrictive in their scope and operation, or to multiply the number of laws unnecessarily, or to promote controversy in regard to the validity of legislative enactments." *Garbade and Boynton v. City of Portland*, 214 P.2d 1000 (1950) (quoting 50 Am.Jur., Statutes, § 194, p. 175).

The principal purpose for the title requirement of Article IV, section 20, is to provide fair notice to legislators (and to others) of the contents of a bill:

> "The constitutional restriction on titles of legislative acts was designed to prevent the use of the title as a means of deceiving members of the legislature and other interested persons as the bill moved through the legislative process. The restriction was intended to assure those who could not examine the body of the act itself that the act did not deal with more than its title disclosed." *Warren v. Marion County et al.*, 353 P.2d 257 (1960).

Those persons who may wish to follow legislation as it moves through the legislative process may include members of the public, the Governor, local government officials, and others.

The principal purpose for the one-subject requirement of Article IV, section 20, for the body of an act is to guard against logrolling. *Nielson (v. Bryson,* 477 P.2d 714 [1970]) reiterates that "one of the principal objects was to 'prevent the combining of incongruous matters and objects totally distinct and having no connection or relation with each other in one and the same bill.'" *Nielson* also defines logrolling as "combining subjects representing diverse interests, in order to unite the members of the legislature who favored either, in support of all."

The Oregon appellate courts have adjudicated at least 90 cases under Article IV, section 20, although none since 1970. The cases are not always clear or consistent in analytical approach. However, several cases examine the body of an act, the title of the act, and the relationship between the body and the title.... After considering the foregoing sources, we conclude that the appropriate analysis of a one-subject challenge to the body of an act, made under Article IV, section 20, should proceed in these steps:

> (1) Examine the body of the act to determine whether (without regard to an examination of the title) the court can identify a unifying principle logically connecting all provisions in the act, such that it can be said that the act "embrace[s] but one subject."

> (2) If the court has not identified a unifying principle logically connecting all provisions in the act, examine the title of the act with reference to the body of the act. In a one-subject challenge to the body of an act, the purpose of that examination is to determine whether the legislature nonetheless has identified, and expressed in the title, such a unifying principle logically connecting all provisions in the act, thereby demonstrating that the act, in fact, "embrace[s] but one subject."

Petitioners have summarized the contents of SB 1156 as follows:

"SB 1156...(1) provides state funding [and land use procedures] for light rail, (2) expands the availability of card-lock service stations, (3) promotes 'regional problem solving' in land use matters, (4) regulates confined animal feeding, (5) preempts local pesticide regulation, (6) adopts new timber harvesting rules, (7) grants immunity to shooting ranges for 'noise pollution,' and (8) protects salmon from cormorants."

We are unable to discern a principle unifying those eight topics. Neither are we able to perceive among the parts of the Act some logical connection relating each to the others. That being so, we move to the next step. We consider whether the legislature nonetheless has identified a unifying principle, logically connecting all provisions in the Act, that we do not yet perceive. If it has, and if the title discloses that unifying principle, then the Act, in fact, embraces but one subject.

In approaching this question, we focus on the title's "relating" clause ("Relating to the activities regulated by state government"), because that is what serves the constitutional function of the title. It is, for example, the relating clause that informs the President of the Senate and the Speaker of the House what amendments to a bill are germane.

The relating clause in the title in this case-the statement that the Act is one "[r]elating to the activities regulated by state government"-fails to identify and express a unifying principle logically connecting all provisions in the Act. It fails to perform that function, because-in this extreme case-the relating clause is so global that it does little more than define the universe with respect to which the legislature is empowered to act.

Respondents argue, however, that the relating clause is not global. They suggest that "the activities regulated" should be read to mean activities already regulated and that "state government" means that activities regulated by local governments are not included.

The "limits" suggested by respondents are illusory. The relating clause for SB 1156, even thus limited, is still so broad and general that it logically connects all provisions in the Act only in the meaningless sense that it announces a connection among nearly all things in the legislative universe. The title does not, in the constitutional sense, express a unifying principle. The phrase "[r]elating to the activities regulated by state government" is too broad and general to unify the disparate topics embraced by SB 1156.

Senate Bill 1156 embraces more than one subject. That being so, a guarantee of Article IV, section 20, was not met, and the process for enacting that legislation was fundamentally flawed. The court is obliged to consider and to remedy violations of Article IV, section 20. In this case, we hold that SB 1156 violates Article IV, section 20, of the Oregon Constitution. That being so, and consistent with the limited grant of jurisdiction in this case, we hold that sections 1 to 17 of SB 1156 are void.

TURNBULL v. FINK
668 A.2d 1370 (Del. 1995)

HARTNETT, J.

This is an Interlocutory Appeal. The Plaintiffs-Appellants challenge pre-trial rulings of the Superior Court as to the extent to which the State waived its sovereign immunity by the purchase of commercial liability insurance covering accidents involving two buses operated by the Delaware Administration for Regional Transit ("DART"). The issue presented to the Superior Court was which statute controls these proceedings: 2 Del.C. § 1329, enacted by 66 Del.Laws C. 360 ("1989 Bond Act"), or 18 Del.C. § 6511. Title 2, Del.C. § 1329 waives the State's sovereign immunity, as to DART, up to a maximum of $300,000 for each occurrence, if DART has in place the commercial insurance coverage authorized to be purchased by the 1989 Bond Act. Title 18, Del.C. § 6511 waives sovereign immunity generally, up to the limit of insurance coverage, if there is in place the insurance authorized to be purchased under that Section.

The Superior Court held that, as between 18 Del.C. § 6511 and 2 Del.C. § 1329, Section 1329 was the more specific and later enacted statute and, therefore, its provisions control. Consequently, the Superior Court determined that 2 Del.C. § 1329 limits the State's waiver of sovereign immunity, as to accidents involving DART, to the lesser of the amount of applicable insurance coverage, or $300,000.

In this Court, Appellants raise for the first time a claim that Section 68 of the 1989 Bond Act, which enacted 2 Del.C. § 1329, is unconstitutional. Specifically, they assert that the Act violated Article II, Section 16 of the Delaware Constitution because it contained more than one subject and that the subject "waiver of sovereign immunity" was not set forth in the title to the bill. The text of Article II § 16 of the Delaware Constitution precludes Appellant's argument. It states: "No bill or joint resolution, except bills appropriating money for public purposes, shall embrace more than one subject, which shall be expressed in its title." Delaware courts have consistently followed the "plain meaning rule" for construction of statutes or the Delaware Constitution. One formulation used by this Court in stating the "plain meaning rule" is: "In the absence of any ambiguity, the language of the statute must be regarded as conclusive of the General

Assembly's intent. The judicial role is then limited to an application of the literal meaning of the words."

As noted by Millard H. Ruud in his article *No Law Shall Embrace More than One Subject*, 42 Minn.L.Rev. 389, 414-452 (1959), the text of the Delaware Constitution is more permissive than any other state constitution because it provides that a bill of the Delaware General Assembly which appropriates money for public purposes is free of the restraint that it be limited to one subject. As Professor Ruud points out, in 1958 18 states had adopted constitutional provisions specifically dealing with the limitation of contents of bills making appropriations-both general appropriations bills and other appropriation bills. The Constitutions of seven of those 18 states (including Pennsylvania) expressly excepted only general appropriation bills from the one subject restriction. There are only four states, including Delaware, in which a "one subject" limitation provision in the State's Constitution is exempted as to all appropriation bills. Of these four states only the Delaware Constitution provides that any bill appropriating money for public purposes is excepted from the one-subject and title requirements.

The 1989 Bond Act is clearly a bill appropriating money for public purposes and its provision relating to the waiver of sovereign immunity in Section 68 relates to the insurance authorized to be purchased in the Act. The 1989 Bond Act is similar to the Annual Budget Act and differs only as to the number of appropriations and its source of funds. The 1989 Bond Act makes over 130 separate appropriations and the money appropriated has several sources including the General Fund, general obligation bonds, revenue bonds, funds made available from the repeal of prior appropriations not yet expended, and certain special funds. As a bill appropriating money for public purposes, the 1989 Bond Act clearly falls within the exception in Article II, § 16 of Delaware Constitution. No other provision in the Delaware Constitution requires a one-subject limitation or a requirement for a title for a bill appropriating money for public purposes. There is, therefore, no requirement in the Delaware Constitution that the 1989 Bond Act be limited to one subject that is expressed in its title. The framers of the Delaware Constitution undoubtedly recognized, even in 1897, the difficulties in limiting an appropriation bill to one subject or setting forth its provisions in a title.

Appellants do not assert that they have been mislead or prejudiced by any deficiencies in the 1989 Bond Act. To the contrary, they are benefitted by the enactment of Section 68 that enacted 2 Del.C. § 1329 because it waives the constitutional doctrine of sovereign immunity, up to $300,000 per occurrence, if DART has in place the insurance coverage authorized to be purchased by the Act. Without Section 68, Appellants would not have the benefit of this waiver.

For the foregoing reasons, the pre-trial rulings of the Superior Court that 2 Del.C. § 1329, enacted by Section 68 of the 1989 Bond Act, applies to this lawsuit and that it limits any recovery to $300,000 per occurrence are AFFIRMED and this proceeding is REMANDED for further action.

HOLLAND, J., dissenting.

The interlocutory judgments of the Superior Court which determined that 2 Del.C. § 1329, rather than 18 Del.C. § 6511, applies to these proceedings and limits any recovery to $300,000 per occurrence should be reversed because § 1329 is unconstitutional....The appellants contend that 2 Del.C. § 1329 is violative of the Delaware Constitution, inter alia, because it was enacted as Section 68 of the 1989 Bond and Capital Improvements Act ("1989 Bond Act"). In support of that contention, the appellants assert that the title of the 1989 Bond Act gave no indication its purpose was to alter the doctrine of sovereign immunity and that it was improper to include substantive legislation in an appropriation bill. The dispositive merit in this challenge to 2 Del.C. § 1329 is contained in three separate provisions that became a part of the Delaware Constitution simultaneously in 1897.

The first provision in the Delaware Constitution is Article II, § 16, which provides:

> No bill or joint resolution, except bills appropriating money for public purposes, shall embrace more than one subject, which shall be expressed in its title.

The second provision in the Delaware Constitution that is relevant to this analysis is Article III, § 18, which provides, in part, that:

> The Governor shall have power to disapprove of any item or items of any bill making appropriations of money, embracing distinct items, and the part or parts of the bill approved shall be the law, and the item or items of appropriation disapproved shall be void, unless repassed according to the rules and limitations prescribed for the passage of other bills, over the Executive veto.

This provision authorizes a line-item veto power for the Governor, but only as to appropriation bills.

The final applicable constitutional provision is Article VIII, § 4, which provides:

> No appropriation of the public money shall be made to, nor the bonds of this State be issued or loaned to any county, municipality or corporation, nor shall the credit of the State, by the guarantee or the endorsement of the bonds or other undertakings of any county, municipality or corporation, be pledged otherwise than pursuant to an Act of the General Assembly, passed with the concurrence of three fourths of all the members elected to each House.

Historical Context

The Single-Subject and Title Rules

The two general provisions in Article II, § 16 of the Delaware Constitution, that a bill contain only one subject and that the title of the bill express its subject, are distinct requirements. Each has different historical origins. Nevertheless, these two requirements are often combined in a single provision, such as Article II, § 16 of the Delaware Constitution, to achieve a common purpose. Before examining the exception for appropriation bills, it is important to understand the history and purpose of the two general requirements.

The potential problem caused by an omnibus bill, which includes unrelated provisions on heterogeneous matters, is an uninformed legislative vote. This was recognized by the Romans. In 98 B.C., the Lex Caecilia Didia was enacted to prohibit the adoption of laws which contained unrelated provisions-the lex satura. The omnibus bill continued to be a cause for concern in colonial America prior to the Revolutionary War. Consequently, the constitution of nearly every state now contains a general requirement that legislation be limited to a single subject.

The other general requirement in Article II, § 16, that the subject matter of a bill be expressed in its title, originated with the Georgia Constitution of 1798. In 1795, the Georgia legislature passed the Yazoo Act, which made grants to private persons that were not reflected in the statute's title. The Georgia Constitution was amended in 1798. The constitution of almost every state now requires that the title of a bill adequately express its subject matter. These provisions are also intended to insure informed legislative action, as the 1897 debates on the Delaware Constitution reflect:

> Oftentimes bills have been introduced in the Legislature with very harmless titles, but amendments have been added to those bills and when they have passed both Houses, they are entirely different from what they were originally. Delaware Constitutional Debates 1897, Vol. 1, p. 264.

Consistent with the foregoing historical background, this Court has recognized that the two general requirements of Article II, § 16 were included in the Delaware Constitution of 1897 in order to "prevent deception of the general public and the members of the General Assembly by titles to bills which give no adequate information of the subject matter of the bills." The single-subject and title provisions in Article II, § 16 are intended to assure sufficient notice that "legislation, the content of which was inadequately brought to the public attention, or so-called sleeper legislation" does not slip through the General Assembly. If a bill contains multiple subjects or the title of the bill is such that it would "trap the unwary into inaction," it must be struck down as a violation of this section of the Delaware Constitution.

a. Single-Subject and Title Rules Appropriation Bills as Limited Exception

Nevertheless, appropriation bills have traditionally been conditionally exempted from both of the general requirements, the single-subject and the title provisions, in state constitutions. In view of the historical fear of omnibus legislation, which led to the constitutional proscriptions against bills with multiple subjects or nondescript titles, however, the exceptions for appropriation bills are always narrow. The condition for exemption is usually a limitation that the provisions in an appropriation bill relate only to appropriations.

While appropriation bills must contain no other substantive provisions than appropriations matters, this does not mean that an appropriation bill must merely be a list of monetary appropriations and respective recipients. Rather, appropriation bills may contain substantive language which relates to the specific appropriations in the appropriation bill. Such language may be found to be "conditional" or "incidental" to an appropriation and, therefore, properly included in an appropriation bill. Factors which indicate that language in an appropriation bill is not merely "conditional" or "incidental," but rather is improperly substantive are: first, the provision is not germane to any appropriation in the appropriation bill; second, the provision amends or repeals an already existing law; and third, the provision is permanent in nature, extending beyond the life of the appropriation act. If an appropriation act contains substantive, non-financial legislation, it then becomes precisely the kind of omnibus bill the single-subject and title rules were meant to prohibit. Accordingly, an appropriation act is an improper place for an enactment of matters unrelated to appropriations. Otherwise, the purpose behind the single-subject and title rules would be meaningless, since they could be circumvented simply by putting a substantive change into legislation otherwise primarily devoted to appropriations. Consequently, those courts which have considered the issue all conclude:

> While under the Constitution general appropriation bills are exempted from the general constitutional provision which requires that all bills must contain but one subject, which must be clearly expressed in the title, it does not follow that general laws may be amended, modified, or repealed by a general appropriation act under such a general title. See, e.g., State v. Cutler, 95 P. 1071, 1072 (Utah 1908).

In Ruud's authoritative analysis of the one-subject rule, he reaches that same conclusion rhetorically regarding the exemption in Article II, § 16 of the Delaware Constitution:

Delaware, making what seems the broadest exception, excepts "bills appropriating money for public purposes." A textual interpretation could lead to the conclusion that any act appropriating money, whether a general or special appropriations act, could contain any number of subjects. The question would be raised, though, whether acts containing more than appropriations and related provisions remain "bills appropriating money for public purposes." Doesn't the exception impose limitation on the bill that it only appropriate money?

Remarkably, no Delaware case dealing with this question was found. Ruud, *"No   Law Shall Embrace More Than One Subject,"* at 434.

The foregoing conclusion by Ruud, that the exemption from the one-subject and title requirements in the Delaware Constitution for appropriation bills limits such legislation to appropriations, is compelled by an examination of the history and context in which Article II, § 16 of the Delaware Constitution was adopted. During the debates on the 1897 Delaware Constitution, Edward G. Bradford proposed that appropriation bills be excluded from the constitutional provision which provided that no bill should embrace more than one subject expressed in its title (the single-subject and title rules).... During the discussion on this proposal, the Pennsylvania Constitution was cited as one of its origins and as persuasive authority for its adoption. In 1894, three years prior to the Delaware constitutional debates, two similar provisions in the Pennsylvania Constitution, along with a provision giving the governor line-item veto power over appropriations, were interpreted by the Pennsylvania Supreme Court to have the same purpose, *i.e.,* to prevent the passage of extraneous matters in appropriation bills. With the benefit of the Pennsylvania Supreme Court's interpretation of its constitutional provisions regarding: appropriation bills; the single-subject rule; and the line-item veto, the drafters of the Delaware Constitution understood that excluding appropriation bills from the single-subject rule meant that such bills would not contain substantive provisions other than appropriations matters.

   b.   Line-Item Veto

Consistent Limited Exception

The narrow exemption for appropriation bills in Article II, § 16 is similar to the limited authorization for the gubernatorial line-item veto in Article III, § 18. In construing the latter provision, this Court has recognized the distinction between bills which have the fundamental purpose of appropriating money for public purposes, and bills which are fundamentally substantive in nature, but which also include an appropriation relating to the substantive issues. As to the former type of bill, the Governor has line-item veto power, but as to the latter, the Governor may only approve or veto the bill in its entirety. The debates on the 1897 Delaware Constitution make this clear:

The Governor shall have power to disapprove of any item or items of any bill, making appropriations of money, embracing distinct items, and the part or parts of the bill approved, shall be the law, and the item or items of appropriation disapproved shall be void unless repassed according to the rules and limitations prescribed for the passage of other bills over the Executive veto. Delaware Constitutional Debates 1897, Vol. 1, p. 282 (emphasis added).

Accordingly, this Court has interpreted the Governor's line-item veto power, as set forth in Article III, § 18 of the Delaware Constitution, to extend "only to a bill containing more than one appropriation and 'embracing distinct items,'" and not to "bills which contain only a single item of appropriation" among other substantive provisions.

c. Limited Appropriation Exceptions

Article II, § 16 and Article III, § 18 of the Delaware Constitution

The provisions in Article II, § 16 and Article III, § 18 of the Delaware Constitution, when viewed in historical context and read in para materia, reflect that to be an appropriation bill the provisions in the legislation must all relate to appropriations. The purpose of exempting appropriation bills from the single-subject and title rules of Article II, § 16 was to allow appropriation bills to designate money for more than one purpose without running afoul of the constitutional mandate that a bill embrace only the one subject expressed in its title. The exception for appropriation bills in Article II, § 16 was not intended to allow substantive provisions other than money appropriations to be included in appropriation bills.

Similarly, the constitutional authority for a line-item veto in Article III, § 18 was limited to appropriation bills only, not legislation that related to substantive subjects and also included appropriations.

Section 68 of 1989 Bond Act Violates Appropriation Exception

Although Article II, § 16 of the Delaware Constitution specifically excludes appropriation bills from its purview, Section 68 of the 1989 Bond Act does not fall within that exclusion. The Constitutional Debates of 1897 reflect that the purpose of excluding appropriation bills from this section was to allow the legislature to make appropriations for many different purposes at once. Those debates also reflect the drafters of Article II, § 16 did not intend to permit the passage of "sleeper" legislation by including substantive non-monetary enactments in an appropriation bill.

Section 68 of the 1989 Bond Act, through which 2 Del.C. § 1329 was enacted, is the type of legislation that was intended to be prevented by Article II, § 16 of the Delaware Constitution. Section 68 of the 1989 Bond Act amends Title 2 of the Delaware Code to waive the State's sovereign immunity for DART operations that are covered by commercial insurance and to impose a liability cap of $300,000. This is a substantive enactment of a permanent nature, which is improper in a bill otherwise completely devoted to "appropriating money for public purposes." Del. Const. art. II, § 16. There is also no indication in the title of the 1989 Bond Act that any change was to be made in the substantive law relating to sovereign immunity. Consequently, as a substantive change to the law of sovereign immunity, which was part of an appropriation bill, Section 68 violated Article II, § 16 of the Delaware Constitution.

What are the ramifications of concluding that Section 68 of the 1989 Bond Act is unconstitutional? The other sections of the 1989 Bond Act are unaffected because of the severability provision in Section 73:

> Section 73. Severability. If any section, part, phrase, or provision of this Act or the application thereof be held invalid by any court of competent jurisdiction, such judgment shall be confined in its operation to the section, part, phrase, provision, or application directly involved in the controversy in which such judgment shall have been rendered and shall not affect or impair the validity of the remainder of this Act or the application thereof.

Therefore, although Section 68 is unconstitutional, it does not invalidate the remaining provisions of the 1989 Bond Act. See 66 Del.Laws c. 360, § 73.

d. Sovereign Immunity Waived

State Insurance Protection Act

This Court first considered the import of the State Insurance Protection Act in *Pajewski v. Perry*, 363 A.2d 429 (1976). We determined that Title 18, Chapter 65, created "a comprehensive insurance program with implementing administrative provisions." We also noted that Chapter 65: mandated that a Committee be formed to determine insurance coverage (Section 6502); specified the forms of coverage (Section 6503); authorized the Insurance Commissioner to promulgate rules and regulations necessary to carry out policy determinations (Section 6504); and formed a State Insurance Coverage Office (Section 6505). We also found that the provisions of the chapter are mandatory, because the word "shall" is used in every significant section... Section 6511 states flatly that the defense of sovereignty "is waived" and "will not be asserted." There is a limitation to that waiver, that is, it extends to "any risk or loss covered by the state insurance coverage program."... In the view we take here of the Statute, the State is not entitled to dismissal of the complaint merely by showing, as it has done, that there is neither commercial nor self-insurance covering the liability for the kind of tortious conduct alleged in the complaint. Immunity is presumptively waived by § 6511 and it is, therefore, incumbent upon the State to provide all of the facts as to how the Committee met its responsibilities under 18 Del.C. ch. 65.

It may be that upon an enlarged record, or at trial, it can be demonstrated that the defense of sovereign immunity is valid because of the absence of liability insurance. On the present record, however, sufficient factual and legal doubt exists as to render inappropriate the grant of summary judgment based on that defense.

For the foregoing reasons, I respectfully dissent.

C.C. DILLON CO. v. CITY OF EUREKA
12 S.W.3d 322 (Mo. 2000)

PRICE, Jr., C. J.

This case involves the constitutionality of section 71.288, RSMo Supp.1999, which allows cities and counties to more restrictively regulate billboards than provided in the Missouri Billboards Act, sections 226.500 to 226.600, RSMo 1994 & Supp.1999 ("Billboards Act"). The City of Eureka ("City") based its billboard regulation ordinance on section 71.288 and denied C.C. Dillon Company's ("Dillon") billboard permit. Dillon claims that the legislative amendments to the several bills establishing and amending section 71.288 were enacted in violation of sections 21, 23, and 28 of article III of the Missouri Constitution. The trial court granted summary judgment for the City. We affirm.

On May 13, 1997, the Missouri Department of Transportation ("MoDOT") granted Dillon a permit to erect a billboard along Interstate 44 Highway within the City. On June 2, 1997, Dillon applied to the City for a permit to erect the billboard. The City Administrator denied the permit application on September 11, 1997, because the billboard did not comply with the City's more restrictive regulations. Dillon subsequently sought a variance from the City's Board of Adjustment, which was also denied.

Dillon filed a declaratory judgment action seeking a ruling that the bills that created and amended section 71.288 authorizing the city's more restrictive regulations were constitutionally invalid. The bills at issue are 1997 House Bill 831, 1998 Senate Bill 883, and 1998 House Bills (combined) 1681 & 1342.

Senate Bill 883 was introduced on February 5, 1998, and was entitled "An Act to repeal section 226.040, RSMo Supp.1997, relating to transportation, and to enact in lieu thereof two new sections relating to the same subject." While the bill was being taken up for the third reading, House Amendment No. 1 was adopted, which revised section 71.288 by stating: "Any city or county shall have the authority to adopt regulations with respect to outdoor advertising that are more restrictive than the height, size, lighting and spacing provisions of sections 226.500 to 226.600, RSMo." The amendment also limited business taxes that cities or counties could impose on billboards to two percent of the gross annual revenue produced by the advertising structure. Numerous other amendments were adopted concerning sections 21.795, 43.030, 226.005, 226.140 as well as sections on fiscal notes. The Senate refused to concur with these House amendments and the bill was sent to a conference committee.

The final version, Conference Committee Substitute for House Committee Substitute for Senate Bill 883 ("CCS HCS SB 883"), was entitled "An Act to repeal sections 43.030, 226.040 and 226.140, RSMo 1994, and sections 71.288 and 226.005, RSMo Supp.1997, relating to transportation, and to enact in lieu thereof seven new sections relating to the same subject." Section 21.795 established the permanent Joint Committee on Transportation Oversight to help account for transportation project funds. Section 43.030 amendments deleted the requirement that highway patrol member salary increases be the same as state merit employees. Amendments to section 226.005 pertained to organizational and salary issues of the Missouri Department of Transportation. Amendments to section 226.040 pertained to the position of the chief executive officer position of the highways and transportation commission and amendments to section 226.140 pertained to audits of that commission. The governor signed CCS HCS SB 883 FN2 into law on July 6, 1998, with an effective date of August 28, 1998. 1998 Mo. Laws 1574.

Article III, section 21 provides, "no bill shall be so amended in its passage through either house as to change its original purpose." Article III, section 23 provides, "[n]o bill shall contain more than one subject which shall be clearly expressed in its title...." The purpose of these two sections is "to keep individual members of the legislature and the public fairly apprised of the subject matter of pending laws and to insulate the governor from 'take-it-or-leave-it' choices when contemplating the use of the veto power."

"The use of these procedural limitations to attack the constitutionality of statutes is not favored. A statute has a presumption of constitutionality." We interpret "procedural limitations liberally and will uphold the constitutionality of a statute against such an attack unless the act clearly and undoubtedly violates the constitutional limitation." "The burden of establishing [a statute's] unconstitutionality rests upon the party questioning it."

Dillon's argument that CCS HCS SB 883 violates section 21's original purpose rule focuses upon the fact that the bill as introduced pertained only to transportation. Thus, Dillon argues that to add provisions to the bill relating to billboards altered the original purpose of the bill. Section 21 seeks to restrict "the introduction of subject matter that is not germane to the object of the legislation or that is unrelated to its original subject. Alterations that bring about an extension or limitation of the scope of the bill are not prohibited; even new matter is not excluded if germane." "The original purpose of the bill must, of course, be measured at the time of the bill's introduction."

Dillon's burden, then, is to demonstrate that billboards are "clearly and undoubtedly" not germane to transportation. "Germane" is defined as: "in close relationship, appropriate, relative, pertinent. Relevant to or closely allied." Black's Law Dictionary 687 (6th ed.). Dillon fails to carry this burden. The very function of billboards is to capture the attention of the traveling public. Billboards have been inextricably linked to highway transportation by federal and state legislation.

In 1958, Congress enacted the Federal-Aid Highway Act, which granted a monetary bonus to those states that passed outdoor advertising control measures. Of the twenty-five states that passed such measures, Missouri chose not to participate.

In May of 1965, then-President Johnson conducted the first ever White House Conference on Beauty. The conference's recommendations spawned the Highway Beautification Act of 1965. This legislation provided that if states did not adopt regulations for the "effective control of the erection and maintenance along the Interstate System and the primary system of outdoor advertising signs, displays, and devices," then those states would lose ten percent of their federal highway funds.

Congress expressed the public policy behind the Act:

> The Congress hereby finds and declares that the erection and maintenance of outdoor advertising signs, displays, and devices in areas adjacent to the Interstate System and the primary system should be controlled in order to protect the public investment in such highways, to promote the safety and recreational value of public travel, and to preserve natural beauty.

Missouri's regulatory response to save its share of federal highway funds is the Missouri Billboards Act, sections 226.500 to 226.600. Important to this case are the Missouri General Assembly's findings and declarations that outdoor advertising is a legitimate commercial use of private property adjacent to the interstate and primary highway systems and that it is necessary to regulate and control same to promote highway safety, to promote convenience and enjoyment of highway travel, and to preserve the natural scenic beauty of highways and adjacent areas. The general assembly further declares it to be the public policy of this state that the erection and maintenance of outdoor advertising in areas adjacent to the interstate and primary highway systems be regulated in accordance with sections 226.500 to 226.600 and rules and regulations promulgated by the state highways and transportation commission pursuant thereto.

Thus, both the federal and Missouri state governments have recognized that the transportation system, specifically the Interstate System and the primary highway system, is impacted by the effective control of outdoor advertising structures. The Missouri Highway and Transportation Commission has adopted administrative rules to implement the Missouri Billboards Act. And, as Dillon did in this case, an outdoor advertising permit must be obtained from MoDOT for placement of a billboard within 660 feet of the Interstate or primary system's right-of-way.

The express public policy decision to place the responsibility of regulating billboards with MoDOT, combined with the historical context of conditioning federal highway funds on effective billboard regulation, is fatal to Dillon's argument that billboards are not clearly and undoubtedly germane to transportation. The United States Congress and the Missouri General Assembly have demonstrated that these subjects are germane to one another. The introduction of billboard regulations into a bill relating to transportation does not change the bill's original purpose. CCS HCS SB 883 does not violate article III, section 21 of the Missouri Constitution.

Section 23 imposes two distinct procedural limitations by which the General Assembly may pass legislation: (1) a bill cannot contain more than one subject and (2) the subject of the bill must be clearly expressed in its title. Mo. Const. art. III, sec. 23.

"The test to determine if a bill contains more than one subject is whether all provisions of the bill fairly relate to the same subject, have a natural connection therewith or are incidents or means to accomplish its purpose." This test does not concern the relationship between individual provisions, but between the individual provision and the subject as expressed in the title. "The determination of whether a bill violates the article III, section 23 single subject requirement is made concerning the bill as it is finally passed. We look first to the title of the bill to determine its subject."

Dillon argues only that the addition of the billboard regulations, as they relate to "transportation," introduces multiple subjects within the bill. The title as enacted reads "An Act to repeal sections 43.030, 226.040 and 226.140, RSMo 1994, and sections 71.288 and 226.005, RSMo Supp.1997, relating to transportation, and to enact in lieu thereof seven new sections relating to the same subject." Assuming that "transportation" is not too broad to identify a single subject, an argument neither made nor addressed here, all of the provisions of the bill must fall within it.

Dillon's argument is exactly the same as its section 21 challenge. As previously noted, the seven new sections concerned the Joint Committee on Transportation Oversight, the Missouri State Highway Patrol, the Department of Transportation, and billboard regulations. Dillon does not develop any argument that any bill provision, except for the billboard provisions, violate section 23's single subject requirement. Our analysis in determining that billboards are germane to transportation also supports our determination here that billboards fairly relate to, or are naturally connected with, transportation. CCS HCS SB 883 does not violate the single subject requirement article III, section 23 of the Missouri Constitution.

We have stated the test for evaluating a clear title challenge as follows:

> The "clear title" provision, like the "single subject" restriction, was designed to prevent fraudulent, misleading, and improper legislation, by providing that the title should indicate in a general way the kind of legislation that was being enacted. If the title of a bill contains a particular limitation or restriction, a provision that goes beyond the limitation in the title is invalid because such title affirmatively misleads the reader. *Fust*, 947 S.W.2d at 429 .

The touchstone of the clear title rule is that the bill's title cannot be underinclusive. "The title to a bill need only indicate the general contents of the act." "The title cannot, however, be so general that it tends to obscure the contents of the act."

Dillon argues the rule was violated because the subject of billboards was not expressed in the title as originally introduced. Dillon miscomprehends the import of the clear title rule. First, the clear title rule necessarily applies to the version of the bill that passed, not the introduced version. Second, the title to this bill, "relating to transportation," includes rather than excludes the bill's provisions. In Missouri at least, billboard regulation is not underinclusive of transportation. Federal highway transportation funds depend on the state's billboard regulations and the state has given regulatory authority of billboards to MoDOT. Third, "[t]he title need not describe every detail contained in the bill."

The judgment of the trial court is affirmed.

NOTE

In cases where a single subject or clear title violation is found, a question may arise concerning the proper remedy for the violation. Should the violation be remedied by severing the offending provisions and allowing the remainder of the statute to stand, or should the entire statute be stricken as unconstitutional? Some state constitutional provisions provide an answer to this question themselves by opting for severability.

For example, the constitutions of both Iowa and Oregon state that "If any subject shall be embraced in an act which shall not be expressed in the title, such act shall be void only as to so much thereof as shall not be expressed in the title." Iowa Const. art III, §29; Oregon Const. art. IV, §20. In other states where constitutional provisions do not specify a remedy, some courts, as a matter of statutory interpretation, have followed a general preference for severability rather than striking down an entire statute. In *Hammerschmidt v. Boon County*, 877 S.W.2d 98 (Mo. 1994), the Supreme Court of Missouri set forth the following criteria for severability:

> Under the usual circumstances, this Court bears an obligation to sever unconstitutional provisions of a statute unless the valid provisions of the statute are so essentially and inseparably connected with, and so dependent upon, the void provision that it cannot be presumed the legislature would have enacted the valid provisions without the void one; or unless the court finds that the valid provisions, standing alone, are incomplete and are incapable of being executed in accordance with the legislative intent.

> Where, as here, the procedure by which the legislature enacted a bill violates the Constitution, severance is a more difficult issue. When the Court concludes that a bill contains more than one subject, the entire bill is unconstitutional unless the Court is convinced beyond reasonable doubt that one of the bill's multiple subjects is its original, controlling purpose and that the other subject is not. In reaching this determination, the Court will consider whether the [additional subject]...is essential to the efficacy of the...[bill], whether it is a provision without which the...[bill] would be incomplete and unworkable, and whether the provision is one without which the...[legislators] would not have adopted the...[bill].

> Where the Court is convinced that the bill contains a "single central [remaining] purpose", we will sever that portion of the bill containing the additional subject(s) and permit the bill to stand with its primary, core subject intact. In determining the original, controlling purpose of the bill for purposes of determining severance issues, a title that "clearly" expresses the bill's single subject is exceedingly important. *Id.* at 103 (citations omitted).

The Supreme Court of Pennsylvania has pointed out that there are significant policy justifications militating against severance in cases where logrolling may have occurred. *Pennsylvanian Against Gambling Expansion Fund, Inc. v. Commonwealth*, 877A.2d 383, 403, n. 14 (Pa. 2005). The practice of logrolling—combining unrelated subjects in one bill in order to obtain majority approval of the entire bill—does not comport with the fair and deliberative process anticipated by single subject and clear title provisions. Where logrolling occurs, the entire law in question may be tainted, and arguably should be struck down in its entirety.

Still, striking down an act in its entirety is a drastic measure that can have serious consequences. In that regard, re-consider the discussion of

People v. Cervantes in the excerpt from Professor Dragich's article at the beginning of this section.

C. PUBLIC PURPOSE REQUIREMENTS

MAREADY v. CITY OF WINSTON-SALEM
467 S.E.2d 615 (N.C. 1996)

WHICHARD, J.

Plaintiff-appellant, William F. Maready, instituted this action against the City of Winston-Salem, its Board of Aldermen, Forsyth County, its Board of Commissioners, and Winston-Salem Business, Inc. Plaintiff contends that N.C.G.S. § 158-7.1, which authorizes local governments to make economic development incentive grants to private corporations, is unconstitutional because it violates the public purpose clause of the North Carolina Constitution and because it is impermissibly vague, ambiguous, and without reasonably objective standards. Plaintiff also argues that the local governing bodies violated the State's Open Meetings Law by voting on and deciding grant matters in closed sessions.

Following a three-day evidentiary hearing and oral argument, the trial court found N.C.G.S. § 158-7.1 unconstitutional, enjoined defendants from making further incentive grants or otherwise committing public funds pursuant to that statute.

This action challenges twenty-four economic development incentive projects entered into by the City or County pursuant to N.C.G.S. § 158-7.1. The projected investment by the City and County in these projects totals approximately $13,200,000. The primary source of these funds has been taxes levied by the City and County on property owners in Winston-Salem and Forsyth County. City and County officials estimate an increase in the local tax base of $238,593,000 and a projected creation of over 5,500 new jobs as a result of these economic development incentive programs. They expect to recoup the full amount of their investment within three to seven years. The source of the return will be revenues generated by the additional property taxes paid by participating corporations. To date, all but one project has met or exceeded its goal.

The typical procedures the City and County observe in deciding to make an economic development incentive expenditure are as follows: A determination is made that participation by local government is necessary to cause a project to go forward in the community. Officials then apply a formula set out in written guidelines to determine the maximum amount of assistance that can be given to the receiving corporation. The amounts actually committed are usually much less than the maximum. The expenditures are in the form of reimbursement to the recipient for purposes such as on-the-job training, site preparation, facility upgrading, and parking. If a proposal satisfies the guidelines as well as community needs, it is submitted to the appropriate governing body for final approval at a regularly scheduled public meeting. If a project is formally approved, it is administered pursuant to a written contract and to the applicable provisions and limitations of N.C.G.S. § 158-7.1.

Article V, Section 2(1) of the North Carolina Constitution provides that "[t]he power of taxation shall be exercised in a just and equitable manner, for public purposes only." In *Mitchell v. North Carolina Indus. Dev. Fin. Auth.*, 273 N.C. 137, 159 S.E.2d 745 (1968), Justice (later Chief Justice) Sharp, writing for a majority of this Court, stated:

> The power to appropriate money from the public treasury is no greater than the power to levy the tax which put the money in the treasury. Both powers are subject to the constitutional proscription that tax revenues may not be used for private individuals or corporations, no matter how benevolent.

In determining whether legislation serves a public purpose, the presumption favors constitutionality. Reasonable doubt must be resolved in favor of the validity of the act. The Constitution restricts powers, and powers not surrendered inhere in the people to be exercised through their representatives in the General Assembly; therefore, so long as an act is not forbidden, its wisdom and expediency are for legislative, not judicial, decision.

In exercising the State's police power, the General Assembly may legislate for the protection of the general health, safety, and welfare of the people. It may "experiment with new modes of dealing with old evils, except as prevented by the Constitution." The initial responsibility for determining what constitutes a public purpose rests with the legislature, and its determinations are entitled to great weight.

The enactment of N.C.G.S. § 158-7.1 leaves no doubt that the General Assembly considers expenditures of public funds for the promotion of local economic development to serve a public purpose.... When making amendments to chapter 158 and adding other provisions designed to promote economic development, the General Assembly mandated: "This act, being necessary for the prosperity and welfare of the State and its inhabitants, shall be liberally construed to effect these purposes." The General Assembly has further demonstrated its commitment to economic development by enacting several other statutes that permit local governments to appropriate and spend public funds for such purposes.... These enactments clearly indicate that N.C.G.S. § 158-7.1 is part of a comprehensive scheme of legislation dealing with economic development whereby the General Assembly is attempting to authorize exercise of the power of taxation for the perceived public purpose of promoting the general economic welfare of the citizens of North Carolina.

While legislative declarations such as these are accorded great weight, ultimate responsibility for the public purpose determination rests with this Court. If an enactment is for a private purpose and therefore inconsistent with the fundamental law, it cannot be saved by legislative declarations to the contrary. It is the duty of this Court to ascertain and declare the intent of the framers of the Constitution and to reject any act in conflict therewith.

This Court has addressed what constitutes a public purpose on numerous occasions. It has not specifically defined "public purpose," however; rather, it has expressly declined to "confine public purpose by judicial definition[, leaving] 'each case to be determined by its own peculiar circumstances as from time to time it arises.'" As summarized by Justice Sharp in *Mitchell*:

> A slide-rule definition to determine public purpose for all time cannot be formulated; the concept expands with the population, economy, scientific knowledge, and changing conditions. As people are brought closer together in congested areas, the public welfare requires governmental operation of facilities which were once considered exclusively private enterprises, and necessitates the expenditure of tax funds for purposes which, in an earlier day, were not classified as public. Often public and private interests are so co-mingled that it is difficult to determine which predominates. It is clear, however, that for a use to be public its benefits must be in common and not for particular persons, interests, or estates; the ultimate net gain or advantage must be the public's as contradistinguished from that of an individual or private entity.

Plaintiff also argues, and the trial court apparently agreed, that this question falls squarely within the purview of *Mitchell v. North Carolina Industrial Development Financing Authority*. There we held unconstitutional the Industrial Facilities Financing Act, a statute that authorized issuance of industrial revenue bonds to finance the construction and equipping of facilities for private corporations. The suit was filed as a test case, before any bonds were issued, to enjoin the appropriation of $37,000 from the State Contingency and Emergency Fund for the purpose of enabling the Authority to organize and begin operations. We find Mitchell distinguishable.

One of the bases for the *Mitchell* decision was that the General Assembly had unenthusiastically passed the enacting legislation, declaring it to be bad policy. The opinion stated:

> At the time the General Assembly passed the Act, it declared in Resolution No. 52 that it considered the Act bad public policy. It explained that it felt compelled to authorize industrial revenue bonds in order to compete for industry with neighboring states which use them. As proof of its reluctance to join the industry-subsidizing group of states, the General Assembly requested the

President and the other forty-nine states to petition Congress to make the interest on all such bonds thereafter issued subject to all applicable income-tax laws.

The resolution recited that the General Assembly passed the act reluctantly, with reservations, and as a defensive measure. The Assembly's obvious apprehension over using public funds to benefit private entities in this manner clearly served to undermine the Court's confidence in the constitutionality of the legislation. The converse is true here in that the Assembly has unequivocally embraced expenditures of public funds for the promotion of local economic development as advancing a public purpose.

Further, and more importantly, the holding in Mitchell clearly indicates that the Court considered private industry to be the primary benefactor of the legislation and considered any benefit to the public purely incidental. Notwithstanding its recognition that any lawful business in a community promotes the public good, the Court held that the "Authority's primary function, to acquire sites and to construct and equip facilities for private industry, is not for a public use or purpose." The Court rightly concluded that direct state aid to a private enterprise, with only limited benefit accruing to the public, contravenes fundamental constitutional precepts… Thus, the Court implicitly rejected the act because its primary object was private gain and its nature and purpose did not tend to yield public benefit.

This Court most recently addressed the public purpose question in *Madison Cablevision v. City of Morganton*, 325 N.C. 634, 386 S.E.2d 200, where it unanimously held that N.C.G.S. § 160A, art. 16, part 1, which authorizes cities to finance, acquire, construct, own, and operate cablevision systems, does not violate the public purpose clause of Article V, Section 2(1). The Court stated that "[t]wo guiding principles have been established for determining that a particular undertaking by a municipality is for a public purpose: (1) it involves a reasonable connection with the convenience and necessity of the particular municipality; and (2) the activity benefits the public generally, as opposed to special interests or persons." Application of these principles here mandates the conclusion that N.C.G.S. § 158-7.1 furthers a public purpose and hence is constitutional.

As to the first prong, whether an activity is within the appropriate scope of governmental involvement and is reasonably related to communal needs may be evaluated by determining how similar the activity is to others which this Court has held to be within the permissible realm of governmental action. We conclude that the activities N.C.G.S. § 158-7.1 authorizes are in keeping with those accepted as within the scope of permissible governmental action.

Economic development has long been recognized as a proper governmental function. In *Wood v. Commissioner of Oxford*, 97 N.C. 227, 2 S.E. 653, this Court upheld the statutory, voter-approved borrowing of money for the purchase of railroad capital stock and donations by towns located along a privately owned, for-profit railroad.

Even subsequent to *Mitchell*, this Court declared that stimulation of the economy involves a public purpose. *State ex rel. Util. Comm'n v. Edmisten*, 294 N.C. 598, 242 S.E.2d 862 (1978), involved a challenge to Utilities Commission approval of a rate increase to subsidize exploration for natural gas by private companies. In upholding the Commission's action, the Court said:

> Stimulation of the economy is an essential public and governmental purpose and the manner in which this purpose is to be accomplished is, within constitutional limits, exclusively a legislative decision.

Further, the activities N.C.G.S. § 158-7.1 authorizes invoke traditional governmental powers and authorities in the service of economic development. For example, subsections 158-7.1(b)(5) and (6) authorize economic development expenditures in connection with local government operation of water, sewer, and other utility systems, matters long considered a proper role of government. Likewise, the power under (b)(1) to acquire land for an industrial park, develop it for its intended use, and then convey it is analogous to the powers granted by the Urban Redevelopment Law (chapter 160A, article 22), which this Court has consistently upheld as meeting the public purpose test. Urban redevelopment commissions have power to acquire property, clear slums, and sell the property to private developers. In that instance, as here, a private party ultimately acquires the property and conducts activities which, while providing incidental private benefit, serve a primary public goal.

As to the second prong of the Madison Cablevision inquiry, under the expanded understanding of public purpose, even the most innovative activities N.C.G.S. § 158-7.1 permits are constitutional so long as they primarily benefit the public and not a private party. "It is not necessary, in order that a use may be regarded as public, that it should be for the use and benefit of every citizen in the community." Moreover, an expenditure does not lose its public purpose merely because it involves a private actor. Generally, if an act will promote the welfare of a state or a local government and its citizens, it is for a public purpose.

Viewed in this light, section 158-7.1 clearly serves a public purpose. Its self-proclaimed end is to "increase the population, taxable property, agricultural industries and business prospects of any city or county." However, it is the natural consequences flowing therefrom that ensure a net public benefit. The expenditures this statute authorizes should create a more stable local economy by providing displaced workers with continuing employment opportunities, attracting better paying and more highly skilled jobs, enlarging the tax base, and diversifying the economy. Careful planning pursuant to the statute should enable optimization of natural resources while concurrently preserving the local infrastructure. The strict procedural requirements the statute imposes provide safeguards that should suffice to prevent abuse.

The public advantages are not indirect, remote, or incidental; rather, they are directly aimed at furthering the general economic welfare of the people of the communities affected. While private actors will necessarily benefit from the expenditures authorized, such benefit is merely incidental. It results from the local government's efforts to better serve the interests of its people. Each community has a distinct ambience, unique assets, and special needs best ascertained at the local level. Section 158-7.1 enables each to formulate its own definition of economic success and to draft a developmental plan leading to that goal. This aim is no less legitimate and no less for a public purpose than projects this Court has approved in the past.

Finally, while this Court does not pass upon the wisdom or propriety of legislation in determining the primary motivation behind a statute, it may consider the circumstances surrounding its enactment. In that regard, a Legislative Research Commission committee made a report to the 1989 General Assembly, warning that:

> The traditional foundations of North Carolina's economy--agriculture and manufacturing--are in decline. And, the traditional economic development tool--industrial recruitment--has proven inadequate for many of North Carolina's communities. Low wages and low taxes are no longer sufficient incentives to entice new industry to our State, especially to our most remote, most distressed areas.

In the economic climate thus depicted, the pressure to induce responsible corporate citizens to relocate to or expand in North Carolina is not internal only, but results from the actions of other states as well. To date, courts in forty-six states have upheld the constitutionality of governmental expenditures and related assistance for economic development incentives.... Thus, by virtue of the trial court's ruling, North Carolina currently stands alone in so holding. Considered in this light, it would be unrealistic to assume that the State will not suffer economically in the future if the incentive programs created pursuant to N.C.G.S. § 158-7.1 are discontinued. As Chief Justice Parker noted in his dissent in *Mitchell*:

> North Carolina is no longer a predominantly agricultural community. We are developing from an agrarian economy to an agrarian and industrial economy.

North Carolina is having to compete with the complex industrial, technical, and scientific communities that are more and more representative of a nation-wide trend. All men know that in our efforts to attract new industry we are competing with inducements to industry offered through legislative enactments in other jurisdictions as stated in the legislative findings and purposes of this challenged Act. It is manifest that the establishment of new industry in North Carolina will enrich a whole class of citizens who work for it, will increase the per capita income of our citizens, will mean more money for the public treasury, more money for our schools and for payment of our school teachers, more money for the operation of our hospitals like the John Umstead Hospital at Butner, and for other necessary expenses of government. This to my mind is clearly the business of government in the jet age in which we are living. Among factors to be considered in determining the effect of the challenged legislation here is the aggregate income it will make available for community distribution, the resulting security of their [sic] income, and the opportunities for more lucrative employment for those who desire to work for it.

The General Assembly thus could determine that legislation such as N.C.G.S. § 158-7.1, which is intended to alleviate conditions of unemployment and fiscal distress and to increase the local tax base, serves the public interest. New and expanded industries in communities within North Carolina provide work and economic opportunity for those who otherwise might not have it. This, in turn, creates a broader tax base from which the State and its local governments can draw funding for other programs that benefit the general health, safety, and welfare of their citizens. The potential impetus to economic development, which might otherwise be lost to other states, likewise serves the public interest. We therefore hold that N.C.G.S. § 158-7.1, which permits the expenditure of public moneys for economic development incentive programs, does not violate the public purpose clause of the North Carolina Constitution. Accordingly, the decision of the trial court on this issue is reversed.

ORR, J., dissenting.

At issue in this case is the City of Winston-Salem and Forsyth County's authorization, pursuant to N.C.G.S. § 158-7.1, to expend public funds directly to, and for the benefit of, selected private businesses as an inducement to these businesses to either expand or locate in the community. The majority opinion sanctions this practice on the theory that since jobs were created and the tax base increased by virtue of the inducements, the expenditures, totalling $13.2 million for the twenty-four challenged projects, were for a public purpose as required by Article V, Section 2 of the North Carolina Constitution. As a result, it appears to me that little remains of the public purpose constitutional restraint on governmental power to spend tax revenues collected from the public. Because I believe that the majority's holding in this case is (1) based on a theory unsupported by the evidence, and (2) contrary to established precedent interpreting the intent of the North Carolina Constitution, I respectfully dissent.

The logic upon which the majority opinion rests its conclusion that the expenditure of these funds was for a public purpose can be stated as follows: The creation of new jobs and an increase in the tax base ipso facto benefits the general public. Therefore, local government expenditure of tax dollars to a private business for its private benefit in order to induce the business to either expand or locate in the community is for a public purpose if it creates new jobs and increases the tax base.

The fallacy of this reasoning begins with the assumption that new jobs and a higher tax base automatically result in significant benefit to the public.... No evidence was presented that incentives paid or committed by the City and County improved the unemployment rate or that they otherwise resulted in meaningful economic enhancement. No evidence was presented that the incentive grants made by the City and County reduced the net cost of government or resulted in a reduction in the amount or rate of property taxes paid by, or the level of services rendered to, the citizens of Winston-Salem and/or Forsyth County.

Although there is undoubtedly some benefit to the general public, as noted with approval in the majority opinion, "direct state aid to a private enterprise, with only limited benefit accruing to the public, contravenes fundamental constitutional precepts." As Justice Sharp (later Chief Justice) stated in *Mitchell v. North Carolina Indus. Dev. Fin. Auth.*, 273 N.C. 137, 159 S.E.2d 745 (1968):

> It is clear, however, that for a use to be public its benefits must be in common and not for particular persons, interests, or estates; the ultimate net gain or advantage must be the public's as contradistinguished from that of an individual or private entity.

In examining the stated purposes of the grants, it is obvious that the $13.2 million was authorized for the specific benefit of the companies in question. The money expended was directly for the use of these private companies to pay for such activities as on-the-job training for employees, road construction, site improvements, financing of land purchases, upfitting of the facilities, and even spousal relocation assistance. In weighing these direct "private benefits" paid for by the taxpayers against the limited "public benefits," only one conclusion can be reached-that the trial court correctly held that the expenditures in question were not for a public purpose. The opposite conclusion reached by the majority can be reached only by ignoring the weight of the private benefits and relying instead on the assumption that simply creating new jobs and increasing the tax base is a public purpose that justifies the payment of tax dollars to the private sector. As previously noted, there is simply no evidence to support such a conclusion, and the majority's position must fail.

The majority also relies on a "changing times" theory to ignore the law as set forth in Mitchell and Stanley. While economic times have changed and will continue to change, the philosophy that constitutional interpretation and application are subject to the whims of "everybody's doing it" cannot be sustained.

Finally, many of the arguments presented to this Court rest on public policy. Advocates for these business incentives contend that without them, North Carolina will be at a significant competitive disadvantage in keeping and recruiting private industry. They further contend that the economic well-being of our state and its citizens is dependent on the continued utilization of this practice. These arguments are compelling, and even plaintiff admits that a public purpose is served by general economic development and recruitment of industry. However, plaintiff and those supporting his point of view argue that direct grants to specific, selected businesses go beyond the acceptable bounds of public purpose expenditures for economic development. Instead, they say that this is selected corporate welfare to some of the largest and most prosperous companies in our State and in the country. Moreover, these opponents contend that the grants are not equitably applied because they generally favor the larger companies and projects and, in this case, under the County's Economic Incentives Program Guidelines, completely eliminate retail operations from being considered. In challenging the actual public benefit, a question also is raised about the economic loss and devastation to smaller North Carolina communities that lose valued industry to larger, wealthier areas. For example, the move of Southern National Bank headquarters from Lumberton to Winston-Salem undoubtedly adversely affected Lumberton.

Also troubling is the question of limits under the majority's theory. If it is an acceptable public purpose to spend tax dollars specifically for relocation expenses to benefit the spouses of corporate executives moving to the community in finding new jobs or for parking decks that benefit only the employees of the favored company, then what can a government not do if the end result will entice a company to produce new jobs and raise the tax base? If a potential corporate entity is considering a move to Winston-Salem but will only come if country club memberships are provided for its executives, do we sanction the use of tax revenue to facilitate the move? I would hope not, but under the holding of the majority opinion, I see no grounds for challenging such an expenditure provided that, as a result of such a grant, the company promises to create new jobs, and an increased tax base is projected.

EMPRESS CASINO JOLIET CORPORATION v. GIANNOULIAS
896 N.E.2d 277 (Ill. 2008)

BURKE, J.

In this case, we are asked to determine the constitutionality of Public Act 94-804 (the Act), which imposed, for a two-year period beginning on the effective date of the amendatory Act, a 3% surcharge on the four riverboat casinos in Illinois that had adjusted gross receipts (AGR) of over $200 million in the calendar year 2004. The remaining five riverboat casinos, all of which had AGRs below $200 million, were not subject to the surcharge. The Act provided that the proceeds of the surcharge were to be distributed to the five horse racing tracks in Illinois. For the reasons that follow, we hold that Public Act 94-804 withstands the constitutional challenges raised, in the circuit court of Will County, by the four casinos subject to the tax.

The Illinois legislature authorized riverboat casinos in 1990 under the Riverboat Gambling Act. There are 10 licenses available for riverboats in Illinois: nine are in use, the tenth is in litigation. The nine riverboat casinos are located in Alton, Aurora, East Dubuque, East St. Louis, Elgin, Joliet, Metropolis, Peoria, and Rock Island. Four casinos have AGRS over $200 million-Empress Casino Joliet, Harrah's Casino Cruises Joliet, Hollywood Casino-Aurora, and Elgin Riverboat Resort-Riverboat Casino. There are five horse racing tracks with live racing in Illinois, located in Arlington Heights, Crete, Collinsville, Stickney/Cicero, and Melrose Park.

In May 2006, the General Assembly passed Public Act 94-804. The Act requires those casinos with AGRs over $200 million to daily contribute 3% of their AGR into the Horse Racing Equity Trust Fund. The Act provides that the monies (along with interest) shall be distributed, within 10 days of deposit into the Fund, as follows: 60% to organization licensees to be distributed at their race meetings as purses and 40% to racetracks "to improve, maintain, market, and otherwise operate [their] racing facilities to conduct live racing, which shall include backstretch services and capital improvements related to live racing and the backstretch." Distribution of the above-described 40% takes place as follows: 11% to Fairmount Park Racetrack and 89% to the other four tracks pro rata based on the aggregate proportion of total handle[1] for

---

[1] The "handle" is the amount of money wagered in the pari-mutuel pool or the total amount of bets taken.

calendar years 2004 and 2005 from wagering on live races conducted in Illinois.

In enacting Public Act 94-804, the legislature made the following findings:

> (1) That riverboat gaming has had a negative impact on horse racing. From 1992, the first full year of riverboat operations, through 2005, Illinois on-track wagering has decreased by 42% from $835 million to $482 million.

> (2) That this decrease in wagering has negatively impacted purses for Illinois racing, which has hurt the State's breeding industry. Between 1991 and 2004 the number of foals registered with the Department of Agriculture has decreased by more th[a]n 46% from 3,529 to 1,891.

> (3) That the decline of the Illinois horseracing and breeding program, a $2.5 billion industry, would be reversed if this amendatory Act of the 94th General Assembly was enacted. By requiring that riverboats agree to pay 3% of their gross revenue into the Horse Racing Equity Trust Fund, total purses in the State may increase by 50%, helping Illinois tracks to better compete with those in other states. Illinois currently ranks thirteenth nationally in terms of its purse size; the change would propel the State to second or third.

> (4) That Illinois agriculture and other businesses that support and supply the horse racing industry, already a sector that employs over 37,000 Illinoisans, also stand to substantially benefit and would be much more likely to create additional jobs should Illinois horse racing once again become competitive with other states.

> (5) That the 3% of gross revenues this amendatory Act of the 94th General Assembly will contribute to the horse racing industry will benefit that important industry for Illinois farmers, breeders, and fans of horseracing and will begin to address the negative impact riverboat gaming has had on Illinois horseracing.

Plaintiffs, Empress Casino Joliet Corporation, Des Plaines Development Limited Partnership d/b/a Harrah's Casino Cruises Joliet, Hollywood Casino-Aurora, Inc., and Elgin Riverboat Resort-Riverboat Casino d/b/a Grand Victoria Casino, filed a four-count complaint for declaratory judgment and injunctive relief against defendants, Alexi Giannoulias as the Treasurer of the State of Illinois and the Illinois Racing Board.

We now turn to plaintiffs' challenge that the surcharge violates article VIII, section 1, of the Illinois Constitution (the public funds clause).

Article VIII, section 1, of the Illinois Constitution of 1970 provides that "[p]ublic funds, property or credit shall be used only for public purposes." "[I]n order to proceed under article VIII, section 1(a) of the Illinois Constitution, facts must be alleged indicating that governmental action has been taken which directly benefits a private interest without a corresponding public benefit...." *In Friends of the Parks,* we reiterated the well-settled principles regarding a public purpose:

This court has long recognized that what is for the public good and what are public purposes are questions which the legislature must in the first instance decide. In making this determination, the legislature is vested with a broad discretion, and the judgment of the legislature is to be accepted in the absence of a clear showing that the purported public purpose is but an evasion and that the purpose is, in fact, private. In the words of Justice Holmes, "a declaration by a legislature concerning public conditions that by necessity and duty it must know is entitled at least to great respect." *Friends of the Parks v. Chicago Park District*, 786 N.E.2d 161 (Ill. 2003), quoting *In re Marriage of Lappe*, 680 N.E.2d 380 (Ill. 1997).

We have further expressed:

What is a 'public purpose' is not a static concept, but is flexible and capable of expansion to meet the changing conditions of a complex society. Moreover, "[t]he power of the State to expend public moneys for public purposes is not to be limited, alone, to the narrow lines of necessity, but the principles of wise statesmanship demand that those things which subserve the general wellbeing of society and the happiness and prosperity of the people shall meet the consideration of the legislative body of the State, though they ofttimes call for the expenditure of public money." The consensus of modern legislative and judicial thinking is to broaden the scope of activities which may be classified as involving a public purpose.

In deciding whether a purpose is public or private, courts are "largely influenced by the course and usage of the government, the object for which taxes and appropriations have been customarily and by long course of legislation levied and made, and what objects have been considered necessary to the support and for the proper use of the government. Whatever lawfully pertains to this purpose and is sanctioned by time and the acquiescence of the people may well be said to be a public purpose and proper for the maintenance of good government." *Hagler v. Small*, 138 N.E. 849 (Ill. 1923)" See also *In re Marriage of Lappe*, 680 N.E.2d 380 (Ill. 1997) ("If the principal purpose of the enactment is public in nature, it is irrelevant that there will be an incidental benefit to private interests"). If the purpose sought to be achieved by the legislation is a public one and it contains elements of public benefit, then the question of how much benefit the public derives is for the legislature, not the courts.

Plaintiffs contend that, from the face of the Act, the primary intended beneficiaries are private parties and, thus, the Act fails the public-purpose test. The standards established above require us to defer to the legislative findings announced in the Act unless plaintiffs have made a showing that the findings are evasive and that the purpose of the legislation is principally to benefit private interests. Plaintiffs have not shown that the legislative findings, as stated in the Act, are evasive or deceptive. Thus, our inquiry turns on whether the surcharge created by the Act serves a public purpose.

Plaintiffs argue that the primary intended beneficiary of the surcharge are private parties, the track owners, and not the public. First, plaintiffs maintain that, because all of the proceeds of the surcharge are turned over to the track owners, this demonstrates the intended beneficiary is private. In a related argument, plaintiffs maintain that, because there is no effective control on how the track owners can use the 40% of the surcharge given to them, this demonstrates the intended beneficiary was private.

The plain language of the Act belies this argument. While it may be true the proceeds go directly to the track owners, the manner in which the owners must utilize the funds is controlled by statute. The Act specifically states how the money must be used: 60% goes to the tracks as purses and 40% goes to the tracks "to improve, maintain, market, and otherwise operate [their] racing facilities to conduct live racing, which shall include backstretch services and capital improvements related to live racing and the backstretch." The track owners cannot simply pocket any of the funds they receive, not even the 40%. The 40% is earmarked for specific purposes and must be used by the tracks for those purposes.

Plaintiffs also maintain that the benefits are conferred on the tracks without regard to need. We disagree. The legislature could reasonably have concluded that the total handle of a track related to how much of a benefit to the economy that track could achieve. Stated differently, the legislature could have believed that the tracks with the larger handles would be able to contribute more benefit to the industry and economy as a whole and, thus, should be entitled to more support.

Plaintiffs' arguments do not support their contention that the Act benefits only private parties. Certainly, the principal purpose of the Act is a public one: to stimulate economic activity, including the creation and maintenance of jobs and the attraction and retention of sports and entertainment, particularly betting on horse racing. We conclude that the Act does, in fact, serve a public purpose. The surcharge will benefit the general well-being of society and the prosperity of the people of the State of Illinois. The emphasis of the Act is to benefit the entire horse racing industry, not simply the track owners, and the collateral businesses associated with that industry. The surcharge will serve to reduce the costs of unemployment and the evils attendant thereto should the industry collapse and the 35,000-plus associated jobs lost. The ultimate result of the surcharge will encourage an increase in industry in this state, including farming, breeding, and training, will stimulate commercial growth, and will revitalize an economically stagnant industry. All of these are objects that enhance the public "weal." Illinois has a strong interest in preserving the viability of industries in this state, which in turn will benefit the economy of the state as a whole.

As we stated in *McMackin*:

We believe that conditions of unemployment within the State are well known and need no documentation. Legislation intended to alleviate these conditions and their inherent problems certainly is in the public interest. New and expanded industry in communities within the State provides work and opportunities not only for those who would be directly employed, but also for others who provide goods and services to those who live and work in the community....The potential impetus to economic development within our State, which otherwise might be lost to other States with financing of this type, likewise serves the public interest. The private benefit resulting from the Act is incidental to the public purpose and benefit to be served, and there is no contravention of the constitution in this regard." *McMackin*, 53 Ill.2d at 358, 291 N.E.2d 807.

The same is true here.

Because we find that plaintiffs have not shown the legislative findings in the Act are evasive nor have they shown that the purpose of the Act is primarily to benefit private interests, we defer to the legislative findings in the Act and the legislature's determination that the Act was necessary. Accordingly, we conclude that the Act does not violate article VIII, section 1.

HOPPER v. CITY OF MADISON
256 N.W.2d 139 (Wis. 1977)

This is an action by the plaintiff, a resident and taxpayer of the city of Madison, for a permanent injunction enjoining the city of Madison and its officials from expending certain funds appropriated for the year 1975. A number of appropriations were challenged by the appellant's action, but only three are involved upon this appeal. They are: (1) $10,000 to the budget of the City Planning Department for human resource services to be provided by the Madison Tenant Union (MTU); (2) $14,000 to the budget of the City Planning Department for human resource services to be provided by the Spanish-American Organization (SAO); and (3) $81,517 to the budget of the City Department of Public Health for a day care program.

The complaint alleged that the appropriations for services provided by MTU and SAO were made contrary to the law because they are to private organizations which benefit only certain citizens and because once the funds are delivered to these organizations, the city will lose all control over their expenditure and use. The complaint further alleged that the appropriation for a day care program was made contrary to the law in that no program outlining the purposes and administration of those funds has been established.

HANLEY, J.

Three issues are presented on appeal:

1. Does the appropriation for services to be provided by the Madison Tenant Union constitute the expenditure of public funds for other than a public purpose?

2. Does the appropriation for services to be provided by the Spanish-American Organization constitute the expenditure of public funds for other than a public purpose?

3. Does the appropriation to the public health department for a day care program constitute the expenditure of public funds for other than a public purpose?

Although not established by any specific clause in the state constitution, the public purpose doctrine is a well-established constitutional tenet. "Public funds may be expended for only public purposes. An expenditure of public funds for other than a public purpose would be abhorrent to the constitution of Wisconsin." This rule applies to the expenditure of public funds by municipalities.

What constitutes public purpose is in the first instance a question for the legislature to determine and its opinion should be given great weight. This court, however, is not bound by the legislature's enactment or declarations regarding its purpose, for it is the court's constitutional burden to examine the challenged legislation and assess its realistic operation.

In so examining a legislative expenditure of public funds, there is a strong presumption that a legislature's acts are constitutional, and it is the duty of this court, if possible, to construe a legislative enactment as to find it in harmony with constitutional principles. In *Hammermill* the court stated, 58 Wis.2d at page 46, 205 N.W.2d at page 792:

It is not enough that respondent establish doubt as to the act's constitutionality nor is it sufficient that respondent establish the unconstitutionality of the act as a probability. Unconstitutionality of the act must be demonstrated beyond a reasonable doubt. Every presumption must be indulged to sustain the law if at all possible and, wherever doubt exists as to a legislative enactment's constitutionality, it must be resolved in favor of constitutionality."

The court is not concerned with the wisdom, merits or practicability of the legislature's enactment, but only with its validity in light of specific constitutional principles. It is constitutionally sufficient if any public purpose can be conceived which might reasonably be deemed to justify or serve as a basis for the expenditure. "A court can conclude that no public purpose exists only if it is 'clear and palpable' that there can be no benefit to the public."

To sustain a public purpose, the benefit to the public must be direct and not merely indirect or remote. However, the fact that the appropriation is made to a private agency does not render it unconstitutional. If an appropriation is designed in its principle parts to promote a public purpose so that its accomplishment is a reasonable probability, private benefits which are necessary and reasonable to the main purpose are permissible.

Appropriation for Services of Madison Tenant Union

The city council appropriated $10,000 to the budget of the City Planning Department to be granted to MTU in exchange for services to be performed pursuant to the terms of a written agreement between the city and MTU. Under this contract, MTU is obligated to "perform services for the City as outlined in the attached Human Resources Funding Application Form and any amendments thereto." MTU's application form describes the service to be provided generally as an information and grievance service for tenants, designed to inform tenants of their rights and assist them with problems in the landlord-tenant relationship. This service will be provided by grievance workers who will answer telephone inquiries and meet with individual tenants. These workers will be familiar with the applicable statutory law and the entire situation of tenants in Madison.

The appellant also contends this appropriation lacks a public purpose generally. In support of this position, the appellant argues that only that part of the city comprised of tenants could benefit from the services purchased from MTU. Although the number of beneficiaries is a pertinent factor in determining whether an appropriation has a public purpose, this court has stated many times "the fact the (appropriation) may benefit certain individuals or one particular class of people, more immediately than other individuals or classes does not necessarily deprive the (appropriation) of its public purpose."

The appellant also makes the argument that the trial court, in concluding the MTU appropriation was for a public purpose, only considered the grievance operation in the most favorable light and failed to consider what MTU would in fact do with the appropriation. The appellant claims evidence of certain MTU activities demonstrates that MTU is not concerned with promoting peaceful and equitable landlord-tenant relations, the adherence to local and state laws controlling these relations, or understanding by tenants of the rights and problems of landlords. The evidence referred to, appellant claims, shows that MTU's only interest is in furthering tenants' rights against those of landlords in any possible manner, including the promotion of rent strikes, picketing, boycotts, and blacklisting of selected landlords. Appellant argues that there is no reason to believe that the Tenant Union would act any differently in the future, simply because it is being subsidized by the city, than it has in the past.

However, the appropriated funds may be used only as provided in the contract between the city and MTU. This contract does not include any of the above-mentioned activities.

The record shows that of all housing units in the city, 49.3 percent are occupied by tenants. MTU's application for funding states that MTU receives approximately 75 telephone calls concerning landlord-tenant problems each week. A community with such a significant tenant segment has an interest in equitable landlord-tenant relations. These relations are a matter of public welfare. The expenditure for informational and grievance services for tenants who lack the expertise held by landlords in landlord-tenant law promotes such equitable relations. This program will also promote adherence to local and state laws governing landlord-tenant relations. Upon this record, it is not clear and palpable that there can be no benefit to the public by this expenditure. It has not been established beyond a reasonable doubt that no public purpose can be conceived which might reasonably justify this expenditure. It is not, therefore, unconstitutional.

Appropriation to Spanish-American Organization

The city appropriated $14,000 to SAO for its program, a bilingual multi-service center. SAO's application, which outlines the services purchased under SAO's contract with the city, states that SAO will provide:

> "(1) bi-lingual outreach and referral services to Spanish-speaking residents of Madison and Spanish-speaking migratory farm workers;

> "(2) employment and educational counseling for migrant workers in the transitional process of resettlement;

> "(3) in cooperation with the Area Technical College, courses in adult basic education and English as a second language;

> "(4) temporary accommodations for migrant families in the process of resettlement and assistance in locating adequate permanent housing; (and)

> "(5) in cooperation with the Wisconsin State Employment Service, bi-lingual job counseling, development and placement services to Spanish-speaking residents."

The appellant further claims that the SAO expenditure generally lacks a public purpose because only a small number of persons will benefit and because some of the persons served will be migrant workers who are not residents of the city. As stated above in respect to the MTU appropriation, the fact a certain group of persons are the immediate beneficiaries of the appropriation does not necessarily deprive the appropriation of its public purpose.

In its application for funding, SAO stated:

> The 1970 U.S. Census indicates that there are over 2,200 residents in Dane County whose principal language is Spanish. The area Spanish-speaking community is one of the fastest growing sub-communities in the State of Wisconsin and in Madison. With the gradual decline of the migrant labor market, many former migrant families, a majority of who are Chicano, have

chosen to resettle in Wisconsin. Although the greater share of resettlement has taken place in the State's south-eastern counties, Madison continues to receive an additional 10 to 20 families each year. 1973-74 public school enrollment data shows that the Spanish-speaking community of Madison is the 5th largest in the State. In addition, nearby food processing plants annually attract several hundred Spanish-speaking migratory workers who travel through Madison on their way to other jobs or in the resettlement process."

The services to be provided under the contract between SAO and the city seek to assist these persons in solving their various problems caused in large part by their language barrier. A community center which provides such assistance serves a public purpose. In the absence of such services, the public may be harmed by the recognized social consequences of poverty and illiteracy. It is a reasonable conclusion that these services will enable Spanish-speaking persons to contribute economically and culturally to the community. These matters are within the objective of the public welfare, the promotion of which will benefit the community as a whole.

In regard to the services provided by SAO to persons in the migrant stream, the citizenry receives the benefit of satisfaction from fulfilling a perceived moral duty by providing temporary assistance to these shelterless, needy persons. Such temporary accommodations also avoid the problem of these persons having nowhere but the streets to go. These benefits are certainly not as significant as those received by the public when the persons receiving the service are residents of the city, and it would be difficult to find a constitutionally sufficient public purpose served by an expenditure for service only for migrants. However, in this case, services provided to migrant workers are only a portion, the record shows, of all the services to be provided by SAO under its program. The SAO program, as a whole, promotes a public purpose, and therefore the expenditure to purchase services provided by that program is constitutional.

Appropriation for Day Care

The city appropriated a total of $198,000 to the budget of the City Department of Public Health for various day care services. $117,000 of this money was designated as tuition aids to be distributed based upon standards of family need. These standards had not been established by the city council at the time of the commencement of the action, and the trial court therefore granted summary judgment to the defendant in respect to this portion of the appropriation for the reason that it could not be determined what persons would be served by the funds. The appellant does not challenge the trial court's decision in respect to this $117,000 appropriation for a day care tuition aids program.

The appellant does claim, however, that the trial court erred in not finding the appropriation of the remaining approximately $81,000 to be for other than a public purpose. Generally stated, these funds are to be allocated for two operations: (1) administration of the city's day care program, which includes salaries and benefits for city employees overseeing the program, and (2) direct aid to day care centers to improve their quality.

The appellant's major challenge to this expenditure for day care is that it lacks a public purpose because it is not to be limited for the benefit of poor and needy families, and therefore will aid families who do not need assistance.

The city's expenditure to ensure the availability of quality day care benefits the community as a whole. The record reasonably supports the conclusion that there is a need for improved day care service. The report of the City Committee on Day Care shows that in the city over 35 percent of women with children under the age of six are in the labor force. The report further states that less than half the children under the age of six who require out of home care may be accommodated in the presently available facilities. The vast majority of children in grades kindergarten through fifth who need extended care are not provided for. The two aspects of the day care program which are challenged here are to a great degree intertwined with the tuition aids program, which provides relief to poor and needy families, enabling the parents to work and contribute economically to the city.

It may not be seriously questioned that the care and supervision of the city's children is a matter of public health and welfare. It is reasonable to conclude that the city's program to improve and make more available day care service promotes these objectives. The appellant's claim that present day care facilities are adequate goes to the wisdom of the legislation, not whether it serves a public purpose.

We conclude that the challenged appropriations were not made contrary to the law. They constituted expenditure of funds for public purposes by promoting the health and general welfare of the public. The trial court correctly granted the defendants' motion for summary judgment dismissing the plaintiff's action.

TOWN OF BELOIT v. COUNTY OF ROCK
657 N.W.2d 344 (Wis. 2003)

CROOKS, J.

Belle Zyla, Marvin Prothero, and the Green-Rock Audubon Society (Intervenors) petitioned for review of a court of appeals decision, which reversed and remanded the decision of the Circuit Court for Rock County, William D. Johnston, Circuit Court Judge. The court of appeals held that the Town of Beloit (town) has the statutory authority to spend public tax monies to develop and sell property in the Heron Bay subdivision, and that the town's goals in developing the subdivision constitute legitimate and valid public purposes.

We affirm the court of appeals decision. In Libertarian Party of Wisconsin v. State, 199 Wis.2d 790, 809, 546 N.W.2d 424 (1996), this court held that creating jobs and enhancing the tax base were legitimate and valid reasons, along with others, for finding a legislative public purpose in the expenditure of public funds to build the Milwaukee Brewers' Miller Park. Accordingly, we hold that the combination of the town's enunciated goals of creating jobs, promoting orderly growth, increasing the tax base, and preserving and conserving an environmentally sensitive area for the benefit of the citizens of the town is a legitimate and valid public purpose under Wisconsin statutes, case law, and the United States and Wisconsin Constitutions.

This case involves a question of whether the Town of Beloit violated the public purpose doctrine. Although there is no specific clause in the Wisconsin Constitution establishing the public purpose doctrine, this court has recognized that the doctrine is firmly accepted as a basic constitutional tenet of the Wisconsin Constitution and the United States Constitution, mandating that public appropriations may not be used for other than public purposes. Courts are to give great weight and afford very wide discretion to legislative declarations of public purpose, but are not bound by such legislative expressions. It is the duty of this court to determine whether a public purpose can be conceived, which might reasonably be deemed to justify the basis of the duty.... Under the public purpose doctrine, "[w]e are not concerned with the wisdom, merits or practicability of the legislature's enactment. Rather we are to determine whether a public purpose can be conceived which might reasonably be deemed to justify or serve as a basis for the expenditure."

Consequently, a conclusion that no public purpose exists can be determined only if it is "clear and palpable" that there can be no benefit to the public. In *State ex rel. Warren v. Reuter*, 44 Wis.2d 201, 211, 170 N.W.2d 790 (1969), this court described the public purpose concept as fluid:

> [T]he concept of public purpose is a fluid one and varies from time to time, from age to age, as the government and its people change. Essentially, public purpose depends on what the people expect and want their government to do for the society as a whole and in this growth of expectation, that which often starts as hope ends in entitlement.

Although courts are not bound by legislative expressions of public purposes, they nevertheless have a constitutional burden to examine legislative actions for the existence of a public purpose pursuant to the Wisconsin Constitution. However, the court's duties are limited to determining whether the legislation contravenes the provisions of the constitution. The presumption of constitutionality is applicable in making such a determination. As such, courts are to give great weight to the opinion of the legislative body, and "[i]f any public purpose can be conceived which might rationally justify the expenditure, the constitutional test is satisfied." Consequently, a court will conclude that there is no public purpose only if it is "clear and palpable that there can be no benefit to the public."

Because of the accepted view that local governments are often in the best position to determine the needs of the public in that locality, Wisconsin municipalities have traditionally been given wide discretion to determine whether a public expenditure is warranted due to public necessity, convenience, or welfare. As such, the public purpose doctrine has been broadly interpreted.

A review of Wisconsin case law illustrates that the trend of Wisconsin courts is to extend the concept of public purpose. In *Bowman*, 34 Wis.2d at 64-65, 148 N.W.2d 683, the industrial development through the creation of separate county agencies and bond issues, pursuant to Wis. Stat. § 59.071, was determined to be a valid constitutional enactment as it related to a declaration of public purpose. In *West Allis v. Milwaukee County*, 39 Wis.2d 356, 159 N.W.2d 36 (1968), construction of incinerators and waste disposal facilities was considered a public purpose. In addition, financial aid to the Marquette School of Medicine (now the Medical College of Wisconsin), a private nonprofit corporation, was upheld on the premise that public health is a public purpose. This court upheld the industrial bonding law under Wis. Stat. § 66.521 (1969), as a public purpose, because the protection of the economic interests of the general public fell within the scope of promotion of the general welfare. Similarly, the elimination of unsafe, unsanitary and overcrowded housing was found to promote the overall public purpose of providing stable residences for those of lower income.

A few years later, this court upheld the creation and operation of the Wisconsin solid waste recycling authority, in part because "recycling can be defined as a means of garbage collection, and, as such, has been denominated as clearly a matter justifying expenditure of public funds."

Wisconsin courts have continued the liberal application of the public purpose doctrine. In 2001, the court of appeals held that the construction of a parking lot to promote rehabilitation of the downtown area was held to be a public purpose. In a similar vein, a city's expenditure of funds to increase the tax base and generally enhance the economic climate of the community was held to satisfy the public purpose doctrine.

Most significantly, this court was recently presented with the question of whether the expenditure of public funds for the construction of the new Milwaukee Brewers' Miller Park satisfied the public purpose doctrine. The purported goals of creating jobs and enhancing the tax base were held to be valid reasons, along with other reasons, by this court. In our analysis, we recognized that enhancing the tax base and creation of new jobs are legitimate and valid public purposes, and held that:

> The purpose of the Stadium Act is to promote the welfare and prosperity of this state by maintaining and increasing the career and job opportunities of its citizens and by protecting and enhancing the tax base on which state and local governments depend upon. It is clear that the community as a whole will benefit from the expenditures of these public funds. Creation of new jobs is of vital importance to the State of Wisconsin and economic development is a proper function of our government. *Libertarian Party*, 199 Wis.2d at 826.

Accordingly, the goal of increasing the tax base, as well as creation of new jobs, has been recognized by this court, and other Wisconsin courts to be a legitimate and valid public purpose justifying the expenditure of public funds.

The record is replete with references to the underlying reasons for the town's decision to develop the Heron Bay Subdivision. In particular, the town was motivated to develop the land by its desire to create jobs, expand the tax base and create an orderly growth of single family housing for the benefit of members of the community.

The town was also concerned with the environmental impact that a subdivision would have in this ecologically sensitive area. As a result of that concern, the town ultimately determined that it was its duty to ensure that an ecologically fragile area was properly developed and that the best way to accomplish this goal was to carry out the development itself.

Thus, contrary to the Intervenors' argument...the record clearly indicates that the town acted on behalf of the public welfare.... Finally, as noted by the town, any profit realized from the sale of the subdivision would in fact benefit the Town of Beloit in that the profit would go into the Town Treasury and ultimately benefit all of the citizens of the town by way of decreased taxes and reduced debt.

In summary...this court has recognized, pursuant to our decision in *Libertarian Party*, that purposes for legislative action such as increasing the tax base and creation of new jobs, along with other reasons, are legitimate public purposes justifying the expenditure of public funds. This court holds that the combination of goals here of creating jobs, promoting orderly growth, enhancing the tax base, and preserving and conserving environmentally sensitive lands is a legitimate and valid public purpose justifying the expenditure of public funds by the Town of Beloit. Accordingly, we affirm the court of appeals decision.

ABRAHAMSON, C. J. (dissenting).

I would affirm the order of the circuit court granting summary judgment to the intervenors on the ground that the town's proposed expenditure for the development of the subdivision did not serve a public purpose.

An expenditure is for a public purpose if it provides a direct advantage or benefit to the public at large. It is not for a public purpose if the advantage to the public is indirect, remote, or uncertain. The constitutional public purpose test is satisfied when the purposes expressed by the legislative body or "conceived" by the court rationally justify the expenditure. In determining whether a public purpose exists the judiciary accords the legislative branch deference and thus plays a limited role. Nevertheless, the court does not merely rubber-stamp government expenditures. The state and federal constitutions demand that courts perform their independent function to assess the realistic operation of the law to protect the public. A court "is not bound by the legislature's enactment or declarations regarding its purpose, for it is the court's constitutional burden to examine the challenged legislation and assess its realistic operation."

The combination of goals enunciated by the majority opinion as constituting a legitimate and valid public purpose for the Town of Beloit's expenditures properly includes a list of benefits that might conceivably, in some circumstances, provide a direct benefit to taxpayers and thereby satisfy the public purpose doctrine. An expenditure of funds that is legitimately designed to create jobs, promote orderly growth, increase the tax base, and preserve an environmentally sensitive area is made for a public purpose.

I dissent in this case, however, to express my conviction that some of the goals on which the majority opinion rests its conclusion are merely assertions unsupported by the facts of this case while others are admittedly hoped for but distant outcomes, not justifications. The public purpose doctrine becomes a charade if a town may justify expenditures by merely offering enough of the proper buzzwords, "job creation," "orderly growth," "increasing the tax base," and "environment concerns," without any facts to back up the assertions. Moreover, judicial review cannot begin and end simply with the recitation of those buzzwords, without any analysis.

I dissent because I conclude on the basis of this record that it is clear beyond a reasonable doubt that the taxpayers of the Town of Beloit will be paying taxes to support the sale of lots for the future construction of private housing from which any benefit to the taxpayers is indirect, remote, and uncertain.

This case is before the court on summary judgment and so our analysis is based upon stipulated facts and affidavits. The parties' stipulation regarding the public purpose states only that the development is based on a policy decision that the town will be able to sell the lots to private individuals, realize a profit, expand the town's tax base, and open up the northwest side of the town in an orderly planned manner. The affidavits do not discuss any particular public purpose except in passing and in conclusory terms. Indeed, analysis of the record exposes the town's asserted justifications and those conceived of by the majority of this court as nothing more than a recitation of buzzwords.

I begin by looking at the four justifications upon which the majority opinion rests its holding: job creation, expanding the tax base, promoting orderly growth, and environmental conservation.

The majority opinion lists job creation as an express goal of the town's expenditure in this case, despite the fact that the town did not articulate that benefit as a goal in its stipulation, brief, or oral argument. Indeed, there is no evidence in the record that the Town of Beloit ever intended the expenditure of monies to develop and sell property in the Heron Bay subdivision to create jobs, let alone that the expenditure would in fact create jobs.

The majority opinion includes this noble public goal based solely upon a single affidavit from the town's attorney, asserting in broad terms, not necessarily related to this subdivision development, that "the Town of Beloit has a history of leading development for the benefit of its citizens. The purpose of development has been to develop jobs, a greater tax base for the community and places for citizens to live."

No evidence appears in the record of the types of jobs that would be created in this case, who would receive those jobs, or how long those jobs would last. The only jobs immediately on the horizon may be jobs related to development of the subdivision. If homes are constructed in the future, one-time construction jobs might be made available in the community. A public purpose cannot rest on conjecture alone.

The court's emphasis on the public purpose of preservation of an environmentally sensitive strip of land along the Rock River also amounts to reliance on buzzwords.... In any event, it is unclear why any expenditure of funds for subdivision improvement is necessary for environmental protection of land the town owns along the river. The monies expended go to the development of the sites, not the creation or enforcement of any environmental easement or covenant. According to the parties' stipulation, the public can access these lands for recreation and enjoyment at the present time. To conclude that the town is justified in expending funds for sewer, water, roads, gas, electricity, storm sewer management and any other appurtenances necessary for development of the subdivision for sale for homes because the public would benefit from no development on a particular strip of town-owned land is doublespeak.

The two other goals in the combination of objectives the majority opinion says supports the expenditures for a public purpose are the promotion of orderly growth and increasing the tax base. The town, however, makes no showing of the relationship of the subdivision to orderly growth. Orderly growth is accomplished by a master plan, zoning codes, and regulation of private land developers. The Town of Beloit has such a master plan in place. How the town is promoting orderly growth by development of the subdivision is therefore unclear. The majority opinion appears to have accepted the town's mere suggestion of promoting orderly growth. It certainly cannot base its conclusion on facts because the record is devoid of any such facts.

The final objective of the expenditures is to increase the tax base. The tax base will increase if the lots are sold and houses are constructed. Yet the stipulation states that the "Town has not sold any portion of the Heron Bay Lands as of this date [December 7, 1999]. The Town has no guarantee that anyone will purchase any of the future residential lots...."

The majority opinion's combination of goals justifying the expenditures in this case thus boils down to this: the expenditure serves an acceptable public purpose because the town's tax base might be enhanced. I disagree with this position. An enhanced tax base from the sale of land and the construction of homes is an indirect, remote, and uncertain benefit of the expenditure in the present case and is not a sufficient public purpose to justify the town's running a for-profit real estate development business and engaging in the non-traditional enterprise of building residential home sites.

Next we turn to the two additional goals the town asserted as justifications for the expenditure in this case that the majority opinion rightly ignores. Both of them are similarly indirect, remote, and too uncertain to constitute public purposes.

First, the town freely admits in the stipulation that it is acting with the hope of making a profit. The town has the power to sell property. The majority opinion goes to great length to explain this statutory authority. Even where a government entity acts pursuant to a valid law, however, it is still subject to the constitution and the public purpose doctrine. The issue in this case is whether the town may expend funds for subdivision development to make a bigger profit on the sale. No evidence was presented analyzing either the expected revenue or market demand for the lots. The justification of a hoped-for profit, pursued to its logical end, would justify the expenditure of public funds for any potentially profitable endeavor in which the town seeks to engage. That cannot be what the public purpose doctrine means.

Second, the affidavit from the town attorney asserts in broad terms, not necessarily related to this subdivision development, that development in the town is to provide places for citizens to live. Nothing in the record evidences a need for single-family residential housing or the lack of private capital to develop such housing. Several private ventures proposed development of the land, but the Town rejected the proposals. In *Heimerl v. Ozaukee County*, 256 Wis. 151, 40 N.W.2d 564 (1949), the court held that building private driveways was not "allied with a public purpose" and declared the expenditures unconstitutional. Similarly, the development of river front lots in and of itself is not allied with a public purpose.

The public purpose doctrine demands deference to the legislative branches of government. Nevertheless, the court must examine the operational facts concerning government expenditures in order to determine whether a direct benefit to the public results. No facts exist in the record in the present case or can be conceived by the court to support a public purpose. I therefore conclude, as did the circuit court, that the possibility of public benefit is too indirect, remote, and uncertain to sustain the expenditures.

For the reasons set forth, I dissent.

D. UNIFORMITY CLAUSES

ALLEGHENY PITTSBURGH COAL v. WEBSTER COUNTY
488 U.S. 336 (1989)

REHNQUIST, C. J.

The West Virginia Constitution guarantees to its citizens that, with certain exceptions, "taxation shall be equal and uniform throughout the State, and all property, both real and personal, shall be taxed in proportion to its value...." Art. X, § 1. The Webster County tax assessor valued petitioners' real property on the basis of its recent purchase price, but made only minor modifications in the assessments of land which had not been recently sold. This practice resulted in gross disparities in the assessed value of generally comparable property, and we hold that it denied petitioners the equal protection of the laws guaranteed to them by the Fourteenth Amendment.

Between 1975 and 1986, the tax assessor for Webster County, West Virginia, fixed yearly assessments for property within the county at 50% of appraised value. She fixed the appraised value at the declared consideration at which the property last sold. Some adjustments were made in the assessments of properties that had not been recently sold, although they amounted to, at most, 10% increases in 1976, 1981, and 1983 respectively.

In 1974, for example, Allegheny Pittsburgh Coal Company (Allegheny) purchased fee, surface, and mineral interests in certain properties for a stated price somewhat in excess of $24 million, and during the tax years 1976 through 1983 its property was assessed annually at half of this figure. In 1982 Allegheny sold the property to East Kentucky Energy Corp. (Kentucky Energy) for a figure of nearly $30 million, and the property thereafter was annually assessed at a valuation just below $15 million. Oneida Coal Company and Shamrock Coal Company participated in similar transactions in Webster County, and the property they purchased or sold was assessed in a similar manner.

Each year, petitioners pursued relief before the County Commission of Webster County sitting as a review board. They argued that the assessment policy of the Webster County assessor systematically resulted in appraisals for their property that were excessive compared to the appraised value of similar parcels that had not been recently conveyed. Each year the county commission affirmed the assessments, and each year petitioners appealed to the state Circuit Court. A group of these appeals from Allegheny and its successor in interest, Kentucky Energy, were consolidated by the West Virginia Circuit Court and finally decided in 1985. Another group of appeals from Shamrock and Oneida were consolidated and decided by the West Virginia Circuit Court early the next year.

The judge in both of these cases concluded that the system of real property assessment used by the Webster County assessor systematically and intentionally discriminated against petitioners in violation of the West Virginia Constitution and the Fourteenth Amendment's Equal Protection Clause. He ordered the county commission to reduce the assessments on petitioners' property to the levels recommended by the state tax commissioner in his valuation guidelines published for use by local assessors. Underlying the judge's conclusions were findings that petitioners' tax assessments over the years were dramatically in excess of those for comparable property in the county. He found that "the assessor did not compare the various features of the real estate to which the high assessment was applied with the various features of land assessed at a much lower rate." "The questioned assessments were not based upon the presence of economically minable or removable coal, oil, gas or harvestable timber in or upon petitioners' real estate, as compared to an absence of the same in or upon [neighboring] properties." Nor were they "based upon present use or immediately foreseeable economic development of petitioners' real estate." Rather, "[t]he sole basis of the assessment of petitioners' real estate was, according to the assessor, the consideration declared in petitioners' deeds."

This approach systematically produced dramatic differences in valuation between petitioners' recently transferred property and otherwise comparable surrounding land. For the years 1976 through 1982, Allegheny was assessed and taxed at approximately 35 times the rate applied to owners of comparable properties. After purchasing that land, Kentucky Energy was assessed and taxed at approximately 33 times the rate of similar parcels. From 1981 through 1985, the county assessed and taxed the Shamrock-Oneida property at roughly 8 to 20 times that of comparable neighboring coal tracts. These disparities existed notwithstanding the adjustments made to the assessments of land not recently conveyed. In the case of the property held by Allegheny and Kentucky Energy, the county's adjustment policy would have required more than 500 years to equalize the assessments.

On appeal, the Supreme Court of Appeals of West Virginia reversed. It found that the record did not support the trial court's ruling that the actions of the assessor and board of review constituted "intentional and systematic" discrimination. It held that "assessments based upon the price paid for the property in arm's length transactions are an appropriate measure of the 'true and actual value' of...property." That other properties might be undervalued relative to petitioners' did not require that petitioners' assessments be reduced: "Instead, they should seek to have the assessments of other taxpayers raised to market value." We granted certiorari to decide whether these Webster County tax assessments denied petitioners the equal protection of the law and, if so, whether petitioners could constitutionally be limited to the remedy of seeking to raise the assessments of others.

We agree with the import of the opinion of the Supreme Court of Appeals of West Virginia that petitioners have no constitutional complaint simply because their property is assessed for real property tax purposes at a figure equal to 50% of the price paid for it at a recent arm's-length transaction. But their complaint is a comparative one: while their property is assessed at 50% of what is roughly its current value, neighboring comparable property which has not been recently sold is assessed at only a minor fraction of that figure. We do not understand the West Virginia Supreme Court of Appeals to have disputed this fact. We read its opinion as saying that even if there is a constitutional violation on these facts, the only remedy available to petitioners was an effort to have the assessments on the neighboring properties raised by an appropriate amount. We hold that the assessments on petitioners' property in this case violated the Equal Protection Clause of the Fourteenth Amendment to the United States Constitution, and that petitioners may not be remitted to the remedy specified by the Supreme Court of Appeals of West Virginia.

The county argues that its assessment scheme is rationally related to its purpose of assessing properties at true current value: when available, it makes use of exceedingly accurate information about the market value of a property-the price at which it was recently purchased. As those data grow stale, it periodically adjusts the assessment based on some perception of the general change in area property values. We do not intend to cast doubt upon the theoretical basis of such a scheme. That two methods are used to assess property in the same class is, without more, of no constitutional moment. The Equal Protection Clause "applies only to taxation which in fact bears unequally on persons or property of the same class." The use of a general adjustment as a transitional substitute for an individual reappraisal violates no constitutional command. As long as general adjustments are accurate enough over a short period of time to equalize the differences in proportion between the assessments of a class of property holders, the Equal Protection Clause is satisfied. Just as that Clause tolerates occasional errors of state law or mistakes in judgment when valuing property for tax purposes, it does not require immediate general adjustment on the basis of the latest market developments. In each case, the constitutional requirement is the seasonable attainment of a rough equality in tax treatment of similarly situated property owners.

But the present action is not an example of transitional delay in adjustment of assessed value resulting in inequalities in assessments of comparable property. Petitioners' property has been assessed at roughly 8 to 35 times more than comparable neighboring property, and these discrepancies have continued for more than 10 years with little change. The county's adjustments to the assessments of property not recently sold are too small to seasonably dissipate the remaining disparity between these assessments and the assessments based on a recent purchase price.

The States, of course, have broad powers to impose and collect taxes. A State may divide different kinds of property into classes and assign to each class a different tax burden so long as those divisions and burdens are reasonable. It might, for example, decide to tax property held by corporations, including petitioners, at a different rate than property held by individuals. In each case, "[i]f the selection or classification is neither capricious nor arbitrary, and rests upon some reasonable consideration of difference or policy, there is no denial of the equal protection of the law."

But West Virginia has not drawn such a distinction. Its Constitution and laws provide that all property of the kind held by petitioners shall be taxed at a rate uniform throughout the State according to its estimated market value. There is no suggestion in the opinion of the Supreme Court of Appeals of West Virginia, or from any other authoritative source, that the State may have adopted a different system in practice from that specified by statute; we have held that such a system may be valid so long as the implicit policy is applied even-handedly to all similarly situated property within the State. We are not advised of any West Virginia statute or practice which authorizes individual counties of the State to fashion their own substantive assessment policies independently of state statute. The Webster County assessor has, apparently on her own initiative, applied the tax laws of West Virginia in the manner heretofore described, with the resulting disparity in assessed value of similar property. Indeed, her practice seems contrary to that of the guide published by the West Virginia Tax Commission as an aid to local assessors in the assessment of real property.

"[I]ntentional systematic undervaluation by state officials of other taxable property in the same class contravenes the constitutional right of one taxed upon the full value of his property." "The equal protection clause ... protects the individual from state action which selects him out for discriminatory treatment by subjecting him to taxes not imposed on others of the same class." We have no doubt that petitioners have suffered from such "intentional systematic undervaluation by state officials" of comparable property in Webster County. Viewed in isolation, the assessments for petitioners' property may fully comply with West Virginia law. But the fairness of one's allocable share of the total property tax burden can only be meaningfully evaluated by comparison with the share of others similarly situated relative to their property holdings. The relative undervaluation of comparable property in Webster County over time therefore denies petitioners the equal protection of the law.

NORDLINGER v. HAHN
505 U.S. 1 (1992)

BLACKMUN, J.

In 1978, California voters staged what has been described as a property tax revolt by approving a statewide ballot initiative known as Proposition 13. The adoption of Proposition 13 served to amend the

California Constitution to impose strict limits on the rate at which real property is taxed and on the rate at which real property assessments are increased from year to year. In this litigation, we consider a challenge under the Equal Protection Clause of the Fourteenth Amendment to the manner in which real property now is assessed under the California Constitution.

Proposition 13 followed many years of rapidly rising real property taxes in California. From fiscal years 1967-1968 to 1971-1972, revenues from these taxes increased on an average of 11.5% per year. In response, the California Legislature enacted several property tax relief measures, including a cap on tax rates in 1972. The boom in the State's real estate market persevered, however, and the median price of an existing home doubled from $31,530 in 1973 to $62,430 in 1977. As a result, tax levies continued to rise because of sharply increasing assessment values. Some homeowners saw their tax bills double or triple during this period, well outpacing any growth in their income and ability to pay.

By 1978, property tax relief had emerged as a major political issue in California. In only one month's time, tax relief advocates collected over 1.2 million signatures to qualify Proposition 13 for the June 1978 ballot. On election day, Proposition 13 received a favorable vote of 64.8% and carried 55 of the State's 58 counties. California thus had a novel constitutional amendment that led to a property tax cut of approximately $7 billion in the first year. Senate Commission Report 28. A California homeowner with a $50,000 home enjoyed an immediate reduction of about $750 per year in property taxes.

As enacted by Proposition 13, Article XIIIA of the California Constitution caps real property taxes at 1% of a property's "full cash value." § 1(a). "Full cash value" is defined as the assessed valuation as of the 1975-1976 tax year or, "thereafter, the appraised value of real property when purchased, newly constructed, or a change in ownership has occurred after the 1975 assessment." § 2(a). The assessment "may reflect from year to year the inflationary rate not to exceed 2 percent for any given year." § 2(b).

Article XIIIA also contains several exemptions from this reassessment provision. One exemption authorizes the legislature to allow homeowners over the age of 55 who sell their principal residences to carry their previous base-year assessments with them to replacement residences of equal or lesser value. § 2(a). A second exemption applies to transfers of a principal residence (and up to $1 million of other real property) between parents and children. § 2(h).

In short, Article XIIIA combines a 1% ceiling on the property tax rate with a 2% cap on annual increases in assessed valuations. The assessment limitation, however, is subject to the exception that new construction or a change of ownership triggers a reassessment up to current appraised value. Thus, the assessment provisions of Article XIIIA essentially embody an "acquisition value" system of taxation rather than the more commonplace "current value" taxation. Real property is assessed at values related to the value of the property at the time it is acquired by the taxpayer rather than to the value it has in the current real estate market.

Over time, this acquisition-value system has created dramatic disparities in the taxes paid by persons owning similar pieces of property. Property values in California have inflated far in excess of the allowed 2% cap on increases in assessments for property that is not newly constructed or that has not changed hands. As a result, longer term property owners pay lower property taxes reflecting historic property values, while newer owners pay higher property taxes reflecting more recent values. For that reason, Proposition 13 has been labeled by some as a "welcome stranger" system-the newcomer to an established community is "welcome" in anticipation that he will contribute a larger percentage of support for local government than his settled neighbor who owns a comparable home. Indeed, in dollar terms, the differences in tax burdens are staggering. By 1989, the 44% of California homeowners who have owned their homes since enactment of Proposition 13 in 1978 shouldered only 25% of the more than $4 billion in residential property taxes paid by homeowners statewide. If property values continue to rise more than the annual 2% inflationary cap, this disparity will continue to grow.

According to her amended complaint, petitioner Stephanie Nordlinger in November 1988 purchased a house in the Baldwin Hills neighborhood of Los Angeles County for $170,000. The prior owners bought the home just two years before for $121,500. Before her purchase, petitioner had lived in a rented apartment in Los Angeles and had not owned any real property in California.

In early 1989, petitioner received a notice from the Los Angeles County Tax Assessor, who is a respondent here, informing her that her home had been reassessed upward to $170,100 on account of its change in ownership. She learned that the reassessment resulted in a property tax increase of $453.60, up 36% to $1,701, for the 1988-1989 fiscal year.

Petitioner later discovered she was paying about five times more in taxes than some of her neighbors who owned comparable homes since 1975 within the same residential development. For example, one block away, a house of identical size on a lot slightly larger than petitioner's was subject to a general tax levy of only $358.20 (based on an assessed valuation of $35,820, which reflected the home's value in 1975 plus the up-to-2% per year inflation factor). According to petitioner, her total property taxes over the first 10 years in her home will approach $19,000, while any neighbor who bought a comparable home in 1975 stands to pay just $4,100. The general tax levied against her modest home is only a few dollars short of that paid by a pre-1976 owner of a $2.1 million Malibu beachfront home.

After exhausting administrative remedies, petitioner brought suit against respondents in Los Angeles County Superior Court. She sought a tax refund and a declaration that her tax was unconstitutional. In her amended complaint, she alleged: "Article XIIIA has created an arbitrary system which assigns disparate real property tax burdens on owners of generally comparable and similarly situated properties without regard to the use of the real property taxed, the burden the property places on government, the actual value of the property or the financial capability of the property owner." Respondents demurred. By minute order, the Superior Court sustained the demurrer and dismissed the complaint without leave to amend.

The California Court of Appeal affirmed. It noted that the Supreme Court of California already had rejected a constitutional challenge to the disparities in taxation resulting from Article XIIIA. Characterizing Article XIIIA as an "acquisition value" system, the Court of Appeal found it survived equal protection review, because it was supported by at least two rational bases: First, it prevented property taxes from reflecting unduly inflated and unforeseen current values, and, second, it allowed property owners to estimate future liability with substantial certainty.

The Court of Appeal also concluded that this Court's more recent decision in *Allegheny Pittsburgh Coal Co. v. County Comm'n of Webster Cty.*, 488 U.S. 336 (1989), did not warrant a different result. At issue in *Allegheny Pittsburgh* was the practice of a West Virginia county tax assessor of assessing recently purchased property on the basis of its purchase price, while making only minor modifications in the assessments of property that had not recently been sold. Properties that had been sold recently were reassessed and taxed at values between 8 and 35 times that of properties that had not been sold. This Court determined that the unequal assessment practice violated the Equal Protection Clause.

The Court of Appeal distinguished *Allegheny Pittsburgh* on the grounds that "California has opted for an assessment method based on each individual owner's acquisition cost," while, "[i]n marked contrast, the West Virginia Constitution requires property to be taxed at a uniform rate statewide according to its estimated current market value." Thus, the Court of Appeal found: "*Allegheny* does not prohibit the states from adopting an acquisition value assessment method. That decision merely prohibits the arbitrary enforcement of a current value assessment method."

The Supreme Court of California denied review. We granted certiorari.

The Equal Protection Clause of the Fourteenth Amendment, § 1, commands that no State shall "deny to any person within its jurisdiction the equal protection of the laws." Of course, most laws differentiate in some fashion between classes of persons. The Equal Protection Clause does not forbid classifications. It simply keeps governmental decisionmakers from treating differently persons who are in all relevant respects alike.

As a general rule, "legislatures are presumed to have acted within their constitutional power despite the fact that, in practice, their laws result in some inequality." Accordingly, this Court's cases are clear that, unless a classification warrants some form of heightened review because it jeopardizes exercise of a fundamental right or categorizes on the basis of an inherently suspect characteristic, the Equal Protection Clause requires only that the classification rationally further a legitimate state interest.

The appropriate standard of review is whether the difference in treatment between newer and older owners rationally furthers a legitimate state interest. In general, the Equal Protection Clause is satisfied so long as there is a plausible policy reason for the classification, the legislative facts on which the classification is apparently based rationally may have been considered to be true by the governmental decisionmaker, and the relationship of the classification to its goal is not so attenuated as to render the distinction arbitrary or irrational. This standard is especially deferential in the context of classifications made by complex tax laws. "[I]n structuring internal taxation schemes 'the States have large leeway in making classifications and drawing lines which in their judgment produce reasonable systems of taxation.'"

As between newer and older owners, Article XIIIA does not discriminate with respect to either the tax rate or the annual rate of adjustment in assessments. Newer and older owners alike benefit in both the short and long run from the protections of a 1% tax rate ceiling and no more than a 2% increase in assessment value per year. New owners and old owners are treated differently with respect to one factor only-the basis on which their property is initially assessed. Petitioner's true complaint is that the State has denied her-a new owner-the benefit of the same assessment value that her neighbors-older owners-enjoy.

We have no difficulty in ascertaining at least two rational or reasonable considerations of difference or policy that justify denying petitioner the benefits of her neighbors' lower assessments. First, the State has a legitimate interest in local neighborhood preservation, continuity, and stability. The State therefore legitimately can decide to structure its tax system to discourage rapid turnover in ownership of homes and businesses, for example, in order to inhibit displacement of lower income families by the forces of gentrification or of established, "mom-and-pop" businesses by newer chain operations. By permitting older owners to pay progressively less in taxes than new owners of comparable property, the Article XIIIA assessment scheme rationally furthers this interest.

Second, the State legitimately can conclude that a new owner at the time of acquiring his property does not have the same reliance interest warranting protection against higher taxes as does an existing owner. The State may deny a new owner at the point of purchase the right to "lock in" to the same assessed value as is enjoyed by an existing owner of comparable property, because an existing owner rationally may be thought to have vested expectations in his property or home that are more deserving of protection than the anticipatory expectations of a new owner at the point of purchase. A new owner has full information about the scope of future tax liability before acquiring the property, and if he thinks the future tax burden is too demanding, he can decide not to complete the purchase at all. By contrast, the existing owner, already saddled with his purchase, does not have the option of deciding not to buy his home if taxes become prohibitively high. To meet his tax obligations, he might be forced to sell his home or to divert his income away from the purchase of food, clothing, and other necessities. In short, the State may decide that it is worse to have owned and lost, than never to have owned at all.

Petitioner argues that Article XIIIA cannot be distinguished from the tax assessment practice found to violate the Equal Protection Clause in *Allegheny Pittsburgh*. Like Article XIIIA, the practice at issue in *Allegheny Pittsburgh* resulted in dramatic disparities in taxation of properties of comparable value. But an obvious and critical factual difference between this case and *Allegheny Pittsburgh* is the absence of any indication in *Allegheny Pittsburgh* that the policies underlying an acquisition-value taxation scheme could conceivably have been the purpose for the Webster County tax assessor's unequal assessment scheme. In the first place, Webster County argued that "its assessment scheme is rationally related to its purpose of assessing properties at true current value" Moreover, the West Virginia "Constitution and laws provide that all property of the kind held by petitioners shall be taxed at a rate uniform throughout the State according to its estimated market value," and the Court found "no suggestion" that "the State may have adopted a different system in practice from that specified by statute."

Even if acquisition-value policies had been asserted, the assertion would have been nonsensical given its inherent inconsistency with the county's principal argument that it was in fact trying to promote current-value taxation.

To be sure, the Equal Protection Clause does not demand for purposes of rational-basis review that a legislature or governing decisionmaker actually articulate at any time the purpose or rationale supporting its classification. Nevertheless, this Court's review does require that a purpose may conceivably or "may reasonably have been the purpose and policy" of the relevant governmental decisionmaker. *Allegheny Pittsburgh* was the rare case where the facts precluded any plausible inference that the reason for the unequal assessment practice was to achieve the benefits of an acquisition-value tax scheme. By contrast, Article XIIIA was enacted precisely to achieve the benefits of an acquisition-value system. *Allegheny Pittsburgh* is not controlling here.

Finally, petitioner contends that the unfairness of Article XIIIA is made worse by its exemptions from reassessment for two special classes of new owners: persons aged 55 and older, who exchange principal residences, and children who acquire property from their parents. This Court previously has declined to hold that narrow exemptions from a general scheme of taxation necessarily render the overall scheme invidiously discriminatory. For purposes of rational-basis review, the "latitude of discretion is notably wide in ... the granting of partial or total exemptions upon grounds of policy." The two exemptions at issue here rationally further legitimate purposes. The people of California reasonably could have concluded that older persons in general should not be discouraged from moving to a residence more suitable to their changing family size or income. Similarly, the people of California reasonably could have concluded that the interests of family and neighborhood continuity and stability are furthered by and warrant an exemption for transfers between parents and children. Petitioner has not demonstrated that no rational bases lie for either of these exemptions.

Petitioner and amici argue with some appeal that Article XIIIA frustrates the "American dream" of home ownership for many younger and poorer California families. They argue that Article XIIIA places startup businesses that depend on ownership of property at a severe disadvantage in competing with established businesses. They argue that Article XIIIA dampens demand for and construction of new housing and buildings. And they argue that Article XIIIA constricts local tax revenues at the expense of public education and vital services.

Time and again, however, this Court has made clear in the rational-basis context that the "Constitution presumes that, absent some reason to infer antipathy, even improvident decisions will eventually be rectified by the democratic process and that judicial intervention is generally unwarranted no matter how unwisely we may think a political branch has acted." Certainly, California's grand experiment appears to vest benefits in a broad, powerful, and entrenched segment of society, and, as the Court of Appeal surmised, ordinary democratic processes may be unlikely to prompt its reconsideration or repeal. Yet many wise and well-intentioned laws suffer from the same malady. Article XIIIA is not palpably arbitrary, and we must decline petitioner's request to upset the will of the people of California.

The judgment of the Court of Appeal is affirmed.

STEVENS, J., dissenting.

During the two past decades, California property owners have enjoyed extraordinary prosperity. As the State's population has mushroomed, so has the value of its real estate. Between 1976 and 1986 alone, the total assessed value of California property subject to property taxation increased tenfold. Simply put, those who invested in California real estate in the 1970's are among the most fortunate capitalists in the world.

Proposition 13 has provided these successful investors with a tremendous windfall and, in doing so, has created severe inequities in California's property tax scheme. These property owners (hereinafter Squires) are guaranteed that, so long as they retain their property and do not improve it, their taxes will not increase more than 2% in any given year. As a direct result of this windfall for the Squires, later purchasers must pay far more than their fair share of property taxes.

As a result of Proposition 13, the Squires, who own 44% of the owner-occupied residences, paid only 25% of the total taxes collected from homeowners in 1989. These disparities are aggravated by § 2 of Proposition 13, which exempts from reappraisal a property owner's home and up to $1 million of other real property when that property is transferred to a child of the owner. This exemption can be invoked repeatedly and indefinitely, allowing the Proposition 13 windfall to be passed from generation to generation. As the California Senate Commission on Property Tax Equity and Revenue observed:

> "The inequity is clear. One young family buys a new home and is assessed at full market value. Another young family inherits its home, but pays taxes based on their parents' date of acquisition even though both homes are of identical value. Not only does this constitutional provision offend a policy of equal tax treatment for taxpayers in similar situations, it appears to favor the housing needs of children with homeowner-parents over children with non-homeowner-parents. With the repeal of the state's gift and inheritance tax in 1982, the rationale for this exemption is negligible." Commission Report 9-10.

The commission was too generous. To my mind, the rationale for such disparity is not merely "negligible," it is nonexistent. Such a law establishes a privilege of a medieval character: Two families with equal needs and equal resources are treated differently solely because of their different heritage.

In my opinion, such disparate treatment of similarly situated taxpayers is arbitrary and unreasonable. Although the Court today recognizes these gross inequities, its analysis of the justification for those inequities consists largely of a restatement of the benefits that accrue to long-time property owners. That a law benefits those it benefits cannot be an adequate justification for severe inequalities such as those created by Proposition 13.

Nor can *Allegheny Pittsburgh* be distinguished because West Virginia law established a market-value assessment regime. Webster County's scheme was constitutionally invalid not because it was a departure from state law, but because it involved the relative "systematic undervaluation...[of] property in the same class" (as that class was defined by state law). Our decisions have established that the Equal Protection Clause is offended as much by the arbitrary delineation of classes of property (as in this case) as by the arbitrary treatment of properties within the same class (as in *Allegheny Pittsburgh*). Thus, if our unanimous holding in *Allegheny Pittsburgh* was sound-and I remain convinced that it was-it follows inexorably that Proposition 13, like Webster County's assessment scheme, violates the Equal Protection Clause. Indeed, in my opinion, statewide discrimination is far more invidious than a local aberration that creates a tax disparity.

In my opinion, Proposition 13 sweeps too broadly and operates too indiscriminately to "rationally further" the State's interest in neighborhood preservation. No doubt there are some early purchasers living on fixed or limited incomes who could not afford to pay higher taxes and still maintain their homes. California has enacted special legislation to respond to their plight. Those concerns cannot provide an adequate justification for Proposition 13. A statewide, across-the-board tax windfall for all property owners and their descendants is no more a "rational" means for protecting this small subgroup than a blanket tax exemption for all taxpayers named Smith would be a rational means to protect a particular taxpayer named Smith who demonstrated difficulty paying her tax bill.

In short, although I agree with the Court that "neighborhood preservation" is a legitimate state interest, I cannot agree that a tax windfall for all persons who purchased property before 1978 rationally furthers that interest. To my mind, Proposition 13 is too blunt a tool to accomplish such a specialized goal. The severe inequalities created by Proposition 13 cannot be justified by such an interest.

The second state interest identified by the Court is the "reliance interests" of the earlier purchasers. Here I find the Court's reasoning difficult to follow. Although the protection of reasonable reliance interests is a legitimate governmental purpose, this case does not implicate such interests. A reliance interest is created when an individual justifiably acts under the assumption that an existing legal condition will persist; thus reliance interests are most often implicated when the government provides some benefit and then acts to eliminate the benefit. In this case, those who purchased property before Proposition 13 was enacted received no assurances that assessments would only increase at a limited rate; indeed, to the contrary, many purchased property in the hope that property values (and assessments) would appreciate substantially and quickly. It cannot be said, therefore, that the earlier purchasers of property somehow have a reliance interest in limited tax increases.

Distilled to its essence, the Court seems to be saying that earlier purchasers can benefit under Proposition 13 because earlier purchasers benefit under Proposition 13. If, however, a law creates a disparity, the State's interest preserving that disparity cannot be a "legitimate state interest" justifying that inequity. As noted above, a statute's disparate treatment must be justified by a purpose distinct from the very effects created by that statute. Thus, I disagree with the Court that the severe inequities wrought by Proposition 13 can be justified by what the Court calls the "reliance interests" of those who benefit from that scheme.

As these decisions demonstrate, the selective provision of benefits based on the timing of one's membership in a class (whether that class be the class of residents or the class of property owners) is rarely a "legitimate state interest." Similarly situated neighbors have an equal right to share in the benefits of local government. It would obviously be unconstitutional to provide one with more or better fire or police protection than the other; it is just as plainly unconstitutional to require one to pay five times as much in property taxes as the other for the same government services. In my opinion, the severe inequalities created by Proposition 13 are arbitrary and unreasonable and do not rationally further a legitimate state interest.

Accordingly, I respectfully dissent.

BETTIGOLE v. ASSESSORS OF SPRINGFIELD
178 N.E.2d 10 (Mass 1961)

CUTTER, J.

These two bills in equity present questions about the validity of the proposed 1961 assessment of property taxes in Springfield. They have been argued together. The Bettigole case is brought by individual, fiduciary, and corporate owners of multi-family dwellings, commercial real estate, and other property in Springfield which it is alleged 'will be in 1961 and subsequent years...deliberately...over-valued and over-assessed both in relation to other classes of taxable real estate for which assessed valuations have been established at lower percentages of fair cash value and in relation to the general average or ratio of valuations to fair cash value of taxable real estate in' Springfield. It is alleged that the board of assessors (the board) has for many years established assessed valuations for different classes of real estate in the city at widely differing percentages of the full fair cash value of such real estate and plans to do so for 1961. The bill seeks a declaration as to the 'lawfulness under the Constitution and laws of [t]he Commonwealth of the policy and practice' just described, and also injunctive relief (a) against continuance of this assessment practice by the assessors, and (b) against action to send out bills for, and to collect, the taxes so assessed.

By August 1, 1961, the board "had determined the sound value [a term used by the board as equivalent to fair cash value] of each parcel of taxable real estate in the [c]ity as of January 1, 1961, and the fair cash value of the personal property owned by each [taxable] person." The board had also classified all parcels of real estate into six categories, set out below, and a majority had voted on September 8 and 15, 1961, "to establish...[1961] assessed valuations of all taxable property in the [c]ity by applying the following percentages to the sound value determined by the...[board] for the following classes of property," respectively, viz., (1) single family residences-50%; (2) two family residences-60%; (3) three family residences-65%; (4) four or more family residences-70%; (5) property of public utilities and commercial and industrial properties-85%; (6) farms, vacant land, and other real estate-70%. Personal property subject to local taxation was to be assessed at 85% of the fair cash value thereof previously determined by the board.

"The [b]oard determined assessed valuations for 1960 in substantially the same manner as it intends to use in 1961 and 1962 and the board's practice of applying varying percentages of sound or fair cash value of different classes of property in arriving at assessed valuations was deliberate and intentional." A table, made a part of each statement of agreed facts...shows, for example, that the fair cash (sound) value of 22,005 parcels of single family residence property was $266,285,568, but that these parcels were assessed at an aggregate of $133,142,792 for only 50% of their fair cash (sound) value. The table indicates that, if all taxable property in the city had been assessed at 100% of fair cash value, these 22,005 parcels would have been subjected to aggregate taxes of $11,223,937 at a tax rate of $42.15 per $1,000 of valuation, whereas they were in fact taxed only $8,601,024 under a tax rate of $64.60. The table also shows that 2,521 parcels of public utility, commercial and industrial properties, assessed at 85% of fair cash value, were in fact taxed $9,602,217, whereas, if all taxable property in the city had been assessed at 100% of fair cash value, the aggregate tax on these 2,521 parcels would have been only $7,370,792. This is the most striking comparison revealed by Annex A, and (although this is not done in the statements of agreed facts) its effect can be shown in tabular form (by a simple mathematical calculation from Annex A) as follows:

	(A) Approximate percentage of total fair cash value of all taxable property	(B) Approximate percentage of all property taxes assessed on non-uniform basis
22,005 single family residence parcels	43%	33%
2,521 public utility, commercial and industrial parcels	28%	37%

It thus appears that 43% of the total fair cash value of taxable property in Springfield is paying only 33% of the property taxes, whereas 28% of the total is paying 37% of the property taxes. The somewhat lesser disparity, produced by the board's assessment method, among various other classes of property is equally susceptible of mathematical demonstration.

The plaintiffs are owners of properties within the classes of four and more family residences, commercial and industrial properties, and farms, vacant land and other real estate, listed in detail in annexes to the bills. Because "they own such property [each of the plaintiffs will] pay substantially more in taxes for 1961 if the [board's assessing] practice described [earlier in this opinion] is followed than if the assessed valuations of all taxable property in Springfield were the fair cash value of such property."

The plaintiffs "insist that, in accordance with the [C]onstitution and laws of the Commonwealth, the assessed valuations of all taxable property in…Springfield should be the fair cash value of such property." A majority of the board insists "upon following…[the above described] practice…and have refused to establish assessed valuations…at the fair cash value of…property."

These cases continue property tax controversies which have existed in Springfield in recent years. The bills present for consideration, upon very complete, precise statements of agreed facts, the question whether the whole 1961 property tax assessment scheme violates the Constitution of the Commonwealth (Part II, c. 1, § 1, art. 4) which empowers the General Court "to impose and levy proportional and reasonable assessments, rates, and taxes, upon all the inhabitants of, and persons resident, and estates lying, within the said commonwealth...." (emphasis supplied). See also art. 10 of the Declaration of Rights, which reads, "Each individual...has a right to be protected...in the enjoyment of his life, liberty and property, according to standing laws. He is obliged, consequently, to contribute his share to the expense of this protection..." (emphasis supplied). It is well settled that the words "his share" in art. 10 of the Declaration of Rights 'forbid the imposition upon one taxpayer of a burden relatively greater or relatively less than that imposed upon other taxpayers.' Similarly, "the expression 'proportional and reasonable' [in Part II, c. 1, § 1, art. 4] forbids the imposition of taxes upon one class of persons or property at a different rate from that which is applied to other classes." This interpretation of these constitutional provisions has been unvarying "from the early days of the Commonwealth to the present time." In *Cheshire v. County Commrs. of Berkshire*, 118 Mass. 386, 389, this court said that the constitutional provision for "proportional and reasonable" taxes "forbids their imposition upon one class of persons or property at a different rate from that which is applied to other classes, whether that discrimination is effected directly in the assessment or indirectly through arbitrary and unequal methods of valuation." The court there recognized that "[p]ractically it is impossible to secure exact equality or proportion in the imposition of taxes" but it pointed out that the statutory "aim [should] be towards that result, by approximation at least." The statements of agreed facts negate any suggestion of "equality or proportion" in the 1961 Springfield assessments, for it is established that disproportion, rising to a maximum of the difference between 50% and 85% of fair cash value, "was deliberate and intentional" and that personal property and one class of real estate was thus to be assessed 170% (85/50) of the level of assessment of another class of real estate. This is not even equality by "approximation," which, at the least, requires attempted equality of assessment in absolute good faith and to the best of the abilities of the public officers charged with making valuations.

Upon the basis of the foregoing authorities, there can be no doubt that the board's proposed 1961 assessment scheme is a complete, widespread, and fundamental failure to comply with either the constitutional or the statutory requirements for proportional assessment.

TOPEKA CEMETARY ASSOCIATION v. SCHNELLBACHER
542 P.2d 278 (Kan. 1975)

PRAGER, J.

This is an action by a taxpayer attacking a statutory tax exemption on the ground that it is discriminatory and hence in violation of the Kansas Constitution. The facts in the case have been stipulated and essentially are as follows: The Topeka Cemetery Association, plaintiff-appellee, is a Kansas cemetery corporation created pursuant to statute. The cemetery association owns property in Topeka which has been platted and dedicated exclusively as a cemetery. The Topeka Cemetery Association has been in existence for many years. The great majority of the lots have been sold to provide individual or family burial lots. A number of the lots have not been sold and are owned by the corporation and available for future sale. The unsold cemetery lots, driveways, lawns, and areas used for maintenance of the cemetery are dedicated to burial purposes and under the association's charter cannot be used for any other purpose.

Prior to 1969 the legislature by statute exempted from taxation all lands used exclusively as graveyards. (K.S.A.1968 Supp. 79-201 Second.) In 1969 the legislature by Chapter 429, Laws of 1969, amended 79-201 Second to provide as follows:

> 79-201.... That the property described in this section, to the extent herein limited, shall be exempt from taxation:
>
>> Second. All lots or tracts of land located within cemeteries, which have been purchased by individual owners and are used or to be used exclusively as a grave site or sites by said individual owner or the family thereof.

Section 3 of Chapter 429 repealed K.S.A.1968 Supp. 79-201 along with other statutes. The effect of the statute was to classify cemetery lands into two groups for tax purposes. Lots or tracts of land owned by individual owners for present or future use as grave sites are declared exempt from ad valorem taxation. Lots or tracts of land owned by a cemetery corporation are not exempt from ad valorem taxation and are required to be assessed and taxed by state taxing officials.

The sole issue presented on this appeal is one of law and simply stated is as follows: Is K.S.A. 79-201 Second unconstitutional as a violation of Article 11, Section 1, of the Kansas Constitution? At the time the case was tried Article 11, Section 1, provided as follows:

> System of taxation; classification; exemption. The legislature shall provide for a uniform and equal rate of assessment and taxation, except that mineral products, money, mortgages, notes and other evidence of debts may be classified and taxed uniformly as to class as the legislature shall provide. All property used exclusively for state, county, municipal, literary, educational, scientific,

religious, benevolent and charitable purposes, and all household goods and personal effects not used for the production of income, shall be exempted from taxation.

This section of the constitution was amended in 1974 but such amendment did not affect the issue presented to the court in this case. The exceptions mentioned in the section are not applicable in the present case and will not be discussed. Specifically, the Topeka Cemetery Association contends the K.S.A. 79-201 Second violates that portion of Article 11, Section 1, which requires the legislature to provide for a uniform and equal rate of assessment and taxation.

This constitutional provision has been before this court for interpretation on many occasions since the provision was adopted as a part of the original constitution of Kansas. It would be helpful to consider some of the general principles of law which this court has followed in applying the constitutional provision to specific taxing statutes enacted by various state legislatures down through the years. As a general proposition all property is subject to taxation except property which is specifically exempted either by the constitution or by statute. Constitutional and statutory provisions exempting property from taxation are to be strictly construed and the burden of establishing exemption from taxation is upon the one claiming it. The constitutional exemptions provided for in Article 11, Section 1, of the Kansas Constitution extend to all property used exclusively for state, county, municipal, literary, educational, scientific, religious, benevolent and charitable purposes and all household goods and personal effects not used for the production of income. We have held that the constitutional exemptions depend solely upon the exclusive use made of the property and not upon the ownership or the character, charitable or otherwise, of the owner.

The legislature has the authority to provide that property other than that named in the constitution may be exempt from taxation, but this exemption must have a public purpose and be designed to promote the public welfare. Some statutory exemptions have been based upon public ownership of property by the United States government. Without congressional action there is immunity from state and local taxation, implied from the United States Constitution itself, of all properties, functions and instrumentalities of the federal government. Statutory exemptions also have been created to apply to property owned by the state or one of its political subdivisions. In *City of Harper v. Fink*, supra, this court stated that under statutes granting tax exemptions to city property, ownership rather than exclusive use is the test of exemption from taxation. It is obvious that statutory exemptions based upon Public ownership of property may have a rational basis and that a public purpose may be served thereby.

Throughout our judicial history a different test has been applied in situations where public property is not involved and where the statutory tax exemption pertains to property owned by private individuals or corporations. We have consistently held that where public property is not involved, a tax exemption must be based upon the use of the property and not on the basis of ownership alone. The reason for the rule is that a classification of private property for tax purposes based solely upon ownership unlawfully discriminates against one citizen in favor of another and therefore is a denial of equal protection of the law. In Associated Rly. Equipment Owners v. Wilson, 167 Kan. 608, 208 P.2d 604, we stated that the equal protection clause of the federal constitution and state constitutional provisions pertaining to equality and uniformity of taxation are substantially similar and that, in general, what violates one will contravene the other and vice versa. In 1887 it was held in M. & M. Rly. Co. v. Champlin, Treas., 37 Kan. 682, 16 P. 222 that a distinction made in the taxation of property in a township belonging to residents and nonresidents was unconstitutional and void and in violation of Article 11, Section 1, of the Kansas Constitution.

The term 'equality' and 'uniformity' were explained in Wheeler v. Weightman, 96 Kan. 50, 149 P. 977, where the court stated as follows:

> The essentials are that each man in city, county, and state is interested in maintaining the state and local governments. The protection which they afford and the duty to maintain them are reciprocal. The burden of supporting them should be borne equally by all, and this equality consists in each one contributing in proportion to the amount of his property. To this end all property in the state must be listed and valued for the purpose of taxation; the rate of assessment and taxation to be uniform and equal throughout the jurisdiction levying the tax. The imposition of taxes upon selected classes of property to the exclusion of others and the exemption of selected classes to the exclusion of others, constitute invidious discriminations which destroy uniformity.

In *Voran v. Wright*, 129 Kan. 1, 281 P. 938, it is declared that the classification permitted by Section 1 of Article 11 of the Kansas Constitution applies to property and not to owners thereof. At page 606 of the opinion on rehearing it is stated: "...A classification as to owners is not now permissible...."

The rule of uniformity may be violated as effectively by arbitrary exemptions from taxation as by arbitrary impositions. In *Mount Hope Cemetery Co. v. Pleasant*, 139 Kan. 417, 32 P.2d 500, this court has before it a factual situation and a statute quite similar to that presented in this case. In that action the Mount Hope Cemetery Co. brought an original proceeding in mandamus in the supreme court to require the state tax commission to order stricken from the tax rolls of Shawnee county certain land lying near Topeka which had been conveyed to the cemetery in trust for cemetery purposes. Prior to 1931 it was provided by statute that all lands used exclusively as graveyards shall be exempt from taxation. In 1931 the legislature enacted R.S.1933 Supp. 17-1314 which reads:

> All lands held and owned by cemetery corporations or associations shall be subject to assessment and taxation: Provided, That where lands are held or owned by municipal corporations for cemetery purposes, such lands shall be exempt from taxation: And provided further, Where such lands are divided or platted in burial lots and the same have been sold to a person for burial purposes, such lot or lots shall be exempt from assessment and taxation, and also shall not be subject to attachment or execution.

This court held that that portion of the statute of 1931 which sought to subject plaintiff's public cemetery to taxation on the ground of corporation ownership of the fee title to the property violated those provisions of the state and federal constitutions which guarantee to all persons, corporate and individual, within the jurisdiction of the state the equal protection of the law, and which forbid unjust discrimination among individuals and corporations in respect to taxation of their properties. In the later case of *Mount Hope Cemetery Co. v. City of Topeka*, 190 Kan. 702, 378 P.2d 30, the earlier case of *Mount Hope Cemetery Co. v. Pleasant*, supra, is cited and it is stated in syllabus 3 that ownership is not the test of whether property is liable to taxation but rather the uses to which property is devoted may exempt it therefrom.

When we turn to the undisputed facts and the statute under consideration in this case and apply the principles of law discussed above, we are compelled to conclude that the statutory classification contained in K.S.A. 79-201 Second is discriminatory and unconstitutional as a violation of Article 11, Section 1, of the Kansas Constitution. All lots and tracts of land contained within the boundaries of a cemetery platted by a cemetery corporation are dedicated exclusively for burial purposes and cannot be used for any other purpose. Since all lands in the cemetery are dedicated exclusively for burial purposes, we find no rational basis for treating differently land owned by individuals and that owned by the corporation, except ownership, which is not a permissible basis for classification. In our judgment the rationale of *Mount Hope Cemetery Co. v. Pleasant*, supra, is controlling in this case.

Since we have determined that the 1969 amendment to 79-201 Second is unconstitutional, we must next determine whether or not the statutory exemption which prior law granted all lands used exclusively as graveyards stands repealed by the repealing clause contained in Section 3 of Chapter 429, Laws of 1969. In this regard the general rule is stated in

City of Kansas City v. Robb, 164 Kan. 577, 190 P.2d 398, to be as follows:

> Where a legislative act expressly repealing an existing statute, and providing a substitute therefor, is invalid, the repealing clause is also invalid unless it appears that the legislature would have passed the repealing clause even if it had not provided a substitute for the statute repealed.

In applying this rule we must determine whether the legislature would have passed the repealing clause even if it had not provided a substitute for the act repealed. We have concluded that that question must be answered in the negative. We think it highly questionable that the legislature would have completely wiped out the statutory exemption heretofore provided for land used exclusively as graveyards. *Mount Hope Cemetery Co. v. Pleasant*, supra, contains a history of the statutory exemption for burial grounds in this state. In the opinion Mr. Justice Dawson points out that from the formation of the state, burial grounds have been exempted from taxation. The underlying philosophy for the statutory exemption for burial grounds is that provision for the decent interment of the dead and for the seemly and dignified maintenance of property set apart for its accomplishment is a public purpose. We have concluded that it is highly unlikely that the legislature would have totally repealed the tax exemption for burial grounds contained in K.S.A.1968 Supp. 79-201 Second without providing a substitute. Hence we hold that the attempted repeal of K.S.A. 1968 Supp. 79-201 Second by Section 3, Chapter 429, Laws of 1969, must fall along with the attempted amendment of said section by Section 1 of Chapter 429. We wish to make it clear that our decision here does not affect in any way other provisions of Chapter 429 which have to do with statutory tax exemptions not involved in this case. We therefore hold that the statutory exemption for lands used exclusively as graveyards as provided by K.S.A.1968 Supp. 79-201 Second as it existed prior to the attempted amendment in 1969 was still in full force and effect for the tax years involved in this case and that the lots and tracts of land owned by Topeka Cemetery Association in its platted cemetery are exempted from ad valorem taxation.

LEONARD v. THORNBURGH
489 A.2d 1349 (Pa. 1985)

FLAHERTY, J.

This is an appeal from an order of the Commonwealth Court which declared unconstitutional Section 359(b) of the Tax Reform Code of 1971, known as the Philadelphia Non-Resident Wage Tax Cap, and Philadelphia

Ordinance No. 1716. The Non-Resident Wage Tax Cap limits to 4 5/16% the rate at which non-residents can be taxed by the City of Philadelphia upon income earned in Philadelphia. Ordinance No. 1716, effective July 1, 1983, amended the City's Wage and Net Profits Tax so as to levy the tax at the rates of 4 5/16% upon non-residents, and 4 96/100% upon residents. Commonwealth Court, in declaring these provisions unconstitutional, reasoned that the differing tax rates applicable to residents and non-residents of the City of Philadelphia violated the Uniformity Clause of the Pennsylvania Constitution, Article VIII, Section I, which provides:

> All taxes shall be uniform, upon the same class of subjects, within the territorial limits of the authority levying the tax, and shall be levied and collected under general laws.

The appellant, Secretary of Revenue James I. Scheiner, contends that the tax provisions in question comport with constitutional requirements, under the Uniformity Clause of the Pennsylvania Constitution, supra, as well as under the equal protection clause of the Fourteenth Amendment. The appellee, Kathleen Leonard, a resident of Philadelphia who is aggrieved by having been assessed higher wage taxes than would have been payable had she not been a resident of Philadelphia, argues that the Uniformity Clause, rather than the Fourteenth Amendment, is the relevant constitutional standard, and that under that standard the tax provisions are invalid. It is well established, however, that in matters of taxation both constitutional standards are relevant, and that allegations of violations of the equal protection clause, and of the Uniformity Clause, are to be analyzed in the same manner.

The principles which govern the analysis of claims of non-uniform taxation are well established. The legislature possesses wide discretion in matters of taxation. The burden is upon the taxpayer to demonstrate that a classification, made for purposes of taxation, is unreasonable. *Amidon v. Kane,* 279 A.2d 53, 60 (1971) ("[T]he challengers of the constitutionality of state or local taxation bear a heavy burden...."). Indeed, tax legislation will not be declared unconstitutional unless it *"clearly, palpably,* and *plainly* violates the Constitution."

Under the equal protection clause, and under the Uniformity Clause, absolute equality and perfect uniformity in taxation are not required. In cases where the validity of a classification for tax purposes is challenged, the test is whether the classification is based upon some legitimate distinction between the classes that provides a non-arbitrary and "reasonable and just" basis for the difference in treatment. Stated alternatively, the focus of judicial review is upon whether there can be discerned "some concrete justification" for treating the relevant group of taxpayers as members of distinguishable classes subject to different tax burdens. When there exists no legitimate distinction between the classes, and, thus, the tax scheme imposes substantially unequal tax burdens upon persons otherwise similarly situated, the tax is unconstitutional.

Applying these principles to the instant case, we find that the tax scheme in question meets constitutional requirements, for there exists the requisite basis for treating residents and non-residents of Philadelphia as separate classes of wage earners subject to different tax rates. The legitimate distinction between those classes rests not upon the superficial fact that one class resides in Philadelphia while the other resides elsewhere, but rather, at a deeper level of analysis, upon significant differences between the two classes of wage earners that provide reasonable and concrete justifications for their being taxed at different rates.

This is not a case, therefore, where mere residence, uncorrelated with concrete justifications related to the situs of residence, has been relied upon by the taxing authority as an asserted basis for differential tax treatment. In the past, it has been held that residence alone is an insufficient basis upon which to sustain differential tax treatment, absent further justifications which correlate with the status of residency. See *Columbia Gas Corp. v. Commonwealth,* 360 A.2d at 595-597 (disparate rates of tax on foreign and domestic corporations invalid where Commonwealth offered no justification for taxing foreign corporations more heavily than domestic ones); *Danyluk v. Johnstown,* 178 A.2d 609 (1962) (city's capitation tax on non-residents held unauthorized and invalid, with dictum indicating that an occupation tax levied only against non-residents would violate constitutional uniformity standards); *Carl v. Southern Columbia Area School District,* 400 A.2d 650 (1979) (school district's tax invalid where, without reasonable justification, taxpayers residing in different counties were charged different amounts for precisely the same educational services).

In the instant case, it may clearly be presumed that non-resident wage earners utilize services provided by the City of Philadelphia to a lesser extent than do residents. Rather than benefit from twenty-four hour and seven day per week availability of such services, non-resident wage earners avail themselves of such services primarily during an eight hour workday on a five day per week basis. Though the exact proportions of the services used by the two classes are not quantifiable, it is clear that differences in the levels of service utilization must necessarily exist. This is true of city-provided services offered to residents and non-residents alike, such as police, fire, sanitation, and other services. As to each of these, the residents' needs are essentially full-time, while the non-residents' needs are merely part-time. These services receive funding from the City of Philadelphia's General Fund, and it is into the General Fund that wage tax revenues are deposited. Further, there are certain services, funded by the General Fund, that are offered only to residents, such as public schools, mental health and retardation services, and child and family welfare services. In short, residents and non-residents are not similarly situated with respect to their needs for services provided by the City of Philadelphia.

An additional justification for differentiating the tax treatment of residents and non-residents is to be found in the extent of the political representation the two classes enjoy. The legislature, in capping the wage tax rate applicable to non-residents, afforded protection to persons who are subject to city wage taxes but who have no voice in the city council. In contrast, residents of the city have recourse through their own elected representatives, the members of city council, in the event that they believe their tax rates are excessive.

We conclude that valid reasons have been offered for imposing a higher tax rate on resident wage earners of the City of Philadelphia than is imposed upon non-resident wage earners. The wage tax scheme in question is, therefore, in compliance with constitutional requirements governing uniformity of taxation. Accordingly, the order of the Commonwealth Court, declaring the tax provisions in question unconstitutional, is reversed.

ALLEGRO SERVICES, LTD. v. METROPOLITAN PIER AND EXPOSITION AUTHORITY
665 N.E. 2d 1246 (Ill. 1996)

NICKELS, J.

This appeal represents our second encounter with the program of taxes imposed by defendant, the Metropolitan Pier and Exposition Authority (Authority), to finance the renovation and expansion of McCormick Place and related infrastructure improvements. In *Geja's Cafe v. Metropolitan Pier & Exposition Authority*, 606 N.E.2d 1212 (1992), this court upheld a retailers' occupation tax imposed by the Authority on certain food and beverage sales. In the instant case we consider the constitutionality of an airport departure tax imposed by the Authority on providers of ground transportation services from Chicago's O'Hare and Midway Airports. Plaintiffs include several suburban and out-of-state businesses which provide bus, van or limousine transportation from the airports, but which do not serve destinations within the City of Chicago. Plaintiffs brought this action in the circuit court of Cook County on behalf of themselves and all others similarly situated, challenging the constitutionality of the tax under the commerce clause and the equal protection clause of the United States Constitution (U.S. Const., art. I, § 8; amend. XIV) and the uniformity clause of the Illinois Constitution of 1970 (Ill. Const.1970, art. IX, § 2). The trial court entered judgment on the pleadings or summary judgment in the Authority's favor on each of the counts in plaintiffs' class action complaint.

In 1992, the General Assembly enacted the Metropolitan Pier and Exposition Authority Act (Act) to provide for a project to renovate and expand McCormick Place (the expansion project). The expansion project includes plans for the renovation of McCormick Place's existing facilities and the construction of a new exhibition hall with a concourse to the existing facilities. It is anticipated that the expanded and improved McCormick Place facilities will lead to a significant increase in tourism to Chicago, thereby boosting certain sectors of the local and regional economy.

To finance the expansion project, the Authority was granted power to issue bonds in an amount not to exceed $937 million. In turn, under section 13 of the Act the Authority is directed to levy a series of local taxes in order to repay the bonds. Section 13(f) provides that "[b]y ordinance the Authority shall...impose an occupation tax on all persons, other than a governmental agency, engaged in the business of providing ground transportation for hire to passengers in the metropolitan area...."

The Authority enacted an ordinance imposing the airport departure tax in accordance with section 13(f), and plaintiffs brought this lawsuit as a class action seeking, inter alia, a declaratory judgment that the airport departure tax is invalid. The trial court conditionally certified four classes of plaintiffs who provide airport transportation service exclusively to destinations outside the City of Chicago. Classes A and C consist of operators of taxicabs or limousines based in Illinois (Class A) or outside the State (Class C) that, from time to time, depart from the airports with passengers for hire, but are not licensed by the City of Chicago to operate within its city limits. Class E consists of all operators of buses or vans regulated by the Interstate Commerce Commission that provide scheduled service from the airports with no destinations within the City of Chicago. Class F consists of bus and van operators providing charter or other unscheduled passenger service from the airports to destinations outside the City of Chicago. Vehicle operators with vehicle licenses issued by the City of Chicago who pay the tax are not included in the plaintiff classes.

Plaintiffs' class action complaint, as amended, consists of 13 counts challenging the airport departure tax under a variety of theories. Several counts raise the theory that, as applied to the members of the plaintiff classes, the airport departure tax violates the constitutional guarantees of equal protection and uniformity in nonproperty taxation because only those vehicle operators serving destinations in Chicago stand to benefit economically from increased tourism related to the expansion and renovation of McCormick Place....

Plaintiffs first contend that the trial court erred in denying their summary judgment motion and granting the Authority's motion on those counts alleging that the airport departure tax violates the equal protection clause of the United States Constitution and the uniformity clause of the Illinois Constitution. The uniformity clause provides:

> In any law classifying the subjects or objects of non-property taxes or fees, the classes shall be reasonable and the subjects and objects within each class shall be taxed uniformly. Exemptions, deductions, credits, refunds and other allowances shall be reasonable. Ill. Const. 1970, art. IX, § 2.

The uniformity clause imposes more stringent limitations than the equal protection clause on the legislature's authority to classify the subjects and objects of taxation. *Geja's Cafe v. Metropolitan Pier & Exposition Authority*, 153 Ill.2d 239, 247, 606 N.E.2d 1212 (1992); *Searle Pharmaceuticals, Inc. v. Department of Revenue*, 117 Ill.2d 454, 467-68, 512 N.E.2d 1240 (1987). "If a tax is constitutional under the uniformity clause, it inherently fulfills the requirements of the equal protection clause." *Geja's Cafe*, 153 Ill.2d at 247. Accordingly, we need only consider the validity of the airport departure tax under the uniformity clause.

To survive scrutiny under the uniformity clause, a nonproperty tax classification must be based on a real and substantial difference between the people taxed and those not taxed, and the classification must bear some reasonable relationship to the object of the legislation or to public policy. The uniformity requirement, as traditionally understood, may be violated by classifications which are either "underinclusive" or "overinclusive." Although the uniformity clause imposes a more stringent standard than the equal protection clause, the scope of a court's inquiry under the uniformity clause remains relatively narrow. Statutes bear a presumption of constitutionality, and broad latitude is afforded to legislative classifications for taxing purposes. One challenging a nonproperty tax classification has the burden of showing that it is arbitrary or unreasonable, and if a state of facts can reasonably be conceived that would sustain the classification, it must be upheld.

In the case at bar, the common characteristic linking the vehicle operators in the plaintiff classes-and forming the basis of plaintiffs' uniformity clause challenge-is that although they provide ground transportation service departing from the airports, they do not transport airport passengers for hire into the City of Chicago. Some of the class members are prohibited by Chicago's ground transportation licensing ordinance from transporting passengers from the airports to destinations in Chicago. Under the ordinance, a Chicago vehicle license is required to provide transportation service wholly within the city. Other class members provide scheduled airport service along routes which do not include destinations in the City of Chicago. Plaintiffs maintain that in terms of the economic impact of the McCormick Place expansion project, there is a real and substantial difference between the vehicle operators in the plaintiff classes and their city-licensed counterparts, because only the operators of city-licensed vehicles enjoy the opportunity to transport passengers from the airports to McCormick Place or nearby downtown hotels. Plaintiffs contend that any positive economic impact from the expansion project for class members is too indirect to support taxing them in the same manner as those operators providing airport transportation to destinations in Chicago, who enjoy a direct benefit by virtue of an increased demand for transportation to McCormick Place and nearby hotels.

Plaintiffs rely on *Geja's Cafe*, where, as previously noted, this court upheld the food and beverage tax imposed by the Authority in connection with the McCormick Place expansion project. The tax applied to certain types of food and beverage sales within a geographic subdistrict in Chicago. One of the arguments raised by its opponents was that pursuant to the uniformity requirement, the tax should have been imposed on food and beverage sales throughout Cook County. This court rejected the argument, finding that "[t]he General Assembly could reasonably conclude that the direct beneficiaries [of the expansion project's economic impact] would be those within the taxing subdistrict, and plaintiffs have not produced anything to suggest that narrowing the taxed area in this fashion was unreasonable." Plaintiffs contend that, like the food and beverage tax in Geja's Cafe, the Authority's airport departure tax should also be limited to the subclass of vehicle operators who benefit most directly from the expansion project.

In response, the Authority notes that in *Geja's Cafe* this court merely held that it was permissible to limit the tax to the geographic subdistrict; the court did not hold or suggest that a more broadly applicable tax would necessarily be unconstitutional. The Authority's observation underscores a basic flaw in plaintiffs' analysis. Plaintiffs' argument rests largely on their understanding that a "real and substantial difference" between the vehicle operators in the plaintiff classes and those who transport passengers from the airports into Chicago would necessarily be fatal to a tax scheme imposing the same taxes on both groups of operators. While *Geja's Cafe* and other decisions under the uniformity clause hold that there must be a real and substantial difference between the people taxed and those not taxed, we are aware of no authority for a converse rule that there may be no real and substantial difference among those taxed. As this court observed in *Geja's Cafe*, "[t]he uniformity clause was not designed as a straitjacket for the General Assembly. Rather, the uniformity clause was designed to enforce minimum standards of reasonableness and fairness as between groups of taxpayers." Accordingly, the "real and substantial difference" standard merely represents the minimum level at which the differences among groups are of a sufficient magnitude to justify taxing the groups differently. However, just because the differences between groups reach this minimum level, it does not follow that identical tax treatment would necessarily be unreasonable.

To apply the real and substantial difference test in the manner plaintiffs propose would transform the uniformity requirement from a minimum standard of reasonableness and fairness to a precise formula for drawing tax lines. Under the analysis that plaintiffs advocate, the relative tax treatment of any two groups of potential taxpayers would be preordained by the existence or nonexistence of a real and substantial difference between the groups. Under such an analysis, the taxing body would be deprived of any range of options in the formulation of tax classifications. We reject such a rigid rule. Instead, we adhere to the view that the existence of a real and substantial difference between groups of taxpayers only establishes that differential taxation may be permissible, not that it is constitutionally essential.

Plaintiffs cite *Northwestern University v. City of Evanston*, 221 Ill.App.3d 893 (1991), in support of their understanding of the real and substantial difference requirement. Plaintiffs' reliance on that decision is misplaced. In *Northwestern*, the appellate court held that pursuant to the uniformity clause, a local hotel-motel tax could not constitutionally be applied to an educational facility simply because the facility included several floors of sleeping rooms primarily for use by students. As we read *Northwestern*, the ratio decidendi was that "[a] taxing body is...prohibited under the uniformity provisions of the Illinois Constitution from defining statutory terms contrary to their common meaning." We express no opinion on the quality of this reasoning. Suffice it to say that the decision has no application here.

We agree with plaintiffs that at some point the differences among taxpayers may be so profound that taxing them as a single class would violate the uniformity requirement. In our view, however, this limitation is embraced within the uniformity clause test's second and more general requirement that tax classifications must bear some reasonable relationship to the object of the legislation or to public policy. In other words, the relevant question here is not whether the differences among vehicle operators serving the airports are "real and substantial," but whether the differences are so great that the General Assembly's decision to tax all such operators as a single class bears no reasonable relationship to the object of the tax. We turn to that question below.

The parties agree that in enacting the scheme of taxation to finance the McCormick Place expansion project, the General Assembly sought to impose the tax burden on certain industries that could be expected to realize significant economic benefits from the large number of visitors the project is expected to bring to the Chicago area. The Authority contends that while not all ground transportation providers who serve the airports will necessarily benefit in precisely the same way or to the same extent, it was still reasonable for the General Assembly to treat all providers as a single class for tax purposes based on anticipated benefits flowing to the class as a whole. The Authority maintains that by focusing exclusively on a limited sector of the market for ground transportation services-the market for transportation from the airports to downtown Chicago-plaintiffs have ignored the broader positive economic impact for the industry in general resulting from the expansion project. Plaintiffs respond that the specific benefits the Authority claims the vehicle operators in the plaintiff classes will enjoy are either nonexistent or "drastically attenuated" and do not support industry wide taxation.

As a prelude to consideration of these arguments, we digress briefly to address certain procedural matters. First, we note that in *Geja's Cafe*, this court clarified the burdens borne by the parties in litigation involving a uniformity clause challenge. While a classification will be upheld if a state of facts can reasonably be conceived to sustain it, the opponent of a tax is not required to come forward with any and all conceivable explanations for the tax and then prove each one to be unreasonable. Rather, upon a good-faith uniformity challenge, the taxing body bears the initial burden of producing a justification for the classifications. Once the taxing body has provided a sufficient justification, the opponent has the burden of persuading the court that the justification is unsupported by the facts.

We also take note of the procedural posture of this case, which is before us on the trial court's ruling in favor of the Authority on the parties' cross-motions for summary judgment. Summary judgment is appropriate where "the pleadings, depositions, and admissions on file, together with the affidavits, if any, show that there is no genuine issue as to any material fact and that the moving party is entitled to a judgment as a matter of law." The purpose of summary judgment is not to try a question of fact, but to determine whether one exists. Plaintiffs are not required to prove their case at the summary judgment stage. However, to survive a motion for summary judgment, the nonmoving party must present a factual basis which would arguably entitle him to a judgment. Accordingly, in the present case, to the extent the Authority has produced a legally sufficient justification for its tax classification, plaintiffs would then be required to present a factual basis negating the asserted justification to survive defendant's motion for summary judgment. Conversely, if the Authority has failed to produce a legally sufficient justification for the classification, plaintiffs would be entitled to a judgment as a matter of law.

Applying these principles, we conclude that the Authority has submitted a legally sufficient justification for imposing the airport departure tax on the members of the plaintiff classes who operate taxicab or limousine services from the airports to destinations outside the City of Chicago (Classes A and C). First, the Authority notes that while suburban and out-of-state operators are precluded from making trips into Chicago, Chicago-licensed operators are permitted to operate outside the city. Hence, both categories of operators compete for the business in taking travellers from the airports to suburban and out-of-state destinations. The Authority maintains that the generally increased demand for transportation from the airports into the city owing to the McCormick Place expansion project will take many city-licensed operators out of competition for the suburban/out-of-state market, thereby increasing the share of this market served by suburban and out-of-state taxicab and limousine operators. In other words, the increased demand for the city market will allow operators without Chicago licenses to take up the slack in the market for airport transportation to destinations outside the city.

Second, the Authority contends that the demand for downtown hotel rooms during major McCormick Place events is likely to divert other visitors to hotels in the suburbs, thereby increasing the demand for transportation from the airports to those hotels. The Authority notes the findings of a marketing study conducted by the firm of KPMG Peat Marwick in conjunction with the McCormick Place expansion project:

> A poorly documented but real effect is the ripple effect. When a large event comes to Chicago, demand currently accommodated in an area may be displaced into outlying areas. A convention oriented hotel which has a strong commercial base may displace regular corporate demand to outlying hotels. Meeting events in Chicago regularly have room in the O'Hare, Oakbrook and Rosemont areas. As delegates stay in these hotels, regular business may be displaced to further outlying areas. In this way the outlying areas are getting demand associated with McCormick Place, but it is not from visitors attending McCormick Place events directly.

Plaintiffs contend that their own informal survey shows that, at present, visitors attending McCormick Place events rarely stay in suburban hotels. However, plaintiffs have offered no evidence contradicting the assertion that McCormick Place events displace other visitors to outlying areas. Nor have plaintiffs offered any evidence to refute the Authority's theory that suburban and out-of-state taxicab and limousine operators will benefit from decreased competition in the market they serve. In essence, plaintiffs simply protest that these benefits are too indirect in comparison with the benefits to city-licensed operators. Be that as it may, the benefits identified are nonetheless tangible and would appear to represent reasonable conclusions about the dynamics of related market forces in the local economy. In this regard, we agree with the observation of our appellate court in *Forsberg v. City of Chicago*, 151 Ill.App.3d 354, 365, 502 N.E.2d 283 (1986), cited by the Authority, that "not all persons burdened by a tax must be benefited in the same way." We cannot say as a matter of law that the inclusion of these vehicle operators bears no reasonable relationship to the object of the tax.

The Authority also points out several potential benefits to the members of the plaintiff classes operating bus or van services (Classes E and F). First, bus and van operators are permitted to transport passengers into Chicago from points outside the city, and do in fact operate both scheduled and charter services with stops in Chicago. The Authority notes deposition testimony that an estimated 30% of the charter business conducted by Sam Van Galder, Inc. (Van Galder)-a Wisconsin-based bus company which is the parent company of plaintiff Alco Bus Corporation (Alco)-consists of trips to museums, baseball games and civic events in Chicago. Thus, the Authority maintains that the expansion project will create new opportunities for bus operators to transport passengers who reside in the suburbs and neighboring states to events at McCormick Place. Moreover, the expansion project includes plans to reroute the northbound lanes of Lake Shore Drive in a manner designed to enhance access to the Field Museum, the Shedd Aquarium and the Adler planetarium, thereby increasing the market for charter services to these already popular attractions. The Authority further notes that bus companies throughout the area enjoy a substantial volume of business as subcontractors in connection with the market for shuttle service between hotels and conventions held at McCormick Place. Business records of one of the major prime contractors for convention shuttle service show subcontracts to suburban and out-of-state companies for over 1,400 buses during a 17-month period.

Plaintiffs' principal objection to the Authority's reasoning is that the particular examples of charter service that the Authority cites involve separately incorporated affiliates of certain plaintiffs rather than the plaintiffs themselves. For instance, plaintiffs dispute the relevance of the charter business conducted by Van Galder, the parent company of plaintiff

Alco. Plaintiffs note that Van Galder's charter business is entirely separate from Alco's airport transportation operation and potential benefits to Van Galder cannot justify imposition of the airport departure tax on Alco. This argument is unpersuasive. The General Assembly cannot be charged with knowledge of the corporate structure of every firm in the ground transportation industry. In formulating tax classifications, the General Assembly is entitled to make reasonable assumptions about the characteristics of the industries subjected to taxation. In this regard, we think it was reasonable for the General Assembly to consider bus companies as integrated enterprises for purposes of appraising the economic impact of McCormick Place and the expansion project.

Plaintiffs also dispute the Authority's contention that suburban and out-of-state bus companies benefit from subcontracting opportunities related to convention shuttle service. Plaintiffs insist that under recent amendments to applicable Chicago ordinances, city-licensed charter operators are prohibited from "affiliating" with unlicensed operators. The provisions that plaintiffs have identified do not resemble the propositions for which they have been cited. We further note that Chicago has provided by ordinance that temporary permits may be issued to operators of licensed charter/sightseeing vehicles for the operation of additional vehicles as charter/sightseeing vehicles. Thus, there is no reason to believe subcontracting opportunities have ceased to exist or will in the future. Plaintiffs' argument is without merit.

As with the taxicab and limousine operators, we conclude that the Authority has submitted a legally sufficient justification for imposition of the bus and van operators in the plaintiff classes. Plaintiffs have not introduced evidence showing that the asserted justifications for taxing the members of the four plaintiff classes are factually erroneous. Accordingly, the trial court properly granted the Authority's motion for summary judgment on the counts brought under the uniformity and equal protection clauses.

For the foregoing reasons, the judgment of the circuit court of Cook County is affirmed.

CHAPTER XV

ORGANIZATION OF STATE GOVERNMENTS

A. INTRODUCTION

The Supreme Court of the United States has made clear on several occasions that the U.S. Constitution has nothing to say about the structure and internal organization of state governments. *See, e.g., Sweezy v. New Hampshire*, 354 U.S. 234, 255 (1957) ("this Court has held that the concept of separation of powers embodied in the United States Constitution is not mandatory in state governments."); *Highland Farms Dairy v. Agnew*, 300 U.S. 608, 612 (1937) ("How power shall be distributed by a state among its governmental organs is commonly, if not always, a question for the state itself."). Thus, the federal constitution does not compel states to allocate certain powers to particular branches of government or, indeed, even to have the traditional three branches. As a result, though many state government systems bear significant similarities to the federal government's structure and organization, there also are significant and interesting differences between the organization of the state governments and the federal system. This chapter explores some of those differences.

B. LEGISLATIVE POWER

1. Introduction

State legislative organization and power generally is defined at some length in state constitutions. All states but Nebraska have a bicameral legislature, not unlike the federal Congress, though the state legislatures vary in their specifics. Generally, state legislatures have responsibility for all lawmaking and exercise traditional police powers, meaning that their actions are limited only by political will and constitutional constraints such as may be found in the federal or relevant state constitution. Thus, state legislatures can and do legislate on a wide array of topics and subject matters. Important topics for legislation in most states include taxation and spending, criminal law, domestic relations, education, and infrastructure such as roads and transportation.

In this section of the chapter, we focus on one potentially significant way in which the state legislatures may differ from the federal Congress – the imposition of term limits on state legislators (and sometimes on local government officials as well).

2. Term Limits for State and Local Officials

The Supreme Court of the United States held in *U.S. Term Limits, Inc. v. Thornton*, 514 U.S. 779 (1995) (excerpted in Chapter III, above), that the States may not impose term limits on their members of Congress, because the Qualifications Clauses in the federal constitution provide the exclusive credentials for determining those qualified to sit in Congress. Thus, there are no enforceable state term limits for U.S. Senators and members of the U.S. House of Representatives.

But there is no federal constraint on the imposition of term limits on members of state legislatures, state executive officials such as governors and attorneys general, local government bodies, or even potentially state judges. Thus, the States have been a fertile laboratory with respect to the adoption and constitutionality of measures limiting the terms of various state and local government officials. Several states have adopted such limits and, in many cases, though not all, term limits have withstood challenge under state constitutions. Below are two examples of state supreme courts interpreting such provisions and assessing their validity under state law.

SECRETARY OF STATE v. BURK
188 P.3d 1112 (Nev. 2008)

GIBBONS, C.J.

Petitioner challenge[s] [various incumbents'] candidacies for state offices or positions on local governing bodies based on the Nevada Constitution's Article 15, Section 3(2) term-limit amendment. That amendment, which became effective in late November 1996, provides that a person may not serve more than 12 years in any state office or as a member of any local governing body. The primary question presented here is whether that amendment applies to an individual who was elected to a term of office before the amendment's effective date but commenced serving in that office thereafter.

No person may be elected to any state office or local governing body who has served in that office, or at the expiration of his current term if he is so serving will have served, 12 years or more, unless the permissible number of terms or duration of service is otherwise specified in this Constitution. Now, nearly 12 years later, several elected officials who have concededly held their positions since 1997 dispute whether the term-limit amendment applies to bar them from serving another term starting in 2009. Thus, in these consolidated writ proceedings, the Nevada Secretary of State...and an elector...challenge the qualifications of eight candidates...currently running for reelection to certain state offices and local governing bodies.

Real parties in interest were originally elected or reelected to their various state offices and local positions in the November 1996 general election. They do not dispute that they commenced serving their respective terms in office in January 1997. Thereafter, real parties in interest retained their offices through reelection; they will have completed their twelfth years of service since the term-limit amendment became effective when their current terms expire at the end of this year, 2008. Nevertheless, real parties in interest have asked...to include their names on the 2008 primary and general election ballots as candidates for the next terms of their offices, beginning in January 2009. [P]etitioners [argue] that if each [incumbent] is reelected and begins serving another term of office in 2009, that year will constitute his or her thirteenth year serving in the same office after the Nevada Constitution's 12-year term-limit provision became effective.

DISCUSSION

Applying term limits prospectively

While the parties generally agree that the term-limit provision applies prospectively from November 27, 1996, they dispute whether the prospective application includes within the years-of-service limitation terms served pursuant to the 1996 election. Specifically, petitioners assert that, even though the term-limit provision did not become effective until after the [1996] election, the term limit applies to terms of office that were filled based on that election, since the elected representatives did not commence serving in their offices until after the provision's effective date. In response, [it is] argue[d] that terms of office filled by virtue of the 1996 election do not count toward the 12-year term limit because the real parties in interest were elected before the term-limit provision became effective.

Article 15, Section 3(2)'s language

Article 15, Section 3(2) provides that "[n]o person may be elected to any state office or local governing body who has served in that office, or at the expiration of his current term if he is so serving will have served, 12 years or more." Here, Article 15, Section 3(2) is clear on its face: if a person "has *served*" in an office or "will have *served*" in that office for 12 years or more by the time his or her current term expires, the person may not be elected to that office. As the Secretary of State...point[s] out, the provision focuses on years of service, not elections. And nothing in it exempts from its purview years of service commencing after its effective date pursuant to the 1996 election. Thus, under Article 15, Section 3(2)'s plain language, so long as a service year commences after the Article's effective date, it constitutes a year of service for limitation purposes.

Nonetheless, real parties in interest argue that…because that provision's first clause uses the phrase "[n]o person may be elected" after 12 years of service, " 'election' is the event that will trigger the 'clock' for term limits." But a provision is ambiguous only when a reasonable alternative interpretation exists, and the phrase "[n]o person may be elected" clearly refers to the result of having already served 12 years in an office, not the commencement of the 12-year service period. Thus, real parties in interest resort to "ingenuity to create ambiguity" that does not exist in the amendment and that cannot serve to defeat the amendment's clear language. Accordingly, Article 15, Section 3(2)'s term limit applies to offices filled pursuant to the 1996 election if the office's term did not commence until after the term limit's November 27 effective date.

Article 15, Section 3(2)'s validity

Having determined that Article 15, Section 3(2) bars real parties in interest from office in 2009, we necessarily address the Legislature's argument that the amendment is invalid and unenforceable. In challenging a voter-enacted constitutional amendment postelection, the Legislature "bear[s] a heavy burden of persuasion," given the presumptive soundness afforded to the vote of the people.

Confusing language

As regards the Legislature's argument that the term-limit ballot question's language confused voters, the Legislature's contention presents us with the unenviable task of determining whether voters were confused or misled by the ballot question when they approved it over a decade ago. Other than pointing to the ballot question's language and posing hypotheticals, however, the Legislature has not provided us with any evidence—much less evidence beyond a reasonable doubt—that voters were indeed confused or misled by that language approximately 12 years ago.

Without strong evidence showing that voters were confused or misled, to now determine, in hindsight, that they were, is nearly impossible. Moreover, the significant consequences of invalidating a voter-enacted constitutional amendment based on the language of the ballot question underlying it, after this state's constituents and would-be candidates have been relying on its existence for over one decade is likewise problematic. These are the very types of problems that the laches doctrine was designed to avoid.

"'Laches is an equitable doctrine which may be invoked when delay by one party works to the disadvantage of the other, causing a change of circumstances which would make the grant of relief to the delaying party inequitable.'" To determine whether a challenge is barred by the doctrine of laches, this court considers (1) whether the party inexcusably delayed bringing the challenge, (2) whether the party's inexcusable delay constitutes acquiescence to the condition the party is challenging, and (3) whether the inexcusable delay was prejudicial to others. According to the Legislature, it did not inexcusably delay bringing this challenge to Article 15, Section 3(2)'s validity because it was not ripe for review until this year, when real parties in interest's candidacies were challenged under Article 15, Section 3(2).

But the Legislature is challenging the clarity of the ballot question's language. This sort of procedural challenge is ripe for judicial review preelection, before the ballot question is presented to the voters, "since the question to be resolved is whether [the] proposal has satisfied all constitutional and statutory requirements for placement on the ballot." To acquiesce to the ballot question's language before the 1994 and 1996 general elections only to challenge now whether it satisfied requirements for placement on the ballot 12 years ago is unconventional. And to consider the challenge and resolve it in the Legislature's favor would be prejudicial to the voters who for the last 12 years have been relying on the amendment that they approved and its now imminent implementation. Had the Legislature successfully challenged the ballot question's language 12 years ago, the voters or the question's proponents potentially could have remedied the question's infirmities by proposing a similar 12-year term-limit amendment in the immediately following general elections. We thus conclude that the doctrine of laches applies and, consequently, precludes the Legislature from challenging the term-limit ballot question's clarity. As no other challenges to the amendment's enactment have been timely made, we conclude that it was validly enacted into law.

CONCLUSION

Article 15, Section 3(2) plainly states that if a person has served, or at the conclusion of his or her current term will have served, 12 years or more in an office or a position on a local governing body, that person may not be reelected to that office or position. Thus, because real parties in interest, at the conclusion of their current terms, will have served at least 12 years in their respective offices, they may not be elected to their current positions. Accordingly,... we direct the clerk of this court to issue a writ of mandamus...[directing that these incumbents' names be excluded] from the 2008 general election ballot.

LEAGUE OF WOMEN VOTERS v. SECRETARY OF THE COMMONWEALTH
681 N.E.2d 842 (Mass. 1997)

WILKINS, C. J.

Before us is a reservation and report, on the pleadings and a statement of agreed facts, of a challenge to the constitutionality of chapter 230 of the

Acts of 1994 (chapter 230), which the people approved as an initiative petition at the November 8, 1994, election under art. 48 of the Amendments to the Constitution of the Commonwealth. Chapter 230 purports (a) to limit the number of consecutive terms for which a public officer may be listed on primary and general election ballots to serve in the same public office and (b) to eliminate the pay, perquisites, and privileges of certain public officers if reelected after serving a number of consecutive terms specified in chapter 230. The plaintiffs contend that a statute adopted by the people pursuant to the initiative process may not legislate qualifications for those public officers in addition to those qualifications that appear in the Constitution.

Chapter 230 has commonly been called a term limits statute. The information for voters, published by the then Secretary of the Commonwealth, concerning 1994 ballot questions described the proposed law, which became chapter 230, under the heading of "Term Limits." The legislative committee's minority report and the argument in favor of the proposal accompanying the voter information characterized the proposal as a term limits measure. Indeed, the statement of agreed facts refers to chapter 230 as a term limits statute. We eschew the characterization, for the moment, because one issue before us is whether chapter 230 establishes limits that are in effect statements of qualifications for office (i.e., is in fact a term limits statute) or whether chapter 230 merely regulates elections. To call chapter 230 a term limits statute, before we decide that issue, would suggest that we have prejudged that question.

We shall summarize portions of chapter 230 that are significant for this case. Important portions...were accurately described by the Attorney General in his summary submitted to the voters in 1994 as follows:

> This proposed law would prevent the name of a person from being printed on a state primary or general election ballot as a candidate for one of a number of specified state and federal public offices, if the person had already served a certain number of consecutive terms in that office within a fixed period preceding the end of the then-current term of office. If such a person were still elected by write-in vote to one of the state offices (except the office of Governor), the person would serve without a salary, and in some of the state offices, without payment for certain expenses.

> Under the proposed law, the name of a person could not be printed on a primary or general election ballot as a candidate for the office of Governor, Lieutenant Governor, Secretary of State, State Treasurer, State Auditor, or State Attorney General, if the person had served two consecutive terms (eight years) in that office in the eleven years prior to the end of the then-current term of office. The name of a person could not be printed on a primary or general election ballot as a candidate for the office of Governor's Councillor, State Representative, State Senator, or United States Representative from Massachusetts, if the person had served four consecutive terms (eight years) in that office in the nine years prior to the end of the then-current term of office. The name of a person could not be printed on a primary or general election ballot as a candidate for the office of

United States Senator from Massachusetts, if the person had served two consecutive terms (twelve years) in that office in the seventeen years prior to the end of the then-current term of office. The proposed law would not prevent any voter from casting a write-in vote for any person as a candidate for any office.

We are not concerned in this case with the offices of United States Senator and United States Representative.

The Attorney General's summary also described the limitations on compensation and benefits that chapter 230 would impose on any person elected in spite of his or her ineligibility to have his or her name printed on the ballot. He stated, "If a person made ineligible by the proposed law to have his or her name printed on the ballot as a candidate for the office of Lieutenant Governor, Secretary of State, State Treasurer, State Auditor, State Attorney General, Governor's Councillor, State Representative or State Senator were still elected to that office by write-in vote, the person would serve without a salary. If such a person were elected to the office of Lieutenant Governor, Governor's Councillor, State Representative or State Senator, the person would also serve without payment for certain expenses."

A person may be elected to a public office established by the Constitution of the Commonwealth only if he or she has the qualifications that the inhabitants of the Commonwealth have established "by their frame of government." The frame of government is Part II of our Constitution. Part II sets forth qualifications for Governor, Lieutenant Governor, Councillor, other constitutional officers, and members of the House of Representatives.

It is well settled that the Legislature may not change qualifications for public office that are prescribed by the Constitution. The Secretary argues that (1) the act does not establish or change any qualification for office because it simply regulates elections and (2) the people, in any event, have the authority to approve qualifications for public offices by acting pursuant to the statutory initiative provisions of art. 48 of the Amendments to the Constitution. We consider each of these arguments in turn and reject them.

The limitations on the right of certain incumbents to have their names printed as candidates for reelection will discourage them, in all reasonable likelihood, from seeking reelection and, if they try, cause their defeat. The difficulties confronting a candidate who seeks election as a "sticker" or "write-in" candidate when other candidates' names are printed on the ballot are substantial. The time, effort, and expense of such a candidacy make the task monumental. The denial of compensation to such a write-in candidate (except a candidate for Governor), if he or she were successful in his or her candidacy, heavily discourages such an official from seeking to run for reelection. Additionally discouraged would be those officeholders (Lieutenant Governor, Governor's Councillor, State Representative, and State Senator) who would also be denied payment for travel and expenses.

Chapter 230 in its effect concerns and prescribes qualifications for elective office and is not simply a ballot access measure.

The question remains whether the Constitution of the Commonwealth authorizes use of the statutory initiative process to adopt the qualifications for those offices that are listed in the challenged portions of chapter 230. The Secretary contends that the initiative process set forth in art. 48 permits the people to add qualifications for office beyond those that appear in the Constitution. This is, of course, an issue that was not involved in the *U.S. Term Limits, Inc.* case.

The Secretary acknowledges correctly that the Legislature has no authority to alter the qualifications for office that are prescribed by the Constitution. He argues that the people may nevertheless use the statutory initiative process of art. 48 to add qualifications for public offices for which the Constitution prescribes qualifications. This argument immediately runs into art. 48, The Initiative, II, § 2, which states that "the limitations on the legislative power of the general court in the constitution shall extend to the legislative power of the people as exercised hereunder." Article 48, therefore, restricts the people from enacting, by statutory initiative, qualifications for those public offices for which the Legislature itself may not enact qualifications. The idea that constitutionally prescribed qualifications may be changed only by constitutional amendment is intuitively sound. Article 48 was a constitutional amendment, but art. 48 disclaims any extension to the people of a right to legislate beyond the right of the Legislature.

The Secretary argues that arts. 8 and 9 of the Declaration of Rights grant the people the right to enact laws, such as chapter 230, and that art. 48 provided the vehicle to exercise that right, a right that had lain dormant from 1780 to 1918 when the people adopted art. 48. When adding art. 48, the people could have granted themselves statutory authority by the initiative process to prescribe qualifications for office beyond those stated in the Constitution, but art. 48 did not do so. Thus, although the people could by a constitutionally authorized statutory initiative measure define (that is, "establish by their frame of government" [arts. 8 and 9]) new qualifications for office, art. 48 disavows any intention to permit a statutory initiative on the subject.

The proponents of term limits, a characterization we may now properly give to chapter 230, have cause for discouragement. It appears from our conclusion in this action that they cannot achieve their goal through a statutory initiative. Efforts to obtain term limits by a constitutional amendment foundered in 1992 because of the refusal of the

Legislature in joint session to take final action on such a proposal as the Constitution of the Commonwealth directed. We concluded in *LIMITS* that this court should not direct the Legislature to exercise its mandated function. We did so based on principles of separation of powers. We noted also that art. 48 "gives the Governor a role in seeing that a joint session carries out its constitutional obligations, but gives to the courts no enforcement role."

We suggested in *LIMITS* that, when the Legislature fails to act in joint session on a proposed initiative to amend the Constitution, and thus frustrates the purpose of art. 48, "the only remedy may come from the influence of public opinion, expressed ultimately at the ballot box." This statement may have had a Delphic quality. The suggestion was not to propose use of the statutory initiative approach but rather to point to the power of the people to elect a sufficient number of legislators who would not defy the requirements of the Constitution so that a joint session would be required to perform its duty.

A judgment shall be entered in the county court declaring St.1994, c. 230, unconstitutional insofar as it seeks to limit access to primary and general election ballots to certain State officers identified in chapter 230 and seeks to eliminate the payment of compensation and benefits to certain of those State officers if they should be reelected in an election in which their names are not printed on the official ballot.

NOTES

1. Probably more state cases uphold term limits than strike them down. For other examples of such litigation, see *Massey v. Secretary of State*, 579 N.W.2d 862 (Mich. 1998) (upholding Michigan term limits); *Bailey v. County of Shelby*, 188 S.W.3d 539 (Tenn. 2006) (upholding term limits imposed on county officials); *Child v. Lomax*, 188 P.3d 1103 (Nev. 2008).

2. Should it matter how the term limits are imposed? In some states, it has been done by constitutional amendment, whether by popular initiative or otherwise, while in others statutes have been enacted.

3. Do term limits make more sense for certain officials but perhaps not others? For example, are the arguments for or against term limits stronger depending on whether the limited officials are state legislators, state-wide executive officers such as the governor, attorney general, or secretary of state, or local officials such as county or city commissioners, or even local mayors?

4. Should some officials be "off limits" in this context? The Nevada proposal discussed above in *Miller v. Burk* originally included state judges, but that aspect of the term limits proposal ultimately was rejected. Colorado also had a vigorous public debate a few years ago and ultimately defeated a proposal to limit the terms of state judges.

5. Can you identify the policy arguments in favor of and against term limits?

C. EXECUTIVE POWER

1. The Selection and Organization of the Executive

The federal constitution deposits all executive authority in the President of the United States. As a result, the President nominates his cabinet members, including the Attorney General, the Secretary of State, and the Secretary of the Treasury. In a real sense, this is a "unitary" executive model, because the President retains control over the important executive branch officials. As one legal scholar recently observed, "[m]any states, however, have diverged from the federal model by having other elected statewide officials, particularly an independently elected state attorney general. Which model is better: the federal or the state? Is a unitary executive optimal in a democracy like ours, or would an unbundled plural executive be better?" Steven G. Calabresi, *The Fatally Flawed Theory of the Unbundled Executive*, 93 Minn. L. Rev. 1696, 1697 (2009).

Thus, although the executive power in the States is often the same or similar to the power exercised in the federal system (with some potentially significant exceptions such as line item veto power, which is addressed in the next section), it is frequently exercised by multiple state officials all of whom are elected, with the result that such officials are not necessarily beholden to the Governor nor subject to the Governor's control and supervision. Indeed, it is quite common for a state to elect its Attorney General, its Secretary of State, and its Treasurer. Such a system obviously can at times lead to conflict between the Governor and these officials. Further complicating the situation, in many states these elected executive officials may to some extent be subject to the will and supervision of the legislature, rather than the Governor, and in some instances may by statute or constitution supersede the Governor's power in some respects.

For example, in some states, the Attorney General may be required to take particular legal action at the direction of the Legislature. Indeed, a legislature may even direct the Attorney General to sue the Governor! *See, e.g., State of Kansas ex rel. Stephan v. Finney*, 836 P.2d 1169) (Kan. 1992) (at the legislature's direction, the Attorney General sued the Governor in a mandamus action in the state supreme court seeking a determination whether the Governor had the constitutional authority to enter into a binding gaming compact with an Indian tribe without approval of the legislature).

Also, in states that elect their Attorney General, it is quite typical that the Attorney General alone (to the exclusion of the Governor) has the constitutional authority to represent the State in court proceedings. Thus, a Governor may even be forced to hire or retain separate counsel to assert the Governor's position in a particular matter in a case of conflict with the Attorney General.

Further, many states do not follow anything like the federal constitution's distinctions between "principal" and "inferior" executive officers, with the corresponding consequence that many executive officials who would be appointed by the President in the federal system are not appointed at all or at least are not appointed by the Governor, nor are many state appointments (such as to the state supreme court) subject to some kind of legislative confirmation process, in contrast to the federal system that requires Senate confirmation of all Article III judges.

The issues here are numerous and sometimes complex, and the variations among states are significant. Our purpose in this section is only to highlight the fact that the executive powers may be exercised by different officials in the States than would be the case in the federal system, with some resulting complications (such as pitting the Governor against the Attorney General) that do not arise in the federal system. One example of such complexities follows.

PERDUE v. BAKER
586 S.E.2d 606 (Ga. 2003)

FLETCHER, C. J.

Governor Sonny Perdue filed a petition for writ of mandamus seeking to compel Attorney General Thurbert Baker to dismiss an appeal filed on behalf of the State of Georgia in a case involving legislative reapportionment under the Voting Rights Act. The trial court denied the Governor's petition, ruling that the Attorney General had exclusive authority to decide whether to continue the State's efforts to enforce a law enacted by the General Assembly and signed by the Governor. The issue presented here is whether the Attorney General has the authority under state law to appeal a court decision invalidating a state redistricting statute despite the Governor's order to dismiss the appeal. Because there is constitutional authority for the General Assembly to vest the Attorney General with specific duties and a state statute vested the Attorney General with the authority to litigate in the voting rights action, we hold that the Attorney General had the power to seek a final determination on the validity of the State Senate redistricting statute under the federal Voting Rights Act.

PRIOR PROCEEDINGS

Following the 2000 decennial census, the General Assembly enacted a bill that reapportioned State Senate districts and Governor Roy Barnes signed the bill into law.... The State then filed a civil action in the United States District Court for the District of Columbia seeking preclearance of the Senate redistricting plan under Section 5 of the Voting Rights Act, a prerequisite to enforcing the law. The State sought a declaratory judgment that the plan did not have the purpose or effect of "'denying or abridging the right to vote on account of race or color' or membership in a language minority group." Denying the State's request for a declaratory judgment, the district court held that the State failed to meet its burden of proof under Section 5 that the State Senate redistricting plan did not have a retrogressive effect on the voting strength of African-American voters in Georgia. It denied preclearance.

The General Assembly enacted a revised Senate redistricting plan, Act 444, and the State submitted the new plan to the district court for preclearance. In June 2002, the three-judge district court approved the revised Senate redistricting plan. Act 444, which was not codified into law, expressly provides that its senatorial districts are contingent and shall take effect only if the original Senate redistricting plan cannot lawfully be implemented under the federal Voting Rights Act. To obtain a final determination, the Attorney General filed a direct appeal in July 2002 to the United States Supreme Court challenging the federal district court's order rejecting the original Senate redistricting plan. The Supreme Court granted review in January 2003.

Ten days later, soon after being installed into office, Governor Perdue requested that Attorney General Baker dismiss the appeal. The Governor contended that the Georgia Constitution vests his office with the chief executive powers to dismiss an appeal pending in the U.S. Supreme Court when the State of Georgia is the sole-named appellant. The Attorney General disagreed, citing constitutional provisions that vest his office with exclusive authority in all legal matters related to the executive branch in state government. Faced with this refusal, the Governor sought a writ of mandamus to require the Attorney General to dismiss the pending appeal in the Supreme Court.

ALLOCATION OF EXECUTIVE POWERS

1. Both the Governor and Attorney General are elected constitutional officers in the executive branch of state government, which is responsible for enforcing state statutes. The Georgia Constitution provides that the Governor is vested with the chief executive powers. Among those powers is the responsibility to see that the laws are faithfully executed. Other executive officers, including the Attorney General, are vested with the

powers prescribed by the constitution and by law. The constitution states that the Attorney General "shall act as the legal advisor of the executive department, shall represent the state in the Supreme Court in all capital felonies and in all civil and criminal cases in any court when required by the Governor, and shall perform such other duties as shall be required by law."

Within the executive branch, both the Governor and Attorney General have statutory authority to direct litigation on behalf of the State of Georgia. Under the State Government Reorganization Act of 1931, which established the Department of Law, the Governor "shall have power to direct the Department of Law, through the Attorney-General as head thereof, to institute and prosecute in the name of the State such matters, proceedings, and litigations as he shall deem to be in the best interest of the people of the State." The Governor also has the power to provide for the defense of any action in which the State has an interest.

OCGA § 45-15-3 sets out the Attorney General's general responsibilities. It repeats his constitutional duties to serve as the executive branch's legal adviser, represent the State in all capital felony appeals, and represent the State in all civil and criminal actions when required by the Governor; it further provides that the Attorney General may give written legal opinions to state departments on request and prepare all state contracts when advisable. Of primary relevance in this case are the last two duties specified in the code section. Subsection (6) gives the Attorney General independent authority to represent the State in any civil action without the Governor's request: "It is the duty of the Attorney General...[t]o represent the state in all civil actions tried in any court." The final subsection is a catch-all phrase similar to the language in the constitution, giving the Attorney General authority to perform "other services as shall be required of him by law."

Construed together, these constitutional provisions and statutes do not vest either officer with the exclusive power to control legal proceedings involving the State of Georgia. Instead, these provisions suggest that the Governor and Attorney General have concurrent powers over litigation in which the State is a party. Both executive officers are empowered to make certain that state laws are faithfully enforced; both may decide to initiate legal proceedings to protect the State's interests; both may ensure that the State's interests are defended in legal actions; and both may institute investigations of wrongdoing by state agencies and officials. Thus, they share the responsibility to guarantee that the State vigorously asserts and defends its interests in legal proceedings.

As a result, we reject the broader claim by each officer that he has the ultimate authority to decide what is in the best interest of the people of the State in every lawsuit involving the State of Georgia. By giving both the

Governor and Attorney General the responsibility for enforcing state law, the drafters of our constitutions and the General Assembly have made it less likely that the State will fail to forcefully prosecute or defend its interests in a court of law or other legal proceeding. This overlapping responsibility is also consistent with the existing practice in state government. Most important, it provides a system of checks and balances within the executive branch so that no single official has unrestrained power to decide what laws to enforce and when to enforce them.

We also reject the dissent's narrow characterization of the Attorney General's role as merely that of legal counsel to the Governor. To imply that the Georgia Rules of Professional Conduct control the Attorney General's relationship to the Governor ignores the important and independent role assigned to the Attorney General under our constitution. Accepting the dissent's argument would eviscerate the Attorney General's separate constitutional role.

The State of Georgia is not one branch of government, one office, or one officer. The State's authority resides with the people who elect many officers with different responsibilities under valid law.

2. Our conclusion that both officers have the duty to enforce state laws is consistent with the language and legislative history of article V of the 1983 Georgia Constitution. The first paragraph on the Governor's duties and powers in the Executive Article states the following: "The chief executive powers shall be vested in the Governor. The other executive officers shall have such powers as may be prescribed by this Constitution and by law."

The Committee to Revise Articles IV and V intended for this paragraph to explain the allocation of powers within the executive branch of state government. First, the drafters wanted to provide a clear statement that the Governor was the chief executive in relationship to other executive officers, both elected and appointed. This clarification was necessary to address the past assertions of some constitutional officers that as elected officers they were not subject to the Governor's power. Second, the drafters wanted to indicate that the Governor had not only express powers, but also had reserved powers. Finally, the drafters wanted to ensure that the Governor did not possess unlimited authority over other executive officers. Immediately after granting executive powers to the Governor, the 1983 Constitution places a restraint on those powers: it grants to the other executive officers "such powers as may be prescribed by this Constitution and by law." This provision means that the other constitutionally elected officers possess powers granted to them by the constitution and other laws.

3. To support his claim that "the Governor, and the Governor alone" is authorized to make decisions related to litigation filed in the State's name,

the Governor relies on the constitutional provision describing the Attorney General's duties and a [statute]. The 1983 Constitution, like all the constitutions since 1868, provides that the Attorney General "shall represent the state ... in all civil and criminal cases in any court when required by the Governor." In addition, OCGA § 45-15-35 vests the Governor with the power to direct the Department of Law to institute and prosecute litigation in the name of the State. The Governor contends that this language means the Attorney General must follow his orders to dismiss or withdraw an appeal in any case regardless of the circumstances.

Contrary to the Governor's contention, we do not read these constitutional or statutory provisions as denying power to the Attorney General in representing the State, but instead interpret them as granting additional power to the Governor. As a result, we decline to address the Governor's contention, adopted by the dissent, that his express right to initiate litigation always includes the implicit right to end any lawsuit. Rather, the dispositive issue is whether any laws of this State grant the Attorney General independent authority to continue the litigation in this case. To decide whether the Governor's powers as chief executive include the absolute right to direct the Attorney General to dismiss the State's appeal, we look to the powers and duties of the Attorney General as prescribed under the Georgia Constitution and statutory law.

THE ATTORNEY GENERAL'S DUTIES

4. The Attorney General is a state executive officer elected at the same time and holding office for the same term as the Governor. As an elected state constitutional officer, the Attorney General has the powers prescribed to him by the 1983 Constitution, statutes, and case law. The General Assembly has given the Attorney General specific authority to act independently on behalf of the State in a variety of civil and criminal cases. For example, the code chapter on the Attorney General empowers that officer to represent the State in all capital felony actions before this Court, prosecute any person for violating a criminal statute while dealing with the State, represent the State in all civil actions in any court, file and prosecute civil recovery actions against any person who violates a statute in dealing with the State, represent the state authorities that are instrumentalities of the State, represent the Comptroller General in collecting or securing any state claim, and represent the State before the United States Supreme Court.

In 1975, there were two changes in the law related to the Attorney General's duties that made explicit what had previously been only implicit: the Attorney General has the power to represent the State in civil actions independently of the Governor's direction. First, this Court held in *Coggin v. Davey* that the Attorney General was authorized to represent legislators in legal actions arising out of their official duties in the General Assembly.

Three months later, the General Assembly amended Ga.Code Ann. § 40-1602 (OCGA § 45-15-3) to expressly grant the Attorney General the authority to represent the State in civil actions without any request from the Governor. The 1975 amendment was enacted "to clarify the duties of the Attorney General and the circumstances under which the Attorney General shall act at the direction of the Governor." Prior to the amendment, the caption of § 40-1602 describing the Attorney General's duties was entitled "Duties required by Governor." The first sentence began, "It is the duty of the Attorney General when required so to do by the Governor," and then listed six separate duties of the State's chief legal officer. The 1975 amendment deleted the words "by Governor" from the caption, "when required so to do by the Governor" in the first sentence, and "when required by the Governor" in subparagraph 6.

Thus, this 1975 amendment resolved, at least in part, the broader issue of the Attorney General's powers that this Court declined to address in *Coggin v. Davey*. The amended code section provides authority for the Attorney General to represent legislators and other state officials "on his own motion" without any request, requirement, or direction from the Governor. We need not decide, however, the full extent of the Attorney General's power to represent the State under this statute or the circumstances, if any, under which the Governor may compel the Attorney General to end his representation. In this case, a more narrowly drawn statute provides authority for the Attorney General to continue the voting rights litigation despite the Governor's order to dismiss the appeal.

ACT 444

5. Act 444 was enacted after the federal district court had denied preclearance to the original Senate redistricting plan, but before the State filed an appeal of that decision to the U.S. Supreme Court. By its terms, Act 444 expresses the legislature's intent that the original redistricting plan for the State Senate should be followed if allowed by federal law. Section 1(d) states that the original plan's provisions are "suspended" until the State can obtain a final determination on the legality of the original plan under the federal Voting Rights Act. At the time the General Assembly enacted Act 444, the first step in the process for the State to obtain a "final determination" on its ability to enforce the reapportionment plan under the federal Voting Rights Act was to file a direct appeal with the Supreme Court seeking to reverse the district court's opinion.

As the State's chief legal officer, the Attorney General is the official charged with representing the State in reapportionment cases. Before any change affecting voting qualifications, standards, practices, and procedures may take effect, the State must obtain preclearance of the change under Section 5 of the Voting Rights Act. One way to obtain preclearance is by instituting a declaratory judgment action in the United

States District Court for the District of Columbia. If preclearance is declined, the State's only remedy is to file a direct appeal to the United States Supreme Court. OCGA § 45-15-9 provides that the Attorney General "shall represent the State in all actions before the Supreme Court."

Accordingly, after the three-judge court denied preclearance, the Attorney General appealed to the Supreme Court. By appealing, the Attorney General was fulfilling his general duty as chief legal officer to execute state law and his specific duty to defend the reapportionment law as enacted by the General Assembly.

SEPARATION OF POWERS

6. We next consider whether Act 444 violates the doctrine of separation of powers by directing that it takes effect only after a final determination is made regarding the enforceability of the provisions of Act 1EX6 under the Voting Rights Act. Because Act 444 does not impermissibly encroach on the power of the executive branch to control litigation, but instead is a proper assertion of legislative power to determine reapportionment, we conclude that it does not violate separation of powers.

A legislative enactment violates separation of powers when it increases legislative powers at the expense of the executive branch, or when the enactment "'prevent[s] the Executive Branch from accomplishing its constitutionally assigned functions,'" even if it does not increase legislative powers. Thus, this Court must examine the respective roles of the legislative and executive branches and determine whether Act 444 inappropriately intrudes upon executive branch powers and functions.

The core legislative function is the establishment of public policy through the enactment of laws. Thus, the expressed intent of the legislative body to prefer one reapportionment scheme over another is plainly proper and within the sphere of legislative power. Nothing prevents the legislature from expressing this intent through a fallback or contingency provision.

On the other hand, the executive branch generally has the power and authority to control litigation as part of its power to execute the laws, and a law that removes from the executive branch sufficient control of litigation may well violate separation of powers. However, the executive branch does not have the authority to decline to execute a law under the guise of executing the laws: "To contend that the obligation imposed…to see the laws faithfully executed, implies a power to forbid their execution, is a novel construction of the Constitution and entirely inadmissible." The power to forbid the execution of the laws would enable the executive branch to nullify validly enacted statutes. In that situation, the executive branch would encroach upon the legislative power to repeal statutes or upon the judicial branch's power of judicial review. What the executive branch cannot do directly, it cannot do indirectly. Thus, even though the executive branch generally has the power and authority to control litigation, it cannot exercise this power in order to prevent the execution of a law.

Balancing these principles in light of this case, we conclude that the legislature may require an appeal to the U.S. Supreme Court so that the legislature's preferred reapportionment scheme be implemented. The intrusion by the legislature into the executive branch function of control of litigation is justified by the limited nature of the encroachment-pursuit of one case-and by the subject matter of the litigation-legislative reapportionment.

Because the legislative encroachment into the executive power of controlling litigation is limited to carrying out the legislature's chosen reapportionment plan, it does not impermissibly intrude into executive branch functions and does not constitute a separation of powers violation. The dissent's dire prediction of a political and constitutional crisis is possible only because it ignores the uniqueness of legislative reapportionment.

CONCLUSION

The Constitution mandates that the Attorney General perform "such other duties as shall be required by law." Act 444 suspends the operation of the new redistricting provisions "pending a final determination of their enforceability under the federal Voting Rights Act of 1965," which requires federal court resolution. Accordingly, when the Attorney General declined to dismiss the appeal, he was fulfilling a duty required by Act 444. Because the Attorney General was acting consistently with his constitutional and statutory duties, we conclude that the Governor does not have a clear legal right to compel the Attorney General to dismiss the appeal or case from the courts. Therefore, the Governor is not entitled to the writ of mandamus.

2. The "Line Item" Veto Power

In *Clinton v. City of New York*, 524 U.S. 417 (1998), the Supreme Court of the United States struck down an Act of Congress that had been described as giving the President a "line item" veto power, in other words giving the President power to strike or cancel individual items within a bill presented for his signature. The Constitution, art. I, § 7, cl. 2, provides no such power to the President explicitly, but instead declares in the Presentment Clause as follows: "Every Bill which shall have passed the House of Representatives and the Senate, shall, before it becomes a Law, be presented to the President of the United States; If he approve he shall sign it, but if not he shall return it, with his Objections...." The Supreme

Court held that the law Congress passed purporting to give the President the power to strike particular items from a bill while permitting the remainder of the bill to become law violated the Presentment Clause.

Interestingly, line item veto powers in state constitutions were not present in the colonial charters but instead appeared much later, notably in the Confederacy's constitution during the Civil War and as late as the 20th century. Well over 40 states now give their Governors such authority. The line item veto provisions vary in their nature and scope, with some being limited for example only to appropriations measures while others authorize broad line item vetoes regarding any legislation and for any reason. Further, the States' line item veto measures have proven a not infrequent source of litigation between Governors and legislatures or legislators, the latter of whom often have been granted standing by state courts to challenge gubernatorial exercises of the power (contrasted with the Supreme Court of the U.S. which held, prior to *Clinton v. City of New York* that individual members of Congress had no standing to challenge the President's exercise of such authority. *Raines v. Byrd*, 521 U.S. 811 (1997)).

Following are two examples of state court litigation over a Governor's exercise of the line item veto power. Note carefully the contexts in which the disputes arise and the parties.

RANTS v. VILSACK
684 N.W.2d 193 (Iowa 2004)

CADY, J.

In this appeal, we consider whether Governor Thomas J. Vilsack (Governor) properly exercised the item veto power granted Iowa's governor by the Iowa Constitution when he vetoed several sections of an economic development bill passed by the general assembly (Legislature). After carefully scrutinizing the Governor's exercise of the item veto power in this case, we determine that his power was impermissibly exercised because the Governor attempted to veto items that were not part of an appropriation bill and thus were not subject to his item veto power. As a result of the Governor's unconstitutional action, his attempted disapproval of portions of the bill has been rendered a nullity and ineffective. Moreover, by operation of the Iowa Constitution, no portion of the bill-including provisions approved by the Governor-became law because the bill as a whole failed to receive the affirmative approval of both the Legislature and Governor.

I.   Background Facts and Proceedings.

During the course of his annual message to the Legislature in January 2003, the Governor outlined several policy positions and initiatives that he hoped to see accomplished during the legislative session. Key among the Governor's priorities was the stimulation and development of the state's economy. The core initiative suggested by the Governor for this purpose was the creation of an "Iowa Values Fund" (Values Fund), a monetary depository from which funds could be provided to certain persons or entities in hopes of stimulating various sectors of the state's economy. While the precise contours of this initiative had yet to take form, at least publicly, the Governor suggested to the Legislature that the program would be most successful if $500,000,000 was committed to the Values Fund over a five-year period.

As is prone to happening, particularly in times of divided government, the Legislature and the Governor had difficulty reaching an agreement on the best methods for economic development and the specific nature of the Values Fund. In particular, some members of the Legislature contended that successful economic development required tax and regulatory reform in addition to a large monetary commitment. While the Governor was not necessarily opposed to tax and regulatory reform in principle, he expressed his clear opinion that any tax reform should be "revenue neutral"-that is, it should not cause a depletion in the state's budget that might force the redistribution of state funds-and any regulatory reform should be equitable.

[Eventually, the Legislature passed two bills, HF 683 and HF 692, that]…created and funded a Values Fund and included provisions for tax and regulatory reform. [T]he Legislature…conveyed both to the Governor, and adjourned sine die. [T]he Governor returned HF 683 and HF 692 to the office of the secretary of state pursuant to the process for consideration of legislation passed "during the last three days of a session." The Governor returned HF 692 with several sections marked "disapproved." In his letter transmitting HF 692, the Governor indicated that he was making several item vetoes to the bill because he believed changes to the tax code present in the bill were not revenue-neutral, various provisions would disrupt the operations of the Governor's office or the department of economic development, and still other provisions would unfairly affect persons injured by unsafe products, seeking redress in the workers' compensation system, or with low or middle incomes. The balance of HF 692, including provisions creating the Values Fund, was approved. *Ultimately, the effect of the Governor's item vetoes was to eliminate the Legislature's economic development priorities while preserving the Governor's economic development priorities, including the Values Fund.* [emphasis added]

Representative Christopher C. Rants, Speaker of the House of Representatives, and Senator Stewart E. Iverson, Jr., Majority Leader of the Senate, as taxpayers, citizens, and representatives of the Legislature, filed suit against the Governor challenging his item vetoes of HF 692. The challenge proceeded to a consideration of dueling motions for summary judgment, and…the district court issued its ruling…determining the item vetoes were constitutional. The Legislature appealed immediately, and we expedited our consideration of its appeal in light of the gravity of the questions presented.

2. The Veto Power Generally

The executive veto power has its origins in ancient Rome. *See* Charles H. Zinn, *The Veto Power of the President,* 12 F.R.D. 207, 210 (1952). The word "veto," derived from Latin, means, "I forbid." Since its inception over fifteen centuries ago, the veto power has evolved and diversified. What was once accomplished by a "single word by the Roman tribune" may now be accomplished in one of three ways.

a. The General Veto Power.

In creating the American form of government, our nation's founders chose to provide a "general" veto power to the national executive. A similar general veto power is found in all but one state constitution. This power features common elements and operates similarly in each jurisdiction. After the legislative body passes a bill, it is presented to the executive for approval or disapproval. The executive may provide affirmative approval of the entire bill by signing it or otherwise approving it, may simply permit the bill to automatically become law by failing to "return" it with a statement of explicit disapproval within a certain number of days, or may affirmatively disapprove the bill. If the executive disapproves the bill, the legislative body then has an opportunity to reconsider the legislation and pass it again-typically by a supermajority-over the executive's veto. This scheme operates to fulfill two purposes of the general veto power: (1) to give the executive suitable opportunity to consider the bills presented to him, and (2) to give the legislature a suitable opportunity to consider the executive's objection to bills and in appropriate cases to seek to pass them over the veto.

b. The Pocket Veto Power.

Very closely related to the general veto power is the "pocket" veto power. This veto power operates almost identically to the general veto power except for special conditions that are triggered when a legislative body passes a bill near the end of its session or when its adjournment prevents the return of a bill by the executive to the legislative body for reconsideration. These conditions typically extend the length of time the executive has to consider a bill, alter the method by which the bill is returned by the executive, and in many cases, change the mechanism of "automatic" approval based upon inaction to a requirement of affirmative approval or automatic *disapproval.*

c. The Item Veto Power.

After the Civil War, a number of states "began to amend their constitutions to allow Governors to veto items in an appropriation bill without having to veto the whole bill." This form of the veto power, which came to be known as "item" or "line item" veto power, apparently originated in the Confederate States Constitution and does not have a federal analogue. Yet, while the national executive has not been provided an item veto power, most state executives have. Brent R. Appel, *Item Veto Litigation in Iowa: Marking the Boundaries Between Legislative and Executive Power,* 41 Drake L.Rev. 1, 5 (1992) ("Today, forty-three state constitutions include item veto or some form of item veto.").

Generally speaking, the item veto power developed "to control logrolling, or the legislators' practice of combining in a single bill provisions supported by various minorities in order to create a legislative majority." In this fashion, the item veto power serves as a companion to "single-subject" constitutional provisions, which are meant "to prevent logrolling by requiring legislatures to limit bills to a single subject." However, the item veto actually "represents the coming together of three widespread state constitutional policies: the rejection of legislative logrolling; the imposition of fiscal restrictions on the legislature; and the strengthening of the governor's role in budgetary matters."

The item veto power provides a substantial limitation on the principle that "[t]he appropriation of money is essentially a legislative function under our scheme of government." In fact, the item veto power grants the governor a limited legislative function in relation to appropriation bills. This legislative function runs contrary to the inherent "power to specify how the money shall be spent" granted the legislature through the general appropriation power. It is also a significant deviation from the traditional separation of powers between the three branches of government. For these reasons, the item veto power is to be construed narrowly, and any doubt over the extent of the power "should be resolved in favor of the traditional separation of governmental powers and the restricted nature of the veto." All of these factors have prompted one commentator to observe, "whatever the veto's successes in dealing with budget problems, by empowering the executive to veto a part of a bill, the item veto opens up a set of knotty legal and conceptual difficulties."

3. The Veto Power in Iowa.

Iowa citizens provided Iowa's governor the item veto power by ratifying an amendment to our constitution in 1968. One need only look to the jurisprudential development of this power in Iowa for proof of the "knotty legal and conceptual difficulties" it presents. Nevertheless, several definitions and principles from our prior cases guide the coordinate branches in the consideration of whether the item veto power may be permissibly exercised. This analysis launches, of course, from the language of our constitution. The item veto power is derived from article three, section sixteen of the Iowa Constitution, which provides, in part:

> The Governor may approve appropriation bills in whole or in part, and may disapprove any item of an appropriation bill; and the part approved shall become a law. Any item of an appropriation bill disapproved by the Governor shall be returned, with his objections, to the house in which it originated, or shall be deposited by him in the office of the Secretary of State in the case of an appropriation bill submitted to the Governor for his approval during the last three days of a session of the General Assembly, and the procedure in each case shall be the same as provided for other bills. Any such item of an appropriation bill may be enacted into law notwithstanding the Governor's objections, in the same manner as provided for other bills.

This constitutional language creates two core considerations that must be part of every analysis of an exercise of the item veto power.

a. Appropriation Bill.

Pursuant to our constitutional language, every analysis of the item veto power must begin with a determination of the nature of the bill that the governor is attempting to item veto. The fundamental prerequisite for the proper exercise of the item veto power is that the bill to be item vetoed is an appropriation bill. This requirement springs from the language of the section and is the primary qualification on the exercise of the item veto power. Its importance is underscored by the very nature of the three veto powers and the deviation from the traditional scheme of separation of powers implicit in the item veto power. Ultimately, this vital determination of whether the bill in question is an appropriation bill in the constitutional sense is for the courts.

Nearly every one of our prior cases in the item veto context has contributed to our definition of an appropriation bill, which is otherwise undefined in the constitution. [W]e [have] observed, "the proper test [of whether a bill is an appropriation bill] is to review each bill on an ad hoc basis and determine whether the bill contains an appropriation which could significantly affect the governor's budgeting responsibility."

[W]e have identified two types of appropriation bills in our item veto cases, both of which allocate funds "whether from the general fund or from a revenue-producing bill, into a separate and distinct fund that the State can no longer utilize for other purposes absent subsequent legislation." The first type, which may be considered a "traditional" appropriation bill, is marked by the inclusion of at least one allocation of a monetary amount on the face of the bill. The second type...is marked by the allocation of funds by either the direct ordering of an expenditure or the commanded alteration to standing allocations within sections of the

Iowa Code resulting in the expenditure of funds absent subsequent legislation to stop the expenditure or somehow redirect it.

b.   Item.

The second key element in the construction of the item veto power arises from the provision of article III, section 16 that provides that the governor "may disapprove any item of an appropriation bill." This language-particularly the term "item"-has caused this court and other courts their greatest interpretive difficulty. In our first consideration of the item veto power, we observed that "[e]ither by circumstance or design, our item veto amendment makes no reference to appropriations 'of money' in its provisions which enable a governor to approve appropriation bills in whole or in part, and permits the disapproval of any 'item' of an appropriation bill." Thus,… we have acknowledged that the governor may constitutionally veto nearly any item in an appropriation bill even if that item is not a monetary allocation.

This broad definition of an item requires a difficult calculation to ensure a proper balance between the executive and legislative branches. "[O]n the one hand, the Governor may not selectively strike words and phrases from 'conditions inextricably linked to an appropriation,' and, on the other hand, the legislature may not block [an] item veto by attaching 'unrelated riders' to an appropriation." In attempting to draw the line…in this area, we have generally defined a condition as "a provision in a bill that limits the use to which an appropriation may be put." A rider, on the other hand, has been generally defined as "an unrelated substantive piece of legislation incorporated in the appropriation bill."

Yet, merely stating these definitions belies the difficulty in defining a condition or a rider or the difference between them. Thus, we have consistently recognized that the fundamental test for determining the validity of an item veto under article III, section 16…is whether the vetoed portion of the legislation may be taken out of a bill without affecting its other purposes and provisions. It is something that can be lifted bodily from it rather than cut out. No damage can be done to the surrounding legislative tissue, nor should any scar tissue result therefrom.

c.   Summary.

In summary, each consideration of the exercise of the governor's item veto power warrants two core considerations. The primary consideration is whether the bill to be item vetoed is an appropriation bill. We have previously recognized two types of appropriation bills, a traditional form which contains at least one allocation of a monetary amount on the face of the bill, and a specialized type…which allocates funds by either directly ordering an expenditure or commanding alterations to standing allocations within sections of the Iowa Code resulting in the expenditure of funds absent subsequent legislation to stop the expenditure or somehow redirect it. If a bill is an appropriation bill, it is subject to the governor's item veto power. If it is not an appropriation bill, it is subject only to the governor's general or pocket veto powers and may not be item vetoed.

Furthermore, the governor may exercise the item veto power only on an item or items in an appropriation bill. We generally recognize three types of items that may be item vetoed. The first is a specific appropriation made on the face of the bill. The second is a rider, "an unrelated substantive piece of legislation incorporated in the appropriation bill." The third is a condition, "a provision in a bill that limits the use to which an appropriation may be put," which may be vetoed *only* if the appropriation accompanying it is vetoed as well. However, a condition, standing apart from its appropriation, may not be item vetoed because such a veto would invade the legislative prerogative to "specify how money shall be spent," granted through the general appropriation power.

   d.   Item Vetoes of HF 692.

[The court examines HF 692 in detail and determines that each disputed provision was not an appropriations measure. Therefore, the Governor lacked the authority to exercise a line item veto of those provisions.]

FORTY-SEVENTH LEGISLATURE OF ARIZONA
v. NAPOLITANO
143 P.3d 1023 (Ariz. 2006)

McGREGOR, C. J.

This case requires us to decide whether the gubernatorial veto of a portion of a bill related to state employee compensation exceeded the Governor's item veto power under Article 5, Section 7 of the Arizona Constitution. We conclude that the vetoed provision is not an item of appropriation subject to the gubernatorial item veto.

I.

On January 25 and 26, 2006, the Forty-seventh Legislature (the Legislature) passed House Bill 2661 (HB 2661) as an emergency measure. Section 1 of HB 2661 expressed the Legislature's intent to grant state employees a pay raise, and Section 6 appropriated money for employee salary adjustments. Section 5...exempted certain employees hired after December 31, 2006, from the state merit system. [T]he Governor vetoed a portion of Section 5. The Governor's veto message stated that the item "would have created an additional expense to the state" because exempt employees accrue leave differently than do merit system employees.

On February 2, 2006, by separate votes, each chamber of the Legislature authorized its presiding officer to bring an action on behalf of the Legislature to challenge the constitutional validity of the Governor's item veto of Section 5. Senate President Ken Bennett and Speaker of the House James Weiers then brought this special action, acting both individually and on behalf of the Legislature.

II.

In deciding whether to accept jurisdiction of this special action, we consider several questions. Because resolution of some of these questions turns on whether this action involves legal or political issues, we define first the nature of the issues raised. The Legislature asks us to determine whether Section 5 constitutes an "item of appropriation of money" within the meaning of Article 5, Section 7 of the Arizona Constitution. The Legislature argues that if the provision is not an item of appropriation, then the Governor's item veto power under the Arizona Constitution does not extend to Section 5. These issues, asserts the Legislature, are purely legal issues and appropriate for this Court's consideration. The Governor in contrast, argues that we can resolve the issues presented only by entering the political arena and that the Legislature has attempted to transform a political dispute into a constitutional question.

We agree with the Legislature that this petition presents purely legal questions. To determine whether a branch of state government has exceeded the powers granted by the Arizona Constitution requires that we construe the language of the constitution and declare what the constitution requires. Such questions traditionally fall to the courts to resolve. Although each branch of government must apply and uphold the constitution, our courts bear ultimate responsibility for interpreting its provisions.

B.

The fact that this action raises issues appropriate for our consideration does not end our inquiry. We next consider whether the Legislature has standing to bring this action. Although "we are not constitutionally constrained to decline jurisdiction based on lack of standing," "[c]oncern over standing is particularly acute" when "legislators challenge actions undertaken by the executive branch." Good reason exists for our caution: "Without the standing requirement, the judicial branch would be too easily coerced into resolving political disputes between the executive and legislative branches, an arena in which courts are naturally reluctant to intrude."

The Governor argues that these petitioners...lack standing. [We disagree.] [First, a] majority of the members of the legislature can pass legislation, subject to the governor's veto power. If, as the Legislature asserts, the Governor's item veto was unconstitutional and thus invalid, the Legislature's right to have the votes of a majority given effect has been overridden and the Legislature, as an institution, has sustained a direct injury to its authority to make and amend laws by a majority vote. Second,...[i]n this case, both the House of Representatives and the Senate authorized the Forty-seventh Legislature to challenge the Governor's item veto of Section 5 of HB 2661, making it clear that the Legislature as a body intended to challenge the Governor's action.

Contrary to the Governor's arguments, the Legislature's failure to attempt to override the item veto does not preclude a finding that it has standing to bring suit. In this case, if the Governor did, in fact, exceed her item veto authority, the Legislature should not be put to the task of attempting to override an invalid veto before being able to challenge an allegedly unauthorized action in court. The alleged injury to the Legislature as a body occurred, if at all, when the Governor vetoed legislation approved by a majority of each house. The existence of the injury does not depend upon and is not affected by whether the Legislature attempted to override the veto.

III.

Article 5, Section 7 of the Arizona Constitution defines the governor's item veto power. Under the terms of the constitution, the governor may veto "items of appropriations of money...while approving other portions of [a] bill." An appropriation is "the setting aside from the public revenue of a certain sum of money for a specified object, in such manner that the executive officers of the government are authorized to use that money, and no more, for that object, and no other." "[N]o specific language is necessary to make an appropriation, for the test is...whether or not the people have expressed an intention that the money in question be paid."

The setting aside of a certain sum of public revenue can occur in two ways: The legislature can authorize spending from the general fund or it can authorize payments of ascertainable amounts from a special fund. If the legislature chooses to appropriate public revenues by setting aside monies from a defined special fund, "no limit need be stated in the act authorizing the expenditures and specifying for what purpose the money is to be expended."

Section 5 amends A.R.S. § 41-771 [which] identifies those groups of employees who are exempt from the state merit system. It adds "correctional officers and juvenile correctional officers, state officers and employees who are appointed or employed after December 31, 2006 and who are at a pay grade of twenty-four or above" to the class of exempt employees. On its face, Section 5 fails to set aside any sum from the general fund. [Further,] Section 5 fails to specify any fund from which payment for accrued leave or, more generally, payment to exempt employees may be made. Instead, it merely defines a class of employees that will be excluded from the state merit system.

The Governor argues that this failure to set aside funds does not disqualify Section 5 from being an appropriation because the "combined effect of the vetoed language and the employment practices statutes [in Title 23]…turns the vetoed language into a spending authorization." She asserts that, under current administrative regulations, exempt employees accrue more leave than do merit system employees and, because the state must pay separating employees for accrued leave, Section 5 will impose additional costs to the state unrelated to employee salaries.

The Governor's argument, however, incorrectly equates the *obligation* imposed by the statutes with an *appropriation* to fulfill the obligation. The employment statutes may obligate the state to make certain payments, but they do not set aside any sum of money from the public revenue and thus cannot be regarded as making an appropriation.

In this case, Section 5, even when considered in conjunction with other statutes, does not set aside a defined amount of public revenue from any specific funding source. We conclude, therefore, that Section 5 was not subject to the Governor's item veto power.

NOTES

1. Do you agree with the Arizona Supreme Court's conclusion that whether the Governor has properly exercised a line item veto is a "legal" rather than "political" question? Can you articulate the arguments for and against the court's involvement?

2. Who should have "standing" to challenge a Governor's line item veto? The Legislature? Individual legislators? Citizens or entities tangibly affected by the veto, such as those who would have received state funds but for the Governor's veto?

3. How difficult is it to define what constitutes an "appropriation" measure for line item veto purposes? What if the Governor vetoes a particular tax deduction or exemption provisions in a major tax system overhaul bill? Or vetoes a provision eliminating mandatory retirement for judges at age 70 (on the ground that the provision will permit judges to serve longer and thus accrue larger retirement benefits that the State will be obligated to pay)? Or vetoes a provision requiring local sheriffs' departments to conduct background checks on all firearms purchases in their counties (on the ground that such a requirement will require more state funding for sheriffs)?

4. For additional commentary on this topic, see Richard Briffault, *The Item Veto In State Courts*, 66 Temple L. Rev. 1171 (1993); Winston David Holliday, Jr., *Tipping the Balance of Power: A Critical Survey of the Gubernatorial Line Item Veto*, 50 S.C. L. Rev. 503 (1999) (discussing South Carolina's experience and comparing it with Iowa, Wisconsin and Virginia).

D. JUDICIAL POWER

By now, the student is familiar with one of the essential tasks of the state judiciary: interpreting the state constitution. That of course is not all that state court judges do. They interpret legislation and regulations (federal and state); they develop state evidentiary, criminal, civil and appellate rules; they regulate the practice of law in their States; and, through their supreme courts, they exercise supervisory authority over the lower state courts.

This section considers three important differences between the federal and state judicial branches: (1) the election of most state court judges; (2) the authority of state court judges to issue advisory opinions; and (3) the authority of federal judges to certify questions of state law to the state supreme courts. And it ends by addressing an issue common to the state and federal courts: implied constitutional remedies.

1. The Election of Judges

One of the key distinctions between the federal and state judiciaries is their manner of selection and tenure of service. Under the United States Constitution, the President nominates federal judges, and the Senate confirms them. Once confirmed, federal judges serve for life or, as Article III puts it, during "good behavior." As the excerpt from the following article shows, that is a distant cry from the way most States choose their judges.

Judith L. Maute, South Texas Law Review (Fall 2000)

SELECTING JUSTICE IN STATE COURTS: THE BALLOT BOX OR THE BACKROOM?

Popular election of judges was virtually unheard of until the early Nineteenth Century. On the federal level, the United States Constitution dictated both the manner of appointment and lifetime tenure without reduction of salary. Andrew Jackson's presidency triggered a new wave of populism which advocated voter control over all aspects of government. Thereafter, several states amended their constitutions, providing for selection by election, or partisan challenges to incumbent judges. Newer states tended to follow uncritically the populist electoral model based on the idea that courts should have some accountability to the electorate. This transformation was achieved "almost completely without regard for the particular considerations of policy and principle which arise out of the nature and functions of the judicial arm of the government." The pendulum swung back towards appointment starting in the 1920s. Missouri was the first state to implement what became known as "merit selection" in 1940.

Currently, there are four basic systems of judicial selection in the United States. Judges are chosen through either partisan or nonpartisan elections in twenty-one states; eleven additional states use elections for some judgeships, usually the lower courts. What has become known as merit selection is the sole selection method in fourteen states. Seven jurisdictions use a combination of merit and election methods with the remaining states using a combination of merit and appointive systems. At present, twenty-two states use merit selection for at least their highest appeals courts. This figure can be misleading. Approximately eighty-seven percent of all state court judges are selected or retained on the basis of popular elections, although about eighty percent of all judicial offices are initially filled by appointment to compete unexpired terms.

A. Appointment

The oldest method of judicial selection in the United States is appointment. In the original thirteen states, to avoid giving exclusive power to one individual, the legislature, or the governor with legislative approval, appointed judges. Today, most states use various combinations of the appointive system. California judges, except for superior court judges, are appointed by the governor, and must then be approved by a commission on judicial appointments. New Hampshire uses an elected executive council to approve appointments by the governor. In New York, only court of appeals judges are appointed by the governor with the consent of the senate, while the remaining judges are chosen in partisan elections. Most states fill interim vacancies by gubernatorial appointment.

B. Partisan Elections

Partisan election of judges began after Andrew Jackson's populist presidency. Some authorities believe the move to elections was a response to widespread dissatisfaction with the perceived elitism of judges. Proponents maintain that judicial elections assure accountability to the people and are the only reliable method for removing judges whose decisions are unacceptable to the populace. Voters may have little information on the individual judicial candidates. Partisan elections can cue voters on a candidate's ideology through the identification of political affiliation. The political party of the judicial candidate can be used for screening purposes. "Although it has been proven otherwise in some cases, it was thought that with the party 'footing the bill' for and controlling recruitment, special interests would be kept at arm's length from the process."

Some voters favor judicial elections because it gives them a choice between parties and a voice in the system. There is a greater electoral turnout when voters have more information on which to make a decision, such as political party cues. One unfortunate method of increasing voter participation is the heightened negativity of judicial campaigns. Wisconsin Supreme Court Justice Shirley Abrahamson faced blistering campaign attacks by opponent Sharren Rose in the 1999 race. Critics of partisan judicial elections claim that increased costs of campaigning and problematic funding sources create an image of justice going to the highest bidder. Special interest groups try to help elect judges favorable to their cause by pouring money into those judges' campaign coffers. Six candidates spent almost six million dollars in 1990 Texas judicial campaigns. Abrahamson and Rose spent over one million dollars on their campaigns.

Another cost of judicial elections is time spent campaigning for office instead of fulfilling the judge's duties. Successful lawyers may be reluctant to run for office, investing their reputation, time, money and effort seeking a job that is neither guaranteed nor highly paid. Additionally, having to answer to political parties and vocal contributors can deter qualified individuals from running for a judicial position.

It is debatable whether partisan elections in fact make judges accountable to the public. Most judges are initially appointed to fulfill vacant positions by the state governor, and run unopposed in the next periodic election. This scenario effectively removes the voter from the equation. Even when there is opposition in a judicial race, voter turnout is typically low. Unless the judicial election takes place during the general election and has become a hotly contested race, most voters either do not vote for the judicial offices or vote with little information, evidenced by the fact that they cannot remember who they voted for immediately afterwards.

C. Nonpartisan Elections

Thirteen states use nonpartisan elections for judicial offices, and seven additional states use it only for selected judicial offices. Ohio is unique in that it nominates judicial candidates in partisan primaries and then places them on a nonpartisan ballot for the general election. Supporters claim that nonpartisan elections remove the problem of politics entailed by partisan elections while keeping accountability to the voters. Adopted in response to the problem of judges controlled by party politics, nonpartisan elections were intended to involve voters in the process and exclude politics and special interests.

"[M]ost commentators contend that, far from being an improvement upon partisan elections, nonpartisan elections are an inferior alternative to partisan elections because they possess all of the vices of partisan elections and none of the virtues." Voters lose their main cue for information on who to vote for and, lacking more relevant information on individual candidates, rely on other factors such as ballot position or name recognition. Candidates who served in prior political offices as prosecutor, legislator or county commissioner, have greater name recognition which helps them in later campaigns for judicial office. Voter apathy may be greater in nonpartisan elections, with lower turn-outs and voter roll-off (not voting in certain races), so that the judicial incumbents usually win. To counter this information problem, some jurisdictions print and distribute voter pamphlets, which greatly increases the election costs. Nonpartisan elections are becoming increasingly expensive and involve many of the same problems with campaign contributions as partisan elections. The most obvious example is the highly politicized, nasty and expensive battle between Ohio Supreme Court incumbent Justice Alice Robie Resnick, a Democrat, and her Republican challenger District Court of Appeals Judge Terrence O'Donnell. Business and insurance groups, with generous backing from the Chamber of Commerce, targeted Resnick for defeat because of her votes in two controversial cases. While ultimately unsuccessful, the bruising fight has prompted state leaders to reconsider selection methods.

D. Merit Selection

Albert Kales, Northwestern University law professor, first called for merit selection of judges in 1914 when the American Judicature Society was founded.

> Kales' plan called for (1) the nomination of judicial candidates based solely on merit by a commission of presiding judges, (2) the selection of judges from this list of nominees by an elected chief justice, and (3) retention elections conducted on a noncompetitive...basis. In 1926, British political scientist Harold Laski suggested that the Kales plan be modified in certain respects. Laski recommended that the Governor rather than the chief justice appoint judges and that the advisory committee consist of a judge or judges from the state supreme court, the attorney general, and the president of the state bar association.

California was the first state to adopt a type of merit plan for its supreme court and intermediate courts; it is still in use today. The governor makes nominations to fill vacant positions which must be approved by a commission including the chief justice, a present justice of the court of appeals and the attorney general. After confirmation, the judges must stand for retention at regular intervals. California is also noteworthy for having been the first state in which hotly contested retention elections resulted in the ouster of judges because of their unpopular decisions.

The most widely known merit selection plan, the "Missouri Plan," was first adopted in 1940. A judicial nominating committee makes recommendations to the governor who then chooses one of the nominees to fill a vacancy. Like many other states, Missouri now uses a "modified" merit system, in which appellate and metropolitan trial courts use a merit appointment process, but elections select the trial bench in rural areas. The judge must thereafter stand for retention at regular intervals. Missouri continues to use this system for its supreme court, courts of appeals and its trial courts in large metropolitan areas such as Kansas City and St. Louis. Three separate nominating commissions are used in Missouri: one for the appellate courts, and one each for Jackson county and St. Louis county circuit courts. Although repeal measures have been regularly introduced, the plan has yet to be revoked. All other state judges are selected in partisan elections.

Alaska was the first state to enact a merit plan for all state judges, in 1959. Rhode Island is the latest state to change to the merit plan for its trial judges in 1994. Delaware, Hawaii, Massachusetts, and Nebraska are the only other states which use merit selection for all judicial appointments.

Judicial nomination committees are composed of lawyers and laypersons. Some jurisdictions require the nominating commission be divided between political parties. Arizona dictates that the names submitted to the governor must be balanced based on political parties. According to Sheldon and Maule, the nomination committee lessens the political pressure on the appointing authority, usually the governor, so that the most qualified persons are submitted as finalists.

Merit selection proponents maintain that it: 1) removes politics from the selection process as much as possible, especially when there are effective controls for politics in the selection of nomination committee members; 2) removes the need to campaign for office and raise contributions; 3) results in more qualified applicants and selections; 4) removes the issue of voter apathy and the problem with ethical restrictions on judicial campaign speech; 5) allows accountability to voters by using retention elections to remove bad judges; and 6) increases minority representation on the bench. They contend it is the best method to reduce the influence of politics in judicial selection.

Opponents disagree with most of these assertions. They contend merit selection is elitist and merely moves the politics outside the light of the electoral system and into the backroom, allowing for private decisionmaking by politically-appointed nomination committees. They assert that retention elections are undemocratic, misleading to voters, and allow little meaningful choice. Campaign contributions must still be addressed if a judge up for retention is targeted by a special interest group based on an unpopular decision. A courageous judge may have a difficult time defending her record against an anonymously funded soft money campaign. In contested judicial elections, at least the voters are presented with a known alternative to the incumbent, enabling them to vote in a more meaningful way.

E.   Hybrid Selection

Eight states use some combination of merit selection, appointment, or elections to fill their judicial positions. In South Carolina, for instance, a merit commission nominates candidates, but the judge is elected by the legislature. The legislature also elects the judges in Virginia. In Maine, judges are confirmed by the Senate after being appointed by the governor. In New Hampshire, judges are appointed by the governor, then confirmed by an elected five member executive council. Floridians recently amended their constitution to provide for counties to vote on whether to "opt-in" to selecting trial court judges through the merit system.

NOTES

1.   Some see the election of judges to a term of years as a threat to judicial independence. How can popularly elected judges, who often must raise considerable campaign funds to win elections, maintain the independence of mind to rule fairly on the issues that come before them? And even when that is not a problem, how can majoritarian-elected judges be entrusted to enforce the counter-majoritarian guarantees of the state constitution. *See* Sandra Day O'Connor, "The Threat to Judicial Independence," The Wall Street Journal, A18 (Sept. 27, 2006); Sandra Day O'Connor, "Judicial Independence and Civics Education," Utah Bar Journal (July 18, 2009). Others see the election of judges in Jacksonian terms—as the only way to place a check on the judiciary, particularly at a time when so many of the most important issues of the day are coming before the courts.

2.   State judicial elections implicate at least two questions of *federal* constitutional law. One, the free-speech guarantees of the First Amendment place significant restrictions on the capacity of state judicial ethics codes to restrict what candidates may say in running for office. *See Republican Party of Minnesota v. White*, 536 U.S. 765 (2002). Two, the substantive due process guarantees of the Fourteenth Amendment require judges to recuse themselves in some settings, most notably when they have directly or indirectly received considerable campaign funds from a party in a case. *See Caperton v. A.T. Massey Coal Co.*, 129 S.Ct. 2252 (2009).

2.   Advisory Opinions

The "case" and "controversy" requirement of Article III of the United States Constitution prohibits federal courts from issuing advisory opinions to the other branches of government. Not so with respect to the state constitutions, which frequently permit their state supreme courts, in appropriate circumstances, to issue advisory opinions about the validity of existing laws or those under consideration. The following cases offer a representative example of the types of issues that may arise in this area.

OPINION OF THE JUSTICES of the Supreme Judicial Court Given Under the Provisions of Section 3 of Article VI of the Constitution.
815 A.2d 791 (Me. 2002)

To His Excellency, Angus S. King, Jr., Governor of Maine:

The Governor's questions ask us to determine whether he may or should evaluate certain ballots from the recent election for the Senate and the House of Representatives before summoning the apparent winners of that election. We respectfully respond, in summary, that neither the Constitution nor the statutes of the State of Maine confer any power, right, or authority upon the Governor to decide whether specific ballots cast in the election of State Senators and Representatives should be counted or rejected in determining who is the "apparent" winner. Our analysis follows.

Preliminarily it is important to understand the questions in context. The Governor recognizes, and we agree, that his role in the election process does not extend beyond his responsibility to summon such persons as shall appear to be elected by a plurality to attend upon their respective houses and take their seats. Following the seating at the Governor's summons, it is ultimately those members of the House and Senate who shall determine who has been elected to the Senate and the House of Representatives of the State of Maine. While we are not unmindful of the role that those summoned may play in determining the ultimate winners of the election, the questions presented here relate not to identifying who has been elected, but rather to determining who are the apparent winners sufficient to summon those persons to Augusta.

We turn then to the first issue that must be addressed: whether or not the questions that the Governor has delivered present us with a solemn occasion involving important questions of law. We conclude that they do.

The doctrine of separation of powers, expressly articulated at Article III of the Maine Constitution, would normally dictate that we decline to answer questions presented by the Governor or the Legislature regarding their respective authority.

A narrow exception to this fundamental principle is created by Article VI, Section 3, which provides: "The Justices of the Supreme Judicial Court shall be obliged to give their opinion upon important questions of law, and upon solemn occasions, when required by the Governor, Senate or House of Representatives." Thus, when we receive a request for an advisory opinion from either house of the Legislature or from the Governor, we first determine whether it is within the scope of our constitutional authority to provide advisory opinions only "upon important questions of law, and upon solemn occasions" pursuant to Article VI, Section 3 of the Maine Constitution.

The following guideposts assist our determination on whether a "solemn occasion" has been presented on an "important question[ ] of law." First, the matter must be of "live gravity," referring to the immediacy and seriousness of the question. "A solemn occasion refers to an unusual exigency, such an exigency as exists when the body making the inquiry, having some action in view, has serious doubts as to its power and authority to take such action under the Constitution or under existing statutes." In addition, the questions presented must be sufficiently precise that we can determine "the exact nature of the inquiry," and we will not answer questions that are "tentative, hypothetical and abstract."

Although an advisory opinion "has no precedential value and no conclusive effect as a judgment upon any party," such opinions provide guidance on present and future controversies. The Justices have previously stated:

> [T]he advice being given to guide the Governor in the performance of a public and constitutional function of government, and having been followed, public policy, at least, requires that strong and compelling reasons be presented before the Court sitting *en banc* will hold an act by the Chief Executive of this nature invalid when taken in pursuance of a construction of the organic law given upon request under the constitution by a majority of the Court.

Thus, the determination that a question presents a "solemn occasion" is of significant import, and we will not find such an occasion to exist except in those circumstances when the facts in support of the alleged solemn occasion are clear and compelling.

A solemn occasion has been presented on the facts before us. Following general elections of the members of the Maine Senate and House, the Secretary of State is required to tabulate the election returns and forward them to the Governor. The Governor is then required by law to issue an election certificate or a notice of an apparent election to individuals who, from his examination of the returns, appear to be the winners of the respective elections by a plurality of the votes cast. Such an election occurred on November 5, 2002, and Governor King must accomplish his duty to issue a certificate or notice at least seven days before December 4, 2002.

The Governor represents that the results of several races are disputed, that recounts have failed to resolve the disputes, and that the number of disputed ballots in more than one such race could determine the outcome of that race. He also represents that the tabulation by the Secretary of State will not include the disputed ballots among those counted.

The essence of the questions can be summarized succinctly: in light of the Governor's uncertainty as to the import of 21-A M.R.S.A. § 739 and other pertinent constitutional and statutory provisions, does the Governor have the authority to investigate and "evaluate disputed ballots in making a determination" independent of the Secretary of State's tabulations. The inquiry is sufficiently precise for us to determine its exact nature, and involves constitutionally mandated conduct on the part of the Governor under circumstances where the Governor has "serious doubts as to [his] power and authority." Moreover, the Justices have historically found similar questions to present a solemn occasion.

We therefore conclude that the Governor's questions present a solemn occasion regarding important questions of law.

RESPONSES TO THE GOVERNOR'S QUESTIONS

QUESTION 1: Must the Governor accept the tabulation of the Secretary of State as the sole basis for his determination of what persons to summon and issue a certificate of election, or does the Governor have authority independent of the Secretary of State to determine the apparent winners of a legislative election?

We answer Question 1 as follows. In the context of the facts presented here, the Governor must accept the tabulation of the Secretary of State as the sole basis for the determination of what persons to summon. The Governor does not have independent authority to examine and accept or reject ballots when determining the apparent winner. The Constitution gives the Governor the authority to examine copies of the lists of votes that have been delivered to the Secretary of State from the towns and cities. From an examination of the copies of the lists, which generate the Secretary of State's tabulation, the Governor then issues a summons to attend the session of the Legislature to those persons who appear to have been elected.

In the 1948 and 1956 Opinions, the Justices said that even though the Legislature had purportedly conferred on the Governor the authority to correct returns by counting votes and hearing testimony, he had no authority to decide which ballots to count or reject. Therefore, because the Legislature has taken away even that purported authority to correct returns, nothing gives the Governor the authority to decide which ballots to count and which to reject in carrying out his responsibility to summon the apparent winners.

QUESTION 2: Does the difference in language between Article IV, Part 1, § 5 and Article IV, Part 2, § 4 result in different responses to Question 1 as between the House of Representatives and the Senate?

We answer Question 2 in the negative. The difference in the language is without significance and makes no difference whatsoever in the Governor's role regarding the election returns. The Governor's role in examining Senate and House elections is the same, and the Governor treats the lists of votes identically.

QUESTION 3: Does 21-A M.R.S.A. § 739 provide the Governor with authority to evaluate disputed ballots in making a determination of who to certify as having apparently received a plurality of votes in a legislative election?

We answer Question 3 in the negative. Section 739 does not give the Governor the authority to evaluate disputed ballots. Its sole function is to require a municipal clerk or the Secretary of State to provide ballots or voting lists to any of the authorities listed in that statute when those authorities make a request for the same. The statute does not confer any authority upon the Governor to examine or count ballots.

QUESTION 4: May the Governor certify and summon persons different from the persons the Secretary of State tabulates as the apparent winner of a legislative election?

In the context of the questions presented and for the reasons stated above, we answer Question 4 in the negative.

In re ADVISORY OPINION TO the GOVERNOR (Casino)
856 A.2d 320 (R.I. 2004)

To His Excellency Donald L. Carcieri, Governor of the State of Rhode Island and Providence Plantations:

We have received from Your Excellency a letter dated July 9, 2004, in which you have requested our written advisory opinion pursuant to article 10, section 3, of the Rhode Island Constitution. In your request, you raise concerns over a recent legislative enactment dealing with a proposed casino in the Town of West Warwick. The enactment at issue, G.L.1956 chapter 9.1 of title 41, entitled "The Rhode Island Gaming Control and Revenue Act," (Casino Act), provides comprehensive guidelines for a casino operation. The Casino Act also calls for a statewide ballot question asking the voters of this state: "Shall there be a casino in the Town of West Warwick operated by an Affiliate of Harrah's Entertainment in association with the Narragansett Indian Tribe?" (referendum question). Section 41-9.1-9. Your Excellency's request asks us: "Do the question and the legislation's establishment of a privately-operated casino violate the

[Rhode Island] constitutional prohibition" on lotteries in this state except those lotteries operated by the state or those previously permitted by the General Assembly. As we said in *Almond v. Rhode Island Lottery Commission,* 756 A.2d 186, 191 (R.I.2000), we say yet again: the General Assembly has plenary power to legislate on all matters pertaining to gambling in this state. Nevertheless, we are of the opinion that both the referendum question and the Casino Act as a whole are constitutionally defective.

Introduction

Before delving into our discussion of the issues raised in Your Excellency's request, we reiterate our role in delivering an advisory opinion. When issuing an advisory opinion, the justices of this Court "do not speak ex cathedra, from the chair of judgment, but only as consultors somewhat like the jurisconsults under the Roman law." Speaking in our individual capacities as legal experts rather than Supreme Court justices, we are unable to exercise the fact-finding power of the Court. Because this opinion is not an exercise of judicial power, it is not binding and "it carries no mandate."

As expected, the Casino Act has proven to be politically charged. Since receiving initial approval from both houses of the General Assembly, the Casino Act met a brief death on the Governor's desk. After the Governor vetoed the legislation on July 1, 2004, the Casino Act was returned to the General Assembly for further action. Expecting his veto to be overridden and betting that the Casino Act is unconstitutional, the Governor submitted the instant request for an advisory opinion. On July 12, 2004, this Court entered an order requesting that the General Assembly notify us of any action taken with respect to the Governor's veto, setting dates for oral argument and issuing a briefing schedule. The Senate and the House overrode the veto on July 23, 2004, and July 30, 2004, respectively, and the Casino Act became law.

Under the terms of the Casino Act, the Rhode Island Lottery Commission (Lottery Commission), the Narragansett Indian Tribe (Narragansett tribe), and Harrah's Entertainment, Inc., or an affiliate thereof (Harrah's), would enter into a "Master Contract" to create a casino in this state. According to its website, Harrah's "is the world's largest casino operator." Patrons of the proposed casino would be able to try their luck at a wide variety of "[g]ambling game[s]," including "any game played with cards, dice, equipment or a machine,…including, but not limited to faro, monte, roulette, keno, bingo fan tan, twenty-one, blackjack, seven and a half, klondike, craps, poker, chuck a luck, Chinese chuck a luck (dai shu), wheel of fortune, chemin de fer, baccarat, pai gow, beat the banker, panguingui, slot machine, any banking or percentage game, or any other game or device approved by the Commission."

The beginning of the casino operation would depend on voter approval. To that end, § 41-9.1-9 of the Casino Act calls for placing the referendum question on the November 2, 2004 ballot; asking: "Shall there be a casino in the Town of West Warwick operated by an Affiliate of Harrah's Entertainment in association with the Narragansett Indian Tribe?"

The Propriety of the Request

We begin our discussion by considering whether it is appropriate to issue an advisory opinion at this time. Our general obligation to issue advisory opinions comes from article 10, section 3, of the Rhode Island Constitution, which provides: "[t]he judges of the supreme court shall give their written opinion upon any question of law whenever requested by the governor or by either house of the general assembly." There are, however, certain procedural hurdles that must be cleared before our duty to issue an advisory opinion arises. "We are constitutionally obligated to give advisory opinions to either House of the General Assembly only when the questions propounded concern the constitutionality of pending legislation, and to the Governor only when the questions propounded concern the constitutionality of existing statutes which require implementation by the Chief Executive." Because the General Assembly has properly overridden the Governor's veto, the Casino Act is an existing statute. Nevertheless, it is clear that executive implementation of the substantive provisions of the Casino Act hinges on voter approval of the casino question through both the local and statewide referendum processes. Unless and until such approval is obtained, the Governor has no present obligation to implement the Casino Act and we are not constitutionally *required* to issue an advisory opinion.

Despite certain procedural infirmities, justices of this Court have been willing to issue advisory opinions if the propounded question raises important constitutional or social questions. There is no clearly defined test for determining whether an improperly presented request for our opinion will be granted. That decision has been made on a case-by-case basis in the exercise of the justices' discretion. For example, in *In re Advisory Opinion (Chief Justice)*, the justices of this Court were presented with a procedurally flawed request for an advisory opinion about the removal of a Supreme Court Chief Justice. Although the request was improperly presented, the justices "exercise[d] [their] discretion and waive[d] the defects" so they could address the important issues raised in the request. Also, in *In re Advisory Opinion to the House of Representatives (Impoundment of State Aid to Cities and Towns)*, despite a procedural flaw in a request for an advisory opinion, justices of this Court issued an advisory opinion about the propriety of a former Governor's refusal to distribute more than $10 million in appropriated money. Because many municipalities adopted operating budgets and entered contracts while relying on the appropriated money, the propounded question raised questions of sufficient public importance to require an immediate answer.

The issues raised in the Governor's request are of great public and constitutional importance. The Casino Act calls for placing the referendum question on the statewide ballot. The Governor's question asks whether the Casino Act and its requirement that the ballot question be submitted to the voters pass constitutional muster. If, as we believe, the question and legislation are void as unconstitutional, then members of the public will waste much money, time, effort, and energy to familiarize themselves with the controversial issues that the proposed casino has raised. This confusion certainly will be intensified by the fact that the Governor and the Attorney General, two general officers of this state, expressly have taken the position that the Casino Act is constitutionally infirm. The issues surrounding a statewide vote on a casino are especially important because, as the Casino Act acknowledges, "[t]here are socio-economic costs that expanded gaming may impose on communities and the state."

Because we believe the question and legislation to be unconstitutional, to delay the issuance of our opinion would only postpone the inevitable. If we were to sit idly by while an unconstitutional question was submitted to the voters, only to later issue a binding decision declaring the Casino Act and the referendum question void, chaos might well ensue.

[T]he Texas Supreme Court has taken the position that

> "[w]hen the Legislature remains silent or denies a right of judicial review, administrative decisions may nevertheless be attacked in court if they adversely affect a vested property right or otherwise violate some provision of the State or Federal Constitution...The right to challenge administrative actions by an original action in district court on the basis that such actions unconstitutionally deprive the plaintiff of a vested property right is a right to judicial review distinctly different from the right to judicial review given by a statute." *Continental Casualty Insurance Co. v. Functional Restoration Associates,* 19 S.W.3d 393, 404 (Tex.2000).

Applying the above cited principles, we would not interpret the Casino Act to impose any restriction on the court's ability to hear and decide constitutional claims relating to the Casino Act or actions taken under it because there is no explicit restriction to that effect.

Even if the Casino Act did contain an explicit limitation on the judiciary's right to hear constitutional claims, we believe that such an attempt would be a violation of the separation of powers doctrine-"an inherent and integral element of the republican form of government."

"The twin purposes of preventing concentrations of power dangerous to liberty and of promoting governmental efficiency are served if we define a constitutional violation of the separation of powers as [1] an assumption by one branch of powers that [is] central or essential to the operation of a coordinate branch, [2] provided also that the assumption disrupts the coordinate branch in the performance of its duties and [3] is unnecessary to implement a legitimate policy of the Government."

A central operation of the judiciary is to determine whether legislative enactments and other governmental actions are constitutionally permissible. Article 6, section 1, of the Rhode Island Constitution provides in part that "[t]his Constitution shall be the supreme law of the state, and any law inconsistent therewith shall be void." Plainly, all laws within this state, including the Casino Act, must conform to the restrictions and limitations set out in this state's constitution. It has long been established that the Supreme Court is the "only...body that is authorized to interpret the statutes of this State with the view of determining their constitutionality." Accordingly, it is for the judiciary alone to determine whether any enactment of the General Assembly is constitutionally repugnant.

Any attempt by the General Assembly to determine for itself whether a law is inconsistent with the constitution is an assumption of this Court's right and obligation under the constitution. This assumption of judicial power disrupts the judiciary as a whole in performing its duties, and serves no legitimate purpose in effectuating governmental policy. Consequently, to the extent that the Casino Act purports to divest the judiciary of its constitutional role, § 41-9.1-9(f) impermissibly usurps the judicial power entrusted to this Court and the trial courts by art. 10, sec. 2, of the Rhode Island Constitution.

It is clear that the General Assembly has the power to establish the jurisdiction of the courts; but that power is not without limits. Although the General Assembly may prescribe requirements for hearing constitutional claims (statute of limitations, venue, etc.), it may not deprive the judiciary of its inherent jurisdiction to hear and decide constitutional issues.

Although we have great regard for the General Assembly and must give great deference to it and the acts it adopts, the General Assembly, like the Supreme Court and the Governor, exists solely by virtue of the state constitution. Under the constitution, "[t]he judicial power of this state shall be vested in one supreme court."

By delivering our advisory opinion before the question is submitted to the voters, we give credence to this Court's recognition of the prevailing public policy in favor of finality and validity of the voting process in this state. In *Cianci,* this Court described the strong preference for resolving election issues before the voters have spoken. Although *Cianci* involved a challenge to a mayor's election to office in Providence, the overriding policy favoring pre-election resolution of issues applies equally to controversial and socially important questions concerning a casino operation in this state.

Because of the public and constitutional importance of the questions before us, we will overlook any procedural deficiencies in the Governor's request and issue an advisory opinion at this time.

Conclusion

For the reasons stated, we answer the first question addressed to us by the Governor, namely whether the proposed ballot question violates the constitution, in the affirmative. We also answer the second question addressed to us by the Governor, namely whether the General Assembly's establishment of the proposed casino violates the constitution, in the affirmative.

In re OPINION OF THE JUSTICES (APPOINTMENT OF CHIEF JUSTICE OF THE SUPREME COURT)
842 A.2d 816 (N.H. 2003)

To His Excellency the Governor and the Honorable Council:

The undersigned justices of the supreme court have considered the questions submitted in your resolution adopted December 3, 2003, and filed on December 9, 2003. You requested our reply on an expedited basis, and, if possible, before December 31, 2003. Time limitations prevented us from complying with our usual practice of allowing interested parties an opportunity to provide memoranda on the questions presented. As time is of the essence, therefore, in response to this resolution, we submit the following:

We have in the past asked to be excused from answering inquiries when they are beyond the spirit or letter of the constitutional provision for advisory opinions. We respectfully ask to be excused from answering the present inquiries.

Part II, Article 74 of the State Constitution empowers the justices of the supreme court to render advisory opinions, outside the context of concrete, fully-developed factual situations and without the benefit of adversary legal presentations, only in carefully circumscribed situations. Part II, Article 74 permits the justices of the supreme court to render advisory opinions only "upon important questions of law and upon solemn occasions" when asked to do so by the legislature or the Governor and Council on matters relating to their official duties. When we issue such opinions, we act not as a court, but as individual constitutional advisors to the legislative or executive branches.

With respect to issuing advisory opinions about existing statutes, as we are asked to do here, our constitutional authority is especially limited. We have no authority under Part II, Article 74 to issue advisory opinions to either branch of the legislature regarding existing legislation. That authority extends only to proposed legislation.

There are occasions where the Governor and Council are entitled to advisory opinions as to their official duty and authority under existing law. This is not such an occasion because there are limitations in the operation of Part II, Article 74. To express our views about the constitutionality of RSA 490:1 would be expressing our views upon questions involving private rights. It would also place us in the position of giving advice in matters that may come before the court for decision.

As we have previously explained, "Where the constitutionality of existing law is ... brought in question, those who may deem their rights infringed...may have recourse to our courts for the protection of their supposed privileges."

In addition, the unusual nature of the private rights involved in this situation make the questions posed particularly ill-suited for an advisory opinion. Among "those who may deem their rights infringed" could be one of our colleagues or one of us. Because of this, we are disqualified from reaching the merits of the questions. Such being the case, the question of whether replacement justices may be appointed under RSA 490:3 arises. That question is addressed by the Chief Justice in his separate opinion.

The justices of the supreme court rarely decline to answer questions posed pursuant to Part II, Article 74. We do so now only after carefully considering our constitutional duties and based upon long-established prior decisions.

For these reasons, we respectfully request to be excused from answering the questions posed.

Separate Opinion of Chief Justice BROCK.

I write separately to explain why I conclude that I am not authorized to appoint replacement justices in this matter. Part II, Article 74 of the New Hampshire Constitution vests in "the justices of the supreme court" the exclusive authority to render advisory opinions upon questions posed by the legislature or the Governor and Council "upon important questions of law." Part II, Article 74 does not vest the authority to issue advisory opinions with the supreme court, as an institution, but rather with the individual supreme court justices. When the justices of the supreme court give an advisory opinion pursuant to Part II, Article 74, they do not act as a court, but as constitutional advisors to the legislative or executive branches.

Only sitting supreme court justices are "justices of the supreme court" for Part II, Article 74 purposes; only sitting supreme court justices may act as constitutional advisors to co-equal branches of the government. Justices appointed to replace sitting members of the court pursuant to RSA 490:3 are not "justices of the supreme court." As we [have] explained a justice appointed to sit in a specific matter pursuant to RSA 490:3 does not become a supreme court justice. A justice appointed to a specific case is "merely enabled to use his power as a judicial officer on a temporary basis, according to RSA 490:3."

Furthermore, RSA 490:3 does not accord a judge assigned to sit temporarily on the supreme court all of the powers of a sitting supreme court justice, but rather only the authority to "hear arguments, render decisions, and file opinions" in one specific matter. In context, the reference to filing an "opinion" does not refer to an advisory opinion, but rather refers to an opinion in a justiciable controversy.

NOTE

The situation on which an advisory opinion was sought in this case was resolved in *In Re Petition of Governor*, 846 A.2d 1148 (N.H. 2004), excerpted below at page 881.

3. Certified Questions

Although federal courts are courts of limited jurisdiction, they frequently entertain questions of state law under their diversity jurisdiction and pendent jurisdiction. When an outcome-dispositive state law question arises in a federal-court case, one or both litigants may wish to ask the court to certify the question to the relevant state supreme court—so that the final dispositor of state law may resolve the question. The process is regulated by the state supreme courts, which generally retain authority to accept or reject the invitation. *See, e.g.*, Rule XVIII of the Rules of Practice of the Supreme Court of Ohio. For like reasons, a federal court on its own initiative may seek to certify the question. The procedure provided by the State of Washington is representative:

> When in the opinion of any federal court before whom a proceeding is pending, it is necessary to ascertain the local law of this state in order to dispose of such proceeding and the local law has not been clearly determined, such federal court may certify to the supreme court for answer the question of local law involved and the supreme court shall render its opinion in answer thereto. WASH. REV.CODE § 2.60.020.

If state court certification is unavailable, a federal court retains the authority to abstain and to require the parties to litigate the question initially in the state courts. *See Kaiser Steel Corp. v. W. S. Ranch Co.*, 391 U.S. 593 (1968).

LEHMAN BROTHERS v. SCHEIN
416 U.S. 386 (1974)

DOUGLAS, J.

The Court of Appeals by a divided vote reversed the District Court. While the Court of Appeals held that Florida law was controlling, it found none that was decisive. So it then turned to the law of other jurisdictions, particularly that of New York, to see if Florida "would probably" interpret Diamond to make it applicable here. The Court of Appeals concluded that the defendants had engaged with Chasen "to misuse corporate property," and that the theory of Diamond reaches that situation, "viewing the case as the Florida court would probably view it." There were emanations from other Florida decisions that made the majority on the Court of Appeals feel that Florida would follow that reading of Diamond. Such a construction of Diamond, the Court of Appeals said, would have "the prophylactic effect of providing a disincentive to insider trading." And so it would. Yet under the regime of *Erie R. Co. v. Tompkins*, 304 U.S. 64 (1938), a State can make just the opposite her law, providing there is no overriding federal rule which pre-empts state law by reason of federal curbs on trading in the stream of commerce.

The dissenter on the Court of Appeals urged that that court certify the state-law question to the Florida Supreme Court as is provided in Fla.Stat.Ann. s 25.031 and its Appellate Rule 4.61. That path is open to this Court and to any court of appeals of the United States. We have, indeed, used it before, as have courts of appeals.

Moreover when state law does not make the certification procedure available, a federal court not infrequently will stay its hand, remitting the parties to the state court to resolve the controlling state law on which the federal rule may turn. Numerous applications of that practice are reviewed in *Meredith v. Winter Haven*, 320 U.S. 228 (1943), which teaches that the mere difficulty in ascertaining local law is no excuse for remitting the parties to a state tribunal for the start of another lawsuit. We do not suggest that where there is doubt as to local law and where the certification procedure is available, resort to it is obligatory. It does, of course, in the long run save time, energy, and resources and helps build a cooperative judicial federalism. Its use in a given case rests in the sound discretion of the federal court.

Here resort to it would seem particularly appropriate in view of the novelty of the question and the great unsettlement of Florida law, Florida being a distant State. When federal judges in New York attempt to predict uncertain Florida law, they act, as we have referred to ourselves on this Court in matters of state law, as "outsiders" lacking the common exposure to local law which comes from sitting in the jurisdiction.

"Reading the Texas statutes and the Texas decisions as outsiders without special competence in Texas law, we would have little confidence in our independent judgment regarding the application of that law to the present situation. The lower court did deny that the Texas statutes sustained the Commission's assertion of power. And this represents the view of an able and experienced circuit judge of the circuit which includes Texas and of two capable district judges trained in Texas law." *Railroad Comm'n v. Pullman Co.*, 312 U.S. 496, 499 (1941).

The judgment of the Court of Appeals is vacated and the cases are remanded so that that court may reconsider whether the controlling issue of Florida law should be certified to the Florida Supreme Court pursuant to Rule 4.61 of the Florida Appellate Rules.

REHNQUIST, J., concurring.

I agree with [the Court], but think it appropriate to emphasize the scope of the discretion of federal judges in deciding whether to use such certification procedures.

Petitioners here were defendants in the District Court. That court, applying applicable New York choice-of-law rules, decided that Florida law governs the case and, finding that the respondents' complaint requested relief which would extend the substantive law even beyond New York's apparently novel decision in *Diamond v. Oreamuno*, 24 N.Y.2d 494 (1969), dismissed the complaint on the merits. The Court of Appeals agreed that Florida law applied, but held that Florida law would permit recovery on the claim stated by respondents. The opinion of the dissenting judge of the Court of Appeals, disagreeing with the majority's analysis of Florida law, added in a concluding paragraph that in light of the uncertainty of Florida law, the Florida certification procedure should have been utilized by the Court of Appeals. On rehearing, petitioners requested the Court of Appeals to utilize this procedure, but they concede that this is the first such request that they made. Thus petitioners seek to upset the result of more than two years of trial and appellate litigation on the basis of a point which they first presented to the Court of Appeals upon petition for rehearing.

The authority which Congress has granted this Court to review judgments of the courts of appeals undoubtedly vests us not only with the authority to correct errors of substantive law, but to prescribe the method by which those courts go about deciding the cases before them. But a sensible respect for the experience and competence of the various integral parts of the federal judicial system suggests that we go slowly in telling the courts of appeals or the district courts how to go about deciding cases where federal jurisdiction is based on diversity of citizenship, cases which they see and decide far more often than we do.

This Court has held that a federal court may not remit a diversity plaintiff to state courts merely because of the difficulty in ascertaining local law; it has also held that unusual circumstances may require a federal court having jurisdiction of an action to nonetheless abstain from deciding doubtful questions of state law. In each of these situations, our decisions have dealt with the issue of how to reconcile the exercise of the jurisdiction which Congress has conferred upon the federal courts with the important considerations of comity and cooperative federalism which are inherent in a federal system, both of which must be subject to a single national policy within the federal judiciary.

At the other end of the spectrum, however, I assume it would be unthinkable to any of the Members of this Court to prescribe the process by which a district court or a court of appeals should go about researching a point of state law which arises in a diversity case. Presumably the judges of the district courts and of the courts of appeals are at least as capable as we are in determining what the Florida courts have said about a particular question of Florida law.

State certification procedures are a very desirable means by which a federal court may ascertain an undecided point of state law, especially where, as is the case in Florida, the question can be certified directly to the court of last resort within the State. But in a purely diversity case such as this one, the use of such a procedure is more a question of the considerable discretion of the federal court in going about the decisionmaking process than it is a question of a choice trenching upon the fundamentals of our federal-state jurisprudence.

While certification may engender less delay and create fewer additional expenses for litigants than would abstention, it entails more delay and expense than would an ordinary decision of the state question on the merits by the federal court. The Supreme Court of Florida has promulgated an appellate rule, which provides that upon certification by a federal court to that court, the parties shall file briefs there according to a specified briefing schedule, that oral argument may be granted upon application, and that the parties shall pay the costs of the certification. Thus while the certification procedure is more likely to produce the correct determination of state law, additional time and money are required to achieve such a determination.

If a district court or court of appeals believes that it can resolve an issue of state law with available research materials already at hand, and makes the effort to do so, its determination should not be disturbed simply because the certification procedure existed but was not used. The question of whether certification on the facts of this case, particularly in view of the lateness of its suggestion by petitioners, would have advanced the goal of correctly disposing of this litigation on the state law issue is one which I would leave, and I understand that the Court would leave, to the sound judgment of the court making the initial choice. But since the Court has today for the first time expressed its view as to the use of certification procedures by the federal courts, I agree that it is appropriate to vacate the judgment of the Court of Appeals and remand the cases in order that the Court of Appeals may reconsider certification in light of the Court's opinion.

HALEY v. UNIVERSITY OF TENNESSEE-KNOXVILLE
188 S.W.3d 518 (Tenn. 2006)

E. RILEY ANDERSON, J.

In addition to the dispute that is the basis of the certified question, the parties have also raised the question of whether the Supreme Court has the authority to answer the certified question. We address that issue first.

Certified Questions

Rule 23 of the Tennessee Rules of the Supreme Court provides:

> The Supreme Court may, at its discretion, answer questions of law certified to it by the Supreme Court of the United States, a Court of Appeals of the United States, a District Court of the United States in Tennessee, or a United States Bankruptcy Court in Tennessee. This rule may be invoked when the certifying court determines that, in a proceeding before it, there are questions of law of this state which will be determinative of the cause and as to which it appears to the certifying court there is no controlling precedent in the decisions of the Supreme Court of Tennessee.

Tenn. Sup.Ct. R. 23, § 1. This Court adopted Rule 23 in 1989 and has since accepted and answered numerous certified questions from the federal courts. In spite of the fact that the rule has been in place for seventeen years, U.T. argues that it is unconstitutional and that this Court lacks jurisdiction to decide the certified question. For the following reasons, we reject U.T.'s argument.

A certification procedure permits a state's highest court to accept and answer a question of state law certified to it by the federal court to assist the federal court in deciding a question of state law. A majority of states have in place a procedure similar to our Rule 23. As the United States Supreme Court recognized in *Erie Railroad Co. v. Tompkins,* 304 U.S. 64, 78 (1938), "[e]xcept in matters governed by the Federal Constitution or by Acts of Congress, the law to be applied in any case [in federal court] is the law of the state." In cases where the "law of the state" is unclear, absent a certification procedure the federal court must either "(1) guess at the law and risk laying down a rule which may later prove to be out of harmony with state decisions...or (2) abstain from deciding the case until the state courts pass upon the point of law involved." Certification procedures assist the federal courts in correctly disposing of state law issues without incurring the delay inherent in the abstention process. Certification thus "save[s] time, energy, and resources and helps build a cooperative judicial federalism." *Lehman Bros. v. Schein,* 416 U.S. 386, 391 (1974).

More importantly, the certification procedure protects states' sovereignty. "To the extent that a federal court applies different legal rules than the state court would have, the state's sovereignty is diminished [because] the federal court has made state law." Such an impact on state sovereignty "is no small matter, especially since a federal court's error may perpetuate itself in state courts until the state's highest court corrects it."

Notwithstanding the strong policy arguments weighing in favor of a certification procedure, U.T. argues that because this Court's jurisdiction is limited by the Tennessee Constitution to appellate jurisdiction, the Court lacks jurisdiction to answer certified questions. Article VI, section 2 of the Tennessee Constitution provides that the jurisdiction of the Supreme Court "shall be appellate only, under such restrictions and regulations as may from time to time be prescribed by law; but it may possess such other jurisdiction as is now conferred by law on the present Supreme Court."

We have consistently held that Article VI, section 2's grant of power limits this Court to adjudicating appellate matters only. In construing the scope of our jurisdiction under Article VI, section 2, however, we have in the past been concerned exclusively with the Court's authority to adjudicate, that is, to finally settle, disputes before this Court. Because answering a certified question is not an adjudicative function, it is not an exercise of this Court's jurisdiction and is not prohibited by Article VI, section 2.

As we have previously explained, "[j]urisdiction is [the] lawful authority of a court to adjudicate a controversy brought before it; jurisdiction of the subject matter is conferred by the constitution and statutes, jurisdiction of the parties is acquired by service of process." In other words, a court only exercises its "jurisdiction" when it is called upon to "adjudicate a controversy." *Id.* To "adjudicate" is not simply to render a decision or an opinion. To "adjudicate" means "[t]o settle in the exercise of judicial authority. To *determine finally.*" *Black's Law Dictionary* 42 (6th ed.1990) (emphasis added). This definition is consistent with the meaning of "adjudicate" as it is used in Tennessee case law and rules.

We do not exercise our jurisdiction unless we finally dispose of a cause. Answering a certified question does not finally dispose of the cause; it merely informs the district court, which retains jurisdiction over the cause, how to interpret the state law at issue. Thus, "[b]y answering a state-law question certified by a federal court, we may affect the outcome of federal litigation, *but it is the federal court who hears and decides the cause.*"

Our power to answer certified questions comes, then, not from the Tennessee Constitution's grant of jurisdiction. Rather, our power to answer certified questions is grounded in Article VI, section 1 of the Constitution.

That section provides that "[t]he judicial power of this State shall be vested in one Supreme Court and in such Circuit, Chancery and other inferior Courts as the Legislature shall from time to time, ordain and establish; in the Judges thereof, and in Justices of the Peace." As the head of the judiciary, this Court is "the repository of the inherent power of the judiciary in this State." As an exercise of that inherent power, it is within the realm of the Court's authority to answer questions certified to us by the federal courts.

The inherent power of the Court consists of all powers "reasonably required to enable a court to perform efficiently its judicial functions, to *protect its dignity, independence and integrity,* and to make its lawful actions effective. These powers are inherent in the sense that they exist because the court exists...."

We have stated that answering certified questions not only furthers judicial efficiency and comity, but also protects this state's sovereignty against encroachment from the federal courts. Answering certified questions thus protects the "dignity, independence and integrity" of not only this Court but of the state as a whole and is therefore within the inherent power of this Court. As a sovereign state, Tennessee has "the power to exercise and the responsibility to protect" the sovereignty granted to it by the United States Constitution. *Scott,* 577 N.E.2d at 1079. We agree with the Ohio Supreme Court's observation that

> The state's sovereignty is unquestionably implicated when federal courts construe state law. If the federal court errs, it applies law other than [state] law, in derogation of the state's right to prescribe a "rule of decision." By allocating rights and duties incorrectly, the federal court both does an injustice to one or more parties, and frustrates the state's policy that would have allocated the rights and duties differently. The frustration of the state's policy may have a more lasting effect, because other potential litigants are likely to behave as if the federal decision were the law of the state. In that way, the federal court has, at least temporarily, made state law of which the state would have disapproved, had its courts had the first opportunity to pass on the question.

We therefore hold that we may answer certified questions consistent with the inherent power of this Court and with our responsibility to protect the sovereignty of the state.

PINO v. UNITED STATES
507 F.3d 1233 (10th Cir. 2007)

GORSUCH, J.

Michael and Amy Pino ask this court to certify to the Oklahoma Supreme Court the question whether a cause of action existed for the wrongful death of a nonviable stillborn fetus as of September 1-2, 2003. We agree that the resolution of this question may well determine the outcome of the Pinos' suit, and that it is a novel and unsettled matter in Oklahoma law. Accordingly, and as specified below, we grant the motion to certify.

I. FACTUAL BACKGROUND

Some twenty weeks pregnant, Ms. Pino arrived at the Carl Albert Indian Health Care Facility in Ada, Oklahoma in the early morning of September 1, 2003, complaining of constant cramping and vaginal bleeding. After evaluation, she was diagnosed with a urinary tract infection and released. Approximately three hours after her discharge, the Pinos called for an ambulance to take Ms. Pino back to the hospital because of her increased bleeding and abdominal pain. Upon her admission to the hospital, Dr. John Harvey, an employee of the hospital, performed a vaginal examination and questioned Ms. Pino about her condition. Dr. Harvey diagnosed Ms. Pino with placental abruption, requested that the pediatrician stand by to attend vaginal delivery of the fetus, and ruptured the amniotic sac. At twenty weeks, the fetus was, the parties stipulate, nonviable given the state of available medical technology. The following day the fetus was delivered stillborn.

Mr. and Ms. Pino sought damages for the wrongful death of their fetus, alleging that Dr. Harvey and the hospital rendered negligent medical care and treatment. Given the federal status of the hospital and Dr. Harvey's employment by the U.S. government, the Pinos first proceeded by filing an administrative claim pursuant to 28 U.S.C. § 2401(b), which the government denied. The Pinos thereafter brought this wrongful death action under the Federal Tort Claims Act (FTCA), 28 U.S.C. § 1346(b) and 2671, in the district court for the Eastern District of Oklahoma. The FTCA provides that the United States shall be liable for "personal injury or death...under circumstances where the United States, if a private person, would be liable to the claimant in accordance with the law of the place where the act or omission occurred." 28 U.S.C. § 1346(b)(1).

With the government's potential liability dependent on state law, the Pinos conceded that it was not clear whether a wrongful death action existed under Oklahoma law for a stillborn and admittedly nonviable fetus as of September 1-2, 2003. Accordingly, they asked the district court to certify the question to the Oklahoma Supreme Court. The district court declined this invitation and instead proceeded to grant summary judgment for the government, concluding Oklahoma would not have allowed such a claim at that time.

Mr. and Ms. Pino now move this court to exercise its independent authority to certify their question to the Oklahoma Supreme Court. Alternatively, they appeal, asking us to reverse the district court's denial of their motion to certify and to reverse its entry of summary judgment.

II. STANDARDS FOR CERTIFICATION

A motion for certification may be brought independently and anew to the court of appeals. *See* 10th Cir. R. 27.1. Such a motion requires us to determine whether certification is appropriate as a *de novo* matter without regard to the district court's assessment. Certification by this court in no way implies an abuse of discretion by the district court in failing to certify, but only indicates our independent judgment on the question.

The standards governing our independent analysis stem from both state and federal law. Under Oklahoma law, the Oklahoma Supreme Court has the power to answer a question certified to it by any federal court "if the answer may be determinative of an issue in pending litigation in the certifying court and there is no controlling decision of the Supreme Court or Court of Criminal Appeals, constitutional provision, or statute of this state." Okla. Stat. tit. 20, § 1602.

Under our own federal jurisprudence, we will not trouble our sister state courts every time an arguably unsettled question of state law comes across our desks. When we see a reasonably clear and principled course, we will seek to follow it ourselves. While we apply judgment and restraint before certifying, however, we will nonetheless employ the device in circumstances where the question before us (1) may be determinative of the case at hand and (2) is sufficiently novel that we feel uncomfortable attempting to decide it without further guidance. In making the assessment whether to certify, we also seek to give meaning and respect to the federal character of our judicial system, recognizing that the judicial policy of a state should be decided when possible by state, not federal, courts. *See Lehman Bros.,* 416 U.S. at 391 .

III. REASONS FOR CERTIFICATION

The Pinos' request for certification meets these criteria. The parties before us are in full agreement that answering the question whether a wrongful death cause of action for a nonviable stillborn fetus existed as of September 1-2, 2003 may well determine the outcome of this litigation. We cannot disagree with their assessment. After all, should no cause of action exist, the government will be entitled to judgment as a matter of law. If a cause of action does exist, the government's primary defense asserted so far in this litigation will fall.

The novelty of the question is likewise apparent for several reasons. First, Oklahoma's legislature in 2005 amended the wrongful death statute expressly to allow claims like the Pinos'. Oklahoma, thus, seems to have a strong public policy preference for claims of this nature. At the same time, though, the 2005 amendment does not have retroactive effect. Thus, one might reasonably question whether the amendment was designed to change preexisting law, and at least tacitly suggests that a cause of action for a nonviable stillborn fetus did not exist prior to its enactment. As it happens, however, such is not necessarily the case in Oklahoma. Under Oklahoma law, it is only "[i]f the earlier version of a statute definitely expresses a clear and unambiguous intent or has been judicially interpreted [that] a legislative amendment is presumed to change the existing law." Meanwhile, "if the earlier statute's meaning is in doubt or uncertain, a presumption arises that the amendment is designed to clarify," rather than change, existing law. In this case, prior to the 2005 amendment, Oklahoma's wrongful death statute did not express a clear and unambiguous intent to exclude nonviable stillborn fetuses, and neither had the Oklahoma Supreme Court interpreted it to do so. Accordingly, the statutory history, suggestive though it may be, affords us no definitive guidance.

Second, there is no authoritative decision of the Oklahoma Supreme Court on the existence or nonexistence of a cause of action under the state's wrongful death statute as of 2003. What law does exist, moreover, underscores that the question is an open one. The Oklahoma Supreme Court long ago held that the pre-2005 wrongful death statute affords a cause of action for negligent prenatal care if a viable fetus is stillborn. The court also definitively held as early as 1993 that a wrongful death action can be predicated on a prenatal injury occurring before viability, at least when a viable fetus is subsequently born alive. And, finally, the Oklahoma Supreme Court held that the pre-2005 wrongful death statute affords a cause of action in cases of nonviable fetuses born alive who subsequently die as the result of medical negligence during pregnancy. Thus, while the Oklahoma Supreme Court has addressed a number of permutations involving viable and nonviable fetuses born alive or stillborn under the law governing as of 2003, it simply has not yet addressed the question whether a cause of action existed in cases combining nonviable fetuses and stillbirth.

Third, *Nealis* highlighted the novelty and difficulty of our question. There, the Oklahoma Supreme Court acknowledged that certain aspects of its reasoning could be read to permit wrongful death actions for nonviable, stillborn fetuses, explaining that "much that we have said could apply equally to nonviable, stillborn fetuses." *Id.* at 455. At the same time, the court explicitly limited its holding to nonviable fetuses born alive, indicating that "[f]actors not considered in today's opinion may bear on whether liability should be extended to the wrongful death of a nonviable, stillborn fetus" under the pre-2005 wrongful death statute. *Id.* This careful acknowledgment and reservation makes it both difficult and unwise for this court to predict how the Oklahoma Supreme Court would decide the question of state law presented by this case.

Fourth, we are aware of only one Oklahoma state court decision directly on point, *Guyer v. Hugo Publishing Co.,* 830 P.2d 1393

(Okla.Civ.App.1991). Because *Evans* only recognized a wrongful death cause of action for a viable unborn child, the Oklahoma Court of Appeals in *Guyer* reasoned that no wrongful death cause of action should exist for the loss of a nonviable stillborn fetus. *Guyer,* 830 P.2d at 1394. But, the appeals court's decision came before *Nealis,* which rather substantially shifted the legal landscape, and the supreme court's explicit reservation in *Nealis* of the exact question presented in *Guyer* indicates that the state's highest court considers it still very much open. Furthermore, the governing Oklahoma statute contemplates certification in exactly these circumstances, where an intermediate court, but not the definitive court of last resort, has spoken to the issue.

IV. QUESTION CERTIFIED

In light of the fact that its resolution may well dispose of the matter before us, as well as its novelty and difficulty, we find the question raised by this appeal to be precisely the sort that calls for us to seek the authoritative guidance of the state supreme court. Therefore, on the Pinos' motion pursuant to 10th Cir. R. 27.1 and Okla. Stat. tit. 20, §§ 1601-1611, the United States Court of Appeals for the Tenth Circuit hereby certifies to the Oklahoma Supreme Court the following question of state law which may determine the outcome in this action pending before the court:

> As of September 1-2, 2003, did the Oklahoma Wrongful Death Statute, Okla. Stat. tit. 12, § 1053, afford a cause of action for the wrongful death of a nonviable stillborn fetus?

4. Implied Constitutional Remedies

KATZBERG v. REGENTS OF THE UNIV. OF CALIFORNIA
58 P.3d 339 (Cal. 2002)

GEORGE, C.J.

We granted review in this matter...to consider whether an individual may bring an action for money damages on the basis of an alleged violation of a provision of the California Constitution, in the absence of a statutory provision or an established common law tort authorizing such a damage remedy for the constitutional violation. In the present case, plaintiff seeks, among other relief, monetary damages based upon defendant's alleged violation of his due process "liberty" interest under article I, section 7, subdivision (a), of the California Constitution (hereafter article I, section 7(a)), by failing to provide him with a timely "name-clearing" hearing after his removal as department chairman at a university medical center. We conclude that an action for damages is not available.[1]

I.

In 1991, plaintiff Richard W. Katzberg was appointed professor of medicine at the University of California at Davis Medical School and Chairperson of the Department of Radiology at the University of California Davis Medical Center. In July 1995, the university commenced an investigation concerning alleged mishandling of funds by the department of radiology. In February 1996, the university issued a press release regarding the investigation, and the Sacramento District Attorney's Office thereafter announced that it would initiate a criminal investigation.

The investigation concerned approximately $250,000 that allegedly had been placed inappropriately in radiology accounts to be used for payment of department expenses. Most of this money came from rebates provided by medical equipment vendors. There never has been any allegation that plaintiff made any personal use of the challenged funds. Instead, the alleged improprieties related to placement of funds in the department's account rather than in the medical center's general funds.

In March 1996, the university announced that "appropriate personnel actions" had been initiated, but did not name any specific employee. Later that month, plaintiff was removed as chairperson of the department. He remained a tenured professor at the medical school and a staff physician at the medical center.

Plaintiff sued various defendants on numerous grounds, and the resulting litigation has moved back and forth between state and federal courts. For present purposes, it is sufficient to note that plaintiff's third amended complaint-the one here at issue-named as defendants the Regents of the University of California (the Regents) and the Chancellor of the University of California at Davis, Larry N. Vanderhoef (hereafter collectively, defendants). The complaint alleged that by making stigmatizing statements about plaintiff in the course of removing him from his position as department chairperson, defendants violated the *liberty* interest of plaintiff protected under article I, section 7(a).

---

[1] [1] We do not here consider the propriety of actions such as those based upon grounds established under common law tort principles-for example, actions for false arrest, false imprisonment, wrongful termination based upon violation of public policy, or the like. In such actions, a breach of duty or violation of public policy may be established by demonstrating a violation of a constitutional provision, and damages properly may be awarded to remedy the tort. We consider here only whether an action for damages is available to remedy a constitutional violation that is not tied to an established common law or statutory action.

Although the department chairmanship was an at-will position, terminable without cause at the discretion of the chancellor of the Davis campus (and hence plaintiff concedes that he had no due process *property* right to that position), it is well established that "an at-will [public] employee's *liberty* interests are deprived when his discharge is accompanied by charges 'that might seriously damage his standing and associations in his community' or 'impose[ ] on him a stigma or other disability that foreclose[s] his freedom to take advantage of other employment opportunities.'" When such a liberty deprivation occurs, a party has a right to a "name-clearing hearing."

The third amended complaint alleged that plaintiff had not been provided with such a hearing at which he could defend himself, either prior to, or since, his removal. The complaint also sought a variety of relief, including an injunction, damages, attorney fees, and costs.

The trial court granted defendants' motion to strike the prayer for relief. Later, in October 1999-three and a half years after plaintiff's removal-defendants offered plaintiff a name-clearing hearing. For the next few months, the parties negotiated unsuccessfully concerning the parameters of such a hearing. In February 2000, defendants revised and renewed the proposal for a name-clearing hearing, but plaintiff rejected that offer, and no such hearing has been held.

Defendants thereafter moved for summary judgment on plaintiff's due-process-liberty-interest claim on the grounds that (i) a liberty interest violation could not be proved, because the "alleged false statements are not stigmatizing as a matter of law," and (ii) even if a liberty interest violation could be proved, the remedy would be limited to a name-clearing hearing, which plaintiff previously had rejected.

The trial judge granted summary judgment to defendants, finding they had offered plaintiff an adequate name-clearing hearing, and that such a postremoval hearing was the sole remedy for the asserted liberty interest violation under the due process clause of article I, section 7(a). The court found that money damages were not available under California law to remedy "infringement of liberty interests," or to remedy any alleged undue delay in the offer of a name-clearing hearing.

In this court, plaintiff contends that article I, section 7(a) affords him a right to damages for the asserted violation of his due process liberty interest. By contrast, defendants assert that a name-clearing hearing is the sole remedy that a court should impose for the alleged constitutional violation. For purposes of analyzing the damages issue upon which we granted review, we shall assume, as did the Court of Appeal, that the facts alleged in the third amended complaint are sufficient to establish a violation of the due process liberty interest under the state Constitution's due process clause.

II.

Article I, section 26 of the California Constitution states: "The provisions of this Constitution are mandatory and prohibitory, unless by express words they are declared to be otherwise." Under this provision, "all branches of government are required to comply with constitutional directives or prohibitions." As we observed more than a century ago, "[e]very constitutional provision is self-executing to this extent, that everything done in violation of it is void."

Accordingly, the question posed in this case is not whether article I, section 7(a) is "self-executing." It is clear that the due process clause of article I, section 7(a) *is* self-executing, and that even without any effectuating legislation, all branches of government are required to comply with its terms. Furthermore, it also is clear that, like many other constitutional provisions, this section supports an action, brought by a private plaintiff against a proper defendant, for declaratory relief or for injunction. The question presented here is whether, assuming the complaint states a violation of plaintiff's due process liberty interest, plaintiff may maintain an action for *monetary damages* to remedy the asserted violation of his due process liberty interests under article I, section 7(a), on the facts alleged.

III.

More than 30 years ago in *Bivens v. Six Unknown Fed. Narcotics Agents*, 403 U.S. 388 (1971), the United States Supreme Court recognized the right of a party to recover damages for the violation of a constitutional right [the Fourth Amendment protection against unreasonable searches and seizures] in an action against federal agents. The court in *Bivens* did not approach the issue as posing a question whether the Fourth Amendment was *intended* to provide an action for damages, or whether such an intent could be *inferred* from that provision; instead, the court viewed the matter as posing a question whether the court should create a cause of action for damages-in effect, a constitutional tort-to remedy a Fourth Amendment violation, even though Congress had not specifically provided such a remedy and even though the Fourth Amendment does not provide for enforcement by an award of damages. The high court reasoned that as a general proposition "'federal courts may use any available remedy to make good the wrong done.'" In support of its conclusion that a damages remedy was warranted, the court emphasized that (i) there existed "no special factors counseling hesitation" to recognize such a right; (ii) there was no equally effective alternative remedy; and (iii) there was no "explicit congressional declaration that persons injured by a federal officer's violation of the Fourth Amendment may not recover money damages from the agents."

Subsequent to *Bivens,* the United States Supreme Court has considered numerous cases in which plaintiffs have sought money damages under a constitutional cause of action premised upon the asserted violation of various federal constitutional provisions. After twice following the lead of *Bivens,* and recognizing the availability of a constitutional tort action for damages on the strength of the considerations set out above, *Davis v. Passman,* 442 U.S. 228, 245 (1979) (*Davis*) (damages allowed to remedy violation by former congressman of equal protection component of Fifth Amendment due process clause); *Carlson v. Green,* 446 U.S. 14, 18-23 (1980) (*Carlson*) [damages allowed to remedy Eighth Amendment violations by prison officials]), the high court for the past two decades repeatedly has refused to recognize a federal constitutional tort action for money damages in cases presenting that issue. *Chappell v. Wallace,* 462 U.S. 296, 305 (1983) (*Chappell*) [alleged equal protection violations by superior officer in United States military]; *Bush v. Lucas,* 462 U.S. 367 (1983) (*Bush*) [alleged First Amendment violation against federal agency employee by superiors]; *United States v. Stanley,* 483 U.S. 669 (1987) [alleged due process violations by military personnel during the course of active military service]; *Schweiker v. Chilicky,* 487 U.S. 412 (1988) (*Schweiker*) [alleged due process violation by government officials, resulting in deprivation of Social Security benefits]; *FDIC v. Meyer,* 510 U.S. 471 (1994) (*Meyer*) [alleged due process violation concerning employment termination by federal agency]; *Correctional Services Corp. v. Malesko,* 534 U.S. 61, 68 (2001) (*Malesko*) [alleged Eighth Amendment violation by private operator of federal prison halfway house].)

In each of these more recent cases, the high court found that the first *Bivens* consideration mentioned above-"special factors" that "counsel hesitation" by a court in recognizing a constitutional tort damages remedy-militated against recognition of that remedy. And in these recent cases, the court also substantially retreated from, and reformulated, the other *Bivens* considerations mentioned above. The court has found that the absence of a "complete" alternative remedy will not support an action for damages, so long as a "meaningful" alternative remedy in state or federal law is available, and it has implicitly discarded the proposition, mentioned in *Bivens,* and emphasized in *Davis* and *Carlson,* that money damages are *presumptively* available unless Congress prohibits that remedy.[2]

The experience in other jurisdictions has been similar. Some out-of-state decisions, often relying upon a combination of (i) the jurisdiction's indigenous common law antecedents, (ii) special legislative history, and (iii) the Restatement Second of Torts section 874A, have recognized a

---

[2] [7] Although the high court has declined to extend *Bivens,* it has not abandoned the core holding of that case, and has recognized the continuing validity of that decision and its progeny.

constitutional tort cause of action and corresponding right to be awarded money damages for various state constitutional violations.[3] A greater number of cases, however, often tracking the reasoning of the most recent United States Supreme Court decisions or pointing to the absence of any historical basis for implying a damages action, have declined to recognize such a constitutional tort or implied damages remedy in a variety of circumstances.[4]

---

[3] [9] See *Brown v. State of New York*, 674 N.E.2d 1129 (N.Y. 1996) (damages allowed for violation of state's search and seizure and equal protection provisions, based upon Restatement Second of Torts, § 874A, early New York case authority recognizing a right to damages for such violations, and the absence of adequate alternative remedies); *Widgeon v. Eastern Shore Hosp. Center*, 479 A.2d 921, 923-925 (Md. 1984) (damages allowed for violation of state's search and seizure provision, based in part upon well-established English and early Maryland common law antecedents); *Moresi v. Dept. of Wildlife & Fisheries*, 567 So.2d 1081, 1091-1093 (La. 1990) (damages permissible to remedy illegal search and seizure, based in part upon English common law); see also *Binette v. Sabo*, 710 A.2d 688, 699 (Conn. 1998) (damages allowed for state constitution search and seizure violation; court found this remedy supported by "compelling policy considerations" and the absence of any special factors counseling against recognition of such an action); *Corum v. University of North Carolina*, 413 S.E.2d 276, 289-291 (N.C. 1992) (suggesting that damages may be allowed to remedy state free speech violation, based upon state common law authority, but noting that courts must defer to alternative remedies); *Old Tuckaway v. City of Greenfield*, 509 N.W.2d 323, 328 n. 4 (Wisc. 1993) (suggesting in dictum that damages may be allowed to remedy violations of state due process clause); see also *Walinski v. Morrison & Morrison*, 377 N.E.2d 242, 243-245 (Ill. App. 1978) (damages allowed to remedy violation of constitutional antidiscrimination clause; court found the drafters of the provision intended to create a right enforceable through damages).

[4] [10] See *Dick Fischer Dev. v. Dept. of Admin.*, 838 P.2d 263, 268 (Alaska 1992) (no damages allowed for asserted violation of state due process provision, based in part upon availability of alternative remedies); *Board of County Com'rs v. Sundheim*, 926 P.2d 545, 549-553 (Colo. 1996) (no damages allowed for asserted violation of state due process provision, based in part upon availability of alternative remedies); *Kelley Property Dev. v. Town of Lebanon*, 627 A.2d 909, 923-924 (Conn. 1993) (no damages allowed for asserted violation of state due process provision, based in part upon availability of alternative remedies and special factors counseling hesitation to recognize such a right); *Garcia v. Reyes*, 697 So.2d 549, 551 (Fla. App. 1997) (summarily holding there is no right to money damages for violation of state due process guarantee); *77th Dist. Judge v. State*, 438 N.W.2d 333, 339-340 (Mich. App. 1989) (no damages for violation of state equal protection rights; court noted, among other things, the availability of alternative relief and deference to legislative policy making expertise); *Moody v. Hicks*, 956 S.W.2d 398, 402 (Mo. App. 1997) (no damages for asserted violation of state search and seizure rights; court noted, among other things, the availability of alternative relief and deference to legislative policy making expertise); *Rockhouse Mountain Prop. v. Town of Conway*, 503 A.2d 1385, 1388-1389 (N.H. 1986) (no damages for alleged state due process and equal protection violations, based in part upon availability of alternative remedies); *Augat v. State* (A.D.1997), 666 N.Y.S.2d 249, 251-252 (N.Y. App. Div. 1997) (declining to extend *Brown, supra*, to allow damages for asserted violation of due process and freedom of association rights, based upon availability of alternative remedies); *Hanton v. Gilbert*, 486 S.E.2d 432, 438-439 (N.C. App. 1997) (no damages for alleged violation of state due

California decisions have followed a similar trend. Putting aside cases recognizing an inverse condemnation action for damages to remedy a violation of the state just compensation clause (a constitutional provision that clearly contemplates an award of damages determined in a judicial proceeding, see Cal. Const., art. I, § 19), only two decisions, each filed two decades ago, have recognized an action for damages to remedy a violation of the state Constitution. All subsequent decisions addressing the issue have declined to find such an action for damages.

In *Gay Law Students Assn. v. Pacific Tel. & Tel. Co.*, 595 P.2d 592 (Cal. 1979) (*Gay Law Students*), this court addressed an action by employees who claimed they were discriminated against by their employer, a state-regulated telephone company, on the basis of their sexual orientation. Our opinion observed that the plaintiffs sought declaratory and injunctive relief, and "also prayed for monetary damages." Without expressly addressing the question of availability of damages in addition to the requested equitable relief, we held that the plaintiffs could maintain a "direct court action" under the California equal protection clause, article I, section 7(a). In the process of announcing this holding we added a "cf." signal and citation to *Bivens*.

Plaintiff suggests that our citation in *Gay Law Students* to those pages of *Bivens* implies approval of a damages remedy for the equal protection violation asserted in *Gay Law Students*. Only the last few of the pages cited from *Bivens* spoke to the question of damages, however, and given the circumstance that in *Gay Law Students*, we did not explicitly address the question of damages, it would be an overstatement to interpret that decision, or its citation to *Bivens*, as directly endorsing such a remedy.

IV.

---

process clause, based in part upon availability of alternative remedies and deference to legislature); *Provens v. Stark Cty. Bd. of Mental Ret.*, 594 N.E.2d 959, 963-965 (Ohio 1992) (no damages for alleged state free speech violation, based in part upon availability of alternative remedies and deference to legislature); *Hunter v. City of Eugene*, 787 P.2d 881, 883-884 (Ore. 1990) (no damages for alleged state "free expression" violations based in part upon absence of textual or historic basis for implying such a right; court concluded that creation of such a right is a task properly left to legislature); *City of Beaumont v. Bouillion*, 896 S.W.2d 143, 148-150 (Tex. 1995) (no damages for alleged state free speech and assembly violations; court noted there was no evidence that violations of the provisions were intended to be remedied by damages, and observed that there was no historical or common law basis for recognizing a damages action); *Spackman ex rel. Spackman v. Board of Educ.*, 16 P.3d 533, 537-539 (Utah 2000) (no damages for asserted state due process and "open education" violations, based in part upon availability of alternative remedies and deference to legislature); *Shields v. Gerhart*, 658 A.2d 924, 929-934 (Vt. 1995) (no damages for asserted state free speech and due process violations, based in part upon availability of alternative remedies).

We conclude it is appropriate to employ the following framework for determining the existence of a damages action to remedy an asserted constitutional violation. First, we shall inquire whether there is evidence from which we may find or infer, within the constitutional provision at issue, an affirmative intent either to authorize or to withhold a damages action to remedy a violation. In undertaking this inquiry we shall consider the language and history of the constitutional provision at issue, including whether it contains guidelines, mechanisms, or procedures implying a monetary remedy, as well as any pertinent common law history. If we find any such intent, we shall give it effect.

Second, if no affirmative intent either to authorize or to withhold a damages remedy is found, we shall undertake the "constitutional tort" analysis adopted by *Bivens* and its progeny. Among the relevant factors in this analysis are whether an adequate remedy exists, the extent to which a constitutional tort action would change established tort law, and the nature and significance of the constitutional provision. If we find that these factors militate against recognizing the constitutional tort, our inquiry ends. If, however, we find that these factors favor recognizing a constitutional tort, we also shall consider the existence of any special factors counseling hesitation in recognizing a damages action, including deference to legislative judgment, avoidance of adverse policy consequences, considerations of government fiscal policy, practical issues of proof, and the competence of courts to assess particular types of damages.

A.

We begin our inquiry by asking whether, when the constitutional provision at issue was adopted, the enactors *intended* that it include a damages remedy for its violation. Such an intent may be quite clear on the face of a particular provision-for example, it is plain that California Constitution article I, section 19, which provides that "[p]rivate property may be taken or damaged for public use only when just compensation, ascertained by a jury unless waived, has first been paid to, or into court for, the owner," supports an action for money damages, and our cases consistently have so held. But with regard to most constitutional provisions, the words of the provision do not on their own manifest any such intent.

The due process clause of article I, section 7(a), falls within this latter category. It states in relevant part: "A person may not be deprived of life, liberty, or property without due process of law...." These words do not explicitly disclose an intent either to authorize or to withhold damages as a remedy for a violation of the provision. Accordingly, we must look further in our attempt to discern whether article I, section 7(a) was intended to include a damages remedy. [The court reviews various materials].

We conclude that there is no indication in the language of article I, section 7(a), nor any evidence in the history of that section, from which we may find, within that provision, an implied right to seek damages for a violation of the due process liberty interest.

B.

This determination, however, does not end our inquiry. Just as we have not discovered any basis for concluding that a damages remedy was contemplated or reasonably might be inferred within article I, section 7(a) for violation of that provision, we also have not discovered any basis for concluding that a damages remedy was intended to be foreclosed. In such circumstances, we, like the United States Supreme Court and the courts of numerous other jurisdictions that have faced similar circumstances, shall proceed to consider whether a constitutional tort action for damages to remedy the asserted constitutional violation should be recognized.

As observed by Friesen, "[*Bivens* and its progeny] actually illustrate[ ] a body of precedent established by state courts, ... [and] expressed in section 874A of the Second Restatement of Torts." Friesen, § 7-5(c), at p. 420. The cited Restatement section provides: "When a legislative [or constitutional] provision protects a class of persons by proscribing or requiring certain conduct but does not provide a civil remedy for the violation, *the court may, if it determines that the remedy is appropriate in furtherance of the purpose of the legislation and needed to assure the effectiveness of the provision,* accord to an injured member of the class a right of action, using a suitable existing tort action or a new cause of action analogous to an existing tort action."

In determining whether to recognize such a constitutional tort, courts have "look[ed] for the policy behind the legislative [or constitutional] provision, attempting to perceive the purpose for which it was enacted, and then, having ascertained that policy or purpose, [have] determine[ed] the most appropriate way to carry it out and identif[ied] the remedy needed to accomplish that result." Rest.2d Torts, § 874A, com. (d), p. 303.

We join the jurisdictions that have endorsed, implicitly or explicitly, the view set out in the Restatement, that courts, exercising their authority over the common law, may, in appropriate circumstances, recognize a tort action for damages to remedy a constitutional violation. We proceed to determine whether a tort action for damages is appropriate here.

1.

We first consider the adequacy of existing remedies. We conclude that this consideration does not support recognition of a constitutional tort cause of action for damages to remedy an asserted violation of the due process "liberty" interest under article I, section 7(a).

2.

We next consider the extent to which a constitutional tort action would change established tort law. [The court concludes traditional tort law would not support a claim for damages here.]

3.

We also consider the nature of the provision and the significance of the purpose that it seeks to effectuate. As a general matter, the due process "liberty" interest of article I, section 7(a) is both important and fundamental.

Although we may agree that this factor, in the abstract, is a consideration that favors recognition of a constitutional tort action for damages, we also find persuasive the cautionary view set out in *Carlsbad Aquafarm, supra,* 83 Cal.App.4th 809[, 823 (italics added)]: "While this factor may be a proper consideration in the overall analysis, it is not one upon which we place great significance. How does one rank the importance of different constitutional provisions? ... [C]an we say a procedural due process right should be accorded more or less dignity [than free speech or voting rights]? We agree that the due process right is fundamental. *But absent the applicability of the other relevant factors discussed here, the relative importance of the constitutional right is of little help in determining the availability of a damages remedy for a violation of that right.*"

The same can be said here. The availability of meaningful alternative remedies leads us to decline to recognize a constitutional tort to remedy the asserted violation of article I, section 7(a) in the case before us.

4.

Because we conclude that the foregoing factors militate against recognition of a constitutional tort to remedy the asserted violation of due process liberty interests in this case, we need not consider, in addition, whether any special factors would counsel hesitation in recognizing such a damages action. If we had found, however, that the considerations discussed above favored recognition of a constitutional tort, we would, before actually recognizing the tort, also consider the existence of any special factors counseling hesitation in recognizing a damages action, including deference to legislative judgment, avoidance of adverse policy consequences, considerations of governmental fiscal policy, practical issues of proof, and competence of courts to assess particular types of damages.

V.

In sum, we discern no evidence from which to infer within article I, section 7(a), an intent to afford a right to seek damages to remedy the asserted violation of the due process liberty interest alleged in this case.

We also find no basis upon which to recognize a constitutional tort action for such damages.

BROWN, J., concurring and dissenting.

I concur in the majority's affirmance of the Court of Appeal's judgment barring plaintiff from seeking damages for any violation of his state constitutional right to due process. In my view, however, it is not only unnecessary but entirely inappropriate to go beyond the short, clear answer to the question presented or to consider anything other than the constitutional history and drafters' intent in determining whether a constitutional provision is enforceable by an action in tort. The majority cites no authority and offers no rationale for applying the "constitutional tort" analysis adopted by the United States Supreme Court in *Bivens v. Six Unknown Fed. Narcotics Agents* to a provision of the California Constitution.

"[I]t is well established that the California Constitution 'is, and always has been, a document of independent force', and that the rights embodied in and protected by the state Constitution are not invariably identical to the rights contained in the federal Constitution. California cases long have recognized the independence of the California Constitution, and article I, section 24, of the California Constitution expressly confirms that the rights 'guaranteed by this Constitution are not dependent on those guaranteed by the United States Constitution.' Past cases make clear that even when the terms of the California Constitution are textually identical to those of the federal Constitution, the proper interpretation of the state constitutional provision is not invariably identical to the federal courts' interpretation of the corresponding provision contained in the federal Constitution."

When a part of our state Constitution has been adopted by initiative, one of our core interpretive principles is that the courts must measure its scope according to the intentions of the voters. The majority correctly concludes there is no evidence the voters intended to create a right to monetary damages in adopting the due process clause set forth in article I, section 7, subdivision (a) of our Constitution. Nevertheless, it declines to end its inquiry with that determination because it finds no basis "for concluding that a damages remedy was intended to be foreclosed." The majority fails to explain this non sequitur, however, and to identify any principle of constitutional interpretation that translates the absence of an express or implied bar to monetary damages into an authorization for a court to determine whether to provide for such a remedy on its own initiative. By its very nature, a constitution orders the relationships of the government and its citizens and serves as a bulwark against encroachment on their rights. The fact that the judicial branch interprets the constitution does not give license to augment its provisions as any shifting majority of judges sees fit. Until now, this court has jealously guarded its role in effectuating legislative intent, particularly with respect to the initiative process. In this case, however, the majority abandons that vigilance.

Moreover, the majority applies an analytical framework based not on our own jurisprudence but a derivation of United States Supreme Court decisions. "The California Constitution is the supreme law of our state-a seminal document of independent force that establishes governmental powers and safeguards individual rights and liberties. As the Supreme Court of California, we are the final arbiters of the meaning of state constitutional provisions. Our authority and responsibility in this regard is part of the basic structure of California government; it cannot be delegated to the United States Supreme Court or any other person or body. When we construe provisions of the California Constitution, we necessarily do so in light of their unique language, purposes, and histories, in accordance with general principles of constitutional interpretation established in our case law. Nor do we act differently when the state constitutional provision in issue contains the same language as a federal constitutional provision. In such a case, we are not bound by a decision of the United States Supreme Court or any other court. We must consider and decide the matter independently."

The majority's lapse of analytical independence-and apparent "assumption that any Supreme Court doctrine is generic constitutional law" (Linde, *Are State Constitutions Common Law?*, 34 Ariz. L.Rev. 215, 227 (1992))-betrays our obligation as final arbiter of state constitutional law in two interrelated ways. First, the majority's approach compounds and perpetuates the misperception that state constitutions are part of common law and that meaningful analysis can be "borrowed wholesale from federal constitutional discourse, as though the language of federal constitutional law were some sort of lingua franca of constitutional argument generally." Unlike the common law, however, constitutional interpretation is bound by text as well as by principles of construction and is decidedly *not* subject-whenever a majority of the court agrees-to judicial extension and innovation in the interest of public policy or national consensus or similar justification. Although in this context "[t]he pull toward a common law of judicial review, toward a vortex of clichés [lifted from United States Supreme Court decisions], is strong", this court must resist if it is to remain faithful to its role as the final arbiter of the meaning of our state Constitution and to respect the demarcations between the respective branches of government-a concern equally of constitutional dimension.

Second, the majority's approach creates a lacuna in our constitutional jurisprudence, adopting without meaningful consideration the United States Supreme Court's interpolation of an unrelated federal constitutional provision in lieu of rigorous substantive analysis of the unique language, purpose and history of our own due process guarantee. Defaulting to the high court fundamentally disserves the independent force and effect of our Constitution. Rather than enrich the texture of our law, this reliance on federal precedent shortchanges future generations.

NOTES

1. Could the plaintiff have argued that a state constitutional "right to a remedy" provision supported his claim for damages as a remedy for a constitutional violation?

2. Who has the better of the argument as to whether state courts should look to analogous federal doctrines when interpreting state constitutions – the majority (which relies heavily on the federal *Bivens* line of cases) or the dissent (which calls for "independent" state court interpretation of state constitutional provisions)?

3. Do you see a separation of powers argument lurking in this case? One could ask the question *which branch* of state government—the courts or the state legislature—should determine what remedies, if any, are to be available for violations of state-created legal rights and interests? That proposition has been raised and discussed explicitly in the federal *Bivens* cases, with the Court and individual Justices more than once arguing that the creation of any federal remedy in a particular circumstance should be left to Congress to decide, rather than the Court.

E. SEPARATION OF POWERS

IN RE PETITION OF GOVERNOR
846 A.2d 1148 (N.H. 2004)

PER CURIAM.

Craig Benson as Governor of the State of New Hampshire, and the Executive Council of the State of New Hampshire, petitioned this court...to exercise original jurisdiction and rule that RSA 490:1...is unconstitutional. The Office of the Attorney General appeared in opposition. The President of the New Hampshire Senate and the Speaker of the New Hampshire House of Representatives filed *amicus* briefs defending the constitutionality of the statute.

The justices of this court recused themselves from participating in the case. In accordance with RSA 490:3 (1997), this panel was assembled, and convened...to hear the matter. The statute in dispute, RSA 490:1 (Supp.2003), provides:

> The supreme court shall consist of 5 justices appointed and commissioned as prescribed by the constitution. On the effective date of this section, the administrative position of chief justice shall be held by the justice with the most seniority on the court for a period of up to 5 years. Each succeeding chief justice shall serve for a period of up to 5 years and shall be the justice with the most seniority of service on the court who has not yet served as chief justice. A justice may decline to serve as chief justice; however, no justice shall be permitted to serve successive terms as chief justice. In the event that all 5 justices have served a term as chief justice, succeeding chief justices shall serve rotating 5-year terms based on seniority.

The petitioners submit two arguments in support of their []position that RSA 490:1 is unconstitutional. First, the petitioners argue [it] is unconstitutional because the legislative branch lacks the requisite constitutional authority to prescribe the method of selection of judicial officers and impermissibly limits the chief justice's term of office. The petitioners advance two sub-arguments in support of that proposition.

First, they argue the legislature does not have any power with respect to the appointment of judicial officers as that power has been expressly committed to the executive branch [in the New Hampshire Constitution]. Part II, Article 46 provides: "All judicial officers ... shall be nominated and appointed by the governor and council[.]" The petitioners contend the legislature is without power to alter this constitutionally prescribed method of selection of judicial officers.

Second, the petitioners claim the chief justice position on the supreme court is a separate and distinct office from that of associate justice. The petitioners argue that, if the term "judicial office" is understood to include administrative functions, the legislature would be without authority to enact RSA 490:1, as the power to appoint the chief justice would lie exclusively with the executive branch pursuant to Part II, Article 46. While the petitioners acknowledge both the chief justice and associate justices have the same adjudicatory powers in common, they submit their judicial powers are not limited to adjudication and in particular that the chief justice has enhanced judicial powers by way of additional and unique constitutionally delegated duties.

> The chief justice of the supreme court shall be the administrative head of all the courts. He shall, with the concurrence of a majority of the supreme court justices, make rules governing the administration of all courts in the state and the practice and procedure to be followed in all such courts. The rules so promulgated shall have the force and effect of law.

The petitioners argue those powers given to the chief justice pursuant to Articles 40 and 73-a are inherent powers that exist in the judicial branch and are not executive or legislative powers and that the exercise of those powers is exclusively a judicial function. For that reason, the petitioners submit that pursuant to the constitution the chief justice position is a separate judicial office.

The petitioners' second argument is that RSA 490:1 encroaches upon the power of the executive branch and the independence of the judicial branch in violation of the separation of powers doctrine under Part I, Article 37 of the New Hampshire Constitution. Article 37 provides in pertinent part: "In the government of this state, the three essential powers thereof, to wit, the legislative, executive, and judicial, ought to be kept as separate from, and independent of, each other, as the nature of a free government will admit[.]" Specifically, the petitioners submit RSA 490:1 violates the separation of powers doctrine because it confiscates the power of appointment from the executive branch and encroaches upon the independence of the judiciary by limiting the tenure of the chief justice. The petitioners warn that legislative enactments such as RSA 490:1, if left unchecked, could pave the way for complete domination by the legislature. The petitioners assert if RSA 490:1 is allowed to stand, the legislature could further diminish the independence of the chief justice by shortening the 5-year term or imposing other restrictions.

A brief history of our judiciary is helpful to an understanding of this issue. The New Hampshire Constitution, as enacted in 1776, did not provide for an independent judicial system-judicial functions were carried out by the legislature. "The government basically consisted of one branch, a bicameral legislature with a house of representatives and a smaller council of twelve." All public officers, including judges, were appointed by the Assembly and Council under the 1776 constitution. It was not until the constitution was amended in 1784 that separation of powers was provided. "Three reforms were enacted with the purpose of fostering an independent judiciary. Judges were given the constitutional right to permanent and honorable salaries, were prohibited from holding plural offices, and were granted tenure during good behavior." The provisions guaranteeing permanent tenure and honorable salaries were "considered particularly important as a means of ending arbitrary removals." The provisions also ensured the independence of the judiciary.

There is no dispute that the constitution explicitly reserves the power of appointment of all judicial officers to the executive branch. Nor can it be disputed that the chief justice is a judicial officer. To say otherwise defies logic, reason and tradition. While there is nothing in the constitution that specifically creates or defines the office of chief justice of the supreme court, the position is assumed to exist as evidenced by Articles 40 and 73-a. Similarly, there is nothing in the United States Constitution which specifically sets out a citizen's right of privacy. Yet, that right is now deeply rooted in federal constitutional law. Like the right of privacy under the federal constitution, the traditional appointment of the chief justice by the governor and council for over two hundred years has effectively rooted that power in our state constitution.

The respondents' position is that the chief justice is not a discrete judicial officer requiring nomination and appointment by the governor and council. This argument is dependent upon the view that the only constitutional duties of a judicial officer are adjudicative. To that end, because the chief justice's adjudicatory duties do not differ from the adjudicatory duties of the associate justices, the respondents contend that the chief justice position is not separate and distinct. The respondents' argument is further dependent upon the view that the chief justice's constitutionally prescribed administrative and legislative duties are not part of his or her judicial duties, but rather are auxiliary and independent.

That the powers allocated to the chief justice in Part II, Articles 40 and 73-a are non-adjudicatory in nature does not suggest that they function in an ancillary fashion to the chief justice's "judicial" powers as the respondents assert. The administrative and legislative powers and duties assigned to the chief justice by the constitution are inextricably bound together with those adjudicatory duties and are incidents of and inherent in that office. This concept, that judicial duties consist of more than just adjudicatory powers, is nowhere more apparent than in Supreme Court Rule 38, the Code of Judicial Conduct. Canon 3 of Rule 38 provides that judges' judicial duties include "*all* the duties of the judge's office prescribed by law." No lines of distinction whatever are drawn between judges' adjudicatory and administrative duties-both are classified as "judicial duties."

Furthermore, a review of the relevant case law draws no distinction between a judge's adjudicatory and administrative duties. In *Mussman*, a case involving the removal of a district court judge from the bench for ethical violations, this court determined that the supreme court's general superintendence power is absolute. We held that the court's superintendence power included not just the power to correct adjudicatory errors made by lower tribunals, but also the power to "approve rules of court and prescribe and administer canons of ethics with respect to such courts[.]" We acknowledged that while this court does not have the power to impeach a judicial officer, as that is solely a legislative function as provided in the constitution, it does have the power "to take disciplinary action short of removal from office under its general power of superintendence[.]" We noted: "It has never been the tradition of the jurisprudence of this court to refuse to exercise *judicial power* when there was an established need for it and there was no constitutional barrier to its exercise."

In *In re Mone,* 719 A.2d 626, 633 (N.H. 1998), we determined that, a statute removing the responsibility for court security from the judiciary and vesting it with the executive branch, violated the separation of powers doctrine because it encroached upon the judiciary's inherent power to control courtroom functions and ensure the fair adjudication of controversies. In discussing the origin of the judiciary's administrative powers, we observed: "Although not specifically set forth in the constitution, *powers reserved for the judiciary arise from its most fundamental duty to interpret and administer the law*." *Id.* at 631 (emphasis added). We noted that the judiciary's exercise of administrative powers to control its courtrooms specifically did not interfere with the separation of powers doctrine because "security is an integral part of the essential adjudicatory function of the courts." Accordingly, we concluded in that instance the judiciary's administrative powers derived from its adjudicatory powers.

While the respondents attempt to draw a distinction between "judicial" duties and the administrative or legislative duties granted separately to the chief justice, we are not convinced that such a distinction exists in fact or in law. We have consistently reiterated that "this court has the responsibility to protect and preserve the judicial system. We have the *inherent authority* to take whatever action is necessary to effectuate this responsibility." This inherent judicial authority includes the use of superintendent powers that flow from and support our essential adjudicatory functions.

Whether the statutory mechanism of rotating 5-year terms for the chief justice position better serves the public than executive nomination and appointment is not a question for this court to consider. The question before us is whether the legislature is empowered by the constitution to declare it so. Our answer to this question is that the legislature is not so empowered. Part II, Article 46 of the New Hampshire Constitution emphatically provides: "*All* judicial officers...shall be nominated and appointed by the governor and council[.]" (emphasis added). There have been no exceptions to this mandatory language. The legislative branch is no less constrained than the other branches of government to stay within the limitations of the constitution. Even if constitutional language appears to leave a vacuum, it does not necessarily follow, as night the day, that the legislature is empowered to fill it.

Because there is no basis for a distinction between this court's adjudicatory duties and its administrative or legislative duties when considering the composition of "judicial power," we agree with the petitioners that the chief justice position is a discrete judicial office. Based on Articles 40 and 73-a, the chief justice inescapably holds separate and unique *judicial powers*. Accordingly, the constitution requires that the chief justice position be filled by executive nomination and appointment, as the separate commissioning of the chief justice historically reflects.

We also agree with petitioners that RSA 490:1 violates the separation of powers doctrine under Part I, Article 37 of the New Hampshire

Constitution. There is no doubt that pursuant to Part II, Article 4 of the constitution, the legislature has "full power and authority to erect and constitute judicatories and courts of record[.]" The appointment of judicial officers, however, is strictly reserved for the executive branch by Part II, Article 46. For over two centuries, governors and executive councils have utilized their Article 46 executive powers to nominate and appoint the chief justice of the supreme court. RSA 490:1 for the first time invades this right of the governor and executive council by categorizing the chief justice as solely an "administrative position." This usurpation of an exclusively executive function violates the separation of powers doctrine.

Moreover, RSA 490:1 impermissibly encroaches upon the prerogative of the judicial branch. While a complete and total separation of powers is neither possible nor contemplated by the constitution, encroachment by one branch into the essential powers of another is impermissible. Here, the legislature impermissibly encroaches on the position of chief justice and upon the independence of the judiciary. First, the constitution specifically conveys upon *all* judicial officers a lifetime appointment to their respective positions, conditioned only upon good behavior and requiring retirement at the age of seventy. RSA 490:1 divests the chief justice position of this lifetime appointment and replaces it with a rotating 5-year term based on seniority. Because the chief justice position is a discrete one, the legislature's enactment of RSA 490:1 is unconstitutional in that it divests the chief justice of the constitutional right to lifetime tenure (subject to the age limitations set forth in Part II, Article 78). Absent a constitutional amendment, the legislature is without authority to do so.

Second, as the petitioners warn, upholding RSA 490:1 would effectively grant the legislature free license to alter the means of appointment and the term of the chief justice based upon the politics of the moment. There is simply nothing to prevent the legislature from further amending the statute at any time to provide for other terms or means of selection of the chief justice by the legislature or otherwise, or to preclude a particular justice from succeeding to the chief justice position. This method of indirectly "addressing" judges out of office, while different in form, is not unfamiliar in theory to the judiciary. In fact, the arbitrary removal of judges from the bench prompted the reforms in 1784 that granted all judges the constitutional right to permanent and honorable salaries and lifetime tenure conditioned only upon good behavior.

While the legislature can no longer abolish the judiciary as a whole, or arbitrarily remove a sitting justice from office, RSA 490:1 would effectively allow it to control the judiciary by manipulating the statute and the chief justice position to its advantage. "It is the [supreme] court's responsibility 'to oversee the operations of the judicial branch for the purposes of maintaining public confidence in the administration of justice.'" This confidence and our independence would be jeopardized if our direction is arbitrarily controlled by the hands of the legislature without specific authority in the constitution to do so.

IN RE REQUEST FOR ADVISORY OPINION FROM HOUSE OF REPRESENTATIVES
961 A.2d 930 (R.I. 2008)

To the Honorable, the House of Representatives of the State of Rhode Island and Providence Plantations:

We have received your request seeking the advice of the justices of this Court, in accordance with the provisions of article 10, section 3 of the Rhode Island Constitution, concerning legislation (2007-H 6266) that is presently pending before the House of Representatives. The questions propounded are as follows:

"(1) Would the proposed act, if duly enacted into law, which permits members of the General Assembly to sit as members of the Coastal Resources Management Council (CRMC)…violate the constitutional amendment to Article IX, Section 5, so called Separation of Powers Amendment, passed by the electorate on November 2, 2004…?

"(2) Would the proposed act, if duly enacted into law, permit the Speaker of the House to appoint public members to the Coastal Resources Management Council (CRMC)…?

Pursuant to the provisions of article 10, section 3 of the Rhode Island Constitution it is our duty to issue an advisory opinion at the request of the House of Representatives when the question concerns the constitutionality of pending legislation.

I

The Separation of Powers Amendments

In November of 2004, the electorate of the State of Rhode Island approved the so-called separation of powers amendments. These amendments ushered in four fundamental changes to the Rhode Island Constitution and, for the first time in Rhode Island's history, clearly and explicitly established three separate and distinct departments of government. Those fundamental changes may be summarized as follows:

(1) Article 3, section 6 was amended to preclude legislators from serving on state boards, commissions, or other state or quasi-public entities that exercise executive power;

(2) Article 5 was amended to provide that the powers of the Rhode Island government are distributed into "three separate and distinct departments";

(3) Article 6, section 10, which had vested broad "continuing powers" in the General Assembly, was repealed; and

(4) Article 9, section 5 was amended to give the Governor appointment power with respect to members of any state or quasi-public entities exercising executive power, subject to the advice and consent of the Senate.

The doctrine of separation of powers, which is now expressly established in the Rhode Island Constitution, declares that governmental powers at the state level are divided among "three separate and distinct departments." In practice, this doctrine operates to confine legislative powers to the legislature, executive powers to the executive department, and judicial powers to the judiciary, precluding one branch of the government from usurping the powers of another.

While there can be no doubt that the separation of powers amendments constitute an important recalibration of the system of checks and balances within our state government, we do not view the amendments as effectuating a wholesale reallocation of power among the executive and the legislative departments. We emphasize, however, that the pendulum has not now swung to the opposite extreme with the adoption of the 2004 constitutional amendments. While the formal incorporation of the doctrine of separation of powers into the Constitution has established a somewhat different balance of power among the departments from that which existed previously, it would be overly simplistic and patently erroneous to view the amendments as somehow *subordinating* the role of the legislative branch to that of the executive.

It is incontestably true that, for most of its history, the Rhode Island General Assembly enjoyed significantly more power than did the legislatures of most of our sister states. "Unlike the United States Congress, the Rhode Island General Assembly does not look to our State Constitution for grants of power.... Accordingly, this court has consistently adhered to the view that the General Assembly possessed all of the powers inhering in sovereignty other than those which the constitution textually commits to the other branches of our state government and that those that are not so committed...are powers reserved to the General Assembly."

As previously noted, in November of 2004 the electorate of Rhode Island approved four such amendments. As a result, separation of powers is now a principle that is firmly established within our state's organic law, whereby the fundamental powers of government are distributed among its three coordinate branches.

The proponents and drafters of the constitutional amendments, which were designed to bring about a greater degree of separation of powers in Rhode Island's governmental structure, manifestly carried out their task with precision. Certain powers of the General Assembly were explicitly curtailed, while others were left largely or entirely unaffected by the amendments.

III

Appointments to the CRMC

The doctrine of separation of powers does not prohibit some overlapping of functions. The resolution of the problems with which government must grapple requires a certain degree of pragmatism; we are not in the pristine realm of algebraic equations, but rather in the complex and infinitely nuanced real world. Accordingly, administrative agencies may combine, to a certain extent, the functions of all three departments of government.

Nevertheless, as the United States Supreme Court has noted, the principle of separation of powers will be violated where the legislative department tries to control the execution of its enactments directly, instead of indirectly by passing new legislation. Direct legislative control of executive powers would be an impermissible usurpation of the central function of a coordinate branch.

Given the language of the separation of powers amendments, it is now our task to ascertain whether or not the CRMC exercises executive power. If it does exercise such power to any meaningful degree, then, pursuant to the plain language of the separation of powers amendments, two significant conclusions ineluctably result: (1) no member of the General Assembly nor an appointee of that body may sit on the CRMC; and (2) appointments to the CRMC are to be made exclusively by the Governor (in the exercise of his or her constitutionally conferred appointment power) with the advice and consent of the Senate.

Upon examination of the CRMC's organic statute, chapter 23 of title 46, it appears that the CRMC combines functions that must properly be characterized as executive with functions that are quasi-legislative and quasi-judicial in nature. This is so even though the CRMC is an independent body not subject to direct gubernatorial supervision or control. The CRMC's organic statute, which was adopted by the General Assembly pursuant to its plenary power over the state's environmental resources, states that its provisions "shall be enforced by the coastal resources management council." Section 46-23-18.4. The CRMC is authorized to "administer...programs" developed pursuant to its quasi-legislative power to develop policy and adopt regulations. The CRMC may also "enforce[ ] and implement[ ] riparian rights[.]"

Furthermore, § 46-23-7(a)(2) authorizes "[CRMC] staff, conservation officers within the department of environmental management, and state and municipal police...to issue written cease and desist orders in any instance where activity is being conducted which constitutes a violation of any provisions of [the] chapter." In addition, CRMC staff, DEM conservation officers, and police are empowered "to apply to a court...for a warrant to enter on private land to investigate possible violations of this chapter." Section 46-23-7(a)(3). The chairperson and the executive director of the CRMC are also authorized "to assess an administrative penalty" of up to $2,500 for certain violations of the chapter. Section 46-23-7.1(1).

It is clear to us that the above-summarized powers and functions of the CRMC are manifestly executive in nature. To state that *all* of the CRMC's powers and functions are legislative would be to blind oneself to that reality. To do so would be to willfully ignore the language of article 5 of the Rhode Island Constitution, which expressly requires the three departments of government to be "separate and distinct." The duties and functions to be conferred on the CRMC pursuant to the proposed legislation are not unconstitutional; the CRMC may constitutionally combine functions that may best be described as quasi-legislative, executive, and quasi-judicial in nature.

In our opinion, the proposed CRMC legislation, which is the subject of the questions posed to us, cannot be reconciled with our Constitution to the extent that it would permit sitting legislators to serve on the CRMC and would allow the General Assembly to make some appointments to that body. In other words, in view of the fact that the CRMC exercises executive power, the Governor has the right to appoint its members with the advice and consent of the Senate.

Without retreating from the foregoing views with respect to the effect of the separation of powers amendments on the appointment process, we would also emphasize that the General Assembly remains fully empowered to carry out its constitutional duty to protect the natural environment of the state through the vigorous and proactive exercise of its legislative powers. Nothing written in this advisory opinion should be construed as implying that the General Assembly does not retain the fullness of its constitutionally bestowed fact-finding powers and oversight responsibility with respect to the protection of the natural environment. We also note that the legislative branch of our state government also retains an important role in the appointment process due to the fact that the Senate may approve or reject gubernatorial appointments.

It is also important to note that the General Assembly retains without diminution its vast constitutional power to enact, revise, or repeal laws concerning coastal management and preservation of natural resources. In the course of exercising its plenary legislative power, the General Assembly may, for example, (1) provide specific criteria with respect to CRMC membership composition and qualifications; (2) narrow or expand the mandate of the CRMC; (3) adopt more elaborate oversight procedures and safeguards; (4) mandate training for new CRMC members; (5) require periodic reports on CRMC activities; (6) retain the right to review CRMC decisions in discrete areas relating to budget or revenue; (7) create a joint subcommittee to oversee coastal resources management; (8) create procedures for the thorough and rigorous vetting of CRMC nominees (including disclosure statements); (9) limit the Governor's removal power; (10) assume performance of the CRMC's rulemaking functions; or (11) restructure the CRMC in to one or more bodies exercising either purely quasi-legislative or purely executive functions.

As discussed above, the CRMC itself routinely combines executive, quasi-legislative, and quasi-judicial powers. We stress, however, that many of the CRMC's functions may be significantly more difficult to classify as strictly executive or legislative in character, and this advisory opinion does not give us occasion to provide a comprehensive classificatory scheme encompassing all of that body's powers and functions.

We conclude by respectfully urging the Governor and the General Assembly to discuss the various subjects addressed in this advisory opinion with the goal of reaching a mutually satisfactory agreement regarding the rights and duties conferred upon each department by the terms of our Constitution.

CHAPTER XVI

AMENDMENT AND REVISION OF STATE CONSTITUTIONS

A. INTRODUCTION

Thomas Jefferson suggested that constitutions should provide each generation with an opportunity to choose its own form of government:

> Let us provide in our Constitution for its revision at stated periods. What these periods should be, nature herself indicates. By the European tables of mortality, of the adults living at any one moment of time, a majority will be dead in about nineteen years. At the end of that period then, a new majority is come into place, or, in other words, a new generation. Each generation is as independent as the one preceding, as that was of all which had gone before. It has then, like them, a right to choose for itself the form of government it believes most promotive of its own happiness;...and it is for the peace and good of mankind, that a solemn opportunity of doing this every nineteen or twenty years, should be provided by the constitution.[1]

That opportunity has been provided for in all state constitutions. Although most state constitutions have not been completely revised every generation, the process of periodic amendments between replacements has been constant for two centuries.

The malleability of state constitutions is a sharp contrast to the stability of the United States Constitution. It has been estimated that between 1776 and 1991 more than 5,800 amendments to state constitutions have been adopted.[2] By 1964, it was estimated that:

> the existing state constitutions had been modified...some 3,718 times - South Carolina with 250, California with 350, Louisiana with 439 - to cite a few of the worst offenders. The constitutions of Alabama, Florida, New Hampshire, New York, Oregon, South Carolina and Texas had each been amended over ninety times. The average number of amendments for each state was seventy-eight.[3]

---

[1] Jefferson to Samuel Kercheval, July 12, 1816, in Thomas Jefferson, Writings: Autobiography; A Summary View of the Rights of British American; Notes on the State of Virginia; Public Papers; Addresses, Messages, and Replies; Miscellany; Letters (New York: Library of America, 1984), 1402.

[2] See Donald S. Lutz, "Toward a Theory of Constitutional Amendment" 88, American Political Science Review 359 (1994). See also James A. Henretta, Foreword: Rethinking the State Constitutional Tradition, 22 RUTGERS L.J. 819, 829 (1991).

[3] W. Brooke Graves, State Constitutional Law: A Twenty-Five Year Summary, 8 WM. & MARY L. REV. 1, 36 (1966).

The writing and amending of state constitutions has been of a distinctively populist and political nature.[4] As of January 1995,

> the American states had held over 230 constitutional conventions and adopted 146 constitutions. They had also adopted over 6,000 statewide amendments to their current constitutions. This last figure, of course, substantially understates the frequency of state constitutional amendment, since it excludes both purely local amendments and amendments to the states' previous constitutions.[5]

Thus, since 1776, the fifty states have had at least 146 constitutions, with thirty-one states having had two or more constitutions.[6] The continual process of state constitution-making has transformed the short, principle-oriented charters of the early republic into "super-legislative" documents.[7] In 1776, state constitutions contained an average of about 7,150 words. In 1985, the average state constitution contained 26,150 words and the longest, the Alabama Constitution, was almost ten times greater than the national average.[8]

State constitutions usually contain common themes: structure of government, separation of powers, individual rights, and responsibilities or limitations on the state in specific subject areas. The solutions to the particular issues raised by those themes are frequently varied and often unique. The differences are attributable to the text and context of each state's historical legal, social, political, and economic landscape.[9]

State constitutions have been the laboratories where many issues have been introduced that were either fused or fractured by the principles of a federal republican democracy. Just as the first state constitutions provided guidance for the United States Constitution, subsequent state constitutions have continued to provide positive and negative examples for each other and the nation. State constitutions pioneered provisions regarding "popular election of judges, women's suffrage, equal rights for women, black

---

[4] James A. Henretta, Foreword: Rethinking the State Constitutional Tradition, 22 RUTGERS L.J. 819, 829 (1991).

[5] G. Alan Tarr, Constitutional Politics in the States, Contemporary Controversies and Historical Patterns, p. 3 (Greenwood Press 1996).

[6] Kermit L. Hall, "Mostly Anchor and Little Sail: The Evolution of American State Constitutions," in Paul Finkelman and Stephen E. Gottlieb, eds., Toward a Usable Past: Liberty Under State Constitutions (Athens: University of Georgia Press, 1991), pp. 394-95.

[7] James A. Henretta, Foreword: Rethinking the State Constitutional Tradition, 22 RUTGERS L.J. 819, 829 (1991).

[8] Kermit L. Hall, "Mostly Anchor and Little Sail" The Evolution of American State Constitutions" in Paul Finkelman and Stephen E. Gottlieb, eds., Toward a Usable Past: Liberty Under State Constitutions (Athens: University of Georgia Press, 1991), pp. 388.

[9] See Truax v. Corrigan, 257 U.S. 312, 344 (1921) (Holmes, J., dissenting).

disfranchisement and suffrage, the income tax," prohibition, the line-item veto, and balanced budget requirements.[10]

Early state constitutions were relatively succinct frameworks of government. Current state constitutions, like Delaware's 1897 Constitution, "contain many of the provisions adopted during the various 'waves' of state constitution-making."[11] Two exceptions are Vermont and Massachusetts, which have kept their state constitutions of 1793 and 1780, respectively.[12] Another exception is the 1784 New Hampshire Constitution. Accordingly, most other state constitutions reflect a "layering" of the concerns of successive generations.[13]

This evolutionary process was never intended for and has not taken place with regard to the United States Constitution. James Madison had argued, in THE FEDERALIST No. 49, that frequent constitutional amendments would be inimical to the national government's stability.[14] According to Madison, the longevity of the United States Constitution, basically as it was enacted originally, would lead to the veneration of its principles and structure.[15]

In a nineteenth century treatise, which was commented upon favorably by Chief Justice John Marshall, Justice Joseph Story, and Chancellor James Kent, it was written:

> The [constitutional] convention did not suppose that their production was perfect…. Changes in the circumstances of the country, might require corresponding alterations in the government…. The Framers of the Constitution were aware of this, and, therefore, wisely provided a method, by which it may be amended, without disturbances of the public tranquility, or injury to the general system.
>
> [The Constitution] contains within itself a provision for amendment, by which to remedy any defects in its original structure, or such as may occur in process of time. But this power should be used with great caution; and always with the

---

[10] Kermit L. Hall, "Mostly Anchor and Little Sail," The Revolution of American and State Constitutions in Paul Finkelman and Stephen E. Gottlieb, eds., Toward a Usable Past: Liberty Under State Constitutions, p. 393-94.

[11] Robert F. Williams, State Constitutional Law: Cases and Materials 19 (2d ed., 1993).

[12] Paul Finkleman and Stephen E. Gottlieb, editors Toward a Usable Part: Liberty Under State Constitutions (Athens: University of Georgia Press 1991) p. 14 n.19.

[13] Robert F. Williams, State Constitutional Law: Cases and Materials 19 (2d ed. Michie, 1993).

[14] The Federalist No. 49, ed. Jacob E. Cooke (Middletown, Conn.: Wesleyan University Press, 1961) p. 340.

[15] Id.

conviction, that *stability* is an important requisite of good government; and that frequent changes are destructive of its utility.[16]

In fact, as a result of the requirements in Article V, the United States Constitution has proven to be difficult to amend.[17] The first ten amendments to the United States Constitution, the Bill of Rights, were submitted collectively and became operative with Virginia's ratification in 1791. Following the ratification of the Twelfth Amendment in 1804, the United States Constitution was not amended again until 1865. It has been estimated that approximately 10,000 amendments to the United States constitution have been proposed.[18] To date, however, there have only been a total of twenty-seven amendments to the United States Constitution and it contains a total of only approximately 7300 words.

B. ALTERING STATE CONSTITUTIONS

ANNE PERMALOFF, ALTERING STATE CONSTITUTIONS, 33 Cumb. L. Rev. 217 (2003)[19]

All of the 50 state constitutions in the United States contain provisions outlining the manner in which they may be altered or revised. State constitutions may be altered through legislatively proposed amendments, constitutional conventions, constitutional initiatives, constitutional commissions, and judicial interpretation. This paper examines the methods of alteration that include direct public representation and involvement at some stage in the alteration process, thus limiting the discussion to the first four methods listed.

There is considerable variation among the states in terms of which methods of alteration are allowed by their existing state constitutions. Furthermore, each method varies greatly in terms of the procedures required for its use. This paper will identify and discuss the variations within each method of alteration, which states use a given method, and the positive and negative factors associated with its use. Some of the philosophical, political, and cultural factors that influenced adoption of specific methods will be discussed as well. Finally, the paper will consider which methods might be appropriate for Alabama and for inclusion in a new Alabama constitution.

---

[16] James A. Bayard, *A Brief Exposition of the Constitution of the United States* 3 (2d ed. 1838), 135-36, 160 (emphasis in Bayard's text).

[17] Donald S. Lutz, Toward a Theory of Constitutional Amendment," *American Political Science Review* 88 (1994): 355.

[18] Richard B. Bernstein with Jerome Agel, *Amending America* (New York: Times Books 1993) p. xii.

[19] Reprinted with permission.

1. The Idea that Constitutions May Be Altered Is Not New

Popular sovereignty or the idea that government is based on popular consent served as the foundation for the Declaration of Independence, the original state constitutions, as well as the U. S. Constitution. Donald S. Lutz who has studied early state constitutional development indicates that an evolutionary process resulted in the gradual adoption of the idea, "... that a doctrine of popular sovereignty required that constitutions be written by popularly selected convention, rather than the legislature, and then ratified by a process that elicited popular consent ideally in a referendum."

Lutz notes that this notion quickly led to American expansion of John Locke's concept that replacement of government and the contract upon which it was based (a constitution) could occur only if those exercising power breached their contract. The American version held that if the public created the governing document and could alter its content by amendment, it also could replace the document at any time.

Lutz and others suggest that at least three other ideas reinforced this conception of constitutional change: human nature though imperfect is educable; faith that deliberative processes of decision-making will lead to the public good; and distinct differences between fundamental or constitutional law and legislative enactments.

Popular sovereignty implies that all constitutional matters should be based upon some form of popular consent, which in turn implies a formal, public process. Human fallibility implies the need for some method of altering or revising the constitution. A distinction between normal and constitutional matters implies that constitutional matters require a distinctive, highly deliberative process and thus implies the need for an amendment procedure more difficult than that used for normal legislation. Together these premises require that the procedure be neither too easy nor to difficult.

Robert F. Williams writes of another basis for the notion that constitutions may be altered--the idea that each generation should have the opportunity to refashion government to meet its needs. He and others quote Thomas Jefferson's views on this point for Jefferson not only advocated amending constitutions through convention, he advocated periodic revisions within set time frames:

> Some men look at constitutions with sanctimonious reverence, and deem them like the arc of the covenant, too sacred to be touched. They ascribe to the men of the preceding age a wisdom more than human, and suppose what they did to be beyond amendment. I knew that age well; I belonged to it, and labored with it. It deserved well of its country. It was very like the present, but without the experience of the present...I am certainly not an advocate for frequent and untried changes in laws and constitutions.... But I know also that laws and institutions must go hand in hand with the progress of the human mind. Let us,

as our sister States have done, avail ourselves of our reason and experience, to correct the crude essays of our first and unexperienced, although wise, virtuous, and well-meaning councils. And lastly, let us provide in our constitution for its revision at stated periods.... Each generation is as independent as the one preceding, as that was of all which had gone before. It has then, like them, a right to choose for itself the form of government it believes most promotive of its own happiness; consequently, to accommodate to the circumstances in which it finds itself, that received from its predecessors; and it is for the peace and good of mankind, that a solemn opportunity of doing this every nineteen or twenty years, should be provided by the constitution; so that it may be handed on, with periodic repairs, from generation to generation, to the end of time, if anything human can so long endure.

Jefferson wrote this passage in response to questions about a constitutional convention to revise the original Virginia constitution. Similar comments from other original signers of the U.S. Constitution could be cited to make the point that from the beginning of this nation's history trust in the public and its ability to grow and learn served as the basis of the argument that constitutions should change over time.

Other contemporaries of Jefferson's such as James Madison and John Adams believed in the ability to alter constitutions by amendment, but they believed that constitutions should not be altered easily. They did not support automatic periodic revision. For Madison the danger to be avoided was use of the amending process to foster factional (interest group) objectives. He believed constitutional change should be reserved for important matters such as the protection of basic rights. He was the major champion of the first amendments to the U.S. Constitution which were proposed by the very first Congress, the Bill of Rights.

Alan Tarr, one of the best known scholars on the development of state constitutions writes:

The United States has not one constitution but fifty-one. These constitutions were drafted at various stages in the nation's history, and their contents (not surprisingly) reflect the constitutional thought regnant at the time of their adoption. The political theory underlying state constitutions has often diverged from the perspective of 1787.

For Tarr, the states have their own constitutional tradition which encompasses not only the constitutional amendment and constitutional convention processes but constitutional initiative as well:

First, the initiative and direct democracy more generally fit comfortably within the state constitutional tradition. Second, this compatibility derives from the belief, basic to the state constitutional tradition, that the primary danger facing republican government is minority faction--power wielded by the wealthy or well-connected few--rather than majority faction. Third, the state tradition's divergence from Federalist #10's diagnosis of the threats to republican government is paralleled by a skepticism about the "republican remedies" proposed in The Federalist Papers. More specifically, the state constitutional tradition is characterized by a distrust of government by elected representatives representation not only fails to solve the problems afflicting republican government, but it may even aggravate those problems by empowering minority factions. If this is so, of course, then direct democracy--or mechanisms designed to approximate it--become much more attractive.

Tarr also reminds us that:

State constitutions of the eighteenth and early nineteenth centuries tended to concentrate power in the state legislature. In addition to enacting laws and imposing taxes, the legislatures in most states selected the governor and state judges and appointed other state officials (and oftentimes local officials as well). Legislators could also remove officials by impeachment and require the removal of judges by address. Moreover, these broad powers existed virtually without check.

The legislative authority was based on the fact that the legislature was considered the only institution that directly represented the citizenry. Even more important,...state constitution-makers sought to approximate direct democracy in their systems of representative government.

2. Legislatively Proposed Amendments

State constitutions are altered most frequently through legislatively proposed amendments. This process first appeared in state constitutions in the 1770s and was a well established principle by the 1780s. Today all 50 state constitutions allow for such amendment. All but one state (Delaware) requires that amendments proposed by the legislature be ratified by a vote of the electorate. Research has repeatedly tied frequent use of the amendment process to the length of a constitution. The longer the constitution, the more it is amended.

Conditions of legislative passage vary from state to state. Seventeen states require that the proposal pass by a simple majority of the membership of each house or 50% plus one. Alabama and seven other states set the bar higher at three-fifths or 60% of the membership of each house while 18 states require a two-thirds vote or 67%. Additional requirements may also apply.

Twelve states (Delaware, Indiana, Iowa, Massachusetts, Nevada, New York, Rhode Island, South Carolina, Tennessee, Virginia, and Wyoming) require that the amendment proposal be passed at two or more separate sessions of the legislature. The conditions of the vote may be different for each session. For example, Connecticut sets the vote at three-fourths (75%) of each house in the first session of passage and then requires passage in two more sessions at a majority level. And, a general election must occur between the two final sessions. South Carolina, Virginia and Tennessee, the only southern states that require passage in two sessions, differ in their procedures. Virginia requires a majority vote in both sessions. In South Carolina, initial passage is set at two-thirds of the membership; second passage is set at a majority but occurs only after ratification of the amendment by the electorate. In Tennessee the number on first passage is set at two-thirds of the senate and a majority of the house and then on second passage the figure is set at two-thirds of both houses.

Only six states place limits on the number or types of amendments that may be presented to the electorate. Arkansas, Kansas and Kentucky limit amendments on a ballot to three, five, and four respectively. In Colorado no more than six articles of the constitution may have amendments proposed in the same legislative session. New Jersey does not limit the number of proposed amendments on the ballot, but a proposal that has been defeated by the electorate may not be put on the ballot until three general elections have passed.

State constitutions either set a specified time and type of election for popular ratification (for example, the next general election) or allow the timing of the vote to be determined by the legislature itself. When the legislature is given the power to determine the timing of the vote as it is in Alabama, the type of election at which the vote occurs (for example, primary vs. general election, presidential election year vs. off-year election, regularly scheduled election vs. a special election) and factors such as likely turnout level and the disposition of voters likely to vote may influence the decision-making. High or low turnout may be the goal depending upon the purpose as well as the beneficiaries of the proposal.

Because legislatively proposed amendments are not normal legislation, they are not sent to the governor for signature or veto. The governor is important to the process, however. As a political party leader, she may work with legislative leaders to facilitate or block passage. Easy access to the media and interest groups may be part of this effort, particularly in attempting to activate supporters or opponents in legislative lobbying efforts. Sometimes governors lead election style campaigns aimed at activating the electorate to vote. Governors engaged in such campaigns may find their potential opponents working the other side of the issue while testing the waters for the next election.

Almost all (44 out of 49) of the state constitutions require a majority popular vote for ratification of an amendment. Most require a majority vote of those voting on the amendment. Three require a majority of those voting in the election while New Hampshire requires a two-thirds vote of those voting on the amendment. Illinois requires a two-thirds vote on the amendment or a majority of those voting in the election. States may add other requirements to these numbers. For example, in Florida any amendment creating a new tax or fee not in effect on November 7, 1994 must pass by a two-thirds vote, and Louisiana requires that amendments that impact five or fewer political subdivisions (for example, parishes or counties) must pass by a majority vote at the state level and a majority in each impacted subdivision. In New Mexico some amendment votes dealing with the right to vote and with education must be approved by 75% of the electorate; they reach the ballot only after 75% of each house have agreed to the proposals. Georgia's current constitution allows only for amendments that are of a general and uniform applicability throughout the state. This eliminates local purpose amendments and keeps the number of amendments down.

3. Constitutional Conventions

The constitutional convention is the oldest and traditional method used for creating constitutions and making major changes in existing constitutions. The convention is often referred to as the most democratic of the alteration procedures because it involves the electorate to the greatest extent.

Tarr, in outlining the Nineteenth Century experience with constitutional conventions, suggests at least three ways in which constitutional conventions then (and now) approximate direct democracy:

> First, the membership of state constitutional conventions tended to mirror the populace of the states. Convention delegates were--like state legislators-- elected by the people, but unlike legislators, they did not tend to be professional politicians.... Second, the people exercised control over the calling of conventions. Whereas the legislature met regularly, a convention came into being only by popular vote, when the people wanted fundamental political issues addressed. Thus when convention delegates met, they had a ready-made agenda of popular concerns to guide their deliberations.... Third, ratification by referendum afforded the people an opportunity to approve or reject the measures proposed by constitutional conventions--not an approximation of direct democracy but the real thing.... Usually voters considered the proposed constitution as a whole rather than voting on particular provisions. Yet in at least some states the practice developed of submitting controversial proposals as separate items, lest opposition to them doom the entire document.

Tarr also writes that often constitutional conventions were initiated in the 1800s in order to create a balance between the branches of government. As legislative bodies came to be viewed as dominated by specific interest groups, the conventions were used to enhance gubernatorial and judicial authority in order to protect the public. Constitutional initiatives which will be addressed in a later section were also used to return power to the people.

4. Constitutional Convention Procedures Today

Forty-two of the 50 states make provisions in their constitutions for constitutional conventions. Generally legislatures are given the right to initiate the constitutional convention call. That call usually requires voter approval. Then, the electorate selects the delegates to the convention using procedures outlined by the state constitution or by the legislature in enabling legislation. The enabling legislation may be outlined to the electorate at the time of its vote on the convention call. The electorate generally must ratify any document or alterations in the existing constitution that are proposed by the convention. As with the amending process, however, there are many variations in this overall pattern.

The standard convention call requirements are a majority vote or a two-thirds (67%) vote of both houses. South Dakota and Illinois require three-quarters (75%) of each house to call a convention.

Fourteen states require an automatic periodic vote by the electorate on whether to hold a convention. New York's 1846 constitution was the first to include such a mandatory referendum provision. Eight states (Connecticut, Illinois, Maryland, Missouri, Nebraska, New York, Ohio, and Oregon) mandate a vote every 20 years. Michigan requires a vote every 16 years. Four states (Alaska, Iowa, New Hampshire, and Rhode Island) use a 10 year cycle while Hawaii's vote must occur every 9 years. For many of these states if a vote for a convention has been called during the interim period, the mandatory vote cycle starts from the date of that vote.

An important factor to be considered in relation to the mandatory vote is whether the constitution includes a self-executing clause for any convention voted for by the electorate. Self-executing clauses may set up procedures for calling the convention, outline delegate selection procedures and delegate requirements, provide for convention location and staff support as well as operating funds all with no action required by the legislature. Without self-execution clauses, the voters may authorize a convention only to find that the legislature may then fail to enact the enabling legislation required, thus forcing the electorate to seek judicial remedies.

State constitutions vary greatly on whether a popular vote is required to ratify the recommendations made by a constitutional convention. When popular ratification procedures are specified in the constitution, the standard requirement for passage is a majority vote of those voting on the proposal. Nine states including Alabama, Florida, Mississippi, and West Virginia do not have specific ratification requirements in their constitutions. The convention call proposal itself usually outlines the procedures to be used for ratification, but the conditions of the ratification vote may also be left to the determination of the convention itself. Seven state constitutions including Kentucky's make no provision at all for popular ratification.

Conventions often are called during crisis periods or periods of major change. For example, the 1968 Florida Constitution was written by a convention called for by the first legislature to take office after reapportionment on a one-person, one-vote basis. One set of political issues its members had to deal with were the tensions between North Florida and South Florida. These tensions not only reflected differences in political party orientations but differences in their economic base. They also were tied to North Florida's domination of the state legislature due to the several decades long failure of the legislature to reapportion itself as the population base grew in South Florida. Similar regional tensions tied to legislative malapportionment aided in making the 1960s the last major decade for state constitutional conventions and total rewriting of state constitutions. The last constitutional convention which was successful in winning voter approval of its recommendations was held in Louisiana in 1974.

5. Strengths and Weaknesses

The greatest strength of the legislatively called convention process is that it maximizes direct citizen participation in the revision process. Citizens are indirectly represented at the legislative vote stage because they decided through the election process who votes on the proposal. They then vote directly on the proposal. They vote again to select convention delegates. Finally, recommendations from the convention must be ratified by the electorate. There is the potential for increasing citizen attention and interest in politics, governmental problems, and possible solutions. There is also the potential for increasing knowledge levels and developing a true public dialogue and debate process.

Several weaknesses or problems with the convention approach to revision are cited by opponents. First, many recent attempts to call conventions have failed due to public suspicion and distrust of politicians and the political process. Second, interest group activity is likely to be high and to create a divisive atmosphere at the delegate selection stage, during convention operations, and at ratification. Some groups will seek to preserve the protected position they have in the current constitution; they will be competing with those who have a vested interest in seeking special treatment for themselves. This is, of course, the democratic process at work. Third, many fear that the ability to spend money or to attract money from interest groups, not competence or concern for the public interest, will drive delegate selection. Others fear that unless specifically barred by the enabling legislation or the constitution, legislators and other elected officials will predominate among the delegates. The previously mentioned items are viewed as reinforcing this possibility.

A major problem exists in the manner by which conventions usually originate by legislative proposal. If the legislature has been captured by interests seeking to preserve the status quo (for example, rural Alabama's dominance of the legislature until the late 1960s), a proposal for a convention will not pass the legislature, and the will of the people may be thwarted. This is precisely the argument advanced by Progressive and Populist reformers during the late 1800s and early 1900s to justify the use of constitutional initiative as a revision method. An automatic periodic vote to determine if a convention should be held is another mechanism for bypassing a recalcitrant legislature.

6. Constitutional Initiatives

An initiative is a form of direct legislation that allows individuals and/or groups to propose public policy through the creation of a constitutional amendment. Currently, 18 states have constitutional initiative powers that allow the public to propose amendments to their constitutions and then submit them to the electorate for ratification. In Florida this process may be used to call a constitutional convention.

Constitutional initiative proposals usually are restricted to single topics and may generally deal with only one article of the constitution. Exceptions include situations where change in one article impacts another article; both may then be changed by the amendment. The general procedures for initiatives begin with the filing of the proposed amendment with the required state office. That office must determine that the amendment and petition meets legal requirements. The sponsors then circulate the petition within the electorate. Numbers of petition signatures required usually are tied to a percentage of the total votes cast in the last gubernatorial election. Currently the numbers range from 3% to 15%. When the requisite number of registered voters have signed the petitions, they are filed with the appropriate state office for review and certification. If the petitions meet all legal requirements, the proposed amendment is placed on the ballot for a vote.

Other requirements than the general format listed above may be set. For example, Mississippi requires petition signatures to be collected within a 12 month period, be equal to at least 12% of the votes for governor in the last gubernatorial election, and have no more than one-fifth (20%) of the signatures from any one congressional district. If a congressional district represents more than one-fifth of the signatures, the Mississippi Secretary of State who must determine whether the petition qualifies for the ballot must eliminate the excess signatures from the signature count.

7. Direct Initiative

Sixteen states, including Arkansas, Florida and Oklahoma use the direct constitutional initiative process. There is no legislative review or revision of the proposed amendment. Once legal requirements are met, the proposed amendment must be placed on the ballot. The timing of the vote is set by the constitution in relation to the date of formal certification of the petitions as legal. The election is usually specified as a general election. In Nevada passage of the constitutional initiative requires a majority vote of the electorate in two successive elections. This provision was established in 1962 with voter acceptance of a legislatively proposed amendment that created the process while simultaneously repealing Nevada's use of the indirect constitutional initiative which will be discussed below.

Many of the direct constitutional initiative states have requirements that specify that if two conflicting amendment proposals pass in the same election, the one with the highest number of votes will go into effect. The effective date of a newly passed amendment may be immediately or 30 days after the official certification of election results or a constitutionally specified day of the year such as January 1 or July 1, the first day of the budget year for most states.

8. Indirect Initiative

Two states, Mississippi and Massachusetts, use the indirect constitutional initiative. Indirect initiatives require that once the petition process is complete and certified as meeting all legal requirements, the proposed amendment must be submitted to the legislature for review. (The Nevada version which was abolished in 1962 in favor of a restrictive direct initiative process required that the proposed amendment also be sent to the governor for review.)

Mississippi's legislature receives constitutional initiative proposals on the first day of the legislative session. The legislature has several options available to it in its review process, but it must act within a four month deadline or the proposed amendment automatically goes on the ballot. The legislature's first option is to accept the proposal by a majority vote of each house; the proposal then goes on the ballot. If the legislature finds the amendment unacceptable and rejects it but without offering an alternative, the proposed amendment is placed on the ballot. If the legislature amends the proposal, both the original proposal and the legislative alternative will appear on the ballot for separate votes. If the proposal is rejected by the legislature which then passes an alternative, a complicated method of presentation and vote counting is specified in the Mississippi constitution:

> both such measures shall be printed on the official ballots that a voter can express separately two (2) preferences: First by voting for the approval of either measure or against both measures, and secondly, by voting for one measure or the other measure. If the majority of those voting on the first issue is against both measures, then both measures fail, but in that case the vote on the second issue nevertheless shall be carefully counted and made public. If the majority voting on the first issue is for the approval of either measure, then the measure

receiving a majority of the votes on the second issue and also receiving not less than forty percent (40%) of the total votes cast at the election at which the measure was submitted for approval shall be law. Any person who votes for the ratification of either measure on the first issue must vote for one (1) of the measures on the second issue in order for the ballot to be valid. Any person who votes against both measures on the first issue may vote but shall not be required to vote for any of the measures on the second issue in order for the ballot to be valid.

All proposals on the ballot carry with them a fiscal analysis outlining their likely financial impacts.

In Mississippi passage of proposed amendments requires a majority of those voting on the proposal. That majority vote count must represent at least 40% of the votes cast in the election. No more than five proposals are allowed on the ballot in any one election, and defeated proposals may not be reconsidered until two years have elapsed.

Massachusetts requires a constitutional initiative to be presented to a joint session of the legislature and to be approved by 25% of the legislature in two successive sessions before it may go on the ballot. If it fails to get the necessary 25%, it will not go to the ballot. During the first review the legislature may amend the proposal if 75% of the legislators vote to do so. The second legislative session may not amend the proposal. Another option available to the legislature is to pass a substitute version of the amendment. The original proposal and the clearly identified legislative alternative then go to the electorate for a vote.

The Massachusetts process has led to legislative approval of only three amendments. The first two were approved by the voters in 1938 and 1974. The third, a 1994 proposal to establish a graduated income tax, failed to receive voter approval.

9. Limitations on Constitutional Initiatives

Constitutional initiatives may be limited by specific provisions of a constitution. What, if any, limitations exist varies greatly from state to state. For example, the Massachusetts constitution places specific restrictions on what portions of the constitution may not be amended through the initiative process. It states that basic citizen rights such as the right to a jury trial, freedom of speech, freedom of the press, the right to peacefully assembly, and religious matters are excluded from initiative action as are some election related matters. The Massachusetts constitution also protects the independence of the judiciary by disallowing constitutional initiatives that alter judicial appointment procedures, judicial qualifications, and the tenure and removal processes for judges. In addition, constitutional initiatives are barred from creating specific appropriations from the state treasury. Illinois's constitution limits constitutional initiatives to structural and procedural subjects found in the

Legislative article. The Mississippi constitution states that the initiative may not be used to alter or repeal the following: the Bill of Rights; Mississippi Public Employees' Retirement System (and laws related to it); right to work provisions; or the constitutional initiative process. California requires that all initiatives must apply to all political subdivisions and be applicable to all subdivisions even if a majority in that jurisdiction voted against the ratified initiative.

Some states may require review of a constitutional initiative by the attorney general of the state for its legality. The opinion that results may be merely advisory in nature or may be given the force of law. Some reviews are accomplished at an initial notice filing that precedes circulation of the petition. This review determines whether all legal requirements have been met for the petition itself including proper format, especially improper or unclear ballot language; it may also determine whether the proposal itself meets constitutional muster. Both federal and state constitutional issues may be involved. Some states require the reviews at the time signed petitions have been filed. These reviews may be undertaken by a state's supreme court. The proposals may become the subject of court cases both before and after they have been approved by the electorate.

10. Strengths and Weaknesses

The constitutional initiative process, particularly in the direct initiative form, returns the power to act to the public. This power may be exercised even when a legislature or one of its houses has been captured by interest groups and blocks all efforts to institute a constitutional convention or to propose amendments. For example, the Oklahoma initiative was created to thwart the power that the railroads held over the state legislature. It is often viewed as a form of direct grass roots democracy.

Weaknesses cited for the initiative process are numerous. One set of complaints focuses on the procedures involved in the petition process. Because states may set the number of required signatures high, require signatures from registered voters, and often limit the time period within which the signatures must be collected, organized groups with large memberships and/or money rather than individual citizens have a distinct advantage. Those with the money are increasingly employing professionals who may not even live in the state to generate and circulate the petitions. In other instances, groups from outside the state that have a national agenda may go into several states with their initiative campaigns. At least one state has attempted to deal with these issues by restricting the right to file and circulate petitions to those who are registered voters in the state. Some states passed laws to make the paying of those who circulate a petition illegal, but a Colorado law to this effect was declared unconstitutional by the U.S. Supreme Court in a unanimous vote. Another problem is that unless the statutory or constitutional requirements require a clear and concise petition statement summarizing the proposal and give a court or the attorney general the authority to police these factors, confusing and purposively misleading information may be disseminated. A similar problem can exist for ballot summaries. Another concern is that majorities voting on initiatives may not be sensitive to minority rights. Both conservative rural interests and African American groups in Mississippi opposed the initiative process on this ground. Minority rights issues are one reason state constitutions may specify that basic rights found in their bill of rights are not alterable by initiative. Constitutions are supposed to serve as the fundamental law of the state. Amendment added by initiative increasingly represent policy issues normally dealt with by legislatures using their lawmaking powers.

A final issue centers around extraordinary majorities; it often is cited by those who are concerned by minority rights. A state that uses constitutional initiative may require a majority vote for passage of the initiative or for passage of a legislatively proposed amendment. An initiative proposal may include within it restrictions on how the proposal once adopted may be changed by future initiatives or amendments. The popular restriction is to require a two-thirds or three-fifths vote. Future generations must come to higher levels of agreement to change proposals made today by a majority vote. They lose the flexibility to create change that was part of the original argument for creation of constitutional initiative authority. A constitutional initiative also may be used to place restrictions on how certain laws may be passed by the legislature. An example is the Florida requirement that new tax proposals pass the legislature by super majority.

11. Constitutional Commissions

Constitutional commissions serve two major purposes: (1) studying the constitution and proposing changes and (2) preparing for a constitutional convention. They have also been used by legislatures as devices to forestall constitutional convention calls.

Commissions may be authorized by law or state constitution to meet on a periodic basis. They may be established by law, executive order, or other means (for example, the Alabama Citizens Commission on Constitutional Reform) to meet for a specified period. They generally report the results of their work to the governor, legislature, or other public authority. In the 1990s both California and New York used the commission system. New York's governor in 1992 created the Temporary New York State Commission on Constitutional Reform to prepare for a convention should the public agree to the automatic convention call set for

1997. The electorate rejected the convention call. California used an executively created commission to make recommendations to the legislature and governor.

One example of the successful use of a commission as an advisory group charged with making recommendations to the legislature may be found in Florida in the 1960s. In 1964 a legislatively proposed amendment received majority support from the Florida electorate. The amendment specified:

> Either branch of the legislature, at any regular session, or at any special or extraordinary session called for the purposes, may propose by joint resolution a revision of the entire constitution or a revision or amendment of any portion or portions thereof and may direct and provide for an election thereon.

The Florida legislature used its new authority to create a revision commission by statute. It met in 1965-1966 and submitted proposals for major revisions of the constitution to the legislature in 1966. These proposals together with legislative revisions were submitted to the voters in the 1968 general election. On passage they became the 1968 Florida Constitution. This new constitution added not only constitutional initiative but a revision commission unlike that used to develop the new constitution. The Florida Constitutional Review Commission is the only constitutionally established commission with the authority to report its recommendations directly to the electorate for a vote.

12. Strengths and Weaknesses

The commission system allows for study and careful deliberation. Its work can be done transparently so that the public is fully informed of all its activities and has numerous opportunities to contribute their concerns and recommendation. If the commission must report to the legislature, its recommendations must be translated into legislatively proposed amendments. Only Florida has a commission that reports recommendations directly to the public. Even when the public has voted against this commission's recommendations, public debate has been increased and change has been generated through later legislative actions.

If commissions are dependent upon legislatures or governors for their call rather than automatically established on a periodic basic, they may never be called into existence. Or if called by a governor, the legislature might ignore their work for partisan reasons. A periodic cycle for automatically calling a commission into session can insure that constitutional reviews are accomplished.

A major problem may be that enabling legislation is not accounted for in the commission process. The Florida CRC worked well in 1998 because of the cooperative efforts of politicians, not existing law.

There are those that critique Florida's CRC and who urge its abolition. For example, Joseph Little finds that the appointment process created the gift of a rich political plum to the politicians who happened to be the incumbents in the designated offices when the time for appointing...rolled abound. He believes the appointees support the political and agendas of those they represent, not the public. In addition, he argues that the public's presentations at the public hearings represent statements of an ideological bent or served as mechanisms for venting displeasure with legislative actions. Little believes that the authority given the CRC is too great, that its proposed amendments often deal with policy issues best handled by the legislature, and that its packaging of recommendations together for a single vote by the electorate forces it to accept revisions it does not want in order to get that does want.

13. Conclusion

Selection of one revision method over another should be based on at least two criteria: an examination of the basic underlying values each reflects and the administrative and political problems associated with each. Some of the administrative problems may be handled through careful constitutional wording and enabling legislation.

Direct democracy and participation by the public is maximized through the use of the constitutional convention. Direct constitutional initiative and required periodic votes by the electorate on whether a constitutional convention should be held also value direct democracy.

Indirect or representative democracy is maximized by legislative involvement in the revisions process. The amendment process usually begins with legislative proposals. Legislatures also serve as the major initiators of constitutional conventions, and in Mississippi and Massachusetts the legislature also reviews constitutional initiatives from the public.

Should a constitutional convention be held in Alabama, the Commission might give consideration to recommending that a new constitution require periodic public votes on whether a constitutional convention should be held. The Florida Constitutional Revision Commission approach should be examined carefully. It combines elements of indirect democracy (appointment of members by public officials) with elements of direct democracy (automatic periodic creation, required public hearing, and sending of recommendations to the public for a vote without legislative intervention). Many of the administrative problems faced by the commission could be overcome through enabling provisions written into the constitution.

C. LEGISLATIVE AMENDMENT – SINGLE OBJECT REQUIREMENT

FORUM FOR EQUALITY PAC v. The Honorable W. Fox McKEITHEN
893 So.2d 715 (La. 2005)

KNOLL, J.

This case concerns a judgment of the district court declaring the constitutional amendment titled "Defense of Marriage," unconstitutional in violation of Article XIII, § 1(B) of the 1974 Constitution of Louisiana. For the following reasons we reverse, finding the district court erred by interpreting the single object requirement narrowly rather than employing a germane approach for a single object with multiple parts. We find each provision of the amendment is germane to the single object of defense of marriage and constitutes an element of the plan advanced to achieve this object.

FACTS AND PROCEDURAL HISTORY

During the 2004 Regular Session, the Louisiana Legislature, by joint resolution with a two-thirds majority of both houses, passed 2004 La. Acts 926. Through the passage of Act 926, the Legislature resolved "that there shall be submitted to the electors of the state of Louisiana, for their approval or rejection in the manner provided by law, a proposal to add Article XII, Section 15 of the Constitution of Louisiana." The amendment was to read as follows:

§ 15. Defense of Marriage

Section 15. Marriage in the state of Louisiana shall consist only of the union of one man and one woman. No official or court of the state of Louisiana shall construe this constitution or any state law to require that marriage or the legal incidents thereof be conferred upon any member of a union other than the union of one man and one woman. A legal status identical or substantially similar to that of marriage for unmarried individuals shall not be valid or recognized. No official or court of the state of Louisiana shall recognize any marriage contracted in any other jurisdiction which is not the union of one man and one woman.

The Legislature "further resolved that this proposed amendment shall be submitted to the electors of the state of Louisiana at the statewide election to be held on September 18, 2004."

Accordingly, the amendment was considered by the voters at the September 18, 2004 election, and the measure was approved by 77.78% of the electorate: 619,908 votes for and 177,067 votes against the amendment.

Following the election, the plaintiffs, Forum for Equality PAC, a registered Louisiana political action committee ("Forum"), Louisiana Log

Cabin Republicans, an unincorporated Louisiana association, Laurence E. Best, Jeanne M. LeBlanc, Gerald W. Thibodeaux, William A. Schultz, and Julie A. Jacobs ("plaintiffs"), filed suit in the Nineteenth Judicial District Court, Parish of East Baton Rouge, against defendants, W. Fox McKeithen, in his official capacity as Secretary of State of Louisiana ("the State"), and the City of New Orleans ("the City").

LAW AND ANALYSIS

Prefatorily we note the issues presented concern strictly a matter of law. As the district court correctly noted in its reasons for judgment, emotions do not govern our resolution of this case. Rather, our role in this state's constitutional scheme as the final judicial authority is to review the district court's legal conclusions. We are called upon to decide whether this amendment to the Constitution of Louisiana conforms to constitutionally established requirements.

Amending the Constitution of Louisiana

"Provisions of a constitution regulating its own amendment,…are not merely directory but are mandatory; and a strict observance of every substantial requirement is essential to the validity of the proposed amendment." This general rule governs the restraints which the people have placed in their Constitution upon themselves, their officers, and agents and representatives. *Id.* Thus, in submitting an amendment to the people, the Legislature is bound by the provisions of our constitution mandating the procedural process for amending the constitution.

Article XIII of the 1974 Constitution of Louisiana sets forth the procedure for proposing and adopting constitutional amendments. Article XIII, § 1 of the Louisiana Constitution provides, in full:

> Section 1. (A) Procedure. An amendment to this constitution may be proposed by joint resolution at any regular session of the legislature, but the resolution shall be prefiled, at least ten days before the beginning of the session, in accordance with the rules of the house in which introduced. An amendment to this constitution may be proposed at any extraordinary session of the legislature if it is within the objects of the call of the session and is introduced in the first five calendar days thereof. If two-thirds of the elected members of each house concur in the resolution, pursuant to all of the procedures and formalities required for passage of a bill except submission to the governor, the secretary of state shall have the proposed amendment published once in the official journal of each parish within not less than thirty nor more than sixty days preceding the election at which the proposed amendment is to be submitted to the electors. Each joint resolution shall specify the statewide election at which the proposed amendment shall be submitted. Special elections for submitting proposed amendments may be authorized by law.
>
> (B) Form of Proposal. A proposed amendment shall have a title containing a brief summary of the changes proposed; shall be confined to one object; and shall set forth the entire article, or the sections or other subdivisions thereof, as proposed to be revised or only the article, sections, or other subdivisions

proposed to be added. However, the legislature may propose, as one amendment, a revision of an entire article of this constitution which may contain multiple objects or changes. A section or other subdivision may be repealed by reference. When more than one amendment is submitted at the same election, each shall be submitted so as to enable the electors to vote on them separately.

(C) Ratification. If a majority of the electors voting on the proposed amendment approve it, the governor shall proclaim its adoption, and it shall become part of this constitution, effective twenty days after the proclamation, unless the amendment provides otherwise. A proposed amendment directly affecting not more than five parishes or areas within not more than five parishes shall become part of this constitution only when approved by a majority of the electors voting thereon in the state and also a majority of the electors voting thereon in each affected parish. However, a proposed amendment directly affecting not more than five municipalities, and only such municipalities, shall become part of this constitution only when approved by a majority of the electors voting thereon in the state and also a majority of the electors voting thereon in each such municipality.

La. Const. art. XIII, § 1(A) thus provides that an amendment to this state's constitution may be proposed by a joint resolution at any regular session of the Legislature.

Joint resolutions propose amendments to the constitution and must "be prefiled, at least ten days before the beginning of the session, in accordance with the rules of the house in which introduced." Joint resolutions are then given bill numbers and are processed as bills, including the designation of an act number by the secretary of state after passage by both houses of the Legislature. However, joint resolutions are not "bills" in the technical sense, because joint resolutions are not presented to the governor for executive action.

A joint resolution must pass both houses of the Legislature by a two-thirds vote of the elected members of each house, and then must be ratified by at least a majority of voters to amend the constitution. Importantly, joint resolutions must contain a title and are generally confined to one object. The joint resolution must also specify the statewide election at which the proposed amendment will be submitted to the voters, and the secretary of state is mandated to timely publish the language of the proposed amendment in the official journal of each parish.

Moreover, joint resolutions routinely include ballot language summarizing the proposed change, despite the language of the constitution requiring the secretary of state to prepare the ballots for all elections. Note, the ballot language need only constitute "sufficient information to identify the proposed amendment which the voter is voting for or against." Further, the publication of the proposed amendment has been deemed as satisfying the due process requirements of notice to voters of its contents. Finally, when the Legislature submits more than one amendment at the same election, each amendment must be submitted so as to enable the voters to vote on them separately.

A JOINT RESOLUTION

Proposing an amendment to the Constitution of Louisiana, to enact

> Article XII, Section 15, relative to marriage; to require that marriage in the state shall consist only of the union of one man and one woman; to provide that the legal incidents of marriage shall be conferred only upon such union; to prohibit the validation or recognition of the legal status of any union of unmarried individuals; to prohibit the recognition of a marriage contracted in another jurisdiction which is not the union of one man and one woman; to provide for submission of the proposed amendment to the electors and provide a ballot proposition; and to provide for related matters.

Section 1: Be it resolved by the Legislature of Louisiana, two-thirds of the members elected to each house concurring, that there shall be submitted to the electors of the state of Louisiana, for their approval or rejection in the manner provided by law, a proposal to add Article XII, Section 15 of the Constitution of Louisiana, to read as follows:

> *§ 15. Defense of Marriage*
>
> *Section 15. Marriage in the state of Louisiana shall consist only of the union of one man and one woman. No official or court of the state of Louisiana shall construe this constitution or any state law to require that marriage or the legal incidents thereof be conferred upon any member of a union other than the union of one man and one woman. A legal status identical or substantially similar to that of marriage for unmarried individuals shall not be valid or recognized. No official or court of the state of Louisiana shall recognize any marriage contracted in any other jurisdiction which is not the union of one man and one woman.*

Section 2. Be it resolved that this proposed amendment shall be submitted to the electors of the state of Louisiana at the statewide election to be held on September 18, 2004.

Section 3. Be it further resolved that on the official ballot to be used at said election there shall be printed a proposition, upon which the electors of the state shall be permitted to vote FOR or AGAINST, to amend the Constitution of Louisiana, which proposition shall read as follows:

> To provide that marriage in this state shall consist of the union of one man and one woman, that legal incidents of marriage shall not be conferred on a member of any union other than such union, and that the state shall not validate or recognize a legal status identical or substantially similar to that of marriage for unmarried individuals or any marriage contracted in any other jurisdiction which is not the union of one man and one woman. (Adds Article XII, Section 15).

Finding that the third sentence of the constitutional amendment contained within this joint resolution, designated as Act 926, constituted a separate and distinct object from that contained within the first, second, and fourth sentences of the amendment, the district court declared the constitutional amendment unconstitutional in violation of La. Const. art.

XIII, § 1(B)'s "single object" requirement. We will now address whether the district court erred in declaring the constitutional amendment unconstitutional.

"Single Object" Requirement

As cited above, La. Const. art. XIII, § 1(B) provides "a proposed amendment shall ... be confined to one object." This provision was adopted in the 1974 Constitution of Louisiana as a restatement of the theretofore existing "single object" rule, which was partially a creature of the jurisprudence arising from the interpretation of various provisions of earlier state constitutions. These earlier provisions provided: "When more than one amendment shall be submitted at the same election, they shall be so submitted as to enable the electors to vote on each amendment separately." Although none of the various Louisiana state constitutions prior to the 1974 Constitution expressly required that every constitutional amendment be confined to one object, Louisiana courts had consistently ruled that constitutional amendments could not pertain to more than one object in their interpretation of the "separate votes" for "separate amendments" provisions noted above.

It was this jurisprudential interpretation that the people sought to continue in their adoption of the first sentence of La. Const. art. XIII, § 1(B). The two leading cases from this Court addressing this rule are *Graham v. Jones,* 198 La. 507, 3 So.2d 761 (1941), and *Miller v. Greater Baton Rouge Port Com'n,* 225 La. 1095, 74 So.2d 387 (1954), which we will discuss in turn.

In *Graham v. Jones,* this Court addressed the validity of 1940 La. Acts 384, a joint resolution of the Legislature proposing a constitutional amendment, which made various changes to state government, including abolishing the Legislative Bureau and reorganizing the executive department. Moreover, as in the instant case, the amendment at issue in *Graham* was approved by the electorate. In its holding, this Court found the Act was without effect because it was not constitutionally adopted, applying a rather narrow construction of the "single object" rule.

In its discussion, the *Graham* court explained the "single object" rule in light of the determination of whether one or more constitutional amendments were contained in a single proposition:

> If the different changes contained in the proposed amendment all cover matters necessary to be dealt with in some manner, in order that the Constitution, as amended, shall constitute a consistent and workable whole on the general topic embraced in that part which is amended, and if, logically speaking, they should stand or fall as a whole, then there is but one amendment submitted. But, if any one of the propositions, although not directly contradicting the others, does not refer to such matters, or if it is not such that the voter supporting it would reasonably be expected to support the principle of the others, then there are in reality two or more amendments to be submitted, and the proposed amendment

falls within the constitutional prohibition. Nor does the rule as stated unduly hamper the adoption of legitimate amendments to the Constitution. Such a document was presumably adopted deliberately, after careful preparation, as a harmonious and complete system of government. Changes suggested thereto should represent the free and mature judgment of the electors, so submitted that they cannot be constrained to adopt measures of which in reality they disapprove, in order to secure the enactment of others they earnestly desire. [quoting *Kerby v. Luhrs,* 44 Ariz. 208, 36 P.2d 549, 554 (1934)]

This provision of the Constitution is a wise one, and is intended to prevent several inconsistent and conflicting propositions from being submitted to the voters in the same amendment, and forcing the voter to approve or reject such amendment as a whole. In other words, it prevents burdening a meritorious proposition with a vicious one, and alike prevents a vicious proposition from having the support of a meritorious one, and gives to the voter the right to have each separate proposition submitted to him in order that he may express his will for or against each separately without being compelled to accept a provision to which he is opposed in order to have adopted a provision which meets his favor."

Numerous cases from other jurisdictions are cited on behalf of relators in which the general rule has been laid down that a constitutional amendment embracing several subjects all of which are germane to the general subject of the amendment, under the requirement for separate submission where more than one amendment is proposed, may be submitted to people as a general proposition.

The question in this case is not whether the rule is sound, but whether it is applicable to the proposed amendment under review by the Court.

Thus, the "single object" rule as restated in La. Const. art. XIII, § 1(B) requires that an amendment to the Constitution embodies a single plan and that every provision therein is germane to that plan. In other words, the judiciary in determining whether the legislative action in submitting a constitutional amendment to the people is constitutional under the "single object" requirement must examine all the provisions of an amendment to ascertain whether every provision relates or is germane to the main purpose or object of the amendment.

The task of this Court is to identify the main purpose or object of the constitutional amendment and then to examine each provision to determine whether the amendment embodies a single plan to accomplish the object and whether every provision is germane to that plan, i.e., to determine "[i]f the different changes contained in the proposed amendment all cover matters necessary to be dealt with in some manner, in order that the Constitution, as amended, shall constitute a consistent and workable whole on the general topic embraced in that part which is amended." We note that "what is 'germane' is that which is in close relationship, appropriate, relevant, or pertinent to the general subject."

"[A]s the branch of government empowered to initiate constitutional amendments, the legislature should be afforded substantial deference to determine both the overall object of a proposed amendment and the changes incidental to and necessarily connected with the object intended." We will afford substantial deference to the Legislature in determining the object of the constitutional amendment, and thus, we will examine the actions of the Legislature in drafting and proposing this amendment in order to ascertain its intended object.

As constitutionally required, "[a] proposed amendment shall have a title containing a brief summary of the changes proposed," La. Const. art. XIII, § 1(B), and the title may be referred to "in order to ascertain generally the scope and object of the proposed changes in the Constitution." ("The title of an act of the Legislature is of the nature of a label, the purpose of which is to give notice of the legislative intent and purpose to those interested in, or who may be affected by, the terms of the act, and to prevent surprise and fraud upon members of the Legislature."). Therefore, in our search for the amendment's intended object, we begin with the title the Legislature adopted for this amendment.

Act 926 titles the constitutional amendment, "Defense of Marriage" and sets forth its purpose as "to enact Article XII, Section 15, relative to marriage; to require that marriage in the state shall consist only of the union of one man and one woman; to provide that the legal incidents of marriage shall be conferred only upon such union; to prohibit the validation or recognition of the legal status of any union of unmarried individuals; to prohibit the recognition of a marriage contracted in another jurisdiction which is not the union of one man and one woman." Given the clear and unambiguous language of the title adopted by the Legislature, one could logically conclude the object of the amendment is "defense of marriage."

However, in further search of the intended object of this amendment and in an abundance of caution, we also look to the committee meeting discussions held by each house of the Legislature. The minutes of the House Civil Law and Procedure Committee indicated a concern that "the Civil Code of law followed in Louisiana" would not be adequate protection for marriage in this state without a constitutional amendment because "Louisiana's Civil Code would yield to provisions of the state constitution that might be found in conflict with it."

Moreover, the minutes of the Senate Committee on Judiciary, Section A also reflect this need for additional protection of our civil law tradition of marriage, noting that the "intent was to put this in the Louisiana Constitution so that the legal issues of law cannot be challenged" because, although the protection of marriage is arguably provided for in our Civil Code, "[t]he constitution has a far greater protection ... than that of a statute." Although the amendment could not protect Louisiana's civil tradition of marriage from all attacks, specifically the United States

Supreme Court's declaration of unconstitutionality, the testimony did note the amendment would provide additional protection to marriage.

The central theme running throughout these committee meetings is the need to protect or defend our civil tradition of marriage through the adoption of a constitutional amendment, which has as its sole object the defense and protection of our civil tradition of marriage.

Thus, as evident from its title as proposed by the Legislature and the discussions in committee meetings, the object of this constitutional amendment is "defense of marriage," i.e., to defend this state's civil tradition of marriage. Notably, this is where the district court erred in that it is apparent from the court's reasoning that the district court, relying on *Graham's* narrow construction rather than *Hotard's* and *Miller's* broad construction, narrowly identified the object of the amendment as a "same-sex marriage ban." Although such a ban is effected by the provisions of the constitutional amendment, the ban itself is not the main purpose or object of the amendment.

Having ascertained the main object of the amendment, we must now determine whether each provision of the constitutional amendment relates to or is germane to this object of "defense of marriage," or rather, constitutes a single plan in "defense of marriage."

Such an examination reveals the amendment contains a single plan to defend our civil tradition of marriage. In effect, the amendment provides the only contract or legal instrument whereby the state is mandated to bestow all or substantially all the rights, civil effects, and legal incidents of marriage upon the parties in recognition of the legal status created or established by said contract or instrument is the contract of marriage between one man and one woman.

We find that each provision constitutes an element of this plan. Specifically, the provisions of sentence one seek to preserve the concept of marriage in its definition, while the provisions of sentences two, three, and four seek to protect and reserve only to marriage the legal incidents and civil effects that necessarily flow to the couple from the state by operation of law based solely on the recognition of their legal status as husband and wife, i.e., their legal union. Moreover, each provision is germane to the object of "defense of marriage" and "constitute[s] a consistent and workable whole on the general topic embraced in that part which is amended," i.e., the "defense of marriage."

Accordingly, we find the constitutional amendment does not violate the "single object" requirement of La. Const. art. XIII, § 1(B), and therefore, we reverse the district court's declaration of unconstitutionality.

NOTES

1. All states require ratification of amendments by a statewide referendum, except Delaware.

2. In 2007, every amendment to a state constitution was proposed by the legislature. None were placed on the ballot of any state by the constitutional initiative process.

D. INITIATIVE

ADAMS v. GUNTER
238 So.2d 824 (Fla. 1970)

DREW, J.

William D. Gunter, Jr., as a taxpayer citizen of the State of Florida, prepared and presented to Tom Adams, Secretary of State of Florida, a 'Petition for a One House Legislature Pursuant to Article XI, Section 3: Initiative' for approval as to form and content before proceeding with the circulation thereof. The Secretary of State declined to approve the petition, whereupon these proceedings for declaratory decree were instituted under Chapter 86, Florida Statutes 1969, for the purpose of resolving the controversy between the parties.

The trial court held:

1.   That the petition submitted by Respondent proposing an amendment by initiative to Section 1, of Article III, of the Constitution of the State of Florida, as amended in 1968, is valid and meets the Constitutional requirements of Article XI, Section 3.

2.   That upon proper signature of petition by the required number of electors, and filing with the Secretary of State in conformity with Article XI, Section 3, of the Constitution, the proposed amendment is in proper form to be submitted to the electors at the next general election held more than ninety (90) days after it is filed.

This direct appeal is from such judgment which construes controlling provisions of the Florida Constitution and presents for the first time the question of whether an initiative petition proposing an amendment to the Constitution of 1968 is defective and unauthorized when the proposed amendment would amend, modify, change or otherwise affect several other provisions of the same constitution.

Article XI of the Constitution of 1968 contains five sections, all relating to amendments. For clarity in the discussion which follows, Article XI in its entirety is set forth below:

ARTICLE XI

AMENDMENTS

§ 1. Proposal by legislature

Amendment of a section or revision of one or more articles, or the whole, of this constitution may be proposed by joint resolution agreed to by three-fifths of the membership of each house of the legislature. The full text of the joint resolution and the vote of each member voting shall be entered on the journal of each house.

§ 2. Revision commission

(a) Within thirty days after the adjournment of the regular session of the legislature convened in the tenth year following that in which this constitution is adopted, and each twentieth year thereafter, there shall be established a constitution revision commission composed of the following thirty-seven members:

   (1) the attorney general of the state;

   (2) fifteen members selected by the governor;

   (3) nine members selected by the speaker of the house of representatives and nine members selected by the president of the senate; and

   (4) three members selected by the chief justice of the supreme court of Florida with the advice of the justices.

(b) The governor shall designate one member of the commission as its chairman. Vacancies in the membership of the commission shall be filled in the same manner as the original appointments.

(c) Each constitution revision commission shall convene at the call of its chairman, adopt its rules of procedure, examine the constitution of the state, hold public hearings, and, not later than one hundred eighty days prior to the next general election, file with the secretary of state its proposal, if any, of a revision of this constitution or any part of it.

§ 3. Initiative

The power to propose amendments to any section of this constitution by initiative is reserved to the people. It may be invoked by filing with the secretary of state a petition containing a copy of the proposed amendment, signed by a number of electors in each of one half of the congressional districts of the state, and of the state as a whole, equal to eight per cent of the votes cast in each of such districts respectively and in the state as a whole in the last preceding election in which presidential electors were chosen.

§ 4. Constitutional convention

(a) The power to call a convention to consider a revision of the entire constitution is reserved to the people. It may be invoked by filing with the secretary of state a petition, containing a declaration that a constitutional convention is desired, signed by a number of electors in each of one half of the congressional districts of the state, and of the state as a whole, equal to fifteen per cent of the votes cast in each such district respectively and in the state as a whole in the last preceding election of presidential electors.

(b) At the next general election held more than ninety days after the filing of such petition there shall be submitted to the electors of the state the question: 'Shall a constitutional convention be held?' If a majority voting on the question votes in the affirmative, at the next succeeding general election there shall be elected from each representative district a member of a constitutional convention. On the twenty-first day following that election, the convention shall sit at the capital, elect officers, adopt rules of procedure, judge the election of its membership, and fix a time and place for its future meetings. Not later than ninety days before the next succeeding general election, the convention shall cause to be filed with the secretary of state any revision of this constitution proposed by it.

§ 5. Amendment or revision election

(a) A proposed amendment to or revision of this constitution, or any part of it, shall be submitted to the electors at the next general election held more than ninety days after the joint resolution, initiative petition or report of revision commission or constitutional convention proposing it is filed with the secretary of state, unless, pursuant to law enacted by the affirmative vote of three-fourths of the membership of each house of the legislature and limited to a single amendment or revision, it is submitted at an earlier special election held more than ninety days after such filing.

(b) Once in the tenth week, and once in the sixth week immediately preceding the week in which the election is held, the proposed amendment or revision, with notice of the date of election at which it will be submitted to the electors, shall be published in one newspaper of general circulation in each county in which a newspaper is published.

(c) If the proposed amendment or revision is approved by vote of the electors, it shall be effective as an amendment to or revision of the constitution of the state on the first Tuesday after the first Monday in January following the election, or on such other date as may be specified in the amendment or revision.

Of assistance also in the resolution of this question are the following excerpts from the Minutes of the Interim Constitutional Revision Committee, viz:

Section 3 discussed next. The section was approved as it reads on page 71 of October 30 draft; however, there is a flag to Style and Drafting that such subcommittee should prepare amendments to be introduced on floor during special session to correct language applying to revision of entire articles as well as amendments to a section. Section 3, until so amended, will read:

Section 3. INITIATIVE.-The power to propose amendments to any section of this constitution by initiative is reserved to the people. It may be invoked by filing with the secretary of state a petition containing a copy of the proposed amendment, signed by a number of electors in each of one half of the congressional districts of the state, and of the state as a whole, equal to eight per cent of the votes cast in each of such districts respectively and in the state as a whole in the last preceding election in which presidential electors were chosen.' (Excerpt from Minutes of the Interim Constitutional Revision Committee on October 30, 1967.)

In Article XI, Representative Pettigrew moved that on page 63, Section 3, line 7, the word 'section' be amended to read 'article.' Senator Friday spoke in opposition to this amendment. Representative Reed offered substitute motion to strike the words 'any section of' on line 7. Representative Sessums offered an amendment to the substitute motion by inserting the words 'article or' before the word 'section.' Mr. Pettigrew withdrew his motion. Mr. Reed's substitute motion as amended by Mr. Sessums would amend the sentence to read: 'The power to propose amendments to any article or section of this constitution by initiative.'...Representative Eddy spoke in opposition to all these amendments and requested that the language remain as it appears in the December 11 Draft. Vote was taken on the motion to amend. MOTION FAILED by vote of 6 yeas and 13 nays (see Roll Call No. 6 attached). Vote taken on motion to amend line 7 by striking the word 'section' and inserting 'article.' MOTION FAILED by voice vote. Representative Wolfson moved that Article XI be adopted as the recommendation of the committee. MOTION CARRIED by voice vote. (Excerpt from Minutes of the Interim Constitutional Revision Committee on June 17, 1968.)

Of pertinence also is the distinction between the words 'amend' and 'revise.' Webster's Collegiate Dictionary, Fifth Edition, defines these words as follows: 'Amend - To change or modify in any way for the better; to improve; to better; hence, to change or alter in any way, esp. in phraseology; Specif., in parliamentary procedure, to alter (as a bill) formally by some addition or modification' and 'Revise - to look at or over again in order to correct or improve; as to revise a printer's proof. To make a new, improved, or up-to-date version of; as to revise the game laws. Act of revising; revision.' That these distinctions were debated and considered at length in selecting the language to be incorporated in Article XI is clear from the Minutes of the Constitutional Revision Committee quoted above.

It has been suggested that these proceedings, brought under the provisions of the Declaratory Judgment Act, are premature and present no question determinable under the Declaratory Judgment Act. The argument in this connection is largely predicated upon the decision of this Court in *Bryant v. Gray*. The same question was raised with reference to the proceedings which culminated in the decision of this Court on June 26, 1970, in the case of *Holley v. Adams*, Fla., 238 So.2d 401. In this decision we swept aside the objections, holding that such action was appropriate and that the circuit court had jurisdiction. What we said in Holley is applicable here. While our Declaratory Judgment Act does not require that there be an actual controversy to form a basis for invoking the provisions of such statute, we find that such a controversy does actually exist in this case. Appellee Gunter presented his petition to the Secretary of State and has alleged in the complaint that the Secretary of State refused to approve it because of alleged legal insufficiencies. To resolve the question these proceedings were instituted. The purpose of the litigation is not only to save the appellee Gunter great sums of money in the promotion of the initiative petition but to resolve the highly pertinent public question involved. The trial court had jurisdiction to entertain the proceedings and enter the decree which is the subject of this appeal.

The provisions of the 1968 Constitution herein quoted at length had no counterpart in any of the previous constitutions of the state. Amendments to the present Constitution may be brought about as follows:

(1) The Legislature may propose an amendment of 'a section' or 'revision of one or more articles' or 'the whole' Constitution;

(2) Ten years after the adoption of the Constitution and every twenty years thereafter a Constitutional Revision Commission, established by the Constitution, shall meet and at such meeting may propose for adoption 'a revision of this Constitution or any part of it.'

(3) The electors of the state may propose amendments to 'any section' of the Constitution by initiative; and

(4) The electors may by petition containing a declaration that a constitutional convention is desired call a convention to consider a revision of the 'entire Constitution.'

The Constitution is divided into twelve Articles and each Article is divided into numbered Sections. Throughout Article XI the words 'amendment' and 'revision' are used to denote entirely different things. The words were carefully and deliberately selected and it is clear from the language of Article XI that the people have reserved the right to bring about an amendment to any Section of the Constitution by following the provisions set forth therein. The people have also reserved unto themselves the power to bring about a complete revision of the Entire Constitution. It is equally clear from Article XI that where more than one section of the Constitution is to be amended it is called a revision, and such revision contemplates deliberative action of either the Legislature or a convention duly assembled in order to accomplish harmony in language and purpose between articles and to produce as nearly as possible a document free of doubts and inconsistencies. Deliberation, discussion, and drafting is a part of the scene of parliamentary procedures and essential when more than one section of a constitution is to be amended.

This case presents a classic example of why Article XI was so framed. Assuming that the petition herein should receive the approval required and become a part of the Constitution, it would be immediately necessary to amend numerous other provisions of the Constitution. This fact is recognized in the proposal itself. Paragraph (c) thereof provides that the Legislature in the General Election of 1972 'shall propose…such further amendment to this Constitution and shall pass such laws as shall be necessary to implement this amendment.' The quoted provision in itself condemns the proposal. It is the type of amendment which this Court condemned in *Rivera-Cruz v. Gray*, which concerned the so-called 'daisy-chain amendments' to the Constitution of 1885. In that case this Court enjoined the submission to the electors of the proposals to revise the Constitution by submitting to the people interlocking amendments to each article thereof (except Article V), with the provision that unless all articles were adopted the election failed. We held in that case that such an attempt to amend the Constitution amounted to a revision without conforming to the then provisions of the Constitution of 1885, concerning revision. We said: 'When the Constitution uses the word 'amendment' it has reference to an article or articles, while the word 'revision' relates to the whole instrument.' Our present Constitution is decidedly analogous. This document uses the word 'amendment' with reference to a section rather than an article as did the 1885 Constitution.

Mr. Justice Thomas in writing for the Court in *Rivera-Cruz* used the following language which is pertinent to the disposition of the problem here:

> If the changes attempted are so sweeping that it is necessary to include the provisions interlocking them, then it is plain that the plan would constitute a recasting of the whole Constitution and this, we think, it was purposed to accomplish only by a convention under Sec. 2 which has not yet been disturbed.

The proposal here to amend Section 1 of Article III of the 1968 Constitution to provide for a Unicameral Legislature affects not only many other provisions of the Constitution but provides for a change in the form of the legislative branch of government, which has been in existence in the United States Congress and in all of the states of the nation, except one, since the earliest days. It would be difficult to visualize a more revolutionary change. The concept of a House and a Senate is basic in the American form of government. It would not only radically change the whole pattern of government in this state and tear apart the whole fabric of the Constitution, but would even affect the physical facilities necessary to carry on government.

Without attempting to enumerate all of the sections of the Constitution which would be affected to a greater or lesser degree by the adoption of this amendment, it is significant to note the following:

1. Section 2 of Article III would have to be rewritten;

2. Sections 3(c)(1), 3(d), 3(e), and 3(f) of Article III would have to be revised to be applicable to the Unicameral theory;

3. Sections 4(a)(b)(c) and (d) of Article III would require revision;

4. Section 5 of Article III would require revision;

5. Sections 8(b) and (c) of Article III would require revision;

6. Section 9 of Article III would require revision;

7. Section 11(a)(21) of Article III would require revision;

8. Sections 15(a)(b) and (c) of Article III would require reconsideration and revision;

9. Substantially all of Section 16 of Article III regarding legislative apportionment would require revision;

10. Perhaps the most sweeping change would have to be made in Section 17 of Article III regarding impeachment. This section would have to be completely recast and revised;

11. Section 6(a) of Article IV would require reconsideration, as would Section 7(b) of the same article;

12. In Article V it would be necessary to change the language in Section 13 and 13(a);

13. Section 1 of Article X relating to amendments to the United States Constitution would require change;

14. It would require a complete revision of Article XI relating to the method of amending the constitution because of the repeated references to the House and Senate throughout that article;

15. Sections 9, 11, 12 and 14 of Article XII would have to be amended.

It is clear from the recitations above that the power reserved to the people to amend any section of the Constitution, includes only the power to amend any section in such a manner that such amendment if approved would be complete within itself, relate to one subject and not substantially affect any other section or article of the Constitution or require further amendments to the Constitution to accomplish its purpose. There are many sections of the Constitution which would lend itself to such amendments; for instance, in Article X of the Constitution there are thirteen sections. An amendment to most, if not all, of these sections could be complete within itself and not substantially affect other provisions of the Constitution or require further amendments thereof. There are many other similar sections in the document.

If it should become necessary in the course of events for the people to bring about such cataclysmic change as that which would result in the adoption of the amendments here under consideration, or Legislature should fail or refuse to act, the people have reserved unto themselves a means of bringing about such a revision by initiating under the provisions of Section 4 of Article XI a convention to consider a revision of the entire Constitution. This Section is available to the people to bring about a Unicameral Legislature if that is their desire.

In *Rivera-Cruz*, this Court cited *McFadden v. Jordan*, 32 Cal.2d 330, 196 P.2d 787, 789. This California case involved a purported initiative amendment to the Constitution of California, the result of which would be to substantially alter or repeal at least fifteen of the twenty-five articles of the California Constitution. The following language used in that decision is highly germane and pertinent:

> The proposal is offered as a single amendment but it obviously is multifarious. It does not give the people an opportunity to express approval or disapproval severally as to each major change suggested; rather does it, apparently, have the purpose of aggregating for the measure the favorable votes from electors of many suasions who, wanting strongly enough any one or more propositions

offered, might grasp at that which they want, tacitly accepting the remainder. Minorities favoring each proposition severally might, thus aggregated, adopt all. Such an appeal might well be proper in voting on a revised constitution, proposed under the safeguards provided for such a procedure, but it goes beyond the legitimate scope of a single amendatory article. There is in the measure itself no attempt to enumerate the various and many articles and sections of our present Constitution which would be affected, altered, replaced, or repealed. It purports only to add one new article but its framers found it necessary to include the omnibus provision (subdivision (7) of section XII) that 'If any section, subsection, sentence, clause or phrase of the constitution is in conflict with any of the provisions of this article, such section, subsection, sentence, clause or phrase is to the extent of such conflict hereby repealed.

We cannot accept such an arbitrary and strained minimization of difference between amend and revise. The differentiation required is not merely between two words; more accurately it is between two procedures and between their respective fields of application. Each procedure, if we follow elementary principles of statutory construction, must be understood to have a substantial field of application, not to be (as argued in intervenors' Answering Memorandum) a mere alternative procedure in the same field. Each of the two words, then, must be understood to denote, respectively, not only a procedure but also a field of application appropriate to its procedure. The people of this state have spoken; they made it clear when they adopted article XVIII and made amendment relatively simple but provided the formidable bulwark of a constitutional convention as a protection against improvident or hasty (or any other) revision, that they understood that there was a real difference between amendment and revision.

We conclude with the observation that if such proposed amendment were adopted by the people at the General Election and if the Legislature at its next session should fail to submit further amendments to revise and clarify the numerous inconsistencies and conflicts which would result, or if after submission of appropriate amendments the people should refuse to adopt them, simple chaos would prevail in the government of this State. The same result would obtain from an amendment, for instance, of Section 1 of Article V, to provide for only a Supreme Court and Circuit Courts-and there could be other examples too numerous to detail. These examples point unerringly to the answer.

The purpose of the long and arduous work of the hundreds of men and women and many sessions of the Legislature in bringing about the Constitution of 1968 was to eliminate inconsistencies and conflicts and to give the State a workable, accordant, homogenous and up-to-date document. All of this could disappear very quickly if we were to hold that it could be amended in the manner proposed in the initiative petition here.

The judgment appealed from is reversed and this cause is remanded for further proceedings in accordance with the views herein expressed.

THE PERILS OF DIRECT DEMOCRACY:

THE CALIFORNIA EXPERIENCE[20]

It is an honor to speak as a representative of the new class of Academy members. I would like to share some thoughts with you on a matter that has been of recent and continued professional concern to me, but that I believe may be of general interest to members of the Academy, because it fundamentally implicates how we govern ourselves. This is the increasing use of the ballot Initiative process available in many states to effect constitutional and statutory changes in the law, especially in the structure and powers of government.

A not-too-subtle clue to my point of view is reflected in the caption I have chosen for these remarks — "The Perils of Direct Democracy: The California Experience." Although two dozen states in our nation permit government by voter Initiative, in no other state is the practice as extreme as in California.

By the terms of its Constitution, California permits a relatively small number of petition signers — equal to at least 8% of the voters in the last gubernatorial election — to place before the voters a proposal to amend any aspect of our Constitution. (The figure is only 5% for a proposed non-constitutional statutory enactment.) If approved by a simple majority of those voting at the next election, the Initiative measure goes into effect on the following day.

The legislature (by two-thirds vote of each house) shares with the voters the power to place proposed constitutional amendments before the electorate. California, however, is unique among all American jurisdictions in prohibiting its legislature, without express voter approval, from amending or repealing even a statutory measure enacted by the voters, unless the Initiative measure itself specifically confers such authority upon the legislature.

The process for amending California's Constitution thus is considerably easier than the amendment process embodied in the United States Constitution, under which an amendment may be proposed either by a vote of two-thirds of each house of Congress or by a convention called on the application of the legislatures of two-thirds of the states. It can be ratified only by the legislatures of (or by conventions held in) three-quarters of the states.

The relative ease with which the California Constitution can be amended is dramatically illustrated by the frequency with which this has

---

[20] Remarks by California's Chief Justice, Ronald M. George, to the American Academy of Arts & Sciences, October 10, 2009 in Cambridge, Massachusetts. Reprinted with permission.

occurred. Only 17 amendments to the United States Constitution (in addition to the Bill of Rights, ratified in 1791) have been adopted since that document was ratified in 1788. In contrast, more than 500 amendments to the California Constitution have been adopted since ratification of California's current Constitution in 1879.

Former United States Supreme Court Justice Hugo Black was known to pride himself on carrying in his pocket a slender pamphlet containing the federal Constitution in its entirety. I certainly could not emulate that practice with California's constitutional counterpart.

One Bar leader has observed: "California's current constitution rivals India's for being the longest and most convoluted in the world.... [W]ith the cumulative dross of past voter initiatives incorporated, [it] is a document that assures chaos."

Initiatives have enshrined a myriad of provisions into California's constitutional charter, including a prohibition on the use of gill nets and a measure regulating the confinement of barnyard fowl in coops. This last constitutional amendment was enacted on the same 2008 ballot that amended the state Constitution to override the California Supreme Court's decision recognizing the right of same-sex couples to marry. Chickens gained valuable rights in California on the same day that gay men and lesbians lost them.

Perhaps most consequential in their impact on the ability of California state and local government to function are constitutional and statutory mandates and prohibitions — often at cross-purposes — limiting how elected officials may raise and spend revenue. California's lawmakers, and the state itself, have been placed in a fiscal straitjacket by a steep two-thirds-vote requirement — imposed at the ballot box — for raising taxes. A similar supermajoritarian requirement governs passage of the state budget. This situation is compounded by voter Initiative measures that have imposed severe restrictions upon increases in the assessed value of real property that is subject to property tax, coupled with constitutional requirements of specified levels of financial support for public transportation and public schools.

These constraints upon elected officials — when combined with a lack of political will (on the part of some) to curb spending and (on the part of others) to raise taxes — often make a third alternative, borrowing, the most attractive option (at least until the bankers say "no").

Much of this constitutional and statutory structure has been brought about not by legislative fact-gathering and deliberation, but rather by the approval of voter Initiative measures, often funded by special interests. These interests are allowed under the law to pay a bounty to signature-gatherers for each signer. Frequent amendments — coupled with the implicit threat of more in the future — have rendered our state government dysfunctional, at least in times of severe economic decline.

Because of voter Initiatives restricting the taxing powers that the legislature may exercise, California's tax structure is particularly dependent upon fluctuating types of revenue, giving rise to a "boom or bust" economic cycle. The consequences this year have been devastating to programs that, for example, provide food to poor children and health care for the elderly disabled. This year's fiscal crisis also has caused the Judicial Council, which I chair, to take the reluctant and unprecedented step of closing all courts in our state one day a month. That decision will enable us to offset approximately one-fourth of the more than $400 million reduction imposed by the other two branches of government on the $4 billion budget of our court system.

The voter Initiative process places additional burdens upon the judicial branch. The court over which I preside frequently is called upon to resolve legal challenges to voter Initiatives. Needless to say, we incur the displeasure of the voting public when, in the course of performing our constitutional duties as judges, we are compelled to invalidate such a measure.

On occasion, we are confronted with a pre-election lawsuit that causes us to remove an Initiative proposal from the ballot because, by combining insufficiently related issues, it violates our state Constitution's single-subject limitation on such measures. At other times, a voter Initiative — perhaps poorly drafted and ambiguous, or faced with a competing or "dueling" measure that passed at the same election — requires years of successive litigation in the courts to ferret out its intended meaning, and ultimately may have to be invalidated in whole or in part.

One thing is fairly certain, however. If a proposal, whatever its nature, is sufficiently funded by its backers, it most likely will obtain the requisite number of signatures to qualify for the ballot, and — if it does qualify — there is a good chance the measure will pass. The converse certainly is true — poorly funded efforts, without sufficient backing to mount an expensive television campaign — are highly unlikely to succeed, whatever their merit.

This dysfunctional situation has led some to call for the convening of a convention to write a new Constitution for California to replace our current 1879 charter, which in turn supplanted the original 1849 document. Yet, although a recent poll reflects that 79% of Californians say the state is moving in the wrong direction, only 33% believe that the state's Constitution requires "major" changes and approximately 60% are of the view that decisions made by Californians through the Initiative process are better than those made by the legislature and the governor.

Add to this mix a split among scholars concerning whether a constitutional convention, if called, could be limited in the subject matter it is empowered to consider. Some argue that a convention would be open to every type of proposal from any source, including social activists and special interest groups. There also is controversy over the most appropriate procedure for selecting delegates for such a convention.

A student of government might reasonably ask: Does the voter Initiative, a product of the Populist Movement that reached its high point in the early 20th century in the mid-west and western states, remain a positive contribution in the form in which it now exists in 21st century California? Or, despite its original objective — to curtail special interests, such as the railroads, that controlled the legislature of California and of some other states — has the voter Initiative now become the tool of the very types of special interests it was intended to control, and an impediment to the effective functioning of a true democratic process?

John Adams — who I believe never would have supported a voter Initiative process like California's — cautioned that "democracy never lasts long…. There is never a democracy that did not commit suicide." The nation's Founding Fathers, wary of the potential excesses of direct democracy, established a republic with a carefully crafted system of representative democracy. This system was characterized by checks and balances that conferred authority upon the officeholders of our three branches of government in a manner designed to enable them to curtail excesses engaged in by their sister branches.

Perhaps with the dangers of direct democracy in mind, Benjamin Franklin gave his much-quoted response to a question posed by a resident of Philadelphia after the adjournment of the Constitutional Convention in 1787. Asked the type of government that had been established by the delegates, Franklin responded: "It would be a republic, if you can keep it." And, as Justice David Souter recently observed in quoting this exchange, Franklin "understood that a republic can be lost."

At a minimum, in order to avoid such a loss, Californians may need to consider some fundamental reform of the voter Initiative process. Otherwise, I am concerned, we shall continue on a course of dysfunctional state government, characterized by a lack of accountability on the part of our officeholders as well as the voting public.

NOTES

1. The State Constitutional initiative was first adopted in Oregon in 1902. Eighteen states now provide for citizens to petition for changes in their state constitutions.

2. The initiative process is referred to as direct democracy, in contrast to representative democracy. When the initiative procedure was challenged

as violating the United States Constitution's guarantee that each state must have a republic form of government, it was held to be a political question for Congress rather than the Supreme Court to decide. *Pacific States Telephone & Telegraph v. Oregon*, 223 U.S. 118 (1912).

3. In *Romer v. Evans*, 517 U.S. 620 (1996), the United States Supreme Court held that an initiated amendment to the Colorado Constitution violated the Equal Protection Clause.

4. A majority of the California Supreme Court held in the *In re Marriage Cases*, 183 P.3d 384 (Cal. 2008), "that same-sex couples, as well as opposite-sex couples, enjoy the protection of the constitutional right to marry embodied in the privacy and due process provisions of the California Constitution, and that by granting access to the designation of "marriage" to opposite-sex couples and denying such access to same-sex couples, the existing California marriage statutes impinged upon the privacy and due process rights of same-sex couples and violated those couples' right to the equal protection of the laws guaranteed by the California Constitution."

Proposition 8, an initiative measure approved by a majority of voters at the November 4, 2008, election, added a new section – section 7.5 – to article I of the California Constitution, providing: "Only marriage between a man and a woman is valid or recognized in California." The measure took effect on November 5, 2008. In *Strauss v. Horton*, 207 P.3d 48 (Cal. 2009), the California Supreme Court held that "Proposition 8, under the governing provisions of the California Constitution, constitutes a permissible change to the California Constitution."

E. CONSTITUTIONAL CONVENTION – REQUIRED FOR REVISION

OPINION OF THE JUSTICES
264 A.2d 342 (Del. 1970)

A question was propounded by the Governor to the Justices of the Supreme Court relating to whether Constitution permitted adoption of amendment or amendments which would revise entire Constitution. The Justices of the Supreme Court were of the opinion that change in Constitution which is mere reorganization, restatement, modernization, abbreviation, consolidation, simplification, or clarification of existing document and which makes no substantial or fundamental change in basic structure of state government can be accomplished by legislative amendment, but changes that do not fall within those lines must be treated as revisions of Constitution which may be accomplished only by constitutional convention, and each situation, as to whether an amendment or revision is involved, must be resolved upon its own facts and circumstances.

Question answered.

General assembly, while permitted to submit question to electorate as to whether unlimited constitutional convention should be called, may also limit question submitted to electorate so as to ascertain its wishes regarding call of a convention for purpose of revising specified parts of Constitution only. Del.C.Ann.Const. art. 16, § 2.

To His Excellency Russell W. Peterson Governor of Delaware

Reference is made to your letter dated January 22, 1970, requesting the opinions of the Justices upon the following question:

> 'Does Article 16, Section 1, of the Delaware Constitution permit the adoption of an amendment or amendments which would revise the entire Constitution?'

As the basis for the question, your letter explains:

> Legislation will soon be introduced in the General Assembly which will contain the proposals of the Constitutional Revision Commission set up by former Governor Charles L. Terry, Jr. This proposed revision concerns the entire State Constitution.

It is further stated that the opinions are requested, under 10 Del.C. § 141, in the interest of public information and to enable you to discharge the duties of your office. We assume that the latter reference relates to the fact that the Report of the Constitutional Revision Commission, established by 56 Del.L.Ch. 189, has been presented to you for your consideration and appropriate action, thus bringing your request within the provisions of 10 Del.C. § 141.

The reply to the question requires consideration of the scope and meaning of Article 16, Sections 1 and 2 of the Delaware Constitution:

> Section 1 of Article 16 provides for change of the Constitution by the agreement of two-thirds of all the members elected to each House of two successive General Assemblies, as follows:

> Section 1. Any amendment or amendments to this Constitution may be proposed in the Senate or House of Representatives; and if the same shall be agreed to by two-thirds of all the members elected to each House, such proposed amendment or amendments shall be entered on their journals, with the years and nays taken thereon, and the Secretary of State shall cause such proposed amendment or amendments to be published three months before the next general election in at last three newspapers in each county in which such newspapers shall be published; and if in the General Assembly next after the said election such proposed amendment or amendments shall upon yea and nay vote be agreed to by two-thirds of all the members elected to each House, the same shall thereupon become part of the Constitution.

> Section 2 of Article 16 provides for change of the Constitution by Convention as follows:

Section 2. The General Assembly by a two-thirds vote of all the members elected to each House may from time to time provide for the submission to the qualified electors of the State at the general election next thereafter the question, 'Shall there be a Convention to revise the Constitution and amend the same?'; and upon such submission, if a majority of those voting on said question shall decide in favor of a Convention for such purpose, the General Assembly at its next session shall provide for the election of delegates to such convention at the next general election. Such Convention shall be composed of forty-one delegates, one of whom shall be chosen from each Representative District by the qualified electors thereof, and two of whom shall be chosen from New Castle County, two from Kent County and two from Sussex County by the qualified electors thereof respectively.

Section 2 then specifies procedures for the conduct of the business of a Convention.

In our judgment, the problem presented by your question is two-fold: (1) does our Constitution, by Article 16, Sections 1 and 2, distinguish between constitutional 'amendments,' on the one hand, and a constitutional 'revision,' on the other, and (2) if so, what is a 'revision' within the meaning of Section 2?

We are of the opinion that a distinction is made by Art. 16 between 'amendments' to the Constitution under Section 1 and a 'revision' thereof under Section 2.

There is ambiguity in the two terms as used in our Constitution. In a sense, every amendment to the Constitution is a revision in that it is a change therein; but a revision, in the larger sense of the word, may be such a basic alteration of the original document as to surmount entirely the ordinary meaning of the word 'amendment.' The two terms are sometimes used interchangeably in constitutional provisions; in other cases, it is said that they are unrelated and should not be confused one with the other. The ambiguity is pointed up by the use of the two words jointly in the question prescribed for the electorate by Section 2: 'Shall there be a Convention to Revise the Constitution and Amend the same?'

In view of the ambiguity, we look to the Delaware Constitutional Debates of 1897 for insight into the intent of the drafters when they formulated Article 16 of the present Constitution and used the terms we are here called upon to construe.

It is clear from the Debates, we think, that the drafters distinguished between 'amendments', on the one hand, and a 'revision' on the other. This conclusion is impelled by the following considerations:

1) Section 1 is, and throughout its evolution was, confined to amendment, whereas Section 2 refers, and throughout its evolution referred, to revision.

2) Throughout the Debates, the drafters referred to amendments under Section 1 as 'changes' or 'alterations' in the present Constitution, whereas they looked upon a 'revision' under Section 2 as the 'making' or the 'manufacture' of a 'new' Constitution; as the 'framing an organic law for the State.'

3) The drafters discussed at great length the standards to be established for the qualification of delegates to a Constitutional Convention charged with the responsibility of 'revising' the Constitution under Section 2, as compared with the constitutency of a General Assembly vested with the power to make constitutional changes legislatively under Section 1. It was generally agreed by the drafters that a Constitutional Convention should be non-partisan, with the major political parties having approximately equal representation; that it should not be limited entirely to representatives of local areas by Representative or Senatorial Districts but should have delegates at large from each of the Counties to assure getting the best qualified people without regard for residence within the County or party lines. And recurrent throughout the Debates was the thought that a Constitutional Convention, specially elected for its expressed purpose, is more the direct agent of the people for that purpose than is a General Assembly. This concept was and is in accord with authorities on the subject. *E.g.*, *Livermore v. Waite*, 102 Cal. 113, 36 P. 424, 25 L.R.A. 312 (1894); *Jackman v. Bodine*, 43 N.J. 453, 205 A.2d 713, 725-726 (1964). It is also consistent with the arrangement whereunder the work- product of a Convention is not required by Section 2 to be submitted to the people for approval; whereas under Section 1 a proposal by a General Assembly for constitutional change is indirectly submitted to the people via the general election which must intervene before a successive General Assembly can effectuate the change.

For these reasons, we are of the opinion that the Constitution differentiates between the procedure for adopting a series of legislative 'amendments' under Section 1 of Article 16, and a 'revision' which can be accomplished only by Constitutional Convention under Section 2 thereof.

We come then to the second question: What is a 'revision' which must be accomplished by Convention under Section 2, and how does it differ from a series of 'amendments' which can be accomplished legislatively under Section 1?

A threshold truism is that the mere Number of changes cannot make the difference. Legislative amendments are not limited in number by Section 1; and a 'revision', to which Section 2 is applicable, does not come into being by reason of the mere number of changes or the mere fact that the changes concern the entire Constitution. It would be unreasonable to conclude that a large number of amendatory changes accomplishable piecemeal under Section 1, could not be accomplished simultaneously under that Section. Rather, it is the nature and scope of the changes contemplated that determine whether there is a 'revision' subject to Section 2 or a series of 'amendments' subject to Section 1.

As has been noted heretofore, in discussing the scope and nature of the 'revision' contemplated under Section 2, the drafters had in mind the 'making' of a 'new' Constitution. This concept of a constitutional 'revision', as contrasted with a series of constitutional 'amendments', is in accord with the views and conclusions of the Supreme Court of California in *Livermore v. Waite*, 102 Cal. 113, 36 P. 424 (1894) and *McFadden v. Jordan*, 32 Cal.2d 330, 196 P.2d 787 (1948). We find the definitions in those cases persuasive. A constitutional 'amendment' was defined therein as 'such an addition or change within the lines of the original instrument as will effect an improvement or better carry out the purpose for which it was framed.' A 'revision' on the other hand, was held in McFadden to be the result of proposed changes in the basic governmental plan because the effect thereof 'would be to substantially alter the purpose and to attain objectives clearly beyond the lines of the Constitution as now cast.' In short, to be a 'revision' the result must be to effect a change in the basic philosophy which has cast our government in its present form.

We think those distinctions are supported by reason and authority. A constitutional 'revision' makes substantial, basic, fundamental changes in the plan of government; it makes extensive alterations in the basic plan and substance of the existing document; it attains objectives and purposes beyond the lines of the present Constitution. A 'revision' is more than a mere reorganization, restatement, modernization, abbreviation, consolidation, simplification, or clarification of the existing document.

The latter type of change, making no substantial and fundamental change or alteration in the basic structure of State government, can be accomplished, we think, by legislative amendment under Section 1, as would any other changes that fall 'within the lines of the original instrument' to constitute 'an improvement or better carry out the purpose for which it was framed.' Any change or changes that fall within such lines should be considered, in our opinion, 'amendments' within Section 1; changes that do not fall within those lines must, in our opinion, be treated as 'revisions' within the scope and application of Section 2.

But it is not enough to distinguish a revision from a series of amendments and to ascertain the tests therefor. Each situation must be resolved upon its own facts and circumstances.

The nature and scope of the changes acceptable to the General Assembly are presently unknown. The ultimate action to be taken by the General Assembly on the proposals of the Constitutional Revision Commission remains to be seen. It is to those ultimate changes that the tests of 'amendment' versus 'revision' must be applied. At that stage, and with its final draft of contemplated changes before it, the General Assembly must determine (1) whether it may proceed legislatively under Section 1 because the proposed changes are amendatory; or (2) whether it must proceed by way of Constitutional Convention under Section 2 because the proposed changes are revisory.

When the General Assembly is confronted with that decision, it may be found that some of the changes contemplated are amendatory while others are revisory. In that event, it is our opinion that the Section1 route may be followed as to the amendatory changes, and the Section 2 route may be simultaneously followed as to the revisory changes. For, in this connection, we are of the opinion that Section 2 permits a partial revision of the Constitution by Convention.

In our view, neither Section 2 nor any other provision of our Constitution prohibits the General Assembly from limiting the question submitted to the electorate so as to ascertain its wishes regarding the call of a Convention for the purpose of revising specified parts of the Constitution only. If the electorate chooses to approve the calling of such limited Constitutional Convention, we are of the opinion that it may do so under Section 2. In such event, the people and not the General Assembly will have limited the work and scope of the Convention; and the authority of such Convention may not exceed the wishes of the people thus expressed. If, on the other hand, the electorate wishes to have the Section 2 question propounded to it by the General Assembly for an unlimited Constitutional Convention, it may make its wishes known to the legislative candidates at any general election.

It would be unreasonable, in our view, to construe Section 2 otherwise. It could not have been the intent of the drafters to deprive the people of the right and method of making a partial revision of the Constitution. Since a 'revision' can be made only by Convention, and since it is unreasonable to assume that a partial revision is impermissible, it necessarily follows that a partial revision by a limited Convention can be decreed by the electorate, if it wishes, in response to an appropriate question propounded by the General Assembly under Section 2. We find support for this view in *Staples v. Gilmer*, 183 Va. 613, 33 S.E.2d 49 (1945). The Supreme Court of Appeals of Virginia there held that a limited Convention could be called under a constitutional provision almost precisely the same as our Section 2. See also Annotation, 158 A.L.R. 512.

We conclude, therefore, that a decision as to the method of constitutional change must await a final ascertainment of the actual changes to be made and an item-by-item determination of whether they are amendatory or revisory in nature.

The foregoing is the unanimous opinion of the undersigned.

NOTE

In 1776, Delaware held the first convention that was ever called for the sole purpose of writing a state constitution.

F. CONSTITUTIONAL COMMISSIONS

PETER J. GALIE AND CHRISTOPHER BOPST, THE CONSTITUTIONAL COMMISSION IN NEW YORK: A WORTHY TRADITION, 64 Alb. L. Rev. 1285 (2001).[21]

---

[21] Reprinted with permission.

In 1997, when New Yorkers decisively defeated a constitutionally mandated ballot proposition to convene what would have been the state's fourth constitutional convention in the twentieth century, they placed the fate of constitutional reform with the state legislature. Not until the year 2017 will the question be required to appear on the ballot, and the likelihood of the legislature proposing a convention vote in the interim is remote. New York does not permit amendments to be submitted to the electorate through constitutional initiative, and no constitutional commission has the power to submit amendments directly to the voters; constitutional reform can only emanate from either a constitutional convention or the state legislature. Since 1938, legislatively proposed amendments have been the only procedure successfully used for revising the state's charter.

Paradoxically, the latest rejection came at a time when many of the state's political actors agreed that systematic constitutional revision was needed. The League of Women Voters, Civil Service Employees Association (C.S.E.A.), American Federation of Labor--Congress of Industrial Organizations (A.F.L.-C.I.O.), National Organization of Women (NOW), and various environmental groups who opposed the calling of a convention in 1997, were, nevertheless, in agreement with proponents of the convention on the need for constitutional reform. Thus, debate has focused on the means for achieving reform. Constitutional conventions, viewed as cumbersome, expensive, and subject to approval by a suspicious, even dangerous, electorate have fallen from favor with citizen groups and politicians. The alternative, the legislature, may not be the ideal agency for providing systematic, regular revision and, in any case, has not been a successful forum for addressing such serious problems as fiscal integrity and state/local relations. Have we reached an impasse? This article examines the use of the constitutional commission, particularly in New York, as a means of achieving constitutional reform.

A study of the constitutional history of New York reveals that the constitutional commission has a long and vital history as a means of proposing meaningful and necessary reform within the state. Some of the most significant constitutional revision in New York has been the product of such commissions, and the most successful commissions were held in the aftermath of constitutional convention defeats.

This article examines the history and tradition of commissions as mechanisms to effectuate constitutional reform in New York, from its origins in the 1870s, when the state was struggling with issues such as corruption, home rule for burgeoning cities, and African-American suffrage, to the present-day, when the state budget process, debt limitations, and social welfare are issues of concern. Each commission will be analyzed, and placed in the historical context from which it emerged. Although a detailed analysis of the results of each commission is outside the scope of this article, an emphasis will be placed on the accomplishments and failures of each commission, as well as each commission's unique contributions to New York's constitutional history. After analyzing the constitutional commission experience of New York State, this article examines the use of constitutional commissions to provide meaningful constitutional reform in several other states, such as Florida, Utah, and Georgia.

1. The New York State Constitutional Commission Experience

Throughout its history, New York has convened ten constitutional commissions. Of these bodies, five were created specifically to prepare for upcoming constitutional conventions, while six were formed to study and propose changes to the existing constitution. As indicated by the appended table, the majority of constitutional commissions were statutorily created, although some were formed by a resolution of one or both houses of the legislature, and others were the product of executive order. The composition of these commissions, both in the number of members and the method of appointment varies. The largest commission was the forty-two member Constitutional Convention Committee of 1937-1938, while the smallest commission was the five member 1914-1915 Constitutional Convention Commission. In marked contrast to constitutional conventions, which typically are composed of over one hundred delegates, six of New York's commissions have had twenty or less members. The maximum amount of funding for an individual commission was $800,000 for the Temporary State Commission on the Constitutional Convention, which was in operation from 1965 through 1967. Although this may appear expensive compared to the earlier commissions, the subsequent convention for which this commission prepared cost taxpayers over six million dollars.

2. The Constitutional Commission Experience in Other States

Resort to the use of constitutional commissions has increased throughout the country since mid-century, and approximately two-thirds of the states have resorted to this procedure in the last thirty years. The composition and function of these commissions varies greatly from state to state. Among the several states achieving considerable success in reforming their state constitutions through constitutional commissions, Florida, Utah, and Georgia provide three different, yet effective, models for constitutional reform using a constitutional commission.

a. Florida

Although Florida has utilized constitutional commissions to effectuate constitutional revision since the 1950s, the Florida Constitution of 1968 represented a unique and historical development in the history of constitutional commissions. In contrast to prior Florida constitutions that had allowed constitutional revision only by legislative amendment or constitutional convention, the new constitution provided an independent constitution revision commission.

The Constitution Revision Commission was mandated to convene in 1978, and every twentieth year thereafter. The thirty-seven member body consists of the attorney general, fifteen members appointed by the governor, nine members each selected by the leaders of both houses of the legislature, and three members chosen by the chief justice of the state supreme court. The chairman of the commission is selected by the governor. When the commission was created, its jurisdiction was plenary, although tax and budget matters were subsequently removed from the province of the body. Proposals from the commission must be filed with the secretary of state at least 180 days before the election, and they do not require legislative approval for ballot placement.

In 1988, Florida voters approved a constitutional amendment that "created a major opportunity to revamp Florida's outdated tax structure." The amendment created a Taxation and Budget Reform Commission with the authority to place proposals on the 1992 ballot without obtaining legislative approval. Unlike its counterpart, the Constitution Revision Commission, the Taxation and Budget Reform Commission is appointed by leaders in only two branches of the government. Taxation and budget processes are the only matters over which the commission has authority, and commission approval of amendments requires a two-thirds vote of the entire body and a majority of each appointed group of members. Sitting legislators are prohibited as voting members of the commission. The body is mandated to meet every ten years, beginning in 1990.

The Florida commissions, the first in history to be afforded the power to submit their proposals directly to the voters, have achieved substantial reform in various areas. The first Constitution Revision Commission submitted many proposals to voters in 1978, recommending a total of eighty-seven constitutional changes to various articles of the constitution. Floridians, unwilling to extensively revise a constitution that had been operating less than ten years, rejected all of the proposals, and even one by a margin of three to one.

Following the rejection of the initial commission's work, the Taxation and Budget Reform Commission in 1992 submitted four proposals to the voters. Of these proposals, one was invalidated by the Florida Supreme

Court as violating statutory requirements on clarity of ballot language, and two were ultimately approved by voters. These amendments represented the first time proposals that had been submitted directly by a constitutional commission were approved by voters. In 1998, after several months of meetings and public hearings, the Florida Constitution Revision Commission submitted thirteen proposals to voters, many of which addressed multiple subjects. Of these proposals, twelve were subsequently approved by the voters, validating the effectiveness of the commission as a permanent, constitutionally prescribed device for achieving meaningful constitutional reform.

b. Utah

Like Florida, Utah has established a permanent commission to propose constitutional changes. Unlike the Florida commission, the Utah commission may not make proposals directly to the voters. Instead of meeting at fixed intervals, such as every ten or twenty years, the commission operates continuously, allowing it to address issues in need of reform without additional legislative activity or within the limits of a fixed time period.

Although the composition of the commission contains heavy legislative representation, safeguards have been placed in the enacting legislation to avoid, or at least minimize, partisan conflict. The commission is composed of sixteen members: three are appointed from each house of the legislature by the respective leader of the house, but no more than two of the members appointed from each house may be members of the same political party; three members of the commission are appointed by the governor, and no more than two of them may be from the same political party; the director of the Office of Legislative Research and General Counsel serves as an ex officio member of the commission; and the remaining six commissioners are chosen by the ten existing members. The term of a commission member is six years, and no commissioner may serve for longer than twelve years. The commission selects its own officers.

In addition to conducting a comprehensive examination of the state constitution and making recommendations to the governor and legislature as to specific proposed constitutional amendments to implement the commission's recommendations for constitutional change, the commission is authorized to advise the governor and legislature on any proposed constitutional amendment or revision. The commission is directed to consider recommendations from the governor, members of the state legislature, state agencies, and "responsible members of the public." The commission must publish and distribute an annual report of its studies and recommendations.

The Utah commission, a permanent body combining legislative influence with the expertise of independent members in a non-partisan manner, has achieved considerable success. The commission has made recommendations on, and the voters have approved, amendments concerning several articles, including the legislature, the executive, corporations, election and rights of suffrage, revenue and taxation, education, and the judiciary. The ability of this commission to achieve success in reforming articles that have traditionally been difficult to amend was a testament to the success of the Utah approach.

c. Georgia

Although Georgia has not utilized a permanent constitutional commission to provide systemic reform of its state charter, it has used a constitutional commission to propose a new constitution. The Georgia Constitution of 1877 was ratified as an attempt to deal with the problems of Reconstruction, and resembled a legislative code in its length and prolixity. By 1900, it became apparent that the constitution needed major revision, and by 1943 it had been amended 301 times. Although all seven of Georgia's previous constitutions had been the product of constitutional conventions, fear of an attempt to reapportion representation had prevented the legislature from obtaining the two-thirds vote of the total membership of both houses of the legislature necessary to call a constitutional convention.

In March of 1943, as an alternative to a constitutional convention, which was not politically feasible at the time, the General Assembly enacted a resolution sponsored by Governor Ellis Arnall for the creation of a twenty-three member constitutional commission. Not only did the creation of this commission circumvent the previous problems with elected conventions, as its proposals would be submitted directly to the General Assembly, but this commission was a product of the belief that constitutional revision could be achieved "'more satisfactorily by a small commission…than through a constitutional convention.'" The membership of the commission included

> the Governor, the President of the Senate, the Speaker of the House of Representatives, three members of the Senate appointed by the President, five members of the House appointed by the Speaker, a justice of the Supreme Court [chosen by the members of that court], a judge of the Court of Appeals [[chosen by the members of that court], the Attorney General, the State Auditor, two judges of the Superior Courts, three practicing attorneys-at-law, and three laymen appointed by the Governor. The resolution creating this commission provided that the commission could submit to the general assembly "proposed amendments to the Constitution or…a proposed new constitution.

This commission convened on January 6, 1944, and adjourned on December 9, 1944. However, many of the subcommittees appointed by

Governor Arnall, who served as chairman of the commission, met and held public hearings prior to the first full commission meeting. The commission submitted a proposed new constitution in January 1945 to the general assembly. The legislature undertook an extensive study of the document and made several revisions, submitting the new constitution to voters at a special election held on August 7, 1945. At that election, "the new Constitution was approved by a vote of 60,065 to 34,417."

The Georgia Constitution of 1945 represents the first time in American history that a constitution was written by a commission and ratified by popular vote. This action was taken following several unsuccessful attempts to pass a resolution that would have convened a constitutional convention, and represents a method for obtaining a complete revision of the constitution while avoiding the negatives of the convention process.

3. Conclusion

The past quarter century has witnessed the decline of the constitutional convention as a mechanism for achieving constitutional change. Although twenty-six state constitutional conventions were held between 1960 and 1995, thirteen of these were held during the 1960s. Only one state constitutional convention was held between 1988 and 1993. A combination of factors has conspired to make it likely that this trend will continue. Conventions are controversial for a number of reasons: they are viewed as "Pandora's box[es]," creating the possibility of dangerous additions to the constitution; they threaten to upset established relationships between the governing institutions and organized interests; and they are viewed as cumbersome, unwieldy and expensive mechanisms. As an example, the rejected convention in New York in 1997 was projected to cost at least fifty million dollars.

The reluctance to resort to conventions, combined with the inability or unwillingness of state legislatures to propose systematic revision, has left states with few options for meaningful constitutional change. The constitutional commission has the potential to break this constitutional logjam. The commission allows an educated, highly specialized group of persons to analyze the problems of the state in a deliberate and relatively nonpartisan manner. When contrasted with constitutional conventions, which in New York have over 150 delegates, it is not surprising that commissions are often viewed as progressive and deliberate in their work. Moreover, the relatively low cost of a commission compared to a constitutional convention makes using a commission a bargain for constitutional reform.

Constitutional reform commissions have played a significant role in New York's constitutional development, providing expertise and impetus for constitutional conventions, the legislature, and the people in the exercise of their respective powers to revise and amend the constitution. Florida, Utah, and Georgia provide models of constitutional commissions that differ from the traditional commission employed in New York. These varied state experiences, and the history of the commission in New York, suggest that a constitutional commission to undertake a comprehensive evaluation of the constitution and provide recommendations to the legislature for its revision, offer the state its best hope for accomplishing needed constitutional reform.

INDEX